GOVERNMENT
in America

- ★ Student Textbook
- ★ Teacher's Annotated Edition
- ★ Teacher's Resources: Blackline Masters

  Skills Practice
  Skills Challenge
  Study Guide/Review
  Chapter Worksheet Review
  Citizenship
  Constitutional Issues
  Comparative Government
  Simulations
  Primary Source Readings
  Supreme Court Decisions
  Tests

- ★ Teaching Transparencies
- ★ Test Generators (IBM, APPLE, MAC)
- ★ Videotape Series

 **Plus**

ANNUAL UPDATES

- ★ Election Analysis
- ★ International Developments
- ★ Domestic Affairs
- ★ Supreme Court Decisions

TEACHER'S ANNOTATED EDITION

GOVERNMENT
in **America**

RICHARD J. HARDY

CONTENTS

McDougal Littell/Houghton Mifflin

Evanston, Illinois
Boston   Dallas   Phoenix

Stay *Up-To-Date* with the 1996 edition of *Government in America*

This **1996 edition** of *Government in America* updates material from the previous (1995) edition to keep students' study of American government as current as possible. The following list highlights the new material.

The Clinton Administration

- *pp. 423-24:* restructuring of executive branch.
- *p. 448:* reorganization of U.S. Department of Agriculture.
- *p. 510-24:* ban on assault weapons.
- *p. 621:* health care reform proposal.

Congress

- *pp. 342–43:* demographic update.
- *p. 356:* 1994 election results.
- *p. 360:* number of congressional committees.

Supreme Court

- *p. 473:* Harry Blackmun retirement and Stephen Breyer appointment.
- *p. 475:* new photo of full court.

Other Domestic Updates

- *p. 416:* presidential approval ratings.
- *pp. 616, 618–19:* Social Security.
- *p. 620:* Medicare.
- *p. 637:* state constitutions.

International Affairs

- *p. 383:* Haiti update.
- *p. 557:* organization of the United Nations.
- *p. 741:* U.S. foreign trade.
- *p. 765:* photo of Mexican President Zedillo, PRI status in new Mexican government.
- *p. 767:* South African democracy.

Student's Edition ISBN: 0–395–73452–5
Teacher's Edition ISBN: 0–395–73453–3

3 4 5 6 7 8 9 VH 99 98 97

SUGGESTED COURSE OUTLINES

Structure of American Government: One Semester Course

		Suggested Time
UNIT 1	**Foundations of American Government**	**4 weeks**
	Chapter 1. Principles of Government	1 week
	Chapter 2. Origins of American Government	4 days
	Chapter 3. The Constitution: Supreme Law of the Land	1 week
	Chapter 4. Federalism: The Division of Power	1 week
	Unit Wrap-Up: Case Studies 1 and 14	1 day
UNIT 4	**National Government: The Legislative Branch**	**2 1/2 weeks**
	Chapter 12. Congress: Its Power, Structure, and Members	1 week
	Chapter 13. The Lawmaking Process	6 days
	Unit Wrap-Up: Case Study 5	1 day
UNIT 5	**National Government: The Executive Branch**	**3 weeks**
	Chapter 14. The Office of President	3 days
	Chapter 15. The Powers of the President	1 week
	Chapter 16. Government at Work	6 days
	Unit Wrap-Up: Case Study 8	1 day
UNIT 6	**National Government: The Judicial Branch**	**2 1/2 weeks**
	Chapter 17. The Supreme Court and the Federal Court System	6 days
	Chapter 18. Law and the Legal Process	6 days
	Unit Wrap-Up: Case Studies 3 and 4	1 day
UNIT 8	**State Government**	**2 1/2 weeks**
	Chapter 24. The Structure of State Governments	6 days
	Chapter 25. State Policies and Finances	1 week
	Unit Wrap-Up: Case Study 11	1 day
UNIT 9	**Local Government**	**2 weeks**
	Chapter 26. The Structure of Local Governments	1 week
	Chapter 27. Local Government Policies and Finances	4 days
	Unit Wrap-Up: Case Studies 7, 12, and 13	1 day
UNIT 10	**Comparative Government**	**1 1/2 weeks**
	Chapter 28. The Role of Government in Economic Systems	4 days
	Chapter 29. Comparing Systems of Government	3 days
	Unit Wrap-Up: Case Study 6	1 day

Citizenship: One Semester Course

		Suggested Time
UNIT 1	**Foundations of American Government**	**3 1/2 weeks**
	Chapter 1. Principles of Government	1 week
	Chapter 2. Origins of American Government	3 days
	Chapter 3. The Constitution: Supreme Law of the Land	1 week
	Chapter 4. Federalism: The Division of Power	4 days
	Unit Wrap-Up: Case Studies 1 and 14	1 day
UNIT 2	**Civil Rights and Civil Liberties**	**3 weeks**
	Chapter 5. Civil Liberties: The First Amendment Freedoms	4 days
	Chapter 6. Civil Liberties: Due Process of Law	6 days
	Chapter 7. Civil Rights: Equal Protection of the Law	4 days
	Unit Wrap-Up: Case Studies 2 and 3	1 day
UNIT 3	**Political Participation: Government by the People**	**3 1/2 weeks**
	Chapter 8. Public Opinion in American Democracy	3 days
	Chapter 9. Interest Groups and Their Influence	3 days
	Chapter 10. Political Parties	1 week
	Chapter 11. Politics in Action	1 week
	Unit Wrap-Up: Case Study 10	1 day
UNIT 4	**National Government: The Legislative Branch**	**1 1/2 weeks**
	Chapter 12. Congress: Its Power, Structure, and Members	3 days
	Chapter 13. The Lawmaking Process	4 days
	Unit Wrap-Up: Case Study 5	1 day
UNIT 5	**National Government: The Executive Branch**	**1 1/2 weeks**
	Chapter 14. The Office of President	2 days
	Chapter 15. The Powers of the President	3 days
	Chapter 16. Government at Work	2 days
	Unit Wrap-Up: Case Studies 6 and 8	1 day
UNIT 6	**National Government: The Judicial Branch**	**1 1/2 weeks**
	Chapter 17. The Supreme Court and the Federal Court System	2 days
	Chapter 18. Law and the Legal Process	4 days
	Unit Wrap-Up: Case Study 4	1 day
UNIT 8	**State Government**	**2 weeks**
	Chapter 24. The Structure of State Governments	1 week
	Chapter 25. State Policies and Finances	4 days
	Unit Wrap-Up: Case Study 11	1 day
UNIT 9	**Local Government**	**1 1/2 weeks**
	Chapter 26. The Structure of Local Governments	3 days
	Chapter 27. Local Government Policies and Finances	3 days
	Unit Wrap-Up: Case Studies 7, 12, and 13	1 day

Government Survey: One Semester Course

Government Survey: Two Semester Course

ESSENTIAL ELEMENTS

The following chart provides the Essential Elements for a course in American government. The chart shows the chapters in the textbook where you will find content related to each Element. In addition, the chart provides examples of ways in which the Essential Elements can be further broken down specifically to meet local district objectives.

Essential Elements	Chapters	Specific Content Objectives
1. Foundations of the United States political system		
1A why governments are established	1–4, 28–29	• keep order • provide national defense • provide public services • promote social standards
1B differences between direct and indirect or representative democracy (Republic)	1–3, 11–13, 24	• Greek origin of direct democracy • citizens act as legislators in direct democracy • town meeting as modern example of direct democracy • elected representatives act as legislators in representative democracy • United States as representative democracy
1C political institutions, processes, and civic values of the United States compared with other governmental systems	1, 28–29	• democracy vs. non-democratic governments (autocracy, oligarchy, authoritarian, totalitarian) • United States (presidential) system vs. other democratic systems (parliamentary) • federalism vs. other ways of dividing authority (unitary government, confederation) • unique American political culture (high degree of national loyalty, pride in democratic government)
1D political ideas and historic documents that formed the foundation for the United States system of government	1–4	• individual rights • rule by law • limited government • representative government • majority rule with minority rights • Magna Charta • English Bill of Rights • Mayflower Compact • Declaration of Independence • Articles of Confederation • United States Constitution, including Bill of Rights and other amendments • *The Federalist*
2. Development of the United States governmental system		
2A purposes of and the political, economic, and social philosophies of the Declaration of Independence, the United States Constitution, the Bill of Rights, and selected Federalist papers and Anti-Federalist writings	2–3, 5–7	• Declaration as colonies' announcement of break with Britain • Constitution as attempt to create stable central government • Bill of Rights as means to ensure individual liberties and gain support for Constitution • belief in human equality • belief in natural rights • belief in social contract theory of government • belief in self-government • support for individual freedoms • respect for private property • support for free enterprise
2B arguments for and against ratification of the Constitution proposed by the Federalists and Anti-Federalists	2	• Antifederalists' worries about protection of individual rights • Antifederalists' complaints about secrecy of Constitutional Convention • Antifederalists' fears of loss of state authority • Federalists' complaints about inadequacy of Articles of Confederation • Federalists' promise of Bill of Rights to protect individual rights
2C notable individuals who played historic roles in establishing and maintaining the government	2–7, 13–15, 17, 24	• Samuel Adams • George Washington • Thomas Jefferson • James Madison • John Marshall • Abraham Lincoln
2D impact of United States Supreme Court decisions on the governmental system	3, 5–7, 17–18	• *Marbury v. Madison* and judicial review • *McCulloch v. Maryland* and supremacy of national law • *Gibbons v. Ogden* and commerce clause • *Texas v. White* and secession • *Baker v. Carr* and redistricting
2E growth of the two-party political system in the United States	10–11	• emergence of Federalist and Democratic-Republican Parties before 1796 election • disappearance of Federalist Party in 1810's • split of Democratic-Republicans in 1820's into Democrats and Whigs • formation of Republican Party in 1850's as antislavery party • rivalry between Democratic and Republican parties through 1900's • similarities between two major parties (both broad-based and centrist) • continuing presence of other, small parties • recent weakening in party support

3. Structures and functions of the United States governmental system at national, state, and local levels

3A	executive, legislative, judicial structures and functions, and authority roles at all levels of government	12–18, 24–27	• executive as enforcer of laws • legislature as maker of laws • judiciary as interpreter of laws • levels of executive authority (President, governor, mayor, etc.) • levels of legislative authority (Congress, state legislature, city council, etc.) • levels of judicial authority (Supreme Court, other federal courts, state courts, municipal courts, etc.)
3B	system of checks and balances of the branches of government at all levels of government	3, 12–18, 24–27	• checks on executive (veto overrides, impeachment, etc.) • checks on legislature (veto, overturning by judiciary, etc.) • checks on judiciary (impeachment, etc.)
3C	division of powers between national and state governments (federalism)	4, 19–25	• distinctions among delegated, concurrent, reserved, implied, and prohibited powers • importance of supremacy clause in Constitution • conflicting views of federalism (states' rights, nationalism, dual federalism, cooperative federalism) • expansion of federal government powers

4. Participation and decision making in civic affairs

4A	factors that influence an individual's political attitudes and actions	8–11	• how greatly an issue affects an individual • how intensely an individual cares about an issue • ideology • political culture (sense of community, support for the democratic process, attitudes toward officials, sense of civic responsibility, political symbols) • political socialization (home and family, schools, peers, mass media)
4B	functions of political parties, interest groups, and the media in the political system	8–11, 15	• providing information • encouraging political participation • simplifying political decisions • raising funds • lobbying • influencing elections • working at the grassroots level • legal action • propaganda • mass media coverage
4C	involvement and participation by individuals in political parties and interest groups	7–11	• voting • signing petitions • participating in caucuses • attending conventions • volunteering • contributing money
4D	reasons why participation and decision making in civic affairs by an individual require knowledge, time, and personal effort	5–7, 9–11	• activities of interest groups (rallies, letter-writing, protests, boycotts, lawsuits) • activities of political parties (running election campaigns, maintaining the organization, organizing political clubs) • need to be informed

5. Respect for self and others

5A	respecting beliefs of other individuals, groups, and cultures	1, 5–10, 28–29
5B	recognizing that some things are valued more in some groups and cultures than in others	1, 5–10, 17, 28–29
5C	recognizing how different societal values and beliefs affect the decision making, political actions, and beliefs of individuals	5–8, 11–12, 15–17, 28–29

6. Democratic beliefs and personal responsibilities

6A	recognizing that individuals should accept the consequences of their beliefs, decisions, and political actions	1–4, 12–18, 21–23, 25
6B	examining open-mindedness, tolerance of differing opinions, civic participation, and compromise as important aspects of democratic behavior	1–2, 5–9, 12–13, 19–21
6C	supporting the rules and laws of the school, community, state, and nation and working responsibly to identify legal means and methods by which unjust laws may be changed	3, 5–7, 13–14, 24–27
6D	evaluating the necessity of balancing legal rights and protections with civic responsibilities	1, 5, 18, 22–24
6E	exploring legal rights and protections afforded citizens (juveniles and adults)	1, 3–7, 18, 23–24
6F	supporting the democratic processes of the republican form of government	1–4, 10–15, 19–20
6G	supporting the basic civic values of American society (e.g., justice, responsibility, religious/political freedom, respect for the law, diversity, equality, privacy, private property rights, and free enterprise)	1–2, 5–7, 11, 18–27
6H	respecting the principles that underlie the United States Constitution (including the Bill of Rights and all other amendments) and the Declaration of Independence	3–7, 11–15, 17, 19
6I	explaining the concepts of "a government of law, not of men," "due process of law," and "equal protection of the law"	1–7, 12, 17, 24

7. Support for the American economic system

7A	recognizing that citizens can influence economic decisions made by government through legal political activities	2, 9–12, 15, 19–25
7B	comparing the taxing and spending functions of national, state, and local levels of government	4, 12, 15, 19, 25–27
7C	analyzing the role of government in regulating competition of both producers and consumers	16, 19, 21–23, 25, 28
7D	recognizi.g that economic self-interest may also serve the economic and political interest of others	16, 19–22, 25, 27–28
7E	comparing the relationship of government and economic systems in the United States to other countries' systems (e.g., capitalism, socialism, communism, etc.)	19, 28–29

8. Application of social studies skills

8A	analyzing, synthesizing, and evaluating information	1–29
8B	interpreting visual materials (e.g., charts, maps, graphs, pictures, etc.)	1–29
8C	organizing and expressing ideas in written forms	1–29
8D	distinguishing fact from opinion	8–13, 17, 19
8E	sequencing data and information	2, 7, 15, 23
8F	perceiving cause/effect relationships	1–29
8G	comparing similarities and differences (e.g., political and economic systems, documents, political parties, and leaders, etc.)	2–3, 8–13, 19–20, 23, 28–29
8H	applying problem-solving and decision-making skills and predicting consequences of decisions	1–29

Teacher's Professional Handbook, pages T11–T22, can be found at the back of the book.

GOVERNMENT
in *America*

RICHARD J. HARDY

McDougal Littell/Houghton Mifflin

Evanston, Illinois
Boston   Dallas   Phoenix

About the Author

RICHARD J. HARDY is Associate Professor of Political Science at the University of Missouri, Columbia. Born in Burlington, Iowa, Dr. Hardy received a B.A. from Western Illinois University, an M.A. from the University of North Dakota, and a Ph.D. in political science from the University of Iowa. He has won numerous teaching awards, is co-author of a book on Missouri state government, and his articles have appeared in many professional journals, including *Teaching Political Science*. Dr. Hardy is a frequent guest on radio and television broadcasts in Missouri as a political analyst and commentator. He has taught social studies courses to eighth, eleventh, and twelfth graders.

Special Curriculum Advisers

Larry Bybee
Secondary Social Studies Supervisor
Northside Independent School District
San Antonio, Texas

Betty Dean
Educational Consultant
Former Social Studies Supervisor, Bellaire H.S.
Houston, Texas

David Depew
Social Studies Consultant
Ector Independent School District
Odessa, Texas

Reviewers

Robert C. Barzdukas
Social Studies Teacher/Curriculum Specialist
Lamar High School, Lamar, CO

Roy Erickson
Social Studies Coordinator
San Juan Unified School District, Carmichael, CA

Lani Evans
Social Studies Teacher/District Consultant
Gunderson High School, San Jose, CA

Jesse Gladden
Social Studies Specialist
Baltimore City Public Schools, Baltimore, MD

Kenneth Hilton
Social Studies Coordinator
Rush-Henrietta Central School District, Henrietta, NY

Paul J. Luckey
History Department Chairperson
Aiken High School, Cincinnati, OH

Steven S. Toda
Social Studies Adviser
Los Angeles Unified School District, Los Angeles, CA

Cover: On March 1, 1792, Secretary of State Thomas Jefferson announced in a letter to the governors of the states ratification of what we now know as the Bill of Rights. The first ten amendments, originally proposed as twelve articles, became part of the Constitution. In Jefferson's circular letter, portions of which are shown on the cover, he transmitted the text of all twelve proposed articles and the text of individual state ratifications showing that only ten of the original twelve articles had been ratified.

Printed in the U.S.A.

Student's Edition ISBN: 0-395-73452-5
Teacher's Edition ISBN: 0-395-73453-3

1 2 3 4 5 6 7 8 9 - VH - 99 98 97 96 95

Readers

Cliff Adams
Shepherd High School
Shepherd, TX

Steve C. Anderson
Georgetown High School
Georgetown, TX

John C. Ashton III
Woodrow Wilson High School
Fairfax, VA

Larry Atkinson
Beech Grove High School
Beech Grove, IN

Carol Baker
Shenandoah High School
Middletown, IN

Karen E. Ball
Titusville High School
Titusville, FL

Everett Ballou
Crown Point High School
Crown Point, IN

Tim M. Bane
Patrick Henry High School
Roanoke, VA

Woody K. Bane, Jr
Halifax County High School
South Boston, VA

Gene Barham
Richmond, VA

Cretia Basham
Burleson High School
Burleson, TX

Bob Bass
Roseburg High School
Roseburg, OR

Darryl B. Belton
Oscoda Area High School
Oscoda, MI

Cecil Blankenship
Brownfield High School
Brownfield, TX

Ralph Booher, Jr.
John S. Battle High School
Bristol, VA

James E. Booth, Jr.
Green Run Senior High School
Virginia Beach, VA

Doris Brandon
Easley High School
Easley, SC

Don J. Branham
West Brook Sr. High School
Beaumont, TX

Jane Ann Breen
Marian Heights Academy
Ferdinand, IN

Edward 0. Bridgewater
Charlestown High School
Charlestown, IN

William A. Brisbois
Green Run Senior High School
Virginia Beach, VA

Gary Broadstreet
South Putnam High School
Greencastle, IN

Tom Brogan
Greenwood, IN

William Brown
James Island High School
Charlestown, SC

Linda Cabell
John Tyler High School
Tyler, TX

Shelvie R. Carr
Turner Ashby High School
Dayton, VA

John D. Cassell
St. Paul High School
St. Paul, VA

Dean Castle
Lebanon, OR

Tamra Clements
Cambridge City, IN

Donald A. Coller
McCutcheon High School
Lafayette, IN

Donald G. Cooper
Langley High School
McLean, VA

James Corey
Miami Killian High School
Miami, FL

Suzanne Crouch
Mauldin, SC

Jacqueline Ann Daley
Lake Taylor High School
Norfolk, VA

Marlene Davis
Airport High School
Cayce-West Colombia, SC

Vernon Defee
Hillcrest High School
Dalzell, SC

Joyce P. Deputy
Mathews High School
Mathews, VA

Ian W. Desborough
Cerritos High School
Artesia, CA

Dan W. Dickerson
Woodruff High School
Woodruff, SC

David L. Donmoyer
Pleasant Hill High School
Hemingway, SC

Richard Erwin
Rogers High School
Michigan City, IN

Rita R. Fletcher
Union, SC

Steven R. Ford
Jay County High School
Portland, IN

Robert J. Franzetti
David Crockett High School
Austin, TX

David E. Freelan
Eastern High School
Greentown, IN

Sue Pinkston Froehner
Livingston High School
Livingston, TX

Andrew Gaddy
St. John's High School
Darlington, SC

Steve Gentry
Crawfordsville High School
Crawfordsville, IN

Mike George
Brookville High School
Lynchburg, VA

Dianne Gibson
L.D. Bell High School
Hurst, TX

Rosemary Gindhart
Delta High School
Muncie, IN

Daniel Goble
Perry Central High School
Leopold, IN

Beverly J. Gore
Boonville, FL

Mary Scifres Grabianowski
Zionsville Community
 High School
Zionsville, IN

Richard D. Graham
Pine Bush High School
Pine Bush, NY

Stuart S. Graham
Washington, IN

Charlotte Griffith
Glenvar High School
Salem, VA

Hilda P. Hagarty
North Charlestown
 High School
Charlestown, SC

Lockwood Hall
Coeburn High School
Coeburn, VA

Mary C. Hanmer
Randolph Henry High School
Charlotte Courthouse, VA

Jon Harper
North Vermillion High School
Cayuga, IN

Pat Harry
Martin High School
Arlington, TX

Bruce Haynes
Frontier High School
Chalmers, IN

Linda Henderson
Falls Church High School
Falls Church, VA

Mildred H. Hinkle
Marion High School
Marion, IN

James E. Hodges, Jr.
Robert E. Lee High School
Staunton, VA

Robert J. Holub
Western Albemarle High School
Crozet, VA

Bobinette Hughes
Albemarle High School
Charlottesville, VA

Harvey Hurst
Penn High School
Mishawaka, IN

Karen G. Jenkins
Frank W. Cox High School
Virginia Beach, VA

Hugh Jeter
Union High School
Union, SC

Bobbie J. Johnson
Park View High School
Sterling, VA

Cheryl P. Johnson
Clintwood High School
Clintwood, VA

Linda Johnson
Nottoway High School
Nottoway, VA

Albert L. Jones
Chicago, IL

Richard C. Kaufman
Cowan High School
Muncie, IN

Patricia A. King
Herndon High School
Herndon, VA

Lisa Klopstock
Saratoga Springs, NY

Rita Koman
Osbourn High School
Manassas, VA

Lou Konig
Bellmont High School
Decatur, IN

Larry Lawlor
Warsaw High School
Warsaw, IN

Bill Lee
Horn Lake High School
Horn Lake, MS

Paul L. Legg
Lloyd C. Bird High School
Chesterfield, VA

Barbara G. Lewis
Monacan High School
Richmond, VA

Francis Libordi
Hornell High School
Hornell, NY

Richard C. Loesch
Mineral Wells High School
Mineral Wells, TX

Kaye B. Lucado
Randolph Henry High School
Charlotte Courthouse, VA

John Lucas
Molalla Union High School
Molalla, OR

William H. Martin, Jr.
Laurel Park High School
Martinsville, VA

Jon Marvin
Kokomo, IN

William H. McCarley
Sulphur Springs High School
Sulphur Springs, TX

John R. McCraw, Jr.
Martinsville High School
Martinsville, VA

Erin M. McCuster
Weston McEwen High School
Athena, OR

George McKinney
Carroll High School
Fort Wayne, IN

John H. McLaughlin
Virginia Beach, VA

Delano McMillin
Rogers High School
Michigan City, IN

Patsy Meeks
Boiling Springs High School
Spartanburg, SC

David E. Meinhard
Cumberland High School
Cumberland, VA

Kathy G. Miller
North White High School
Monon, IN

Delores Moreland
North Eugene High School
Eugene, OR

Phil Morgan
Tipton High School
Tipton, IN

James R. Morley
Huntsville High School
Huntsville, TX

Edward G. Motley
Tunstall High School
Dry Fork, VA

Wilbert G. Mueller
St. Helens High School
St. Helens, OR

Terry W. Mulins
North Tazewell, VA

Ralph Mundt
Portage High School
Portage, IN

Gavin Murdoch
Amsterdam, NY

Madeline Murphy
Chantilly High School
Chantilly, VA

Thomas V. Murphy
Tottenville High School
Staten Island, NY

Dorothy B. Neals
Dan River High School
Ringgold, VA

Mike E. Neilson
Danville Community
  High School
Danville, IN

Gary Nelson
Klein Oak High School
Spring, TX

Bruce I. Oliver
Northrop High School
Fort Wayne, IN

David A. Olson
Angola High School
Angola, IN

Linda Backmeyer Paust
Richmond, IN

Les Payne
Heppner High School
Heppner, OR

Jack Perry
Gulfport High School
Gulfport, MS

Martin Perry
Locust Valley High School
Locust Valley, NY

Jerry Petro
Union County High School
Liberty, IN

Robert E. Philbert
Marion High School
Marion, IN

Michael Pittman
Franklin High School
Franklin, OH

Anita J. Pitts
Milan High School
Milan, IN

John E. Poindexter
Summerville High School
Summerville, SC

Susan L. Portlock
Orange, VA

Kenneth I. Prowell
Chantilly High School
Chantilly, VA

Zandy Pustay
A&M Consolidated High School
College Station, TX

Julia N. Raap
J.L. McCullough High School
The Woodlands, TX

Donald G. Ray
Griffith High School
Griffith, IN

David Reves
Denver City High School
Denver City, TX

William B. Riffe
Middletown, IN

Mildred B. Rivers
Wade Hampton High School
Hampton, SC

Les Ross
Clatskanie High School
Clatskanie, OR

Roberto Salinas
Martin High School
Laredo, TX

Gloria Scanlon
Tampa Catholic High School
Tampa, FL

Susan Sharpe
Irmo High School
Columbia, SC

Jamie Shealy
Ninety Six High School
Plain City, OH

Donald Bruce Smith
Brownsburg High School
Brownsburg, IN

Gilbert Smith III
Gate City High School
Gate City, VA

Ray H. Smith
Patrick County High School
Stuart, VA

Joan L. Spence
Spotswood High School
Penn Laird, VA

David M. Stacy
Charlottesville High School
Charlottesville, VA

Michael Stanley
Spencer, IN

Robert E. Stevens
Airport High School
Cayce-West Columbia, SC

Bert Stewart
J.R. Tucker High School
Richmond, VA

Kenneth F. Stewart
Madison High School
Portland, OR

Kenneth G. Stuart
Frankfort, IN

James V. Sullivan
Jackson Public Schools
Jackson, MS

James Swaney
Winamac Community High
School
Winamac, IN

Terry L. Swindell
Monroe Central High School
Parker City, IN

William Tatom
Bedford-North Lawrence
 High School
Bedford, IN

Hubert D. Thomas
Gaffney High School
Gaffney, SC

Cheryl Tosch
Columbia High School
West Columbia, TX

Mary Jane Trefil
Albemarle High School
Charlottesville, VA

Joan Tretham
Merritt Island High
Merritt Island, FL

Tony L. Trimble
Arthur Campbell High School
Plainfield IN

Azmi A. Uthman
John Handley High School
Winchester, VA

Douglas M. Vermillion
Anderson, IN

June Walker
Christiansburg High School
Christiansburg, VA

Marie Waller
E.C Glass High School
Lynchburg, VA

David Walls
Jefferson High School
Lafayette, IN

Hattie Lois Watkins
Polytechnic High School
Fort Worth, TX

Sandra Weatherholtz
Page County High School
Shenandoah, VA

Joseph Weaver
Oak Hill High School
Converse, IN

Robert A. Weaver
R. Nelson Snider High School
Fort Wayne, IN

Edward M. Wessel
Evansville, IN

Greg Whaley
Jac-Cen-Del High School
Osgood, IN

Susan White-Trivette
Laurel Hill, NC

Nancy Whitley
Virginia High School
Bristol, VA

James S. Whitmer
Flagler Palm Coast High School
Bunnell, FL

David Willett
Cradock High School
Portsmouth, VA

Gene Wilson
Saginaw, MI

Dennis Wingfield
Sperryville, VA

Robert Worthy
Thomas Jefferson High School
Port Arthur, TX

Harold D. Wright
Warren County High School
Front Royal, VA

Hazel M. Young
Glen Oak High School
Canton, OH

Ronald D. Young
Buffalo Gap High School
Swoope, VA

CONTENTS

Patriotic celebration

The Supreme Court building

UNIT 3	Political Participation: Government by the People	223

Political convention

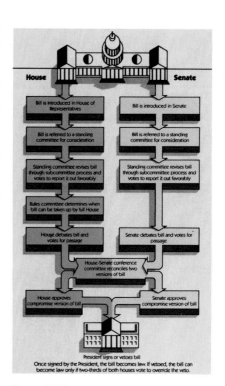

How a bill becomes law

Federico Peña,
U.S. Secretary of
Transportation

Justice Sandra Day O'Connor

CASE STUDIES
of Controversial Issues

510-1

**Warning label
on CD**

**Ben Johnson,
Olympic sprinter**

Delegates, United Farm Workers convention

Christine Todd Whitman, governor of New Jersey

Toppled statue, Moscow

Government in America

This text helps you learn about the many people, institutions, and processes that make up the government of the United States—from the President and Congress to your state and local governments. This is knowledge that you—and all Americans—need to become informed, involved citizens.

Chapter Openers
Chapters begin with a dramatic photograph, significant quotation, absorbing introduction, and full outline of chapter content.

Section Openers
Sections form the basis of chapter organization. Each section begins with questions directing you to the main ideas.

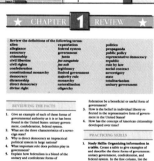

Chapter Reviews
At the end of each chapter you will find a Chapter Review with questions that will help you check your comprehension and challenge your understanding of the chapter.

FEATURES

Government in America *includes several high-interest features. These features not only complement and enrich the narrative, but also give you additional skills practice.*

Citizenship Skills
In this feature, lessons focus on practical, everyday ways in which citizens and government interact.

As Others See Us
This feature provides you with a foreign perspective on key American government issues or practices.

You Decide
Actual legal cases, along with controversial issues, give you a chance to act as a decision-maker.

Your Turn
Students from across the country share their opinions and experiences on government.

Critical Thinking
These case studies give you practice in the skills needed to make reasoned decisions about matters of public concern.

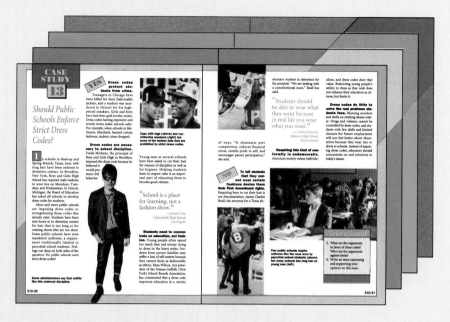

Case Studies of Controversial Issues This special 32-page section enables you to involve yourself emotionally and practically in many of the real-life controversies that decision-makers face today. From gun control to mandatory drug testing, from women in combat to special schools for African American males, you get to see all sides of an issue—and decide what your position is.

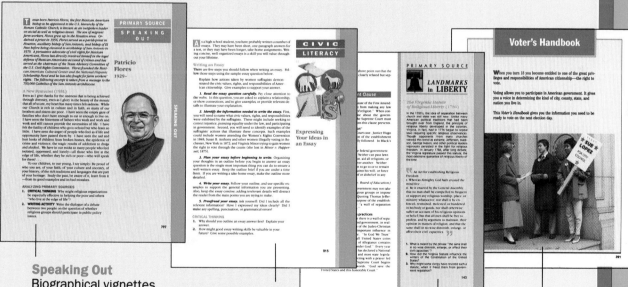

Speaking Out
Biographical vignettes of well-known figures highlight personal involvement in the nation's political life.

Civic Literacy
This feature makes the connections between government and other disciplines and activities.

Landmarks in Liberty
Excerpts from documents, speeches, and Supreme Court decisions give you a chance to work with primary sources.

Voter's Handbook
A special section on the registration and voting processes with practical information for both new and experienced voters.

Dear student:

Although many years have passed since I was in high school, I can still recall those days quite vividly. I often reflect with fondness upon the many fine teachers, friends, and events that have had a profound impact on my life.

I was just an average student, concerned with extracurricular activities such as listening to music, playing sports, or working after school. Like most high school students, I too was required to take a course in American government. Why, I thought, did I have to take a government course? After all, wasn't government something dirty? Or boring? Or both?

Although my government textbook was boring, Mr. Clifford Dodds, my high school government teacher, was not. Mr. Dodds had the ability to arouse even the most disinterested students. His uncanny knack of drawing upon just the right anecdotes made his classes come alive!

However, it was Mr. Jack Anderson, my first college history and government teacher, who had the greatest impact upon me. Mr. Anderson, a former high school teacher, was a gifted orator and an inspirational leader. Each lecture was like a magnificent symphony, as students hung on his every word. More importantly, Mr. Anderson treated each student with the utmost respect while he challenged us to live up to our potential. This was the person I wanted to be like.

In writing this book, I have tried to capture that same spirit and enthusiasm that Mr. Dodds and Mr. Anderson brought to their classrooms. More specifically, the text contains three interrelated themes that I believe embody my mentors' philosophies.

First, you must understand that government and politics are not something evil, but are great human endeavors. The vast majority of government employees are honest, hardworking people who strive to alleviate society's problems. Of course, not everyone can agree upon just how to solve those problems. Rather than fighting about it, we compromise, and that's what politics is all about.

Second, you need to become aware of our political system, because it affects virtually every aspect of your life. Turning on a light, making a phone call, buying a loaf of bread, driving your car, or mailing a letter are just a few activities regulated by government. You need to know what government does and how much it costs. As Thomas Jefferson once wrote, "If a nation expects to be ignorant and free . . . it expects what never was and will never be."

And finally, you have an obligation to participate in our political system, and if you don't like what's going on, do something about it. In America you have the freedom to vote, run for public office, contribute to political candidates, bring lawsuits, form associations, write letters, and even to protest.

I only hope that when you finish using **Government in America**, you will have a better understanding of and appreciation for our dynamic political system. It is without question a singularly priceless, matchless, and magnificent form of government. Long may it wave!

Sincerely,

UNIT
★ 1 ★

FOUNDATIONS of AMERICAN GOVERNMENT

1

Foundations of American Government
(pp. 1–138)

Unit Overview

Unit One introduces students to the basic elements of American government. Chapter 1 opens by discussing the characteristics of states (in the sense of nations) and then focuses on theories of government, the functions of governments, their different forms, the principles that guide American democracy, and the concept of citizenship. Chapter 2 deals with the origins of American government. It describes English political traditions brought to America, forms of colonial government, the upheaval and aftermath of the American Revolution, and the drafting and ratification of the Constitution. Chapter 3 explains the principles that form the foundation of the Constitution, describes the amendment process, and discusses informal methods of changing the Constitution. In Chapter 4, the division of power between the national and state governments is discussed, along with the responsibilities of both levels. The chapter explains how the national government's power has increased over time, and discusses the ways in which federalism links the fifty states.

Photo
Washington, D.C.

CHAPTER 1
PRINCIPLES OF GOVERNMENT
(pp. 2–27)

	Section Objectives	**Section Resources**

Section 1
Government Is Necessary in Every Society

☐ list the characteristics of states
☐ explain the different theories about government

Section 2
Governments Act Through a Political System

☐ explain the duties of government
☐ describe some causes of political conflict

Section 3
Government Takes Many Forms

☐ explain the different ways in which political authority can be divided
☐ describe the different forms of political leadership

▲ SKILLS PRACTICE WORKSHEET **1**

● CITIZENSHIP WORKSHEET **1**

▲ TRANSPARENCY **1**

Section 4
Principles Guide American Democracy

☐ describe the rights that Americans have as individuals
☐ list four basic political ideals of American government

■ SKILLS CHALLENGE WORKSHEET **1**

Section 5
Citizenship Is a Special Status

☐ explain how American citizenship is defined
☐ explain how a person can gain or lose American citizenship
☐ describe the categories of non-citizen residents

Essential Elements

The list below shows Essential Elements relevant to this chapter.
(The complete list of Essential Elements appears in the introductory
pages of this Teacher's Edition.)

Section 1: 1A, 1C, 1D, 2A, 8B, 8F

Section 2: 1A, 4A, 5A, 6B

Section 3: 1B, 1C, 1D, 3C, 6F

Citizenship Skills feature (p. 17): 4C, 4D

Section 4: 1D, 6A, 6B, 6D, 6F, 6G, 6I, 8H

Section 5: 1C, 3C, 5A, 6D, 6E, 6G

Chapter Review: 1A, 1D, 3C, 4D, 5A, 6D, 6F, 6G, 8A, 8B, 8C

Section Resources are keyed
for student abilities:
▲ = Basic
● = All Levels
■ = Average/Advanced

Homework Options

Each section contains activities labeled "Guided/Independent Practice," "Reteaching/Correctives," and "Enrichment/Extension." You may wish to choose from among these activities when assigning homework.

Students Acquiring English Activities

Have students use newspapers to find evidence of the government services listed on p. 10. Form six groups to look for and cut out articles related to: (1) public health; (2) public safety; (3) public transportation; (4) public communications; (5) public education; (6) general welfare. Each group will be responsible for one category. Use the categories as titles for differently colored bulletin-board sections around the room. For two to three weeks, students should post articles under the appropriate category. Then have each group present its articles to the class and explain which issues may most affect them or their parents now or in the near future.

LISTENING/SPEAKING: Invite a naturalized citizen to your class to describe how and why he or she decided to become an American citizen. Have students prepare questions in advance and provide the speaker with these questions before he or she meets with the class.

Case Studies

When teaching this chapter, you may use Case Study 10, which debates mandatory national service, or Case Study 14, which deals with making English the official language. (Case Studies may be found following p. 510.)

Teacher Bibliography

Austin, Erik W. and Jerome M. Chubb. *Political Facts of the United States Since 1789.* Columbia University Press, 1986. Statistics on American political history and life.

Mason, Alpheus and Gordon E. Baker, eds. *Free Government in the Making.* 4th ed. Oxford University Press, 1985. An overview of American political philosophy.

Student Bibliography

Hobbes, Thomas. *Leviathan.* Many editions. Famous seventeenth-century treatise that describes the origins of government and defines politics and political institutions.

Social Contract: Essays by Locke, Hume, and Rousseau. Oxford University Press, 1962.

Literature

Lewis, Sinclair. *It Can't Happen Here.* NAL-Dutton, 1970. A demagogue becomes the dictator of the United States.

Meer, Fatima. *Higher than Hope: The Authorized Biography of Nelson Mandela.* HarperCollins, 1991.

Meltzer, Milton. *George Washington and the Birth of Our Nation.* Franklin Watts, 1986.

Orwell, George. *Animal Farm.* Harcourt Brace Jovanovich, 1954. After the farm animals revolt against the humans, a new tyranny replaces the old.

Zamyatin, Yevgeny. *We.* Translated by Mirra Ginsburg. Avon, 1983. A future state is run mathematically and people have numbers instead of names.

CHAPTER RESOURCES

Study Guide/Review 1
Workbook Chapter 1
Chapter 1 Test, Forms A–C

Films and Videotapes*

Government and Law. Rev. ed. (Series title: *Debt To The Past.*) 14 min. MIS, 1976. f. Examines the American system of government.

A World of Ideas with Bill Moyers: Henry Steele Commager. 28 min. PBS, 1988. v. Professor Commager discusses American democracy as based on the Founding Fathers' belief in individual honor and in posterity.

Software*

American Government I (Apple, IBM, Macintosh). Queue. Students learn about the development and processes of the American governmental system through interactive tutorials. Three programs cover American democracy, popular sovereignty, representative government, separation of powers, checks and balances, the Supreme Court, the Constitution, and the American political system.

U.S. Government (Apple, IBM). Queue. Students explore the historical significance of each of the three branches of government as well as the functions and limits of power. Provides practice in research skills.

---

* For a complete guide to audiovisual sources, see page T22.

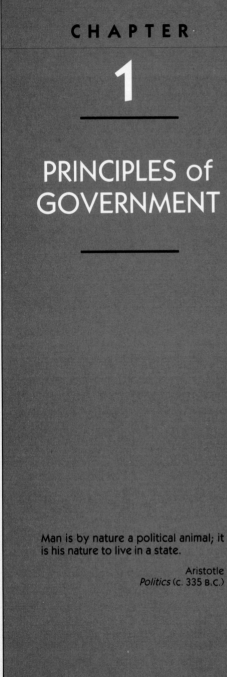

CHAPTER

1

PRINCIPLES of
GOVERNMENT

Man is by nature a political animal; it
is his nature to live in a state.

Aristotle
Politics (c. 335 B.C.)

Photo
Naturalization ceremony.

T homas Paine called government "a necessary evil." Thomas Jefferson remarked that he would rather have newspapers without a government than a government without newspapers. Ralph Waldo Emerson wrote, "The less government we have the better." Ronald Reagan declared, "Government is not the solution to our problem. Government is the problem."

Such statements suggest that while Americans are justifiably proud of our own form of government, we have traditionally been suspicious of government in general. Does government protect freedom, or stifle it? Will government bring prosperity, or strangle it? In order to answer these questions, we must begin by looking at the reasons why governments were established in the first place. This chapter will explore why and how governments developed, and what governments mean to their citizens.

3

CHAPTER SUPPORT MATERIAL

Skills Practice Worksheet 1

Skills Challenge Worksheet 1

Citizenship Worksheet 1

Transparency 1

Study Guide/Review 1

Workbook Chapter 1

Chapter 1 Test, Forms A-C

Government Is Necessary in Every Society *(pp. 4–8)*

Section Objectives
☐ list the characteristics of states
☐ explain the different theories about government

Vocabulary
state, sovereignty, citizenship, allegiance, government, public policy, legitimacy, divine right, social contract

FOCUS
● Write the section title on the board—"Government Is Necessary in Every Society." Next to it write "Why?" See if every student can list a different reason why government is necessary, and write these reasons on the board. (Remind students that *government* refers to political authority at the local as well as state and national levels.)

Ask if any students believe that government is *not* necessary in every society. Have them explain their views.

1A, 1C, 1D, 2A, 8B, 8F

SECTION 1 — Government Is Necessary in Every Society

ACCESS	The Main Ideas
1	**What are the characteristics of states?** *pages 4–7*
2	**What are the different theories about government?** *pages 7–8*

The Greek scholar Aristotle, who is quoted in the introduction to this chapter, was one of the first people to study the workings of government. His ideas about people and politics were based on his own experience with the *polis,* the city-state of ancient Greece. These city-states were small and fiercely independent communities. For their time in history, they were also unusual, because they were self-governing.

For Aristotle, a political unit like the *polis* seemed the only natural way for people to live. He could not imagine people living without the laws and orderly society that government can provide. (The word *politics,* in fact, comes from *polis.*) Although the Greek city-state differed in many ways from modern nations, we still take many of Aristotle's ideas as a guide for studying politics and government.

Political units called states all share the common features of population, territory, government, and sovereignty. One distinguishing feature of the United States is the diversity of its population.

4

Background: *Cultural Literacy* Aristotle (384–322 B.C.) explored the fields of drama, biology, and rhetoric as well as political science.

He invented the word *democracy* and many other government terms. Aristotle spent part of his career as a tutor to Alexander the Great.

1A, 1C

States in the Modern World

The modern equivalent of Aristotle's *polis* is an independent political unit called the **state.** Although *state* is the most correct term, people more commonly use the terms *nation, country,* or even *nation-state* to mean generally the same thing. There are about 170 states or nations in the world today, including the United States. While these states are very different, they share four basic characteristics: population, territory, government, and **sovereignty** (SAHV-ur-en-tee) — the state's right to rule itself.

This kind of "state" must not be confused with the political subdivisions of the United States. California, Iowa, Texas, Vermont, Illinois, North Carolina, and the other "states" are not sovereign. They cannot negotiate treaties with foreign countries, coin money, or overturn laws of the United States government. Before the adoption of the Constitution in 1788, the original thirteen states behaved in many ways like small separate countries, and so the name continued.

Population

Obviously, all nation-states must have people. Their population may be large or small. For example, Iceland has about 260,000 people, and tiny Liechtenstein's population is about a tenth of that. By contrast, the United States has about 260 million people. India has close to a billion people, and China's population is over a billion.

The people in a country may be very similar or very diverse in language, race, customs, and culture. Although the American people represent an amazing variety of different races, religions, and backgrounds, most Americans think of themselves primarily as "Americans." For this reason, the United States has been described as a "melting pot" that blends many cultures into one. On the other hand, Americans are also proud of their differing backgrounds. Their own religions and cultures are important in their lives. From this point of view, the United States has been compared to a "salad bowl" with many different, but separate, ingredients.

Figure 1–1 shows the different ancestry groups of many Americans. Because the United States is both a "melting pot" and a "salad bowl," many Americans have ancestors from two or more different places.

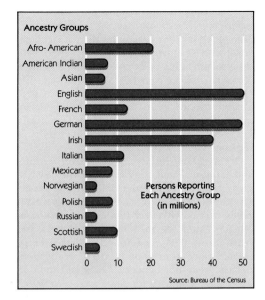

Figure 1–1 AMERICANS' ANCESTRY In a recent census, Americans were asked where they traced their ancestors. This graph shows the nationalities they named most frequently. 8B

No matter how diverse its population is, each nation makes a legal distinction between its own people and those of foreign countries. All states confer a special status, usually called **citizenship,** on their own people. This special status includes both rights and responsibilities. A citizen's responsibility to his or her country begins with loyalty, or **allegiance.** Other duties may include paying taxes, obeying the laws, and serving the state in some capacity. The benefits of citizenship usually include the right to take part in the political system and protection against outside attack.

Territory

Every nation-state occupies a particular territory, or geographic area on the earth's surface. The term *territory* refers to the area within a definite, recognizable boundary that separates one state from another. Territory includes not only land but also coastal waters, inland waters (lakes and rivers), the air above the land, and all natural resources on or under the land (such as timber, coal, and iron ore).

5

EXPLANATION

After reviewing the content of the section, you may want to consider the following activities:

Cultural Literacy

● CRITICAL THINKING The word *government* is derived from the Latin verb *gubernare,* which means "to direct, or steer." **How does this help define the term government?** (The purpose of government is to direct, or steer, the state.) Ask students to think of other words related to *government.* (Govern, governor.)

👥 Multiculturalism

Together with the class, create a chart similar to Figure 1–1 showing the ancestry groups of members of the class.

▲ **Why has the United States been called both a "melting pot" and a "salad bowl"?** (A melting pot blends many cultures into one; a salad bowl contains different, but separate, cultures.)
● CRITICAL THINKING **What are the advantages of such a diverse population?** (The country can benefit from the skills and practices of a wide range of people.) **What are the possible disadvantages?** (Differences among people could lead to tension and conflict unless everyone learns to accept and respect other groups.)

Check for Understanding
▲ Make sure that students understand the difference between a "state" as an independent country and a "state" as a part of the United States.

Figure 1–1
● **According to the graph, where do most Americans trace their ancestors?** (England, Germany, and Ireland.) **What is the ancestry of students in the class?**

Background: *Civic Participation* Students should recognize the term *allegiance* from the Pledge of Allegiance.

The symbol 👥 denotes active participation strategies.

Activities are keyed for student abilities:
▲ = Basic
● = All Levels
■ = Average/Advanced

Global Awareness

In strictly technical terms, the word *country* refers to land and territory, while *nation* means people sharing the same language and culture, or *nationality*. *Nation-state,* then, technically refers to a political state in which most people have the same language and culture.

● **Is the United States a nation-state?** (No.) **Is Japan?** (Yes.) **How does geography help or hinder the development of nation-states?** (States in isolated territories, such as islands, are more likely to contain a single people; states in territories easily reached by foreign peoples are more likely to contain several nations.)

Values

● CRITICAL THINKING Throughout history, political leaders have often also been spiritual and religious leaders. Church and state, in other words, have been intertwined. The separating of the two, which started in the American colonies in the 1600's, was a bold idea. **How has the separation of church and state affected the development of religion in this country?** (It has allowed a variety of religious groups to practice in freedom.)

Cooperative Learning

● CRITICAL THINKING Divide the class into small groups. Have each group draw up a list of ways in which their lives would be different if government did not exist. (It might help to suggest categories, such as *Safety* and *Education,* to get students started.) Then have groups compare their lists.

The countries of the modern world vary as much in territory as they do in population. Among the smallest geographically are Liechtenstein, with 62 square miles, and San Marino, with 23.6 square miles. (For comparison, the city of Houston, Texas, covers 579 square miles.) The United States is among the largest countries, with a land area of more than 3,600,000 square miles. Canada is still larger. Our northern neighbor counts more than 3,800,000 square miles of territory within its borders.

Throughout history, disputes over territory and national boundaries have been the cause of many conflicts. While the United States was acquiring its territory, for example, there were disputes over nearly every border, from Maine to Oregon. More recently, the state of Israel has been involved in numerous conflicts over its borders since its creation in 1948. Border skirmishes broke out between China and India in 1959 and continued for three years. In 1980, Iran and Iraq renewed a long-standing military fight over their common border. Clearly, the political boundaries of its territory are important to any country.

Government

All states also must have **government**. In any state or nation, government can be defined as the *people* and *institutions* with authority to establish and enforce *public policies*. Most of the rest of this book will be concerned with investigating some aspect of this definition as it applies to American government.

In more general terms, the *people* who run a nation may be called by a variety of titles — king, queen, premier, president, governor, emperor, shah, or dictator, to name just a few. The *institutions* can include a constitution, a court system, a legislature, an army, and other established parts or practices of the state. A **public policy** is any course of government action directed toward a national goal. Protecting consumers, providing medical care, and competing in space technology are all examples of public policy goals.

To make policy, the people and institutions of the government need to have *authority*. They must have the right to make decisions that others will follow. Many people, of course, have some

type of authority. An umpire has the authority to call players "safe" in a baseball game. A teacher has authority to award grades on a test or report. Neither an umpire nor a teacher, however, has authority to license automobiles or to make people pay taxes. Only a government has the authority to make and enforce such public policies.

The idea of "authority" must include the ability to make people accept the government's rules or policies, by using rewards or punishment if necessary. This is *power*. Without it, the government will not be strong enough to carry out its authority. For example, if a person refuses to pay her taxes, the U.S. government has the power to seize her bank account, impose a fine, or take other steps to collect the taxes. So, to maintain its authority, a government must be able to use significantly greater power than any other group, individual, or organization in the state.

Power and authority are not the only reasons people comply with the policies of their government. People follow these policies because they believe the government has **legitimacy**. That is, people *accept* its authority and its right to lead them. A government with enough power can exist for a while, usually by force, even if the people do not accept it. But legitimacy is necessary if the government is to be stable, effective, and lasting.

Sovereignty

The last characteristic that all nation-states share is sovereignty — the political authority to act independently. There are three conventional tests for determining whether a state is sovereign.

First, a state must be able to decide and carry out its own foreign policy. Second, a state must be able to send and receive diplomats or ambassadors. Finally, a state must be able to protect its own territory and keep foreigners out if it wishes to do so. By these criteria, the United States has been a sovereign state since 1776, when the Declaration of Independence announced that the former colonies now had all the powers of independent states.

In reality, sovereignty is a relative term. The United States, Germany, China, Great Britain, France, Japan, and other major powers clearly are sovereign states. Some states, however, are subject to greater outside influence than

Background: *History*
Students tend to think of government and the state as being the same thing. Governments, however, come and go, while the state continues to exist. For example, France has had thirteen governments since 1789, while the United States has only had one.

others. Until a few years ago, for instance, the Soviet Union controlled the foreign policies of the
countries that were part of the "Soviet bloc" —
Hungary, Poland, Romania and other Eastern European states. Even so, despite Soviet control,
those countries were considered sovereign.

1A, 1D, 2A

Origins of Government

The beginnings of organized government
took place more than 5,000 years ago, along with
the development of early civilizations. Four
places in the world are considered the birthplaces of civilization — Mesopotamia in western
Asia; Egypt, along the Nile in northern Africa; the
Yellow River plains in northern China; and the
Indus Valley in northeast India. In each of these
river valleys, wandering people settled down to
build villages, plant and cultivate crops, and
tame herds of animals.

Even tribes who moved from place to place
had developed rules or laws in order to travel and
live together. With this new, more settled life-
style, people now had to work together even

more closely. Leaders — usually priests or war-
riors — emerged to organize workers for large
projects, such as making canals to control floods,
building walls for defense, and constructing temples for worship. To get the work done and to
keep order among the people in growing cities,
the leaders issued orders and made laws. Leaders
also went to war to protect the people and the
territory they ruled. All the characteristics of organized government were being shaped in these
early river valley civilizations.

Theories of government

Aristotle, who studied the politics of the
Greek city-state, was among the first to look
closely at how governments work. He asked himself: How do rulers gain (and keep) authority and
power? What is the relationship between the
people and their government? As modern states
developed in Europe, later scholars and historians asked these same basic questions about
government. They developed several different
theories, or explanations.

Some thought that the state was a natural
stage in the evolution of human society, growing

Figure 1–2 BIRTHPLACES OF CIVILIZATION Early forms of government
developed in the four river valley civilizations shown on this
map. 8B

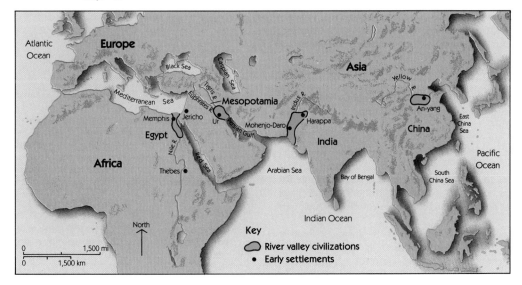

● Have students write a brief
essay comparing the divine right
and social contract theories of
government from the point of
view of the average citizen.

RETEACHING/CORRECTIVES
▲ Write the following equation
on the board: *State = Population
+ Territory + Government +
Sovereignty.* Have students copy
the equation on a sheet of paper
and then define each of the
terms in the equation.

ENRICHMENT/EXTENSION
■ Have students select one of
the four river valley civilizations
shown in Figure 1–2 and write a
brief report about it—the years it
existed, its government and
economy, its major cultural
achievements, and so on. Then
discuss with the class the similarities and differences among the
four civilizations.

Figure 1–2
● *In what areas are the four
river valleys shown on the
map located?* (Egypt,
Mesopotamia, India, and
China.) *What are the names
of the rivers?* (Nile, Tigris
and Euphrates, Indus, and
Yellow River.) *On what
continents are they found?*
(Africa and Asia.)

The symbol ⁞ denotes
active participation strategies.

Activities are keyed for
student abilities:
▲ = Basic
● = All Levels
■ = Average/Advanced

Section 1 Review Answers

1. Population, territory, government, sovereignty.
2. A legitimate government does not need to force people to obey it.
3. **(a)** From God. **(b)** Selection by the governed.
4. Locke said that people have "natural rights." A ruler must protect these rights and, failing to do so, can be replaced.

Critical thinking If other governments do not recognize it as legitimate, they might not respect its borders or might seek to overthrow it.

CLOSURE

● Have students consider Aristotle's statement, "Man is by nature a political animal; it is his nature to live in a state." Ask them if, on the basis of the information in the section, they agree with Aristotle, and why or why not. Then have students read Section 2, noting the general duties of government.

out of the family relationship between parents and children. Rulers were seen as "parents," with authority to guide and punish their "children" — the people of the state.

Another theory saw a strong leader as the most important element in the state. Such rulers would take power by force, creating myths and legends proving to the people that they were "superior" and their rule could not be challenged.

Political thinkers in 17th-century Europe developed a similar theory — the **divine right** of kings. Royal power, they said, came from God, and no authority on earth could take it away. People therefore were obliged to obey their ruler without question, as they would obey God. Although it was European rulers who used the term "divine right," this explanation of power was very old. Rulers in many ancient civilizations — China and Egypt, for example — had claimed either to be gods or to have the gods' favor.

The social contract

Most of these theories of government focused only on the rulers, not the people of a state. The idea of a social contract was the first to acknowledge that the people themselves had any rights or powers. In 1651, the English philosopher Thomas Hobbes suggested in his book *Leviathan* that, long before government developed, humans lived in a "state of nature." There people had complete freedom to do as they pleased, provided they were powerful and resourceful enough to do so. Only the strongest and fittest survived. In Hobbes's words, life in the state of nature was "solitary, poor, nasty, brutish, and short."

To improve their lives (Hobbes continued), people came together to create a state. They made, in effect, a social contract, or agreement, in which one superior person was selected to rule over the rest. The contract was rather one-sided, for the people agreed to surrender all their freedoms to this sovereign ruler in exchange for protection. Nevertheless, Hobbes's theory was the first in which the people voluntarily took part in creating a state.

Hobbes lived and wrote during a time of great political turmoil in England. Many people rejected the monarch's claim of "divine right" and demanded more rights for themselves. In

1690 another English philosopher, John Locke, took a different and more optimistic view of the social contract. Locke believed that people had "natural rights" to life, liberty, and property. In making a social contract, people agreed to obey the government or ruler, to pay taxes, and to follow any reasonable laws. But in return, the ruler was obliged to protect their "natural rights." If the ruler did not, said Locke, the contract was broken. The people would be free to revolt and establish a new social contract — a new government.

The social contract theory, especially Locke's idea of "natural rights," had a remarkable impact on political thinkers of the eighteenth century. At the time of the American Revolution, many American leaders had studied these ideas and been influenced by them. As Chapter 2 will show, these principles would help shape American government.

SECTION 1 REVIEW

Vocabulary and key terms

state (5)   public policy (6)
sovereignty (5)   legitimacy (6)
citizenship (5)   divine right (8)
allegiance (5)   social contract (8)
government (6)

For review

1. Identify the four basic features of a nation-state. **1A**
2. Why is it important for a government to have legitimacy? **1A**
3. (a) According to the "divine right" theory, where did rulers get their power? (b) How did a ruler or government gain power in Hobbes's idea of the social contract? **1A**
4. What new ideas did Locke add to the "social contract" theory? **1A**

Critical thinking

THINKING ABOUT BASIC IDEAS   Why is it important for a government to be seen as legitimate by other governments as well as by its own people? **8F**

SECTION 2
Governments Act Through a Political System

ACCESS	The Main Ideas

1 What are the duties of government?
pages 9–11

2 What are some causes of political conflict?
page 11

According to the definition of *government* given in Section 1, governments "establish and enforce public policies." Policies are a government's plans for action, which are aimed at certain goals such as a stronger defense, better health care, quality education, or a growing economy.

The actions (or policies) taken by modern governments fall into four broad areas: social order, national defense, public services, and social standards. To fulfill their functions and carry out their responsibilities in these areas, governments must work through the processes of conflict and compromises that make up **politics**.

1A

Areas of Government Action

Keeping order in society

Perhaps the first responsibility of government, as suggested long ago by Aristotle, is to keep the society orderly and peaceful. The need for rules and laws to help maintain order was one reason that government developed as soon as many people began to live close together. As the English political leader Edmund Burke (1729–1797) put it, "Good order is the foundation of all good things." Burke meant that only in an orderly society can people achieve their individual and collective goals. In a society torn by violence and disorder, people can achieve little.

To maintain order among the people in a state, governments pass laws to prevent crime and ensure people's safety. They set up courts to settle disputes, employ police to capture criminals, and build prisons to punish offenders.

Crimes and illegal actions are not the only threats to an orderly society. Governments also

ensure order in other ways — such as issuing money, enforcing legal contracts, making traffic regulations, and licensing drivers and doctors.

Providing national defense

To protect the nation's sovereignty, government must establish a defense system that provides security for the nation and its people. To guard against threats of attack, modern governments maintain well-trained, well-equipped military forces. They also watch for internal threats such as treason or rebellion. To discourage spying and protect military secrets, they establish intelligence-gathering agencies.

In addition, governments rely on negotiations, agreements, and treaties with foreign nations to help protect national security. These agreements are part of what is called "foreign policy." Sovereign states also take responsibility for protecting their citizens who are traveling or working outside the country.

General Colin Powell, Chairman of the Joint Chiefs of Staff from 1989 to 1993, here speaks at a press conference during the Persian Gulf War (1991).

9

Governments Act Through a Political System *(pp. 9–11)*

Section Objectives
☐ explain the duties of government
☐ describe some causes of political conflict

Vocabulary
politics

 FOCUS

● Have students consider the following questions: *Can you imagine a life without choice? Give some examples of choices you make every day.*

Now imagine that you and nine other people choose the same thing, but there is only one of these things to go around. What happens next?

What happens next is politics in its basic human sense.

EXPLANATION
After reviewing the content of the section, you may want to consider the following activities:

Politics
● CRITICAL THINKING *Why is keeping order considered the first responsibility of government?* (Without order, a society and its members would not be able to meet any of their other goals.)

Economics

Have students review the list of public services provided by government.

● CRITICAL THINKING **Why would it be difficult or impractical for individuals to provide most of these services?** (They are complicated and expensive.) **Could private companies provide some of these services? What would be the advantages and disadvantages?** (Yes. Contracting private companies might save money by introducing competition, but it also might affect services if these companies tried to cut corners.)

Cooperative Learning

● Practice compromise as a way of solving conflicts. Divide the class into three groups: two will be opposing sides in a dispute and the third will devise a compromise solution acceptable to both sides. See p. 11 for possible topics of dispute.

GUIDED/INDEPENDENT PRACTICE

● Ask students to examine newspapers, magazines, or television for examples of the four areas of government action outlined on pp. 9–11. Students should bring examples to class for discussion.

RETEACHING/CORRECTIVES

▲ Have students outline the section. They should include the four areas of government action in their outline and give examples of public services. Remind them to use the boldface headings in the section as clues for important concepts.

ENRICHMENT/EXTENSION

■ Have students write a letter to the editor giving their opinion on

Public services provided by government touch many aspects of daily life. What essential services do you notice in this city street scene?

Providing public services

Governments provide their citizens with many essential services that would be difficult or impractical for individuals to provide for themselves. Some of these services also contribute to keeping society orderly. In the United States, for example, governments act in these important areas of public services:

- Public health — *clean water supply, solid waste management, polio vaccinations, meat inspection, restaurant licensing, quarantines, drug testing, mental health programs, licensing of physicians.*
- Public safety — *traffic control, building codes, highway construction standards, fire prevention, regulation of air traffic, highway speed limits, licensing drivers.*
- Public transportation — *constructing and maintaining highways, canals, harbors, bridges, mass transit systems.*
- Public communications — *broadcasting regulations, postal services, licensing radio and television stations.*

- Public education — *establishing school systems, licensing teachers, paying teachers' and bus drivers' salaries, supporting research, offering scholarships, promoting adult education.*
- General welfare — *retirement pensions, veterans' hospitals, public housing, protection of natural resources, special programs for the disabled, unemployment compensation, agricultural assistance, parks, libraries, and museums.*

Not every government in the world provides the same public services for its citizens. Some offer more services, some fewer, than the United States does. Moreover, public service functions usually are shared by national, state, and local governments.

Promoting social standards

A final area of government action is the promotion of certain standards of behavior. It is frequently said that "government cannot legislate morality." In other words, it is difficult for any

10

Photo
Government-provided services illustrated in the picture include fire protection, traffic control (stoplights, street signs, crosswalks), license plates, streets and gutters, buses.

Background: *Economics*
In *Wealth of Nations,* economist Adam Smith argued that the state should perform limited functions (defense, justice) that individuals could not provide for a profit.

government to prevent actions that an over-whelming number of its citizens want to do. Nevertheless, governments are seldom neutral on such matters. They can — and do — pass laws to enforce the standards of the leaders or the majority.

In the United States, the Constitution firmly protects individuals' rights. Nonetheless, government may take action to prevent certain individual actions. It may, for example, outlaw cocaine, destroy marijuana crops, ban slot machines, restrict pornography, require marriage licenses, limit divorces, and impose age limits on drinking alcohol.

4A, 5A, 6B

Conflicts and Politics

Conflicts over values

People everywhere have conflicts and disagreements. Social conflicts range from arguments in a restaurant to riots in the street. These conflicts seem to have many causes. Basically, though, most conflicts arise from disputes over things of value — objects or ideas that people believe are desirable or worthwhile.

Some values are tangible — that is, they are things that can be touched, such as gold, oil, cars, money, or land. One reason for their value is that they are scarce or hard to obtain. Gold, for instance, is a very valuable metal because it is both scarce and beautiful. If gold were as plentiful as sand, it would not bring high prices, nor would people be tempted to steal it.

Many values, on the other hand, are intangible. These include such things as respect, affection, recognition, social status, power, educational opportunities, and religious freedom. Because these things also may be hard to obtain, people want them intensely.

Resolving social conflicts

In a society, conflicts arise when people think they are not getting their "fair share" of scarce values, tangible or intangible. Rival political parties want to place their own candidates in office. Two neighborhood groups disagree over whether a piece of land should be used for a park or for an office building. Civil rights groups want a local supermarket to end discrimination in hiring. Farmers want bankers to lend money at lower interest rates. To keep society orderly and carry out its other jobs, government must be able to resolve these disputes. Otherwise, such conflicts can carry the threat of violence, such as riots, bombings, or assassinations.

To resolve conflict, every organized government in history has operated within a political system. While it is very difficult to define what politics *is*, it is easier to describe what politics *does*. Politics is to government what muscles are to the human body — it allows the government to move and stretch and take action. Politics includes the struggles between people or groups seeking control and influence over the government. An equally important part of politics is a process of compromise — finding solutions in which each side gives up some of the things it wants. Without these compromises, the struggle might destroy the government.

In short, politics is the civilized way for individuals and groups in a state to settle their differences. Politics and political processes are essential to the functioning of government. We will be looking at various aspects of politics throughout this book.

SECTION 2 REVIEW

Vocabulary and key terms

politics (9)

For review

1. What four functions do all modern governments perform? **1A**
2. Give an example of government action in each of these areas: health, safety, transportation, communications, education, general welfare. **1A**
3. What is (a) a tangible value? (b) an intangible value? **5A**
4. Why are compromises an important part of politics? **6B**

Critical thinking

APPLYING KEY CONCEPTS What are some of the intangible values that are important in your school? How might these cause conflicts? How could these conflicts be resolved? **6B**

11

whether government should try to promote social standards. Students should take into account the following issues: **Who decides what standards government will promote? Who would promote standards if government did not?**

Section 2 Review Answers

1. Social order, national defense, public services, social standards.
2. Answers may include licensing physicians, meat inspection, highway speed limits, building codes, highways, mass transit, broadcasting regulations, establishing school systems, public housing, museums.
3. **(a)** Something that can be touched or seen. **(b)** Something that cannot be touched, such as respect, power, or opportunity.
4. Without them, conflicts might destroy government.

Critical thinking Answers may include grades, the teacher's approval, a role in the school play, or to be chosen for a team. In these situations, students are in competition with other students. Tests, tryouts, and the impartial judgments of teachers resolve these conflicts.

CLOSURE

● Remind students of the pre-reading objectives at the beginning of the section. Post one or both of these questions again. Then have students read Section 3, noting the differences among types of government.

The symbol ♟ denotes active participation strategies.

Activities are keyed for student abilities:
▲ = Basic
● = All Levels
■ = Average/Advanced

SECTION 3

**Government Takes
Many Forms** *(pp. 12–16)*

Section Objectives

☐ explain the different ways in
which political authority can
be divided

☐ describe the different forms of
political leadership

Vocabulary

unitary government,
confederation, federal system,
autocracy, oligarchy, democracy,
monarchy, constitutional
monarchy, dictatorship, *junta,*
totalitarianism, propaganda,
direct democracy, representative
democracy, republic

FOCUS

● Vocabulary is central to an
understanding of this section. To
reinforce students' knowledge of
vocabulary, divide terms in this
section according to the following classifications:

1. word pairs that compare
similarities and differences:
autocracy and *democracy,
oligarchy* and *monarchy, direct*
and *representative democracy.*
2. pairs of contrasting words:
democracy and *dictatorship.*
3. words with "telling" roots:
*totalitarianism, unitary,
republic.*

Government Takes Many Forms

> **ACCESS** The Main Ideas
>
> **1** In what different ways can political
> authority be divided?   *pages 12–13*
> **2** What are the different forms of political
> leadership?   *pages 13–16*

Because the Greeks were the first to write ana-
lytically about government, many of the words
we use to describe governments are Greek in origin. With the suffixes *-cracy* and *-archy,* the
Greeks went to the heart of the matter: *power* and
rule. The fundamental questions of government
are: (1) Where is power located? and (2) Who
rules, or makes the final decisions about the use
of power? This section describes how governments have answered these basic questions.

1C, 3C

How Authority Is Divided

In every government, authority must be divided between the state and its political subdivisions. These political subdivisions may be called
by many different names: *states,* as in the United
States, Mexico, and India; *counties,* as in Great
Britain; *departments,* as in France; *prefectures,*
as in Japan; *provinces,* as in China and Canada.
There are only three basic ways in which government authority is divided. It is important to look
at all three forms briefly, because all have existed
at some time in the United States.

Centralized power: unitary government

In states such as Great Britain, France, Japan,
and China, government power is very centralized. That is, the central government has authority over all political subdivisions within the
state. Because there is essentially *one* government, it is termed a **unitary government**. The
political subdivisions of such countries have only
the limited authority that the central government
grants them.

Unitary governments have both advantages
and disadvantages. The main advantage is that a
unitary government can have relatively uniform,
consistent policies, which apply basically to
every person in the state. This factor, however,
also contributes to the chief disadvantage of a unitary system — its inflexibility. Policies are applied to all political subdivisions without regard
for local differences or special needs. For this
reason, most experts think that unitary systems
work best in relatively small countries where
there are few regional or ethnic differences
among people.

It should be noted that all fifty American
states have unitary forms of government. As we
will discuss later in this book, each state government has some control over the local governments — cities, counties, and townships — in
that state.

Sovereign states: the confederation

In a **confederation**, or confederate form of
government, two or more independent states join
together to achieve some common goal, such as
mutual defense or foreign trade. In a way, the
confederation is the opposite of a unitary government. Each state retains its own sovereignty,
giving only limited powers to the central government. Confederate governments are considered
very unstable, and modern nations are generally
not organized in this way.

In American history, confederacies for defense or trade were a common form of alliance
among Indian peoples. During the American
Revolution, the first government of the thirteen
new "states" was formed under the Articles of
Confederation. The flaws and weaknesses of the
Confederation government prompted American
leaders to invent a new governmental system.
During the Civil War, the Southern states retained
their sovereignty when they left the Union and
formed the Confederate States of America.

Divided powers: federalism

The Constitution of 1787 was the framework
for the world's first **federal system**. In a federal
system, political authority is divided between a
national, or federal, government and its political
subdivisions. How these powers are divided

Cross-reference
Unit 9 discusses the structure, policies, and finances
of local governments.

Background: *Global
Awareness* The United
Nations is similar to a confederate form of govern-
ment. Each member nation
retains sovereignty, and the
organization has very limited
powers.

varies in different federal systems. In the United States, the division is defined in the Constitution. The national government and the state governments each are granted some powers. Some powers are *shared* by both governments, and some are *denied* to either government. (This division will be examined in greater detail in Chapter 4.)

Federalism represents a nice blend of the unitary and confederate forms. On the one hand, a federal system enables a strong central government to handle common problems. At the same time, smaller subdivisions can retain their local pride, traditions, and laws and give attention to regional problems. This type of system works especially well in countries with a large or varied population. Other modern nations that use federal systems include Canada, Australia, India, Mexico, Switzerland, and the Federal Republic of Germany.

1B, 1C, 1D, 6F

Who Rules the State?

When Aristotle studied the governments and politics of ancient Greece, he classified governments according to the *number* of people who have power — who rule the state. This time-tested classification is still accepted by most political scientists — scholars who study government structure and processes. New categories have been added to describe modern developments.

Aristotle's names for three basic kinds of rule are also still used. The first term is **autocracy**, or rule by one person. (This word comes from the Greek *auto*, meaning "self.") The second is **oligarchy** — rule by a small group (from *oligos*, meaning "few"). The third is **democracy**—rule by the people (*demos*).

Autocracy

In an autocracy, a single individual holds both political power and authority. Throughout history, the most common form of autocracy has been **monarchy**. While this term also means "one ruler," it is used to describe a government in which the ruler acquires his or her position through inheritance or family ties. Monarchs may be called kings, queens, princes, sultans, czars, nizams, empresses, or other regal names.

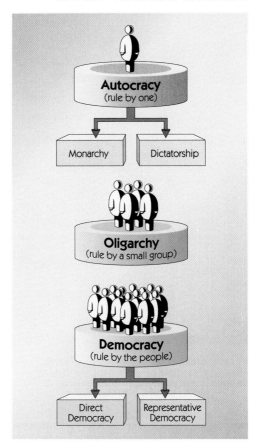

Figure 1–3 FORMS OF POLITICAL RULE 1C

Until the late 1700's, most monarchies in the world tended to be "absolute." That is, their rulers had total, unlimited authority and power. A trend toward limiting the monarch's power, however, began in England as early as the thirteenth century. In a limited monarchy, the ruler's power can be checked by law and by the authority of a lawmaking body or legislature. The last absolute monarch in a major Western nation was the czar of Russia, who was overthrown in 1917. The only remaining absolute monarch is the king of Saudi Arabia.

Today most nations with hereditary rulers are **constitutional monarchies**. Their rulers share authority with elected legislatures and

EXPLANATION

After reviewing the content of the section, you may want to consider the following activities:

Cultural Literacy

The suffix *-cracy* is derived from the Greek *krateia*, meaning "power"; *-archy* is derived from the Greek *arkhon*, meaning "rule" or "ruler."

■ *What other words do you know with these endings? What do they mean?* (Possibilities include *plutocracy*—rule by the wealthy; *gerontocracy*—rule by elders; *anarchy*—chaos.)

Global Awareness

● The British royal family is well known and widely followed, in the United States as well as Britain. *What actions of the royal family have been in the news recently? Why is the royal family so popular in this country?* (The United States has historic ties with Britain. Also, many Americans find the pomp and ceremony associated with the English monarchy interesting.)

13

Critical Thinking
● *What are some national issues in the news? What are some state issues? Can you see the advantages of the federal arrangement in handling these issues?*

Figure 1–3
■ *Select one of the forms of government shown and explain how it might change into another one of the forms.* (*Example:* An oligarchy might become an autocracy if one member of the

oligarchy eliminated the other members.)

Background: *History* The trend toward limiting the monarch's powers began with the Magna Charta in 1215.

The symbol ⅱ denotes active participation strategies.

Activities are keyed for student abilities:
▲ = Basic
● = All Levels
■ = Average/Advanced

As czarina (empress) of Russia, Catherine the Great ruled with absolute power from 1762 to 1796, expanding and strengthening the empire.

must follow their country's laws and constitution. Most constitutional monarchs, in fact, are mainly ceremonial heads of state. They preside at state ceremonies and are important symbols for their people, but they have little to do with making policies or actually running the state. That is, they "reign but do not rule." King Carl XVI Gustaf of Sweden and Queen Elizabeth II of England are modern constitutional monarchs.

Another form of autocracy is **dictatorship** Dictators acquire and maintain leadership in the state through fear and force — war, revolution, assassination. Some dictators gain power legally in times of crisis, when people believe that a strong ruler is necessary. Once in office, dictators typically try to strengthen their rule by suppressing all opposition through strict controls and through terror. Usually they depend on police or military forces to stay in power. Free speech, a free press, and open elections are limited in a dictatorship.

14

Oligarchy

In Aristotle's second category, an oligarchy, a small group of powerful people — not one ruler — rule in the state. Such forms of government have been fairly common throughout history. What has varied is the make-up of the ruling group. Some oligarchies have been based on wealth and social position, with their leaders being known as an "aristocracy." Some states have been ruled by religious leaders or by a council of older people.

Modern-day oligarchies most commonly are based on military or political power. The Spanish word *junta* (HOON-tah) often is used for a small group of military officers who seize a state and establish their own government. Such military takeovers have been fairly common in Latin America, Africa, and other parts of the world in the past 100 years. A junta known simply as "the colonels" ruled Greece from 1967 to 1975. Today it is not unusual for one member of the ruling group to assume more and more power and eventually become a dictator.

China represents yet another type of oligarchy. In that country, political power rests with a group composed of top Communist Party leaders. That is, both Party leadership and government authority are concentrated in the hands of a small group of people.

Totalitarian rule

Neither autocracies nor oligarchies are obliged to follow the wishes of the people. Even though some monarchs and some dictators have made efforts to improve people's lives and rule wisely, these forms of government are *authoritarian*. The rulers have enough power and authority to control many aspects of society and of people's personal lives.

In the twentieth century, authoritarian government developed into a form more extreme than Aristotle could have imagined. The term **totalitarianism** was invented to describe a government in which the rulers attempt to reshape the state, the people, and the society *totally,* to conform to an idea or plan. Government tries to change and control every aspect of public and private life, often through terror or violence. Individuals exist only to serve the state.

Totalitarianism could not exist before the twentieth century because it depends greatly on modern technology — mass communications and advanced military weapons. Totalitarian dictators use radio, television, newspapers, and the schools to spread propaganda, emotional appeals designed to persuade people to believe in the government. The ruling political party also controls businesses, transportation, housing, jobs, labor unions, churches, youth groups, and even sporting events.

The first totalitarian dictatorships arose in the 1920's and 1930's under Benito Mussolini in Fascist Italy, Adolf Hitler in Nazi Germany, and the Communist rule of Joseph Stalin in the Soviet Union. Following the establishment of the People's Republic of China, that country became a totalitarian Communist state under Mao Zedong, who ruled from 1949 to 1976.

Dictators in some smaller countries have also tried to establish totalitarian rule. In the island nation of Haiti, François Duvalier (known as "Papa Doc") was elected president in 1957 but soon set up a dictatorship that used fear and violence to remain in power till Duvalier's death in 1971. In 1979 the Ayatollah Khomeini in Iran set up a totalitarian state based on a return to the strict religious laws and traditions of Islam.

Democracies

The last kind of government that Aristotle described was the one in which he lived — a democracy. As explained earlier, *democracy* means "rule by the people." Unlike governments in which all power remains with the leaders, democratic governments are selected by the state's adult citizens and respond to their wishes. As Abraham Lincoln described it eloquently in his 1863 Gettysburg Address, democracy is "government of the people, by the people, for the people."

Democracy began in the city-states of ancient Greece, several thousand years ago. The kind of democracy described by Aristotle, therefore, is its original form — direct democracy. In a direct, or "pure," democracy, all citizens have a chance to participate in government on a first-hand basis. Every citizen can attend public meetings, vote on all legislation, and so establish public policy. In ancient Greece, in fact, each citizen was expected to do some job for the state.

It is clear why direct democracies are practical only in relatively small communities like the ancient Greek city-state. It would be impossible for the people of a large country to come together at a given time and place to settle complex social issues. (Imagine trying to bring the 186 million Americans of voting age into one meeting!) No nation in the world today has a direct democracy, though the form exists in a few cantons in Switzerland and the New England town meetings in the United States.

Democracy movements enjoyed huge public support and undermined governments in the Communist nations of Eastern Europe during late 1989 and early 1990. But in China in June 1989, a pro-democracy protest that began peacefully ended in a government-ordered bloodbath. Before the violence began, students gathered in Beijing's Tiananmen Square displaying the "Goddess of Democracy" statue, which was later crushed by a tank.

15

Background: *History* The "ideal" size for the Greek *polis* was 5,000 free male citizens, who were the only people counted in official records.

Section 3 Review Answers

1. (a) From the central government. **(b)** Yes, the states.
2. (a) The Constitution. **(b)** In countries with a large or varied population.
3. No. The monarchs are ceremonial heads of state and do not actually rule.
4. (a) By fear and force—war, revolution, or assassination. **(b)** Most are based on military force.
5. Totalitarian governments attempt to reshape every aspect of people's public and private lives to conform to an idea or plan.

Critical thinking It is *of* the people in that it is made up of elected citizens. It is *by* the people in that it was set up by their representatives. It is *for* the people in that its actions aim to benefit them.

CLOSURE

● Have students review the content of the section by rereading the headings and subheadings. Be sure that students understand the meanings of the words used. Then have students read Section 4, paying special attention to the distinction between individual rights and individual responsibilities.

In a republic the people choose representatives to act for them in governing. Here, voters in New Hampshire cast their ballots for President.

The people of the United States, like those in Canada, France, Israel, and other modern democracies, live under **representative democracy**. As the term suggests, representative, or *indirect,* democracy is a form of government in which the people elect a relatively small group of citizens to represent them in making laws and establishing public policies. The people's representatives may be called by a variety of names, such as legislature, congress, council, general assembly, house, or parliament. How they are chosen and how the government is organized also vary.

Republic or democracy?

Just as direct democracy originated in ancient Greece, representative democracy developed later in ancient Rome. The Romans used the term **republic** to describe any government in which the people exercise their political power through elected representatives, and no public offices are inherited. Sweden, for example, has a constitution, an elected legislature, and a king or

queen who inherits the throne. Though Sweden is a democracy, it is not a republic.

The United States is both a democracy and a republic, but its founders preferred the terms *republic* and *republican government* for the new nation. They distrusted the word *democracy* because to them it meant direct rule by an undisciplined mob. At the same time, they wanted to make it clear that no hereditary aristocracy or monarchy would ever develop. Today Americans do not have this negative reaction to the word *democracy*. On the contrary, as the next section will show, Americans today place great value on the principles underlying democracy.

SECTION 3 REVIEW

Vocabulary and key terms

unitary government(12)	dictatorship(14)
confederation(12)	junta(14)
federal system(12)	totalitarianism(14)
autocracy(13)	propaganda(15)
oligarchy(13)	direct democracy(15)
democracy(13)	representative
monarchy(13)	democracy(16)
constitutional	republic(16)
monarchy(13)	

For review

1. (a) In a unitary government, where do political subdivisions get their power? (b) Are there any unitary governments in the United States? **1C**
2. (a) What determines the way powers are divided between state and national governments in the United States? (b) In what kinds of states does a federal system work best? **3C**
3. Is a constitutional monarchy an autocracy? Why or why not? **1C**
4. (a) How do dictators usually gain power? (b) How are most modern oligarchies similar to dictatorships? **1C**
5. How does a totalitarian dictatorship differ from other forms of dictatorship? **1C**

Critical thinking

ANALYZING A QUOTATION   Explain how the American government is, in Lincoln's words, "of the people, by the people, for the people." **6F**

16

Organizing a Meeting

4C, 4D

Suppose you belong to a club with fifty members, and you have an idea for raising money. When you present your idea at a meeting, some members like it but want to change it a little. Others think they have better ideas. How can fifty people come to a single decision? The result might be chaos — unless the club follows an organized decision-making procedure.

One decision-making method that has been used for centuries is called *parliamentary procedure*. This set of rules for conducting organized debate is based on the practices of the English Parliament. It has worked so well that nearly all decision-making groups, from student councils to the United States Congress, use it to conduct meetings. Many groups use a version of parliamentary procedure published in 1876, called *Robert's Rules of Order*.

Parliamentary procedure is a formal process based on the following principles:

- *Fair and complete discussion.* Members on every side of an issue have the opportunity to speak.
- *Orderly discussion.* Members consider only one subject at a time, and only one person may speak at a time.
- *Majority rule.* A decision supported by more than half the members is binding on all.

An important part of this process is the *motion* — the proposal that members will consider and act upon. To make a motion, a member must ask the person in charge of the debate (the chairperson) for permission to speak. The chairperson formally ''recognizes'' the member, and the member states the motion, ''I move that. . . .'' Some motions require a second member's support, ''I second the motion.'' The chairperson may then either invite debate or call for a vote.

Think about how this procedure might work with fifty people trying to decide how to raise money for their club. Parliamentary procedure may seem awkward at first, but it does ensure that decisions are made in an organized, democratic manner.

Follow-up

1. Contact a local club or organization to find out whether they run their meetings by parliamentary procedure. If they do, ask if they use *Robert's Rules of Order*. If they don't, find out how they keep their meetings running smoothly.
2. Find a copy of *Robert's Rules of Order* in the library. Read the introduction and skim the rest of it. Then begin a meeting of your own using parliamentary procedure. One student should be assigned to be the chairperson, and others should take opposing sides to debate an issue.

Follow-up Answers

1. Possibilities include civic organizations, fraternal organizations, and political organizations.

2. During student debates, see that students follow parliamentary procedure in solving procedural problems as they arise.

SECTION 4

Principles Guide American Democracy
(pp. 18–20)

Section Objectives
- ☐ describe the rights that Americans have as individuals
- ☐ list four basic political ideals of American government

Vocabulary
civil liberties, civil rights, majority rule

FOCUS
● Demonstrate the need for limits on individual liberty and majority rule.

First, have one student take an object belonging to another student. Ask the class why this is not an acceptable way to exercise individual liberty.

Next, poll the class to see how many students support the Republicans and how many support the Democrats. Suggest that only those views of the more popular party will be permitted in class discussion. Ask the class why this is not an acceptable way to exercise majority rule.

EXPLANATION
After reviewing the content of the section, you may want to consider the following activities:

Cultural Literacy
Write the words *civil, liberties,* and *rights* on the board. Have students look up these words in the dictionary.

● ***How is the meaning of civil as "polite" consistent with its political meanings?*** (To be polite is to behave as a citizen should —obeying society's rules of

---

SECTION 4

1D, 6A, 6B, 6D, 6F, 6G, 6I, 8H

Principles Guide American Democracy

ACCESS The Main Ideas

1. **What rights do Americans have as individuals?** *pages 18–19*
2. **What are four basic political ideals of American government?** *pages 19–20*

Writer and critic George Bernard Shaw once said, "*Democracy* is a word all public men use and none understand." In the last section we learned that *democracy* means "rule by the people." Yet what exactly does "rule by the people" mean?

To be truly a democracy, a government must follow certain principles, or rules of conduct. In the United States these principles concern the institutions that make up the American government. However, these principles also affect the values and attitudes that Americans have long believed to be important.

1D, 6A, 6D, 6F, 6G, 6I

The Rights of Individuals

Individual worth

One basic principle of American democracy is the belief in ***individual worth.*** That is, Americans assume that each person knows what is best for himself or herself and generally has the right to make personal choices and decisions. Naturally, everyone makes some bad choices or decisions. Nevertheless, it is a democratic belief that it is far better for individuals to make their own mistakes than to entrust their choices to a monarch, or dictator, or oligarchy.

In the United States, individuals have great freedom to make choices. Americans are allowed to make their own decisions concerning what to eat, what to wear, what to read, where to live, where to travel, what schools to attend, and so on. Americans have economic freedom, too —

Americans of all ages are free to travel where they wish and follow the individual interests they enjoy. Such freedoms are unknown in many countries of the world.

Critical Thinking

● ***Is it possible for an individual to have too much freedom? What sorts of problems and challenges does freedom create for an individual?*** (Students should note that with freedom comes responsibility for one's life and actions.)

we can choose to start a business, learn the skill or profession we want, spend our money as we wish. In non-democratic states, people often cannot make such decisions. Rather, the government assumes *it* knows what is best for individuals and makes these decisions for them.

Individual liberty

The freedom to choose is what liberty is all about. For one thing, it means that individuals can make decisions in life without undue interference from government authorities. The protections that the law gives to people's freedom of thought and action are called **civil liberties**. They include the freedoms to write and speak freely and to choose one's own religion.

Individual liberty does not mean total, unrestricted freedom, however. In a democracy, laws are made by a majority of the people for the benefit of all. Therefore, although Americans cherish such civil liberties as the freedoms of speech and religion, each individual's freedom is still limited by *other* people's rights. John Stuart Mill, an English political philosopher, put the idea like this: "Your freedom to move your arm ends where my nose begins." (We will look at civil liberties in detail in Chapters 5 and 6.)

The rights of citizens

Every member of a democratic society is also entitled to **civil rights** — the rights of a citizen. This term is used in two related ways. One meaning is that government must treat each citizen equally. That is, every citizen has a vote, and each person's vote counts equally. Laws are applied fairly, and government does not discriminate against certain people or groups. This is "equality under the law."

But the term *civil rights* has also taken on a broader meaning that goes beyond government action. It means that every individual has an equal chance to develop to his or her maximum capabilities, without discrimination. This is "equality of opportunity."

5A, 6B, 6I

Political Principles

In addition to placing great value on the rights of individuals, American democracy emphasizes some basic political ideals and responsibilities.

"Rule by law"

In a democracy, no person, no matter how important, is above the law. That is, the law applies to government and government officials as much as to ordinary citizens. In the words of John Adams, we have "a government of laws, and not of men." Public officials must make decisions based on the law, not only on their own opinions or wishes. Moreover, if officials break the law, they must be treated as other citizens would be.

It is also important in a democracy that laws be public and that citizens know the basic law of the land. This is a principle that most Americans take for granted, but it is an important protection against the government. In the United States, the basic law is the Constitution of 1787. Most other modern democracies also have written constitutions.

Throughout history, the governments not bound by such fundamental laws have been most likely to fall into the hands of tyrants. Dictators such as Hitler and Stalin made arbitrary decisions that cost millions of lives. Such leaders, like the absolute monarchs of earlier times, have thought that their wishes *were* the law. Colonial Americans had had long experience with arbitrary decisions by the English king and royal officials. This led Thomas Jefferson to declare, "In questions of power, then, let no more be heard of confidence in man, but bind him down from mischief by the chains of the Constitution."

Limits on government power

Closely related to rule by law is the principle of limited government. As we will discuss in Chapter 4, the Constitution of the United States sets many limits on government actions. These limits help to ensure individual liberties and equality under the law.

Representative government

Part of the basic meaning of democracy is the people's right to elect representatives who make their laws. Free elections ensure that these elected representatives carry out the wishes and opinions of those who voted for them. If the representatives fail to do so, people have the right to choose other representatives in the next election.

Many Americans do not exercise this right to choose. In fact, in recent U.S. elections, only 50 percent of those eligible turned out to vote.

19

conduct.) **How do civil rights differ from civil liberties?** (Civil liberties are the protections of people's freedom of thought and action. Civil rights are each person's right to fair treatment and equal opportunity.)

Constitutional Heritage
Direct students' attention to the statement by Thomas Jefferson on this page. Help students see that *man* refers to people who hold government power.
● CRITICAL THINKING **Why did Jefferson have little confidence in such people?** (Because of the colonies' experience with British leaders.) **What did he mean when he suggested binding such leaders by "the chains of the Constitution"?** (Restricting by law the authority of any one individual.)
■ CRITICAL THINKING **In what way would the Constitution restrict an individual's power?** (By providing for elected officials, majority rule, and a system of checks and balances, as well as by protecting civil rights and liberties.)

Cooperative Learning
● Divide the class into groups, each of which should create a poster dealing with Americans' belief in individual worth. Students should scan the text for examples of personal freedom. Students may draw or cut pictures from magazines to compose the posters. Display the posters in the classroom.

Background: *Values* Freedom of religion is one of the most important principles of American government. See the text of the First Amendment, p. 128, and the Virginia Statute of Religious Liberty, p. 143. Ask students how their lives would be different without this kind of freedom.

Cross-reference
Chapter 11 compares U.S. voter turnout with that of other democratic nations. See the graph on p. 312.

The symbol ▮▮ denotes active participation strategies.

Activities are keyed for student abilities:
▲ = Basic
● = All Levels
■ = Average/Advanced

GUIDED/INDEPENDENT PRACTICE

● Have students compose a dialogue between two persons, one arguing that the low American voter turnout endangers democracy, and the other one disagreeing.

RETEACHING/CORRECTIVES

▲ Have students transform the headings in the section into questions and then use the subheadings to answer those questions.

ENRICHMENT/EXTENSION

■ Have students complete **Skills Challenge Worksheet 1,** which contains a political cartoon on the subject of voting.

Section 4 Review Answers

1. Individual worth means that people know what is best for them. Liberty gives them the right to act on their beliefs.
2. (a) Even the government must abide by the law. **(b)** By the Constitution.
3. To be re-elected, officials must carry out the people's wishes.
4. Lawmakers are selected, and laws are passed, by majority vote.

Critical thinking Students should recognize that failure to protect minority rights would violate the people's right to have a voice in government, a central part of democracy.

CLOSURE

● Remind students of the pre-reading objectives at the beginning of the section. Pose one or both of these questions again. Then have students read Section 5, noting the steps in the naturalization process.

20

YOU DECIDE 8H

Crescent Elementary School in Anaheim, California, is the home for Pack 519 of the Cub Scouts of America. William and Michael Randall, nine-year-old twins, were expelled from Pack 519 after announcing that they did not believe in God and would not say the word "God" during the recitation of the Cub Scout Promise. James Randall, father of the two boys, contends that the Cub Scouts do not have the right to dismiss his sons.

Do the Randalls have a case? Why or why not?

Although this may seem alarming, it is nevertheless the people's choice to exercise this right. In non-democratic governments, voting turnout may reach 99 percent, but the people are forced to vote. As there is often no real choice among the candidates, such voting is purely symbolic. The government does not really represent the people.

"Majority rule with minority rights"

In a democracy, most decisions are made by **majority rule.** According to this idea, people agree to abide by decisions on which more than half of them agree. In the United States, for instance, lawmakers are selected by majority (or plurality) vote in free elections. They, in turn, pass legislation by majority vote.

At the same time, however, *minority rights* are respected in a democracy. Civil liberties such as freedom of speech, press, and assembly exist in part to permit minority groups to express their viewpoints. Political minorities may lose an election, but their opinions and actions will not be banned or censored by the winning party. Moreover, the protection of minority rights assures the legitimacy of the government. As long as all groups have the right to be heard and take part in government, they are more likely to accept the government's authority.

20

Putting principles into practice

These principles of American democracy are closely linked and dependent on one another. It would be difficult, for example, to have limited government without rule by law. It would probably be impossible to maintain civil liberties if there were no limits on government power.

In addition, these principles sometimes collide. Individuals' rights may conflict. Majority rule may mean that some people's opinions are not represented in the government. Rule by law may put limits on individuals' choices.

Finally, it is often easier to believe in some principles than to put them into effect. For example, Americans generally believe in the freedom of speech, yet some Americans would prefer that certain groups — whose views they oppose — not be accorded that right.

One of the main responsibilities of being a citizen in a democracy is to understand the principles on which democracy is based. Another is to see that the principles are in fact carried out. The next section looks more closely at what it means to be a citizen in a democracy.

SECTION 4 REVIEW

Vocabulary and key terms

civil liberties (19)   limited government (19)
civil rights (19)   majority rule (20)
rule by law (19)

For review

1. How does the principle of individual worth relate to the idea of individual liberty? **1D**
2. (a) How does "rule by law" relate to "limited government"? (b) How is government power limited in the United States? **6I**
3. How do democratic elections help make the government representative of people's wishes? **6F**
4. Give examples of majority rule in the U.S. government. **6F**

Critical thinking

APPLYING KEY CONCEPTS   Why are minority rights a fundamental idea of democracy? **1D**

You Decide Answer
Students should defend their answers. A county superior court judge ruled that the boys could not be barred from attending Scout meetings until a trial decided whether Scout leaders can legally expel them.

1C, 3C, 5A, 6D, 6E, 6G

Citizenship Is a Special Status

ACCESS **The Main Ideas**

1 How is American citizenship defined?
pages 21–22

2 How can a person gain or lose American citizenship?
pages 22–24

3 What are the categories of non-citizen residents?
pages 24–25

If you and your family were born in this country, the statement, "I am a United States citizen," might not seem like a big deal. Citizenship is something you were born with and take for granted.

In that case, you need to hear from a recent immigrant—someone in your class, your school, or your neighborhood perhaps. Such a person will tell you that being a citizen of the United States means becoming part of this nation, something many people value so greatly they will risk their lives for it.

1C, 3C, 5A, 6D, 6E

Who Is a Citizen?

Although American citizenship and the rights of citizens are precious, these important concepts are not defined in the basic text of the Constitution. It states only that candidates for national office must have been citizens for a certain number of years.

At the time the Constitution was written in 1787, the laws of each state determined who would be eligible to vote, to hold office, or to have other rights of citizenship. Neither black slaves nor American Indians were considered citizens under the Constitution. Free black men had the right to vote in some states, but these rights were increasingly denied after 1800, in both the North and the South. Women of both races had some civil rights, but though they owned property and paid taxes, not until 1890 did states begin permitting them to vote. In the early years of the country, then, many Americans were denied the rights of citizens on the basis of race, sex, lack of property, and other factors.

The Fourteenth Amendment

The first definition of American citizenship was given in the Fourteenth Amendment, enacted in 1868 following the Civil War. Its intent was to ensure newly freed blacks the rights of American citizens. One provision of this amendment clearly grants citizenship with no exceptions: "All persons born or naturalized in the United States, and subject to the jurisdiction thereof, are citizens of the United States and of the State wherein they reside." Other rules concerning citizenship have been established by laws passed by Congress.

Citizenship by birth

According to the provisions of the Fourteenth Amendment, almost everyone born in United States territory is an American citizen. This follows a principle of international law called *jus soli* (yoos SO-lee), which means literally "the right of the soil." That is, one's *place* of birth determines citizenship. United States "soil" includes not only the territory of the fifty states but also most American overseas territories, such as Puerto Rico and Guam, and American embassies in other countries.

Children born on foreign ships in American waters or to high-ranking foreign diplomats serving in the United States probably would not be considered U.S. citizens. (Diplomats are usually treated as if they carry a part of their home country with them wherever they are.)

Children born to American citizens living or traveling abroad also automatically become United States citizens. This follows another legal principle — *jus sanguinis* (yoos sang-GWY-nus), meaning "the right of citizenship by *blood*." If only one of the child's parents is an American citizen, that parent must have lived in the United States for at least 10 years — five of them after the age of 14. To keep his or her American citizenship, the child also must live in the United States for two years after turning 14. (Requirements for citizenship have changed frequently over the years.)

21

SECTION 5

Citizenship Is a Special Status *(pp. 21–25)*

Section Objectives
☐ explain how American citizenship is defined
☐ explain how a person can gain or lose American citizenship
☐ describe the categories of non-citizen residents

Vocabulary
jus soli, jus sanguinis, naturalization, expatriation, alien

FOCUS
● Ask the class why citizenship is an important concept. *How is the life of a citizen different from the life of a non-citizen?* (Citizens have rights, such as voting, that non-citizens do not have. Citizens also have special obligations.) *Why is citizenship an especially important concept in a democracy?* (Citizens of a democracy have a role in the government of their country.)

EXPLANATION
After reviewing the content of the section, you may want to consider the following activities:

Constitutional Heritage
The Fourteenth Amendment contains several other important provisions, including the "due process" clause, which has been the basis for extending Bill of Rights protections, and the

"equal protection" clause, which has been the basis of laws and court decisions providing equal opportunities.

● **What was the main purpose of the Fourteenth Amendment?** (To ensure newly freed blacks the rights of American citizens.)

● CRITICAL THINKING Have students reread the passage from the Fourteenth Amendment on p. 21. **How is state citizenship linked to national citizenship?** (Citizens of the United States are automatically citizens of the state in which they live.) **Has this linkage always existed in the United States?** (No; when the Constitution was written, state citizenship was granted by the states alone.)

Civic Participation

Direct students to Figure 1–4 on p. 24.

● **What are the three basic requirements for citizenship?** (Legal entry into the United States, residency for five years, age of 18.) **Proof of what other qualifications is required during the naturalization process?** (Good moral conduct, knowledge of English, an understanding of American government and history.)

● After discussing Figure 1–4, you may wish to ask students to use the information in the chart (and caption) to draw their own flow charts of the naturalization process. Several of the charts may be used for a bulletin-board display.

Cultural Literacy

▲ See whether any words in the citizenship oath are unfamiliar to students. (Possibly *abjure, fidelity, potentate, noncombatant.*) If so, have students use a dictionary to find the meanings of the new words.

22

Dual citizenship

Most nations of the world follow one or both of these legal principles of citizenship. But because laws vary from country to country, it is not uncommon for a person to hold dual citizenship. Say, for instance, that a child is born in the United States to Italian parents. By the principle of *jus soli,* that child automatically becomes a United States citizen. However, Italy and most other European countries recognize the principle of *jus sanguinis.* The child therefore becomes an Italian citizen too.

In cases of dual citizenship, most countries (including the United States) require the person to make a formal declaration of allegiance to *one* country when he or she turns 18. Otherwise, complications are likely to arise over taxes, military service, and other duties of adult citizens.

Becoming an American Citizen

The Constitution gives Congress the power to establish rules for granting U.S. citizenship to someone who has not acquired it by birth. This process, called **naturalization**, has been particularly important in the United States because of the large numbers of people who have immigrated to this country.

Except for members of native American Indian groups, *all* Americans have roots in other countries of the world. This is the origin of the "melting pot" idea mentioned in Section 1. Even today, about 600,000 people enter the United States as legal immigrants each year. They are drawn by the freedoms and opportunities that the United States offers its citizens.

For more than fifty years, Ellis Island in New York Harbor was the first stop for European immigrants entering the United States. Since 1965 it has been a national monument along with the nearby Statue of Liberty.

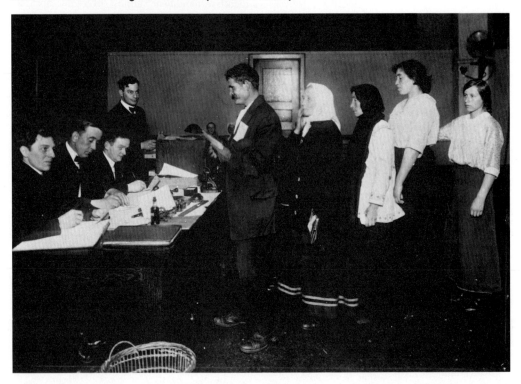

22

Check for Understanding
▲ *Do any students in the class hold dual citizenship?*

Cross-reference
A chart showing immigration by continent since 1940 can be found on p. 207.

Check for Understanding
▲ *Do any students in the class have ancestors who entered the U.S. at Ellis Island, as shown in the picture?*

Requirements for naturalization

To be eligible for individual naturalization, adult immigrants must meet certain requirements. These include five years of residence in the United States (three years if married to an American citizen), the ability to read, write, and speak English, and an understanding of American government and history. A final requirement is "good moral character." This allows the government to refuse citizenship for a variety of political and social reasons. The steps each immigrant must follow to become an American citizen are outlined in Figure 1–4.

Young people under 18 can become citizens when their parents are naturalized. Parents who are citizens can apply for citizenship for children under the age of 18. About 230,000 persons from other countries are naturalized each year in the United States.

Naturalized citizens may lose their citizenship if it is proved that they lied or misrepresented themselves during the naturalization process. Otherwise, the Supreme Court has ruled that they have the same rights as natural-born citizens.

Collective naturalization

Sometimes a large group of people are granted citizenship at the same time. For example, at several times in American history, Congress has passed laws for the *collective naturalization* of people in various U.S. overseas territories — Hawaii (1900), Puerto Rico (1917), the Virgin Islands (1927), and Guam (1950). Most recently, citizenship was granted in 1986 to the people of the Northern Marianas, a small group of islands in the Pacific.

When the United States has acquired territory by treaty with another country, the people in that territory have gained U.S. citizenship at the same time. This occurred in the Louisiana Purchase (1803) and the acquisition of Florida (1819) and Alaska (1867). When Texas, formerly an independent republic, became a state in 1845, its citizens became U.S. citizens.

In two cases, citizenship was granted to large groups of Americans whose rights had previously been denied. As we have just noted, the Fourteenth Amendment officially granted all black Americans the citizenship that many state laws

Taking the oath of allegiance to the United States is a solemn and important moment for those who have worked and studied to become naturalized American citizens.

had withheld. Many members of native American Indian tribes also were not considered citizens under the Constitution. Over the years, some became citizens by treaties and acts of Congress. In 1924, the Citizenship Act declared that *all* Indians born in U.S. territory were citizens and entitled to full voting rights.

Losing citizenship

Losing one's American citizenship is rare, but may happen in certain circumstances. Because loss of citizenship is a serious step, it has become a complicated legal question.

There is no question that everyone has the right to surrender his or her citizenship voluntarily. For example, a person who marries someone from another country might choose to live abroad and formally give up American citizenship. This process is termed **expatriation**.

Whether the government can legally take away a person's citizenship is a more difficult issue. In the Immigration and Nationality Act of 1952, Congress listed a number of actions that could result in losing one's citizenship — for example, voting in a foreign election or leaving the country to avoid the military draft.

23

Controversial Issues

● CRITICAL THINKING Discuss with students the issue of whether the government can legally take away a person's citizenship. Remind students that the Immigration and Naturalization Act, which listed a number of offenses punishable by loss of citizenship, was passed in 1952. *What issues or concerns might have led Congress in 1952 to pass such a law?* (The Korean War was going on, and fear of communism at home as well as abroad was strong in the United States.) *Why might support for such a law not be as strong today?* (Fear of communism within the United States has diminished, and the cold war has ended.)

Ask students to list the kinds of offenses, if any, for which loss of citizenship would be an appropriate punishment.

Cooperative Learning

● Divide the class into small groups. Give each group a sheet of paper containing a list of individuals, and have the group decide which of those persons would be United States citizens. (Possibilities include: person born in Mexico to American parents; native of Hawaii in 1889; foreign student studying in an American university.) Check the groups' answers for accuracy.

Check for Understanding
▲ *Are there any naturalized American citizens in the class?* Ask them to relate their experience.

Background: *Civic Participation* Naturalized citizens

are entitled to all the rights of natural born citizens except one: they may not serve as President or Vice President.

Background: *History* Citizenship was not ex-

tended to black persons in the Louisiana Territory, Florida, or Texas when these areas became part of the United States because the Fourteenth Amendment had not yet been ratified.

The symbol ▮▮ denotes active participation strategies.

Activities are keyed for student abilities:
▲ = Basic
● = All Levels
■ = Average/Advanced

Some provisions of this law have been declared unconstitutional by the Supreme Court. Members of the Court have questioned whether Congress has power to take away a person's citizenship. The justices have also disagreed sharply about what actions — if any — justify the loss of the "priceless right" of citizenship. In a 1958 case, Chief Justice Earl Warren declared, "The basic right of American citizenship has been too dearly won to be so lightly lost."

Rules for aliens

While many people from other countries come to the United States intending to become citizens, many others come temporarily — as students or workers, for instance. Most are citizens of other countries, but while in the United States, they are considered **aliens**.

Depending on their circumstances, aliens fall into different legal categories. A *resident alien* is a citizen of a foreign nation living permanently in the United States, usually with the intention of becoming an American citizen. A *non-resident alien,* on the other hand, plans to reside in the United States for a limited time only. Many foreign students, for example, study at an American university and then return to their home country. In wartime, people from countries at war with the United States are considered *enemy aliens.* Their rights and freedoms within this country are likely to be limited because of the state of war.

Illegal aliens are people who enter the United States without permission, usually to find work or escape political troubles. The number of illegal aliens increased dramatically in the

Figure 1–4 BECOMING AN AMERICAN CITIZEN In general, any immigrant who has legally entered the United States, has lived here for at least five years, and is 18 years old may become a naturalized American citizen by following these steps: 6D

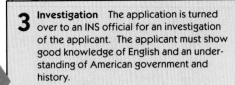

1 Declaration of intention An immigrant may announce his or her intention to become a citizen by filing a declaration with the office of the Attorney General. This step is optional.

2 Petition for citizenship The immigrant must file a petition requesting citizenship. The application is filed with the Attorney General. The petition must be accompanied by a sworn, written declaration signed by two American citizens. In this declaration, the Americans must swear to the applicant's good moral conduct.

3 Investigation The application is turned over to an INS official for an investigation of the applicant. The applicant must show good knowledge of English and an understanding of American government and history.

4 Oath of allegiance If the application is approved, the applicant attends a final hearing. He or she then must take the following oath:

"I hereby declare, on oath, that I absolutely and entirely renounce and abjure all allegiance and fidelity to any foreign prince, potentate, state, or sovereignty, of whom or which I have heretofore been a subject or citizen; that I will support and defend the Constitution and laws of the United States against all enemies, foreign and domestic; that I will bear true faith and allegiance to the same; that I will bear arms on behalf of the United States when required by the law; or that I will perform noncombatant service in the armed forces of the United States when required by the law; or that I will perform work of national importance under civilian direction when required by the law; and that I take this obligation freely without any mental reservation or purpose of evasion; so help me God."

24

Figure 1–4
● *Why must a person, in swearing the oath of allegiance, renounce his or her loyalty to any foreign leader?*

(Because a United States citizen must be loyal to the United States above all other nations.)

1980's and became a serious national concern. Congress in 1986 acted to grant resident-alien status to those who entered before 1982.

Unlike many other countries, the United States grants aliens many of the civil rights and civil liberties of citizens. Legal aliens can own property, run a business, use public services, and attend public schools. They are guaranteed due process and legal protection. In return, aliens are obliged to pay taxes and obey the laws. On the other hand, aliens do not have the political rights of citizens. They cannot vote, serve on a jury, or hold public office.

Congress establishes certain laws regulating aliens and immigration, and the United States Immigration and Naturalization Service (INS) administers them. All aliens must register yearly with the INS and keep this information up-to-date. Aliens who break the INS rules or other laws may be deported — forced to leave the United States. Illegal aliens, of course, may be deported at any time.

SECTION 5 REVIEW

Vocabulary and key terms

jus soli (21)   expatriation (23)
jus sanguinis (21)   alien (24)
naturalization (22)

For review

1. (a) By what laws were people granted the rights of citizenship at the time the Constitution was written? (b) What two groups were not considered citizens? **3C**
2. What law first defined United States citizenship? **3C**
3. (a) According to the principle of *jus soli,* who is an American citizen? (b) What are the requirements for naturalization? **6E**
4. (a) What rights do most aliens have in the United States? (b) What rights are they denied? **5A**

Critical thinking

APPLYING KEY CONCEPTS Could democracy exist without minority rights? Give reasons for your answer. **6G**

Chapter Summary

The state is the world's basic political unit. It is defined by four features: territory, population, government, and sovereignty. (The words *country, nation,* or *nation-state* are often used to mean the same thing as *state.*) The fifty states in the United States are not truly "states," although they once acted independently.

Many philosophers attempted to explain the origins of the state. The idea of the social contract, developed by Hobbes and Locke in 17th-century England, had the strongest effect on American government.

Governments serve four basic functions in the state: social order, national defense, public services, and social standards. In carrying out these functions, governments must find ways to satisfy different people competing for things of value. Politics enables governments to settle conflicts in a civilized manner through a political system.

Governments can be classified as unitary, confederate, or federal systems, according to how authority is distributed between the state and its geographic subdivisions. States are also classified by the number of people that have power. Autocracy refers to rule by one person, and oligarchy is rule by a small group of people. In a democracy, all citizens participate in governing, either directly or through their representatives. The United States can correctly be called a republic or a representative democracy.

The rights of individuals — including civil liberties and civil rights — play an important role in American democracy. Other principles, such as rule by law, limited government, and majority rule with minority rights are the bases of the political system of the United States.

Citizens enjoy the full rights and privileges of American democracy. Almost everyone born either on American soil or to American parents is automatically a citizen. Others can become American citizens through naturalization. Citizens can also lose their status by expatriation. Aliens living in the United States receive many, but not all, of the rights of American citizens.

---

4. (a) Many civil rights and liberties of citizens—the right to own property, to run a business, to use public services, to attend public schools, and the rights of due process and legal protection. (b) The political rights of citizens.

Critical thinking Students may note that the United States is a nation of immigrants and may therefore be more sympathetic to immigrants. Furthermore, pride and confidence in our system, along with a belief in individual worth, may keep Americans from supporting repressive policies.

CLOSURE
● Remind students of the pre-reading objectives at the beginning of the section. Pose one or all of these questions again. Then have students read the next assigned lesson.

CHAPTER 1 CORRECTIVES
● To review the content of Chapter 1, you may want to have students complete **Study Guide/Review 1** or **Workbook Chapter 1.**

The symbol 👥 denotes active participation strategies.

Activities are keyed for student abilities:
▲ = Basic
● = All Levels
■ = Average/Advanced

25

Answers

Vocabulary See pp. T19–T21 for suggested vocabulary activities.

Reviewing the Facts

1. *Unitary*—individual state of United States. *Confederation*— American Indian alliances; first U.S. government under Articles of Confederation; Confederate States of America. *Federal*—national government of United States under Constitution.
2. A sovereign state can decide and carry out its own foreign policy, send and receive ambassadors, and defend its own territory.
3. It would be impossible for all the people of large countries—or even large cities—to gather in one place to make political decisions.
4. Politics, a civilized way to settle disagreements, allows a government to remain stable while conflicts are resolved.
5. Federalism allows for a strong central government while at the same time giving some independence to the smaller political subdivisions.
6. A majority of the people must agree to any decision. However, the rights of the minority to disagree must be protected.
7. A child born in one country to parents who are citizens of another country may be considered a citizen of both countries.

Thinking Critically About Key Concepts

1. Students should support their answers.
2. (a) The federal system can combine stability and flexibility.
(b) A confederation might be helpful if a group of independent states wished to cooperate on a matter of common concern, such as defense.
3. If individuals do not agree with the actions of their representatives, they can vote against them

★ CHAPTER 1 REVIEW ★

● **Review the definitions of the following terms:**

alien	expatriation	politics
allegiance	federal system	propaganda
autocracy	government	public policy
citizenship	junta	representative democracy
civil liberties	*jus sanguinis*	republic
civil rights	*jus soli*	rule by law
confederation	legitimacy	social contract
constitutional monarchy	limited government	sovereignty
democracy	majority rule	state
dictatorship	monarchy	totalitarianism
direct democracy	naturalization	unitary government
divine right	oligarchy	

● **REVIEWING THE FACTS**

---

1. Give an example of each of these forms of governmental authority as it is or has been found in the United States: unitary government, confederation, federal system. **3C**
2. What are the three characteristics of a sovereign state? **1A**
3. Why is direct democracy an impractical political system in large nations? **6F**
4. What important role does politics play in government? **6B**
5. Explain how federalism is a blend of the unitary and confederate forms of government. **3C**
6. How is the principle of "majority rule with minority rights" applied in a democracy? **1D**
7. Under what circumstances might a child hold dual citizenship? **6D**

▲ **THINKING CRITICALLY ABOUT KEY CONCEPTS**

---

1. Do you think the United States is more like a "melting pot" or a "salad bowl"? Explain. **5A**
2. (a) What advantage does the federal system of government have over the confederation? (b) Under what circumstances might a con-

26

federation be a beneficial or useful form of government? **3C**
3. How is the belief in individual liberty reflected in the representative form of government in the United States? **6F**
4. How has the concept of American citizenship developed over time? **6G**

▲ **PRACTICING SKILLS**

---

1. **Study Skills: Organizing information in a table.** Create a table to give examples of and describe the three forms of government: unitary government, confederation, and federal system. In the first column, list the forms of government. In the second column, list two examples of each. In the third column, write a brief description of each. Give each column a heading. **8C**
2. **Study Skills: Analyzing a photograph.** Examine the photograph on page 22. Try to imagine the thoughts of the persons in line to speak with immigration officials, and write down what they might have been. **8B**
3. **Critical Thinking Skills: Making generalizations.** Refer to Figure 1–2 (page 7). Make a general statement connecting the rise of civilization with the development of government. Why does this connection exist? **8A**

---

in the next election or work for an opposing candidate.
4. American citizenship was not defined in the Constitution as it was written in 1787. State laws determined who would have the rights of citizenship. Over

time, groups once denied citizenship, such as African Americans and women, were made citizens.

Practicing Skills

1. Unitary government/ Great Britain, France, Japan,

China/Central government has authority over all political subdivisions. Confederation/Confederate States of America, United States under Articles of Confederation, American Indian alliances/ Two or more independent

27

▲ PARTICIPATORY CITIZENSHIP

1. **Locating information.** Write the Immigration and Naturalization Service to ask what knowledge of U.S. government and history is required of naturalized citizens. **4D**
2. **Analyzing the media.** Listen to a news program or examine a newspaper. Which stories concern tangible values and which concern intangible values? Note several examples of each. Explain why each represents tangible or intangible values. **1A**

■ WRITING ABOUT ISSUES

1. **Writing an essay.** The revolutionary improvements in transportation and communication in the world today might eventually affect the sovereignty of states. Write a brief essay explaining why this might happen, whether you think this will happen, and why. Provide your own ideas regarding how the world might change in the future. **8C**
2. **Writing a letter.** Imagine that a friend in a non-democratic country writes you asking what American democracy is all about. Write a letter explaining the principles of American democracy as outlined in Section 4 in simple, basic terms. **6F**
3. **Composing an editorial.** During World War II, thousands of Japanese Americans were classified as enemy aliens and moved from their homes to internment camps until the end of the war. Imagine that you are a newspaper editor during the war, and write an editorial expressing your view of this policy. Your editorial should explain why the policy is or is not consistent with the ideals of a democratic society. **6G**

▲ ANALYZING A POLITICAL CARTOON

Poet Emma Lazarus wrote the famous inscription on the Statue of Liberty: "Give me your tired, your poor, your huddled masses yearning to breathe free." Despite this generous invitation, the United States has often set quotas on immigration. These quotas remain a subject of political controversy.

Look at the cartoon below and answer the following questions.

1. What does the Statue of Liberty stand for in the cartoon? **8B**
2. How does the cartoon portray the way in which immigration is currently affecting the United States? **8B**

AUTH copyright 1989 Philadelphia Inquirer. Reprinted with permission of Universal Press Syndicate. All rights reserved.

Participatory Citizenship
1. Students may want to make additional suggestions to the list of required knowledge.
2. You might want to list the various tangible and intangible values from students' responses on the board.

Writing About Issues
1. Students should explain that the ability of people, ideas, and goods to move freely from one state to another makes it harder for any state to act independently. Possible suggestions as to other future developments include the creation by states of regional confederations or, conversely, the breakup of states into small, inward-looking units.
2. Students' letters should explain the principles of rule by law, limits on government power, representative government, and majority rule with minority rights.
3. Students' answers should take into account the fact that the Japanese Americans were interned simply for having Japanese ancestry, not for committing a crime.

Analyzing a Political Cartoon
1. The American people.
2. The United States is being overrun by immigrants.

---

states join together to pursue a common goal. Federal system/United States, Australia, India, Mexico, Switzerland, Germany/Authority is divided between the government and its subdivisions.

2. Students may suggest thoughts of excitement at new opportunities in the United States and thoughts of sadness and uncertainty as families and homes are left behind.

3. The development of government naturally accompanies the rise of civilization. The connection exists because the rise of civilization created needs, such as keeping order, that governments arose to meet.

Chapter Review exercises are keyed for student abilities:
▲ = Basic
● = All Levels
■ = Average/Advanced

CHAPTER 2
ORIGINS OF AMERICAN GOVERNMENT
(pp. 28–59)

	Section Objectives	Section Resources
Section 1 **Political Traditions Are Brought from England**	☐ explain why the English influence on American politics was dominant ☐ describe what cornerstones of American political thought originated in England	● PRIMARY SOURCE WORKSHEET **1** ▲ TRANSPARENCY **2**
Section 2 **Government Develops in the Colonies**	☐ explain how England's American colonies were governed ☐ explain how England's policy toward the colonies changed during the 1760's ☐ describe how the new English policy affected the colonies	● PRIMARY SOURCE WORKSHEETS **2–3** ▲ TRANSPARENCIES **3–4**
Section 3 **The New Nation Is Established**	☐ describe the structure of the Declaration of Independence ☐ explain how the Confederation government was put together and the problems it faced	▲ TRANSPARENCIES **5–8**
Section 4 **The Constitution Is Written and Ratified**	☐ list the delegates to the Constitutional Convention ☐ explain how the process of compromise led to agreement on the new Constitution ☐ describe the debate over ratification of the Constitution	▲ SKILLS PRACTICE WORKSHEET **2** ■ SKILLS CHALLENGE WORKSHEET **2** ■ CONSTITUTIONAL ISSUES WORKSHEET **1** ● PRIMARY SOURCE WORKSHEET **4** ▲ TRANSPARENCY **9**

Essential Elements

The list below shows Essential Elements relevant to this chapter. (The complete list of Essential Elements appears in the introductory pages of this Teacher's Edition.)

Section 1: 1C, 1D, 2A, 6G, 6I, 8B, 8G

Section 2: 1D, 2C, 4A, 5C, 6G, 6H, 7A, 8F

Section 3: 1C, 1D, 2A, 2C, 4A, 6A

Declaration of Independence: 1D, 2A, 2C

Section 4: 2A, 2B, 2C, 3A, 3C, 5A, 6B, 8E, 8H

Chapter Review: 1D, 2A, 2B, 3C, 4A, 6B, 8A, 8B, 8C, 8E, 8F, 8G

> Section Resources are keyed for student abilities:
> ▲ = Basic
> ● = All Levels
> ■ = Average/Advanced

Homework Options

Each section contains activities labeled "Guided/Independent Practice," "Reteaching/Correctives," and "Enrichment/Extension." You may wish to choose from among these activities when assigning homework.

Students Acquiring English Activities

The following activity may make the concept behind the slogan, "No taxation without representation," more accessible to students. Have students review the information on pp. 32 and 38–39. Bring to class (or have students bring) newspapers, playing cards, legal documents, calendars, paint, and tea. Ask if taxes are paid on these items today. If these items are taxed, have students consider whether this constitutes taxation without representation.

LISTENING/SPEAKING: Invite a government official to talk to the class about how taxes affect the community. Have students prepare questions in advance. (Possible questions include: Are these taxes determined by representatives of the people? If so, who are the representatives for your community at the local/state/national level? Who can vote for these representatives? How can taxes be increased, decreased, or protested? Are there any persons or groups that are not taxed, and if so, why?)

Case Studies

When teaching this chapter, you may use Case Study 1, which addresses the relevance of the Constitution today. (Case Studies may be found following p. 510.)

Teacher Bibliography

Carroll, Peter N., ed. *Religion and the Coming of the American Revolution.* Ginn & Company, 1970. Documents the religious background of the split between Great Britain and the American colonies.

Foner, Eric. *Tom Paine and Revolutionary America.* Oxford University Press, 1976.

Rossiter, Clinton. *1787: The Grand Convention.* Norton, 1987. Describes how the delegates to the Constitutional Convention worked together to create the Constitution.

Student Bibliography

Bowen, Catherine Drinker. *Miracle at Philadelphia.* Rev. ed. Little, Brown, 1986. New edition of a classic account of the Constitutional Convention.

Hamilton, Alexander, James Madison, and John Jay. *The Federalist.* Many editions. Eighty-five essays presenting the Federalist arguments for ratification of the Constitution.

Paine, Thomas. *Common Sense.* Many editions. This pamphlet persuaded many colonists to support the call for independence.

Literature

Bowen, Catherine Drinker. *The Most Dangerous Man in America: Scenes from the Life of Benjamin Franklin.* Little, Brown, 1986. An excellent biography of Franklin.

Dickens, Charles. *Bleak House.* Many editions. A classic that describes the nineteenth-century English court system.

Fast, Howard. *Citizen Tom Paine: A Play in Two Acts.* Houghton Mifflin, 1986. An amusing tribute to Thomas Paine.

Winslow, Ola. *Master Roger Williams.* Macmillan, 1957. A biography of the founder of Rhode Island.

CHAPTER RESOURCES

Study Guide/Review 2
Workbook Chapter 2
Chapter 2 Test, Forms A–C

Films and Videotapes*

The Constitution of the United States. 2nd ed. 19 min. EBEC, 1982. f, v. The Constitutional Convention through the eyes of James Madison.

Federalism. (Series title: *Focus on the Constitution.*) 19 min. MTI (Coronet), 1986. f, v. Reviews the arguments over how much power the federal government can exercise.

George Washington and the Whiskey Rebellion: Testing the Constitution. 27 min. LCA (Coronet), 1974. f, v. The Constitution meets its first challenge—enforcement of a federally imposed tax on whiskey in 1791.

Software*

Colonial Merchant (Apple). EDACT. Students become colonial merchants in Boston and try to increase their wealth through trading while avoiding pirates, shipwreck, and the Royal Navy. The program simulates the economic concepts and causes of the American Revolution.

The U.S. Constitution: Nationalism and Federalism (Apple). Focus. Students act as farmers or manufacturers living under the Articles of Confederation in the 1780's and write their own Constitution.

* For a complete guide to audiovisual sources, see page T22.

27B

Origins of American Government *(pp. 28–59)*

This chapter outlines the development of the American system of government, including the origins of American political thought, the development of government in the American colonies, and the establishment of an independent United States.

Chapter Objectives
After students complete this chapter, they will be able to:

1. Explain why the English influence on American politics was dominant.

2. Describe what cornerstones of American political thought originated in England.

3. Explain how England's American colonies were governed.

4. Explain how England's policy toward the colonies changed during the 1760's.

5. Describe how the new English policy affected the colonies.

6. Describe the structure of the Declaration of Independence.

7. Explain how the Confederation government was put together and the problems it faced.

8. List the delegates to the Constitutional Convention.

9. Explain how the process of compromise led to agreement on the new Constitution.

10. Describe the debate over ratification of the Constitution.

CHAPTER

2

ORIGINS of AMERICAN GOVERNMENT

When in the Course of human events, it becomes necessary for one people to dissolve the political bands which have connected them with another, and to assume among the powers of the earth, the separate and equal station to which the Laws of Nature and of Nature's God entitle them, a decent respect to the opinions of mankind requires that they should declare the causes which impel them to the separation.

The Declaration of Independence
(July 4, 1776)

28

Photo
Colonial militia
re-enactment,
Yorktown, Virginia.

Thomas Jefferson suggested that John Adams write the draft. "I will not," Adams declared. "You should do it," said Jefferson. "Oh! no," Adams replied. "Why will you not? You ought to do it," said Jefferson. "I will not," Adams repeated. "Why?" asked Jefferson. "Reasons enough," said Adams firmly. "What can be your reasons?" Jefferson inquired. "Reason first—You are a Virginian, and a Virginian ought to appear at the head of this business. Reason second—I am obnoxious, suspected, and unpopular. You are very much otherwise. Reason third—You can write ten times better than I can." "Well," said Jefferson, "if you are decided, I will do as well as I can." In this way, according to Adams, it was decided that Jefferson would draft the Declaration of Independence.

In writing the Declaration, Jefferson drew upon nearly 200 years of colonial history and more than 500 years of English history. As this chapter will explain, English ideas about government, transplanted to North America and modified to meet new conditions, were used by Americans to create a new kind of government.

CHAPTER OUTLINE

1 Political Traditions Are Brought from England

Colonization in North America
The English Political Heritage

2 Government Develops in the Colonies

Colonial Governments
Britain's Colonial Policies
Steps Toward Colonial Unity

3 The New Nation Is Established

Debate over Independence
The Confederation Period

4 The Constitution Is Written and Ratified

The Constitutional Convention
Plans and Compromises
The Struggle for Ratification

29

SECTION 1

Political Traditions Are Brought from England

(pp. 30–33)

Section Objectives

☐ explain why the English influence on American politics was dominant

☐ describe what cornerstones of American political thought originated in England

Vocabulary

parliament, common law, precedent

FOCUS

● Tell students to imagine that they are about to write up a plan of government for the class. Ask them where they would get their ideas about how this new government would be structured.

Explain that the people who established the American system of government drew from existing forms of government—specifically, the English political tradition.

SECTION 1 — Political Traditions Are Brought from England

ACCESS **The Main Ideas**

1 Why was the English influence on American politics dominant?

pages 30–31

2 What cornerstones of American political thought originated in England?

pages 31–33

The United States has existed as a nation for about 200 years. For nearly 200 years before that, however, settlers from England and other countries had come to the American colonies. The people who established the new nation in 1776 were about as far removed in time from the first colonies as you are from the American Revolution.

From the 1500's on, France, Spain, Holland, and England competed for territory in North America. The English eventually won control of nearly all the Atlantic coast. Colonists from England brought with them long-established traditions of politics, law, and government. These traditions would deeply influence the forms of government that developed in the new land.

1D, 6G

Colonization in North America

English explorers and adventurers began to stake claims and settle colonies in North America in the late 1500's, during the reign of Queen Elizabeth I. England's first successful colony was Jamestown, settled in 1607 by members of the Virginia Company of London, an English trading corporation. Beginning in 1620, colonies were established in Massachusetts by Pilgrims and Puritans who wanted to escape religious persecution. English colonization in North America continued for 125 years. The thirteenth colony, Georgia, was established in 1732 to give debtors from England a chance for a new life.

Colonial rivalry

France was England's main rival for colonies in eastern North America. The French claim included the Great Lakes, the St. Lawrence River, and the entire Mississippi Valley. Explorers from Holland, Sweden, and Spain also claimed land along the Atlantic coast. Yet it was the British who finally took control.

Figure 2–1 THE THIRTEEN ENGLISH COLONIES 8B

30

Figure 2–1

▲ *What were the thirteen English colonies?* (Massachusetts, New Hampshire, Rhode Island, Connecticut, New York, New Jersey, Pennsylvania, Delaware, Maryland, Virginia, North and South Carolina, Georgia.)

Background: *Geography* Other important, but non-English, settlements were founded in North America during this time. The oldest permanent European settlement is St. Augustine, Florida, settled by the Spanish in 1565, some 42 years before Jamestown.

In 1664, England took over the Dutch colonies at New Netherland (later called New York). At the end of the French and Indian War in 1763, Great Britain acquired the French territories in Canada and the Great Lakes region. It also gained control of Florida from Spain. On the eve of American independence, the British dominated all of North America east of the Mississippi River.

1C, 1D, 2A, 6I, 8G

The English Political Heritage

The American colonies drew people from England, Scotland, Wales, and Ireland. Many settlers also came from the continent of Europe, particularly France and Germany. Not all came voluntarily. People from western and central Africa were brought as slaves. Despite this variety of settlers, it was England's political heritage that most deeply influenced government in the American colonies.

The English colonists brought with them four important principles that became cornerstones of American political thought. These principles are (1) *limited government,* (2) *representative government,* (3) *individual liberty,* and (4) *rule by law.* These ideas had developed over hundreds of years of English history.

Limits on the monarchy

From the time of William the Conqueror in 1066, English rulers had tried to establish a strong central government. They never acquired the total, unrestrained power of absolute monarchy, however. Nobles and landowning families kept considerable authority.

In 1215, rebellious English nobles placed definite limits on royal power by forcing King John to accept the Magna Charta, or "Great Charter." The Magna Charta is considered the foundation of English constitutional freedoms. In this document, King John conceded several important rights, such as limits on taxation, protection of private property, trial by jury, and certain religious freedoms. Although the Magna Charta guaranteed these rights only to nobles, the document was an important step in establishing the principle of limited government.

Representative government

Other changes also were occurring in the government of England during the 1200's. One

Amid splendor and pageantry, Queen Elizabeth I of England presides at a meeting of Parliament. In Elizabeth's reign (1558-1603), the House of Lords was the more powerful chamber.

of the most important was the emergence of a **parliament**, a representative body with power to make laws. Parliament in England developed out of the council of nobles and bishops who advised the ruler. In the late 1200's, as towns grew more important, knights (who held small estates) and townspeople were sometimes invited to parliamentary meetings. As this custom continued, the members of Parliament began to meet separately, as two "houses."

The House of Lords, or upper house, was made up of bishops and great nobles who either inherited their seats or were appointed. This house dominated Parliament until the early 1700's. The House of Commons, or lower chamber, included knights and townsmen who were elected by other knights and townspeople.

31

■ CRITICAL THINKING **What do the examples of the Magna Charta and Parliament tell you about the growth of individual rights in England?** (Early limitations on government power helped only nobles, but these limitations established principles that were eventually used to protect the rights of common people as well.)

Cooperative Learning

● Divide the class into six groups, and assign each group one of the rights listed under the English Bill of Rights. Have each group find and copy the reference to this right in the United States Constitution (pp. 112–138), and discuss the importance of that right. Groups should present their findings to the class.

GUIDED/INDEPENDENT PRACTICE

● Have students complete **Primary Source Worksheet 1,** which contains excerpts from the Magna Charta.

RETEACHING/CORRECTIVES

▲ Have students construct a time line of the following events mentioned in this section: beginnings of English common law (1100's); Magna Charta (1215); founding of Jamestown (1607); Petition of Right (1628); Glorious Revolution (1688); publishing of *Two Treatises on Government* (1690); end of French and Indian War (1763). Review each of these events with students.

You may also want to use **Transparency 2,** which reviews changes in English law and government between 1100 and 1300.

Only a few people had the right to vote for representatives to Parliament. For years, voting was limited to property-owning men who were members of the Anglican Church. Nevertheless, an important principle had been established: certain English citizens had the right to choose people to represent them in the legislature. This principle of representative government carried over into the legislatures of the colonies and, later, the United States Congress.

Individual liberty

The principle of personal freedom is also firmly anchored in English history. The Magna Charta made it clear that British subjects possessed certain rights that not even the monarch could violate. One important section, for instance, states that ''No free man shall be arrested or imprisoned . . . except by the lawful judgment of his peers or by the law of the land.'' The phrase ''judgment of his peers'' meant that a noble could be accused or tried only by a jury of his social equals — the other nobles. This right gradually was broadened to give *all* English citizens the right to trial by jury and the protection of the law.

A struggle for parliamentary power

The English Parliament continued to demand more rights for the people — and more limits on the monarch. The Petition of Right in 1628 was another landmark in this process. Although King Charles I claimed to rule by ''divine right,'' Parliament refused to grant him any money until he agreed to the demands listed in the Petition of Right. For example, the king would no longer be able to declare martial law in peacetime, imprison citizens without a legal reason, or impose taxes without the approval of the House of Commons.

King Charles signed the Petition of Right but soon ignored these promises. Moreover, he dismissed Parliament and attempted to rule as an absolute monarch. This struggle between king and Parliament finally erupted into civil war in 1642. Royalist forces were defeated, Charles I was beheaded, and a republic was set up. Although England returned to a monarchy in 1660, Parliament had decisively established its supremacy over the ruler.

32

The English Bill of Rights

In 1688, in a peaceful revolt known as the Glorious Revolution, Parliament chose new rulers for England. Parliament also drafted a Bill of Rights, which Queen Mary II and King William III willingly signed. In this historic document, the newly crowned rulers recognized certain basic rights of the people. Some of these rights would later be incorporated into the Constitution of the United States. The English Bill of Rights includes these guarantees:

● The right of British subjects to petition the monarch to answer their grievances.
   The First Amendment to the Constitution gives citizens the right to petition the government.

An 18th-century children's history book shows this woodcut drawing of William and Mary. The king holds the Bill of Rights in his hand; the queen has the orb, a symbol of royal power.

XXVIII. WILLIAM the THIRD and MARY the SECOND, from 1688 to 1702.

WILLIAM the hero, with MARIA mild,
(He James's nephew, she his eldest child)
Fix'd freedom and the church, reform'd the coin;
Oppos'd the French, and settled Brunswick's line.

Photo
The verse below the woodcut explains the relationships: Mary was the daughter of King James II. William was her cousin; his mother was James II's sister, his father a Dutch prince of the House of Orange.

- The right of British subjects to be protected from excessive bail and from cruel and unusual punishment.
  The Eighth Amendment grants American citizens this same protection.
- The right of Parliament (not the monarch) to approve keeping a standing army in peacetime.
  Article I, Section 8 of the Constitution gives Congress the right to establish and support an army and navy.
- The right of British subjects to a fair and speedy trial.
  This same provision appears in the Sixth Amendment.
- The right of free speech and debate in meetings of Parliament.
  Members of Congress are given this same protection by Article I, Section 6 of the Constitution.
- The right of certain subjects to keep and bear arms.
  This provision is found in the Second Amendment.

Locke and the "social contract"

To explain and defend these great changes in England's government, the philosopher John Locke (page 8) developed ideas that would later have great impact in America. His book *Two Treatises on Government* was published in 1690, soon after the Glorious Revolution put William and Mary on the throne.

In this work, Locke put forth his view of the "social contract" — that the purpose of government is to protect people's "natural rights" to life, liberty, and property. If the government fails to do so, then the people have the right to rebel and overthrow it. Locke's classic work greatly influenced the ideas of American leaders, especially Thomas Jefferson, James Madison, and Benjamin Franklin. If Locke's ideas sound familiar, it is because they are echoed in the Declaration of Independence.

The principle of "rule by law"

Along with their belief in individual liberty, the English had come to believe deeply in rule by law. The English **common law** began to develop in the 1100's as kings tried to establish one system of justice throughout the whole country. The common law was not based on specific laws or statutes passed by a legislature. Instead, it was built up gradually from the decisions of judges, based on custom and tradition. These decisions served as a **precedent** (PRESS-eh-dent), or model, for later judgments. Although Parliament was the official law-making body, judges had great influence on the ways that laws were interpreted and applied.

Because the common law grew out of custom — not royal command — the English valued it as a safeguard of their rights. One basic principle of the common law was that the law applied to the monarch as well as to his or her subjects. The Magna Charta, the Petition of Right, and the English Bill of Rights all carried out this principle. When English colonists migrated to North America, they brought with them the belief that rule by law was necessary. Common-law principles would play an important part in the governments established in the colonies.

SECTION 1 REVIEW

Vocabulary and key terms

Magna Charta (31)	English Bill of Rights (32)
parliament (31)	common law (33)
Petition of Right (32)	precedent (33)

For review

1. What four political principles did English settlers bring to the American colonies? **1D**
2. What groups of people were represented in (a) the House of Lords? (b) the House of Commons? **1D**
3. What was the purpose of the Petition of Right of 1628? **1D**
4. (a) What unusual action did Parliament take in the Glorious Revolution? (b) What political writer explained and defended the Glorious Revolution? **1D**

Critical thinking

FORMING AN OPINION Which of the four political principles brought from England do you believe is most important? Why? **1D**

33

Cross-reference
Chapter 17, p. 480, discusses the role of precedent in Supreme Court decision-making. Chapter 18, p. 492, discusses the influence of common law in the American legal system.

ENRICHMENT/EXTENSION

■ Have students read the Declaration of Independence (pp. 46–48), looking for the ideas from John Locke explained on p. 33. Students should write down the relevant excerpts and then explain them in their own words.

Section 1 Review Answers

1. Limited government, representative government, individual liberty, rule by law.
2. **(a)** Bishops and nobles. **(b)** Knights and townspeople.
3. To limit the king's power by preventing him from declaring martial law in peacetime, prohibiting the unlawful arrest of citizens, and requiring Parliament's approval on taxes.
4. **(a)** Parliament chose England's new rulers, William and Mary. **(b)** John Locke.

Critical thinking Students should select limited government, representative government, individual liberty, or rule by law, and then defend their selection.

CLOSURE

● Have students review the content of the section by restating the headings in the section as questions and answering them. Then have students read Section 2, noting the kinds of government that developed in the colonies.

The symbol ⅱ denotes active participation strategies.

Activities are keyed for student abilities:
▲ = Basic
● = All Levels
■ = Average/Advanced

SECTION 2

Government Develops in the Colonies
(pp. 34–39)

Section Objectives

☐ explain how England's American colonies were governed

☐ explain how England's policy toward the colonies changed during the 1760's

☐ describe how the new English policy affected the colonies

Vocabulary

charter, proprietor, assembly, burgess

FOCUS

● Ask students whether, in their opinion, the American Revolution was inevitable. Discuss the answers given. Then tell students to keep the question in mind as they review the section.

EXPLANATION

After reviewing the content of the section, you may want to consider the following activities:

Structure of Government

● *Who chose most colonial governors?* (The monarch, or the proprietor with the monarch's approval.) *Who chose the council of advisers?* (The governor.) *What roles did the council play?* (Upper house of the legislature and colony's highest court.)

● *What was the first colonial lawmaking assembly?* (House of Burgesses, in Virginia.) *Who could vote in elections for colonial assemblies?* (White males who owned property.) *How powerful were these assemblies? Why?* (Very powerful, because they had the backing of public opinion and had control over taxation and the governor's salary.)

34

Government Develops in the Colonies

> **ACCESS** The Main Ideas
>
> **1** How were England's American colonies governed? *pages 34–36*
>
> **2** How did England's policy toward the colonies change during the 1760's? *pages 36–37*
>
> **3** How did the new English policy affect the colonies? *pages 37–39*

For New Yorkers in the early 1700's, meeting the colonial governor could be an unsettling experience. Governor Edward Hyde liked to put on women's clothes, hide behind trees, and pounce on passers-by and pull their ears. He also stole from the treasury, which led England's Queen Anne (his cousin) to remove the unbalanced governor from office.

By the mid-1700's, there was a conflict between colonists and Crown-appointed officials that went deeper than strange pranks or even corruption. The colonists had grown used to ruling themselves. When Britain tried to tighten its control, the colonists fought back.

1D, 6G, 6H, 8G

Colonial Governments

Royal control over colonies

Anyone who wanted to establish a colony in English North America had to get both land and permission from the English monarch. This authorization was in the form of a **charter** — a legal document issued by the monarch to trading companies, to individuals, or to groups of settlers wishing to start a colony.

The earliest colonies, in New England and Virginia, were originally established by trading companies. Their charters allowed the colonists considerable self-government. Most of the southern and middle Atlantic colonies were granted to individuals, usually friends or relatives of the king. These individuals, called **proprietors**, organized their colonies as they wished. They were limited only by the terms of their charters and their obligations to the king.

34

Having granted a charter, the monarch also could take it back. By the early 1700's, most of the colonies established by trading companies had lost their charters. They became royal colonies ruled directly by the monarch. Only a few colonies kept their charters up to the time of American independence.

The governor and council

Colonial governments were similar in that all had a governor, a council of advisers, and a court system. They differed in the way these officials were chosen. In most colonies, the governor was an English aristocrat appointed by the king or by the proprietor with the king's approval. The governor chose his own council of advisers, picking men who agreed with his political views.

The governor and council, then, were a link with England and with British official policy. Gradually the council came to serve both as the upper house of the colonial legislature and as the colony's highest court.

Representative assemblies

The governor and his council represented British authority in the colonies. The English settlers, however, still strongly believed in representative government. Early in colonial history, colonists claimed their right to choose elected **assemblies**, or legislatures.

The first colonial law-making assembly was established in the Virginia Colony in 1619, only twelve years after the settlement of Jamestown. Each settlement chose delegates, just as towns in England chose representatives, or **burgesses**, to Parliament. The Virginia assembly was thus known as the House of Burgesses. Although King James I revoked the Virginia Company's charter a few years later, the House of Burgesses was allowed to continue.

A tradition of self-government was also established early in New England. In 1620, shortly before they landed at Plymouth, 41 of the colonists aboard the *Mayflower* drew up an agreement, or compact, establishing their own government.

Background: *Economics* One reason the monarch revoked the charters of trading companies was that once the difficult and risky job of establishing a colony had been accomplished, the king could make a profit by selling the newly profitably land at high prices.

Background: *History* All those who signed the Mayflower Compact were male.

The houses, barns, and dusty streets of a colonial New England village are re-created at Plimoth Plantation, southeast of Boston, Massachusetts. Plymouth Colony was established in 1620 by the Pilgrim settlers who had traveled on the *Mayflower*.

The signers of the Mayflower Compact agreed to live under a government that would make "just and equal laws . . . for the good of the colony." After the signing, the group elected one of its members the colony's first governor.

The backers of other colonies soon realized that, in order to attract new settlers, they too would have to allow representative assemblies. An assembly was set up in nearly every colony soon after its founding. Members were elected by white males who owned property — usually a fairly small group of the settlers. Voting requirements varied from colony to colony. In general, though, a larger percentage of men could vote in the New England colonies, where many settlers owned their own small farms and businesses. In the southern colonies, a relatively small number of people owned large farms or plantations.

Self-governing colonies

In two of the thirteen colonies, representative government began early and lasted throughout the colonial period. Both Rhode Island and Connecticut were established by settlers who had left the Massachusetts Bay Colony. Because they were independent of any proprietor or trading company, these colonists had an unusual amount of control over their own governments.

Rhode Island was founded by Roger Williams and other religious dissenters who had

been forced to leave Massachusetts by church leaders. Williams and his companions set up a civil government clearly separate from the church. The English monarchy was restored in 1660, and in 1663 King Charles II granted Rhode Island an unusually generous charter. It let the colonists elect the governor and his assistants, as well as members of the assembly. Moreover, the governor could not overturn the actions of the assembly, as he could in most colonies.

The settlers in Connecticut's early towns also took great strides toward self-government. In 1639 the colony was organized under the first written constitution in America — the Fundamental Orders. This document called for "an Orderly and decent Government" and made the freemen of the towns the colony's highest authority. The governor and court officials were to be elected, and the freemen could call a meeting of the assembly. In 1662 Connecticut also secured a royal charter from Charles II. This generous document let the Connecticut colonists keep the basic rights listed in the Fundamental Orders.

By the 1750's, Rhode Island and Connecticut were the only colonies still allowed to choose their own governors. Colonists in these two colonies treasured their charters. After making small changes during the Revolutionary War, both Connecticut and Rhode Island kept their colonial charters as their state constitutions.

35

Background: *History* The Mayflower Compact was deemed necessary because the Pilgrims had landed outside the area designated by their charter.

Background: *Constitutional Heritage* Roger Williams and his followers, considered "radical" in Massachusetts, fervently believed in religious liberty and separation of church and state. The beliefs embedded in Rhode Island's government became an important part of the democratic tradition eventually expressed in the United States Constitution.

👥 History

■ CRITICAL THINKING Draw the following chart on the board. Help students understand the events leading to the American Revolution in cause-effect terms by having them come to the board and fill in the missing causes or effects:

1. *Cause:* French and Indian War. *Effect:*＿＿＿＿＿＿ (Britain controls eastern North America; Britain imposes new taxes on colonies to pay debts.)

2. *Cause:* Stamp Act Congress. *Effect:*＿＿＿＿＿＿ (Colonists refuse to buy or sell British goods; Sons of Liberty organized; Stamp Act repealed.)

3. *Cause:*＿＿＿＿＿＿ (Colonists' anger at Townshend Acts and at presence of British troops in Boston.) *Effect:* Boston Massacre.

4. *Cause:* Boston Tea Party. *Effect:*＿＿＿＿＿＿ (Parliament closes port of Boston, limits self-government in Massachusetts, passes Quartering Act.)

5. *Cause:*＿＿＿＿＿＿ (Anger over "Intolerable Acts.") *Effect:* Colonists call First Continental Congress.

■ CRITICAL THINKING Ask
students to sum up the events of the 1760's and early 1770's in one sentence. (The harder that Britain tried to tighten its control over the American colonies, the harder the colonists resisted.)

Comparative Government

● Remind students that one issue in the clash between Parliament and King Charles I (p. 32) was Parliament's demand that it approve taxes. *What similar powers did the colonial assemblies have?* (They could set the governor's salary and impose local taxes.)

■ *What was the effect, both in England and in the colonies, of the legislature's possession of this power?* (The power of the executive—the monarch or the governor—was kept in check.)

Cooperative Learning

■ Divide the class into small groups, and divide each small group into pro-Britain and anti-Britain subgroups. Have each group debate the issues dividing Britain and the colonies in the 1770's.

When Williamsburg was the capital of colonial Virginia (1699-1780), this was the Royal Governor's Palace. Williamsburg today has been restored to look as it did in the 1700's.

Freedom in the colonies

It may seem that England kept a very tight rein on most of the American colonies through royal governors, appointed councils, and other controls. In fact, the Americans had great freedom in governing their own towns and colonies. By the early 1760's, the elected assemblies — the lower houses — dominated the legislature in nearly every colony.

There were three reasons for this shift in power. First, colonial legislators had the backing of public opinion. Because the assemblies were made up of elected representatives, people considered them the legitimate government. Second, following the tradition set by Parliament, the assemblies claimed the right to set the governor's salary and impose local taxes. Legislators often could get what they demanded by threaten-

ing to cut off their governor's funds. Finally, the colonial assemblies generally had their way because the British government's colonial policies allowed them to do so.

8F

Britain's Colonial Policies

"Salutary neglect"

From the British point of view, there were specific purposes in having colonies. The American colonists were expected to provide a market for goods from British merchants, supply material for British factories, and remain loyal subjects of the Crown. Generally, they did so, although American merchants and manufacturers did compete with the British. Otherwise, the British generally maintained a "hands-off" policy toward the colonies. One official called this policy "salutary neglect"; that is, neglect that would be helpful. This attitude was partly a matter of geography. England was more than 3,000 miles away from the American colonies. Any communications or instructions sent by British officials took months to arrive. It was therefore impossible for the Crown to keep control over day-to-day events in the colonies.

While the American colonists were loyal, they went against British colonial policy in some ways. For example, they started their own factories and traded in competition with British merchants. Still, they also benefited from colonial policy. The British government gave the colonies a basic legal system. British troops protected them from foreign powers, particularly Spanish pirates and French soldiers. In addition, the colonists enjoyed a great deal of freedom and paid fairly low taxes.

War debts and George III

Relations between the colonies and the British government changed suddenly in the 1760's. One major cause for this change was the French and Indian War. Although fighting began on American soil in 1754, this war was actually the result of a long and bitter rivalry between Britain and France over colonial possessions throughout the world. Hostilities soon spread to Europe and to India as well, becoming the conflict known as the Seven Years' War. Eventually, the British were victorious in every part of the world. In the

---

Background: *Geography* English colonists established Williamsburg in 1633. They chose the site because it had better soil drainage and, therefore, fewer mosquitoes than did the area around Jamestown.

Background: *History* The term *salutary neglect* was coined by a member of Parliament, Edmund Burke: "Through a wise and salutary neglect [of the colonies], a generous nature has been suffered to take her own

way to perfection. . . ." Burke advocated increased colonial freedom.

Treaty of Paris in 1763, France ceded to Britain nearly all its territory in North America.

The war, however, left Great Britain saddled with a tremendous financial problem. The British national debt had more than doubled during the many years of fighting. More important, Britain now had vast new North American territories to oversee and protect. The cost of administering and defending the colonies was five times greater after the war. British taxpayers resented this burden and began to clamor for Americans to pay their "fair share" of defense costs.

The king of England, George III, was a brash 22-year-old when he came to the throne in 1760, during the Seven Years' War. Faced with a huge war debt and angry British taxpayers, King George sought to make the Americans pay for their own defense. Under his leadership, Parliament passed a series of trade acts to bring in greater revenues from the colonies. Colonial officials also were told to enforce existing laws more strictly, particularly those against smuggling foreign goods to avoid paying taxes on them.

1D, 2C, 4A, 5C, 6G, 7A

Steps Toward Colonial Unity

A plan for union

The French and Indian War not only changed British colonial policies but also had a significant impact within the American colonies. In 1754, at the outbreak of the war, the British called a meeting of colonial representatives at Albany, New York, to discuss the war effort. At this convention, Benjamin Franklin offered a plan for uniting the colonies. Known as the Albany Plan of Union, it called for a colonial confederation to levy taxes, regulate Indian affairs, and establish an army and navy.

The delegates adopted the Albany Plan, but it was never carried out. The colonial assemblies rejected it because they feared a strong central government. British officials, on the other hand, thought it gave the colonists too much power. Nevertheless, the Albany Plan was one of the earliest attempts at colonial unification.

The Stamp Act Congress

The next move toward unity among the colonies resulted from Parliament's passage of new trade laws. Of these regulations, the Stamp Act of 1765 was most upsetting to the colonists. This law placed a tax on all printed material, including newspapers, merchants' bills, legal documents, and even playing cards and calendars.

The colonists protested vigorously. Parliament could regulate trade, they said, but only their own elected representatives had the right to impose taxes within the colonies. Because the colonists could not send delegates to Parliament, they claimed that the Stamp Act was "taxation without representation." This was a violation of one of the basic rights of English citizens. Opposition to the Stamp Act was so intense that delegates from nine colonies assembled at the Stamp Act Congress in New York City in October 1765.

Delegates at the Stamp Act Congress denounced the new taxes and petitioned the king and Parliament to repeal the act. They also called for a ban on buying or selling British goods. To make this protest effective, groups of patriots known as the Sons of Liberty organized throughout the colonies to put pressure on merchants. In 1766 Parliament repealed the Stamp Act after merchants in Britain complained that the drop in trade was seriously harming their business. The success of this protest convinced some colonists that unity was the only effective way to resist Parliament's actions.

The 1765 Stamp Act required an official mark like this to be stamped on all printed material to show that colonists had paid the tax.

37

GUIDED/INDEPENDENT PRACTICE

● Have students complete **Primary Source Worksheet 2,** which contains the Mayflower Compact, and **Primary Source Worksheet 3,** which contains excerpts from the Fundamental Orders of Connecticut.

RETEACHING/CORRECTIVES

▲ Draw on the board a diagram of the structure of colonial government, including the governor, governor's council, elected assembly, and the voters. Have students copy the diagram and explain how the system worked.

You may also want to use **Transparency 3,** which lists causes and effects of colonial self-government, and **Transparency 4,** which deals with the repeal of the Stamp Act.

Background: *History* To support his plan of union, Benjamin Franklin published one of the earliest political cartoons. Entitled "JOIN, or DIE," it appears in Study Skill 5 on p. 781.

Background: *Cultural Literacy* The Stamp Act Congress did not use the term *boycott* to describe their ban on buying and selling English goods because the term had not yet been invented. It was coined in 1880 by the Irish Land League after Captain Boycott, the original victim of the tactic.

The symbol ⅱ denotes active participation strategies.

Activities are keyed for student abilities:
▲ = Basic
● = All Levels
■ = Average/Advanced

Taxes and protests

Parliament, however, was still resolved to increase revenue from the colonies by imposing taxes. The Townshend Acts, passed in 1767, taxed such everyday items as paper, window glass, paint, and tea. In addition, as a warning, Parliament ordered the suspension of New York's colonial assembly.

These actions brought new protests throughout the colonies. Another ban on trade cut British imports by nearly half. In several letters to British officials, members of the Massachusetts assembly complained that Parliament's acts violated the colonists' rights as British subjects.

At first the British refused to repeal the taxes. Instead, they sent additional troops to Boston, Massachusetts, where colonial resistance was most vigorous. The citizens of Boston detested the British soldiers patrolling their streets and resented having to house and feed them. Tempers flared, and in March 1770, street fighting broke out between British soldiers and Bostonians. Five colonists were killed in what was termed the Boston Massacre.

The violence temporarily broke the tensions. New leaders in Parliament repealed all the Townshend Acts except the tea tax, which was left as a reminder of Parliament's power. The colonists, in turn, began to buy British goods again. Nevertheless, many people in England regarded the colonists and their assemblies as annoying and disobedient. Some colonial leaders, on the other hand, felt that resistance to British policies should be even stronger.

An artist's engraving of the Boston Tea Party shows a crowd of patriots cheering enthusiastically as others — dressed like Indians — board the East India Company ships and toss crates of tea into Boston Harbor.

38

Colonial resistance

In 1772, Samuel Adams of Boston began to organize a network of committees throughout the colonies to oppose British policies. These Committees of Correspondence provided a way to exchange information and coordinate plans for resistance. They operated independently of the colonial governments.

The Tea Act, passed by Parliament in 1773, caused the colonists' next act of open resistance. This law granted the financially troubled East India Company special advantages in selling tea in America. Colonial tea merchants were furious at losing business to the East India Company. Other colonists were angry at paying the tax on tea. Protests took place in many port cities but were most intense in Boston. On the evening of December 16, 1773, about sixty colonists, disguised as Indians, boarded the three East India Company ships and dumped more than 300 crates of tea into Boston Harbor.

The destructiveness of the "Boston Tea Party" brought widespread disapproval, even from colonists who opposed the tea tax. Nevertheless, Parliament's angry reaction increased colonial resentment again and helped unify the colonists. In a series of new laws, Parliament closed the port of Boston (until the tea was paid for) and strictly limited self-government in Massachusetts. A Quartering Act ordered colonists to house British soldiers in their inns or private homes.

The colonists termed these laws the "Intolerable Acts." Throughout the colonies, they met to protest Parliament's "unconstitutional" actions and to organize aid for Boston. Leaders in Massachusetts and Virginia called for a convention of colonial representatives to discuss the colonies' situation.

A demand for "American rights"

On September 5, 1774, representatives from every colony except Georgia met in Philadelphia to consider the colonies' relations with Great Britain. Delegates to this First Continental Congress included such distinguished leaders as George Washington, John Adams, Samuel Adams, Patrick Henry, Richard Henry Lee, John Rutledge, John Jay, and Roger Sherman. These men represented a wide range of political views. Some sought a colonial union allied with Britain (like the Albany Plan) and the establishment of an American branch of Parliament. Others were ready to call for independence from Britain.

The First Continental Congress debated strategy for almost two months. Before adjourning, the delegates drew up a Declaration of Rights. It stated that the American colonists were entitled to the same rights and liberties as people in England, and that Parliament had violated these rights. The Congress also agreed on the "Continental Association," an organized ban on imports from any British territory. Finally, the Congress decided to meet again the following spring (May 1775) unless Parliament had satisfactorily answered their complaints.

SECTION 2 REVIEW

Vocabulary and key terms

charter (34)	Fundamental Orders (35)
proprietor (34)	"salutary neglect" (36)
assembly (34)	Albany Plan of Union (37)
burgess (34)	Stamp Act (37)
Mayflower Compact (35)	"Intolerable Acts" (39)

For review

1. In what ways did the English monarch have control over the American colonies? **1D**
2. (a) When and where was the first representative assembly established in the American colonies? (b) Why did elected assemblies come to dominate colonial governments? **6H**
3. What significant steps toward self-government were taken by Americans in the colonies of (a) Plymouth? (b) Rhode Island? (c) Connecticut? **6H**
4. How did the French and Indian War change British policies toward the colonies? **8F**
5. (a) Why did the colonists object to the Stamp Act? (b) What actions did they take? **7A**
6. What were the short-term and long-term effects of the Boston Tea Party? **8F**

Critical thinking

DRAWING INFERENCES What role did emotions play in the growing split between the colonies and Britain? Explain. **8F**

4. Heavy war debts, increased defense expenses, and the resentment of English taxpayers forced the king to levy taxes on the colonies.

5. **(a)** They claimed it was taxation without representation. **(b)** They petitioned the king and Parliament to repeal the act and called for a boycott of English goods.

6. *Short-term*—Parliament closed Boston's port, limited self-government in Massachusetts, and passed the Quartering Act. *Long-term*—Increased colonial resentment, unified colonists, caused First Continental Congress to meet.

Critical thinking British efforts to tighten control over the colonies, such as sending troops to patrol Boston, angered colonists and increased their desire to resist.

CLOSURE

● Remind students of the pre-reading objectives at the beginning of the section. Pose one or all of these questions again. Then have students read Section 3, focusing on the content of the Declaration of Independence and the Articles of Confederation.

The symbol 👥 denotes active participation strategies.

Activities are keyed for student abilities:
▲ = Basic
● = All Levels
■ = Average/Advanced

The New Nation Is Established *(pp. 40–45)*

Section Objectives

☐ describe the structure of the Declaration of Independence

☐ explain how the Confederation government was put together and the problems it faced

Vocabulary

bicameral, unicameral, bill of rights, ratification

FOCUS

● Ask if any students can recall a phrase of the Articles of Confederation. Then ask if any can recall a phrase of the Declaration of Independence. (Probably no student will know the Articles, but students may be familiar with at least the opening lines of the Declaration.) Discuss with students the reasons why the Declaration is so much better known.

The New Nation Is Established

ACCESS | The Main Ideas

1 What is the structure of the Declaration of Independence? *pages 40–43*

2 How was the Confederation government put together and what problems did it face? *pages 43–45*

To Parliament and the king, the Americans' actions looked like rebellion, and rebellion could not be tolerated. Britain might lose important income, and such a precedent might lead other British colonies to rebel. Britain therefore answered the demands of the First Continental Congress with even harsher policies. In April 1775, British soldiers were sent to the Massachusetts towns of Lexington and Concord. Their mission was to destroy the colonists' supply of weapons and arrest John Hancock and Samuel Adams for treason. The colonial militia resisted, and the battles of Lexington and Concord marked the start of the American Revolution. Against this background, colonial leaders met again to decide on their next steps.

1D, 2A, 2C, 6A

Debate over Independence

The Second Continental Congress

On May 10, 1775, three weeks after the battles of Lexington and Concord, the Second Continental Congress met in Philadelphia. This time all thirteen colonies were represented, although Georgia's delegates arrived late. John Hancock was elected president of the Congress, and each of the colonies was accorded one vote. Executive committees carried out all of the decisions and policies.

Because war had begun, the Congress was forced to take on the powers of a government and organize the colonies' defense. It immediately established an army to carry on the war against the British and named George Washington as commander. As the war continued, the Continental Congress borrowed and issued money, negotiated treaties with foreign states, and created a

navy. In effect, it served as the first American government until 1781.

Although the Continental Army was fighting the king's soldiers, the Continental Congress at first tried to find a policy that would maintain the colonies' ties with Britain. Only a few Americans, the most fervent patriots, really wanted to break completely with Britain. Both in the Congress and throughout the colonies, people debated the issue of independence.

The most persuasive arguments for independence were advanced by Thomas Paine in a popular and widely read pamphlet, *Common Sense*. (You can read parts of Thomas Paine's pamphlet in the Speaking Out feature on page 794.) Paine insisted that Americans had no choice except to cut their ties with royal tyranny. Paine's stirring words, combined with the opinions of respected patriot leaders and the continued fighting, had a great effect on public opinion. By the spring of 1776, many of the colonists were demanding independence.

A decision for independence

On June 7, 1776, the Second Continental Congress considered this resolution from Virginia's Richard Henry Lee:

> *Resolved,* That these United Colonies are, and of right ought to be free and independent States, that they are absolved from all allegiance to the British Crown, and that all political connection between them and the State of Great Britain is, and ought to be, totally dissolved.

To draft a proclamation of independence based on this resolution, the Congress appointed a committee. John Adams, Roger Sherman, Benjamin Franklin, Robert Livingston, and Thomas Jefferson were all members. The actual writing, however, was almost exclusively the work of the scholarly young Jefferson. On July 2, 1776, the Congress approved Lee's resolution, and the entire Declaration of Independence was approved on July 4, 1776.

Check for Understanding

● *In what ways did the Second Continental Congress act as a government during the Revolutionary War?* (It created an army and named Washington its commander, borrowed and issued money, negotiated treaties, and created a navy.)

Critical Thinking

■ *Why might many colonists not have wanted to break with Britain?* (They might have been proud of their status as British citizens, felt a loyalty toward the monarchy, or feared the death and destruction a war for independence would cause.)

*I*n the years after the Revolution, Americans struggled to create a lasting system of government. That system is the one under which you live. How well does this government work today? And how does it affect your life? Three students give their opinions below: John R. Garza, from Pharr-San Juan-Alamo Upper Level High School in Pharr, Texas; Tanika Chapman from Paul Laurence Dunbar Community High School in Baltimore, Maryland; and Jacob Medow who attends Highland Park High School in Illinois. Think about your own response to the questions.

John Garza

I like my congressman [Kika de la Garza] because he took time to come to a classroom and talk to the students. He tries. He came from this area, he sees the poverty here in the Rio Grande Valley. But many in Congress, they get out of touch with what's going on. What it all boils down to is that people forget where they come from, they forget what's going on. When I'm old enough, I plan to go into law, and then run for office and change things. This guy asked me, what were my plans. I answered that I planned to come back and help the Hispanic community. And he told me, "You can't do that, you can't be successful from down here." And I said, "Wait a minute, how do you define success?" It's not about money. You don't forget your roots, you don't forget where you're from.

Tanika Chapman

I think speaking out makes a difference. That's why we have two student commissioners on the school board. If there's anybody that knows what we need, that can represent us, it's us. My organization has a legislative lobbying program and we lobby on educational bills that affect us as students. We have student interns in the administration building for Baltimore City. We also have a student on the state board of education. We go to Annapolis [Maryland's capital] and we give our opinions about how we think bills should be handled. We have had some success, we have changed some legislators' minds. We are represented and we are heard.

Jacob Medow

I would have to say that the bureaucracy is a real disadvantage. The strength is that people have the choice to elect to office anyone they want. I think that when you elect someone, you elect their views also. When you vote for candidates, you're putting your trust in them and you expect that they will make the choices that you want. You reinforce that by writing letters to them.

STUDENT PARTICIPATION

1. What do Jacob, Tanika, and John see as the strengths of American government today? Its weaknesses? Do you agree?
2. What methods of influencing the government do they suggest? What are other possible methods?

4A

Three Students Discuss American Government

John Garza

Tanika Chapman

Jacob Medow

41

YOUR TURN

Background

John Garza, 17 years old, has been involved in student theater as well as community political activities. Tanika Chapman, also 17, is a member of the Associated Student Congress of Baltimore City and plans a career in medicine. Jacob Medow, 16 years old, is a sophomore.

♊ Constitutional Heritage

● Ask for volunteers to role-play such leaders of the Revolution and framers of the Constitution as Samuel Adams, Patrick Henry, James Madison, Thomas Jefferson, and Alexander Hamilton. Have the volunteers form a panel. Ask other members of the class to represent the points of view of the students quoted here, as well as their own points of view, and ask the panel questions about how close the members of the panel think today's government is to the one they originally envisioned.

Student Participation Answers

1. The students agree that the system of representation and the ability to speak out and lobby legislators are strengths. Weaknesses are the fact that many in Congress forget whom they are representing, and the fact that there are conflicts between points of view.
2. John believes representatives must not forget their roots, and Tanika and Jacob both stress the importance of contacting and lobbying government officials. Students may suggest becoming involved in political campaigns as well as introducing such government reforms as term limitation and strict campaign financing controls.

The symbol ♊ denotes active participation strategies.

Activities are keyed for student abilities:
▲ = Basic
● = All Levels
■ = Average/Advanced

EXPLANATION

After reviewing the content of the section, you may want to consider the following activities:

Historic Documents

Compare the two central documents in this section, the Declaration of Independence and the Articles of Confederation.

● **What was the basic purpose of each document?** (The Declaration announced the colonies' independence from Britain; the Articles created the framework of a league of independent states.)

● CRITICAL THINKING **In what way did the Articles of Confederation answer a question left open by the Declaration of Independence?** (The Declaration did not specify whether the new nation was one or thirteen independent states; the Articles created a confederation of thirteen independent states.)

■ CRITICAL THINKING **What evidence suggested that this answer was not the wisest one?** (The Confederation government was too weak to deal effectively with many of the nation's problems.)

Sometimes called the "birth certificate" of the United States of America, the Declaration of Independence was, and still is, a unique document. The Declaration served several crucial functions. First, it explained the ideas and philosophy that justified America's break with Great Britain. Second, it rallied world sentiment in favor of the American colonists. It was praised by supporters of democracy throughout the world and later influenced the French Revolution of 1789. Perhaps most important, the Declaration helped unify American public opinion.

The Declaration of Independence

The Declaration of Independence, given in full on pages 46–48, has several parts. Jefferson began the document with an explanation of *why* it was being written and the basic principles on which it was based. Drawing on the heritage of English political history, Jefferson listed many of the basic principles of American democracy — limited government, representative government, individual liberty, and rule by law. The Declaration also echoes John Locke's ideas about people's "natural rights" and the "social contract" between the government and the people. Instead of the rights to "life, liberty, and property," however, Jefferson added the words "the pursuit of Happiness":

> We hold these truths to be self-evident, that all men are created equal, that they are endowed by their Creator with certain unalienable Rights, that among these are Life, Liberty, and the pursuit of Happiness. That to secure these rights, Governments are instituted among Men, deriving their just powers from the consent of the governed. . . .

The middle part of the Declaration consists of a detailed list of charges against King George III. These were intended to show exactly how the British government had violated basic rights that the colonists, as British subjects, possessed. The Declaration charges, for example, that the king has quartered British soldiers in civilian homes, imposed taxes without the consent of the people, denied the right to trial by jury, and abolished elected legislatures.

The final part of the Declaration explains the colonists' efforts to achieve a peaceful settlement, the British government's stubbornness, and the Americans' resolve to be free. The Declaration concludes with a restatement of Lee's earlier resolution, stating:

> That these United Colonies are, and of Right ought to be Free and Independent States; that they are Absolved from all Allegiance to the British Crown, and that all political connection between them and the State of Great Britain, is and ought to be totally dissolved; and that as Free and Independent States, they have full Power to levy War, conclude Peace, contract Alliances, establish Commerce, and do all other Acts and Things which Independent States may of right do.

The Congress then approved the document, and John Hancock, as president, signed first with his famous bold stroke. Over the next several months, 55 others signed the Declaration, pledging "our Lives, our Fortunes, and our sacred Honor." In the eyes of the British government, this action made them traitors. Benjamin Franklin observed that if the signers did not "hang together" in pursuing independence, they would "most assuredly hang separately." Behind Franklin's wit lay real fear and the risk of danger.

Organizing new state governments

Even before the Declaration was issued, most of the colonies had begun to organize as states. New Hampshire was the first to replace its royal charter with a constitution, in January 1776. South Carolina followed suit in March. On May 10, 1776, almost two months before the Declaration of Independence, the Continental Congress urged the remaining colonies to adopt "such governments as shall, in the opinion of the representatives of the people, best conduce to the happiness and safety of their constituents."

During the next few years, all the colonies adopted written constitutions. As the new state governments emerged, Americans began to think of them as independent, sovereign states. Although there were wide variations among the new state constitutions, there were even more similarities. These reflected the colonists' shared heritage of English politics, as well as their experience with colonial rule.

All the new states established three separate branches of government — legislative, executive, and judicial. Like the English Parliament,

42

Cross-reference
As Chapter 24, p. 634, explains, Connecticut and Rhode Island created state constitutions by revising their colonial charters. The chart on p. 637 provides more details on state constitutions.

the legislatures in most states were **bicameral**, with two houses. (Only Georgia and Pennsylvania had one-house, or **unicameral**, legislatures.) Executive branches were generally weak, while the popularly elected lower houses had the most authority.

Remembering their difficulties with colonial rule, seven states included a **bill of rights**. These listed the basic civil liberties of citizens. All states limited voting rights to adult male property owners. It is important to remember these key features, because many became part of the national government created under the Constitution.

1D, 2A, 2C

The Confederation Period

Although written charters and constitutions were a basic feature of colonial and state governments, neither the First nor the Second Continental Congress had such a written plan to follow. In the midst of the Revolutionary War, members of the Congress realized that a more permanent form of central government was needed to bring together the new states.

The first national constitution

While Thomas Jefferson was writing the Declaration of Independence, another committee (composed of one member from each colony) was appointed to prepare "the form of a confederation to be entered into between the colonies." The Congress debated the committee's plan for the Articles of Confederation for seventeen months before approving it in November 1777. In order to take effect, the plan required **ratification**, or final approval, by all thirteen of the new states. A disagreement over western lands delayed Maryland from ratifying until March 1781. The Articles then went into effect, becoming America's first national constitution. (Excerpts from the Articles appear in Landmarks in Liberty on this page.)

The Declaration of Independence had given no clear guide as to the form of government of the new nation. Did the Declaration create *one* nation-state or *thirteen* separate states? Its words could be read in several ways. It refers to "the united States of America," but it also asserts that "these United Colonies are . . . free and independent states. . . ."

LANDMARKS in LIBERTY

The Articles of Confederation (1781)

In June 1776, even before the Declaration of Independence had been issued, the Second Continental Congress appointed a committee to set up a plan of government for the new nation. On November 15, 1777, the Congress adopted the committee's proposal for "certain articles of Confederation and perpetual Union between the States." The Articles were ratified on March 1, 1781.

❝ ARTICLE II. Each state retains its sovereignty, freedom and independence, and every Power, jurisdiction and right, which is not . . . expressly delegated to the United States. . . .

ARTICLE IX. . . . The United States . . . shall never engage in a war, nor grant letters of marque and reprisal in time of peace, nor enter into any treaties or alliances, nor coin money, nor regulate the value thereof, nor ascertain the sums and expenses necessary for the defence and welfare of the United States, . . . nor emit bills, nor borrow money on the credit of the United States, nor appropriate money, nor agree upon the vessels of war, to be built or purchased, or the number of land or sea forces to be raised, nor appoint a commander in chief of the army or navy, unless nine states assent to the same: nor shall a question on any other point . . . be determined, unless by the votes of a majority of the United States in congress assembled. ❞

1. What is meant by the word *sovereignty* in Article II?
2. What was the delegates' intent in placing such specific limitations on the defense powers of the central government?
3. What provision was made for deciding issues not covered by the Articles?

43

Economics
● CRITICAL THINKING Ask students to look for ways in which the weakness of the Confederation government harmed the United States economy. Have students write their answers on the board in the form of cause-and-effect statements. (*Examples:* Congress's inability to levy taxes kept the public debt high; Congress's lack of control over commerce harmed interstate trade and domestic manufacturers; Congress's inability to prevent states from coining their own money harmed interstate trade.)

Cooperative Learning
● Divide the class into small groups. Within each group, have students take turns reading a sentence from the Declaration of Independence (pp. 46–48). Other students in the group should then rephrase that sentence in their own words.

GUIDED/INDEPENDENT PRACTICE
● Have students imagine that they are among those Americans of the 1780's who supported the creation of a stronger central government. Have students write a letter to the editor listing the failures of the Confederation government and explaining the need for stronger central control.

Landmarks in Liberty Answers

1. The word *sovereignty* in Article II indicates that the states' rule was supreme over the central government's rule under the Articles.

2. They intended to prevent the central government from waging war in any form without the states' consent.

3. Every power that was not expressly delegated to the central government belonged to the states.

The symbol ♟♟ denotes active participation strategies.

Activities are keyed for student abilities:
▲ = Basic
● = All Levels
■ = Average/Advanced

▲ Draw the following chart on the board. Have students come to the board and fill in the chart with information about the Declaration of Independence and the Articles of Confederation.

	Dec.	Art.
Who?		
What?		
Where?		
When?		
Why?		

You may also want to use **Transparencies 5-8,** which deal with different aspects of the American Revolution and the Articles of Confederation.

ENRICHMENT/EXTENSION

■ Have students write an essay on the following theme: *The importance to this nation of the Declaration of Independence extended far beyond the Revolutionary War, and in fact can still be seen today.*

Section 3 Review Answers

1. (a) The outbreak of war (Lexington and Concord).
(b) It established military forces, borrowed and issued money, negotiated treaties, and drafted the Declaration of Independence.
2. The first section explains its purpose and lists principles of American democracy; the second lists charges against the king; the third explains colonists' attempts to settle their disputes peacefully

The Articles of Confederation temporarily answered this question. As the term *confederation* indicates, the states joined together to meet certain common goals. In the words of the Articles, they formed a "firm league of friendship" to ensure "their common defense, the security of their liberties, and their mutual and general welfare." On the other hand, each state retained its "sovereignty, freedom, and independence." The Articles of Confederation thus created only an association among thirteen independent states.

A weak central government

For such a league, only a weak central government was needed or wanted. A unicameral Congress was the only official government body. Congressional committees tried to carry out executive duties, and most judicial functions were left to the states. Representatives were appointed and paid (if at all) by their respective state legislatures. Although the number of representatives from each state ranged from two to seven, each state cast only one vote in the Confederation Congress.

Under the Articles, all the powers of the central government belonged to the Congress. There was no separate executive branch to coordinate or carry out the government's duties. On paper, the Congress could conduct foreign relations, declare war, negotiate treaties, settle conflicts between states, borrow money, set up post offices, establish armed forces, fix weights and measures, direct Indian affairs, and set national policies.

In reality, the structure of the Articles often made it impossible for the government to carry out these functions. The votes of seven states (a majority) were needed to pass any law. All thirteen states had to agree on any changes in the Articles, so that it was almost impossible to amend them.

These were some of the many areas of weakness of the Confederation government:

- *Congress was powerless to levy or collect taxes,* although the public debt was more than $40 million.

- *Congress was unable to maintain an army or navy* because it could not pay for them. Without an army, settlers on the frontier had difficulty with the Indians, the British, and the Spanish. Without a navy, American merchant ships were easy prey for pirates.

- *Congress had no control over foreign or interstate commerce.* The states imposed taxes and other barriers on trade with neighboring states. In addition, American merchants could not compete with European rivals because they were not protected by taxes on imports.

- *Congress was, therefore, unable to establish a sound economy.* States coined their own money, making trade difficult. States also interfered with the obligations of contracts, which made business risky.

- *Congress lacked authority to enforce its own laws.* It could not prevent states from negotiating with foreign nations and conducting their own Indian affairs.

- *Congress could not effectively settle disputes between states,* because there was no national court system. States often refused to recognize or enforce the laws and court decisions of other states. Fugitives could escape criminal prosecution by crossing state lines.

Successes of the Confederation

Despite its severe weaknesses, the Confederation government made some lasting achievements. It managed somehow to keep the states together, win the American Revolution, and successfully negotiate the Treaty of Paris with Great Britain, signed in 1783. It established a diplomatic corps that sent to Europe such outstanding representatives as Benjamin Franklin, Thomas Jefferson, and John Adams.

The government also set up permanent congressional committees to handle administrative duties. The committees for foreign, military, and financial affairs were the forerunners of the present Departments of State, Defense, and Treasury.

The Northwest Ordinance

Another lasting achievement of the Confederation government was a workable plan for the vast lands to the West, spelled out in the Northwest Ordinance of 1787. This landmark act outlined a governmental structure for the Northwest Territory, the land north of the Ohio River and westward to the Mississippi River.

The Ordinance guaranteed religious freedom and prohibited slavery in the territory. It also established the method by which three to five new states would be carved from these lands and would enter the union "on an equal footing with the original states." This procedure became the model for admitting all new states.

Economic troubles

In spite of the accomplishments of the Confederation, many people soon saw the need for a stronger central government than the Articles could provide. The new country's economic problems were rapidly growing worse. States issued their own paper money, but inflation soon made it worthless. A serious postwar depression hurt small businesses and lowered the prices farmers got for their crops. By 1786, people in many states were on the verge of rebellion.

In Massachusetts, for example, farmers and townspeople met in their town meetings to protest high taxes and other economic problems. They wanted the state government to make reforms and issue paper money to help them pay their taxes and debts. The government, though, was led mainly by prosperous merchants and property-owners, and they ignored these pleas. Led by Daniel Shays, a veteran of the Revolution, hundreds of angry farmers and laborers banded together, marched on courthouses, and freed imprisoned debtors from jail. Shays's Rebellion was quelled by the state militia, but it made leaders in every state realize that changes in the government must be made soon. Some feared that people might even turn to a dictator or king who promised to restore order.

The Annapolis Convention

Several meetings of state leaders led up to a full-scale convention for making necessary changes. Prominent Virginians, such as George Washington and James Madison (both supporters of a stronger central government), took the lead. They persuaded the Virginia legislature to call a convention of all the states to discuss trade, commerce, and "the state of the union."

Only five states sent delegates to the meeting at Annapolis, Maryland, in September 1786. They issued a strong recommendation for a meeting of all the states to consider the critical problems facing the country. In February 1787, the Congress officially urged all the states to send delegates to Philadelphia on the second Monday in May

> . . . for the sole and express purpose of revising the Articles of Confederation and reporting to Congress and the several legislatures such alterations and provisions therein as shall . . . render the federal constitution [the Articles of Confederation] adequate to the exigencies of Government & the preservation of the Union.

The message stated specifically that the "sole and express purpose" of this meeting was to be the "revising" of the Articles of Confederation. Nonetheless, many states chose as their delegates prominent statesmen who supported a stronger national government. It was clear that discontent with the Articles was deep and significant.

SECTION 3 REVIEW

Vocabulary and key terms

bicameral (43)   Articles of Confederation (43)
unicameral (43)   ratification (43)
bill of rights (43)   Northwest Ordinance (44)

For review

1. (a) What forced the Second Continental Congress to take on the duties of a government? (b) What were the Congress's major achievements? **1D**
2. Describe the major sections of the Declaration of Independence and the purpose of each. **1D**
3. What were four characteristics shared by most of the new state constitutions? **1D**
4. (a) What were the main weaknesses of the government under the Articles of Confederation? (b) What did this government accomplish? **2A**

Critical thinking

ANALYZING A QUOTATION Reread the comment by Benjamin Franklin on page 42. Though made during the Revolutionary War, the comment remained relevant during the period of the Confederation government. Explain why. **1C**

and declares the colonies to be independent.
3. Three branches of government; a bicameral legislature with a popularly elected, powerful lower house; a bill of rights; voting limited to adult male property owners.
4. (a) It could not levy or collect taxes, maintain armed forces, control commerce, enforce its own laws, or settle disputes among the states.
(b) It won the Revolutionary War, negotiated the Treaty of Paris, and enacted the Northwest Ordinance.

Critical thinking Just as the signers of the Declaration needed to work together to ensure independence, the newly independent states needed to work together to ensure the success of the United States.

CLOSURE

● Briefly review the major events in the section by having students name a key event in each of the following years: 1775 (battles of Lexington and Concord), 1776 (Declaration of Independence), 1781 (Articles of Confederation ratified), 1783 (Treaty of Paris), 1787 (convention meets to revise Articles of Confederation). Then have students read Section 4, paying special attention to the role compromise played in the Constitutional Convention.

The symbol 👥 denotes active participation strategies.

Activities are keyed for student abilities:
▲ = Basic
● = All Levels
■ = Average/Advanced

THE DECLARATION OF INDEPENDENCE

Historic Documents

Remind students that the Declaration of Independence is *not* the official act by which the Continental Congress separated from Britain. Richard Henry Lee's June 7 resolution, cited on p. 40, declared that "these United Colonies are, and of right ought to be free and independent States." The committee to "prepare a declaration to the effect of the said first resolution" was appointed on June 11.

● CRITICAL THINKING **Why is the Declaration better remembered than Lee's June 7 resolution?** (The Declaration was the means by which the Continental Congress announced to the world that the colonies were independent.)

The Declaration of Independence

When in the Course of human events, it becomes necessary for one people to dissolve the political bands which have connected them with another, and to assume among the powers of the earth, the separate and equal station to which the Laws of Nature and of Nature's God entitle them, a decent respect to the opinions of mankind requires that they should declare the causes which impel them to the separation.*

[Principles of American Democracy]

We hold these truths to be self-evident, that all men are created equal, that they are endowed by their Creator with certain unalienable Rights, that among these are Life, Liberty and the pursuit of Happiness. That to secure these rights, Governments are instituted among Men, deriving their just powers from the consent of the governed, That whenever any Form of Government becomes destructive of these ends, it is the Right of the People to alter or to abolish it, and to institute new Government, laying its foundation on such principles and organizing its powers in such form, as to them shall seem most likely to effect their Safety and Happiness. Prudence, indeed, will dictate that Governments long established should not be changed for light and transient causes; and accordingly all experience hath shown, that mankind are more disposed to suffer, while evils are sufferable, than to right themselves by abolishing the forms to which they are accustomed. But when a long train of abuses and usurpations, pursuing invariably the same Object evinces a design to reduce them under absolute Despotism, it is their right, it is their duty, to throw off such Government, and to provide new Guards for their future security.

[List of Grievances]

Such has been the patient sufferance of these Colonies; and such is now the necessity which constrains them to alter their former Systems of Government. The history of the present King of Great Britain is a history of repeated injuries and usurpations, all having in direct object the establishment of an absolute Tyranny over these States. To prove this, let Facts be submitted to a candid world.

He has refused his Assent to Laws, the most wholesome and necessary for the public good.

He has forbidden his Governors to pass Laws of immediate and pressing importance, unless suspended in their operation till his Assent should be obtained, and when so suspended, he has utterly neglected to attend to them.

He has refused to pass other Laws for the accommodation of large districts of people, unless those people would relinquish the right of Representation in the Legislature, a right inestimable to them and formidable to tyrants only.

He has called together legislative bodies at places unusual, uncomfortable, and distant from the depository of their Public Records, for the sole purpose of fatiguing them into compliance with his measures.

* In punctuation and capitalization the text of the Declaration follows accepted sources.

He has dissolved Representative Houses repeatedly, for opposing with manly firmness his invasions on the rights of the people.

He has refused for a long time, after such dissolutions, to cause others to be elected; whereby the Legislative powers, incapable of Annihilation, have returned to the People at large for their exercise; the State remaining in the mean time exposed to all the dangers of invasion from without, and convulsions within.

He has endeavoured to prevent the population of these States; for that purpose obstructing the Laws for Naturalization of Foreigners; refusing to pass others to encourage their migrations hither, and raising the conditions of new Appropriations of Lands.

He has obstructed the Administration of Justice, by refusing his Assent to Laws for establishing Judiciary powers.

He has made Judges dependent on his Will alone, for the tenure of their offices, and the amount and payment of their salaries.

He has erected a multitude of New Offices, and sent hither swarms of Officers to harass our People, and eat out their substance.

He has kept among us, in times of peace, Standing Armies without the Consent of our legislatures.

He has affected to render the military independent of and superior to the Civil power.

He has combined with others to subject us to a jurisdiction foreign to our constitution, and unacknowledged by our laws; giving his Assent to their Acts of pretended Legislation:

For quartering large bodies of armed troops among us:

For protecting them, by a mock Trial, from Punishment for any Murders which they should commit on the Inhabitants of these states:

For cutting off our Trade with all parts of the world:

For imposing Taxes on us without our Consent:

For depriving us in many cases, of the benefits of Trial by Jury:

For transporting us beyond Seas to be tried for pretended offenses:

For abolishing the free System of English Laws in a neighbouring Province, establishing therein an Arbitrary government, and enlarging its Boundaries so as to render it at once an example and fit instrument for introducing the same absolute rule into these Colonies:

For taking away our Charters, abolishing our most valuable Laws, and altering fundamentally the Forms of our Governments:

For suspending our own Legislatures, and declaring themselves invested with power to legislate for us in all cases whatsoever.

He has abdicated Government here, by declaring us out of his Protection and waging War against us.

He has plundered our seas, ravaged our Coasts, burnt our towns, and destroyed the lives of our people.

He is at this time transporting large Armies of Foreign Mercenaries to compleat the works of death, desolation and tyranny, already begun with circumstances of Cruelty & perfidy scarcely paralleled in the most barbarous ages, and totally unworthy the Head of a civilized nation.

He has constrained our fellow Citizens taken Captive on the high Seas to bear Arms against their Country, to become the executioners of their friends and Brethren, or to fall themselves by their Hands.

History

● Explain that during the 1700's, kings claimed to rule by divine right. According to that notion, rebellion could never be justified. The writers of the Declaration, therefore, needed a case against kings in general. The paragraph in the Declaration labeled "Principles of American Democracy" was intended to provide a theory of government that made rebellion respectable.

Ask students to write this paragraph in their own words.

Historic Documents

▲ The Declaration is as interesting for what it omits as for what it includes. **Is there any mention of the British Parliament?** (No, only as "others.")

■ **Do you think this was intentional? Why?** (Yes. The writers wanted to blame the monarch, not representative government.)

The symbol 👥 denotes active participation strategies.

Activities are keyed for student abilities:
▲ = Basic
● = All Levels
■ = Average/Advanced

He has excited domestic insurrections amongst us, and has endeavoured to bring on the inhabitants of our frontiers, the merciless Indian Savages, whose known rule of warfare, is an indistinguished destruction of all ages, sexes and conditions.

[The Colonists' Efforts]

In every stage of these Oppressions We have Petitioned for Redress in the most humble terms: Our repeated Petitions have been answered only by repeated injury. A Prince, whose character is thus marked by every act which may define a Tyrant, is unfit to be the ruler of a free people.

Nor have We been wanting in attentions to our British brethren. We have warned them from time to time of attempts by their legislature to extend an unwarrantable jurisdiction over us. We have reminded them of the circumstances of our emigration and settlement here. We have appealed to their native justice and magnanimity, and we have conjured them by the ties of our common kindred to disavow these usurpations, which, would inevitably interrupt our connections and correspondence. They too have been deaf to the voice of justice and of consanguinity. We must, therefore, acquiesce in the necessity, which denounces our Separation, and hold them, as we hold the rest of mankind, Enemies in War, in Peace Friends.

[The Declaration]

We, therefore, the Representatives of the united States of America, in General Congress, Assembled, appealing to the Supreme Judge of the world for the rectitude of our intentions, do, in the Name, and by Authority of the good People of these Colonies, solemnly publish and declare, That these United Colonies are, and of Right ought to be Free and Independent States; that they are Absolved from all Allegiance to the British Crown, and that all political connection between them and the State of Great Britain, is and ought to be totally dissolved; and that as Free and Independent States, they have full Power to Levy War, conclude Peace, contract Alliances, establish Commerce, and to do all other Acts and Things which Independent States may of right do. And for the support of this Declaration, with a firm reliance on the protection of divine Providence, we mutually pledge to each other our Lives, our Fortunes and our sacred Honor.

John Hancock

[NEW HAMPSHIRE]	[CONNECTICUT]	[PENNSYLVANIA]	[MARYLAND]	[NORTH CAROLINA]
Josiah Bartlett	Roger Sherman	Robert Morris	Samuel Chase	William Hooper
William Whipple	Samuel Huntington	Benjamin Rush	William Paca	Joseph Hewes
Matthew Thornton	William Williams	Benjamin Franklin	Thomas Stone	John Penn
	Oliver Wolcott	John Morton	Charles Carroll	
[MASSACHUSETTS]		George Clymer	of Carrollton	[SOUTH CAROLINA]
Samuel Adams	[NEW YORK]	James Smith		Edward Rutledge
John Adams	William Floyd	George Taylor	[VIRGINIA]	Thomas Heyward, Jr.
Robert Treat Paine	Philip Livingston	James Wilson	George Wythe	Thomas Lynch, Jr.
Elbridge Gerry	Francis Lewis	George Ross	Richard Henry Lee	Arthur Middleton
	Lewis Morris		Thomas Jefferson	
[RHODE ISLAND]		[DELAWARE]	Benjamin Harrison	[GEORGIA]
Stephen Hopkins	[NEW JERSEY]	Caesar Rodney	Thomas Nelson, Jr.	Button Gwinnett
William Ellery	Richard Stockton	George Read	Francis Lightfoot Lee	Lyman Hall
	John Witherspoon	Thomas M'Kean	Carter Braxton	George Walton
	Francis Hopkinson			
	John Hart			
	Abraham Clark			

SECTION 4
The Constitution Is Written and Ratified

The Main Ideas

1 Who were the delegates to the Constitutional Convention? *pages 49–50*

2 How did the process of compromise lead to agreement on the new Constitution? *pages 51–54*

3 What was the debate over ratification of the Constitution like? *pages 54–57*

The task facing the delegates assembled in Philadelphia in 1787 was mind-boggling. No other nation in the world at that time had a written constitution describing a complete framework of government. Even the Articles of Confederation, weak as they were, were unique. In the course of one summer, the Constitutional Convention would debate and decide many issues, framing the document that still guides the United States. That document, the Constitution of the United States, was later called by British politician William Gladstone "the most wonderful work ever struck off at a given time by the brain and purpose of man."

2C

The Constitutional Convention

A choice of delegates

Following the Congress's call for a convention, eleven states soon appointed delegates. New Hampshire, beset with internal problems, did not send delegates until the convention was well in session. Rhode Island did not participate at all, for its politics were dominated by people opposed to strengthening the central government. Altogether, 74 delegates were appointed. Of those, 55 actually attended, but only 39 signed the final document.

Figure 2–2 lists some of the prominent delegates to the Convention, along with information about each one. You may notice that many well-known political figures of the Revolution were conspicuously absent. Samuel Adams and John Hancock were not chosen as delegates because of

their hostility to the idea of a strong national government. Patrick Henry suspected that the delegates would do more than just revise the Articles and so refused his appointment, saying he "smelt a rat." John Adams and Thomas Jefferson were on diplomatic missions in Europe.

As a whole, the delegates were fairly young and well educated. They ranged in age from 26 to 81, with the average age being 42. Roughly half had attended college, and a similar number were trained in law. (Lawyers at this time usually learned their profession by working with an experienced lawyer, not by going to law school.) Others were merchants, physicians, landowners, and one famous inventor — Benjamin Franklin.

Most of the delegates had considerable political experience in colonial and state legislatures and the Continental Congress. Seven had been state governors. Many had been officers in the American Revolution.

Organizing the Convention

Only a few delegates gathered at Independence Hall in Philadelphia on the chosen day, May 14, 1787. The Constitutional Convention did not get under way until May 25, when enough delegates arrived to make up a **quorum** — the minimum number needed to conduct business. The Convention then elected leaders and adopted rules for its meetings.

Given his reputation as the country's elder statesman, Benjamin Franklin appeared to be the logical choice to preside over the Convention. Because of his age and health, however, Franklin gave his support to George Washington, who was nominated and elected unanimously. Major William Jackson was then chosen secretary, and other minor officers were appointed. The rules were simple: Although the states had sent different numbers of delegates, each state got one vote. A majority of states (seven) constituted a quorum, and proposals could be passed by a majority of those present. The delegates also decided that all proceedings were to be kept secret, a decision that allowed everyone to speak freely.

49

EXPLANATION

After reviewing the content of the section, you may want to consider the following activities:

👥 Constitutional Heritage

● Draw the following diagram on the board. Have students fill in each of the circles with the specific ideas in each plan. When the ideas have been filled in, have a volunteer sum up the process by which a compromise was reached.

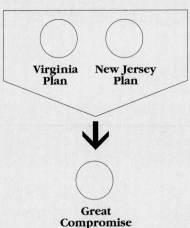

Virginia Plan   New Jersey Plan

Great Compromise

Figure 2–2 MEN WHO MADE THE CONSTITUTION 2C

NAME BORN-DIED/BIRTHPLACE	AGE	DELEGATE FROM	ACCOMPLISHMENTS BEFORE AND AFTER THE CONVENTION
Jonathan Dayton 1760–1824/N.J.	26	N.J.	Served in Revolution; member N.J. legislature; youngest delegate to Convention; Speaker of the House; U.S. Senator.
John Dickinson 1732–1808/Md.	54	Del.	Member Del. and Penn. legislatures; author *Letters from a Farmer in Pennsylvania.*
Oliver Ellsworth 1745–1807/Conn.	42	Conn.	Delegate to Continental Congress; U.S. Senator; Supreme Court chief justice; minister to France.
Benjamin Franklin 1706–1790/Mass.	81	Penn.	Member Penn. legislature; drafter of Albany Plan of Union; signer of Declaration of Independence; first U.S. Postmaster; minister to France, England; author *Poor Richard's Almanac.*
Elbridge Gerry 1744–1814/Mass.	43	Mass.	Member Mass. legislature; signer of Declaration of Independence; U.S. representative; governor Mass.; U.S. Vice President.
Alexander Hamilton 1755–1804/ British West Indies	32	N.Y.	Secretary to General Washington; member N.Y. legislature; co-author *The Federalist;* first Secretary of the Treasury (under Washington); killed in duel with Aaron Burr.
James Madison 1751–1836/Va.	36	Va.	Member Va. legislature; co-author *The Federalist;* U.S. representative; Secretary of State (under Jefferson); fourth U.S. President.
Alexander Martin 1740–1807/N.J.	47	N.C.	Member N.C. legislature; governor N.C.; U.S. senator.
Robert Morris 1734–1806/England	53	Penn.	Member Penn. legislature; signer of Declaration of Independence; U.S. senator.
Gouverneur Morris 1752–1816/N.Y.	35	Penn.	Member N.Y. legislature; delegate to Continental Congress.
William Paterson 1745–1806/Ireland	42	N.J.	N.J. attorney general; U.S. senator; governor N.J.; Supreme Court justice.
Charles Pinckney 1757–1824/S.C.	30	S.C.	Member S.C. legislature; governor S.C.; U.S. senator and representative; minister to Spain.
Edmund Randolph 1753–1813/Va.	34	Va.	Va. attorney general; governor Va.; first U.S. Attorney General; Secretary of State.
Roger Sherman 1721–1793/Mass.	66	Conn.	Member Conn. legislature; signer of Declaration of Independence; mayor of New Haven; U.S. representative and senator.
George Washington 1732–1799/Va.	55	Va.	Member Va. House of Burgesses; Commander-in-chief Continental Army; president Constitutional Convention; first U.S. President.
James Wilson 1742–1798/Scotland	44	Penn.	Delegate to Continental Congress; signer of Declaration of Independence, Supreme Court justice; first professor of law at Univ. of Penn.

50

Figure 2–2
● *What do the accomplishments of the framers of the Constitution tell you?* (The framers had wide political experience.) *Did the framers of the Constitution represent a cross-section of American society?* (No, they all were prominent white males.)

Both the Constitution and the Declaration of Independence were written at the Pennsylvania State House in Philadelphia, now better known as Independence Hall. Young James Madison (inset) of Virginia was a leader in the framing and ratifying of the Constitution.

Even though this pledge of secrecy was later ended by Congress, there are only a few sources of information about the Convention. One is Jackson's formal Journal. His notes, however, were messy and incomplete. The Convention gave the notes to Washington, who deposited them with the State Department in 1796. (In 1819 Congress had them printed.) Several delegates also took notes for their private papers.

The most complete account of the Convention is James Madison's diary. Of all the delegates, Madison had the most influence. He is often called "the Father of the Constitution." In addition, throughout the meetings, he sat near the front of the room and took excellent, detailed notes on each speech and opinion. Congress purchased the diary after Madison's death in 1836 and made it public four years later.

2A, 3A, 3C, 5A, 6B

Plans and Compromises

As soon as the Convention began to discuss business, on May 29, delegates faced a major decision. Governor Edmund Randolph of Virginia immediately proposed a list of sweeping changes to strengthen the central government. These went far beyond merely making changes in the existing Articles of Confederation. The effect of Randolph's plan was to turn the convention toward creating a federal system, a new government structure that set up a different relationship between the states and the federal government.

The Virginia Plan

Randolph's plan showed the ideas and influence of other Virginia leaders who favored a strong national government. Its fifteen specific proposals brilliantly set the tone for the Convention. The Virginia Plan included these ideas:

- Three separate branches of government — legislative, executive, and judicial. The legislative branch would select the officials in the executive and judicial branches.

- A bicameral legislature. Representation would be based upon state population, money contributions, or both. The lower house would be popularly elected and then would select the upper house.

- The national legislature would have authority to cancel conflicting state laws and make the states comply with national laws.

51

Economics

■ CRITICAL THINKING Review the effects of sectional disputes on the Constitutional Convention. **Why did northern and southern states have different perspectives on the issue of counting slaves?** (Slavery still existed in the South, while most northern states had abolished it.) **Why did southern states object to the northern plan to give the national government power over international trade and domestic commerce?** (Southerners worried that the national government, if given such powers, would interfere with agricultural exports and imports of slaves.)

👥 Values

● Conduct a class debate over the issue of slavery and the Constitution. **Why did the Constitution not include a ban on slavery?** (Southern delegates would not have supported it.)

● CRITICAL THINKING **Suppose you were an antislavery delegate at the Convention. Would you have refused to support the Constitution if it did not contain a ban on slavery? Explain.** (Some students might argue that no constitution at all was preferable to one permitting slavery. Others might argue that a new constitution was vital to the survival of the United States as a democratic society, and that the survival of the United States was in the interest of all Americans, including slaves.)

The symbol 👥 denotes active participation strategies.

Activities are keyed for student abilities:
▲ = Basic
● = All Levels
■ = Average/Advanced

Controversial Issues

Read aloud the following argument, made by Patrick Henry, against the proposed Constitution: "That this is a consolidated government is demonstrably clear; and the danger of such a government is, to my mind, very striking. I have the highest veneration for those gentlemen [the framers of the Constitution]; but, sir, give me leave to demand. What right had they to say, *We, the people?* . . . Who authorized them to speak the language of *We, the people,* instead of, *We, the states?* . . . The federal Convention ought to have amended the old system; for this purpose they were solely delegated; the object of their mission extended to no other consideration. . . ."

● Have students write down in their own words the three main points that Henry was making in the passage you just read. (The proposed new government would be too powerful. The delegates to the Convention had no authority to speak on behalf of the people, only on behalf of the states. The Convention should merely have revised the Articles of Confederation, not proposed a new government.) Then call on selected students to read their statements to the class. (A longer excerpt from Henry's speech appears in **Primary Source Worksheet 4.**)

YOU DECIDE

Imagine that a new constitutional convention has just been called, and you have been selected as a delegate to represent your state. Before the convention can begin, you and other delegates need to consider the following: who should preside; how should votes be counted (each state receiving delegate votes equal to state population or each state having just one vote); what items should be on the agenda; and should the convention be held in secrecy or open to the media?

How would you vote on these questions? Why?

For two weeks, the delegates discussed this well-thought-out plan. The main objection was that the Virginia Plan favored the interests of larger, more populous states. The states with smaller populations feared that they would have little or no power in such a government. Delaware, Rhode Island, and Georgia, for example, would have only two or three representatives in the proposed legislature, while Virginia would get sixteen. This situation led to the most basic disagreements of the Convention.

The New Jersey Plan

To counter the Virginia Plan, William Paterson of New Jersey — a small state — offered a new proposal on June 15. In many ways the New Jersey Plan, or "small state" plan, closely resembled the Articles of Confederation. It provided for a government with these central features:

- A one-house national legislature with representatives selected by the state legislatures. Each state would cast one vote.

- A plural executive — that is, two or more chief executive officers — selected by the national legislature (Congress).

- A supreme court appointed for life by the executive officers.

The large states rejected this proposal after only four days of debate. Other counterproposals were then offered by Charles Pinckney of South Carolina and Alexander Hamilton of New York, but they too were rejected.

A crisis in the Convention

The next five weeks were a critical period at the Convention. The question of representation for the large and small states was a central problem. But it was not the only issue. Delegates also debated how officials should be chosen, how frequently elections should be held, how many "executives" there should be, and what powers they should have. From time to time, some delegates seemed ready to give up the whole idea of a united country. On June 28 Luther Martin, a delegate from Maryland, reported that the Convention was "scarce held together by the strength of a hair."

The Great Compromise

Just when it appeared that the Convention would break up, the delegates began to make compromises about major issues. The first of these resolved the question of state representation in Congress, the most basic problem in uniting the states. The smaller, less populated states feared they would consistently lose to the larger states in the legislature. They wanted equal representation regardless of population (as in the New Jersey Plan). The large-state delegates understandably wanted congressional representation to be based on population (as proposed in the Virginia Plan).

When the Convention was clearly deadlocked, a separate committee was set up to work out a compromise. After days of heated debate, the Connecticut delegation — Roger Sherman, Oliver Ellsworth, and Dr. William Samuel Johnson — suggested a compromise that would combine the opposing viewpoints. As Johnson explained this new approach: "In one branch the *people* ought to be represented; in the other, the *States.*"

After more argument, the delegates agreed to what became known as the Great Compromise or Connecticut Compromise. Members in the lower house (House of Representatives) would be apportioned among the states according to population and elected by the people. In the

52

You Decide Answer
Students should defend their answers.

Critical Thinking
■ *How would the United States be different today if the Convention had adopted the features of the New Jersey Plan dealing with the legislative and executive branches?*

(State governments would be more powerful, since they would have the power to appoint members of Congress. The chief executive would have less power than the current President.)

upper house (Senate), each state would have an equal number of representatives, who would be chosen by the state legislatures.

The House of Representatives thus would tend to favor the states with large populations. Moreover, the House was given the power to originate all bills for raising or spending money. The smaller states were favored in the Senate. With two senators each, every state had equal representation in the upper house.

The "three-fifths compromise"

Even when the make-up of Congress had been decided, there remained another deep-seated issue involving representation and taxation. At the time of the Convention, more than half a million of the nearly four million Americans were slaves. (About 60,000 black Americans were free.) Nearly all of the northern states had abolished slavery by 1787. Most of the slaves, therefore, lived in the six southern states,

Figure 2–3 STEPS TOWARD SELF-GOVERNMENT IN COLONIAL AMERICA 8E

1619	**House of Burgesses** America's first representative assembly, is established in Virginia.
1620	**Mayflower Compact** sets forth an agreement by which the Plymouth colonists will govern themselves.
1639	**Fundamental Orders** of Connecticut, America's first written constitution, is adopted.
1754	**Albany Plan of Union** proposes a colonial confederation.
1765	**Stamp Act Congress** petitions for repeal of the Stamp Act, calls for a boycott of British goods.
1772–1776	**Committees of Correspondence** organize and carry out colonial resistance to British policies.
1774	**First Continental Congress** declares that Britain has no right to make laws for the colonies without their consent, organizes a boycott of British imports.
1775	**Second Continental Congress** which becomes the first national government, convenes.
1776	**Declaration of Independence** is signed.
1776–1780	**State constitutions** outlining powers and principles of state governments, are adopted.
1781	**Articles of Confederation** the first national constitution, is adopted.
1786	**Annapolis Convention** calls for the revision of the Articles of Confederation.
1787	**Northwest Ordinance** establishes a model for admitting new states to the Union.
1787	**Constitutional Convention** writes the Constitution of the United States.

53

Cooperative Learning
● Divide the class into small groups and have the members of each group work together to create a graphic organizer of the events described in this section. Possibilities include a cause-and-effect chart and a time line. Show the graphic organizers to the class, asking which one is most effective and why.

GUIDED/INDEPENDENT PRACTICE
● Have students complete **Primary Source Worksheet 4,** which contains excerpts of a speech given by Patrick Henry in opposition to the Constitution.

Background: *Constitutional Heritage* The Seventeenth Amendment (1913) provided for the direct election of senators.

Figure 2–3
● *Into what three historical periods could the events listed in the table be divided?*
(Colonization: 1619–1639; independence: 1754–1776; nation-building: 1776–1787.)

The symbol 👥 denotes active participation strategies.

Activities are keyed for student abilities:
▲ = Basic
● = All Levels
■ = Average/Advanced

RETEACHING/CORRECTIVES

RETEACHING/CORRECTIVES

▲ Have students outline the section. They should provide details of the various issues discussed and resolved at the Constitutional Convention, as well as the opposing arguments made during the debate over ratification.

Have students complete **Skills Practice Worksheet 2,** which lists milestones in the formation of the United States government.

You may also want to use **Transparency 9,** which lists causes and effects of the Constitutional Convention.

where their labor was thought to be essential to the plantation economy.

Southern delegates naturally wanted to count their slaves for the purpose of determining state representation in Congress, but not for allocating direct taxes. Delegates from the North, however, argued that counting slaves for representation would give southern states an unfair advantage and encourage them to import even more slaves. Because slaves contributed to the southern economy, however, some northern delegates thought they should be counted when direct taxes were imposed on the states.

Ultimately, the "three-fifths compromise" was reached. Northern delegates agreed that three-fifths of the slave population would be counted in determining representation, but they also were to be counted in figuring direct taxes. (American Indians were not to be counted in either situation.)

Economic compromises

The slavery issue showed that there were regional divisions between North and South as well as conflicts between large and small states. Another sectional dispute arose over the question of commerce. Northern delegates had interests in shipping and manufacturing. They wanted the national government to have power to regulate foreign commerce and trade among the states, which it had not been able to do under the Articles of Confederation. Southern delegates, however, feared that a central government with such powers would interfere too much with commerce — particularly exports of agricultural products and imports of slaves.

Once again, an important compromise was reached. Northern interests were satisfied by giving Congress the exclusive authority to regulate foreign trade and interstate commerce. The President was given the power to negotiate treaties with foreign states. Southern interests, on the other hand, were met by three provisions: (1) the slave trade was not to be prohibited for twenty years; (2) Congress could not impose duties on exports; and (3) treaties must be approved by two-thirds of the Senate.

The final meeting

By making compromises, the delegates had basically agreed on the substance of the Constitution by September 8, 1787. A Committee on

54

Style, dominated by Gouverneur Morris, was appointed to arrange and write the final document. The handwritten text of the Constitution was presented on September 12. After four months of intense work, the delegates were finally ready to approve the completed document.

George Washington called the final meeting to order on September 17, 1787. Secretary Jackson then read the text of the entire Constitution. After the reading, Benjamin Franklin rose to address the Convention, first asking James Wilson to read his written speech:

> I confess that there are several parts of this constitution which I do not at present approve . . . but . . . having lived long, I have [often been] obliged by better information, or fuller consideration, to change opinions. . . .
>
> It therefore astonishes me, Sir, to find this system approaching so near perfection as it does. . . . I cannot help expressing a wish that every member of the Convention who may still have objections to it, would with me, on this occasion doubt a little of his own infallibility, and to make manifest our unanimity, put his name to this instrument.

Franklin's solemn motion was approved overwhelmingly by all the states. Most of the delegates present then stepped forward and signed. (Three men — Edmund Randolph, Elbridge Gerry, and George Mason — chose not to sign, for varying reasons.) The delegates then adjourned to the City Tavern to celebrate the creation of a glorious new government.

2A, 2B, 2C

The Struggle for Ratification

The Convention delegates had argued and debated for months to create the new structure of government. Now the Constitution's backers faced another hurdle — obtaining approval by the states. To make ratification possible, the framers, in Article VII, had made only *nine* states' agreement necessary. Moreover, the Constitution was not to be ratified by the legislatures but by special conventions called for that purpose in all the states. The existing state legislatures, it was thought, were likely to turn down a docu-

Background: *Constitutional Heritage* The Civil War and the subsequent ratification of the Thirteenth (1865) and Fourteenth (1868) Amendments would later render the "three-fifths" compromise obsolete.

Background: *History* Randolph, Gerry, and Mason refused to sign the Constitution because they wanted a bill of rights, a less powerful Congress, and a second constitutional convention.

ment that reduced their powers by creating a strong national government.

Supporters of the new Constitution feared specifically that New York and Rhode Island might block final approval. Some of New York's delegation had stormed out of the Convention in protest, while Rhode Island had not even sent delegates. A reluctant Congress therefore agreed to the nine-state requirement and submitted the Constitution to the states for ratification on September 28, 1787.

Federalists and Antifederalists

The debate over ratification throughout the country was as heated and dramatic as the arguments in Philadelphia. Those who favored the creation of the new federal system of government were called Federalists. Those who opposed it were known as Antifederalists.

Antifederalists included Patrick Henry, Samuel Adams, John Hancock, Richard Henry Lee, George Mason, and Elbridge Gerry. Some of them disliked the secrecy of the Constitutional Convention and thought the framers had gone too far. Patrick Henry asked:

> Who authorized them to speak the language of *We, the people,* instead of, *We, the states?*
> . . . The federal Convention ought to have amended the old system; . . . the object of their mission extended to no other consideration.

Others worried that a national judiciary would overrule state laws. They also wanted a bill of rights. Without one, they feared, the government would violate individual liberties.

Federalists included Alexander Hamilton, John Jay, Gouverneur Morris, and James Madison. They argued that the Constitution would remedy the Articles of Confederation's most glaring problems. A bill of rights was not necessary, they said, because many state constitutions already had them. Yet to ease their opponents' fears, they promised to include a bill of rights once the Constitution was adopted.

Voters in each of the states chose delegates to the ratifying conventions that would decide the fate of the Constitution. Support for the Federalists was greatest in Delaware, Connecticut, Georgia, Maryland, and New Jersey. These less

Figure 2-4 RATIFICATION OF THE CONSTITUTION This chart shows the final Yes-No vote of the delegates at each state's ratifying convention. 8E

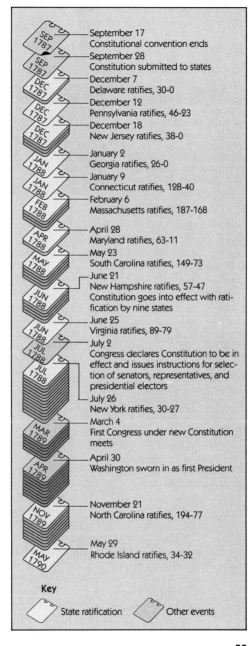

SEP 1787 — September 17
Constitutional convention ends

SEP 1787 — September 28
Constitution submitted to states

DEC 1787 — December 7
Delaware ratifies, 30-0

DEC 1787 — December 12
Pennsylvania ratifies, 46-23

DEC 1787 — December 18
New Jersey ratifies, 38-0

JAN 1788 — January 2
Georgia ratifies, 26-0

JAN 1788 — January 9
Connecticut ratifies, 128-40

FEB 1788 — February 6
Massachusetts ratifies, 187-168

APR 1788 — April 28
Maryland ratifies, 63-11

MAY 1788 — May 23
South Carolina ratifies, 149-73

JUN 1788 — June 21
New Hampshire ratifies, 57-47
Constitution goes into effect with ratification by nine states

JUN 1788 — June 25
Virginia ratifies, 89-79

JUL 1788 — July 2
Congress declares Constitution to be in effect and issues instructions for selection of senators, representatives, and presidential electors

JUL 1788 — July 26
New York ratifies, 30-27

MAR 1789 — March 4
First Congress under new Constitution meets

APR 1789 — April 30
Washington sworn in as first President

NOV 1789 — November 21
North Carolina ratifies, 194-77

MAY 1790 — May 29
Rhode Island ratifies, 34-32

Key

State ratification   Other events

55

ENRICHMENT/EXTENSION
■ Have students complete **Skills Challenge Worksheet 2,** which contains an editorial supporting ratification of the Constitution.

You may also want students to complete **Constitutional Issues Worksheet 1,** which concerns the division of power among the national government, the states, and the people.

Check for Understanding
▲ *Why was a bill of rights added to the Constitution?*
(To ease the fears of Antifederalists, who complained about the Constitution's lack of a bill of rights.)

Figure 2-4
▲ *Why did the Constitution take effect before its ratification by New York, North Carolina, and Rhode Island?*
(The approval of only nine states was needed for the Constitution to take effect.)

The symbol 👥 denotes active participation strategies.

Activities are keyed for student abilities:
▲ = Basic
● = All Levels
■ = Average/Advanced

His hand on the Bible, George Washington takes the oath of office as the United States' first President. Washington's inauguration, on April 30, 1789, was at Federal Hall in New York City, then the nation's capital.

Section 4 Review Answers

1. (a) They were fairly young, well-educated lawyers and politicians. **(b)** They opposed a strong central government.

2. (a) Three branches of government, bicameral legislature with proportional representation, national legislature empowered to cancel conflicting state laws. **(b)** Unicameral legislature with one vote per state, a plural executive, and a supreme court.

3. (a) Equal representation versus proportional representation by population. **(b)** Representation and taxation of states with large slave populations.

4. Because federal regulation might harm their exports of agricultural products and imports of slaves.

populated states especially favored the Constitution because it guaranteed them equal representation in the Senate. The Federalists also enjoyed the backing of merchants and people in seaport cities.

Antifederalist sympathies, on the other hand, were strongest in Rhode Island, Virginia, North Carolina, and New York. Opposition also was strong among westerners and small farmers. Public opinion was divided in four states — South Carolina, New Hampshire, Massachusetts, and Pennsylvania.

Key states in ratification

On December 7, 1787, Delaware became the first state to ratify (as the timeline in Figure 2–4 shows). It was followed by Pennsylvania, New Jersey, Georgia, Connecticut, Massachusetts, Maryland, and South Carolina. With New Hampshire's vote on June 21, 1788, the Constitution was officially ratified. The Federalists knew, however, that a strong and stable government would be impossible without the support of Virginia and New York, the richest and largest states.

In Virginia, the debate over ratification was sharp and passionate. Antifederalist forces were led by the fiery orator Patrick Henry. Henry's supporters included Richard Henry Lee, William Grayson, George Mason, and James Monroe. The Federalist position was advanced by quick-witted

James Madison, backed by John Marshall and Edmund Randolph (who had not signed the document but now gave it his support). George Washington also used his influence to help the Federalists prevail. Virginia ratified within four days of New Hampshire.

The Federalist

In New York, the campaign for ratification was equally intense. In the Philadelphia Convention, Alexander Hamilton had openly voiced his dislike for the new plan of government. He had signed the Constitution only because he feared the alternative was anarchy. Now Hamilton argued convincingly for the Federalists.

Throughout the winter and spring of 1787–1788, Hamilton, Madison, and John Jay published in the New York newspapers a series of 85 essays defending the Constitution. These essays, signed "Publius" and known collectively as *The Federalist,* helped turn the tide. On July 26, 1788, New York ratified the Constitution by a margin of three votes. Even today, the essays in *The Federalist* are considered among the finest political documents ever written.

A new government

Once Virginia and New York had ratified, the Confederation Congress made plans to inaugurate the new government. Federal Hall, on Wall

56

Cross-reference
Excerpts from *The Federalist,* No. 10 appear on p. 353.

Street in New York City, was selected as the temporary national capitol. Elections were set for the first Wednesday in February 1789, and the first Congress was to convene on March 4, 1789. Its members would be the 22 senators and 59 representatives chosen by the eleven states that had ratified the Constitution.

The new government did not actually get under way until April 1789. Congress met as scheduled but lacked a quorum until April 6. George Washington, the unanimous choice for first President, was inaugurated in New York City on April 30. As the Federalists had promised, on June 8, 1789, James Madison introduced a number of amendments to make up a Bill of Rights. Within a year, North Carolina and Rhode Island ratified the Constitution and joined the ranks of the states. At long last, the "more perfect union" had been established.

SECTION 4 REVIEW

Vocabulary and key terms

quorum (49)   Great Compromise (52)
Virginia Plan (51)   Federalists (55)
New Jersey Plan (52)   Antifederalists (55)

For review

1. (a) What characteristics were typical of delegates to the Constitutional Convention? (b) Why did such patriots as John Hancock and Sam Adams not attend? **2C**
2. What were the main features of (a) the Virginia Plan? (b) the New Jersey Plan? **2A**
3. What were the issues in (a) the Connecticut Compromise? (b) the three-fifths compromise? **6B**
4. Why did southern states fear national government regulation of trade and commerce? **3C**
5. (a) What were the main objections of the Antifederalists? (b) Who wrote the essays in *The Federalist*? **2B**

Critical thinking

LINKING PAST AND PRESENT Senators are now elected by the voters, not the states. Does this violate the Great Compromise? Explain. **2A**

Chapter Summary

The documents upon which the United States government was founded — the Declaration of Independence, the Articles of Confederation, and the Constitution — were influenced by centuries of English tradition. The Magna Charta, Petition of Right, English Bill of Rights, and the works of John Locke set forth the principles of limited government, representative government, individual liberty, and rule by law, which the colonists incorporated into colonial governments and eventually into the new United States government.

Early colonies acquired royal charters that allowed considerable self-government through elected assemblies. Colonists felt independent and separate from Britain, which Britain tolerated under its policy of "salutary neglect." When Parliament taxed the colonists to pay off war debts and provide for colonial defense, the colonists united in protest. Additional parliamentary acts, called the "Intolerable Acts" by colonists, provoked them to send representatives to the First Continental Congress to demand their rights as British subjects.

When war broke out, the Second Continental Congress convened and acted as the government. Congress drafted and approved the Declaration of Independence, which outlined the principles and reasons for the new country. States adopted new constitutions that provided for bicameral legislatures and included bills of rights. Congress adopted a national constitution, the Articles of Confederation. The articles created a confederation of thirteen independent states.

The new government and its unicameral legislature had many weaknesses. A Constitutional Convention was called to draft a new government framework. Many delegates argued for a stronger central government. Antifederalists, small states, and southern states opposed them. Congress approved the Constitution only after many compromises had been made over the issues of state rights, representation, and taxation. With the promise of a bill of rights to safeguard the rights of individuals, the thirteen states ratified the new Constitution.

5. (a) Secrecy surrounding the Constitutional Convention, fear of a national judiciary overruling state laws, and lack of a bill of rights. (b) Hamilton, Madison, and Jay.

Critical thinking Most students should answer that although the states no longer choose senators, the smaller states still are favored in the Senate; in this sense, the Great Compromise has not been violated.

CLOSURE
● Remind students of the pre-reading questions at the beginning of the section. Pose one or all of these questions again. Then have students read the next assigned lesson.

CHAPTER 2 CORRECTIVES
● To review the content of Chapter 2, you may want to have students complete **Study Guide/Review 2** or **Workbook Chapter 2.**

The symbol ⚏ denotes active participation strategies.

Activities are keyed for student abilities:
▲ = Basic
● = All Levels
■ = Average/Advanced

★ **CHAPTER** **2** **REVIEW** ★

Answers

Vocabulary   See pp. T19–T21 for suggested vocabulary activities.

Reviewing the Facts

1. It made clear that British subjects had certain rights that not even the monarch could violate.
2. The elected assembly.
3. The British enforced trade laws more strictly and levied new taxes.
4. The first part states why it is being written and the basic principles on which it is based. The middle part lists charges against King George III. The final part explains the colonists' efforts to achieve a peaceful settlement, Britain's resistance, and the Americans' resolve to be free.
5. All the new states established the executive, legislature, and judiciary as three separate branches of government. Most set up bicameral legislatures. Seven states included bills of rights. All states limited voting rights to adult male property owners.
6. A confederation, or association of independent states.
7. The Great Compromise called for a bicameral legislature with membership in the lower house determined by state population and two seats per state in the upper house. The "three-fifths" compromise counted three-fifths of the slave population for purposes of representation and taxation. Economic compromises were made regarding regulation of trade and the slave trade.
8. Nine.

Thinking Critically About Key Concepts

1. (a) The Magna Charta made clear that British subjects possessed certain rights that could not be violated. These rights were further defined in the Petition of Right and the English Bill of Rights. The principle of rule by

● **Review the definitions of the following terms:**

Albany Plan of Union	Federalists	precedent
Antifederalists	Fundamental Orders	proprietor
Articles of Confederation	Great Compromise	quorum
assembly	"Intolerable Acts"	ratification
bicameral	Magna Charta	"salutary neglect"
bill of rights	Mayflower Compact	Stamp Act
burgess	New Jersey Plan	unicameral
charter	Northwest Ordinance	Virginia Plan
common law	parliament	
English Bill of Rights	Petition of Right	

● **REVIEWING THE FACTS**

1. What was the significance of the Magna Charta? **1D**
2. What sort of governing body came to dominate in the colonies? **1D**
3. How did British policy toward the colonies change after the French and Indian War? **8F**
4. What is the purpose of each major section of the Declaration of Independence? **2A**
5. What were the main similarities among the constitutions written by the new states? **8G**
6. What was the relationship among the states under the Articles of Confederation? **3C**
7. What compromises contributed to the final form of the Constitution? **6B**
8. How many states were needed to ratify the Constitution? **2B**

▲ **THINKING CRITICALLY ABOUT KEY CONCEPTS**

1. (a) How did the basic concepts of limited government and rule by law develop in England? **(b)** How did Parliament gain power from the monarch? **1D**
2. Suppose the British government had allowed colonists to elect representatives to Parliament, but all British policies toward the

colonies had remained unchanged. Would the American Revolution have occurred? Explain. **8A**
3. Reread the quotation from Benjamin Franklin on page 42 regarding the need for the signers of the Declaration of Independence to support one another. In what way did Franklin's statement apply to the states as well during the Confederation period? **8G**

▲ **PRACTICING SKILLS**

1. Study Skills: Making a time line. To get a sense of the events leading up to the American Revolution, make a time line of major developments mentioned in the chapter, beginning with the French and Indian War. **8E**
2. Study Skills: Organizing information in a table. Review the subsection "The English Political Heritage" (pages 31–33). Make a four-column table labeled *Constitutional Rights, Magna Charta, Petition of Right,* and *English Bill of Rights.* In the first column, list five of the rights or protections mentioned in the Constitution (such as trial by jury, or the right of legislators to speak freely). Place checks in the next three columns to show which of the rights listed in the first column are mentioned in each document. **8A**

law was based on English common law, which grew out of custom and precedent. **(b)** Parliament first emerged in the 1200's as a representative body with lawmaking powers. Later, Parliament used its control

over the king's finances to force him to sign the Petition of Right, increasing Parliament's power. After the Glorious Revolution, the English Bill of Rights gave Parliament specific powers over the monarch.

2. Some will argue that representation in Parliament would have cemented colonists' loyalty toward Britain. Others will argue that the physical separation of the colonies from Britain would eventually have created a

3. **Critical Thinking Skills: Analyzing Arguments.** Read the excerpt from Thomas Paine's pamphlet *Common Sense* ("Speaking Out," page 794). What might Paine have hoped to achieve by giving his pamphlet that title? **8A**

▲ PARTICIPATORY CITIZENSHIP

1. **Locating historic documents.** Find out more about the original copies of the Declaration of Independence and United States Constitution. Where are they kept? What special efforts are made to preserve them? Are they ever moved? **1D**
2. **Doing historical research.** How did common citizens react to the start of the American Revolution, or to the drafting of the United States Constitution? Consult your library to find information about how either of these events changed the life of an average American. **4A**

■ WRITING ABOUT ISSUES

1. **Researching a historical figure.** Research one of the following people and write a short report on his or her life and career: King John, King Charles I, Queen Mary II, Roger Williams, William Penn, Lord Baltimore, Samuel Adams, Crispus Attucks. **8C**
2. **Writing an essay.** Write an essay on the following topic: "The weakness of the Confederation government was not accidental; rather, it was a deliberate attempt to correct past abuses." **8A**

▲ ANALYZING A POLITICAL CARTOON

In the two hundred years since the Constitution was drafted, attitudes towards the political rights of various groups in society have become more inclusive. However, older, less inclusive attitudes remain relevant and influential. Look at the cartoon below and answer the following questions.

1. What is the setting of the cartoon? **8B**
2. Explain the cartoon's message in your own words. **8B**
3. Is the cartoon effective? Why, or why not? **8A**

MIKE PETERS reprinted by permission of UFS, Inc.

CHAPTER 3
THE CONSTITUTION: SUPREME LAW OF THE LAND
(pp. 60–83)

	Section Objectives	Section Resources
Section 1 **The Constitution Follows Basic Principles**	☐ list the six basic principles of the Constitution	▲ SKILLS PRACTICE WORKSHEET **3** ● PRIMARY SOURCE WORKSHEET **5** ■ CONSTITUTIONAL ISSUES WORKSHEET **2** ■ SUPREME COURT DECISION **1** ▲ TRANSPARENCIES **10–11**
Section 2 **Formal Amendments Change the Constitution**	☐ describe the methods of proposing constitutional amendments ☐ describe the methods of ratifying amendments ☐ explain why some proposed amendments are ratified and others are rejected	■ SKILLS CHALLENGE WORKSHEET **3** ▲ TRANSPARENCY **12**
Section 3 **The Constitution Remains Flexible**	☐ explain the difference between fundamental law and statutory law ☐ describe the informal changes that have been made in the United States government	■ CONSTITUTIONAL ISSUES WORKSHEET **3**

Essential Elements

The list below shows Essential Elements relevant to this chapter. (The complete list of Essential Elements appears in the introductory pages of this Teacher's Edition.)

Section 1: 1C, 2A, 2D, 3A, 3B, 3C, 6E, 6F, 6H, 8H

Section 2: 2A, 3C, 4B, 4C, 6C, 6E, 6F, 6H, 8B

Critical Thinking feature (p. 77): 8A, 8G

Section 3: 2A, 2D, 2E, 3A, 6F

Chapter Review: 2A, 3A, 3B, 3C, 4A, 4D, 6C, 6F, 6H, 8A, 8B, 8C

> Section Resources are keyed for student abilities:
> ▲ = Basic
> ● = All Levels
> ■ = Average/Advanced

Homework Options

Each section contains activities labeled "Guided/Independent Practice," "Reteaching/Correctives," and "Enrichment/Extension." You may wish to choose from among these activities when assigning homework.

Students Acquiring English Activities

Use Figure 3–1 (p. 65) to create a variation of a tick-tack-toe game on the system of checks and balances. Have students create their own game boards with headings for each column (for example: *Executive, Judicial, Legislative*). List each of the checks mentioned in Figure 3–1 on a separate index card. Call out the checks one at a time without listing the branch. Students must remember the branch to which the check applies, then write the name of the check in the appropriate column. The first student to identify a check in each of the three columns wins.

LISTENING/SPEAKING: Have students watch several segments of a national TV news broadcast and identify the branches of the federal government discussed. Use the game board to keep track of the number of times that each branch is in the news.

Case Studies

When teaching this chapter, you may use Case Study 1, which addresses the relevancy of the Constitution today; Case Study 8, which examines the issue of women in combat; or Case Study 14, which deals with the question of whether English should become the official language of the United States. (Case Studies may be found following p. 510.)

Teacher Bibliography

Barbash, Fred. *The Founding: A Dramatic Account of the Writing of the Constitution.* Simon & Schuster, 1987. Traces the development of the Constitution through primary sources.

Beeman, Richard, Stephen Botein, and Edward C. Carter II, eds. *Beyond Confederation: Origins of the Constitution and American National Identity.* University of North Carolina Press, 1987. Examines the impact and viability of the Constitution today.

Kurland, Philip B. and Ralph Lerner, eds. *The Founders' Constitution.* University of Chicago Press, 1987. Presents documents from the seventeenth, eighteenth, and nineteenth centuries that were important to the development of the Constitution.

Student Bibliography

Bender, David L., ed. *American Government: Opposing Viewpoints.* Greenhaven Press, 1988. Questions are asked of and answered by a variety of experts on the subject of the Constitution and whether it should be revised.

Garraty, John A., ed. *Quarrels That Have Shaped the Constitution.* Harper & Row, 1987. Discussion of sixteen Supreme Court decisions that established historic interpretations.

Kammen, Michael. *A Machine That Would Go of Itself: The Constitution in American Culture.* Knopf, 1986. Examines the relationship of the American people to the Constitution.

Literature

Stites, Francis N. *John Marshall: Defender of the Constitution.* Edited by Oscar Handlin. Little, Brown, 1981. Describes Chief Justice Marshall's impact on the power of the Supreme Court.

CHAPTER RESOURCES

Study Guide / Review 3
Workbook Chapter 3
Chapter 3 Test, Forms A–C

Wise, William. *Alexander Hamilton.* Putnam, 1963. A biography that emphasizes Hamilton's belief in a strong central government.

Films and Videotapes*

The Constitution: That Delicate Balance. 13 one-hour video programs on 13 cassettes. Annenberg, 1984.

Marbury vs. Madison. (Series title: *Equal Justice Under Law.*) 36 min. NAVC, 1979. f, v. Dramatization of the 1803 Supreme Court decision.

Prayer in the Classroom. (Series title: *This Constitution: A History.*) 28 min. PSUAVS, 1987. v. The philosophical origins, drafting, and interpretation of the Constitution are shown in this chronological and conceptual approach to issues raised by the First Amendment. Several Supreme Court cases are outlined as well.

The Rise and Fall of Prohibition. (Series title: *This Constitution: A History.*) 28 min. PSUAVS, 1987. v. The tension that exists between social demands and constitutional authority are described with reference to the Eighteenth Amendment.

Software*

The U.S. Constitution: Our Guarantee of Liberty (Apple, IBM). Queue. Simulations and interactive exercises dealing with the Constitution, Preamble, and the Bill of Rights.

To Preserve, Protect and Defend (Apple). MECC. Students must protect the Constitution until it is signed.

---

* For a complete guide to audiovisual sources, see page T22.

59B

The Constitution: Supreme Law of the Land *(pp. 60–83)*

This chapter examines the content of the Constitution, highlighting its basic principles, and explains the process of amending the Constitution as well as informal methods of change.

Chapter Objectives

After students complete this chapter, they will be able to:

1. List the six basic principles of the Constitution.
2. Describe the methods of proposing constitutional amendments.
3. Describe the methods of ratifying amendments.
4. Explain why some proposed amendments are ratified and others are rejected.
5. Explain the difference between fundamental law and statutory law.
6. Describe the informal changes that have been made in the United States government.

CHAPTER

3

THE CONSTITUTION: Supreme Law of the Land

In framing a government which is to be administered by men over men, the great difficulty lies in this: you must first enable the government to control the governed; and in the next place oblige it to control itself.

James Madison
The Federalist (1787–1788)

60

Photo
The Constitution on display in the National Archives, Washington, D.C.

S eptember 1787 — John McLean read the Constitution, liked it, and vowed to do what he could to get it ratified. As a newspaper publisher, he could do a lot. McLean printed the Constitution as a supplement to his twice-weekly New York paper, the *Independent Journal*. Readers got a chance to read the document for themselves and make up their own minds about it. Moreover, when the New York ratifying convention met, McLean's supplement served as the official copy on which delegates cast their votes. In other states as well, newspapers spread word of the Constitution to average citizens and convention delegates alike.

It seems appropriate that a popular newspaper helped get the Constitution ratified. For here was a plan for a *people's* government, one answerable to them and dedicated to the protection of their rights. In the two centuries since its creation, the Constitution has done its work amazingly well. This chapter will explore the Constitution's principles and the ways in which it has adapted to changing times.

CHAPTER OUTLINE

1 The Constitution Follows Basic Principles

Popular Sovereignty
Separation of Powers
Checks and Balances
Federalism
Supremacy of National Laws
Civilian Control of Government

2 Formal Amendments Change the Constitution

Proposing Amendments
Ratifying Amendments
Politics and Amendments
Why Amendments Are Passed

3 The Constitution Remains Flexible

The Value of Fundamental Law
Informal Methods of Change

61

CHAPTER SUPPORT MATERIAL

Skills Practice Worksheet 3

Skills Challenge Worksheet 3

Primary Source Worksheet 5

Constitutional Issues Worksheets 2–3

Supreme Court Decision 1

Transparencies 10–12

Study Guide/Review 3

Workbook Chapter 3

Chapter 3 Test, Forms A-C

SECTION 1

The Constitution Follows Basic Principles *(pp. 62–69)*

Section Objective

☐ list the six basic principles of the Constitution

Vocabulary

popular sovereignty, Preamble, separation of powers, legislative, executive, judicial, constituency, presidential government, parliamentary government, prime minister, checks and balances, veto, supremacy clause, judicial review

█▌ FOCUS

● Write on the board, *The single most important thing about the Constitution is. . . .* Have students come to the board and write down suggested ways of completing the statement.

SECTION 1
The Constitution Follows Basic Principles

ACCESS The Main Idea

What are the six basic principles of the Constitution? *pages 62–69*

In 1857 the Supreme Court, in the landmark case *Dred Scott v. Sanford,* declared: "The right of property in a slave is distinctly and expressly affirmed in the Constitution." Frederick Douglass, himself a former slave, was enraged but not discouraged:

> I base my sense of the sure overthrow of slavery upon the nature of the American government, the Constitution, and the character of the American people — and this in spite of the decision of Judge Taney [Chief Justice of the United States]. *All I ask of the American people is that they live up to the Constitution, adopt its principles, and enforce its provisions.* [emphasis added]

Read that last sentence again and think about it for a minute. What makes it so remarkable? Even as the federal government was reaffirming

its support of slavery, Douglass reaffirmed his faith in the Constitution. Douglass believed, correctly, that the ideals on which our government is based would one day be used to destroy slavery.

This section examines the six fundamental principles of government contained within the Constitution. They are:

(1) popular sovereignty,
(2) separation of powers,
(3) checks and balances,
(4) federalism,
(5) supremacy of national laws, and
(6) civilian control of government.

2A, 6E, 6H

Popular Sovereignty

Government by the people

Perhaps the most striking feature of the Constitution is the basic principle of **popular sovereignty.** Popular sovereignty means, simply, that the power to govern belongs to the people. The people, in turn, entrust this power to a

In 1992 Carol Moseley Braun of Illinois became the first African American woman to be elected to the U.S. Senate. Her election demonstrated the idea of popular sovereignty — the idea that "we the people" have the right to choose the officials and representatives who will run our government.

62

Cross-reference
The background of the *Dred Scott* case can be found on p. 194.

Cross-reference
The complete text of the Constitution, annotated and illustrated, begins on p. 112. In this book, articles of the Constitution are referred to by Roman numerals, and

sections by Arabic numerals, as in the original document. Clause numbers are given for reference when appropriate.

government under their control. The **Preamble**, or introduction, to the Constitution states this idea clearly: "*We the people* of the United States . . . do ordain and establish this Constitution for the United States of America." It is the people who establish and change the fundamental rules of American government.

Several provisions in the Constitution ensure popular sovereignty. For example, the Constitution states that members of the House of Representatives are to be elected directly by the people. It also guarantees each state a "republican form of government" (Article IV, Section 4). In this way, the people are guaranteed that state government officials will be their elected representatives. Most important, the Constitution is flexible enough that, over the years, more and more Americans have gained the chance to take part in government.

Extending popular sovereignty

Although they believed in popular sovereignty, the delegates to the Constitutional Convention wanted to make sure that the people's wishes were carried out wisely by qualified representatives. They did not entrust the selection of the President, senators, and judges to the people directly. The only national officials elected directly by the voters were members of the House of Representatives.

Determining who could vote was left up to the states. State laws varied but at first generally allowed only white male property owners or taxpayers to vote. During the first half of the 19th century, some states dropped their property, tax, and religious requirements for voting. Nevertheless, by the mid-1800's, voting was still limited to white males over 21.

Several amendments to the Constitution expanded popular sovereignty. The Fifteenth Amendment (1870) guaranteed black Americans the right to vote. The Seventeenth Amendment (1913) called for senators to be elected directly by the voters, rather than by state legislatures. Beginning in 1869, some states and territories gave the right to vote to women. In 1920, the Nineteenth Amendment guaranteed this right to women in every state. The 24th Amendment (1964) outlawed poll taxes in federal elections, and the 26th Amendment (1971) extended the vote to 18-year-olds. These amendments, cou-

pled with Supreme Court rulings and acts of Congress, have truly established a "government of the people, by the people, for the people."

1C, 3A

Separation of Powers

Three branches of government

The framers of the Constitution wanted to create a strong central government. At the same time, they feared that individuals or groups might acquire too much power or stay in power too long. To prevent the concentration of power in the hands of a few, the delegates adopted the idea of **separation of powers**. That is, they divided the powers of government among three separate branches.

The idea that government powers ought to be split in this way was originally put forward by the Baron de Montesquieu, a French political philosopher. Montesquieu's book *The Spirit of the Laws* (1748), like the ideas of Locke, greatly influenced political thought in the American colonies. Even before the delegates met in 1787, many state constitutions already included some form of separation of powers.

The first three articles of the Constitution spell out how the powers of government are to be divided. Article I establishes the **legislative**, or lawmaking, branch of government. Article II creates the **executive**, or law-enforcing, branch. Article III provides for the **judicial**, or law-interpreting, branch of government. The following sections assign the branches specific powers:

LEGISLATIVE BRANCH "All legislative powers herein granted shall be vested in a Congress of the United States, which shall consist of a Senate and a House of Representatives" (Article I, Section 1). This section grants Congress the authority to enact laws and establish policies for the national government.

EXECUTIVE BRANCH "The executive power shall be vested in a President of the United States of America" (Article II, Section 1). This section confers upon the President the authority to carry out, administer, and enforce the policies of the national government.

JUDICIAL BRANCH "The judicial power of the United States shall be vested in one Supreme Court and in such inferior courts as the Congress may from time to time ordain and establish"

63

EXPLANATION

After reviewing the content of the section, you may want to consider the following activities:

Constitutional Heritage

● *What was the aim of separation of powers?* (To prevent the concentration of power in the hands of a few individuals.)

▲ CRITICAL THINKING *How is the principle of checks and balances different from the principle of separation of powers?* (Separation of powers refers to the division of the government into three branches; checks and balances refers to the division of power among those three branches.)

Background: *History*
Wyoming Territory established women's suffrage in 1869. Prior to the Nineteenth Amendment, women had full voting rights in Ariz. (since 1912), Calif. (1911),

Colo. (1893), Idaho (1896), Kansas (1912), Mich. (1918), Mont. (1914), Nev. (1914), N.Y. (1917), Okla. (1918), Ore. (1912), S.D. (1918), Utah (1896), and Wash. (1910).

Cross-reference
Chapter 7 traces the struggles of African Americans and of American women to gain full civil rights.

The symbol ⅱ denotes active participation strategies.

Activities are keyed for student abilities:
▲ = Basic
● = All Levels
■ = Average/Advanced

(Article III, Section 1). This section gives the Supreme Court final authority in cases involving national laws. The Court thus interprets the laws and policies of the national government.

Responsibility to the people

In addition to creating three separate branches, the delegates also made each branch responsible to a different **constituency**. The term *constituency* refers to the people who choose government officials and to whom these officials are directly accountable. Even though officials represent all the people, they are responsible to different sets of people. The delegates thus hoped to keep any one group from having too much influence in the government. Therefore, officials in the three branches are selected in slightly different ways.

The President of the United States is not chosen directly by popular vote but by the Electoral College. This is a group of people elected by the voters in each state for the express purpose of choosing the President. (The Electoral College system is discussed in detail in Chapter 14.)

Senators today represent all the voters of their state as a whole. While they originally were chosen by the state legislatures, the Seventeenth Amendment (1913) provided for their direct popular election. Members of the House of Representatives represent the qualified voters of each congressional district within the states.

Supreme Court justices and other federal judges are not elected. They are appointed by the President and must be confirmed by a majority vote of the Senate. Once in office, they are therefore quite independent.

Length of term

Not only do officials in each branch represent different constituencies, they also serve for different lengths of time. A President is elected for a four-year term but is limited to two full terms (eight years) by the 22nd Amendment. If a person has completed the term of another President of two years or less, it is possible to be President for a total of ten years.

Senators serve for six years. Their terms expire at different times, so that one-third of the senators come up for election every two years. All members of the House of Representatives, however, must seek re-election every two years. At the other extreme, federal judges hold office

"during good behavior," which almost always means for life or until retirement.

These different terms of office — two years, four years, six years, a lifetime — were discussed in great detail at the Constitutional Convention. The delegates wanted stability but, at the same time, did not want any person or group to stay in power too long. It was suggested, for instance, that the President also hold office "during good behavior." This proposal alarmed delegates who feared the President might become virtually a king. On the other hand, too frequent elections would bring confusion and constant changes in the government. The system of "staggered" terms ensures that some people with experience remain in office to provide continuity while new officials are elected.

Cooperation between the branches

Although the duties of the three branches are technically separate, in practice the branches share many responsibilities. For example, Congress works closely with the executive branch in making laws. Much of the legislation that Congress enacts originates with the President. On the other hand, Congress often gives an executive department specific lawmaking powers, such as the authority to make rules and regulations in certain policy areas. Supreme Court decisions often decide the direction national policy will take. In addition, the executive branch sometimes steps in to ensure that court orders are followed. Thus, though separation of powers is a cornerstone of the Constitution, government would be unworkable without some cooperation between the branches.

Other systems of government

Dividing government powers among separate branches is very rare. The United States government is among a handful of systems with what is called **presidential government**. The term, of course, comes from the title of the executive leader. Under a presidential government, the executive officers act independently of the legislature. Members of the executive branch cannot hold office in the legislature. Regardless of whether Congress approves of their actions, Presidents hold office for a fixed term (unless they commit a crime).

By contrast, most democratic governments throughout the world combine the legislative

64

and executive functions into a single body. These systems are known as **parliamentary governments**. The government of Great Britain is perhaps the most familiar example. In Britain, governmental authority is held by Parliament (the elected legislature) and a Cabinet of advisers headed by a **prime minister**. The prime minister is not elected separately but chosen from among leaders in the House of Commons. He or she then chooses Cabinet ministers.

Checks and Balances

While making the three branches separate, the delegates also wanted to be sure that no one branch could act completely without restraints. They therefore set up a system of **checks and balances**. As Figure 3–1 shows, under this system, each branch of government exercises some control over the other two. The system of checks and balances prevents the accumulation of too

Figure 3–1 THE SYSTEM OF CHECKS AND BALANCES Each of the three branches can check actions by the other two. 3A, 3B

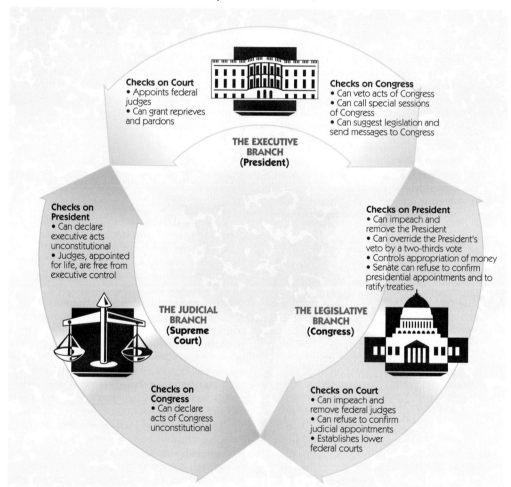

Checks on Court
• Appoints federal judges
• Can grant reprieves and pardons

Checks on Congress
• Can veto acts of Congress
• Can call special sessions of Congress
• Can suggest legislation and send messages to Congress

THE EXECUTIVE BRANCH (President)

Checks on President
• Can declare executive acts unconstitutional
• Judges, appointed for life, are free from executive control

Checks on President
• Can impeach and remove the President
• Can override the President's veto by a two-thirds vote
• Controls appropriation of money
• Senate can refuse to confirm presidential appointments and to ratify treaties

THE JUDICIAL BRANCH (Supreme Court)

THE LEGISLATIVE BRANCH (Congress)

Checks on Congress
• Can declare acts of Congress unconstitutional

Checks on Court
• Can impeach and remove federal judges
• Can refuse to confirm judicial appointments
• Establishes lower federal courts

Constitutional Heritage

● *What constitutional safeguards preserve civilian rule?* (The President is commander-in-chief; Congress alone can declare war and approve defense funding; the government cannot force private citizens to house soldiers.)

■ Point out that several Presidents, such as Washington, Grant, and Eisenhower, were former military leaders. *Should former members of the armed forces be barred from running for President? Explain.* (*Pro*—Former members of the armed forces might be too sympathetic to military interests. *Con*—The fact that a person once served in the armed forces does not mean that he or she will support only the interests of the armed forces. Also, some former soldiers, such as Washington and Eisenhower, have made very successful Presidents.)

Cross-reference
Chapter 29, pp. 756–758 and 760, examines the structure of the British government.

Figure 3–1
● *What is the major benefit of the system of checks and balances?* (No one branch can become too powerful.)

What is the potential drawback? (If the branches disagree, the government could become paralyzed.)

The symbol 👥 denotes active participation strategies.

Activities are keyed for student abilities:
▲ = Basic
● = All Levels
■ = Average/Advanced

much power in the hands of a few self-interested people. As James Madison succinctly put it, "Ambition must be made to counteract ambition."

Checks on Congress

Congress, of course, makes national laws. Yet it can be checked in numerous ways by the President and the Supreme Court. For example, every bill passed by Congress is sent to the President, who can either approve the bill or **veto** it. The veto, which is a Latin word meaning "I forbid," prevents a bill from becoming law. (Congress can sometimes pass the bill again despite the President's veto, however.) The President may also call special sessions of Congress. The Supreme Court, for its part, has the power to overturn acts of Congress by declaring them unconstitutional.

In addition, the two houses of Congress check each other. All bills, for instance, must pass both the Senate and the House of Representatives in identical form before they can be sent to the President for signing. In other words, all bills passed by the Senate must be approved by the House, and vice versa.

Checks on the President

The President has the authority to execute policy, but presidential power can be checked both by Congress and by the Supreme Court. Congress, for instance, may pass laws that the

President opposes, override the President's veto, or cut items from the President's budget. The Senate can turn down the President's nominations of ambassadors, judges, or department heads, or refuse to ratify treaties the President has negotiated. Congress can even remove the President from office if there is cause. The Supreme Court also can check the President, by declaring presidential orders or actions unconstitutional.

Checks on the Supreme Court

The Supreme Court is the most independent of the three branches, but it too can be checked by the President and Congress. Supreme Court justices are appointed by the President with the approval of the Senate. Congress sets the number of judges who sit on the Supreme Court and establishes lower courts. In addition, Congress may remove federal judges for misbehavior through the impeachment process (page 335). Even if the Supreme Court rules a law unconstitutional, Congress can alter the law to meet the Court's requirements, or propose a constitutional amendment to counteract the Court's decision.

3C

Federalism

National and state powers

To solve the problem of the relationship between the national government and the state governments, the delegates at the Constitutional Convention created a federal system. The confederation system of government under the Articles had proven too weak. On the other hand, a unitary government, favored by Alexander Hamilton, seemed too strong. The states would not surrender control of their internal affairs to a powerful, centralized government. Moreover, a unitary government would have created administrative nightmares. Transportation and communication among the states was slow and difficult, and each region of the country had its own interests and problems.

Only federalism seemed to meet the challenge of creating a strong central government without endangering the identities and functions of the states. In this system, some powers are given (delegated) to the national government, and some powers are kept (reserved) by the

YOU DECIDE

8H

The Constitution empowers the President to appoint members of the Supreme Court "with the advice and consent" of the Senate. In the early days of the republic, senatorial confirmation was simple. Questions concerning a nominee's politics were rare. More recently, nominees Robert Bork and Clarence Thomas were closely questioned about their judicial philosophies and political views.

Are these questions appropriate?

The center of our federal system is the nation's capital — Washington, D.C. Federalism tries to reach a balance between the federal government's powers and those kept by the states. (The Capitol is in the foreground. Other government buildings line both sides of the Mall, which leads to the Washington Monument.)

states. The states retain their own constitutions and political identities. They make their own laws, have their own courts, and elect their own officials. On the other hand, the national government is granted sufficient powers to govern and protect the nation as a whole and to settle disputes among the states. (The specific powers granted to the national and state governments by the Constitution are detailed in Chapter 4.)

2A, 2D, 3A, 3C

Supremacy of National Laws

The "supreme law of the land"

The framers of the Constitution anticipated that national laws and state laws might sometimes contradict each other. Article VI, Clause 2 was written to prevent such conflicts:

This Constitution, and the laws of the United States which shall be made in pursuance thereof, and all treaties made, or which shall be made, under the authority of the United States, shall be the supreme law of the land; and the judges in every state shall be bound thereby, anything in the Constitution or laws of any state to the contrary notwithstanding.

This single statement, known as the **supremacy clause**, is what makes federalism work. The supremacy clause declares that where the national government has constitutional authority, the states may not challenge or contradict it. Consequently, all state courts must uphold national laws.

The supremacy clause offers a straightforward solution to conflicts between national and state laws. If a state constitution conflicts with the Constitution of the United States, the state constitution must give way. If a state constitution or law clashes with a law passed by Congress, the state must yield. If a state constitution or law runs contrary to a national treaty, the state again must concede.

Judicial review

The supremacy clause clearly declares that state laws may not violate the Constitution. But what if Congress or the President does something that is forbidden by the Constitution? This question is not answered specifically in the Constitution but was resolved in 1803 by the Supreme Court's decision in the case of *Marbury v. Madison*. In this landmark case, the Supreme Court for the first time asserted its right to declare an act of Congress unconstitutional.

67

Check for Understanding
▲ *What happens if a state law conflicts with a national law?* (The state law must yield.)

Cross-reference
All Supreme Court decisions mentioned in the text are listed in the Index of Supreme Court Cases on pp. 820–824. The Citizenship Skills lesson on p. 149, "Understanding the Language of the Law," explains basic legal terms to help students understand court cases.

RETEACHING/CORRECTIVES
▲ Have students write a six-sentence paragraph that summarizes the structure of the United States government. Students should devote one sentence to each of the six principles outlined in the section.

Have students complete **Skills Practice Worksheet 3,** which deals with the principles of separation of powers and checks and balances.

You may also want to use **Transparency 10,** which shows how American government has been influenced by Enlightenment philosophers, and **Transparency 11,** which presents the three branches of the federal government and their main powers.

ENRICHMENT/EXTENSION
■ Have students complete **Constitutional Issues Worksheet 2,** which deals with separation of powers.

Have students complete **Supreme Court Decision 1,** which deals with *Marbury v. Madison*.

The symbol 👥 denotes active participation strategies.

Activities are keyed for student abilities:
▲ = Basic
● = All Levels
■ = Average/Advanced

Section 1 Review Answers

1. (a) Through the words "We the People," the direct election of representatives, and the guarantee of a "republican form of government." **(b)** By amendments, Supreme Court rulings, and acts of Congress.

2. By creating separate legislative, executive, and judicial branches.

3. Presidential government separates legislative and executive powers; parliamentary government combines them.

4. Answers may include any of the checks listed in Figure 3–1, p. 65.

5. (a) State laws cannot contradict or challenge national laws. **(b)** The Supreme Court can declare state laws unconstitutional.

A few years after John Marshall (inset) became Chief Justice, the Supreme Court moved into this gracefully arched chamber in the Senate wing of the Capitol building. Many important decisions were made in this room, where the Court met until 1860.

The case of *Marbury v. Madison* began as a political battle. Defeated in the election of 1800, outgoing President John Adams hastily appointed many of his fellow Federalists to judgeships and other government positions. Adams also named John Marshall (his Secretary of State) to the Supreme Court as Chief Justice. Some of the official commissions for the new appointments were quickly handwritten on Adams's last night as President. They had not yet been delivered when the new President, Thomas Jefferson, was sworn in on March 4, 1801.

Jefferson and the incoming Republicans in Congress hoped to put more of their own supporters into federal offices. Jefferson therefore declared that the "midnight judges" and other last-minute Federalist appointees would not be sent their commissions. One of them, William Marbury, decided to fight for his promised job as justice of the peace for Washington, D.C. Marbury brought a lawsuit asking for a court order that would force the new Secretary of State, James Madison, to give him the commission. The Supreme Court had been given the power to issue orders such as these by the Judiciary Act of 1789.

Led by Chief Justice Marshall, the Court reached a unanimous decision. Marbury did have a right to his job, they said, because his commission had been legally signed and approved. On the other hand, the Supreme Court could not order Madison to deliver it. Issuing such an order, Marshall said, was not one of the powers that the Constitution gave the Supreme Court. Congress could not give the Supreme Court this power by passing a law, and so this part of the Judi-

68

Background: *History*
John Marshall was a distant cousin, and constant rival, of Thomas Jefferson.

ciary Act was unconstitutional. Enforcing a law that was contrary to the Constitution, Marshall said, would undermine the basic idea of having a written constitution. (Marshall's eloquent explanation is quoted on page 465.)

The ruling in *Marbury v. Madison* established the concept known as **judicial review**. As Marshall said, it is the judicial branch's duty "to say what the law is." The Supreme Court can therefore declare acts of government — national, state, or local — invalid because they violate the Constitution. Judicial review backs up the statement that the Constitution is the supreme law of the land. All federal and most state courts may exercise judicial review, but the United States Supreme Court remains the ultimate authority on what is or is not constitutional.

Judicial review is an American invention. Prior to *Marbury v. Madison,* no other government in the world gave its judicial branch such authority. Despite possessing this powerful weapon, the Supreme Court has exercised remarkable restraint. In the 190 years since the *Marbury* decision, the Supreme Court has declared only about 125 national laws and about 1,100 state laws unconstitutional. These figures average out to fewer than one national law and about six state laws per year.

6F

Civilian Control of Government

Limits on military power

The writers of the Constitution believed (as did Locke and Montesquieu) that control of the government by military leaders would seriously endanger representative democracy. The colonists' experience with British military officials had reinforced this belief. The charges leveled against George III in the Declaration of Independence echoed the Americans' opposition to military domination: "He has kept among us, in times of peace, Standing Armies without the Consent of our legislatures. He has affected to render the military independent of and superior to the Civil power."

With this background, the delegates included numerous safeguards in the Constitution to ensure that elected government officials would control the military. The President, a civilian, is commander-in-chief of the armed services. Congress alone can declare war and approve money for defense spending. Such military funding must be reconsidered at least every two years. The Third Amendment prohibits the federal government from forcing citizens to house soldiers. With these provisions, the writers of the Constitution sought to ensure that military leaders would never control government officials or threaten the freedom of the people.

SECTION 1 REVIEW

Vocabulary and key terms

popular sovereignty (62)
Preamble (63)
separation of powers (63)
legislative (63)
executive (63)
judicial (63)
constituency (64)
presidential government (64)
parliamentary government (65)
prime minister (65)
checks and balances (65)
veto (66)
supremacy clause (67)
Marbury v. Madison (67)
judicial review (69)

For review

1. (a) How does the Constitution guarantee popular sovereignty? (b) How was popular sovereignty later extended? **6H**
2. How does the Constitution provide for the separation of powers? **3A**
3. What is the main difference between presidential government and parliamentary government? **1C**
4. Give one example of how each branch of government is checked by the other two. **3B**
5. (a) How does the "supremacy clause" resolve conflicts between national and state laws? (b) How does judicial review uphold the supremacy of national laws? **3C**
6. What safeguards against military control does the Constitution provide? **6F**

Critical thinking

THINKING ABOUT BASIC IDEAS Give evidence to support the following sentence: "The Supreme Court is at once the strongest and the weakest of the three branches that make up the federal government." **3A**

---

6. The President, a civilian, is commander-in-chief. Only Congress can declare war. Citizens cannot be forced to house soldiers.

Critical thinking It is the strongest in that it alone makes the final decision as to the constitutionality of acts and laws. It is the weakest in that it cannot propose legislation and its members must be approved by both other branches.

CLOSURE

● Have students review the content of the section by restating the red headings in the section as questions and then answering them. Then have students read Section 2, focusing on the different means of proposing and ratifying amendments.

The symbol ♟ denotes active participation strategies.

Activities are keyed for student abilities:
▲ = Basic
● = All Levels
■ = Average/Advanced

SECTION 2

Formal Amendments Change the Constitution *(pp. 70–76)*

Section Objectives

☐ describe the methods of proposing constitutional amendments

☐ describe the methods of ratifying amendments

☐ explain why some proposed amendments are ratified and others are rejected

FOCUS

● Begin by asking students to suggest reasons why it might be necessary to amend the Constitution. (To deal with new situations unforeseen by the framers of the Constitution; to clarify issues left vague in the Constitution.) Then ask what makes a constitutional amendment more durable than a state or federal law. (Once ratified, it can be overturned only by another amendment.)

SECTION 2 | Formal Amendments Change the Constitution

| ACCESS | The Main Ideas |

1 What are the methods of proposing constitutional amendments?
pages 70–72

2 What are the methods of ratifying amendments?
pages 72–73

3 Why are some proposed amendments ratified and others rejected?
pages 73–76

Historian Stewart Holbrook described the attack on the saloon in this way:

> Her first missile smashed the large mirror behind the bar. The second was a perfect strike that shattered every glass on the back bar and also broke several bottles. Now sure of herself, she poured a torrent of paper-wrapped stones at the surviving bottles of liquor, then turned to address the poor proprietor. "Now, Mr. Dobson," she said, "I have finished. God be with you."

"She" was Carry Nation, the famous crusader against alcohol. Nineteen years later, in 1919, the struggle against alcoholic beverages became part of the Constitution with the passage of the Eighteenth Amendment.

The delegates at the Constitutional Convention wanted the Constitution to be flexible enough to change with the times. Article V, sometimes called the "amending article," explains how the Constitution can be amended. Following the principles of federalism, Article V declares that an amendment must be proposed at the *national* level and then ratified by the *states*. Methods for proposing and for ratifying amendments are shown in Figure 3–2.

3C, 6C

Proposing Amendments

Proposals by Congress

The first, and by far the most common, method of proposing constitutional amendments is by an act of Congress. A two-thirds vote in each

house is necessary to approve a proposed amendment. All the amendments added to the Constitution so far were proposed in this way.

The number of amendments passed by Congress is a tiny percentage of all those introduced. Scores of amendments are proposed in Congress each year. Since 1789, in fact, there have been more than 10,000 proposals. Nearly half of those have been introduced since 1962.

Many of the proposed amendments that Congress considers border on the ridiculous. For example, there have been proposals to create four regional Presidents, to legalize dueling, and to change the nation's name to the "United States of the World." Most proposals, however, are serious ideas for altering the structure of the U.S. government. For example, amendments have been proposed to limit the President to a single six-year term and members of Congress to twelve years in office. Some other controversial proposals would balance the federal budget, institute voluntary prayer in public schools, and end affirmative action programs.

There are several reasons why so many proposals have been introduced in Congress. One obvious reason is that many people feel there are problems in government that need to be solved. Another reason is that some groups are upset with the Supreme Court's interpretation of the Constitution. These groups seek to override Supreme Court decisions by amending the Constitution. A final reason is that the other method of proposing amendments is extremely difficult.

Proposals by constitutional conventions

The alternative method for proposing constitutional amendments is through a national convention called by Congress at the request of the legislatures of two-thirds (34) of the states. Although more than 300 attempts to call a constitutional convention have been made since 1789, none has ever been successful.

On one occasion, however, a constitutional convention appeared almost certain. In 1964 the Supreme Court ruled in *Reynolds v. Sims* that

70

Cross-reference
The issues of voluntary school prayer, affirmative action, and a balanced federal budget are discussed in Chapters 5, 7, and 19, respectively.

both houses of a state legislature must be elected from districts with equal populations. This decision upset many Americans, who claimed that the Supreme Court had interfered with the right of the states to decide their own internal affairs. To override the *Reynolds* decision, Senator Everett M. Dirksen of Illinois led a petition drive calling for a constitutional convention. Thirty-three state legislatures (one less than needed) had voted for a convention when the petition drive came to an end with Dirksen's death in the fall of 1969.

Another active campaign to call a constitutional convention was prompted by the growing federal budget deficit. The United States Constitution does not require the government to balance its yearly budget. In other words, the national government can, and does, spend more money than it collects. In 1976 the national debt was approximately $600 billion. It passed the $3 trillion mark in 1990 and continues to rise.

The movement to place a balanced-budget amendment in the Constitution began in 1976. In 1982 the proposed amendment was voted down in the House. Its supporters then organized a drive to call for a convention. Thirty-two state legislatures, two short of the number required, voted in favor of calling a convention to prepare a balanced-budget amendment. In 1992 the proposed amendment was brought up once again in the House. It was defeated in a close vote.

Rules for a constitutional convention?

Because a national convention for amending the Constitution has never been held, the possibility of such a convention raises many questions. How would delegates to the convention be selected? Would states get one vote each, or would votes be assigned according to population? Who would preside over the convention?

The most important question may be whether Congress can limit the purpose of the

Figure 3–2 **AMENDING THE CONSTITUTION** Only one of the four methods of amending the Constitution has been used more than once. 3C, 6C

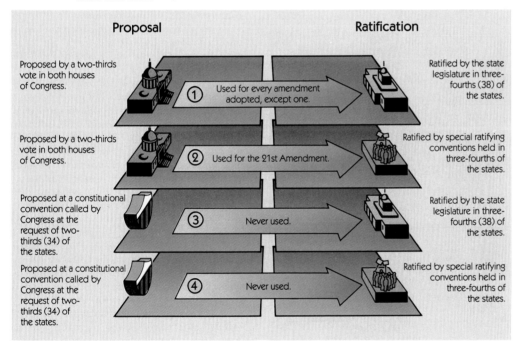

Proposal

Proposed by a two-thirds vote in both houses of Congress.

① Used for every amendment adopted, except one.

Proposed by a two-thirds vote in both houses of Congress.

② Used for the 21st Amendment.

Proposed at a constitutional convention called by Congress at the request of two-thirds (34) of the states.

③ Never used.

Proposed at a constitutional convention called by Congress at the request of two-thirds (34) of the states.

④ Never used.

Ratification

Ratified by the state legislature in three-fourths (38) of the states.

Ratified by special ratifying conventions held in three-fourths of the states.

Ratified by the state legislature in three-fourths (38) of the states.

Ratified by special ratifying conventions held in three-fourths of the states.

EXPLANATION
After reviewing the content of the section, you may want to consider the following activities:

Constitutional Heritage
▲ *When was the last time a national convention met to discuss constitutional changes?* (In 1787, at the Constitutional Convention in Philadelphia.)

■ CRITICAL THINKING *In what way could both supporters and opponents of another national convention point to this precedent to back their arguments?* (Supporters could point to the fact that the Constitutional Convention put together a more effective form of government for the United States; opponents could point to the fact that the Convention went beyond its stated purpose by approving a new form of government rather than making changes to the Confederation government.)

■ CRITICAL THINKING *Suppose a new national convention did meet, and it became a "runaway" convention as discussed on page 72. What safeguard exists to protect against the addition to the Constitution of unwise amendments?* (Any amendment proposed by the convention would still have to be ratified by three-fourths of the states.)

Background: *History* Prior to *Reynolds v. Sims* (1964), seats in many state legislatures were assigned by county. A sparsely populated rural county then had the same representation as a densely populated urban one; therefore, state legislatures were dominated by rural interests.

Figure 3–2
● Note that an amendment must receive two-thirds approval at the proposal stage and three-fourths approval at the ratification stage. *Why is more than a simple majority required?* (Because the Constitution is the supreme law of the land, any change must have overwhelming support.)

The symbol 👥 denotes active participation strategies.

Activities are keyed for student abilities:
▲ = Basic
● = All Levels
■ = Average/Advanced

Politics

● **What was the aim of the District of Columbia Amendment?** (It would give the District two senators and two representatives.) **What was the primary argument in favor of the amendment?** (To give residents of Washington, D.C., voting representation in Congress.) **Why did some members of Congress oppose the amendment?** (Some Republicans feared that the new representatives would be Democrats; some representatives from rural areas and small towns feared the amendment would increase big-city influence.) Ask students which arguments they find most persuasive, and why.

convention to a single issue, such as the balanced budget. What would prevent a "runaway" convention at which the delegates proposed a new constitution? After all, the Constitutional Convention of 1787 was called for the "sole and express purpose of revising the Articles of Confederation." These questions will remain unanswered until a constitutional convention is held.

3C, 6C

Ratifying Amendments

Once an amendment has been proposed, either by Congress or by a constitutional convention, it must be ratified by the states. Three-fourths (38) of the states must ratify an amendment for it to take effect. Amendments can be ratified in two ways — either by the state legislatures or by special ratifying conventions held in the states.

Federal government agents in the 1920's destroy barrels of illegal beer as they try to enforce Prohibition and the Eighteenth Amendment.

The role of Congress

The Constitution states that Congress shall choose the method of ratification. But it does not indicate how much time the states should be given to consider proposed amendments. Congress, therefore, also sets a time limit.

Starting with the Eighteenth Amendment, Congress began including a seven-year limit in the text of proposed amendments. Since the 23rd Amendment, however, Congress has imposed the seven-year limit through a separate resolution, rather than in the amendment itself. This change may seem like a mere technicality, but it can actually determine the success or failure of an amendment. If the time limit is part of the amendment itself, it can be changed only by a two-thirds vote of Congress. If it is separate, Congress can grant additional time by a simple majority vote. Congress can in this way give an amendment a second chance to be ratified.

The state-legislature method

Most commonly, Congress has called on the state legislatures to ratify amendments. All the amendments but one were ratified in this manner. Over the years, however, several questions concerning this method have arisen.

One crucial issue is whether a state legislature can change its vote once it has ratified an amendment. This question first arose in 1868. After voting to ratify the Fourteenth Amendment, the legislatures of New Jersey and Ohio decided to withdraw their approval. Because a change by either state would have prevented the amendment from taking effect, Congress refused to recognize either withdrawal. It thereby established the precedent that once a state legislature has ratified an amendment, it cannot later retract its vote. On the other hand, if a state legislature at first *rejects* a proposed amendment, it may later vote to ratify it. (The Supreme Court generally has left questions of ratifying amendments up to Congress.)

Another question about the state-legislature method is how much voice the voters themselves should have in the ratification process. Under this method, it is the state legislators, not the voters, who decide the fate of proposed amendments. It can be argued that the voters have chosen legislators who share their views on proposed amendments. Yet most people vote for a legisla-

---

Background: *History* There was no seven-year limit for the Nineteenth Amendment.

Critical Thinking
■ *What might be the reasoning behind letting a state change a "No" vote to a "Yes" vote, but not letting a state rescind a "Yes" vote?*

(Permitting states to rescind "Yes" votes would create chaos by making it possible for any amendment to be "unratified.")

tor on the basis of numerous state and local issues, not just his or her stand on a particular amendment. Moreover, a constitutional amendment is likely to be presented to the states after legislators have been elected.

The state-convention method

The second method of ratifying constitutional amendments — by special ratifying conventions — has been used only once. Congress deliberately chose this method for the ratification of the 21st Amendment, which repealed an earlier amendment.

The Eighteenth Amendment, passed in 1919, established Prohibition, a nationwide ban on the manufacturing, sale, or transportation of alcoholic beverages. The amendment proved impossible to enforce. Americans continued to consume liquor, and bootleggers reaped large profits from illegal sales. By 1932, many Americans, especially city dwellers, were calling for an end to Prohibition.

The 21st Amendment — repealing Prohibition — won approval from Congress in February 1933. Supporters of the amendment, known as "wets," feared it would not be ratified by the state legislatures, many of which were dominated by legislators from rural "dry" areas. To improve the amendment's chances for ratification, Congress called for holding ratifying conventions in the states.

Each state legislature was allowed to organize its own ratifying convention. In all cases, delegates were chosen in a statewide election, rather than district-by-district. Furthermore, each delegate was pledged to vote a certain way. Therefore, a vote for a particular delegate was in fact a vote for or against the amendment. By December 5, 1933, ratification was complete, and the 21st Amendment went into effect.

4B, 4C

Politics and Amendments

Congress has passed seven proposed amendments that failed to be ratified by the states. The difficulty of changing the Constitution by formal amendment is demonstrated by the political battles over two amendments — the Equal Rights Amendment and a proposal to give the District of Columbia representation in Congress.

The Equal Rights Amendment

Since 1923, numerous amendments to end sex discrimination have been introduced in Congress. Before the 1960's, proposals for such an amendment received scant support, either inside or outside Congress. During the social upheavals of the 1960's, the women's rights movement gained momentum. Led by the National Organization for Women (NOW), supporters of an Equal Rights Amendment (ERA) put pressure on Congress. They argued that a constitutional amendment was the only way to end sex discrimination in employment. Moreover, public opinion appeared to favor ERA.

By 1972 ERA had passed easily in both houses of Congress. A separate bill gave the amendment seven years to be ratified. The text of the entire proposal reads as follows:

Section 1. Equality of rights under the law shall not be denied or abridged by the United States or by any State on account of sex.

Section 2. The Congress shall have power to enforce, by appropriate legislation, the provisions of this article.

Section 3. This amendment shall take effect two years after date of ratification.

The battle over ERA

When ERA was submitted to the states, it seemed likely to pass within the seven-year time limit. Twenty-two states ratified the amendment by the end of 1972, in some instances without hearings. Opposition began to mount, however, under the leadership of a group called Stop-ERA. The Stop-ERA forces argued that the amendment would force women into military service. They also believed that women would lose certain legal privileges, such as alimony benefits and preference in child-custody cases.

In the fall of 1978, it was evident that ERA would fall three states short of ratification by the March 22, 1979, deadline. Furthermore, five state legislatures that had ratified ERA changed their vote. To prevent defeat of the amendment, Congress, by a simple majority vote, extended the deadline to June 30, 1982. This controversial move was possible because the time limit was in a separate bill. (A case challenging both Idaho's withdrawal of ratification and Congress's

Cooperative Learning
● Divide the class into four groups, one each supporting the ERA and the District of Columbia Amendment and one each opposing it. Each group should do research to assemble the arguments made by the side it represents, and then use these arguments in a classroom debate on the two amendments. Have class members vote on each amendment before and after the debate to see if the debate changed any opinions.

GUIDED/INDEPENDENT PRACTICE
● Have students read the following amendments: 1–10, 13–15, 19, 24, 26. Students should choose one of these amendments that has affected, or will affect, their lives in a clearly positive way and write a paragraph explaining the importance to them of that amendment.

Critical Thinking
● *Why is the state-convention method of ratification more responsive to the people than the state-legislature method?* (It gives the people a more direct choice.)

Background: *History*
Stop-ERA was led by Phyllis Schlafly. NOW was led by Betty Friedan and later by Eleanor Smeal.

The symbol ⅱ denotes active participation strategies.

Activities are keyed for student abilities:
▲ = Basic
● = All Levels
■ = Average/Advanced

RETEACHING/CORRECTIVES

▲ Have students transform the information in Figure 3–2 into a paragraph that explains the four different ways in which the Constitution can be amended.

You may also want to use **Transparency 12,** which reviews the methods of proposing and ratifying amendments.

A march in July 1978 demonstrates support for the proposed Equal Rights Amendment, whose deadline for ratification was March of the following year.

extension of the time limit was appealed to the Supreme Court, but it never ruled on the case.)

Between 1979 and 1982, states that had not ratified the amendment became political battlegrounds. To pressure legislators in Illinois, Georgia, Florida, Missouri, and Louisiana, NOW called for an economic boycott of those states. Hundreds of companies and organizations that favored ERA refused to hold their annual meetings in non-ratifying states. To counter these actions, Stop-ERA waged a publicity campaign. Both sides debated, held rallies, and pressured key legislators. By the time the final deadline arrived, ERA was still three states short of becoming the 27th Amendment.

Two weeks later, ERA was re-introduced into Congress. In November 1983, the proposal was defeated in the House of Representatives, just six votes short of the necessary two-thirds majority. ERA remained a major political issue, backed by the Democratic Party platform, NOW, and many other supporters. Nevertheless, the proposed amendment never received the support it needed to become part of the Constitution.

The District of Columbia Amendment

Another amendment that failed concerned the voting rights of residents of the District of Co-lumbia. Until 1961, the citizens of Washington, D.C., could not vote in federal elections. The 23rd Amendment, however, allowed them to cast votes for President. It gave the District three electoral votes, equal to the vote of the smallest state. Yet the District of Columbia still had no voting representation in Congress, even though its population is greater than that of three states — Alaska, Vermont, and Wyoming.

The District of Columbia Amendment, proposed in 1978, would have given the District two senators and two representatives (based on its population). It would have, in effect, repealed the 23rd Amendment, because it would have given the District one additional electoral vote. Finally, the amendment would have permitted the District to participate in ratifying constitutional amendments. (This would not have changed the number of states needed for ratification: three-fourths of 51 is still 38.)

Washington, D.C., an urban area with a large black population, has tended to vote Democratic. Opposition to the amendment, therefore, included Republican legislators, who feared it would give the Democrats additional strength in Congress. Legislators from rural areas and small towns also opposed the amendment because it would increase big-city influence. On August

Background: *History*
In the Idaho ERA case, an Idaho judge had ruled that states do have the right to withdraw ratification of ERA. The Supreme Court never made a formal ruling on the case because the time limit for ratification expired and the question became moot. The Court did issue an order staying the impact of the judge's decision.

Cross-reference
Each state has as many electors as it has senators and representatives combined. The Electoral College is discussed in detail on pp. 387–393.

22, 1985, the seven-year time limit expired, with only sixteen states having ratified the amendment. Unlike the proposed Equal Rights Amendment, the time limit was in the text of the amendment and so could not be extended.

2A, 6E, 6H

Why Amendments Are Passed

Each of the 27 amendments passed since the ratification of the Constitution in 1788 was the result of specific circumstances and events. To identify some basic trends in American government, however, it is useful to group some of the amendments together according to the general areas they have affected.

The Bill of Rights: basic freedoms

The first ten amendments, known as the Bill of Rights, were added to the Constitution in 1791. Much of the debate over ratifying the Constitution had centered on the lack of such a bill of

Figure 3–3 LATER CONSTITUTIONAL AMENDMENTS Since the Bill of Rights, the Constitution has been amended to . . . 8B

Reverse Supreme Court decisions.

Amendment 11 (1798) Protects a state from being sued by citizens of other states or foreign countries. Overrides the Supreme Court decision (1793) in *Chisholm v. Georgia.*
Amendment 14 (1868) Defines American citizenship. Prohibits the states from depriving any citizen of due process of law, equal protection of the law, or any other privilege guaranteed to United States citizens. Overrides the *Dred Scott* decision.
Amendment 16 (1913) Allows Congress to place a tax on incomes. Overrides the Supreme Court decision (1895) in *Pollock v. Farmers' Loan & Trust Co.,* which declared a federal income tax unconstitutional.

Change the selection of the President, Vice President, and Congress.

Amendment 12 (1804) Requires electors to cast separate ballots for President and Vice President.
Amendment 17 (1913) Calls for the direct popular election of United States senators.
Amendment 20 (1933) Changes the date of the presidential inauguration from March 4 to January 20 and changes the date on which Congress convenes from March 4 to January 3. This is to prevent "lame ducks" — members of Congress defeated in the November elections — from serving nearly four months.
Amendment 22 (1951) Limits the President to two full terms or no more than ten years in office.
Amendment 25 (1967) Stipulates the conditions under which the Vice President assumes the duties of President and the method by which vacancies in the office of Vice President shall be filled.

Extend the right to vote.

Amendment 15 (1870) Prohibits the national or state governments from denying anyone the right to vote on account of race, color, or previous condition of servitude. This amendment was passed after the Civil War to protect the voting rights of former slaves and other black Americans.
Amendment 19 (1920) Prohibits the national or state governments from denying anyone the right to vote on account of sex.
Amendment 23 (1961) Grants the people of Washington, D.C., the right to vote in presidential elections by giving the District of Columbia three votes in the Electoral College.
Amendment 24 (1964) Prohibits poll taxes (fees to be paid as a condition of voting) in federal elections.
Amendment 26 (1971) Grants 18-year-olds the right to vote in federal and state elections.

Reflect changing social values.

Amendment 13 (1865) Prohibits slavery and involuntary servitude, except as punishment for crime.
Amendment 18 (1919) Known as *Prohibition,* prohibits the manufacture, sale, or transportation of alcoholic beverages in the United States.
Amendment 21 (1933) Repeals Amendment 18.
Amendment 27 (1992) Prohibits congressional pay changes from taking effect before the next House election.

75

Figure 3–3

▲ *What evidence does the table give that a constitutional amendment can be overturned even after ratification?* (Amendment 21 repealed Amendment 18.)

Cross-reference

Chapters 5 and 6 deal with specific protections of the Bill of Rights. All other amendments are fully explained in later chapters (e.g., the Eleventh Amendment is explained in the discussion of federal court jurisdiction in Chapter 17).

ENRICHMENT/EXTENSION
■ Have students complete **Skills Challenge Worksheet 3,** which deals with the ratification of a hypothetical constitutional amendment.

The symbol 👥 denotes active participation strategies.

Activities are keyed for student abilities:
▲ = Basic
● = All Levels
■ = Average/Advanced

Section 2 Review Answers

1. (a) By Congress. **(b)** By a constitutional convention.

2. (a) By state legislatures or by state ratifying conventions. **(b)** Three-fourths, or 38, states.

3. (a) Congress. **(b)** If the time limit is included in a separate resolution, it can be extended by a simple majority vote.

4. The state-convention method. Because delegates are chosen in a statewide election and are pledged to vote a certain way, voters can in effect vote directly on the amendment.

5. (a) Basic freedoms. **(b)** Reverse Supreme Court decisions; change selection of the President, Vice President, and Congress; extend suffrage; reflect changing social values.

Critical thinking Direct popular vote would reflect the principle of popular sovereignty. On the other hand, state legislators are professional lawmakers and may be better judges of constitutional change.

CLOSURE

● Remind students of the pre-reading objectives at the beginning of the section. Pose one or all of these questions again. Then have students read Section 3, noting the difference between formal and informal methods of constitutional change.

---

rights, and the Federalists had promised to add it immediately. Madison actually proposed more than ten amendments, and Congress sent twelve to the states. The ten that were then approved became the Bill of Rights. The Bill of Rights was originally intended to ensure that a strong national government would not violate the people's basic rights. In recent years, most of its provisions have been extended to protect citizens against infringements by state governments as well.

The First Amendment provides for freedom of expression. Specifically, it guarantees the freedoms of religion, speech, press, and assembly, as well as the right "to petition the government for a redress of grievances." This amendment guarantees Americans the right to speak out for or against government policies.

The next two amendments in the Bill of Rights protect citizens from domination by the military. The Second Amendment guarantees the states the right to have a militia and the people the right "to keep and bear arms." The Third Amendment prohibits the quartering of soldiers in private homes during peacetime.

Amendments 4 through 8 protect citizens from arbitrary actions by the police or the courts. The Fourth Amendment protects people's homes, prohibiting unreasonable searches and seizures and requiring warrants for searches. The Fifth Amendment provides a number of protections for persons accused of a crime, while the Sixth Amendment sets up rules for a fair trial and guarantees the right to have a defense lawyer. The Seventh Amendment ensures a jury trial in certain civil cases. The Eighth Amendment prohibits excessive bail, excessive fines, and cruel or unusual punishments.

The last two amendments in the Bill of Rights re-emphasize the principle of "government by the people." The Ninth Amendment states that the rights of the people are not limited to those spelled out in the Constitution. The Tenth Amendment guarantees that the powers not expressly given to the national government or denied to the states by the Constitution belong to the states or to the people.

Later changes in government

The Bill of Rights may to some extent be considered part of the original Constitution, because these amendments were added as a condition of ratification. The remaining seventeen amendments, adopted separately over a period of 194 years, truly represent changes in the framework of government.

The later amendments can be grouped into four categories, as shown in Figure 3–3. The first category includes amendments that were written to override Supreme Court decisions. The second group of amendments alters how the President, Vice President, and members of Congress are selected. Several amendments extending voting rights make up the third category. The last category includes amendments that reflect changes in the social values and ideas of the American people.

SECTION 2 REVIEW

Vocabulary and key terms

Equal Rights
   Amendment (73)
District of Columbia
   Amendment (74)
Bill of Rights (75)

For review

1. (a) By what method have all constitutional amendments been proposed? (b) How else can they be proposed? **6C**
2. (a) What are the two methods by which proposed amendments can be ratified? (b) How many states are needed to ratify an amendment? **6C**
3. (a) Who determines which method of ratification will be used? (b) How can the means of including the time limit for ratification affect an amendment's chances of being ratified? **6C**
4. Which method of ratification gives voters a stronger voice? Why? **6C**
5. (a) What rights are promised the people in the Bill of Rights? (b) Into what four categories can the remaining seventeen amendments be classified? **2A**

Critical thinking

FORMING AN OPINION Should constitutional amendments be proposed and ratified by direct popular vote? Why or why not? **6F**

CRITICAL THINKING
Finding the Main Point

When you read about a controversial subject you might sometimes feel overwhelmed. Many facts are presented, arguments are made, and conclusions are drawn. The first thing you must do to sort out this information is to make sense of what you read. Ask yourself this question: What is the author's main point?

As you read, try to translate what the author says into your own words. This will help you make his or her arguments clear in your mind. Next, try to determine the relative importance of the information given. Which are the author's main points, and which are supporting ideas? Good places to look for main ideas are opening paragraphs, which usually state the problem, and closing paragraphs, which often state final conclusions.

★ ISSUE: Immigration Reform

Battles over immigration policy are a regular feature of American politics. In the mid-1980's, the immigration controversy centered on the large number of illegal immigrants entering the United States each year.

Some Americans called on the federal government to crack down on illegal immigration. They charged that illegal aliens took jobs from American citizens and that the aliens placed a burden on taxpayers to provide social welfare programs. Supporters of immigration argued that illegal immigrants often took low-paying jobs that Americans did not want. They also pointed out that many people coming to this nation were fleeing starvation or oppression.

The following two columns express opinions on an immigration reform bill passed by Congress in 1986. As you read the editorials, look for main ideas and supporting points.

Business Week, column by Gary S. Becker (12/1/86)

. . . [T]he principal shortcoming of the new law is its silence on legal immigration. It does not consider . . . raising the number of people admitted legally and . . . changing the criteria for selecting legal immigrants. . . .

While large numbers of illegal aliens receive amnesty, many students and other immigrants who have been here legally will be forced to leave because they do not qualify for legal immigration status. . . .

To cope with illegal immigration in the future, the new law establishes fines and prison sentences for employers convicted of hiring illegal aliens. . . . Punishing illegal aliens would be far more effective in deterring illegal immigration than any system of employer sanctions.

. . . I view the law as a missed opportunity for sensible immigration. It will probably do more harm than good.

Houston Post, column by Jody Powell (7/9/86)

. . . [T]he legislative record of the past five years suggests that there is no workable solution that will satisfy opponents [of immigration reform]. The deeper one digs into the political maneuvering and repeatedly unsuccessful offers of compromise, the more compelling becomes the conclusion that their goal is not a fair bill but no bill.

. . . The charge that this country is about to abandon its ideals and close its door to the oppressed and afflicted is a baseless slander. . . . We accept more legal immigrants for permanent resettlement than the rest of the world combined. . . .

Those who blindly oppose all effort to regain control of our national borders would do well to consider whether immigration reform may not be the salvation of rather than a threat to the ideals and traditions represented by [the Statue of Liberty].

Analyzing the Issue

1. What are the two writers' positions on the bill?
2. What is the main point of the *Business Week* column?
3. What supporting point does the *Houston Post* column make with regard to opponents of the bill?

77

CRITICAL THINKING

Values
● CRITICAL THINKING **Why is immigration policy such a controversial issue in the United States?** (Most Americans are descended from immigrants. Also, the United States has historically been a popular destination for emigrants from all over the world.)
● CRITICAL THINKING **The Houston Post column refers to "the ideals and traditions" represented by the Statue of Liberty. What are these?** (Accepting large numbers of immigrants into American society and offering them a chance to build new lives here.)

Analyzing the Issue Answers

1. Gary Becker opposes the bill; Jody Powell favors it.

2. That because the law failed to raise the number of legal immigrants, it will do more harm than good.

3. That they are opposed to immigration reform in general, not just to any one bill.

The symbol 👥 denotes active participation strategies.

Activities are keyed for student abilities:
▲ = Basic
● = All Levels
■ = Average/Advanced

The Constitution Remains Flexible
(pp. 78–81)

Section Objectives

☐ explain the difference between fundamental law and statutory law

☐ describe the informal changes that have been made in the United States government

Vocabulary

fundamental law, statutory law, enabling act, executive agreement, Cabinet, senatorial courtesy, executive privilege

FOCUS

● To dramatize the Constitution's effectiveness as fundamental law, ask students to list the ways in which the United States of today differs from the United States of the late 1700's. Then point out that in spite of these changes, our nation's fundamental law remains largely unchanged.

EXPLANATION

After reviewing the content of the section, you may want to consider the following activities:

Historic Documents

● CRITICAL THINKING **Is there a sense in which the Constitution is "timeless"? Explain.** (Yes. The fundamental principles upon which the United States government is based are not bound to any single historical period.)

Constitutional Heritage

● CRITICAL THINKING **Why might informal change sometimes be preferable to amending the Constitution?** (Because informal methods of change do not require

78

ACCESS **The Main Ideas**

1 **What is the difference between fundamental law and statutory law?**
page 78

2 **What informal changes have been made in the United States government?**
pages 78–81

Have you and your friends ever made up a game? Usually you begin with a general idea of how you want the game to work, and then you figure out the specific rules. You do not, however, try to handle in advance every possible situation that might emerge in the game. You understand that as the game progresses, minor changes can be made as needed. Similarly, while the basic principles of the Constitution remain fixed, experience and custom have adjusted how our government operates.

2A

The Value of Fundamental Law

The flexibility of the Constitution can be explained by the fact that the Constitution represents **fundamental law**. Fundamental law outlines the basic principles, powers, and structures of a government. **Statutory law**, on the other hand, is made up of the detailed rules of government — the laws, or *statutes,* passed by a legislature.

Unlike the national Constitution, many state constitutions go beyond basic ideas. They tend to be very long and overloaded with details that could be covered by statutes. The Kentucky constitution, for example, lists official salaries, while that of South Dakota specifies what vines shall grow on the walls of the state prison. Such details go out of date quickly, and state constitutions therefore must be amended frequently or replaced altogether.

By contrast, the Constitution of the United States has only a few provisions so specific that they have become dated. Because the delegates at the Constitutional Convention were careful to

78

create fundamental law, the Constitution has been amended only 27 times in 200 years.

Flexibility of the Constitution

The "commerce clause" of the Constitution is a good example of the flexibility of fundamental law. Article 1, Section 8, Clause 3 of the Constitution states that Congress has the power "to regulate commerce . . . among the several states." The Constitution, fortunately, does not define *commerce.* In 1787 the members of the Constitutional Convention might have defined *commerce* as "the buying and selling of goods transported by horse and wagon or by ship." They could not have envisioned that, 200 years later, there would be jet airplanes, trucks, vans, television, telephones, and communications satellites. Had the Constitution included a precise definition of *commerce,* Congress could probably not regulate interstate commerce without the passage of many formal amendments.

By contrast, one of the few detailed provisions in the Constitution is found in the Seventh Amendment. It stipulates, "In suits at common law, where the value in controversy shall exceed twenty dollars, the right of trial by jury shall be preserved. . . ." While twenty dollars was a considerable sum in 1791, it is not today. It would probably not even pay for a pair of running shoes or a bag of groceries. Because of this specific reference, the Seventh Amendment now seems out of date.

Because most of the Constitution *is* flexible, it enables the national government to "breathe." It allows the government to change with the times. As Henry Clay said, "The Constitution was made not merely for the generation that then existed, but for posterity."

2D, 2E, 3A

Informal Methods of Change

Although the Constitution sets out the basic rules of American government, every President, every Congress, and every Supreme Court has interpreted these rules differently. Moreover,

---

Cross-reference
A chart containing information about each state's constitution appears on p. 637.

Check for Understanding
▲ **Is the Constitution fundamental law or statutory law?**
(Fundamental law.)

political parties and customs have affected the development of government institutions in ways not foreseen in 1787. Even though these developments have not altered a single word of the document, they have changed the meaning of parts of the Constitution.

Legislative acts

Article I of the Constitution provides a general framework for the legislative branch and gives Congress certain powers and duties. These powers, however, are described in general terms — for example, "to lay and collect taxes," "to regulate commerce," and "to raise and support armies." The Constitution does not say what items should be taxed, how commerce should be regulated, or how many people should be in the army. It is left up to Congress itself to fill in the details. To make this possible, the Constitution authorizes Congress "to make all laws which shall be necessary and proper" for carrying out its constitutional duties and powers.

For example, Article III, Section 1 states that the judicial branch shall consist of "one Supreme Court" and "such inferior [lower] courts as the Congress may from time to time ordain and establish." On the basis of this phrase, acts of Congress have established ninety federal district courts, twelve circuit courts of appeal, and a handful of special courts throughout the country.

Many formal constitutional amendments also grant Congress considerable scope in interpreting the fundamental law. They contain the phrase, "Congress shall have the power to enforce this article by appropriate legislation." This provision, known as an **enabling act**, authorizes Congress to pass whatever laws are necessary to make the amendment effective.

Executive actions

Over the years, Presidents have assumed many powers that are mentioned nowhere in the Constitution. Many of these actions have become standard and accepted practice, while some have led to fears of a too-powerful presidency. For example, the Constitution gives Congress the power to declare war and to call forth the state militia (the National Guard). Yet Presidents have sometimes called on the National Guard to carry out federal laws.

In addition, several Presidents have used their authority as commander-in-chief to engage American troops overseas without a formal declaration of war by Congress. The Korean and Vietnam wars are two conspicuous examples. Congress sought to limit this expansion of presidential powers in 1973 with the War Powers Act.

Another practice that has become common in recent years is the **executive agreement**. Executive agreements are informal accords between leaders of nations. Presidents often prefer executive agreements over treaties because they can be negotiated and concluded quickly, whereas treaties must be approved by the Senate. Although executive agreements are not mentioned in the Constitution, the Supreme Court has held that they have the same force as treaties.

Supreme Court decisions

Many provisions of the Constitution are stated in general terms. When questions arise about their meaning and application, the Supreme Court must interpret them. In a sense, this gives the Court a part in the lawmaking process. With its power of judicial review, the

Most years since 1913, Presidents have delivered a State of the Union Address to Congress outlining their legislative priorities for that session. Before then, Presidents had simply sent Congress the message in writing. Here President Bush addresses Congress.

79

formal ratification, they are more flexible. They can be made, and unmade, as changing circumstances require.)

● CRITICAL THINKING **What might be the risks of executive agreements and executive privilege?** (A President could use them to limit Congress's ability to check the presidency.)

■ CRITICAL THINKING **Using the information in this section, what can you conclude about the future use of informal change in our government?** (Because it helps keep the Constitution up to date, informal change is likely to continue.)

History

● **What quotations in the section demonstrate that the framers of the Constitution expected the Constitution to evolve over time?** (Clay's statement on p. 78: "The Constitution belongs . . . to posterity." Washington's statement on p. 80: "Time and habit are at least as necessary to fix the true character of governments as of other human institutions.")

■ CRITICAL THINKING **If you were one of the framers of the Constitution, would you approve of the fact that some of these changes have been informal, not through amendment? Explain.** (Some may argue that all changes should follow the amendment process. Others may argue that the informal changes made have been consistent with the Constitution.)

Cross-reference
Chapter 15 discusses the President's powers in detail.

The symbol ♙♙ denotes active participation strategies.

Activities are keyed for student abilities:
▲ = Basic
● = All Levels
■ = Average/Advanced

Cooperative Learning

● Divide the class into six groups and assign two groups to each of the first three subheadings under the heading "Informal Methods of Change." Then have each set of groups stage a debate for the class on the issue of whether that kind of change is good for the United States. Each debate should be followed by a class vote on the issue.

GUIDED/INDEPENDENT PRACTICE

● Have students create a two-column chart comparing formal and informal methods of change in the United States government. After the charts have been completed, have students compare them and discuss which ones are the most useful and effective, and why.

RETEACHING/ CORRECTIVES

▲ On the board draw a box labeled *United States Constitution.* Draw two arrows, labeled *Formal Changes* and *Informal Changes,* extending outward from the box. Then select students to come to the board and draw and label boxes representing the formal (amendment) and informal (legislative acts, executive actions, Supreme Court decisions, political parties, custom) changes in American government.

ENRICHMENT/EXTENSION

■ Have students complete **Constitutional Issues Worksheet 3,** which deals with methods of changing the Constitution.

President Washington (right) began the custom of meeting with the heads of the executive departments — Secretary of the Treasury Alexander Hamilton (next to Washington), Secretary of War Henry Knox (seated), and Secretary of State Thomas Jefferson (center, standing). Edmund Randolph, the Attorney General (behind Knox's chair), also met with the Cabinet.

Supreme Court holds actions of the states, Congress, and the executive branch up to the light of the Constitution to see if they can be justified.

In many cases, the Supreme Court must judge issues that the Constitution never mentions. In recent years the Court has ruled, for example, that racially segregated schools are unconstitutional and that wiretaps are illegal without a search warrant. These rulings are final, unless they are reversed by a later Supreme Court decision or overturned by a constitutional amendment. Such decisions have, therefore, almost the same impact as formal amendments.

Political parties

The Constitution nowhere mentions political parties, for they were not part of the political scene in 1787. Yet party politics have added a new dimension to the election process, the organization of Congress, the appointment of judges, and nearly all the other workings of government. Even the role of the President is not quite as described in the Constitution, for it now includes the leadership of a national political party. Thus, political parties, without altering the Constitution, have caused many changes in American government.

Changes through custom

George Washington remarked, in his Farewell Address, "Time and habit are at least as necessary to fix the true character of governments as

of other human institutions." In two hundred years of "time and habit," customs have developed within the United States government that have almost the same force as written constitutional provisions.

An outstanding example of constitutional change through custom is the development of the **Cabinet** — the President's formal group of advisers, comprising the heads of the executive departments. The Constitution does not provide for such a Cabinet but states only that the President can call on the heads of the "executive departments" for their opinions. Congress in 1789 set up the departments of State, Treasury, and War, along with an Attorney General and a Postmaster General. As President, George Washington often called his department heads together for consultation on important decisions. All Presidents since have entrusted many executive decisions to members of their Cabinets.

Another custom that has grown up over time is the practice of **senatorial courtesy.** Senators will not confirm a presidential nomination that is opposed by both senators from the state of the appointee or by the senior senator of the President's party. For instance, in 1951 President Harry Truman, a Democrat, nominated two federal district judges from Illinois but did not consult with Senator Paul Douglas, an Illinois Democrat. When Douglas objected to Truman's nominees, the Senate rejected them.

Cross-reference
Chapter 16 discusses the organization of the Executive Office of the President and other executive agencies. The Guide to Executive Departments, pp. 447-460, lists the many functions and duties of the Cabinet departments.

A third illustration is the unwritten custom of **executive privilege**, which is the President's right to withhold information from Congress and the courts. The Constitution does not grant the President this right. Rather, this time-honored tradition is based on the principle of separation of powers. The independence of the presidency might be seriously undermined if all its records were open to the other branches.

Unlike formal amendments, these informal changes have not altered the basic framework established in the Constitution. They have, however, allowed the government to adapt to the growth and change of the United States. This ability to adapt to changing times is one important reason why the Constitution — and the governmental system that it established — remain vital after 200 years.

SECTION 3 REVIEW

Vocabulary and key terms

fundamental law (78)   Cabinet (80)
statutory law (78)   senatorial courtesy (80)
enabling act (79)   executive privilege (81)
executive agreement (79)

For review

1. What is the difference between fundamental law and statutory law? **2A**
2. How is Congress able to expand on provisions of the Constitution? **3A**
3. Give examples of ways in which Presidents have enlarged the power of the executive branch. **3A**
4. How did the Cabinet begin? **3A**
5. (a) Under what circumstances is senatorial courtesy followed? (b) On what principle of government is the custom of executive privilege based? **3A**

Critical thinking

EXAMINING BASIC PRINCIPLES Some informal methods of constitutional change, such as executive agreements, seem to contradict the basic principles of the Constitution. Should this be a cause for concern? Why or why not? **6F**

Chapter Summary

The Constitution of the United States incorporates six key principles of government. The principle of popular sovereignty ensures the people of the United States ultimate authority over their government. The powers of government are divided among three branches — legislative, executive, and judicial. To ensure that no branch gains too much power, a system of checks and balances gives each branch some leverage over the other two.

The principle of federalism further divides the powers of government between the national government and the governments of the states. To make federalism work, the supremacy clause (Article VI, Clause 2) settles conflicts between state and national laws. Using the power of judicial review, the Supreme Court decides whether state and national laws are constitutional. Finally, a number of safeguards in the Constitution ensure that civilian officials are able to maintain control over the military.

To change any of the basic principles or structures set up by the Constitution, a formal amendment is necessary. Amendments can be proposed by a two-thirds vote of Congress or by a convention called at the request of two-thirds of the states. To go into effect, an amendment must be ratified either by the state legislatures or by ratifying conventions in three-fourths of the states. Several notable attempts to amend the Constitution have failed in recent years.

The Bill of Rights, ratified in 1791, comprises the first ten amendments, which protect people's basic rights from a strong government. Later amendments have made some changes in government structure.

As fundamental law, the Constitution establishes basic principles and structures for the government of the United States, with enough flexibility to meet changing needs and circumstances. A number of informal changes in American government have been made without altering the basic framework set up by the Constitution. Acts of Congress, Presidents, and the Supreme Court have served to enlarge and clarify many areas of the Constitution. In addition, political parties and customs have been a force in changing American government.

Section 3 Review Answers
1. Fundamental law outlines basic principles, powers, and structures of government. Statutory law, passed by legislatures, is more detailed.
2. By passing specific legislation under its broadly worded powers; also by enabling acts in amendments.
3. Sending troops overseas, making executive agreements.
4. Congress set up three executive departments; Washington frequently called the department heads together for consultation.
5. (a) When the Senate is considering presidential appointments within a state.
(b) Separation of powers.

Critical thinking Students should recognize the potential for abuse, resulting in an imbalance of power between branches. Conversely, students might cite the importance of "time and habit" and the importance of flexibility to adapt with the times.

CLOSURE
● Have students outline the section, using the headings and subheadings and filling in any details. Then have students read the next assigned lesson.

CHAPTER 3 CORRECTIVES
● To review the content of Chapter 3, you may want to have students complete **Study Guide/Review 3** or **Workbook Chapter 3**.

The symbol 👥 denotes active participation strategies.

Activities are keyed for student abilities:
▲ = Basic
● = All Levels
■ = Average/Advanced

CHAPTER 3 REVIEW

Answers

Vocabulary See pp. T19–T21 for suggested vocabulary activities.

Reviewing the Facts

1. The executive branch (President), legislative branch (Congress), and the judicial branch (Supreme Court and other federal courts).

2. Refer to the chart on p. 65 for possible answers.

3. The supremacy clause (Article VI, Clause 2) declares that all state courts must uphold national laws because the states may not challenge the constitutional authority of the national government.

4. The President, a civilian, is commander-in-chief of the armed forces. Only Congress may declare war and authorize defense spending. Such spending must be reconsidered every two years. The Third Amendment prohibits the federal government from forcing citizens to house soldiers.

5. A constitutional amendment may be proposed either by Congress or by a national convention called by Congress at the request of two-thirds of the state legislatures.

6. The Bill of Rights, which was intended primarily to ensure that the people's rights would not be violated by a strong national government, was passed in order to overcome opposition to the Constitution.

7. Answers might include the Cabinet, political parties, and executive privilege.

Thinking Critically About Key Concepts

1. The Constitution states that powers not delegated to the national government are reserved by the states.

2. (a) Less efficient. **(b)** No. In a more efficient system, such as one in which the chief executive

---

● Review the definitions of the following terms:

Bill of Rights	executive agreement	Preamble
Cabinet	executive privilege	presidential government
checks and balances	fundamental law	prime minister
constituency	judicial	popular sovereignty
District of Columbia	judicial review	senatorial courtesy
Amendment	legislative	separation of powers
enabling act	*Marbury v. Madison*	statutory law
Equal Rights Amendment	parliamentary	supremacy clause
executive	government	veto

● REVIEWING THE FACTS

1. What are the three branches of government? **3A**

2. Name one control, or check, that each branch has over the other two branches. **3B**

3. What is the supremacy clause? **3C**

4. How does the Constitution ensure that the federal government will not be controlled by the military? **6F**

5. What are two methods of proposing constitutional amendments? **6C**

6. What was the purpose of adding the Bill of Rights to the Constitution? **2A**

7. What are two examples of informal changes in government that have developed through custom? **3A**

▲ THINKING CRITICALLY ABOUT KEY CONCEPTS

1. What prevents the federal government from using the supremacy clause to take all powers away from the states? **3C**

2. (a) Does the system of checks and balances make the federal government more efficient or less efficient? **(b)** If a more efficient system than checks and balances could be found, should it be instituted? Explain. **3B**

3. What reasons might explain why the Constitution has been formally amended only 27 times? **2A**

▲ PRACTICING SKILLS

1. Study Skills: Reading a diagram. Refer to Figure 3–1 (page 65) to answer the following questions. **(a)** Which branch of government controls appropriations? **(b)** In what two ways can the President check the actions of the judiciary? **(c)** What is the means by which judges are kept free from executive control? **(d)** Does the President's veto power always act as a check on the powers of Congress? **8B**

2. Critical Thinking Skills: Finding the main idea. Reread the subsection "Rules for a constitutional convention?" (pages 71–72) to answer the following questions. **(a)** What is the main idea of this subsection? **(b)** What details are used to support this idea? **(c)** Which detail is the most significant? **(d)** How is the Constitutional Convention of 1787 used as an example of what might happen? **8A**

▲ PARTICIPATORY CITIZENSHIP

1. Writing an essay. Select one of the amendments to the Constitution (pages 128–138) and write an essay describing the ways in which this amendment directly affects you or your family. **4A**

---

operated without legislative or judicial restraint, the rights of the people would not be as well protected.

3. The amendment process is long and difficult. Also, many changes that might have been made in the

Constitution appeared instead in the form of statutory law.

Practicing Skills

1. (a) Legislative. **(b)** The President appoints Supreme Court justices and other

federal judges, and can also grant reprieves and pardons. **(c)** They are appointed for life. **(d)** No, because Congress can override a presidential veto.

2. (a) There are potential problems with a constitu-

2. **Making an argument.** Suppose someone said to you, "The beauty of the American system of government is that it is designed to run by itself. All its parts are perfectly balanced so that Americans do not have to get involved in their government." How would you respond to this statement? Organize your ideas into an argument. **4D**

■ WRITING ABOUT ISSUES

1. **Creating a pamphlet.** Imagine that you are preparing a pamphlet on the Constitution for immigrants wishing to gain United States citizenship. Write five questions (with answers) that focus on the most important aspects of the Constitution. **8C**
2. **Writing an essay.** Review the constitutional amendments listed in Figure 3–3 on page 75. Then select one of the amendments and write a brief essay explaining why, in your opinion, that amendment is or is not consistent with the principles that underlie the United States Constitution. **6H**
3. **Writing a report.** Do research and write a report on Prohibition, focusing on the arguments used to secure passage of the amendment establishing Prohibition and the amendment repealing it. Explain how, if at all, the debate over Prohibition changed between the 1910's and the 1930's. **8C**
4. **Composing an editorial.** Review the ways in which the roles of each of the branches of government have changed informally (pages 78–81). Then decide which branch has gained the most power from these changes and write a newspaper editorial warning that this branch is becoming too powerful. **8C**

▲ ANALYZING A POLITICAL CARTOON

According to the Constitution, only Congress can declare war. However, the President is the commander-in-chief of the military. In this role, Presidents have sent troops into combat without Congress declaring war. Look at the cartoon below and answer the following questions.

1. What group of people do the four individuals in the cartoon represent? **8B**
2. According to the cartoonist, who decides if the United States will declare war? **8B**
3. Explain how this cartoon suggests that the government does not always follow the provisions of the Constitution. **8B**

© 1990 William Costello / The Lowell Sun.

Participatory Citizenship

1. Essays should list the amendment by number, describe the amendment, and then explain the practical effect of the amendment on the student or family.
2. Students must explain that direct citizen involvement, through voting, office-holding, and other activities, is central to the American system of government.

Writing About Issues

1. Possible questions include: Which body can declare a law unconstitutional? How are laws made? How can the Constitution be changed? Do states have to obey federal laws? What is the relationship between the armed forces and the civilian government?
2. Students should defend their opinions.
3. These reports might serve as the starting point for a class discussion about legislating social values.
4. Editorials should be supported by specific examples.

Analyzing a Political Cartoon

1. The authors of the Constitution.
2. The President as well as Congress.
3. Even though Congress is supposed to declare war, in reality Presidents often, in effect, declare war first by exercising their power as commander-in-chief.

tional convention. **(b)** The details are the questions that would have to be answered: How would delegates be selected? Would states get one vote each, or would votes be assigned according to population? Who would preside over the convention? Can Congress limit the purpose of a convention to a single issue? **(c)** The ability of Congress to limit the convention to a single issue. **d)** The Constitutional Convention of 1787 was supposed to revise the Articles of Confederation, but it instead created an entirely new Constitution.

Chapter Review exercises are keyed for student abilities:
▲ = Basic
● = All Levels
■ = Average/Advanced

CHAPTER 4
FEDERALISM: THE DIVISION OF POWER
(pp. 84–109)

	Section Objectives	Section Resources
Section 1 **The Constitution Establishes a Federal System**	☐ list the powers of the national government under the Constitution ☐ explain the relationship between state power and national power	▲ SKILLS PRACTICE WORKSHEET **4** ● PRIMARY SOURCE WORKSHEET **6** ■ CONSTITUTIONAL ISSUES WORKSHEET **4** ■ SUPREME COURT DECISION **2** ▲ TRANSPARENCY **13**
Section 2 **State and Federal Governments Have Specific Duties**	☐ describe the duties of the federal government ☐ describe the responsibilities of state governments ☐ explain how views of federalism have changed	■ SKILLS CHALLENGE WORKSHEET **4** ● PRIMARY SOURCE WORKSHEET **7** ▲ TRANSPARENCY **14**
Section 3 **The National Government's Powers Have Increased**	☐ explain how the national government has increased its power through regulation of interstate commerce and extension of civil liberties ☐ explain how the federal government influences state and local affairs through financial aid	■ SUPREME COURT DECISION **3**
Section 4 **Federalism Links the Fifty States**	☐ describe how the Constitution encourages cooperation between states ☐ list examples of conflict and cooperation between states	

Essential Elements

The list below shows Essential Elements relevant to this chapter. (The complete list of Essential Elements appears in the introductory pages of this Teacher's Edition.)

Section 1: 2C, 2D, 3A, 3C, 6E, 6I

Section 2: 3A, 3C, 4C, 6F, 8B, 8H

Section 3: 2A, 2D, 3A, 3C, 7B

Section 4: 2A, 3A, 3C, 6A, 6E

Chapter Review: 3A, 3C, 4D, 8A, 8B, 8C, 8D

> Section Resources are keyed for student abilities:
> ▲ = Basic
> ● = All Levels
> ■ = Average/Advanced

Homework Options

Each section contains activities labeled "Guided/Independent Practice," "Reteaching/Correctives," and "Enrichment/Extension." You may wish to choose from among these activities when assigning homework.

Students Acquiring English Activities

How does your state use the powers reserved to it in the areas of public health, safety, welfare, morals, convenience, and education? Have students write letters to the state agency responsible for something of interest to them (for example, licensing of cars, marriages, pharmacists, etc.). Ask for pamphlets for the entire class if possible. Select students to report to the class on the information they have received.

LISTENING/SPEAKING: Ask for volunteers to follow the directions for two cake mixes to make the "all-American cakes" shown on p. 98. Have students make a marble cake and a layer cake to eat in class as part of the discussion on p. 98. Use strawberry and vanilla in the cake and blue food coloring in the frosting to show the contrast between the two kinds of federalism. As students eat the cakes, have them compare and contrast the two kinds of federalism.

Case Studies

When teaching this chapter, you may use Case Study 6, which deals with defense budget cuts or Case Study 11, which addresses the issue of gun control. (Case Studies may be found following p. 510.)

Teacher Bibliography

Sexton, John and Nat Brandt. *How Free Are We? What the Constitution Says We Can and Cannot Do.* M. Evans, 1986. Examines the powers of the legislative, executive, and judicial branches and the curbs on those powers.

Walker, David Bradstreet. *Toward a Functioning Federalism.* Scott, Foresman, 1981. Appraises the federal system from its beginnings to its present expanded condition and suggests ways in which its effectiveness could be enhanced.

Student Bibliography

Feldman, Daniel L. *The Logic of American Government: Applying the Constitution to the Contemporary World.* Greenwillow, 1990. The different roles played by the Constitution in American history are examined by looking at contemporary controversies.

Goode, Stephen. *The New Federalism: State's Rights in American History.* Franklin Watts, 1983. A historical look at federalism from the Constitutional Convention to the Reagan administration.

Tocqueville, Alexis de. *Democracy in America.* Many editions. Originally published in the 1830's, this is the classic philosophical text on democracy in the United States.

Literature

Bober, Natalie. *Thomas Jefferson: Man on a Mountain.* Atheneum, 1988. An excellent, detailed biography of Jefferson.

CHAPTER RESOURCES

Study Guide/Review 4
Workbook Chapter 4
Chapter 4 Test, Forms A–C

Films and Videotapes*

South Carolina and the United States. (Series title: *This Constitution: A History.*) 28 min. PSUAVS, 1987. v. A survey and analysis of the division of sovereignty between the federal and state governments, using South Carolina as an example.

The Federal City. (Series title: *This Constitution: A History.*) 28 min. PSUAVS, 1987. v. The development of Washington, D.C., as our capital and how it exemplifies the principles of the Constitution.

Software*

American Government II (Apple, IBM, Macintosh). Queue. Students learn about the development and processes of American government through interactive tutorials covering federalism, the First Amendment, Civil Rights, and state and federal rights.

The U.S. Constitution: Nationalism and Federalism (Apple). Focus. Students act as farmers or manufacturers living under the Articles of Confederation in the 1780's and write their own Constitution.

* For a complete guide to audiovisual sources, see page T22.

83B

CHAPTER 4

Federalism: The Division of Power
(pp. 84–109)

This chapter examines the division of power between the federal and state governments, explaining their different responsibilities and describing Americans' changing views of federalism.

Chapter Objectives

After students complete this chapter, they will be able to:

1. List the powers of the national government under the Constitution.

2. Explain the relationship between state power and national power.

3. Describe the duties of the federal government.

4. Describe the responsibilities of state governments.

5. Explain how views of federalism have changed.

6. Explain how the national government has increased its power through regulation of interstate commerce and extension of civil liberties.

7. Explain how the federal government influences state and local affairs through financial aid.

8. Describe how the Constitution encourages cooperation between states.

9. List examples of conflict and cooperation between states.

CHAPTER

4

FEDERALISM: The Division of Power

The federal system was devised to combine the various advantages of large and small size for nations. A glance at the United States of America will show all the advantages derived from adopting that system.

Alexis de Tocqueville
Democracy in America (1835)

84

Photo
Interstate highway under construction.

Over a century and a half ago, Alexis de Tocqueville, a French statesman, journeyed to the United States to study our political system. Following his trip in 1831–1832, he wrote his most famous book, *Democracy in America*. This classic work, quoted on the facing page, is considered one of the most insightful accounts of American government by an outside observer. Tocqueville, however, was familiar only with the monarchies and centralized governments of Europe. He marveled at the fact that American federalism actually worked. It was, after all, the first government in the world to divide governmental powers between the national government and the separate states.

To those unfamiliar with American government, the workings of the federal system may appear quite complicated. How *does* the Constitution divide authority? What happens when conflicts arise between national and state powers? How does the Constitution resolve conflicts between the states? These are some of the questions to be answered in Chapter 4.

CHAPTER OUTLINE

1 The Constitution Establishes a Federal System

National Government Powers
State Government Powers

2 State and Federal Governments Have Specific Duties

Federal Government Duties
State Responsibilities
Changing Views of Federalism

3 The National Government's Powers Have Increased

Using the Commerce Clause
Extending Civil Liberties
Using Economic Influence

4 Federalism Links the Fifty States

Cooperation Between States

85

The Constitution Establishes a Federal System

ACCESS **The Main Ideas**

1 What are the powers of the national government under the Constitution?
pages 86–90

2 What is the relationship between state power and national power?
pages 90–91

In *The Federalist* (No. 46), James Madison wrote, "The federal and state governments are in fact but different agents and trustees of the people, instituted with different powers, and designated for different purposes." In other words, the United States government and the governments of the states exist side by side within our federal system, each performing different functions. Americans actually live under *two* governments at the same time.

The Constitution provides a framework for dividing authority between the national government and the states. This section outlines how the powers of government are distributed between these two levels.

2C, 2D, 3A, 3C, 6E, 6I

National Government Powers

Before the Constitution was ratified, the states acted as thirteen small, independent nations. Each elected its own officials, made its own laws, and had its own army. (This is why they are still called "states.") To enable the United States government to protect *all* the states and to ensure the stability of the new nation, the states had to give up many of their powers. The powers given to the federal, or national, government are very carefully spelled out in the Constitution.

The delegated powers

The powers specifically granted to the national government in the Constitution are called **delegated powers**. They are also sometimes called "enumerated" or "expressed" powers (see Figure 4–1).

86

The delegated powers are divided among the three branches of the federal government. Article I, Section 8 gives the legislative branch (Congress) the powers to tax, to regulate commerce, to prescribe rules for naturalization, to coin money, to establish weights and measures, to grant patents, to declare war, and many others.

Article II, Section 2 grants the executive branch (the President) the power to appoint and receive ambassadors and to command the army and navy and state militias.

Article III, Section 2 gives the judicial branch (the Supreme Court) the responsibility for deciding lawsuits between states and court cases that affect foreign ambassadors. Because the delegated powers are stated explicitly in the Constitution, there is no question that they belong to the national government.

The implied powers

The national government also has many powers that are not specifically stated in the Constitution but result logically from the delegated powers. These are the **implied powers**.

The basis of the implied powers is the last clause in Article I, Section 8, sometimes called the "necessary and proper" clause. This clause gives Congress the power "to make all laws which shall be *necessary and proper* for carrying into execution the foregoing powers, and all other powers vested by this Constitution in the government of the United States, or in any department or officer thereof." This clause is sometimes known as the **elastic clause** because it has allowed the national government to stretch its powers.

The elastic clause became a source of controversy in George Washington's first term as President. Debate over its meaning began when Congress in 1791 passed an act to create the Bank of the United States. Before acting on the bill, Washington sought advice from Alexander Hamilton, his Secretary of the Treasury, and Thomas Jefferson, his Secretary of State. These two brilliant statesmen held completely opposite views.

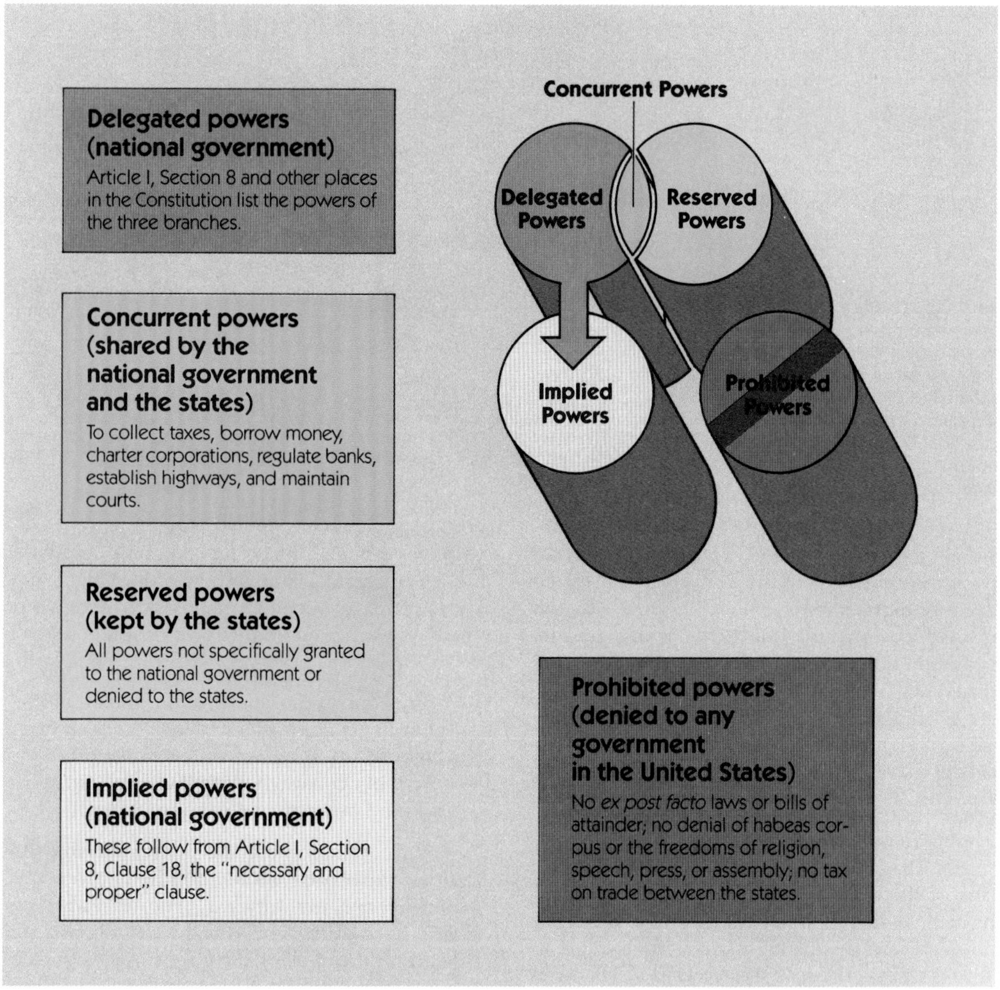

Delegated powers (national government)

Article I, Section 8 and other places in the Constitution list the powers of the three branches.

Concurrent powers (shared by the national government and the states)

To collect taxes, borrow money, charter corporations, regulate banks, establish highways, and maintain courts.

Reserved powers (kept by the states)

All powers not specifically granted to the national government or denied to the states.

Implied powers (national government)

These follow from Article I, Section 8, Clause 18, the "necessary and proper" clause.

Concurrent Powers

Delegated Powers

Reserved Powers

Implied Powers

Prohibited Powers

Prohibited powers (denied to any government in the United States)

No *ex post facto* laws or bills of attainder; no denial of habeas corpus or the freedoms of religion, speech, press, or assembly; no tax on trade between the states.

Figure 4–1 THE DIVISION OF POWERS IN THE FEDERAL SYSTEM   The Constitution divides powers between the national government and the state governments.   **3C**

Hamilton favored a strong national government. He interpreted the words "necessary and proper" to mean that, in carrying out a delegated power, the national government could do anything not prohibited by the Constitution. This broad view of the meaning of the Constitution is known as **loose construction**, or loose interpretation. A national bank, Hamilton argued, would help carry out the national government's powers to lay taxes, borrow money, and regulate commerce. These powers, he said, implied the power to create a bank.

Jefferson disagreed absolutely with Hamilton's approach. Wishing to limit the national government's powers, he interpreted the elastic clause differently. "The Constitution," Jefferson wrote, "allows only the means which are 'necessary,' not those which are merely 'convenient' for

87

EXPLANATION

After reviewing the content of the section, you may want to consider the following activities:

Constitutional Heritage

▲ CRITICAL THINKING *Why does the Constitution permit both state and federal governments to tax?* (Both state and federal governments require a source of revenue in order to function.)

● CRITICAL THINKING *Suppose the Constitution denied the federal government the right to tax, relying instead on state contributions to fund the federal government. What problem would this arrangement create?* (The federal government would be held hostage to the states and would lose its independence.) Remind students that a major weakness of the Confederation government was its inability to tax (p. 44).

Figure 4–1
▲ *Why is the symbol for implied powers connected to the symbol for delegated powers but not to the symbol for reserved powers?* (Only the federal government possesses implied powers.)

The symbol 👪 denotes active participation strategies.

Activities are keyed for student abilities:
▲ = Basic
● = All Levels
■ = Average/Advanced

Cultural Literacy

▲ Discuss John Marshall's well-known statement, "The power to tax involves the power to destroy." **What did Marshall mean?** (By levying very high taxes on a person or institution, the government could bankrupt that person or institution.)

■ CRITICAL THINKING **What prevents state and federal governments from using their powers of taxation to "destroy"?** (Both state and federal lawmakers are elected by the voters, and can be voted out of office.)

Law

▲ **What is a bill of attainder?** (A law that declares a person or group guilty and inflicts punishment without a trial.) **What does the Constitution say about bills of attainder?** (Neither Congress nor state legislatures may enact them.)

● **Why are bills of attainder contrary to American principles of government?** (They allow the government to convict and punish people without holding trials, thereby violating the principle that all persons are "innocent until proven guilty.")

Even though they disagreed on how the Constitution should be interpreted, Alexander Hamilton (left) and Thomas Jefferson both played essential roles in establishing the United States as a nation.

effecting the enumerated powers.'' This narrower interpretation of the Constitution is called **strict construction**. Jefferson argued that the national government could lay taxes, borrow money, and regulate commerce without creating a bank.

Washington agreed with Hamilton's view and signed into law the bill establishing the First Bank of the United States. The controversy, however, was far from over.

McCulloch v. Maryland

In 1816 Congress established the Second Bank of the United States. Many states resented the Bank, which they saw as a federal government intrusion into the states' affairs. In an effort to close the Bank, the state of Maryland in 1818 imposed a heavy tax on its Maryland branch.

James McCulloch, a cashier at the Baltimore branch of the Bank of the United States, refused to pay the $15,000 state tax. Maryland took him to state court, and he was convicted. In 1819, however, McCulloch appealed his case to the Supreme Court.

In *McCulloch v. Maryland* (1819), the Supreme Court supported McCulloch's action and dismissed the charges against him. Chief Justice John Marshall criticized those who favored strict construction and held that Congress did have the authority to create a bank. In the Court's opinion, Congress's powers to control the nation's

money supply and to collect taxes did imply the power to create a bank. The words of Marshall's decision have become famous as a defense of broad construction of the Constitution.

> Let the end be legitimate, let it be within the scope of the Constitution, and all means which are appropriate, which are plainly adopted to that end, which are not prohibited, but consistent with the letter and spirit of the Constitution, are constitutional.

With this decision, the Court officially recognized the broad notion of implied powers that Hamilton had put forward. Future lawmakers would have great flexibility in interpreting the Constitution and using the government's powers to meet the country's changing needs.

McCulloch v. Maryland had several other important consequences. By upholding the national law that created the bank over Maryland's tax law, Marshall restated the principle of the supremacy of national law. In addition, he ruled that a state cannot tax any agency of the federal government, for this might endanger national sovereignty. ''The power to tax,'' Marshall said, ''involves the power to destroy.''

The prohibited powers

While the elastic clause provided a way for the government to deal with changing conditions, the framers of the Constitution also wanted

Photo

These portraits are by the well-known American artists John Trumbull (Hamilton) and Gilbert Stuart (Jefferson).

to limit government power in certain areas. The **prohibited powers** (sometimes called "restricted" powers) are those that are denied to the national government, the state governments, or both. Most of the prohibited powers are found in Sections 9 and 10 of Article I. Section 9 places limits on the powers of Congress, and Section 10 lists the specific powers that are denied to the states.

Protection of legal rights

Some of the prohibited powers can be traced to the colonists' experiences with harsh laws, arbitrary arrests, unfair judges, and punishment without a trial. The writers of the Constitution therefore included various provisions to protect people's legal rights. (The Bill of Rights later extended these protections.)

For example, the Constitution states that neither Congress nor the state legislatures may enact a **bill of attainder**. A bill of attainder is a law that declares a specified person or group guilty and inflicts punishment without a trial. Such laws had been used in England but are rare in American history. In 1865, however, Congress passed the Test Oath Act, which kept former Confederate soldiers or officials from practicing law in federal courts. Two years later, this law was declared unconstitutional. It both singled out a particular group (former Confederates) and punished individuals in the group (by loss of privileges) without a trial. Therefore, the Supreme Court ruled, it was a bill of attainder (*Ex parte Garland*, 1867).

Congress is also prohibited from suspending the writ of **habeas corpus** (HAY-bee-us KOHR-puhs) except in times of war or national emergency. This protection comes from the common-law tradition. A writ of habeas corpus requires law-enforcement officials to bring a person being held in custody before a court. (Its literal translation is "you have the body.") The judge then determines whether there are legal reasons for keeping the person in jail. Habeas corpus is a valuable protection because if government officials could suspend it, they would be able to keep people in jail indefinitely without legal justification.

Another legal protection is the provision that neither Congress nor the states may pass an *ex post facto* **law**. (This Latin term means "after the deed.") An *ex post facto* law punishes an individual for an action committed before the law was passed. For example, a state may not pass a law prohibiting jaywalking and then arrest all those who jaywalked during the previous year. Similarly, a federal prisoner serving ten years for robbery cannot be given an additional five-year sentence because Congress imposes a harsher penalty for that crime. Both would be examples of *ex post facto* laws. (Legislatures may, however, enact laws that decrease punishments for past actions.)

The *ex post facto* rule applies only to criminal laws, not other kinds of laws. For instance, Congress could pass a law increasing taxes and make the increased rates apply to an earlier period.

With the writing of the Constitution, the states gave up some powers to the new federal government. In 1774 the colony of Maryland issued this bank note, but under the Constitution the power of issuing money belongs only to Congress.

89

Cooperative Learning
● Divide the class into groups of two for debates. Within each group, one person should represent strict construction and the other should represent loose construction. Then have all the "strict constructionists" (and all the "loose constructionists") meet to compare their arguments and select the most effective ones. Finally, conduct a class-wide debate on the issue.

GUIDED/INDEPENDENT PRACTICE

● Have students complete **Primary Source Worksheet 6,** which contains excerpts from the Supreme Court decision in *McCulloch v. Maryland.*

Photo
■ *What clues on the bill shown, besides the date, tell you that it was printed before the Revolution?* (It is payable in London and is linked in value to British currency.)

Background: *History* The *ex post facto* law was first interpreted in 1798 in *Calder v. Bull.* This case involved the distribution of property from an invalid will. Because this case involved a retroactive change in a *civil* procedure, the Supreme Court ruled that it did not involve an *ex post facto* law.

The symbol **ⅱ** denotes active participation strategies.

Activities are keyed for student abilities:
▲ = Basic
● = All Levels
■ = Average/Advanced

▲ Several vocabulary terms in this section deal with the various powers of government shown in Figure 4–1. Write these terms on the board and circle the modifiers (*delegated, concurrent,* etc.) Help students understand and remember the terms by asking students to write definitions of the modifiers on the board. Have students consult a dictionary if necessary. Then ask students to use these definitions in giving definitions of the various powers of government.

Have students complete **Skills Practice Worksheet 4,** which deals with the principles of federalism.

You may also want to use **Transparency 13,** which reviews the division of powers under the federal system.

ENRICHMENT/EXTENSION

■ Have students complete **Constitutional Issues Worksheet 4,** which deals with issues relating to federalism.

You may also want to have students complete **Supreme Court Decision 2,** which deals with *McCulloch v. Maryland.*

The inherent powers

The national government possesses other powers not mentioned in the Constitution. The **inherent powers** are those that the national government is assumed to have just because it is the government of a sovereign state. For example, the national government has the power to make foreign policy and to pass laws controlling immigration and citizenship.

Likewise, any government is assumed to have the power of **eminent domain**. That is, it can, by legal means, buy private property to use for public projects. For example, the government may use private property to build a highway or extend an airport runway, or it can flood farmland in building a dam.

Even though this power is not specifically mentioned in the Constitution, the Fifth Amendment places limits on it. One clause in this amendment states that private property shall not "be taken for public use without just compensation." That is, whenever the government takes someone's property for public use, it must pay a fair price.

State Government Powers

The reserved powers

According to the Tenth Amendment the **reserved powers** are all powers except those specifically delegated or prohibited. This amendment does not *grant* the states and the people these powers. It simply affirms that the national government will not interfere with them.

There is, therefore, no complete list of reserved powers. Over the years, Supreme Court decisions have generally acknowledged state power in six broad categories, listed below with some examples of each:

- public health — *licensing medical personnel, inspecting food and drugs*
- public safety — *regulating building codes, passing motor vehicle laws*
- public welfare — *regulating utilities, prohibiting discrimination*
- public morals — *restricting obscenity, regulating sales of tobacco and alcohol*

Using the power of eminent domain, government can take land for projects such as dams and roads. Theodore Roosevelt Dam, in Arizona, diverts the Salt River for irrigation and electricity.

Background: *Constitutional Heritage* Eminent domain is and has been an inherent right of government. In Anglo-American law, it is derived from the fact that all land in England once belonged to the monarch, who allowed others to use it subject to his or her authority.

Background: *Civic Participation* The legal process of taking over property that the owner refuses to sell is called *condemnation.*

- public convenience — *providing public parks and transportation*
- public education — *providing compulsory education, certifying teachers*

The concurrent powers

Although certain powers are given to either the national government or to the states, *both* possess the **concurrent powers**. For example, both state and national governments have the power to tax, to borrow money, to charter corporations, to regulate banks, to establish highways, and to maintain court systems. They carry out these powers separately and independently, however. For example, residents of most states must fill out two tax forms each year — one for federal and one for state taxes.

The Constitution does not list the concurrent powers. It does, however, deny the states certain powers and grant others (such as issuing money) *exclusively* to the national government. Otherwise, the states in general have the same powers as the national government. In exercising these powers, of course, the states may not pass any law that conflicts with national law.

The supremacy clause in action

With the rather complex division of powers in the federal system, it is not surprising that conflicts sometimes occur. As Chapter 3 pointed out, the supremacy clause in Article VI clearly resolves such disagreements. If a state clashes with the national government in carrying out one of its powers, the state must yield to national law.

A state law or constitution and a national law may rule differently on the same issue. For example, one article of the Virginia constitution, which was written in the late 1940's, required voters to pay a poll tax in order to vote in presidential elections. The 24th Amendment, ratified in 1964, prohibited poll taxes as a voting requirement in any federal election. Virginia's provision was therefore unconstitutional, as were similar provisions in the laws of other states.

State laws may also be contrary to international agreements. In a 1916 treaty, the United States and Canada agreed to protect migratory birds such as ducks and geese. Congress then passed a law forbidding the capturing, selling, or killing of certain migratory wildfowl. When Ray Holland, a United States game warden, tried to enforce this regulation, the state of Missouri brought suit to stop him. Missouri argued that the power to regulate wildfowl was not specifically delegated to Congress in the Constitution. The national law, it said, violated the state's reserved powers.

In *Missouri v. Holland* (1920), however, the state lost its case. The Supreme Court ruled that the treaty represented the "supreme law of the land" and that congressional action to implement the treaty was "necessary and proper." In other words, Congress was exercising an implied power, and Missouri had to yield. Thus, the supremacy clause allows such conflicts to be settled without threatening the federal system.

SECTION 1 REVIEW

Vocabulary and key terms

delegated powers (86)	prohibited powers (89)
implied powers (86)	bill of attainder (89)
"necessary and proper" clause (86)	habeas corpus (89)
elastic clause (86)	*ex post facto* law (89)
loose construction (87)	inherent powers (90)
strict construction (88)	eminent domain (90)
McCulloch v. Maryland (88)	reserved powers (90)
	concurrent powers (91)

For review

1. What is the relationship between the delegated powers and the implied powers? **3C**
2. (a) What is the constitutional basis for the implied powers? (b) What were some effects of the Supreme Court's decision in *McCulloch v. Maryland*? **2D**
3. What are three prohibited powers intended to protect the legal rights of citizens? **6I**
4. (a) Who holds the reserved powers? (b) Name the categories into which these powers generally fall. **3C**
5. What is the rule for settling disputes between conflicting state and national laws? **3C**

Critical thinking

COMPARING AND CONTRASTING In ratifying the Constitution, the states gave up many of their powers to the federal government. How does this compare with Locke's idea of the social contract (page 8)? **3C**

91

Section 1 Review Answers

1. Delegated powers are specifically granted by the Constitution; implied powers result logically from delegated powers.
2. **(a)** The elastic clause. **(b)** It recognized the broad notion of implied powers, gave lawmakers flexibility in interpreting the Constitution, re-emphasized the supremacy of national law, and prohibited states from taxing any federal agency.
3. Enacting bills of attainder, suspending the writ of habeas corpus, and passing *ex post facto* laws are all prohibited.
4. **(a)** The states. **(b)** Public health, safety, welfare, morals, convenience, and education.
5. State laws must yield to federal laws.

Critical thinking It is comparable because, in the social contract, individuals give up certain freedoms for state protection. Likewise, states give up powers for national unity.

CLOSURE

● Have students review the main point of the section by copying down the information in Figure 4–1. Then have students read Section 2, paying special attention to the changing views of federalism.

The symbol 👥 denotes active participation strategies.

Activities are keyed for student abilities:
▲ = Basic
● = All Levels
■ = Average/Advanced

State and Federal Governments Have Specific Duties

(pp. 92–98)

Section Objectives

☐ describe the duties of the federal government

☐ describe the responsibilities of state governments

☐ explain how views of federalism have changed

Vocabulary

militia, apportionment, redistrict, states' rights, secede, nationalism

 FOCUS

● Point out to students that the federal government has duties that relate to the individual states, and that state governments have responsibilities concerning the nation as a whole.

Ask students to imagine that they are the President. Would they be alarmed by threats to republican government in an individual state? Why or why not? (Students should understand that popular rule in the nation as a whole is inseparable from popular rule within each state.)

3A, 3C, 4C, 6F, 8B, 8H

SECTION 2
State and Federal Governments Have Specific Duties

ACCESS	The Main Ideas

1 What are the duties of the federal government? *pages 92–95*

2 What responsibilities do state governments have? *pages 95–96*

3 How have views of federalism changed? *pages 96–98*

Imagine that a political crisis is taking place in your state. The governor disbands the state legislature, suspends the state constitution, and cancels elections. Then the governor announces that he or she has decided to rule alone for an indefinite period.

Who would prevent such a situation? That task falls to the federal government. The idea behind federalism is that the federal government and the state governments have certain duties — such as protecting republican government — to carry out for each other. This "give-and-take" between the federal and state governments is crucial to making federalism work.

3A, 3C, 6F

Federal Government Duties

The Constitution gives the federal government five specific responsibilities toward the states. These carry out some of the national aims stated in the Preamble — to "form a more perfect union," "provide for the common defense," and "insure domestic tranquillity." The national government must ensure that each state has a republican form of government and that all states are represented equally in the Senate. It cannot take a state's territory to form a new state without the original state's permission. In addition, the national government must protect each state against foreign invasion and internal violence.

Protecting republican government

Article IV, Section 4 of the Constitution provides that "the United States shall guarantee to every state in this Union a republican form of

government." This pledge may seem unnecessary today, but it was prompted by the delegates' fear that a strong leader might take over one of the states and turn it into a monarchy or dictatorship.

The national government was first called upon to enforce this pledge after the "Dorr Rebellion" challenged the legitimacy of Rhode Island's government. In the early 1840's, Rhode Island was still using its 1663 colonial charter as the state constitution. The charter's strict property requirements prevented about half the men in the state from voting. To gain the right to vote, Thomas Dorr and his followers rebelled, wrote a new constitution, and set up a government with Dorr as governor. The former governor then declared military rule and called on President John Tyler to quell the revolt. The President promised federal help to support the old charter government, but Dorr and his followers were eventually arrested by the state militia.

The issue came to the Supreme Court after Borden, a state militia officer, tried to arrest Luther, one of Dorr's supporters. Luther then sued Borden for trespassing on his property, charging that the arrest was unlawful because Borden did not represent a "republican form of government." In *Luther v. Borden* (1849), Chief Justice Roger B. Taney (pronounced TAH-nee) refused to decide between the two Rhode Island governments. Taney ruled that the issue was a "political question." It was up to Congress, not the Supreme Court, to decide whether Rhode Island's government was "republican." Congress never had to act in the case, however. Dorr's rebellion brought about the adoption of a new, more democratic constitution in Rhode Island.

Congress did act on the question of "republican government" during the ratification of the Fourteenth Amendment to the Constitution. This amendment was passed by Congress after the Civil War to ensure the civil rights of black Americans, especially former slaves. When the amendment was sent to the states, it was obvious that

92

National Guard troops worked with federal troops and local law-enforcement officials to quell violence in Los Angeles in the spring of 1992.

the southern states were not going to ratify it. Congress then declared that the former Confederate states did not have republican forms of government because so many people (namely the former slaves) could not vote and so were not represented. Congress therefore refused to admit representatives or senators from the South until those states wrote new constitutions and ratified the Fourteenth Amendment.

Providing for the common defense

When the Constitution was written, the delegates feared the states might not unite if any one state were attacked by foreign forces. This feeling was due not only to lack of national unity but also to slow communication and the great distances between some states. Therefore, Article IV, Section 4 included the provision that the national government "shall protect each of them [the states] against invasion." Today there is no question about this guarantee. An invasion of any state would be considered an attack on the entire United States.

Ensuring domestic tranquility

Constitutional Convention delegates also feared the Union might be endangered by rebellion or unrest within a state. They included in Article IV, Section 4 a promise that the national government would protect each state against unrest if asked by the state legislature (or, in emergencies, the governor). For example, any state legislature may request federal help to end civil disturbances such as riots or looting. Although the Constitution suggests that the state legislature should make such a request, in practice it is usually the governor who asks for federal assistance.

The writers of the Constitution foresaw more trouble within the states than has actually occurred. The states ask for federal help only occasionally. The Dorr Rebellion in 1842 was one example, though federal troops were never used. In 1967 Governor George Romney of Michigan asked for federal troops to be sent into Detroit to help stop unrest. In 1992 President Bush ordered Marines and Army troops into Los Angeles to help National Guard troops restore order following an outbreak of violence.

More often, the national government sends troops without being asked. This authority stems from Article II, Section 3, which states that the President "shall take care that the laws be faithfully executed." This clause allows the President to send troops, with or without a state's permission, whenever federal laws are being violated.

In 1894 President Grover Cleveland ordered troops to Chicago when railway workers went on strike in sympathy with workers at the Pullman Company. Although Illinois Governor John P. Altgeld objected, the President justified his actions because the strike had halted the flow of interstate commerce and the U.S. mail.

Likewise, in 1957, a federal court had ordered school integration at Little Rock Central High School in Arkansas. President Dwight Eisenhower declared that his responsibility to uphold this court order was "inescapable." To ensure that black students could enroll and attend classes, he sent both federal troops and the Arkansas National Guard to Little Rock, even though Governor Orval Faubus and local authorities strongly opposed the action.

Equal representation in the Senate

Another responsibility of the national government is stated in Article V, the "amending article." This article not only sets up rules for amending the Constitution but also prohibits one kind of amendment: "No state, without its consent, shall be deprived of its equal suffrage in the

93

EXPLANATION
After reviewing the content of the section, you may want to consider the following activities:

Constitutional Heritage
● *How was the Constitution's requirement that the federal government "insure domestic tranquillity" designed to help the states?* (It empowered the federal government to send troops into states threatened by unrest.)

● CRITICAL THINKING *In what circumstances might state officials themselves feel threatened by this requirement?* (Sometimes the federal government sends troops into a state even over the objections of the governor.)

Check for Understanding
● Looting often occurs after floods, earthquakes, tornadoes, and other natural disasters. Ask students if they can recall any recent "states of emergency" when the National Guard was called in to help.

The symbol ♟ denotes active participation strategies.

Activities are keyed for student abilities:
▲ = Basic
● = All Levels
■ = Average/Advanced

Geography

▲ Have students use the text and the map on this page to answer the following questions: *Which of the following was not one of the original thirteen states, New Hampshire or Vermont?* (Vermont.) *Parts of which states besides Texas were created from the Texas Annexation?* (Colorado, Kansas, New Mexico, Oklahoma, Wyoming.) *Which states were enlarged by land acquired in the Gadsden Purchase?* (Arizona and New Mexico.) *By what year did the United States stretch "from sea to shining sea"?* (1846.)

Senate." Added to make the smaller states feel more secure, this phrase means that the national government cannot reduce the number of senators from a state unless that state grants permission. (This, of course, would never happen.) Because this provision is the only part of the Constitution that may *never* be amended, it is often called the "entrenched" clause.

Protecting state boundaries

Congress alone has the authority to admit new states into the Union. At the same time, Congress has a constitutional obligation to respect the territorial rights of existing states. Specific guidelines are set out in Article IV, Section 3 of the Constitution:

No new state shall be formed or erected within the jurisdiction of any other state; nor any state be formed by the junction of two or more states, or parts of states, without the consent of the legislatures of the states concerned, as well as of the Congress.

That is, a new state may not be carved out of an existing state unless that state approves. While this is an unlikely event today, it was an immediate problem in 1787, when several states claimed land to the west.

Since the Constitution was written, 37 states have joined the Union. Five of those were formed from the territory of existing states under the guidelines. They are Vermont (1791) from

Figure 4–2 U.S. TERRITORIAL EXPANSION, 1783–1898 As the United States expanded westward from the original thirteen states, it acquired land by purchase and by treaty.

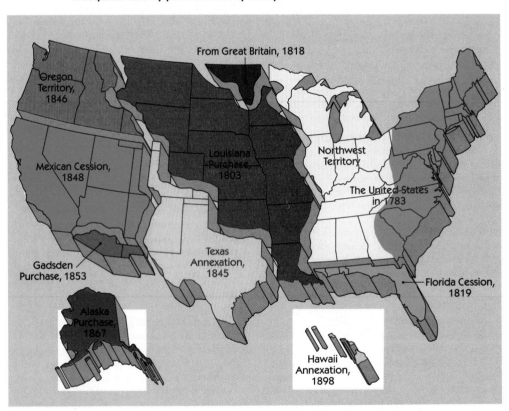

94

Background: *Geography* Though Vermont and Maine did not exist as states in 1783, the territories they occupy did belong to the United States. Vermont was created out of land formerly claimed by New Hampshire and New York. What is now Maine belonged to Massachusetts. (Figure 4–2 does not show minor border adjustments.)

Figure 4–2
▲ *When did your state become part of the United States?*

land held by New York and New Hampshire; Kentucky (1792) from Virginia; Tennessee (1796) from North Carolina; Maine (1820) from Massachusetts; and West Virginia (1863) from Virginia. (Because Virginia had left the Union to join the Confederate States of America, it was not asked to consent to the admission of West Virginia.)

Two states, Texas and California, were separate political units before their admission as states. California was ceded from Mexico in 1848, and Texas, annexed in 1845, had been an independent republic.

Admitting new states

The Constitution does not describe how new states are to be formed; it says only that new states cannot be carved from existing states. The rules for admitting new states actually derive from the Northwest Ordinance of 1787, passed under the Articles of Confederation.

Most states have followed a similar admission process. First, the territory wishing to become a state organizes a government. The territorial government then applies to Congress for admission, and Congress passes an "enabling act" stating conditions for admission. The territorial government next draws up a constitution, which the voters in the territory must approve. Congress then approves an act of admission. The President must approve both the enabling act and the act of admission.

Both Congress and the President have used their powers to delay the admission of states until certain conditions were met. For example, Utah was admitted in 1896 only after it agreed to outlaw polygamy (having more than one spouse) and church-run public schools. In 1905, voters in the two halves of Oklahoma — the Oklahoma Territory and the Indian Territory — petitioned for admission as two separate states. (The second was to be named "Sequoyah.") Congress rejected the idea and insisted the territories join as one state. Alaska was admitted in 1959 under the condition that land be reserved for the federal government and for the Eskimo, Aleut, and Indian populations.

There are limits on the qualifications that Congress can impose on would-be states. For instance, as another condition for Oklahoma's admission in 1907, Congress said that the state capital could not be moved from Guthrie before 1913. Despite this ruling, in 1910 the Oklahoma legislature moved the capital to Oklahoma City. In the lawsuit that resulted, the Supreme Court upheld Oklahoma's right to make such a move. The Court ruled that while Congress can impose any conditions *before* statehood, afterward it can no longer interfere in a state's affairs. In other words, once a state is admitted to the Union, it is on "equal footing with the original states."

3A, 3C

State Responsibilities

The Constitution requires each state to contribute to the workings of the country as a whole. The state governments are required to provide militia to aid the national defense. They also establish election machinery for national elections and set new boundaries for congressional districts after the national census taken every ten years.

The state militia

Each state is entitled to maintain its own **militia** (mih-LISH-uh), a volunteer civilian army. In 1903 these armies were reorganized as the National Guard. The National Guard is most commonly called up by the state governor during emergencies. For example, the National Guard has been called on to put down riots, assist victims of natural disasters, and substitute for striking police officers and firefighters.

Although separate militia units are located in each state, Congress can mobilize any or all of them into service for the nation (Article I, Section 8, Clause 15). In practice, however, it is the President, as commander-in-chief, who "nationalizes" the National Guard. National Guard units were called up for military service in World War II, Korea, and Vietnam. In the 1980's, President Reagan ordered several state militias on training missions in Honduras.

On occasion, the President calls on the National Guard to enforce a federal law or court order, even if the state governor objects. This was the case in Little Rock in 1957 (page 93). Similarly, in 1965 President Johnson ordered the Alabama National Guard to protect thousands of civil-rights marchers on their way from Selma to Montgomery.

Controversial Issues

● CRITICAL THINKING Explain to students that support for states' rights has reappeared from time to time since the Civil War. *Who would be attracted to the states' rights theory?* (Someone opposed to a federal government policy but unable to change it.) *How would the United States be different today if individual states had the right to nullify federal acts?* (The federal government would be much weaker; the states would be much stronger; differences among state laws might be greater.)

Cooperative Learning

● Divide the class into groups and have each group prepare a brief report describing the history of your state's admission to the United States.

Cross-reference
Chapter 2, pp. 44–45, discusses the Northwest Ordinance of 1787.

Background: *Constitutional Heritage* The Supreme Court's ruling in the Oklahoma case occurred in *Coyle v. Smith* (1911).

The symbol 👥 denotes active participation strategies.

Activities are keyed for student abilities:
▲ = Basic
● = All Levels
■ = Average/Advanced

GUIDED/INDEPENDENT PRACTICE

● Have students complete **Primary Source Worksheet 7,** which contains excerpts from the joint resolution of Congress to annex Texas.

Members of the state militia, or National Guard, must be ready to help out when emergencies or disasters occur. Here, Virginia National Guard members bring help to citizens stranded by floodwaters.

The states' role in elections

The Constitution gives each state the right — and responsibility — to handle the details of electing U.S. senators, representatives, and the President. Subject to certain federal restrictions, the state legislatures have authority to register voters, print ballots, establish polling places, supervise voting, count votes, punish voter fraud, and publish election returns.

Drawing congressional districts

Under Article I, Section 2, Congress determines both the size of the House of Representatives and the number of representatives each state may have. This **apportionment**, or distribution, of representatives among the states is based on the national census taken every ten years.

Based on the number of representatives, each state is required by law to divide the state into congressional districts. These districts must be approximately equal in population. Changes in population may mean that the state must **redistrict**, or draw new boundaries for its congressional districts. (Chapter 12 provides a complete explanation of this process.)

3C, 4C

Changing Views of Federalism

The relationship between the states and the national government has changed drastically in the two centuries since the Constitution was written. Many theories about the nature of federalism have been advanced. These theories emerged at different times and so reflect the political issues and attitudes of other eras.

States' rights

Since the nation began, individual states had been wary of the national government's power. In the Kentucky and Virginia Resolutions of 1798, for example, Thomas Jefferson and James Madison had argued that the states could declare laws passed by Congress unconstitutional. In 1814, representatives of the New England states, dismayed by their financial losses during the War of 1812, met in protest in Hartford, Connecticut. The Hartford Convention proposed several amendments to the Constitution and declared that states should fight federal actions they thought were unconstitutional. Support for their position withered when the war ended.

After 1828, certain southern states became increasingly upset over the national government's economic policies, especially the high taxes the government levied on imported goods. As southern opposition grew, it was expressed in the **states' rights** theory. The leading spokesman for states' rights was John C. Calhoun of South Carolina.

Calhoun argued (as Jefferson had) that the Constitution is only a *compact* among the states. That is, the states created the national government and established all of its powers. Calhoun, however, took this argument one step further. In his view, any time the national government's actions ran contrary to the states' interests, the

96

Background: *Civic Participation* The first census was conducted in 1790. The U.S. census attempts to count everyone in the country at a certain time through questionnaires sent to every household asking for the number of persons living there.

Background: *History* The Hartford Convention convened to protest what the Federalists saw as inept management by Jefferson's Democratic-Republicans. The convention resulted in charges of treason from the Democratic-Republicans and the demise of the Federalist Party outside of the New England states.

states had the right to "nullify," or cancel, those acts. A constitutional amendment would be required to override such "nullification."

As the controversies surrounding slavery and tariffs grew more heated during the 1840's and 1850's, this theory was carried even further. Calhoun's followers believed that the states also had a right to break the compact and **secede**, or leave the Union. After the election of Abraham Lincoln in 1860, seven states did secede, forming the Confederate States of America. Four others joined them when the Civil War began. Echoing Calhoun's thesis, the constitution of the Confederacy began, "We, the people of the Confederate States, each State acting in its sovereign and independent character, . . ."

Nationalism

The strongest response to Calhoun's ideas came from Daniel Webster, a Massachusetts senator famous for his powerful speeches. In 1830, as Congress was debating nullification, Webster defended **nationalism**. He argued that the people — not the states — had created the Constitution: "It is, sir, the people's Constitution, the people's government made for the people, made by the people, answerable to the people." His fiery speech ended with the words, "Liberty *and* Union, now and forever, one and inseparable."

The states' rights issue came to a dramatic climax in the Civil War (1861–1865) and the secession of the southern states. The North's victory ensured that the Union would remain unbroken. The question that remained was, does a state have the legal right to secede? This question came to the Supreme Court in the case of *Texas v. White* (1869), which raised the issue of whether Texas (or the other states) had ever left the Union. The Court decision stated:

> When, therefore, Texas became one of the United States, she entered into an indissoluble relation. . . . The act which [completed] her admission into the Union was something more than a compact; it was the incorporation of a new member into the political body. And it was final. The union between Texas and the other States was as complete, as perpetual, and as indissoluble as the union between the original States.

In summing up the Court's position, Chief Justice Salmon P. Chase stated: "The Constitution . . . looks to an indestructible Union, composed of indestructible States." In other words, once a state enters the Union, it is there to stay.

Dual federalism

After the bitter clash between the backers of states' rights and nationalism, a new view of federalism emerged. This interpretation, known as "dual federalism," was popular from the late 1800's through the 1930's. In dual federalism, there is a clear-cut, constitutional division between the powers of the national government and

Daniel Webster, standing in the old Senate chamber, delivers his famous "Liberty and Union" speech in January 1830 as visitors watch from the gallery. At the far left, John C. Calhoun, then Vice President, is presiding over the Senate. (The painting is by the 19th-century American artist G.P.A. Healy.)

97

RETEACHING/CORRECTIVES
▲ Have students outline the section, using both the headings and subheadings as entries and listing supporting details under each subheading.

You may also want to use **Transparency 14,** which illustrates the organization of western lands.

ENRICHMENT/EXTENSION
■ Have students complete **Skills Challenge Worksheet 4,** which contains excerpts on the issue of federalism and states' rights.

Background: *Geography*
The seven seceding states were South Carolina, Mississippi, Florida, Alabama, Georgia, Louisiana, and Texas. Joining them were Virginia, North Carolina, Arkansas, and Tennessee.

Background: *Constitutional Heritage* *Texas v. White* dealt with the meaning of "state" and the nature of the Union. The case involved the selling of U.S. bonds by the Confederate government in Texas to George White.

After the war, the Supreme Court ruled that Texas could recover the title to the bonds because the actions of the Confederate government were not binding.

The symbol 👥 denotes active participation strategies.

Activities are keyed for student abilities:
▲ = Basic
● = All Levels
■ = Average/Advanced

Section 2 Review Answers

1. Half the state's men were ineligible to vote.

2. Write new state constitutions and ratify the Fourteenth Amendment.

3. During strikes or violations of federal laws and court orders.

4. The territory organizes a government and applies to Congress for admission; Congress states conditions for admission; a constitution is written and approved by the voters; Congress and the President approve the admission.

5. Register voters, print ballots, establish polls, supervise voting, punish voter fraud, publish election returns.

6. **(a)** States' rights supporters believed that states could secede; nationalists believed the Union was permanent. **(b)** Dual federalism divides state and national powers clearly, whereas cooperative federalism intermixes the powers.

Critical thinking Factors possibly causing a shift toward the federal government include the growing economic interdependence of the states and the need for federal solutions to such problems as pollution. Factors suggesting a shift toward the states include the federal government's inability to fund new programs and popular dissatisfaction with the growth of the federal government.

CLOSURE

● Remind students of the pre-reading objectives at the beginning of the section. Pose one or all of these questions again. Then have students read Section 3, noting the means by which the federal government has expanded its power.

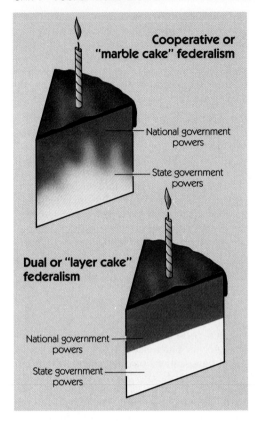

Cooperative or "marble cake" federalism

National government powers

State government powers

Dual or "layer cake" federalism

National government powers

State government powers

Figure 4–3 DUAL AND COOPERATIVE FEDERALISM   3C

those of the states. Like the "layer cake" in Figure 4–3, the national and state governments were thought of as having separate layers of authority. When conflicts did occur between the two levels, the Supreme Court settled the disputes. In other words, dual federalism stressed the formal, legal relationships between two very distinct levels of government.

Cooperative federalism

Since the Great Depression of the early 1930's, still another theory of federalism has developed. It has been described as "cooperative federalism." In this view, national and state activities are intermixed, rather than being split into two distinct levels of authority. One political scientist, Morton Grodzins, compared this

98

mixture to the "marble cake" in Figure 4–3. Cooperative federalism is characterized by greater national involvement in state and local affairs.

The 1980's saw a swing back toward dual federalism. President Ronald Reagan's policies reflected the opinions of many people that the federal government was becoming too involved in the affairs of the states. Reagan called for a "New Federalism" to reduce the size and cost of the federal government. Under his administration, the federal government played a smaller role in social programs and turned over more responsibility to the states. During his first term in office, President Bush basically followed the same policy.

SECTION 2 REVIEW

Vocabulary and key terms

militia (95)	secede (97)
apportionment (96)	nationalism (97)
redistrict (96)	dual federalism (97)
states' rights (96)	cooperative federalism (98)

For review

1. Why did Thomas Dorr believe that Rhode Island's government was not a "republican form"? **6F**
2. What conditions did Congress set up after the Civil War for admitting members from former Confederate states? **3A**
3. Under what circumstances have Presidents sent federal troops into a state? **3A**
4. What is the general procedure for admitting new states to the Union? **3C**
5. What are the responsibilities of the states in federal elections? **3C**
6. (a) How did supporters of states' rights and nationalism disagree over the nature of the Union? (b) Distinguish between dual federalism and cooperative federalism. **3C**

Critical thinking

MAKING PREDICTIONS Name one reason why power might in the future shift from the states to the federal government, and one reason why power might shift from the federal government to the states. **8H**

Figure 4–3
▲ **Which kind of federalism entails greater national government involvement in state affairs?** (Cooperative federalism.)

SECTION 3

The National Government's Powers Have Increased

ACCESS **The Main Ideas**
1 How has the national government increased its power through regulation of interstate commerce and extension of civil liberties? *pages 99–101*
2 How does the federal government influence state and local affairs through financial aid? *pages 101–103*

When you get a part-time job for weekends or afternoons after school, you take for granted the fact that you will earn at least the minimum wage. You probably never ask why the minimum wage exists, or why it is the same from state to state.

The answers to both questions reflect the growth of the power of the federal government. Since the early days of the Republic, the federal government has gradually and continually extended its authority into areas that were once considered to be the exclusive domain of the states.

Reasons for government expansion

The growth of the national government is not the result of a conspiracy or the ambitions of politicians in Washington. The reason is that, over the past two hundred years, the United States has changed from a relatively simple farming nation to a complex technological society.

The duties of government have also become more complex. In 1789 the national government concerned itself with the affairs of thirteen states, separated from the rest of the world by an ocean and a vast frontier. Today the national government must contend with fifty states and the responsibility of being a world power. The states cannot effectively manage the nation's economy or foreign policy, nor can they efficiently regulate interstate transportation and communication. Imagine, for example, the inconvenience if passengers on a cross-country bus had to stop at each state border to pay a new fare.

The increased importance of the national government does not mean that the states have lost their powers. If anything, state and local governments also have become more important. As Units 8 and 9 will explain, state and local governments carry out more programs and employ more people than ever before. Many of their activities, however, result from national policies and directives.

To understand the development of federalism, it is important to examine the various ways in which the national government has grown. The national government has increased its authority mainly through the regulation of interstate commerce, the extension of the Bill of Rights, and the use of economic influence.

2D, 3A, 3C

Using the Commerce Clause

The commerce clause of the Constitution (Article I, Section 8, Clause 3) gives Congress the exclusive power to regulate commerce "among the several states." Yet it does not define precisely what is meant by "commerce." Over the years, this term has expanded to involve the federal government in a wide range of activities.

Gibbons v. Ogden

The broadening of the commerce clause began in 1824 with the Supreme Court's decision in *Gibbons v. Ogden.* This case concerned two companies that operated steamboats on the Hudson River. The state of New York had granted exclusive rights for a steamboat line to inventor Robert Fulton and his partner, Robert Livingston. They made an agreement with Aaron Ogden, who set up a ferryboat service across the Hudson River between New York and New Jersey. Then Thomas Gibbons, with a license granted by the United States government, began running a competing steamboat line. When the New York state courts found Gibbons guilty of violating Ogden's contract, he appealed his case to the Supreme Court.

The Supreme Court reversed New York's ruling. The Court held that travel by ship on the Hudson River between New Jersey and New York

---

Cross-reference
The minimum wage is discussed on p. 577.

SECTION 3

The National Government's Powers Have Increased
(pp. 99–103)

Section Objectives
☐ explain how the national government has increased its power through regulation of interstate commerce and extension of civil liberties
☐ explain how the federal government influences state and local affairs through financial aid

Vocabulary
grant-in-aid, categorical grant, block grant, revenue sharing

FOCUS
● Say the following sentence to the class: *The government announced a new policy today.* Ask students what they assumed you meant by *government*—local, state, or federal government. Most students will probably think of the federal government.

Next discuss the reasons for this. Point out that as a world power, the United States is heavily involved in international affairs, and that local and state governments have very minor roles in such matters. Another reason, however, is the growing role of the federal government in domestic affairs.

The symbol ☷ denotes active participation strategies.

Activities are keyed for student abilities:
▲ = Basic
● = All Levels
■ = Average/Advanced

EXPLANATION

After reviewing the content of the section, you may want to consider the following activities:

Controversial Issues

● CRITICAL THINKING Recall with students the debate between strict and loose constructionists over interpreting the Constitution (pp. 87–88). *In broadening the commerce clause, has the national government been adhering to strict or loose construction?* (Loose.)

● CRITICAL THINKING Recall with students the discussion in Chapter 3 relating the flexibility of the Constitution to its durability (p. 78). *Is the concept of flexibility more likely to be associated with strict or loose construction?* (Loose.) *What is the major result of loose construction?* (Extension of the national government's powers.)

■ CRITICAL THINKING *Given the examples cited in the text (pages 100–101), which of the following groups might be opposed to a broad interpretation of the commerce clause: transportation companies, unions, insurance companies, civil rights activists?* (Transportation and insurance companies.)

Robert Fulton's steamboats were covered by the commerce clause, according to *Gibbons v. Ogden.* This ruling gave Congress authority over navigation.

was *interstate* commerce. The power to regulate this travel therefore belonged to Congress, not the New York state legislature. In making this decision, the Court redefined commerce as not only the transportation of goods, but the movement of services and people as well. Since this decision, the definition of commerce has become increasingly broad.

Regulating interstate commerce

Some examples of the laws passed by Congress under the commerce clause illustrate how the definition of interstate commerce has expanded. In 1935 the Wagner Act gave protection to labor unions and ensured workers the right to bargain collectively. Three years later, the Fair Labor Standards Act set minimum wages, maximum hours, and limits on child labor. These laws used the commerce clause to extend the authority of Congress into areas once under state law.

Supreme Court decisions have supported Congress in challenges of its broad use of the commerce clause. For instance, in 1937 the Supreme Court upheld the Wagner Act and Congress's right to regulate business and labor relations (*National Labor Relations Board v. Jones & Laughlin Steel Corp.*) In the 1940's, the Court extended the commerce clause to allow regulation of agriculture and insurance companies.

100

Civil rights and the commerce clause

A broad definition of "commerce" was also used to uphold the Civil Rights Act of 1964. In that year Congress passed the Civil Rights Act. Among its many provisions, this act banned discrimination in public accommodations and forbade discrimination in employment. Congress was assuming authority in all these areas because of the commerce clause. Its authority to do so was challenged in two test cases — *Heart of Atlanta Motel v. United States* and *Katzenbach v. McClung* (both in 1964).

In the first case, the national government sued the Heart of Atlanta Motel for refusing to rent rooms to black customers. The motel argued that Congress had no authority to prevent discrimination by private firms and, furthermore, that the motel was not engaged in interstate commerce. The federal government, however, proved that the motel *was* engaged in interstate commerce. It was near two interstate highways, advertised nationally, and drew 75 percent of its guests from out of state. The motel lost the case.

The second case involved Ollie's Barbeque, a family-owned restaurant in Birmingham, Alabama, that refused to seat blacks. Unlike the Atlanta motel, the restaurant was eleven blocks from an interstate highway and over a mile away from the nearest railroad or bus station. More-

Background: *Constitutional Heritage* The two Supreme Court decisions regarding regulation of agriculture and insurance were, respectively, *Wickard v. Filburn* (1942) and *U.S. v. Southeastern Underwriters Association* (1944).

Cross-reference Chapter 7, pp. 203–204, includes a fuller discussion of the Civil Rights Act of 1964.

over, nearly all of Ollie's customers were from Birmingham. The owners therefore maintained that they were not engaged in interstate commerce. The Court ruled, however, that because 46 percent of Ollie's food was purchased outside Alabama, the restaurant actually *was* involved in interstate commerce. The Civil Rights Act of 1964 was thus upheld as a legitimate application of the commerce clause.

3C

Extending Civil Liberties

When the Constitution was written, many people feared that a strong national government would abuse citizens' legal rights and civil liberties. They insisted that a Bill of Rights be added to the Constitution. The guarantees in these ten amendments were designed to limit the powers of the national government. They were not applied to the states, many of which had their own bills of rights. This limited interpretation of the Bill of Rights was upheld by the Supreme Court in *Barron v. Baltimore* (1833).

The Fourteenth Amendment
In time it became apparent that most abuses of civil rights came not from the national government but from the states. In particular, after the Civil War, many southern states quickly passed "black codes" to restrict the rights of black Americans in employment, property-owning, and other areas. In an attempt to end such state-sanctioned discrimination, the Fourteenth Amendment was passed in 1868.

The Fourteenth Amendment defined U.S. citizenship and declared that "no state shall make or enforce any law which shall abridge the privileges or immunities of citizens of the United States; nor shall any state deprive any person of life, liberty, or property, without due process of law; nor deny . . . the equal protection of the laws." Many of the members of Congress who proposed this amendment intended it to apply the protections in the Bill of Rights to every state.

Extending the Bill of Rights
For many years, the Supreme Court refused to recognize this broader interpretation of the Fourteenth Amendment. It was not until 1925, in the case of *Gitlow v. New York,* that the Court reversed itself. The justices ruled that the Four-teenth Amendment's guarantee of due process protected the rights of free speech and a free press from both state and federal law.

To the Court in the 1920's and 1930's, the First Amendment freedoms — speech, religion, the press, assembly, petition — seemed the most basic. Justice Benjamin Cardozo, in a 1937 decision, said that "neither liberty nor justice would exist if they [these freedoms] were sacrificed." The First Amendment protections, then, were the only ones to be applied to the states under the Fourteenth Amendment.

By the 1960's, however, national concern about civil rights focused on other Bill of Rights protections. The Court has now extended most of the guarantees in the Bill of Rights to protect citizens from violations by *both* the national and the state governments. By doing so, the Court has given the national government more and more authority over the state governments.

3C, 7B

Using Economic Influence

Perhaps the most effective power the national government has over the states is the "power of the purse." The national government collects billions of tax dollars each year, and many of these dollars are set aside for the states. The national government can use its financial powers to influence state and local affairs through grants-in-aid and threats of withholding federal funds. Until recently, it could also use revenue sharing.

Financing local programs
Money given to a state or local government by the national government for a particular program or project is called a **grant-in-aid**. The national government specifies the purpose of each grant it makes and so can take a direct part in state and local affairs. Grants-in-aid operate on a "matching" basis. That is, for every dollar the national government spends, the state must put up a specified amount, typically twenty cents. In 1990 the federal government spent more than $136 billion on grants-in-aid. Grants come in many kinds of packages, but most are either *categorical* or *block* grants.

A **categorical grant** is given for a specific purpose — the construction of a highway or a

Politics
● CRITICAL THINKING *Why would the federal government want to maintain restrictions on the way federal aid to the states is used?* (To ensure that federal aid is used in ways the federal government would like.) *Why would states want few restrictions on federal aid?* (To give them the flexibility to use the money where it could do the most good.) *How might a political party use federal aid to increase its strength?* (By trying to channel federal aid to groups that support, or might be persuaded to support, that party.)

👥 Cooperative Learning
● Divide the class into small groups. Have members of each group work together to write a statement supporting or opposing the increase in the federal government's powers. Students should use the information presented in the section to support their arguments. Each group should then read its statement to the class.

GUIDED/INDEPENDENT PRACTICE
● Have students make a time line listing developments from this section—laws, court cases, and amendments—related to the growth of federal power. Next to each development, students should write a brief explanation of its significance.

Background: *Constitutional Heritage* In *Barron v. Baltimore* the Court rejected the effort of a wharf owner to invoke the Fifth Amendment to compel the city of Baltimore to compensate him for the value of his

wharf, which he claimed was useless as a result of a city action. The precise finding stands to this day.

Background: *History* Benjamin Gitlow led the left wing of the Socialist Party

and advocated the government's violent, unlawful overthrow. His conviction was upheld on the grounds that New York need not wait until the spark "burst into a sweeping and destructive conflagration."

The symbol 👥 denotes active participation strategies.

Activities are keyed for student abilities:
▲ = Basic
● = All Levels
■ = Average/Advanced

hospital, for example. Categorical grants may carry many restrictions, such as what cities the highway must go through or how many beds the hospital must have. About two-thirds of all federal grants are of this variety.

Because categorical grants are so specific, they give the national government a good deal of control over local programs. Supporters point out that such grants enable the national government to set priorities for the country as a whole and establish uniform standards. Critics, however, argue that categorical grants encourage spending and undercut state authority.

In response to criticism of categorical grants, **block grants** have become more popular. Block grants channel federal money through the states for general purposes, such as "law enforcement" or "community development." The detailed distribution of funds and planning of programs are left to state officials. During the Reagan administration, most grants-in-aid were in the form of block grants. Opponents of block grants include big-city mayors and minority groups. They fear their needs will be ignored because federal funds distributed by the state governments are less likely to be given to the cities than to other interests within the state.

Controlling state use of federal funds

Because many state programs rely heavily on federal funds, the national government can exert influence by withholding money unless certain conditions are met. The Hill-Burton Act of 1946, for example, prohibits the use of federal construction money for state hospitals that practice racial discrimination. The power to withhold funds thus allows the national government to extend its influence over the states.

Revenue sharing

To cut federal "strings" and help financially troubled state and local governments, **revenue sharing** was established in 1972. In this form of government financing, a portion of the money collected in federal income taxes was automatically returned to state and local governments. The amount each governmental unit received was based on its population, income, and local tax revenues. Under revenue sharing, state and local governments had almost complete control over spending. The national government set far fewer guidelines than for grants-in-aid.

In 1986 Congress stopped revenue-sharing. Because of the large federal budget deficit, there was just not enough revenue to share.

Federal grant money often is used for large and expensive local projects such as building and equipping a hospital.

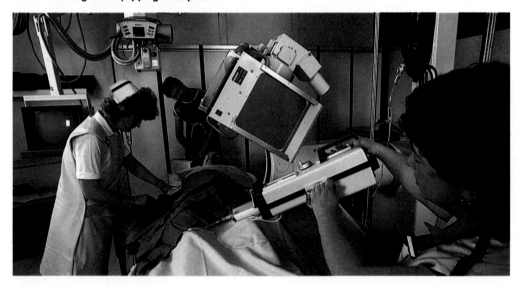

102

SECTION 3 REVIEW

Vocabulary and key terms

Gibbons v. Ogden (99)   block grant (102)
grant-in-aid (101)   revenue sharing (102)
categorical grant (101)

For review

1. (a) How was commerce defined in *Gibbons v. Ogden*? (b) What are some areas that Congress regulates on the basis of the commerce clause? (c) How did Congress use the commerce clause to defend civil rights laws? **2D**

2. (a) What was the original purpose of the Bill of Rights? (b) How have recent interpretations of the Fourteenth Amendment changed this aim? **2A**

3. (a) What kind of federal grant gives the national government the greatest influence in state affairs? (b) What kind of federal financing gives state governments the greatest independence? **7B**

Critical thinking

DRAWING INFERENCES What problems might arise from increased federal government participation in the affairs of the states? From less federal participation? **3C**

SECTION 4 2A, 3A, 3C, 6A, 6E

Federalism Links the Fifty States

ACCESS   **The Main Ideas**

1 **How does the Constitution encourage cooperation between states?**
pages 103–106

2 **What are some examples of conflict and cooperation between states?**
pages 106–107

So far in this chapter we have looked at the relationship between the national government and the states. Now we turn to the relationships among the states.

2A, 3A, 3C, 6A, 6E

Cooperation Between States

Full faith and credit

A recurring problem for the government under the Articles of Confederation was that citizens could flee from one state to another to avoid debts and court judgments. Under these circumstances, contracts and state judicial orders often became meaningless. To remedy this problem, the "full faith and credit" clause was included in the Constitution. Article IV, Section 1 provides,

Full faith and credit shall be given in each state to the public acts, records, and judicial proceedings of every other state. And the Congress may by general laws prescribe the manner in which such acts, records, and proceedings shall be proved, and the effect thereof.

This clause means that such documents as contracts, wills, deeds, mortgages, birth certificates, and civil court judgments of one state must be recognized as legal by all other states.

As an example of full faith and credit, suppose that Mary Rossi sues Cliff Baker over a contract in Colorado, and the court awards her $500. Soon thereafter, Baker moves to Indiana and refuses to pay the settlement. Based on the principle of full faith and credit, Indiana must recognize the Colorado judgment and force Baker to pay Rossi. Or suppose that Ed Johnson, a resident of Iowa vacationing in Florida, injures Tony Rodriguez, a Florida resident. When his vacation is over, Johnson returns to Iowa. Following some rather complicated legal actions, Rodriguez could file a civil suit against Johnson in Florida. Should Rodriguez win, the Iowa

103

(side column)

2. (a) To limit the national government's power. (b) They have been extended to protect citizens from state and national violations.
3. (a) Categorical grants. (b) Revenue sharing.

Critical thinking With too much federal participation, local concerns could be ignored. With too little, fundamental rights and broader issues might be ignored.

CLOSURE

● Have students write a paragraph summarizing the section. The paragraph should begin with a question based on the section title. Students should use the headings from the section to answer the question, and include specific details for each heading. Then have students read Section 4, noting the formal and informal ways in which states cooperate.

SECTION 4

Federalism Links the Fifty States *(pp. 103–107)*

Section Objectives

☐ describe how the Constitution encourages cooperation between states

☐ list examples of conflict and cooperation between states

Vocabulary

extradition, interstate compact, reciprocity

The symbol 👥 denotes active participation strategies.

Activities are keyed for student abilities:
▲ = Basic
● = All Levels
■ = Average/Advanced

104

FOCUS

● Ask students if they have heard recently of cases involving the extradition of criminals to or from your state. (Be sure that all students understand the meaning of the word *extradition*.) Hold a class discussion on the importance of extradition as a law enforcement tool.

EXPLANATION

After reviewing the content of the section, you may want to consider the following activities:

Constitutional Heritage

▲ Point out that this final section of the chapter deals with relationships among the states themselves. (The earlier sections dealt with relationships between the states and the national government.) *What document has provided a framework for cooperation among the states?* (The Constitution.) *What other kinds of cooperation have developed?* (Informal methods.)

courts would have to uphold the Florida decision and make Johnson pay damages.

Problems with full faith and credit

Although the "full faith and credit" provision works reasonably well, there are several problem areas. One problem is that in practice the process is very time-consuming. It is relatively easy for a person to use legal tactics to delay paying a debt or obeying a court settlement, particularly from another state. Some cases drag on for years without any final resolution. If the amount in question is fairly small, the wronged person may simply give up.

A second problem is whether the "full faith and credit" clause applies to divorce cases. For example, while Rhode Island has a one-year residence requirement for couples seeking a divorce, Nevada's residence requirement is only six weeks. What happens if a Rhode Island couple moves to Nevada, lives there for six weeks, gets a divorce, and then moves back to Rhode Island? Does Rhode Island have to recognize the Nevada divorce?

Over the years some states — particularly New York, Massachusetts, and North Carolina — have successfully challenged the legality of "quickie" divorces granted in other states. The Supreme Court has ruled that divorces do not always have to be accorded full faith and credit. The Court has set up two general guidelines for recognition of divorce. First, both husband and wife must participate in the divorce proceedings. Second, both must have ample opportunity to contest the divorce. If a divorce meets these two requirements, it must be given full faith and credit in any state.

Cooperation in criminal cases

The principle of full faith and credit covers contracts, divorces, and similar cases, but it does not apply to criminal cases. What may be a crime in one state may not be recognized as a crime in another or may carry a different penalty. Another provision in the Constitution, however, does deal with the question of persons who have committed a crime in another state (Article IV, Section 2):

A person charged in any state with treason, felony, or other crime who shall flee from justice and be found in another state shall,

on demand of the executive authority [the governor] of the state from which he fled, be delivered up, to be removed to the state having jurisdiction of the crime.

This procedure for returning an accused person to the scene of the alleged crime is called **extradition**. It follows the legal tradition (restated in the Sixth Amendment) that a person charged with a crime can be prosecuted and tried only in "the state and district wherein the crime shall have been committed."

Recognizing that the extradition process was likely to cause difficulties, Congress in 1793 established a set of basic procedures for state governors to follow. In addition, nearly every state has adopted the Uniform Criminal Extradition Act, which provides specific steps for handling interstate fugitives. These steps are shown in Figure 4–4.

Refusing extradition

As with full faith and credit, extradition proceedings do not always run smoothly. Although governors nearly always honor extradition requests, the Supreme Court held in *Kentucky v. Dennison* (1861) that they cannot be forced to do so. In that case, Willis Lago, a free black, had helped a slave escape from Kentucky, then a slave state. Lago himself then fled across the river into Ohio, a free state. The governor of Kentucky requested Lago's extradition for helping a slave escape, but William Dennison, the Ohio governor, refused to comply because he was morally opposed to slavery. The Court upheld Dennison's right to make this choice.

The belief that another state's laws are harsh or unfair is one reason a governor may refuse extradition. Governors also may refuse to cooperate because the alleged offense is not a crime in their state, because the accused has "turned over a new leaf," or because public opinion opposes extradition. On the average, each state requests over a hundred extraditions a year. Only about a half dozen of these requests are denied.

The rights of all citizens

By including provisions for full faith and credit and extradition, the delegates at the Constitutional Convention hoped to increase cooperation among the states. The "comity" clause was also included in Article IV, Section 2 to encour-

Critical Thinking
● *Article IV, Section I was called "the Lawyer's Clause of the Constitution" by Justice Robert H. Jackson. Why might this be an accurate description?*

(Because the passage is open to interpretation, despite its apparent simplicity and clarity.)

age national unity. (The word *comity* means "courtesy" or "friendship.") This clause states, "The citizens of each state shall be entitled to all privileges and immunities of citizens in the several states." In other words, each state must grant the residents of all other states the same rights its own residents enjoy.

The Constitution, however, does not state exactly what "privileges and immunities" the comity clause covers. Again, the Supreme Court has established some general guidelines. The Court has held that all United States citizens are entitled to travel through any state or take up residence there, to buy and sell property, to attend public schools, and to use the courts. And, of course, in every state all citizens must be accorded equal protection of the law.

Exclusive rights of state citizens

Some privileges, however, are not protected by the comity clause. One exception is what are known as "beneficial services." These are the resources and institutions in which a state has special investments. The courts have held that states can reserve these special services for their own citizens. For example, a state may charge out-of-state residents additional fees for hunting and fishing licenses or admission to state parks and beaches. Out-of-state students usually pay higher tuition to attend state universities.

Another exception is political rights. A state may require new residents to live in the state for a specified time before they can vote or run for public office. In addition, states are not obligated to give nonresidents equal treatment in

Figure 4–4 STEPS IN THE EXTRADITION PROCESS 3A

1 The accused must first be formally charged with a crime. This can be done only in the state where the alleged crime was committed.

2 Police in the *requesting state* (the state in which the charges have been filed) ask the police in the *asylum state* (the state to which the fugitive has fled) to detain the accused until the necessary paperwork is completed.

3 The governor of the requesting state sends a copy of the charge, along with a formal request for extradition, to the governor of the asylum state.

4 The governor of the asylum state checks the charges and may then ask the state's attorney general (chief legal officer) for advice. Occasionally, a governor holds a public hearing before honoring a request.

5 When extradition is granted, the requesting state sends officers to the asylum state to bring back the fugitive. All expenses incurred in the process (such as transportation and food) are paid by the requesting state.

6 Once the accused has been returned to the requesting state, he or she is accorded due process of law.

105

Science and Technology
● CRITICAL THINKING Have students list the ways in which new forms of technology—advances in transportation and communications, the invention of the computer, and so on—have influenced the state-to-state issues discussed in this section. (Faster transportation makes it easier for people to move or flee to new states; improved communications and the invention of the computer allow states to keep better track of their residents.) *Do these advances work to increase, or decrease, cooperation among states?* (Increase.)

Cooperative Learning
● Divide the class into groups of five and have each group act out the six steps in the extradition process as outlined in Figure 4–4. Within each group, students should be selected to represent the accused, the police in the requesting state, the police in the asylum state, the governor of the requesting state, and the governor of the asylum state.

Background: *Civic Participation* The principle of "hot pursuit" circumvents the extradition process. States respect the right of out-of-state police to cross state lines in high-speed chases of alleged criminals.

Figure 4–4
■ *Why must the formal charging of a crime take place in the state where the alleged crime was committed?* (Because that is where the defendant will be tried.)

The symbol 👥 denotes active participation strategies.

Activities are keyed for student abilities:
▲ = Basic
● = All Levels
■ = Average/Advanced

GUIDED/INDEPENDENT PRACTICE

● Have each student describe a series of hypothetical situations, each illustrating one of the following concepts: the "full faith and credit" clause, extradition, the "comity" clause, "beneficial services," reciprocity.

RETEACHING/CORRECTIVES

▲ Have students review the list of vocabulary terms in the Section Review and use each of the terms in a sentence.

ENRICHMENT/EXTENSION

■ Have students write a description of how life would be different in the United States if there were no formal means of cooperation among the states—no "full faith and credit" clause, no extradition, and so on.

some business and professional activities. For example, a state does not have to recognize professional licenses, such as teaching certificates or pharmacists' licenses, which are granted by other states.

Interstate agreements

Sometimes two or more states wish to work together to solve some common problem. In some cases they join in an **interstate compact**, a formal agreement between two or more states. Article I, Section 10 of the Constitution calls for the consent of Congress in such cases, but it fails to specify how or when this consent should be given. In practice, the states assume consent unless Congress states otherwise.

More than 160 interstate compacts are currently in operation. These agreements deal with issues such as flood control, forest fire protection, health services, and waste disposal. Two good examples are the New York Port Authority of 1921 and the Red River Compact of 1979. The New York Port Authority is an agreement between New York and New Jersey to handle their common transportation needs. Together the two states have constructed bridges, tunnels, airports, and bus and truck terminals. The Red River Compact

is an agreement between Arkansas, Louisiana, Texas, and Oklahoma to distribute the waters of the Red River fairly.

Disagreements between states

States may clash as well as cooperate. In fact, when the Constitution was written, ten of the original thirteen states were having territorial disputes. The responsibility for settling all such conflicts was given solely to the Supreme Court (Article III, Section 2).

Most lawsuits between states have involved contract obligations, boundary disputes, and water rights. For example, in 1980 the Supreme Court decided a long-standing boundary dispute between Ohio and Kentucky. Since Kentucky joined the Union in 1792, its northern border has been the low-water mark on the opposite side of the Ohio River (Ohio's shore). The state of Ohio asked that the boundary be moved to the middle of the river. The Supreme Court, however, refused the request; the Ohio River remains wholly in Kentucky.

Fortunately, the states do not have to rely on the Supreme Court for every conflict. Many interstate conflicts can be, and are, settled informally.

Working together through the Port Authority, the states of New York and New Jersey have cooperated in such projects as this bridge at Outerbridge Crossing, which links Perth Amboy, N.J., with Staten Island, N.Y.

Background: *Civic Participation* Explain the rights your teaching certificate gives you and tell whether any other states recognize your teaching certificate.

Informal cooperation between states

The simplest form of interstate cooperation is **reciprocity** (reh-sih-PROSS-ih-tee), meaning mutual action or respect. To put it another way: "We'll respect your state laws if you'll respect ours." Some states, such as North Dakota and Minnesota, allow each other's citizens to enroll as residents in their state university systems. All states temporarily honor out-of-state drivers' licenses with the knowledge that other states will honor theirs.

There are many other ways in which the states cooperate. There are also many areas where conflicts arise. As the federal system in the United States continues to develop, conflicts will be solved and new methods of cooperation will evolve, either formally — through acts of Congress, Supreme Court rulings, and constitutional amendments — or informally — through interstate organizations and agreements.

SECTION 4 REVIEW

Vocabulary and key terms

"full faith and credit" clause (103)
extradition (104)
comity clause (104)
interstate compact (106)
reciprocity (107)

For review

1. What kinds of state actions must be given full faith and credit, and which are not covered by the "full faith and credit" clause? **2A**
2. (a) What rights are considered "privileges and immunities" available to all U.S. citizens? (b) What privileges and immunities can be reserved for state citizens? **6E**
3. What proceedings between states involve the participation (a) of Congress? (b) of the Supreme Court? **3C**
4. Give two examples of how the states cooperate informally. **3A**

Critical thinking

APPLYING KEY CONCEPTS   What kinds of problems would arise if the states did not accept one another's "public acts, records, and judicial proceedings" (for example, contracts, wills, marriages, court settlements, etc.)? **3C**

Chapter Summary

The Constitution sets up the basic framework for the federal system by dividing authority between the national government and the states. The delegated powers are specifically assigned to the national government. The implied powers allow the national government to do anything that is "necessary and proper" to carry out its delegated powers. The prohibited powers prevent both levels of government from interfering with some basic legal rights. Both national and state governments exercise the concurrent powers, while the reserved powers are kept by the states. The national government also possesses inherent powers as the government of a sovereign state.

The national government must ensure that the states have a republican form of government and equal representation in the Senate. The national government protects the states from foreign invasion and violence from within. The states, in turn, provide militia, oversee national elections, and set boundaries for congressional districts. Throughout U.S. history, the ideas of states' rights, nationalism, dual federalism, and cooperative federalism have been used to describe the relationship between the national government and the states.

Since the writing of the Constitution, the national government has taken on a larger role in the federal system. Through the commerce clause, it plays a role in almost every aspect of American business and trade. Through the Fourteenth Amendment, it makes sure that many of the provisions of the Bill of Rights are followed by the states. Also, the federal government uses financial powers — grants-in-aid and threats of withholding federal funds — to influence the programs and policies carried out by the states.

The Constitution also provides for relations among the states themselves. The states must recognize one another's public acts and legal decisions. Through extradition, they cooperate in capturing accused criminals attempting to flee prosecution. The comity clause requires states to extend to all U.S. citizens most of the privileges that they grant their own citizens. The Constitution allows interstate compacts and provides for settling disputes between states. The states also cooperate informally through reciprocity.

Section 4 Review Answers

1. Contracts, wills, deeds, mortgages, birth certificates, and civil court judgments must be given full faith and credit. Criminal cases and certain divorces are not covered.
2. (a) The right to travel through or to take up residence in any state, to buy and sell property, to attend public schools, to use the courts, and to receive equal protection under the law. (b) Beneficial services.
3. (a) Interstate compacts. (b) Lawsuits.
4. Honor out-of-state drivers' licenses, allow out-of-state students to enroll in each other's universities.

Critical thinking Legal and procedural chaos would surely result if states did not honor each other's laws and judgments. The enforcement of certain laws and the guarantee of rights would be impossible.

CLOSURE

● Remind students of the pre-reading objectives at the beginning of the section. Pose one or both of these questions again. Then have students read the next assigned lesson.

CHAPTER 4 CORRECTIVES

● To review the content of Chapter 4, you may want to have students complete **Study Guide/Review 4** or **Workbook Chapter 4.**

The symbol 👥 denotes active participation strategies.

Activities are keyed for student abilities:
▲ = Basic
● = All Levels
■ = Average/Advanced

Answers

Vocabulary See pp. T19–T21 for suggested vocabulary activities.

Reviewing the Facts

1. Hamilton interpreted the clause to mean that the national government could take any action not expressly prohibited by the Constitution. Jefferson argued that the national government's powers extended only to those actions absolutely necessary for carrying out the delegated powers.
2. The national government has supremacy.
3. Organize a government.
4. It has used the clause to regulate interstate transportation and communication, regulate business and labor relations, and extend civil rights protections.
5. Extradition.

Thinking Critically About Key Concepts

1. The Constitution delegates certain powers to the three branches of the federal government. The implied powers give the national government the flexibility to carry out the delegated powers. The national government possess inherent powers as the government of a sovereign state. The states hold the reserved powers— those not expressly delegated to the national government. The national and state governments share concurrent powers, while the prohibited powers are denied to both the national and state governments in order to protect the rights of the people.
2. States would exert more power, while the national government would be limited in its scope of action and would have less flexibility in carrying out laws.
3. **(a)** It now prevents the abuse of citizens' rights and liberties by state governments as well as by the national government. **(b)** The

---

 CHAPTER REVIEW

● **Review the definitions of the following terms:**

apportionment	extradition	nationalism
bill of attainder	"full faith and credit"	"necessary and proper"
block grant	clause	clause
categorical grant	*Gibbons v. Ogden*	prohibited powers
comity clause	grant-in-aid	reciprocity
concurrent powers	habeas corpus	redistrict
cooperative federalism	implied powers	reserved powers
delegated powers	inherent powers	revenue sharing
dual federalism	interstate compact	secede
elastic clause	loose construction	states' rights
eminent domain	*McCulloch v. Maryland*	strict construction
ex post facto law	militia	

● **REVIEWING THE FACTS**

1. Briefly restate Jefferson's and Hamilton's different interpretations of the "necessary and proper" clause. **3C**
2. What happens when a state and the national government conflict in carrying out a concurrent power? **3C**
3. Before a territory can apply to Congress for admission as a new state, what must that territory do? **3C**
4. How has the national government used the commerce clause to extend its power over the states? **3C**
5. How can one state retrieve a criminal who has fled to another state? **3A**

▲ **THINKING CRITICALLY ABOUT KEY CONCEPTS**

1. Explain, in general terms, how the Constitution distributes the power to govern among the following three groups: the federal government, the states, and the people. **3C**
2. Describe some changes you might expect in the relationship between the federal government and the states if strict construction of

the Constitution became the general policy of the nation. **3C**
3. (a) How has the purpose of the Bill of Rights changed since the Constitution was written? (b) How did the Fourteenth Amendment, *Gitlow v. New York,* and the civil rights movement each contribute to this change? **3A**
4. Why is it important that the states recognize each other's laws? **3A**

▲ **PRACTICING SKILLS**

1. **Study Skills: Outlining.** Refer to Figure 4–1 (page 87), and review Section 1 (pages 86–91). Make an outline showing how different types of powers are distributed in our federal system. Include two specific examples of each type of power. (To review outlining skills, see Study Skill 7 in the back of the book.) **8C**
2. **Study Skills: Analyzing a chart.** Look at Figure 4–1 again. Suppose the powers listed in the chart as concurrent powers were held by the national government but *not* by the states. How would you redraw the chart to reflect this change? **8B**
3. **Critical Thinking Skills: Drawing conclusions.** Refer to Figure 4–3 (page 98).

Fourteenth Amendment was intended to apply the protections in the Bill of Rights to every state. In *Gitlow v. New York,* the Supreme Court ruled that First Amendment freedoms (free speech and a free press)

were protected from both state and federal law. When the civil rights movement focused on other protections in the Bill of Rights, the Court extended most Bill of Rights guarantees to protect citizens from violations by

both the state and national governments.
4. Cooperation is necessary to permit the enforcement of laws and smooth operation of state government and interstate activity.

During the Great Depression, the federal government devised many special programs to create jobs for the unemployed and to encourage business and industry. Why did the theory of cooperative federalism emerge in the period following the Depression? **8F**

▲ PARTICIPATORY CITIZENSHIP

1. **Contacting the National Guard.** Write, call, or visit the nearest headquarters of the National Guard to find information regarding its structure, its members, and its recent activities in or near your community. Report your findings to the class. **4D**
2. **Delivering a speech.** Prepare selections from Daniel Webster's famous speech in reply to Robert Y. Hayne, and present them to the class. The speech can be found in many anthologies. **8A**
3. **Contacting your state representative.** Write a letter to your state senator or representative about cooperation among states. In it, request information on one of the following topics: (a) What interstate agreements does our state have with other states? (b) Is our state involved in any disagreements with other states? If so, what is the conflict? **3C**

■ WRITING ABOUT ISSUES

1. **Writing an essay.** Write an essay on the following statement, agreeing or disagreeing with it and explaining your reasons: "A loose construction of the Constitution was necessary for American leaders to deal with the issues raised by this nation's growth in size and power." **8C**
2. **Creating dialogue.** Review the discussion of federal aid to the states (pages 101–102). Then write a dialogue between two persons over the issue of federal aid. One person should argue that the federal government should strictly limit the uses to which its aid is put. The other person should argue for fewer restrictions. **8C**
3. **Writing an article.** Write a newspaper story

based on the issue involving the extradition of William Lago, as described on page 104. The story should open with a report of the Supreme Court's decision in the case, and should close with a statement regarding the long-term importance of the decision. **8C**

▲ ANALYZING A POLITICAL CARTOON

State reapportionment—the process by which state legislative and other seats are reassigned on the basis of population changes—seems routine, even boring. However, because reapportionment can directly affect who gets elected, it often causes a surprising amount of controversy. Look at the cartoon below and answer the following questions.

1. What image does the cartoonist use to portray legislative districts? **8B**
2. According to the cartoon, what effect does reapportionment have for incumbents? For referendum voters? **8B**
3. How does the cartoonist view the reapportionment process? **8D**

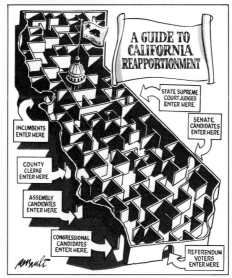

Cartoon by Dennis Renault, Sacramento Bee. Reprinted by permission.

109

Participatory Citizenship
1. You might invite a representative of the National Guard to speak to the class.
2. To ensure that students comprehend the speech, have the reader pause occasionally and ask students to restate selections in their own words.
3. Brief the students on the form and appropriate content of a business letter before they begin writing.

Writing About Issues
1. Students should explain and defend their positions.
2. The proponent of tight restrictions should argue for uniform standards from state to state. The proponent of loose restrictions should argue that the states can better determine how money should be spent.
3. Newspaper stories should explain the facts of the case, the Court's decision that Dennison was not required to turn over Lago, and the precedent that this case sets regarding extradition.

Analyzing a Political Cartoon
1. A maze.
2. It puts incumbents closer to the capital. It puts referendum voters far away from the capital.
3. The cartoonist views reapportionment as confusing and unfair.

Practicing Skills
1. Students should give appropriate examples of each type of power.
2. The circles "Delegated Powers" and "Reserved Powers" would not overlap; there would be no label "Concurrent Powers"; the powers listed under "Concurrent powers" would be listed instead under "Delegated powers."
3. Students may comment that more federal involvement was needed, or that the state governments alone were unable to handle the extraordinary demand for social and economic services during the Depression.

Chapter Review exercises are keyed for student abilities:
▲ = Basic
● = All Levels
■ = Average/Advanced

Vocabulary

Ayub and Yahya Khan, Zia ul-Haq—all dictators in Pakistan at various times.

Background

Benazir Bhutto's father, Zulfikar Ali Bhutto, was executed by the government of Zia ul-Haq in 1979. Benazir Bhutto herself was dismissed from office in August 1990 on charges of corruption. National elections were held in October of that year, and her party was defeated. In October 1993, Bhutto's party won a plurality in parliamentary elections, and she again became Prime Minister.

History

● Working with partners or in small groups, have students do research on the Watergate scandal. Then have students imagine that they are television reporters from a country other than the United States. Have them write a television editorial on Watergate for their viewers back home and present it to the class.

Benazir Bhutto

A Pakistani Leader Views the Constitution

Benazir Bhutto was studying at Harvard in 1971 when her father became prime minister of Pakistan. Six years later the army seized power in Pakistan. Benazir Bhutto became the focus of a democracy movement in her home country. In 1988 Bhutto became prime minister and the first woman to lead a modern Muslim nation.

Pakistan. By studying government at Harvard I began to understand more about Pakistan than I ever had by living there. "When a policeman holds up his hand in the street and says 'Stop!' everybody stops. But when you or I hold up our hands and say 'stop,' nobody stops. Why?" Professor John Womack queried the small group of us in his freshman seminar on "revolution." "Because the policeman is authorized by the Constitution, by the government, to enforce laws. He has the mandate, the legitimacy to say 'stop' and you and I don't."

I remember sitting spellbound in Professor Womack's study, where I was probably the only student who actually lived in a dictatorship. With one example, Professor Womack had pinpointed the state of lawlessness and contempt in Pakistan under Ayub and Yahya Khan, and later, Zia ul-Haq. The authority of these dictators to govern was self-imposed, not a mandate from the people. I saw clearly for the first time why the people in Pakistan saw no reason to obey the regimes, no reason to "stop." Where there was no legitimate government, there was anarchy. . . .

As I prepared to leave Harvard in the spring of 1973, the strength of the United States Constitution was being graphically demonstrated. In spite of the balmy weather and the Frisbee games in Harvard Yard, many

of us were rooted to the televised Watergate hearings. My God, I thought. The American people are removing their president through democratic, constitutional means. Even a powerful president like Richard Nixon . . . could not escape the law of his land. I had read Locke, Rousseau, and John Stuart Mill on the nature of society and the state, the need to guarantee the rights of the people. But theory was one thing. Seeing it unfold in practice was quite another.

The Watergate process left me with a profound sense of the importance of nationally accepted laws, rather than whimsical or arbitrary laws imposed by individuals. When President Nixon resigned his office a year later in August 1974, the succession of power was smooth and peaceful. The leaders in a democracy like America's come and go, but the U.S. Constitution remained.

From *Daughter of Destiny* by Benazir Bhutto. Copyright © 1989 by Benazir Bhutto. Reprinted by permission of Simon & Schuster, Inc.

CRITICAL THINKING

1. In a democracy, where do officials get their power? What did Bhutto realize about the authority claimed by dictators?
2. For Benazir Bhutto, what did the Watergate process demonstrate about constitutional government in the United States?

Critical Thinking Answers
1. Leaders in a democracy get their power from popular support, while dictators impose their authority and are therefore less likely to truly control the population.

2. She was impressed that the law was more important than the person in power, and that presidential succession was peaceful.

The Constitution of the United States

*T*he complete text of the Constitution of the United States begins on the following page. The actual text of the Constitution appears in the inside column on each page, while the other column explains specific parts or provisions. Headings and subheadings have been added to the Constitution to help you find the topics discussed. Those parts of the original document that are no longer in effect are in lighter type. Some spellings and punctuation have been modified for modern readers.

A DIRECTORY TO THE CONSTITUTION

111

THE CONSTITUTION OF THE UNITED STATES

● After students have reviewed the text of the Constitution, have them complete the **Workbook** exercises on the Constitution.

An 1801 engraving of the new "Federal City" of Washington, then only a small town on the Potomac River.

The Preamble states the purposes for which the Constitution was written: (1) to form a union of states that will benefit all, (2) to make laws and establish courts that are fair, (3) to maintain peace within the country, (4) to defend the nation against attack, (5) to ensure people's general well-being, and (6) to make sure that this nation's people and their descendants remain free.

The opening words of the Constitution make clear that it is the people themselves who have the power to establish a government or change it.

The first branch described is the legislative, or law-making, branch. Congress is made up of two houses—the Senate and the House of Representatives.

Section 2
Note that the states establish qualifications for voting. Any person who has the right to vote for representatives to the state legislature has the right to vote for the state's representatives in the House of Representatives. This is the only qualification for voting listed in the original Constitution. It made sure that the House would be elected by the people themselves.

Preamble

We the people of the United States, in order to form a more perfect union, establish justice, insure domestic tranquility, provide for the common defense, promote the general welfare, and secure the blessings of liberty to ourselves and our posterity, do ordain and establish this Constitution for the United States of America.

ARTICLE I   Legislative Branch

SECTION 1   Congress

All legislative powers herein granted shall be vested in a Congress of the United States, which shall consist of a Senate and House of Representatives.

SECTION 2   The House of Representatives

Clause 1. Election and term of members   The House of Representatives shall be composed of members chosen every second year by the people of the several states, and the electors in each state shall have the qualifications requisite for electors of the most numerous branch of the state legislature.

Clause 2. Qualification of members   No person shall be a representative who shall not have attained to the age of twenty-five years, and been seven years a citizen of the United States, and who shall not, when elected, be an inhabitant of that state in which he shall be chosen.

112

Clause 3. Appointment of representatives and direct taxes Representatives [and direct taxes] shall be apportioned among the several states which may be included within this Union, according to their respective numbers, [which shall be determined by adding to the whole number of free persons, including those bound to service for a term of years, and excluding Indians not taxed, three-fifths of all other persons]. The actual enumeration shall be made within three years after the first meeting of the Congress of the United States, and within every subsequent term of ten years, in such manner as they shall by law direct. The number of representatives shall not exceed one for every thirty thousand, but each state shall have at least one representative; [and until such enumeration shall be made, the State of New Hampshire shall be entitled to choose three; Massachusetts, eight; Rhode Island and Providence Plantations, one; Connecticut, five; New York, six; New Jersey, four; Pennsylvania, eight; Delaware, one; Maryland, six; Virginia, ten; North Carolina, five; South Carolina, five; and Georgia, three].

Clause 4. Filling vacancies When vacancies happen in the representation from any state, the executive authority thereof shall issue writs of election to fill such vacancies.

Clause 5. Officers; impeachment The House of Representatives shall choose their Speaker and other officers; and shall have the sole power of impeachment.

SECTION 3 The Senate

Clause 1. Number and election of members The Senate of the United States shall be composed of two senators from each state, chosen [by the legislature thereof,] for six years; and each senator shall have one vote.

Clause 3
Several amendments have changed these provisions. All the people of a state are now counted in determining the number of representatives a state shall have, based on a census taken every ten years. The House of Representatives cannot have more than one member for every 30,000 persons in the nation. But each state is entitled to one representative, no matter how small its population. In 1910 Congress limited the number of representatives to 435.

Amendment 16 made the income tax an exception to the rule against direct taxes not based on population.

Clause 4
When a state does not have all the representatives to which it is entitled—for example, when a representative resigns or dies—the governor of the state may call an election to fill the vacancy.

Clause 5
Only the House can impeach, that is, bring charges of misbehavior in office against a U.S. official.

Section 3
Senators are no longer chosen by state legislatures but elected by the people (Amendment 17).

Senators in the 1st Congress were divided into three groups so that their terms would not all end at the same time. Today all senators are elected for six-year terms, but only one-third are elected in any election year.

A bird's-eye view of the nation's capital in 1880, when the Washington Monument was still being built.

Daniel Webster in a tense Senate debate, 1850.

Clauses 6 and 7
The Senate tries the case when a federal official is impeached by the House of Representatives. The Senators must formally declare that they will be honest and just. If the President of the United States is on trial, the Chief Justice presides over the Senate. Two-thirds of the senators present must agree that the charge is true for the impeached person to be found guilty.

If the Senate finds an impeached official guilty, the only punishment is removal from office and disqualification for ever holding a government job again. Once out of office, however, the former official may be tried in a regular court and, if found guilty, punished like any other person.

Clause 2. Choosing senators   Immediately after they shall be assembled in consequence of the first election, they shall be divided as equally as may be into three classes. [The seats of the senators of the first class shall be vacated at the expiration of the second year, of the second class at the expiration of the fourth year, and of the third class at the expiration of the sixth year,] so that one-third may be chosen every second year; [and if vacancies happen by resignation, or otherwise, during the recess of the legislature of any state, the executive thereof may make temporary appointments until the next meeting of the legislature, which shall then fill such vacancies.]

Clause 3. Qualifications of members   No person shall be a senator who shall not have attained to the age of thirty years, and been nine years a citizen of the United States, and who shall not, when elected, be an inhabitant of that state for which he shall be chosen.

Clause 4. Senate President   The Vice President of the United States shall be President of the Senate, but shall have no vote, unless they be equally divided.

Clause 5. Other officers   The Senate shall choose their own officers, and also a President pro tempore, in the absence of the Vice President, or when he shall exercise the office of President of the United States.

Clause 6. Impeachment trials   The Senate shall have the sole power to try all impeachments. When sitting for that purpose, they shall be on oath or affirmation. When the President of the United States is tried, the Chief Justice shall preside; and no person shall be convicted without the concurrence of two-thirds of the members present.

Clause 7. Impeachment convictions   Judgment in cases of impeachment shall not exceed further than to removal from office, and disqualification to hold and enjoy any office of honor, trust, or profit under the United States; but the party convicted shall nevertheless be liable and subject to indictment, trial, judgment, and punishment, according to law.

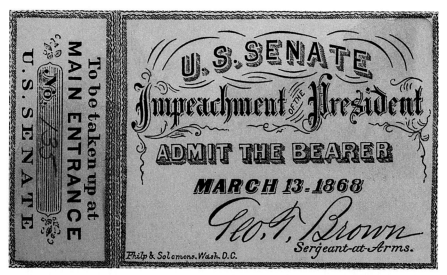

A visitor's ticket to the Senate gallery for the 1868 impeachment trial that acquitted President Johnson.

SECTION 4 Congressional Elections and Meetings

Clause 1. Elections The times, places, and manner of holding elections for senators and representatives shall be prescribed in each state by the legislature thereof; but the Congress may at any time by law make or alter such regulations, [except as to the places of choosing senators.]

Clause 2. Meetings of Congress The Congress shall assemble at least once in every year, [and such meeting shall be on the first Monday in December, unless they shall by law appoint a different day.]

SECTION 5 Organization and Rules

Clause 1. Organization Each house shall be the judge of the elections, returns, and qualifications of its own members, and a majority of each shall constitute a quorum to do business; but a smaller number may adjourn from day to day, and may be authorized to compel the attendance of absent members, in such manner, and under such penalties as each house may provide.

Clause 2. Rules Each house may determine the rules of its proceedings, punish its members for disorderly behavior, and with the concurrence of two-thirds, expel a member.

Clause 3. Journal Each house shall keep a journal of its proceedings, and from time to time publish the same, excepting such parts as may in their judgment require secrecy; and the yeas and nays of the members of either house on any question shall, at the desire of one-fifth of those present, be entered on the journal.

Section 4
The legislature of each state has the right to determine how, when, and where senators and representatives are elected, but Congress may pass election laws that the states must follow. For example, a federal law requires that secret ballots be used. Congress must meet at least once a year. Amendment 20 made January 3 the day for beginning a regular session of Congress.

Andrew Johnson, the only U.S. President impeached.

Clause 3
Each house of Congress keeps and publishes a record of what goes on at its meetings. The *Congressional Record* is issued daily during sessions of Congress. Parts of the record that the members of Congress believe should be kept secret may be withheld. How members of either house vote on a question may be entered in the record if one-fifth of those present wish it.

115

Clause 4
When Congress is meeting, neither house may stop work for more than three days without the consent of the other house. Neither house may meet in another city without the consent of the other house.

Section 6
Senators and representatives are paid out of the United States Treasury and have a number of other privileges.

Until their terms have ended, senators or representatives may not hold offices created by the Congress of which they are members. The same restriction applies to jobs for which Congress has voted increased pay. No person may be a member of Congress without first giving up any other federal office he or she may hold.

Section 7
Bills for raising money for the federal government must start in the House of Representatives, but the Senate may make changes in such bills. Actually, the Senate now has as much influence over revenue bills as does the House. Other bills may start in either the Senate or the House of Representatives. However, exactly the same bill must be passed by a majority vote in both houses of Congress. (Chapter 13 details how a bill becomes law.)

President Gerald Ford signs a tax bill into law.

Clause 4. Adjournment Neither house, during the session of Congress, shall without the consent of the other adjourn for more than three days, nor to any other place than that in which the two houses shall be sitting.

SECTION 6 Privileges and Restrictions

Clause 1. Pay; Congressional immunity The senators and representatives shall receive a compensation for their services, to be ascertained by law, and paid out of the Treasury of the United States. They shall in all cases, except treason, felony, and breach of the peace, be privileged from arrest during their attendance at the session of their respective houses and in going to and returning from the same; and for any speech or debate in either house, they shall not be questioned in any other place.

Clause 2. Restrictions No senator or representative shall, during the time for which he was elected, be appointed to any civil office under the authority of the United States which shall have been created, or the emoluments whereof shall have been increased during such time; and no person holding any office under the United States shall be a member of either house during his continuance in office.

SECTION 7 Method of Passing Laws

Clause 1. Revenue bills All bills for raising revenue shall originate in the House of Representatives; but the Senate may propose or concur with amendments as on other bills.

Clause 2. How bills become law Every bill which shall have passed the House of Representatives and the Senate shall, before it become a law, be presented to the President of the United States; if he approves he shall sign it, but if not he shall return it, with his objections, to that house in which it shall have originated, who shall enter the objections at large on their journal, and proceed to reconsider it. If after such reconsideration two-thirds of that house shall agree to pass the bill, it shall be sent, together with the objections, to the other house, by which it shall likewise be reconsidered, and if approved by two-thirds of that house, it shall become a law. But in all such cases the votes of both houses shall be determined by yeas and nays, and the names of the persons voting for and against the bill shall be entered on the journal of each house respectively. If any bill shall not be returned by the President within ten days (Sundays excepted) after it shall have been presented to him, the same shall be a law, in like manner as if he had signed it, unless the Congress by their adjournment prevent its return, in which case it shall not be a law.

Clause 3. Presidential approval or disapproval Every order, resolution, or vote to which the concurrence of the Senate and House of Representatives may be necessary (except on a question of adjournment) shall be presented to the President of the United States; and before the same shall take effect, shall be approved by him, or being disapproved by him, shall be repassed by two-thirds of the Senate and House of Representatives, according to the rules and limitations prescribed in the case of a bill.

SECTION 8   Powers Granted to Congress

The Congress shall have power
Clause 1. To lay and collect taxes, duties, imposts, and excises; to pay the debts and provide for the common defense and general welfare of the United States; but all duties, imposts, and excises shall be uniform throughout the United States;

Clause 2. To borrow money on the credit of the United States;

Clause 3. To regulate commerce with foreign nations, and among the several states, and with the Indian tribes;

Clause 4. To establish a uniform rule of naturalization, and uniform laws on the subject of bankruptcies throughout the United States;

Section 8
This section lists the many delegated powers of Congress.

Clause 3
Under this "commerce clause," the national government has broadened its powers.

The harbor at Philadelphia — an important center for American commerce and shipping — in 1800.

Clause 8
Congress may pass copyright and patent laws that make it illegal for a person to use the work of an artist, musician, author, or inventor without permission.

U.S. gold "quarter eagle" coins, minted in 1796.

Clauses 11–16
These provisions ensure civilian control of the military.

Clause 5. To coin money, regulate the value thereof and of foreign coin, and fix the standard of weights and measures;

Clause 6. To provide for the punishment of counterfeiting the securities and current coin of the United States;

Clause 7. To establish post offices and post roads;

Clause 8. To promote the progress of science and useful arts by securing for limited times to authors and inventors the exclusive right to their respective writings and discoveries;

Clause 9. To constitute tribunals inferior to the Supreme Court;

Clause 10. To define and punish piracies and felonies committed on the high seas and offenses against the laws of nations;

Clause 11. To declare war, grant letters of marque and reprisal, and make rules concerning captures on land and water;

Clause 12. To raise and support armies, but no appropriation of money to that use shall be for a longer term than two years;

Clause 13. To provide and maintain a navy;

Clause 14. To make rules for the government and regulation of land and naval forces;

Clause 15. To provide for calling forth the militia to execute the laws of the Union, suppress insurrections, and repel invasions;

Clause 16. To provide for organizing, arming, and disciplining the militia, and for governing such part of them as may be employed in the service of the United States, reserving to the states respectively the appointment of the officers and the authority of training the militia, according to the discipline prescribed by Congress;

The first American dollar bill, an 1862 "greenback."

Clause 17. To exercise exclusive legislation in all cases whatsoever over such district (not exceeding ten miles square) as may, by cession of particular states and the acceptance of Congress, become the seat of the government of the United States, and to exercise like authority over all places purchased by the consent of the legislature of the states in which the same shall be for the erection of forts, magazines, arsenals, dock-yards, and other needful buildings; and

Clause 18. To make all laws which shall be necessary and proper for carrying into execution the foregoing powers, and all other powers vested by this Constitution in the government of the United States, or in any department or officer thereof.

SECTION 9   Powers Denied to the Federal Government

Clause 1. [The migration or importation of such persons as any of the states now existing shall think proper to admit shall not be prohibited by the Congress prior to the year one thousand eight hundred and eight, but a tax or duty may be imposed on such importation, not exceeding ten dollars for each person.]

Clause 2. The privilege of the writ of habeas corpus shall not be suspended, unless when in cases of rebellion or invasion the public safety may require it.

Clause 3. No bill of attainder or ex post facto law shall be passed.

Clause 4. No capitation or other direct tax shall be laid, unless in proportion to the census or enumeration herein before directed to be taken.

Clause 5. No tax or duty shall be laid on articles exported from any state.

Clause 6. No preference shall be given by any regulation of commerce or revenue to the ports of one state over those of another; nor shall vessels bound to or from one state be obliged to enter, clear, or pay duties in another.

Clause 7. No money shall be drawn from the treasury, but in consequence of appropriations made by law; and a regular statement and account of the receipts and expenditures of all public money shall be published from time to time.

Clause 8. No titles of nobility shall be granted by the United States; and no person holding any office of profit or trust under them shall, without the consent of Congress, accept of any present, emolument, office, or title, of any kind whatever, from any king, prince, or foreign state.

Clause 17
Congress has the power to make laws for the District of Columbia, the national capital. Congress also makes laws regulating the use of all other property belonging to the national government—forts, arsenals, national parks, etc.

Clause 18
The "necessary and proper" clause, or elastic clause, is the basis for the implied powers.

Section 9
This is the first list of prohibited powers—those denied to the federal government.

Clause 1
Congress could not take action against slavery until 1808, when it prohibited further importation of slaves.

The shelling of Ft. McHenry, Baltimore, in 1814, which inspired the words of the "Star-Spangled Banner."

Clause 8
The United States may not grant a title of nobility. Federal officials may not accept titles, gifts, or honors from any foreign ruler or government unless Congress gives its permission.

Section 10
This is the listing of powers prohibited to the states.

Clause 2
States cannot tax goods leaving or entering their territory but may charge fees to cover the costs of inspection. Any profit from such inspection fees must be turned over to the United States Treasury. Congress has the power to change the inspection laws of a state.

Clause 3
Unless Congress gives permission, a state may not tax ships entering its ports, keep an army or navy— except the militia — in time of peace, make treaties with other states or foreign countries, or make war except when it is invaded.

The second branch is the executive branch, which carries out the laws.

GENERAL ANDREW JACKSON.
The Hero, the Sage and the Patriot.

Clause 2
This provision sets up the Electoral College: The President and Vice President are elected by electors chosen by the states according to rules established by the legislatures. Each state has as many electors as it has senators and representatives in Congress.

This clause did not work well in practice and was changed by Amendment 12.

SECTION 10   Powers Denied to the States

Clause 1. No state shall enter into any treaty, alliance, or confederation; grant letters of marque and reprisal; coin money; emit bills of credit; make any thing but gold and silver coin a tender in payment of debts; pass any bill of attainder, ex post facto law, or law impairing the obligation of contracts; or grant any title of nobility.

Clause 2. No state shall, without the consent of the Congress, lay any imposts or duties on imports or exports, except what may be absolutely necessary for executing its inspection laws; and the net produce of all duties and imposts, laid by any state on imports or exports, shall be for the use of the treasury of the United States; and all such laws shall be subject to the revision and control of the Congress.

Clause 3. No state shall, without the consent of Congress, lay any duty of tonnage; keep troops or ships of war in time of peace; enter into any agreement or compact with another state or with a foreign power; or engage in war, unless actually invaded or in such imminent danger as will not admit of delay.

ARTICLE II   Executive Branch

SECTION 1   President and Vice President

Clause 1. Term of office   The executive power shall be vested in a President of the United States of America. He shall hold his office during the term of four years, and, together with the Vice President chosen for the same term, be elected as follows:

Clause 2. Electoral College   Each state shall appoint, in such manner as the legislature thereof may direct, a number of electors, equal to the whole number of senators and representatives to which the state may be entitled in the Congress; but no senator or representative, or person holding an office of trust or profit under the United States, shall be appointed an elector.

[The electors shall meet in their respective states and vote by ballot for two persons, of whom one at least shall not be an inhabitant of the same state with themselves. And they shall make a list of all the persons voted for and of the number of votes for each; which list they shall sign and certify, and transmit sealed to the seat of government of the United States, directed to the President of the Senate. The President of the Senate shall, in the presence of the Senate and House of Representatives, open all the certificates, and the votes shall then be counted. The person having the greatest number of votes shall be the President, if such number be a majority of the whole number of electors appointed; and if there be more than one who have such majority, and have an equal number of votes, then the House of Representatives shall immediately choose by ballot one of them for President; and if no person have a majority, then from the five highest on the list the said house shall in like manner choose the President. But in choosing the President the votes shall be taken by states, the representation from each state having one vote; a quorum for this purpose shall consist of a member or members from two-thirds of the states, and a majority of all the states shall be necessary to a choice. In every case, after the choice of the President, the person having the greatest number of votes of the electors shall be the Vice President. But if there should remain two or more who have equal votes, the Senate shall choose from them by ballot the Vice President.]

Clause 3. Time of elections The Congress may determine the time of choosing the electors, and the day on which they shall give their votes; which day shall be the same throughout the United States.

Clause 4. Qualifications for President No person except a natural-born citizen, [or a citizen of the United States, at the time of the adoption of this Constitution] shall be eligible to the office of President; neither shall any person be eligible to that office who shall not have attained the age of thirty-five years, and been fourteen years a resident within the United States.

Clause 5. Succession In case of the removal of the President from office or of his death, resignation, or inability to discharge the powers and duties of the said office, the same shall devolve on the Vice President; and the Congress may by law provide for the case of removal, death, resignation, or inability, both of the President and Vice President, declaring what officer shall then act as President; and such officer shall act accordingly, until the disability be removed or a President shall be elected.

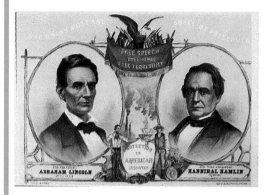

An 1860 poster for candidates Lincoln and Hannibal Hamlin.

Clause 3
Congress determines when electors are chosen and when they vote. The day is the same throughout the United States. The popular vote for electors takes place on the Tuesday after the first Monday of November every four years. In mid-December the electors meet in their state capitals and cast their electoral votes.

Clause 5
If the presidency becomes vacant, the Vice President becomes the President of the United States. If neither the President nor the Vice President is able to serve, Congress has the right to decide which government official shall act as President. Amendment 25 practically assures that there always will be a Vice President to succeed to the presidency.

The White House — the presidential mansion — in 1848.

Section 2
Presidential powers are described very generally (unlike those of Congress).
Clause 1
The President is commander-in-chief of the armed forces and of the militia when it is called out by the national government. This is another provision to ensure civilian control of the military. No provision is made in the Constitution for the Cabinet or for Cabinet meetings, but the existence of executive departments is implied in this clause.

Clause 2
The President is the nation's chief diplomat, with the power to make treaties. All treaties must be approved in the Senate by a two-thirds vote of the senators present. The President also can appoint important government officials, who must be approved in the Senate by a majority.

Clause 6. Salary The President shall, at stated times, receive for his services a compensation, which shall neither be increased nor diminished during the period for which he shall have been elected, and he shall not receive within that period any other emolument from the United States, or any of them.

Clause 7. Oath of office Before he enter on the execution of his office, he shall take the following oath or affirmation: "I do solemnly swear (or affirm) that I will faithfully execute the office of President of the United States, and will to the best of my ability, preserve, protect, and defend the Constitution of the United States."

SECTION 2   Powers of the President

Clause 1. Military powers; Cabinet; pardons The President shall be Commander-in-Chief of the Army and Navy of the United States, and of the militia of the several states, when called into the actual service of the United States. He may require the opinion, in writing, of the principal officer in each of the executive departments, upon any subject relating to the duties of their respective offices, and he shall have power to grant reprieves and pardons for offenses against the United States, except in cases of impeachment.

Clause 2. Diplomatic powers; appointments He shall have power, by and with the advice and consent of the Senate, to make treaties, provided two-thirds of the senators present concur; and he shall nominate and, by and with the advice and consent of the Senate, shall appoint ambassadors, other public ministers and consuls, judges of the Supreme Court, and all other officers of the United States, whose appointments are not herein otherwise provided for, and which shall be established by law; but the Congress may by law vest the appointment of such inferior officers as they think proper in the President alone, in the courts of law, or in the heads of departments.

Past and future Presidents and their families at the inauguration of John F. Kennedy. (The front row includes the Eisenhowers, Lady Bird Johnson, Jacqueline Kennedy, Lyndon Johnson, Richard Nixon, and the Trumans.)

Clause 3. Filling vacancies The President shall have power to fill up all vacancies that may happen during the recess of the Senate, by granting commissions which shall expire at the end of their next session.

SECTION 3   Duties of the President

He shall from time to time give to the Congress information of the state of the Union, and recommend to their consideration such measures as he shall judge necessary and expedient; he may, on extraordinary occasions, convene both houses, or either of them, and in case of disagreement between them with respect to the time of adjournment he may adjourn them to such time as he shall think proper; he shall receive ambassadors and other public ministers; he shall take care that the laws be faithfully executed, and shall commission all the officers of the United States.

SECTION 4   Impeachment

The President, Vice-President, and all civil officers of the United States shall be removed from office on impeachment for, and conviction of, treason, bribery, or other high crimes and misdemeanors.

Clause 3
If the Senate is not meeting, the President may make temporary appointments to fill vacancies.

Section 3
The Constitution imposes only a few specific duties on the President. One is to give a "State of the Union" message, which Presidents now deliver once a year.

Section 4
This section makes all Federal officials subject to the impeachment process described in Article I.

The Supreme Court held its first two sessions in this New York building, known as the Exchange.

ARTICLE III   Judicial Branch

SECTION 1   The Federal Courts

The judicial power of the United States shall be vested in one Supreme Court and in such inferior courts as the Congress may from time to time ordain and establish. The judges, both of the Supreme and inferior courts, shall hold their offices during good behavior and shall, at stated times, receive for their services a compensation which shall not be diminished during their continuance in office.

Article III gives the power to interpret the laws of the United States to the third branch, the judicial, which includes the Supreme Court and the other federal courts established by Congress. District courts and courts of appeal are now part of the regular court system. Federal judges are appointed by the President with the approval of the Senate.

123

Section 2

The federal courts have jurisdiction in certain kinds of cases (described in Chapter 17).

Roger B. Taney, Chief Justice of the United States in the crucial years between 1836 and 1864.

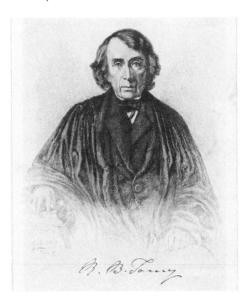

Section 3

The Constitution defines treason and places limits on how it can be punished.

The Supreme Court building today.

SECTION 2 Federal Court Jurisdiction

Clause 1. Federal cases The judicial power shall extend to all cases, in law and equity, arising under this Constitution, the laws of the United States, and treaties made, or which shall be made, under their authority; to all cases affecting ambassadors, other public ministers, and consuls; to all cases of admiralty and maritime jurisdiction; to controversies to which the United States shall be a party; to controversies between two or more states; [between a state and citizens of another state;] between citizens of different states; between citizens of the same state claiming lands under grants of different states, and between a state, or the citizens thereof, and foreign states, citizens, or subjects.

Clause 2. Supreme Court jurisdiction In all cases affecting ambassadors, other public ministers, and consuls, and those in which a state be a party, the Supreme Court shall have original jurisdiction. In all the other cases before mentioned, the Supreme Court shall have appellate jurisdiction, both as to law and fact, with such exceptions and under such regulations as the Congress shall make.

Clause 3. Trial rules The trial of all crimes, except in cases of impeachment, shall be by jury; and such trial shall be held in the state where the said crimes shall have been committed; but when not committed within any state, the trial shall be at such place or places as the Congress may by law have directed.

SECTION 3 Treason

Clause 1. Definition Treason against the United States shall consist only in levying war against them or in adhering to their enemies, giving them aid and comfort. No person shall be convicted of treason unless on the testimony of two witnesses to the same overt act, or on confession in open court.

Clause 2. Punishment The Congress shall have power to declare the punishment of treason, but no attainder of treason shall work corruption of blood, or forfeiture except during the life of the person attainted.

ARTICLE IV The States and the Federal Government

SECTION 1 State Records

Full faith and credit shall be given in each state to the public acts, records, and judicial proceedings of every other state. And the Congress may by general laws prescribe the manner in which such acts, records, and proceedings shall be proved, and the effect thereof.

SECTION 2 Rights of Citizens

Clause 1. Privileges and immunities The citizens of each state shall be entitled to all privileges and immunities of citizens in the several states.

Clause 2. Extradition A person charged in any state with treason, felony, or other crime who shall flee from justice and be found in another state shall, on demand of the executive authority of the state from which he fled, be delivered up, to be removed to the state having jurisdiction of the crime.

[**Clause 3. Fugitive workers** No person held to service or labor in one state, under the laws thereof, escaping into another shall, in consequence of any law or regulation therein, be discharged from such service or labor, but shall be delivered upon claim of the party to whom such service or labor may be due.]

SECTION 3 New States and Territories

Clause 1. Admission of new states New states may be admitted by the Congress into this Union; but no new state shall be formed or erected within the jurisdiction of any other state; nor any state be formed by the junction of two or more states, or parts of states, without the consent of the legislatures of the states concerned, as well as of the Congress.

Clause 2. Federal territory The Congress shall have power to dispose of and make all needful rules and regulations respecting the territory or other property belonging to the United States; and nothing in this Constitution shall be so construed as to prejudice any claims of the United States, or of any particular state.

SECTION 4 Federal Duties to the States

The United States shall guarantee to every state in this Union a republican form of government, and shall protect each of them against invasion; and on application of the legislature, or of the executive (whom the legislature cannot be convened), against domestic violence.

Article IV sets out many of the principles of the federal system, describing relations among the states and between the national government and the states. Section 3 tells how new states may be admitted to the Union. Section 4 outlines the national government's duties to the states.

Section 2
The provisions of this section extend most privileges of state citizenship to *all* citizens. (Some exceptions are made.) It also establishes the extradition process.

Clause 3
Amendment 13 abolished slavery and made this clause obsolete.

Dakota Territory applying to Uncle Sam for statehood, in an 1880's cartoon.

125

Article V sets up two ways of amending the Constitution and two ways of ratifying amendments (see page 71).

ARTICLE V Amending the Constitution

The Congress, whenever two-thirds of both houses shall deem it necessary, shall propose amendments to this Constitution, or, on the application of the legislatures of two-thirds of the several states, shall call a convention for proposing amendments, which, in either case, shall be valid to all intents and purposes, as part of this Constitution, when ratified by the legislatures of three-fourths of the several states or by conventions in three-fourths thereof, as the one or the other mode of ratification may be proposed by the Congress; provided that [no amendments which may be made prior to the year one thousand eight hundred and eight shall in any manner affect the first and fourth clauses in the ninth section of the first article; and that] no state, without its consent, shall be deprived of its equal suffrage in the Senate.

ARTICLE VI Supremacy of National Law

Article VI makes the Constitution the "supreme law of the land." If state law is in conflict with national law, it is the national law that must be obeyed.

Clause 1. Public debt All debts contracted and engagements entered into, before the adoption of this Constitution, shall be as valid against the United States under this Constitution as under the Confederation.

Clause 2. Supreme law of the land This Constitution, and the laws of the United States which shall be made in pursuance thereof, and all treaties made, or which shall be made, under the authority of the United States, shall be the supreme law of the land; and the judges in every state shall be bound thereby, anything in the Constitution or laws of any state to the contrary notwithstanding.

Clause 3. Oath of office The senators and representatives before mentioned, and the members of the several state legislatures, and all executive and judicial officers, both of the United States and of the several states, shall be bound by oath or affirmation to support this Constitution; but no religious test shall ever be required as a qualification to any office or public trust under the United States.

Clause 1
The framers of the Constitution agreed that the United States would be responsible for all debts contracted by the government under the Articles of Confederation.

Present-day courtroom, Newport, Rhode Island.

The signing of the Constitution, September 17, 1787.

ARTICLE VII Ratification of the Constitution

The ratification of the conventions of nine states shall be sufficient for the establishment of this Constitution between the states so ratifying the same.

Article VII established that the Constitution would go into effect when nine states voted to accept it. This occurred on June 21, 1788, with New Hampshire's ratification.

George Washington —
    President and
    delegate
    from Virginia

New Hampshire
John Langdon
Nicholas Gilman

Massachusetts
Nathaniel Gorham
Rufus King

Connecticut
William Samuel
    Johnson
Roger Sherman

New York
Alexander Hamilton

New Jersey
William Livingston
David Brearley
William Paterson
Jonathan Dayton

Pennsylvania
Benjamin Franklin
Thomas Mifflin
Robert Morris
George Clymer
Thomas FitzSimons
Jared Ingersoll
James Wilson
Gouverneur Morris

Delaware
George Reed
Gunning Bedford, Junior
John Dickinson
Richard Bassett
Jacob Broom

Maryland
James McHenry
Daniel of St. Thomas
    Jenifer
Daniel Carroll

Virginia
John Blair
James Madison, Junior

North Carolina
William Blount
Richard Dobbs
    Spaight
Hugh Williamson

South Carolina
John Rutledge
Charles Cotesworth
    Pinckney
Charles Pinckney
Pierce Butler

Georgia
William Few
Abraham Baldwin

127

AMENDMENTS to the Constitution

Amendments 1–10 make up the Bill of Rights.

Amendment 1 protects citizens from government interference with their freedoms of religion, speech, press, assembly, and petition. These are the basic civil liberties.

Amendment 2 guarantees that the federal government cannot deny states the right to enlist citizens in the militia and to provide them with training in the use of weapons.

Amendment 3 was included because of the troubles caused when the British sought to quarter and supply their troops in colonists' homes. The amendment guarantees that in time of peace the federal government may not force people to have soldiers live in their homes. Even in time of war, people cannot be compelled to do this unless Congress passes a law requiring it.

Amendment 4 extends the people's right to privacy and security by setting limits on authorities' power to search property and seize evidence.

AMENDMENT 1   Freedom of Religion, Speech, Press, Assembly, and Petition (1791)

Congress shall make no law respecting an establishment of religion or prohibiting the free exercise thereof; or abridging the freedom of speech, or of the press; or the right of the people peaceably to assemble, and to petition the government for a redress of grievances.

AMENDMENT 2   Right to Bear Arms (1791)

A well-regulated militia being necessary to the security of a free state, the right of the people to keep and bear arms shall not be infringed.

AMENDMENT 3   Quartering of Soldiers (1791)

No soldier shall, in time of peace, be quartered in any house without the consent of the owner, nor in time of war, but in a manner to be prescribed by law.

AMENDMENT 4   Search and Seizure (1791)

The right of the people to be secure in their persons, houses, papers, and effects, against unreasonable searches and seizures, shall not be violated, and no warrants shall issue but upon probable cause, supported by oath or affirmation and particularly describing the place to be searched and the persons or things to be seized.

AMENDMENT 5   Rights of the Accused (1791)

No person shall be held to answer for a capital or otherwise infamous crime, unless on a presentment or indictment of a grand jury, except in cases arising in the land or naval forces, or in the militia, when in actual service in time of war or public danger; nor shall any person be subject for the same offense to be twice put in jeopardy of life or limb; nor shall be compelled in any criminal case to be a witness against himself, nor be deprived of life, liberty, or property, without due process of law; nor shall private property be taken for public use without just compensation.

Amendment 5 ensures certain rights for people accused of crimes. It says that no person may be tried in a federal court unless a grand jury decides that the person ought to be tried. (Members of the armed forces may be tried in military court under military law.) Other provisions guarantee due process of law. Finally, a person's private property may not be taken for public use without a fair price being paid for it.

AMENDMENT 6   Requirements for Jury Trial (1791)

In all criminal prosecutions, the accused shall enjoy the right to a speedy and public trial by an impartial jury of the state and district wherein the crime shall have been committed, which districts shall have been previously ascertained by law, and to be informed of the nature and cause of the accusation; to be confronted with the witnesses against him; to have compulsory process for obtaining witnesses in his favor; and to have the assistance of counsel for his defense.

Amendment 6 lists additional rights of an individual accused of a crime. A person accused of a crime is entitled to a prompt public trial before an impartial jury. The trial is held in the district where the crime took place. The accused must be told what the charge is. The accused must be present when witnesses give their testimony. The government must help the accused bring into court friendly witnesses. The accused must be provided with legal counsel.

AMENDMENT 7   Rules of Common Law (1791)

In suits at common law, where the value in controversy shall exceed twenty dollars, the right of trial by jury shall be preserved, and no fact tried by a jury shall be otherwise reexamined in any court of the United States than according to the rules of common law.

Amendment 7 is somewhat out of date. Today, cases involving lawsuits are not tried before federal courts unless large sums of money are involved.

The draft of the Bill of Rights — twelve amendments sent to the states in 1789 — only ten of which were approved.

Amendment 8 provides that persons accused of crimes may in most cases be released from jail if they or someone else posts bail. Bail, fines, and punishments must be reasonable.

Amendment 9 was included because of the impossibility of listing in the Constitution all the rights of the people. The mention of certain rights does not mean that people do not have other fundamental rights, which the government must respect. These include the right to privacy.

Amendment 10 establishes the reserved powers. It states that the powers that the Constitution does not give to the United States and does not deny to the states belong to the states and to the people.

This amendment was the first that was enacted to override a Supreme Court decision. It confirms that no federal court may try a case in which a state is being sued by a citizen of another state or of a foreign country. Amendment 11 changes a provision of Article III, Section 2.

AMENDMENT 8   Limits on Criminal Punishments (1791)

Excessive bail shall not be required, nor excessive fines imposed, nor cruel and unusual punishments inflicted.

AMENDMENT 9   Rights Kept by the People (1791)

The enumeration in the Constitution of certain rights shall not be construed to deny or disparage others retained by the people.

AMENDMENT 10   Powers of the States and the People (1791)

The powers not delegated to the United States by the Constitution, nor prohibited by it to the states, are reserved to the states respectively, or to the people.

AMENDMENT 11   Lawsuits Against a State (1798)

The judicial power of the United States shall not be construed to extend to any suit in law or equity commenced or prosecuted against one of the United States by citizens of another state or by citizens or subjects of any foreign state.

A southern jury in 1867 included blacks who, for the first time, had the rights of citizens.

AMENDMENT 12 Election of President and Vice President (1804)

The electors shall meet in their respective states and vote by ballot for President and Vice President, one of whom, at least, shall not be an inhabitant of the same state with themselves; they shall name in their ballots the person voted for as President, and in distinct ballots the person voted for as Vice President, and they shall make distinct lists of all persons voted for as President, and of all persons voted for as Vice President, and of the number of votes for each, which lists they shall sign and certify, and transmit sealed to the seat of the government of the United States, directed to the President of the Senate; the President of the Senate shall, in the presence of the Senate and House of Representatives, open all the certificates and the votes shall then be counted; the person having the greatest number of votes for President shall be the President, if such number be a majority of the whole number of electors appointed; and if no person have such majority, then from the persons having the highest numbers not exceeding three on the list of those voted for as President, the House of Representatives shall choose immediately, by ballot, the President. But in choosing the President, the votes shall be taken by states, the representation from each state having one vote; a quorum for this purpose shall consist of a member or members from two-thirds of the states, and a majority of all the states shall be necessary to a choice. And if the House of Representatives shall not choose a President whenever the right of choice shall devolve upon them, [before the fourth day of March next following] then the Vice President shall act as President, as in the case of the death or constitutional disability of the President. The person having the greatest number of votes as Vice President shall be the Vice President, if such number be a majority of the whole number of electors appointed, and if no person have a majority, then from the two highest numbers on the list, the Senate shall choose the Vice President; a quorum for the purpose shall consist of two-thirds of the whole number of senators, and a majority of the whole number shall be necessary to a choice. But no person constitutionally ineligible to the office of President shall be eligible to that of Vice President of the United States.

AMENDMENT 13 Slavery Abolished (1865)

Section 1. Abolition of slavery Neither slavery nor involuntary servitude, except as a punishment for crime whereof the party shall have been duly convicted, shall exist within the United States or any place subject to their jurisdiction.

Section 2. Enforcement Congress shall have the power to enforce this article by appropriate legislation.

Amendment 12 changed the Electoral College procedure for choosing a President. The most important change made by this amendment was that the presidential electors would vote for President and Vice President on separate ballots. In 1800, when only one ballot was used, Thomas Jefferson and Aaron Burr received the same number of votes, and the election had to be decided by the House of Representatives. To guard against this possibility in the future, Amendment 12 calls for separate ballots.

Chapter 14 describes the present-day Electoral College in action.

Thomas Jefferson, third President of the United States.

Amendment 13 is the first of three amendments that were a consequence of the Civil War. It states that slavery must end in the United States and its territories.

Congress may pass whatever laws are necessary to enforce Amendment 13. This statement, called an *enabling act*, is now commonly included in amendments.

By the definition of citizenship in Amendment 14, black Americans were granted citizenship. The first section provides that all persons born or naturalized in the United States and subject to this country's laws are citizens of the United States and of the state in which they live. State governments may not deprive anyone of due process of law or equal protection.

This section abolished the provision in Article 1, Section 2, which said that only three-fifths of the slaves should be counted as population.

Section 3 was designed to bar former leaders of the Confederacy from holding federal office.

Following emancipation, most Southern blacks became sharecroppers, working land owned by others.

AMENDMENT 14   Civil Rights Guaranteed (1868)

Section 1. Definition of citizenship   All persons born or naturalized in the United States, and subject to the jurisdiction thereof, are citizens of the United States and of the state wherein they reside. No state shall make or enforce any law which shall abridge the privileges or immunities of citizens of the United States; nor shall any state deprive any person of life, liberty, or property, without due process of law; nor deny to any person within its jurisdiction the equal protection of the laws.

Section 2. Apportionment of representatives   Representatives shall be apportioned among the several states according to their respective numbers, counting the whole number of persons in each state, [excluding Indians not taxed.] But when the right to vote at any election for the choice of electors for President and Vice President of the United States, representatives in Congress, the executive and judicial officers of a state, or the members of the legislature thereof, is denied to any of the [male] inhabitants of such state, [being twenty-one years of age] and citizens of the United States, or in any way abridged, except for participation in rebellion, or other crime, the basis of representation therein shall be reduced in the proportion which the number of such [male] citizens shall bear to the whole number of [male] citizens [twenty-one years of age] in such state.

Section 3. Restrictions on holding office   No person shall be a senator or representative in Congress, or elector of President and Vice President, or hold any office, civil or military, under the United States, or under any state, who, having previously taken an oath as a member of Congress, or as an officer of the United States, or as a member of any state legislature, or as an executive or judicial officer of any state, to support the Constitution of the United States, shall have engaged in insurrection or rebellion against the same, or given aid or comfort to the enemies thereof. But Congress may by vote of two-thirds of each house remove such disability.

Black members of Congress elected after the Civil War.

Section 4. Valid public debts of the United States The validity of the public debt of the United States, authorized by law, including debts incurred for payment of pensions and bounties for services in suppressing insurrection or rebellion, shall not be questioned. But neither the United States nor any state shall assume or pay any debt or obligation incurred in aid of insurrection or rebellion against the United States, or any claim for the loss or emancipation of any slave; but all such debts, obligations, and claims shall be held illegal and void.

This section was included to settle the question of debts incurred during the Civil War. All debts contracted by the United States were to be paid. Neither the United States nor any state government, however, was to pay the debts of the Confederacy. Moreover, no payment was to be made to former slave owners as compensation for slaves who were set free.

Section 5. Enforcement The Congress shall have power to enforce by appropriate legislation the provisions of this article.

AMENDMENT 15   Black Voting Rights (1870)

Section 1. The right of citizens of the United States to vote shall not be denied or abridged by the United States or by any state on account of race, color, or previous condition of servitude.

Amendment 15 sought to protect the right of citizens, particularly former slaves, to vote in federal and state elections.

Section 2. The Congress shall have power to enforce this article by appropriate legislation.

AMENDMENT 16   Income Tax (1913)

The Congress shall have power to lay and collect taxes on incomes, from whatever source derived, without apportionment among the several states and without regard to any census or enumeration.

Amendment 16 authorizes Congress to tax incomes. An amendment was necessary because in 1895 the Supreme Court had decided that an income tax law, passed by Congress a year earlier, was unconstitutional.

133

Amendment 17 changed Article I, Section 3, to allow the direct election of senators by popular vote. Anyone qualified to vote for a state representative may vote for United States senators.

AMENDMENT 17   Direct Election of Senators (1913)

Section 1. Election by the people   The Senate of the United States shall be composed of two senators from each state, elected by the people thereof, for six years; and each senator shall have one vote. The electors in each state shall have the qualifications requisite for electors of the most numerous branch of the state legislatures.

Section 2. Senate vacancies   When vacancies happen in the representation of any state in the Senate, the executive authority of such state shall issue writs of election to fill such vacancies: provided that the legislature of any state may empower the executive thereof to make temporary appointments until the people fill the vacancies by election as the legislature may direct.

Section 3. Effective date   This amendment shall not be so construed as to affect the election or term of any senator chosen before it becomes valid as part of the Constitution.

AMENDMENT 18   Prohibition (1919)

[**Section 1.**   After one year from the ratification of this article the manufacture, sale, or transportation of intoxicating liquors within, the importation thereof into, or the exportation thereof from the United States and all territory subject to the jurisdiction thereof for beverage purposes is hereby prohibited.

Section 2.   The Congress and the several states shall have concurrent power to enforce this article by appropriate legislation.

Section 3.   This article shall be inoperative unless it shall have been ratified as an amendment to the Constitution by the legislatures of the several states, as provided in the Constitution, within seven years from the date of the submission hereof to the states by the Congress.]

Amendment 18 forbade the manufacture, sale, or shipment of alcoholic beverages within the United States. Importing and exporting such beverages was also forbidden. Amendment 18 was later repealed by Amendment 21.

Federal agents destroying a still to enforce Prohibition.

AMENDMENT 19   Women's Voting Rights (1920)

Section 1.   The right of citizens of the United States to vote shall not be denied or abridged by the United States or by any state on account of sex.

Section 2.   The Congress shall have power to enforce this article by appropriate legislation.

AMENDMENT 20   Terms of Office and Presidential Succession (1933)

Section 1. Terms of office   The terms of the President and Vice President shall end at noon on the 20th day of January, and the terms of senators and representatives at noon on the 3rd day of January, of the years in which such terms would have ended if this article had not been ratified; and the terms of their successors shall then begin.

Section 2. Sessions of Congress   The Congress shall assemble at least once in every year, and such meeting shall begin at noon on the 3rd day of January, unless they shall by law appoint a different day.

Section 3. Presidential succession   If, at the time fixed for the beginning of the term of the President, the President-elect shall have died, the Vice President-elect shall become President. If a President shall not have been chosen before the time fixed for the beginning of his term, or if the President-elect shall have failed to qualify, then the Vice President-elect shall act as President until a President shall have qualified; and the Congress may by law provide for the case wherein neither a President-elect nor a Vice President-elect shall have qualified, declaring who shall then act as President, or the manner in which one who is to act shall be selected, and such person shall act accordingly until a President or a Vice President shall have qualified.

Section 4. House election of President   The Congress may by law provide for the case of the death of any of the persons from whom the House of Representatives may choose a President whenever the right of choice shall have devolved upon them, and for the case of the death of any of the persons from whom the Senate may choose a Vice President whenever the right of choice shall have devolved upon them.

Section 5. Effective date   Sections 1 and 2 shall take effect on the fifteenth day of October following the ratification of this article.

[**Section 6. Ratification**   This article shall be inoperative unless it shall have been ratified as an amendment to the Constitution by the legislatures of three-fourths of the several states within seven years from the date of its submission.]

Amendment 19 provides that women citizens may not be denied the right to vote in a federal or state election.

A suffragist rally.

When the Constitution was written, transportation and communication were slow. There was a long period, therefore, between the President's election (November) and inauguration (March). One purpose of Amendment 20 was to shorten that waiting period. The amendment established that the terms of the President and Vice President end at noon on January 20 following a presidential election. The terms of one-third of the senators and of all representatives, meanwhile, end at noon on January 3 in years ending in odd numbers. The new terms begin when the old terms end.

Section 2 provides that Congress must meet at least once a year, with the regular session beginning on January 3 unless Congress sets a different day.

Section 3 provides ways of filling the office of President in several emergencies.

Because the House of Representatives chooses the President if no candidate receives a majority of the electoral votes, Section 4 also gives Congress power to make a law to decide what to do if one of the candidates dies.

135

Amendment 21 repealed Amendment 18, putting an end to Prohibition. It was the only amendment submitted to special ratifying conventions instead of state legislatures.

Section 2 allows states or local governments to continue prohibition if they wish.

Amendment 22 set limits on the time a President may serve. No person may be elected President more than twice. A person who has served more than two years in the place of an elected President may be elected President only once. This limitation did not apply to President Truman, who was in office when Amendment 22 was proposed.

Presidents Washington, Jefferson, and Madison set the pattern of serving only two terms in office. Although Ulysses S. Grant and Theodore Roosevelt sought third terms, the precedent of serving only two terms was not broken until 1940, when Franklin D. Roosevelt was elected for a third term.

AMENDMENT 21   Repeal of Prohibition (1933)

Section 1. The eighteenth article of amendment to the Constitution of the United States is hereby repealed.

Section 2. State laws. The transportation or importation into any state, territory, or possession of the United States for delivery or use therein of intoxicating liquors, in violation of the laws thereof, is hereby prohibited.

[**Section 3.** This article shall be inoperative unless it shall have been ratified as an amendment to the Constitution by conventions in the several states, as provided in the Constitution, within seven years from the date of the submission hereof to the states by the Congress.]

AMENDMENT 22   Limits on Presidential Terms (1951)

Section 1. No person shall be elected to the office of the President more than twice, and no person who has held the office of President, or acted as President, for more than two years of a term to which some other person was elected President shall be elected to the office of the President more than once. But this article shall not apply to any person holding the office of President when this article was proposed by the Congress, and shall not prevent any person who may be holding the office of President, or acting as President, during the term within which this article becomes operative from holding the office of President, or acting as President during the remainder of such term.

[**Section 2.** This article shall be inoperative unless it shall have been ratified as an amendment to the Constitution by the legislatures of three-fourths of the several states within seven years from the date of its submission to the states by the Congress.]

A victorious Franklin D. Roosevelt with congratulatory mail after his sweeping 1936 election victory.

Celebrating the bicentennial of the Constitution, 1987.

AMENDMENT 23 Voting in the District of Columbia (1961)

Section 1. The District constituting the seat of government of the United States shall appoint, in such manner as the Congress may direct:

A number of electors of President and Vice President equal to the whole number of senators and representatives in Congress to which the District would be entitled if it were a state, but in no event more than the least populous state; they shall be in addition to those appointed by the states, but they shall be considered, for the purposes of the election of President and Vice President, to be electors appointed by a state; and they shall meet in the District and perform such duties as provided by the twelfth article of amendment.

Section 2. The Congress shall have power to enforce this article by appropriate legislation.

This amendment gave the residents of the District of Columbia the right to vote in presidential elections. Before Amendment 23 was adopted, residents of the District of Columbia had not voted for President and Vice President because the Constitution provided that only states should choose presidential electors.

AMENDMENT 24 Poll Tax Illegal (1964)

Section 1. The right of citizens of the United States to vote in any primary or other election for President or Vice President, for electors for President or Vice President, or for senator or representative in Congress, shall not be denied or abridged by the United States or any state by reason of failure to pay any poll tax or other tax.

Section 2. The Congress shall have power to enforce this article by appropriate legislation.

Amendment 24 prohibited using the poll tax to deny voting rights in federal elections. (The poll tax was a device used in some southern states to keep black voters from the polls.) In 1966, the Supreme Court ruled that payment of poll taxes was also an unconstitutional precondition for voting in state and local elections.

AMENDMENT 25 Presidential Disability (1967)

Section 1. Vice President In case of the removal of the President from office or of his death or resignation, the Vice President shall become President.

Amendment 25 clarifies Article 2, Section 1, which deals with filling vacancies in the presidency. It also establishes procedures to follow when the President is too ill to serve and when there is a vacancy in the office of Vice President.

137

With ratification of the 26th Amendment, the voting age was lowered to eighteen years.

Section 2. Replacing the Vice President Whenever there is a vacancy in the office of the Vice President, the President shall nominate a Vice President who shall take office upon confirmation by a majority vote of both Houses of Congress.

Section 3. Presidential inability to act Whenever the President transmits to the President pro tempore of the Senate and the Speaker of the House of Representatives his written declaration that he is unable to discharge the powers and duties of his office, and until he transmits to them a written declaration to the contrary, such powers and duties shall be discharged by the Vice President as Acting President.

Section 4. Determining presidential disability Whenever the Vice President and a majority of either the principal officers of the executive departments or of such other body as Congress may by law provide, transmit to the President pro tempore of the Senate and the Speaker of the House of Representatives their written declaration that the President is unable to discharge the powers and duties of his office, the Vice President shall immediately assume the powers and duties of the office as Acting President.

Thereafter, when the President transmits to the President pro tempore of the Senate and the Speaker of the House of Representatives his written declaration that no inability exists, he shall resume the powers and duties of his office unless the Vice President and a majority of either the principal officers of the executive department or of such other body as Congress may by law provide, transmit within four days to the President pro tempore of the Senate and the Speaker of the House of Representatives their written declaration that the President is unable to discharge the powers and duties of his office. Thereupon, Congress shall decide the issue, assembling within forty-eight hours for that purpose, if not in session. If the Congress, within twenty-one days after receipt of the latter written declaration, or, if Congress is not in session, within twenty-one days after Congress is required to assemble, determines by two-thirds vote of both Houses that the President is unable to discharge the powers and duties of his office, the Vice President shall continue to discharge the same as Acting President; otherwise, the President shall resume the powers and duties of his office.

AMENDMENT 26   Voting Age (1971)

Section 1. The right of citizens of the United States who are eighteen years of age or older to vote shall not be denied or abridged by the United States or by any state on account of age.

Section 2. The Congress shall have power to enforce this article by appropriate legislation.

AMENDMENT 27   Congressional Pay (1992)

No law, varying the compensation for the services of the Senators and Representatives, shall take effect, until an election of Representatives shall have intervened.

UNIT ★2★

CIVIL RIGHTS and CIVIL LIBERTIES

CHAPTER

5 CIVIL LIBERTIES: The First Amendment Freedoms

6 CIVIL LIBERTIES: Due Process of Law

7 CIVIL LIBERTIES: Equal Protection of the Law

139

UNIT 2

Civil Rights and Civil Liberties *(pp. 139–222)*

Unit Overview
Unit Two examines the civil rights and liberties enjoyed by United States citizens. In Chapter 5, students learn about the First Amendment freedoms of religion, speech, press, and assembly—what they are and how their meaning has been interpreted by the Supreme Court. Chapter 6 deals with the civil liberties guaranteed through "due process of law." These include limited investigation, rights of the accused, right to a fair trial, and right to privacy. Chapter 7 traces the progress in civil rights that has been made in this century. It describes the civil rights movement and discusses how, more and more, equal protection under the law is applied to all Americans.

CHAPTER 5
CIVIL LIBERTIES: THE FIRST AMENDMENT FREEDOMS
(pp. 140–165)

	Section Objectives	Section Resources
Section 1 **The First Amendment Guarantees Religious Freedom**	☐ describe how the First Amendment prevents the government from supporting specific religions ☐ explain how the "free exercise" clause has been interpreted	▲ SKILLS PRACTICE WORKSHEET **5** ● PRIMARY SOURCE WORKSHEETS **8–9** ● CITIZENSHIP WORKSHEET **2** ■ CONSTITUTIONAL ISSUES WORKSHEET **5** ■ SUPREME COURT DECISIONS **4–12**
Section 2 **The First Amendment Ensures Freedom of Speech**	☐ explain the three categories of free speech identified by the Supreme Court ☐ describe the legal limits of freedom of speech	■ SKILLS CHALLENGE WORKSHEET **5** ▲ TRANSPARENCY **15** ■ SUPREME COURT DECISIONS **13–17**
Section 3 **The First Amendment Protects Freedom of the Press**	☐ explain the importance of freedom of the press in a democracy ☐ distinguish between the protections given to the printed press and those given to radio and television	■ SUPREME COURT DECISIONS **18–19**
Section 4 **The First Amendment Allows Freedom of Assembly**	☐ describe the kinds of assembly given First Amendment protection ☐ describe the limits of freedom of assembly	■ SUPREME COURT DECISIONS **20-21**

Essential Elements

The list below shows Essential Elements relevant to this chapter.
(The complete list of Essential Elements appears in the introductory
pages of this Teacher's Edition.)

Section 1: 1D, 2A 2C, 2D, 5A, 5B, 5C, 6G, 6H, 8A

Citizenship Skills feature (p. 149): 6E

Section 2: 2A, 2D, 6B, 6E, 6H

Section 3: 1C, 4B, 4D, 5A, 6A, 6G, 6H

Section 4: 2D, 5C, 6B, 6C, 6D

Chapter Review: 2A, 2D, 5C, 6A, 6B, 6G, 6H, 8A, 8B, 8C, 8E

> Section Resources are keyed for student abilities:
> ▲ = Basic
> ● = All Levels
> ■ = Average/Advanced

Homework Options

Each section contains activities labeled "Guided/Independent Practice," "Reteaching/Correctives," and "Enrichment/Extension." You may wish to choose from among these activities when assigning homework.

Students Acquiring English Activities

Divide the class into groups and have them use the following outline to chart two important cases in each of the following areas: freedom of religion, freedom of speech, freedom of the press, and freedom of assembly.

(1) Issue:
(2) Civil or Criminal?
(3) Names of opposing sides:
(4) Verdict:
(5) Appeal:
(6) Final verdict (and date):
   Have students dramatize at least one of the cases by portraying the individuals involved and writing dialogues to explain the opposing sides.

   LISTENING/SPEAKING: Have students use this same outline as they watch the videotape, *The Road to the Supreme Court: The Webster Case.* Students should complete the outline and make notes to prepare for a classroom discussion on the case.

Case Studies

When teaching this chapter, you may use Case Study 2, which debates censorship of rock albums; Case Study 3, which addresses the issue of religion in public schools; or Case Study 13, which deals with dress codes in public schools. (Case Studies may be found following p. 510.)

Teacher Bibliography

Abernathy, M. Glenn. *Civil Liberties Under the Constitution.* 5th ed. University of South Carolina Press, 1989. Covers the Bill of Rights and its guarantees.

_____. *The Right of Assembly and Association.* 2nd ed., rev. University of South Carolina Press, 1981. A close look at First Amendment rights.

McBrien, Richard P. *Caesar's Coin: Religion and Politics in America.* Macmillan, 1987. Discusses the role and limits of religion in public life.

Student Bibliography

Hentoff, Nat. *The First Freedom.* Delacorte, 1988. Discusses the history of free speech in America.

Miller, William Lee. *The First Liberty: Religion and the American Republic.* Knopf, 1986. Studies the constitutional guarantees of religious liberty.

Warsaw, Thayer S. *Religion, Education, and the Supreme Court.* Abingdon, 1979. An examination of what the Supreme Court has said concerning religion in the schools.

Literature

Bradbury, Ray. *Fahrenheit 451.* Simon & Schuster, 1967. In a futuristic Fascist state, books are burned.

Hobson, Laura Keane Zametkin. *Gentleman's Agreement.* Simon & Schuster, 1947. A magazine editor poses as a Jew and experiences anti-Semitism firsthand.

Woods, Donald. *Asking for Trouble: Autobiography of a Banned Journalist.* Peter Smith, 1988. Woods, a journalist who spoke out forcefully against apartheid in South Africa, had his writing censored, travel restricted, and was prohibited from meeting with more than one person even in his own home.

CHAPTER RESOURCES

Study Guide/Review 5
Workbook Chapter 5
Chapter 5 Test, Forms A–C

Films and Videotapes*

Freedom of Speech. Rev. ed. (Series title: *Bill of Rights in Action.*) 17 min. Barr, 1982. f, v. The complexities of constitutional freedoms and guarantees are examined, using the case of an unpopular speaker charged with disturbing the peace and inciting a riot.

Life and Liberty . . . For All Those Who Believe. 28 min. Films, 1983. f, v. Questions whether religious groups can use religious freedom to ban books, thereby curtailing others' freedom of speech.

Religious Freedom in America's Beginnings. 14 min. Coronet, 1971. f. A brief look at the relation between church and state in the sixteenth century in various countries and in the American colonies. The roles of Penn, Locke, Madison, Jefferson, and others in upholding the principle of religious freedom are explored.

Software*

The Research Companion: Supreme Court Decisions (Apple). Focus. Students become legal assistants to a Supreme Court justice, with access to a database on landmark cases.

U.S. Constitution Then and Now (Apple). Scholastic. Students assume the role of delegates to the Constitutional Convention.

* For a complete guide to audiovisual sources, see page T22.

139B

CHAPTER 5

Civil Liberties: The First Amendment Freedoms *(pp. 140–165)*

Chapter 5 examines the individual freedoms guaranteed in the First Amendment, including religious freedom, freedom of speech, freedom of assembly, and freedom of the press, as well as limitations on these freedoms.

Chapter Objectives

After students complete this chapter, they will be able to:

1. Describe how the First Amendment prevents the government from supporting specific religions.

2. Explain how the "free exercise" clause has been interpreted.

3. Explain the three categories of free speech identified by the Supreme Court.

4. Describe the legal limits of freedom of speech.

5. Explain the importance of freedom of the press in a democracy.

6. Distinguish between the protections given to the printed press and those given to radio and television.

7. Describe the kinds of assembly given First Amendment protection.

8. Describe the limits of freedom of assembly.

CHAPTER

5

CIVIL LIBERTIES: The First Amendment Freedoms

If there is any fixed star in our constitutional constellation, it is that no official, high or petty, can prescribe what shall be orthodox in politics, nationalism, religion, or other matters of opinion. . . .

Justice Robert H. Jackson
West Virginia Board of Education v. Barnette (1943)

140

Photo
Church service.

In 1958 the Herricks School District of New York voted to require students and teachers to recite a 22-word, nondenominational prayer written by the state Board of Regents. For Mary Harte, school board member, the decision was a victory. She believed that school prayer was an exercise of free religious expression and an important tradition in American education. To Lawrence Roth, the father of two students, public prayer had no place in public schools. "My basic feeling," he explained, "was that if the state could tell us what to pray and when to pray and how to pray, there was no stopping."

Lawrence Roth and Mary Harte agreed that the Bill of Rights guaranteed freedom of religion, but they disagreed on what that meant. Their disagreement went to the Supreme Court in *Engel v. Vitale* (1962), which outlawed prayer in public schools. Freedom of religion is a civil liberty mentioned in the First Amendment, which also guarantees freedom of speech, the press, and assembly. This chapter discusses how these liberties have been defined.

CHAPTER OUTLINE

1 The First Amendment Guarantees Religious Freedom

Roots of Religious Tolerance
The Establishment Clause
Religion and the Schools
The Free Exercise Clause

2 The First Amendment Ensures Freedom of Speech

Principles of Free Speech
Limits on Free Speech

3 The First Amendment Protects Freedom of the Press

Press Censorship
Motion Pictures, Radio, and TV
Other Free Press Issues

4 The First Amendment Allows Freedom of Assembly

The Right to Meet Peacefully
Unpopular Assemblies

141

SECTION 1

The First Amendment Guarantees Religious Freedom *(pp. 142–148)*

Section Objectives

☐ describe how the First Amendment prevents the government from supporting specific religions

☐ explain how the "free exercise" clause has been interpreted

Vocabulary

civil liberties, establishment clause, free exercise clause, conscientious objector

FOCUS

● Ask volunteers to suggest laws and public policies that involve questions of religious freedom. (Prayer in the legislature, tax exemption for churches, prayer in school, laws requiring people to swear on a Bible in a trial, laws exempting clergy from the military draft, religious groups preaching in public parks, etc.)

Do you think that the "wall of separation" between church and state in the United States is too high? Not high enough? At the right level? Explain your position.

SECTION 1

The First Amendment Guarantees Religious Freedom

ACCESS **The Main Ideas**

1 How does the First Amendment prevent the government from supporting specific religions?   *pages 142–146*

2 What has the "free exercise" clause been interpreted to mean?   *pages 147–148*

When Thomas Jefferson died, the great President, architect, statesman, and diplomat asked that he be remembered for writing two documents. In keeping with his wishes, Jefferson's tombstone memorializes his great gifts to this country: "Here was buried Thomas Jefferson, Author of the Declaration of American Independence, of the Statute of Virginia for religious freedom. . . ."

Jefferson's great pride in the Virginia Statute of Religious Liberty, quoted on the next page, was well founded. The document served as the basis of the constitutional guarantee of freedom of religion—the first civil liberty mentioned in the Bill of Rights. (**Civil liberties** are the personal rights of individuals that are protected from government interference.)

1D, 2A, 2C, 6G

Roots of Religious Tolerance

Though many of the early New England colonists crossed the Atlantic to escape religious persecution, they did not themselves tolerate differing religious beliefs. Most colonies had an official church, and people who held different beliefs were generally unwelcome. Only a few colonies, such as Rhode Island, Maryland, and Pennsylvania, were fairly tolerant of different religions.

An increase in religious freedom

The idea of toleration for *all* beliefs developed gradually. By the time of the Revolutionary War, many people thought there should be fewer ties between the church and the government. For example, in 1776 Virginia proclaimed a Declaration of Rights, which included an article providing religious freedom. Nevertheless,

prominent Virginians such as George Washington and Patrick Henry favored a tax to support all Christian churches in the state. Yet Thomas Jefferson and James Madison were able to convince the Virginia legislature to pass the Statute of Religious Liberty.

Constitutional provisions

The principle of religious toleration established in Virginia influenced the writers of the Constitution. The text of the Constitution includes the promise that "no religious test shall ever be required as a qualification to any office or public trust under the United States." That is, government posts cannot be limited to members of a certain religion.

Many people still feared, however, that the new government might establish an official church and abridge religious freedom. A constitutional guarantee of freedom of religion was the first thing to be mentioned when the Bill of Rights was added in 1791. The First Amendment begins, "Congress shall make no law respecting an *establishment* of religion or prohibiting the *free exercise* thereof. . . ."

The motto "In God We Trust" was first used on a U.S. two-cent piece in 1864, at the request of Treasury Secretary Salmon P. Chase. Today both bills and coins must carry these words.

Background: *History*
Rhode Island, Maryland, and Pennsylvania offered haven for Roman Catholics, Jews, Quakers, and Protestant minorities from various European countries.

The words italicized above point out that the First Amendment has two closely related but separate provisions — the **establishment clause** and the **free exercise clause**.

2D, 6G, 6H

The Establishment Clause

The establishment clause of the First Amendment forbids government from making any law about "an establishment of religion." When constitutional questions arise about the government's role in religion, the Supreme Court must decide what specific actions this clause prevents.

"A wall of separation"

In a 1947 Supreme Court case, Justice Hugo Black set forth a definition of the establishment clause that is still generally followed. In Black's words,

> Neither a state nor the federal government can set up a church. Neither can pass laws which aid one religion, aid all religions, or prefer one religion over another. Neither can force . . . a person to go to or to remain away from church against his will, or force him to profess a belief or disbelief in any religion.
>
> *(Everson v. Board of Education)*

In addition, said Black, government may not take part in the affairs of religious groups or impose taxes to support them. Quoting Thomas Jefferson, Black said that the purpose of the establishment clause is to create "a wall of separation between church and state."

Traditional religious practices

Although in principle there is a wall of separation between religion and government, in reality the beliefs and values of the Judeo-Christian tradition have been an important influence in American life and culture. "In God We Trust" has been inscribed on United States coins since 1864. The Pledge of Allegiance contains the words "one nation, under God." Most years since 1957, the President has declared a National Day of Prayer. Congress and most state legislatures open each day's meeting with a prayer led by their chaplain. The Supreme Court begins each session with the words, "God save the United States and this honorable Court."

The Virginia Statute of Religious Liberty (1786)

In the 1700's, the idea of separation between church and state was still new. Unlike many American political traditions that had been brought over from England, the principle of religious liberty developed in the colonies. Virginia, in fact, had in 1776 begun to repeal laws requiring specific religious observances. Though opponents from many churches viewed this trend as extreme, Jefferson, Madison, George Mason, and other political leaders vigorously persisted in the fight for religious freedom. In January 1786, after long debate, the Virginia legislature passed this statute, the most extensive guarantee of religious liberty of the time.

> An Act for establishing Religious Freedom
> I. Whereas Almighty God hath created the mind free. . .
> II. Be it enacted by the General Assembly, that no man shall be compelled to frequent or support any religious worship, place, or ministry whatsoever, nor shall it be enforced, restrained, molested, or burdened in his body or goods, nor shall otherwise suffer on account of his religious opinions or belief; but that all men shall be free to profess, and by argument to maintain, their opinion in matters of religion, and that the same shall in no wise diminish, enlarge, or affect their civil capacities.

1. What is meant by the phrase "the same shall in no wise diminish, enlarge, or affect their civil capacities"?
2. How did the Virginia Statute influence the writers of the Constitution of the United States?
3. Why might some clergy have resisted such a statute, when it freed them from government regulation?

143

● CRITICAL THINKING Ask students to paraphrase Justice Black's opinion in the Supreme Court ruling in *Engel v. Vitale*. (The establishment clause forbids the government to write official prayers.) Tell them that the only dissent came from Justice Potter Stewart, who said: "I cannot see how an 'official religion' is established by letting those who want to say a prayer say it. On the contrary, I think that to deny the wish of these school children to join in reciting this prayer is to deny them the opportunity of sharing in the spiritual heritage of our Nation." **Do you agree with Black or Stewart? Why?**

Do practices like these amount to "an establishment of religion"? This question came to the Supreme Court in a 1983 case about whether the Nebraska state legislature could legally employ a chaplain (*Marsh v. Chambers*). The Court observed that the custom of starting legislative sessions with a prayer had become "part of the fabric of our society." Chief Justice Warren Burger said that the practice simply acknowledged "beliefs widely held among the people of this country."

The same reasoning applied in a 1984 case concerning a Christmas display in Pawtucket, Rhode Island. For forty years Pawtucket's city officials had put up a nativity scene, a Christmas tree, and a Santa Claus with reindeer near the downtown shopping center. Several residents objected to the nativity scene, saying that it amounted to government support of religion. The Supreme Court, however, ruled that the display did not directly benefit any religion. Because it included non-religious symbols of Christmas, such as Santa Claus and reindeer, it was simply an acceptable observance of a national holiday.

Tax exemptions

In judging questions involving the establishment clause, the courts must look carefully at whether the result of government actions is toleration for religion or actual encouragement. Historically, neither federal, state, nor local governments impose taxes on church-owned property used for religious purposes. This policy is based on the belief that taxing churches would threaten religious freedom. In John Marshall's famous words, "the power to tax involves the power to destroy." (Church-owned property used for business or profit-making activities *is* taxed.) On the other hand, some people charge that by allowing tax exemptions, the government is encouraging religion.

In a 1970 case, Frederick Walz, a New York City taxpayer, challenged a law that made churches exempt from paying local property taxes. Walz maintained that such tax exemptions not only raised his own property taxes but also represented public support for religion. The Supreme Court, however, ruled that such tax exemptions are not intended to *support* religion, only to show government's "benevolent neutral-

ity." Therefore, tax exemptions do not violate the Constitution's establishment clause (*Walz v. Tax Commission of the City of New York*).

A similar controversy arose a few years later in Hardenburgh, New York, a small community in the Catskill Mountains. Between 1971 and 1976, Hardenburgh's property taxes soared. Because the town had become a haven for religious and nonprofit organizations, thousands of acres of land were no longer taxable. A group of Zen Buddhists bought 1,000 acres. Dungkar Gompa, an order of Tibetan monks, purchased 780 acres. The Jehovah's Witnesses owned 8,000 acres. The lost property tax revenues had to be made up by the townspeople, who suddenly found that their taxes had more than tripled.

Angered by the increase in taxes, most of Hardenburgh's 236 residents became "ordained ministers" in the Universal Life Church, a mail-order religious organization. As ministers, they declared their homes, barns, and land as church property — and therefore tax exempt. The state of New York quickly challenged this action in

One of the issues raised by the establishment clause is whether the government can provide transportation for parochial school students.

Cross-reference
The chapters in this unit cite many Supreme Court cases, opinions, and dissents. The Citizenship Skills lesson on p. 149, "Understanding the Language of the Law,"

guides students in reading and understanding these cases.

Background: *Constitutional Heritage* The Pawtucket Christmas-display case was

Lynch v. Donnelly (1984). Critics referred to the decision as the "two-reindeer rule."

court and won. The court held that the residents were more concerned with avoiding taxes than with practicing religion. (In 1984, the Internal Revenue Service declared that the Universal Life Church itself would no longer be recognized as a religious organization for tax purposes.)

5B, 5C, 6H

Religion and the Schools

The greatest number of controversies over the establishment clause have concerned religion and the schools, both public and private. There are several different issues: Can government use tax money to aid private religious schools? Are religion courses, prayers, and Bible readings allowed in state-supported public schools? In judging these emotional issues, the courts decide where the wall of separation is to be built.

Government aid to parochial schools

The Supreme Court first considered the question of state aid for parochial (church-supported) schools in 1947, in the case of *Everson v. Board of Education.* Under a New Jersey law that provided transportation for children to and from school, the state reimbursed parents of parochial school students for their bus fare. Some taxpayers objected that these payments were government aid to religion, but the Supreme Court upheld the state law. The Court reasoned that the primary purpose of the law was to ensure the safety of children, not to aid religion. This reasoning became known as the "child benefit theory." (It was in this case that Justice Black gave the definition of the establishment clause quoted on page 143.)

The Court later set up guidelines for determining how government can aid church-affiliated schools without violating the establishment clause (*Lemon v. Kurtzman,* 1971). Such aid must neither promote nor harm religion. In addition, the government must avoid "excessive entanglement" with religion.

Under these guidelines, the courts have ruled that tax money may be used to provide children in parochial schools with free lunches, health services, and textbooks (except for courses in religion). On the other hand, public schools may not lend maps, projectors, and record players to parochial schools, for this equipment could be used to teach religion. The

Religious instruction, such as the lessons Jewish students receive in this class, must be given outside public school property.

Court has also not allowed the states to pay the salaries of parochial school teachers, ruling that it is "excessive entanglement" with religion.

Religious instruction in public schools

Another issue involving religion and schools is the constitutionality of "released-time" religious education programs. In these programs, public school students can receive religious instruction at certain times during school hours. The first case questioning this practice arose in the late 1940's in Champaign, Illinois. There, public school children, with their parents' consent, took religious education classes once a week on school grounds. Children attended either Protestant, Catholic, or Jewish religion courses or went to study hall. The teachers were supervised by school officials.

In *McCollum v. Board of Education* (1948), the Supreme Court held that giving such instruction on public school property violated the establishment clause. Justice Black declared that the program unquestionably used the "tax-supported public school system to aid religious groups to spread their faith." The *McCollum* decision sent shock waves through many communities with similar programs.

145

Critical Thinking

● *Do you agree with the Supreme Court's decision that giving religious instruction on public school property violates the establishment clause? Explain your answer.* (Students who agree may claim that using public property for religious instruction constitutes support of that religion; students who disagree may claim that if all religions are taught, then no one religion is being "established.")

A few years later, New York City's released-time program was challenged in a seemingly similar case (*Zorach v. Clauson,* 1952). The Court's decision in this case shows the careful distinctions that it must make in First Amendment cases. New York's program was constitutional, the Court said, because students left school to attend religious classes *off* the school grounds. Therefore, the program involved "neither religious instruction in public school classrooms nor the expenditure of public funds."

The Court later made some exceptions to the ban on using school property for religious activities. In 1977 an evangelical Christian group, Cornerstone, sued the University of Missouri (Kansas City) for the right to hold religious services on campus. Cornerstone argued that religious groups deserved the same freedom of expression given other campus groups. The Supreme Court agreed (*Widmar v. Vincent,* 1981). In addition, Congress in 1984 passed a law that granted student religious groups the right to hold meetings on elementary and secondary school grounds during non-school hours.

Prayer in the schools

One very emotional church-state issue is the question of prayer in the public schools. For years, children in many public schools began each day with a prayer. In New York state, the Board of Regents wrote a prayer for school use.

The parents of ten public school children in New Hyde Park, N.Y., objected to the Regents' prayer and began the first case on this issue. In *Engel v. Vitale* (1962), the parents argued that the prayer violated the establishment clause. A majority of the Supreme Court agreed. Justice Black delivered the majority opinion:

> We think that by using its public school system to encourage recitation of the Regents' prayer, the state of New York has adopted a practice wholly inconsistent with the establishment clause. . . . We think that . . . in this country it is no part of the business of government to compose official prayers for any group of the American people to recite. . . .

In 1992 the Court further restricted school prayer by ruling that prayers at public school graduations were unconstitutional (*Lee v. Weisman,* 1992).

Other school issues

Closely related to the school prayer issue is the question of Bible readings in public schools, also a tradition in some places. In 1963 the Supreme Court banned this practice in two companion cases — *Abington School District v. Schempp* and *Murray v. Curlett.*

The *Abington* case involved a Pennsylvania state requirement that "at least ten verses from the Holy Bible, shall be read without comment, at the opening of each . . . school day." The Schempps were Unitarians and objected to certain literal readings from the Bible. In the second case, the Murrays, who were atheists, objected to a Baltimore law that called for the "reading, without comment, of a chapter in the Holy Bible and/or the use of the Lord's Prayer."

In both cases the Court ruled that reading from the Bible in public schools violated the establishment clause, even if students could be excused from the readings. The Court again emphasized that government must be neutral — it must neither support nor oppose religion. It pointed out also that students could study the Bible as literature or history, but it could not be used in a form of worship.

Several other state laws on education have been declared unconstitutional under the establishment clause. In 1968 the Court struck down an Arkansas statute that prohibited public schools from teaching evolution rather than the Biblical story of creation. The Court ruled that the law was not "religiously neutral." In 1985 the Court overturned an Alabama law that allowed teachers to hold moments of silent prayer in class (*Wallace v. Jaffree*). This decision affected similar laws in 23 states. Moments of silence not designated for prayer, however, were not affected by that decision.

A constitutional amendment?

The Supreme Court has consistently ruled that public school prayers, Bible readings, and the like violate the establishment clause. In an effort to overturn the Court's interpretation, several groups have supported a constitutional amendment to allow "voluntary prayers" in public schools. That amendment has failed to secure the necessary two-thirds approval in Congress. Nevertheless, the controversy over school prayer and other religious issues continues.

Background: *Constitutional Heritage* The case that allowed the teaching of evolution was *Epperson v. Arkansas* (1968).

Cross-reference
The methods of proposing and ratifying amendments to the Constitution are discussed in Chapter 3, pp. 70–73.

The Free Exercise Clause

The right to worship freely

A Wisconsin law once required all parents to send their children to high school. This law brought protests from the Amish, a Protestant group whose centuries-old religious beliefs compel them to remain apart from modern society. In 1972 the Supreme Court declared that the state of Wisconsin could not require Amish children to attend school past the eighth grade (*Wisconsin v. Yoder*). The Court ruled that the law interfered with the Amish people's freedom to put their religious beliefs into practice. Similarly, in *Sherbert v. Verner* (1963), the Court ruled that a Seventh-Day Adventist could not be denied unemployment benefits because she refused to work on Saturday (her Sabbath day).

These two rulings were based on the free exercise clause of the First Amendment. While the establishment clause keeps the government from supporting religion, the free exercise clause prevents the government from *restricting* people's religious practices. It guarantees people the right to believe and worship as they wish, without government interference.

Limits on freedom of religion

Despite the First Amendment guarantee of religious freedom, the courts have consistently allowed some limits on the free exercise of religion. Religious freedom does not give anyone the right to infringe on the health, safety, welfare, or morals of other people or of society as a whole. The first significant ruling of this kind was more than a century ago, in *Reynolds v. United States* (1879).

Reynolds, a Mormon living in Utah, was convicted of marrying two women, thus breaking a federal law. Because the Mormon church at that time approved of polygamy (having more than one spouse), Reynolds contended that the law violated his religious freedom. In this case, the Supreme Court ruled that religious freedom does have its limits. The Court held that "It was never intended that the First Amendment . . . could be invoked as protection for the punishment of acts inimical to the peace, good order, and morals of society."

Since *Reynolds,* other laws that seemed to limit religious freedom have been upheld. Figure 5–1 lists some of them. In many such cases, individual religious beliefs come into conflict with other deeply held principles or with the concerns of society or the nation. In wartime, for example, the country's need for military personnel may be given precedence over the personal beliefs of a **conscientious objector**, who refuses military service because of his opposition to war.

The flag-salute cases

During the 1930's and 1940's, seventeen states passed laws requiring public school children to salute the American flag at the beginning of each school day. This practice was challenged by members of Jehovah's Witnesses, a religious sect that interprets the Bible very strictly. To the

Court decisions have protected Amish families' freedom to raise their children in a traditional religion and way of life.

ENRICHMENT/EXTENSION

■ Ask students to create a political cartoon reflecting their opinion about the value and nature of the "wall of separation" between church and state. Suggest that they refer to Study Skill 5 in the Handbook of Basic Skills on pp. 781–782.

Have students complete **Constitutional Issues Worksheet 5,** which has them examine the limits on individual rights.

You may also want students to complete **Supreme Court Decisions 4–10,** which deal with cases involving the establishment clause, **Supreme Court Decision 11,** which deals with *Wisconsin v. Yoder,* and **Supreme Court Decision 12,** which deals with *Reynolds v. United States.*

Background:

Multiculturalism A famous conscientious objector was four-time heavyweight boxing champion Muhammad Ali, who first won the championship under the name Cassius Clay. In 1967 Ali was stripped of his title for refusing to be inducted into the armed forces. In 1971 the Supreme Court reversed his conviction for draft evasion, holding that his religious beliefs qualified him as a conscientious objector and prevented him from fighting in a war.

The symbol ♟ denotes active participation strategies.

Activities are keyed for student abilities:
▲ = Basic
● = All Levels
■ = Average/Advanced

Section 1 Review Answers

1. (a), (b), and **(c)** Establishment clause.

2. (a) Yes, but church-owned property used for profit is taxable. **(b)** Yes. **(c)** No. **(d)** No, but courses in religion may be taught off school grounds and religious groups may meet on school property after hours. **(e)** No.

3. When they infringe on public health, safety, welfare, or morals.

4. (a) Whether the government's interest in requiring a flag salute outweighed the students' right to freedom of religion. **(b)** Although the government has a legitimate interest in encouraging patriotism, citizens cannot be forced to act a certain way.

Critical thinking Students should justify their opinions on the basis of the establishment clause or the free exercise clause, and may wish to refer to Justice Black's statement on p. 143.

CLOSURE

● Have students write a thesis statement for each of the three headings in this section. Then have students read Section 2, noting the types of, and limits on, free speech.

★ Parents who deny medical treatment to their sick children on religious grounds may be prosecuted as criminals. (*People v. Pierson*, 1903)

★ Poisonous snakes may not be used in religious ceremonies. (*Bunn v. North Carolina*, 1949)

★ Orthodox Jewish merchants may be compelled to observe Sunday closing laws (so-called "blue laws") even though Sunday is not their Sabbath. (*Braunfeld v. Brown*, 1961)

★ The Amish cannot avoid paying Social Security taxes even though paying taxes is against their faith. (*United States v. Lee*, 1982)

★ Religious leaders who evade paying income taxes are subject to imprisonment. (*United States v. Sun Myung Moon*, 1982)

★ Religious colleges that practice racial discrimination can be denied tax exemptions. (*Bob Jones University v. United States*, 1983)

★ Jewish men may not wear yarmulkes (skullcaps) in violation of military uniform regulations. (*Goldman v. Weinberger*, 1986)

Figure 5–1 LIMITS SET BY THE COURTS ON RELIGIOUS PRACTICES 5B

Gobitis family, saluting the flag seemed like worshipping a pagan idol, and they told their children not to comply. When Lillian and William, who were 10 and 12, refused to salute the American flag, they were expelled from school.

The Gobitis family argued that the law violated the free exercise clause. They cited the Biblical commandments, "Thou shalt have no other gods before me" and "Thou shalt not make unto thee any graven image." But in *Minersville [Pa.] School District v. Gobitis* (1940), the Supreme Court ruled that the flag-salute law promoted "national unity," which was "the basis of national security."

The *Gobitis* ruling was widely criticized by legal scholars and the news media. Just three years later, the Court dramatically reversed its decision. (Three of the justices, in fact, stated that the *Gobitis* decision had been a mistake.) The 1943 case, *West Virginia Board of Education v. Barnette,* involved other Jehovah's Witnesses, who refused to obey West Virginia's flag-salute law. In this case, the Court noted the importance of national unity but declared that government

should not force citizens to carry out "patriotic ceremonies" unless they wanted to. According to Justice Jackson (who was quoted at the beginning of this chapter),

> We think the action of the local authorities in compelling the flag salute and pledge transcends constitutional limitations on their power and invades the sphere of intellect and spirit which it is the purpose of the First Amendment to our Constitution to reserve from all official control.

SECTION 1 REVIEW

Vocabulary and key terms

civil liberties (142) establishment clause (143)
freedom of religion (142) free exercise clause (143)
Virginia Statute of conscientious objector (147)
  Religious Liberty (142, 143)

For review

1. Which clause in the First Amendment prevents government from (a) forcing a person to attend church? (b) requiring prayers in public schools? (c) buying textbooks used for teaching religion? 6H
2. What did the Supreme Court decide in each of the following cases? Explain any special conditions. (a) Can the government exempt a church from paying property tax? (b) Can a city put up a Christmas display? (c) Can state government pay the salaries of parochial school teachers? (d) Can religion courses be taught in public school classrooms? (e) Can state officials write a prayer for students to say in school? 2D
3. According to the Supreme Court, when can the government place limits on religious practices? 6G
4. (a) What was the issue in the *Gobitis* and *Barnette* cases? (b) What was the Court's reason for changing its opinion on this issue? 8A

Critical thinking

EXAMINING BASIC PRINCIPLES Review the five cases referred to in question 2. Do you disagree with the Supreme Court decision in any of them? Why? 8A

Figure 5–1
● Ask different students to choose one practice from the list and explain how it infringes on public health, safety, welfare, or morals.

Understanding the Language of the Law

If you watch television programs about lawyers or police, you are probably familiar with quite a few legal terms. As you read about the many court cases in this textbook, you will need to know the exact meaning of these and many other words.

In general, court cases fall into two categories: criminal and civil. In a *criminal case,* a law has been broken, which is considered a crime against society. The person accused of the crime is the *defendant.* The government, which protects society, is always the *prosecution* in criminal cases. The prosecution tries to prove that the defendant is guilty.

Civil cases involve disputes between individuals or businesses. One party, the *plaintiff,* believes it has been wronged and brings a suit, or *sues,* in court to settle its claim. As in criminal cases, the party brought to court is the defendant.

All court cases are identified by the names of the parties involved (such as *Marbury v. Madison*). The *v.* stands for the Latin word *versus,* meaning "against," but it is usually pronounced simply as "v." In criminal cases, the name of the prosecution is always listed first, and the defendant last. Because it is the government that prosecutes criminal cases, the first party named in a criminal case is always either a state or the United States. Thus, in a case called *Nevada v. Jones,* Nevada is the prosecution and Jones is the defendant. In civil cases, the plaintiff's name comes before the defendant's.

After the court hands down its decision, or *verdict,* one of the parties may want a higher court to review the judgment. This is called an *appeal,* and the party who seeks the appeal is called the *appellant.* The name of the appellant comes first in the case name. If, in the example above, Jones were to appeal his conviction, the case name would become *Jones v. Nevada.* Almost all cases that reach the U.S. Supreme Court are appeals.

The Supreme Court has nine judges, or *justices* (including the Chief Justice). A simple majority, five justices, must agree for a decision to stand. Important Supreme Court decisions are accompanied by a written explanation, called the *majority opinion,* which gives the reasons for the Court's verdict. A justice who disagrees with the verdict may write a *dissenting opinion,* explaining why he or she disagrees. Supreme Court opinions and dissents are often eloquently written and widely quoted documents.

Follow-up

1. Make up a likely name for (a) a civil case, (b) a criminal case, and (c) an appeal. Explain your answers.
2. Make a table of five Supreme Court cases discussed in this unit. Who are the plaintiffs and the defendants? Write a sentence or two to summarize the majority opinion in each.

CITIZENSHIP SKILLS

149

Follow-up Answers
1. **(a)** (*Plaintiff's name*) v. (*defendant's name*).
(b) (*State name or U.S.*) v. (*defendant's name*).
(c) (*Appellant's name*) v. (*other party's name*).

2. Students may choose from Chapters 5–7, and may wish to refer to the Supreme Court Cases list on pp. 820–824.

The symbol 👥 denotes active participation strategies.

Activities are keyed for student abilities:
▲ = Basic
● = All Levels
■ = Average/Advanced

SECTION 2

The First Amendment Ensures Freedom of Speech *(pp. 150–155)*

Section Objectives

☐ explain the three categories of free speech identified by the Supreme Court

☐ describe the legal limits of freedom of speech

Vocabulary

pure speech, speech-plus, symbolic speech, sedition, defamation, slander, libel

 FOCUS

● Have each student come to the board and write one sentence explaining why free speech is important in a democracy. (*Example:* Freedom of speech gives people a chance to debate issues and criticize officials, both necessary to a healthy democracy.)

 SECTION 2

The First Amendment Ensures Freedom of Speech

ACCESS | **The Main Ideas**

1 What are the three categories of free speech identified by the Supreme Court?
pages 150–151

2 What are the legal limits of freedom of speech?
pages 151–154

In the 1930's, the Supreme Court considered the question of which rights guaranteed by the Constitution were most fundamental to the American people. To Justice Benjamin Cardozo, a brilliant and influential legal mind, the answer was clear. "Freedom of expression is the matrix, the indispensable condition, of nearly every other form of freedom," he wrote.

Do you agree? What do you think of when you think of your most fundamental rights?

Principles of Free Speech

The founders of the United States believed that free speech was a cornerstone of democracy. To support this principle, the First Amendment was written to include the promise that no law passed by Congress would abridge "the freedom of speech." In a 1927 ruling, Supreme Court Justice Louis D. Brandeis eloquently explained this idea:

> [The Founders] believed that freedom to think as you will and to speak as you think are means indispensable to the discovery and spread of political truth; that without free speech and assembly, discussion would be futile; . . . that public discussion is a political duty; and that this should be a fundamental principle of . . . government.

What "freedom of speech" actually means has been an issue in many Supreme Court cases. One important point has been made clear: "speech" can involve different forms of expression. Specifically, the Supreme Court has distinguished three types of speech: *pure speech, speech-plus,* and *symbolic speech.*

150

Pure speech

Communication by the spoken word alone is called **pure speech**. It includes face-to-face discussions, speeches at public meetings, telephone conversations, classroom debates, and most things said on television or radio. Pure speech may be dry and boring or dramatic and emotional. Two elements set it apart from other types of speech. First, pure speech relies solely on *words* to convey ideas or emotions. Second, the listener or audience usually participates voluntarily. Therefore, pure speech typically does not interfere with other people's rights.

Speech plus action

Speech combined with some kind of action is called, not surprisingly, **speech-plus**. The "plus" may take the form of marching, singing, picketing, or chanting slogans. These actions are intended to call attention to the speech—to involve bystanders, uninterested people, or even hostile groups. The "speech" component of speech-plus generally is constitutionally protected. The "plus," however, may be subject to reasonable regulations. For example, unauthorized marching on city sidewalks, football fields, or public parks may not be constitutional, because the main function of such places is not communications.

Picketing is one of the most controversial of speech-plus activities. Strikes by labor unions often include picketing outside stores, factories, or schools. People protesting the policies of other organizations also may form picket lines, carry signs, and march in an orderly way. In *Thornhill v. Alabama* (1940), the Supreme Court gave peaceful picketing the full protection of the First Amendment. A year later, however, the Court qualified its position somewhat. In *Milk Wagon Drivers Union v. Meadowmoor Dairies* (1941), the Court held that the right to picket can be restricted when there is a threat of violence. Since then, the Court has also held that picketing may be limited if it conflicts with valid state laws.

Check for Understanding
▲ *What is the difference between pure speech and speech-plus?* (Pure speech is the spoken word. Speech-plus includes actions taken to call attention to what is said.)

In June 1989 the Supreme Court ruled that burning the American flag was an acceptable form of free speech. This decision was unpopular with many Americans, such as this group in Chicago, who felt the flag was a sacred symbol of the nation and should not be desecrated in any way.

Symbolic speech

The third category of speech is **symbolic speech**. Here, actions and objects replace words in conveying ideas or emotional appeals. The courts have found some forms of symbolic speech constitutional but have restricted others.

Several cases from the era of protests against the Vietnam War illustrate how the courts reason about such issues. To show their objections to military service, four young men burned their draft cards and were arrested. In 1968, the Supreme Court's decision in *United States v. O'Brien* upheld their arrest. The following year, however, the Court ruled that school officials could not dismiss students for wearing black armbands as an antiwar protest (*Tinker v. Des Moines School District*).

Why was wearing an armband a legitimate form of symbolic speech when burning a draft card was not? According to the Court, the students wearing armbands were merely expressing an opinion, but the protesters burning draft cards were disrupting a legitimate function of government — raising an army for national defense.

In *Texas v. Johnson* (1989), the Court determined that flag burning was protected under freedom of speech. Outraged, Congress passed a law against flag burning. The Supreme Court struck down that law, stating "punishing desecration of the flag dilutes the very freedom that

makes this emblem so revered." A constitutional amendment banning flag desecration was introduced in Congress, but defeated.
6E, 6H

Limits on Free Speech

Even though freedom of speech is a basic constitutional principle, it has been limited in special cases. A well-known quotation from Justice Oliver Wendell Holmes points out, "The most stringent protection of free speech would not protect a man in falsely shouting 'Fire!' in a theater and causing a panic." The courts must sometimes weigh the principle of free speech against other factors, such as public safety, public welfare, or national security.

Limits on political criticism

Words that stir up rebellion or advocate overthrowing the government are called **sedition** (sih-DISH-un) or seditious speech. Americans recognize that government has the right to protect itself against outright destructive acts (sabotage), spying (espionage), and betrayal to an enemy (treason). But since colonial times, Americans have believed that the right to criticize the government and public officials is basic to a free society. At what point does political criticism become "sedition"? Should it be limited? Does the First Amendment protect it?

151

History

▲ CRITICAL THINKING Have students review the circumstances of *Schenck v. United States*. **Why might certain expressions of speech be permitted in peacetime but not in wartime?** (During wartime, the country is at greater risk and the "clear and present danger" of certain speech is increased.)

▲ CRITICAL THINKING **Why did many of the free speech cases in the 1950's involve Communist Party members?** (The cold war was at its peak, and Americans were worried about Communist advances.)

Cooperative Learning

● Divide the class into small groups and have each group paraphrase Brandeis's 1927 ruling (p. 150). Then have the groups create a chart, political cartoon, or other image illustrating Brandeis's ideas on the importance of free speech.

Until World War I, there had been only one major law against sedition — the highly unpopular Sedition Act of 1798. More than a hundred years later, the Espionage Act of 1917 was passed. It outlawed interfering with the draft. A year later, the Sedition Act made it illegal to "utter, print, write, or publish any disloyal . . . or abusive language about the form of government in the United States."

A "clear and present danger"

In 1918 Charles T. Schenck, an official of the Socialist Party, was convicted under the Espionage Act for printing and mailing 15,000 pamphlets urging men to evade the military draft. He appealed the conviction, arguing that the Espionage Act violated his First Amendment right to free speech. The Supreme Court, however, upheld the validity of the Espionage Act and Schenck's conviction (*Schenck v. U.S.,* 1919). The Court believed that writing and distributing such material would ordinarily be protected under the First Amendment. But, said Justice Holmes, these circumstances were different:

Words can be weapons. . . . The question in every case is whether the words used are used in such circumstances and are of such a nature as to create a clear and present danger that they will bring about the . . . evils that Congress has a right to prevent.

This statement became known as the "clear and present danger" doctrine. Judges have used it to decide whether the danger to public welfare outweighs the right to freedom of speech.

The Smith Act and American Communists

In free speech cases since the *Schenck* decision, the Supreme Court justices have modified Holmes's doctrine. Once again, the classic cases have involved a sedition law, the Smith Act. Under the Smith Act, it became a crime to (1) advocate the violent overthrow of any government in the United States, (2) attempt or conspire to commit a rebellion, or (3) organize or join any organization advocating rebellion.

Eleven leaders of the American Communist Party who were convicted under the Smith Act

The First Amendment right of free speech is guaranteed even though that speech may tell listeners to riot or otherwise break the law. The law protects this speaker at a Ku Klux Klan rally up to the point where police judge the danger of lawbreaking to be both "clear" and "imminent."

152

Background: *Constitutional Heritage* The *Schenck* case is also important because it ruled that free speech is not absolutely protected by the First Amendment. The case marked the beginning of the Court's efforts to define standards concerning the curtailment of free speech.

took their case to the Supreme Court. In *Dennis v. United States* (1951), the Supreme Court upheld their conviction by a 6–2 vote. The majority agreed that advocating the overthrow of the government created a "clear and present danger," which justified government action.

Justices William O. Douglas and Hugo Black, however, disagreed. In their opinion, the Court's decision was a more serious threat to democracy than the actions of the American Communists. Douglas argued that where people actually have the freedom to discuss ideas, communism is unlikely to gain supporters.

A few years later, the Court reconsidered the question of whether teaching and advocating rebellion constituted a "clear and present danger." The case was brought by Oleta O'Connor Yates and other members of the Communist Party, who also had been charged with violating the Smith Act.

Reversing Yates's conviction, the Court made a distinction between speech that expresses an idea and speech that encourages others to break the law or commit violence (*Yates v. United States,* 1957). The Court held that believing and teaching an idea — even the idea of revolution — was not a crime, but that urging others to break the law could be. Membership in subversive organizations and discussions of abstract principles are, therefore, protected by the First Amendment. Organizing a revolution or planning a bombing is not.

Justices Douglas and Black agreed in part with the *Yates* ruling but continued to oppose the Smith Act as being contrary to a strict reading of the First Amendment. Justice Black remarked:

Doubtlessly, dictators have to stamp out causes and beliefs which they deem subversive to their evil regimes. But governmental suppression of causes and beliefs seems to me to be the very antithesis [opposite] of what our Constitution stands for. . . . The First Amendment provides the only kind of security system that can preserve a free government.

"Imminent danger"

Most free speech cases in the 1950's involved members or alleged members of the Communist Party. Other groups have also been judged by the "clear and present danger" test.

Clarence Brandenburg, a Ku Klux Klan leader in Ohio, staged a rally and cross-burning to show his contempt for blacks and Jews. When he refused to follow a police order to clear the street, he was arrested. In *Brandenburg v. Ohio* (1969), the Supreme Court said that these actions were protected by the First Amendment. Even though Brandenburg was encouraging others to break the law, there was no "imminent," or immediate, danger that the crowd would follow him. That is, a speaker who talks about rioting is constitutionally protected up to the point where a riot seems likely to start. Danger must be both "clear" and "imminent" before the police can curb free speech.

Restrictions on verbal attacks

The First Amendment does not protect the use of free speech to damage someone's reputation. **Defamation** is the general term for attacks on another person's good name and reputation. For instance, it would be defamatory to say falsely that Senator X takes bribes, that the local bank is bankrupt, that Doctor Y is a "butcher," or that a contractor uses unsafe materials.

Defamation can be either written or spoken. If it is spoken, as in a public speech or on the radio, it is **slander**. A defamatory remark in written form—newspapers, magazines, cartoons, signs, billboards, statues, movies, and television—is called **libel**. Libel and slander are generally not legal because such accusations can harm someone's professional or personal life.

Criticism of public figures

On the other hand, valid criticism of public officials is not considered defamation but a legitimate use of free speech. This protection was established in the 1964 landmark case of *New York Times v. Sullivan.* The *New York Times* printed an advertisement paid for by a civil rights group. The ad stated, in part, that police in Montgomery, Alabama, had conducted a "wave of terror" against student protesters. L. B. Sullivan, the police commissioner of Montgomery, contended that the ad was wrong and that he had been libeled. An Alabama court awarded him damages of $500,000. (Other officials also sued the *Times,* asking for more than $5 million in damages.)

When the *Times* appealed the case, the Supreme Court decided unanimously against Sullivan. It held that criticism of public officials —

153

GUIDED/INDEPENDENT PRACTICE

● Have students check newspapers, magazines, or news broadcasts to identify and learn about a recent case involving free speech. Have them report on their case to the class, describing the issues and type of speech involved in the case.

RETEACHING/CORRECTIVES

▲ Write the vocabulary and key terms listed in the Section Review on the board and have students define them and suggest examples for each term (except the Smith Act).

You may also want to use **Transparency 15,** which shows a political cartoon dealing with the issue of flag burning.

The symbol 👥 denotes active participation strategies.

Activities are keyed for student abilities:
▲ = Basic
● = All Levels
■ = Average/Advanced

like criticism of the government — is a basic First Amendment right. The fact that the ad contained some errors did not matter. The Court reasoned that if citizens could be sued for "good faith" criticism of public officials, they might be afraid ever to voice their criticisms. The only exception to this blanket extension of free speech is statements made with "actual malice" or "reckless disregard for the truth."

Since the *New York Times* case, the courts have held that the Constitution also protects statements — including insults — about "public figures" other than politicians. "Public figures" include people who voluntarily achieve fame or notoriety, such as professional athletes or entertainers. The Court reasons that such people, like public officials, have access to the media that most people do not possess and so are better able to contest false statements.

Celebrity cases

It is still possible for celebrities to win libel suits against the media. For example, in 1981 entertainer Carol Burnett was awarded $1.6 million in a libel suit against the *National Enquirer,* a nationally circulated tabloid. In 1976 the paper had published an untrue story that Burnett had drunkenly insulted Secretary of State Henry Kissinger at a Washington restaurant. Referring back to the *New York Times* decision, the jury ruled that the *Enquirer* article showed a "reckless disregard for the truth."

The *Burnett* decision was praised by those who felt that the press was abusing its power. Critics of the decision, however, argued that it might bring a flood of defamation suits against the media, limiting free speech and freedom of the press.

Though several such lawsuits did occur, few have been successful. For example, Baptist minister and televangelist Jerry Falwell sued the publisher of a pornographic magazine that printed a vicious and clearly false parody of Falwell. Though Falwell won $200,000 in a lower court, that award was overturned by the Supreme Court. Criticism of public figures is protected by the First Amendment, the Court ruled, no matter how offensive or cruel the criticism is.

This does not give reporters the right to distort information, however. Jeffrey Masson, a psychoanalyst, had a libel suit reinstated in 1991

The Supreme Court upheld the First Amendment right to criticize public figures in its ruling against the Reverend Jerry Falwell (right).

when the Supreme Court found that he may have been misquoted by a reporter. In *Masson v. New Yorker Magazine, Inc.* the Court ruled that, while writers can make slight changes to a quote, they cannot change its meaning. Any false or greatly altered quote is grounds for libel.

In general, to win a libel or slander suit, a person must convince a jury that his or her reputation has suffered harm as a result of a spoken or printed statement. Private individuals do not have to prove that actual malice was intended, but public figures do. Finally, in most cases, truth is an absolute defense against a defamation suit. If a defamatory statement is true, it is protected by the First Amendment.

"Fighting words"

One very narrow legal category of speech is "fighting words" — words that are so insulting or offensive that their very utterance causes immediate violence. In *Chaplinsky v. New Hampshire* (1942), the Supreme Court ruled that such language is not protected by the guarantee of free speech. Cases involving "fighting words" are rare. A statement must be more than just annoying or offensive. It must be directed to a particular person or group *and* "have a direct tendency to cause acts of violence."

SECTION 2 REVIEW

Vocabulary and key terms

freedom of
  speech (150)
pure speech (150)
speech-plus (150)
symbolic speech (151)
sedition (151)

"clear and present
  danger" (152)
Smith Act (152)
defamation (153)
slander (153)
libel (153)

For review

1. (a) What part of speech-plus may be restricted? (b) Give an example of symbolic speech. **6H**

2. (a) What is the "clear and present danger" doctrine? How was this standard modified by (b) the *Yates* decision? (c) the *Brandenburg* decision? **2D**
3. What is the difference between libel and slander? **6E**
4. Is criticizing public officials considered defamation? Why or why not? **6H**

Critical thinking

INTERPRETING A PRIMARY SOURCE What did Justice Black mean by the statement (page 153): "The First Amendment provides the only kind of security system that can preserve a free government"? **6H**

1C, 4B, 4D, 5A, 6A, 6G, 6H

The First Amendment Protects Freedom of the Press

ACCESS **The Main Ideas**

1 **Why is freedom of the press important in a democracy?** *pages 155–159*
2 **How are the protections given to the printed press different from those given to radio and television?** *pages 155–159*

Robert Reynold, principal of a high school in Hazelwood, Missouri, was unhappy with articles on the subjects of teenage pregnancy and divorce that were to appear in the school's newspaper. He felt that several references were not proper for younger students to read and that some quotes were one-sided and unfair. The articles, he ruled, could not be published as written.

Three student editors argued that Reynolds was violating the constitutional guarantee of freedom of the press. They took their case to the Supreme Court—and lost. In *Hazelwood School District v. Kuhlmeier* (1988) the justices decided that First Amendment rights "must be applied in light of the special characteristics of the school environment." In other words, school administrators could censor school publications.

The Court's decision was limited to official school publications, however. Freedom of the press continues to be a pillar of democracy. In the words of the noted political writer Walter Lippman, "A free press is not a privilege, but a . . . necessity in a great society."

1C, 4B, 5A, 6H

Press Censorship

Protecting the right to publish

Many governments of the world strictly control the press and other media. They may destroy printing presses, prevent stories from being printed, shut down newspapers that criticize the government, require approval of books before distribution, or ban motion pictures before they are shown. In the United States, however, the First Amendment guarantee of freedom of the press generally prohibits such forms of government **censorship**.

William Blackstone, a famous British judge and lawyer, once wrote that "the liberty of the press consists in laying no previous restraints on publications." The term **prior restraint** refers to government censorship of a work *before* it is published. The state of Minnesota, for example,

155

● Tell students to imagine that they are the news staff of the local newspaper meeting to discuss a story that quotes an anonymous source attacking the local police chief. *What freedom of the press issues are involved?* (Libel and the right to protect sources.) *Should the newspaper print the article? Would your decision be different if printing the article would compromise an important criminal investigation? Would you print the name of the source if that person were a criminal under investigation?*

EXPLANATION

After reviewing the content of the section, you may want to consider the following activities:

Values

▲ CRITICAL THINKING *What are the dangers of a completely free press?* (Journalists could publish or broadcast information that might threaten national security, damage an innocent person's reputation, or do some other kind of harm.)

Ask students to consider this statement by James Fenimore Cooper: "If newspapers are useful in overthrowing tyrants, it is only to establish a tyranny of their own." *What did he mean?* (Though the press can bring down undemocratic governments, the press can become too powerful.) *Do you agree?*

Civic Participation

● Have students consider the Supreme Court's decision to allow censorship of school newspapers. *Do you agree with that decision? Why or why not?*

If your school has a newspaper, have students investigate your school's policy toward it.

156

---

had in the 1920's a law forbidding the publication of any "malicious, scandalous, or defamatory" periodicals. Under this law, state courts could stop the publication of any periodical labeled as a "nuisance." When the *Saturday Press,* a weekly Minneapolis paper, ran a series of articles charging the chief of police and other local officials with graft and corruption, a state court issued an **injunction** to prevent further publication. (An injunction is a court order that forbids a specific activity.)

In *Near v. Minnesota* (1931), the Supreme Court held that the law and the injunction represented unconstitutional prior restraint. Charles Evans Hughes, who was then Chief Justice, stated that upholding this law "would be but a step to a complete system of censorship." The Court warned, however, that it might allow prior restraint in special cases, such as those relating to national security.

The *Pentagon Papers*

Prior restraint and national security were the issues forty years later, when the *Near* ruling met its stiffest challenge. The case of *New York Times Co. v. United States* (1971) was fought over the *Pentagon Papers.* These documents

Freedom of the press ensures Americans great freedom of choice in what they can read and see.

156

were part of a multi-volume report by the Defense Department on the circumstances leading to American involvement in the Vietnam War. The report was classified as secret. Daniel Ellsberg, a government employee, violated security rules and furnished copies to the *New York Times* and the *Washington Post.* After some deliberation, the newspapers began publishing the documents.

Immediately, the administration of President Richard Nixon went to court seeking an injunction to stop further publication. But in keeping with the *Near* decision, the Supreme Court ruled against the government. The majority felt that the government had failed to meet the "heavy burden" of justifying prior restraint by proving that publication would cause direct and serious harm to the nation. Justice Hugo Black was most adamant: "In the First Amendment, the [Founders] gave the free press the protection it must have to fulfill its essential role in our democracy. The press was to serve the governed, not the governors."

Obscene publications

One type of publication that has never been given First Amendment protection is **obscenity**, a legal category that includes pornography. There has always been a problem, however, in defining exactly what obscenity is. For example, is foul language obscene? Are X-rated movies obscene? Justice Potter Stewart's comment is famous: "I can't define it [obscenity], but I know it when I see it."

The Supreme Court has attempted in many cases to clarify the meaning of obscenity. One standard definition was given in *Miller v. California* (1973), a case involving "adult" books sold by mail. The Court set three criteria for finding a work obscene: (1) An "average person, applying contemporary community standards," would find that the work as a whole appeals to a "prurient interest" in sex. (2) The work depicts sexual conduct in a manner that local law or the courts define as offensive. (3) The work, taken as a whole, lacks "serious literary, artistic, political, or scientific value."

The *Miller* decision was refined in 1987. In *Pope v. Illinois* the Supreme Court held that in obscenity cases, the jury must determine "whether a reasonable person would find such

---

value in the material taken as a whole."

In practice, decisions on obscenity have varied widely. In 1990, the director of Cincinnati's Contemporary Arts Center was arrested when his museum exhibited photographs that some people called obscene. The director, Dennis Barrie, was acquitted when the prosecutor failed to prove that the photographs met the *Miller* definition of obscenity. At the same time, a record store owner in Ft. Lauderdale, Florida, was convicted for selling a nationally famous rap group's recordings found to be obscene.

The Supreme Court has the final word on censorship. For example, the Supreme Court ruled in 1969 that booksellers cannot be punished for selling obscene materials unless they do so knowingly. It also ruled that state and local authorities cannot stop citizens from having obscene materials in their own homes for their own private use. State and local governments may, however, prohibit people under 18 from entering "adult" bookstores or movies.

Laws passed by Congress also have made it difficult for people to buy or sell pornography. For example, it has been illegal for more than a hundred years to send obscene materials by mail. In addition, obscene material cannot be shipped from one state to another. These laws have been upheld by the Supreme Court.

Limits on advertising

Advertising, known legally as "commercial speech," has only limited First Amendment protection. In fact, because of the need to protect consumers, the government controls advertising to an extent. The Federal Trade Commission (FTC), created by Congress in 1914, has the primary responsibility for overseeing the content of advertising. For instance, cigarette ads were forbidden on radio and TV in 1971, and tobacco companies were required to list tar and nicotine content in their printed advertising. Other advertisers have been stopped from making false claims.

The FTC also tries to make advertising more informative. For years, state laws and the rules of professional groups prevented certain kinds of advertising. In the mid-1970's the courts and the FTC began to loosen this control. For example, in 1977 the Supreme Court struck down a law that prohibited lawyers from advertising their services and fees (*Bates v. Arizona Bar Associa-*

Though American radio does not have censors, both college and commercial stations must follow government regulations and broadcast standards.

tion). The same year, the Court overturned a New York state law banning the advertisement of contraceptives. Bans on advertising contact lenses, dental clinics, and other medical services have also been removed.

5B, 6B

Motion Pictures, Radio, and TV

The basic principle of freedom of the press grew up in England and the American colonies to protect newspapers and books from government censorship. As **mass media** such as film, radio, and television developed, new and complex questions about press freedom arose.

Movie censorship

In 1915, when the motion picture industry was new, the Court ruled in *Mutual Film Corporation v. Ohio* that state and local authorities had complete freedom to censor movies. Movies were not considered to be either part of the press or "organs of public opinion." As a result of this decision, thousands of state and local censorship boards sprang up throughout the country, with the power to prevent movies from being shown in their areas.

157

GUIDED/INDEPENDENT PRACTICE

● Have students create charts comparing newspapers, books, movies, television, and radio on the following issues: obscenity (banned in all media, but more closely regulated in movies, TV, and radio); government regulation (movies, TV, and radio are regulated, books and newspapers are not), fairness doctrine (required of broadcasters only).

RETEACHING/CORRECTIVES

▲ Have students list items mentioned under the heading "Press Censorship" (p. 155) that illustrate the types of things the United States government is *not* allowed to do to censor the press. (Destroy printing presses, prevent stories from being printed, shut down newspapers critical of the government.)

ENRICHMENT/EXTENSION

■ Have students contact a local radio or TV station and invite a representative to address the class on free press issues as they affect the station. Have students prepare questions in advance to ask the representative, and review those questions with the class.

Have students complete **Supreme Court Decisions 18–19,** which deal with cases involving press censorship.

Freedom of the press first went on trial in America in 1735, in the case of John Peter Zenger, a New York printer who published articles that criticized the British colonial governor. Zenger's lawyer defended him by arguing against arbitrary government power. The jury quickly freed Zenger.

As time passed, the Court viewed the film industry differently. In 1952 it ruled that motion pictures are partially protected by the First Amendment (*Burstyn v. Wilson*). In this case, the New York Board of Regents had refused to license an Italian film entitled *The Miracle* because they found it "sacrilegious." The Court ruled that such prior censorship of the film was unconstitutional because the law's definition of "sacrilege" was too vague. To be valid, the Court held, movie licensing laws must set forth definite standards and be applied fairly.

Since the *Burstyn* decision, the Court's strict requirements have made it extremely difficult for licensing boards to ban films. As a result, there are few state or local film licensing boards today. Obscenity is the only permissible grounds for withholding a license. Even then, obscenity laws must be worded very carefully.

In addition, the motion picture industry itself now classifies or rates films, as a way of avoiding government intervention. The rating system is familiar: *G,* for general audiences; *PG,* parental guidance suggested; *PG-13,* parental guidance suggested for those under 13; *R,* restricted; and *NC-17,* no children under 17 admitted.

Regulating public airwaves

Even more limits are involved in applying freedom of the press to television and radio. Like newspapers, these broadcast media are important forums for news and debates on public issues. But because TV and radio stations operate on publicly owned airwaves, the federal government licenses each station to use only a certain broadcast frequency. (Too many stations would mean overlapping transmissions and constant interference.) Government licensing thus means some government control.

The Federal Communications Commission (FCC) is the government agency responsible for broadcast licensing. Although the FCC is not allowed to censor broadcasts or interfere with free speech, it can set standards through licensing. Licenses are granted for three years and must then be renewed. A station that fails to observe FCC standards may lose its license.

One FCC regulation, the **fairness doctrine**, required stations to present all sides of an important issue. The FCC later repealed the doctrine, claiming that it violated the First Amendment rights of broadcasters. In 1990 the Supreme Court upheld the FCC decision.

158

Other Free Press Issues

Freedom of information

The public's right to know what government does is an important element of freedom of the press. Therefore, in 1966 Congress passed the Freedom of Information Act. This act, as amended in 1974, requires the government to allow journalists and other interested persons to inspect federal records, such as budgets, records of expenses, maps, and photographs. Certain "classified" documents are not made available.

Furthermore, the federal government and state governments have adopted **sunshine laws**. Sunshine laws require government agencies to open their meetings to the press and public. The Sunshine Act of 1976, for example, made public the operations of approximately fifty federal agencies, boards, and commissions. Under the law, an agency must notify the public of its meetings at least one week in advance. While some meetings may be conducted behind closed doors, the public is entitled to view the written reports of such meetings.

Protecting news sources

Freedom of the press and government interests also conflict over revealing the sources of news stories. Reporters argue that being forced to testify in court interferes with freedom of the press. The Supreme Court, however, has repeatedly refused to extend the First Amendment to allow journalists to protect their sources. A major decision on this issue was handed down in 1972 in *United States v. Caldwell.* Earl Caldwell, a reporter for *The New York Times,* had refused to testify before a federal grand jury about the operation of the Black Panthers, a radical black political group. Caldwell maintained that his appearance would destroy confidential sources that he had worked hard to establish.

A federal appeals court agreed that freedom of the press protected Caldwell's right not to appear or testify, but a narrow majority of the Supreme Court did not. By a 5–4 vote, the Court ruled that law enforcement and the investigation of crimes outweigh a reporter's confidentiality. The four dissenting justices, however, believed that this decision undermined "the historic independence of the press."

Since *Caldwell,* numerous reporters have chosen to go to jail rather than testify in court. In an effort to protect journalists, 27 states have now passed **shield laws**. These laws establish the conditions under which news reporters are not required to testify in state courts. Thus, shield laws protect confidential sources of information in some states. In other states and in federal cases, journalists are still required to name their sources.

A 1991 Supreme Court decision put even those journalists protected by shield laws in a tough spot. In *Cohen v. Cowles Media Co.,* the Court ruled that reporters who agree to protect confidential sources and then publish their sources' names can be sued for breach of promise.

SECTION 3 REVIEW

Vocabulary and key terms

freedom of the
   press (155)
censorship (155)
prior restraint (155)
injunction (156)
obscenity (156)

mass media (157)
fairness doctrine (158)
Freedom of
   Information Act (159)
sunshine law (159)
shield law (159)

For review

1. (a) What did the Nixon administration attempt to do in the Pentagon Papers case? (b) What was the Supreme Court's ruling in this case? **6G**
2. Under what circumstances can booksellers be punished for selling obscene material? **6G**
3. For what reasons does the government regulate advertising? **6H**
4. How did attitudes toward movie censorship change between 1915 and the 1950's? **5B**
5. Why do radio and TV have less First Amendment protection than the printed press? **6H**
6. What are the arguments of (a) journalists and (b) law-enforcement officials in the controversy over confidential sources? **5B**

Critical thinking

ANALYZING AN ISSUE What are reasons *for* and *against* giving radio and television the same First Amendment protection as newspapers and books? **5B**

159

SECTION 4

The First Amendment Allows Freedom of Assembly *(pp. 160–163)*

Section Objectives

☐ describe the kinds of assembly given First Amendment protection

☐ describe the limits of freedom of assembly

 FOCUS

● Have a volunteer read aloud the first paragraph of this section, and ask students to suggest why the assemblies described might be offensive. *Do you think these assemblies should be allowed? Explain your answer.*

EXPLANATION

After reviewing the content of the section, you may want to consider the following activities:

Constitutional Heritage

■ CRITICAL THINKING Have students consider the potential conflict between freedom of assembly and the right to a fair trial. *Why would ensuring a fair trial be more important than the public's right to assemble?* (Students might suggest that an individual's freedom or even life may be at stake in a trial. A group, on the other hand, can have other opportunities to express itself.)

2D, 5C, 6B, 6C, 6D

SECTION 4 — The First Amendment Allows Freedom of Assembly

ACCESS **The Main Ideas**

1 What kinds of assembly are given First Amendment protection? *pages 160–163*

2 What are the limits of freedom of assembly? *pages 161–162*

The American Nazi Party marches in a town where survivors of Nazi camps live. The Communist Party holds a rally attacking private business. The Ku Klux Klan marches in an African American neighborhood. Are these actions legal?

According to the last section of the First Amendment, the government cannot abridge "the right of the people peaceably to assemble, and to petition the government for a redress of grievances." Freedom of assembly includes the right to meet, protest, march, parade, or picket. Like the other First Amendment freedoms, the right to assemble may sometimes be limited for the public's welfare and safety. On the other hand, people cannot be stopped from assembling just because the views they hold are unpopular.

2D, 6B, 6C, 6D

The Right to Meet Peacefully

The First Amendment refers specifically to "peaceable" assemblies. Nobody has the right to storm the jails, break down doors, take over public offices, throw rocks at pedestrians, start fires, loot stores, or overturn automobiles in the name of free assembly. Nor do people have the right to parade on bridges, gather on airport runways, or disrupt rush hour traffic. There is a time and a place for peaceful assembly.

Assembly in public places

The Supreme Court has held that peaceful assembly is guaranteed in public places. In general, these are areas supported by tax dollars, where people normally gather. They include parks, streets, sidewalks, city halls, state capitol buildings, and national monuments.

The right to assemble peacefully on public grounds was put to the test in 1963 when a group

of black students gathered on the lawn of the South Carolina state capitol to protest racial segregation policies. The protesters sang songs and danced. When the students ignored a police order to disperse, they were arrested and later convicted of disturbing the peace. The Supreme Court, however, overturned the conviction because the students were protected by the First Amendment (*Edwards v. South Carolina*, 1963). According to the Court, the protesters' peaceful meeting on public grounds represented

The First Amendment protects the rights of Americans to assemble in order to present their views. Here, state employees in Austin, Texas, protest job cuts.

Background: *Law* Note that public gatherings can be (and often are) restricted in the interest of public safety and welfare. Alcohol use can be regulated and curfews can be set, for example, on public property.

Photo
▲ *For what other kinds of reasons might people gather together in a public place?* (Political demonstrations, public prayer, to watch a performance, to publicize an economic boycott, etc.)

"basic constitutional rights in their most pristine and classic form."

Not all publicly owned property is open to the public, however. For example, Harriett Louise Adderly was a student at Florida A & M University in Tallahassee. She and 31 other students, without permission, entered the nearby county jail grounds to protest the earlier arrest of some fellow students. When the local sheriff asked the protesters to leave, they refused. They were then arrested and charged with trespassing. In *Adderly v. Florida* (1966), the Supreme Court upheld their conviction, distinguishing this case from the *Edwards* decision. The Court reasoned, "Traditionally, state capitol grounds are open to the public. Jails, built for security purposes, are not."

Assembly on private property

People's rights to their private property are another important principle, and the First Amendment does not grant others the right to trespass on such property. This limit may include areas such as shopping malls that appear to be public but are in fact privately owned. In *Lloyd Corporation Ltd. v. Tanner* (1972), for instance, the Supreme Court ruled that an anti-Vietnam War group did not have the right to gather and distribute handbills in a large, privately owned shopping mall. The Court noted, however, that the group could have passed out the leaflets legally on nearby city sidewalks and streets, which were public property.

Regulations on assemblies

The First Amendment does not prohibit state or local officials from establishing rules for gatherings in public places. To be constitutional, such rules must be reasonable, precise, and fair. For instance, a city may require parade permits and set the conditions under which assemblies may take place. On the other hand, authorities cannot arbitrarily decide who may or may not be issued a permit.

Deciding whether regulations are "reasonable" is not always easy. A few Supreme Court decisions demonstrate how the standards are applied. For example, a local law in Birmingham, Alabama, allowed the city to deny a group a parade permit on the grounds of "decency, . . . morals or convenience." In *Shuttlesworth v. City of Birmingham* (1969), the Supreme Court found this law so unclear that it was an unreasonable restriction on freedom of assembly. In another case, a city law prohibited all demonstrations near school buildings except picketing by labor unions. The Supreme Court held that this law unfairly discriminated against particular types of assemblies and so was unconstitutional (*Police Department of Chicago v. Mosley*, 1972).

In *Coates v. City of Cincinnati* (1971), the Court struck down an ordinance making it illegal for "three or more persons to assemble on the sidewalks . . . in a manner annoying to persons passing by." The Court ruled that "mere public intolerance or animosity" did not justify restricting a First Amendment right.

Conflicts with other rights

Among the cases that are most difficult to decide are those in which a lawful assembly interferes with a function of government. As in other situations where basic rights conflict, the courts must weigh freedom of assembly against the public interest. For example, the Supreme Court upheld a Louisiana state law that made it illegal to parade near a courthouse in an attempt to influence judges, jurors, or witnesses. In this case, ensuring a fair trial was considered more important than guaranteeing freedom of assembly. In another case, the Court upheld a law that banned demonstrations that were staged near schools during school hours and intended to disrupt classwork. The Court considered that the students' right to an education outweighed others' right to demonstrate.

5C, 6B

Unpopular Assemblies

Potential violence

Even in gatherings where the demonstrators are "peaceable," bystanders may become angry or even violent. This situation is sometimes termed the "heckler's veto." A heckler's veto is the ability of hostile onlookers (hecklers) to disrupt a peaceful speech or assembly by jeering, shouting insults, or physically interfering with demonstrators. By threatening violence, an angry crowd can force police to stop an otherwise lawful assembly in order to protect public safety or welfare.

RETEACHING/CORRECTIVES

▲ Have students outline the section, using the headings and subheadings as guides for their outlines.

ENRICHMENT/EXTENSION

■ Have students bring in articles about recent demonstrations in your state or community and summarize them for the class. The class should discuss where the assembly was held, whether it was peaceful, how it ended, what its goals were, and whether it achieved its goals.

Have students complete **Supreme Court Decisions 20-21,** which deal with cases involving freedom of assembly. **Decision 58** also involves freedom of assembly.

When should police interfere with an assembly? On one hand, if police do not have the right to disperse rallies when violence is imminent, then the public may be endangered. On the other, if police are allowed to break up any potentially dangerous assembly, they could invent reasons to discriminate against certain controversial groups.

The case of *Feiner v. New York* (1951) clearly illustrates this conflict. Irving Feiner was a sidewalk speaker in Syracuse, New York. One evening, as a crowd gathered, Feiner hurled verbal assaults against President Harry Truman, the American Legion, and local officials. The crowd grew angry, and the police were called. Believing that violence was imminent, the officers ordered Feiner to stop talking. Feiner refused and was convicted of breaching the peace. Chief Justice Fred M. Vinson defended Feiner's conviction:

> It is one thing to say that the police cannot be used as an instrument for the oppression of unpopular views, and another to say that, when, as here, the speaker passes the bounds of argument and undertakes incitement to riot, they are powerless to prevent a breach of the peace.

The Dick Gregory case

Decisions in cases like this may depend on the courts' judgment about who actually caused the violence. In another case, Dick Gregory, an entertainer and social activist, led a group of marchers from Chicago's City Hall to the home of Mayor Richard Daley. The group was protesting unfair treatment of black students in the city's public schools. As the group marched peacefully in front of the mayor's house, a thousand residents of the all-white neighborhood began shouting obscenities and throwing rocks and eggs at the marchers. On hand to protect the marchers were approximately 175 police officers. Sensing immediate danger, the police asked Gregory and his group to leave. They refused and were charged with "disorderly conduct."

In contrast to the *Feiner* case, the Supreme Court unanimously overturned Gregory's conviction (*Gregory v. Chicago,* 1969). The Court believed that Gregory and his followers were, in fact, assembling peacefully. It was the angry

Demonstrating their opposition to a planned march by American Nazis, residents of Skokie, Illinois, carry placards bearing reminders of the Nazi persecution of Jews in World War II.

neighbors who had acted in a disorderly manner. The Court added that the marchers might have been guilty of violating city laws governing public demonstrations, but they were not guilty of disorderly conduct.

The Skokie march

In 1977 a small band of American Nazi Party members planned a demonstration in Skokie, Illinois, a suburb of Chicago with a large Jewish population. Many residents were survivors of the Holocaust and had been in Nazi concentration camps in World War II. In an effort to stop the Nazis, the city of Skokie passed laws that banned wearing military-style uniforms in parades and passing out "hate literature." In addition, they demanded that the Nazis post a bond of $350,000 to insure against the outbreak of violence.

The American Civil Liberties Union, despite opposition from many of its members, found itself in the awkward position of defending the Nazis. The ACLU, an organization concerned

162

with maintaining the Bill of Rights, argued that all groups must be granted the right to assemble peacefully. As Justice Holmes once put it, the purpose of the First Amendment is not to protect "free thought for those who agree with us but freedom for the thought that we hate."

In 1978 the U.S. Seventh District Court threw out the Skokie ordinances, holding that they were intended not to protect public safety but to restrict the activities of a particular group. The Supreme Court soon after denied an appeal filed by opponents of the Nazis to postpone the march. Gaining far more publicity from the court hearings than they stood to gain from a demonstration, the Nazis eventually abandoned their plans and held a poorly attended march in another suburb of Chicago.

Thus, any peaceful assembly, whether popular or unpopular, must be given equal protection under the First Amendment. Although regulation of assemblies is permitted, such legislation must not be used to favor one group over another.

SECTION 4 REVIEW

Vocabulary and key terms

freedom of assembly (160)   heckler's veto (161)

For review

1. What is the main reason for placing limits on freedom of assembly? Give an example in which this happened. **6B**
2. How did the Supreme Court rule on freedom of assembly for (a) students at the state capitol? (b) students at the county jail? (c) protesters at a shopping mall? **6D**
3. Why did the courts allow a march by the American Nazi Party? **6B**

Critical thinking

EXAMINING BASIC PRINCIPLES Why is it important in a democracy for even unpopular groups (such as Nazis) to have the right to assemble? Why might a non-democratic government limit this right? **6B**

Chapter Summary

Some of the most important civil liberties enjoyed by Americans are listed in the First Amendment to the Constitution: freedom of religion, speech, press, and assembly.

Freedom of religion has two aspects. The establishment clause prevents government from requiring or supporting the practice of any religion. This clause is the basis for the "wall of separation" between church and state and plays an important role in many cases involving religion and public schools. The free exercise clause guarantees Americans the freedom to practice whatever religion they choose without government interference. Religious practices may be restricted if they conflict with public health, safety, or welfare.

Freedom of speech is basic to a democracy but is not absolute. The courts classify speech as pure speech, speech-plus, or symbolic speech and give different levels of protection to each.

Speech attacking the government (sedition) can be limited if it creates a "clear and present danger" to the public interest. The courts must decide, however, if such a danger really exists. The right to free speech does not allow the defamation — libel or slander — of private citizens. Public officials and other public figures, however, are generally not protected from defamatory speech, unless it is made with "actual malice."

Freedom of the press applied originally to newspapers, books, and magazines, which are free to publish without prior restraint. Local communities, however, can restrict materials they judge to be obscene. Other kinds of media have less First Amendment protection. For example, radio and television broadcasts are subject to government regulation. Protecting reporters' sources is a controversial issue; in some states, shield laws protect journalists.

The First Amendment also guarantees freedom of assembly. Citizens may gather peacefully on public property to express their views. Government can pass reasonable laws to regulate assemblies, and officials can interfere if violence occurs. The right to assemble applies equally to people with unpopular and popular views, so long as the assembly remains peaceful.

Section 4 Review Answers

1. To keep assemblies from interfering with public safety and welfare or interfering with other rights. Examples include the Louisiana law forbidding assemblies near courthouses, and the heckler's veto.
2. (a) The right to assemble on public property was upheld. (b) The right to assemble at the county jail—which is not usually open to the public—was denied. (c) The right to assemble on private property was denied.
3. Any group has the right to assemble peacefully.

Critical thinking The right to assemble protects freedom of expression as well as the free exchange of ideas. A non-democratic government might restrict assemblies to suppress ideas that it considered threatening to its power.

CLOSURE

● Remind students of the pre-reading objectives at the beginning of the section. Pose one or both of these questions again. Then have students read the next assigned lesson.

CHAPTER 5 CORRECTIVES

● To review the content of Chapter 5, you may want to have students complete **Study Guide/Review 5** or **Workbook Chapter 5.**

163

The symbol 👥 denotes active participation strategies.

Activities are keyed for student abilities:
▲ = Basic
● = All Levels
■ = Average/Advanced

CHAPTER 5 REVIEW

Answers

Vocabulary See pp. T19–T21 for suggested vocabulary activities.

Reviewing the Facts

1. Government cannot interfere with the practice of religion.
2. People have the right to practice their own religion.
3. If they interfere with public safety, welfare, health, or morals.
4. The "clear and present danger" doctrine asserts that freedom of speech can be limited if it endangers public welfare or creates a risk to national security.
5. This type of censorship is prohibited by the guarantee of freedom of the press.
6. Advertising can be limited to prevent deception or false claims. Motion pictures can be limited by licensing boards, usually to restrict obscenity. Radio and TV, because they operate on publicly owned airwaves, are regulated by the FCC to serve the public interest and present both sides of an issue.
7. The First Amendment protects peaceable assemblies such as meetings, protests, marches, parades, and pickets. Freedom of assembly may be limited to protect public welfare and safety.

Thinking Critically About Key Concepts

1. Taxing religious groups would involve the government in the finances and operations of these religions. Also, religious groups are non-profit, often with limited resources, and could be prevented from operating by high taxes.
2. Possible answer: forcing people to salute the flag and say the pledge of allegiance denies their freedom of conscience, a freedom guaranteed by the First Amendment.
3. Public officials carry out the policies of the government, and the First Amendment guarantees

● Review the definitions of the following terms:

censorship	freedom of the press	slander
"clear and present danger"	freedom of religion	Smith Act
civil liberties	freedom of speech	speech-plus
conscientious objector	heckler's veto	sunshine law
defamation	injunction	symbolic speech
establishment clause	libel	Virginia Statute of
fairness doctrine	mass media	Religious Liberty
free exercise clause	obscenity	
freedom of assembly	prior restraint	
Freedom of Information Act	pure speech	
	sedition	
	shield law	

● REVIEWING THE FACTS

1. What is meant by "a wall of separation" between church and state? **6H**
2. What is the basic guarantee of the free exercise clause? **6B**
3. When are religious practices not protected by the First Amendment? **6G**
4. How does the "clear and present danger" doctrine relate to freedom of speech? **6B**
5. Why is prior restraint illegal in the United States? **6H**
6. What are the reasons for government limits on advertising, motion pictures, and radio and television broadcasts? **2A**
7. What kinds of assembly are protected by the First Amendment, and when can limits be placed on freedom of assembly? **6G**

▲ THINKING CRITICALLY ABOUT KEY CONCEPTS

1. How does the establishment clause of the First Amendment support the government policy of not taxing church-owned property used for religious purposes? **6G**
2. In your own words, restate Justice Jackson's

ruling on *West Virginia Board of Education v. Barnette* quoted on page 148. **2D**
3. Why is criticism of individual public officials a First Amendment right? **6H**
4. Why are state and local governments empowered to prohibit those under 18 years old from entering "adult" bookstores? **6H**
5. Do you agree with the ACLU's defense of the American Nazi Party's march in Skokie? Why or why not? Which groups, if any, should not be allowed to demonstrate peacefully? Explain your answer. **6B**

▲ PRACTICING SKILLS

1. **Study Skills: Organizing information in a table.** Create a table in three columns, based on the following Supreme Court cases: *Walz v. Tax Commission of the City of New York, Abington School District v. Schempp, Chaplinsky v. New Hampshire, U.S. v. Caldwell, Edwards v. South Carolina.* In the first column, list the case. In the second column, list the constitutional issue in question. In the third column, state the decision. You may wish to add more cases to your table. Refer to the chapter or the Supreme Court Cases index (page 820). **8E**

164

all citizens the freedom to criticize the government if they wish to.
4. The First Amendment does not give people the right to publish and distribute obscene material, so state and local governments

are allowed to regulate who can buy obscene material.
5. While some students may answer that every group has the right to assemble peacefully, others may say that groups that advocate hatred or racism

are inherently violent and should not be allowed to demonstrate.

Practicing Skills
1. *Walz*/Freedom of religion/Tax exemption of religious groups does not

2. Critical Thinking Skills: Posing questions. For each of the following court cases, pose one question that expresses the basic issue on which the Supreme Court had to decide: *McCollum v. Board of Education, Engel v. Vitale, New York Times v. Sullivan, Near v. Minnesota.* **8A**

3. Understanding political motivation. Interview someone who has participated in a public demonstration on some issue. Ask the person for a description of the demonstration, its aim and results, why the participant became involved, and how he or she felt about the experience. **6A**

▲ PARTICIPATORY CITIZENSHIP

1. Conducting a poll. Ask students in your class or school the following question: "Should the school day begin with a moment of silence during which students can pray?" Write an editorial for the school newspaper based on the results of the poll. **5C**

2. Analyzing freedom of the press. Read through a newspaper, marking the articles that would be censored by a government that did not allow freedom of the press. **6H**

■ WRITING ABOUT ISSUES

1. Presenting a legal argument. Write the closing arguments for the attorneys for either Johnson or Texas in the 1989 flag-burning case *Texas v. Johnson.* **8C**

2. Writing an essay. In a short essay, explain what Justice Holmes meant when he said that the purpose of the First Amendment is to allow "freedom for the thought we hate." Illustrate your essay with examples. **8C**

▲ ANALYZING A POLITICAL CARTOON

Freedom of expression was a controversial topic during the early 1990's. Americans were divided over whether forms of expression which they found offensive should still be protected against censorship. Look at the cartoon below and answer the following questions.

1. Who do the couple represent? **8A**
2. What problems, if any, might arise if the government adopted the man's attitude? **6B**
3. What is the cartoonist's point of view on this issue? How can you tell? **8B**
4. If you wanted to create an opposing cartoon, what might you draw? **8H**

"WELL IF YOU ASK ME, THE FIRST AMENDMENT SHOULD ONLY PROTECT UNCONTROVERSIAL EXPRESSION."

Cartoon by Jim Borgman, 1990, Cincinnati Enquirer. Reprinted with special permission of King Features Syndicate, Inc.

165

Participatory Citizenship

1. Student editorials may address the issue of respect for the minority under majority rule.

2. Students should mark articles critical of the government, and any that make officials look incompetent or corrupt.

3. Interviews may be of strikers or demonstrators.

Writing About Issues

1. Students arguing for Johnson may claim that the Bill of Rights guarantees freedom of symbolic speech, that the flag is a symbol, and that no harm is caused by its burning. Students arguing for Texas may argue that the flag is so meaningful to so many Americans that it is more than a symbol.

2. Essays might suggest that "the thought we hate" is the one that needs protection because it is the thought most likely to be attacked.

Analyzing a Political Cartoon

1. Average Americans.

2. Students may suggest that because most expression is controversial to some degree, such a policy would render the First Amendment meaningless.

3. The cartoonist probably favors protection of controversial speech. The man in the cartoon is drawn in an unflattering way.

4. Students may suggest drawing a cartoon showing some controversial form of speech being protected.

violate the establishment clause. *Schempp*/Freedom of religion/Reading from the Bible in public schools violates the establishment clause. *Chaplinsky*/Freedom of speech/"Fighting words" are not protected under the First Amendment. *Caldwell*/Freedom of the press/Law enforcement requirements outweigh a reporter's need to keep sources confidential. *Edwards*/Freedom of assembly/Peaceful meeting on public grounds is protected by the First Amendment.

2. Possible answers: *McCollum*—Does religious education on public school property violate the establishment clause? *Engel*—Does prayer in public schools violate the

Chapter Review exercises are keyed for student abilities:
▲ = Basic
● = All Levels
■ = Average/Advanced

CHAPTER 6
CIVIL LIBERTIES: DUE PROCESS OF LAW
(pp. 166–191)

	Section Objectives	Section Resources
Section 1 **The Due Process Clause Ensures Civil Liberties**	☐ describe the rights protected by the Second and Third Amendments ☐ explain the importance of "due process of law"	▲ SKILLS PRACTICE WORKSHEET **6** ■ CONSTITUTIONAL ISSUES WORKSHEET **6**
Section 2 **The Fourth Amendment Limits Investigations**	☐ explain how the Fourth Amendment limits searches and seizures ☐ describe how the exclusionary rule can conflict with the need for evidence ☐ describe the limits on electronic surveillance	■ SKILLS CHALLENGE WORKSHEET **6** ■ SUPREME COURT DECISIONS **22–28**
Section 3 **The Fifth Amendment Protects the Rights of the Accused**	☐ detail the limits set on the legal system's ability to charge a suspect ☐ describe the Fifth Amendment's protection from self-incrimination	
Section 4 **The Sixth Amendment Ensures a Fair Trial**	☐ list the Sixth Amendment's requirements for a fair trial ☐ describe the cases leading to the expansion of the right to legal advice	● PRIMARY SOURCE WORKSHEET **10** ■ SUPREME COURT DECISIONS **29–34**
Section 5 **Due Process Includes Other Rights**	☐ describe the Eighth Amendment guarantee of fair treatment for those convicted of crimes ☐ describe the U.S. Supreme Court rulings regulating capital punishment	■ SUPREME COURT DECISIONS **35–36**
Section 6 **The Right to Privacy Is Protected**	☐ determine the constitutional basis for the right to privacy ☐ define the "zones of privacy" that are protected from government interference	▲ TRANSPARENCY **16** ■ SUPREME COURT DECISIONS **37–38**

Essential Elements

The list below shows Essential Elements relevant to this chapter. (The complete list of Essential Elements appears in the introductory pages of this Teacher's Edition.)

Section 1: 2A, 2D, 3C, 6E, 6I, 8A

Section 2: 2D, 6E, 6I, 8B

Section 3: 2D, 6E, 6I, 8H

Critical Thinking feature (p. 179): 8A

Section 4: 2A, 2D, 6E, 6I

Section 5: 2A, 2D, 3A, 6E, 6H

Section 6: 2A, 6E, 6H, 8H

Chapter Review: 1D, 2A, 2D, 5A, 6E, 6H, 6I, 8A, 8B, 8C, 8E, 8H

Section Resources are keyed for student abilities:
▲ = Basic
● = All Levels
■ = Average/Advanced

Homework Options

Each section contains activities labeled "Guided/Independent Practice," "Reteaching/Correctives," and "Enrichment/Extension." You may wish to choose from among these activities when assigning homework.

Students Acquiring English Activities

Write on the board the phrase, "innocent until proven guilty." Have students copy the phrase on a sheet of paper, write a phrase or sentence restating that concept in their own words, and then list three specific ways in which that concept is reflected in the American system of justice. (Examples include limitations on the gathering of evidence and the right not to testify against oneself.)

LISTENING/SPEAKING: Ask for volunteers to tell the class about situations in their own lives involving the concept "innocent until proven guilty."

Case Studies

When teaching this chapter, you may use Case Study 4, which discusses mandatory drug testing; Case Study 7, which addresses the legality of curfews for young people; or Case Study 11, which debates the issue of gun control. (Case Studies may be found following p. 510.)

Teacher Bibliography

Brigham, John. *Civil Liberties and American Democracy.* CQ Press, 1984. Offers a clear presentation of current themes in civil rights and liberties, with paraphrased Supreme Court decisions.

Forer, Lois G. *A Chilling Effect.* Norton, 1987. Examines the growing threat that invasion-of-privacy and libel suits present to the First Amendment.

Student Bibliography

Draper, Thomas, ed. *Capital Punishment.* Wilson, 1985. Pro and con opinions on the issue from a variety of sources are examined, and the laws and judicial decisions made since 1977 are reviewed.

Lewis, Anthony. *Gideon's Trumpet.* Random House, 1989. An account of the prisoner whose letter to the Supreme Court ultimately resulted in the guarantee of counsel regardless of income.

McClellan, Grant S., ed. *The Right to Privacy.* Wilson, 1976. The political, social, and philosophical aspects of the right to privacy are explored in a variety of essays.

Films and Videotapes*

Justice Is a Constant Struggle. 30 min. UCEMC, 1988. v. The key role played by the National Lawyers Guild in helping to maintain civil rights for more than fifty years is outlined.

Justice Under Law: The Gideon Case. (Series title: *Our Living Bill of Rights.*) 22 min. EBEC, 1966. f. Describes how Gideon, while in jail, managed to reach state and federal authorities to secure the legal representation he had been denied in court.

CHAPTER RESOURCES

Study Guide/Review 6
Workbook Chapter 6
Chapter 6 Test, Forms A–C

A Question of Balance: Fair Trial, Free Press. 27 min. EBEC, 1984. f. The conflict between two constitutional rights—to a free press and a fair trial—is explored using dramatizations of landmark cases.

The Road to the Supreme Court—The Webster Case. 40 min. HMCO, 1991. v. A well-balanced discussion of the landmark abortion case, *Webster v. Reproductive Health Services,* that includes the leading players in the case.

Software*

The Research Companion: Supreme Court Decisions (Apple). Focus. Students become legal assistants to a Supreme Court justice, with access to a database on landmark cases.

The Constitutional Amendments: What They Mean to You (Apple, IBM). Queue. This program uses color graphics and animations to teach students the content, purpose, and history of Amendments 11-26.

Criminal Procedure (Apple, IBM, Macintosh). Queue. Students use an interactive tutorial program to learn about the rights of the accused, bail and bond procedures, public defenders, plea-bargaining, trial procedures, and parole and probation.

* For a complete guide to audiovisual sources, see page T22.

165B

Civil Liberties: Due Process of Law

(pp. 166–191)

Chapter 6 deals with the due process of law guaranteed in the Bill of Rights to those suspected or accused of a crime, as well as the Ninth Amendment guarantee of rights not specifically mentioned in the Constitution.

Chapter Objectives

After students complete this chapter, they will be able to:

1. Describe the rights protected by the Second and Third Amendments.

2. Explain the importance of "due process of law."

3. Explain how the Fourth Amendment limits searches and seizures.

4. Describe how the exclusionary rule can conflict with the need for evidence.

5. Describe the limits on electronic surveillance.

6. Detail the limits set on the legal system's ability to charge a suspect.

7. Describe the Fifth Amendment's protection from self-incrimination.

8. List the Sixth Amendment's requirements for a fair trial.

9. Describe the cases leading to the expansion of the right to legal advice.

10. Describe the Eighth Amendment guarantee of fair treatment for those convicted of crimes.

11. Describe the U.S. Supreme Court rulings regulating capital punishment.

12. Determine the constitutional basis for the right to privacy.

13. Define the "zones of privacy" that are protected from government interference.

166

CHAPTER

6

CIVIL LIBERTIES: Due Process of Law

Under our constitutional system, courts stand against any winds that blow as havens of refuge for those who might otherwise suffer because they are helpless, weak, outnumbered. . . . No higher duty, or more solemn responsibility, rests upon this Court than that of . . . maintaining this constitutional shield deliberately planned and inscribed for the benefit of every human being subject to our Constitution. . . .

Justice Hugo Black
Chambers v. Florida (1940)

Photo
Courtroom, Newport,
Rhode Island.

O n December 25, 1990, Rahila Tiwana, a student in Karachi, Pakistan, was arrested. Taken to police headquarters, she was tortured, starved, and forced to sign papers that could be used against her. No charges were registered by the police until weeks later.

Rahila Tiwana was not read her rights or informed of the charges. She did not have legal advice. She could not refuse to testify against herself. And she suffered from "cruel and unusual punishment."

Americans are protected from these kinds of injustices. The authors of the Bill of Rights knew that few people are more vulnerable to an abuse of governmental power than those accused of crimes. Chapter 6 examines the constitutional guarantees they included to prevent such abuses.

CHAPTER OUTLINE

167

CHAPTER SUPPORT MATERIAL

Skills Practice Worksheet 6

Skills Challenge Worksheet 6

Primary Source Worksheet 10

Constitutional Issues Worksheet 6

Supreme Court Decisions 22–38

Transparency 16

Study Guide/Review 6

Workbook Chapter 6

Chapter 6 Test, Forms A-C

 VIDEOTAPE SERIES

This would be an appropriate place to use Houghton Mifflin's videotape, *The Road to the Supreme Court—The Webster Case.*

SECTION 1

The Due Process Clause Ensures Civil Liberties

(pp. 168–170)

Section Objectives

☐ describe the rights protected by the Second and Third Amendments

☐ explain the importance of "due process of law"

Vocabulary
due process of law

👥 FOCUS

● Have volunteers serve as narrator, suspect, and officials and dramatize an arrest or trial in a country that does not guarantee due process of law. Ask class members to recall and describe similar scenes of arbitrary arrest they might have seen in a film or on television.

EXPLANATION

After reviewing the content of the section, you may want to consider the following activities:

Civic Participation

● [CRITICAL THINKING] Have students discuss how due process is applied to school rules. Have them consider school procedures and divide these procedures into two categories: those that reflect substantive due process and those that reflect procedural due process.

👥 Constitutional Heritage

● Ask interested students to research one or more of the Supreme Court decisions listed in Figure 6–1 and make a short oral report on the details of the case or cases.

SECTION 1 — The Due Process Clause Ensures Civil Liberties

1 What rights are protected by the Second and Third Amendments? *page 168*

2 What is the importance of "due process of law"? *pages 168–170*

Suppose uniformed officials came to your door, put you in handcuffs, and took you to prison. "What am I being charged with?" you might ask. "I want to speak to a lawyer. I have my rights!"

Those rights are based on constitutional guarantees of fairness and equality under the law. These basic civil liberties are called **due process of law**. This section examines the concept of due process, as well as limits to federal power imposed by the Second and Third Amendments.

A salesman at a Florida gun shop demonstrates a pistol to a customer. Relaxed gun laws in the state contributed to a rise in the sale of handguns in the early 1990's.

Limits on Federal Power

During colonial times, Americans had often been forced to house and feed British troops. The Third Amendment guarantees that no homeowner will be required to quarter (house) troops in peacetime. During a war, only a duly enacted law can force Americans to house soldiers.

The Second Amendment, a simple sentence, also limits federal power. It reads:

> A well-regulated militia being necessary to the security of a free state, the right of the people to keep and bear arms shall not be infringed.

Some people argue that this amendment merely prevents the federal government from outlawing state militias. It has nothing to do with gun control, they say. Others define "militia" as every able-bodied citizen—much like the minutemen of colonial times. These people say the amendment defines gun ownership as a right.

The Supreme Court has upheld Congress's right to pass gun control laws. In *United States v. Miller* (1939), the Court unanimously allowed a federal law requiring owners to pay a tax on such weapons as sawed-off shotguns and machine guns. In a 1980 decision, *Lewis v. United States,* the Court went further: "These legislative restrictions . . . [do not encroach] upon any constitutionally protected liberties."

The Principle of Due Process

Constitutional guarantees

The original text of the Constitution protects citizens from certain arbitrary or unjustified government actions that would deprive them of due process. As you read in Chapter 4, state and national governments are prohibited from passing bills of attainder or *ex post facto* laws. To prevent unlawful arrests, citizens also have the right to ask for a writ of habeas corpus. The Bill of

---

Cross-reference

Bills of attainder, *ex post facto,* and habeas corpus are defined and discussed in Chapter 4, p. 89.

Figure 6–1 THE RIGHTS OF THE ACCUSED These protections now apply in state cases because of Supreme Court decisions "incorporating" them in the Fourteenth Amendment. **2D**

BILL OF RIGHTS PROTECTION	COURT CASE	YEAR
Fourth Amendment Unreasonable search and seizure	Mapp v. Ohio	1961
Fifth Amendment Grand jury hearing (serious crimes) Double jeopardy Self-incrimination	Not required in state cases Benton v. Maryland Malloy v. Hogan	 1969 1964
Sixth Amendment Speedy trial Public trial Trial by jury in criminal cases Knowing the charges Confronting witnesses Calling defense witnesses Right to legal counsel	Klopfer v. North Carolina In re Oliver Duncan v. Louisiana Cole v. Arkansas Pointer v. Texas Washington v. Texas Powell v. Alabama (capital crimes) Gideon v. Wainwright (all felonies) Argersinger v. Hamlin (jail sentences)	1967 1948 1968 1948 1965 1967 1932 1963 1972
Eighth Amendment Excessive fines and bail Cruel and unusual punishment	Included in most state constitutions Robinson v. California	 1962

Rights adds still more safeguards of people's legal rights.

Due process itself is considered so important that it is restated in two amendments. Both the Fifth and the Fourteenth Amendments state that the government shall not deprive any person of "life, liberty, or property, without due process of law." The Fifth Amendment's due process clause protects people from actions of the *federal* government. The Fourteenth Amendment guards against civil liberties violations by *state* (or local) government authorities.

Two aspects of due process

The principle of due process protects people's civil liberties in two ways. First, the laws themselves must be reasonable and fair. For example, the law cannot say that only blue-eyed, left-handed people must have drivers' licenses. Nor can it prohibit one labor union and allow others. Because this kind of due process refers to the content, or substance, of the law, it is called *substantive* (SUB-stun-tiv) *due process.*

In addition, due process includes the methods by which laws are carried out. Laws must be applied fairly and equally. They cannot be enforced more strictly for some people than for others. Every individual accused of a crime has the right to legal advice and a jury trial. Police officers cannot torture suspects to force them to confess. Such rules of conduct, or procedure, for police officers, judges, lawyers, and courts are called *procedural* (pruh-SEE-juhr-ul) *due process.* Most of the amendments in the Bill

Figure 6–1
▲ *Write a sentence explaining when and how one of the protections listed was incorporated into the Fourteenth Amendment.* (*Example:* In 1961, in the case *Mapp v. Ohio,* the Supreme Court incorporated the Fourth Amendment's protection against unreasonable search and seizure into the Fourteenth Amendment.)

Background: *Law* Procedural due process is also called procedural protections.

The symbol ⅱ denotes active participation strategies.

Activities are keyed for student abilities:
▲ = Basic
● = All Levels
■ = Average/Advanced

Cooperative Learning
● Divide the class into groups and have each group assemble an argument in the case of *United States v. Miller,* presenting their opinion on federal laws regulating gun ownership. Have the groups choose a presenter to make their arguments to the class.

GUIDED/INDEPENDENT PRACTICE
● Using Figure 6–1 on this page, have students create an annotated time line of Supreme Court cases incorporating the rights of the accused.

RETEACHING/CORRECTIVES
▲ Have students suggest the two main principles of due process. (Laws must be fair and laws must be carried out fairly.)
Have students complete **Skills Practice Worksheet 6,** which reviews the key terms and concepts of due process of law.

ENRICHMENT/EXTENSION
■ Have students complete **Constitutional Issues Worksheet 6,** which examines the issue of suspects' rights.

Section 1 Review Answers

1. To protect people from due process violations by the federal government (Fifth Amendment) and by the states (Fourteenth Amendment).

2. By ruling that the protections are necessary aspects of procedural due process, not only in federal government cases, but also in state and local government cases.

3. Procedural due process.

Critical thinking The Second Amendment prevents the federal government from being the only organization with military power, thereby limiting abuse of that power. Students arguing that the amendment bans gun control laws may note that the words "the right of the people" implies individuals, not just states. Those who believe that gun control laws are not banned might point to the opening clause.

CLOSURE

▲ Remind students of the pre-reading objectives at the beginning of the section. Pose one or both of these questions again. Then have students read Section 2 for the next class, noting the limits on investigators' powers.

SECTION 2

The Fourth Amendment Limits Investigations
(pp. 170–175)

Section Objectives

☐ explain how the Fourth Amendment prohibits unreasonable searches and seizures

---

of Rights are intended to make sure that every citizen enjoys the protection of this second kind of due process.

Extending civil liberties

As Chapter 4 pointed out, most of the amendments in the Bill of Rights originally applied only to the national government, not to the states. The Sixth Amendment, for example, guarantees citizens a "speedy and public trial" only in federal courts. In recent years, however, the Supreme Court has held that this and other Bill of Rights protections are necessary aspects of procedural due process *everywhere*. That is, state and local governments cannot violate these rights. They are considered part of the due process clause in the Fourteenth Amendment.

Figure 6–1 (on the preceding page) lists the amendments that have thus been "incorporated" under the Fourteenth Amendment's due process clause. It also names the Supreme Court decisions that extended these civil liberties to apply to state law.

SECTION 1 **REVIEW**

Vocabulary and key terms

due process of law (168)
substantive due process (169)
procedural due process (169)

For review

1. Why is there a due process clause in both the Fifth and the Fourteenth Amendments? **6E**
2. How has the Supreme Court extended the protections in the Bill of Rights? **2D**
3. Which kind of due process ensures that laws will be carried out fairly? **6E**

Critical thinking

ANALYZING AN ISSUE How does the Second Amendment serve as a limit on federal power? Do you believe that it bans gun control laws? Why or why not? **8A**

2D, 6E, 6I, 8B

SECTION 2
The Fourth Amendment Limits Investigations

ACCESS	The Main Ideas

1 How does the Fourth Amendment protect against unreasonable searches and seizures? *pages 170–173*

2 How can the exclusionary rule conflict with the need for evidence? *page 173*

3 What are the limits on electronic surveillance by law-enforcement officials? *pages 174–175*

In 1761 a fiery young lawyer named James Otis spoke out in a Massachusetts courtroom: "One of the most essential branches of English liberty is the freedom of one's house. A man's house is his castle; and whilst he is quiet, he is as well guarded as a prince in his castle."

Otis's protest was against "writs of assistance," legal documents that allowed British offi-

cials to search colonists' houses whenever they pleased. The authorities ignored Otis, but his arguments were not forgotten by the colonists. When the Bill of Rights was added to the Constitution in 1791, the Fourth Amendment was intended precisely to guard against such arbitrary police power.

2D, 6E, 6I

Searches and Seizures

The words of the Fourth Amendment are a strong declaration of private rights. The amendment includes two guarantees:

The right of the people to be secure in their persons, houses, papers, and effects, against unreasonable searches and seizures, shall not be violated, and no warrants shall issue

---

Background: *History* James Otis (1725–1783) was a representative from Boston to the Massachusetts colonial legislature in 1761. His proposal for a meeting of representatives of all the colonies led to the Stamp Act Congress of 1765. After publicly criticizing certain British officials, Otis was physically attacked by British revenue officers. Head injuries caused by the attack led him to lose his mind before he was killed by lightning in 1783.

U.S. customs officials at border stations and international airports have the right to search the luggage of both Americans and visitors.

☐ describe how the exclusionary rule can conflict with the need for evidence
☐ describe the limits on electronic surveillance

Vocabulary
warrant, probable cause, exclusionary rule, surveillance

FOCUS
● Present the following scenario to the class: The police suspect a woman of smuggling drugs into the country and selling them here. Have the class list the types of actions law-enforcement officials can legally take to investigate the woman. (If they can prove probable cause, they can get a warrant to search her house or tap her telephone; customs officials can search her when she comes into the country; if the police are pursuing her on the way to a suspected drug sale, they can search her car.)

but upon probable cause, supported by oath or affirmation and particularly describing the place to be searched and the persons or things to be seized.

This amendment protects people and their possessions wherever they have a legitimate right to expect privacy — houses, hotel rooms, and even telephone booths. This protection is directed primarily against searches and seizures by police officers and other law-enforcement officials. It also applies, though less strictly, to government workers such as health inspectors, fire marshals, safety inspectors, or agents of the Internal Revenue Service.

Authorization for searches and seizures

One clear limit that the Constitution places on searches and seizures is the need to have a **warrant**. A warrant is a court order that authorizes law-enforcement officials to make an arrest, search a person or place, or take property as evi-

dence. To secure a valid warrant, police officers must follow three basic steps.

1. Police must appear before a judge or magistrate. The magistrate need not have formal legal training but must be a "neutral and detached" observer.
2. The police must swear under oath that they have **probable cause**, a reasonable belief that a particular crime has been or is being committed.
3. The judge or magistrate must issue a warrant that describes the exact place to be searched. The warrant must also describe the specific persons or items to be seized. A random search is unconstitutional.

Searches without warrants

The intent of the Fourth Amendment was to protect people's rights, but not to prevent the police from obtaining needed evidence. Therefore, not all searches and seizures are outlawed, only

171

Background: *Civic Participation* Probable cause is more specifically defined as "less than evidence which would justify condemnation," including *belief* that a law was violated on the

premises to be searched and *facts* that would lead a "reasonably discreet and prudent person" to believe that the charged crime was committed.

The symbol ♦♦ denotes active participation strategies.

Activities are keyed for student abilities:
▲ = Basic
● = All Levels
■ = Average/Advanced

EXPLANATION

After reviewing the content of the section, you may want to consider the following activities:

Law

▲ CRITICAL THINKING Ask students to suggest why law enforcement officials would want to make random checks of motorists. (To check for drunk drivers; to uncover other illegal activities.) Tell the class that in *Delaware v. Prouse* (1979) the Court ruled that state police could not randomly stop motorists to check drivers' licenses or registrations without probable cause.

▲ *Why, according to the Court, do random checks violate the Fourth Amendment?* (They are searches and seizures without probable cause.)

Controversial Issues

● CRITICAL THINKING Read aloud the following statement about the exclusionary rule, made by Benjamin Cardozo before he was named to the Supreme Court: "The criminal is to go free because the constable has blundered." *What might Cardozo have thought of the "good faith exception"?* (He would probably have approved of it.) *Do you agree with Cardozo's assessment of the exclusionary rule? Explain your answer.*

unreasonable ones. Over the years, the courts have made many close and controversial decisions about what is or is not "unreasonable." As Supreme Court Justice Lewis Powell, Jr., commented, "Searches and seizures are an opaque [cloudy] area of the law."

In general, a search without a warrant is considered reasonable if police have good reason to believe a suspect will escape, destroy evidence, or harm others. For example, in *Terry v. Ohio* (1968) the Court held that police may "stop and frisk" a suspect without a warrant or probable cause. But they must believe the suspect is armed or dangerous, or have a "reasonable suspicion" that a crime is about to take place.

Many cases of searches and seizures without warrants involve moving vehicles. If police officers had to get a warrant to search an automobile, the driver could easily flee to another state. In 1925, Chief Justice William Howard Taft pointed out that there was a practical "difference between a search of a store, dwelling house, or other structure . . . and a search of a ship, motor boat, wagon, or automobile."

Nonetheless, many questions remain: Can police stop cars at random to check licenses, search for drugs, or test for drunk driving? Is a camper a "home" or a "motor vehicle"? Such decisions are likely to be made case-by-case. Figure 6–2 describes a number of such cases in which warrants were not required.

Searches by other officials

There are other situations when officials may make searches without warrants. For instance, inspectors at airports and border crossings do not need a warrant or probable cause to search for weapons, explosives, or drugs. Mere suspicion is enough to justify a search. Customs agents may also open the mail if they have "reasonable cause" to believe it contains illegal merchandise. In 1986 the Court decided that investigators for the Environmental Protection Agency could fly over private property to search for toxic

Figure 6–2 "REASONABLE" SEARCHES WITHOUT WARRANTS These are typical cases in which the Supreme Court has allowed searches without warrants. 8B

★ Police may search an automobile without a warrant, provided they have probable cause to believe it contains illegal items. The search may include any packages in the automobile, and even a locked trunk. (*United States v. Ross,* 1982)

★ Police may make warrantless searches of persons who give consent voluntarily—even though they are not told they have the right to refuse. (*U.S. v. Matlock,* 1974)

★ Searches and seizures without warrants are permissible if police are in "hot pursuit." In a 1976 case, a woman sold heroin to an undercover agent, then fled to her home to avoid arrest. Without a warrant, police followed the suspect inside her home and searched her. Heroin and marked bills found during the search were used to convict her. (*United States v. Santana,* 1976)

★ Police do not need a warrant to seize evidence in "plain view." Police had seized a bag of marijuana they spotted in a car they had impounded for parking violations. (*South Dakota v. Opperman,* 1976)

★ Police looking for marijuana plants can fly over a fenced-in yard. (*California v. Ciraolo,* 1986)

★ Officers may approach passengers of long-distance buses at random and ask to search their belongings. The argument against this procedure was that in the confines of a bus, people may not feel free to say no to the police. (*Florida v. Bostick,* 1991)

Background: *Constitutional Heritage* The case that established the right to search without probable cause at airports was *U.S. v. Davis* (1973). *U.S. v. Ramsey* (1977) established the right of customs agents to open mail that might contain illegal merchandise.

Figure 6–2
● *Do you disagree with the Court's reasoning in any of these cases? Explain.*

waste dumps or other forms of pollution (*Dow Chemical Co. v. United States*).

Also in 1985 the Court held (6 to 3) that school administrators and teachers do not need either a warrant or probable cause before searching a student they suspect. The case involved a New Jersey high school vice principal who searched a 14-year-old student's purse for cigarettes and found marijuana and drug paraphernalia (*New Jersey v. T.L.O.*). (The three justices who voted against this ruling believed it weakened the Fourth Amendment.)

2D, 6E, 6I

The Use of Evidence

Illegal evidence

What if officials do use illegal methods to find evidence? In 1914 the Supreme Court decided a landmark Fourth Amendment case on this question. Federal agents had arrested Fremont Weeks and searched his home without a warrant. According to the court report, they took "books, letters, money, papers, . . . deeds, bonds, candies, clothes, and other property." Weeks protested that his rights under the Fourth Amendment had been violated and demanded that his property be returned. Instead, some of the letters and documents were used to convict him of a federal crime — sending lottery tickets through the mail.

In *Weeks v. United States,* however, the Supreme Court overturned his conviction — not because Weeks was innocent, but because the evidence used to convict him had been obtained without a warrant. Justice William R. Day explained the Court's decision:

> If letters and private documents can thus be seized and held and used as evidence against a citizen accused of an offense, the protection of the Fourth Amendment . . . is of no value . . . and might as well be stricken from the Constitution.

By this ruling, the Court established what is called the **exclusionary rule**, the principle that evidence obtained illegally cannot be used in federal court cases. The *Weeks* decision applied this rule only to federal cases. For more than forty years, state courts continued to allow evidence gathered by illegal searches.

Extending the exclusionary rule

On May 23, 1957, police in Cleveland, Ohio, knocked on the door of 19-year-old Dollree Mapp who, they believed, was hiding a man wanted for bombing a house. The police asked to search her house but did not have a warrant, and Mapp refused to let them in. A few hours later, the police broke into Mapp's house, looked through her personal belongings, and seized some obscene books and pictures. On the basis of this evidence, Mapp was tried and convicted for possessing obscene materials.

In *Mapp v. Ohio* (1961), the Supreme Court overturned her conviction because the evidence had been obtained illegally. The Court, for the first time, applied the exclusionary rule to state governments. The Court ruled that due process includes both the exclusionary rule and the Fourth Amendment protection against unreasonable searches and seizures. Because of the Fourteenth Amendment's due process clause, these protections apply to the states.

Exceptions to the exclusionary rule

As Justice Day pointed out in the *Weeks* case, the Fourth Amendment would be practically meaningless without the exclusionary rule. Critics, on the other hand, claim that criminals are often allowed to go free just because of technicalities about illegal evidence.

In response to complaints that accused criminals had too much protection, the Supreme Court in the 1970's began to whittle away at the exclusionary rule. The Court ruled in several cases that evidence obtained through illegal searches and seizures can sometimes be used in court. Two such decisions were made in 1984. In *Nix v. Williams,* the Court held that illegally obtained evidence is admissible if it would have "inevitably" been discovered by lawful means. In *United States v. Leon,* the Court permitted a "good faith" exception. The police in this case had used a warrant containing legal errors. But since the police had good reason to believe their search was legal, the Court ruled that the evidence could be used. In *California v. Hodari D.* (1991) the Court ruled that evidence discarded by a fleeing suspect can also be used. The police may use such evidence even if they did not believe the person had committed the crime when the chase began.

173

Science and Technology

● Have students suggest recent technological innovations that could be used by law enforcement officials to conduct surveillance without physically entering a suspect's home or office. (Possible answers include computers, high-resolution video cameras, sensitive microphones.)

♙♙ Cooperative Learning

● Divide the class into groups and have the groups debate the merits of the exclusionary rule. Members of each group should keep track of arguments for and against the exclusionary rule. Then reassemble the class and have groups compare their arguments.

GUIDED/INDEPENDENT PRACTICE

● Assign each student one of the cases described in Figure 6–2. Then have the students write a "police report" of a warrantless search that would be allowed under the circumstances described in the case they were assigned.

The symbol ♙♙ denotes active participation strategies.

Activities are keyed for student abilities:
▲ = Basic
● = All Levels
■ = Average/Advanced

▲ Have a volunteer read aloud the passage from the Fourth Amendment quoted on pp. 170–171. Then have another student paraphrase the passage. **What are the two main points of the amendment?** (Authorities cannot search or seize property without a good reason. To make searches and seizures, authorities must have specific warrants based on reasonable causes for the search.)

ENRICHMENT/EXTENSION

■ Have students complete **Skills Challenge Worksheet 6,** which has them determine different attitudes toward due process.

Have students complete **Supreme Court Decisions 22–28,** which deal with cases involving searches and seizures.

Section 2 Review Answers

1. (a) Yes, under almost all circumstances; it is a basic protection of the Fourth Amendment. **(b)** No; a boat could sail away before a warrant was obtained. **(c)** No; the suspect must be prevented from escaping. **(d)** Yes; an act of Congress requires it.
2. Evidence obtained illegally.
3. Criminals may go free because of technicalities.

Law enforcement agencies, such as the FBI (shown here), must have a warrant to set up surveillance. The inset shows tiny electronic "bugging" devices used to listen in on private conversations.

2D, 6E, 6I

Electronic Surveillance

Threats to privacy

Modern technology has given "search and seizure" a new meaning. Law-enforcement officials can now eavesdrop, or listen in, on private conversations with telephone wiretaps or electronic listening devices ("bugs"). They can keep someone under **surveillance** (ser-VAY-lunts), or observation, with hidden cameras or tape recorders. Ultra-sensitive microphones can pick up private conversations miles away.

Does the use of modern technology to gather criminal evidence violate the Fourth Amendment? Many people contend that the use of such methods represents serious government intrusion into private affairs. Many law-enforcement officials, however, argue that these devices are valuable weapons for fighting kidnappers, spies, and organized crime rings.

The first case to bring this issue before the public eye was *Olmstead v. United States* in 1928. Olmstead, a bootlegger, had been convicted in federal court on the basis of evidence gained by wiretapping his telephone. The Supreme Court upheld Olmstead's conviction, even though police had not obtained a warrant for the wiretap. Taking a very literal interpretation of the Fourth Amendment, the Court ruled that the wiretap was legal because it did not involve either entering Olmstead's house or seizing his property. The *Olmstead* decision remained the rule of law for nearly four decades.

Limits on surveillance

In 1967, however, the Court decided that the Fourth Amendment prohibits more than just *physical* intrusions and seizures. Charles Katz, a Los Angeles gambler, used a public telephone to place bets with bookmakers in Miami and Boston, which violated federal law. Without Katz's being aware of it, the Federal Bureau of Investigation (FBI) had placed a microphone on top of the phone booth and recorded his bets on college basketball games. Katz claimed that his rights had been violated.

Agreeing with Katz, the Court ruled that eavesdropping does not have to involve physical trespass to violate the Fourth Amendment (*Katz v. U.S.*). Justice Potter Stewart explained that the Fourth Amendment protects "people, not places." Stewart then went on to explain this distinction:

174

Cross-reference

"Speaking Out" on p. 801 quotes Justice Brandeis on *Olmstead v. United States.*

What a person knowingly exposes to the public, even in his own home or office, is not a subject of Fourth Amendment protection. . . . But what he seeks to preserve as private, even in an area accessible to the public, may be constitutionally protected. . . . What [Katz] sought to exclude when he entered the booth was not the intruding eye — it was the uninvited ear.

The Court's decision in the *Katz* case did not prohibit electronic surveillance entirely but made a valid warrant necessary. The following year, Congress passed a law controlling electronic surveillance. The Omnibus Crime Control and Safe Streets Act of 1968 requires court approval before law-enforcement officials may set up a wiretap or other "bug." Some emergency exceptions are permitted in organized crime or national security cases. Even then, authorities must apply for a warrant within 48 hours after installing the device. Under this law, several government wiretaps were found illegal.

A later act of Congress required warrants to bug or wiretap foreign agents operating in the United States. Because of the *Katz* ruling and these two laws, practically all electronic surveillance by government officials now requires a valid warrant.

SECTION 2 REVIEW

Vocabulary and key terms

warrant (171)
probable cause (171)
exclusionary rule (173)
surveillance (174)

For review

1. Is a warrant required (a) to search someone's home? (b) to search someone's boat? (c) to arrest a suspect fleeing from a crime? (d) to "bug" the hotel room of a suspected spy? Explain your answers. **6E**
2. What kind of evidence may not usually be used in court? **6E**
3. What is the main criticism of the exclusionary rule? **6E**
4. (a) What reasons did the Supreme Court give for allowing a wiretap in *Olmstead v. United States*? (b) Why did the Court reverse this decision in *Katz v. United States*? **2D**

Critical thinking

ANALYZING AN ISSUE When and how might the Fourth Amendment interfere with law enforcement? Should searches and seizures be restricted even if it means that some criminals go free? **6I**

4. **(a)** The wiretap did not involve entering Olmstead's house or seizing his property. **(b)** It ruled that the Fourth Amendment protects anything meant to be private, including conversations on public telephones.

Critical thinking When important evidence cannot be used because it was obtained illegally. In answering the second question, students should weigh the right to be secure in one's home and property against the need to punish criminals.

CLOSURE

● Have students define the vocabulary terms in their own words and use each term in a sentence describing an important concept discussed in the section. Then have students read Section 3, defining vocabulary terms as they encounter them.

2D, 6E, 6I, 8H

SECTION 3 The Fifth Amendment Protects the Rights of the Accused

> **ACCESS** The Main Ideas
> 1 What are the limits set by the Fifth Amendment on the legal system's ability to charge a suspect? *pages 176–177*
> 2 How does the Fifth Amendment protect suspects from self-incrimination? *pages 177–178*

In Great Britain, police officers read criminal suspects their rights when they are arrested. "You are under arrest," the officer says. "Any-thing you say may be taken down and used against you."

In the United States, the list of rights read after an arrest begins quite differently. The first right of every person accused of a crime is to remain silent, to refuse to give authorities the evidence necessary for conviction. On the stand in court, witnesses can refuse to answer questions that would prove they were guilty of a crime. This right is guaranteed by the Fifth Amendment, which adds more safeguards for people suspected or accused of crimes:

SECTION 3

The Fifth Amendment Protects the Rights of the Accused
(*pp. 175–178*)

Section Objectives

☐ detail the limits set by the Fifth Amendment on the legal system's ability to charge a suspect

☐ describe the Fifth Amendment's protection from self-incrimination

The symbol 👥 denotes active participation strategies.

Activities are keyed for student abilities:
▲ = Basic
● = All Levels
■ = Average/Advanced

Background: *Law* The act of Congress that makes a warrant necessary for bugging foreign agents is the Foreign Intelligence Surveillance Act of 1978.

175

Vocabulary

grand jury, capital crime, prosecuting attorney, indictment, true bill, presentment, double jeopardy, self-incrimination, immunity

 FOCUS

● On the board, write the following statements: *1. Protection against double jeopardy allows criminals to go free. 2. The Fifth Amendment's protection from self-incrimination subverts true justice. 3. "Pleading the Fifth" makes a witness appear guilty.*

Poll the class on their opinions of these statements by asking them to write on a blank piece of paper whether they strongly agree, agree, disagree, or strongly disagree with each of the statements. Have volunteers tally the results and report back to the class. Then discuss the results with the class.

EXPLANATION

After reviewing the content of the section, you may want to consider the following activities:

Constitutional Heritage

■ CRITICAL THINKING Justice Cardozo developed a two-question test to determine whether a right should be incorporated in the Fourteenth Amendment or if it should apply only to federal cases. Cardozo's test asks if the right is the "very essence of a scheme of ordered liberty" and a principle "so rooted in the traditions and conscience of our people as to be ranked as fundamental."

Ask students to consider how certain rights delineated in the Bill of Rights—freedom of religion and speech and protection from cruel and unusual punishment, for example—pass Justice Cardozo's test.

176

No person shall be held to answer for a capital, or otherwise infamous crime, unless on a presentment or indictment of a grand jury . . . nor shall any person be subject for the same offense to be twice put in jeopardy of life or limb; nor shall be compelled in any criminal case to be a witness against himself, nor be deprived of life, liberty, or property, without due process of law. . . .

6E, 6I

Limits on Criminal Charges

Grand jury investigations

To protect citizens from being unfairly charged with serious crimes, the Fifth Amendment states that there must first be a **grand jury** investigation. This procedure is not a trial, and the grand jury does not decide the person's guilt or innocence. Rather, this group of people is called together to look at the evidence and decide whether it is sufficient to justify a criminal trial. The right to such a grand jury hearing is guaranteed in all cases involving a serious federal crime, particularly a **capital crime** — one for which the death penalty may be given.

Usually the grand jury meets in secret to examine evidence that has been collected by the **prosecuting attorney**, the lawyer who represents the government. The prosecutor also presents an **indictment** (in-DYT-ment), a formal statement charging the accused person with certain crimes. If the members of the grand jury agree that the prosecutor's evidence is strong enough, they return a **"true bill** of indictment" calling for a trial. If they think the evidence is too weak, the charges are dropped.

Less commonly, a grand jury conducts its own investigation. The jury can call witnesses and gather evidence. Based on these findings, the grand jury may then issue a formal written accusation, or **presentment**.

Although many state constitutions allow for grand jury hearings, this provision of the Fifth Amendment is one that has not been "incorporated" in the Fourteenth Amendment. Therefore, states do not have to call a grand jury in order to bring someone to trial.

Double jeopardy

Another clause in the Fifth Amendment prevents the government from bringing a person to trial over and over again in an attempt to convict him or her of a crime. That is, it protects against

When a trial is under way, the judge, the lawyers, and other court officials must be concerned with protecting the rights of a person accused of a crime.

176

Background: *History* Since the early 1800's, most executions have resulted from murder convictions, as well as kidnapping and rape convictions. In 1977, however, rape was determined not to be a capital crime in *Coker v. Georgia.* Recently, there has been a move on the federal level and in several states to attach the death penalty to drug-related crimes.

double jeopardy (JEH-per-dee). The amendment states that no one shall "be subject for the same offense to be twice put in jeopardy [danger] of life or limb." The phrase "life or limb" is meant literally, for even a few hundred years ago, someone accused of a relatively small crime (such as stealing a loaf of bread) might be punished by hanging or by having a hand cut off.

The double jeopardy clause protects people from being prosecuted twice for the same crime, whether they have been convicted or found not guilty. A person who has been convicted and wants to appeal for another trial must officially give up, or waive, this protection. People are also protected against "multiple punishments" for the same offense — for instance, both a fine and a jail sentence, if the law demands only one or the other.

There are many cases that appear to be exceptions to the double jeopardy rule. For example, a person can be tried for the same act in both state and federal courts. This is legal because many serious crimes — such as bank robbery — are against both state and federal laws. A person can also be tried in both civil and criminal courts for the same act. If X deliberately hits Y over the head with a baseball bat, X may be taken to criminal court and charged with "battery." In addition, Y can sue X in civil court to recover damages and medical costs for the injuries. (The Supreme Court has also ruled that a person may be brought to trial both in an Indian tribal court and in state or federal court.)

In addition, a single crime may involve several criminal acts — for example, breaking and entering, murder, and robbery. The person may be tried separately for each of these acts, or the prosecution may choose to charge him or her with only the most serious one.

Other decisions depend on how "jeopardy" is defined. For instance, if a jury cannot agree on a verdict (a "hung jury") and the judge dismisses them, the defendant is not considered to have been in jeopardy. He or she can, and probably will, be brought to trial again.

In 1980 the Supreme Court narrowly upheld (by a 5–4 vote) the Organized Crime Control Act of 1970. This law was aimed at securing stiffer penalties against organized crime. It allows federal prosecutors to appeal cases in which they believe the jury has given a penalty that is too light

for the seriousness of the crime. The Court's ruling weakened the double jeopardy protection by letting the prosecution, as well as the defendant, appeal a case to a higher court (*United States v. DiFrancesco*).

2D, 6E, 6I

Protecting Witnesses

Freedom from self-incrimination

Perhaps the best-known Fifth Amendment protection is the right *not* to testify against oneself. That is, people do not have to give testimony in court that might "incriminate" them — reveal their personal involvement in criminal activity. A person may "take the Fifth Amendment" and refuse to answer a question on "grounds of self-incrimination."

Because the amendment says that no one "shall be compelled in any criminal case to be a witness against himself," this protection originally was applied only to defendants in federal criminal cases. Now, however, it has been extended to defendants and witnesses in grand jury investigations, civil trials, and congressional or legislative investigating committees. (In *Malloy v. Hogan* [1964], freedom from self-incrimination also was extended to state courts.)

Numerous complex restrictions apply to the right to "take the Fifth." Essentially, individuals can only refuse to give evidence that incriminates *themselves.* That is, they do not have the right to refuse to answer embarrassing questions or to withhold evidence that might incriminate someone else. Defendants who choose to testify at their own trials automatically give up their right to protect themselves.

Moreover, the courts have the final word on when and if the Fifth Amendment may be invoked. People who refuse to testify may be held in "contempt of court." This means that a person may be punished for obstructing the judicial process.

In an effort to avoid overuse of the Fifth Amendment, authorities may compel witnesses to testify but grant them **immunity**. This is a promise that witnesses' own testimony will not be used to prosecute them for crimes. In the 1950's the Supreme Court upheld this practice in several cases involving congressional investigations of people alleged to be Communists.

177

Law
● Ask volunteers to research your state's drunk-driving laws and report their findings to the class. Ask the class to apply what it has learned about Fifth Amendment protections to these laws. *Does a person have a right to refuse to take a breath test? If a person does refuse, what are the consequences? How does the principle of "innocent until proven guilty" apply to these laws?*

Cooperative Learning
● Divide the class into groups and have the groups pretend that they are grand juries conducting an investigation into either a case of local interest, or one of the cases described earlier in the chapter. Have students draw up a list of the kinds of witnesses they would like to hear from, and the kind of evidence they believe it is necessary to gather.

GUIDED/INDEPENDENT PRACTICE
● Have students create flow charts illustrating the grand jury procedure.

RETEACHING/ CORRECTIVES
▲ Write each vocabulary term on a slip of paper, put the slips in a bag, and ask students to reach into the bag and select one of the slips. Have the students write the definition of their vocabulary term (but not the term itself) on the board. Then choose students to identify the terms.

Background: *Law*
Protection against self-incrimination is not an absolute right to silence; it must be claimed. It is considered waived unless invoked, and when it is claimed, a judge must decide whether the claim is justified.

The symbol denotes active participation strategies.

Activities are keyed for student abilities:
▲ = Basic
● = All Levels
■ = Average/Advanced

ENRICHMENT/EXTENSION

■ Have students do research and write a report on the use of immunity during congressional hearings. Some suggested topics include the House Committee on Un-American Activities in the late 1940's and early 1950's and the investigation of the Iran-*contra* affair in the 1980's.

Section 3 Review Answers

1. To determine whether the evidence justifies a criminal trial.
2. Yes, because robbery and murder are two separate crimes. Double jeopardy is trying someone twice for the same crime.
3. The witness refuses to answer because he or she has the right not to testify against himself or herself.

Critical thinking Students opposed to forcing people to testify may quote Justice Douglas's arguments that the Fifth Amendment was intended to allow people to decide for themselves whether to testify. Students in favor of immunity may argue that the Fifth Amendment is intended to protect people from being forced to help the prosecution make its case against them.

CLOSURE

● Have each student write one question covering information in the chapter, and have students take turns asking the rest of the class the questions in an informal "college bowl." Then have students read Section 4, noting the factors that make a trial "fair."

Police may legally use a number of testing devices similar to this one to measure the level of alcohol in a person's blood and judge whether he or she should be charged with drunk driving.

Several justices, however, disagreed. They considered threats against unwilling witnesses to be contrary to the spirit of the Fifth Amendment. In a dissenting opinion written in 1956, Justice William O. Douglas said that the intent of the amendment was in part to "prevent any Congress, any Court, and any prosecutor from prying open the lips of an accused. . . ."

Physical evidence

The Fifth Amendment protects people from incriminating themselves by their *words*. But can evidence from a person's body, such as blood or hair, be used in a court of law? Under what conditions, if any, can the police take such evidence? This question involves both self-incrimination and illegal searches.

One morning in 1949, without warning, three Los Angeles County deputy sheriffs entered the house of Antonio R. Rochin, a suspected drug dealer. They found Rochin in bed, partially dressed, with two capsules on the nightstand next to him. Before the police could reach the nightstand, Rochin grabbed and swallowed the capsules. Unable to find other evidence, the deputies rushed Rochin to the hospital where his stomach was pumped. The morphine capsules found in Rochin's stomach were then used as evidence to convict him.

In *Rochin v. California* (1952), the Supreme Court unanimously overturned Rochin's

178

conviction as a violation of due process under the Fourteenth Amendment. Writing for the Court, Justice Felix Frankfurter said that the deputies' actions "do more than offend some fastidious squeamishness or private sentimentalism about combating crime too energetically. This is conduct that shocks the conscience."

In a concurring opinion, Justice Hugo Black argued that Rochin's case also involved his Fifth Amendment rights: "I think a person is compelled to be a witness against himself not only when he is compelled to testify, but also when as here, incriminating evidence is forcibly taken from him by a contrivance of modern science."

The question, then, is *how* evidence is obtained from a person's body. The Court has ruled that accused persons may be required to submit to "reasonable physical examinations." It also has allowed certain kinds of physical evidence: fingerprints and handwriting samples; blood, urine, or breath tests to show drugs or alcohol; and voice analysis, photographs, or police line-ups. These procedures are constitutional if they are conducted without force or brutality.

SECTION 3 REVIEW

Vocabulary and key terms

grand jury (176)	true bill (176)
capital crime (176)	presentment (176)
prosecuting	double jeopardy (177)
attorney (176)	self-incrimination (177)
indictment (176)	immunity (177)

For review

1. What is the purpose of a grand jury investigation? **6E**
2. Can a bank robber who kills a security guard be tried for both robbery and murder, or is that double jeopardy? Why or why not? **6E**
3. What does it mean when a witness "takes the Fifth"? **6E**

Critical thinking

EXAMINING BASIC PRINCIPLES Several Supreme Court justices believed that forcing witnesses to testify (even with immunity) is against the spirit of the Fifth Amendment. Do you agree? **8H**

Background: *Constitutional Heritage* Blood tests were allowed by *Schmerber v. California* (1966).

CRITICAL THINKING
Determining Relevance

To understand an issue, form your own opinion, and back your opinion with facts, you need sufficient information. Having *too much* information, however, can be just as troubling as not having enough. In analyzing any complex current issue, you must be able to sift through articles, editorials, talk shows, and interviews to pick out which information is useful and which is not. In other words, you must determine which information is **relevant**, or pertains to the issue at hand.

To take a simple example, suppose you want to know whether Mary Johnson thinks that people accused of crimes should be given more protection in investigations by police. You know three things about Mary: she has two children; she is a criminal defense lawyer; and she has favored Supreme Court decisions that sided with police officials over suspects.

Knowing that Mary has two children may tell you something about her, but the fact is **irrelevant**, or unrelated, to your question. Knowing that she is a criminal lawyer is certainly relevant, but that does not necessarily tell you her opinion on the issue. Knowing how she feels about Supreme Court decisions on the rights of the accused is the best indicator of her opinion.

★ ISSUE: The *Miranda* Decision

In 1966, Chief Justice Earl Warren wrote the majority opinion for a landmark Supreme Court decision, *Miranda v. Arizona.* The Court's decision has been a source of controversy ever since. Basically, *Miranda* requires police to inform criminal suspects of certain rights before police may begin questioning. (The "*Miranda* warnings" are listed on page 184.) Supporters of *Miranda* praised it as a needed protection of the rights of the accused. Critics claimed the decision "handcuffed" police, making it more difficult for them to do their job.

The following statements about the *Miranda* decision are all true. Read them carefully before answering the questions that follow.

A. Before the *Miranda* ruling, most police departments routinely read suspects their rights.

B. Statistics show that less than 1 percent of criminal convictions are reversed because of illegal confessions.

C. Most suspects waive their *Miranda* rights and speak with police voluntarily.

D. Many criminal lawyers believe *Miranda* is an important protection of the rights of the accused.

E. After the *Miranda* decision, some members of Congress called for Earl Warren's impeachment.

F. Not many Americans sympathize with accused criminals.

G. The *Miranda* rights do not mean that a suspect will go free. Ernest Miranda himself was retried and reconvicted.

H. Criminal justice systems in other countries require all questioning to be done in the presence of a neutral magistrate.

Analyzing the Issue

1. Which of the statements above support the assertion that *Miranda* protects the rights of the accused?

2. Does Statement A show that the Miranda rule is necessary? Why or why not?

3. Which of the statements could be used to discuss how the American people feel about the *Miranda* decision?

4. Which statements could be used both by supporters and opponents of the *Miranda* decision? Why?

5. Which statement would be relevant in arguments for further extending the rights of the accused?

6. Write a short paper either defending or opposing the *Miranda* decision. Use the statements above to support your argument.

179

CRITICAL THINKING

Law
A lawyer for the suspect does not have to be present during questioning. According to the *Miranda* warning, the suspect has the right to have a lawyer present if he or she wishes.

● CRITICAL THINKING ***Would you favor requiring a lawyer to be present during questioning? Explain.*** (Some students will argue that requiring a lawyer's presence would ensure that suspects' rights were protected. Others will argue that if a suspect is willing to talk to the police without a lawyer present, he or she should be allowed to do so.)

Analyzing the Issue Answers
1. D.
2. It implies that *Miranda* is unnecessary, but does not state that *all* police departments read *all* suspects their rights.
3. D and E indicate how some parts of the population feel about *Miranda.* F tells how people feel about criminals, from which one might infer people's opinion of *Miranda.*
4. A, B, C, and G could be used by opponents to argue that *Miranda* is unnecessary or by supporters to argue that it does not interfere with the criminal justice system.
5. H.
6. Students should use supporting statements that are relevant to their topics.

The symbol ♟♟ denotes active participation strategies.

Activities are keyed for student abilities:
▲ = Basic
● = All Levels
■ = Average/Advanced

SECTION 4

The Sixth Amendment Ensures a Fair Trial
(pp. 180–184)

Section Objectives

☐ list the Sixth Amendment's requirements for a fair trial

☐ describe the cases leading to the expansion of the right to legal advice

Vocabulary

petit jury, subpoena, counsel, public defender, felony, misdemeanor

🏃 FOCUS

● Have the class debate whether an accused person who is too poor to hire a lawyer should be given free legal help. One side of the class should give arguments in favor of free legal help, while the other side of the class should provide arguments against it.

EXPLANATION

After reviewing the content of the section, you may want to consider the following activities:

🏃 Civic Participation

● Have students imagine that they are prospective jurors for a current criminal case of local significance. Ask for four volunteers to serve as the lawyers in this case: two prosecuting attorneys and two defense attorneys. You will serve as the judge. Have groups of six students stand in front of the class and answer questions put to them by the prosecutors and defenders about their background, legal experiences, and feelings about the case. After everyone has been questioned, have the class

180

SECTION 4
The Sixth Amendment Ensures a Fair Trial

ACCESS The Main Ideas

1 What are the requirements for a fair trial established by the Sixth Amendment?
pages 180–182

2 Which cases led to the expansion of the right to legal advice?
pages 182–184

In the late 1960's a series of decisions by the Supreme Court expanded the rights of the accused — and received a strong reaction from the press and public officials. The *Washington Star* editorialized against one decision by claiming it would be "received with rejoicing by every thug in the land." Billboards went up across the country calling for the impeachment of Chief Justice Earl Warren. Congress tried to overrule the Court by passing the 1968 Crime Control and Safe Streets Act. Richard Nixon, the Republican presidential candidate in 1968, attacked the Court's rulings in his speeches. He claimed their interpretation of the Sixth Amendment would make it almost impossible for the police to restore "law and order." He won the election.

Have Supreme Court decisions given the accused too many rights? The Sixth Amendment guarantees the right to a "fair" trial: one that occurs quickly before an impartial jury, where the accused can be represented by a lawyer, face prosecution witnesses, and call witnesses of his or her own. This section examines these guarantees and how they have been interpreted by the Supreme Court in recent decades.

6E, 6I

A Fair Trial

"A speedy and public trial"

An old saying in law is that "justice delayed is justice denied." For this reason, the Sixth Amendment guarantees a "speedy" trial — that is, no undue delay between a person's arrest and trial. A prompt trial is important for several reasons. For society and the victims of crime, it means the swift administration of justice. For the

180

accused person — especially one who is innocent — it lessens the difficulties, financial losses, and public disgrace associated with facing criminal charges. Finally, a prompt trial reduces the chances that witnesses will move away, forget their testimony, or even die.

The Supreme Court has never defined "speedy" but has made decisions on a case-by-case basis. In *Barker v. Wingo* (1972), the Court set forth a "balancing test" based on four factors: (1) the length of delay, (2) the reason for delay, (3) whether the accused demanded the right to a speedy trial, and (4) whether the accused was harmed by the delay.

Following this case, Congress passed the Speedy Trial Act of 1974, which limited the time between arrest and trial in federal cases to 100 days (extra time can be allowed for illness or psychiatric examination). In most cases, if this deadline is not met, the judge is to dismiss the charges.

The right to a *public* trial is also one of the basic freedoms in English and American law. It was seen as an essential protection against unjust decisions made in secret by judges or other officials. This safeguard is for the benefit of the accused, not the general public. For this reason, a judge may restrict the number of spectators at a trial or clear the courtroom of noisy or disturbing witnesses.

News coverage of trials

Several important civil rights may conflict when journalists are reporting the events of a trial — freedom of the press, the right to privacy, the right to a fair trial. In some highly publicized trials, the Court has decided that too much media coverage can interfere with a trial.

For example, in 1954, Dr. Samuel H. Sheppard, a Cleveland, Ohio, physician, was accused of bludgeoning his wife to death in their home. Sheppard insisted he was innocent, claiming that a "bushy-haired intruder" had broken in and committed the crime. Months before his trial, however, local newspaper editorials had said

---

Background: *Constitutional Heritage* The Seventh Amendment ensures trial by jury in most federal *civil* cases.

Critical Thinking
● *How might justice delayed be justice denied?* (Delays increase the time the accused lives under the stress of possible punishment. Delays also increase the possibility that vital witnesses or evidence will become unavailable.)

Sheppard was guilty. During the trial, reporters talked freely with witnesses and jurors, many of whom had read the damaging news reports. Sheppard was convicted but appealed his case. In *Sheppard v. Maxwell* (1966), the Supreme Court reversed Sheppard's conviction and ordered a new trial. The Court agreed that the publicity and "carnival atmosphere" had denied Sheppard a fair and impartial trial. Shortly thereafter, he was retried and acquitted.

In other cases, however, the Court has given more weight to freedom of the press and has upheld the right of news reporters to cover trials. In 1980, the Court ruled that "a trial courtroom also is a public place where the people generally — and the representatives of the media — have a right to be present." A year later, the Court upheld the right of states to permit televised trials, even when defendants object. Today, over half the states allow television coverage of trials.

Choosing an impartial jury

The Sixth Amendment also states a jury must be *impartial*. The members of a trial jury, called a **petit** (or petty) **jury**, should evaluate evidence fairly and then decide an accused person's guilt or innocence. The Sheppard case shows one example of a situation in which the jury could not be impartial — the jurors were biased against the defendant before they heard any evidence.

Another requirement for an impartial jury is that jurors must represent a cross-section of the community. In principle, this means all adult citizens should have equal chances to be called for jury duty. In practice, however, jurors are usually chosen from the list of registered voters. Moreover, laws in some states automatically disqualify certain groups of people — attorneys, military personnel, people who are mentally ill or unable to read, write, or speak English. Other laws permit the exemption of elderly persons, doctors, dentists, teachers, journalists, clergy, government employees, or persons whose jobs might be jeopardized by spending time on jury duty.

Other sorts of limits on jurors are not allowed. The Supreme Court has ruled that exclusions based on race, sex, or national origin are unconstitutional. In 1986, for example, the Court ruled that a prosecutor could not reject potential jurors simply on the basis of their race. Such exclusion, claimed the Court, violated the defendant's right to equal protection of the law. This rule applies regardless of the race of the defendant or the potential jurors.

The right to know the charges

Not knowing *why* you have been arrested or jailed is a frightening prospect. To protect people against this, the Sixth Amendment says that people must be told "the nature and cause of the accusation." This right means, first, that criminal laws must be drawn precisely so that accused persons know the legal reasons for their arrest. Second, it means that an accused person must be given a copy of the official charges. An additional protection is a prisoner's right to demand a writ of habeas corpus (page 89).

The right to confront witnesses

In addition to knowing the crimes with which they are charged, people have the right to see and hear the witnesses who are testifying against them. One intent of this Sixth Amendment provision was to allow both the jury and the accused to observe witnesses in person, not merely hear their written accusations read in

Once members of a jury have been chosen, they are sworn in by the bailiff, a court official.

consider whom the prosecutor would choose to serve on the jury, and whom the defense attorney would choose.

Multiculturalism

● The Scottsboro case (p. 182), a landmark case in the civil rights movement, was brought to the Supreme Court again in 1935, when the Court overturned the conviction of two of the young men on the grounds that African Americans were not allowed to serve on juries in Alabama.

Have students do research on the case and present their findings to the class.

Law

▲ *Why is the suspect's right to know the charges so important?* (It is almost impossible to prepare a good case for the defense without knowing the charges.)

Discuss how the provisions for a fair trial relate to the assumption that a person is "innocent until proven guilty." (These protections are concerned with giving defendants all possible means to prove their innocence.)

181

Background: *Constitutional Heritage* The case in which televised trials were allowed was *Richmond Newspapers, Inc. v. Virginia* (1980). The case in which a defendant's objection to such trials was denied was *Chandler [and Granger] v. Florida* (1981).

Background: *Constitutional Heritage* The cases involving the exclusion of jurors on the basis of race were *Batson v. Kentucky* (1986) and *Powers v. Ohio* (1991).

The symbol ⫯⫯ denotes active participation strategies.

Activities are keyed for student abilities:
▲ = Basic
● = All Levels
■ = Average/Advanced

Cooperative Learning

● Divide the class into groups and have the groups write a question for each subheading in the section. Then have the groups compete as teams in a "fair trial bowl," with each group asking the other groups its questions and gaining or losing points based on the ability of the group to answer the questions correctly or to stump the other groups.

GUIDED/INDEPENDENT PRACTICE

● Have students complete **Primary Source Worksheet 10,** which examines Justice Hugo Black's opinion in *Gideon v. Wainwright.*

The right to discuss one's case with a lawyer is a basic civil liberty under the Constitution.

court. (The protection applies only in jury trials, not grand juries or preliminary hearings.)

The accused person, then, has the right to be in court when adverse testimony is given. The defense lawyer (or the defendant) also must have a chance to cross-examine witnesses to weaken or discredit their statements. Defendants can lose this right if they are voluntarily absent from the courtroom or disrupt the trial so much that the judge removes them (*Allen v. Illinois,* 1970).

The right to call defense witnesses

Until the eighteenth century, British subjects accused of crimes were not permitted to introduce witnesses in their own defense. To avoid this situation in the American legal system, the Sixth Amendment requires the government to call witnesses to testify *for* the accused person. The government does this by issuing a **subpoena** (suh-PEA-nah), a court order requiring a person to appear as a witness. The court can punish persons who do not appear.

Although nearly all state constitutions have similar guarantees, this Sixth Amendment protection was not applied to the states until 1967 (*Washington v. Texas*). In this case, the Court overturned a Texas law that forbade an accused person's accomplices to testify on his or her behalf. Today, all state courts must make "good faith" efforts to secure defense witnesses.

182

The Right to Legal Advice

An old saying among lawyers is, "The man who is his own lawyer has a fool for a client." That is, even the best trained legal minds might have trouble defending themselves in court. People untrained in law would have little or no chance of proving their innocence. For this reason, the Sixth Amendment guarantees persons accused of crimes the right to have an attorney who can give legal advice, or **counsel**. Until recently, few defendants benefited from this right.

Originally, the guarantee of legal counsel applied only to people charged under federal law with a crime punishable by death (capital crime). In 1938, in a case involving counterfeit money, the Court extended this right to people charged with any federal crime.

Crimes against state law

The sensational "Scottsboro cases" of the 1930's resulted in a Supreme Court decision that also granted the right to counsel in *state* capital crimes. A group of black teenagers had been arrested and charged with raping two young white women on a freight train near Scottsboro, Alabama. The youths were from out of town, and the court named local lawyers to defend them. But the lawyers and the defendants never met until the trial began. An all-white jury quickly convicted the so-called "Scottsboro boys" and asked for the death penalty. In *Powell v. Alabama* (1932), the Supreme Court ordered a new trial, ruling that the defendants had been denied due process.

Except in special circumstances, however, the Court did *not* extend the right to counsel for state offenses that did not carry the death penalty. This decision was made by the Court in *Betts v. Brady* (1942), and stood for more than twenty years, until the landmark decision of *Gideon v. Wainwright* (1963).

The *Gideon* case

In June 1961, Clarence Earl Gideon was arrested and charged with breaking into a poolroom in Panama City, Florida, and stealing wine, beer, and some small change from the jukebox. Gideon, a drifter with a prison record, was too poor to hire a lawyer. The state court refused to appoint one for him. Convicted of breaking

Background: *Constitutional Heritage* The case in which the Court extended the right to legal counsel to everyone accused of a federal crime was *Johnson v. Zerbst* (1938).

and entering, he was sentenced to five years in the Florida State Prison. After studying law books in the prison library, Gideon became convinced that he had been denied his constitutional rights. He wrote an appeal by hand and sent it directly to the Supreme Court.

The Court looked into the case and then appointed Abe Fortas, a prominent lawyer (later a Supreme Court justice), to represent Gideon. The state of Florida was represented by an inexperienced lawyer who had never appeared before the Court. After hearing both sides, the Court voted unanimously to reverse Gideon's conviction because he had been denied counsel. This decision, they said, was a return to principles intended to achieve "a fair system of justice."

Drawing on both the Sixth and Fourteenth Amendments, Justice Hugo Black wrote the Court's opinion that a person on trial "who is too poor to hire a lawyer, cannot be assured a fair trial unless counsel is provided for him." Gideon was given a new trial several months later. This time, with the aid of a local court-appointed lawyer, he was acquitted. Because of Gideon's stubborn determination, thousands of other prisoners who had been convicted without having the advice of an attorney were set free.

His study of law in prison inspired Clarence Earl Gideon to take his case to the Supreme Court.

Public legal assistance

Today, all levels of American government provide legal counsel for people who cannot afford to hire an attorney. In 1964, Congress enacted legislation to hire court-appointed attorneys in federal cases. Many states now employ **public defenders**, who serve as defense lawyers for poor people charged with state crimes. Other states pay private attorneys.

The *Gideon* ruling extended the right to counsel only to those charged with state **felonies** — serious crimes for which the prison sentence is at least a year and a day. The question of what to do with suspects charged with less serious crimes, or **misdemeanors**, had not been answered. In 1972 (*Argersinger v. Hamlin*), the Court unanimously held that, because any jail sentence is a serious matter, the right to counsel should extend to any offense for which a defendant can be imprisoned. Later it ruled that a person cannot actually be sent to jail without having legal counsel (*Scott v. Illinois,* 1979).

Legal counsel for suspects

Sixth Amendment protections were intended to ensure accused persons both a fair trial and adequate legal advice. As these protections were broadened, the next question was whether they apply to police investigations and questioning *before* a person comes to trial.

In 1960 Danny Escobedo, a Chicago laborer, was picked up by police and questioned about the fatal shooting of his brother-in-law. Escobedo was then released, but he was picked up again ten days later and interrogated for several hours. He asked to talk to his lawyer but was not allowed to; the lawyer was told to wait until the interrogation was over. During the four hours of questioning, Escobedo — handcuffed and kept standing — made statements that incriminated him. This evidence led to his conviction.

Four and a half years later, the Supreme Court overturned Escobedo's conviction in a 5–4 decision (*Escobedo v. Illinois,* 1964). Writing for the majority, Justice Arthur Goldberg explained that once "the [questioning] process shifts from investigatory to accusatory," the accused is entitled to an attorney under the Sixth Amendment. Because Escobedo had not had access to a lawyer during questioning, his confession was not legal evidence.

183

RETEACHING/CORRECTIVES

▲ Have students write a paragraph describing the conditions necessary for a fair trial. (The trial should take place soon after arrest; it should not be secret but also not be surrounded by a "carnival atmosphere"; the jury should be impartial; the defendant should have a lawyer; the defendant should know and understand the charges; the defendant should be able to face the witnesses against him or her and to call other witnesses.)

ENRICHMENT/EXTENSION

■ Have students arrange for the class to attend local court proceedings and view the legal system in action. Ask them to try to arrange to speak with the judge following the court session. Students might also write a short essay describing the trial and their reactions to it.

You may also want students to complete **Supreme Court Decision 29,** which deals with *Sheppard v. Maxwell,* and **Supreme Court Decisions 30–34,** which deal with cases involving the right to legal advice.

Background: *Law* Not all courts draw the same distinctions between felonies and misdemeanors. In general, a felony involves murder, manslaughter, arson, burglary, and rape. Convicted felons can lose certain legal rights, such as the right to vote or to bear arms. Misdemeanors generally include gambling, assault and battery, reckless driving, and petty larceny (theft). Felons are usually sent to state prisons, while persons convicted of misdemeanors are usually sent to city or county jails.

The symbol ii denotes active participation strategies.

Activities are keyed for student abilities:
▲ = Basic
● = All Levels
■ = Average/Advanced

Section 4 Review Answers

1. A speedy, public trial by an impartial jury.

2. The right to know the charges, to confront witnesses, to call defense witnesses, and to receive counsel.

3. (a) Because people untrained in law may have a difficult time preparing a good defense. (b) It ruled that any accused felon who cannot afford a lawyer has the right to free defense counsel.

4. *Escobedo* required police to admit lawyers to accusatory interrogations; *Miranda* required police to advise suspects of their rights before questioning.

Critical thinking In their answers, students should weigh the importance of protecting the innocent against the need to punish the guilty.

CLOSURE

● Have students define the vocabulary terms in their own words. Then have them read Section 5, noting the Supreme Court's interpretation of the Eighth Amendment.

Arresting officers must read suspects their rights under the *Miranda* decision.

The *Miranda* rule

The *Escobedo* ruling opened up new questions. What if suspects do not know they have the right to legal counsel? Should suspects be told an attorney will be appointed for them if they cannot afford one? When should suspects be told they have a right to remain silent? These questions were addressed two years later in *Miranda v. Arizona* (1966).

Ernesto Miranda was a mentally disturbed drifter who kidnapped and raped an 18-year-old woman near Phoenix, Arizona. Ten days after the crime, the victim picked Miranda out of a police line-up. He was interrogated for two hours and confessed. At no time during the interrogation was Miranda informed that he had the right to remain silent or to have an attorney. The confession was used as evidence to convict him.

The Supreme Court overturned Miranda's conviction in a 5–4 decision. It also set forth new rules for police procedure, based on both the Fifth Amendment protection against self-incrimination and the Sixth Amendment right to counsel. Chief Justice Earl Warren issued specific guidelines for what came to be called the "*Miranda* warnings." Prior to any questioning, accused persons must be clearly told:

184

1. They have the right to remain silent.
2. If they give up the right to remain silent, anything they say can and will be used against them in a court of law.
3. They have the right to consult with a lawyer before and during questioning.
4. Their failure to request legal counsel does not mean they give up the right to counsel.
5. Counsel will be appointed if they cannot afford legal fees.

The *Miranda* decision, both in principle and in practice, has caused great debate. Supporters maintain that it is not too much to ask police officers to inform accused persons of their rights. Further, they believe that it is better to set a guilty person free than to put an innocent person in jail without due process. Critics, however, believe that the rule hampers police work and lets criminals avoid prosecution through legal technicalities. (In 1976, Miranda was stabbed to death during a barroom brawl in Phoenix. The person arrested for the killing was read the *Miranda* warnings.)

SECTION 4 REVIEW

Vocabulary and key terms

petit jury (181)   felony (183)
subpoena (182)   misdemeanor (183)
counsel (182)   *Miranda* warnings
public defender (183)   (184)

For review

1. According to the Sixth Amendment, what kind of trial is a person entitled to have? **6E**
2. What rights does the Sixth Amendment give an accused person during a criminal trial? **6E**
3. (a) Why is the right to legal counsel important? (b) What effect did the *Gideon* case have on this right? **6E**
4. How did the *Escobedo* and *Miranda* cases change police procedures? **2D**

Critical thinking

FORMING AN OPINION Critics of Supreme Court decisions on the Fifth and Sixth Amendments argue that criminals are allowed to go free because of "technicalities." Is it better to let criminals escape justice than to jail innocent people? **6**

Background: *Controversial Issues* The *Miranda* decision was so unpopular that it led to calls for the impeachment of Chief Justice Earl Warren. The case was an election issue in 1968, when presidential candidate Richard Nixon, campaigning on a "law and order" platform, strongly criticized the decision.

SECTION 5

2A, 2D, 3A, 6E, 6H

Due Process Includes Other Rights

> **ACCESS** **The Main Ideas**
>
> 1 How does the Eighth Amendment guarantee fair treatment for those convicted of crimes?   *pages 185–186*
> 2 How have Supreme Court rulings regulated capital punishment?   *pages 186–187*

Should the death penalty be legal? For more than 100 years, the Supreme Court has considered aspects of that question. The Court's decisions have been based on the Eighth Amendment, which bans excessive bail and fines as well as "cruel and unusual punishment." But the questions remain: What is excessive? And what is "cruel and unusual"?

2D, 3A, 6E

Eighth Amendment Rights

Innocent until proven guilty

A man once spent 54 days in a Washington, D.C., jail awaiting trial for a traffic violation. Had he been convicted, the maximum sentence would have been only five days! Unfortunately, the man in this case could not afford to post **bail**. That is, he lacked a certain sum of money to leave with the court as security to go free until the start of the trial.

The Eighth Amendment was intended to avoid cases such as this one. The idea of posting bail follows the principle of American and English law that people are presumed innocent until proven guilty in a court of law. To put people in jail before they have been tried for their crime would violate this principle. Furthermore, releasing accused persons on bail gives them a better chance to prepare their defense. At the same time, bail is a guarantee that the accused, once free, will not attempt to escape justice. If the person does not appear for the trial, the bail is forfeited.

Limits on bail

To ensure that someone accused of a crime is not deprived of this right, the Eighth Amendment states that "excessive bail shall not be required, nor excessive fines imposed."

How much bail is "excessive" has never been precisely defined but varies from case to case. In general, the amount depends on both the person's ability to pay and the seriousness of the crime. For example, someone arrested for armed robbery would probably have to pay more bail than someone arrested for shoplifting. In setting bail, the court also considers such factors as the accused person's age, family status, employment record, and residency. A person who has a job, family, and home within the court's jurisdiction is considered more likely to show up for trial than someone who does not.

Like other constitutional protections, the right to post bail is not absolute. The court is likely to deny bail to suspects accused of capital crimes or those believed to be highly dangerous to the community. Furthermore, this provision of the Eighth Amendment has never been incorporated in the Fourteenth Amendment and so applies only to federal crimes. Most state constitutions, however, include similar protections.

The Bail Reform Act

One drawback of the bail system is that it does not treat all people fairly. People with low incomes, unable to raise enough money for bail, must remain in jail until their trial is held. To address this problem, Congress passed the Bail Reform Act of 1966. This law requires federal officials to release people who cannot meet bail payments, unless they are accused of a capital crime or there is good reason to believe they will fail to appear in court.

This law also provides that the time a person spends in jail awaiting trial is subtracted from any sentence given later. For example, suppose a man spends 34 days in prison awaiting trial. If he is then convicted and sentenced to 90 days, he must remain in jail for only 56 more days. Although the Bail Reform Act does not apply to state courts, many follow similar procedures.

185

Section Objectives

☐ describe the Eighth Amendment guarantee of fair treatment for those convicted of crimes

☐ describe the U.S. Supreme Court rulings regulating capital punishment

Vocabulary
bail, capital punishment

FOCUS

● On the board, write the word *fair.* Ask students to suggest legal provisions mentioned in the section that have to do with fairness and ask them to explain their suggestions. (Possible suggestions include bail, the Bail Reform Act, *Weems v. U.S., Trop v. Dulles,* objective standards for the death penalty.)

EXPLANATION

After reviewing the content of the section, you may want to consider the following activities:

Values

▲ Have students create political cartoons that express their point of view on capital punishment.

Background: *Law* Money for bail may come from the accused or from family and friends, or a professional bondsman or bondswoman may provide the money for a fee. A judge may accept a person's promise to appear in court in lieu of money; this is known as releasing a person on his or her *own recognizance.*

The symbol **ii** denotes active participation strategies.

Activities are keyed for student abilities:
▲ = Basic
● = All Levels
■ = Average/Advanced

Cooperative Learning

● Divide the class into groups and assign each group to examine either the *Weems* or the *Trop* case. Have the groups determine whether the original punishment was "cruel and unusual" and then create a short presentation explaining their decision.

GUIDED/INDEPENDENT PRACTICE

● Have students create an outline of this section. They may wish to refer to Study Skill 7, "Writing an Outline," on p. 784.

RETEACHING/CORRECTIVES

▲ Have students find evidence in the text to support the following statements: *(1) Because accused persons are presumed innocent until proven guilty, they may be released on bail* (p. 185). *(2) The right to post bail is not absolute* (p. 185). *(3) Cruel and unusual punishments are unconstitutional* (p. 186). *(4) In order for the death penalty to be constitutional, states must set up objective criteria for its implementation* (p. 187).

"Cruel and unusual punishment"

Due process extends beyond the rights of the accused to include other aspects of criminal justice. To ensure that punishments for convicted criminals are carried out fairly, the Eighth Amendment forbids "cruel and unusual punishment."

What kind of punishment is "cruel and unusual"? The Supreme Court has held that barbaric punishments and tortures — such as burning at the stake, starvation, or beheading — are unconstitutional. Moreover, any punishment that is obviously out of line with the nature of the crime may be considered cruel and unusual.

In the early 1900's, Paul Weems was a U.S. Coast Guard officer stationed at Manila in the Philippines, then a United States possession. In keeping accounts for the captain of the port, Weems wrongly recorded payments of about 600 pesos to lighthouse keepers. He was found guilty of "falsifying government documents." The Philippine legal code, styled after Spanish law, prescribed the following punishment: "They shall always carry a chain at the ankle, hanging from the wrists; they shall be employed at hard and painful labor." For his bookkeeping error, Weems was sentenced to fifteen years at hard labor. In *Weems v. United States* (1910), the Supreme Court ruled that this was indeed excessive punishment.

In a similar case, Albert Trop, a soldier stationed in French Morocco during World War II, was stripped of his American citizenship for trying to desert. Trop had escaped from a stockade in Casablanca, but turned himself in the following day. In *Trop v. Dulles* (1958), the Supreme Court ruled that this punishment was too severe. Trop's citizenship was reinstated.

The Eighth Amendment not only applies to the method and severity of punishment, but also restricts the types of conduct that can be punished. For example, in 1962 the Court struck down a California state law that made it a crime for a person to be a drug addict. The Court ruled that it was cruel and unusual to punish a person for being ill. (This was the first time that a state law was overturned as "cruel and unusual punishment"; see Figure 6–1.) Later, though, the Court made it clear that people can be punished for behavior, such as public drunkenness or possession of drugs.

Background: *Constitutional Heritage* The decision that struck down California's law against being a drug addict was *Robinson v. California* (1962).

The Death Penalty Controversy

Whether **capital punishment**, or the death penalty, is cruel and unusual has long been a constitutional issue. For many people it is also a serious moral or religious question. Even those who support the death penalty as a deterrent to crime often do so reluctantly.

The Supreme Court first ruled on the question of capital punishment over a hundred years ago, in *Wilkerson v. Utah* (1878). In this case the Court ruled that execution by firing squad was constitutional because it was carried out swiftly, without cruelty. Twelve years later, the Court upheld the use of electrocution as a method of capital punishment (*In re Kemmler*, 1890). Years later, in a bizarre Louisiana case, a condemned prisoner, Willie Francis, was strapped to the electric chair, but when the executioner threw the switch, nothing happened. Francis appealed, but the Supreme Court ruled 5–4 that it was not cruel and unusual to subject him to electrocution twice (*Louisiana ex rel. Francis v. Resweber*, 1947).

Court rulings on capital punishment

For years, opponents of capital punishment pressured the Supreme Court to abolish it on legal grounds. The Court's decision in *Furman v. Georgia* (1972) appeared to do so. In this decision, the Court ruled 5 to 4 that the death penalty, as it was carried out everywhere in the United States and its territories, violated both the Eighth and the Fourteenth Amendments.

Several justices believed that the death penalty, in modern times, is always "cruel and unusual punishment." Others stressed that state laws allowed judges and juries too much discretion in deciding between the death penalty or a prison term. Justice Potter Stewart declared that the death penalty was "wantonly" and "freakishly" imposed, in a way that discriminated against racial minorities and the poor. (At the time of the *Furman* decision, 329 of the 600 people awaiting execution were black, and 14 were Hispanic or American Indian.)

The *Furman* decision invalidated all existing state and federal death penalty laws, but it did not outlaw the death penalty itself. Hence, the Court left open the possibility that states could again enact death penalty laws, provided such

Although prison conditions may be harsh, prisoners' rights also are protected by the Constitution's forbidding of "cruel and unusual punishment."

laws followed the *Furman* guidelines in setting up objective, non-discriminatory standards. Within four years, more than thirty states passed new death penalty laws. In 1976 the Court heard a series of cases challenging the laws.

New death penalty standards

In one of these cases, *Gregg v. Georgia* (1976), the Court ruled that "punishment of death does not invariably violate the Constitution." To pass the constitutional test, however, a law must not be arbitrary. Consideration must be given to the facts of the case, the accused's past record, and events surrounding the crime. The death penalty cannot be mandatory.

In 1977, the country's first execution since the *Furman* decision took place when Gary Gilmore was executed by a Utah firing squad. Executions remained rare at first, but by the second half of the 1980's there were roughly twenty executions per year. Several Supreme Court decisions made in the late 1980's and early 1990's have limited opportunities for appeals from death row.

SECTION 5 REVIEW

Vocabulary and key terms

bail (185)   capital
Bail Reform Act (185)   punishment (186)

For review

1. (a) What is the principle that allows posting bail? (b) Why did Congress pass the Bail Reform Act? **6H**
2. What kinds of punishment are considered cruel and unusual? **6E**
3. According to the Supreme Court decisions in *Furman v. Georgia* and *Gregg v. Georgia,* is the death penalty unconstitutional? Explain. **2D**

Critical thinking

ANALYZING AN ISSUE What constitutional arguments can be made against and in favor of the death penalty? **2A**

187

Background: *Controversial Issues* Since the late 1960's, public support for the death penalty has increased dramatically. Public opinion was quoted by the Supreme Court in the *Gregg* decision. The Court also noted that punishment by death itself does not violate the Constitution.

ENRICHMENT/EXTENSION
■ Have students do research on the status of capital punishment in your state: whether it is legal, for what crimes, by what method, how many have been executed in the last year, and how many prisoners are waiting on death row.

You may also want students to complete **Supreme Court Decisions 35–36,** which deal with cases involving the death penalty.

Section 5 Review Answers
1. (a) People are presumed innocent until proven guilty in a court of law. (b) People with low incomes were usually unable to post bail and had to remain in jail until trial.
2. Barbaric punishments, torture, and punishments out of line with the nature of the crime.
3. No, but it must be carried out in an objective way and not be mandatory.

Critical thinking Arguments should revolve around the constitutional issues of whether the death penalty is either "cruel and unusual" or denies due process. Some arguments may involve moral, religious, or philosophical issues.

CLOSURE
● Have students determine the main idea of the passages under each subheading. Then have students read Section 6, analyzing the Supreme Court's interpretation of the right to privacy.

The symbol ⅱ denotes active participation strategies.

Activities are keyed for student abilities:
▲ = Basic
● = All Levels
■ = Average/Advanced

The Right to Privacy Is Protected *(pp. 188–189)*

Section Objectives
☐ determine the constitutional basis for the right to privacy
☐ define the "zones of privacy" that are protected from government interference

FOCUS
● Discuss with the class the concept of "unalienable rights." *How well does the Bill of Rights protect our "unalienable rights"?*

EXPLANATION
After reviewing the content of the section, you may want to consider the following activities:

Constitutional Heritage
● Create a chart of the "zones of privacy." Have students list the zones and suggest which amendments, Court cases, and laws fall under each zone.

Cooperative Learning
■ Divide the class into groups and ask each group to make a list of rights that they believe exist though these rights are not specified in the Bill of Rights.

GUIDED/INDEPENDENT PRACTICE
● Have students write a short essay stating their opinion on whether there should be a constitutional amendment guaranteeing the right to privacy.

RETEACHING/CORRECTIVES
▲ *Which amendment implies the right to privacy?* (Ninth Amendment.) *What are the three main zones of privacy?* (Thoughts and beliefs, personal information,

---

2A, 6E, 6H, 8H

The Right to Privacy Is Protected

> **ACCESS** The Main Idea
> **What are the "zones of privacy" that are protected from government interference?**
> *pages 188–189*

Suppose that at school you were given a list of rules, which included things you were allowed to do as well as those that were prohibited. Would you assume that anything *not* included on the list was banned? That if driving to school was not noted, for example, you had to walk?

Of course not. A list that attempted to include all rights and privileges would be enormous. Yet the authors of the Bill of Rights worried that the government might act as though civil rights not specifically spelled out did not exist. To end that threat, they added the Ninth Amendment: "The enumeration in the Constitution of certain rights shall not be construed to deny or disparage others retained by the people."

2A, 6E, 6H

Zones of Privacy

What exactly are the "rights retained by the people"? Do they include the right to breathe fresh air, the right to marry, the right to have children, the right to die, or the right to read? The Supreme Court has made very few rulings that clarify the Ninth Amendment, but it has consistently upheld one unmentioned right — the right to privacy. In these decisions, the justices have drawn not only on the Ninth Amendment but also on interpretations of the First, Fourth, Fifth, and Fourteenth amendments.

Supreme Court decisions have established certain "zones of privacy," where Americans can expect to be free from government interference in their lives. For example, the Fourth Amendment protection against surveillance without a warrant also entitles people to have private conversations. People also have the right to privacy (1) in their thoughts and beliefs, (2) about personal information, and (3) in family and personal relationships.

188

Personal information
A necessary function of government is the keeping of records — for taxes, for government programs, for the census. On the other hand, individuals have the right to privacy in their personal affairs. Therefore, in 1974 Congress passed two important laws that protect the privacy of personal records.

The Privacy Act of 1974 stipulates that certain information about private individuals may not be made public without their consent. For example, employment, financial, health, and criminal records are protected. Individuals, however, generally have access to government files about themselves. In addition, the Family Educational Rights and Privacy Act of 1974 prevents school boards from disclosing their records to other agencies of government. Parents have the right to examine their children's school files, such as test scores and teachers' reports. Students over 18 may check their own records.

Privacy in personal relationships
The Supreme Court has also strongly upheld the right to privacy in family matters, especially the relationship of a married couple. Justice William O. Douglas described this area as "a right of privacy older than the Bill of Rights."

In 1965 the Supreme Court made one of its first rulings that specifically cited the Ninth Amendment. Under a Connecticut law that made birth control devices illegal, a marriage counselor was arrested for giving a married couple information about the use of birth control. In *Griswold v. Connecticut,* the Court declared the Connecticut law unconstitutional. The privacy of a marriage, the Court ruled, was a right within the "penumbra," or shadow, of specific guarantees of the Bill of Rights. In addition, the Court ruled that the right to privacy was one of the fundamental rights retained by the people under the Ninth and Fourteenth amendments.

Abortion
A far more controversial ruling based on the Ninth Amendment was made eight years later. In

Roe v. Wade (1973), the Court overturned a Texas law that made abortion illegal. They found the law a violation of the right to privacy under the Ninth and Fourteenth Amendments. Specifically, the Court ruled that in the first three months of pregnancy, women have the right to decide for themselves, without government interference, whether to have an abortion. States were allowed to set limits on abortion in the later months of pregnancy, however.

In the years since *Roe*, the controversy surrounding legal abortion has grown. In 1986 the Supreme Court reaffirmed a woman's right to seek an abortion *(Thornburgh v. American College of Obstetricians and Gynecologists)*. Yet in 1991 the Court ruled that federal regulations could prevent workers in federally funded clinics from discussing abortion with their patients *(Rust v. Sullivan)*. Just two years before, the Court had upheld a Missouri statute in *Webster v. Reproductive Health Services* (1989). That law barred public funds from being spent on abortion and ordered doctors to perform fetal-viability tests on women seeking abortions after 20 or more weeks of pregnancy.

In one of the most long-awaited decisions in recent years, the Court upheld *Roe* in *Planned Parenthood of Pennsylvania v. Casey* (1992). However, in the same ruling, the Court gave states new powers to restrict access to abortions.

SECTION 6 REVIEW

Vocabulary and key terms

zones of privacy (188)   Privacy Act (188)

For review

1. What does the Ninth Amendment guarantee? **2A**
2. What important "zones of privacy" have been established by Supreme Court decisions? **6H**
3. How did the two privacy acts passed in 1974 protect individual rights? **6H**

Critical thinking

THINKING ABOUT BASIC IDEAS How might the right to privacy conflict with other rights or with the powers of government? **8H**

Chapter Summary

The Bill of Rights contains several guarantees of procedural due process that protect the legal rights of citizens suspected, accused, or convicted of crimes. Under the due process clause of the Fourteenth Amendment, many of these provisions apply to the states as well as the federal government.

The Fourth Amendment prohibits government from making unreasonable searches of individuals' homes or seizures of their property. Law-enforcement officials, upon probable cause, must obtain a warrant to make a legal search. In certain situations, some searches without warrants are allowed. Under the exclusionary rule, evidence found in an illegal search may not be used in court. The Fourth Amendment also protects individuals from electronic surveillance except with a warrant.

The Fifth and Sixth Amendments guarantee many important legal rights. The Fifth Amendment requires a grand jury investigation before people can be charged with federal crimes. It also protects individuals against double jeopardy and self-incrimination. The Sixth Amendment guarantees the accused a speedy, fair, and public trial by an impartial jury. People on trial also have the right to legal counsel, to know the charges, to confront witnesses who testify against them, and to call witnesses on their own behalf. Because of the *Miranda* decision, suspects must be warned of their rights as soon as they are arrested.

The Eighth Amendment guarantees that citizens held in jail have a reasonable opportunity to be released on bail. It also protects convicted criminals from "cruel and unusual punishment." The Eighth Amendment does not prohibit capital punishment; however, laws calling for the death penalty must not be arbitrary, unfair, or discriminatory.

The Ninth Amendment protects the rights "retained by the people" — all the rights not specifically listed in the Constitution. This includes the right to be free from government interference in private matters. Citizens have the right to privacy in their thoughts and beliefs, personal records, and relationships.

189

family and personal relationships.) *In which of these was Griswold decided?* (Family and personal relationships.)

You may also want to use **Transparency 16,** which shows what policies states might adopt if *Roe v. Wade* were overturned.

ENRICHMENT/EXTENSION
■ Have students complete **Supreme Court Decisions 37–38,** which deal with cases involving abortion.

Section 6 Review Answers
1. Rights not listed in the Constitution are still protected.
2. Privacy of thoughts and beliefs, about personal information, and in family and personal relationships.
3. They protect the privacy of an individual's records.

Critical thinking It might conflict with the need of government to find evidence or protect people's welfare and health.

CLOSURE
● Have students define the vocabulary terms and explain how they relate to the section. Then have students read the next assigned lesson.

CHAPTER 6 CORRECTIVES
● To review the content of Chapter 6, you may want to have students complete **Study Guide/Review 6** or **Workbook Chapter 6.**

Background: *Constitutional Heritage* *Roe v. Wade* ruled that states can regulate abortions during the second trimester and forbid abortions during the third trimester, except abortions necessary to save the mother's life.

The symbol **ïi** denotes active participation strategies.

Activities are keyed for student abilities:
▲ = Basic
● = All Levels
■ = Average/Advanced

CHAPTER 6 REVIEW

Answers

Vocabulary See pp. T19–T21 for suggested vocabulary activities.

Reviewing the Facts

1. During wartime if a duly enacted law is passed.
2. The Supreme Court has decided that the Constitution does not guarantee the absolute right to own firearms, with no restrictions.
3. They must appear before a magistrate, swear that they have probably cause, and state exactly what they wish to search and seize.
4. Officials now can eavesdrop on private conversations with telephone wiretaps or listening devices, and they can maintain surveillance with hidden cameras and tape recorders.
5. Only to avoid revealing personal responsibility in a crime.
6. An impartial jury, the right to know the charges, the right to call and cross-examine witnesses, and the right to legal counsel.
7. It gave felony defendants the right to legal advice, even if they could not afford a lawyer.
8. To allow persons accused of crimes to be released from prison so that they can prepare their defense. The amount of bail depends on the seriousness of the crime as well as the accused's age, employment, family status, and residency.
9. Death penalty laws left too much discretion to judges and juries and tended to discriminate against racial minorities and the poor.
10. Privacy in thought and belief, of personal information, and in personal relationships.

Thinking Critically About Key Concepts

1. Most are thought to be essential aspects of due process, and thus apply to the states through the Fourteenth Amendment.

● **Review the definitions of the following terms:**

bail	immunity	public defender
Bail Reform Act	indictment	self-incrimination
capital crime	*Miranda* warnings	subpoena
capital punishment	misdemeanor	substantive due process
counsel	petit jury	surveillance
double jeopardy	presentment	true bill
due process of law	Privacy Act	warrant
exclusionary rule	probable cause	zones of privacy
felony	procedural due process	
grand jury	prosecuting attorney	

● **REVIEWING THE FACTS**

1. Under what circumstances can Americans be forced to house soldiers? **1D**
2. What is the Supreme Court's stand on local gun control laws? **2D**
3. What steps must law-enforcement officials take to acquire a warrant? **6E**
4. How does modern technology give new meaning to "search and seizure"? **6I**
5. Under what conditions can a person "take the Fifth"? **2A**
6. Under the Sixth Amendment, what elements are necessary for a fair trial? **6I**
7. What was the significance of the Supreme Court case *Gideon v. Wainwright?* **2D**
8. What is the purpose of bail, and how is the amount of bail set? **6E**
9. In *Furman v. Georgia,* why did the Supreme Court invalidate all state death penalty laws? **2D**
10. What are three zones of privacy protected by the Ninth and other amendments? **6H**

▲ **THINKING CRITICALLY ABOUT KEY CONCEPTS**

1. Why have most provisions for due process in the Bill of Rights been incorporated under

the Fourteenth Amendment's due process clause? **6I**
2. Why might the Supreme Court have ruled that school officials can search students without probable cause? **6E**
3. Does the practice of granting immunity to witnesses contradict the spirit of the Bill of Rights? Explain your answer. **6H**
4. What generalizations can you make about the way Supreme Court decisions have changed the procedures for due process? **2D**
5. How would you describe people's right to privacy in their thoughts and beliefs? **5A**

▲ **PRACTICING SKILLS**

1. **Study Skills: Reading a table.** Refer to Figure 6–1 (page 169) to answer the following questions. (a) What do the court cases in the chart illustrate? (b) What decision extended the self-incrimination clause of the Fifth Amendment to state courts? (c) By what date had all the provisions of the Sixth Amendment been extended to state courts? (d) What protections are not guaranteed in all state cases? **8B**
2. **Critical Thinking Skills: Predicting consequences.** Refer to Section 4 (pages 180–184) to answer the following questions. (a) What might a federal court judge decide if a

---

2. The safety and well-being of other students are more important than protection of the individual against search and seizure.
3. Students may argue that compelling a person to testify is always wrong.

Other students may claim that no harm is caused so long as immunity is granted.
4. Students may note that, in general, the Court has strengthened the rights of the accused.

5. Students may note that the government cannot force you to declare what religion you are, or require you to state your point of view on a political or social issue.

suspect were arrested on April 7 but did not come to trial until September 14? Why? (b) What might a judge decide if it were discovered during a trial that the arresting officer never informed the suspect of the right to remain silent? Why? **8H**

▲ PARTICIPATORY CITIZENSHIP

1. **Drawing a chart.** Develop a flow chart which illustrates due process. The chart should follow an accused person from the moment of arrest for a federal crime, through grand jury proceedings, the trial, and subsequent treatment (presuming conviction). You may wish to refer to Study Skill 2 in the *Handbook of Basic Skills* (page 778). **8E**
2. **Developing research skills.** Working with others, list the various ways by which you might determine your state's laws and record

concerning capital punishment. The group should then evaluate the list. What are the good and bad points about each method? Which would you use if you needed to find this information for a report? **8A**

■ WRITING ABOUT ISSUES

1. **Organizing an essay.** Write an essay explaining the importance of protecting people accused of crimes. Address the question of whether such protections interfere with society's need to punish lawbreakers. **6I**
2. **Connecting with theater.** A number of plays have been written in which crucial scenes take place at a trial: for example, *The Caine Mutiny, The Crucible, Inherit the Wind,* and *Twelve Angry Men.* Read one of these plays and write a report on the fairness of the trial described in the play. **8C**

▲ ANALYZING A POLITICAL CARTOON

During the 1980's, widespread use of dangerous, illegal drugs prompted some people to call for mandatory drug testing. Look at the cartoon below and answer the following questions.

1. What kind of a classroom does the cartoon show? **8B**
2. Why is the age of the children involved related to the cartoon's effectiveness? **8B**
3. Do you think that the cartoonist favors mandatory drug tests? Explain. **8B**

Cartoon by Scott Stantis. Reprinted by permission of The Commercial Appeal.

191

CHAPTER 7
CIVIL RIGHTS: EQUAL PROTECTION OF THE LAW
(pp. 192–221)

	Section Objectives	Section Resources
Section 1 **African Americans Struggle for Equal Rights**	☐ identify the provisions and purposes of the Thirteenth, Fourteenth, and Fifteenth Amendments ☐ trace the development of legalized discrimination against African Americans through the 1940's	● PRIMARY SOURCE WORKSHEET **11** ■ CONSTITUTIONAL ISSUES WORKSHEET **7** ■ SUPREME COURT DECISIONS **39–42** ▲ TRANSPARENCY **17**
Section 2 **The Civil Rights Movement Gains Momentum**	☐ explain the consequences of the Supreme Court decision in *Brown v. Board of Education* ☐ describe the goals and achievements of the civil rights movement	■ SKILLS CHALLENGE WORKSHEET **7** ● PRIMARY SOURCE WORKSHEETS **12–13** ■ SUPREME COURT DECISIONS **43–44** ▲ TRANSPARENCY **18**
Section 3 **Civil Rights Policies Seek Equality for All Americans**	☐ describe how other ethnic groups besides African Americans gained fuller civil rights ☐ detail the two main points of view on the affirmative action issue	● PRIMARY SOURCE WORKSHEET **14** ■ CONSTITUTIONAL ISSUES WORKSHEET **8** ■ SUPREME COURT DECISIONS **45–49**
Section 4 **American Women Seek the Rights of Citizens**	☐ describe how women in the United States gained the right to vote ☐ name the areas in which laws and Supreme Court decisions have reduced discrimination against women	▲ SKILLS PRACTICE WORKSHEET **7** ● PRIMARY SOURCE WORKSHEET **15** ■ CONSTITUTIONAL ISSUES WORKSHEET **9** ■ SUPREME COURT DECISIONS **50–52** ▲ TRANSPARENCIES **19–20**

Essential Elements

The list below shows Essential Elements relevant to this chapter.
(The complete list of Essential Elements appears in the introductory
pages of this Teacher's Edition.)

Section 1: 2D, 5C, 6C, 6H, 6I, 8E

Your Turn feature (p. 199): 5A, 5B

Section 2: 2D, 5A, 6B, 6C, 6G, 6I

Section 3: 2D, 5A, 6B, 6E, 6G, 6I, 8B

Section 4: 1D, 2C, 2D, 5C, 6B, 6C, 6E, 6G, 6I, 8A, 8B, 8H

Chapter Review: 2D, 5A, 5C, 6A, 6C, 6F, 6G, 6I, 8B, 8C, 8D, 8E

Section Resources are keyed
for student abilities:
▲ = Basic
● = All Levels
■ = Average/Advanced

Homework Options

Each section contains activities labeled "Guided/Independent Practice," "Reteaching/Correctives," and "Enrichment/Extension." You may wish to choose from among these activities when assigning homework.

Students Acquiring English Activities

Remind students that the United States is a nation of immigrants. Have students study their family's heritage to find their own roots. If possible, students should report the year their ancestors came to the United States and where they first settled. Ask students to learn at least one phrase in the native language of their ancestors and then say it to the class.

LISTENING/SPEAKING: Have students ask someone who has learned English as a second language to describe the process. Also have students discuss the advantages of knowing more than one language.

Case Studies

When teaching this chapter, you may use Case Study 1, which addresses the relevancy of the Constitution; Case Study 8, which discusses the question of women serving in combat; or Case Study 12, which deals with the issue of special public schools for African American males. (Case Studies may be found following p. 510.)

Teacher Bibliography

Cagin, Seth and Philip Dray. *We Are Not Afraid.* Macmillan, 1988. A compelling account of the murders of the civil rights workers who went to Mississippi in the summer of 1964 to register black voters.

Deloria, Vine, Jr. and Clifford M. Lytle. *The Nations Within: The Past and Future of American Indian Sovereignty.* Pantheon, 1984. Discusses Native Americans' attempts to gain their civil rights.

Faludi, Susan. *Backlash: The Undeclared War Against American Women.* Crown, 1991. Pulitzer Prize-winning journalist documents the response to women's progress.

Student Bibliography

Becker, Susan D. *The Origins of the Equal Rights Amendment: American Feminism Between the Wars.* Greenwood Press, 1981. Looks at the history of equal rights from the 1920's to today.

Coles, Robert. *Children of Crisis, Vol. I.* Little, Brown, 1967. Experiences of African American students at the forefront of desegregation.

Williams, Juan. *Eyes on the Prize: America's Civil Rights Years, 1954–1965.* Viking, 1987. Chronicles the civil rights movement.

Literature

Barry, Kathleen. *Susan B. Anthony: A Biography of a Singular Feminist.* New York University Press, 1988. Traces Anthony's political evolution.

Ellison, Ralph. *Invisible Man.* Random House, 1952. The story of a young black man during the Depression. A powerful classic.

Morrison, Toni. *The Bluest Eye.* Holt, Rinehart & Winston, 1970. A moving story of a poor, African American girl's dream of having blue eyes.

Shange, Ntozake. *Betsey Brown.* St. Martin's, 1985. A 13-year-old black girl encounters prejudice when she attends an all-white school.

Styron, William. *The Confessions of Nat Turner.* Random House, 1967. Narrative of the slave rebellion in Virginia, by its instigator. A Pulitzer Prize winner.

CHAPTER RESOURCES

Study Guide/Review 7
Workbook Chapter 7
Chapter 7 Test, Forms A–C

Films and Videotapes*

The Pursuit of Equality. (Series title: *This Constitution: A History.*) 28 min. PSUAVS, 1987. v. The historical development of the idea of equality is shown by looking at federal civil rights policies in the past twenty years.

Eyes on the Prize. 60 min. each. PBS, 1986. v. A prize-winning, six-program documentary that covers the civil rights movement from 1954 to 1966.

Software*

Visions of American History: Struggles for Justice (Amiga). Scholastic. This interactive videodisc program uses stills, maps, animation, speeches, biographies, music, and text. Volume 1 portrays the struggle of Native, Latino, and African Americans. Volume 2 focuses on women, labor, and immigrants.

Law in American History I (Apple, IBM). Queue. Using the case study method, students are presented with landmark Supreme Court cases. Includes seven programs: The case of Peter Goodman, the Intolerable Acts, the Bill of Rights, a vigilante mock trial, *Brown v. Board of Education, Tinker v. Des Moines,* and a mock sex discrimination trial.

African American History (Apple, IBM). TS. Students and teachers can create a variety of historical time lines covering slavery, the civil rights movement, and notable African Americans.

* For a complete guide to audiovisual sources, see page T22.

CHAPTER 7

Civil Rights: Equal Protection of the Law *(pp. 192–221)*

Chapter 7 opens with a discussion of the historical background of African Americans' struggle for civil rights and then traces the history of the expansion of voting rights and desegregation, closing with accounts of the efforts of other groups inspired by the civil rights movement.

Chapter Objectives
After students read this chapter, they will be able to:

1. Identify the provisions and purposes of the Thirteenth, Fourteenth, and Fifteenth Amendments.

2. Trace the development of legalized discrimination against African Americans through the 1940's.

3. Explain the consequences of the Supreme Court decision in *Brown v. Board of Education.*

4. Describe the goals and achievements of the civil rights movement.

5. Describe how other ethnic groups besides African Americans gained fuller civil rights.

6. Detail the two main points of view on the affirmative action issue.

7. Describe how women in the United States gained the right to vote.

8. Name the areas in which laws and Supreme Court decisions have reduced discrimination against women.

CHAPTER 7

CIVIL RIGHTS: Equal Protection of the Law

I have a dream that one day on the red hills of Georgia, the sons of former slaves and the sons of former slave-owners will be able to sit together at the table of brotherhood. . . . That my four children will one day live in a nation where they will not be judged by the color of their skin but by the content of their character.

Dr. Martin Luther King, Jr.
"I Have a Dream,"
Washington, D.C. (1963)

192

Photo
Coretta Scott King and other civil rights activists mark the 30th anniversary of the historic "March on Washington."

On the morning of August 28, 1963, close to thirty special trains pulled into Union Station in Washington, D.C. Thousands of chartered buses rolled into the city, and thousands more cars arrived, parking where they could. Over a quarter of a million Americans gathered, marching through the streets of the capital. Their aim: to press Congress for passage of the Civil Rights Act.

The huge crowd assembled before the Lincoln Memorial. Martin Luther King, Jr., a minister who had led the drive to integrate public buses in Montgomery, Alabama, took the podium. Quoting from the Declaration of Independence and the Bible, he spoke of racial equality and an end to discrimination. His voice rising with emotion, he ended with a call for a day when all people could say, ''Free at last! Free at last! Thank God almighty, we are free at last!''

The March on Washington was part of a long struggle by African Americans to win their civil rights. Other groups in the United States have also fought for equal opportunity and equal treatment under the law. This chapter examines the response to this call for equality.

CHAPTER OUTLINE

1 African Americans Struggle for Equal Rights

The Civil War and Civil Rights
Legalized Discrimination
Early Gains in Civil Rights

2 The Civil Rights Movement Gains Momentum

Public School Desegregation
The Civil Rights Movement

3 Civil Rights Policies Seek Equality for All Americans

The Rights of Other Minorities
Ensuring Fair Laws
Affirmative Action

4 American Women Seek the Rights of Citizens

The Right to Vote
Discriminatory Laws
Ending Sex Discrimination

193

African Americans Struggle for Equal Rights *(pp. 194–198)*

Section Objectives

☐ identify the provisions and purposes of the Thirteenth, Fourteenth, and Fifteenth Amendments

☐ trace the development of legalized discrimination against African Americans through the 1940's

Vocabulary

discrimination, segregation, "Jim Crow" laws

FOCUS

● Copy the following statement, made by Frederick Douglass in October 1883, on the board: "No man can put a chain about the ankle of his fellow man without at last finding the other end fastened about his neck." Ask students to read the statement and explain it. (Limiting opportunities for one group of people ultimately limits opportunities for all people.) Then ask students to suggest the ways in which laws and customs segregating African Americans harmed American society.

You may wish to end the discussion with the following quotation by Hubert Humphrey: "The struggle for equal opportunity in America is the struggle for America's soul. The ugliness of bigotry stands in direct contradiction to the very meaning of America."

SECTION 1

African Americans Struggle for Equal Rights

ACCESS The Main Ideas

1 What are the provisions and purposes of the Thirteenth, Fourteenth, and Fifteenth Amendments? *pages 194–195*

2 How did legalized discrimination against African Americans develop? *pages 195–198*

Olaudah Equiano was about ten years old and living in what is now the country of Nigeria when he was kidnapped. Along with hundreds of others he was put in chains in the hold of a ship, whipped when he refused to eat, and kept awake by the groans of the sick and dying. After this nightmarish voyage, Equiano arrived in the Americas — and was sold as a slave.

Equiano's experience, which took place in the mid-1750's, was shared by millions of Africans. The Civil War freed their descendents from the horrors of slavery, but the war did not end segregation and prejudice. Laws passed in the 1860's and 1870's extending full rights to African Americans were often ignored. Discrimination against African Americans was a fact of life in both the North and South. It was nearly 100 years before the issue of black civil rights again became a national concern.

The Civil War and Civil Rights

The *Dred Scott* case

Even before the Civil War, the issue of slavery threatened to divide the nation. One of the earliest legal battles over the rights of black Americans was the famous 1857 case of *Dred Scott v. Sanford.* Dred Scott, a slave born in Virginia, had lived both in Illinois, where slavery was forbidden, and in Minnesota, a territory declared free by the terms of the Missouri Compromise of 1820. In 1846, Scott filed a lawsuit to gain his freedom, claiming that his residence in the free territories made him a free citizen.

The case eventually came to the Supreme Court, which ruled 7 to 2 against Scott after months of bitter debate. The Court's opinion,

194

written by Chief Justice Roger B. Taney, was that blacks, whether free or slave, could not become citizens, because they were not considered citizens by the Constitution. Therefore, Scott did not even have the right to bring a lawsuit in federal courts. The Court also ruled that the Missouri Compromise's ban against slavery was unconstitutional. Slavery, it said, was a matter of *state* law.

Rather than settling the question of slavery, the *Dred Scott* decision increased tensions between the North and South. It would take a bloody Civil War and three constitutional amendments to overturn the Court's decision.

The Civil War amendments

President Lincoln's Emancipation Proclamation of 1863 freed slaves in the Confederate states. After the Civil War ended, the Constitution was amended to give former slaves not only their freedom but also the rights of citizens. The Thirteenth Amendment, passed in 1865, declared that "neither slavery nor involuntary servitude" could exist anywhere in U.S. territory except as punishment for a crime.

The Fourteenth Amendment, passed in 1868, clearly defined citizenship: "All persons born or naturalized in the United States, and subject to the jurisdiction thereof, are citizens of the United States and of the State wherein they reside." The amendment promised all black Americans not only United States citizenship but also the "equal protection of the laws." Jacob Howard, a Michigan senator who fought for the amendment in Congress, said that it was intended to give "to the humblest . . . , the same rights and the same protections before the law as it gives to the most powerful, the most wealthy, or the most haughty."

The seemingly straightforward provisions of the Fourteenth Amendment led to endless legal disputes. Nearly a hundred years later, the question of "equal protection" became the focus of the modern civil rights movements.

One final result of the Civil War was the Fifteenth Amendment, ratified in 1870. This

---

Background: *History* When Abraham Lincoln became President, he considered supporting a constitutional amendment to

protect slavery in the South. As the abolitionists' views spread, however, Lincoln changed his position.

amendment stated that the right of all U.S. citizens to vote cannot be denied "on account of race, color, or previous condition of servitude." This amendment was aimed clearly at ensuring black Americans and former slaves the right to vote. Many states, however, soon found ways to get around the Fifteenth Amendment.

The first civil rights laws

Some hopes were fulfilled in the decades after the Civil War, and black Americans did witness some political gains. In the South, a few black officials were elected to both state and national government posts. Blacks also made modest inroads in employment, entering the building trades and other skilled crafts.

Under the authority of the Thirteenth Amendment, Congress quickly enacted the nation's first civil rights legislation — the Civil Rights Act of 1866. Like the amendments, this law seemed to hold great promise. It offered blacks the same rights enjoyed by white citizens "to inherit, purchase, lease, sell, hold, and convey real and personal property." It also made punishable **discrimination** — treating one person or group differently from another — "by reason of his color or race." But to many people's bitter disappointment, the law had little real effect. Most sections were either repealed by later Congresses, declared unconstitutional by the Supreme Court, or simply never enforced.

In fact, it was not until 102 years later in the case of *Jones v. Mayer* (1968) that the Supreme Court upheld the 1866 Civil Rights Act. In this case a land developer had refused to sell a house to Jones because he was black. Ruling for Jones in the 1968 decision, Justice Potter Stewart proclaimed that "the freedom that Congress is empowered to secure under the Thirteenth Amendment includes the freedom to buy whatever a white man can buy, the right to live wherever a white man can live."

2D, 5C

Legalized Discrimination

Limits on the Fourteenth Amendment

Unsympathetic Supreme Court rulings made most early civil rights laws ineffective. They also weakened the three constitutional amendments that had been meant to ensure black civil rights. One clause in the Fourteenth Amendment was specifically intended to prevent discrimination by state governments. It provides that "No State shall make or enforce any law which shall abridge the *privileges or immunities* of citizens of the United States."

This provision was soon challenged in a group of court cases that had no real connection with civil rights. In the *Slaughterhouse Cases* of 1873, the Supreme Court upheld a Louisiana law that granted a monopoly to one butcher in the

A contemporary engraving shows President Abraham Lincoln and his Cabinet at the first reading of the Emancipation Proclamation, issued in 1863.

195

Background: *Economics*
Real property includes land, buildings, and improvements to the land. *Personal* property includes tangible items such as jewelry and furniture, as well as intangible possessions such as bank accounts and stocks.

Check for Understanding
▲ *Why did the Civil Rights Act of 1866 not end discrimination against African Americans?* (Much of it was repealed, not enforced, or declared unconstitutional.)

EXPLANATION
After students have read the section, you may want to consider the following activities:

Constitutional Heritage
● Have students read the Thirteenth, Fourteenth, and Fifteenth Amendments on pp. 131–133. *What rights do these amendments guarantee to African Americans?* (Freedom from slavery, rights of citizenship and equal protection under the law, right to vote.) *How did* Plessy v. Ferguson *allow segregation to exist despite these guarantees?* (It declared that separating the races was constitutional as long as the separate facilities were equal.)

Discuss with the class how prevailing attitudes may have influenced the Supreme Court's decision in that case.

Multiculturalism
● Ask students to list some of the effects of segregation on African Americans in the South. (African Americans had to attend separate schools and restaurants, and use separate public facilities; they could not vote.)

The symbol ꙮ denotes active participation strategies.

Activities are keyed for student abilities:
▲ = Basic
● = All Levels
■ = Average/Advanced

History

▲ Have students list important national and international events occurring during the late 1930's and 1940's, the period when the Supreme Court began to show greater concern for individual rights and liberties. (The Great Depression and World War II.)

● CRITICAL THINKING **How might these events have influenced the Court?** (During the Depression, more Americans looked to the government to solve problems. African Americans made important contributions to the war effort. The United States was fighting for democracy abroad, causing some Americans to re-examine democracy at home.)

Cooperative Learning

● Divide the class into groups and ask each group to choose one of the Supreme Court cases mentioned in the section. Have the groups prepare arguments for both sides in the case and choose representatives to present these arguments to the class.

Patterns of racial separation set by the Jim Crow laws of the late 1800's persisted for many decades in all regions of the country. When this picture was taken, stores were still racially segregated, especially in the South.

state. Other butchers had claimed that the law violated their rights to equal protection under the Fourteenth Amendment.

The Court's decision severely narrowed the protections of the Fourteenth Amendment and allowed state governments to continue limiting civil rights. Legislators, especially in the southern states, soon began to pass discriminatory laws. Legal devices such as literacy tests and poll taxes were developed to prevent blacks from voting. Once blacks lost their right to vote, it became easy for employers, as well as state and local governments, to discriminate against them.

Segregation laws

Other state legislation actually represented a step backward for blacks in the South. These laws gave official support to the **segregation**, or separation, of blacks and whites in public places. Such **"Jim Crow" laws** (named after a minstrel-show song) actually increased segregation as well as making it lawful. State laws required that blacks and whites attend separate schools, be treated in different hospital wards (or in different hospitals), and even be buried in separate cemeteries. There were "Jim Crow" cars on passenger trains. Likewise, many local ordinances did not allow blacks to use the same drinking fountains, restrooms, or hotels as whites. Housing also was segregated by law.

196

The Civil Rights Cases

The courts continued to give support to state laws that legalized segregation. Although Congress passed several more civil rights acts, they also were ineffective. The last of these, the Civil Rights Act of 1875, tried to eliminate segregation, promising all persons, regardless of race and color, the "full and equal enjoyment" of any public accommodations and facilities.

In 1883, five cases under this law came before the Supreme Court as the *Civil Rights Cases.* They involved incidents in both northern and southern states. One, for example, involved a black woman who was refused admission to the "ladies' car" on a passenger train in Tennessee. Two were against theaters, in New York and California, that would not admit blacks.

In a single decision on all five cases, the Court declared the 1875 Civil Rights Act unconstitutional. The Fourteenth Amendment, said the Court, prohibited discrimination only by state governments. Because railroads and theaters were *private* enterprises, Congress had no authority to limit discrimination in them.

"Separate but equal"

Legal support for segregation laws was established even more firmly in the landmark 1896 case of *Plessy v. Ferguson.* Homer Plessy, who was one-eighth black, challenged a Louisiana

---

Background: *Cultural Literacy* The term *Jim Crow* originated in the early 1800's.

Background: *Constitutional Heritage* Justice John Marshall Harlan objected to the Supreme Court's ruling in the *Civil Rights Cases.* During his Supreme Court career, Harlan delivered 316 dissents, far more than any other justice.

"Jim Crow" law that required blacks and whites to ride in separate coaches on trains. Plessy bought a ticket in New Orleans and took a seat in a "whites only" car. When he refused to move, he was arrested and convicted of violating state law. Plessy then sued, contending that the Louisiana law violated the equal protection and due process clauses of the Fourteenth Amendment.

The Supreme Court's 8–1 decision in *Plessy v. Ferguson* established the notorious "separate but equal" doctrine. According to the Court, segregation under state law was constitutional as long as the public facilities provided for blacks and whites were equal. While the accommodations provided for blacks were in fact never "equal," the majority of the Court said that any discrimination existed only in the mind of the black community.

The lone dissent in *Plessy v. Ferguson* was voiced by Justice John Marshall Harlan, a former Kentucky slave-owner. In Harlan's stinging words, "Our Constitution is color-blind, and neither knows nor tolerates classes among citizens. . . . The thin disguise of 'equal' accommodations . . . will not mislead any one, nor atone for the wrong done this day."

Despite Harlan's harsh warning, most white Americans at the turn of the century had little concern for black civil rights. The "separate but equal" doctrine would remain law for nearly sixty years.

2D, 5C, 6C

Early Gains in Civil Rights

The NAACP

Despite many setbacks, blacks and some concerned whites still continued their efforts to secure and protect civil rights. An important milestone was the founding of the National Association for the Advancement of Colored People (NAACP) in 1909 (the centennial of Abraham Lincoln's birth). Its founders were sixty leading Americans, both black and white, who were dedicated to securing social and political rights for blacks. Among the NAACP's early leaders and supporters were social worker Jane Addams, philosopher John Dewey, novelist William Dean Howells, law professor W.E.B. Du Bois (doo-BOYS), and lawyer Clarence Darrow. The thrust of the NAACP was to increase public awareness, exert

pressure on Congress, and, above all, initiate legal action in the courts. One of the group's earliest targets was segregation in schools, especially colleges and universities.

Gains in higher education

Beginning in the late 1930's, some Supreme Court justices — led in particular by Justice Hugo Black — began to show a greater concern for individual rights and civil liberties.

In 1938 Lloyd Gaines, a qualified undergraduate, was denied admission to the University of Missouri Law School, which did not accept black students. Missouri had no black law schools, but the state offered to pay his tuition to attend a non-segregated law school in a neighboring state. With legal assistance from the NAACP, Gaines sued, contending that the law violated his right to equal protection.

The Court, in part, agreed (*Missouri ex rel. Gaines v. Canada*). Justice Charles Evans Hughes pointed out that the state had created a "privilege" for white law students that it denied to black students. Missouri was given the option of either admitting Gaines to the state's law school or creating a "separate but equal" law school for blacks. The state gave in and chose to admit Gaines to its existing law school.

Separate but not equal

The question of whether "separate" schools were in fact "equal" did not come before the Court until 1950, in two cases decided the same day. Heman Sweatt, a black student, was denied admission to the all-white law school at the University of Texas. Texas set up a separate law school for blacks, but Sweatt argued that it provided an inferior education. In *Sweatt v. Painter,* the Supreme Court ruled unanimously that the two law schools were far from equal in professional training.

In the second case, a court order had forced the University of Oklahoma to admit G. W. McLaurin, a black graduate student. The school tried to maintain segregation, however. McLaurin had to sit by himself in class and use separate tables in the library and cafeteria. Hearing McLaurin's charges, the Supreme Court again unanimously ruled against the university (*McLaurin v. Oklahoma State Regents,* 1950).

Although these Court decisions affected only segregation in higher education, they did repre-

197

GUIDED/INDEPENDENT PRACTICE

● Have students complete **Primary Source Worksheet 11,** which contains excerpts from the Emancipation Proclamation.

RETEACHING/CORRECTIVES

▲ Have students examine Figure 7–1 on p. 198. Ask them to identify the branch of government taking action to end discrimination in each entry. They should also note which actions were taken by private citizens. Then have them create separate time lines for each branch and for private citizens.

You may also want to use **Transparency 17,** which charts the causes and effects of the Civil War.

ENRICHMENT/EXTENSION

■ Have students do research and write a report on the early history of the NAACP. Volunteers might contact the nearest office of the NAACP to find out what its priorities are today. If the office is in your community, students may arrange to have a representative come to speak to the class.

Have students complete **Constitutional Issues Worksheet 7,** which has them examine attitudes toward civil rights.

You may also want students to complete **Supreme Court Decisions 39–42,** which deal with civil rights.

Background: *Values* Other decisions illustrating the Court's increasing concern for individual rights during the 1930's: In 1932 the Court ruled that several convicted black men ("the Scottsboro boys," see p. 182) had a right to legal counsel in state as well as federal court (*Powell v. Alabama*). In 1935 the Court held that the Scottsboro defendants were denied their rights when they were tried by an all-white jury in a state that excluded African Americans from jury duty (*Norris v. Alabama*).

The symbol 👥 denotes active participation strategies.

Activities are keyed for student abilities:
▲ = Basic
● = All Levels
■ = Average/Advanced

Section 1 Review Answers

1. Scott was not considered a citizen under the Constitution, and thus could not sue; the Missouri Compromise ban on slavery was unconstitutional.

2. The Thirteenth Amendment made slavery illegal. The Fourteenth Amendment defined citizenship and guaranteed equal protection under the laws. The Fifteenth Amendment gave African Americans the vote.

3. **(a)** The Court, by allowing state governments to continue limiting civil rights, undermined the "privileges and immunities" clause. **(b)** It allowed discrimination by private enterprises.

4. **(a)** By "Jim Crow" laws requiring separate facilities for blacks and whites. **(b)** *Plessy v. Ferguson.*

5. To secure social and political rights for African Americans by increasing public awareness, by pressuring Congress, and by taking legal action.

Critical thinking Students may argue that forced segregation is inherently unequal.

CLOSURE

● Review the section, asking students to suggest the main idea of each of the subheadings in the section. Then have them read Section 2, noting the major victories of the civil rights movement.

Figure 7–1 **STEPS TOWARD EQUAL RIGHTS**
More than 100 years were needed for black Americans to achieve full civil rights. **8E**

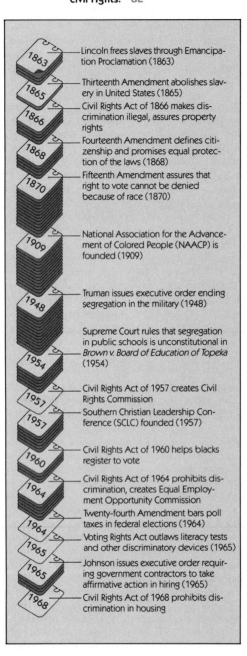

- Lincoln frees slaves through Emancipation Proclamation (1863) — 1863
- Thirteenth Amendment abolishes slavery in United States (1865) — 1865
- Civil Rights Act of 1866 makes discrimination illegal, assures property rights — 1866
- Fourteenth Amendment defines citizenship and promises equal protection of the laws (1868) — 1868
- Fifteenth Amendment assures that right to vote cannot be denied because of race (1870) — 1870
- National Association for the Advancement of Colored People (NAACP) is founded (1909) — 1909
- Truman issues executive order ending segregation in the military (1948) — 1948
- Supreme Court rules that segregation in public schools is unconstitutional in *Brown v. Board of Education of Topeka* (1954) — 1954
- Civil Rights Act of 1957 creates Civil Rights Commission — 1957
- Southern Christian Leadership Conference (SCLC) founded (1957) — 1957
- Civil Rights Act of 1960 helps blacks register to vote — 1960
- Civil Rights Act of 1964 prohibits discrimination, creates Equal Employment Opportunity Commission — 1964
- Twenty-fourth Amendment bars poll taxes in federal elections (1964) — 1964
- Voting Rights Act outlaws literacy tests and other discriminatory devices (1965) — 1965
- Johnson issues executive order requiring government contractors to take affirmative action in hiring (1965) — 1965
- Civil Rights Act of 1968 prohibits discrimination in housing — 1968

198

sent a break from the past. Moreover, World War II had brought some advances in civil rights in other areas of society. In 1941 President Franklin D. Roosevelt issued Executive Order 8802, forbidding racial discrimination in defense industries. His successor, Harry Truman, proposed a strong civil rights program, but Congress blocked most legislation. In 1948, President Truman sent a special message to Congress urging an end to discrimination, which, he said, was "utterly contrary to our ideals." Truman also issued Executive Order 9981, ending segregation throughout the military. (Some branches had been integrated during the war.)

The next step for the NAACP was to seek a complete reversal of *Plessy v. Ferguson.* It would contend that racial segregation, in and of itself, constitutes inequality under the Fourteenth Amendment.

SECTION 1 REVIEW

Vocabulary and key terms

Dred Scott case (194)   *Plessy v. Ferguson* (196)
discrimination (195)   "separate but equal" (197)
segregation (196)   NAACP (197)
"Jim Crow" laws (196)

For review

1. What two reasons did the Supreme Court give for denying Dred Scott his freedom? **2D**
2. Briefly describe the aims of the Thirteenth, Fourteenth, and Fifteenth Amendments. **6H**
3. How did the Supreme Court limit the scope of the Fourteenth Amendment in the (a) *Slaughterhouse Cases*? (b) *Civil Rights Cases*? **2D**
4. (a) How was segregation established by law in the South? (b) What Supreme Court case established the doctrine of "separate but equal"? **5C**
5. What were the main goals of the NAACP? **6C**

Critical thinking

EXAMINING BASIC PRINCIPLES If the "separate" public facilities for blacks and whites had really been "equal" in quality and comfort, would segregation have been justified? Why or why not? **5C**

Figure 7–1
● Ask students to choose the two events listed on the chart that they consider to be the most important steps toward equal rights. Have them explain their choices.

198

The population of the United States is becoming more diverse, and that can sometimes lead to misunderstandings and discrimination. What can young people do to fight prejudice? In Woonsocket, Rhode Island, a group of students meet each week to talk about how people from different cultures and races can learn to respect each other. They have this to say about what they have learned.

Students at Woonsocket High School, Rhode Island

Irene Briggs: People in America are occupied with prejudice, because they are afraid. They have stereotypes. They don't see that there are black people, Hispanic people, who are doing things. And Asian people who are trying to do something for themselves and make themselves proud.

Thongkhoon Pathana: When I came to the United States, there were people who called me names. I heard about this group, so I came. Maybe I could help out. Because when you have so many things in your heart, sometimes you have to speak out.

Phalatsamy Vongvisay: The Asians, all the people pick on them. It gets us really mad. All we can do is ignore them. I think this is a good place to let it all out. To let them know how we feel and what they're doing to us and how it hurts us.

Heriberto Roman: We're trying to get as many people involved as possible. You talk to some people and they turn away from you. They say, "That's weak," or "I got no time for that." That's how people are. We just talk to them and talk to them.

Susana Rivera: We try to make up activities and stuff. Bring people together and show them that we can all have fun, no matter what race you are.

Ahmad Morris: Last year I was writing rhymes, raps. I asked [friends] to join me. So we wrote some raps expressing ourselves about prejudice and hatred.

Irene Briggs: Everything starts with education. They have to teach in school about other people, their history—Asian, Hispanics, African, everybody.

Mary Lynch: We have to start by getting people together to understand each other.

Susana Rivera: Don't be ignorant. Try to learn about what other people have been through and what they go through.

Destiny Harmon: Don't look at anybody and make judgments. You have to get to know them, their culture, what they are really about—not just what they look like.

STUDENT PARTICIPATION

1. What suggestions do these students have for fighting prejudice? What else can teenagers do to end prejudice?
2. Write a letter to the editor of the local newspaper describing race relations in your community.

Students Talk About Fighting Prejudice

Front row, left to right: Susana Rivera, Irene Briggs, Mary Lynch. Back row, left to right: Thongkhoon Pathana, Phalatsamy Vongvisay, Heriberto Roman, Destiny Harmon, Ahmad Morris.

Background

The students quoted here are members of a school club called the Human Rights Squad. It was formed following a presentation on issues of discrimination. The presentation was made by sports figures working for Project Teamwork, sponsored by Northeastern University's Center for the Study of Sport in Society program. For more information on this program, write to: Dexter Jenkins; Center for the Study of Sport in Society; Northeastern University; 360 Huntington Avenue, Suite 161 CP; Boston, MA 02115.

Prejudice Reduction

▲ Ask students if they think that prejudice is a problem in their lives. You may wish to bring up the issue of discrimination on the basis of religion and gender, as well as race and national origin.

● CRITICAL THINKING Ask students if their attitude toward this issue has changed over time. *What makes people change their attitudes toward prejudice?* (Possible answers include education, personal experience, and changing attitudes in the community.)

199

Student Participation Answers

1. These students suggest that people need to talk to each other, to learn about different cultures and to educate others, to interact socially with others, and to avoid prejudging people.

2. Letters should be concise and should use examples if possible.

The symbol 👥 denotes active participation strategies.

Activities are keyed for student abilities:
▲ = Basic
● = All Levels
■ = Average/Advanced

Section Objectives
☐ explain the consequences of
the Supreme Court decision in
Brown v. Board of Education
☐ describe the goals and
achievements of the civil
rights movement

Vocabulary
integration, civil disobedience,
restrictive covenant

FOCUS
● Ask if any students had heard
of the case *Brown v. Board of
Education* before taking this
course. Then have these students
explain when and how they
learned about the case, what
their first opinion about it was,
whether their opinion has
changed, and how the case
might have affected their lives.

EXPLANATION
After students have read the
section, you may want to consider the following activities:

Civic Participation
● *How did students participate in
the civil rights movement?* (They
were involved in the integration
of schools, held sit-ins, and were
"Freedom Riders.") *What social
concerns have gained the support
of students in recent times?*

2D, 5A, 6B, 6C, 6G, 6I

SECTION 2 The Civil Rights Movement Gains Momentum

ACCESS **The Main Ideas**

1 What were the consequences of the
Supreme Court decision in *Brown v. Board
of Education*?
pages 200–202

2 What were the goals and achievements of
the civil rights movement?
pages 202–204

If you were an African American living in the
South in the 1950's, your school system would
be segregated, you would have to drink from
"colored" water fountains, and eat at "colored"
restaurants. This had been true when your grandparents were young, but around you is a growing
movement to change this unfair world.

2D, 5A, 6G

Public School Desegregation

In the early 1950's the state of Kansas, like
many other states, required "separate but equal"
segregated public schools. In the city of Topeka,
the segregated schools appeared to be fairly
equal in terms of books, equipment, and the
like. But it was the *intangible* factors in segregation — those that could not easily be measured

**In 1953, Linda Brown was attending an all-black
school in Topeka, Kansas. Her family's protest
led to the court case ending legal segregation.**

200

— that the NAACP wanted the Supreme Court to
consider. For this reason, civil rights activists
chose Topeka as the site to take their stand against
segregated schools.

An end to "separate but equal"

The landmark case of *Brown v. Board of Education of Topeka* (1954) centered on an 8-year-
old black girl named Linda Carol Brown.
Although there was a "white" public school just
seven blocks from her home, Linda Brown had to
travel 20 blocks to attend a "black" grade
school. With the help of the NAACP, Linda's
father, Oliver Brown, sued the school district,
charging that segregated schools violated the
equal protection clause of the Fourteenth
Amendment.

When the case reached the Supreme Court, it
was presented by Thurgood Marshall, general
counsel for the NAACP. (Later, Marshall became
the first black Supreme Court justice.) The
Court voted unanimously to support Brown and
overturn *Plessy v. Ferguson,* thus rejecting the
"separate but equal" doctrine. Writing for the
Court, Chief Justice Earl Warren asked,

> Does segregation of children in public
> schools solely on the basis of race, even
> though the physical facilities and other
> "tangible" factors may be equal, deprive
> children of the minority group of equal
> educational opportunities? We believe that
> it does. . . . To separate [school children]
> from others of similar age and qualifications
> solely because of their race generates a feel-
> ing of inferiority as to their status in the
> community that may affect their hearts and
> minds in a way unlikely ever to be un-
> done. . . . We conclude that in the field of
> public education the doctrine of "separate
> but equal" has no place. Separate educa-
> tional facilities are inherently unequal.

Enforcing the *Brown* decision

The Court did not immediately decide how
the landmark *Brown* decision would be carried

Background: *Constitutional
Heritage* Ideal cases, or
"test cases," are selected
carefully. Note that the
NAACP chose to challenge a
school system whose segregated schools appeared to
be of the same quality.

Critical Thinking
● *How is the rejection of the
"separate but equal" doc-
trine a reaffirmation of American ideals?* (Students may
suggest that it is an American ideal to bring together

many cultures, not to separate them.)

Federal troops were required to protect African American schoolchildren from violent mobs opposed to integrated schools in Little Rock, Arkansas. Norman Rockwell portrayed the social tensions over school desegregation in a painting entitled *The Problem We All Live With.*

out. The following year, the Court ordered all public school districts to move promptly toward "full compliance" and end segregation "with all deliberate speed." The task of overseeing this sweeping change was assigned to federal district court judges in the states with segregation laws.

School districts in some states obeyed the federal court orders quickly. But in others the opposition to court-ordered desegregation was strong, emotional, and sometimes violent. Over 100 Southern members of Congress issued a "declaration of constitutional principles" protesting the Supreme Court's actions.

In response to the violence in some school districts, President Dwight Eisenhower in 1957 used the power of the federal government to back up the court orders. In Little Rock, Arkansas, a mob had gathered as nine black students tried to enroll in the previously all-white Central High School. Although Governor Orval Faubus had called out the Arkansas National Guard to stop the students, Eisenhower put the Guard under federal control. He also sent army paratroopers to help oversee the students' safe enrollment.

Federal action was needed again in 1962 when James Meredith, a black veteran, tried to enroll in the University of Mississippi at Oxford. President John Kennedy dispatched 16,000 federal troops, and federal marshals escorted Meredith to classes. The next year, Alabama Governor George Wallace declared he would "stand in the schoolhouse door" to prevent **integration** — the mixing of students of all races. Wallace personally stopped two black students from enrolling at the University of Alabama. This time Kennedy ordered the Alabama National Guard to ensure that the students were admitted.

Delays in desegregation

Even where there was no violence, desegregation in the southern states progressed at a snail's pace. Ten years after the *Brown* decision, some southern states had not achieved even one percent integration. In 1964, an impatient Court ruled that it would no longer tolerate unnecessary delay or open disregard for its ruling. In Prince Edward County, Virginia, the public schools had been closed to avoid integration, and all-white "private" schools were being run with public funds. The Court declared, "there has been entirely too much deliberation and not enough speed" (*Griffin v. Prince Edward County School Board,* 1964). In another Virginia case four years later, the Court ordered a school board to make a desegregation plan that "promises realistically to work *now*."

Court-ordered busing

Nearly twenty years after *Brown v. Board of Education,* segregated school systems still existed in many places. Some, mainly in the South, were those established by law, or *de jure* (dee JOO-ree). In many other places — particularly in

---

GUIDED/INDEPENDENT
PRACTICE

● Have students complete
**Primary Source Worksheets
12–13,** which contain excerpts
from Martin Luther King, Jr.'s, "I
Have a Dream" speech and the
Voting Rights Act of 1965.

RETEACHING/CORRECTIVES

▲ Have students work in pairs
to create a time line of civil
rights legislation.

You may also want to use
Transparency 18, which reviews the causes and effects of
the civil rights movement.

large cities — schools tended to be segregated because of housing and neighborhood patterns. Such actual, or *de facto,* segregation required a different solution.

In 1971 the Court directed the school board in Charlotte, North Carolina, either to (1) redraw school district boundaries, (2) impose racial quotas in public schools, or (3) order busing across school districts in order to break up "all-white" and "all-black" schools (*Swann v. Charlotte-Mecklenburg Board of Education*).

Courts began ordering forced busing in northern cities too. For example, in 1973 the Supreme Court upheld an order from a federal district judge calling on Denver, Colorado, to begin busing, because officials had purposely segregated a "substantial portion" of its students. Likewise, in 1974 Boston, Massachusetts, was instructed to bus students. There a federal judge ruled that school authorities had systematically segregated the public schools.

Busing, however, aroused criticism and controversy. Many parents and students, both black and white, preferred the "neighborhood school" and objected to the extra time and travel. In *Oklahoma City Board of Education v. Dowell* (1991) the Supreme Court ruled that school districts can be released from court-ordered busing if they have taken all "practicable" steps to eliminate segregation.

6B, 6C, 6I

The Civil Rights Movement

A new national leader

The crusade to win social and political rights for black Americans gained strength and speed after the 1954 *Brown* decision. Small incidents grew into major events. In December 1955, Rosa Parks, a 42-year-old black dressmaker, boarded a crowded bus in Montgomery, Alabama. Tired from her day's work, she refused to give up her bus seat when a white person got on, as the law required. Parks's arrest and quiet resolve inspired the 50,000 black residents of Montgomery to a year-long boycott of the city's segregated bus system. Out of the boycott emerged an inspiring new leader — a 27-year-old Baptist minister named Martin Luther King, Jr.

The Montgomery boycott propelled Dr. King to national prominence. In 1957, he and

other leaders formed the Southern Christian Leadership Conference (SCLC). This group organized orderly, persistent protests throughout the country.

King's charismatic leadership gave the movement a new set of tactics — nonviolent resistance, or **civil disobedience,** to discriminatory laws. This approach derived from King's own philosophy, which followed the ideas of Mohandas K. Gandhi, the Indian nationalist leader, and Henry David Thoreau, an American philosopher of the 1800's. King's followers, many of them students, held "sit-ins" at segregated lunch counters and boarded segregated buses as "Freedom Riders." Sympathizers in other parts of the country boycotted discriminatory companies and their products.

Despite King's insistence on nonviolent methods, violence frequently erupted. Marchers and protesters in a number of cities were attacked by police using dogs and fire hoses. Several civil rights leaders and workers in the South were killed. Riots in black urban ghettos marked the summers during the mid-1960's.

Nevertheless, peaceful protests and demonstrations played a major role in increasing national awareness of civil rights. One of the most dramatic moments of the movement was the "March on Washington," on August 28, 1963, which drew more than 200,000 demonstrators to Washington, D.C. The high point was King's famous "I Have a Dream" speech, quoted at the beginning of this chapter.

Civil rights strategies

Other civil rights battles were won in the courtroom and the legislatures. The *Brown* decision cleared the way for the Supreme Court to overturn state and local laws that established segregation in other areas. For example, the Court soon ruled against segregation at public beaches and parks, on local buses, and in state and local jails. The Court also ruled against laws that forbade interracial marriage.

Civil rights groups also used political pressure to win new civil rights laws from Congress. Since the late 1800's, numerous states had used various legal devices to discourage or stop blacks from voting. Securing the right to vote became a major goal, for once blacks could vote in large numbers, elected officials would pay more atten-

202

Background: *Global Awareness* Mohandas K. Gandhi (1869–1948) is often called Mahatma ("great soul") because he was held in such high respect by his followers. Born in India, Gandhi was trained as a lawyer in England and later moved to South Africa. There he worked against racial discrimination and developed his concept of nonviolent resistance to unjust government. In 1915 he returned to India, where he was repeatedly imprisoned for leading opposition to British rule. Gandhi often used hunger strikes as part of his resistance. His philosophy and tactics have influenced civil rights workers around the world.

In 1963, thousands flocked to the March on Washington, where Martin Luther King, Jr., made an eloquent plea for racial justice.

ENRICHMENT/EXTENSION
■ Ask students to find out how your school district deals with the issue of desegregation.

Have students complete **Skills Challenge Worksheet 7,** which examines support for the Voting Rights Act.

You may also want students to complete **Supreme Court Decisions 43–44,** which deal with cases involving segregation.

tion to their demands. Moreover, leaders also believed there would be less resistance to *political* change than to changes in social patterns, such as housing or employment. Congress responded by passing two civil rights acts.

The Civil Rights Act of 1957 was the first civil rights legislation passed since 1875. It created a six-person Civil Rights Commission to investigate civil rights violations and established a Civil Rights Division within the Justice Department. The federal government now could seek court orders against anyone who interfered with citizens' right to vote. Between 1957 and 1960, however, the Justice Department filed only ten cases charging voting discrimination.

The Civil Rights Act of 1960 also relied on federal court action. Court-appointed federal referees were to assist blacks in registering to vote and in voting. In addition, the act made it a federal crime to use violence in attempting to prevent school integration.

The Civil Rights Act of 1964

The civil rights movement continued to grow in intensity and gain widespread public and political support. In June 1963, President Kennedy proposed a strong, comprehensive civil rights bill. Following Kennedy's assassination on November 22, 1963, President Lyndon Johnson took on the responsibility of persuading Congress to pass the new law. "We have talked long enough in this country about civil rights," Johnson said. "We have talked for one hundred years or more. It is time now to write the next chapter — and to write it in the books of law."

Southern senators vigorously opposed the bill in months of debate and speeches. The far-reaching Civil Rights Act of 1964 finally passed with support from both Democrats and Republicans. These are some provisions of the act's major sections, called "titles":

- Bars arbitrary discrimination in voter registration (Title I).
- Outlaws discrimination in public accommodations, such as motels, restaurants, theaters, and sports arenas (Title II).
- Gives the Attorney General the power to bring lawsuits to desegregate public facilities and schools (Titles III and IV).

203

The symbol ii denotes active participation strategies.

Activities are keyed for student abilities:
▲ = Basic
● = All Levels
■ = Average/Advanced

Section 2 Review Answers

1. (a) Whether segregated public schools, even with similar facilities, are truly equal. **(b)** Segregation is inherently unequal.

2. (a) It ordered desegregation and assigned federal district judges to oversee integration. **(b)** They used federal troops and the National Guard to carry out integration.

3. The *de facto* segregation of housing patterns.

4. Nonviolent civil disobedience and boycotts.

5. Public beaches, parks, and buses; state and local jails; marriage laws.

6. (a) It barred discrimination in voter registration, public accommodations, and employment, expanded the Civil Rights Commission, and established a Community Relations Service and the EEOC. **(b)** It allowed federal examiners to protect black voting rights, eliminated discriminatory voting devices, and imposed penalties for interfering with voters.

Critical thinking To provide further opportunities for African Americans, thereby enabling them to have greater prosperity and influence in the future.

CLOSURE

● Have students define the vocabulary and key terms in their own words. Then have them read Section 3, noting the expansion of civil rights for different groups.

- Calls for the withholding of federal funds from public or private programs (including school programs) that practice discrimination (Title VI).
- Prohibits job discrimination by private employers or unions on account of race, color, religion, national origin, or sex (Title VII).
- Expands the power of the Civil Rights Commission, creates a Community Relations Service to conciliate racial disputes, and establishes the Equal Employment Opportunity Commission (Titles VII, X).

The broad provisions of the 1964 act clearly showed how the federal government was prepared to act to override discriminatory state laws. As Chapter 4 explained, lawsuits quickly challenged the new Civil Rights Act. The Supreme Court upheld it, however, on the basis of both the commerce clause and the Fourteenth Amendment (page 100).

The Voting Rights Act

Even after three Civil Rights Acts, many black citizens in parts of the South were still being kept from voting. In Selma, Alabama, state and local police used violence to stop a 1965 drive to register voters. To protest this action, Martin Luther King, Jr., organized a march from Selma to the capitol at Montgomery, 54 miles away. Several hundred state troopers stopped the march with clubs and tear gas. Throughout the rest of the country, thousands of people, shocked by the brutality, flocked to join the Selma marchers. To protect the marchers from attack, President Johnson called out the Alabama National Guard. Johnson also urged Congress to pass new legislation.

The Voting Rights Act was passed in the summer of 1965. It allowed federal examiners to ensure blacks the right to vote, eliminated discriminatory devices to discourage minority voting, and imposed stiff criminal penalties on those who interfere with voters. In 1982 Congress strengthened this act and extended it for 25 years.

Open housing

Political rights, education, and employment were the first major priorities of the civil rights movement. Serious discrimination still existed in housing, despite several Supreme Court rul-

204

ings. So-called **restrictive covenants** in leases and sales agreements prevented many members of minorities from buying or renting homes. (These private agreements were directed not only against blacks, but also against Jews and other religious or ethnic minorities.)

The Civil Rights Act of 1968, also known as the Open Housing Act, prohibits discrimination in the sale or rental of most housing. This new civil rights legislation was passed quickly by Congress in April 1968, following the assassination of Martin Luther King, Jr. The 1968 law, however, required would-be buyers or tenants to prove discrimination. While it brought some improvements, black Americans were still frequently limited in their choice of houses or apartments.

SECTION 2 REVIEW

Vocabulary and key terms

Brown v. Board of Education (200)	Civil Rights Act (1964) (203)
integration (201)	Voting Rights Act (1965) (204)
de jure (201)	restrictive covenant (204)
de facto (202)	
civil disobedience (202)	

For review

1. (a) What was the issue in *Brown v. Board of Education*? (b) What did the Supreme Court decide? **2D**
2. (a) How did the Supreme Court act to enforce the *Brown* decision? (b) What actions did Presidents Eisenhower and Kennedy take? **2D**
3. What form of school segregation was busing supposed to remedy? **6B**
4. What methods did Dr. Martin Luther King, Jr., use in the civil rights movement? **6C**
5. In what new areas did Supreme Court decisions help end segregation? **2D**
6. What were the major provisions of (a) the Civil Rights Act of 1964? (b) the Voting Rights Act of 1965? **6G**

Critical thinking

ANALYZING AN ISSUE Why were political rights and equal education the first major goals of the civil rights movement? **6C**

Check for Understanding
● *How did the attacks on the Selma marchers help win passage of the Voting Rights Act?* (Americans were shocked by the brutality of the state troopers and threw their support behind the marchers.)

Background: *Civic Participation* In the four years following the passage of the Voting Rights Act of 1965,

the number of southern black voters tripled. In Mississippi, the percentage of African American registrants rose from less than 10 percent to roughly 60 percent.

2D, 5A, 6B, 6E, 6G, 6I, 8B

SECTION 3
Civil Rights Policies Seek Equality for All Americans

ACCESS **The Main Ideas**

1 How have other ethnic groups, besides African Americans, gained fuller civil rights?
pages 205–209

2 What are the two main points of view on the affirmative action issue?
pages 209–211

During the mid-1940's, the town of Pearland, Texas, had two schools. One was a modern school with a teacher for each grade, attended by Anglo-American children. The other had only one room, with no running water, where one teacher taught all grade levels. Mexican-American students attended that school.

The Mexican-American community protested this inequality. Through hard work and organization they successfully changed the system. In the future, all Pearland students, whatever their background, would attend the modern school.

In the decades after World War II, many ethnic communities organized to demand rights they had been denied. The 1964 Civil Rights Act was a victory for all those groups who had been discriminated against on the basis of their "race, color, religion, or national origin."

5A, 6E, 6G
The Rights of Other Minorities

The rights of ethnic minorities

Throughout its history, the United States has been a "nation of immigrants." Each new group to arrive has, for a time, been a new minority that encountered social and economic discrimination. Until quite recently, most immigrants came from Europe. As Figure 7–2 shows, this pattern changed radically in the 1960's. Since then, many newcomers to the United States have come from Southeast Asia, the Middle East, the Caribbean area, and other parts of the Americas.

One of the fastest growing minorities in America today are Hispanics — people who trace their heritage to Spanish-speaking nations. They total 22.4 million people, or about 9 percent of the population. In general, Hispanic Americans comprise four separate groups: Mexican-Americans, often called *Chicanos* (roughly 13.5 million); Puerto Ricans (about 2.75 million living in the U.S.); Cuban Americans (over one million), and those from South or Central America (more than 3 million). Leaders of this large Hispanic community are concerned with protecting a range of civil rights. They also seek to end discrimination in housing and employment.

The 1964 Civil Rights Act offered such protection to *all* racial, religious, and ethnic minorities, not just black Americans. Similarly, the Voting Rights Act promised that citizens could not be denied their right to vote because they could not speak English. In areas where large numbers of minority voters live, ballots and voting instructions must be printed in both their native language and English.

Bilingual education

An important and controversial issue for Hispanics and other culture groups is **bilingual education** — classroom instruction in students'

With two "language minority" groups among its voters, the city of San Francisco gives election information in English, Spanish, and Chinese.

205

SECTION 3

Civil Rights Policies Seek Equality for All Americans *(pp. 205–211)*

Section Objectives
☐ describe how other ethnic groups besides African Americans gained fuller civil rights
☐ detail the two main points of view on the affirmative action issue

Vocabulary
bilingual education, affirmative action, reverse discrimination

FOCUS
● Write the following questions on the board: *Is it ever proper for the law to discriminate against one group of people? If so, when?* Instruct students to write a one-paragraph response to the questions. Collect all the responses and read selected ones aloud, asking for the class's response to each.

Background:
Multiculturalism Economic organizations such as the United Farm Workers, founded by Cesar Chavez in 1962, have worked for improvements for Hispanic Americans.

The symbol ♀♀ denotes active participation strategies.

Activities are keyed for student abilities:
▲ = Basic
● = All Levels
■ = Average/Advanced

EXPLANATION

After students have read the section, you may want to consider the following activities:

Multiculturalism

● CRITICAL THINKING Discuss bilingual education with the class, asking students if they think immigrants should learn such topics as social studies and math in their native language. *Do you think English should be made the country's official language? Why or why not?* (Students favoring the idea might argue that it would improve communication among groups. Students opposing the idea might argue that it would encourage hostility toward recent immigrants.)

Prejudice Reduction

● Ask two pairs of students to prepare a debate over whether Americans should be forced to retire at a certain age. Have the pairs present their viewpoints in a five-minute speech and then give a short rebuttal. Afterward, ask other class members if their attitudes toward mandatory retirement have changed.

native language as well as in English. Learning in their own language, supporters say, helps children learn faster and instills pride in their own cultures.

Bilingual education in Spanish has become a particularly important issue in California, Florida, and the Southwest. Giving instruction in Spanish, Vietnamese, Chinese, Arabic, and other languages is a question for many big-city school systems. In 1974, the Supreme Court decided a case involving Chinese students in San Francisco. The Court ruled that the Civil Rights Act of 1964 (Title VI) obliges a school district with a substantial number of non-English-speaking students to offer instruction to overcome language difficulties (*Lau v. Nichols*). The growing number of such students, however, created a "backlash" against bilingual education. Some argued that it led to cultural separateness and even suggested that English be made the country's only official language.

The rights of American Indians

The only Americans who are *not* immigrants make up another important minority. American Indians, or Native Americans, have a unique legal status among American citizens. In effect, they hold a form of dual citizenship. On the one hand, they are American citizens (and citizens of the states where they reside). This entitles them to all the rights of other Americans. On the other hand, Native Americans are also members of some 400 different tribes or nations. Each has its own form of government with power to regulate its internal affairs free from state control. Although about two-thirds of the almost 2 million Native Americans do not live on their tribal reservations, most maintain voting rights with their own tribe.

Like black Americans, American Indians have suffered severe discrimination, both legal and social, over the centuries. The Constitution grants Congress authority to supervise Indian tribes, and this supervision has long been handled by the Bureau of Indian Affairs (part of the Interior Department). Government policies varied over the years, but few Indians had "equal opportunities."

In the 1960's, one offshoot of the civil rights movement was more political activism by Native Americans, led by groups such as the American Indian Movement (AIM). Demonstrations, law-

suits, and public attention brought the extension of Indian rights. Courts considered violations of past treaties, and many tribes regained valuable mineral and water rights as well as hunting and fishing rights. Land taken illegally was returned, and millions of dollars were paid to Native Americans to compensate for past wrongs. The Self-Determination Act of 1975 now permits Indian tribal governments to administer their own federally supported programs in education, health, welfare, and housing.

The rights of older Americans

Throughout American history, numerous laws have made distinctions based upon age. Nearly all of these set a *minimum* age for certain acts — voting, driving an automobile, getting married, buying alcoholic beverages, running for senator, or joining the armed forces. While there are few laws that actually discriminate against older Americans, many social practices and attitudes have encouraged "ageism." Congress, therefore, has prohibited certain forms of discrimination against people beyond middle age.

The Age Discrimination in Employment Act of 1967, for example, protects many employees between the ages of 40 and 65 from being discriminated against in hiring and promotion. The law covers jobs in government and in companies that do business in several states. Exceptions may be made for jobs where it can convincingly

Since the 1960's, American Indians have gained more political rights and self-government. This district representative takes part in an Apache tribal council in Arizona.

206

Background: *History* Indian activists took over the island of Alcatraz in San Francisco Bay in 1969 and the town of Wounded Knee, South Dakota, in 1973, to protest government seizures of Indian land, restrictions on Indian hunting and fishing rights, and pollution.

Check for Understanding
▲ *Which schools do not have to provide instruction to overcome language difficulties for students who do not speak English?* (Schools that do not have a substantial number of those students.)

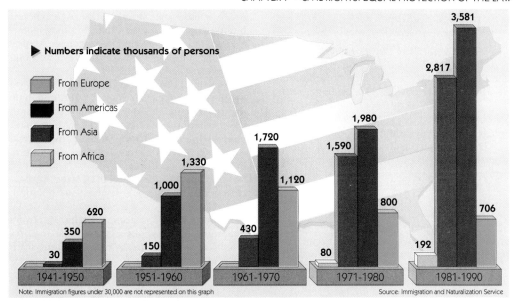

▶ Numbers indicate thousands of persons

☐ From Europe
■ From Americas
▮ From Asia
▯ From Africa

Note: Immigration figures under 30,000 are not represented on this graph

Source: Immigration and Naturalization Service

**FIGURE 7–2 IMMIGRATION TO THE UNITED STATES   The pattern of immi-
gration to the United States from different continents has
changed dramatically in recent decades. 8B**

be shown that age is related to doing the job well. In 1978 this act was amended to prohibit forced retirements before the age of 70 for most workers. In addition, the Age Discrimination Act of 1975 (amended in 1978) authorizes the federal government to withhold federal funding from any program that discriminates unreasonably because of a person's age.

The rights of disabled Americans

For years, opportunities for disabled Americans were severely restricted. Physical barriers were one problem; social discrimination was another. The Rehabilitation Act of 1973 tried to provide genuinely equal opportunities. For example, under this act, programs that receive federal funds must make public facilities accessible to people with physical disabilities. As a result, public buildings have installed ramps and elevators for wheelchair users, the elderly, and those temporarily disabled. In addition, the act requires federal contractors to take affirmative action to promote and hire handicapped people.

Congress has also tried to ensure equal educational opportunities for school-aged children with mental or physical disabilities. The Education for All Handicapped Children Act of 1975 provides federal money to assist state and local agencies in giving such children the right to a "free and appropriate public education" at no extra cost to their parents. In general, schools must provide individualized programs for each child with a disability. As far as possible, schools must also "mainstream" these children — that is, teach them in regular school classes with other children.

Also in 1975, Congress enacted the Developmentally Disabled Assistance and Bill of Rights Act. Under this act, the federal government provides states with grants to help care for those with developmental handicaps. It includes a "bill of rights" guaranteeing mentally retarded persons the right to appropriate treatment and care in the safest and least restrictive setting possible.

In 1990 Congress passed the Americans with Disabilities Act, which made it illegal to discriminate against the disabled. Regulations drawn up under the Act require companies employing more than fifteen people to have made modifications for disabled workers by July 1994.

Controversial Issues

● ▢CRITICAL THINKING▢ AIDS (Acquired Immune Deficiency Syndrome) has raised several important civil rights questions. Ask the class to consider the following issue: ***Should AIDS tests be mandatory? Would such tests constitute a violation of privacy?*** Have students explain their views.

Values

● ▢CRITICAL THINKING▢ Have students consider the fact that all three branches of the federal government approved the relocation of Japanese Americans during World War II. ***How could all branches agree on a policy that was later declared unconstitutional?*** (The strong emotions of wartime led the three branches to ignore the unconstitutional aspects of the policy.)

■ Interested students may wish to read one of the following books about Japanese internment: *Journey into Topaz* and *Desert Exile* by Yoshiko Uchida, *Behind Barbed Wire* by Daniel Davis, and *Years of Infamy* by Michi Weglyn. Ask students to report to the class what they learned.

Figure 7–2
● Note that immigration figures under 30,000 are not shown. Ask students to summarize the information provided for each time period. ***What major developments in immigration are shown?*** (The number of immigrants from Europe has been declining since 1960, while the Americas and Asia have become the overwhelming source of new immigrants since the 1960's.)

The symbol ⅱ denotes active participation strategies.

Activities are keyed for student abilities:
▲ = Basic
● = All Levels
■ = Average/Advanced

Ensuring Fair Laws

While the purpose of civil rights legislation is to prevent *discrimination,* this term is more complex than it may seem at first. Some forms of discrimination are obvious. For example, saying "You may not stay at this hotel because you are Mexican" or "We never hire women for this job" are clear cases of discrimination.

On the other hand, suppose that a black woman is told, "We cannot hire you as a union printer because you are not skilled enough." Does discrimination play a part in this situation? Perhaps she does lack training. But perhaps, too, the printers' union has purposely excluded blacks or women (or both) from training programs. That is, this worker's present opportunities are limited by *past* discrimination. The solutions to this situation are even more difficult than eliminating obvious discrimination.

A promise of "equal protection"

One aim of the Fourteenth Amendment was to end the bias and inconsistencies common among the laws of the states. The amendment's guarantee of "equal protection" means that state laws may not make unfair or unreasonable distinctions between people. Individuals must be judged on the basis of their abilities or conduct, rather than on their race, sex, age, color, religion, heritage, or physical attributes. This is one important aspect of substantive due process (page 169). The Constitution does not forbid government from making *any* distinctions between people, however. The law may sometimes group or "classify" people in certain ways, *if* there is an acceptable reason for doing so.

Tests for discriminatory laws

Over the years, the Supreme Court has developed several tests to judge whether laws that treat certain groups differently are allowable under the "equal protection" clause. The traditional test of equal protection is whether the distinction between people is based on common sense and promotes a proper aim of government, such as public health or safety.

For example, a state might pass a law prohibiting red-haired persons from driving motorcycles. This law is not reasonable because having red hair does not relate to driving a motorcycle

safely. On the other hand, a state law *could* forbid those under 12 years old from riding motorcycles. This law discriminates against children under 12, but there is a reasonable connection between age and public safety.

A stricter test looks at the effects of a law on people's "fundamental rights." These include the right to vote, the right to privacy, the right to travel where one wishes, and the right to speak freely. Interfering with such constitutional rights is a serious matter, one that the government must prove is necessary.

Perhaps the strictest test of all is the "suspect classification" test. A "suspect," or questionable, classification is one based on race or national origin. Its constitutionality is always doubtful. For example, a policy that requires schools to be segregated by race would automatically be "suspect."

Applying these tests for discrimination in actual cases has not been simple or clear-cut, however. The courts have had to consider many factors and questions in each case charging discrimination.

Japanese Americans' relocation

Despite legal protection, injustices sometimes occur. Two months after the Japanese attack on Pearl Harbor in 1941, President Franklin D. Roosevelt, backed by Congress, issued an executive order severely curtailing the civil rights of people of Japanese descent living on the West Coast. More than 100,000 Japanese Americans were forced to relocate from their homes to what amounted to prison camps further inland. No distinction was made between aliens and American citizens.

Fred Korematsu and several other Japanese Americans resisted the President's orders and were arrested. They protested that the order violated their rights as American citizens. The Supreme Court, however, upheld the orders (*Hirabayashi v. U.S.,* 1943; *Korematsu v. U.S.,* 1944). Although the Court pointed out that any law directed at a specific racial group was automatically "suspect," the justices decided that the President and Congress had the authority to take such action in wartime.

The injustice of the treatment of Japanese Americans continued to disturb Americans for years after the war ended. In 1984 the courts

---

● Divide the class into groups and ask each group to prepare a bulletin-board display entitled *Equality in America.*

GUIDED/INDEPENDENT PRACTICE

● Have students complete **Primary Source Worksheet 14,** in which they examine the plea from the Cherokee nation not to be relocated from Georgia to the West.

Background: *History* The government of Canada also forcibly relocated people of Japanese ancestry during World War II.

Critical Thinking
● *Should the peacetime rights of citizens ever be curtailed during wartime? Why or why not?* (Students arguing in favor of rights limitations may note that war is an extraordinary circumstance, when the rights of individuals matter less than national security. Other students may argue that civil rights are fundamental to a free society and should never be curtailed.)

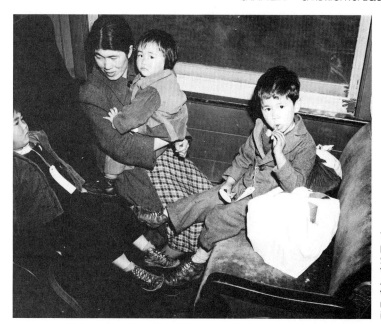

Wartime fears in the 1940's prompted the federal government to order thousands of Japanese American families to leave their West Coast homes for relocation camps further inland.

RETEACHING/CORRECTIVES
▲ Ask students to change the section's three headings into questions that ask for the main idea of each part of the section. Then have the class answer the questions.

overturned Korematsu's original conviction. Four years later, Congress offered tax-free payments of $20,000 to each of the 60,000 surviving veterans of wartime camps.

2B, 6B, 6G

Affirmative Action

The goals of civil rights policies gradually broadened to include "equal opportunity" as well as "equal protection." The *Brown v. Board of Education* ruling, as well as the civil rights laws passed in 1964, 1965, and 1968, tried to break down the barriers of discrimination. But civil rights legislation in practice still did not give all Americans an equal chance to compete in life. President Lyndon B. Johnson remarked,

> You do not take a person who for years has been hobbled by chains and liberate him, bring him up to the starting line of a race, and then say, "You are free to compete with all the others," and still justly believe that you have been completely fair. Thus it is not enough just to open the gates of opportunity. All our citizens must have the ability to walk through those gates.

Other kinds of policies were used in an attempt to make "equal opportunity" a reality. Their intent was to give disadvantaged Americans a better chance to compete on an equal footing.

New federal policies

The federal government led the way in adopting policies of **affirmative action**. That is, businesses, unions, schools, and governments at all levels, were encouraged — and in some instances required — to recruit millions of blacks, women, and other minorities. This extra, *positive* (or affirmative) effort was intended to compensate for past negative policies that had limited people's opportunities.

To implement affirmative action, the federal government used the powers of both the presidency and the courts. In 1965, President Johnson issued Executive Order 11246, which required all contractors and unions doing business with the federal government to take "affirmative action" in hiring minorities. Two years later this was amended to extend affirmative action to women.

The federal courts played a strong role in encouraging affirmative action. The courts often agreed that a very low percentage of minority em-

Check for Understanding
▲ *How were interned Japanese Americans compensated for their losses?* (In 1988 Congress offered tax-free payments of $20,000 to surviving veterans of relocation camps.)

Background:
Multiculturalism Executive Order 11246 also created the Office of Federal Contract Compliance to oversee federal contracts and directed the Civil Service Commission to investigate all charges of racial or sex discrimination.

The symbol ⁇ denotes active participation strategies.

Activities are keyed for student abilities:
▲ = Basic
● = All Levels
■ = Average/Advanced

ENRICHMENT/EXTENSION

■ Have students complete **Constitutional Issues Worksheet 8,** which examines the meaning and applications of equality.

You may also want students to complete **Supreme Court Decisions 45–46,** which deal with minority rights, and **Supreme Court Decisions 47–49,** which deal with affirmative action.

In many industries, affirmative action plans have given women and minorities new job opportunities. The woman on the left is a supervisor in a steel-making plant.

ployees was evidence of job discrimination. For example, Duke Power Company, in North Carolina, required job applicants either to have a high school diploma or pass a general intelligence test. In *Griggs v. Duke Power Co.* (1971), the Supreme Court unanimously ruled that this test was discriminatory, because it kept many black job applicants from being hired. As the tests did not have a direct bearing on the job, the policy violated the Civil Rights Act of 1964.

In a number of similar cases, the courts found that employers had discriminated against women and minorities both in hiring and in pay. Companies were ordered to pay back wages and establish quotas for future job recruitment.

One effect of these court decisions was to encourage affirmative action policies. Another result, however, was a "backlash" of resentment by those who felt that affirmative action denied them opportunities they deserved. They charged that preferential treatment for women and minorities led to **reverse discrimination**. Controversies arose particularly in the areas of higher education and employment.

The *Bakke* case

In an effort to train more doctors from racial and ethnic minority groups, the medical school at the University of California (Davis) set up a special admissions program. It reserved 16 out of 100 places each year for minority students —

blacks, American Indians, and people of Mexican or Asian descent. Allan Bakke, a 34-year-old white male, was twice rejected for admission to the medical school in favor of minority applicants. Both Bakke's grades and his Medical College Admission Test scores were higher than the average for the minority students who were admitted. Believing that his rejection was reverse discrimination, Bakke sued the university.

In *Regents of the University of California v. Bakke* (1978), the Supreme Court handed down a two-part decision. In the first ruling, five justices sided with Bakke. Their opinion was based on the Fourteenth Amendment's equal protection clause: "Preferring members of any one group for no reason other than race or ethnic origin is discrimination for its own sake." That is, the university's strict racial quota system was not acceptable.

In the second part of this decision, Justice Lewis Powell, Jr., switched sides and joined the four justices who had ruled against Bakke. These five justices ruled that a school could adopt an admissions program in which "race or ethnic background is simply one element . . . in the selection process." This part of the decision upheld the goals of affirmative action policies.

Some justices also pointed out that when race is used to give whites preference over members of minorities, it must always be questioned as a "suspect classification." But giving preference to those who have long been discriminated against is a different matter. Justice Blackmun said, with regret, that "in order to get beyond racism, we must first take account of race."

Decisions for affirmative action

Since *Bakke,* the Supreme Court has upheld a number of affirmative action policies. For example, to increase the number of blacks in skilled positions, the Kaiser Aluminum plant in Gramercy, Louisiana, along with the steelworkers union, developed a special training program. Half the positions in the program were set aside for blacks. Brian Weber, a production worker, applied for the program several times but was bypassed in favor of black employees who had less seniority. Weber sued the union, charging reverse discrimination under Title VII of the 1964 Civil Rights Act. (This provision makes it illegal to consider race, religion, sex, or national origin as a factor in hiring or promoting workers.)

A majority of the Supreme Court believed, however, that the 1964 Civil Rights Act was designed to help minorities, not to prohibit private affirmative action programs. In *United Steelworkers of America v. Weber* (1979), the Court ruled against Weber:

> It would be ironic indeed if a law triggered by a Nation's concern over centuries of racial injustice and intended to improve the lot of those who had "been excluded from the American dream for so long" . . . constituted the first legislative prohibition of all voluntary, private . . . efforts to abolish traditional patterns of racial segregation.

Limits on affirmative action

The Court has also put limits on the scope of affirmative action. The city of Memphis laid off some employees because of budget problems, including three white firefighters with more seniority than some blacks who kept their jobs. This violated the union contract, and the white firefighters sued. In *Firefighters Local Union No. 1784 v. Stotts* (1984), the Court ruled, in essence, the last hired should be the first fired. Similarly, in 1986 the Court rejected a Jackson, Michigan, union plan to lay off white teachers before less experienced black teachers in order to achieve racial balance (*Wygant v. Jackson Board of Education*).

Setbacks for affirmative action

In June 1989, the Supreme Court ruled in *Wards Cove Packing Co. v. Atonio* that minorities seeking legal redress for discrimination in employment must provide proof that they had been discriminated against. This ruling dealt a blow to previous civil rights legislation. National Urban League President John Jacob stated "The court we once looked to as the protector of minority rights has itself become a threat to our rights." President Bush defended the ruling, saying that in the 1990's there would be "more than enough jobs and too few people qualified to fill them," making affirmative action programs unnecessary.

President Bush opposed Congress's attempts to reverse the Supreme Court's ruling on *Wards Cove* until 1991, when a compromise civil rights bill was passed. The bill required employers to prove that their hiring practices were not discriminatory. It also gave victims of racial and sexual discrimination—including sexual harrassment—the right to win cash damages.

SECTION 3 REVIEW

Vocabulary and key terms

bilingual education (205) equal opportunity (209)
equal protection (208) affirmative action (209)
suspect classification reverse discrimination
(208) (210)

For review

1. What grounds besides "race" does the Civil Rights Act outlaw as a basis for discrimination? **6G**
2. What is a "suspect classification"? **6B**
3. What is the citizenship status of American Indians? **5A**
4. How did the Supreme Court's decision in the Bakke case (a) support affirmative action? (b) support Bakke's claim? **6I**
5. Why did the Supreme Court rule against Weber and in favor of the steelworkers' training program? **2D**

Critical thinking

ORGANIZING AN ARGUMENT What are the arguments for and against the fairness of affirmative action programs? **6B**

Section 3 Review Answers

1. Color, religion, or national origin.
2. One that is based on race or national origin.
3. They hold dual citizenship: U.S. and tribal.
4. **(a)** It held that race can be a factor in selecting applicants. **(b)** It held that race could not be the only factor.
5. The 1964 Civil Rights Act was designed to help minorities, not to prohibit private affirmative action programs.

Critical thinking *For*—Affirmative action only gives people the opportunities that they would have had if they had not been discriminated against. *Against*—Affirmative action gives preferential treatment to certain groups and thereby discriminates against others.

CLOSURE

● Remind students of the pre-reading objectives at the beginning of the section. Pose one or both of these questions again. Then have students read Section 4, creating a time line of the women's rights movement.

Background: *Constitutional Heritage* In the *Firefighters* case, the Court ruled that layoffs did not have to proceed by seniority if minority employees could demonstrate that they were actual victims of discrimination. This meant that the minority firefighters would have the difficult task of proving that they would have been employed if not for the city's discrimination.

The symbol 👥 denotes active participation strategies.

Activities are keyed for student abilities:
▲ = Basic
● = All Levels
■ = Average/Advanced

SECTION 4

American Women Seek the Rights of Citizens
(pp. 212–219)

Section Objectives

☐ describe how women in the United States gained the right to vote

☐ name the areas in which laws and Supreme Court decisions have reduced discrimination against women

Vocabulary

suffragist, comparable worth

 FOCUS

● Ask members of the class to create on the board a checklist of rights that women enjoy today that they did not have 100 years ago. (Suffrage, equal opportunity for most jobs, equality for many social and economic opportunities, equal school sports teams.)

1D, 2C, 2D, 5C, 6B, 6C, 6E, 6G, 6I, 8A, 8B, 8H

American Women Seek the Rights of Citizens

ACCESS The Main Ideas

1 How did women in the United States gain the right to vote? *pages 212–213*

2 In what ways have laws and Supreme Court decisions reduced discrimination against women? *pages 213–219*

When the Founding Fathers gathered at the Continental Congress to debate the principles of their new country, one woman tried to have them address the concerns of their wives and daughters. Abigail Adams wrote to her husband, John, to "remember the ladies." Her plea carried a threat: "If particular care and attention is not paid to the ladies, we are determined to foment a rebellion, and will not hold ourselves bound by any laws in which we have no voice, or representation." Despite Abigail Adams's efforts, women's political rights were ignored. The revolution she promised became a long struggle for rights for women.

1D, 2C, 5C

The Right to Vote

For 130 years after the Constitution, women in most of the United States could neither vote nor hold political office. Although Wyoming Territory gave women the vote in 1869, it took time and vigorous effort for women nationwide to gain this basic right of citizenship. Before 1920, only sixteen states and territories, mainly in the West, extended full voting rights to women. The first woman member of Congress, Jeannette Rankin, was elected from Montana in 1916 — before women in the rest of the country could vote.

The suffrage movement

During the late 1800's, **suffragists** such as Susan B. Anthony and Elizabeth Cady Stanton began to organize a movement that sought full voting rights (or *suffrage*) as well as social and economic reforms. They used protests, parades,

Carrying banners in support of votes for women, suffragists march along Fifth Avenue, New York City, in a 1913 parade.

212

Cross-reference
More information about the career of Jeannette Rankin appears on p. 331.

and civil disobedience to draw attention to their cause. The first Woman's Rights Convention, held in 1848 at Seneca Falls, N.Y., issued a *Declaration of Sentiments* based on the Declaration of Independence, saying "We hold these truths to be self-evident: that all men and women are created equal. . . ." The convention also set forth a number of resolutions, including the following:

> *Resolved,* That it is the duty of the women of this country to secure to themselves their sacred right to the elective franchise.

In the early 1870's, women in several states went to the polls and tried to cast their ballots. In most places, the women's ballots were placed in separate boxes and never counted. Risking a fine or prison sentence, Susan B. Anthony and fifteen other women registered and voted in Rochester, New York, in the 1872 presidential election. They were arrested for "illegal voting," a federal offense. Anthony again quoted the Declaration of Independence. How, she asked, "can the consent of the governed be given if the right to vote be denied?" She was not allowed to testify at her trial and was fined $100 (which she refused to pay).

Other women also went to court to claim their right to vote — and lost. In 1875, the Supreme Court ruled against Virginia Minor, a St. Louis woman who claimed her right to vote under the Fourteenth Amendment (*Minor v. Happersett,* 1875). Neither the Fourteenth nor the Fifteenth Amendment was considered to apply to women, black or white. Not until 1920 did the suffragists' efforts fully succeed, when the Nineteenth Amendment guaranteed all adult American women the right to vote.

2D, 6C, 6G, 6I

Discriminatory Laws

During most of the nation's history, social and economic discrimination against women also was both accepted and legal. Laws tended to "protect" and restrict women, reflecting the traditional view that their place was only "in the home." In the late 1800's, the Supreme Court several times upheld the constitutionality of legal classifications based on sex.

Myra Colby Bradwell, for example, was trained in law and ran a well-known legal news-

YOU DECIDE

8H

Nina Wu, a sophomore at the University of Connecticut, thought she was joking when she put a sign on her dormitory door attacking "preppies," "bimbos," and various other kinds of persons. Wu was evicted from the dorm for violating the student-behavior code, which prohibited "making personal slurs based on race, sex, ethnic origin, disability, religion or sexual orientation."

Advise Ms. Wu.

paper in Chicago in the 1860's. She herself could not practice law in Illinois. In *Bradwell v. State of Illinois* (1873), the Supreme Court upheld the Illinois law that denied any woman the right to practice law. As part of the ruling, Justice Joseph P. Bradley explained, "The natural and proper timidity and delicacy which belongs to the female sex evidently unfits it for many of the occupations of civil life."

"Equal protection" for women

Not until 1971 did the Supreme Court, for the first time, rule that a law based on classification by sex violated the "equal protection" clause of the Fourteenth Amendment. Sally and Cecil Reed, who were separated, both sought to administer the estate of their child who had died. An Idaho law automatically gave the father preference over the mother in such cases. In *Reed v. Reed,* the Court overturned this law, saying that the parent's sex had no relation to his or her ability to manage money.

On the heels of *Reed* the Court heard a series of cases challenging laws based on sex discrimination. As Figure 7–3 shows, these involved both economic and social inequalities.

The Equal Rights Amendment

Many women's groups in the 1960's believed that a constitutional amendment would be the only real guarantee of "equality of rights under the law" for women. As detailed in

213

EXPLANATION

After students have read the section, you may want to consider the following activities:

History

Have students reread the statement by Abigail Adams at the beginning of this section.

● **What is Abigail Adams saying?** (Women's rights should not be neglected in setting up the new country or women will rebel.)

● ┃CRITICAL THINKING┃ **Did history bear out Adams's prediction?** (For the most part, women did obey the laws, but many protested their lack of rights.)

■ ┃CRITICAL THINKING┃ **If Abigail Adams were alive today, how do you think she would feel about women's position in America?** (Some students might argue that she would be pleased and surprised at the advances women have made. Others might disagree, claiming that Adams would not be satisfied unless women had complete social and economic equality with men.)

You Decide Answer
Students should defend their answers. Threatened with a federal lawsuit, the university later let Wu move back onto campus and revised its student-behavior code.

Cultural Literacy

■ In recent years, various groups have objected to the use of male-oriented language. Ask students to suggest terms and words that have come under fire for being "sexist" and the terms that can be used to replace them. (Possible answers include fireman—firefighter; chairman—chair; freshman—first year student; fisherman—fisher.)

👥 History

● Draw the time chart below on the board. Call on individual students to come to the board and fill in the event next to each of the years. Then have students suggest other events mentioned in the section and explain why they think these events are comparable in importance to the events already listed.

| 1848: |
| 1916: |
| 1920: |
| 1964: |
| 1972: |
| 1982: |

(1848—Woman's Rights Convention at Seneca Falls; 1916—First woman member of Congress elected; 1920—Nineteenth Amendment gives women the vote; 1964—Civil Rights Act of 1964 prohibits sex discrimination in employment; 1972—ERA passed by Congress; 1982—ERA ratification deadline.)

Economic distinctions found unconstitutional

★ A provision of the Social Security Act that allowed widows greater benefits than widowers. (*Califano v. Goldfarb*, 1977)

★ A policy that allowed employers to deduct larger pension contributions from the paychecks of female workers than from those of male workers. (*Los Angeles Department of Water and Power v. Manhart*, 1978)

★ A law that favored women over men in awarding alimony. (*Orr v. Orr*, 1979)

★ An Air Force ruling that husbands had to prove they were dependents of officers, while wives were automatically assumed to be dependent. (*Frontiero v. Richardson*, 1973)

★ The exclusion of women from membership in the Junior Chamber of Commerce or Rotary International, even though both are private associations. (*Roberts v. United States Jaycees*, 1984; *Board of Directors of Rotary International v. Rotary Club of Duarte* [Cal.], 1987)

Social distinctions found unconstitutional

★ A Louisiana practice of routinely excluding women from jury duty. (*Taylor v. Louisiana*, 1975)

★ A policy that barred girls from Little League baseball teams. (*Fortin v. Darlington Little League*, 1975)

★ An Oklahoma law that called for different legal drinking ages for males (age 21) and females (age 18). (*Craig v. Boren*, 1976)

★ A New York law that permitted unwed mothers, but not unwed fathers, to prevent the adoption of their children. (*Caban v. Mohammed*, 1979)

★ A women-only admissions policy at a state-supported nursing school. (*Mississippi University for Women v. Hogan*, 1982)

Figure 7–3 DISTINCTIONS BASED ON SEX FOUND UNCONSTITUTIONAL 2D

Chapter 3, this was the intent of the proposed Equal Rights Amendment (ERA). Passed by Congress in 1972, this amendment was still three states short of ratification when its extended time limit ran out in 1982. ERA continues to be reintroduced in every session of Congress.

Allowable sex-based laws

In the absence of a specific constitutional provision such as the ERA, the Supreme Court has stopped short of declaring that *all* laws treating women as a separate group must be questioned. Some justices, such as Justice Brennan, have argued that such laws relegate women to "inferior legal status" without considering their capability as individuals. A majority of the justices, however, have not agreed.

In some cases, therefore, the Supreme Court has upheld laws discriminating between women and men. In two cases, for instance, the Court took into consideration both women's lower average salaries and the years in which few women worked outside the home. They therefore allowed women to receive greater social security benefits "to compensate for past economic discrimination" (*Califano v. Webster*, 1977). They also upheld a Florida law that granted widows, but not widowers, a yearly $500 tax exemption (*Kahn v. Shevin*, 1974).

Considering past discrimination, the Court also found other laws reasonable. For example, women in the Navy are barred from combat and most sea duty and so have few chances to show their skills and be promoted. Because of this, the

214

Figure 7–3

■ *How did the sex-based distinctions described in the chart once favor women? How did they harm women?* (Women benefited from receiving greater Social Security benefits and greater alimony; women could prevent the adoption of their children; women were given all openings at a state-supported school. Women were hurt by paying larger amounts in pension plans, by being denied membership in the Jaycees, and by being barred from serving on juries.)

As a high school student, you have probably written a number of essays. They may have been short, one-paragraph answers for a test, or they may have been longer, take-home assignments. Writing concise, well-organized essays is a skill you will value throughout your lifetime.

Writing an Essay

There are five steps you should follow when writing an essay. Follow those steps using the sample essay question below.

> Explain how actions taken by women suffragists demonstrated the civic values, rights, and responsibilities of American citizenship. Give examples to support your answer.

1. Read the essay question carefully. Pay close attention to the verbs. In this question, you are asked to *explain* a relationship, or show connections, and to *give examples,* or provide relevant details to illustrate your explanation.

2. Identify the information needed to write the essay. First, you will need to name what civic values, rights, and responsibilities were exhibited by the suffragists. These might include seeking to correct injustice, pursuing equality under the law, and participating in government. Second, you will need to identify examples of the suffragists' actions that illustrate these concepts. Such examples could include women attending the Woman's Rights Convention in 1848; Susan B. Anthony and other women illegally voting in Rochester, New York in 1872; and Virginia Minor trying to gain women the right to vote through the courts (she lost in *Minor v. Happersett,* 1875).

3. Plan your essay before beginning to write. Organizing your thoughts in an outline before you begin to answer an essay question is the single most important thing you can do to ensure a well-written essay. Keep the outline brief if you are under a time limit. If you are writing a take-home essay, make the outline more detailed.

4. Write your essay. Follow your outline, and use specific examples to support the general information you are presenting. Also, keep the essay concise; adding irrelevant details will distract the reader from the main points you are trying to make.

5. Proofread your essay. Ask yourself: Did I include all the relevant information? Have I expressed my ideas clearly? Did I make any spelling, punctuation, or grammatical errors?

CRITICAL THINKING

1. Why should you outline an essay answer first? Explain your answer.
2. How might good essay-writing skills be valuable in your future? Give some possible examples.

CIVIC
LITERACY

8B

Expressing Your Ideas in an Essay

215

Although women in the military work in non-combat jobs, they may still face the dangers of combat. Army flight surgeon Major Rhonda Cornum was held captive in early 1991 by Iraqi forces during the Persian Gulf War. It is believed her arms were broken when the helicopter she was riding in crashed. Here, she is greeted by General H. Norman Schwarzkopf upon her release.

Supreme Court upheld a Navy policy giving female officers more time than male officers to acquire a promotion before being discharged (*Schlesinger v. Ballard,* 1975).

In a California case, the Supreme Court found other reasonable grounds for a sex-based law. It upheld a law that punished males, but not females, for statutory rape. (Statutory rape is defined as having sexual relations with a person who is under age 18.) The court's reason for this decision was that young women suffered "virtually all of the significant harmful and inescapably identifiable consequences of teen-age pregnancy," (*Michael M. v. Superior Court of Sonoma County,* 1981).

The all-male military draft remains controversial. The case of *Rostker v. Goldberg* (1981) challenged a federal draft law. The Court, however, believed that women were not "similarly situated" with men in terms of military fitness. It ruled that Congress did not have to make "gestures of superficial equality" by drafting women. Draft laws may change, however. After the Persian Gulf War, in which women were killed and taken prisoner by the enemy, Congress overturned a law barring women from flying warplanes in combat. Congress also established a commission to consider opening combat positions to women—a commission that could study whether women should register for a future draft.

Protective labor legislation

Many long-standing laws that treated women as a distinct group aimed to protect working women and children. During the 1800's, women and children often worked 16 hours a day under harsh conditions. One result of the reform movements at the turn of the century was the passage of state laws limiting the number of hours that women and children could work.

Employers challenged these laws, claiming that *their* right to equal protection had been violated. But in 1908 the Supreme Court upheld an Oregon law limiting female laundry workers to 10-hour days (*Muller v. Oregon*), stating:

> It is impossible to close one's eyes to the fact that she [women] still looks to her brother and depends upon him. . . . The two sexes differ in structure of body, . . . in the amount of physical strength, in the capacity for long-continued labor, . . . the self-reliance which enables one to assert full rights, and in the capacity to maintain the struggle for subsistence. This difference justifies a difference in legislation. . . .

216

After the Oregon case, most states passed laws limiting the hours that women could work and the amount of weight they could lift. In addition, restrictions were placed on night work and employment in certain businesses, such as bars and restaurants. These laws were well-intentioned, for working conditions at the time were harsh and dangerous. Nevertheless, they became convenient excuses to deny women jobs, overtime pay, and equality in the workplace.

6B, 6E

Ending Sex Discrimination

Bans on job discrimination

As in other areas of civil rights, the first major legislative efforts to prohibit job discrimination based on sex came in the 1960's. The Equal Pay Act of 1963 forbids using different pay scales for women and men who do equal work under similar conditions. The bill's coverage, though, effectively excluded millions of women and permitted wage differences for a number of reasons. Until it was amended in 1972, the law applied only to large interstate companies.

Many of these shortcomings were addressed in the Civil Rights Act of 1964. As mentioned earlier, Title VII of this act prohibits sex (as well as racial) discrimination in employment. This provision was not in the bill first introduced in Congress. Southern Congressmen — the principal opponents of the Civil Rights Act — introduced an amendment on sex discrimination in hopes of weakening its chances of passage. Both the act and the amendment passed, bringing about the first comprehensive legislation on sex discrimination.

Many cases of sex discrimination in the workplace came before the Supreme Court. The Court ruled against a company that would not hire women with preschool-age children, while employing men with young children (*Phillips v. Martin Marietta Corp.,* 1971). The Court also rejected arbitrary height and weight limits (*Dothard v. Rawlinson,* 1977) and policies treating maternity leave differently from other leaves (*Nashville Gas v. Satty,* 1977). In *International Union, United Auto., etc. v. Johnson Controls* (1991), the Court outlawed a policy of banning women of child-bearing age from working with materials that could harm a fetus.

Controversy over "comparable worth"

The issue of **comparable worth** aroused reactions much like those to affirmative action (page 209). According to this concept, women and men should receive equal pay for jobs that require the same, or comparable, levels of skills and responsibilities, even though they are not the *same* skills. The issue arose because many jobs that have traditionally been held by women have also traditionally been low-paying. Statistics show that, on the average, women with four years of college are paid less than men without high school diplomas. Supporters of comparable worth argue that it is necessary to overcome the unequal pay scales that now exist because of sex discrimination in the past (Figure 7–4).

Figure 7–4 A COMPARISON OF EARNINGS FOR MEN AND WOMEN 8B

Education	MEDIAN EARNINGS 1990	
	Men	Women
Elementary: 8 years or less	$16,840	$11,831
High school: 1 to 3 years	$20,452	$13,858
4 years	$25,872	$17,412
College: 1 to 3 years	$30,865	$21,324
4 years	$37,283	$26,828
5 years or more	$47,131	$31,969

Source: *Current Population Reports*

Figure 7–4
■ *What are some factors that might account for these differences in pay?* (Discrimination; more women than men work part time; women take time out from work to have children.)

Background: *History*
Representative Howard W. Smith of Virginia proposed an amendment to the Civil Rights Act of 1964 barring employment discrimination based on gender in an attempt to ridicule the law, causing laughter in the House during the debate. Martha Griffiths, a representative from Michigan, threw her support behind the amendment, helping it—and the Act—to pass.

Federal legislation in the 1970's opened up many more opportunities for high school women athletes. With more funding and better equipment, women's teams also won larger audiences and more public recognition.

In the mid-1980's, a number of lawsuits were brought by workers in predominantly "female" jobs, such as clerks, secretaries, bank tellers, and librarians. In 1983, for instance, a district court judge in Washington state ordered the state to make up the back pay of some 15,000 women workers. A study had shown that workers in "men's jobs" earned about 20 percent more than those in "women's jobs." In 1985, however, a federal appeals court reversed the ruling, saying that the "worth" of different jobs could not be compared objectively.

On the other hand, in May 1985 the city of Los Angeles took steps to achieve "comparable pay." The city raised the salaries of librarians and clerks 10 to 15 percent so that they would match the earnings of gardeners and maintenance workers.

Critics of comparable worth maintain that the market, not the government, should dictate wages. They also point out that women are now free to apply for higher-paying jobs. Under the Reagan administration, the federal government strongly opposed the concept of comparable worth. In June 1985, the Equal Employment Opportunity Commission (EEOC) ruled against administrative clerks and secretaries in the municipal housing authority of Rockford, Illinois. They had sought pay equal to that of maintenance workers.

Sex discrimination in schools

Until the mid-1970's, sex discrimination in education was common. Many schools, for example, would not allow boys to enroll in home economics or permit girls to take industrial arts or drafting. School athletics were generally dominated by boys-only team sports. Girls' teams were poorly equipped, often ignored, and sometimes nonexistent. In the classroom, there were often pay differences between male and female teachers with similar qualifications. These practices changed dramatically with the passage of the Education Amendments of 1972.

Title IX of the act requires all schools receiving federal funds to give male and female students equal opportunities in instruction and extracurricular activities. For instance, academic courses must be available to all students regardless of sex. Thus, home economics courses must be open to boys, while vocational training courses must be open to girls. In addition, Title IX mandates that schools must provide equal opportunities for girls and boys in sports, and treat women's athletics equally. Finally, the Court has ruled that Title IX prohibits sex discrimination in educational employment (*North Haven Board of Education v. Bell,* 1982).

To assure compliance, Title IX authorizes the withholding of federal funds from institutions that discriminate. Questions arose about

218

whether discrimination in one program — a tennis team, for instance — would cause the whole school to lose its federal funding. In *Grove City College v. Bell* (1984), the Supreme Court ruled that Title IX applies only to specific programs or departments. But in 1988 Congress passed legislation that denied all federal funds for discrimination in any program.

Sex discrimination in credit

It was once very difficult for women to get credit cards, buy houses, or otherwise get credit on their own. Single women were likely to be denied credit altogether. Married women often had to be "junior partners" in their husband's credit plans. The Equal Credit Opportunity Act of 1974, however, tried to end such practices. The law prevents banks, retail stores, savings and loan associations, government agencies, and credit card companies from denying credit on account of sex. It also prohibits creditors from asking questions regarding a person's sex or marital status. Credit is to be given, or loans made, purely on the basis of the borrower's own income and credit rating.

SECTION 4 REVIEW

Vocabulary and key terms

suffragist (212)   Title IX (218)
comparable worth (217)

For review

1. (a) What right of citizenship were women denied until 1920? (b) Who were some leaders of the suffragist movement? **2C**
2. (a) Why was the Idaho law overturned in *Reed v. Reed*? (b) Why did the Court allow women to be excluded from the military draft? **2D**
3. (a) What was the original aim of laws limiting women's working hours and jobs? (b) What other effects did these laws have? **5C**
4. What are the legal limitations on sex discrimination in (a) schools? (b) credit? **6E**

Critical thinking

ANALYZING AN ISSUE What are the issues involved in deciding whether jobs are of "comparable worth"? **8A**

Chapter Summary

All United States citizens are entitled to the political rights and privileges called civil rights, but for many years large groups of Americans were denied these rights. In the 1857 *Dred Scott* case, the Supreme Court ruled that blacks were not considered citizens by the Constitution. After the Civil War, the Fourteenth Amendment clearly extended the rights of citizenship to black Americans, but early civil rights laws were soon ignored or overturned in court cases. Many states passed "Jim Crow" laws, which legally enforced the segregation of blacks and whites. *Plessy v. Ferguson* in 1896 upheld the idea of "separate but equal" accommodations. In the early 1900's, the NAACP led a movement to challenge segregation laws.

In *Brown v. Board of Education* (1954), the Supreme Court rejected the "separate but equal" doctrine as unconstitutional. Federal troops enforced court-ordered integration of public schools in the South; however, the busing of students to end de facto segregation met strong opposition. Under the leadership of Martin Luther King, Jr., a broad-based civil rights movement using nonviolent methods of civil disobedience called national attention to racial discrimination. Legislation passed by Congress further extended black civil rights.

The civil rights movement also brought attention and improvements in the rights of Hispanics, older Americans, the disabled, Native Americans, and other minorities. To enforce the Fourteenth Amendment's promise of "equal protection," legal tests have developed to judge laws that classify people by age, race, nationality, or sex. Moreover, the federal government has encouraged affirmative action in education and employment to correct past discrimination. Critics, however, complain that such policies create reverse discrimination.

Through the efforts of suffragists, women gained the right to vote with the passage of the Nineteenth Amendment in 1920. The Supreme Court has struck down many laws that treat women differently from men, although some laws that make distinctions have been found "reasonable." Women have also made gains in education, employment, wages, and credit.

219

Section 4 Review Answers

1. **(a)** The vote. **(b)** Susan B. Anthony, Elizabeth Cady Stanton.
2. **(a)** Because a person's sex is not relevant to his or her ability to handle money. **(b)** Because women are not considered "similarly situated" with men in terms of military fitness.
3. **(a)** To protect them. **(b)** Women were denied jobs, overtime pay, and equality in employment.
4. **(a)** There can be no discrimination in athletics, employment, or educational opportunities. **(b)** Credit cannot be denied on account of sex or marital status.

Critical thinking Issues include the education and skills needed for the jobs; the difficulty, desirability, usefulness, and responsibility of the jobs; the possibilities for promotion; and competition for the jobs.

👥 CLOSURE

● Divide the class into groups and assign each group a different subsection. Groups should take turns quizzing the class on their assigned subsection. Then have students read the next assigned lesson.

CHAPTER 7 CORRECTIVES

● To review the content of Chapter 7, you may want to have students complete **Study Guide/Review 7** or **Workbook Chapter 7.**

Background: *Economics*
Other legislation that has improved the economic situation for women is the Equal Pay Act of 1963, which requires equal pay for men and women doing equal work in industries engaged in commerce or producing goods for commerce.

The symbol 👥 denotes active participation strategies.

Activities are keyed for student abilities:
▲ = Basic
● = All Levels
■ = Average/Advanced

CHAPTER 7 REVIEW

Answers

Vocabulary See pp. T19–T21 for suggested vocabulary activities.

Reviewing the Facts

1. Whether living in a free territory made Dred Scott a free man. The Court ruled that African Americans were not citizens. It also ruled that the Missouri Compromise's ban on slavery was unconstitutional.

2. Whether a law requiring blacks and whites to ride in separate train cars violated the Fourteenth Amendment. The Court established the "separate but equal" doctrine.

3. It overturned the "separate but equal" doctrine.

4. The goals were equality of education and voting rights for African Americans. Methods included pressuring Congress, taking legal action in courts, and nonviolent protests.

5. It is legal if the distinction is based on common sense or promotes the aim of government, if it does not interfere with a "fundamental right," and if it is not a "suspect classification."

6. It called into question some affirmative action policies.

7. Protests, parades, legal actions, and civil disobedience.

8. Women were weaker and less self-reliant than men.

9. Schools must provide equal opportunities for girls and boys in sports.

Thinking Critically About Key Concepts

1. Students should note that passing laws did not immediately erase years of prejudice, and that prejudice remains a problem today.

2. He was noting that years of racism had hurt African Americans and that the effects had to be considered until equality has been achieved.

 ★ CHAPTER **7** REVIEW ★

● **Review the definitions of the following terms:**

affirmative action
bilingual education
Brown v. Board of Education
civil disobedience
Civil Rights Act of 1964
comparable worth
de facto
de jure

discrimination
Dred Scott case
equal opportunity
equal protection
integration
"Jim Crow" laws
NAACP
Plessy v. Ferguson
restrictive covenant

reverse discrimination
segregation
"separate but equal"
suffragist
suspect classification
Title IX
Voting Rights Act (1965)

● **REVIEWING THE FACTS**

1. What was the issue in the *Dred Scott* case, and what did the Supreme Court decide? **2D**

2. What was the issue in *Plessy v. Ferguson,* and what did the Court decide? **2D**

3. What was the significance of *Brown v. Board of Education?* **2D**

4. What were the main goals and strategies of the civil rights movement? **6C**

5. How does the government determine if it is legal for a certain group to be treated differently? **6G**

6. What was the significance of the Supreme Court's decision in *Regents of the University of California v. Bakke?* **2D**

7. What strategies did suffragists use to win women's right to vote? **6C**

8. What was the justification for laws in the early 1900's limiting the hours and jobs in which women could work? **5C**

9. How has Title IX of the Education Amendments affected school sports? **6I**

▲ **THINKING CRITICALLY ABOUT KEY CONCEPTS**

1. Why did it take so long to make real progress in civil rights for African Americans? What barriers still stand in the way? **6F**

2. Explain Justice Blackmun's statement (p. 211) that "in order to get beyond racism, we must first take account of race." **5C**

3. What are the arguments for and against bilingual education? With which stand do you agree? Why? **5C**

4. What laws discriminate against people on the basis of age? Do you think they are reasonable? **6F**

5. Are there any employment situations where women should be treated differently from men? **5C**

▲ **PRACTICING SKILLS**

1. **Study Skills: Reading a time line.** Refer to Figure 7–1 (page 198) to answer the following questions. (a) Which amendment abolished slavery? (b) Which steps toward equal rights had to do with voting? (c) Which came first, affirmative action or the Civil Rights Commission? (d) There is a long segment of this time line that is interrupted only by the founding of the NAACP. What does this gap suggest to you? **8E**

2. **Study Skills: Reading a bar graph.** Refer to Figure 7–2 (page 207) to answer the following questions. (a) In the 1940's and 1950's, from which continent did most of the immigrants come to the United States? (b) About how many Asians had immigrated

---

3. Those in favor say bilingual education helps students learn faster and gives them pride in their heritage, while those opposed say it leads to cultural separateness and may hurt students in later life.

4. Minimum ages are set for voting, driving, drinking alcohol, getting married, running for Congress and the presidency, and complete legal rights. Students should note that these restrictions take into account

certain physical and mental capabilities.

5. Students may suggest dealing with materials that cause birth defects, infertility, or miscarriages.

to the United States from 1981 to 1990? (c) According to the graph, were there no African immigrants in the 1960's? Explain your answer. (To review graph skills, see Study Skill 3 in the back of the book.) **8B**

3. **Study Skills: Analyzing a photograph.** Referring to the photograph on page 216, answer the following questions. (a) What is the attitude of the soldiers shown greeting Major Rhonda Cornum when she was released by Iraqi forces? What is her expression? (b) How does this picture illustrate changes in the status of women since the time when the photograph on page 212 was taken? **8B**

4. **Critical Thinking Skills: Identifying assumptions.** Refer to the excerpt from the Supreme Court's opinion in *Muller v. Oregon* (page 216) to answer the following questions. (a) What assumptions did the justices make about the abilities of women? (b) How did these assumptions affect women's opportunities and rights? (c) In what ways are assumptions about women different today? (d) How has this changed women's role in society? **8D**

▲ PARTICIPATORY CITIZENSHIP

1. **Developing strategies.** Imagine that you are a member of a coordinating committee of a student civil rights group in the early 1960's. Develop a proposal for a plan of action to call attention to and protest against segregated facilities in the country. **6A**

2. **Illustrating an issue.** With others, choose one of the groups discussed in the chapter and create a visual display of how the civil rights of that group has changed in recent years. You may wish to create a poster, bulletin board, or mural showing "before" and "after" the legislation and Supreme Court cases of the last few years. **5A**

■ WRITING ABOUT ISSUES

1. **Writing an article.** Write a newspaper account of the integration of one of the schools mentioned in the section. **8C**

2. **Organizing a legal argument.** Prepare a defense for Fred Korematsu and other Japanese Americans resisting President Franklin Roosevelt's order to relocate them from the West Coast. **6C**

3. **Expressing an opinion in an essay.** Write an essay explaining your opinion on whether a constitutional amendment is necessary to guarantee equal rights for women. **8C**

▲ ANALYZING A POLITICAL CARTOON

More women are in the work force today than ever before. Despite legal action over the past twenty years that aimed to reduce job discrimination, many women still find that they hold lower-paid, less-prestigious jobs than men. Look at the cartoon below and answer the following questions.

1. In the cartoon, what is the difference between the routes that men and women take "to the top"? **8B**

2. How does the cartoonist portray the men's reaction to the situation? **8B**

3. Judging from the cartoon, would you predict that the cartoonist would favor a policy of leaving rules on sex-based discrimination up to private employers? Why, or why not? **8B**

Clay Bennett, St. Petersburg Times. Reprinted by permission of the artist.

4. **(a)** That women depend on men, are physically weaker, are less self-reliant, and are unable to maintain the effort to earn a living. **(b)** Laws were passed limiting the hours and jobs of working women. **(c)** Women are generally assumed to be equal to men in most fields of work. **(d)** Many women have jobs outside the home with financial and political responsibilities.

Participatory Citizenship

1. Students may plan a Freedom Ride to protest segregation of transportation or a sit-in to protest segregated facilities.
2. Displays may include drawings, clippings, photographs, and cartoons.

Writing About Issues

1. Students may wish to do research to find out more about integration in Little Rock, Virginia, North Carolina, Denver, or Boston.
2. Students should argue that the law is "suspect," that there was no evidence that Japanese Americans were helping Japan, and that the racial bias of the law violated the Fourteenth Amendment.
3. Students should defend their opinions.

Analyzing a Political Cartoon

1. Men have the easy way up—just riding together on an elevator—while women must climb their way to success by themselves.
2. One man is shown smiling, amused at the woman's situation.
3. The cartoonist would probably not favor leaving these rules up to employers because the cartoon shows how unfair employers have been.

Practicing Skills

1. **(a)** Thirteenth. **(b)** Fifteenth Amendment, Civil Rights Act of 1960, 24th Amendment, Voting Rights Act. **(c)** Civil Rights Commission. **(d)** Students may suggest that civil rights were not a high national priority during this period.

2. **(a)** Europe. **(b)** 2.8 million. **(c)** Not necessarily, because immigration figures under 30,000 are not represented on the graph.

3. **(a)** Soldiers seem happy, respectful, and approving. Cornum is very happy. **(b)** Cornum is dressed in pants like the men. She is an accepted part of the military, respected by male soldiers.

Chapter Review exercises are keyed for student abilities:
▲ = Basic
● = All Levels
■ = Average/Advanced

AS OTHERS SEE US

Vocabulary

diaspora—the dispersed community of a people who originally shared a homeland.

Background

Cheryl McCourtie's father was an agricultural economist with the Food and Agriculture Organization of the UN. She was three years old in 1966 when he took his family from Kingston, Jamaica, to Monrovia, Liberia. In Swaziland, McCourtie went to school with Winnie and Nelson Mandela's daughters. She was sent to boarding school in the United States in 1977.

Geography

Using a classroom map or the world map on pp. 808–809, have students locate the countries mentioned in this feature. Ask for volunteers to do research on one of these countries, and to make a short presentation to the class describing the country. After each description, ask students to suggest how their life might be different if they lived there.

AS OTHERS SEE US

1C, 5C

Cheryl McCourtie

A Jamaican's Sense of African American Identity

Cheryl McCourtie, whose parents are Jamaican, grew up in the African nations of Liberia, Swaziland, and Malawi, where her father worked for the United Nations. As a high school and college student, she lived in the United States.

Africa. After six years in Liberia, my father was assigned to Swaziland, a beautiful, tiny, landlocked kingdom bordering the Republic of South Africa and Mozambique. . . .

At my new school . . . I was constantly teased for having an "American" accent. And worse, I was immediately identifiable as an outsider wherever I went. I wore my natural hair in pigtails while most southern African girls wore their hair close-cropped. . . .

Some of the Swazis we met did not have a clear sense of the African diaspora. . . . Once a cab driver asked my mother and me what our "real" names and language were. He didn't understand that, as people of the Americas, we had lost our names in slavery.

United States. At . . . a Quaker school in . . . Pennsylvania, I was ill-equipped to deal with the racial environment. When one of the Black students was suspended from the school for stealing jewelry, the white victim, supposedly a friend of mine, informed me that the perpetrator would go to jail if she decided to press charges "because she is Black." This incident was one of many that helped introduce me to American-style racism.

When I was growing up in Africa, I was painfully and guiltily aware of how much suffering surrounded me: poverty, malnutrition, disease. Despite my privileged upbringing, the proof of this suffering was always evident.

. . . But as the product of developing countries, I grieve when I see how much

Black Americans take for granted. Because for all the misery Black people have endured in this country, they are still the richest Black people in the world. This potential must be realized and made to work on behalf of Black people everywhere.

This, however, does not affect the reality that in America I am defined (and subsequently have learned to define myself) first by race. It is the primary and perhaps only quality many white Americans see. One of the most difficult aspects of being a Black American is that in addition to my ever-pervasive otherness, I have also become identityless. Outside my community, I become just another Black face in the masses. . . .

In Africa, I did not have to wake up every morning defining myself by race. My pride in who and what I am was quietly evident. . . . Because I was raised in Africa, I had the luxury of being myself without first having to declare a position. For that I am forever grateful.

From "Where I Enter" by Cheryl McCourtie. Copyright © 1989 by Essence Communications, Inc. Reprinted by permission.

CRITICAL THINKING

1. What kinds of experiences made the author feel like she was an outsider in African society?
2. How was the author primarily defined by others in America?
3. Why will the author always be grateful for having lived in Africa?

222

Critical Thinking Answers
1. The way that people noted her appearance and accent, and the taxi driver asking her and her mother their real names.

2. She feels that white Americans see her only as a black person, not as an individual.
3. In Africa, surrounded by other black people, McCour-

tie did not have to define herself by her race. She was able to experience the identity of just being herself.

UNIT
★ 3 ★

POLITICAL PARTICIPATION: Government by the People

223

Photo
Town Hall, Wenham, Massachusetts.

Political Participation: Government by the People *(pp. 223–328)*

Unit Overview

Unit Three examines the role of citizens in the political system of the United States. In Chapter 8 students learn how public opinion affects government policy. This chapter discusses American ideology and political culture, as well as methods of measuring public opinion. Chapter 9 investigates interest groups: why they are formed and how they influence public officials. Included are descriptions of the various types of groups and the ways such groups exert their influence through lobbying and other persuasive techniques. Chapter 10 presents political parties as essential American institutions. It describes their historical development and their roles in a democracy, and compares the Democratic and Republican parties. Chapter 11 describes the political process, from nomination to election day. It examines the legal basis for suffrage and provides a detailed look at the American voter.

CHAPTER 8
PUBLIC OPINION IN AMERICAN DEMOCRACY
(pp. 224–245)

	Section Objectives	**Section Resources**
Section 1 **What Is Public Opinion?**	☐ identify the factors that determine how much public opinion influences government policy ☐ describe the usefulness and limitations of such ideological labels as *liberal* and *conservative*	▲ TRANSPARENCY **21**
Section 2 **Many Factors Shape Political Opinions**	☐ identify the ways political culture affects how Americans think about government and politics ☐ describe how political socialization takes place	● PRIMARY SOURCE WORKSHEET **16**
Section 3 **Public Opinion Is Measured in Several Ways**	☐ describe the traditional methods of measuring public opinion ☐ identify the advantages of scientific polling	▲ SKILLS PRACTICE WORKSHEET **8** ■ SKILLS CHALLENGE WORKSHEET **8** ● CITIZENSHIP WORKSHEET **3** ▲ TRANSPARENCY **22**

Essential Elements

The list below shows Essential Elements relevant to this chapter.
(The complete list of Essential Elements appears in the introductory pages of this Teacher's Edition.)

Section 1: 4A, 4D, 5B, 5C, 6B, 8F

Section 2: 4A, 5B, 5C

Section 3: 4A, 4B, 4C, 8D, 8G, 8H

Chapter Review: 1C, 4A, 4B, 4C, 8A, 8B, 8C, 8D, 8E, 8F, 8H

> Section Resources are keyed for student abilities:
> ▲ = Basic
> ● = All Levels
> ■ = Average/Advanced

Homework Options

Each section contains activities labeled "Guided/Independent Practice," "Reteaching/Correctives," and "Enrichment/Extension." You may wish to choose from among these activities when assigning homework.

Students Acquiring English Activities

Have students choose partners and create posters divided into three sections. The first section should tell the best thing about the United States; the second section should tell the best thing about your state; the third section should tell the best thing about your community. Students should use drawings, photos, slogans, etc., to make their posters attractive and informative. Select the top three posters for awards.

LISTENING/SPEAKING: Invite a person who has lived outside the United States (for example, a member of the armed forces who was based in a foreign country) to describe how living abroad affected his or her perceptions of the United States.

Case Studies

When teaching this chapter, you may use Case Study 10, which addresses the issue of mandatory national service, or Case Study 14, which debates the idea of making English the official language of the United States. (Case Studies may be found following p. 510.)

Teacher Bibliography

Denton, Robert E. and Gary C. Woodward. *Political Communication in America*. 2nd ed. Greenwood Press, 1990. Examines the role of communication in shaping the power of politicians.

Graber, Doris A. *Mass Media and American Politics*. 3rd ed. CQ Press, 1988. An examination of the contributions of the media to public policy and public opinion.

Rubin, Bernard. *When Information Counts: Grading the Media*. Free Press, 1985. Selected readings on the themes of political information and democracy, endangered free speech, and the role of the news media.

Student Bibliography

Bennett, W. Lance. *Public Opinion in American Politics*. Harcourt Brace Jovanovich, 1980. An analysis of the links between politics and public opinion.

Broder, David S. *Behind the Front Page: A Candid Look at How the News Is Made*. Simon & Schuster, 1988. A discussion of the performance of the press — its failures and successes — by a *Washington Post* political correspondent.

Literature

Ayer, A. J. *Thomas Paine*. Macmillan, 1989. Covers the effect of *Common Sense* on public opinion.

Vidal, Gore. *Empire*. Random House, 1987. A woman newspaper owner joins the inner circle of the Washington, D.C., power elite.

CHAPTER RESOURCES

Study Guide/Review 8
Workbook Chapter 8
Chapter 8 Test, Forms A–C

Films and Videotapes*

Media Probes: Political Spots. 30 min. Time-Life, 1981. f, v. Techniques used by political media designers to produce vote-winning television commercials.

Software*

American Government III (Apple, IBM). Queue. Students learn about the development and processes of the American governmental system through interactive tutorials. Three programs cover the role of public opinion, the electoral system, voting, selection of candidates, and the process of running for office.

Television: A Study of Media Ethics (Apple, IBM, Macintosh). TS. Students use a decision-making model to assess the impact of popular media on American life.

---

* For a complete guide to audiovisual sources, see page T22.

CHAPTER 8

Public Opinion in American Democracy *(pp. 224–245)*

Chapter 8 defines public opinion, explains how it is formed—how home and family, schools, friends, and mass media shape Americans' political attitudes—and how it is measured.

Chapter Objectives
After students complete this chapter, they will be able to:

1. Identify the factors that determine how much public opinion influences government policy.

2. Describe the usefulness and limitations of such ideological labels as *liberal* and *conservative*.

3. Identify the ways political culture affects how Americans think about government and politics.

4. Describe how political socialization takes place.

5. Describe the traditional methods of measuring public opinion.

6. Identify the advantages of scientific polling.

CHAPTER
8

PUBLIC OPINION in AMERICAN DEMOCRACY

Public opinion stands out, in the United States, as the great source of power, the master of servants who tremble before it.

James Bryce
The American Commonwealth (1888)

224

Photo
Earth Day celebration.

In colonial America, denying the existence of God, and cursing one's parents were crimes punishable by death. Despite changes in law and society, most Americans continued to support capital punishment until the 1960's. In 1966, however, surveys showed that a majority of Americans opposed use of the death penalty. States began to impose it less frequently. In 1972 the Supreme Court, citing public opposition, ruled Georgia's death penalty unconstitutional. But public opinion had swung back in favor of the death penalty and in 1976 the Court approved a revised death penalty law. States performed more executions.

This chapter explores how public opinion affects public policy. More basically, what is public opinion, how is it formed, and how is it measured?

CHAPTER OUTLINE

1 What Is Public Opinion?

Judging Public Opinion
Ideology and Public Opinion

2 Many Factors Shape Political Opinions

American Political Culture
Political Socialization

3 Public Opinion Is Measured in Several Ways

Traditional Methods
Scientific Polling

CHAPTER SUPPORT MATERIAL

Skills Practice Worksheet 8

Skills Challenge Worksheet 8

Citizenship Worksheet 3

Primary Source Worksheet 16

Transparencies 21–22

Study Guide/Review 8

Workbook Chapter 8

Chapter 8 Test, Forms A–C

 VIDEOTAPE SERIES

This would be an appropriate place to use Houghton Mifflin's videotape, *Media and Politics: Inside TV News*. You may also want to use Houghton Mifflin's videotape, *Public Opinion and the Presidency*.

SECTION 1

What Is Public Opinion? *(pp. 226–230)*

Section Objectives
☐ identify the factors that determine how much public opinion influences government policy
☐ describe the usefulness and limitations of such ideological labels as *liberal* and *conservative*

Vocabulary
public opinion, ideology, radical, liberal, moderate, conservative, reactionary

FOCUS
● Select a current issue of community or state interest. Possible issues include taxes, employment, pollution, an election campaign, or controversial actions by an elected official. Ask students how "the public" feels about the issue.

If students disagree about public opinion on this issue, focus discussion by asking students what they mean by "the public." Then ask the class how *they* formed views about public opinion on this issue. How do students know the public's feelings on this issue?

What Is Public Opinion?

> **ACCESS** **The Main Ideas**
>
> **1** What kinds of factors determine how much public opinion influences government policy? *pages 227–228*
>
> **2** What are the uses and limitations of such ideological labels as *liberal* and *conservative*? *pages 228–230*

If you loved a certain movie, you will probably tell your friends about it and encourage them to see it. If enough people feel the way you do, there will be a visible result — perhaps a blockbuster hit. Likewise, if you hated it and discouraged everyone you know from seeing it, your reaction could help make the film a flop.

Your reactions to politics can have similar effects. You can discuss your political views with the people around you. If enough people share your ideas and take organized action, together you may be able to influence the actions and policies of government officials.

Public opinion makes a difference in a democracy. It is especially influential in areas that affect many people, such as abortion, job discrimination, pollution, or prayer in public schools. Domestic public opinion may even change the government's policy in cases such as war or international trade. This section analyzes the components that make up public opinion and the factors that make it more or less influential.

4A, 5C

Judging Public Opinion

Public and private opinions

Preferring soccer to tennis is an opinion. So is preferring one presidential candidate over another. The first, however, is a strictly private, or personal, feeling that you might express to your family, neighbors, and friends. The second opinion involves a public concern — it has to do with government and politics.

Public concerns can be expressed in many ways. People can discuss them in the community, write letters to members of Congress, call a radio talk show, speak at a PTA meeting, or vote. All these actions are part of **public opinion** — the combination of many individuals' expressed feelings about government and political issues.

It is important to realize that one person's opinion — even on a political question — is still not *public* opinion. A substantial number of people must share and express the same feeling, or it will not have any effect on government actions. In the classic definition given by political scientist V. O. Key, public opinion is "those opinions held by private persons which governments find it prudent to heed."

From public opinion, government officials can gain a picture of what the American people are thinking. Like a photograph, public opinion can be clear or blurred, vibrant or dull. These qualities or characteristics play a large role in determining how much influence public opinion actually will have on government actions and policies.

Are people personally concerned?

How greatly an issue affects people personally is one factor that determines whether public opinion has an effect on government actions. Usually people have the strongest opinions about issues directly related to their health, welfare, or economic security. For instance, in a community whose water supply is polluted, people will have sharp, strong opinions about pollution control, because this situation threatens their families' health. In a time of recession, people worry about losing their jobs and incomes.

Such personal concerns change over time. During the Great Depression of the 1930's, for example, the most important issues for the vast majority of Americans were unemployment and economic security. In the 1940's, World War II became the public's greatest concern. In the 1960's, civil rights, the Vietnam War, and environmental problems moved to the foreground. During the 1970's, people were concerned about inflation, unemployment, and the questions raised by the Watergate scandal. Concerns

226

Public support for the issues of the 1963 March on Washington was still strong twenty years later, as this anniversary rally in 1983 shows. (Speaker Bella Abzug's words are being "signed," or interpreted for the hearing-impaired, by the woman on the right.)

in the 1980's included economic security, the threat of nuclear war, and terrorism.

How many people agree on the issue?

Once an issue has been raised, most people find it difficult to be neutral. Instead, they usually express some preference — "for or against," "agree or disagree," "right or wrong." The number of people who line up on one side or the other of an issue indicates the direction that public opinion is taking. Sometimes, of course, public opinion is sharply divided, and it is not possible to judge its direction clearly.

In addition, there is no single "public opinion." Rather, public opinion is made up of the views of many different "publics." Parents, students, veterans, nurses, farmers, Baptists, Hispanics, and business owners are examples of different publics that are likely to be concerned about different issues. Even within a particular public there is often a wide range of opinion.

How intensely do people care?

The sheer number of people who take a particular side on an issue is one gauge of public opinion. How strongly they believe in that position is also an important factor. A relatively small number of people may be passionately for or against a policy, while most people hold views in between those extremes. The issue of gun control illustrates this point. Most hunters and gun collectors vehemently oppose any effort to regulate handguns. Victims of crimes involving handguns strongly favor efforts to regulate or outlaw them. Most other Americans have an opinion about gun control, but they are not intensely committed to acting on their feelings.

How stable are people's opinions?

Some opinions resist change and endure over a long period of time. People whose opinions on issues remain stable are likely also to be those whose lifestyles stay much the same. They live in the same neighborhood, stay on the same job, and associate with like-minded friends for a long time. Enduring opinions also stem from strong identification with an ethnic group, a religion, a political party, or a region of the country. For example, most black Americans have long favored strong civil rights legislation. Most union workers have steadfastly supported increased minimum wage laws. Because of such stability, it is often possible to predict the opinions that members of a particular group will hold on certain issues.

How widespread is an opinion?

The final way of judging public opinion is by its distribution. Is it spread out over a wide sector of the population or concentrated in one region or group? For example, limiting imports of shoes may be an important issue for many

227

EXPLANATION

After students have read the section, you may want to consider the following activities:

Civic Participation

Examine with the class the difference between public and private opinion.

▲ Begin by asking each student to make a list of eight topics about which he or she has a strong opinion (e.g., music, clothing, sports, capital punishment, or freedom of speech). Students need not state their opinions on these subjects.

● Next ask each student to make a two-column chart. Have students label the columns *Private Opinion* and *Opinions About Public Issues* and place each of the topics they have listed in the appropriate column. Then have students read aloud some of the topics they have put in the second column. Students should explain the criteria they used to classify these topics.

Politics

● CRITICAL THINKING Have students list five public policy issues about which they have strong opinions and five questions about which they are not concerned. Then ask them to write a two-paragraph analysis of why some issues are of more concern to them than others, and to draw conclusions about factors that influence public opinion generally.

Critical Thinking
● *Why do the issues at the forefront of public opinion change over time?* (New problems arise; old problems are solved or the public loses interest in them.)

What issues might be prominent in the 1990's? (Students might suggest the environment, economic growth, and changes in international relations.)

The symbol ᴛ̈ denotes active participation strategies.

Activities are keyed for student abilities:
▲ = Basic
● = All Levels
■ = Average/Advanced

workers and businesses in the Northeast, but not for farmers in the South and West. Similarly, farm dwellers are not likely to have strong opinions about problems of the inner city.

On the other hand, when fanatic students in Iran held dozens of Americans hostage in 1979, Americans all across the nation favored action to free the hostages. Similarly, high unemployment due to a recession concerns people in all parts of the country and at every economic level.

Public opinion and government action

In American democracy, public opinion serves as a message from the people to their government. But government officials do not heed, or pay equal attention to, all opinions. There are no ironclad rules that determine the link between public opinion and government actions. Still, some generalizations are possible.

An opinion on which many people throughout the country agree intensely is likely to be heard and considered. When public opinion is less intense, more localized, or sharply divided, the message to government is less clear.

For example, in 1941, after the bombing of Pearl Harbor, American public opinion in favor of the war effort was strong and united. The government waged a vigorous campaign to defeat Germany and Japan. During the final years of the Vietnam War, on the other hand, public opinion on how to bring the war to an end was intense and emotional, but it was also deeply divided. Government policies seemed to mirror this mixed opinion. While the United States took part in peace talks and began to withdraw troops, it also carried out bombing raids, ground fighting, and the invasion of Cambodia.

In judging public opinion on an issue, government officials must look closely at *all* its qualities. For example, a majority of people may take the same side on an issue, but it may not be very important to them. In this situation, a deeply committed, well-organized minority may have greater influence on government action.

5C, 6B

Ideology and Public Opinion

Public opinion is made up of the combined opinions of millions of Americans on hundreds of subjects. Do all these opinions fall into any familiar patterns? An organized pattern of looking at the political world is known as an **ideology**. More precisely, an ideology is a systematic set of ideas that is used to justify a particular point of view. It is a way of bringing together attitudes and opinions into a consistent whole.

Most Americans tend to take positions issue by issue, not following any strict ideology. Because of this tendency, it is often said that Americans are "less ideological" than the citizens of other nations.

Figure 8–1 THE IDEOLOGICAL SPECTRUM Political points of view can be arranged along a spectrum. 5C

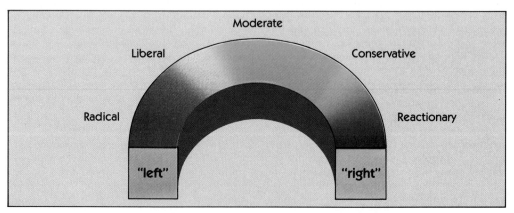

The range of ideologies

Probably you have heard someone described as a "radical" or a "conservative," or as being "left-leaning" or "right-wing." These terms are used to describe different ideologies. They are difficult to define exactly, however, because they have developed and taken on new meanings over the years. Moreover, such labels often reflect the point of view of the person who uses them.

Because some ideologies overlap, and some seem to include conflicting positions, it is difficult to categorize them precisely. Political scientists usually arrange political points of view along a range, or spectrum, as in Figure 8–1. Today, the terms most commonly used to describe ideological positions have these meanings:

Radicals (on the far left) favor rapid, fundamental change in the existing social, economic, or political order. They may be willing to resort to extreme means, even violence and revolution, to accomplish such change.

Liberals are those who think that the government should actively promote social reform to increase individuals' well-being. Liberals generally view change as a good thing. The change desired by liberals, however, is peaceful change within the existing political system — not the rapid change desired by radicals.

Moderates are people whose attitudes and opinions on issues are located somewhere between liberal and conservative and may include some of both. Moderates usually are thought of as people who are tolerant of others' opinions and not likely to hold extreme views on issues.

Conservatives favor the *status quo*, that is, keeping things as they are. Although not totally opposed to change, conservatives are cautious and hesitant about new policies. They feel that the government should, as much as possible, stay out of private citizens' lives and businesses.

Reactionaries (on the far right) are people who advocate a return to a previous state of affairs, often a social order or government that existed earlier in history. Reactionaries, like radicals, may be willing to go to extremes to attain their goals.

As you can see, the term *right* generally refers to people who hold traditional views, and *left* refers to those who favor change in society. Between the extreme left and the far right, there are several in-between points of view.

Historically, the terms *left* and *right* originated in the French National Assembly of 1789. In the Assembly chambers, aristocrats and those favoring the policies of the past French monarchs were seated to the right of the speaker. The revolutionaries, those favoring swift and far-reaching change, were seated on the left. Although "left" and "right" no longer describe the same political groups, they have kept similar meanings (and still influence seating arrangements in many European legislatures).

Figure 8–2 POLITICAL IDEOLOGIES In response to a poll on ideology, most Americans considered themselves moderates. **5C**

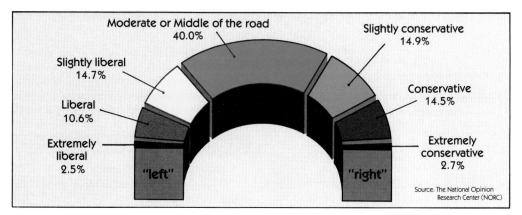

Moderate or Middle of the road
40.0%

Slightly conservative
14.9%

Slightly liberal
14.7%

Conservative
14.5%

Liberal
10.6%

Extremely liberal
2.5%

"left"

"right"

Extremely conservative
2.7%

Source: The National Opinion Research Center (NORC)

GUIDED/INDEPENDENT PRACTICE

● Have students identify national or local political figures or organizations and describe where they stand on the ideological spectrum. For each individual or organization, students should state the reasons why they chose the label they did.

RETEACHING/CORRECTIVES

▲ Have students copy down the five subheadings under the heading "Judging Public Opinion" that are in the form of questions. For each subheading, students should explain how that factor will affect government policy. (For example, if people are personally concerned about an issue, public opinion is more likely to influence government action.)

You may also want to use **Transparency 21**, which shows a cause-and-effect chart of the rise of conservatism in the 1980's.

ENRICHMENT/EXTENSION

■ Ask students to research issues in their community that are currently giving rise to strong public opinion. Have them report on the means through which people are expressing opinions on these issues.

Figure 8–2

■ *What is a moderate?* (Someone whose views fall between liberal and conservative.) *Why might people with little interest in politics be more likely to see themselves as moderates?* (The other labels imply more sharply defined political viewpoints.)

The symbol 👥 denotes active participation strategies.

Activities are keyed for student abilities:
▲ = Basic
● = All Levels
■ = Average/Advanced

Section 1 Review Answers

1. **(a)** Issues related to their own health, welfare, or economic security. **(b)** Stable lifestyles and a strong identification with an ethnic group, a religion, a political party, or a region of the country.
2. **(a)** Public opinion was united in favor of entering World War II. **(b)** The government launched an all-out war effort.
3. *Left* generally refers to those who favor change; *right* refers to those who favor the status quo.

Critical thinking Students should identify these issues, then note whether these issues are related to their health, welfare, or economic security.

CLOSURE

● Review the Section 1 vocabulary with students to reinforce key concepts from the section. Then have students read Section 2, noting how political opinions are formed.

SECTION 2

Many Factors Shape Political Opinions

(pp. 230–235)

Section Objectives

☐ identify the ways political culture affects how Americans think about government and politics
☐ describe how political socialization takes place

Vocabulary

culture, political culture, political symbol, political socialization, peers

---

The vast majority of Americans are concentrated somewhere between liberal and conservative on the political spectrum. This is less true in European democracies, where there are numerous political parties that represent "far left" or "far right" opinions. While the United States does have both radicals and reactionaries, they represent only a small minority of the total population. Figure 8–2 shows how Americans describe their own political views.

Avoiding ideological labels

There are several reasons to be very cautious in applying any of these ideological labels to groups or individuals, particularly in the United States. First, they originated in political systems with greater differences between parties than exist in American politics. Second, the meanings of some terms have changed over the years. For example, in Great Britain in the 19th century, a "liberal" was someone who opposed government interference in the economy. A 19th-century "liberal" would probably be labeled a "conservative" today. Third, not everyone fits neatly into such categories. A person may be conservative on economic issues but liberal on civil rights issues, or vice versa. Finally, as mentioned earlier, labels commonly reflect the speaker's own political position.

SECTION 1 REVIEW

Vocabulary and key terms

public opinion (226)	conservative (229)
ideology (228)	status quo (229)
radical (229)	reactionary (229)
liberal (229)	"left" (229)
moderate (229)	"right" (229)

For review

1. (a) About what kind of issues are people likely to feel most involved? (b) What are some factors that promote stable opinions? **4A**
2. (a) What were the qualities of American public opinion at the time of the bombing of Pearl Harbor? (b) How did government react? **8F**
3. In describing ideologies, to what kind of attitudes do the terms *left* and *right* generally refer? **5B**

Critical thinking

FORMING AN OPINION   Page 226 mentions issues that have been prominent in certain decades. What issues today concern the members of your government class? What issues do you think will be important in ten years? **4D**

SECTION 2
4A, 5B, 5C

Many Factors Shape Political Opinions

ACCESS	The Main Ideas
1	What are some of the ways political culture affects the way Americans think about government? *pages 230–233*
2	How does political socialization take place? *pages 233–235*

A national survey asked the following question in 1942: "Should white and black students go to the same schools or separate schools?" Poll results showed that only 30 percent of white respondents favored students attending school together. When the same question was posed in 1984, 90 percent of whites favored integrated schools. What factors shape people's ideas about politics and society? Why, as this example suggests, can people's views also change over time? **5B, 5C**

American Political Culture

Effects of political culture
What makes Americans different from Canadians, Russians, Egyptians, or Japanese? Obviously, each country has a complex combination

---

Background: *History* The meaning of some ideological labels has changed over the years. For example, in Great Britain in the 19th century, a "liberal" was someone who opposed government interference in the economy. A 19th-century liberal would probably be labeled a "conservative" today.

By honoring those Americans killed or missing in action in Vietnam, the Vietnam Veterans Memorial in Washington, D.C., is part of our nation's political culture.

ïï FOCUS

● To introduce this section, ask each student to complete the following sentences on a sheet of paper: *I believe the United States is . . . . I believe the American government is . . . . I believe voting is . . . .* Ask students how they think the opinions reflected in their statements were formed. Students might make a list of the people, organizations, events, or ideas that have influenced their political views. Ask students to retain their lists until they have completed this section. At that time, they can review their lists to see whether they left out any important influences.

of traits that are unique to its population. These make up the nation's **culture**, which includes language, religion, music, history, food, economics, geography, climate, art, sports, and many other things. Not all Americans share *exactly* the same culture. Nonetheless, there is a basic culture that distinguishes people raised in the United States from those who have grown up in other countries.

One aspect of culture is **political culture** — those elements related to a nation's government and politics. These include its legal system, constitution, political leaders and institutions, customs, traditions, patriotic songs, and flags. The political culture that surrounds us exerts a profound influence on the ways we think about government and politics.

Sense of community

One of the first contacts that children have with their political culture is a sense of identification with their own community. At a very young age, children are aware that they are part of a city, region, state, or country. They learn they are "Americans," or "Texans," or "Midwesterners," or "New Yorkers." This sense of being part of a community continues into adult life.

Most Americans, regardless of age, are proud of their country and feel that the United States is the best place in the world to live. Such deeply rooted feelings of pride and loyalty are reflected in Americans' basic attitudes. These attitudes

may be expressed in many ways: "America means freedom," "America is the land of opportunity," "God bless America," "America is the great melting pot," or "United we stand, divided we fall." There are times, of course, when many Americans disagree with the government's policies. Then, we feel free to criticize government leaders without weakening our basic loyalty to the country. Compared even with people in other democratic nations, only a tiny percentage of Americans say they would like to live permanently in another country.

Support for the democratic process

Another important part of our political culture is that Americans strongly support the democratic political system. In the early 1960's, political scientists asked people in five countries what they were proudest of about their country. Of the Americans surveyed, 85 percent named their political system and government. (Figure 8–3 shows the answers to this survey.) Some years later, in 1973, a Gallup Poll asked Americans what they would tell foreigners was the "best thing about the United States." An overwhelming majority of responses referred to "democracy" and "freedom."

Closely related to this positive feeling about democracy are other basic attitudes toward the political process. In general, Americans believe in and strongly support the following policies and ideas: free elections, universal suffrage, ma-

231

The symbol ïï denotes active participation strategies.

Activities are keyed for student abilities:
▲ = Basic
● = All Levels
■ = Average/Advanced

EXPLANATION

After students have read the section, you may want to consider the following activities:

Cultural Literacy

▲ Ask a class member to define the term *political culture.* (The elements of a nation's culture related to government and politics.)

Point out that political culture, like other aspects of culture, is of two types. *Material* political culture consists of tangible objects such as the flag, the White House, patriotic songs, or the Capitol building. *Nonmaterial* political culture consists of the rules, ideas, and attitudes that influence the behavior of Americans and their beliefs about political events.

▲ Have each student make a list of the elements of American political culture discussed on pp. 231–233. The list should include both concrete political symbols and ideas or beliefs.

jority rule with minority rights, rule by law, due process of law, freedom of speech, "innocent until proven guilty," and "liberty and justice for all." These beliefs underscore the principles of American government discussed in this book.

Attitudes toward officials

In some countries, citizens commonly express mistrust, disdain, or fear of their political leaders. In the American political culture, however, most people have relatively strong confidence and trust in public officials. Studies of very young American children generally show that they have deep affection for government leaders — especially the President and police officers, the two authority figures with whom children are most familiar. Young people usually do not start to become critical of government leaders until their early teens.

Despite Americans' general confidence in their political leaders, there have been periods when many adults felt deep disillusionment with politics and politicians. This was certainly true in the mid-1970's, when the Watergate break-in and the events following it seemed to involve President Richard Nixon and White House staff members in illegal actions. Public opinion polls at the time showed that most citizens had lost some of their confidence in *all* political leaders. By 1990, the public's lack of confidence in political officials led to movements to set mandatory limits on terms in office.

At the same time, Americans since colonial times have distrusted the power and authority of government. This long-held mistrust is the reason for the many safeguards for individual rights provided in the Constitution.

Civic responsibility

Political culture also affects what people consider to be their responsibilities as citizens. For example, Americans believe that it is their duty to take part in the political system — to vote, serve on a jury, and the like. One political scientist's research showed that by the eighth grade, most students think they ought to vote and take an interest in current events. Although many Americans do not participate actively in politics, most feel that they *should.*

Political symbols

Most Americans also respect patriotic symbols like the American flag and the national anthem. Even at sports events, spectators remove their hats and stand at attention for the playing of "The Star Spangled Banner." Such distinctive **political symbols** are an important part of a nation's political culture. They are objects or expressions that represent abstract ideas like "freedom," "democracy," or even "America" itself.

In general, political symbols serve three functions. First, they help people recognize and respond directly to political objects or ideas.

Figure 8–3 SOURCES OF NATIONAL PRIDE
(Percentage of Respondents)* 5B

WHAT MAKES YOU MOST PROUD OF YOUR COUNTRY?	UNITED STATES	GREAT BRITAIN	WEST GERMANY	ITALY	MEXICO
Government, political system	85	46	7	3	30
Economic system	23	10	33	3	24
Social legislation	13	18	6	1	2
Characteristics of people	7	18	36	11	15
Beauty of country	5	10	17	25	22
Contributions to science	3	7	12	3	1
Contributions to the arts	1	6	11	16	9

* Figures represent the percentage of people surveyed in each country who named this characteristic. Some people gave more than one response, so each column may total more than 100%.

232

Figure 8–3
■ *Why do Americans have more pride in their government than people in other nations?* (The United States has had a long history of stable democracy.)

Second, they help people identify with their own group or nation. Third, political symbols evoke emotions and thus help shape attitudes. The American flag, the Statue of Liberty, and the Lincoln Memorial, for example, are all powerful political symbols. They not only represent the nation but also stir feelings of pride, hope, and respect.

Political symbols can generally be divided into four classes: personal, verbal, visual (or pictorial), and authority symbols.

PERSONAL SYMBOLS   People who are national heroes and heroines, as represented in portraits, photographs, statues, and biographical films or books. Examples include George Washington, Abraham Lincoln, Susan B. Anthony, Eleanor Roosevelt, and Dr. Martin Luther King, Jr. Because they are readily identifiable, personal symbols are especially important to young children.

Personal symbols do not have to represent individuals. Monuments such as the Vietnam Memorial or Arlington National Cemetery are very emotional personal symbols of a group.

VERBAL SYMBOLS   Written or spoken expressions of patriotism, such as songs, speeches, and pledges of allegiance — for example, ''The Star-Spangled Banner'' and Lincoln's ''Gettysburg Address.'' We learn some verbal symbols in school, and they are publicly reinforced in political campaigns, parades, and sports events. Such symbols are important to citizens of all ages.

VISUAL SYMBOLS   Visual representations such as flags, emblems, maps, medals, and colors (red, white, and blue, for example), or objects like the Statue of Liberty. Visual symbols often stand for a nation or a specific group.

AUTHORITY SYMBOLS   Objects that convey the idea of legitimacy and generate respect. Examples include the Constitution, the Capitol building, judges' robes, and military uniforms.

4A, 5C

Political Socialization

At the beginning of this section, we asked how people acquire their political attitudes. Where do we learn the political culture of our own country? John Locke, the 17th-century English philosopher, noted that when a child enters the world, his or her mind is like a *tabula rasa* (TAB-yoo-luh RAH-suh), a ''blank slate.'' Children

Parades and national celebrations are part of political culture. Even small children respond to political symbols such as flags.

are born without any attitudes, opinions, or knowledge and must gain them through education and experience. The process by which citizens acquire their sense of political identity is called **political socialization** .

Political socialization starts when we are very young. In fact, by the time most of us reach high school, our political beliefs are basically set. Although we continue to gather information and develop opinions about government during adulthood, the basic attitudes we learn as children remain with us throughout our lives.

Where do these attitudes come from? The political culture around us plays an important role in political socialization. In addition, we gain specific beliefs from certain other sources, or ''agents,'' of political socialization. In general, there are four main agents: the family, the school, peer groups, and the mass media.

233

Home and family

The earliest, and perhaps the most important, agent of political socialization is the family. Just as children observe and copy their family's language, religious beliefs, and social actions, so too do they acquire their parents' political attitudes. For instance, if parents discuss politics, keep up with current events, and vote regularly, their children are likely to feel that participating in politics is the natural thing to do. If families take no part in politics, their children are likely to carry on this pattern.

Furthermore, families filter information from the outside world and pass on their specific political opinions to their children. For example, if parents discuss their good opinion of a particular public official, their children are likely to feel the same way. If, on the other hand, parents grumble that taxes are too high or that the President's economic policy is unreasonable, their children will probably accept this belief.

The clearest evidence of the family's role in political socialization is the way political party identification is transmitted from parents to children. Studies reveal that by age 7 or 8 many children begin to support their parents' political party. Roughly two-thirds of Americans continue to favor their parents' party into adulthood.

The schools

After the family, schools are the next important early agent of political socialization. Societies have long relied on schools to teach about citizenship and transmit society's values. Jean Jacques Rousseau, an 18th-century French philosopher, wrote, "It is education that should put the national stamp on children's minds and give their opinions and tastes the direction that will make them patriots."

Political socialization is an important part of most schools' social studies programs. In the primary grades (kindergarten–3), social studies programs focus on the individual, family, neighborhood, and community. During the middle grades, students usually learn about their home state, the United States, and their rights and responsibilities as citizens. Other areas of study may include geography and the cultures of other nations. Finally, high school students are usually required to study American history and American government. Most of you are reading this book to

234

meet such requirements. In addition, high school students are often given a choice of studying other social sciences, including economics, sociology, world history, law, anthropology, and contemporary issues.

Besides actual courses, students learn a number of other things inside and outside the classroom. Political scientist Robert D. Hess and psychologist David Easton have described these events:

> The school reinforces attitudes toward law, government, and citizenship in a number of informal ways. Pledging allegiance to the flag, singing the national anthem, celebrating the birth of Washington and Lincoln, and observing Veterans Day are some of the most frequent occasions for teaching the young respect for law and a feeling of national loyalty and pride. By such informal and unsystematic means the school continues the process of political socialization begun in the home.

These early agents — families and schools — play contrasting roles in political socialization. While families influence their children's choice of political party, elementary and secondary schools try to give an unbiased view of politics. They make every effort to remain impartial. Textbooks and teachers stress the importance of democratic principles and the American two-party system but try not to take sides on controversial issues. Education therefore encourages good citizenship but seems to have little impact on whether students become Democrats or Republicans, liberals or conservatives.

Peer groups

Our attitudes and opinions on many subjects may also be influenced by our **peers**. These are the people around us who have similar backgrounds and beliefs and may be near us in age. Peers affect opinions and attitudes about politics as well as tastes in clothing, books, music, and other things. Because we see many of our peers on a daily basis — classmates, neighbors, co-workers, and close friends — these people have a direct influence on us. By discussing issues and exchanging ideas with them, we often arrive at similar conclusions. Peer group influence is particularly important for teenagers.

Television news programs are the most important source of political news for many Americans. Newscasters such as Connie Chung are familiar faces to millions of people.

Other groups are less a part of our day-to-day lives but still affect our opinions. These "secondary" peer groups include labor unions, religious groups, and professional associations. As Chapter 9 will discuss, people usually join an organized group because they agree with its aims, attitudes, and tactics. Belonging to such a group, therefore, usually reinforces attitudes and opinions that people already have.

Mass media

The mass media — magazines, newspapers, radio, and television — are the fourth important agent of political socialization. In the United States there are an estimated 1,800 daily newspapers, 11,000 magazines, and 9,000 radio and television stations. Nearly every household has at least one television set, and the average American watches roughly 30 hours of television per week. The mass media are very much a part of our lives.

The media, especially television, have become a principle source of political information for most Americans. Studies also suggest that the mass media have an impact on public opinion. A television documentary, a segment on a program like *60 Minutes,* or even a brief interview on local news can create interest in a particular issue or generate a reaction to a particular candidate. Media coverage of specific topics such as missing children, drug abuse, violence in the home, and care for the elderly have aroused nationwide concern about these subjects.

But Americans do not believe everything they read or hear, nor do they unquestioningly accept every television program or editorial comment. Rather, most people tend to read and hear what they want or expect to read and hear. In addition, most people tend to remember only what they want to remember about politics. The mass media, therefore, may be more effective in reinforcing people's opinions and attitudes than in actually changing them.

SECTION 2 REVIEW

Vocabulary and key terms

culture (231)
political culture (231)
political symbol (232)
political socialization (233)
peers (234)

For review

1. In American political culture, what are people's general attitudes about (a) the political system? (b) public officials? (c) the responsibilities of citizens? **4A**
2. List at least five political symbols that you see each day. **4A**
3. What are the four major agents of political socialization? **4A**

Critical thinking

TRACING CAUSE AND EFFECT What is your earliest memory of being aware of politics? Have your attitudes toward politics changed over the years? In what ways have individuals, groups, or events affected your attitudes? **4A**

235

Section 2 Review Answers
1. **(a)** Underlying sense of pride and support. **(b)** Relative confidence and trust despite many political scandals of the last two decades. **(c)** Citizens believe they should take an active role in the political system, such as by voting or serving on juries.
2. The flag, the American eagle (on money), portraits of such Presidents as George Washington and Abraham Lincoln (on money), police uniforms.
3. Family, school, peer groups, the mass media.

Critical thinking Students should specify what attitudinal changes they have experienced, as well as any individuals, groups, or events that have caused these changes.

CLOSURE
● Remind students of the pre-reading objectives at the beginning of the section. Pose one or both of these questions again. Then have students read Section 3, focusing on the different ways of measuring public opinion.

Background: *History* The *Harrisburg Pennsylvanian* conducted one of the first recorded polls in the United States in 1824. When the newspaper asked voters to predict the presidential election outcome, Andrew Jackson was the popular choice. John Quincy Adams eventually won that extremely close election after a vote in the House of Representatives.

The symbol 👥 denotes active participation strategies.

Activities are keyed for student abilities:
▲ = Basic
● = All Levels
■ = Average/Advanced

SECTION 3

Public Opinion Is Measured in Several Ways *(pp. 236–243)*

Section Objectives

☐ describe the traditional methods of measuring public opinion

☐ identify the advantages of scientific polling

Vocabulary

interest group, mandate, straw poll, scientific polling, sample, probability, random sample, sampling error

FOCUS

● Tell the class that President James Garfield reportedly once said that the President is "the last person in the world to know what the people really want and think." ***Why is it important for the President to know the people's wishes and thoughts?*** (The President is supposed to serve as the leader of all the people and carry out their wishes.)

Why would it be easy for the President to become isolated from public opinion? (The President is busy talking with advisers, foreign heads of state, and congressional leaders. There are few opportunities for the President to hear the views of average citizens.)

Why is it in the nation's interest for public opinion to be accurately measured? (Leaders will be better able to serve their constituents if they understand the views that their constituents hold.)

Public Opinion Is Measured in Several Ways

> **ACCESS** **The Main Ideas**
>
> **1** What are the traditional methods of measuring public opinion?
> *pages 236–238*
>
> **2** What are the advantages of scientific polling?
> *pages 238–243*

What questions might come to mind if you hear about an interesting poll result? For example, "Polls show that 63 percent of Americans favor prayer in public schools." If you see or hear about the results of a public opinion poll, you may wonder who were the Americans surveyed. How were they selected? How were the survey questions worded? How should the results of the poll be interpreted?

Researchers today conduct polls on almost every possible subject. This section describes the methods they use.

4A, 4B, 8D

Traditional Methods

In the course of American political history, public officials have gauged public opinion through some time-tested techniques. These traditional methods include making personal contacts, listening to interest groups, monitoring the mass media, assessing election returns, and using informal polls. Each of these methods has its unique advantages as well as problems.

Personal contact

Nearly all elected officials, from city council members to Presidents, sometimes gather information about public opinion simply by talking with people. Personal contact with the public can include conversing over the telephone, shaking hands at rallies or local events, or taking trips to meet with constituents. Letters sent by constituents also can provide a gauge of individual opinions. For many elected officials, these are helpful ways to learn about public opinion. Indeed, some politicians seem to have a "sixth sense," or intuition, for getting accurate and useful information directly from the people.

236

The use of personal contact to determine public opinion has certain drawbacks. First, it is physically impossible for most officials to meet person-to-person with every constituent. In addition, the people an official talks to may not accurately represent the entire population and so cannot indicate the intensity or importance of issues. Finally, because of politeness or shyness, people tend to tell an important official what they think he or she wants to hear, not necessarily what they truly feel.

Interest groups

Government officials can also learn about public opinion by paying attention to the activities of **interest groups**. Interest groups are organizations of people with shared attitudes who attempt to influence public policy. They make their views known in a variety of ways, including writing letters, demonstrating, and contributing money to candidates. One main goal of an interest group, in fact, is to make its members' opinions known to officials and to the public in general. (The activities of interest groups are discussed in detail in Chapter 9.)

Elected officials must be careful about basing their idea of public opinion solely on interest group activity. An interest group may represent only a small, but vocal, minority of people with a strong, special interest in one issue, such as nuclear energy, gun control, or automobile safety. Many more people may hold different views but not be represented by a well-organized interest group. Therefore, government officials cannot safely rely on interest groups as indicators of general public opinion.

Mass media

Public officials may also try to interpret public opinion by keeping an eye on the mass media. Headline news, magazine cover stories, television newscasts, syndicated columns, editorials, "letters to the editor," and radio talk shows all reflect issues that are foremost in people's minds.

But the media, also, may not always be an accurate guide to public opinion. In the mass media today, as Section 2 pointed out, headline news, cover stories, and TV "specials" tend to concentrate on sensational events, unusual people, and outspoken interest groups. Editorials and commentaries may reflect opinions that readers or listeners do not share. People who write "letters to the editor" or place calls to radio talk shows may be either personally involved or intensely interested in a particular issue. They may not represent broader public views. For all these reasons, the media can give a distorted view of public opinion.

Election results

After an election, winning candidates — especially those who win by wide margins — often claim they have the "mandate of the people." A **mandate** here means the support of the people as expressed by their votes. An elected official who claims to have a mandate is assuming, however, that people's votes mean they support all of the opinions and policies he or she discussed in the campaign.

Election results, however, may or may not indicate public opinion on specific policies. Many factors typically go into a voter's decision to vote for a certain candidate. The candidate's stand on one issue could be a factor, but so could the candidate's experience, party affiliation,

charm, good looks, or his or her stand on another issue altogether. The merits of other candidates also matter. Therefore, elections may not be a reliable barometer of public opinion on particular issues.

Straw poll results

The **straw poll** was first introduced in the late 1800's by newspapers and magazines as a way to liven up their political coverage. In a straw poll, a group of people are questioned informally to determine public opinion. Today, straw polls may include mail surveys, "person-on-the-street" interviews, or telephone call-ins. Members of Congress frequently conduct straw polls by mailing questionnaires to their constituents. While straw polls make interesting conversation, they are unreliable indicators of public opinion. They are based on the incorrect assumption that public opinion can be assessed accurately merely by interviewing a large group of people.

The election of 1936 provided a dramatic example of how seriously wrong straw polls can be. *Literary Digest* was a widely circulated popular magazine that was known for its straw polls. During the 1936 presidential campaign, it mailed over 10 million postcard ballots asking people to register their choice for President.

Making personal contact with voters is still an effective way for politicians to gauge popular support and influence voters. Here Colorado Senator Ben Nighthorse Campbell (left), the first Native American elected to the U.S. Senate, campaigns in 1992.

237

Background: *Cultural Literacy* The term *straw poll* derives from the phrase "a straw in the wind." By tossing a straw in the wind (taking a poll), you can tell which way the wind (opinion) is blowing.

EXPLANATION

After students have read the section, you may want to consider the following activities:

Civic Participation

● CRITICAL THINKING Make a three-column table on the board. Label the columns *Traditional Methods of Measuring Public Opinion, How Measured, Limitations of Method*. In the first column list the following entries: *personal contact, interest groups, mass media, assessing election returns, using straw polls*. Have students complete the table by describing briefly how public opinion is measured using each of these methods, and assessing the drawbacks or limitations of each method.

● CRITICAL THINKING When the table is completed, the class should recognize that all traditional methods are biased and lack reliability. Ask students why objectivity and reliability are important in measuring public opinion.

■ CRITICAL THINKING Then have students explain why scientific polling methods are more reliable than each of the traditional polling methods listed in the table.

The symbol 👥 denotes active participation strategies.

Activities are keyed for student abilities:
▲ = Basic
● = All Levels
■ = Average/Advanced

Civic Participation

● Invite an elected official (or an aide) to talk to the class about methods used to sample public opinion on local or national issues. The speaker can be asked to describe both the traditional and scientific methods his or her staff use to determine public opinion. The speaker might also provide examples of the ways he or she has used straw polls or other traditional and scientific polling methods.

Have the students prepare questions for the speaker in advance.

Politics

■ Have students find an example of a poll in a newspaper or magazine and write a two-paragraph report on that poll. The first paragraph should summarize the methods used in the poll. In the second paragraph, students should evaluate these methods to determine the poll's reliability. Have students attach to their reports copies of the polls they selected.

Based upon the 2.4 million ballots returned, *Literary Digest* confidently predicted that Alf Landon, the Republican challenger, would soundly defeat President Franklin D. Roosevelt. The forecast stated, moreover, that Landon would win 54 percent of the vote and carry 32 states. Instead, Roosevelt won a landslide victory, taking 61 percent of the vote and winning all but two states.

Experts agree that the *Literary Digest* made two major errors. First, the people polled did not represent a true cross-section of the American population. Those surveyed were drawn from telephone directories, automobile registration lists, and subscribers to *Literary Digest.* In 1936, in the midst of the Great Depression, only those who were well off financially could afford telephones, cars, and magazine subscriptions. The views of the less fortunate, particularly blue collar workers and the unemployed, were not recorded. Unluckily for *Literary Digest,* these groups made up the base of Roosevelt's support. The second error was the failure to detect shifts in public opinion. The straw poll relied upon one mass mailing early in the campaign. Changes in opinion later in the race were ignored.

Ironically, several newcomers to public opinion polling correctly predicted Roosevelt's victory. These pioneers relied upon the sampling of just a few thousand carefully selected people.

Taking a reliable opinion poll requires a sympathetic, skillful interviewer, who can make people feel at ease.

238

Scientific Polling

The use of precise sampling and statistical methods is the basis for **scientific polling**. Today such methods are used by over a thousand polling agencies in the United States. Perhaps the best known are the Gallup Organization, Inc. (the Gallup poll), Louis Harris & Associates, Inc. (the Harris poll), and the Roper Organization (the Roper poll). Moreover, scientific surveys are now widely used by businesses, governments, political candidates, interest groups, and scholars to acquire information about public opinion. These remarkably accurate polls are based on a few relatively simple principles.

Sampling

The first step in measuring public opinion is to determine the "universe." In polling jargon, the universe is the population to be studied. The universe could be small — for example, the students in your government class. In that case, it would be a simple matter merely to ask each person his or her opinions. In most cases, however, the universe is too large for that. For example, if one state — say, Illinois or Florida — were the universe, it would obviously be impractical to interview every person in that state. A better way to find out what people in Illinois or Florida are thinking is to take a representative sample.

A cook does not have to drink an entire pot of soup to determine if it needs more seasoning. He or she merely sips. Likewise, it is unnecessary for a poll to interview every person in a universe when a sample can be taken. In scientific polling, the term **sample** refers to a small group of people who accurately represent a universe. The Gallup and Harris polls normally use a sample of only 1,500 to 1,600 people to determine public opinion nationwide.

Mathematical laws for polling

How can such a small sample represent the opinions of 160 million adult Americans? The answer can be explained by the mathematical law of **probability** — the likelihood that something will happen. Imagine a large jar containing 1,000 marbles — 500 red and 500 blue. If you mix the marbles thoroughly and scoop up ten, chances are that you will pick out five red and five blue marbles.

The 1948 election produced a classic example of mistaken public opinion polling. Weeks before the election, both Roper and Gallup polls predicted an easy victory for Republican candidate Thomas E. Dewey. Voter opinion changed late in the campaign — too late for pollsters (or newspaper editors) to realize that incumbent President Harry Truman would, in fact, win.

Scientific polling merely turns this principle around. If you picked ten marbles out of a jar and found that you had picked five red and five blue, you might make an educated guess that the jar contains 50 percent red marbles and 50 percent blue marbles. The key to scientific polling is that the sample is made at *random*. In other words, every member of the universe (or every marble in the jar) must have an equal chance, or probability, of being selected. If all the blue marbles were at the top of the jar, this sample would not be a **random sample**; the red marbles would not have an equal probability of being selected. Only by using random samples is it possible to determine the true characteristics of a population. Non-random surveys (such as the one used by *Literary Digest*) tend to be biased and, therefore, inaccurate.

The probability of drawing a random sample of all Americans has been calculated mathematically. The results show that a random sample of just 339 people will reflect a population of 160 million, with a **sampling error** of plus-or-minus 7 percentage points. That is, if 339 people are surveyed and 40 percent prefer Brand X, the actual percentage of American adults preferring Brand X is between 33 and 47 percent.

A poll could decrease its sampling error by increasing the sample size. For example, a poll could sample 1,843 people and be accurate within plus-or-minus 3 percent.

Short-cut methods

A true random sample often is not possible, especially if the universe is large. First, a researcher must identify every person in a universe. Obtaining a reliable list of names may be difficult. At that point, it also may be very costly to seek out and interview those who are selected. To overcome these obstacles, pollsters have developed some short cuts.

One common short cut is the *quota sample*. A quota sample is chosen based upon characteristics found in a population: race, income, religion, occupation, and the like. For example, the population of City X may be 70 percent Mormons and 30 percent Methodists. A quota sample based on religion, then, would include numbers of Mormons and Methodists in the same proportion — seven Mormons and three Methodists in every ten people surveyed. This technique is fairly simple, but always has a potential for bias. Characteristics may overlap, and interviewers often cannot select their sample at random.

239

GUIDED/INDEPENDENT PRACTICE

● Have students put together a glossary of terms relating to the measuring of public opinion. Glossaries should include the vocabulary terms and any other terms in the section that students find relevant. Students should then use each of these terms in a sentence.

RETEACHING/CORRECTIVES

▲ Ask students what features a poll must have to be as accurate as possible. (It must have a sample that is random but still represents a cross-section of the population; it must be timely; it must ask questions clearly.)

Have students complete **Skills Practice Worksheet 8,** which asks them to analyze a public opinion poll.

You may also want to use **Transparency 22,** which shows two political cartoons on the subject of opinion polling.

ENRICHMENT/EXTENSION

■ Have students complete **Skills Challenge Worksheet 8**, which asks them to use a poll to predict the outcome of a class election.

Figure 8–4 A CLUSTER SAMPLE A cluster sample focuses on smaller and smaller geographical units. 8H

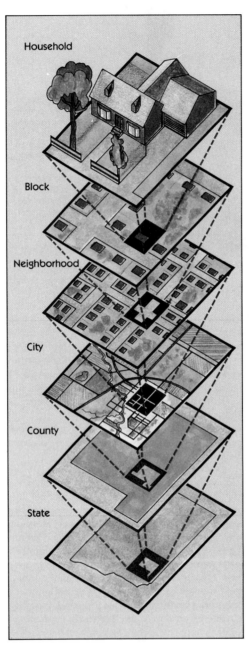

Household

Block

Neighborhood

City

County

State

240

Perhaps the most widely used technique is the *cluster sample.* A cluster sample is one that groups (or "clusters") people by geographical area to make interviewing easier. For example, to cover a particular state, a poll might first pick several counties. Within those counties, some cities would be chosen, then neighborhoods in those cities, followed by blocks, houses, and, finally, individuals. (See Figure 8–4.) At each stage, selections are made at random to avoid bias.

Asking the right questions

The sampling technique is not the only thing to consider when conducting a poll. The way questions are stated is equally important. Questions must be clear, fair, and unbiased. A valid survey should avoid pitfalls such as these:

- Vague or ambiguous questions: *Do you support our current policies?*
- Embarrassing questions: *How much money do you make in a year?*
- Double-negatives: *Why didn't you decide not to vote in the last city election?*
- Technical questions: *Should the city auditor use accrual accounting procedures?*
- Emotionally charged questions: *Would you vote for a candidate who supports legalizing murder through the death penalty?*
- Loaded questions: *Do you support this bill that would let industry pollute our water?*

Obviously, the way questions are worded can significantly affect the way people answer. Take this classic example. In 1971 the Gallup Poll asked people if they favored a policy "to bring home all U.S. troops [from Vietnam] before the end of the year." Two-thirds of those interviewed said they favored the policy. Gallup then rephrased the question: "Do you agree or disagree with a proposal to withdraw all U.S. troops [from Vietnam] by the end of the year, *regardless of what happens there after the troops leave?*" This time, less than half of the people agreed.

Survey methods

The method of conducting a public opinion poll also can affect the results. Many polling agencies now rely almost exclusively on telephone interviews. Because over 93 percent of all Americans now have telephones, this method no

Figure 8–4
▲ *What is the smallest unit in the cluster sample illustration?* (Household.)

Critical Thinking
● *In the 1971 Gallup poll described above, how does the clause "regardless of what happens there after the troops leave" affect the fairness of the question?*

(It gives the impression that the situation might deteriorate once the American troops are withdrawn.)

Taking an Opinion Poll

In the upcoming school election, your friend Louis is running against Karen for class president but is afraid he will lose by a land-slide. To reassure Louis, you decide to take an informal poll. After a class assembly, you stand by the door and ask your classmates this question as they leave: "Do you think Louis would make a good president?" The results of your poll reveal that 40 percent think Louis would make a good president, 40 percent think he would not, and 20 percent do not know. You report back to Louis that the race is even.

How reliable are the results of your poll? You know that to be accurate a poll must account for all the voters, and the questions must be properly worded. Were you able to talk to *all* your class-mates as they left the assembly? Was anyone absent? Were most of the students you polled Louis's friends? How much do you think the wording of your question affected the poll? Is it possible that stu-dents who think Louis "would make a good president" will not vote for him? What if they also think Karen would make a good presi-dent? For these reasons, the results of your poll probably were not valid.

How can you formulate a question that *will* give you an accurate response? First, you must know exactly what you want to find out. In the class-election poll, for example, what is the one bit of infor-mation that you want to get from each person you question? You want to know how he or she is going to vote. Next, think about the kind of answers you expect to get. Your answers should be names of people — specifically, Louis or Karen (or neither). Now you can formulate a question that will lead only to those responses. One possible question is this: *In the upcoming class election, will you vote for Louis or for Karen?*

Before you conduct your poll, you might find it helpful to test your question on some friends or relatives. If anyone does not un-derstand your question or gives an answer that you did not expect, you should rewrite your question and retest it before conducting the poll.

Follow-up

1. Imagine that there is a small park in your neighborhood that is about to be converted into a parking garage. Formulate a ques-tion to find out how your classmates feel about this controversial situation.
2. Formulate two or three questions to find out what your classmates think about a real issue in your school or community. Have sev-eral of your classmates respond to the poll.

CITIZENSHIP SKILLS

Civic Participation
● *What type of poll is this an example of?* (A straw poll.) *Besides the polling methods used, what factors help a poll's reliabil-ity?* (Carefully worded questions, well-trained interviewers.)
▲ CRITICAL THINKING *How does the timing of an election poll affect its accuracy as a predictor of the election's outcome?* (The closer to the election the poll is taken, the more likely it is to be an accurate predictor.)
● Have students complete **Citizenship Worksheet 3,** which presents a sample poll.

Follow-up Answers

1. Students' questions should avoid the pitfalls listed on p. 240.
2. Issues could be selected by the students or assigned by you.

The symbol ♯♯ denotes active participation strategies.

Activities are keyed for student abilities:
▲ = Basic
● = All Levels
■ = Average/Advanced

Section 3 Review Answers

1. **(a)** The media can reflect public opinion through syndicated columns, letters to the editor, editorials, and radio talk shows. **(b)** They can create public opinion through the selection of headline news and cover stories. The media tend to concentrate on sensational events, unusual people, and outspoken interest groups; editorials and commentaries may not reflect broader public views.

2. **(a)** They show the people's support for a candidate in a general sense, but not necessarily for particular issues. **(b)** The candidate's qualifications, party affiliation, personality, positions on various issues, and campaign tactics.

3. Scientific polling uses random samples. Straw polling uses a large sample size that may or may not be random.

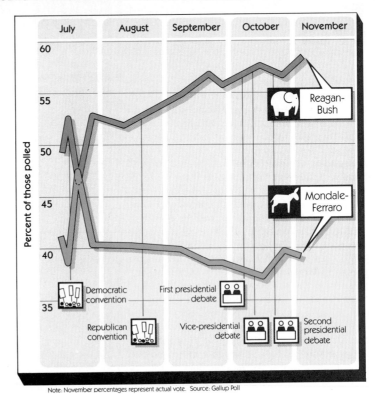

Note: November percentages represent actual vote. Source: Gallup Poll

Figure 8–5 THE 1984 PRESIDENTIAL RACE A Gallup poll asked how people would vote if the election were held on that day. 8H

longer carries the bias it did in the 1936 *Literary Digest* poll. In fact, people are sometimes more willing to be interviewed over the phone than in person. Other polling agencies, however, including Gallup and Roper, rely almost entirely upon personal interviews conducted in the homes of those surveyed.

The success of these methods often hinges upon the ability of the interviewers. A phone interviewer's voice must be pleasant. In person-to-person interviews, tone of voice, body gestures, and facial expressions can all influence the answers given. Good interviewers make people feel relaxed and confident, not embarrassed or ashamed of their answers.

Many public opinion polls are conducted by mail. Mail surveys, like telephone and personal interviews, must be carefully structured to be ac-

curate. People chosen to respond to the poll should be notified in advance of the survey and its purpose. The survey itself should not be too long, directions must be clear, and questions should be arranged carefully. The order of the questions can affect the answers people give.

Interpreting poll results

The final step in any poll is to report the results. A reliable polling organization will include in its report both the method of survey — personal, telephone, or mail — and the type of sample — random, cluster, or quota. For mail surveys, the agency should report the return rate — the percentage of questionnaires sent out that were actually completed and returned. For a probability poll, the sampling error must be reported. Finally, because events can influence

Figure 8–5
▲ *In what month was public opinion most closely divided?* (July.) *What was the general trend in the months leading up to the election?* (The Republican ticket gained support, while the Democratic ticket held steady or lost support.)

public opinion, a reliable poll should indicate exactly when the survey was conducted. The events surrounding the election of 1984 demonstrate the importance of timely polling.

As Figure 8–5 shows, a Gallup Poll after the Democratic National Convention on July 19, 1984, indicated that enthusiasm for the Democratic ticket of Walter Mondale and Geraldine Ferraro was running slightly ahead of support for Republicans Ronald Reagan and George Bush. Over the next few months, however, Reagan's support increased and that for Mondale and Ferraro declined. Gallup prudently waited until a few days before the November election to make any projections. The final Gallup Poll predicted Reagan would win with 59.0 percent of the vote. He actually received 59.2 percent.

Other nationwide polls also predicted the outcome correctly, with only a few percentage points of error. Largely because of modern methods, presidential polls since the 1960's have been very accurate in predicting winners.

SECTION 3 REVIEW

Vocabulary and key terms

interest group (236) sample (238)
mandate (237) probability (238)
straw poll (237) random sample (239)
scientific polling (238) sampling error (239)
universe (238)

For review

1. How do the mass media (a) reflect public opinion? (b) create public opinion? **4B**
2. (a) What do election results reveal about public opinion? (b) What other factors contribute to election results? **4C**
3. In what ways is scientific polling more accurate than taking a straw poll? **8G**
4. Describe the kinds of samples used in scientific polling. **4B**

Critical thinking

MAKING A JUDGMENT   Under what circumstances are public opinion polls a good idea? Under what circumstances might they be misleading? Cite examples to support your views. **4B**

Chapter Summary

Public opinion plays a major role in American democracy. How much public opinion influences government policies and actions depends on several factors — whether opinions are intense or half-hearted, widespread or narrowly held, stable or changeable.

Organized systems of political opinions are called ideologies. Ideologies can generally be classified (from "left" to "right") as radical, liberal, moderate, conservative, or reactionary. Such labels must be used with caution, however. Americans in particular tend not to follow ideologies rigidly but to formulate opinions issue by issue.

Each nation has a unique political culture, which influences its people's attitudes toward government. Political symbols are a part of this culture, as are institutions, legal systems, and major documents. American political culture emphasizes national pride, strong support of democracy, respect for public officials, and a sense of civic duty. Learning one's political culture and developing attitudes about government and politics are called political socialization. Family, schools, peer groups, and the mass media are the main agents of political socialization.

For government officials to act on public opinion, they must be able to determine what it is. Traditionally, public officials have measured opinion by talking to individuals and interest groups, monitoring election returns and the mass media, and taking straw polls. Straw polls are inaccurate, however, because they are based on the incorrect assumption that public opinion can be measured simply by interviewing a large enough group of people.

More recently, scientific polling has provided an accurate way to gauge public opinion. This method is based on the mathematical law of probability, which states that a small, random sample can accurately assess a much larger "universe." Polls are taken in person, over the phone, or by mail. A reliable poll depends on carefully worded questions and well-trained interviewers. The reports of a scientific poll should include details on method, timing, and sampling error.

4. *Random sample*—All members have an equal probability of being selected. *Cluster sample*—Choice is by geographic area. *Quota sample*—Choice is based on population characteristics (race, income, religion, occupation).

Critical thinking Students may cite cases in which public opinion polls made politicians aware of public attitudes toward an issue. However, students may argue that over-reliance on public opinion polls might make politics superficial and might frighten politicians away from taking unpopular, yet principled, stands.

CLOSURE
● Review the Section 3 vocabulary with students to help reinforce key concepts from the section. Then have students read the next assigned lesson.

CHAPTER 8 CORRECTIVES
● To review the content of Chapter 8, you may want to have students complete **Study Guide/Review 8** or **Workbook Chapter 8**.

The symbol ⅈⅈ denotes active participation strategies.

Activities are keyed for student abilities:
▲ = Basic
● = All Levels
■ = Average/Advanced

Answers

Vocabulary See pp. T19–T21 for suggested vocabulary activities.

Reviewing the Facts

1. A private political opinion belongs only to one person. Public opinion is the combination of many individuals' feelings.
2. Issues related to their health, welfare, and economic security.
3. Americans tend to take positions issue by issue instead of adhering to a strict ideology; both major political parties share many values.
4. Children usually identify with their parents' political party as well as their political opinions.
5. The mass media are principal sources of political information for most Americans and can focus attention on a particular issue.
6. An interest group may represent only a small (but vocal) minority of people who share an opinion. Their opinions may not be shared by the many others who are not part of the interest group.
7. Cluster and quota samples.
8. Events occurring after a poll is taken can have a significant influence on public opinion. Depending on the issue, a poll's results can vary greatly over time.

★ CHAPTER 8 REVIEW ★

● **Review the definitions of the following terms:**

conservative	peers	reactionary
culture	political culture	"right"
ideology	political socialization	sample
interest group	political symbol	sampling error
"left"	probability	scientific polling
liberal	public opinion	status quo
mandate	radical	straw poll
moderate	random sample	universe

● REVIEWING THE FACTS

1. What is the difference between a private political opinion and public opinion? **4A**
2. What kinds of issues bring out the strongest opinions in people? **4A**
3. Why might Americans be "less ideological" than the citizens of other nations? **1C**
4. How are children socialized politically by their families? **4A**
5. Why are the mass media considered important agents of political socialization? **4B**
6. Why are interest groups often poor indicators of public opinion? **4C**
7. What are two short-cut methods that are used to determine public opinion when a true random sample is not possible? **8H**
8. Why should a poll indicate exactly when the survey was conducted? **8A**

▲ THINKING CRITICALLY ABOUT KEY CONCEPTS

1. (a) How have Americans usually viewed public officials? (b) Under what circumstances might this feeling change? **8F**
2. What are the five traditional methods public officials use to assess public opinion, and what are the main weaknesses of each? **8A**
3. How did the 1936 election poll conducted by the *Literary Digest* point out the potential for error in straw polls? **8C**

▲ PRACTICING SKILLS

1. **Study Skills: Reading a graph.** Refer to Figure 8–2 (page 229) to answer the following questions. (a) Which label did most Americans choose? (b) Do more Americans label themselves "conservative" or "liberal"? (c) What percentage of Americans label themselves "extremely liberal"? (d) What percentage label themselves "extremely conservative"? (To review graph skills, see Study Skill 3 on page 779.) **8B**
2. **Critical Thinking Skills: Evaluation.** Why might most respondents to the survey represented in Figure 8–2 describe themselves as "moderate or middle of the road"? For what reasons might the design of this particular survey be criticized? **8A**

▲ PARTICIPATORY CITIZENSHIP

1. **Opinion poll.** Create a survey question based on the author's statement that Americans have strong confidence and trust in public officials ("Attitudes toward officials," page 232). Conduct a poll of relatives and friends to find out how they feel toward public officials. You might wish to compare attitudes toward local, state, and national officials. Combine your results with others' and present them to the class. What conclusions can you draw from the poll? **8E**

Thinking Critically About Key Concepts

1. **(a)** In general, with trust and confidence. **(b)** When evidence of public betrayal or political corruption surfaces, people may lose their confidence in public officials, such as during the Watergate scandal.
2. *Personal contacts*—Officials cannot meet with every single constituent. *Interest groups*—They may be small and not representative of widespread opinion. *Mass media*—May concentrate more on sensational events than everyday occurrences that affect public opinion. *Election results*—Voter choice may be related to factors other than the candidate's stand on a

2. Current events. Search through newspapers or news magazines to find an article that includes the results of an opinion poll. Note the question asked in the poll, the results, and any interesting conclusions drawn concerning those results. From the question posed and the sampling method, how would you evaluate the poll results? **8A**

▲ WRITING ABOUT ISSUES

1. Writing an essay. Suppose someone said this to you: "We form our political attitudes while at home and in school; those attitudes are then confirmed by our peers and the mass media." Would you agree? Why or why not? Write an essay explaining your view of how political attitudes are formed. **8C**

2. Writing an editorial. Write a short editorial on whether or not polling organizations should be prohibited from releasing any results of presidential election polls on the day of the election. How might such a poll affect voters if it showed that one candidate either had a huge lead or if it showed that the race was very close? Could the release of such a poll affect the outcome of an election? If so, what policies should be adopted toward the release of polling data? **8C**

▲ ANALYZING A POLITICAL CARTOON

In 1989 the Supreme Court decided that deliberately burning an American flag is a constitutionally protected form of political speech. The decision raised a squall of controversy in the United States. Around the same time, Chinese students were carrying out protests against their government. Look at the cartoon below and answer the following questions.

1. Who is being shown in the picture on the right? Who is shown on the left? **8B**
2. Does the cartoon show the two protesters to be more similar or different? **8B**
3. Whose voice is supposedly represented in the captions? **8A**
4. What is the cartoonist's point? Is he successful? Why, or why not? **8D**
5. If you had a different point of view, what kind of cartoon might you draw? **8H**

Chris OBrion, courtesy Potomac News.

245

state the centrist positions and underrepresent more extreme positions.

Participatory Citizenship
1. Check to see that survey questions are clear and unbiased.
2. Students may wish to conduct their own opinion poll about an issue of local interest and publicize their findings in a school or local newspaper.

Writing About Issues
1. Some students may agree, citing people's tendency to associate with peers of like opinions. Others may argue that their attitudes are formed independently of peers and the mass media.
2. Some students may conclude that releasing a public opinion poll on the day of an election might affect voter turnout and thus the outcome of the election.

Analyzing a Political Cartoon
1. A Chinese pro-democracy protester. An American protester.
2. Similar.
3. The voice of American public opinion.
4. Students should note that the protesters are doing the same thing, yet they are viewed differently by the American public.
5. Students may wish to illustrate their points of view to share with the class.

particular issue. *Straw poll results*—Group polled may not be representative of the entire population.
3. First, the people did not represent a true cross-section of the country. Second, the poll was

conducted too early in the race, before people had made their decisions.

Practicing Skills
1. (a) Moderate or Middle of the road. **(b)** Conservative. **(c)** 2.5%. **(d)** 2.7%.

2. People may be liberal in some views and conservative in others. Additionally, even if they hold "radical" or "extremely conservative" views, people may not see themselves as extremists. Thus, the results may over-

CHAPTER 9
INTEREST GROUPS AND THEIR INFLUENCE
(pp. 246–265)

	Section Objectives	Section Resources
Section 1 Interest Groups Are a Part of American Politics	☐ define an interest group and identify factors that make interest groups effective ☐ identify criticisms that have been made of interest groups	■ SKILLS CHALLENGE WORKSHEET **9**
Section 2 Interest Groups Have Diverse Goals	☐ identify the major categories of interest groups and explain how their aims differ ☐ explain the concerns raised by the increase in single-issue interest groups	■ CONSTITUTIONAL ISSUES WORKSHEET **10** ▲ TRANSPARENCY **23**
Section 3 Interest Groups Use Varied Tactics	☐ explain what is meant by lobbying and describe the techniques used by lobbyists ☐ explain how interest groups try to influence elections ☐ identify other techniques used by interest groups to influence public policy	▲ SKILLS PRACTICE WORKSHEET **9** ▲ TRANSPARENCIES **24–25**

Essential Elements

The list below shows Essential Elements relevant to this chapter. (The complete list of Essential Elements appears in the introductory pages of this Teacher's Edition.)

Section 1: 4B, 4C

Section 2: 4B, 4C, 6B, 6C, 7A, 8A

Section 3: 4B, 4C, 4D, 8A, 8D

Chapter Review: 4B, 4C, 8A, 8B, 8C, 8D, 8E, 8F, 8G, 8H

Section Resources are keyed for student abilities:
▲ = Basic
● = All Levels
■ = Average/Advanced

Homework Options

Each section contains activities labeled "Guided/Independent Practice," "Reteaching/Correctives," and "Enrichment/Extension." You may wish to choose from among these activities when assigning homework.

Students Acquiring English Activities

Invite members of student interest groups on campus to describe how such groups are organized, what ideas they share, and how they try to influence school activities. Such groups might include the student council and athletic teams. Groups should also explain their rules for membership and the stated purpose of the group. Then ask students how the activities of these groups parallel those of political interest groups.

LISTENING/SPEAKING: Have students review campaign literature or TV political campaign commercials for evidence of propaganda. Students should identify which of the seven propaganda techniques described in Figure 9–4 (p. 262) are being used in each case.

Case Studies

When teaching this chapter, you may use Case Study 3, which discusses religion in public schools; Case Study 9, which examines the question of a lower minimum wage for teenagers; or Case Study 11, which debates the issue of gun control. (Case Studies may be found following p. 510.)

Teacher Bibliography

Conway, M. Margaret. *Political Participation in the United States.* 2nd ed. CQ Press, 1991. An overview of the many ways citizens can influence the government.

Hrebenar, Ronald J. and Ruth K. Scott. *Interest Group Politics in America.* 2nd ed. Prentice-Hall, 1990. Explains the composition and influence of interest groups and their lobbying methods.

Schlozman, Kay Lehman and John T. Tierney. *Organized Interests and American Democracy.* Harper & Row, 1986. Describes the nature and role of interest groups on the basis of interviews with organized groups.

Student Bibliography

Caplan, Marc. *Ralph Nader Presents a Citizens' Guide to Lobbying.* Dembner, 1983. This clear and concise guide takes the would-be lobbyist through the steps needed to organize support, use the media, and participate in hearings.

Drew, Elizabeth. *Politics and Money: The New Road to Corruption.* Macmillan, 1983. The author exposes corruption in raising campaign finances by special interest groups and proposes reforms.

The Washington Lobby. 5th ed. CQ Press, 1987. An examination of what lobbyists do and the roles they play in the U.S. political process. Detailed case studies are included.

Literature

Thomas, Michael. *Hard Money.* Viking, 1985. A retired television mogul returns to the station to bring back responsible programming and to prevent the President from being re-elected.

Wilkins, Roy. *Standing Fast.* Penguin, 1984. A grandson of slaves and proponent of integration, Wilkins recounts his growing awareness of racial discrimination and eventual leadership of the NAACP.

CHAPTER RESOURCES

Study Guide/Review 9
Workbook Chapter 9
Chapter 9 Test, Forms A–C

Films and Videotapes*

Lobbying: A Case History. 19 min. EBEC, 1977. f, v. Demonstrates how the lobbying system can influence national government policy.

Software*

"And if Re-elected . . ." (Apple, IBM). Focus. Students play the role of an incumbent President running for re-election. They are presented with twelve crises and must decide which crises directly influence special interest groups.

On the Campaign Trail (Apple, IBM, Macintosh). TS. Students assume the role of a third-party candidate for President. They learn about the Electoral College, campaign strategies and costs, special interest groups, and political action committees.

Television: A Study of Media Ethics (Apple, IBM, Macintosh). TS. Students use a decision-making model to assess the impact of popular media on American life. As sponsors of a controversial television program, they deal with objections of special interest groups and must consider such issues as media responsibility, censorship, and their effect on public opinion and social behavior.

---

* For a complete guide to audiovisual sources, see page T22.

Interest Groups and Their Influence

(pp. 246–265)

Chapter 9 examines the role of interest groups in the American political system, describing the goals of three major types of interest groups and then looking at lobbying, electioneering, and other techniques used by interest groups to influence public policy.

Chapter Objectives
After students complete this chapter, they will be able to:

1. Define an interest group and identify factors that make interest groups effective.
2. Identify criticisms that have been made of interest groups.
3. Identify the major categories of interest groups and explain how their aims differ.
4. Explain the concerns raised by the increase in single-issue interest groups.
5. Explain what is meant by lobbying and describe the techniques used by lobbyists.
6. Explain how interest groups try to influence elections.
7. Identify other techniques used by interest groups to influence public policy.

CHAPTER

9

INTEREST GROUPS and THEIR INFLUENCE

In no other country of the world has the principle of association been more successfully used or applied to a greater multitude of objects than in America.

Alexis de Tocqueville
Democracy in America (1835)

246

Photo
Demonstrators protest budget cuts in public education.

The battle was on. In July 1991, President George Bush named Clarence Thomas to fill the Supreme Court seat vacated by Thurgood Marshall. Thomas proved to be a controversial choice, and interest groups lined up for and against the nominee. Large organizations such as the AFL-CIO, the American Association of Retired Persons, and the NAACP, the country's largest civil rights group, voiced their opposition to Thomas. These groups called on their members to pressure key senators to vote against his confirmation. The White House and groups such as the American Conservative Union, the Traditional Values Coalition, and the U.S. Chamber of Commerce fought for Thomas. They pressed members of the Senate Judiciary Committee to approve him. One group even ran television ads attacking senators who opposed Thomas. The Thomas nomination involved interest groups in a high-visibility battle. In fact, interest groups play key roles in almost every political decision.

CHAPTER OUTLINE

1 Interest Groups Are a Part of American Politics

The Nature of Interest Groups
Interest Groups: Pro and Con

2 Interest Groups Have Diverse Goals

Economic Interest Groups
Social Action Groups
Single-Issue Groups

3 Interest Groups Use Varied Tactics

Lobbying
Influencing Elections
Other Persuasive Techniques

CHAPTER SUPPORT MATERIAL

Skills Practice Worksheet 9

Skills Challenge Worksheet 9

Constitutional Issues Worksheet 10

Transparencies 23–25

Study Guide/Review 9

Workbook Chapter 9

Chapter 9 Test, Forms A-C

SECTION 1

Interest Groups Are a Part of American Politics *(pp. 248–251)*

Section Objectives

☐ define an interest group and identify factors that make interest groups effective

☐ identify criticisms that have been made of interest groups

👥 FOCUS

● Introduce the section by having students list the types of organizations they might belong to, such as youth groups, pep groups, religious groups, sports teams, political groups, and hobby clubs. Have students suggest reasons why people might belong to such groups.

Then ask a student to synthesize a definition of *interest group* from the description on this page and read it aloud to the class. (Organizations of people with shared attitudes who attempt to influence public policy.) Have class members circle all of the groups on their lists that fit this definition. Ask students what part of the definition eliminated most of the groups on their lists. (Attempt to influence public policy.)

EXPLANATION

After students have read the section, you may want to consider the following activities:

Politics

▲ Have students describe the factors that contribute to an interest group's effectiveness. List them on the board. (Size, geographic distribution, cohesion, intensity, degree of organization, access to government officials, funding, prestige.)

248

SECTION 1

Interest Groups Are a Part of American Politics

| ACCESS | The Main Ideas |

1 What is an interest group? *pages 248–249*

2 What factors help make interest groups effective? *pages 249–250*

3 What criticisms have been made of interest groups? *pages 250–251*

What are some political or social issues that you care deeply about? Some people believe strongly in protecting the environment, preventing crime, fighting racism, or promoting free enterprise. In each of these areas, and in many others, Americans have formed groups for the purpose of addressing the issues they believe to be important. In fact, nearly two-thirds of all Americans are members of some type of interest group. So if there is an issue that interests you, you probably do not have to start your own group. It is likely that one exists whose interests overlap with your own.

Interest groups try to gain public support for their agendas by making their views known to the public and by working behind the scenes to influence decision-makers in government. This section examines the origin and nature of interest groups and the various roles they play in American government.

4B, 4C

The Nature of Interest Groups

What is an interest group?

Not every group of people who get together because of common interests actually form an *interest group*. An interest group has three basic characteristics. First, it must be organized, with some sort of structure, leadership, and rules. Second, members of an interest group are people who share certain ideas and feel strongly enough about them to join together. Finally, an interest group seeks to influence public policy by affecting the actions of government.

Joining interest groups

People join interest groups for a variety of reasons. Some join primarily for the social con-

tacts. They want to be around like-minded people, to laugh, talk, or complain together. The political influence of the group is important, but so is the comradeship

Many people join interest groups for economic reasons. Higher wages, protection from foreign competition, increased medical coverage, greater retirement benefits, lower taxes, new roads, and government subsidies are examples of demands that such interest groups might make.

Moral causes attract other people. They may want to protest discrimination, change drinking laws, fight worldwide hunger, protect the environment, or engage in other causes.

Most people, of course, join interest groups for a combination of reasons. For example, women who have encountered job discrimination may join the National Organization for Women (NOW). They do so not only because they believe sex discrimination is morally wrong,

Members of interest groups work together to support causes they consider important. For these hikers in Oregon, preserving wilderness and the environment would be important issues.

248

---

but also to work with a group in securing fair pay and to share their attitudes with other women who feel the same way. Likewise, Vietnam War veterans may be drawn together for fellowship, but they may also unite to press for increased government benefits or to secure funds for a war memorial to honor fallen comrades.

Joining a group does not necessarily mean getting actively involved. A small percentage of members may spend hours on the front lines — making speeches, writing letters, organizing membership drives. Other members may simply send in their dues once a year.

Conflicting interests

It is not uncommon for a person to belong to many groups and organizations, some of which take conflicting sides on an issue. Citizen Z, for example, may simultaneously be a member of the National Urban League, the Veterans of Foreign Wars, and the Parent Teachers Association (PTA). Citizen X, on the other hand, may belong to the American Bar Association, the League of Women Voters, the Audubon Society, and the Gray Panthers.

Americans tend to take sides issue by issue, rather than following a rigid ideology or pattern. When a person belongs to several different interest groups, it is even more difficult to predict his or her position on any given issue. In Citizen Z's case, for instance, the National Urban League might favor a school policy that the PTA opposes. Citizen X may have to choose between political candidates favored by the Bar Association and by the Gray Panthers.

Judging a group's effectiveness

Not all interest groups have the same amount of influence on public policy. The *size* of an interest group can be one important indication of its strength. A 14-million-member labor union like the AFL-CIO is more likely to influence labor laws than the National Doorknob Polishers Union, with only 200 members. Along with size, a group's *geographic distribution* is also important. The National Farmers' Union, with members across the country, naturally has more influence over national farm policy than, for example, the Iowa Bee Keepers Association. The bee keepers, nevertheless, might still be influential in the Iowa General Assembly.

Against the background of the Capitol in Washington, speakers address a rally of Mothers Against Drunk Driving, an interest group dedicated to a single cause.

Even a large, widely distributed group will be powerless if its members are not united. *Cohesion,* the tendency to stick together, contributes to a group's effect on public policy. For example, in the 1940's the labor movement was split into two camps — one led by the American Federation of Labor, the other led by the Congress of Industrial Organizations. Largely because they were divided, the unions were unable to mount effective opposition to the passage in 1947 of the Taft-Hartley Act, a law that restricted union power.

Intensity, or how strongly the members of a group feel about an issue, can also contribute to a group's effectiveness. A small, intense, and outspoken group can often exert more influence on public policy than a large group whose members do not express their opinions as strongly.

Organization and resources

The success of an interest group also depends on how well it is organized and financed. Interest groups with skilled, energetic, and experienced leaders are generally more influential than those headed by inexperienced people.

The skill of its leaders can help a group gain *access* to government officials. Without such

---

● CRITICAL THINKING **Why is each of these factors important to an interest group's effectiveness?** (When the class has considered each factor individually, have them note relationships among factors as well. Point out that well-organized and well-financed groups are more likely to build a large and widely distributed membership than groups that must spend most of their time and energy raising funds. Also, interest groups that have large memberships and plentiful funds are likely to have greater access to government officials.)

👥 Politics

■ Divide the class into two groups. Have each group review pp. 250–251 on the advantages and disadvantages of interest groups. Then hold a class debate on the following proposition: *Interest groups hurt the American political system more than they help it.*

One group should prepare arguments supporting this statement, the other group opposing it. As part of their preparation, have each group summarize the arguments on this issue. Each group should select a spokesperson to carry out the debate.

Background: *History* The AFL and CIO were separated for many years, in part because of a dispute over whether to group skilled and unskilled workers together in unions. (The CIO wanted to; the AFL did not.) In 1955 the organizations resolved their differences and merged into a single association.

Critical Thinking
● **What qualities besides intensity might enable a small group to influence public policy more than a large group?** (Strong financial base, close ties to lawmakers, etc.)

The symbol 👥 denotes active participation strategies.

Activities are keyed for student abilities:
▲ = Basic
● = All Levels
■ = Average/Advanced

Interest groups on both sides of the issue have organized protests and other forms of political pressure to influence the legal status of abortion.

4B

Cooperative Learning

● Divide the class into groups and ask each group to make a plan for forming an interest group. Groups will need to decide what common interests to focus on and a name for the group. They should plan how to publicize their interests, promote issues, and influence public policy. (For example, public service announcements in the media are one way to gain publicity.) Groups should also consider how to raise and spend funds. Have groups present their reports to the class.

GUIDED/INDEPENDENT PRACTICE

● Ask students to compare the factors that determine the effectiveness of an interest group with those that determine the effectiveness of public opinion (as discussed in Chapter 8).

RETEACHING/CORRECTIVES

▲ Have students create a two-column chart on a sheet of paper. One column should be titled *Interest Groups: Pro,* and the other *Interest Groups: Con.* Students should fill in the chart with at least four factors in each column.

ENRICHMENT/EXTENSION

■ Have students complete **Skills Challenge Worksheet 9,** which asks them to analyze the effectiveness of two hypothetical interest groups.

access, even the most electrifying leader may have difficulty influencing public policy. Most public officials — especially members of Congress and the President — do not have the time to meet with everyone who seeks their attention. Therefore, interest group representatives who can approach public officials personally have an advantage over those who cannot. The American Bar Association, for instance, would find it easy to present its ideas to members of Congress — many of whom are lawyers and ABA members.

An interest group also must have plentiful *funds* to be effective. Many groups have begun on a small scale, with a few concerned people meeting in someone's living room. But as a group grows, it needs money to staff an office, set up computers, mail letters, collect information, advertise, hire lawyers, and hold conventions. Without good resources, a group will have difficulty making its voice heard in the public policy arena.

Finally, the more *prestige* an interest group has, the more power it can wield and the more easily it will gain officials' attention. The American Medical Association (AMA), for example, is a very prestigious organization, probably because of the respect most Americans have for doctors. When the AMA pushes for a policy — a change in drug laws, for example — lawmakers are likely to listen.

250

Interest Groups: Pro and Con

Interest groups are intricately woven into America's political fabric. Because they are such a powerful force, their influence is frequently the subject of heated debate. Critics are quick to point out the negative qualities of American interest groups.

Speaking for the few

One major criticism is that small groups may have more influence on public policy than they should. Their success can upset the balance between majority rule and minority rights, giving a misleading picture of public opinion. Interest groups generate publicity about issues that concern them. Through their efforts, these issues may get a lot of attention from the media. In this way, an issue that affects a relatively small group may take on national importance. In other words, an interest group may seem bigger than it really is.

Money may play an important role also. For example, a well-financed group that represents only a small number of people may speak with a booming voice and influence public policy. Or a group that will benefit greatly from a policy — say, through higher profits or lower taxes — can put intense pressure on legislators. Large groups with fewer resources or less motivation may go unheard. In politics it is quite often true that "the wheel that squeaks the loudest gets the grease."

A related criticism of interest groups is that they do not truly represent even their own members' opinions. Many groups are run by a small, active minority of their members, who make decisions for the entire group. Often, it is argued, the leaders do not consult with the group's "rank and file" members. It is difficult to tell whether the leaders' decisions represent the views of the group as a whole. This problem is particularly important for large, broad-based groups.

Harming the public interest

Some critics maintain that interest groups simply have become too powerful in the United States. Elected public officials may be afraid to speak candidly or take decisive action, for fear of offending significant interest groups. The results are stalemate, inaction, and weak policies rather than coherent, effective decision-making.

Another serious charge against interest groups is that they sometimes use unethical tactics to influence public policy. Incidents of bribery, blackmail, illegal campaign funding, and even violence have been associated with interest groups. Such practices usually stem from abuse of power or fanatical belief in a cause. Fortunately, they are not common. Nevertheless, they remain a serious threat to honest and orderly government.

Contributions of interest groups

The criticisms of interest groups must be weighed realistically against the contributions that such groups make to American democracy. First, interest groups provide a channel for public opinion and a link between citizens and public officials. It is very difficult for an individual, all alone, to change the course of public policy. The average American just does not have the time, money, or ability to influence government leaders. Collectively, people can pool their resources, develop strategies, and exert pressure on public officials.

Second, interest groups provide policymakers and officials with useful information. Even though they may overemphasize their own points of view, interest groups can also be a useful gauge of public opinion. Equally important, interest groups furnish governmental officials with expert knowledge — data, studies, and reports — in many fields, from nuclear power to popular music. All three branches of government at times rely on the expertise of interest groups.

Third, interest groups stimulate political participation. Interest groups encourage political activism through protests, boycotts, lawsuits, letter-writing, and other tactics. They keep their members informed about the issues and encourage them to vote for candidates who share their views. At the very least, interest groups generate political discussions among their members.

Finally, interest groups serve as a stabilizing force in American democracy. Opposing interest groups are naturally suspicious of each other and often serve as public watchdogs. If one interest group gets out of line, there is usually another interest group to "blow the whistle." These counteracting forces may serve to prevent a few groups from exerting too much influence on public policy. Therefore, the competition and compromise between interest groups may not harm the public interest but actually result in sound, balanced public policy.

SECTION 1 **REVIEW**

Vocabulary and key terms

interest group (248)

For review

1. What are three reasons that people join interest groups? **4C**
2. Explain how each of these factors contributes to an interest group's influence: (a) geographic distribution; (b) cohesion; (c) access to officials; (d) prestige and resources. **4B**
3. For what reasons have interest groups been criticized? How have they been praised? **4B**

Critical thinking

ORGANIZING AN ARGUMENT Some people argue that the competition among interest groups weakens public policymaking. Others believe it results in more balanced policies. What evidence is there to support each point of view? **4B**

251

SECTION 2

Interest Groups Have Diverse Goals
(pp. 252–258)

Section Objectives

☐ identify the major categories
of interest groups and explain
how their aims differ

☐ explain the concerns raised by
the increase in single-issue
interest groups

Vocabulary

gross national product,
public-interest group

▮▮ FOCUS

● Have students name five or
six interest groups with which
they are familiar and write them
on the board. Then ask them to
classify the groups as economic
interest groups, social action
groups, or single-issue groups.
Ask students to give reasons for
their classifications. You may
wish to point out that many
groups span categories. For
example, social action groups
often try to influence economic
policy; some single-issue groups
are active in economic matters as
well.

Interest Groups Have Diverse Goals

ACCESS	The Main Ideas

1 What are the major categories of interest
groups and how do their aims differ?
pages 252–257

2 What are some concerns raised by the
increase in single-issue interest groups?
pages 257–258

What do the National Midas Dealers Association, the Society for the Advancement of Fission Energy, and the National Family Farm Coalition have in common? Not much, except that they are all interest groups. They exist to advance the interests of their members. About 100,000 interest groups are active in the United States. Interest groups can be divided into three broad and sometimes overlapping categories: economic, social action, and single-issue. This section highlights some of the important interest groups in each category.

4B, 7A

Economic Interest Groups

In 1993, the United States **gross national product** (GNP) — the total value of all goods and services produced — was about $6.5 trillion. Private individuals control the spending and investing of much of this money. But the government also plays a great role in determining where the money goes. Governments spend great amounts of money — over $2.5 trillion in 1993 alone. Businesses and individuals must pay taxes to federal, state, and local governments.

Economic interest groups, therefore, try to influence government economic policy, which includes how government spends its money and from whom it collects taxes. These interest groups fall into four major categories — business, professional, agricultural, and labor. (Figure 9–1 lists some of these organizations.)

Business and trade associations

There are thousands of business and trade associations — both national and local — in the United States. These interest groups have one

underlying goal — to create the most favorable climate for their businesses to prosper.

Some of these groups, such as Chambers of Commerce, look out for the interests of the business community in general. They work to reduce government regulation and corporate taxes, to offset the power of labor unions, and to promote free enterprise. These groups might, for example, exert pressure to prevent Congress from raising the minimum wage.

Competing companies that operate in one industry set up a *trade association* to set standards and influence policies that affect their particular industry. For example, an association of clothing manufacturers might work for higher tariffs or import quotas on blue jeans or jackets made overseas. Examples of trade associations include the American Petroleum Institute and the Chocolate Manufacturers Association of the United States.

Professional groups

Nearly every profession has an interest group that seeks to protect and advance the field. These groups publish journals, give awards, hold conferences and seminars, and, of course, communicate their opinions to government officials. Among the many professional interest groups operating in the United States are the American Dental Association, the National Society of Professional Engineers, the Academy of Motion Picture Arts and Sciences, and the National Education Association.

One of the ways that professional associations interact with government is to establish standards for entering the profession. State governments sometimes give these organizations authority to regulate who can practice the profession in that state. For example, in many states, law schools must be approved by the American Bar Association.

Agricultural interests

Today farm families make up only about 2 percent of the United States population. Nevertheless, they feed hundreds of millions of people

Critical Thinking
● *Why would companies
that compete against each
other for sales want to work
together in setting up trade
associations?* (Such associations work toward goals,

such as import tariffs, that
would benefit all companies
in a particular industry.)

Figure 9-1 SOME ECONOMIC INTEREST GROUPS   6B

GROUP	FOUNDED	MEMBERSHIP REPORTED 1992	STATED PURPOSE
Business			
Chamber of Commerce of the United States	1912	180,000 businesses	To represent the interests of small businesses.
National Association of Manufacturers	1895	13,500 corporations	To represent the interests of large businesses.
Business Roundtable	1972	200 largest U.S. businesses	To promote business interests in general.
Professional			
American Bar Association (ABA)	1878	360,000 attorneys	To improve the administration of justice; to make recommendations concerning legal reform and the nomination of judges.
American Medical Association (AMA)	1847	271,000 physicians	To represent the medical profession in Congress and in government organizations; to set standards for medical schools and hospitals.
National Education Association (NEA)	1857	2 million teachers	To improve the quality of education and increase teacher salaries.
Agriculture			
American Farm Bureau Federation	1919	3.3 million farmers (large farms)	To promote free trade, oppose price support programs; to help members achieve educational, economic, and social advancement.
United Farm Workers of America	1962	100,000 farmers (small farms)	To achieve collective bargaining rights for U.S. farm workers; to improve working and safety conditions and wages.
National Grange	1867	365,000 farmers	To promote the welfare of rural families through legislation, higher price supports, insurance, and credit union programs.
Labor			
American Federation of Labor–Congress of Industrial Organizations (AFL–CIO)	1955	14.1 million workers	To represent the interests of skilled and unskilled wage-earners in crafts and industries.
International Brotherhood of Teamsters	1903	2 million workers	To represent the interests of truck drivers and other workers.
National Association of Government Employees	1961	195,000 employees	To represent the interests of government employees.

SOURCE: *Encyclopedia of Associations*

EXPLANATION

After students have read the section, you may want to consider the following activities:

Controversial Issues

Have students discuss this statement: *The recent increase in the number of single-issue groups is cause for concern.*

● ⬜ CRITICAL THINKING ⬜ *What effects can such groups have on the way in which voters select candidates?* (They may try to influence voters to support a candidate on the basis of his or her views on a single issue.)

■ ⬜ CRITICAL THINKING ⬜ *What are the drawbacks of voting for a candidate solely on the basis of his or her stand on a single issue?* (Through discussion, students should recognize that an elected official is asked to make decisions on a range of issues, not just one.)

Figure 9-1

▲ Ask students which groups are most familiar to them. **Why might those groups be more familiar?** (Large memberships, active in community, recent publicity.)

Background: *History* The National Grange is the popular name of the Order of the Patrons of Husbandry, the oldest general farm organization in the nation. Its original function was to provide lectures and entertainment to isolated farm men and women. Today, the Grange works with the U.S. Department of Agriculture (USDA) in education, as well as with legislators.

The symbol 👥 denotes active participation strategies.

Activities are keyed for student abilities:
▲ = Basic
● = All Levels
■ = Average/Advanced

Politics

● Have groups of students select particular interest groups for further study. Ask students to write a letter to the interest group they have selected, requesting information about its purpose, methods, support of particular candidates, and long-term goals.

Students might also ask whether the group has a paid professional staff or is staffed by volunteers and whether it has organizations at the local, state, or national level. A useful reference for this activity is *The Encyclopedia of Associations,* an annual publication. Students can also consult the *Readers' Guide to Periodical Literature* for articles on the groups they have chosen.

Civic Participation

■ Assign each of the following topics to a different group of students: business or trade associations, professional groups, agricultural interest groups, labor unions, civil rights groups, religious groups, public-interest groups, and single-issue groups. Ask students to find and list names of groups in their category within the community. To obtain this information, students can scan local newspapers or look in the yellow pages of the local telephone directory under such headings as *Associations, Unions,* and *Trade Groups.* The Chamber of Commerce and the public library are also useful resources.

Then, with the class, compile a master list of interest groups in the community. If certain categories contain large numbers of interest groups, have the class speculate about reasons for this.

To draw attention to their problems and concerns, farmers from around the nation rallied in front of the Department of Agriculture in Washington, D.C.

in this country and abroad. As a vital part of the American economy, agriculture receives a lot of attention from government policy-makers.

Many groups speak for the interests of American farmers. Some, like the Maine Potato Board and the Southeastern Poultry and Egg Association, include farmers engaged in a specific activity (just as a trade association represents firms in a certain industry). Other interest groups are tied together for broader reasons. The American Farm Bureau Federation is made up of the managers of large farms. The National Farmers Union includes mostly small, independent farm owners.

Because they represent different segments of the farm population, agricultural interest groups may have conflicting aims. The Farmers Union generally favors government price supports for crops. The Farm Bureau, on the other hand, opposes government intervention in agriculture.

Labor unions

Perhaps the best-known and most active economic interest groups are labor unions. Since the early 1800's, American labor unions have called public attention to the needs of working people. Largely because of labor union pressure, federal and state governments have instituted policies such as the eight-hour day, child labor laws, and workplace health and safety measures.

254

Unions are most often organized in one of two ways. A *craft* union is made up of workers with a similar skill, such as plumbers, bricklayers, or carpenters. An *industrial* union includes both skilled and unskilled workers in the same industry, such as the United Automobile Workers and the United Steel Workers.

On some key issues, organized labor is relatively united. Most labor groups favor increased minimum wage laws, full employment, and restrictions on imports. On other issues, however, labor is badly divided. Conflicts between skilled and unskilled workers have plagued labor unions for years. There are also regional differences and urban-rural rivalries. Within a union, members may disagree about hiring practices, especially affirmative action programs.

Public-employee unions

For many years, neither federal nor state government employees were permitted to join unions. This policy began to change in 1962, when President John F. Kennedy issued an order that recognized the right of federal employees to form unions and bargain for wages and benefits. (Federal employees have never been granted the right to strike.) Most states adopted similar policies. Since that time, the number of public-employee interest groups has risen dramatically.

Critical Thinking
■ *Why might two farm groups have differing opinions on such matters as price supports?* (The Farm Bureau, composed of owners of large farms, probably opposes price supports because the high volume of these farms allows them to be profitable without supports. The smaller farmers of the Farmers Union, however, want government help in order to sell their smaller quantities for a profit.)

Major public-employee unions include the American Federation of Teachers (a member of the AFL-CIO), the American Federation of State, County, and Municipal Employees, and the American Federation of Government Employees.

4B, 6C

Social Action Groups

The second broad category of interest groups includes those that try to bring about changes in society or public goals because of principles and ideas their members believe to be important. Many racial and ethnic groups, for example, have organized to seek equal rights and opportunities. Other groups try to influence public policy to reflect their religious beliefs. Still others aim to protect the environment, to advocate consumer rights, or simply to educate people. Figure 9–2 lists some typical groups.

Civil rights groups

Beginning with the abolitionist movement in the early 1800's, civil rights groups have struggled to establish, defend, and extend the rights that the Constitution promises all Americans. (Chapter 7 describes this movement and the role of groups such as the NAACP.) As Martin Luther King, Jr., once said, "Freedom is never voluntarily given by the oppressor; it must be demanded by the oppressed."

Many civil rights groups are organized along racial or ethnic lines. They represent, for instance, black Americans, Hispanics, American Indians, Croatians, Italian Americans, or Asian Americans. Several interest groups, such as NOW, work for the goals of the women's rights movement. Groups like the American Association of Retired Persons (AARP) and Older Americans, Inc., speak for the rights of older people. Groups representing people with disabilities seek goals such as easier access to public buildings.

Veterans' rights

Several groups represent the interests of men and women who are veterans of military service. These groups seek compensation for time and opportunities lost while they were serving in the armed forces. The most significant veterans' groups since World War I have been the American Legion and the Veterans of Foreign Wars, each with membership above two million; and the Dis-

abled American Veterans, with 1,100,000 members. Together these groups have pressured Congress to increase funding for the Department of Veterans Affairs, to provide free health care for veterans, to offer a variety of loans, and to help veterans with educational expenses.

Religious groups

Although the United States has a long tradition of separating religion and politics, religious groups or their representatives have often expressed definite views on certain public policy issues. Quakers (the Society of Friends), for example, have long voiced opposition to war. Members of the Jehovah's Witnesses spurred the overturn of mandatory flag-salute laws.

In recent years, however, religious and church-affiliated groups have become directly involved in politics and public policy issues. Their members support laws that conform with their religious beliefs and combat laws that do

One of the religious leaders who took an active role in political issues was television evangelist Pat Robertson.

255

Controversial Issues

● [CRITICAL THINKING] Ask students whether they believe religious groups should take an active role in political campaigns. Have them give reasons for their views.

Politics

■ Ask students to identify interest groups that oppose each other on a major local or national issue. (Examples include utility rate increases, budget priorities, gun control, health care, abortion, and drug policy.) Students should research the opposing positions and the tactics each side is using to influence lawmakers. Students should report their findings to the class.

Cross-reference
The Supreme Court ruled that mandatory flag-salute laws violated First Amendment freedoms (Chapter 5, pp. 147–148).

Background: *Constitutional Heritage* The "wall of separation between church and state" was established in the Virginia Statute of Religious Liberty by Thomas Jefferson and later defined by Justice Black in the 1947 case of *Everson v. Board of Education* (Chapter 5, pp. 142–143).

The symbol 👥 denotes active participation strategies.

Activities are keyed for student abilities:
▲ = Basic
● = All Levels
■ = Average/Advanced

Cooperative Learning

■ Have interested students work in groups to start a school or area chapter of an existing public-interest group. Students might begin by holding a school-wide organizational meeting, coordinating activities with the regional or national organization and developing committees for membership and planning.

GUIDED/INDEPENDENT PRACTICE

● Ask students to compare social action and single-issue groups from the standpoint of politicians, noting the special problems that each kind of group might pose for a politician. (Some social action groups are highly motivated because of their members' consensus on a matter of principle. Single-issue groups often base their position on a politician entirely on the politician's stand on one issue.)

Figure 9–2 SOME SOCIAL ACTION INTEREST GROUPS 6B

GROUP	FOUNDED	MEMBERSHIP REPORTED 1992	STATED PURPOSE
Civil Rights			
National Organization for Women (NOW)	1966	250,000	To end sex discrimination in all aspects of American life.
American Civil Liberties Union (ACLU)	1920	375,000	To protect the freedoms of speech, press, religion, assembly, due process, and equal protection for all.
National Association for the Advancement of Colored People (NAACP)	1909	400,000	To obtain full civil rights for African Americans; to eliminate racial discrimination.
League of United Latin American Citizens	1929	110,000	To help all Hispanic Americans achieve full civil rights.
National Congress of American Indians	1944	155 tribes	To protect and develop natural and human resources and serve the legislative interests of Indian tribes.
National Alliance of Senior Citizens	1974	375,000	To present the views and needs of senior citizens before Congress; to study government policies.
Religion			
National Conference of Catholic Bishops	1966	377 bishops	To advocate government policies that are consistent with the doctrines and policies of the Roman Catholic Church.
American Baptist Black Caucus	1968	13,000	To encourage Baptist support for job and educational opportunities for minorities.
American Jewish Committee	1906	45,000	To protect religious and civil rights; to combat bigotry.
Public Interest			
Common Cause	1970	265,000	To get citizens involved in government; to expand voting rights.
League of Women Voters	1920	110,000	To educate the public on political matters and promote participation in government.
Public Citizen	1971	100,000	To promote consumer rights and safe energy and environmental policies.
Environmental Protection			
National Audubon Society	1905	600,000	To promote conservation; to protect endangered wildlife.
Sierra Club	1892	565,000	To preserve and protect wilderness areas.

SOURCE: *Encyclopedia of Associations*

Figure 9–2

● ***Why are there so many different civil rights groups?*** (Different groups represent different portions of the population, such as women, Hispanic Americans, or senior citizens.)

Background: *Multiculturalism* Senior citizens are a growing political force in the United States, accounting for nearly 30 percent of all voters.

not. Religious interest groups also have supported or opposed political candidates on the basis of their positions on such issues. Some Christian groups, for example, have supported a constitutional amendment to allow voluntary prayer in public schools, but others have opposed the idea as violating the separation of church and state.

Programs on national radio and television have provided a forum for the leaders of some religious interest groups. The so-called "media ministers" have taken strong policy positions, urging their followers to write letters to elected officials and work for or against certain candidates for office.

Public-interest groups

Numerous interest groups are made up of people working for goals that bring them no direct benefits but are, they believe, for the common good. These **public-interest groups** include, for example, environmental groups that seek to protect endangered animals and to preserve wilderness areas for all citizens to enjoy. Other public-interest groups seek such diverse goals as voter education, consumer protection, and restoration of historic buildings.

Single-Issue Groups

Some interest groups focus their attention almost entirely on one issue. One of the oldest such groups is the Woman's Christian Temperance Union, formed in 1874 to oppose the consumption and sale of alcohol. In recent years, the number of such groups has increased dramatically. (Figure 9–3 lists some leading single-issue groups.)

People who join single-issue groups usually have very intense feelings about that issue and support their group with determination. Often, when a single-issue group forms on one side of a controversial issue, another group supports the opposite opinion. For example, the Abortion Rights Action Committee is countered by the National Right-to-Life Committee.

The increase in the number of single-issue groups in recent years has caused some political concern. Many public officials fear that powerful single-issue groups can cause people to vote for or against a candidate without considering his or her overall record. For instance, suppose Voter P belongs to a single-issue group that opposes nuclear power plants. Candidate Q favors

Figure 9–3 SOME SINGLE-ISSUE INTEREST GROUPS   6B

GROUP	FOUNDED	MEMBERSHIP REPORTED 1992	STATED PURPOSE
Mothers Against Drunk Driving (MADD)	1980	2.8 million	To curb drug- and alcohol-related automobile accidents through strict drunk-driving laws and educational campaigns.
National Abortion Rights Action League	1969	400,000	To maintain the right of all women to legal abortions.
National Right-To-Life Committee	1973	unreported	To make abortion illegal.
National Rifle Association (NRA)	1871	3 million	To uphold the right of people to bear arms for recreation and self-defense.
Handgun Control, Inc.	1974	250,000	To promote government regulations on the manufacturing, sale, and possession of handguns.

SOURCE: *Encyclopedia of Associations*

257

Figure 9–3
■ *In the areas of abortion and gun control, one group heavily outnumbers the opposing group. What conclusions can you draw from this fact?* (The imbalances may indicate, but do not necessarily indicate, an imbalance in public opinion. They may also indicate a stronger organizational structure on one side of each issue. In the case of gun control, another cause of the imbalance may be the fact that the National Rifle Association has been in existence much longer than Handgun Control, Inc.)

RETEACHING/CORRECTIVES
▲ Ask students to create a table with the following headings: *Economic Interest Groups, Social Action Groups,* and *Single-Issue Groups.* Ask them to list at least four features unique to each category.

You may also want to use **Transparency 23,** which shows a political cartoon on the subject of gun control.

ENRICHMENT/EXTENSION
■ Have students complete **Constitutional Issues Worksheet 10** on the role of interest groups.

The symbol ⅱ denotes active participation strategies.

Activities are keyed for student abilities:
▲ = Basic
● = All Levels
■ = Average/Advanced

Section 2 Review Answers

1. (a) Business, professional, agricultural, labor. **(b)** Civil rights, veterans, religious, public-interest.

2. (a) To create the best business environment. **(b)** To protect constitutional rights. **(c)** To achieve goals that serve society.

3. They fear the influence of single-issue groups on voting.

Critical thinking Students should support their answers with specific information.

CLOSURE

● Remind students of the pre-reading objectives at the beginning of the section. Pose one or both of these questions again. Then have students read Section 3, paying special attention to the tactics interest groups use to achieve their goals.

SECTION 3

Interest Groups Use Varied Tactics

(pp. 258–263)

Section Objectives

☐ explain what is meant by lobbying and describe the techniques used by lobbyists

☐ explain how interest groups try to influence elections

☐ identify other techniques used by interest groups to influence public policy

Vocabulary

lobbying, electioneering, political action committee, grassroots, litigation, class action suit, propaganda, initiative, referendum

---

the use of nuclear energy. Although Voter P may agree with Candidate Q's stance on practically every other issue, P may vote against the candidate because of this one issue.

SECTION 2 REVIEW

Vocabulary and key terms

gross national product (252) public-interest group (257)
craft union (254)   single-issue group (257)
industrial union (254)

For review

1. What are the major types of (a) economic interest groups? (b) social action groups? **4C**

2. What is the underlying goal of (a) business and trade associations? (b) civil rights groups? (c) public-interest groups? **4C**

3. Why are some public officials concerned about the increasing number of single-issue groups? **4C**

Critical thinking

DRAWING INFERENCES   Section 1 described some factors that make interest groups effective, such as size and intensity (pages 249–250). Which of these factors would be most important in the success of a business group? a labor union? a civil rights group? a religious group? a public interest group? a single-issue group? Use the information in Figures 9–1, 9–2, and 9–3 to support your answers. **8A**

4B, 4C, 4D, 8A, 8D

SECTION 3   Interest Groups Use Varied Tactics

> **ACCESS**   The Main Ideas
>
> **1** What is meant by lobbying and what techniques are used by lobbyists?
> *pages 258–259*
>
> **2** How do interest groups try to influence elections?
> *pages 259–260*
>
> **3** What other techniques do interest groups use to influence public policy?
> *pages 260–263*

The National Right-To-Life Committee and the National Abortion and Reproductive Rights Action League (NARAL) are both highly organized, active interest groups. Right-to-life groups have tried to discourage abortions and make them illegal. Members have blocked entrances to abortion clinics and helped bring cases against abortion-rights groups to court. The actions of one right-to-life group, Operation Rescue, led Congress to pass a bill in 1994 that made it a federal crime to use the threat of force to intimidate women seeking to enter abortion clinics.

NARAL also asks its members to write members of Congress. The group makes contributions to the election campaigns of candidates who support abortion rights. Like the National Right-to-Life Committee, NARAL organizes mass rallies in support of its cause.

4B

Lobbying

The rowdy, popular politics of President Andrew Jackson's era encouraged more people to take part in government. Beginning in the 1830's, citizens who backed a cause would gather in the lobbies of legislative chambers and outside government offices. There they waited for a chance to talk to officials entering or leaving the building — seeking votes for a bill or new legislation.

From this custom came the term **lobbying**, which now refers to efforts to influence legislation or other government decisions through personal persuasion. Professional lobbyists represent not only interest groups but also major corporations, foreign businesses, and foreign governments.

258

Seeking jobs in the new administration, political supporters crowd into the White House lobby and wait near the doorway of President Rutherford B. Hayes's private office. An 1877 engraving shows these "lobbyists" at work.

Lobbying techniques

Lobbyists use many forms of persuasion. They supply information to policy-makers personally. Lobbyists also testify before congressional committees or executive agencies. Finally, lobbyists do favors for public officials, such as buying dinners or drafting speeches.

To be effective, a lobbyist must be thoroughly familiar with the legislative process. He or she must also be able to gain access to key decision-makers, especially congressional leaders and committee chairpersons. This is why many Washington lobbyists are former members of Congress or executive departments. Furthermore, the information a lobbyist provides to policy-makers must be accurate. Careless or dishonest lobbyists will lose their contacts.

Controls over lobbying

Occasionally, a lobbyist may try to bribe an official or use other questionable tactics. For this reason, Congress in 1946 passed the Federal Regulation of Lobbying Act. About half the states also have established rules for lobbying.

Among the important provisions of the 1946 federal law are the following: (1) Any person or group paid to influence federal legislation must be registered with the Senate and the House. (Agents of foreign firms or governments also must register with the Justice Department.) (2) Lobbyists must give, under oath, their correct name, address, employer, and salary. There are about 6,000 registered lobbyists in Washington, D.C., but it is estimated that some 20,000 people are actually involved in lobbying efforts in the federal government. (3) Registered lobbyists must provide quarterly reports on their income and expenditures. (4) Lobbyists who fail to comply with the law can receive a five-year prison term plus a fine of up to $10,000.

4B

Influencing Elections

Lobbying is not the only technique that interest groups use to influence public officials. At election time, interest groups can either rally behind a candidate or mount tremendous oppo-

259

FOCUS

● Refer students to the chapter opener on p. 247. *What were some of the tactics each side used in the fight over the Thomas nomination?* List them on the board and explain that Section 3 will focus on the processes interest groups use to influence legislation.

EXPLANATION

After students have read the section, you may want to consider the following activities:

Politics

▲ Have students list the four major provisions of the Federal Regulation of Lobbying Act (described on this page).

● CRITICAL THINKING Ask class members to explain why lawmakers considered such a law necessary and to speculate about the reasons for each provision of the law.

■ CRITICAL THINKING Tell students that lobbyists have sometimes been called the "third house of Congress." Ask students to explain why. Then ask students if they think the framers of the Constitution would have been pleased by the creation of an unofficial "third house." (Students should recognize that lobbyists are not elected representatives, but do represent the interests of certain American citizens.)

Check for Understanding
● *How would previous membership in Congress or in an executive branch department help a lobbyist?* (It would give that person an intimate knowledge of the workings of the institution, as well as personal contacts within that institution.)

Background: *Historic Documents* Lobbyists' quarterly reports are published in the *Congressional Record.* As required by the Constitution, the *Record* publishes daily accounts of everything said in Congress (except executive sessions of the Senate). Anyone can subscribe to or buy separate parts of the *Record.*

The symbol ⅱ denotes active participation strategies.

Activities are keyed for student abilities:
▲ = Basic
● = All Levels
■ = Average/Advanced

sition. This strategy, called **electioneering**, can be defined informally as "the attempt to elect political friends and defeat political enemies."

Interest groups typically scrutinize candidates for major offices to see whether they have been or are likely to be sympathetic to the group's position on key issues. Many interest groups send questionnaires to candidates for office in an effort to assess their views. A candidate may, in fact, be swamped with hundreds of such surveys. If the candidate is an office-holder running for re-election, interest groups will examine his or her voting record.

Based upon voting records, surveys, public statements, party affiliation, and other factors, interest groups then decide which candidates to support. Support may come in the form of campaign contributions, endorsements, computer services, mailing lists, and information. Of course, in many cases, interest groups work just as hard to *prevent* an opposition candidate from winning the election.

Political action committees

A dramatic development in recent years has been the rise of **political action committees**. These committees, commonly known as *PACs* (pronounced "packs"), are legal entities set up by interest groups to collect and spend funds for political purposes. In 1974 about 600 PACs spent a total of $12.5 million in congressional elections. By 1990, the number of PACs had swelled to more than 4,000, which spent over $125 million.

The reason behind the sudden growth of PACs lies in federal legislation. Federal law has long prohibited corporations from using their operating funds to support political candidates. In 1974, however, an amendment to the federal election laws permitted both corporations and labor unions to set up special committees (PACs) to collect *voluntary* contributions for political campaigns. PACs were limited to giving up to $5,000 per election to the campaign funds of a candidate for national office. There was no limit, however, on what PACs could spend independently on behalf of a candidate. That is, the PAC itself can pay for a TV spot or billboard supporting a candidate.

The immense financial power of some PACs has been challenged in court. In 1985, however,

a Supreme Court ruling overturned limits on PAC spending in presidential elections as a violation of freedom of speech (*Federal Election Commission v. National Conservative Political Action Committee*). In this decision, Justice William Rehnquist said that putting a limit on such spending was "much like allowing the speaker in a public hall to express views while denying him the use of an amplifying system."

4B, 4C

Other Persuasive Techniques

Working at the grassroots

Rather than relying on lobbyists or PACs, an interest group may try to influence public policy by mounting a **grassroots** campaign. In politics, the term *grassroots* refers to a movement started and carried out by ordinary people, not professional politicians. An interest group may ask its members to write letters, send telegrams, or telephone public officials, creating the image of a groundswell of opinion for or against a policy. Using computers and high-speed printers, interest groups today can notify their members quickly and generate an avalanche of letters.

Grassroots pressure may or may not bring desired results. In 1982, for example, the Motion Picture Association mailed to Congress over 20,000 form letters and telegrams. Its goal was to force the makers of home video recorders (VCRs) to pay royalties to filmmakers. This grassroots effort failed. The National Rifle Association (NRA), however, has used grassroots methods very successfully. Whenever gun control laws have been proposed, Congress has been swamped with thousands of NRA letters, mainly hand-written ones, opposing them. As a general rule, public officials are more likely to heed a few personally written letters than a flood of computer-generated form letters.

Legal action

When interest groups fail to change public policy in the legislative or executive branches of government, they frequently turn to **litigation** in the judicial branch. Litigation means, simply, bringing a lawsuit. Interest groups file suits in hopes that a judge or jury will either overturn an unfavorable law or decision, or rule that a law must be enforced.

Bumper stickers, T-shirts, and buttons are popular ways for people to show "grassroots" support for an interest group or an issue. The National Rifle Association is one group that has consistently marshalled such support effectively.

One common tactic is to bring a **class action suit**. This is a lawsuit brought by one person or a group on behalf of all people who would benefit directly from the court's decision. Bringing such a case would probably be too difficult for most individuals to undertake.

Class action lawsuits have been especially important to environmental, consumer, and civil rights groups. The National Audubon Society, Common Cause, and NOW (Figure 9-2) are three groups that have successfully used class action suits in recent years. *Brown v. Board of Education* (page 200) was a class action suit brought by the NAACP to end school segregation. A class action suit brought on behalf of the Japanese Americans relocated during World War II won them the right to sue for damages (page 209).

Interest groups can also become indirectly involved in litigation by filing *amicus curiae* briefs. (*Amicus curiae* [uh-MEE-kuhs KYOOR-ee-eye] is Latin for "a friend of the court.") These briefs are legal arguments that are delivered voluntarily to a court to give testimony for or against a decision. One group that files many such briefs with the Supreme Court each year is the American Civil Liberties Union (ACLU). In the Bakke "reverse discrimination" case (page 210), more than fifty interest groups filed *amicus* briefs — including 37 for the university and 16 for Bakke.

Propaganda
Interest groups also use **propaganda** to influence public policy. The term *propaganda* is

often used negatively to mean only false or misleading types of persuasion. In fact, propaganda is any persuasive communication intended to influence people's opinions, emotions, or actions in a certain direction. It may use every tactic from factual evidence to outright lies. (See Figure 9-4.)

Interest groups are not the only users of propaganda. All governments, for example, use propaganda of some sort to generate public support for their policies. Political parties, candidates for office, advertisers, and a variety of organizations also use propaganda techniques. Learning to recognize propaganda is important in making intelligent decisions.

Direct legislation
Interest groups that fail to get the attention of legislators have still another way of expressing their members' concerns. Since the turn of the century, many of the states have set up procedures that let citizens participate directly in proposing and enacting legislation. These processes derive from voters' constitutional right to petition the government.

One such procedure is the **initiative**. In the initiative process, the voters start, or initiate, the lawmaking process by signing a petition proposing a law or constitutional amendment. A more common procedure is the **referendum**. It allows voters to approve or disapprove an amendment to the state constitution or a law already passed by the legislature.

261

Background: *History* Nazi leader Adolf Hitler declared, "All propaganda has to be popular and has to adapt its spiritual level to the perception of the least intelligent."

Background: *Civic Participation* In a *direct* initiative, the proposal is placed on the ballot after gaining the required number of signatures. In an *indirect* initiative, the proposal goes first

to the state legislature. If the legislature does not pass the proposal, it then goes on the ballot. Chapter 24, Section 2 (pp. 644–645), discusses direct legislation in detail.

👥 Cooperative Learning
● Have the class list ten major problems faced by citizens today. Divide the class into small groups and ask each group to research one of these problems.

Groups can then be asked to imagine that they are lobbyists working for an interest group that wants to convince an uninterested legislator to accept its point of view. Members of each group can take the part of lobbyists, while another student acts as the lawmaker, asking questions and challenging the lobbyists on occasion.

👥 GUIDED/INDEPENDENT PRACTICE
● Discuss with the class the seven propaganda techniques described in Figure 9–4 (p. 262). Then have students create collages illustrating these techniques. Students can use magazines, newspapers, direct mail advertisements, or political campaign literature, or create their own examples. Examples can be combined for a bulletin-board display on propaganda.

The symbol 👥 denotes active participation strategies.

Activities are keyed for student abilities:
▲ = Basic
● = All Levels
■ = Average/Advanced

262

RETEACHING/CORRECTIVES

▲ Have students outline the section, using the headings and subheadings and supplying other information as necessary.

Have students complete **Skills Practice Worksheet 9,** which asks them to analyze common political propaganda techniques.

You may also want to use **Transparencies 24–25,** which show political cartoons on the subjects of PAC contributions and the influence of special interests over Congress.

ENRICHMENT/EXTENSION

■ Have students research and report to the class on the current role of political action committees in national politics. Reports can focus on the growth in the number of PACs and the amount of money PACs spent in the most recent presidential election year.

You may also want students to complete **Supreme Court Decision 58,** which deals with interest groups.

Section 3 Review Answers

1. **(a)** Supplying information, testifying, doing favors for public officials, providing electoral support. **(b)** Being familiar with the legislative process, having access to key decision-makers, supplying accurate information.

Figure 9–4 COMMON PROPAGANDA TECHNIQUES   8D

BANDWAGON

This technique creates the impression of wide-spread support. It plays upon people's desire to conform, or "climb on the bandwagon."

"We have the #1 product."

"Policy X is the clear choice of all Americans."

TRANSFER

Used to associate a policy or product with an object that is honored and respected.

A presidential candidate links himself with a historical figure such as Thomas Jefferson or Abraham Lincoln, quoting their words in speeches.

A group pictures the Statue of Liberty in its brochures.

TESTIMONIALS

Well-known people are used to endorse a product, candidate, or proposal. It is hoped that the audience will follow their example.

A professional basketball player advertises a pair of shoes.

A movie star speaks in favor of a balanced federal budget.

NAME CALLING

A substitute for arguing the merits of an issue or product. This tactic is used to appeal to fears and prejudices.

"Anyone who opposes this policy is supporting communism."

"Candidate J is a Nazi."

PLAIN FOLKS

An attempt to win public confidence by showing that you are "just like everyone else."

A city politician attempts to win farm votes by wearing overalls and carrying a pitchfork.

A large corporation advertises how much its research helps the poor.

GLITTERING GENERALITIES

The most common propaganda technique, which uses vague, sweeping statements that gloss over details. Policies or products are described in lofty terms.

An official says, "Policy X is in the public interest."

A company argues its opposition to government regulation by saying "America's freedom is at stake."

CARD STACKING

Presenting only one side of the argument. It may involve juggling, distorting, or omitting facts.

Unemployment has remained constant for two consecutive years; a politician argues that there has been "a dramatic decline in the rate of increase" of unemployment.

An interest group points out that Candidate W voted against "every Social Security increase" last session, when there was only one such bill presented.

Even though not all the states allow the initiative and referendum, the number of such special ballot issues has increased remarkably. Interest groups play the major role in circulating the necessary petitions to get their proposals before the voters. For instance, interest groups have been successful in passing special ballot measures that restored the death penalty in Oregon, limited property taxes in California, and permitted a state lottery in Missouri.

Public protests

In 1966, ninety unemployed blacks from Mississippi pitched tents in Lafayette Park in

262

Figure 9–4

■ *Select one of the techniques in the figure and explain how you would counter it.* (*Example:* In response to the testimonial technique, one could point out that the celebrity spokesperson is not an expert in the area about which he or she is speaking.)

Background: *Historic Documents* The right to petition, which can be traced to the English Bill of Rights, is guaranteed in the First Amendment to the Constitution.

Washington, D.C., across from the White House. The "camp-in" was called to protest the government's delay in providing promised aid to families living in poverty. In 1979 the American Agricultural Movement organized a "tractorcade" through the streets of Washington to protest farm policies. About 2,000 tractors and trucks disrupted rush-hour traffic.

Such peaceful protests are another way that interest groups dramatize their concerns and try to attract public interest. Protests can take many forms, such as boycotts, marches, and sit-ins. They may be legal public assemblies or a form of civil disobedience. While protesting is very effective in generating publicity, its impact on government is difficult to assess. Some groups have used protests successfully to achieve their goals. Other groups use protests only as a last resort, when traditional methods will not work.

SECTION 3 REVIEW

Vocabulary and key terms

lobbying (258)	class action suit (261)
electioneering (260)	*amicus curiae* (261)
political action	propaganda (261)
committee (260)	initiative (261)
grassroots (260)	referendum (261)
litigation (260)	

For review

1. (a) What are some activities of lobbyists? (b) What are some of the qualities of effective lobbyists? **4B**
2. (a) What are some ways that interest groups influence election results? (b) What is the role of political action committees? **4B**
3. (a) How do interest groups use the judicial branch of government to gain their goals? (b) How can people directly influence legislation? **4D**

Critical thinking

ORGANIZING AN ARGUMENT Regulations on lobbying and on political action committees have been challenged as violations of the First Amendment right to freedom of speech. Can this argument be justified? Why or why not? **8A**

Chapter Summary

An interest group is a structured organization of people with shared attitudes who attempt to influence public policy. People join interest groups for social, economic, and moral reasons. The effectiveness of a group depends on the size, geographic distribution, cohesion, and intensity of its membership. In addition, the ability of its leaders, their access to public officials, the group's financial resources, and its prestige are important factors. Interest groups have been criticized for giving a few individuals too much influence over government, for distorting the issues, for damaging the effectiveness of government officials, and for unethical practices. On the other hand, they have been praised for encouraging participation in government, providing useful information to policy-makers, and stabilizing American politics.

Interest groups pursue a wide variety of goals and purposes. Many are organized around economic concerns; business groups, professional associations, agricultural interests, and labor unions are the most important of these. A number of groups are formed to influence social issues; some examples include civil rights, religious, and public-interest groups. Single-issue groups, which focus on one cause, have become a major force in recent years.

Interest groups use many tactics to influence public policy. Many groups hire lobbyists to influence government officials through personal persuasion. Through electioneering, interest groups rally support for candidates who favor their views and try to defeat candidates who oppose them. Many groups have political action committees (PACs) to channel campaign contributions. Some groups organize grassroots movements, urging their members to write letters, make phone calls, and send telegrams urging legislators to vote a certain way on an issue that affects the group. Legal action (litigation) is a useful method for opposing unfavorable laws or policies. Interest groups can also use the initiative or referendum processes to back legislation supporting their goals. Finally, groups can resort to propaganda or engage in public protests to call attention to their point of view.

2. (a) By electioneering and by funding political action committees. (b) To collect and spend funds to support or defeat candidates.
3. (a) Through litigation or *amicus curiae* briefs. (b) Through the initiative process or the referendum.

Critical thinking Students should discuss the rights of individuals to express themselves in effective ways, the narrow focus of interest groups, and interest groups' power to influence government officials.

CLOSURE

● Review key concepts from Section 3 by asking students to make brief arguments for both sides of the following question: *Do lobbying practices distort the democratic process?* (Some students may argue that lobbyists are just representing the interests of constituents; others may argue that they represent narrow interests and not those of the majority of citizens.) Then have students read the next assigned lesson.

CHAPTER 9 CORRECTIVES

● To review the content of Chapter 9, you may want to have students complete **Study Guide/Review 9** or **Workbook Chapter 9.**

263

The symbol ♟ denotes active participation strategies.

Activities are keyed for student abilities:
▲ = Basic
● = All Levels
■ = Average/Advanced

★ CHAPTER **9 REVIEW ★**

Answers

Vocabulary See pp. T19–T21 for suggested vocabulary activities.

Reviewing the Facts

1. The diversity of the people encourages a variety of attitudes and opinions, which find expression through interest groups.

2. Factors include size, geographic distribution, cohesion, intensity, leadership, access to government officials, funds, and prestige.

3. Such leaders may not accurately represent the opinions of most members because they do not consult the majority when making decisions.

4. They provide important information and expert knowledge in many fields.

5. To create a more favorable climate for their business to prosper.

6. Union organization of federal and state employees was forbidden before 1962.

7. They know the legislative process and have access to decision-makers.

8. Federal election laws now permit corporations and labor unions to set up PACs to collect contributions for campaigns. Also, the Supreme Court in 1985 refused to put a limit on PAC spending in presidential elections.

9. By initiating class action suits and *amicus curiae* briefs.

● **Review the definitions of the following terms:**

amicus curiae	**industrial union**	**propaganda**
class action suit	**initiative**	**public-interest group**
craft union	**interest group**	**referendum**
electioneering	**litigation**	**single-issue group**
grassroots	**lobbying**	
gross national product	**political action committee**	

● **REVIEWING THE FACTS**

1. Why, according to the author, does the United States have so many interest groups? **4C**

2. Name three of the factors that help make an interest group more effective in influencing policies. **4C**

3. Why are some interest groups criticized for being run by a small, active minority of their members? **4C**

4. How do interest groups help policy-makers and public officials? **4B**

5. What is the general goal of business and trade associations? **4B**

6. Why were there no unions of public employees before 1962? **4B**

7. Why are former members of Congress or of executive departments often hired as lobbyists? **4C**

8. What are some of the reasons behind the growth of PACs? **4B**

9. What are some of the ways in which interest groups can become involved in legal action? **4B**

▲ **THINKING CRITICALLY ABOUT KEY CONCEPTS**

1. Americans tend to take sides according to issues rather than ideology. How might this cause conflicts for a person who belongs to several different interest groups? Give an example of such a conflict. **8H**

264

---

2. Explain how the saying "The wheel that squeaks the loudest gets the grease" applies to interest groups. **8C**

3. How might the success of interest groups upset the balance between majority rule and minority rights? **8F**

▲ **PRACTICING SKILLS**

1. **Study Skills: Organizing information.** Reread the subsections "Economic Interest Groups" and "Social Action Groups" (pages 252–257). Make a list that shows one success or positive effect that each of the following interest groups has had on public policy: professional groups, labor unions, public-employee unions, veterans' rights groups. **8A**

2. **Study Skills: Reading a table.** Refer to Figure 9–3 (page 257) to answer the following questions. (a) Which of these groups has the largest membership? (b) Which group is the oldest? (c) Which groups listed probably find themselves on opposite sides of the same issue? **8G**

3. **Critical Thinking Skills: Recognizing propaganda.** Refer to Figure 9–4 (page 262) to identify the technique represented by each of the following descriptions. (a) A candidate for office wears an American flag pin in his lapel. (b) A campaign worker tells a voter, "All your neighbors are supporting this bill." (c) A lobbyist tells a key official, "It's for the good of the country." **8D**

Thinking Critically About Key Concepts

1. These interest groups may disagree on a specific issue. For example, a person might belong to an anti-abortion single-interest group and also to a social action interest group that supports the right of abortion.

2. Groups that keep their issue and viewpoint in the public spotlight will gain the attention of lawmakers and gain influence.

3. Interest groups often do not represent the views of the majority of voters, yet they have tremendous resources to influence government policy.

1. **Analyzing a newspaper.** Examine a newspaper to find all the interest groups that are mentioned in news stories, letters to the editor, editorial pages, or other parts of the paper. List all the groups, and in a sentence or two, explain why each group appeared in the paper. **4B**

2. **Researching an oral report.** Research an interest group concerned with veterans' rights, such as the American Legion, the Disabled American Veterans, or the Veterans of Foreign Wars. In your report, describe the group, its goals, issues or legislation in which the group is currently active, and the group's major achievements. **8E**

1. **Writing a position paper.** All citizens are guaranteed equal rights by the Constitution. Is there a need, therefore, for social action groups to work for the rights of blacks, women, American Indians, and others? Imagine that you are a candidate for public office. Write a policy paper on this issue. **8C**

2. **Writing an editorial.** How do the initiative and referendum procedures reflect the principle of "government by the people"? Is this principle supported or undermined when such direct legislation is organized and financed by powerful interest groups? Write an editorial on this subject, giving reasons for your opinion. **8C**

▲ ANALYZING A POLITICAL CARTOON

Members of Congress have often been accused of being more responsive to the concerns of special interests than to those of the average voter. Indeed, few in Congress can afford to ignore special-interest groups which donate large amounts of money to re-election campaigns. Look at the cartoon below and answer the following questions.

1. How does the cartoon portray Senator Ziltch's attitude towards the voter? **8B**
2. Under what circumstances would the Senator have welcomed his visitor? **8A**
3. Who is the man at left to whom Senator Ziltch is speaking? **8B**
4. What might the cartoonist be implying by the Senator's name? **8A**

" I THOUGHT HE WAS A MEMBER OF A SPECIAL INTEREST GROUP...
BUT I FOUND OUT HE'S ONLY A VOTER ! "

© 1989 Wayne Staykal, Tampa Tribune. Reprinted by permission of Wayne Staykal.

265

Participatory Citizenship

1. You may want to list students' responses on the board and ask the class which groups are concerned with issues that affect or concern them personally.
2. Students may also investigate the involvement of local veterans' groups in the community, or conduct an interview with a veteran to present to the class.

Writing About Issues

1. Students supporting such social action groups may point to evidence of past discrimination against the people mentioned. Students opposing such groups may argue that they encourage divisions within American society.
2. You may want to have students read their editorials aloud, and then organize a debate on interest groups.

Analyzing a Political Cartoon

1. He is unresponsive.
2. If he had been a member of a special-interest group.
3. A member of a special-interest group, or perhaps another senator.
4. That the senator does not care at all about voters.

Practicing Skills

1. *Professional groups*—Established standards for practicing a profession within a state. *Labor unions*—Child labor laws, eight-hour work days, workplace health and safety measures. *Public-employee unions*—Won right of public employees to establish unions. *Veterans' rights groups*—Increased funding for the VA, veterans' loans.
2. **(a)** National Right-To-Life Committee. **(b)** National Rifle Association. **(c)** Handgun Control, Inc. and NRA; National Right-To-Life Committee and National Abortion Rights Action League.
3. **(a)** Transfer. **(b)** Bandwagon. **(c)** Glittering generalities.

Chapter Review exercises are keyed for student abilities:
▲ = Basic
● = All Levels
■ = Average/Advanced

CHAPTER 10
POLITICAL PARTIES
(pp. 266–289)

	Section Objectives	Section Resources
Section 1 **Political Parties Play Many Roles**	☐ explain the roles of parties in the American system of government ☐ explain how parties affect political participation	
Section 2 **Two Parties Dominate American Politics**	☐ identify the three types of party systems ☐ explain the barriers third parties face in the American political system ☐ describe the roles third parties have played in American politics	
Section 3 **Politics Are Part of American History**	☐ describe how political parties developed ☐ explain how the Civil War and the Great Depression affected party politics	▲ TRANSPARENCY **26**
Section 4 **How Do Democrats and Republicans Differ?**	☐ describe the major similarities and differences between the Democratic Party and the Republican Party ☐ identify recent trends in party politics	▲ SKILLS PRACTICE WORKSHEET **10** ■ SKILLS CHALLENGE WORKSHEET **10** ▲ TRANSPARENCY **27**

Essential Elements

The list below shows Essential Elements relevant to this chapter. (The complete list of Essential Elements appears in the introductory pages of this Teacher's Edition.)

Section 1: 4B, 4C, 6F, 8H

Section 2: 1C, 2E, 4B, 4C, 8C

Section 3: 1D, 2A, 2C, 2E, 8G

Section 4: 2E, 4B, 4C, 5B, 8A, 8G

Chapter Review: 1C, 2E, 4A, 4C, 4D, 5A, 8A, 8B, 8C

> Section Resources are keyed for student abilities:
> ▲ = Basic
> ● = All Levels
> ■ = Average/Advanced

Homework Options

Each section contains activities labeled "Guided/Independent Practice," "Reteaching/Correctives," and "Enrichment/Extension." You may wish to choose from among these activities when assigning homework.

Students Acquiring English Activities

Divide the class into two groups, "Democrats" and "Republicans." Have students review overnight "their" party's positions on major issues, as outlined on pp. 284–285. Create a spinner showing the categories *Agriculture, Economic Policy, Education, Labor, Business, Social Programs, Energy, AIDS, Crime, Defense, Foreign Affairs,* and *Women.* Have the two groups reassemble and spin the spinner. Pick one person in each group to give their party's position on the issue.

LISTENING/SPEAKING: Invite a precinct captain or other party official to speak to the class about his or her party's positions on major issues.

Case Studies

When teaching this chapter, you may use Case Study 5, which examines the issue of limitations on Congressional terms. (Case Studies may be found following p. 510.)

Teacher Bibliography

Kayden, Xandra and Eddie Mahe, Jr. *The Party Goes On: The Persistence of the Two-Party System in the United States.* Basic, 1987. Depicts the shift in the two-party system from grassroots to Washington-based organizations.

Woll, Peter. *Behind the Scenes in American Government.* 8th ed. HarperCollins, 1991. Portrays the people who shape politics.

Student Bibliography

Archer, Jules. *Winners and Losers: How Elections Work in America.* Harcourt Brace Jovanovich, 1984. The workings of the electoral process are explained as the author discusses the role of American political parties.

National Party Conventions, 1832–1988. CQ Press, 1991. Written portraits of the candidates of all parties are given, along with the major events and issues of the times.

Salmore, Stephen A. and Barbara G. Salmore. *Candidates, Parties, and Campaigns: Electoral Politics in America.* CQ Press, 1985. Examines the roles of professional consultants, political action committees, and political parties in elections.

Literature

Cohen, Dan. *Undefeated: The Life of Hubert H. Humphrey.* Lerner Publications, 1978. A look at the career of the former Vice President, emphasizing his Minnesota roots and political savvy.

Liddy, G. Gordon. *Will: The Autobiography of G. Gordon Liddy.* St. Martin's, 1991. A personal account by a Watergate conspirator.

Remini, Robert Vincent. *The Life of Andrew Jackson.* Harper, 1988. A condensed and updated book by the author of a three-volume biography of Jackson.

CHAPTER RESOURCES

Study Guide/Review 10
Workbook Chapter 10
Chapter 10 Test, Forms A–C

Films and Videotapes*

Political Parties in the United States. 17 min. Phoenix, 1976. f, v. Provides a history of the American political party system emphasizing the importance of third parties and splinter groups.

Politics at the Grass Roots. 21 min. Parthenon (Paramount), 1973. f. A thorough examination of grassroots politics, focusing on the process and importance of precinct work.

A World of Ideas with Bill Moyers: James MacGregor Burns. 29 min. PBS, 1988. v. This political scientist, teacher, and historian discusses his theory that creative policies stem from strong party loyalty.

Software*

On the Campaign Trail (Apple, IBM, Macintosh). TS. Students assume the role of a third-party candidate for President. They learn about the Electoral College, campaign strategies and costs, special interest groups, and political action committees.

Presidential Campaign! (Apple). Queue. Using this simulation of a national presidential campaign, students must select a candidate, raise and allocate funds, and decide where and how to campaign.

* For a complete guide to audiovisual sources, see page T22.

Political Parties
(pp. 266–289)

Chapter 10 examines the role of political parties in American life, describing the many functions political parties have in the American political system, tracing the growth of political parties from the nation's earliest years to the present, and comparing the two dominant parties in the nation today.

Chapter Objectives

After students complete this chapter, they will be able to:

1. Explain the roles of parties in the American system of government.

2. Explain how parties affect political participation.

3. Identify the three types of party systems.

4. Explain the barriers third parties face in the American political system.

5. Describe the roles third parties have played in American politics.

6. Describe how political parties developed.

7. Explain how the Civil War and the Great Depression affected party politics.

8. Describe the major similarities and differences between the Democratic Party and the Republican Party.

9. Identify recent trends in party politics.

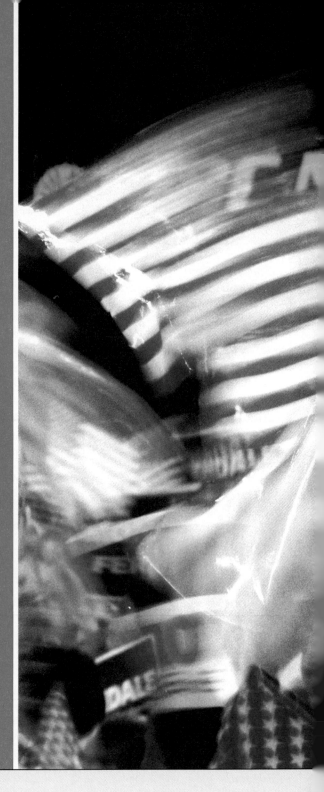

C H A P T E R

10

POLITICAL PARTIES

A party of order or stability, and a party of progress or reform, are both necessary elements of a healthy state of political life.

John Stuart Mill
On Liberty (1859)

266

Photo
Political convention.

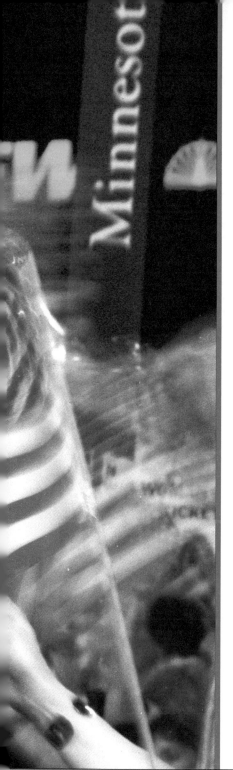

Thomas Jefferson thought political parties were a bad idea. In the 1790's he flatly stated, "If I could not go to heaven, [except] with a political party, I would not go there at all." Jefferson and other early leaders, such as George Washington, John Adams, and James Madison, feared that parties would divide the nation and lead to "intrigue, favoritism, and cabal." In other words, parties were a recipe for bad government. Nevertheless, Jefferson himself helped found the present-day Democratic Party.

This contradiction is perhaps typical of America's ambivalent attitude toward political parties. On the one hand they play no part in the fundamental political structure of our government. The Constitution does not even mention them. And yet political parties have been with us since the early days of the republic. We have come to rely on them in choosing public officials, determining national policies, and encouraging political participation. It is hard to imagine the political process without them.

Chapter 10 examines the development of political parties and the roles they play in American democracy.

CHAPTER SUPPORT MATERIAL

Skills Practice Worksheet 10

Skills Challenge Worksheet 10

Transparencies 26-27

Study Guide/Review 10

Workbook Chapter 10

Chapter 10 Test, Forms A-C

CHAPTER OUTLINE

1 Political Parties Play Many Roles

Parties in Government
Parties and the People

2 Two Parties Dominate American Politics

Party Systems
America's Two-Party System
The Role of Third Parties

3 Politics Are Part of American History

Early Political Rivalries
Modern Political Parties

4 How Do Democrats and Republicans Differ?

Party Similarities
Party Differences
Trends in Party Politics

267

SECTION 1

Political Parties Play
Many Roles

(pp. 268–270)

Section Objectives

☐ explain the roles of parties
in the American system of
government

☐ explain how parties affect
political participation

Vocabulary

political party, opposition party,
coalition

FOCUS

● Write on the board the following statement: "Let me now . . .
warn you in the most solemn
manner against the baneful
effects of the spirit of party." Ask
students to explain the quotation. (*Baneful* means "destructive.") Then tell them that the
quotation comes from George
Washington's Farewell Address
on September 17, 1796.

Ask students to write a
one-paragraph reply to Washington, explaining why they believe
Washington's warning was or
was not correct. Tell students
that they will write another reply
at the end of the chapter and
then compare the two.

EXPLANATION

After students have read the
section, you may want to consider the following activities:

Politics

● CRITICAL THINKING List on the
board the functions of political
parties in the United States. Then
have students rank these functions by importance and give
reasons for their rankings.

Political Parties Play Many Roles

 ACCESS **The Main Ideas**

1 What roles do parties play in the
American system of government?
pages 268–269

2 How do parties affect political
participation? *pages 269–270*

For most people, the very word *politics* brings
up ideas connected with political parties —
Democrats and Republicans, the symbols of a
donkey and an elephant, rallies and debates, campaign slogans, and the hype and excitement of
political conventions.

The role of political parties in American government, however, is much deeper and more
basic. Clinton Rossiter, an American political
scientist, has said, "No America without democracy, no democracy without politics, no politics
without parties, no parties without compromise
and moderation."

4B

Parties in Government

According to Rossiter, democratic government would not work without political parties.
What do parties do that make them so necessary?

A **political party** is a group of citizens who
are organized to win elections, control government, and set public policy. These goals make
political parties quite different from the interest
groups discussed in Chapter 9. While interest
groups may endorse or oppose political candidates, they do not run candidates for office or try
to gain control of the government.

Providing government leadership

Providing experienced and competent
leaders for government is one of a party's most
important functions. In the United States, the
parties act as huge personnel agencies to help select and recruit such leaders. Through party
politics, candidates are nominated and elected to
public office. Imagine how difficult and confusing this task would be without some way to sift
through the thousands of potential officeholders.

268

Once officials are elected, party politics play
a role in organizing and managing the government. Presidents, state governors, and many city
mayors appoint or hire people from their own
parties to administer policies. Likewise, both
Congress and the state legislatures are organized
along party lines. Party leaders set priorities for
lawmaking and organize their followers to vote
along party lines.

The "loyal opposition"

In non-democratic countries, the losers in an
election may find themselves powerless or even
in serious danger. They may use military force or
start a civil war to try to overthrow the government of the winners. In a democracy, however,
the party that loses an election still has a vital role
to play. The **opposition party** — the party out
of office — serves as a watchdog on the party
holding office.

In British politics, the term for this group is
the "loyal opposition." That is, they are *loyal* to

**The donkey and the elephant have been cartoon
symbols for the two major political parties for
more than a hundred years.**

IT'S A CUTE TRICK, BUT IT DOESN'T GET ANY APPLAUSE

Photo
In the cartoon, the Demo-
cratic machine is using its
control over Chicago politics
to make the local Republicans "roll over."

Background: *History*
Rutherford B. Hayes de-
clared in his Inaugural Address (March 5, 1877), "He
serves his party best who
serves the country best."

the nation while *opposing* the policies of the party in power. For example, if the Democrats hold a majority in Congress, the Republicans become the opposition. They criticize the majority party, propose alternative policies, and provide an informal check and balance. By expressing the minority view, the "loyal opposition" makes the majority party more responsible to all the people.

Guiding public policy

Interest groups, other concerned citizens, and the media focus public attention on certain issues or problems. It is up to political parties to translate these popular concerns into practical, workable plans and programs for government action. Again, Clinton Rossiter put it well: "Because they [political parties] are the only truly national, multi-interest, broadly based organizations active in our society, they are uniquely situated to originate public policies."

Moreover, there is a great diversity of viewpoints and interests among Americans. Political parties help to bring together people with differing views and reduce conflict among them. Parties arrange compromises and try to soften the clash between extreme viewpoints. In their efforts to win elections, political parties often put together **coalitions** — temporary alliances between groups that have different interests. This process of compromises is why politics has been called "the art of the possible."

4C
Parties and the People

Outside the actual workings of the government, political parties have other important roles in a democracy.

Providing information

Political debates, campaign speeches, newspaper ads, press conferences, and television talk shows all give the public information about current issues in their government. Such public information, of course, may be quite biased in favor of one party's aims. Nevertheless, parties do identify and publicize issues.

Encouraging political participation

The citizens who make up a party are not all equally involved in that party. For some people,

YOU DECIDE

Convinced that both the Democratic and Republican parties have failed to address women's needs, members of the National Organization for Women have proposed the formation of a women's political party. However, members of the National Women's Political Caucus, a group comprised mainly of elected officials, oppose a separate feminist political party.

Would such a third party be helpful or harmful to women's concerns? Explain.

party membership means only that they cast their vote for the party's candidates at election time. Others make politics their life's work. They may run for election and win important and influential offices in the national, state, or local government. They speak publicly for the party and influence government policy.

Still other party members work actively in the day-to-day party organization. They are the activists or professionals who give the party time, money, and expertise.

Both major parties also have organized service clubs that encourage a wider group of people to take part in politics. For example, for high school and college students, there are the Teen Age Republicans, College Republicans, and Young Democrats. The two parties have adult service organizations such as the Pachyderm Clubs (Republican) and the Muleskinners (Democratic). While women today play a central role in party politics, there are also separate women's organizations in each party — the Democratic Women's Clubs and the National Federation of Republican Women.

Party workers also encourage people to vote by spearheading voter registration drives and offering services such as rides to the polls on election day. The effects of party efforts can be seen in the higher voter turnouts in cities where party organization is strong.

269

270

ENRICHMENT/EXTENSION

■ Have students collect a series of political cartoons that feature caricatures of one or both major political parties and ask them to prepare an analysis of differences in the way the parties are depicted. Students should examine the stereotypes used to portray the parties.

Section 1 Review Answers

1. Political parties run candidates for office.
2. Parties provide competent, experienced leaders for government office. Also, elected officials appoint or hire people from their own parties to administer policies; political parties organize Congress and state legislatures along party lines; party leaders set priorities and organize voting along party lines.
3. By holding debates, giving speeches, advertising, and distributing literature; through voter registration drives; and by taking people to the polls.

Critical thinking Most students may suggest that an opposition party serves a crucial role as a watchdog, as well as a source of alternative ideas. Some students may suggest that a system without an opposition party might work if the party in power were composed of various factions that could check one another yet work well together.

CLOSURE

● Have students write three "I learned . . ." statements to show what they learned in this section. Then have students read Section 2, noting how the two-party system functions.

In a democracy, political party organizations encourage people to take an active part in the day-to-day work of political campaigning and electioneering.

Simplifying political decisions

Loyalty to a party can make political decisions easier for voters. In a typical election, people are asked to choose among dozens of candidates. Many citizens unfortunately lack the time, ability, or interest to study thoroughly each candidate's qualifications and positions on issues. Most Americans, however, feel a tie with one of the major parties. By casting a vote for that party, voters can feel they have chosen candidates who share their attitudes on many issues. In 1908, Graham Wallas, a British political scientist, described this feeling in *Human Nature in Politics*:

> Something is required simpler and more permanent, something which can be loved and trusted, and which can be recognized at successive elections as being the same thing that was loved and trusted before; and a party is such a thing.

Loyalty to a party thus helps people identify and deal with the complex ideas and information involved in government.

It is important to realize that not all political parties fulfill all these functions. In the United States, only the two major parties carry out all of them. Many minor parties fulfill only a few. Even the major parties differ in how well they carry out these roles. Such differences help explain why one major party is often more successful than the other.

SECTION 1 REVIEW

Vocabulary and key terms

political party (268)   "loyal opposition" (268)
opposition party (268)   coalition (269)

For review

1. How are political parties different from interest groups? **4B**
2. What functions do political parties play in the government? **4B**
3. How do parties encourage participation in politics? **4B**

Critical thinking

EXAMINING BASIC PRINCIPLES Could a democracy function without a "loyal opposition"? Explain your answer. **6F**

270

SECTION 2

Two Parties Dominate American Politics

ACCESS The Main Ideas

1 What are the three types of party systems? *pages 271–272*

2 What barriers do third parties face in the American political system? *pages 272–273*

3 What roles have third parties played in American politics? *pages 273–275*

Throughout its history, American politics has been essentially a **two-party system**. This idea was never stated in a law or document, but it is basic to American government. Over the years many minor or third parties have formed in the United States. Some of these third parties have influenced policies and election results. Still, two major parties have remained dominant. How did the two-party system originate and why has it prevailed? What does it reveal about American politics?

1C

Party Systems

While the two-party system seems normal to Americans, it is not the most common political pattern in the world. Every nation's party system is unique, a part of its political culture. For simplicity, however, most countries can be classified as having one-party, multi-party, or two-party systems.

One-party systems

One-party systems are most typically found in nations with authoritarian governments. In such countries, the party in power *is*, in effect, the government. Only one party appears on the ballot, and the state tolerates no political opposition. Such one-party systems commonly exist where a party has gained power by force. This occurred in the Soviet Union after the Russian Revolution of 1917, and in Fascist Italy and Nazi Germany in the 1930's. Cuba and China today have one-party systems. One-party systems are often imposed in non-Communist countries after

a military government takes power. Examples of this situation include Iraq and Zaire. In monarchies such as Saudi Arabia or Kuwait, a royal family holds all political power.

A different sort of one-party system can develop in a country where elections are held but one party consistently wins. There, voters have a real choice among parties, but election contests are still one-sided. This type of one-party control occurs in Mexico, for example. Some American states have had similar situations, in which either Democrats or Republicans traditionally controlled the state.

Multi-party systems

Political systems with many rival parties are most common throughout the world. All the democracies in Western Europe, for example, have **multi-party systems**. France and Germany each have four major parties and several minor ones. Italy has ten. Multi-party systems typically are divided along sharp ideological lines, representing the range of opinions from "right" to "left." Parties also may be linked with different religious, regional, or social class groupings.

Some nations with multi-party systems, such as Sweden, Belgium, and Germany, have very stable governments, but most are unstable. Seldom can one party capture a majority of the votes. Usually the system is held together by fragile coalitions of parties, with frequent changes in the government.

The rare two-party system

Two-party systems have their roots in British politics and so are found almost exclusively in English-speaking countries. Only about a dozen nations have two-party systems, notably Great Britain, Canada, New Zealand, and the United States. Although minor parties form regularly in these democracies, two major parties generally dominate. The major parties in Canada are the Progressive Conservative and Liberal, in Britain, Labour and Conservative.

The United States has perhaps the strongest two-party system of all. Since 1800, two major

271

SECTION 2

Two Parties Dominate American Politics
(pp. 271–276)

Section Objectives

☐ identify the three types of party systems

☐ explain the barriers third parties face in the American political system

☐ describe the roles third parties have played in American politics

Vocabulary

two-party system, multi-party system, consensus, single-member district, proportional representation, at large

FOCUS

● Poll class members on the party affiliation (if any) of their parents. Write the results on the board. Then discuss the results with the class. If any parties other than Democratic or Republican receive any "votes," ask students to provide information about the third parties. If no third parties are mentioned, ask students to comment on the monopoly held by the two major parties.

Background: *Comparative Government* In Italy numerous parties compete for seats in the legislature. Parliament chooses the president, who appoints the premier. In the years since World War II, more than 40 premiers have been named to office.

The symbol 👥 denotes active participation strategies.

Activities are keyed for student abilities:

▲ = Basic

● = All Levels

■ = Average/Advanced

EXPLANATION

After students have read the section, you may want to consider the following activities:

Comparative Government

● CRITICAL THINKING Discuss with the class the differences among one-party, two-party, and multi-party systems. Focus discussion on reasons for the stability of the two-party system in the United States. Have students explain how each of the factors identified on pp. 272–273 has helped stabilize this system.

parties have accounted for over 90 percent of the popular vote in the United States. Since 1860, when both modern parties had formed, only Democrats and Republicans have been elected President. While minor parties have sometimes won strong electoral support, their successes have been short-lived. In fact, only Democrats or Republicans win national offices. For example, seventeen minor party candidates ran for President in 1988. Together, they accounted for less than one percent of the total vote.

2E

America's Two-Party System

Why does the United States have such a stable two-party system? The answer probably lies in a combination of factors that both created the system and gave it the strength to last.

Historical and cultural tradition

Modern political parties, which began in England in the 1600's, were part of the political heritage the American colonists brought with them. When the first American political organizations formed, they continued the two-party tradition and it soon became part of our political culture. As a result, American families help perpetuate the two-party system, teaching it as part of their children's political socialization. Most American children tend to identify with their parents' political party, learning early in life that their families are Republicans or Democrats. Comparatively few American children are socialized to be members of minor parties.

Agreement on basic ideas

Multi-party systems tend to develop where people's political views diverge greatly. By contrast, most Americans generally agree on basic principles of democratic government. Relatively few hold extreme radical or reactionary ideologies. Americans early on reached **consensus**, or general agreement, on fundamental issues such as freedom of speech, rule by law, and free enterprise. They are not likely to join a party that supports abolishing free speech, or setting up a dictatorship, or ending all private property.

There are, of course, differences — sometimes deep ones — among Americans' political beliefs. But the differences are not usually about

basic issues or goals but how they will be accomplished. For example, there is consensus among Americans on the fundamental idea of private ownership of businesses. Hence, both the Democratic and Republican parties support private enterprise and oppose government ownership of, for example, oil companies. Americans disagree, however, on secondary issues, such as how much businesses should be taxed, and the two parties also divide on this question. Democrats generally tend to favor higher taxes on businesses. Republicans, on the other hand, have generally favored lower taxes on business.

If our society became deeply divided on basic issues of government or economics, such as private ownership, then third parties advocating some form of public ownership, such as a Socialist party, would probably gain support. However, as long as Americans agree on such fundamental issues, strong third parties are less likely to develop.

Legal barriers for minor parties

Our two-party system has existed so long that laws and custom now ensure its stability. Minor parties face many legal barriers. First, it is extremely difficult for third parties to get on the ballot in most states. The names of Democratic and Republican candidates are automatically placed on state ballots, but those of third-party candidates are not. For example, Pennsylvania in 1972 required all third-party candidates to secure 36,000 signatures from registered voters within 21 days in order to have their names placed on the ballot. Likewise, in 1980, California law did not allow the name of John Anderson, Independent Party candidate for President, to appear on the ballot unless he could obtain a total of 101,300 signatures between the dates of June 3 and August 8.

Money is another obstacle to the success of third parties. Some states set high filing fees to enter an election. In Louisiana, for instance, all third-party candidates were once required to pay $5,000 filing fees. Most third parties simply do not have enough money to wage effective campaigns. Although recent federal laws make it possible for third-party candidates to secure matching federal funds, these laws still favor the major parties.

272

Check for Understanding
▲ *What are some of the legal obstacles facing minor parties?* (The need to collect signatures in order to be placed on the ballot, high filing fees, and "winner-take-all" voting rules.)

Independent candidate Ross Perot greets enthusiastic supporters at a 1992 campaign rally. Perot won 19 percent of the popular vote, the best showing by a third-party candidate since Theodore Roosevelt in 1912.

Patterns of voting

American voting patterns, set by law, cause the greatest problem for minor parties. Almost all elected public officials in the United States are chosen to represent the voters in one **single-member district**. That is, the one candidate who receives the most votes in his or her district is elected to office.

By contrast, most multi-party systems use an electoral system that is based on **proportional representation**. Several political party candidates are elected **at large** to represent a given area or district. Each party gets legislative seats in proportion to the votes it receives. For instance, one election area in Germany might be entitled to ten seats in the legislature. If Germany's leading party, the Christian Democrats, received 60 percent of the vote in this district, it would send six representatives to the legislature. The rest of the vote might be divided like this: Social Democrats, 20 percent (two people);

Free Democrats, 10 percent (one person); "Green" Party, 10 percent (one person).

Proportional representation has been tried in the United States. For example, in 1936 New York City switched to proportional representation. In 1945, the new system produced 14 Democrats, 3 Republicans, 2 Communists, 2 Liberals, and 2 American Labor Party aldermen. Alarmed by the success of minor parties, the city returned to the winner-take-all system. In the 1949 election, 24 Democrats and 1 Republican were elected.

4B, 4C

The Role of Third Parties

Despite the handicaps they face, minor parties do play important roles. Some parties serve as safety valves, giving people a legitimate outlet for their anger at "the system." Minor parties have often been sources of new political ideas and indicators of change. An increase in their

273

Politics

● Have students review pp. 273–275 and write a short essay explaining the following statement: *Third parties play an important role in the American political system.* Essays should describe third-party roles in American politics and explain how these roles contribute to the functioning of the democratic system.

♟ Cooperative Learning

● Have students work in groups to create a poster or chart illustrating several differences among one-party, two-party, and multi-party systems. Students might also include information on the circumstances in which the different systems develop and which nations around the world use each system.

support may indicate growing public concern over an issue. Minor parties, in fact, were the first to advocate such policies as the graduated income tax, child labor laws, antitrust laws, unemployment compensation, and woman suffrage. Major parties adopt these ideas as they see growing public support for them.

Third-party successes

Occasionally a third party makes a strong showing in a presidential election, usually because of a candidate's personal popularity or an issue that splits a major party. The Populist Party got 8.5 percent of the popular vote in 1892; Teddy Roosevelt's Bull Moose Party won 27.4 percent in 1912; Robert LaFollette's Progressive Party had 16.6 percent in 1924; and George Wallace (American Independent Party) received 13.5 percent in 1968. None, however, had much effect on the Electoral College voting.

Nevertheless, some third parties have acted as "spoilers" to prevent one of the major parties from winning. Certainly this was the case in 1912, when the votes given to Teddy Roosevelt's Bull Moose Party prevented Republican William Howard Taft from winning re-election. The vote for Wallace in 1968 cut into Democrat Hubert Humphrey's support.

Parties based on issues

Most minor political parties in the United States have formed in support of social, moral, or economic issues. Before the Civil War, for instance, a number of antislavery parties formed, such as the Liberty (1840–1848) and Free Soil parties (1848–1854). The American or "Know-Nothing" Party (1856) opposed the immigration of "foreigners," particularly Irish Catholics. Most parties focused on a single issue are short-lived. An exception is the Prohibition Party, which opposes alcoholic beverages. Founded in 1869, it has run a presidential candidate in every election since then. The party's only real success was the ratification in 1919 of the Eighteenth Amendment to the Constitution (later repealed).

Economic crises have spurred numerous regional protest parties, some of which have had a lasting impact on public policy. For example, the Greenback Party (1876–1884) called for the issuance of paper money, the end of the gold standard, and the graduated income tax. The Populists (1892–1908) called for government ownership of railroads and utilities, a graduated income tax, and the free coinage of silver. Some Populist ideas were adopted by the Democrats; in 1896 both Populists and Democrats named William Jennings Bryan as their candidate for President.

Ideological parties

Parties based on an ideology (rather than current issues) advocate far-reaching plans for change. In American politics, ideological parties may represent either end of the ideological spectrum but tend to be on the left.

Parties on the far left advocate varying degrees of socialism and communism. The Socialist Party supports collective ownership of basic industries but (like Western European Socialist parties) works through democratic election processes. Socialist candidates ran for President regularly from 1912 until the 1950's and have been the largest vote-getters among minor-party candidates. The Socialist Labor Party also has run presidential candidates in most 20th-century elections, though it has gained fewer votes. The Communist Party advocates the overthrow of capitalism by force if necessary. Communist candidates for President have never gathered more than a few thousand popular votes out of millions cast.

Parties on the far right include the Libertarians (founded in 1971), who stress individualism and an end to government intervention in citizens' lives. At the worst extreme, the American Nazi Party advocates the policies practiced by Adolf Hitler.

Splinter parties

Some minor parties form when disagreements within a major party become so serious that a group splits off, or "splinters." Often such a party is formed around a popular hero who fails to win the major party's nomination. Two notable Republican Party spin-offs were Teddy Roosevelt's Bull Moose Party of 1912 and Robert LaFollette's Progressive Party of 1924. The Democratic Party has split twice over the issues of states' rights and desegregation: the States' Rights Democratic (Dixiecrat) Party of 1948, and the American Independent Party of George Wallace in 1968. A further Democratic split in 1948 came when party liberals followed Henry A. Wallace to form the Progressive Party.

274

Critical Thinking

■ *Why is the life span of a third party not a good indicator of its success?* (Some third parties may find their ideas co-opted by the major parties, a development that could destroy the minor party yet promote that party's long-term agenda.)

Check for Understanding

● *How do parties based on issues differ from parties based on an ideology?*

(Single-issue groups concentrate on one specific item, while ideological groups consider a broad agenda.)

Figure 10-1 SIGNIFICANT THIRD PARTIES IN AMERICAN POLITICS   4B

PARTY	GOALS
Liberty (1840–1848)	Abolition of slavery
Free Soil (1848–1854)	No extension of slavery into newly acquired territories, free homesteads for settlers, easier immigration process
American or "Know Nothing" (1856)	Curtailed immigration, exclusion of Catholics and foreigners from public office, 21-year residency requirement for citizenship
Constitutional Union (1860)	Preservation of the Constitution and the Union of the states
Prohibition (1872–present)	Prohibition of the production, sale, and use of alcoholic beverages
Greenback (1876–1884)	Increased money supply, income tax, eight-hour work day, women's suffrage
Socialist Labor (1892–present)	Worker control of production
People's or "Populist" (1892–1908)	Increased money supply (free silver), greater government regulation of business, graduated income tax, direct election of senators
Socialist (1901–present)	Collective ownership of the means of production, social security, welfare legislation
Roosevelt Progressive or "Bull Moose" (1912)	Government anti-trust action, minimum wage standards, women's suffrage
Communist (1924–present)	Overthrow of capitalism, government controlled by the working class
LaFollette Progressive (1924)	Breakup of corporate monopolies and trusts, public control of the nation's resources, reduced income taxes, farm relief
States' Rights Democratic or "Dixiecrat" (1948)	Rejection of Democrats' civil rights program
Henry Wallace Progressive (1948–1952)	Reversal of Truman's anti-Communist policies, strengthening of civil rights laws
American Independent (1968–present)	Opposition to civil rights legislation, restoration of states' rights
Libertarian (1971–present)	Increased individual liberties, limited government, private enterprise, neutral foreign policy

Finally, some minor parties successfully establish a base in a single state and may elect members of Congress. The most successful one-state parties are the Conservative Party and the Liberal Party in New York and the Farmer-Labor Party in Minnesota. Other one-state parties have included the Progressive Party in Wisconsin (which became national in the 1924 presidential election) and La Raza Unida, organized by Chicanos in Texas and California.

275

Figure 10–1

■ *Which goals once held by a third party have now been achieved?* (Slavery abolished, women's suffrage, the eight-hour work day, greater government control of business, graduated income tax, minimum wage, direct election of senators, social security, welfare legislation, strengthening of civil rights laws.)

GUIDED/INDEPENDENT PRACTICE

● Have students write an essay comparing the American two-party system with both one-party and multi-party systems. *What advantages do the other systems have? What disadvantages? Are there ways you think the two-party system could be improved? How?*

RETEACHING/CORRECTIVES

▲ Have students identify three reasons why third parties have formed in the United States and then identify at least three functions that third parties might serve in a democracy.

ENRICHMENT/EXTENSION

■ Have students choose an existing third party and research its history, its level and sources of support, and its plans for the future. Students should report their findings to the class.

Section 2 Review Answers
1. **(a)** One-party.
(b) Multi-party.
2. **(a)** The colonists brought the tradition from England to America. **(b)** Children identify with their parents' political party.
(c) It eliminates the demand for third parties and frees the two parties to focus on secondary issues.

The symbol 👥 denotes active participation strategies.

Activities are keyed for student abilities:
▲ = Basic
● = All Levels
■ = Average/Advanced

3. Legal barriers to getting on the ballot, high campaign costs and, sometimes, filing fees; single-member election districts.
4. A split from a major party; social, moral, or economic issues.

Critical thinking Students should recognize that third parties are sources of alternative ideas, indicators of public concern over an issue, and outlets for discontented political groups.

CLOSURE

● Review the Section 2 vocabulary with students to help reinforce key concepts from the section. Then have students read Section 3, noting the origins of today's Democratic and Republican parties.

SECTION 3

Politics Are Part of American History
(pp. 276–280)

Section Objectives

☐ describe how political parties developed

☐ explain how the Civil War and the Great Depression affected party politics

👀 FOCUS

● Ask each student to write on the board the name of a famous American political leader from the 1700's, 1800's, or 1900's. Then have students return to the board and write next to that name the person's party affiliation if students know it.

SECTION 2 REVIEW

Vocabulary and key terms

two-party system (271)
multi-party system (271)
consensus (272)
single-member district (273)

proportional representation (273)
at large (273)

For review

1. Which party system is most common in (a) authoritarian states? (b) other democratic nations of the world? **1C**

2. How is the two-party system strengthened by (a) American history? (b) family background? (c) general agreement on basic principles? **4C**

3. What obstacles do most minor political parties face? **4C**

4. What kinds of issues have led to the founding of most minor parties? **4C**

Critical thinking

FORMING AN OPINION Even though third parties almost never win national offices in the United States, are they necessary and helpful in a democracy? Why or why not? **8C**

SECTION 3

1D, 2A, 2C, 2E, 8G

Politics Are Part of American History

ACCESS The Main Ideas

1 How did America's political parties develop? *pages 276–278*

2 How did the Civil War and the Great Depression affect party politics? *pages 278–280*

Do you think that American political parties are older or newer than those in the rest of the world? Since the United States is a relatively young country, we might think that its political parties are also relatively new. Actually, they are among the oldest. In fact the Democratic Party, founded in 1828, may be the world's oldest party. Both the Democratic and Republican parties have changed greatly over time.
2A, 2C, 2E

Early Political Rivalries

American statesmen at the time of the Constitution regarded a political party as nothing more than a large "faction," or interest group. Factions were thought to be destructive to national unity. Prominent statesmen such as Benjamin Franklin, Madison, and John Adams openly expressed their disdain for political parties.

276

The Federalist Party

Despite these leaders' fears, the emergence of political parties was unavoidable. Deep rivalries and economic problems in the new nation made it difficult for President Washington and the first Congress to establish a coherent policy. Washington's personal dignity, however, made him unwilling to get involved in political squabbles. He therefore gave the Secretary of the Treasury, Alexander Hamilton, the job of building a coalition among the factions.

The coalition that Hamilton built became America's first political party — the *Federalists.* (The name "Federalists" had been used earlier for those who supported the Constitution.) The Federalists favored a strong central government. They therefore advocated interpreting the Constitution broadly, to allow high tariffs (to protect American shipping and manufacturing) and the creation of a national bank. Support for the Federalist party came largely from New England merchants and manufacturers.

The Democratic-Republicans

Opponents of Hamilton's plans found a natural leader in Thomas Jefferson, Washington's Secretary of State. His outlook and political

Background: *Constitutional Heritage* Loose constructionists, such as the Federalists, favor a broad interpretation of the Constitution (usually in order to expand the powers of the federal government). Strict constructionists, such as the Democratic-Republicans, favor a literal interpretation of the document and often cite "the intent of the framers" to support their interpretations.

philosophy had always been the opposite of Hamilton's. Jefferson, Madison, and their supporters became the *Democratic-Republican* Party. It was a coalition of small farmers, laborers, Western pioneers, and Southern planters. Like Jefferson himself, the Democratic-Republicans feared a strong central government. They favored a strict interpretation of the Constitution, called for low tariffs, and opposed the creation of a national bank.

The election of 1796

The first heated contest between the newly formed parties was the presidential election of 1796. Washington chose to retire from politics, and John Adams, the Federalist candidate, defeated Jefferson by only three electoral votes. Adams, however, was the only Federalist President. Federalist policies, Adams's unpopularity, and strong organization by Jefferson and Madison brought a Democratic-Republican victory in the bitterly fought election of 1800. This began a period of Democratic-Republican domination. Jefferson won again in 1804, followed by Madison (1808 and 1812) and James Monroe (1816).

The "Era of Good Feelings"

James Monroe's election in 1816 began what one Boston newspaper called the "Era of Good Feelings." The Federalist Party, whose support had dwindled to New England, nominated its last presidential candidate in 1816, then died out. The Democratic-Republicans were now essentially the only national political party. In 1820, Monroe ran unopposed. Thus, the Era of Good Feelings was a short, tranquil period, characterized by personal, rather than party, politics.

Whigs and Democrats

Regional loyalties and personality differences soon brought a new period of party politics. In the election of 1824, none of the presidential candidates ran under a party label, but each was supported by one state or region. Andrew Jackson won the popular vote, gaining votes from nearly every region. John Quincy Adams, whose support was mainly in New England, was second. But since none of the four candidates had a majority of votes in the Electoral College, the election was decided in the House of Representatives, and Adams became President. A determined Jackson then set about to build a new

PRIMARY SOURCE

LANDMARKS in LIBERTY

Jefferson's Inaugural Address (1801)

Thomas Jefferson, leader of the emerging Democratic-Republican Party, was elected to his first term as President amidst controversy in 1801. In his inaugural address, given on March 4, 1801, he urged citizens to disregard party differences that had disrupted the election and to unite behind the democratic principles common to all Americans.

❝ During the contest of opinion through which we have passed, the animation of discussions and of exertions has sometimes worn an aspect which might impose on strangers unused to think freely and to speak and write what they think; but this being now decided by the voice of the nation, . . . all will, of course, arrange themselves under the will of the law. . . . All, too, will bear in mind this sacred principle, that though the will of the majority is in all cases to prevail, that will to be rightful must be reasonable. . . . Let us, then, fellow-citizens, unite with one heart and one mind. . . . We are all Republicans, we are all Federalists. . . .

You should understand what I deem the essential principle of our government. . . . Equal and exact justice to all men . . . ; peace, commerce, and honest friendship with all nations . . . ; the support of the State governments in all their rights . . . ; a jealous care of the right of election by the people . . . ; freedom of religion; freedom of the press, and freedom of person. . . . ❞

1. What aspects of American politics did Jefferson think might surprise someone from another country?
2. What does Jefferson mean by "We are all Republicans, we are all Federalists"?
3. What limitations does Jefferson put on majority rule?

277

Have students check the answers on the board for accuracy. Then, with the class, try to explain why the party affiliation was known in some cases but not known in others. **Was party affiliation known only for more recent political figures? Did some of the earlier political figures belong to parties no longer in existence? Is the notoriety of some of these figures not related to their party affiliation?** (For example, James Madison is remembered more for his prominent role in the Constitutional Convention than for his accomplishments as a Democratic-Republican President.)

EXPLANATION

After students have read the section, you may want to consider the following activities:

Politics

▲ Write the following statement from p. 279 on the board: "The Great Depression of the 1930's, like the Civil War, drastically changed the balance between parties." Ask students to write a short essay during the class period explaining this statement and giving examples from the text to support it. You may prefer to have some students outline the material.

Landmarks in Liberty Answers

1. Jefferson thought that some people might be surprised by Americans' freedom to speak and write openly and by the liveliness of debates.

2. He means that all Americans are citizens of one nation and, despite political differences, share the goals of fair government and protection of the rights of the individual.

3. He says that majority rule must not violate the rights of the minority; the law must protect the majority and minority equally.

The symbol ⚏ denotes active participation strategies.

Activities are keyed for student abilities:
▲ = Basic
● = All Levels
■ = Average/Advanced

Civic Participation

● Invite a Democratic or Republican candidate or party official to address the class. Students may wish to prepare questions beforehand, such as the speaker's view of the local balance between the two parties and the history of party competition in your area.

Politics

● In Section 1, students learned that an important role of American political parties has been to reduce conflict through the building of coalitions. This section provides several examples of the ways in which new political parties were created or strengthened through consensus and coalition building. Have students identify such examples.

Cooperative Learning

● Divide the class into groups. Each group should predict the result of an upcoming election. Groups should list at least four advantages and disadvantages that each candidate or party will have going into the election and analyze which factors will be decisive. Groups should take into account recent political trends and public opinion.

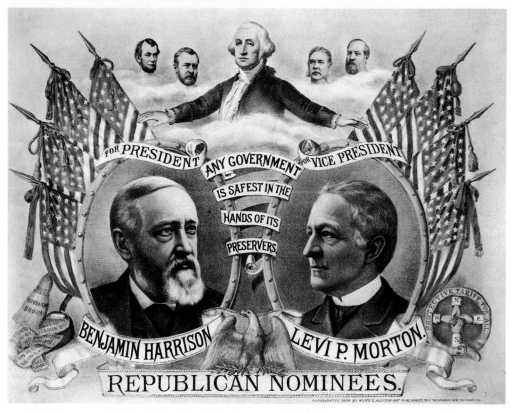

A Republican Party poster from the 1888 presidential election calls on patriotic symbols and past national heroes to support its platform.

coalition. By the election of 1828, the Democratic-Republicans had splintered into two camps — the Democrats and the Whigs.

The "new" Democrats were strongest in the South and West, especially among slave owners, small farmers, and those who owed money. As frontier territories became states, men without property gained the vote. Much of this new popular support went to Andrew Jackson, who won the presidency in 1828 and 1832. This coalition remained the dominant political force until the Civil War.

Jackson's opponents, who referred to him as "King Andrew," took the name "Whigs." (In England, the Whigs were the party that opposed the king's power.) Whig leaders included John Quincy Adams, Daniel Webster, and Henry Clay.

278

The party was a strange, often contradictory, mixture of groups. It included, for example, eastern bankers, southern plantation owners, and anti-slavery forces. Although the Whigs were not as cohesive as the Democrats, they were able to elect two Presidents, William Henry Harrison (1840) and Zachary Taylor (1848).

2E

Modern Political Parties

The Republican Party

In the years leading up to the Civil War, the two major parties, the Democrats and the Whigs, were torn apart by the intense issues of slavery and sectionalism. Many small political parties formed and soon disappeared.

Background: *Cultural Literacy* The Whig Party was formally organized in 1834. Before 1834, Whigs were called *National Republicans*.

Background: *History* Both Whig Presidents, Harrison and Taylor, died in office and were succeeded by their Vice Presidents, John Tyler and Millard Fillmore, respectively.

In 1854, a new coalition of antislavery groups formed the Republican Party. Republicans quickly drew strength, especially in the North and West, and swept the 1854 congressional elections. The Republican candidate, Western hero John C. Frémont, was a close second in the 1856 election. In 1860 the Republican Abraham Lincoln defeated rival candidates from the badly split Democrats and the Constitutional Union Party (mostly former Whigs).

A new two-party system

In the later 1800's, the deep emotional scars left by the Civil War were reflected in the development of a new two-party system. For the most part, northern supporters in the Civil War became Republicans, while backers of the South became Democrats. Many states became virtually one-party states. Georgia, South Carolina, Louisiana, and other southern states became the "solid South," voting overwhelmingly for Democratic candidates. Ohio, Wisconsin, and other northern states identified, though not quite as "solidly," with the Republican Party. Because of this regional split, many short-lived third parties surfaced periodically. The Republican Party nevertheless dominated national politics. Their new coalition consisted of farmers, bankers, business owners, former Union soldiers, and blacks who now had the right to vote.

With some minor changes, this Republican coalition held firm for many years. About 1880, political speakers began to refer to it as the "Grand Old Party" or "Gallant Old Party," soon shortened to "GOP." From 1860 until 1932, the GOP captured the White House in all but four elections. Democrat Grover Cleveland won in 1884 and again in 1892. Twenty years later, a badly split Republican Party allowed Woodrow Wilson victories in 1912 and 1916. After Wilson, however, the Republicans regained control, electing Warren G. Harding (1920), Calvin Coolidge (1924), and Herbert Hoover (1928).

The Depression and the New Deal

The Great Depression of the 1930's, like the Civil War, drastically changed the balance between parties. This time it was the Democratic Party that became dominant. In 1933, a time of deep economic trouble, Democrat Franklin D. Roosevelt became President. Under Roosevelt's astute leadership, the Democrats promised Amer-

icans a "New Deal." The major theme of Roosevelt's policies was that government must assume a more active role in regulating the economy and providing badly needed jobs and money. The program drew votes not only from those hard-hit economically but also from a mix of ethnic groups, Catholic and Jewish voters, intellectuals, and many black voters.

This New Deal coalition, the backbone of the Democratic Party, dominated national politics for many years. Roosevelt went on to win three more elections (1936, 1940, and 1944), and his Democratic successor, Harry S Truman, won in 1948. In 1952 and 1956, Dwight Eisenhower, a well-known war hero, snapped the Democrats'

Figure 10–2 HISTORY OF MAJOR POLITICAL PARTIES Though party names have changed, there have been two major political parties throughout U.S. history.

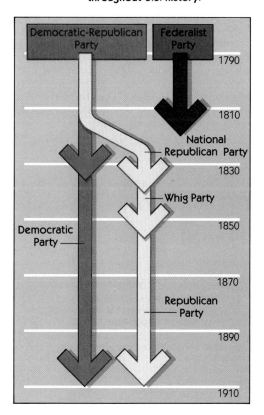

279

GUIDED/INDEPENDENT PRACTICE

● Have students create a chart summarizing the differences between the Federalists and the Democratic-Republicans. Charts should also indicate who were each party's leaders and who were its major supporters.

RETEACHING/CORRECTIVES

▲ Have students construct a time line, containing at least six entries, that charts the development of American political parties.

You may also want to use **Transparency 26,** which identifies differences between Republicans and Federalists.

ENRICHMENT/EXTENSION

■ Have students research and report on the history of party politics in your state. *Has one party traditionally dominated? How did that party come to power and how has it kept power? Is the situation changing at the moment? Why or why not?*

Figure 10–2
▲ *Which party was the common ancestor of today's Democratic and Republican parties?* (The Democratic-Republican Party.)

Background: *History* The Republican Party split in 1912 when Theodore Roosevelt wanted a third term as President but was not nominated at the Republican convention. He responded by forming a third party. (See p. 274 and Figure 10-1, p. 275.)

The symbol ⅱ denotes active participation strategies.

Activities are keyed for student abilities:
  ▲ = Basic
  ● = All Levels
  ■ = Average/Advanced

Section 3 Review Answers

1. Federalists, Alexander Hamilton; Democratic-Republicans, Thomas Jefferson and James Madison.

2. **(a)** Jefferson. **(b)** Hamilton.

3. **(a)** Democrats and Whigs. **(b)** Democrats.

4. **(a)** Slavery. **(b)** Abraham Lincoln.

5. **(a)** People in economic difficulty, intellectuals, Catholics, Jews, blacks, and other ethnic groups. **(b)** The federal government should increase its regulation of the economy, and thus provide jobs and money.

Critical thinking Students should contrast the regional differences highlighted by the Civil War with the national impact of the Depression and the government's response to it.

CLOSURE

● Remind students of the pre-reading objectives at the beginning of the section. Pose one or all of these questions again. Then have students read Section 4, noting recent trends in popular support for political parties.

SECTION 4

How Do Democrats and Republicans Differ? *(pp. 280-287)*

Section Objectives

☐ describe the major similarities and differences between the Democratic Party and the Republican Party

☐ identify recent trends in party politics

280

victory streak. Eisenhower's popularity, however, did not carry over to his Republican Party. With the exception of two years, the Democrats maintained control of both houses of Congress. In 1960, the voters turned back to the Democrats, electing John F. Kennedy. Following Kennedy's assassination, Democrat Lyndon Johnson succeeded to the presidency and was elected in his own right in 1964.

Recent presidential contests

Republican Richard Nixon scored election victories in 1968 and 1972, but resigned in 1974 following Watergate. Nixon's successor, Gerald R. Ford, lost the 1976 election to Democrat Jimmy Carter. Carter was defeated by Republican Ronald Reagan in 1980. That same year, the Republicans gained control of the Senate. Reagan easily won re-election in 1984. In 1986, the Democrats won back the Senate and maintained control of the House.

In the 1988 presidential election, Republican George Bush handily defeated Democrat Michael Dukakis. In 1992 Democrat Bill Clinton broke the twelve-year Republican hold on the presidency by defeating Bush and independent candidate Ross Perot. Clinton defeated Bush by six percentage points in the popular vote tally. The Democrats also maintained their majority in both houses of Congress. In 1994, the Republicans gained control of both houses for the first time since the 1950's.

SECTION 3 REVIEW

Vocabulary and key terms

Federalists (276)

Democratic-Republicans (276)

Whigs (278)

Democrats (278)

Republicans (278)

"solid South" (279)

For review

1. Name the two parties in the 1796 election and their leaders. **2E**

2. Which of the party leaders in 1796 favored (a) a weak central government? (b) high tariffs? **2E**

3. (a) Which two parties were active between 1828 and the Civil War? (b) Which party was dominant? **2E**

4. (a) What issue led to the founding of the Republican Party? (b) Who was the first Republican to win the presidency? **2E**

5. (a) What groups were part of the Democratic "New Deal coalition"? (b) What was the main theme of New Deal policies? **2E**

Critical thinking

ANALYZING CAUSE AND EFFECT Why did the Civil War drastically change party politics? How would you compare these changes with those resulting from the Depression? **8G**

2E, 4B, 4C, 5B, 8A, 8G

SECTION 4 · How Do Democrats and Republicans Differ?

ACCESS **The Main Ideas**

1 What are the major similarities and differences between the Democratic Party and the Republican Party?

pages 280–285

2 What are some recent tends in party politics?

pages 285–287

A newcomer to American politics might ask, "What is the difference between Democrats and Republicans?" There is no simple answer. A Republican might characterize the Democrats as the "party of high taxes." Likewise, a loyal Democrat might describe the Republicans as the "party of the rich."

Such generalities, however, leave much out. There are real differences between the two parties, but there are also many areas of similarity. This chapter will look at both, as well as recent trends in party politics.

280

4B, 5C

Party Similarities

The strength of the American two-party system rests largely on qualities that the two major parties share. Both parties are (1) broad-based in support, (2) **centrist**, or middle-of-the-road, in ideology, and (3) very decentralized in organization. These shared qualities make the Democratic and Republican parties a rarity among the world's political parties.

Broad-based support

The two major American parties have perhaps the most broadly based support of any political parties in democratic nations. Any person is welcome to join either party just by declaring his or her choice. Neither membership dues nor formal approval by the organization is needed for a person to become a Democrat or a Republican.

Both parties therefore draw support from many groups. For instance, both Democratic and Republican parties contain wealthy people, middle-income people, and poor people.

The political center

Most Americans describe themselves as being somewhere between liberal and conservative on the ideological spectrum. Only a few lean to the far right or far left. Politicians realize that they must appeal to this large middle ground if they expect to win elections. Both major parties, therefore, are centrist in ideology.

While the parties as a whole are in the political center, they still allow room for individual viewpoints. Both parties provide an umbrella for liberals and conservatives. One of these viewpoints may even dominate a party for a time. Usually, though, politicians with views far out of the mainstream find a home in a minor party.

One could say therefore that major American political parties — like most Americans — are "less ideological" than parties in other countries. They can be termed "broker parties." (A broker is someone who acts as a go-between in a business deal.) Broker parties are more concerned with gaining votes than with maintaining rigid ideologies. They will alter their policies to build a winning coalition.

In contrast, some political parties are highly ideological, firmly devoted to a system of political attitudes. They seek converts or followers more than votes, and so are termed "missionary parties." Missionary parties — such as the Communist Party or the Nazi Party — do, of

Over the past five decades, voter affiliation with Independent political candidates has grown steadily. Here, Connecticut's Independent Governor, Lowell P. Weicker Jr., and Lieutenant Governor Eunice Groark celebrate their victory over Democratic and Republican candidates in November 1990.

Check for Understanding

▲ *How do missionary parties differ from broker parties?* (If the missionary party's ideology is unpopular, it will try to persuade voters to change their attitudes. It will not change its ideology.)

Vocabulary

centrist, national committee, nominating convention, platform, straight party ticket, split ticket, independent, patronage, merit employment

👥 FOCUS

● Ask students to raise their hands if they agree with the following statement: *From the standpoint of the average citizen, it really makes no difference which political party is in power.* Tell those who raised their hands that some Americans share their view, and ask them to explain their position.

Then have students list on the board some major policy issues in the nation today, such as civil rights, environmental protection, abortion, taxation, and defense. Ask students whether (and how) the two major parties differ in these areas. (You may want to use Figure 10–4 on p. 285 as the basis for such a comparison.)

If there are significant differences between the two parties on important issues, why do many people still believe that it makes no difference which party is in power? (Possible answers include the belief that neither party can achieve its goals in any major policy area, and the belief that compromises during the lawmaking process blur differences between the parties.)

The symbol 👥 denotes active participation strategies.

Activities are keyed for student abilities:
▲ = Basic
● = All Levels
■ = Average/Advanced

course, desire votes. But a missionary party will not alter its ideology just to get more votes.

Decentralized party organization

Parties can also be classified according to the way authority is distributed. In Great Britain, for example, the Conservative and Labour parties are both highly centralized. The national party organizations keep tight control over the local agencies. A local politician who ignores the party leadership is likely to lose the party's nomination at the next election.

The United States' two major parties, by contrast, are perhaps the most decentralized in the world. Although both parties choose national committees and maintain national headquarters, state and local party officials have a great deal of independence and freedom of action.

As Figure 10–3 shows, the parties are formally organized in pyramid style. On paper, this organization seems neat and orderly, giving the national party organizations clear lines of authority over the state and local organizations. In practice, however, the three levels of party organization often operate independently of one another. In a sense, there is not just one Democratic Party and one Republican Party. There are really fifty Democratic and fifty Republican parties, one in each state.

NATIONAL PARTY ORGANIZATION Each party has two principal bodies — the national committee and the national nominating convention.

The **national committee** provides continuing leadership and direction between elections. It is headed by a chairperson, who is selected by the party's candidate for President and then ap-

Figure 10–3 POLITICAL PARTY ORGANIZATION National political parties are organized in a pyramid form, with the national officers at the top and the voters at the base. 4B

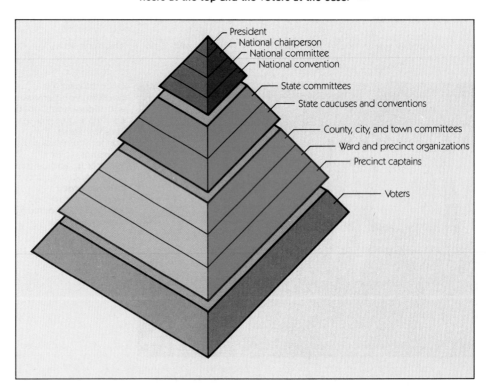

- President
- National chairperson
- National committee
- National convention
- State committees
- State caucuses and conventions
- County, city, and town committees
- Ward and precinct organizations
- Precinct captains
- Voters

Figure 10–3

■ *Why is the party organization presented in the shape of a pyramid rather than a cube?* (The pyramid shape reflects the fact that there are many more people involved in the lower levels of the party than the higher levels.)

proved by the national committee. As the national committees meet just twice a year, everyday details of party business are left to the chairperson and his or her staff in the Washington, D.C., office. The national committee's main responsibility is choosing a convention site and planning the national **nominating convention**.

National conventions are a good illustration of party decentralization. Although they can generate excitement and popular support, they have little real power. They select only two candidates — President and Vice President. Candidates for Congress and state governorships are all selected by state party organizations or statewide primaries. If the national leaders dislike their party's state or local candidates, they are usually helpless to do anything about it. Moreover, neither national party organization can effectively compel members to follow its party **platform** — the statement of goals and principles adopted at the national convention.

After the convention, the national committees must raise funds, promote the party, and above all, help elect the party's candidate for President. Both parties maintain congressional and senatorial campaign committees to help re-elect incumbents to Congress and fill seats of retiring members. In recent years, the national committees also have helped state and local candidates with training, legal assistance, and fund-raising.

STATE PARTY COMMITTEES The major party organization in each of the fifty states is the state committee or state central committee, which enjoys a great deal of independence from the national organization. Because state organizations are governed by state law, their structures vary.

Most state committees are made up of equal numbers of men and women chosen from the local party organizations. Like any political organization, they spend time on fund-raising and promoting the party. On a statewide level, their major responsibilities include drafting the state party platforms, adopting by-laws and party emblems, apportioning delegates to the state party conventions, and preparing for state election campaigns. The state committees work with local party groups, advising local candidates and coordinating local committee activities. They also choose representatives to the national party convention.

LOCAL PARTY ORGANIZATIONS At the base of the party "pyramid" are thousands of local party organizations. These local groups vary both in name and in function. Typically, there is a party committee for each election unit — county, city, township, ward, and precinct. Some of these grassroots committees are well organized and operate year-round. Many are inactive and poorly financed, and come to life only just before elections.

Local committees are busiest in their own home territory. There they recruit local party candidates, organize political campaigns and rallies, and raise funds. Staffed mainly by volunteers, local party organizations canvass voters and conduct voter registration drives.

4B

Party Differences

What, then, are the differences between the two major parties? Comparing the Democrats and Republicans, Governor George Wallace of Alabama once remarked, "There's not a dime's worth of difference between them." It is true that both parties are broadly based, ideologically middle-of-the-road, and highly decentralized in organization. There *are,* however, major differences between Democrats and Republicans.

Electoral support

While both Democrats and Republicans draw support from virtually every group in America, certain people are more likely to support one or the other party. For instance, Democrats have generally drawn support from the "New Deal coalition," including organized labor, Catholics, Jews, people in the South and Northeast, residents of urban areas, and those with less education. Strong Democratic support also has come from blacks and ethnic groups, including Puerto Ricans and Americans of Mexican, Irish, and Slavic descent. This varied mixture once led humorist Will Rogers to joke, "I don't belong to any organized political party; I'm a Democrat."

Republicans, on the other hand, tend to draw more support than Democrats from business and professional groups; Protestants; people in the West and Midwest and parts of New England; residents of suburbs, small towns, and rural areas; and persons with more education. In

283

Background: *History*
The term "New Deal coalition" originated during the administration of Franklin Roosevelt.

ᵛᵛ Politics
▲ Make a three-column table on the board, labeling the columns *Political Party, Electoral Support,* and *Policy Differences*. In the first column list the Democratic and Republican parties. Have students complete the table by adding (1) the groups within society that have traditionally supported each party, and (2) the ways in which the two parties differ in terms of their general view of the role of government and their approach to specific issues.
● CRITICAL THINKING When the table is completed, have the class note relationships between the groups supporting each party and the party's positions on policy issues.

The symbol ᵛᵛ denotes active participation strategies.

Activities are keyed for student abilities:
▲ = Basic
● = All Levels
■ = Average/Advanced

Civic Participation

■ CRITICAL THINKING Have students speculate about the long-term effects of the decline in support for the two major political parties. **What might be the effects on the two-party system of this decline?** (Third parties might gain strength; the efficiency of government might suffer as party discipline weakened.) **Would it benefit or harm the American political system?** (Students should support their views.)

ethnic background, Republicans are more commonly white persons of northwest European heritage (sometimes termed "WASPs," or "White Anglo-Saxon Protestants"). Republicans in general, then, tend to be somewhat more alike and financially better-off than Democrats.

It is essential to remember that these are generalizations. Many Americans do not fit these traditional partisan "profiles." Not all laborers, Catholics, or southerners are Democrats, and not all business people, Protestants, or Midwesterners are Republicans.

Moreover, these generalizations are on the national level. Other differences exist in specific states. For example, most states in the South are considered strongly Democratic, because Democrats control most state government offices. Yet southern voters overwhelmingly chose Republican presidential candidates in 1972, 1980, 1984, and 1988.

Policy differences

Clear differences exist between Democrats and Republicans over the direction of public policy. The central issue is whether private activity or government activity can be used most effectively to solve the nation's problems. Democrats tend to favor government action, while Republicans usually lean toward private action. Specific differences can be seen in several areas:

AGRICULTURE Democrats have favored greater agricultural supports (for example, crop insurance, parity payments) than Republicans.

ECONOMIC POLICY Republicans have favored less government spending and fewer taxes as ways to stimulate the economy. Democrats have advocated increased government spending to stimulate the economy. For Republicans, inflation is the nation's most serious economic problem; for Democrats, unemployment.

EDUCATION Democrats have tended to favor greater federal aid to education. Republicans have maintained that state and local governments should be responsible for education.

LABOR Democrats have favored increasing minimum wage laws and other policies that benefit labor. Republicans have generally opposed such policies as being harmful to business.

BUSINESS Republicans have favored lower corporate taxes and fewer government regulations on business. Democrats have favored increased corporate taxes and greater regulation of business.

SOCIAL PROGRAMS Democrats have been more likely to launch new social programs, such as social security, Medicare, food stamps, or public housing programs. Democrats have argued that government must spend more to help those who cannot help themselves. Republicans have opposed spending for such programs, urging the use of incentives to get people away from government support.

ENERGY Republicans have stressed reliance on supply and demand to control energy use. They feel that profits should be the incentive to determine the price and production of scarce resources. Democrats have favored greater regulation of energy sources and increased spending for alternative sources of energy, such as solar energy and synthetic fuels.

These, too, are only generalizations. They do not hold true for every Democrat or every Republican. Moreover, party policies can change. For example, Republicans have historically favored higher taxes on foreign imports than have Democrats. In recent years, however, these positions have generally been reversed. Because of competition from cheap foreign labor, most Democrats now feel that higher import tariffs are needed to protect American workers.

Party platforms

Perhaps the best indicators of the policy differences between Democrats and Republicans are their party platforms. This document, which summarizes a party's principles and goals, comprises many *planks,* or statements of position on specific issues. Figure 10–4 shows some of the differences between planks in the 1992 Democratic and Republican platforms.

Many people think that platforms are vague, meaningless documents, part of the show at a national party convention. Harry Truman, however, once said, "To me party platforms are contracts with the people." This may be a truer picture. For example, one political scientist conducted a study of both parties' platforms from 1968 to 1978. Of the 1,795 planks in their platforms, both parties kept their promises about three-fourths of the time. There *is* more than "a dime's worth of difference" between the two major parties.

284

Figure 10–4 COMPARISON OF THE 1992 DEMOCRATIC AND REPUBLICAN PLATFORMS

	DEMOCRATIC PARTY	REPUBLICAN PARTY
AIDS	• Supports targeted prevention and education campaigns • Promises increased research, and supports speeding-up of the drug-approval process	• Promotes education stressing marital fidelity, abstinence, and a drug-free lifestyle • Encourages research and speeding-up of the drug-approval process
Environment	• Calls for protection of forests and wetlands • Opposes new oil, gas, and mineral exploration	• Promotes mining, oil and gas exploration, and other economic uses of public lands in ways compatible with conservation
Health Care	• Supports giving all Americans universal access to health care	• Opposes government control of health care
Taxes	• Favors higher taxes on the wealthiest Americans	• Opposes any attempt to increase taxes
Women	• Supports an Equal Rights Amendment to the Constitution • Backs a national law to protect a woman's abortion rights	• Asserts a commitment to the rights of women; does not mention the Equal Rights Amendment • Opposes public funds for abortion • Supports a constitutional amendment banning abortion

Trends in Party Politics

Americans sometimes seem to have a "love-hate" relationship with party politics. On the one hand, political parties are necessary in American democracy. Many people have deep political loyalties and enjoy the excitement of political campaigns and conventions. On the other hand, many Americans distrust party politics. They feel that politics is "sneaky" or "tricky" and that politicians are motivated by self-interest and concerned mainly with being re-elected. Given these conflicting attitudes, what does the future hold for the two-party system?

Weakening party support?

Popular support for the major parties evidently has decreased in recent years. Two closely related indicators suggest this trend.

First, fewer voters now choose the **straight party ticket** — a vote for all the candidates of one party. Instead, they vote a **split ticket**, choosing candidates of different parties. A voter may, for instance, cast her vote for the Democratic candidate for President but a Republican candidate for Congress. The decline in straight-ticket voting is clear. In 1960, for example, only 27 percent of voters split their tickets for state and local races. By 1974 a full 61 percent of Americans split their votes between candidates from the two parties.

The second indicator is the increase in the number of **independents** — people who are not affiliated with any political party. This group has grown steadily in the past five decades. According to the Gallup Poll, in 1940 only 20 percent of all Americans classified themselves as independents. The changes over time are shown in Figure 10–5.

Changes in politics

Several changes in the political system have been suggested as reasons for the apparent weakening of party support.

First, there has been a significant decline in **patronage** (PAY-truh-nij). This is the practice of

Cooperative Learning

● Divide the class into groups to identify current examples of the ways major American political parties act as broker parties. Students should identify liberal and conservative positions on selected issues and identify members of Congress who support each position. Have groups follow media coverage of these issues to see how dissenting views within the party are resolved. Groups can also look for examples of issues on which the Democratic and Republican parties attempt to cooperate. Have groups write a report of their observations or present them to the class.

Figure 10–4
■ *Select one of the issues listed and explain whether a person could fully support both the Democratic and the* *Republican platform positions on that issue.*
(*Example:* The two parties' positions on AIDS were not necessarily contradictory.)

The symbol ♟♟ denotes active participation strategies.

Activities are keyed for student abilities:
▲ = Basic
● = All Levels
■ = Average/Advanced

GUIDED/INDEPENDENT PRACTICE

● Have students create a chart showing the activities associated with the three levels of party organization—national, state, and local. (*National*—Run national convention, raise funds, lead party between elections. *State*—Draft platform, adopt by-laws, apportion delegates to state party conventions, prepare for campaigns. *Local*—Recruit local party candidates, organize campaigns and rallies, raise funds.)

RETEACHING/CORRECTIVES

▲ Have students make a chart listing the major similarities and the major differences between the Democratic and Republican parties.

Have students complete **Skills Practice Worksheet 10,** which asks them to analyze a cartoon concerning political parties.

You may also want to use **Transparency 27,** which shows a political cartoon about the Democrats' tax policy.

ENRICHMENT/EXTENSION

■ Have students complete **Skills Challenge Worksheet 10,** in which they analyze two political speeches.

awarding public jobs to people who have worked hard for the party. For many years, almost all government workers — particularly at the local level — were hired and fired on the basis of partisanship. Patronage was considered the glue that kept the parties together.

Today, fewer jobs are available for officials to give to their supporters. Many more government jobs are based on **merit employment** — hiring and promoting on the basis of objective testing such as civil service examinations. Indeed, the Supreme Court held in 1980 that public employees generally cannot be fired solely on the basis of party affiliation.

Changing political methods also have lessened the parties' control over nominating and electing candidates. For many years, candidates for public office were nominated at party conventions. Usually they were politicians who had worked their way up through the party ranks and "paid their political dues." Today, however, many candidates are nominated by direct primaries — that is, by popular vote. No longer do candidates have to be party "regulars." Instead they can appeal directly to the people. Critics maintain that this trend weakens the parties. It gives an advantage to candidates with a familiar name and to those who are famous in other fields, such as actors, astronauts, business leaders, or sports heroes.

Candidates campaigning for office also once had to rely almost entirely upon the party organization for funds, skills, and information. Now candidates can hire their own public relations people, media consultants, and pollsters. They can use slick television ads, sophisticated voter targeting, mass mailings, direct telephone contacts, and high-speed computers. Contributions come from PACs and other interest groups. Many candidates can thus direct their own campaigns almost independently of the formal party organizations.

The tremendous growth in powerful interest groups has also diluted the party influence. Join-

Figure 10–5 **POLITICAL PARTY AFFILIATION The percentage of Americans who identify themselves as independents has nearly doubled since the 1930's.** 2E

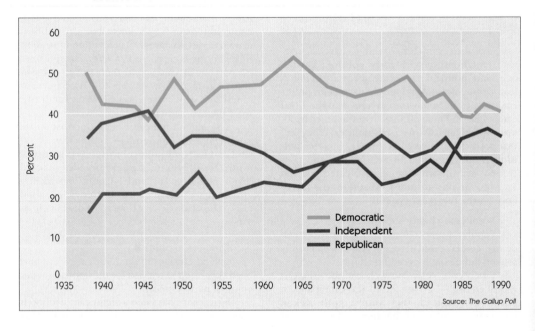

Source: *The Gallup Poll*

Cross-reference
Chapter 16, Section 4 (pp. 438-443), discusses the civil service system and government jobs.

Figure 10–5
■ *Which events correlate with the high and low points of membership in the two parties?* (The period following the Watergate scandal in the mid-1970's, for example, correlates with the decline of affiliation with the Republican Party. Membership in the Democratic Party declined sharply during the 1980's, when Republicans controlled the White House.)

ing a political party is no longer the only way to have a voice in making public policy. As part of an interest group, people can lobby, organize public protests, or form political action committees to support their cause.

The parties' future?

Despite these recent trends, it is highly unlikely that political parties will go the way of the dinosaurs. As a basic part of our political culture, the two-party system will probably remain an essential part of American democracy. According to political scientist E.E. Schattschneider, ''The rise of political parties is indubitably one of the principal distinguishing marks of modern government. . . . The two-party system is the Rock of Gibraltar of American politics.''

SECTION 4 REVIEW

Vocabulary and key terms

centrist (281)
''broker party'' (281)
''missionary party'' (281)
national
  committee (282)
nominating
  convention (283)

platform (283)
straight party
  ticket (285)
split ticket (285)
independent (285)
patronage (285)
merit employment (286)

For review

1. What three qualities are shared by the Democratic and Republican parties? **8G**
2. What are the functions of (a) the national nominating convention? (b) state party committees? **4B**
3. Which of the two parties would be more likely to support the following policies? (a) Social programs such as Medicare. (b) Lower taxes on corporations. (c) State and local control over education. (d) Government regulations on business and energy sources. **8G**
4. What trends among voters suggest that party loyalties are weakening? **8A**

Critical thinking

DRAWING INFERENCES What do the similarities between the Republican and Democratic parties reveal about American politics? **8A**

Chapter Summary

Political parties are groups of citizens organized to win elections, control government, and set public policy. Political parties serve many purposes: they recruit leaders and organize the executive and legislative branches; they identify and publicize issues; they encourage political participation; they simplify political choices; and they reduce conflict by forming coalitions.

The United States has a strong two-party system because of historical and cultural tradition, consensus among the American people over basic issues, and restrictions on minor parties. Nevertheless, minor parties have gained attention from time to time and have been sources of important reforms in American government.

The first political parties in the United States were the Federalists and the Democratic-Republicans. These parties reflected the basic differences between Alexander Hamilton's and Thomas Jefferson's ideas of government. Major changes in party politics occurred in two critical periods — the Civil War and the Depression of the 1930's. The two major modern parties, Republicans and Democrats, emerged after the Civil War. Their support changed, however, with the forming of the Democrats' ''New Deal coalition.'' There were indications that another shift in party support might be occurring in the 1980's.

Both the Republican and Democratic parties have broad-based support, hold moderate views, and have decentralized organizations. A national committee in each party provides leadership and direction between elections and organizes the nominating convention to write the party platform and nominate candidates for President and Vice President. The parties differ, however, in their stances on social and economic issues. An increase in independents and in split-ticket voting seems to indicate a decline in support for political parties today. Merit employment, direct primaries, and interest groups may partly explain this trend.

Section 4 Review Answers

1. Broad-based support, centrist ideology, decentralized organization.
2. **(a)** Write platform, nominate candidates for President and Vice President. **(b)** Raise funds, write state party platform and by-laws, conduct state campaigns, coordinate local activities.
3. **(a)** Democrats. **(b)** Republicans. **(c)** Republicans. **(d)** Democrats.
4. Increase in split tickets; increase in number of independents.

Critical thinking Students should note that most citizens share a basic set of values. You may wish to use this opportunity to compare the strength of the American two-party system with a less stable system.

CLOSURE

● Remind students of George Washington's warning against political parties, to which they replied in Section 1. (See the "Focus" activity on p. 268.) Have students write another reply and explain why this reply differs from the first one they wrote (if it does). Then have students read the next assigned lesson.

CHAPTER 10 CORRECTIVES

● To review the content of Chapter 10, you may want to have students complete **Study Guide/Review 10** or **Workbook Chapter 10.**

The symbol ✸ denotes active participation strategies.

Activities are keyed for student abilities:
  ▲ = Basic
  ● = All Levels
  ■ = Average/Advanced

Answers

Vocabulary   See pp. T19–T21 for suggested vocabulary activities.

Reviewing the Facts

1. They organize service clubs, encourage young people to join, and organize voter-registration drives.

2. Historical and cultural tradition, consensus among Americans on basic issues, and restrictions on third parties.

3. Federalists represented New England manufacturers, merchants, and other wealthy property owners. Democratic-Republicans represented small farmers, laborers, Western pioneers, and Southern planters.

4. They serve as an alternative "outlet" for the views of people disenchanted with the major parties, and advocate reforms often adopted later by the major parties.

5. It has hurt parties because patronage motivated people to work harder for their parties.

  CHAPTER **10** REVIEW

● **Review the definitions of the following terms:**

at large	merit employment	proportional
"broker party"	"missionary party"	representation
centrist	multi-party system	Republicans
coalition	national committee	single-member district
consensus	nominating convention	"solid South"
Democratic-Republicans	opposition party	split ticket
Democrats	patronage	straight party ticket
Federalists	platform	two-party system
independent	political party	Whigs
"loyal opposition"		

● **REVIEWING THE FACTS**

1. How do political parties encourage people to vote? **4C**

2. What factors contribute to the stability of the two-party system in America? **2E**

3. Whose interests were represented by the two original U.S. parties, the Federalists and the Democratic-Republicans? **2E**

4. What important roles do third, or minor, parties play in the U.S. political system? **2E**

5. How has the decline in patronage affected the strength of political parties? **4C**

▲ **THINKING CRITICALLY ABOUT KEY CONCEPTS**

1. (a) What are some basic political issues on which most Americans agree? (b) Generally, what aspect of dealing with such issues causes disagreements to arise among Americans? **5A**

2. (a) What issues led to the formation of the first political parties in the United States? (b) What economic issues have led to the creation of some of the third parties? (c) What other types of issues have led to the formation of third parties? **2E**

288

3. How do the goals of the modern Republican and Democratic parties differ in the areas of (a) economic policy and (b) social programs? **2E**

4. Why are the parties in a two-party system more ideologically centrist, while those in a multi-party system are usually sharply divided along ideological lines? **1C**

5. How can the work of political parties lead to a more aware voting public? How can it lead to less aware voters? **4C**

▲ **PRACTICING SKILLS**

1. Study Skills: Reading a time line. Refer to Figure 10–2 (page 279) to answer the following questions. (a) About when did the Democratic-Republican Party split into two separate parties? (b) Which party was active in the early years of the nation and then disappeared? (c) Which formed earlier, the modern Democratic Party or the modern Republican Party? **8B**

2. Critical Thinking Skills: Drawing conclusions. Refer to Figure 10–5 (page 286). In 1980 about 26 percent of voters were Republicans, 44 percent were Democrats, and 30 percent were Independents. How

Thinking Critically About Key Concepts

1. (a) Freedoms protected by the Constitution, rule of law, free enterprise.
(b) How to protect freedoms and how to encourage free enterprise.

2. (a) Federalists favored a strong central government; Democratic-Republicans did not. The two sides also differed over tariff and bank issues. **(b)** Demands for paper money, free coinage of silver, government owner-

ship of railroads and utilities, and a graduated income tax. **(c)** Social and moral issues.

3. (a) Republicans favor less government spending and lower taxes, and are primarily concerned about inflation. Democrats favor

did Ronald Reagan, a Republican, win 51 percent of the popular vote with such a low percentage of Republican voters? **8A**

office. In your account, be sure to describe what you learned about the workings of the U.S. election system. **8C**

▲ PARTICIPATORY CITIZENSHIP

1. **Conducting an interview.** Interview a number of people to find out what beliefs they hold about the two major political parties. Do they support one party over the other? If so, why? Try to interview a variety of people to get different responses. What conclusions can you draw from the responses you received? **4A**
2. **Personal account.** Write a fictional or factual account based on your own involvement in politics, whether in school, in the community, or at the state or federal level. Perhaps you have passed out leaflets for a candidate or worked in a local campaign

■ WRITING ABOUT ISSUES

1. **Writing a research paper.** Research one of the third parties mentioned in the chapter. Write a report describing the party's history, its reasons for forming, its policies, and its leaders. **8C**
2. **Reporting.** Write a news article on a campaign taking place either locally, or on a state or national level. Include information on the main issues that have come up during the campaign. Are the candidates' personalities playing a role in the campaign? What conclusions can you draw based on the way the campaign has proceeded? **4D**

▲ ANALYZING A POLITICAL CARTOON

In the late 1980's the style and substance of American political campaigns appeared to be turning increasingly ugly. Candidates talked less about how to make America better and spent more energy attacking their opponents. Some political strategists suggested that such negative campaigning was the best way to win elections. Others disagreed.

Look at the cartoon below and answer the following questions.

1. Who is the man on the right? Who is the man on the left? **8B**
2. What are the two men discussing? **8B**
3. What impression does the cartoonist convey about the advice being given? **8A**

Dan Wasserman. Copyright 1984, Boston Globe. Distributed by Los Angeles Times Syndicate. Reprinted with permission.

greater government spending, and are concerned primarily about unemployment. **(b)** Democrats generally support new programs to help the needy; Republicans prefer to use incentives to move needy people out of government programs.
4. In a two-party system, each party must seek votes from the mass of people at the center of the ideological spectrum.

5. Through debates, advertisements, and public appearances, parties provide the public with current information. Yet they also can present biased information that may lead voters to make unwise decisions.

Practicing Skills
1. **(a)** Between 1810 and 1830. **(b)** Federalist Party. **(c)** Democratic Party.
2. He must have drawn support from some independents and Democrats as well as Republicans.

Participatory Citizenship
1. Students should try to determine which issues influence people the most when choosing a party.
2. You may want to have students visit a local campaign headquarters, or have a local politician visit the class to discuss his or her most recent campaign.

Writing About Issues
1. Ask volunteers to summarize their reports for the class.
2. Students should make sure to present their findings objectively and address all sides of the issues.

Analyzing a Political Cartoon
1. The candidate. A campaign adviser.
2. Strategy for a political campaign.
3. It will result in a negative, morally dubious campaign.

Chapter Review exercises are keyed for student abilities:
▲ = Basic
● = All Levels
■ = Average/Advanced

CHAPTER 11
POLITICS IN ACTION
(pp. 290–319)

	Section Objectives	Section Resources
Section 1 **Candidates Are Chosen to Run for Office**	☐ explain the arguments in favor of closed and open primaries ☐ identify other common means by which candidates are nominated for office	
Section 2 **National Conventions Name Presidential Candidates**	☐ identify the factors that affect a candidate's chances of nomination for President ☐ explain the two basic methods of selecting delegates to nominating conventions ☐ describe the highlights of national conventions	■ PRIMARY SOURCE WORKSHEET **17** ▲ TRANSPARENCY **28**
Section 3 **Election Campaigns Are Complex and Costly**	☐ identify important considerations in planning a political campaign ☐ identify the major sources of campaign funds	■ SKILLS CHALLENGE WORKSHEET **11**
Section 4 **Laws Ensure Fair Elections**	☐ explain how federal laws guard against discriminatory voting restrictions ☐ explain how federal and state governments regulate voting procedures	
Section 5 **American Voting Behavior Is Unique**	☐ identify major factors that affect whether people vote ☐ identify major factors that affect how people vote	▲ SKILLS PRACTICE WORKSHEET **11** ● CITIZENSHIP WORKSHEET **4**

Essential Elements

The list below shows Essential Elements relevant to this chapter. (The complete list of Essential Elements appears in the introductory pages of this Teacher's Edition.)

Section 1: 4B, 4C, 8A, 8G

Section 2: 4B, 4C, 4D, 8H

Your Turn feature (p. 301): 4C

Section 3: 2E, 4B, 4C, 4D, 7A

Critical Thinking feature (p. 307): 8D

Section 4: 2D, 4C, 6G, 6H, 8A

Section 5: 1C, 4A, 4C, 4D, 5C, 8H

Chapter Review: 2E, 3C, 4A, 4B, 4C, 4D, 5B, 6C, 7D, 8A, 8B

> Section Resources are keyed for student abilities:
> ▲ = Basic
> ● = All Levels
> ■ = Average/Advanced

Homework Options

Each section contains activities labeled "Guided/Independent Practice," "Reteaching/Correctives," and "Enrichment/Extension." You may wish to choose from among these activities when assigning homework.

Students Acquiring English Activities

Explain to students that the language of American politics contains many colorful expressions. Have students make sketches to depict the literal meaning of a few expressions. Below each sketch, students should write the expression and then its political meaning. (Students may have to consult outside sources.) Some suggested expressions: *Throwing your hat into the ring* (entering a political campaign); *dark horse candidate* (candidate not expected to win); *favorite son/daughter* (candidate nominated by his or her own constituents); *whistle-stop campaign* (stopping in many small towns to campaign).

LISTENING/SPEAKING: View the Houghton Mifflin videotape *Anatomy of a Campaign.* Have students write down any political expressions used in the videotape, and then discuss their meanings.

Case Studies

When teaching this chapter, you may use Case Study 5, which examines the issue of limitations on congressional terms or Case Study 10, which addresses the question of mandatory national service for all eighteen-year-olds. (Case Studies may be found following p. 510.)

Teacher Bibliography

Archer, J. Clark and Fred M. Shelley. *American Electoral Mosaics.* Association of American Geographers, 1986. Analyzes regional and national voting patterns in presidential and congressional elections.

Carroll, Susan J. *Women as Candidates in American Politics.* Indiana University Press, 1985.

Student Bibliography

Barber, James David. *The Pulse of Politics: Electing Presidents in the Media Age.* Norton, 1980. Examines the media's contribution to presidential politics and elections.

Bernards, Neal, ed. *The Mass Media: Opposing Viewpoints.* Greenhaven Press, 1988. Journalists, politicians, communications experts, and others discuss the media's influence on society.

Nie, Norman, Sidney Verba, and John Petrocik. *The Changing American Voter.* Harvard University Press, 1980. A study of electoral behavior in the United States.

Literature

Drury, Allen. *Capable of Honor.* Doubleday, 1966. A columnist and his supporters try to take over a national convention.

Ferraro, Geraldine A. *Ferraro: My Story.* Bantam Books, 1986. The first woman vice-presidential candidate of a major political party describes life on the campaign trail.

Wicker, Tom. *Facing the Lions.* Viking, 1973. The story of a cynical political reporter and an ambitious senator in search of the presidency.

Films and Videotapes*

Electing the President. 29 min. EBEC, 1983. f, v. Follows the change and growth of the American electoral process from the eighteenth century to modern times.

CHAPTER RESOURCES

Study Guide/Review 11
Workbook Chapter 11
Chapter 11 Test, Forms A–C

Elections in the United States. 19 min. Phoenix, f, v. Shows how the right to vote was originally conceived and how it has changed throughout history.

Elections in the United States. 15 min. BFA (Phoenix), 1976. f, v. Several kinds of elections are covered, from the start of the process to the presidential race itself. Coverage includes how the right to vote was originally conceived, how it has changed throughout our history, and how citizens can affect government beyond the ballot box.

Software*

The '88 Vote: Campaign for the White House (Macintosh). OD. This videodisc is an interactive documentary of the 1988 race for the presidency. Coverage begins before the primaries, includes party platforms, conventions, election tallies, and ends with George Bush's victory speech.

"And if Re-elected . . ." (Apple, IBM). Focus. Students play the role of an incumbent President running for re-election. They are presented with twelve crises and must decide which crises directly influence special interest groups.

On the Campaign Trail (Apple, IBM, Macintosh). TS. Students assume the role of a third party candidate for President. They must develop a platform and campaign strategies, and learn about the Electoral College, special interest groups, and political action committees.

* For a complete guide to audiovisual sources, see page T22.

289B

Politics in Action
(pp. 290–319)

Chapter 11 describes how political parties select candidates for office, looks at how campaign strategies are planned and carried out, and considers factors that influence whether citizens vote and for whom they vote.

Chapter Objectives
After students complete this chapter, they will be able to:

1. Explain the arguments in favor of closed and open primaries.
2. Identify other common means by which candidates are nominated for office.
3. Identify the factors that affect a candidate's chances of nomination for President.
4. Explain the two basic methods of selecting delegates to nominating conventions.
5. Describe the highlights of national conventions.
6. Identify important considerations in planning a political campaign.
7. Identify the major sources of campaign funds.
8. Explain how federal laws guard against discriminatory voting restrictions.
9. Explain how federal and state governments regulate voting procedures.
10. Identify major factors that affect whether people vote.
11. Identify major factors that affect how people vote.

CHAPTER

1.1

POLITICS in ACTION

The right to vote is the basic right without which all others are meaningless. It gives people — individual people — control over their own destinies.

Lyndon B. Johnson
Speech in the U.S. Senate (1957)

290

Photo
Polling place, San Francisco.

290

V oter registration drives played an important role in the civil rights movement of the early 1960's. Many civil rights leaders believed that the power of the ballot box could produce social change. African American voters could help elect politicians who would be more responsive to concerns such as housing, education, and an end to racial discrimination.

However, several states still tried to keep African Americans from voting. President Lyndon Johnson pushed for legislation to overcome these restrictions. Finally, in August 1965, with Martin Luther King, Jr., Rosa Parks, and other civil rights leaders present, Johnson signed the Voting Rights Act of 1965. Calling the act "one of the most monumental laws in the entire history of American freedom," Johnson declared, "The vote is the most powerful instrument ever devised by man for breaking down injustice."

CHAPTER OUTLINE

1 Candidates Are Chosen to Run for Office

Primary Elections
Other Nomination Methods

2 National Conventions Name Presidential Candidates

Entering the Race
Winning Convention Delegates
The National Convention

3 Election Campaigns Are Complex and Costly

Planning the Campaign
Financing the Campaign

4 Laws Ensure Fair Elections

Guaranteeing Suffrage
Voting Procedures

5 American Voting Behavior Is Unique

The American Voter
Trends in Voting Behavior
Voting Decisions

291

CHAPTER SUPPORT MATERIAL

Skills Practice Worksheet 11

Skills Challenge Worksheet 11

Citizenship Worksheet 4

Primary Source Worksheet 17

Transparency 28

Study Guide/Review 11

Workbook Chapter 11

Chapter 11 Test, Forms A-C

 VIDEOTAPE SERIES

This would be an appropriate place to use Houghton Mifflin's videotape, *Anatomy of a Campaign.* You may also want to use Houghton Mifflin's videotape, *Media and Politics: Inside TV News.*

SECTION 1

Candidates Are Chosen to Run for Office

(pp. 292–294)

Section Objectives

☐ explain the arguments in favor of closed and open primaries

☐ identify other common means by which candidates are nominated for office

Vocabulary

nomination, primary election, direct primary, general election, closed primary, plurality, open primary, nominating petition, caucus, write-in candidate

FOCUS

● Ask students if they think primaries are necessary. **What would happen if there were only a general election without primaries?** (There might be dozens of candidates, and the winner might only receive a small percentage of the popular vote, which would harm his or her credibility as a representative of the people.)

EXPLANATION

After students have read the section, you may want to consider the following activities:

 Politics

■ Discuss with students the differences between open and closed primaries. Then write the following debate topic on the board: *The closed primary is unfair and should not be allowed in a democracy.* Select teams of students or individuals to debate this topic, or ask all class members to write short papers agreeing or disagreeing with the statement.

 SECTION 1

Candidates Are Chosen to Run for Office

| ACCESS | **The Main Ideas** |

1 Explain the arguments in favor of closed and open primaries. *pages 292–293*

2 Identify other common means by which candidates are nominated for office. *pages 293–294*

Political parties spend much of their time and energy trying to get party members elected to public office. How do parties choose their candidates and what role do voters play?

The first — and perhaps most important— step a party takes is to choose candidates who will run for election. The process of naming candidates, or **nomination**, usually begins within the party organization. However, political party conventions name candidates for only two offices — President and Vice President. Candidates for other offices must usually first win a preliminary, or **primary election**. Independent candidates may also seek election.

4B

Primary Elections

Direct primaries

The most common method for nominating candidates for office today is the **direct primary** election, first adopted in Wisconsin in 1903. The term *primary* is used because the primary elections come first, before the **general election** in which all the voters choose the winners for each office. Each of the fifty states now uses some form of direct primary. The direct primary is used to nominate candidates for Congress, governor, state legislature, as well as for many state and local offices.

Direct primaries are unique to American government. No other nation in the world has ever adopted this democratic method of allowing all party members a voice in choosing candidates. In most countries, the people have no part in selecting candidates. Either the government or the political party leaders retain total control over the nomination process.

292

Types of direct primary

Because each of the fifty states makes its own election rules, several types of direct primary have developed.

The most common is the **closed primary**, used in 35 states. In a closed primary, voters must declare their party affiliation — Democratic, Republican, or independent — before entering the voting booth. On election day, they can vote only for candidates running in that party's primary.

The candidate who receives a **plurality**, the highest number of votes, usually wins the nomination. In some states, however, a candidate must receive a majority (more than half) of the votes. If no candidate does, these states hold a run-off primary between the two highest vote-getters. Run-off elections are particularly important in states where one political party dominates. Whoever wins the nomination of the dominant party almost certainly will win the general election. Closed primaries have strong political support because they encourage party loyalty and the two-party system.

Twelve states (Hawaii, Idaho, Michigan, Minnesota, Missouri, Montana, South Carolina, Tennessee, Utah, Vermont, Virginia, and Wisconsin) hold **open primaries**. Voters do not choose a party in advance, but simply decide in the voting booth which party to support. They then can vote only for that party's nominees.

A modified form of the open primary, used in Washington, Louisiana, and Alaska, is the blanket primary (sometimes called the "wide-open" primary). In a blanket primary, voters are free to cast their votes back and forth for candidates of any party.

Nonpartisan primaries are common in local government. In these primary elections, party labels are not used. Only the candidates' names appear on the ballot, and the top two finishers in the primary advance to the general election. Nebraska is the only state in which state legislators are nominated and elected on nonpartisan ballots.

Critical Thinking

● *How do closed primaries encourage both the two-party system and party loyalty?* (Voters must declare their affiliation before they vote and can only vote for those candidates who are members of their party.)

Other Nomination Methods

Nomination by petition

In many elections for local office, candidates must be nominated by petition. To get on the ballot in other elections, third-party or independent candidates also must usually be backed up by **nominating petitions**. These petitions contain the signatures of a certain number of qualified voters who support putting the candidate's name on the ballot.

State and local laws determine how petitions must be obtained, how many signatures must be gathered, and when the petition must be delivered to election officials. If a candidate can secure enough valid signatures within the specified time, his or her name is placed on the ballot for the next general election.

The caucus method

Early in American political history, most political candidates were nominated by **caucus**, a small group meeting. This practice originated in New England, where influential citizens met secretly to decide who would run for various local offices. With the rise of organized political parties, the caucus became an important tool of party decision-making. Party members in the state legislatures met to decide party strategy and to suggest candidates for Congress and state of-fices. Beginning in 1800, legislative caucuses also were held in Congress. The congressional caucuses nominated candidates for President until 1824. (State legislators and members of Congress still meet in legislative caucuses, but only to decide on strategies for handling legislation.)

The secret bargains made in the caucus by powerful party leaders soon drew bitter criticism for being undemocratic. When Andrew Jackson was denied nomination by the Democratic-Republican caucus of 1824, he began a campaign against what he called "King Caucus." With Jackson's election as President in 1828, the use of the party caucus for nominating presidential candidates came to an end.

As a nominating device, the caucus is used today mainly to choose delegates to the national party convention and candidates for a few local offices, mainly in New England. These open, public meetings bear little resemblance to the secret caucuses of the 1800's.

The convention method

The nominating convention was developed in the 1830's as a more democratic method of choosing candidates than the caucus. Political parties held conventions at the local, county, and state levels. The state conventions nominated candidates for Congress and state offices. They

The nominating petition enables candidates to get their names on the ballot in many election contests, particularly at the local level. Here, qualified voters sign a candidate's petition.

Background: *History*
Andrew Jackson was seen as a champion of the common citizen. He shunned the aristocratic attitude that had prevailed in previous presidencies, and the word *democracy* became synonymous with his two terms in office.

Cross-reference
The selection of national convention delegates is discussed in Section 2, pp. 297–298.

Cultural Literacy

▲ CRITICAL THINKING *Caucus* may be derived from an Algonquin Indian word meaning "counselor" or "elder." Make sure the class recognizes the difference between a legislative caucus and a caucus used to nominate candidates.

👥 Cooperative Learning

● To help students learn the differences among the various nomination methods discussed in this section, divide the class into small groups. Have each group write, for each of the vocabulary terms in this section, a question that can be answered by that term. Have groups take turns asking their questions in class.

GUIDED/INDEPENDENT PRACTICE

● Have students write a short essay explaining why the nominating convention replaced the caucus method of nomination, and why the direct primary replaced the nominating convention.

RETEACHING/CORRECTIVES

▲ Ask each student to create a three-column table with columns labeled *Nomination Method, Requirements,* and *Level of Government Where Used.* Students should then complete their tables using information in the section.

The symbol 👥 denotes active participation strategies.

Activities are keyed for student abilities:
▲ = Basic
● = All Levels
■ = Average/Advanced

ENRICHMENT/EXTENSION

■ Assign several students to research and report to the class on the nomination methods used in your local and state elections. The League of Women Voters and the county election board can provide information on these topics. The local Republican and Democratic headquarters are other sources of information.

Section 1 Review Answers

1. Political parties usually begin the process of nominating candidates. State governments pass laws to regulate primary elections in those cases where the public chooses the nominees.
2. In closed primaries, voters receive only the ballot of their party choice. In open primaries, voters do not have to declare a party choice.
3. (a) It was undemocratic.
(b) The nominating convention.
4. By nonpartisan primaries, where party labels are not used.

Critical thinking Students might discuss the various methods of nominating a candidate and the ways in which these methods reflect the wishes of the people. Students should then compare the election and nominating processes.

CLOSURE

● Review the Section 1 vocabulary with students to help reinforce key concepts from the section. Then have students read Section 2, noting the activities that make up a convention.

Whig campaign organizers used the theme of a log cabin and hard cider to portray candidate William Henry Harrison as a folksy "man of the people," opposing the wealthy Martin Van Buren.

also designated delegates to the national party convention.

In time, these conventions were also criticized for being undemocratic. A handful of powerful party "bosses" tended to control the choice of delegates and, hence, the party nominees. Decisions were not made on the convention floor but through wheeling and dealing behind closed doors. Ordinary party members had little voice in the nominating process.

As a result of growing criticism, most states eventually abandoned nominating conventions in favor of direct primaries. A few states still hold state party conventions but provide for elections too. If a losing candidate has a certain percentage of the convention votes (20–25 percent), he or she can call for a challenge primary against the

294

winner. National party conventions, of course, are still used (as we will see in Section 2) to nominate presidential and vice-presidential candidates.

Self-announcement

The oldest method of entering the race for office is self-announcement, "throwing your hat in the ring" and declaring you are a candidate. Self-announcement is practical only when few people are competing for nomination and is rarely used today except for minor offices in local government. Most state election laws require a would-be candidate to have at least a nominating petition in order to be listed on the ballot.

A person who fails to get on the ballot through traditional methods may run as a **write-in candidate**. His or her supporters must insert the candidate's name in the appropriate place on the ballot, either by hand or with a sticker supplied by the candidate. (Most ballots leave a place for write-in votes.) Write-in campaigns are usually last-ditch efforts and rarely succeed.

SECTION 1 REVIEW

Vocabulary and key terms

nomination (292)	plurality (292)
primary election (292)	open primary (292)
direct primary (292)	nominating petition (293)
general election (292)	caucus (293)
closed primary (292)	write-in candidate (294)

For review

1. How do parties and state governments share control of nominating candidates? **4B**
2. What is the difference between a closed and an open primary? **8G**
3. (a) What was the major criticism of the caucus as a nominating method? (b) What replaced it? **4C**
4. How are most candidates for local offices nominated? **4C**

Critical thinking

EXAMINING BASIC PRINCIPLES Is the nomination process more democratic than the election process? Why or why not? **8A**

SECTION 2
National Conventions Name Presidential Candidates

ACCESS The Main Ideas

1 What factors affect a candidate's chances of nomination for President? *pages 295–297*

2 Which two basic methods are used to select delegates to nominating conventions? *pages 297–298*

3 What are some of the highlights of national conventions? *pages 298–300*

Chicago, 1920. The Republican national convention is meeting to choose a presidential candidate. No clear winner has emerged. Then party leaders adjourn to a smoky back room. According to legend, a deal is struck. The candidate will be Warren G. Harding, a little-known Ohio senator.

Conventions in recent times have contained more pomp and pageantry than back-room deci-sion-making and compromise. Modern conventions are pure political theatre. Their intent is to display party unity and gloss over divisions within the party. Occasionally, however, conventions dramatically reflect such divisions. For example, the 1948 Democratic convention split over the issue of the party's support for civil rights. Likewise, protests against the Vietnam War helped cause divisions among the Democrats at their 1968 convention.

4B, 4C

Entering the Race

Announcing a candidacy

A candidate's campaign for the presidential nomination process formally begins when he or she declares an intention to seek the presidency.

George Bush, shown here addressing the 1988 Republican convention, lost the 1992 presidential race to Bill Clinton.

295

Background: *Politics* The first national convention to nominate a presidential candidate was held in 1831 by a minor party, the Anti-Masons.

EXPLANATION

After students have read the section, you may want to consider the following activities:

Politics

▲ CRITICAL THINKING Have students come to the board and list the factors that increase a candidate's chances of winning the presidential nomination of a major political party. (Name recognition, experience in high public office, time, ambition, willingness to make personal sacrifices.)

● CRITICAL THINKING Then have students suggest additional factors that might help a candidate win nomination. (Possible answers: personal wealth or substantial sources of campaign funds, charm, a good speaking voice, an attractive television image.)

■ CRITICAL THINKING Finally, ask students if factors that make a good presidential candidate and campaigner also help to make a good President. Have students defend their conclusions.

In 1984 Jesse Jackson mounted the first significant campaign for President by a black candidate. He made an even better showing in 1988, amassing 6.7 million votes, and finishing second at the Democratic convention in Atlanta to Michael Dukakis. Here, Jackson brings his message — "Together, We Can Win" — to voters in the crucial New Hampshire primary.

This announcement, however, comes only after months, or even years, of careful thought and planning.

The timing of the announcement is very important. Candidates dare not declare their intention to run too early, for their campaign may run out of steam before the nominating convention. Nor can they afford to make their announcement too late, for some convention delegates may already be pledged to other candidates.

Springboards to the presidency

It is often said that anyone born in the United States can grow up to be President. Nevertheless, certain factors increase a candidate's chances. For instance, nearly every candidate to receive a major party's nomination in this century has had experience in high public office, particularly as senator, Vice President, or governor. Franklin Roosevelt, Jimmy Carter, Ronald Reagan, and Bill Clinton all served as state governors before advancing to the White House. Challengers Alf Landon (1936), Thomas Dewey (1944, 1948), and Adlai Stevenson (1952, 1956) also had been governors. From the U.S. Senate came President John Kennedy and nominees Barry Goldwater and George McGovern. Harry Truman, Lyndon Johnson, Hubert Humphrey, Richard Nixon, Gerald Ford, Walter Mondale, and George Bush all served both in Congress and as Vice President before running for President.

Name recognition

Candidates must be well known to the general public if they expect to have any chance of winning. Public office is one good source of name recognition, but other occupations can also attract political interest. Ronald Reagan, for example, was a movie and television actor before entering California politics. Dwight Eisenhower commanded the Allied Forces in Europe during World War II and became a national hero with the D-Day invasion in 1944. John Glenn, who sought the Democratic nomination in 1984, won fame as the first American astronaut to orbit the earth. (Glenn also served as senator from Ohio.) Jesse Jackson, another Democratic hopeful in 1984 and in 1988, was a well-known civil rights leader and minister.

Time and ambition

Running for President can be a full-time job. Candidates must be ambitious and ready to make personal sacrifices. Once a candidate has announced his or her candidacy, there is little privacy until the election is over. Even before the actual campaign begins, candidates must meet rigorous deadlines, sacrifice family activities, travel constantly, and smile on command. Adlai Stevenson, the Democratic nominee in 1952 and 1956, noted that, "At least for an inexperienced candidate," there are "few more exciting ordeals than a presidential campaign."

296

Background: *Politics*
Candidates who wait too long to announce their intention to run also get a late start on fund-raising, a critical aspect of a presidential campaign.

Background: *History*
Franklin Roosevelt had been governor of New York, Jimmy Carter had been governor of Georgia, Ronald Reagan had been governor of California, and Bill Clinton had been governor of Arkansas.

Furthermore, a presidential campaign can cost a candidate millions of dollars — even to lose. After running a close second to Walter Mondale in the Democratic contest in 1984, Gary Hart came out of his campaign with $3.5 million in debts to show for it.

4C

Winning Convention Delegates

Serious candidates for nomination must concentrate first on winning the support of delegates to the national party convention. Several thousand delegates attend each convention. In 1992, for example, the Democrats had over 4,250 convention delegates, the Republicans over 2,200. To win nomination, a candidate needs a majority of the convention delegates.

Rules for delegate selection

The two national party organizations use a complex formula to allot each state a certain number of delegates. Typically, the number of delegates depends on the state's population and on its past support of the party ticket, with extra "bonus" delegates for important past election victories. In 1992, the Democrats also invited 771 high-ranking Democratic officials to attend as uncommitted "super delegates."

Each state legislature sets rules for how convention delegates are to be chosen, but two basic methods are used — *primary elections* and *caucuses.* Delegates chosen according to state rules can still be challenged at the national convention, however. For example, in 1972 the Democrats' rules for delegates required that women, minorities, and young persons (ages 18 to 30) be represented in state delegations "in reasonable relationship to the group's presence in the population of the state." The Illinois delegation was challenged for not including enough women, blacks, and youths, and the Democratic National Convention refused to grant the delegation its full voting rights. (A 1981 Supreme Court decision, *Democratic Party v. LaFollette,* confirmed the national committee's right to overrule a state's selection of delegates.)

Choosing delegates by primary elections

The **presidential primary** is the most common way of choosing convention delegates, used by over 35 states in 1992. Like other primary elec-

tions (page 292), these are organized differently from state to state. As a result, they have different impacts on the actual nomination process.

The *presidential preference* primary can help a candidate's campaign and image, but it does not guarantee delegates. The voters indicate the candidate they prefer, but delegates are actually chosen later at a state party convention. The number of delegates each candidate gets may or may not reflect the popular vote.

The results of a *binding* presidential preference primary are quite different. On the basis of the popular vote, delegates who are bound, or pledged, to vote for certain candidates are selected. Delegates may be assigned in proportion to the vote each candidate receives, or they may all go to the winner.

In a *delegate selection* primary, party members vote directly for the convention delegates. In some states, each delegate's name appears on the ballot beside the name of the candidate he or she supports. In other states, only the delegates' names are listed.

Choosing delegates by caucus

Presidential nominations, like those for other offices, were once made mainly by caucus. But because of low turnout, many states turned to

The Iowa caucuses are the earliest tests of a presidential bid. Here, Iowa Senator Tom Harkin campaigns for the 1992 Democratic nomination.

297

History

● Have the class review the subsection "The National Convention" (pp. 298–300). Ask students to identify ways in which media coverage has influenced conventions.

👥 Cooperative Learning

● Divide the class into groups and assign each group a Republican or Democratic presidential ticket from a past election. Each group should speculate about the way in which each vice-presidential candidate "balanced" his or her party's ticket.

GUIDED/INDEPENDENT PRACTICE

● Have students make a chart comparing different means of choosing delegates. Charts should include the presidential preference primary, the binding presidential preference primary, the delegate selection primary, and the caucus. Charts should list the features of each process that make it unique.

presidential primaries instead. The caucus is still used in several midwestern and mountain states. The Iowa caucuses, in fact, draw record numbers of participants because they are held early in the presidential election year.

Caucus rules and procedures vary from state to state. Typically, though, the process begins with voter meetings in hundreds of precincts throughout the state. Neighborhood caucuses may be held in schools, libraries, or any other convenient places. At each local caucus, citizens who want to serve as delegates announce the candidate they support. A vote is taken, and the winning delegates move on to the next level of caucusing, usually the county or district conventions. Delegates chosen there attend the state convention, which selects those who will attend the national nominating convention.

The contest for delegates

Competition for convention delegates officially begins in late February or early March of election years, when the Iowa caucuses and the New Hampshire primary are held. It ends in June with primaries in five states — North Dakota, New Mexico, Montana, New Jersey, and California.

Most candidates run in Iowa and New Hampshire hoping to take an early lead. Candidates who do poorly in these states sometimes drop out of the race, as did Democrats Edmund Muskie in 1972 and Alan Cranston in 1984. Candidates who do well, such as Jimmy Carter in 1976, may gain momentum and find it easier to raise money.

Some candidates decide to run in all states, but this strategy requires much money and skillful organization. Other candidates concentrate their efforts in states where they know they will do well. In 1984, for example, Democrat Jesse Jackson concentrated his efforts in the South and in states with many black voters. A candidate who feels sure of the nomination may ignore certain primaries, but this strategy may offend local political leaders.

Conversely, candidates sometimes enter state races they are not expected to win. In 1960 John F. Kennedy, a Roman Catholic, entered the West Virginia primary to demonstrate that he could win support in a predominantly Protestant state. His victory helped his candidacy seem possible. Likewise, Alabama Governor George Wal-

298

lace entered the Wisconsin primary in 1968 to show that a southerner could do well in a northern state. (Wallace lost, but drew some support.)

Any serious candidate, however, must compete in the big states with many convention delegates — California, New York, Texas, Pennsylvania, Illinois, Ohio, Florida, and Wisconsin.

4B

The National Convention

The convention begins

Plans for the national conventions are made well in advance by the national party committees, who consider factors such as hotel accommodations, transportation, security, and media coverage. Politics also plays a part in the choice of a convention site. Both parties wanted to strengthen their support in the South in 1988, so the Republicans chose New Orleans and the Democrats picked Atlanta. In 1992 the Republicans again held their convention in the South, this time choosing Houston. The Democrats, meanwhile, held their convention in New York City.

To the public, national nominating conventions have a carnival atmosphere, with rituals, rallies, demonstrations, and debates. On the first day, the convention is called to order by the national committee chairperson, and convention officers are elected. The highlight of the day is the **keynote speech**, a rousing, colorful address praising the party's virtues and criticizing the opposition's faults. Keynote speeches can greatly influence the mood of a convention. Speakers are chosen for both their ability to stir an audience and their political position.

Day two: Committee reports

Usually on the second day, the convention hears reports from two important committees. The credentials committee formally examines the qualifications of the delegations from each state. At this time, delegations may be challenged, or rival delegations may each claim the right to represent a state. Candidates who trail in the delegate count may try to challenge the credentials of their opponents' delegates.

The platform committee, which has been meeting for several months, now presents the party's platform, its official stand on the issues. The "planks" in the platform identify these poli-

Critical Thinking
▲ *Why is it particularly important for candidates to do well in early primaries?* (To gain momentum, enhance name recognition, and improve fund-raising potential.)

Political conventions are designed to win support for a party's candidates through extensive media coverage and exciting speeches. Delegates from all over the country participate.

cies, which help distinguish the two parties. Parts of the platform, however, may cause sharp disagreement and debate among delegates. The 1968 Democratic convention, for example, was nearly torn apart by a platform fight over the party's Vietnam War policy.

Day three: Choosing the nominee

The selection of the party's presidential candidate is the main business of the third day. Candidates' names are "placed in nomination," and nominating speeches are given. In addition to the leading candidates, the names of "favorite sons" or "favorite daughters" may be placed in nomination as a courtesy by their home states. Occasionally a "dark horse" candidate is suggested — a relative unknown who backers think might win a surprise victory. Parades and demonstrations usually follow nomination speeches.

Finally, state-by-state balloting begins. In 1992 Governor James Blanchard of Michigan announced his delegation's votes for Bill Clinton in this way: "Madam Chairman, the great state of Michigan, home of the Great Lakes and great people . . . proudly casts 120 votes for the next President of the United States, Governor Bill Clinton!"

As mentioned earlier, both the Republican and Democratic parties now require a simple majority vote of the delegates. If there is no clear winner on the first ballot, another roll-call vote is taken. In the meantime, candidates with poor showings may bow out of the contest. They may either urge their delegates to support another candidate or leave them uncommitted. In recent years, most winning candidates had enough delegates before the convention to ensure nomination on the first ballot. To boost party unity, nominations now are generally given the unanimous vote of the convention.

Until 1936, the rules for balloting were quite different. The Democratic Party, for example, had a two-thirds rule, which meant that as few as one-third of the delegates could block a nomination. Conventions frequently needed many ballots to decide on a nominee. In the last-minute bargaining, "dark horse" candidates sometimes won nominations when the front-runners became deadlocked.

Balancing the ticket

After securing the nomination, the party's nominee selects a vice-presidential running

299

RETEACHING/CORRECTIVES
▲ Have students make a chart outlining the events that take place over the course of a national political convention.

You may also want to use **Transparency 28,** which examines the media coverage given to different states during presidential campaigns.

ENRICHMENT/EXTENSION
■ Have students read **Primary Source Worksheet 17,** which presents excerpts from Barbara Jordan's address to the 1976 National Democratic Convention.

Check for Understanding
▲ *Why do parties believe that it is important to unanimously nominate the victorious candidate?* (A unanimous nomination shows that the party is united behind one candidate for the national election.)

The symbol 👥 denotes active participation strategies.

Activities are keyed for student abilities:
▲ = Basic
● = All Levels
■ = Average/Advanced

Bill Clinton chose Senator Al Gore of Tennessee as his running mate in 1992. Gore's combination of youth and experience appealed to many voters.

mate. Most vice-presidential candidates are chosen to "balance the ticket" geographically or ideologically, or to appeal to a particular group. For example, Richard Nixon, a conservative politician from California, was the Republican nominee in 1960. To widen the appeal of his ticket, Nixon chose Henry Cabot Lodge, a liberal Republican from Massachusetts, as his running mate. However, in 1992 Bill Clinton of Arkansas felt he would strengthen his ticket by choosing a fellow southerner, Senator Al Gore of Tennessee. Gore helped Clinton win the presidency.

The final day of the convention

The party officially nominates the vice-presidential candidate on the final day of the convention. This balloting usually just confirms the candidate's choice. Adlai Stevenson in 1956 was the only presidential nominee in modern times to allow the convention to pick his running mate.

The last day of the convention is also a chance to mend any rifts in the party that may have occurred during the nomination process. Battles for nomination and platform fights can cause serious splits among party members. If the party fails to reunite behind its chosen nominee, it has little chance of winning the election.

300

Losing candidates usually deliver concession speeches that urge party unity. Gary Hart, Jesse Jackson, and George McGovern all made such speeches at the 1984 Democratic convention. In 1980 George Bush, the runner-up in a bitter fight for the Republican nomination, appealed to the convention to unite behind Ronald Reagan. Reagan, in turn, chose Bush as his running mate.

Finally, the nominees make their acceptance speeches, timed for national television coverage, amidst outpourings of cheers, flagwaving, and music. When an incumbent President is nominated for a second term, the speech is punctuated with shouts of "Four more years" from the convention floor. In their speeches, candidates traditionally praise the losers, call for party unity, outline their proposals, and try to set the tone for the upcoming campaign.

SECTION 2 REVIEW

Vocabulary and key terms

presidential primary (297)   "dark horse"
keynote speech (298)   candidate (299)
favorite son/daughter (299)

For review

1. What backgrounds and experience do most presidential candidates have? **4C**
2. What roles do (a) the national party committees and (b) the states play in selecting convention delegates? **4C**
3. (a) What does each kind of presidential primary determine? (b) What decisions must candidates make about entering primaries? **4D**
4. What are the steps in the actual nomination process at the convention? **4C**
5. By what method is the vice-presidential candidate chosen? **4B**

Critical thinking

ANALYZING CAUSE AND EFFECT Explain how the following factors might help or hurt a candidate's chances of winning presidential nomination: experience in Congress; family wealth; residence in a populous state; an active history in party politics; experience as a TV talk-show host; a loss in a previous presidential election; one previous term in office as President. **8H**

Have you ever worked on a political campaign? Or do you think campaigning is just not worth it? In 1991 some seniors at Bellaire High School (Texas) worked for candidates in Houston's mayoral election. They performed tasks at campaign headquarters, put up signs, and distributed leaflets. The following are their thoughts on their experiences on the frontlines of a political campaign.

Seniors at Bellaire High School, Texas

Diana Sims: The reason we did this was to find out about the political process and how it works. I found out it's a lot of hard work, a lot of manual labor to get people to know about the candidate.

Marnie Rose: I never realized how much thought goes into every single step and detail, that just blew my mind.

Bryan Pate: I did block walks. They assigned us a precinct, divided us up, and we went house to house, hung things on the doors, and had a chance to talk to people.

Janet Thompson: It can be very tiring. I was block walking for four hours. It could be frustrating, and it got to be hard.

Rachael McDonell: It was obvious to me that it really takes a lot of money to run. It's kind of a shame. If candidates don't have a lot of money to begin with, they're at a disadvantage and that's unfair. I think there should be a limit set on spending.

Michael Shepherd: The head of volunteers mentioned that the minimum amount of money to run for mayor of Houston was a million dollars. The candidate I worked for barely had a million, so he couldn't do things that cost a lot of money. He had to pass out flyers and make personal appearances instead of buying television time.

Angela Walter: But that is more personal, it makes more of an impact than commercials.

Diana Sims: The volunteers I coordinated were students. I don't think adults are as interested. You don't see them walking house to house.

Bolivar Fraga: I think it's a general attitude in American society. People don't even go to vote, much less help campaign. Everyone takes it for granted.

Mary Chang: I think there isn't high voter turnout because people don't know about the candidates. If you go work in a campaign office you know more about what they stand for. You feel like you have an obligation to vote.

STUDENT PARTICIPATION
1. What criticisms did these students have about political campaigning in the United States? Do you agree?
2. Create a list of different methods used in campaigning in order of effectiveness.

YOUR TURN

Houston Students Participate in a Political Campaign

Left to right: Marnie Rose, Diana Sims, Michael Shepherd, Angela Walter, Rachael McDonell, Bryan Pate, Bolivar Fraga, Janet Thompson, and Mary Chang.

Background
The students quoted here were all in a government class taught by Pam Young. They participated in campaigns as part of an assignment to apply political concepts to the real world. Other possible activities included writing a position paper, attending a lecture on a political issue, and attending a meeting of local government.

Civic Participation
● Ask students to imagine that they are volunteer coordinators for a local campaign office. Tell them that a group of high school students has volunteered to help the campaign for a week, and have the class brainstorm activities that the volunteers could do to help the campaign. (Block walks, clerical work, phone banks, handing out campaign literature outside stores and commuter stations, etc.)

Politics
■ Have students write editorials on what sorts of changes to the campaign financing system they think are necessary.

301

Student Participation Answers
1. The students feel that it takes too much money to run for office, that it can be physically tiring, and that adults are not sufficiently involved.

2. Students should be able to defend the order of their list, which may include television commercials, personal appearances, distributing campaign literature, calling possible voters, and press conferences.

The symbol ♊ denotes active participation strategies.

Activities are keyed for student abilities:
▲ = Basic
● = All Levels
■ = Average/Advanced

SECTION 3

Election Campaigns Are Complex and Costly *(pp. 302–306)*

Section Objectives

☐ identify important considerations in planning a political campaign

☐ identify the major sources of campaign funds

Vocabulary

canvass, endorsement

FOCUS

● Ask students to suggest the single biggest change in presidential campaigning in the last fifty years. (Television.)

Then have the class speculate about the ways in which national conventions and presidential campaigns may be conducted twenty or fifty years from now. Focus discussion on the ways in which new technologies, such as electronic mail and interactive television, may change the process.

EXPLANATION

After students have read the section, you may want to consider the following activities:

Controversial Issues

● CRITICAL THINKING *Do you think that it is proper for newspapers to endorse political candidates? Explain your view.* (Students opposed to newspaper endorsements might argue that such endorsements undermine the impartiality of the press. Students in favor of newspaper endorsements might argue that newspapers perform a public service by announcing their preferences.)

302

SECTION 3

Election Campaigns Are Complex and Costly

> **ACCESS** — **The Main Ideas**
>
> **1** What are some important considerations in planning a political campaign? *pages 302–304*
>
> **2** What are some major sources of campaign funds? *pages 304–306*

Abraham Lincoln described his 1846 run for Congress as follows: "I made the canvass on my own horse; my entertainment, being at the houses of friends, cost me nothing; and my only outlay was 75¢ for a barrel of cider, which some farm-hands insisted that I treat them to."

Today's election campaigns are far more complex and expensive. They require teams of advisers, detailed strategy, and glitzy advertising. Modern campaigns also require big money. In 1990 for example, Senator Jesse Helms of North Carolina spent over $13 million in his campaign for re-election. Helms's opponent, Harvey Gantt, spent nearly $8 million. That's a lot of cider!

4B, 4C, 7A

Planning the Campaign

Both before and after the nomination, candidates and their advisers map out campaign strategies. They must consider many things: the candidate's strengths and weaknesses, the financial support he or she can attract, the type of campaign they want to wage, the image they want to project, the issues they will stress. Should the candidate vigorously attack opponents or largely ignore them? What interest groups must be courted — labor, business, Catholics, Protestants, farmers, women, minorities? What use should be made of television advertising?

Candidates for President have a special set of decisions to make: Should the candidates concentrate on just the populous states or try to visit all fifty? What should be the role of the vice-presidential candidates be — highly visible or low-key? Should the candidate agree to a nationally televised debate?

302

Campaign organizations

No candidate can expect to win either the nomination or the election without a solid campaign organization. A candidate running for local office may have only a small staff of volunteers to help with campaign chores. Those seeking state or national office — such as governor, Congress, or the presidency — usually rely on paid political consultants and professional staff as well as volunteers. A large campaign organization generally includes the following people.

- *Campaign manager* — coordinates the entire campaign; develops strategy; schedules activities.

- *Treasurer* — handles campaign contributions; pays the bills; maintains complete financial records; files official reports as required by state or federal law.

- *Press secretary* — serves as official spokesperson for the candidate; writes press releases; keeps in contact with the media.

- *Media consultant* — "markets" the candidate; creates radio and television commercials; schedules advertising; conducts public opinion surveys; monitors the candidate's popularity; advises the candidate.

- *Speech writers* — draft speeches; coin phrases; help the candidate communicate effectively.

- *Policy advisers* — analyze complex social and economic problems; clarify issues; give policy advice.

- *Fund raisers* — raise campaign money from a variety of sources, including neighborhood coffees, dinner parties, computerized mailing lists, and political action committees.

- *Volunteers* — establish grassroots contacts; conduct door-to-door canvassing; maintain phone banks; type letters; help register voters; provide rides to the polls.

In smaller campaign organizations, staff members may take on more than one of these tasks.

Critical Thinking
▲ *Do you know anyone who has worked on a political campaign? Has a campaign worker ever come to your house?* (Students answering yes to either question could describe their experiences.)

Critical Thinking
● *Why have media consultants played an increasingly important role in recent years?* (Achieving a popular image, as projected through TV, radio, and other media forms, has taken on major

importance for political candidates.)

Information-gathering

Reliable information is crucial for a successful campaign. Candidates must study the issues, determine the stand they will take, and be able to defend their positions publicly. Voters do not trust a candidate who appears "fuzzy" on the issues or makes inaccurate statements about current policies.

A strong stand in favor of an unpopular issue, however, can also gravely harm the campaign. This is why many campaign organizations spend time and money conducting public opinion polls to find out voters' opinions. A poll might reveal, for example, that 90 percent of the voters favor Policy Q. Based on such information, it would be foolish for any candidate to oppose Policy Q.

Finding the voters

The secret to winning most elections lies in knowing where one's supporters are and getting them out to vote. This is known as targeting voters.

One way to target voters is to study previous voting results. Wise candidates identify specific areas that consistently vote for one party or another. For example, it would be a waste of time for a Republican candidate for mayor to campaign in a neighborhood or precinct that consistently votes 70 percent Democratic. Instead, the candidate would first make sure of the Republican precincts, then campaign in the "marginal" areas — those that tend to split their votes between Democrats and Republicans.

Cross-country train trips with speeches at every "whistle stop" were long a feature of presidential campaigning, as in Harry Truman's 1948 tour. Candidates today are more likely to travel by airplane or bus.

Politics

▲ *What are the three general sources of campaign funds?* (The candidates themselves, other individuals, and political action committees.)

▲ *What limits are there on contributions by private individuals?* (It is illegal to donate more than $1,000 per election to any one campaign, or more than $25,000 per year to a number of campaigns.)

▲ *What government funds go to political campaigns?* (Voluntary deductions from federal income taxes are paid out to major candidates.)

● ⬛CRITICAL THINKING⬛ List one argument for, and one argument against, the proposal that the federal government fund *all* presidential campaigns equally and fully. (*For*—The influence of money on campaigns would be diminished. *Against*—The cost would be prohibitive.)

Critical Thinking

■ *Is it ever in a candidate's interest to appear "fuzzy" on an issue? Explain.* (It could be, if the public itself is fuzzy on the same issue or, conversely, if the public is so deeply polarized that taking any clear stand would cost a candidate the support of the other side.)

The symbol 👥 denotes active participation strategies.

Activities are keyed for student abilities:
▲ = Basic
● = All Levels
■ = Average/Advanced

A door-to-door **canvass**, or survey, is a traditional method of targeting. Precinct captains and volunteers survey each household to determine the occupants' party identification and their opinion of the candidate. At election time, campaign workers can then concentrate on known party supporters.

Establishing a phone bank is a more modern way of canvassing voters. Using a computerized list of registered voters, volunteers call each one on the phone. Usually, the caller politely asks, "If the election were held today, would you vote for Candidate X or Candidate Y?" On election day, volunteers can call back their candidate's supporters and urge them to vote. Computerized lists now let campaign workers target voters according to personal preferences and tastes — favorite TV shows or magazines, contributions to interest groups, and many others.

Mass media coverage

The quickest and easiest way for candidates to reach the most voters is through the mass media. Attracting the attention of newspaper and television journalists has become a must, particularly for candidates in state, congressional, and presidential races. A carefully timed 30-second TV commercial, for example, will probably reach more voters than 30 days of door-to-door canvassing.

One important form of media coverage is the editorial **endorsement**, or support, of a major newspaper. During the 1992 presidential election, for example, over 180 daily newspapers — among them the *Detroit Free Press, New York Times,* and *Washington Post* — endorsed Bill Clinton for President. Over 130 daily newspapers, including the *Chicago Tribune, Dallas Morning News,* and *Cincinnati Enquirer,* supported George Bush.

Paid political advertising has become a vital part of most major political campaigns. Candidates use newspaper, radio, and television advertising, but TV is unquestionably the most potent tool for conveying a candidate's message. Television advertising is also the most expensive, and it is now the single largest campaign expense in congressional and presidential campaigns.

Appearances on television news programs are another important form of mass media coverage. For most Americans, television newscasts have become the major source of political information. To get coverage on the evening news, candidates schedule rallies, "whistle-stop" tours, press conferences, or meetings with farmers, factory workers, or minority groups early in the day. Candidates also like to appear on political talk shows such as "Meet the Press" or "Face the Nation." These appearances amount to free advertising, a tactic campaign experts call "visuals."

Visuals, however, can be a double-edged sword. Media exposure may harm, not help, the candidate. The camera may reveal the candidate being heckled by angry onlookers. A microphone can pick up thoughtless, off-the-cuff remarks that prove both embarrassing and costly in terms of votes.

Presidential debates

Televised debates — staged for the first time in 1960 — play a controversial role in presidential campaigns. In the 1960 series of debates, John F. Kennedy successfully projected a positive, youthful image, in contrast with Richard Nixon, who appeared tired and sullen. In 1976, when Gerald Ford mistakenly stated in a debate that Poland was not under the influence of the Soviet Union, viewers gave the edge to challenger Jimmy Carter. But in 1980, Ronald Reagan's ease and charm helped him score an unofficial television "victory" over Carter. The results of the 1984 and 1988 debates were mixed. In 1992 Bill Clinton, George Bush, and Ross Perot held three debates. The debates were often lively, but no candidate emerged a clear winner.

It is difficult to measure the actual impact of TV debates on voters' choices. Voters who are wavering between the candidates, however, may be influenced by what they see on television. Whatever their impact, televised debates are likely to be a part of future presidential campaigns.

4B, 4C, 7A

Financing the Campaign

To wage a successful campaign, candidates must be able to attract financial backers. Money is the oil that keeps campaign machinery running. It costs money for office rental, supplies,

The second 1992 presidential debate used a "town-hall" format. Undecided voters, rather than reporters, asked the candidates questions. Bill Clinton felt especially comfortable in this setting since he had often used the format during the Democratic primaries.

GUIDED/INDEPENDENT PRACTICE

● Have each student imagine that he or she is a veteran of many successful political campaigns. A close friend has been nominated to run for a high political office and has asked for advice on how to run a campaign. Have each student write a memorandum to the nominee giving advice on key points to remember while campaigning. Memoranda can indicate how to attract voters and obtain media coverage, and should describe strategies the writer considers most important to a successful campaign.

RETEACHING/CORRECTIVES

▲ Ask students to compare the various means by which candidates finance presidential campaigns. Have students indicate the advantages or drawbacks of each method.

ENRICHMENT/EXTENSION

■ Have students complete **Skills Challenge Worksheet 11,** which asks them to analyze an editorial that discusses some of the problems with presidential campaigns.

salaries, postage, advertising, chartered airplanes, telephone lines, printing, computer services, and much more. The cost of printing and mailing 100,000 brochures, for example, may be more than $10,000. A 30-second network TV commercial during prime time often exceeds $200,000.

Moreover, each election seems to cost more than the previous one. According to one authority, Herbert Alexander, total campaign spending for all national, state, and local offices rose from $200 million in 1964 to an estimated $1.8 billion in 1984. On the average, a candidate for the House of Representatives can expect to spend $300,000, while a Senate campaign averages $2 million. The Bush and Clinton presidential campaigns in 1992 cost over $90 million each. This is a far cry from the 75 cents that Abraham Lincoln spent for cider in his 1846 campaign for Congress.

Sources of campaign funding

There are three general sources of campaign funds. One source is the candidates themselves. Some candidates are wealthy enough to finance large parts of their own campaigns. For instance, Nelson Rockefeller, a New York Republican, spent $5 million to become governor. In 1970 Richard Ottinger, a Democrat from New York, spent $3.9 million in an unsuccessful bid for the Senate. Perhaps this is why a comedian once joked, "America is the only country in the world where any millionaire can grow up to be President." (Actually, even millionaires have to borrow money to run for national office.)

Contributions from individuals are a second way to secure funds. Until recently, individuals were allowed to contribute as much as they wanted to candidates. In 1972, for instance, about forty people gave President Nixon more than $100,000 each in campaign contributions.

Many people believed that such large contributions gave wealthy persons too much influence over public officials. These criticisms increased after the Watergate scandal, which uncovered illegal tactics in Nixon's 1972 campaign. In response, the Federal Election Campaign Acts of 1971, 1974, and 1976 were passed to limit campaign contributions. Today, one person can give only $1,000 per election to any candidate's campaign. (Primaries and general elections are considered separate elections.) The top limit for an individual's total contributions to all candidates is $25,000 in a year.

A third source of campaign funding is political action committees (PACs), the special organizations created by interest groups to channel money to political candidates. Federal laws also limit PAC contributions to $5,000 per candidate

305

Check for Understanding
▲ *Why were the Federal Election Campaign Acts of 1971, 1974, and 1976 passed?* (To combat fears that the rich were using campaign contributions to influence candidates.)

Background: *Constitutional Heritage* Except for presidential candidates who receive federal funds, there are no restrictions on how much a candidate can contribute to his or her own campaign. (*Buckley v. Valeo,* 1976.)

Cross-reference
Chapter 9, p. 260, explains the development and regulation of PACs.

The symbol 👥 denotes active participation strategies.

Activities are keyed for student abilities:
▲ = Basic
● = All Levels
■ = Average/Advanced

Section 3 Review Answers

1. **(a)** Candidates must assess their strengths and weaknesses, the type of campaign they want to wage, the image they seek to project, and the issues they will stress. **(b)** Whether to debate on national television, the role their running mate should play, whether to visit every state.

2. **(a)** Paid political advertisements, appearances on news programs, televised debates. **(b)** Through mass media.

3. The candidate's personal wealth, individual contributions, political action committees, federal funding.

4. The candidate must raise $5,000, in contributions of $250 or less, in a minimum of twenty states.

Critical thinking Students should consider what kind of role advertising plays in influencing voters. They may wish to cite examples to support their opinions.

CLOSURE

● Have students write three "I learned . . ." statements to show what they learned in this section. Then have them read Section 4, paying special attention to efforts to guarantee suffrage.

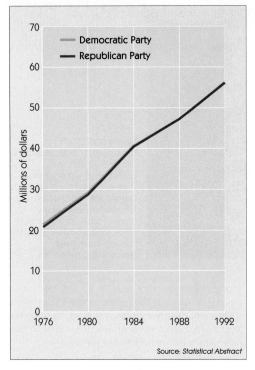

Source: *Statistical Abstract*

Figure 11-1 PRESIDENTIAL ELECTION FUNDS The two major parties have received almost equal amounts of federal money since federal funding was introduced in 1976. **4C**

per election. Acting on its own, however, a PAC can spend unlimited amounts to show its support for a candidate — buying newspaper or TV ads, for instance. The Supreme Court ruled in 1985 that limiting such expressions would violate the PAC's freedom of speech (*Federal Election Commission v. National Conservative Political Action Committee*).

Federal funding

Because the high cost of campaigning could make it difficult for anyone but the very wealthy to run for President, the federal government now contributes to presidential campaigns. Taxpayers actually supply these campaign funds through voluntary deductions from their federal income taxes. A box on the tax form asks taxpayers whether they want $1.00 of their taxes to

306

go into the Presidential Election Campaign Fund. (Checking "Yes" neither increases one's tax nor reduces one's refund.)

In election years since 1976, these federal funds have been distributed to presidential hopefuls in both the primaries and general election. To be eligible to receive money for the presidential primaries, a candidate must first raise $5,000 (in contributions of $250 or less) in at least twenty states. The government then matches any further contributions the candidate receives (up to $250 for each giver).

In presidential elections, major party nominees are automatically eligible for campaign funding. In 1992 Bill Clinton and George Bush both received $55.2 million. If candidates accept federal funds, they may not take contributions from any other source. Minor party candidates are reimbursed for part of their campaign costs if they receive at least 5 percent of the popular vote. For example, in 1980, Independent presidential candidate John Anderson got 6.6 percent of the popular vote. He therefore was repaid $4.2 million in federal funds after the election.

SECTION 3 REVIEW

Vocabulary and key terms

canvass(304)   endorsement(304)

For review

1. (a) What are some strategy decisions that a candidate for office must make? (b) What special considerations must presidential candidates take into account? **4D**
2. (a) What are three ways that political campaigns can make use of the media? (b) What is the most effective way to reach voters? **4B**
3. What are four sources of campaign funds? **4C**
4. What criteria must presidential candidates meet to be eligible for federal funding in the general election? **2E**

Critical thinking

DRAWING INFERENCES How does TV advertising affect political campaigning? Are its effects on elections good or bad? Why? **4B**

Figure 11-1
● *Approximately how much federal funding did each party receive in 1984? In 1992?* (About $40 million; about $55 million.) *Should presidential election campaigns be supported by*

federal funds? Explain.
(Students should note that taxpayers' contributions to federal election funds are voluntary.)

Background: *Politics* The voluntary deduction originated in the Revenue Act of 1971.

★☆ CRITICAL THINKING
Recognizing Propaganda

Any communication intended to influence the opinions or actions of its listeners is **propaganda**. Propaganda is all around you — television commercials telling you to buy a product, speeches by public figures urging you to support a particular policy, or statements by candidates seeking your vote. Although propaganda usually has a negative connotation, it is neither good nor bad; it is simply a part of political life.

Propagandists use a variety of techniques to persuade you to think or do something. (Some of these techniques are listed on page 262.) Propaganda may appeal to logic and reason, but more often it relies on appeals to emotion, prejudice, and fear. To make intelligent judgments and decisions, you should be aware of propaganda and the forms in which it comes.

★ ISSUE: Negative Political Advertising

Recent political campaigns have stirred controversy because of the increased use of negative advertising. Instead of aiming to give a favorable impression of the candidate paying for the ad, negative advertising aims to give a negative impression of his or her opponent.

Critics charge that negative ads do not give voters the information they need to make rational political choices. Instead, negative ads often focus on personalities. Critics also charge that negative campaigns lower the quality of American politics. Many able and respected individuals refuse to take part in politics because of the scrutiny their private lives must undergo.

Many observers defend negative advertising, however. First of all, they say, a candidate's personality should be important to voters. Knowing that a candidate has cheated on taxes or has done political favors for campaign contributors may be just as important as knowing his or her positions on the issues. Moreover, many negative ads do discuss policy issues. Such ads help voters make informed decisions by alerting them to the differences between candidates. Finally, negative ads are entertaining and may actually spark interest in politics.

Read the following cases of political advertising. As you are reading, look for instances of propaganda.

Case A
In the 1964 presidential campaign, challenger Barry Goldwater was criticized for his apparent willingness to use nuclear weapons. Lyndon Johnson's supporters ran an ad showing a little girl playing peacefully in a flower-filled meadow. Suddenly a nuclear mushroom cloud loomed up behind her. The only words in the commercial appeared at the end: "Re-elect President Johnson."

Case B
A candidate for the Senate (the challenger) appears on the television screen saying, "I'll have more time each day to work on Oklahoma's problems because I won't spend my time using one of these." He then produces a whirring hair-dryer and points it at his balding head.

Case C
Imagine the following ad: "Candidate A *says* he supports a strong defense, but has voted against every appropriation for the Strategic Defense Initiative. Vote for Candidate B."

Analyzing the Issue

1. What emotions does the advertisement in Case A try to evoke?
2. What is the candidate in Case B saying about his opponent?
3. What reasons does the ad in Case C give to vote against Candidate A? What does it leave out?
4. Which of the cases above deal mostly with issues? With personalities? Which is most helpful to voters trying to decide for whom they should vote?
5. Study Figure 9-4 on page 262. Which of the methods of propaganda listed in the figure are used in the cases above?

307

Laws Ensure Fair Elections

In her autobiography, Fannie Lou Hamer told how as a black person in Mississippi, she was denied her constitutional right to vote in 1962.

> There was eighteen of us who went down to the courthouse that day [to register to vote] and all of us were arrested. Police said the bus was painted the wrong color — said it was too yellow. After I got bailed out I went back to the plantation where Pap and I had lived for eighteen years. My oldest girl met me and told me that Mr. Marlow, the plantation owner, was mad and raising sand. He had heard that I had tried to register. That night he called on us and said "We're not going to have this in Mississippi and you will have to withdraw. . . . I will give you until tomorrow morning and if you don't withdraw, you will have to leave." So I left. . . . Ten days later they fired into Mrs. Tucker's house where I was staying.

Fanny Lou Hamer's experience of discrimination led her to work for changes in voting laws. For decades, the federal government had permitted states to discriminate against minority citizens' voting rights. She and others in the civil rights movement pressured Congress to prohibit discrimination at the polls. In passing the Voting Rights Act of 1965, Congress did just that.

2D, 4C, 6G, 6H

Guaranteeing Suffrage

The national government has had the greatest impact on elections through its actions to extend the right to vote — also called *suffrage* or the **franchise**. Under national laws, women,

blacks, and American Indians have all finally won their right to vote. As Chapter 7 discusses, the ratification of the Fifteenth Amendment in 1870 legally extended suffrage to black male Americans. Despite this amendment, many states invented legal devices to prevent blacks and other minorities from voting. These discriminatory laws, which were one target of the civil rights movement, have gradually been eliminated by federal action.

Ending discriminatory laws

One device used by the states to limit voting rights was the **poll tax**, a fee that had to be paid as a condition for voting. Intended to replace property requirements, poll taxes were originally meant to encourage voting. In time, however, they became a discriminatory tool, used mainly against blacks in the South. The 24th Amendment, ratified in 1964, put an end to poll taxes in national elections. Two years later, the Supreme Court ruled that poll taxes were also unconstitutional in state or local elections (*Harper v. Virginia State Board of Elections,* 1966).

Another technique some states developed to discourage voting was the **literacy test**. A literacy test is a written or oral examination designed to determine a voter's ability to read and to understand documents. Literacy tests were first used in the late 1800's to prevent immigrants from voting. Some groups even proposed using a literacy test to keep immigrants from entering the country at all.

In the South, however, literacy tests were used mainly to discourage black voters. The tests included highly detailed, technical questions on the Constitution, law, and government. White election examiners applied the tests unfairly to keep even well-educated blacks from voting.

With the Voting Rights Act of 1965, Congress tried to eliminate such tests as a barrier to voting. This act was quickly challenged as interference with state law but upheld by the Supreme Court (*South Carolina v. Katzenbach,* 1965). The act was later extended several times to add safeguards for the voting rights of other ethnic

308

minorities. An amendment in 1975 called for bilingual ballots in areas where a sizable percentage of voters speak a language other than English.

When literacy tests were first used in the South, they disqualified many whites as well as blacks. To get around this, South Carolina in 1895 introduced the **grandfather clause**. According to this legal provision, anyone who was qualified to vote before January 1, 1867, or whose father or grandfather was qualified at that time, did not have to pass a literacy test. Obviously, only whites could satisfy this requirement. Other states quickly followed South Carolina's lead. In a 1915 Oklahoma case, the grandfather clause was declared unconstitutional (*Guinn v. U.S.*).

Another device used to deny blacks the right to vote was the **white primary**. In 1923, Texas passed a law that prohibited blacks from voting in the Democratic Party primary, on the grounds that the Fifteenth Amendment applied only to general elections. But because the Democratic Party dominated Texas politics at that time, candidates who won the primary almost always won the general election. The effect of the white primary was essentially to deprive blacks of their vote. In 1944, the Supreme Court ruled that white primaries violated the Fifteenth Amendment (*Smith v. Allwright*).

Votes for 18-year-olds

Before 1971, nearly all the states required voters to be at least 21 years old. Georgia, in 1943, was the first to let 18-year-olds vote. During the 1960's, a nationwide movement to lower the voting age to 18 gained momentum, spurred in part by the Vietnam War. The movement's chief argument was that if 18-year-olds were old enough to fight for their country, they were old enough to have a say in its government.

Congress responded by enacting the Voting Rights Act of 1970. This act gave 18-year-olds the right to vote in both federal and state elections. The law was quickly challenged, and in *Oregon v. Mitchell* (1970) the Supreme Court ruled that Congress could not regulate state elections. The 1970 Voting Rights Act, therefore, applied only in national elections. States with voting ages over 18 had to keep two voting lists — one for national elections and one for state elections.

To override the Court's decision and eliminate the confusion, Congress quickly proposed the 26th Amendment: "The right of citizens of the United States, who are eighteen years of age or older, to vote shall not be denied or abridged by any state on account of age." This amendment was soon ratified by the states, becoming effective in 1971.

Vigorous efforts by the civil rights movement removed many of the legal barriers that had long kept blacks from registering and voting in many parts of the South.

309

EXPLANATION

After students have read the section, you may want to consider the following activities:

History

▲ *Why did many states pass laws that discriminated against African Americans?* (The states' white populations wanted to keep African Americans from gaining political power.) *How were these discriminatory laws done away with?* (Through Supreme Court decisions.)

Civic Participation

▲ Have students read the relevant parts of the Voter's Handbook that are referred to within the section. Then have students find the information for your state under the registration requirements table on p. 324. *Compared to those of other states, are your state's requirements strict, loose, or average?*

👥 **Civic Participation**

● | CRITICAL THINKING | Have class members imagine that they have been asked to prepare voting requirements for the next election. Have students meet in groups to deal with the following questions: *Should the restrictions on eligibility be more or less stringent than those now in existence? Who would be eligible to vote? Who would not? Would literacy be a requirement? Speaking English? Completing junior or senior high school? Participating in military or community service?*

The symbol 👥 denotes active participation strategies.

Activities are keyed for student abilities:
▲ = Basic
● = All Levels
■ = Average/Advanced

Voting Procedures

Today 18-year-olds can vote in all elections in the United States. Certain rules and procedures, however, vary from place to place. The Voter's Handbook, found at the end of this chapter (page 321), gives you the information you need to prepare to vote in your state. This section summarizes current American election procedures.

Registration

In nearly every state, people must register in order to vote. **Registration** is the act of signing up with election officials in order to qualify for voting. To register, potential voters are required to give their name, address, and, in states with closed primaries, party preference.

As the table on page 324 of the Voter's Handbook shows, registration rules vary from state to state. Most states also have **residency** requirements, meaning that a voter must have lived in the state for a certain period of time. These laws are intended to make sure that voters are familiar with local issues and to prevent outsiders from trying to swing elections. Under the Voting Rights Act of 1970, residency requirements cannot be used to discriminate.

The secret ballot

Early in American history, political parties printed their own ballots. Each party's ballot had a distinctive color, size, or marking. When a voter selected a ballot, onlookers could easily identify the candidates for whom he was voting. This practice not only deprived voters of privacy, it also made it easy for corrupt politicians to bribe or intimidate voters.

The **Australian ballot** (or secret ballot), named after the country where it originated, was introduced in the United States in 1888 and is now used in every state. To ensure secrecy, the Australian ballot is printed, paid for, and distributed by state or local governments. Only qualified voters can obtain ballots and (except for absentee voters) can vote only at polling places established by state law. General election ballots list the candidates of every party, rather than having separate ballots for each party. Most importantly, all ballots are cast in the privacy of a voting booth.

There are several variations of the Australian ballot. The two most common are the party-column ballot (or "Indiana" ballot) and the office-group (or "Massachusetts") ballot. Both of these ballots are shown on page 326 of the Voter's Handbook.

Figure 11–2 WARDS AND PRECINCTS   Urban voters are assigned to wards and precincts as shown in this map of Boston. 4C

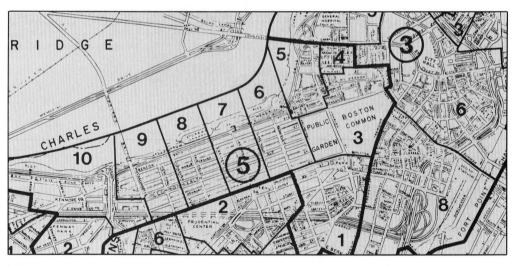

ments has been singled out as one of the most effective ways of increasing voter participation.

Figure 11–2
● *Why are some of the black lines drawn on the map thicker than the others?* (The thick lines represent ward boundaries; the thin ones represent precincts.)

The polling place

Both state and local laws govern where a person votes. The state sets up voting districts, and local governments divide them into smaller areas, usually the **ward** and then the **precinct** (PREE-sinkt). There are about 160,000 precincts in the United States, each with about 1,000 voters. Voters in each precinct are assigned to a specific polling place. Polling places may be in public schools, fire stations, libraries, private homes, apartment lobbies, church basements, or even storefronts.

State or local officials also determine the hours for voting. Typically, polling places are open from 7 A.M. to 7 P.M., giving most voters a chance to vote. If people must be away from their home precincts because of illness, business, vacation, school, or military service, all states allow them to vote by casting **absentee ballots**. Absentee ballots must be requested, filled out, and mailed in to the proper election official within a specified time prior to the election.

Finally, state or local officials determine the type of voting apparatus used. Many places still use paper ballots, which the voter simply marks with a pencil. Paper ballots, though easy to use, are difficult to tally. To reduce counting time and errors, most precincts now use some type of computerized voting machine. The most widely used voting machines use either punch-cards or small levers by which voters can record their choices.

Ensuring honest elections

The quality of American government depends on free and honest elections. Besides the secret ballot, officials take other precautions to prevent vote fraud. For example, election judges from both parties are assigned to each polling place. These judges distribute and count ballots and check registration lists to determine who is qualified to vote. In some places, a police officer also is assigned to each polling place.

Poll watchers may also be present in the polling place to ensure honest elections. These persons can represent any participating political party, including minor parties. When the judge reads each voter's name aloud from a master voting list, the poll watchers, seated nearby, check the name on their own lists. If a person has already voted or is listed as having moved or died, the poll watcher may challenge his or her right to vote. The election judges must then decide if the voter is qualified.

As soon as the polls close, the results from each precinct are tallied and forwarded to the appropriate local or state canvassing board. (The actual ballots, cards, or machine records may also be taken to a secure place.) The canvassing board is an official body that tabulates the votes and certifies the election winners. Most canvassing boards are also **bipartisan**, with members from both major parties. In extremely close elections, the losers may call for a recount or another election. The final decision on the validity of election results rests with the courts.

SECTION 4 REVIEW

Vocabulary and key terms

franchise (308)	party-column ballot (310)
poll tax (308)	office-group ballot (310)
literacy test (308)	ward (311)
grandfather clause (309)	precinct (311)
white primary (309)	absentee ballot (311)
registration (310)	poll watcher (311)
residency (310)	bipartisan (311)
Australian ballot (310)	

For review

1. What election rules are established by (a) the states? (b) the national government? **6H**
2. How were voting rights denied by (a) literacy tests? (b) the grandfather clause? (c) the poll tax? **6G**
3. What was the effect on voting procedures of (a) the 24th Amendment? (b) the 26th Amendment? **6H**
4. What are some reasons voters are required to register? **4C**
5. What precautions are taken at the polls to ensure an honest election? **6G**

Critical thinking

ORGANIZING AN ARGUMENT   What are some arguments that might have been made in favor of the constitutional amendment to give 18-year-olds the vote? What arguments might have been made against the proposal? **8A**

discrimination, and the election of House members from single-member districts.

2. (a) The detailed, technical questions that were asked about the Constitution, laws, and government disqualified many voters. **(b)** It disqualified many former slaves because their fathers and grandfathers had not qualified to vote before January 1, 1867, as required by this clause. **(c)** The required fee disqualified poorer voters.

3. (a) It outlawed poll taxes in national elections. **(b)** It lowered the voting age to 18.

4. Registration ensures that voters meet age and residency requirements as well as disclose party preferences (in states with closed primaries).

5. Secret ballots, election judges, and poll watchers.

Critical thinking *In favor—* Anyone old enough to be drafted and treated as an adult in other ways should be allowed to vote. *Against—*Teenagers are too young to be responsible; they may not be aware of local issues because they are in school or are not generally well informed.

CLOSURE

● Have students reread the statement by Fannie Lou Hamer on p. 308 and use it to explain the need for laws ensuring fair elections. Then have students read Section 5, noting changes in voting behavior.

311

The symbol 👥 denotes active participation strategies.

Activities are keyed for student abilities:
▲ = Basic
● = All Levels
■ = Average/Advanced

SECTION 5

American Voting Behavior Is Unique
(pp. 312–317)

Section Objectives

☐ identify major factors that affect whether people vote

☐ identify major factors that affect how people vote

Vocabulary

socioeconomic

FOCUS

● Introduce the section by writing the following statement on the board: *Most young people in America are far more interested in obtaining a drivers' license than in gaining the right to vote.* **Do you agree or disagree with this statement? Why or why not?**

Why is voter participation in America so low? Focus discussion on the reasons why voting should be important to American citizens of all ages and the reasons why so many eligible citizens, especially younger ones, do not vote.

ACCESS | **The Main Ideas**

1 **What are some major factors that affect whether people vote?** pages 312–316

2 **What are some major factors that affect how people vote?** pages 316–317

If you ask people you know who are eligible voters, "So, why didn't you vote in the last election?" you may hear answers like "I forgot." "I didn't have time." "I thought the candidates were bad." "It doesn't make any difference if I vote." "I had to work on my car."

A surprisingly small number of Americans actually vote. In presidential elections, only about half of all eligible voters participate. In other elections, such as those for Congress, turnout is even lower (see the graph below). As the chart on the opposite page shows, those who vote generally have more education, earn more money, and are older than those who do not. Many poorer, less-educated people doubt whether voting will make much difference in their lives.

Each of the millions of Americans of voting age faces the choices of whether to vote and how to vote. Many factors influence these decisions.

4A, 4C, 4D, 5C

The American Voter

During the past 125 years, voter turnout in presidential elections has dropped severely. In 1876, for example, over 80 percent of those eligible went to the polls. By 1936, that figure had dropped to around 56 percent. It continued to decline, reaching 50 percent in 1988, until 1992, when turnout increased to 55 percent.

Figure 11–3 **VOTER TURNOUT IN FEDERAL ELECTIONS   The percentage of eligible voters who go to the polls drops sharply in years when there is not a presidential election.** 4D

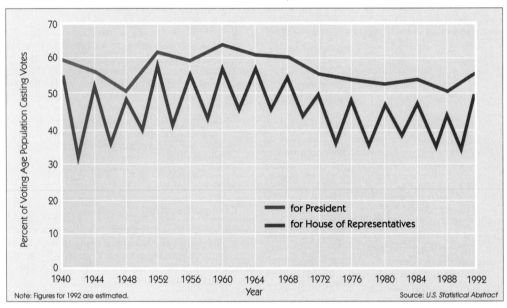

Note: Figures for 1992 are estimated.   Source: *U.S. Statistical Abstract*

Background: *Civic Participation* Government figures for the number of Americans of voting age include non-citizens.

Figure 11–3
● *Why is voter turnout lower for most off-year elections than in years with presidential elections?* (Presidential elections get more media coverage, only occur once every four years, and determine who will lead the entire nation.)

Moreover, as Figure 11–3 shows, voter turnout is even lower for off-year elections — races for Congress and governor in years when there is not a presidential election. Even in presidential elections, millions of people who vote for President ignore the congressional races. In many county and city elections, voter turnout of less than 25 percent is not uncommon.

Who were the 114 million Americans who decided to vote in 1992? Who were the 71 million who chose *not* to vote? A look at Americans' voting behavior can give an interesting picture of American voters.

Social and economic characteristics

One way of looking at voting behavior is to analyze **socioeconomic** factors. This term refers to a combination of an individual's *social* characteristics, such as age and education, and *economic* status, such as occupation and income. Figure 11–4 shows how these factors influenced voting behavior in the presidential election of 1992.

EDUCATION AND INCOME   It is very clear that the more education and wealth people have, the more likely they are to vote. In 1992, 40 percent of people who had not finished high school voted. By contrast, college graduates had the highest rate of any group surveyed — 81 percent. People with higher incomes are also more likely to vote. Over 78 percent of families earning more than $35,000 voted.

OCCUPATION   The most significant effect of occupation on voting is being out of a job. In 1992, over 60 percent of those employed voted, compared with 46 percent of the unemployed. People who work for the government had the best voter turnout of any working group — 75 percent.

AGE   The older the person, the more likely it is that he or she will vote. The age group with the lowest voter participation is 18- to 24-year-olds. One reason may be that young people tend to be much more mobile — leaving home, attending college, traveling, or serving in the armed forces, for example — and may for reasons like this fail to meet residency requirements or be out of town on election day.

RACE   Historically, racial background has played a part in voter turnout, with whites more likely to vote than blacks or other minority

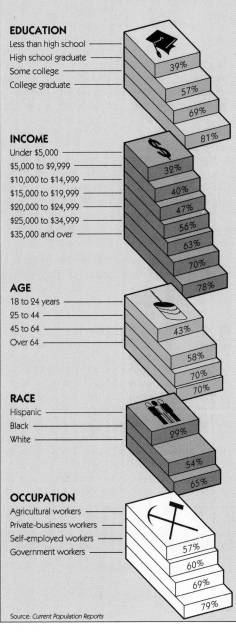

Figure 11–4 CHARACTERISTICS OF VOTERS
As these 1992 statistics show, turnout is related to several social and economic characteristics. 4A

EDUCATION
Less than high school
High school graduate — 39%
Some college — 57%
College graduate — 69%
81%

INCOME
Under $5,000
$5,000 to $9,999 — 32%
$10,000 to $14,999 — 40%
$15,000 to $19,999 — 47%
$20,000 to $24,999 — 56%
$25,000 to $34,999 — 63%
$35,000 and over — 70%
78%

AGE
18 to 24 years
25 to 44 — 43%
45 to 64 — 58%
Over 64 — 70%
70%

RACE
Hispanic
Black — 29%
White — 54%
65%

OCCUPATION
Agricultural workers
Private-business workers — 57%
Self-employed workers — 60%
Government workers — 69%
79%

Source: *Current Population Reports*

313

EXPLANATION

After students have read the section, you may want to consider the following activities:

♟ Politics

● Have students write a three-paragraph editorial proposing a plan to increase voter turnout in the United States. Ask for volunteers to read their editorials to the class.

♟ Civic Participation

● Stage a debate in class on the issue of voter turnout. Topics for debate include: *(1) America's low voter turnout is actually a sign of a healthy political system. (2) In a democracy, citizens should have the right not to vote. (3) American citizens should be fined for not registering and voting.*

Figure 11–4
■ *Select one of the socioeconomic characteristics and write a hypothesis to explain the differences in voter turnout.*

(*Example:* Government workers probably have greater political interest and awareness than other groups; this might explain their relatively high turnout.)

The symbol ♟ denotes active participation strategies.

Activities are keyed for student abilities:
▲ = Basic
● = All Levels
■ = Average/Advanced

Comparative Government

● CRITICAL THINKING **What might be the reason why some countries require their citizens to vote?** (They might regard voting as a civic duty or want to ensure that election results are as representative of public sentiment as possible.)

Civic Participation

Some voters suffer from "ballot fatigue." They are overwhelmed by the seemingly endless list of names and issues on the ballot. Some voters do not complete their ballots and others are discouraged from voting altogether.

■ CRITICAL THINKING **List one argument for and one argument against shortening the ballot.** (*For*—It would reduce "ballot fatigue." *Against*—Any limitations on the number of ballot issues would interfere with voters' right to decide important issues.)

Cooperative Learning

● Have students work in groups to produce cartoons or posters on the subject of voter apathy in America.

groups. In 1980, for example, 60.9 percent of whites voted, compared to 50.5 percent of blacks and 29.9 percent of Hispanics. By 1992, the numbers had not changed significantly. The percentage of whites who voted was 65 percent. The black vote increased slightly to 54 percent, while the Hispanic vote was about the same percent.

SEX Even after the passage of the Nineteenth Amendment, American men were for many years more likely to vote in elections than women. There no longer, however, appears to be any significant difference between the two groups. In fact, in the 1992 election, the 65 percent voter turnout for women was higher than the 63 percent for men.

RESIDENCE Where people live may also have some bearing on whether they vote. Regionally, the Midwest and Northeast record higher turnouts than the South or West. People living in suburbs and small towns also are more likely to vote than those in metropolitan areas.

Voter attitudes

Despite these generalizations, each voter is an individual who must make his or her personal decision to vote or not vote. Many Americans vote out of a sense of civic duty. Others vote because they have a sense of political efficacy (EHF-ih-kuh-see), or effectiveness. They believe that their opinions and votes really matter and can make a difference in how the country is run.

Low voter turnout figures, on the other hand, show that there is considerable political apathy, or indifference, among American voters. According to a survey taken by the U.S. Census Bureau, about 27 percent of registered voters in 1980 failed to vote because they didn't want to vote, didn't prefer any of the candidates, or were simply uninterested. Another 41.3 percent of nonvoters claimed they were unable to get to the polls on election day. Excuses included illness, travel, or lack of transportation.

4C, 5C

Trends in Voting Behavior

International comparisons

America's voter turnout figures are even more meaningful when compared with those in other countries. Figure 11–5 shows comparative voter turnouts in a number of democratic na-

tions. Only Switzerland, with 46.1 percent, is lower than the United States. The highest percentage of voters turn out in Australia, Belgium, Italy, and Greece.

These comparisons do not necessarily mean that American democracy is in trouble. They clearly show, however, that many countries have a more politically active population than does the United States. In these countries, the people are clearly more interested in the outcome of elections than we are in the United States.

More voters, fewer votes

Oddly, voter turnout has declined as suffrage has been extended to more Americans. Each time a new group of Americans is given the vote, the *percentage* of eligible voters who go to the polls has decreased. For example, the 26th Amendment gave 11 million Americans between the ages of 18 and 21 the right to vote. In 1972, however, less than half that newly enfranchised group actually voted. Between the 1968 and 1972 elections, the total number of voters increased from 73.2 to 77.7 million, but the percentage of voter turnout decreased from 61 to 55. Thus, the extension of voting rights — clearly a sign of a democratic government — may be one cause of a decrease in voter turnout.

Voter interest

A number of simple political factors affect voter turnout. As we have seen, presidential elections draw more voters than congressional, state, or local elections. General elections usually bring out more voters than primary elections. This is especially true in close races and in states where two-party competition is strong. Voters in these situations are more likely to believe that their vote does make a difference. In predominantly one-party states, primaries sometimes generate more votes than general elections, because the primaries are where the true contest is fought. Finally, the more media coverage an election attracts, the greater the turnout.

Easier voting

Despite the removal of barriers like the poll tax and literacy tests, legal restrictions on residency and voter registration still prevent some people from voting. People who move just before election day, for example, are likely to lose their chance to vote.

Check for Understanding
▲ *Why do primaries in predominantly one-party states often generate a higher voter turnout than general elections?* (The candidate who wins the dominant party's primary usually is heavily favored to win the general election. Some voters, expecting that candidate to win the general election handily, do not vote.)

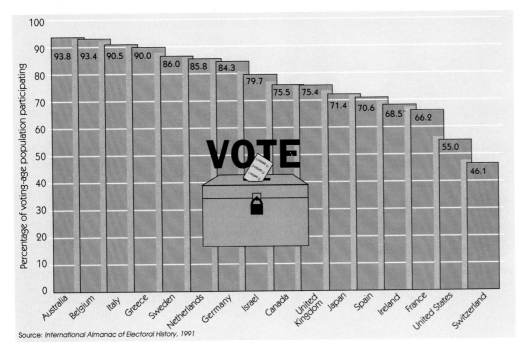

Source: International Almanac of Electoral History, 1991

Figure 11–5 **VOTER TURNOUT IN DEMOCRATIC NATIONS** Voter turnout in the United States is lower than that in most other democratic nations. 1C

In states requiring long residency and registration in person, voting turnout is quite low. Such is the case in Nevada and North Carolina, for example, where the turnout in 1992 was 48.0 and 44.5 percent, respectively. Conversely, voter turnout is much greater in states where it is easier to register. For instance, North Dakota has no voter registration, while voters in Maine and Minnesota can register on election day. Voter turnout in those states in 1992 was 66.6, 71.4, and 69.8 percent — well above the national average.

Some observers have recommended making voter registration easier. While the United States leaves registering up to the individual voter, in some other nations the government mails out registration forms to its citizens. In some countries, such as Austria and Belgium, citizens can be fined for not registering and voting. Americans would probably object to that kind of law. But political scientists estimate that by simplifying registra-

tion voter turnout could be increased about 9 percent.

In 1993 Congress passed a registration-simplification law. Under the Motor Voter Act, states must allow citizens to register to vote by mail and when they apply for driver's licenses or for federal or state benefits. Other suggestions for increasing voter turnout include extending voting hours and making election day a holiday.

Election predictions

Media coverage can heighten voter interest, but election night coverage may hurt voter turnout, particularly in the West. Television networks compete to be the first to report election results and predict the outcomes accurately.

In 1980, for example, one network declared a Reagan victory at 8:15 P.M. (Eastern time). This was based upon early returns and exit polling. Even in New York, polls were open for another hour. In the West, it was only 5:15, and many

315

Figure 11–5

■ In some of the nations with the highest turnouts, voting is required. Ask students to suggest other reasons for the differences in turnout between the United States and other democratic nations. (Widespread unhappiness with government policies, few registration rules.)

GUIDED/INDEPENDENT PRACTICE

● Have students select one of the three graphics in this section and write a two-paragraph summary of the information it presents.

RETEACHING/CORRECTIVES

▲ Have students write three paragraphs, each one summarizing the material under one of the red headings.

Have students complete **Skills Practice Worksheet 11**, which asks them to analyze a graph of voter turnout in congressional elections.

The symbol ⅱ denotes active participation strategies.

Activities are keyed for student abilities:
▲ = Basic
● = All Levels
■ = Average/Advanced

4A, 4B, 4C

Making registration easier and more convenient may be one way of increasing voter turnout.

voters had not yet gone to the polls. Many people believed that the early television reports kept some westerners from voting, making them think that their vote was too late to affect the results. To avoid this situation, the networks agreed not to project any state's results until its polls had closed. It was also suggested that polls throughout the nation close at the same time.

The right *not* to vote

It has been suggested, on the other hand, that America's low voter turnout is actually a sign of a healthy political system.

A low voter turnout may mean that people are relatively satisfied with the government and its policies. Americans may not bother to vote because they are confident about the stability of their political system and sure that no candidate will make radical changes. America's two major parties are middle-of-the-road in political ideology. In countries with multi-party systems, the range of political possibilities is much wider. In Italy, for instance, an election may represent a choice between a Communist, Socialist, liberal, or conservative government.

Finally, people in the United States are given the choice whether to vote or not to vote. The ability to choose, in itself, is a freedom that Americans cherish.

316

Voting Decisions

Political scientists and politicians have long tried to figure out not only why people vote, but also why they vote in a certain way. There are three major factors that appear to influence voting decisions: political party identification, candidate image, and campaign issues.

Party identification

One indicator of how people will vote is political party identification. In the 1976 presidential election, 82 percent of all Democrats voted for Democrat Jimmy Carter, and 91 percent of all Republicans voted for Republican Gerald Ford. In the 1992 race, an estimated 77 percent of all Democrats voted for Democrat Bill Clinton, while an estimated 73 percent of all Republicans voted for Republican George Bush.

Party loyalty — especially voting a "straight ticket" — contributes to the "coattail effect." That is, if a very popular candidate, such as a governor or President, heads the party ticket, straight-party voting may bring other candidates in the same party into office "on the coattails" of this leader.

The impact of political parties, however, seems to have lessened. First, the number of independent voters has increased steadily in recent years. By 1990, nearly one-third of the voters declared themselves independent. Ticket-splitting is another sign that party identification has less influence on voting. Between 1952 and 1992, registered Democrats outnumbered Republicans. During that same period, however, Republican candidates won seven of eleven presidential elections. Republicans were able to win because many Democrats voted for them.

The candidates' image

The image that candidates project — their personality, appearance, and reputation — certainly affects how people vote. The importance of these qualities explains why modern presidential candidates hire media consultants. The presidential elections of 1952 and 1956 provide a striking example of "image." Both elections were landslide victories for Republican Dwight D. Eisenhower over Democrat Adlai Stevenson. Eisenhower, a military hero in World War II, had an engaging smile and a "fatherly" image that ap-

Critical Thinking
▲ *Those who do choose to vote tend to be better informed and more concerned about the issues than those who do not vote. In what ways can people make an effort to become better informed?* (Read newspapers, discuss issues with others.)

pealed to many voters. By contrast, the brilliant and scholarly Stevenson projected the image of an intellectual or "egghead."

The importance of candidate image was also apparent in 1984. From a public relations viewpoint, Democratic challenger Walter Mondale was no match for President Ronald Reagan. Reagan, a former Hollywood actor, was charming and confident in public appearances. Mondale, though a political veteran, had less audience appeal than the incumbent President.

Campaign issues

Issues are another important factor in voters' decision-making. Voters cast their ballots for candidates whose positions on one or several issues most closely resemble their own. Among the issues that have been crucial in recent elections are inflation, taxes, unemployment, civil rights, social programs, defense spending, and the threat of nuclear war. Candidates may win or lose not only because of their stands on issues but also by the way they present issues and solutions to the voters.

SECTION 5 REVIEW

Vocabulary and key terms

off-year election (313)   socioeconomic (313)

For review

1. About what percentage of voting-age Americans vote in presidential elections today? **4A**
2. Which socioeconomic factors are usually related to high voter turnout? **4A**
3. How might changing voter residency and registration laws affect voter turnout? **4A**
4. (a) What factor is the best indicator of how a person will vote? (b) How has this factor changed in recent elections? **8H**

Critical thinking

DRAWING INFERENCES Figure 11–4 shows some socioeconomic factors and their effects on voter turnout. How are these factors interrelated? What reasons might explain them? For example, why are educated people more likely to vote than uneducated people? Why do fewer unemployed people vote? **8H**

Chapter Summary

Nominating candidates for office is one of the most important functions of political parties. In the direct primary, voters in each party elect the party's nominees. In some states, a run-off primary is held if no candidate receives a majority vote. Local governments often have nonpartisan primaries, in which party labels are not used. Other nomination methods include petitions, caucuses, conventions, and self-announcement.

Candidates seeking presidential nomination enter primary elections and caucuses throughout the states to gain delegates who will support them. In the summer of election years, each party holds a national nominating convention, in which delegates from each state vote on the party platform and select its presidential and vice-presidential nominees.

Candidates for major office and their campaign staffs decide on strategies, gather information, advertise, arrange television appearances, and raise money. Candidates can give unlimited amounts to their own campaigns; contributions from individuals and PACs are regulated by federal law. Federal funds are available for presidential candidates in both the primaries and the general election.

The national government has extended the franchise to all citizens over 18 and has put an end to discriminatory voting practices. The states are responsible for overseeing voter registration, printing ballots, and determining voting districts. Local governments divide districts into wards and precincts. Bipartisan poll watchers and election judges ensure fairness at the polls.

Only slightly more than half of eligible voters in the United States participate in presidential elections, and many fewer in off-year elections. Socioeconomic factors, such as age, income, and occupation, affect voter turnout. Education is probably the most important factor; the more education people have, the more likely they are to vote. Voters are usually people with a sense of political efficacy, while apathy is common among nonvoters. Some observers believe that making registration and voting easier would increase U.S. voter turnout. The most important factors in determining how people vote are the candidates' party, image, and positions on issues.

317

Section 5 Review Answers
1. About 55 percent.
2. Education and income.
3. Making registration easier and shortening the residency requirements in most states might increase voter turnout.
4. **(a)** Party identification. **(b)** It has decreased in importance due to the growing number of independent voters and the increase in ticket-splitting.

Critical thinking Students should consider such factors as awareness of issues, as well as the sense of involvement each group feels with the government.

CLOSURE
● Remind students of the pre-reading objectives at the beginning of the section. Pose one or all of these questions again. Then have students read the Voter's Handbook on pp. 321–328 and complete **Citizenship Worksheet 4.**

CHAPTER 11 CORRECTIVES
● To review the content of Chapter 11, you may want to have students complete **Study Guide/Review 11** or **Workbook Chapter 11.**

The symbol 👥 denotes active participation strategies.

Activities are keyed for student abilities:
▲ = Basic
● = All Levels
■ = Average/Advanced

CHAPTER 11 REVIEW

Answers

Vocabulary   See pp. T19–T21 for suggested vocabulary activities.

Reviewing the Facts

1. Primary elections and caucuses.

2. To prevent wealthy persons from gaining too much influence over public officials.

3. It enables them to vote.

4. Factors include education, income, occupation, age, race, sex, and residence. Those with higher incomes are more likely to vote; those unemployed are less likely to vote; whites have historically been more likely to vote. Gender has little influence on voter turnout.

5. Television advertising.

6. (a) Presidential preference primary, binding presidential preference primary, and delegate selection primary. **(b)** Delegate selection primary. **(c)** Presidential preference primary.

● **Review the definitions of the following terms:**

absentee ballot	general election	poll tax
Australian ballot	grandfather clause	poll watcher
bipartisan	keynote speech	precinct
canvass	literacy test	presidential primary
caucus	nominating petition	primary election
closed primary	nomination	registration
"dark horse" candidate	office-group ballot	residency
direct primary	off-year election	socioeconomic
endorsement	open primary	ward
favorite son/daughter	party-column ballot	white primary
franchise	plurality	write-in candidate

● **REVIEWING THE FACTS**

1. What two methods are used to choose delegates to a national party convention? **4B**

2. Why is there a limit on how much money one person may give to a political campaign? **4C**

3. Why is the 26th Amendment important to 18-year-olds? **4D**

4. Name two socioeconomic factors that influence voter turnout, and tell how they influence it. **4A**

5. What is the single largest expense in a modern presidential campaign? **4D**

6. (a) What are the three kinds of presidential primaries? (b) In which one are delegates voted for directly? (c) In which is only the candidate's popularity tested? **2E**

▲ **THINKING CRITICALLY ABOUT KEY CONCEPTS**

1. How are PACs able to sidestep the law that limits their contributions to candidates? Should this practice be curtailed? Why, or why not? **7D**

2. (a) Why did states' attempts to limit the suffrage of blacks and other minorities, even

after the Fifteenth Amendment, necessitate action by Congress and the Supreme Court? (b) What conflicts might arise if different states could keep some groups of people from voting? **3C**

3. Which is more important, image or issues? Can a candidate with a strong public image but a poor grasp of important issues win a presidential election over a candidate with an unappealing image but a thorough grasp of the issues? Explain your answer. **5B**

▲ **PRACTICING SKILLS**

1. **Study Skills: Reading a line graph.** Refer to Figure 11–3 (page 312). Which statements are true and which are false? (a) In presidential election years, there are fewer voters for House of Representatives than in off years. (b) In presidential election years, the voter percentage for House of Representatives follows a curve similar to that for President but is always a number of percentage points lower. (c) Voter participation did not reach 70 percent in the elections shown. (d) The percent of voter participation in presidential elections has steadily increased over the last fifty years. **8B**

318

Thinking Critically About Key Concepts

1. PACs can spend unlimited amounts to help a candidate. Students should defend their opinions.

2. (a) Those states were violating the guarantee of equal protection of the laws, made by the Fourteenth Amendment. **(b)** Conflicts among racial, age, and

ethnic groups and between the sexes over issues such as representation.

3. Students should consider the links between candidates' images and their grasp

2. Critical Thinking Skills: Summarizing information. Refer to Figure 11–1 (page 306). Summarize the data presented in this graph. Make a general statement about any trends you see. **8B**

▲ PARTICIPATORY CITIZENSHIP

1. Voter registration drive. Form groups to plan a voter registration drive in your area. Groups should plan how to find eligible voters and how to provide registration information and forms. How do you plan to convince people of the importance of voting? Your class may wish to discuss and combine the best features of different plans and put them into action. **4D**

2. History re-created. Research the literacy tests used to discriminate against blacks in the South. Make up your own literacy test, based on the information you find. Then give the test to classmates as if you were an election official and they wished to vote. **6C**

■ WRITING ABOUT ISSUES

1. Writing an editorial. Write an editorial on the following questions: Is the campaign for President too long, too complex, and too expensive? Do these factors prevent many qualified individuals from running? Or does this system ensure that only the most suitable candidates will be nominated? **4D**

2. Analyzing a problem. Do research on the question of low voter turnout in the United States. What theories exist about the causes and solutions to this situation? You may wish to interview friends of voting age to find out why they do or do not vote. Write an analysis based on your research. **4D**

▲ ANALYZING A POLITICAL CARTOON

Although it is often seen as the world's leading democracy, the United States has one of the poorest voter participation rates among democratic nations. Look at the cartoon below and answer the following questions.

1. Explain the title, "Bald Eagle." **8A**
2. Judging from the cartoon, what do you think the cartoonist might say is the relationship between voter participation and American democracy? **8B**

Cartoon by Richard Crowson. Copyright © 1991. Reprinted by permission of the Wichita Eagle.

Participatory Citizenship
1. You may want to help students target important local issues to help them convince people of the power of voting.
2. Students should discuss the results of the test, examining how the results could influence a real election.

Writing About Issues
1. Students may want to research a recent presidential campaign to obtain specific information for their editorials.
2. Students should realize that people fail to vote for a variety of reasons.

Analyzing a Political Cartoon
1. The bald eagle represents the United States. However, if it keeps losing voters, the eagle of American democracy will be doubly bald.
2. Lower voter participation endangers democracy.

of issues. They might also want to consider the difference between understanding important issues and appearing able to deal with those issues.

Practicing Skills
1. **(a)** False. **(b)** True. **(c)** True. **(d)** False.
2. Federal election funds for both parties increased dramatically from 1976 to 1992. The Republican and Democratic parties have

received approximately the same amount in federal funds in every presidential election campaign since 1976.

Chapter Review exercises are keyed for student abilities:
▲ = Basic
● = All Levels
■ = Average/Advanced

AS OTHERS SEE US

Background

You may wish to point out that the United States has one of the lowest voter turnout records among democratic nations. (See Figure 11–5, p. 315.)

Civic Participation

● Have students write letters to the editor of the *Globe and Mail* giving their opinions of this article.

Politics

● CRITICAL THINKING Remind students that this article was written during the 1992 presidential primaries. **Did the theme of this article hold true for the general election in November 1992? Explain your answer.** (Some students may suggest that voters were apathetic in 1992 because only a little more than half actually voted in the general election. Others may note that voter turnout in the 1992 presidential election was the highest since 1968.

Politiken/Copenhagen

A Canadian Newspaper Explores Voter Apathy in the U.S.

Many foreign observers are puzzled by the low voter turnout in the United States. This article from the Globe and Mail, *a Toronto newspaper, addresses the issue of voter participation during the 1992 presidential primaries.*

Victor and Betty Peterfreund have voted in every U.S. election and primary since the Second World War. The retired couple follows politics closely and votes Democratic religiously. "We were sort of born into it," Betty Peterfreund said with a laugh as she made her way out of a campaign event for Bill Clinton in Sunrise, Florida.

A few miles down Interstate 95, Fred Stokes shakes his head when asked if he plans to vote. "Doesn't change a thing," the retired railway worker said as he sat on his North Miami porch. "Never has."

In the U.S. primary season, the Stokeses outnumber the Peterfreunds by a huge margin. Candidates roar around the country pleading for support, viewers are bombarded with commercials and newscasts, and readers are submerged in acres of politics-related newsprint. All this activity does little to lure people to the polls. Only rarely do more than 30 percent of the voters in most states turn out to cast ballots in primaries, and in Rhode Island this year, only 12 percent made it to the polling booths. . . .

In many ways, this drought of primary voters is merely an extension of the chronically weak U.S. election turnout. Only a bare majority, 50.1 percent, of the voting-age population cast ballots in the 1988 election, continuing a steady downward drift that started in 1960. Only in 1924, when many women did not use their newly won right to vote, was the turnout as low.

There appears to be no one reason for the United States having one of the lowest voter-participation rates in the world. Awkward registration procedures, lackluster campaigns and candidates, the irrelevance of politics in many people's lives, and the traditional U.S. mistrust of government have all been advanced as explanations. . . .

"All of the above," says Ruy Teixeira, who is writing a book on U.S. voting, "but mainly the fact that people feel disconnected from government. It's hard to get excited about doing something if you don't think it matters. . . ."

Unlike Canada, where enumerators seek out prospective voters, the United States requires its residents to sign up to vote. In most states, this usually requires nothing more than filling out a form at the post office. But that is apparently deterrent enough for the roughly 30 percent of those eligible who are not registered.

"Why Americans Avoid the Polls" by Colin MacKenzie. Copyright © 1992 by Thomson Newspapers. Reprinted by permission of *The Globe and Mail,* Toronto.

CRITICAL THINKING

1. Do you agree with Fred Stokes's view of voting? Why or why not?
2. Voter turnout in 1992 was about 55 percent. Do you think that signals a future upward trend in voter turnout?
3. What arguments would you use to convince people to vote?

Critical Thinking Answers
1. Some may agree, saying individual votes do not matter and all politicians are the same. Others may disagree, saying that every vote counts in a democracy.

2. *Yes*—the 1992 turnout proved more people are taking an interest in their government and their role in it. *No*—the turnout was due to a popular third-party candidate, and does not signal an upward trend in voting.

3. Students might note that the success of a democracy depends on the participation of its citizens.

When you turn 18 you become entitled to one of the great privileges and responsibilities of American citizenship—the right to vote.

Voting allows you to participate in American government. It gives you a voice in determining the kind of city, county, state, and nation you live in.

This *Voter's Handbook* gives you the information you need to be ready to vote on the next election day.

Voter's Handbook

This Voter's Handbook explains the registration and voting processes and encourages students to exercise their suffrage rights. Once students have reviewed these pages, have the class go through the "Voter's Checklist" on p. 328. Answers to most of the Checklist questions will depend on the next election in your state and on local circumstances.

Emphasize that information about elections, including registration and voting, can be secured from the county election commission or board, the League of Women Voters, or the local headquarters of the major political parties.

321

Who Can Vote?

To vote in the United States, you must be:

1. an American citizen

2. at least 18 years old

If you meet these two requirements (and are not a convicted felon or legally insane), your right to vote cannot be taken away, regardless of your race, sex, religion, national origin, or income. The 26th Amendment, ratified in 1971, lowered the voting age to 18 in both federal and state elections.

> **Are you eligible to vote now?**
>
> **When will you be?**

GRAPH SKILLS This graph shows that younger American voters have a lower turnout at the polls than all eligible voters. **CRITICAL THINKING** What factors might explain this?

VOTER TURNOUT FOR AMERICANS, AGES 18 TO 20

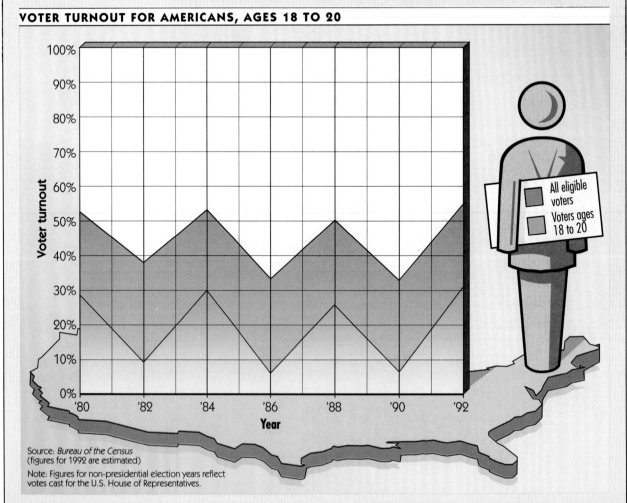

All eligible voters

Voters ages 18 to 20

Source: *Bureau of the Census*
(figures for 1992 are estimated)

Note: Figures for non-presidential election years reflect votes cast for the U.S. House of Representatives.

How Do You Register to Vote?

In every state except North Dakota you must register to vote. Registration is a simple procedure intended to ensure honest elections. Registration forms are easy to fill out.

In most states you can register at a government office, such as a town or municipal hall. Registration booths are sometimes set up in public places — shopping centers, for example. Some states let you register by mail. In 1993 Congress passed a law requiring states to let people register when they apply for a driving license or for government benefits. Whatever way you choose to register, remember to bring along proof of your age (such as a birth certificate) and your address.

The detailed requirements for registering to vote vary considerably from state to state. In most states you must register a certain number of days before the election is held. To ensure that voters are knowledgeable about local issues, many states have a minimum residency requirement, usually around 30 days. (The details for registering to vote in each state are shown in the table on the next page.)

Where can you register to vote?

A SAMPLE VOTER REGISTRATION FORM In areas where a certain number of voters speak a language other than English, election materials are printed in several languages.

For primary elections, you may have to give a party preference.

Such warnings ensure honest elections.

What Are the Requirements for Registration?

STATE	How long before the election must I register?	What is the residency requirement?	Must I declare party preference for the primaries?[1]	Is there registration by mail?[4]
Alabama	10 days	none	yes; at the polls	no
Alaska	30 days	30 days	no; blanket primary	yes
Arizona	29 days	50 days	yes; at registration	yes
Arkansas	20 days	none	yes; at the polls	no
California	29 days	20 days	yes; at registration	yes
Colorado	25 days	32 days	yes; at registration	no
Connecticut	14 days/1 day[2]	none	yes; at registration	yes
Delaware	24 days/21days[2]	none	yes; at registration	yes
Florida	30 days	none	yes; at registration	no
Georgia	30 days	none	yes; at the polls	no
Hawaii	30 days	none	yes; at the polls	yes
Idaho	10 days[3]	30 days	yes; at the polls	no
Illinois	29 days	30 days	yes; at the polls	no
Indiana	29 days	30 days	yes; at the polls	yes
Iowa	10 days	none	yes; at the polls	yes
Kansas	14 days	20 days	yes; at the polls	yes
Kentucky	28 days	30 days	yes; at registration	yes
Louisiana	24 days	none	no; blanket primary	no
Maine	election day	none	yes; at the polls	yes
Maryland	29 days	none	yes; at registration	yes
Massachusetts	28 days	none	yes; at the polls	no
Michigan	30 days	30 days	yes; at the polls	no
Minnesota	election day	20 days	yes; at the polls	yes
Mississippi	30 days	30 days	yes; at the polls	yes
Missouri	28 days	none	yes; at the polls	no
Montana	30 days	30 days	yes; at the polls	yes
Nebraska	10 days	none	yes; at registration	yes
Nevada	30 days	30 days	yes; at registration	yes
New Hampshire	10 days	10 days	yes; at registration	no
New Jersey	29 days	30 days	yes; at the polls	yes
New Mexico	28 days	none	yes; at registration	yes
New York	25 days	30 days	yes; at registration	yes
North Carolina	16 business days	30 days	yes; at registration	yes
North Dakota	no registration	30 days	yes; at the polls	—
Ohio	30 days	30 days	yes; at the polls	yes
Oklahoma	10 days	none	yes; at registration	no
Oregon	20 days	20 days	yes; at registration	yes
Pennsylvania	30 days	30 days	yes; at registration	yes
Rhode Island	30 days	30 days	yes; at the polls	no
South Carolina	30 days	none	yes; at the polls	yes
South Dakota	15 days	none	yes; at registration	no
Tennessee	30 days	20 days	yes; at the polls	yes
Texas	30 days	none	yes; at the polls	yes
Utah	5 days	30 days	yes; at the polls	yes
Vermont	17 days	none	yes; at the polls	yes
Virginia	2 days	none	yes; at the polls	no
Washington	30 days	30 days	no; blanket primary	yes
West Virginia	30 days	30 days	yes; at registration	yes
Wisconsin	election day	10 days	yes; at the polls	yes
Wyoming	30 days	none	yes; at the polls	no
District of Columbia	30 days	none	yes; at registration	yes
Puerto Rico	50 days	none	yes; at the polls	no
Virgin Islands	30 days	45 days	yes; 30 days in advance	no

1. for first-time voters **2.** general election/primary election **3.** with county clerk; 17 days with precinct registrar
4. The motor-voter bill of 1993 calls on states to allow registration by mail for all federal elections.

When and Where Are Elections Held?

When Do You Vote?

National elections are held on the Tuesday following the first Monday in November of even-numbered years. Elections for House of Representatives and one-third of the Senate seats are held every two years. Presidential elections are held every four years. Election day in 1996 is November 5.

Elections for state and local offices are often held on the same day as the national elections. However, states may call their own elections at any time they wish. Voters may also be asked to vote "Yes" or "No" on ballot measures such as bond issues and referendums.

A preliminary round of elections, called primary elections, usually precedes the general elections. The primaries decide which candidates' names will go on the ballot in November. The dates of primary elections differ from state to state.

Election judges are allowed to assist voters with disabilities, helping to ensure that everyone will have the chance to vote.

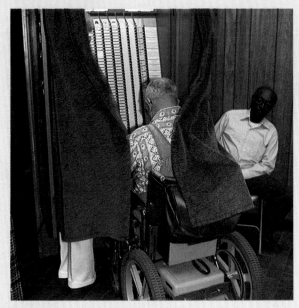

Where Do You Vote?

Based on your home address, you will be assigned to the polling place in your precinct. Although voting hours vary from place to place, polls are generally open from 7 A.M. to 7 P.M.

Before the day of the election, find where your polling place is located and how to get there. If your polling place is not within walking distance of your home, make travel arrangments in advance. Make sure to plan on getting to the polls during voting hours.

At the poll, the names of all registered voters appear on a list. (A few states allow you to register at the polling place on election day.) When you arrive, tell the election officials your name. A judge will check your name off the list, hand you a ballot or punch card (if you need one), and direct you to a voting booth. If you have questions about voting procedures, don't hesitate to ask one of the officials.

You cast your vote in secret, in a private booth behind a closed curtain. Take your ballot or card with you into the voting booth and close the curtain behind you. Now you are free to vote as you choose, without fear or intimidation or pressure. Take your time, read the ballot carefully, and then cast your vote.

Do you know the date of the next election in your state? How can you find out?

How Do You Read the Ballot?

Two kinds of ballots are most common in the United States. They are illustrated and explained on this page.

The Office-Group Ballot

The office-group (or "Massachusetts") ballot lists candidates together by the office they are seeking. Their party affiliation is listed beside their name.

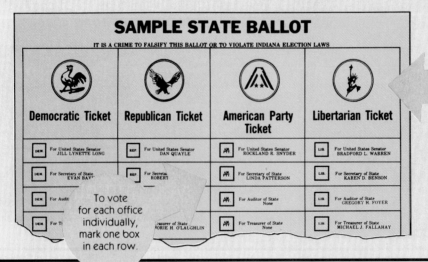

Select one pair of candidates

Select one candidate for treasurer.

The Commonwealth of Massachusetts
STATE ELECTION
SPECIMEN BALLOT

GOVERNOR - LIEUTENANT GOVERNOR

☐ DUKAKIS and MURPHY · · · · · · · · · · · · · · · · Democratic **3**
☐ KARIOTIS and NIKITAS · · · · · · · · · · · · · · · Republican **4**

ATTORNEY GENERAL   Vote for ONE

☐ EDWARD F. HARRINGTON · 732 Great Plain Ave., Needham   Republican **7**
☐ JAMES M. SHANNON · 401 Prospect St., Lawrence · · · · · Democratic **8**

SECRETARY OF STATE   Vote for ONE

☐ MICHAEL JOSEPH CONNOLLY · 42 Cordan Ave., Boston · Democratic **11**
      Candidate for Re-election
☐ DEBORAH R. COCHRAN · 962 High St., Dedham · · · · · Republican **12**

TREASURER

☐ ROBERT Q. CRANE · 7 ...
☐ L. JOYCE HAMPERS · 92 ... th La., ...

The Party-Column Ballot

The party-column (or "Indiana") ballot lists all the candidates from each party in a single row or column. The parties are identified by symbols at the top of the column. You may vote for one party's entire slate of candidates or office by office, selecting candidates from any party.

To vote for all the candidates of one party, mark one circle.

To vote for each office individually, mark one box in each row.

SAMPLE STATE BALLOT

IT IS A CRIME TO FALSIFY THIS BALLOT OR TO VIOLATE INDIANA ELECTION LAWS

Democratic Ticket	Republican Ticket	American Party Ticket	Libertarian Ticket
DEM For United States Senator JILL LYNETTE LONG	REF For United States Senator DAN QUAYLE	AM For United States Senator ROCKLAND R. SNYDER	LIB For United States Senator BRADFORD L. WARREN
DEM For Secretary of State EVAN BAY...	REF For Secretar... ROBERT...	AM For Secretary of State LINDA PATTERSON	LIB For Secretary of State KAREN D. BENSON
DEM For Audit...		AM For Auditor of State None	LIB For Auditor of State GREGORY H. FOYER
DEM For T...	...asurer of State ...ORIE H. O'LAUGHLIN	AM For Treasurer of State None	LIB For Treasurer of State MICHAEL J. FALLAHAY

How Do You Use a Voting Machine?

If your polling place uses paper ballots, simply mark your choices directly on the ballot with a pencil in the secrecy of the voting booth. Follow the ballot instructions for marking inside the squares. When you are through, fold your ballot and deposit it in the locked ballot box.

Many polling places now use voting machines to count ballots more quickly and accurately. The most common are the lever and punch-card machines, illustrated on this page.

The Lever Machine

The lever machine is both the ballot and the voting booth. Enter the booth and pull the large lever to one side, which closes a curtain around you. Next, turn down the small levers by the names of candidates you prefer. On a lever machine, you can reset the levers and change your vote up to the last moment. Once you are sure you have turned all the levers you want, a second pull on the large lever records your vote, opens the curtain, and resets the machine for the next voter.

The Punch-Card Machine

In some states, you will be handed a punch-card to use as your ballot. Once you are inside the private booth, insert your card in the voting machine. This lines up the card with the names of the candidates. To vote, use the stylus provided to punch holes at the appropriate places on the ballot. Once you have punched the card, your vote is final. Place your completed card in its envelope and give it to the election judge, who puts it in the ballot box. Your votes will later be counted electronically.

The United States was the first country to use voting machines in elections. The lever machine (below) and punch-card machine (bottom) both have improved the accuracy and lowered the cost of administering elections.

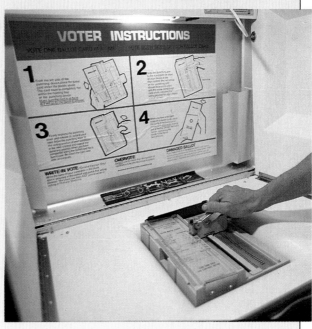

How Do You Decide How to Vote?

Your first important voting decision should be *deciding to vote.* Then, to vote intelligently, you must keep informed. This means reading the newspaper, learning about the candidates and the issues, and discussing the election with friends, family, and others. You can get information from the media, from candidates' headquarters, and nonpartisan organizations like the League of Women Voters. The ultimate decision on how you vote, however, is your own.

Most states provide sample ballots well before the elections are held. These give you a chance to become familiar with the candidates and the issues. (Usually you can take your sample ballot into the voting booth.) Before you enter the voting booth, you should know what your choices are. And you should have the information that will help you choose wisely when you finally cast your vote.

> Make sure you know the answer to all of these questions before election day.

★ Voter's Checklist

- Do you know the date of the next primary election in your state?
- The date of the next general election?
- Do you know the requirements for registering in your state?
- Do you know where you can register?
- Are you registered to vote?
- Do you know where your polling place is?
- Do you know when the polls are open?
- Do you know what kind of voting method is used at your polling place?
- Do you know who the candidates are and where they stand on issues you care about?
- Are there any other questions (such as a referendum) on the ballot?
- Do you know where to get more information if you need it?
- Have you carefully read and understood the sample ballot?

UNIT
★ 4 ★

NATIONAL GOVERNMENT: The Legislative Branch

CHAPTER

12 CONGRESS: Its Powers, Structure, and Members

13 The LAWMAKING PROCESS

329

National Government: The Legislative Branch *(pp. 329–376)*

Unit Overview

Unit Four presents a discussion of Congress—its powers, members, and procedures. Chapter 12 begins by clarifying for students the powers of the legislative body and then examines the roles of the members of Congress. Chapter 13 concentrates on lawmaking, describing the step-by-step process from the introduction of a bill to its final passage or veto. Together, these chapters familiarize students with the organization of Congress and also with its functions.

Photo
The Capitol.

CHAPTER 12
CONGRESS: ITS POWERS, STRUCTURE, AND MEMBERS
(pp. 330–349)

	Section Objectives	Section Resources
Section 1 **Congress Has Many Powers**	☐ identify the lawmaking powers of Congress ☐ identify the non-lawmaking powers of Congress	▲ TRANSPARENCIES **29–30**
Section 2 **Congress Is an Elected Assembly**	☐ explain how membership in the House and Senate is determined ☐ explain how congressional districts are established	■ SUPREME COURT DECISIONS **53–55**
Section 3 **Who Are the Members of Congress?**	☐ list the qualifications for Congress ☐ describe the privileges and benefits that members of Congress have ☐ consider how members of Congress are supposed to represent their constituents	▲ SKILLS PRACTICE WORKSHEET **12** ■ SKILLS CHALLENGE WORKSHEET **12** ● CITIZENSHIP WORKSHEET **5**

Essential Elements

The list below shows Essential Elements relevant to this chapter. (The complete list of Essential Elements appears in the introductory pages of this Teacher's Edition.)

Section 1: 1D, 2A, 3A, 3B, 7B

Section 2: 1D, 2D, 3A, 4B, 6F, 6H, 8A, 8B

Section 3: 3A, 4A, 5C, 6A, 6B, 6F, 6G, 6I, 7A, 8A, 8G, 8H

Chapter Review: 1D, 2D, 3A, 3B, 4A, 4C, 8A, 8B, 8C, 8H

> Section Resources are keyed for student abilities:
> ▲ = Basic
> ● = All Levels
> ■ = Average/Advanced

Homework Options

Each section contains activities labeled "Guided/Independent Practice," "Reteaching/Correctives," and "Enrichment/Extension." You may wish to choose from among these activities when assigning homework.

Students Acquiring English Activities

Have students convert the information in Figure 12–3 (p. 342) into a pictograph. Students should draw figures representing each of the occupations listed; the size of each figure should be determined by the percentage of members of Congress holding that occupation. (That is, the larger the percentage, the larger the figure.) An alternate activity is for students to create a pictograph comparing the make-up of Congress with the make-up of the general population, using the information in the paragraph underneath the heading "A statistical view" on p. 343.

LISTENING/SPEAKING: Have students watch on TV news programs or C-SPAN members of Congress speaking on the floor of Congress. Have students summarize their impressions of the speakers and note any differences they see in members' speaking styles.

Case Studies

When teaching this chapter, you may use Case Study 5, which examines the issue of limitations on congressional terms. (Case Studies may be found following p. 510.)

Teacher Bibliography

Fisher, Louis. *Constitutional Conflicts Between Congress and the President.* 3rd ed. University Press of Kansas, 1991. Considers from a historical and practical perspective the many points on which Congress and the President clash.

Mann, Thomas E. and Norman J. Ornstein. *The New Congress.* American Enterprise Institute, 1981. Eleven articles by various contributors provide a solid introduction to Congress.

Powers of Congress. 2nd ed. CQ Press, 1982. Reviews the constitutional powers of Congress using historical background and contemporary issues.

Student Bibliography

Coffey, Wayne R. *How We Choose a Congress.* St. Martin's, 1980. A clear and concise description of the process of running for and getting elected to Congress.

Galloway, George B. *History of the House of Representatives.* 2nd ed. Crowell, 1976. A lively history of the House from 1787 through the Watergate era.

Literature

Just, Ward. *Jack Gance.* Houghton Mifflin, 1989. A seasoned political staffer returns to Illinois to run for the Senate.

Smith, Margaret Chase. *Declaration of Conscience.* Edited by William C. Lewis, Jr. Doubleday, 1972. An autobiography presenting important speeches with appropriate capsule histories of the background and effect of each.

Twain, Mark, and C.D. Warner. *The Gilded Age.* Many editions. A satiric look at Washington and Congress by an easterner and a westerner.

Williams, T. Harry. *Huey Long.* Knopf, 1969. The definitive biography of this flamboyant Louisiana politician; winner of the Pulitzer Prize and National Book Award.

CHAPTER RESOURCES

Study Guide/Review 12
Workbook Chapter 12
Chapter 12 Test, Forms A–C

Films and Videotapes*

"And if Elected . . ." (Series title: *Congress: We the People.*) 30 min. Films, 1983. v. Compares elections of senators and members of the House of Representatives.

Power of the Purse. (Series title: *Congress: We the People.*) 30 min. Films, 1983. v. Presents the budget process as an example of the kinds of conflicts and cooperation between Congress and the President.

Software*

How a Bill Becomes a Law (Apple, IBM, Macintosh). Queue. Students become members of Congress trying to get a bill passed.

* For a complete guide to audiovisual sources, see page T22.

329B

CHAPTER 12

Congress: Its Powers, Structure, and Members *(pp. 330–349)*

Chapter 12 examines the legislative and non-legislative powers of Congress, the differences between the House and the Senate, the qualifications required of members of Congress, and the pay and benefits they receive.

Chapter Objectives
After students complete this chapter, they will be able to:

1. Identify the lawmaking powers of Congress.
2. Identify the non-lawmaking powers of Congress.
3. Explain how membership in the House and Senate is determined.
4. Explain how congressional districts are established.
5. List the qualifications for Congress.
6. Describe the privileges and benefits that members of Congress have.
7. Consider how members of Congress are supposed to represent their constituents.

CONGRESS: Its Powers, Structure, and Members

A people who know their minds and can get real representatives to express them are a self-governed people, the practiced masters of constitutional government.

Woodrow Wilson
Constitutional Government in the United States (1908)

Photo
Joint congressional committees at the Iran-*contra* hearings.

April 2, 1917 — Applause and shouts of approval echoed through the House chamber as the newly elected representative from Montana was sworn in. This opening day of the 65th Congress was a time of celebration for women's rights advocates. Suffragists jammed the visitors' gallery to cheer Jeannette Rankin, the first woman elected to Congress.

Four days later Rankin, a committed pacifist, voted against United States entry into World War I. Returning to Congress in 1941, she was the only member to oppose United States entry into World War II. Though her complete opposition to war eventually ended her political career, Rankin never changed her beliefs.

Today, women are regularly elected to Congress, though their numbers remain disproportionately small. This chapter looks at how the membership of Congress has changed since Congress first assembled in 1789. It also examines the roles and the constitutional powers of the men and women who make laws for the United States.

CHAPTER OUTLINE

1 Congress Has Many Powers

Legislative Functions
Non-Legislative Functions

2 Congress Is an Elected Assembly

The House and the Senate
"One Person, One Vote"

3 Who Are the Members of Congress?

Qualifications for Congress
Privileges and Penalties
Compensation and Benefits
Representing the People

331

SECTION 1

Congress Has Many Powers (pp. 332–335)

Section Objectives

□ identify the lawmaking powers of Congress

□ identify the non-lawmaking powers of Congress

Vocabulary

expressed powers, duty, impost, excise tax, post roads, copyright, patent, legislative veto, impeach

FOCUS

● Use a sports analogy to help students understand why Congress's powers go beyond those expressly stated in the Constitution. *When was the first rule book written for major league baseball?* (About 100 years ago.) *Have the rules changed since then?* (The basic rules have stayed the same, but there have been many minor changes.) *Why have there been changes?* (As time passes, refinements are made, needs change, and the rules must change to keep up with the times. For example, the American League created the designated hitter to increase offense and please the fans.)

The Constitution lists the rules by which Congress makes laws. Are those rules ever refined? (Yes, through the elastic clause.) *Why?* (So Congress can keep up with changing times.)

EXPLANATION

After reviewing the content of the section, you may want to consider the following activities:

Constitutional Heritage

■ *What prevents Congress from making laws for the states?* (The

Congress Has Many Powers

> **ACCESS** **The Main Ideas**
>
> **1** What are the lawmaking powers of Congress? *pages 332–334*
>
> **2** What powers does Congress have that are not related to lawmaking? *pages 334–335*

Turn to the text of the Constitution on page 112 and look at Article I. It is no accident that Congress is the first of the three branches of government to be described. The authors believed that the legislature should play the leading role in government. (Remember that both in England and the American colonies, the legislature was closest to the will of the people. Executives, such as the English monarch or most colonial governors, were not democratically chosen.) The long list of specific, or enumerated, powers that follows also shows the central role of Congress in American government.

1D, 2A, 3B, 7B

Legislative Functions

Although Congress has a great many lawmaking powers, these powers are not unlimited. For example, Congress cannot make laws for the states. It cannot pass laws that deny citizens their legal rights or violate the civil rights and liberties protected in the Bill of Rights. Most of the lawmaking powers that the Constitution specifically gives to Congress are listed in detail in Article I, Section 8. These are called enumerated powers, or **expressed powers.**

Sovereign powers

Many of the lawmaking powers given to Congress in the Constitution are those that belong to any sovereign nation. For instance, Clause 1 gives Congress the power "to provide for the common defense and general welfare of the United States." What purpose would any government serve if it could not defend its land and ensure its citizens' well-being?

Congress has a number of other sovereign powers. It can, for example, make rules for natu-

332

ralization, deciding the requirements for becoming a citizen of the United States.

Congress also has the power to create, equip, and fund the armed forces. Clause 12 gives Congress the authority to raise and support an army; Clause 13 provides for the navy. According to Clause 11, only Congress can formally declare war. American Presidents, however, have often sent troops to fight in "undeclared wars." This power has caused conflicts between the legislative and executive branches.

Clause 17 grants Congress exclusive authority to make laws for the "seat of government," which today is Washington, the District of Columbia (D.C.). Although today the residents of the District of Columbia enjoy a measurable degree of self-government, Congress nevertheless remains the final authority over the District's laws. Similarly, Article IV gives Congress the right to govern the territories of the United States.

Financial powers

One of the biggest problems facing the national government under the Articles of Confederation was that it could not raise money or regulate trade. To address these problems, the Constitution grants Congress financial powers so that it can raise the immense sums of money needed to pay for the government and all it does.

The first clause of Article I, Section 8 gives Congress the power "to lay and collect taxes, duties, imposts, and excises." **Duties** and **imposts** here mean taxes collected on goods imported into the United States from other countries. **Excises** are taxes on the production and sale of particular goods, such as alcohol, tobacco, or gasoline. Because Clause 2 allows Congress "to borrow on the credit of the United States," Congress can sell Treasury bonds, notes, and certificates. Furthermore, only Congress can authorize the federal government to spend money.

Regulating and promoting trade

An important clause of Article I, Section 8 allows Congress "to regulate commerce with

---

Cross-reference
Naturalization procedures are discussed in Chapter 1, pp. 23–25. Chapter 15, pp. 411–412, discusses "undeclared wars."

Background: *History*
Congress actually met in eight different cities, including New York, Philadelphia, and York (Pennsylvania), before finally settling on its

permanent site—Washington, D.C.—in 1800. A contemporary (1801) engraving of the newly chosen "Federal City" appears on p. 112.

foreign nations, and among the several states, and with the Indian tribes'' (Clause 3). As Chapters 4 and 7 explain, a broad interpretation of the commerce clause has greatly expanded the role of Congress in national affairs.

A number of specific powers allow Congress to set uniform standards for commerce and trade. For example, only Congress can coin money and establish its value (Clause 5). Similarly, Congress has the power to fix standards of weights and measures, such as yards, feet, inches, ounces, pounds, and bushels.

Also as an encouragement to business and trade, Clause 7 gives Congress the power to establish post offices and **post roads**, routes over which the mail is carried. Finally, "to promote the progress of science and useful arts," Congress may issue **copyrights** and **patents**. A copyright is the exclusive right to publish, distribute, or sell a literary or artistic work, such as a book, film, song, or videocassette. Under the Copyright Act of 1976, a copyright lasts for the life of the owner plus 50 years. A patent is the exclusive right to produce, sell, or use an invention. Depending on the invention, patents last up to seventeen years.

Powers over the courts

The Constitution specifically gives Congress some power over the judicial branch. While the Constitution sets up a Supreme Court, it gives Congress the power to establish the other federal courts. Since 1789, Congress has established the entire system of federal courts. Congress also sets the number of associate justices in the Supreme Court.

The implied powers

All the powers discussed above are mentioned specifically in the Constitution. In addition, the elastic clause gives Congress the right to pass any laws that are "necessary and proper" to carry out these functions. The Supreme Court's decision in *McCulloch v. Maryland* (page 88) has allowed Congress great flexibility in using the *implied powers,* which are based on the elastic clause.

The Court's broad interpretation of "necessary and proper" meant that Congress can pass any law that is reasonably related to the expressed powers. Examples of how far Congress has stretched the elastic clause range from establishing the Bank of the United States to creating

Tourists gaze at the massive dome above the statue-lined Great Rotunda of the U.S. Capitol building. Funeral ceremonies for eminent Americans, such as Presidents Abraham Lincoln and John F. Kennedy, have been held in the Rotunda.

333

Tenth Amendment reserves such powers for the states.)

■ *Why did the writers of the Constitution allow state governments to make their own laws?* (They feared a too-powerful central government; each region had its own needs.)

Constitutional Heritage

▲ List on the board the non-legislative functions of Congress: advice and consent, impeachment, admitting new states, proposing amendments, counting the electoral vote, overseeing executive agencies.

▲ CRITICAL THINKING *Which of these powers reflect checks on the President?* (Advice and consent, impeachment, overseeing executive agencies.) *On the judiciary?* (Impeachment.)

● CRITICAL THINKING *Which power was probably more important in the past than it is today?* (Admitting new states.) *Are there any that you think are more important today?* (Overseeing executive agencies.)

👥 Cooperative Learning

● Divide the class into groups and assign each group several of the clauses in Article 1, Section 8 of the Constitution. Have each group present its clauses to the class as follows: one student reads the clause as stated, and then a second student rephrases the clause in his or her own words.

Critical Thinking
● *What if Congress did not set standards for weights and measures? For example, what might happen if a quart of orange juice were a different size in Florida than in Texas?* (Because so many products are consumed in states other than the ones in which they are produced, massive confusion would result.)

Background: *Constitutional Heritage* Copyright law was expanded in *Sony v. Universal City Studios* (1984). The Court ruled that home taping of copyrighted TV programs and movies is legal as long as the tapes are not sold for profit.

The symbol 👥 denotes active participation strategies.

Activities are keyed for student abilities:
▲ = Basic
● = All Levels
■ = Average/Advanced

GUIDED/INDEPENDENT PRACTICE

● Have students read articles about Congress and categorize its activities as lawmaking or non-lawmaking, expressed or implied power, or reflecting checks and balances.

RETEACHING/CORRECTIVES

▲ Have students graphically organize the information in the section by creating a web. To do so, they should write *Congress* inside a circle and then draw two circles connected by lines to the original circle. Have them write the two kinds of congressional functions in these circles (*Legislative Functions, Non-Legislative Functions*). Finally, have them draw other circles connected to the two circles in order to show all the specific functions noted in the section.

You may also want to use **Transparency 29,** which shows a cutaway drawing of the Capitol, and **Transparency 30,** which presents a political cartoon dealing with Congress and foreign policy.

ENRICHMENT/EXTENSION

■ Assign students to report to the class on the reasons for the involvement of the House of Representatives in the presidential elections of 1800 and 1824.

Section 1 Review Answers

1. To provide for the general welfare and the common defense; set requirements for citizenship; create, equip, and fund the armed forces; declare war; make laws for Washington, D.C., and territories.

2. Collecting duties, imposts, excises, taxes, and selling Treasury bonds, certificates, and notes.

In 1987 a joint House-Senate committee investigated the involvement of White House officials in the Iran-*contra* affair. Lt. Col. Oliver L. North (inset) was a key witness before the committee.

an air force. The Supreme Court is the final authority on whether a law passed by Congress falls within the limits of the elastic clause.

The legislative veto

One controversial area of congressional power is the so-called **legislative veto**. In a number of bills, Congress has included a provision that allows one or both houses to review or cancel an action taken by the President or any agency or department in the executive branch. Legislative vetoes were used sparingly until the Watergate scandal in 1972. Thereafter, Congress tried to exert more authority over the executive branch. By 1981, there were more than 200 laws containing some sort of legislative veto.

A landmark Supreme Court case in 1983 brought all "legislative veto" provisions into question. In *Immigration and Naturalization Service v. Chadha,* the Supreme Court ruled that Congress could not reverse a decision by the Justice Department to grant permanent resident status to an alien. The constitutionality of other laws with legislative vetoes has not been tested before the Court.

334

3A, 3B

Non-Legislative Functions

Congress also has powers that are not related to lawmaking. Many of these are set out in the Constitution as part of the system of checks and balances, allowing Congress to oversee certain actions of the executive and judicial branches. Other powers have developed informally.

"Advice and consent"

The President appoints many major federal officials, including ambassadors, Cabinet members, Supreme Court justices, and other federal judges. Presidential appointments, however, must be made "with the advice and consent of the Senate." That is, a majority of the Senate must approve key presidential appointments. Furthermore, the President may not make any treaties or other formal agreements with foreign nations without the approval of two-thirds of the Senate.

Impeachment

Congress also has the power to remove federal officials from office for crimes or serious misconduct. The House of Representatives, by a majority vote, may **impeach**, or bring criminal charges against, any official in the executive or judicial branch. This includes even Supreme Court justices and the President. If two-thirds of the Senate membership votes to convict the impeached official, that official is then removed from office.

Other non-legislative powers

Congress has various other functions and duties outside its lawmaking powers. One of these is to admit new states into the Union. Another is to propose amendments to the Constitution or, at the request of the states, call a convention for proposing amendments. Congress also counts the electoral vote in presidential elections. If no candidate receives a majority of the electoral vote, the House of Representatives elects the President. Congress also must approve the appointment of a Vice President if that office is vacant.

Finally, though this role is nowhere specified in the Constitution, Congress acts as a ''watchdog'' over government activities. Congressional committees may act somewhat like special courts to conduct investigations, hold hearings, call witnesses, and make recommendations. Among the areas Congress has investigated are military spending, NASA, organized crime, the 1972 Watergate scandal, and the 1986 Iran-*contra* affair.

SECTION 1 REVIEW

Vocabulary and key terms

expressed powers (332) patent (333)
duty (332) elastic clause (333)
impost (332) implied powers (333)
excise tax (332) legislative veto (334)
post roads (333) impeach (335)
copyright (333)

For review

1. What are the sovereign powers of the United States Congress? **3A**
2. What methods does the Constitution allow Congress for raising money? **3A**
3. Besides the power to regulate commerce, in what other ways can Congress help trade and communication? **3A**
4. (a) What actions of the President must the Senate approve? (b) What checks does Congress have over the judicial branch? **3A**
5. What powers does Congress have in relation to electing the President? **3B**

Critical thinking

DRAWING CONCLUSIONS Why did the writers of the Constitution think it important to list the powers of Congress? What might have happened if there were no listing of these powers? **2A**

3. Coining money, fixing standards of weights and measures, establishing post offices and post roads, and issuing copyrights and patents.
4. **(a)** Federal appointments, treaties. **(b)** Congress can establish federal courts and set the number of Supreme Court justices.
5. Congress counts the electoral vote. If no candidate receives a majority of the electoral vote, the House elects the President.

Critical thinking The framers enumerated the powers of Congress to prevent infringement on state and individual rights.

CLOSURE

● Remind students of the pre-reading objectives at the beginning of the section. Pose one or all of these questions again. Then have students read Section 2, paying special attention to redistricting.

SECTION 2

1D, 2D, 3A, 4B, 6F, 6H, 8A, 8B

Congress Is an Elected Assembly

ACCESS	The Main Ideas
1	How is membership in the House and Senate determined? *pages 336–337*
2	How are congressional districts established? *pages 337–340*

Humorist Will Rogers once joked:

You see, they have two of these bodies — Senate and House. . . . If there is nothing funny happening in one, there is sure to be in the other; and in case one body passes a good bill, why, the other can see it in time and kill it.

Actually, as you recall from Chapter 2, the structure of Congress is a result of the Great Compromise. The Senate was to represent the *states,* while the House was to represent the *people* and the principle of popular sovereignty. These functions have led to differences in membership between the two bodies.

SECTION 2

Congress Is an Elected Assembly *(pp. 335–340)*

Section Objectives

☐ explain how membership in the House and Senate is determined

☐ explain how congressional districts are established

Background: *Constitutional Heritage* The constitutionality of the legislative veto remains an unsettled issue. A landmark Supreme Court case in 1983 brought all "legislative veto" provisions into question. In *Immigra-tion and Naturalization Service v. Chadha,* the Supreme Court ruled that Congress could not reverse a decision by the Justice Department to grant permanent resident status to an alien. The constitutionality of other laws with legislative vetoes has not been tested before the Court.

The symbol ᵲ denotes active participation strategies.

Activities are keyed for student abilities:
▲ = Basic
● = All Levels
■ = Average/Advanced

Vocabulary
at large, census, reapportionment, redistrict, gerrymander, sunbelt

FOCUS

● Select a controversial issue and ask students to show, by raising their hands, which side they favor regarding that issue. (Be sure that the class is fairly evenly divided.) Then have a volunteer representing one of the two sides divide the class into four "districts" in such a way that will benefit his or her position (by a 3–1 vote). Explain that this exercise is an example of gerrymandering.

EXPLANATION

After reviewing the content of the section, you may want to consider the following activities:

Civic Participation

■ Gauge students' knowledge of your state's congressional delegation by asking questions such as the following: *How many senators represent our state? Who are they? How many representatives does this state have? Who represents the district in which we live?* (Information on these topics can be found in current almanacs, the *Congressional Directory,* or the *Washington Information Directory.*)

■ *When is the next general election? How many senators and how many representatives will be up for election that year?* (All representatives are up for election every two years. Senatorial elections are staggered.)

The House and the Senate

Length of terms

Members of the House of Representatives are elected every two years. Short terms with frequent elections ensure that representatives are in close touch with those they represent.

Senators, on the other hand, serve six-year terms. This longer term allows senators to gain more experience, and to be less concerned about elections and more independent in their decisions. To further increase continuity and stability, Senate terms are staggered so that only one-third of the senators come up for re-election every two years.

At any given time, one-third of the senators have at least two years of experience, and another third have been in Congress for at least four years. There has been no limit on the number of terms a senator or representative may serve. However, in late 1990, Colorado set a twelve-year limit for senators and House members.

Filling vacancies

Occasionally members of Congress resign, die in office, or (very rarely) are expelled by their fellow members. According to the Seventeenth Amendment, when vacancies occur in the Senate, the governor of the state that the senator represented may call a special election to fill the empty seat. Alternatively, the state legislature may grant the governor the power to make a temporary appointment. The person appointed then serves until the next regular general election.

When a House seat becomes vacant, the governor may call a special election to fill the empty seat. Alternatively, the states can leave the office vacant until the next regularly scheduled election. Because House elections are held so frequently, states thus can avoid the enormous expense of holding a special election.

Changes in congressional terms?

Over the years, a number of proposals have been made to change the constitutional provisions for terms of office in Congress. A recurring suggestion is to lengthen House terms from two to four years, and to have representatives elected at the same time as the President. Advocates claim that the longer term would help attract better candidates, reduce the costs of elections, and allow representatives time to gain legislative experience. On the other hand, it would reduce representatives' direct contact with the people.

A limit on the number of terms members of Congress may serve, like Colorado's initiative, has also been a suggestion. It is difficult to vote senators and representatives out of office and some people feel term limits could make elections more fair.

Senate representation

The Constitution guarantees each state two senators, regardless of population. Since the admission of Alaska and Hawaii in 1959, there have

The number of women in Congress rose from 30 to 53 as a result of 1992 elections. Senators in this photo with Hillary Rodham Clinton (center) are Carol Moseley-Braun of Illinois, Patty Murray of Washington, Barbara Mikulski of Maryland, Barbara Boxer and Dianne Feinstein of California, and Nancy Landon Kassebaum of Kansas.

336

Background: *Historic Documents* The idea that House members should be in close touch with those they represent dates from the founding of the nation. James Madison noted in *The Federalist,* No. 52, that representatives ought to have "an immediate dependence on, and an intimate sympathy with, the people."

been 100 senators — two from each of the 50 states. A state's representation in the Senate cannot be reduced, even by constitutional amendment, without that state's consent — an unlikely situation. Vermont, with a population of about a half a million, is thus entitled to as many senators as California, with more than 29 million people.

The writers of the Constitution intended for the Senate, the upper house, to be one step removed from the people. Therefore, besides serving longer terms than representatives, senators were originally chosen by the state legislatures. As suffrage increased, so did demands for the direct election of senators by the voters. In 1913 the Seventeenth Amendment, calling for the popular election of Senators, was ratified. Today, senators from each state are elected **at large**, that is, by all the voters of the state as a whole.

Representation in the House

Seats in the House of Representatives, or lower house, are distributed among the states according to population. Each state is guaranteed at least one representative. Beyond that minimum, Congress determines the size of the House, and how the seats are to be divided.

When the first House of Representatives met in 1789, it had 59 members. As the population grew and new states were added, the size of the House also increased. It currently has a maximum size of 435 members.

In addition, the District of Columbia, Puerto Rico, Guam, American Samoa, and the Virgin Islands each send one elected delegate to the House of Representatives. These delegates may serve on committees, take part in debate, and introduce some motions. They have no voting rights on the floor of the House.

2D, 4B, 6F, 6H

"One Person, One Vote"

To determine each state's population and the number of representatives it may send to the House, Congress is required to conduct a **census** every ten years. The census is an official survey of United States population. Today the Bureau of the Census, in the Department of Commerce, conducts the census. Based on these figures, it recommends a plan for **reapportionment**, which is the redistribution of House seats among the states.

Drawing district boundaries

Congress determines how many seats each state is entitled to, but it is up to the state legislatures to divide the state into election districts. When a state gains or loses a representative, it must **redistrict**, or redraw boundaries so that legislative districts are all approximately equal in population. Although states are required to redistrict after every census, many states did not do so for many years. As a result, by the early 1900's, fast-growing cities and urban areas were underrepresented in Congress, while rural areas were overrepresented.

Until 1962, however, the courts refused to hear lawsuits protesting unfair representation. These were considered "political" questions, to be settled by the legislative and executive branches or by the voters. In the 1962 case of *Baker v. Carr*, however, the Supreme Court reconsidered. The state of Tennessee had not redistricted its state legislature since 1901, even though its cities had been growing rapidly. By 1961, 42 percent of the state's population lived in four urban counties, but they elected only 18 percent of the state senators and 20 percent of the state representatives. Moreover, these counties were receiving less than their fair share of educational aid and other state funds.

The Court in this case decided, for the first time, that people's right to fair representation was part of the Fourteenth Amendment's promise of equal protection. Voters claiming to be underrepresented could therefore take their complaint to court.

The *Baker* decision did not say on what basis such cases would be judged. This issue was settled in another case two years later, when the Court decided that Georgia's unequal congressional districts were unconstitutional (*Wesberry v. Sanders*, 1964). Justice Hugo Black pointed out that the Constitution clearly intended to have "equal representation for equal numbers of people" — in short, to guarantee that ". . . one man's vote in a congressional election is to be worth as much as another's."

What Justice Black put forth became known as the "one person, one vote" principle. Thereafter, congressional districts were required to be of nearly equal population. (In the same year, this principle was also applied to apportionment in state legislatures by *Reynolds v. Sims*.)

337

Politics

● CRITICAL THINKING *When a governor chooses someone to fill a vacancy in Congress, from which party will the appointee likely come?* (From the governor's own party.) *What effect might this have?* (It might give one party excessive power.)

Politics

Refer students to Figure 12–1 (p. 338), which shows the effects of gerrymandering on redistricting. To make sure students understand the concept of gerrymandering, ask the following questions:

● *What group of citizens lost representation in the House due to redistricting?* (Republicans.)

● CRITICAL THINKING *Why could this be construed as an unfair practice?* (Because although Republicans still made up a large part of the population, they were denied party representation in Congress.)

● CRITICAL THINKING *Which political party probably dominated the state legislature that made the redistricting decision in this case? How can you tell?* (The Democratic Party, because the redistricting ensured that no Democratic representation was lost.)

Background: *Controversial Issues* The 25 least populated states, with roughly 16 percent of the U.S. population, hold half the Senate seats.

Background: *History* When the first House of Representatives met in 1789, North Carolina and Rhode Island had not yet ratified the Constitution.

Background: *History* Though the maximum size of the House is 435 members, two representatives were temporarily added when Alaska and Hawaii joined the Union in 1959.

The symbol ⚎ denotes active participation strategies.

Activities are keyed for student abilities:
▲ = Basic
● = All Levels
■ = Average/Advanced

Economics

▲ **What is the main reason so many people have been moving into the sunbelt?** (People follow jobs; many industries have found that they can save money by relocating to the South.)

● CRITICAL THINKING **The "snowbelt" region of the North is also often referred to as the "rustbelt." Why?** (Many of its factories, once so productive, have been idle so long that they are rusting away.)

■ Ask students whether your state is in the sunbelt, the snowbelt, or somewhere in between. Then ask them to summarize the condition of the state's economy.

👥 Cooperative Learning

● Divide the class into three groups. Ask one group to write an editorial favoring lengthening House terms to four years and having representatives elected at the same time as the President. Another group should propose limiting the number of terms members of Congress may serve. The third group should favor preserving the traditional terms.

GUIDED/INDEPENDENT PRACTICE

● Have students explain what the effects on representation in Congress would be if a U.S. territory gained statehood. (The Senate would add two members; the House would have to reapportion to accommodate the new members from the new state.)

RETEACHING/CORRECTIVES

▲ Write the terms *reapportionment* and *redistricting* on the board. Ask students to distinguish between the terms. **When is reapportionment most likely to take place?** (After a census.) **How are reapportionment decisions**

Gerrymandering

Although state legislatures must provide for districts of approximately equal populations, they can still **gerrymander** the district. Gerrymandering, named after Massachusetts politician Elbridge Gerry, is the practice of drawing odd-shaped boundary lines to favor a particular candidate or political party, or to reduce the voting power of a racial or ethnic group.

Figure 12–1 shows a hypothetical example of gerrymandering. Suppose that State X has four representatives in Congress, each elected from a congressional district with roughly the same number of voters. The voters in three districts are primarily Democrats, while the fourth district has mostly Republicans. Thus, State X usually elects three Democrats and one Republican to the House of Representatives. After the census, Congress determines that State X must lose one seat. The state legislature, dominated by Democrats, draws the three new districts so that the Republican voters are split up among the Democratic districts. As a result, State X elects only Democratic representatives to the House.

Gerrymandering along party lines benefits the party with a majority in the state legislature. This practice was challenged by the Democratic Party in Indiana. It challenged that the state's Re-publican-dominated legislature had gerrymandered legislative districts to the Democrats' disadvantage. A federal court in 1984 ruled the practice unconstitutional, but the Supreme Court later overruled the decision. In *Davis v. Bandemer* (1986), the Court ruled that this instance of political gerrymandering did not violate the principle of "one person, one vote."

Redistricting has also been used both to weaken and to strengthen the voting power of certain groups. In *Gomillion v. Lightfoot* (1960), the Supreme Court ruled that gerrymandering in a way that disadvantaged African Americans violated the Fifteenth Amendment. In *Thornburg v. Gingles* (1986), the Court upheld a law that enabled minority groups to challenge gerrymandering. In *Reno v. Shaw* (1993), however, the Court warned that bizarrely shaped districts drawn to achieve racial representation may be unconstitutional.

Shifts in representation

Redistricting and reapportionment have remained important issues because of shifts in America's population. Since World War II, millions of Americans have moved from the so-called "snowbelt" states of the North to the **sunbelt** states. The sunbelt is the region stretching across

Figure 12–1 POLITICAL PARTY GERRYMANDERING 8B

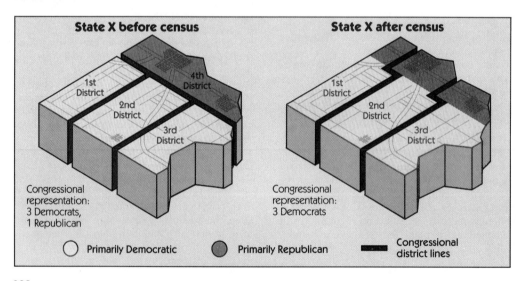

State X before census

1st District
2nd District
3rd District
4th District

Congressional representation:
3 Democrats,
1 Republican

State X after census

1st District
2nd District
3rd District

Congressional representation:
3 Democrats

○ Primarily Democratic   ● Primarily Republican   ▬ Congressional district lines

338

Background: *Cultural Literacy* The word *gerrymander* was coined to title a caricature of a Massachusetts election district formed during Elbridge Gerry's governorship. The district's irregular shape reminded the artist of a salamander.

Figure 12–1
● **Which party—majority or minority—has the power to gerrymander along party lines in a state legislature?** (The majority party.) **Why would it do this?** (To increase the party's number of elected officials.)

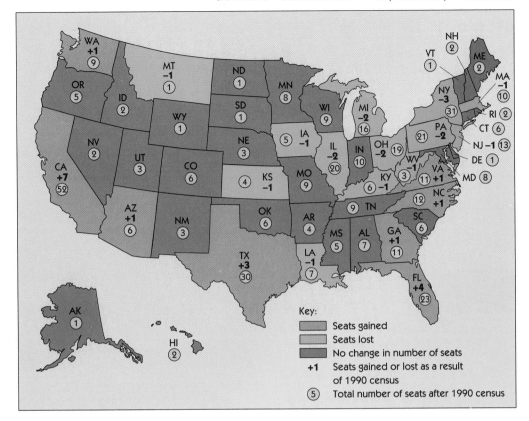

Key:
- ▨ Seats gained
- ▨ Seats lost
- ▨ No change in number of seats
- **+1** Seats gained or lost as a result of 1990 census
- ⑤ Total number of seats after 1990 census

Figure 12–2 SHIFTS IN THE HOUSE OF REPRESENTATIVES The reapportionment of seats in the House of Representatives after the 1990 census reflects a shift in the population from the "snowbelt" to the "sunbelt" states. 6F

the country from the southeastern Atlantic coast to southern California. In the past decade, the population of the West has grown by 22.3 percent and the South by 13.4 percent, whereas the Northeast has grown only 3.4 percent.

A major reason for this trend is economics. Many heavy industries in the Midwest and Northeast have closed. This has resulted in the loss of millions of jobs. At the same time, many new industries have sprung up in the South and West, partly because of lower taxes and lower labor costs. As manufacturing moves south, so do jobs and people. In addition, the sunbelt's warm climate and cheap energy have been a drawing card — especially for retired people.

The political consequences of the population shift can be clearly seen in the map in Figure 12–2, showing changes in the House of Representatives following the 1990 census. Eight states, mostly in the sunbelt, won seats. Thirteen states, mostly in the snowbelt, lost representatives in Congress. The biggest loser among the snowbelt states was New York, with a loss of three seats. By contrast, new representatives from the sunbelt included seven for California, three for Texas, and four for Florida. The long-term trends in California and New York are particularly striking. Since 1950 California has gained a total of twenty-two seats in the House, while New York has lost twelve.

---

made? (On the basis of population.) *Which is more likely to come first: reapportionment or redistricting?* (Reapportionment.) *Why?* (Congress determines, on the basis of the census, how many House seats a state will gain or lose. State legislatures then redraw district boundaries as needed.)

ENRICHMENT/EXTENSION

■ Have students find out how many congressional election districts there are in your state, which election district your community belongs to, and whether your state has undergone reapportionment as a result of the most recent census. You may also have students use a state almanac to find out the approximate number of people in your congressional election district.

Have students complete **Supreme Court Decisions 53–55,** which deal with apportionment.

Section 2 Review Answers
1. (a) 100 members. **(b)** 435 members.
2. Senators represent the interests of the entire state; House members represent the interests of their district.
3. The census determines each state's population. Congress determines the number of House seats for each state, based on the census.
4. (a) State legislatures.
(b) Equal populations.

Figure 12–2
● *Is your state in the snowbelt, sunbelt, or another region? Has the population shift of recent decades affected your town and state? For instance, have large numbers of people been moving in or have long-time residents been moving away?*

Critical Thinking
■ *Why do additional congressional seats in the sunbelt give those states more influence in presidential elections?* (Their number of electoral votes increases.)

The symbol 👥 denotes active participation strategies.

Activities are keyed for student abilities:
- ▲ = Basic
- ● = All Levels
- ■ = Average/Advanced

5. Gerrymandering can strengthen a political party or a particular candidate as well as weaken the voting power of certain groups.

Critical thinking Students should note that the frequency of elections necessitates frequent trips home in order to stay in close touch with constituents. The consequence of not doing so could be loss of office.

CLOSURE

● Review with students the vocabulary for the section. Have them define or describe each term or use it in a sentence. Then have students read Section 3, after which they should be able to describe a typical member of Congress.

SECTION 3

Who Are the Members of Congress?

(pp. 340–347)

Section Objectives

☐ list the qualifications for Congress

☐ describe the privileges and benefits that members of Congress have

☐ consider how members of Congress are supposed to represent their constituents

Vocabulary

congressional immunity, censure, code of ethics, perquisite, franking privilege, incumbent, pork-barrel program, casework

---

SECTION 2 REVIEW

Vocabulary and key terms

at large (337)   redistrict (337)
census (337)   gerrymander (338)
reapportionment (337)   sunbelt (338)

For review

1. What is the present membership of (a) the Senate? (b) the House? **3A**
2. What is the main difference between representation in the House and the Senate? **3A**
3. What is the purpose of the census with regard to Congress? **6F**
4. (a) Who is responsible for drawing congressional district boundaries? (b) What are the legal requirements for representation in these districts? **3A**
5. What are the effects of gerrymandering on congressional districts? **4B**

Critical thinking

EXAMINING BASIC PRINCIPLES   How might running for re-election every two years make a representative closely attuned to the people of his or her district? **8A**

SECTION
3

3A, 4A, 5C, 6A, 6B, 6F, 6G, 6I, 7A, 8A, 8G, 8H

Who Are the Members of Congress?

| ACCESS | The Main Ideas |

1 What are the qualifications for Congress?
pages 340–343

2 What privileges and benefits do members
pages 343–346

3 How are members of Congress supposed to represent their constituents?
pages 346–347

Congress is supposed to represent the people, yet the make-up of Congress does not reflect the nation as a whole. It has proportionately fewer women, African Americans, and Hispanics than the population at large. Does this matter? If so, in what ways?

In defending the Constitution in *The Federalist,* James Madison pointed out that Americans were free to use their own judgment in electing their representatives. The Constitution set up "no qualification of wealth, of birth, of religious faith, or of civil profession." The people, said Madison, could choose any citizen who deserved their "esteem and confidence." This section examines the kind of people we choose to represent us in Congress, their qualifications and compensation, and how they view their job.

340

3A, 6G

Qualifications for Congress

Constitutional requirements

As Madison noted, the Constitution sets up only a few qualifications for Senate and House membership. A senator must be 30 years old when he or she takes office and have been a citizen of the United States for nine years. A representative must be 25 years old and a United States citizen for seven years. Senators and representatives both must live in the state from which they are elected. Custom also dictates that representatives live in their own districts, although the Constitution does not require it.

Judging members' qualifications

Each house of Congress has the right to judge the "elections, returns, and qualifications of its own members" (Article 1, Section 5). This means that Congress alone has the right to resolve disputes over congressional election results. For example, in 1984, Democrat Frank McCloskey defeated Republican Richard D. McIntyre in Indiana's Eighth District by only a handful of votes. When the state recounted the ballots, however, McIntyre had won. Nevertheless, in

When was the last time you read a newspaper? Today? Last week? Over a year ago? When you read a newspaper, do you read only certain sections? Is a newspaper your main source of news?

Americans have been reading newspapers for close to 300 years, beginning with the *Boston News-Letter,* which was first published in 1704. The United States now boasts over 1,800 daily newspapers, with a total circulation of over 65 million. And there are thousands more non-daily newspapers! Reading a newspaper can be enjoyable; it can also make you a better citizen. Still, readers may face certain challenges when they pick up a newspaper.

Issues for Readers

1. I don't feel like I understand some of the articles I read. Newspaper reporters assume that their readers have a shared background knowledge, or **cultural literacy**, that allows them to comprehend the main point of a story, even though they may not understand all of the details. For example, the following excerpt appeared in *The New York Times* on September 24, 1991:

> The nation's savings rate is slumping again, despite the common view that the baby boomers would become thriftier in middle age. Not only do baby boomers save less than experts had hoped, but the number of retired people is growing, and they spend more than they earn.

The reporter who wrote the excerpt expects the reader to understand what significance the nation's savings rate might have; who baby boomers are; and why a lower savings rate among baby boomers combined with a higher spending rate among retired people is not good for the economy. Reading a newspaper frequently can help you to learn and store this background knowledge.

2. I'm only interested in the sports section. Why should I read the stories on the front page? The front page contains the major international and national news stories of the previous day. Reading or even skimming these stories will help you to keep up with current events and, most importantly, will help to expand your cultural literacy.

3. How can reading a newspaper make me a better informed citizen? Newspapers offer their readers a wealth of information. Let's take an example of how you can use this information: Your town is holding an election for mayor. Your newspaper can tell you who the candidates are; what they stand for; where you can see them debate; and where an election rally will be held. By gathering this information, you can make an informed vote, fulfilling one of your responsibilities as an American citizen.

CRITICAL THINKING
1. What role can cultural literacy play in reading a newspaper?
2. How can education be a part of expanding your cultural literacy?

CIVIC LITERACY

8A

Reading a Newspaper

CIVIC LITERACY

Cooperative Learning
● Divide the class into groups of four or five and have each group bring to class a copy of the news section of a local newspaper. Each group should prepare summaries of three of the articles—one dealing with international affairs, one dealing with national affairs, and one dealing with a state or local issue. Once the groups have submitted their summaries, discuss with the class the differences among the three kinds of stories they read. See whether students were more familiar with state or local issues than with national or international ones, and, if so, how this affected their summaries.

Critical Thinking Answers
1. It helps a reader understand the main point of a story.

2. Education provides a person with the many different kinds of knowledge—political, historical, literary, etc.—that help one understand news stories.

The symbol **ii** denotes active participation strategies.

Activities are keyed for student abilities:
▲ = Basic
● = All Levels
■ = Average/Advanced

FOCUS

FOCUS

● Ask each student to compose a profile (occupation, education, ethnic background, gender, religion, age, and income) of an ideal community leader. Then have each student read his or her profile to the class. The class should then decide to what degree that profile fits the average member of Congress.

EXPLANATION

After reviewing the content of the section, you may want to consider the following activities:

Multiculturalism

There are many instances in recent congressional history in which one group's interests have been represented by another group. The Civil Rights Act of 1964, for example, was passed by a predominantly white Congress.

● CRITICAL THINKING   *In deciding issues, should a member of Congress consider the views of the other members of his or her gender, ethnic, or other group? Explain.* (Some students might argue that members of Congress, as members of particular social groups, should consider the views of other members. Other students might argue that members of Congress should consider only their own views and those of their constituents.)

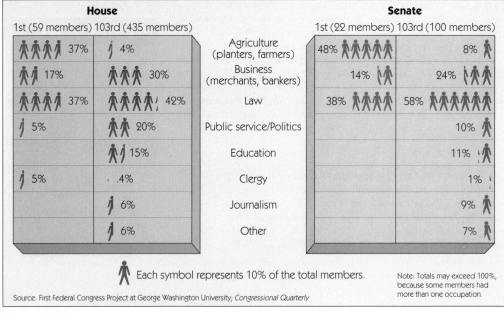

	House				Senate	
	1st (59 members)	103rd (435 members)			1st (22 members)	103rd (100 members)
Agriculture (planters, farmers)	37%	4%			48%	8%
Business (merchants, bankers)	17%	30%			14%	24%
Law	37%	42%			38%	58%
Public service/Politics	5%	20%				10%
Education		15%				11%
Clergy	5%	.4%				1%
Journalism		6%				9%
Other		6%				7%

Each symbol represents 10% of the total members.

Note: Totals may exceed 100%, because some members had more than one occupation.

Source: First Federal Congress Project at George Washington University; *Congressional Quarterly*

Figure 12–3 THE FIRST AND 103RD CONGRESSES: COMPARING OCCUPATIONS   8G

1985, the House — controlled by the Democrats — voted 236–190 to seat McCloskey.

While only Congress can determine whether one of its members meets the constitutional qualifications, it cannot impose extra qualifications. In 1967, for example, the House refused to seat Representative Adam Clayton Powell, Jr., of New York because of alleged "financial misconduct." Powell sued to be seated and won. The Supreme Court held in *Powell v. McCormack* (1969) that Congress could not require new members to satisfy more than the qualifications established by the Constitution.

A "profile" of the U.S. Congress

Although the members of Congress represent the American people, they by no means resemble a cross-section of the population. In reality, senators and representatives tend to be older, wealthier, and better-educated than their constitutents. The 103rd Congress had the following characteristics:

OCCUPATION Law was still the most common profession among members of Congress, but

backgrounds in politics and business were becoming more common. The 103rd Congress had 58 lawyers in the Senate and 181 in the House. Banking and business ranked second, with 24 people in the Senate and 131 in the House. Other occupations represented in Congress were journalism, professional sports, and the ministry.

EDUCATION Almost all of the members were college graduates. A majority had professional and advanced degress.

ETHNIC BACKGROUND There were 96 white senators, 2 Asians, 1 African American, and 1 Native American. In the House, there were 39 African Americans, plus 19 Hispanics, and 7 of Asian or Hawaiian descent.

GENDER Seven senators in the 103rd Congress were women, as were 48 representatives (about 11 percent).

RELIGION Nearly half the members of Congress were either Methodists, Episcopalians, Presbyterians, or Baptists. Among senators, 63 were Protestant, 23 Roman Catholic, 10 Jewish, 1 Greek Orthodox, and 3 Mormon. In the House, there were 265 Protestant, 118 Roman Catholic,

342

Check for Understanding
▲ *What principle did the Supreme Court reaffirm in Powell v. McCormack?* (Congress could not require new members to satisfy more than the actual constitutional requirements.)

Figure 12–3
● *Why were there so many fewer people in the 103rd Congress involved in agriculture than there were in the First Congress?*

(Much smaller percentages of the nation's workers and wealth are involved in agriculture.)

32 Jewish, 4 Greek Orthodox, and 9 Mormon representatives.

AGE The average senator was 58.0 years old; the average representative was 51.7 years old.

INCOME Congress members are substantially wealthier than the average American. A 1991 report, for example, revealed that 26 members of the Senate and 51 members of the House were millionaires.

A statistical view

Because Congress does not reflect a true cross-section of Americans, some argue that it is undemocratic. From a purely statistical viewpoint, some groups appear to be greatly overrepresented. For instance, fewer than half (49 percent) of all Americans are men, but Congress is nearly entirely male (about 90 percent). Lawyers make up 45 percent of Congress, but are less than 1 percent of the labor force. Whites, who represent 80 percent of all Americans, make up over 87 percent of Congress. From a purely statistical standpoint, here is what Congress ought to look like: 51 percent women, 12 percent African Americans, 9 percent Hispanics, 3 percent Asians, and 1 percent Native Americans. Moreover, 27 percent would be blue-collar workers and only 1 percent lawyers.

6A, 6F, 6I

Privileges and Penalties

Because of the nature of their job, members of Congress are entitled to certain legal rights that ordinary citizens do not have. They are also subject to rules of conduct and penalties that do not apply to all Americans.

Freedom from arrest

In 16th- and 17th-century England, members of Parliament were frequently arrested on false charges. The monarch used this tactic to prevent political opponents from attending Parliament. To avoid a similar situation in America, the Constitution grants members of Congress freedom from arrest while they are attending legislative sessions or traveling to and from them. This privilege is called **congressional immunity**.

For example, in 1984 Senator Roger Jepsen of Iowa was stopped by a police officer while driving to Congress from his home in Alexandria, Virginia. Jepsen had been driving alone in a lane restricted for buses and carpools. The senator claimed congressional immunity, and the charges were dropped.

Although they are exempt from minor traffic violations, jury duty, and civil suits, Congress members can be arrested, tried, and convicted on criminal charges.

Some members of Congress have been caught taking bribes, using official funds for personal pleasure, and evading income tax. One of the worst scandals in recent years was the "Abscam" case in 1980. Six House members and one senator were videotaped accepting payments as high as $50,000 from undercover FBI agents posing as Arab sheiks. The congressmen, in return, agreed to help the "sheiks" gain entry into the United States and get licenses for gambling casinos and other businesses. All seven were convicted in federal court for accepting bribes.

Freedom of expression

Congressional immunity also gives members of Congress the right to speak freely about political questions. They cannot be prosecuted or sued for libel or slander for speeches made in committees or on the floor of Congress, or for reports printed in the *Congressional Record.* Defamatory speech and writing outside of Congress, however, are not constitutionally protected.

For example, Senator Mike Gravel of Alaska had the *Pentagon Papers,* secret documents relating to U.S. involvement in Vietnam, entered in the *Congressional Record,* even though the White House had said their publication would harm national security. The Supreme Court ruled that Gravel's action was protected as "privileged speech." Senator William Proxmire of Wisconsin, however, was found to have libeled a hospital researcher by ridiculing the researcher's federally funded research on monkeys. The Supreme Court ruled that Proxmire's remarks were not connected with his job as a senator.

Penalties for misconduct

Like society at large, Congress sometimes has members who abuse their power and privileges. Congress itself has many possible ways of dealing with wrongdoing by its members. The Constitution provides that "each house may . . . punish its members for disorderly behavior, and, with

343

Multiculturalism

▲ CRITICAL THINKING Discuss with the class the reasons why Congress generally does not represent a cross-section of Americans. *Why would a law degree be helpful to a member of Congress?* (Congress's job is to make law.) *Why are a disproportionate number of members of Congress millionaires?* (Running for office is very expensive.)

● CRITICAL THINKING *What might account for the underrepresentation of women and minorities in the House and Senate?* (Fewer women and minority group members have the money or the organizational network needed to run a successful political campaign.)

Law

● CRITICAL THINKING Assign each student a different special privilege given to members of Congress (congressional immunity, franking privilege, etc.). Students should write down one reason why the privilege is appropriate and one reason why it is inappropriate, then make their own decision. Review the privileges and the arguments for and against them with the class.

Background: *Cultural Literacy* ABSCAM is an acronym for "Arab scam." *Scam* is slang for a phony business scheme. The word was also used to describe the 1986 scandal surrounding the arms sales to Iran ("Iranscam").

Background: *Controversial Issues* In *Hutchinson v. Proxmire* (1979), the Court found Senator Proxmire guilty of libel because he had ridiculed Hutchinson (the hospital researcher) in a press release. This action was found to be libelous because the statement was not made in Congress.

The symbol ♯♯ denotes active participation strategies.

Activities are keyed for student abilities:
▲ = Basic
● = All Levels
■ = Average/Advanced

Cooperative Learning
● Have students reread the subsection "The representative's dilemma" (p. 346). Divide the class into four groups and assign each group the role of representative, factory worker, cotton producer, or House leader. Each group should prepare its arguments for or against the bill described in the subsection. Have each group field questions from the other groups.

GUIDED/INDEPENDENT PRACTICE
● Have students consider the compensation, benefits, and privileges of members of Congress as well as the rigors of the job and write a short essay describing why they would or would not want to run for Congress some day.

---

the concurrence of two-thirds, expel a member." One form of punishment is to **censure** a member, officially declaring disapproval. Censure may carry with it a loss of privileges, but the member's reputation suffers the greatest damage.

Very few members have been expelled. In fact, the first since the Civil War was Representative Michael Myers from Pennsylvania, who had been convicted in the "Abscam" case. Two other representatives and the one senator involved in "Abscam" chose to resign rather than face the public embarrassment of expulsion. The three other representatives involved did not have to face this decision — they were all defeated when they ran for re-election in 1980.

Codes of ethics
To prevent members of Congress from taking undue advantage of their position, both houses have drawn up **codes of ethics** These are rules and guidelines for the behavior of congressional members, particularly in financial matters. New guidelines that went into effect in 1991 eliminated outside honoraria, or speaking fees, for House members. New restrictions were also placed on the receiving of gifts by House members. In the Senate, a precise limit was placed on the amount of money that members could earn from outside sources.

3A

Compensation and Benefits

Salaries
Though senators and representatives represent their states, they are paid out of the national treasury. Congress, therefore, determines its own salaries and benefits. In 1789, the first Congress set each of its members' pay at $6 per day. As times changed, so did congressional pay. In 1993, compensation for senators and representatives was about $130,000. In addition, members can receive income from outside sources, such as stock dividends and interest.

Many Americans dislike the fact that members of Congress set their own salaries. Members of Congress recognize that voting themselves a raise could jeopardize their chances of re-election. In 1989 they avoided this problem by passing an increase quickly with little time for debate. Members justified the hike by setting restrictions on their outside income.

344

The issue of congressional pay is not new. In 1789 James Madison proposed a constitutional amendment that said no increase in congressional pay would take effect until an election had taken place. Although this amendment passed Congress and went to the states, it failed to win the necessary two-thirds state vote. In the late 1980's, as opposition to congressional pay raises grew, states began to ratify this "lost" amendment. In 1992, Michigan became the 38th and final state to ratify the 27th Amendment, more than 200 years after it was proposed.

Fringe benefits
Members of Congress also receive a number of **perquisites** (or "perks") — benefits, allowances, and services in addition to their regular salaries. For example, each member of Congress is given a suite of offices in one of the Senate or House office buildings adjacent to the Capitol. They receive generous expense accounts for staff and supplies, as well as allowances to maintain offices in their home district.

In addition, stationery, long-distance telephone calls (up to 15,000 minutes per year), and postage are free. The free postal service, known as the **franking privilege**, costs taxpayers $100 million yearly. Congress members also have access to a computer service for contacting constituents and interest groups, assistance in taping television or radio broadcasts, and free photographs.

Members of Congress also receive an allowance for travel. Representatives and senators travel a number of times each year between Washington, D.C., and their home states in order to keep in touch with their constituency. In addition, members of Congress and their families may travel to foreign countries at the expense of the government, often in military planes. These trips are supposed to be for official business, such as fact-finding missions or meetings with foreign dignitaries. Critics, who see many of these trips as unnecessary vacations, sometimes refer to them as "junkets."

While no longer receiving free prescription drugs, Congress members do have access to low-cost hospitalization. Each member gets a low-cost life insurance policy. A generous pension plan can lead to substantial retirement income. Other benefits include free research service at the

---

Background: *Structure of Government* Congress wrote the initial Ethics in Government Act in 1978, partly in response to Watergate.

Critical Thinking
● *How could the franking privilege help incumbents?*
(It allows them to keep in touch with their constituents at no cost, a privilege not available to their challengers.)

Expressing Your Political Opinions

6B, 7A

One evening while watching the news on TV, you see a senator from your state talking about a bill that is up for a vote in Congress. You suddenly realize that this bill will affect both the number of jobs in your community and the wages that teenagers will receive next summer. "Wait a minute," you think, "that's my summer job they're deciding about. That senator should listen to me and my friends before voting on anything!"

The right to express your opinion about what your government is doing is one of your important rights as a citizen in a democracy. If you are eighteen, you can express your opinion by voting for or against a candidate. But any American, of any age, can write an *opinion letter* to any public official — from your mayor up to the President of the United States. Public officials welcome letters from the people they represent. Such letters are an important way of learning "grassroots" feelings about bills and issues.

There are several things to remember when you write a letter to a public official:

- *Be sure of what you want to say.* Look into the issue thoroughly. Gather enough facts to back up your opinion, and then state it thoughtfully.

- *Write your opinion briefly and clearly.* If you take time to organize your ideas carefully, it will be easier to write them clearly. Keep your letter short. Two or three well-written paragraphs are more effective than several long, rambling pages.

- *Write your letter correctly.* An opinion letter is a business letter. It begins with a heading giving the name, title, and address of the person to whom it is written. For example, a letter to Senator Elizabeth Lee would be headed, "The Honorable Elizabeth Lee." The greeting of your letter may take the form, "Dear Senator Lee:" or "Dear Ms. (or Mrs.) Lee:" The body of your letter should be typed or written neatly in ink. Sign your letter with your full name.

Following these guidelines will help ensure that your letter will be read and appreciated — and that your opinion will be heard.

Follow-up

1. Check your local telephone book to find out whether the members of Congress from your state have local offices. (Simply look under the senator's or representative's name.) From these offices, find their correct mailing addresses.
2. Suggest one or more current issues that affect you as a student or as a member of your community. Working alone or in a small group, draft a letter on one of these topics. Make a final copy following the guidelines given above.

CITIZENSHIP SKILLS

Civic Participation
One incentive for people to write to their representative or senator is that they will most likely receive a response. Congressional staffs try to reply to all inquiries and opinions.

▲ CRITICAL THINKING **Why do members of Congress try to reply to all letters from constituents?** (Meeting the needs of constituents is one of a member's jobs. Also, failure to respond to constituents could hurt a member of Congress in the next election.)

● Have students complete **Citizenship Worksheet 5,** in which they examine a letter that expresses a political opinion.

Follow-up Answers
1. You might begin by writing the names of these members of Congress on the board.
2. Letters should be read aloud to the class.

The symbol ♥♥ denotes active participation strategies.

Activities are keyed for student abilities:
▲ = Basic
● = All Levels
■ = Average/Advanced

RETEACHING/CORRECTIVES

▲ Have students create an outline of the section, using both the red headings and the black subheadings. Outlines should provide as much detail as is necessary to understand the main points in the section.

Have students complete **Skills Practice Worksheet 12,** in which they study a chart to make generalizations about House re-election bids.

ENRICHMENT/EXTENSION

■ Have students complete **Skills Challenge Worksheet 12,** which discusses a vote by Senator Sam Houston.

Section 3 Review Answers

1. **(a)** Representatives must be 25 years old and U.S. citizens for seven years; senators must be 30 years old and citizens for nine years. **(b)** Congress.

2. Members are mostly lawyers, male, and white and are usually older, richer, and better educated than the general population.

3. Freedom from arrest in legislative sessions or on the way to and from sessions; freedom from prosecution for libel and slander while speaking in committee or on the floor or for reports in the *Congressional Record;* freedom from minor traffic violations, jury duty, and civil suits.

4. The member can be censured or expelled.

5. **(a)** National treasury.
(b) Congress determines its salaries.

Figure 12–4 INCIDENTAL BENEFITS FOR MEMBERS OF CONGRESS **3A**

★ Free use of health facilities, gymnasium, and pool

★ Free parking

★ Free flowers and plants from the U.S. Botanic Garden

★ Free "We the People" wall calendars, complete with the member's name, to be given to constituents

★ Special barbershop and beauty salon

★ Low-cost meals at the Senate and House dining rooms

★ Free research service at the Library of Congress

★ Free prints from the National Gallery

★ Free funeral arrangements and undertaker services

Library of Congress, low-cost meals in the House and Senate dining areas, and free use of excellent health facilities. (See Figure 12–4.)

Staying in office

Another fringe benefit of holding office is that once members are elected to Congress, they are usually able to be re-elected again and again. Many **incumbents** — those already in office — occupy what are called "safe seats." In these districts, one political party tends to dominate. An incumbent from the leading party is almost guaranteed re-election. In 1992, for example, 348 incumbents sought re-election to the House, and only 24 were defeated.

Congressional "perks" and privileges can give incumbents an advantage at election time. Members of Congress gain name recognition from press releases, television appearances, trips to the home district, attendance at football games, state fairs, and the like. They usually find it easy to raise funds for campaigns, for individuals and interest groups are more likely to contribute to candidates with proven track records. Voters also are more likely to remember candidates who have been able to secure **pork-barrel programs** — projects or grants that chiefly benefit the home district, such as a new dam, a federal office building, highway funds, or grants for the local college.

Having an office and staff in Washington and at home is another advantage. One of the tasks of a congressional staff is **casework.** Casework involves doing personal favors for constituents, such as cutting bureaucratic red tape, finding lost government checks, or helping individuals enroll in federal programs. This kind of activity helps cultivate friends and supporters.

At election time, Congress members can make use of stationery and the franking privilege to mail questionnaires, newsletters, and the like to their constituents. Challengers argue that these mailings are really campaign brochures and give incumbents an unfair advantage.

4A, 5C, 8H

Representing the People

Because the United States is a representative democracy, the members of Congress represent the people. But how do they carry out this job? Which people do they represent — their home district, the entire state, or the nation as a whole? What about the wishes of interest groups, of the President, or of their political party?

The representative's dilemma

Representatives frequently face the following kind of situation: You are a member of the House of Representatives. You favor free trade and are philosophically opposed to limiting imports. Your home district depends economically on producing cotton and manufacturing shoes. Because of an influx of cheap shoes from Brazil, several factories in your district have shut down and many constituents are now unemployed. Workers and factory owners want you to support legislation to restrict the import of shoes from Brazil. The cotton producers, however, are afraid that such import quotas will cause Brazil to retaliate by buying less cotton. The House leadership and a PAC that contributed heavily to your election want you to support the bill. The President, however, says the bill could harm the U.S. economy. *How would you vote?*

A representative's roles

Political scientists have found that members of Congress — and elected representatives in general — think of "representative" in three dif-

Figure 12–4
● *Would you eliminate any of these benefits? Which ones? Why?*

Critical Thinking
▲ *Why would a member of Congress attend such non-political events as a football game or county fair?* (To gain free publicity, generate good will, and keep in touch with the people.)

Background: *Cultural Literacy* The term *pork barrel* predates the Civil War, when salt pork (a valuable product) was stored in barrels.

ferent ways, and make their decisions accordingly. Some representatives see themselves as *delegates*. They feel compelled to follow the desires of their constituents. No matter what they personally believe, they usually vote the way they think the "folks back home" would want them to. Other representatives act as *trustees*. They feel the voters have entrusted them with the job of making independent judgments.

The most common point of view combines the trustee and delegate roles. This is sometimes called the *politico* role. On some issues, where there is no strong public sentiment, a representative makes independent judgments, acting as a trustee. But on highly visible or controversial issues, this representative tries to be a delegate and reflect the desires of his or her constituents.

SECTION 3 REVIEW

Vocabulary and Key Terms

congressional immunity (343)
censure (344)
code of ethics (344)
perquisite (344)
franking privilege (344)
incumbent (346)
pork-barrel program (346)
casework (346)

For review

1. (a) What are the constitutional requirements for membership in the House and Senate? (b) Who judges the qualifications of new members? **3A**
2. How does Congress differ from the general population in terms of occupation, sex, and racial or ethnic background? **6F**
3. What special legal privileges and freedoms do members of Congress have? **3A**
4. What actions can Congress take to punish a member? **6A**
5. (a) Who pays the members of Congress? (b) How are their salaries determined? **3A**

Critical thinking

ORGANIZING AN ARGUMENT What are some arguments in favor of the following statement: "Congress should represent a true cross-section of the population"? How would one defend the composition of the 103rd Congress? **8A**

Chapter Summary

The Constitution gives Congress many powers. As the lawmaking branch of a sovereign nation, it makes rules for becoming a citizen, provides for an army and a navy, and regulates U.S. properties and territories. It has the power to tax, borrow, and spend money for the national government and to promote and regulate trade among the states. It also establishes federal courts, approves presidential appointments and treaties, <u>impeaches</u> and tries federal officials, and acts as a "watchdog" over governmental activities.

Members of the House of Representatives serve two-year terms and are closely attuned to the people. Senators serve for six years and are more independent. Two senators are elected <u>at large</u> from each state; representation in the House is decided by state population. State legislatures draw the boundaries of congressional districts. After a <u>census</u> they may have to <u>redistrict</u> to ensure "one person, one vote." However, they may not <u>gerrymander</u> districts to deprive minority groups of their fair representation. Current representation in Congress reflects shifts in population toward the <u>sunbelt</u>.

Qualifications for Congress members are set by the Constitution and judged by each house. A senator must be 30 years old and a U.S. citizen for 9 years before taking office. A representative must be 25 years old and a citizen for 7 years. <u>Congressional immunity</u> makes members free from arrest while attending Congress, but they can be <u>censured</u> or, in rare cases, expelled for misconduct. The <u>perquisites</u> (or "perks") of membership include large staffs, generous travel budgets, and the <u>franking privilege</u>.

Some activities of members of Congress — such as securing <u>pork-barrel</u> programs or doing <u>casework</u> — give <u>incumbents</u> an advantage in bids for re-election. Members of Congress view their role as a representative differently. Some believe they are entrusted by the voters to make decisions according to their personal judgment; others rely more upon the opinions of their constituents.

Critical thinking The statement that Congress should represent a cross-section of the population rests on the argument that a more diverse Congress would better represent the people. In defending the composition of the 103rd Congress, one might argue that congressional elections are fair and that a member of Congress should not be judged by such criteria as ethnic background or occupation.

CLOSURE

● Tell students to reread the quotation by James Madison in the opening paragraph of the section and decide if the theory stated there applies to today's Congress. Then have students read the next assigned lesson.

CHAPTER 12 CORRECTIVES

● To review the content of Chapter 12, you may want to have students complete **Study Guide/Review 12** or **Workbook Chapter 12.**

347

Critical Thinking
● *As a citizen, how do you view the role of elected officials? Should they be delegates, trustees, or a combination of both (politicos)? Why?*

(Students should show a clear understanding of the three terms in their answers.)

The symbol ⅱ denotes active participation strategies.

Activities are keyed for student abilities:
▲ = Basic
● = All Levels
■ = Average/Advanced

CHAPTER 12 REVIEW

Answers

Vocabulary See pp. T19–T21 for suggested vocabulary activities.

Reviewing the Facts

1. *Sovereign*—Provide for defense and general welfare; make rules for naturalization; create, equip, and fund the armed forces; declare war; make laws for Washington, D.C., and U.S. territories. *Financial*—Lay and collect taxes. *Trade*—Coin money and establish its value; fix standards of weights and measures; establish post offices and post roads; issue copyrights and patents.

2. The right to pass any laws that are "necessary and proper" to carry out the powers specifically enumerated in the Constitution.

3. They are part of the system of checks and balances.

4. The Senate must approve, by a majority vote, presidential appointments. Therefore, the President may first seek the "advice" of the Senate in making nominations.

5. In the Senate, which represents the states, each state has equal membership. In the House, which represents the people, membership is apportioned according to population.

6. The Senate is unaffected; states may lose or gain seats in the House, depending on changes in population.

7. Differences in population among congressional districts became unconstitutional.

8. A representative must be 25 years old, a U.S. citizen for at least seven years, and a resident of the state that elected him or her. A senator must be 30 years old, a U.S. citizen for at least nine years, and a resident of the state that elected him or her.

9. Financial matters.

348

● **Review the definitions of the following terms:**

at large	excise tax	patent
casework	expressed powers	perquisite
censure	franking privilege	pork-barrel program
census	gerrymander	post roads
code of ethics	impeach	reapportionment
congressional immunity	implied powers	redistrict
copyright	impost	sunbelt
duty	incumbent	
elastic clause	legislative veto	

● **REVIEWING THE FACTS**

1. Give one example of a lawmaking power granted to Congress in each of the following areas: sovereign powers, financial powers, and powers to regulate and promote trade. **3A**

2. What right does the elastic clause give to Congress? **3A**

3. What is the primary function of the non-legislative powers granted to Congress by the Constitution? **3B**

4. Explain the significance of Congress's power to "advise and consent" in presidential appointments. **3A**

5. How does the different representation in the Senate and House help balance the various interests of society? **3B**

6. How does a census affect representation in Congress? Explain the recent increase in representation from the sunbelt states. **3A**

7. How did the "one person, one vote" principle affect the make-up of congressional districts? **4A**

8. What are the constitutional requirements for membership in the House of Representatives? What are the requirements for membership in the Senate? **1D**

9. Which major area of conduct is addressed by the codes of ethics of the House and Senate? **4A**

▲ **THINKING CRITICALLY ABOUT KEY CONCEPTS**

1. Why does the Congress have non-legislative functions? Do these give the Congress too much power? **3B**

2. Do you agree with the Court decision in *Davis v. Bandemer* (1986) that allows gerrymandering along party lines as long as the resulting congressional districts have equal populations? Explain your answer. **2D**

3. In what ways does the system of perquisites give an edge to an incumbent at election time? **4C**

▲ **PRACTICING SKILLS**

1. **Study Skills: Reading a special-purpose map.** Refer to Figure 12–2 (page 339) to answer the following questions. (a) How many congressional seats did your state have before the 1990 census? (b) How many seats did your state have after the 1990 census? (c) Did your state show a gain, a loss, or no significant change in population? **8B**

2. **Study Skills: Reading a pictograph.** Refer to Figure 12–3 (page 342) to answer the following questions. (a) Which Congress had a greater variety of occupations? (b) What

Thinking Critically About Key Concepts

1. These functions are part of the checks and balances system built into the Constitution. Sometimes they may give Congress considerable power over the other branches, but, over time, the various powers of the three branches have kept each other in check.

2. Many students may find the concept of gerrymandering distasteful. Others may say that because both parties can do it, there is a balance of sorts; besides, the Supreme Court has ruled in support of the practice.

3. Incumbents can make their names and faces well known through public appearances; they can find

statement can you make about the number of lawyers in Congress? **8B**

3. **Critical Thinking Skills: Distinguishing fact from opinion.** Reread the subsection ''A statistical view'' (page 343). (a) What opinion is presented in this paragraph? (b) Find three statistics that seem to support this opinion. **8A**

▲ PARTICIPATORY CITIZENSHIP

1. **Creating a display.** With the help of classmates, create a display showing the different members of Congress who have represented your community. The display might show photographs or portraits of the representatives, biographical information about them, lists of their legislative accomplishments, and accounts of their visits to your community. **4C**

2. **Contacting your representative.** Write a letter to your representative in Congress asking for his or her position on the issue of term limits. When you receive the response, discuss it with your classmates. **4A**

■ WRITING ABOUT ISSUES

1. **Writing a letter to the editor.** Write a letter to the editor for or against term limits for members of Congress. Be sure to explain and defend your position. **8C**

2. **Writing a letter to Congress.** Could a congressional committee abuse its oversight function? Write a letter to a committee chairperson as if you were the head of an executive agency. In your letter, describe what you see as abuse of the committee's oversight function. **8H**

▲ ANALYZING A POLITICAL CARTOON

Congress has been criticized for being reluctant to lead or take unpopular, but principled, stands on issues. Instead, its critics claim, its members strive to avoid any action that might prove politically unpopular. Look at the cartoon below and answer the following questions.

1. How does the cartoon portray the heritage of Congress? **8B**
2. How does the cartoon portray Congress today? **8B**
3. What might account for members of Congress today seeming more fearful than members of the past? **8A**

Cartoon by Jim Borgman, 1990, Cincinnati Enquirer. Reprinted with special permission of King Features Syndicate, Inc.

349

some argue that it is undemocratic. **(b)** Statistics include the following: Fewer than half of all Americans are men, yet Congress is nearly entirely male; lawyers are less than 1 percent of the labor force, but make up 45 percent of Congress; 80 percent of all Americans are white, but whites make up over 87 percent of Congress.

Participatory Citizenship
1. The display could be set up in the classroom or in the hall.
2. Students' letters might also inquire about a representative's position on current issues.

Writing About Issues
1. Letters supporting term limits should mention the difficulty of voting incumbents out of office and the danger of corruption posed by long tenures in office. Letters opposing term limits should note that voters retain the ability to vote incumbents out of office, and may suggest that term limits would deprive Congress of its most experienced members.
2. Letters should specify which agency and which committee are involved and should clearly describe the nature of the abuse.

Analyzing a Political Cartoon
1. It depicts Congress as having a noble and distinguished heritage, exemplified by Webster and Clay, two bold leaders.
2. As paralyzed by fear.
3. Students might suggest that current members of Congress are overly concerned with re-election or with maintaining a positive media image.

financial support more easily because they have an established voting record; they can make friends among the voters by using their office staff to do casework; they can send newsletters and brochures to voters with the help of free stationery and the franking privilege.

Practicing Skills
1. Students should use the key to help them determine their answers.

2. (a) the 103rd Congress. **(b)** Lawyers held a consistently high percentage of seats in both houses and in both Congresses.
3. (a) Because Congress does not reflect a true cross-section of Americans,

CHAPTER 13
THE LAWMAKING PROCESS
(pp. 350–375)

	Section Objectives	Section Resources
Section 1 **How Is Congress Organized?**	☐ explain the rules governing the operation of Congress ☐ explain how the leadership of Congress is organized ☐ describe the support services that Congress has	
Section 2 **Committees Play a Key Role in Lawmaking**	☐ identify the different kinds of committees in Congress ☐ explain how the members of committees are chosen	
Section 3 **How Does a Bill Become Law?**	☐ explain how a bill gets to be voted on by the entire legislative chamber ☐ describe what happens once a bill reaches the floor of a chamber	▲ SKILLS PRACTICE WORKSHEET **13** ■ SKILLS CHALLENGE WORKSHEET **13** ● SIMULATION **1** ▲ TRANSPARENCIES **31–32**

Essential Elements

The list below shows Essential Elements relevant to this chapter. (The complete list of Essential Elements appears in the introductory pages of this Teacher's Edition.)

Section 1: 1B, 1C, 2A, 2E, 3A, 6B, 6C, 6F, 8A, 8B, 8G

Section 2: 3A, 4C, 8A, 8F, 8G

Section 3: 3A, 6B, 6F, 8G, 8H

Critical Thinking feature (p. 373): 8D

Chapter Review: 3A, 6A, 6F, 8A, 8B, 8C, 8F, 8H

Section Resources are keyed for student abilities:
▲ = Basic
● = All Levels
■ = Average/Advanced

Homework Options

Each section contains activities labeled "Guided/Independent Practice," "Reteaching/Correctives," and "Enrichment/Extension." You may wish to choose from among these activities when assigning homework.

Students Acquiring English Activities

Have each student make two cards, one labeled *Senate* and the other labeled *House of Representatives*. Read to the class a list of distinguishing features of each house, one item at a time. (Figure 13–1 on p. 355 supplies several such features; others are located in the chapter narrative.) After each item is called out, students should hold up the appropriate card. Have students keep track of the number of correct responses they make.

LISTENING/SPEAKING: Have students condense the information in Figure 13–4 (p. 365) into a brief summary of the lawmaking process. Students should read their summaries to the class. After all summaries have been read, have students write a new summary adopting the best features of the summaries they have heard.

Case Studies

When teaching this chapter, you may use Case Study 9, which discusses the issue of a special minimum wage for teenagers. (Case Studies may be found following p. 510.)

Teacher Bibliography

Keefe, William J. and Morris S. Ogul. *The American Legislative Process: Congress and the States.* 7th ed. Prentice-Hall, 1989. An exposition of the American way of making law.

O'Neill, Thomas P., Jr., and William Novak. *Man of the House: The Life and Political Memoirs of Speaker Tip O'Neill.* St. Martin's, 1988. The retired Speaker of the House and long-term member of Congress writes about his life and congressional career.

Student Bibliography

How Congress Works. CQ Press, 1991. A survey of the dynamics of congressional action, including the committee system and the power of lobbyists.

Hutson, James H. *To Make All Laws: The Congress of the United States, 1789–1989.* Houghton Mifflin, 1990. An illustrated history of the first 200 years of Congress that focuses on its achievements and the personalities who helped shape it.

Maass, Arthur. *Congress and the Common Good.* Basic, 1983. Traces the response of Congress to its committees and other internal institutions.

Literature

Drury, Allen. *Advise and Consent.* Doubleday, 1959. The response of Washington insiders to the nomination of a new Secretary of State. The novel gives a good picture of how the Senate works and the political scene in Washington.

Films and Videotapes*

Congress in Committee. (Series title: *Congress: We the People.*) 30 min. Films, 1983. v. Focuses on how congressional committees are responsible for shaping public policy.

The Legislative Branch. (Series title: *Government As It Is.*) 26 min. Pyramid, 1980. f, v. Presents the history of Congress and its day-to-day role governing our nation.

Legislative Process—Who or What Makes the Wheels Turn? (Series title: *Upon Reflection.*) 29 min. UWA, 1985. v. A candid discussion by Senator Daniel Evans of the homework and staff work that supports the behind-the-scenes activity of the legislative process.

Software*

American Government IV (Apple, IBM, Macintosh). Queue. Students learn about the development and processes of the American government through interactive tutorials. Three programs cover the roles and organization of political parties, the presidency, the White House, Congress, and the lawmaking process.

The Congressional Bill Simulator (Apple). Focus. A realistic simulation of the legislative process. Student legislators write bills to introduce into the House of Representatives and shepherd a bill through committee, the Senate vote, and presidential approval or veto.

How a Bill Becomes a Law (Apple, IBM, Macintosh). Queue. Students become members of Congress trying to get a bill passed. They must make decisions on moral and political issues while bargaining for support.

* For a complete guide to audiovisual sources, see page T22.

349B

The Lawmaking Process *(pp. 350–375)*

Chapter 13 examines the process by which Congress makes laws for the nation, explaining the formal and informal rules that affect the operation of the legislative branch, the role of congressional leaders and committees, and the steps by which a bill becomes law.

Chapter Objectives

After students complete this chapter, they will be able to:

1. Explain the rules governing the operation of Congress.
2. Explain how the leadership of Congress is organized.
3. Describe the support services that Congress has.
4. Identify the different kinds of committees in Congress.
5. Explain how the members of committees are chosen.
6. Explain how a bill gets to be voted on by the entire legislative chamber.
7. Describe what happens once a bill reaches the floor of a chamber.

CHAPTER 13

THE LAWMAKING PROCESS

Like a vast picture ... Congress is hard to see satisfactorily and appreciatively at a single view and from a single standpoint. ... It is too complex to be understood without an effort, without a careful and systematic process of analysis.

Woodrow Wilson
Congressional Government (1885)

350

Photo
House Foreign Affairs Committee in session.

C ongress called him "Mr. Sam." Sam Rayburn grew up on a small farm near Flag Springs, Texas, in the late 1800's, and learned the value of hard work and personal integrity from his parents, both strict Baptists. After several years of teaching, Rayburn entered state politics. In 1912 he was elected to the House of Representatives, where he served for the next 48 years. Widely respected for his political and personal qualities, Rayburn was Speaker of the House — the most powerful member of Congress — for seventeen years, far longer than any other person.

Rayburn's best-known saying was, "If you want to get along, go along." It meant that Congress runs best on tolerance and compromise. Making laws, Congress's primary job, is a complicated process that requires the cooperation of many different people and interests. This chapter looks at how Congress works.

CHAPTER OUTLINE

1 **How Is Congress Organized?**

Terms and Sessions
Congressional Rules
Congressional Leadership
Support Services

2 **Committees Play a Key Role in Lawmaking**

Types of Committees
Committee Assignments

3 **How Does a Bill Become Law?**

Proposing a Law
Consideration by Committee
Scheduling Bills
Floor Action

CHAPTER SUPPORT MATERIAL

Skills Practice Worksheet 13

Skills Challenge Worksheet 13

Transparencies 31–32

Simulation 1

Study Guide/Review 13

Workbook Chapter 13

Chapter 13 Test, Forms A-C

 VIDEOTAPE SERIES

This would be an appropriate place to use Houghton Mifflin's videotape, *Portrait of a Congressman.*

☐ explain the rules governing the operation of Congress
☐ explain how the leadership of Congress is organized
☐ describe the support services that Congress has

Vocabulary
floor action, recess, special session, joint session, seniority, floor leader, whip

FOCUS
● Have students speculate about problems that might arise from having 435 people in the House and 100 people in the Senate working as a group to make laws for the millions of people of the United States. Have them consider how difficult it would be for just two students to agree on all the details of an important decision that would affect the entire class; for the members of the class to make rules for the entire school; for all the members of the school to work together to formulate policies that would affect all the students in the state.

How can the members of Congress function as a lawmaking body without breaking down into chaos?

> **ACCESS** **The Main Ideas**
> 1 What rules govern the operation of Congress? *pages 352–355*
> 2 How is the leadership of Congress organized? *pages 356–359*
> 3 What support services does Congress have? *pages 359–360*

In 1808 Thomas Jefferson described Congress as "the great commanding theater of this nation." This is still true today. The Capitol building, where the two houses meet, is constantly swarming with scores of lobbyists and tourists, as well as senators, representatives, and their staffs. Reporters and film crews from nations around the world are always present, searching for a late-breaking story.

The Capitol is a scene of drama, power, and conflict, where lawmakers strive to solve the seemingly endless problems of a large and complex nation. At the same time, members of Congress are influenced by the way their actions are received in their home states or districts.

3A, 6C

Terms and Sessions

A congressional term — sometimes called simply "a Congress" — extends over a two-year period following the election of members (one-third of the senators and all members of the House). Each term begins (and ends) on January 3 of odd-numbered years, about two months after the November elections. Thus, the term of the 102nd Congress ran from January 3, 1991, to January 3, 1993. Each congressional term is divided into two regular sessions, or meetings to carry on business. The first session of the 102nd Congress, for example, was in 1991; the second in 1992.

The "lame duck amendment"
Congressional terms originally began on March 4 of odd-numbered years. This date provided a four-month lag between the day members

352

were elected and the day they actually took office. In 1789 this time lag was necessary because it took some members many weeks to travel from their home states to the nation's capital. As communications and transportation improved, however, such a lag was no longer justified. The incumbents defeated in November became known as "lame ducks" because they held office for four months without the voters' support.

Critics charged that "lame ducks" often passed self-serving laws and went on spending sprees just before their terms expired. To end this practice, the Twentieth Amendment was passed in 1933. This "lame duck amendment" established the January 3rd starting date for congressional terms. (The amendment also moved the President's inauguration date from March 4 to January 20.)

Scheduled meetings of Congress
Each house of Congress has its own meeting room, or *chamber*. Although senators and representatives meet separately and fix their own meeting times, the two houses follow similar schedules. The normal workweek in both chambers is Monday through Friday, but most **floor action** takes place between Tuesday and Thursday. This is the time when all members discuss and vote on legislation. Members spend the rest of their time in committee work or in their home districts. Customarily, floor action begins at noon and lasts until five or six o'clock.

Although the Constitution stipulates when Congress meets, it does not say when sessions must formally end, or adjourn. According to the Constitution, neither house may adjourn for more than three days without the consent of the other chamber. Furthermore, the Senate and House must agree on a final date for each session. If they cannot settle on a time for adjournment, the President chooses the date. (This has never happened.) Either chamber may **recess**, or take a temporary break. Normally, both chambers recess for a few weeks during the Christmas and Easter seasons.

Critical Thinking
● *Today, are defeated members of Congress still "lame ducks"?* (They can still pass laws in the two months they have before their terms expire, but for part of that time, Congress is usually in recess for the Christmas season.)

Check for Understanding
▲ *What is the difference between a congressional "term" and a "session"?* (Each two-year term is divided into two regular sessions, or business meetings.)

In the 1800's Congress met only about six months of the year. But the work of Congress has increased as the nation has grown. Since World War II, it has held much longer sessions. Current law specifies that Congress is to adjourn on the last day of July. Sessions can be extended, however, if Congress has unfinished business. Such extensions have become quite common. For example, the 1977 session of the 95th Congress lasted until December, and the 1978 session adjourned in mid-October. Normally, the first session of Congress (odd-numbered years) adjourns in the late summer. The second session (even-numbered years) ends in early summer, for these are election years. Members want to have ample time to campaign for re-election.

Special sessions

Emergencies occasionally occur when Congress has recessed or adjourned. In such cases, the Constitution allows the President to call either or both houses for a **special session**. In 1933, for example, President Franklin Roosevelt called Congress into special session to pass legislation badly needed to counteract the severe economic depression. This session, known as the "Hundred Days," marked a dramatic beginning to Roosevelt's New Deal program. Presidents have also called special sessions of the Senate to confirm appointments and ratify treaties.

Periodically, both houses meet together in a **joint session**. Joint sessions are not part of the lawmaking process but are used for special occasions, such as when the President delivers the annual State of the Union Address or when Congress gathers to count Electoral College votes.

1C, 6B

Congressional Rules

Newly elected members of Congress are sometimes overwhelmed by the complexity of the rules. The Senate's formal rules run about 100 pages, while those for the House of Representatives take up nearly 400. The House, because of its size, needs strict rules to govern legislative conduct. As one first-term Congress member put it, "Imagine a school board with 435 members trying to hire a football coach." The Senate can afford to be less formal because it has fewer members.

PRIMARY SOURCE

1B, 2A, 2B

LANDMARKS in LIBERTY

The Federalist, No. 10 (1787)

Representative government, rather than direct democracy, is the basis of the U.S. political system. In *The Federalist* (No. 10), James Madison argued the virtues of the Constitution's plan for electing representatives to Congress.

> The two great points of difference between a democracy and a republic are: first, the delegation of the government, in the latter, to a small number of citizens selected by the rest; secondly, the greater number of citizens and greater sphere of country, over which the latter may be extended.
>
> The effect of the first difference is, on the one hand, to refine and enlarge the public views, by passing them through the medium of a chosen body of citizens, whose wisdom may best discern the true interest of their country and whose patriotism and love of justice will be least likely to sacrifice it to temporary or partial considerations. . . .
>
> By enlarging too much the number of electors, you render the representative too little acquainted with all their local circumstances and lesser interests; as by reducing it too much, you render him unduly attached to these, and too little fit to comprehend and pursue great and national objects. . . .
>
> Extend the sphere and you take in a greater variety of parties and interests; you make it less probable that a majority of the whole will have a common motive to invade the rights of other citizens. . . .

1. In what two areas do a democracy and a republic differ?
2. What is the disadvantage of having one representative speak for many voters?
3. According to Madison, how does republican government protect the rights of minority interests?

353

EXPLANATION

After reviewing the content of the section, you may want to consider the following activities:

History

During World War II, Congress remained in session almost continuously to handle the many issues that resulted from United States involvement in the war. In the mid-1970's, Congress averaged 20 months for every 24-month term.

● CRITICAL THINKING **List an argument for, and an argument against, the idea that Congress should be in session continuously.** (*For*—Increasing the time Congress spends in session would allow Congress to look more closely at issues facing the nation. *Against*—Longer sessions would only produce more bad and costly legislation and would further isolate members of Congress from their constituents.)

Landmarks in Liberty Answers

1. In a republic, a small number of citizens represent the rest, and a republic can effectively govern a larger area than a democracy.

2. It becomes impossible for the representative to understand the many different interests of his or her constituents.

3. Because a republic can encompass a large territory and population, too many diverse interests will be represented for one group to exercise arbitrary power over another.

The symbol 👥 denotes active participation strategies.

Activities are keyed for student abilities:
▲ = Basic
● = All Levels
■ = Average/Advanced

Politics

▲ CRITICAL THINKING Have students decide which category of informal rules and traditions best describes each of the following situations:

(1) Senator A wants to fund a study of plant pests but needs the support of Senator B. Senator B agrees to co-sponsor such a bill as long as Senator A votes against closing a military base in Senator B's home state. (Reciprocity, or log-rolling.)

(2) A former television producer now in Congress becomes responsible for writing bills dealing with the Federal Communications Commission. (Specialization.)

Have students imagine events or situations that fit the categories *loyalty, civility,* and *compromise.*

All the members of Congress gather in the House chamber when a joint session is called. Joint sessions, like this one for the President's State of the Union Message, are called for special occasions.

Informal rules

In addition to the formal rules, Congress also has a number of traditions, or unwritten standards of conduct. New members need to become thoroughly familiar with these unwritten rules if they expect to accomplish anything in Congress.

One important congressional tradition is *loyalty* to one's own chamber — that is, the House or the Senate. There is often rivalry between the Senate and the House, particularly when they are controlled by different political parties. Members are expected to avoid publicly criticizing their own house. They are also expected to defend it against verbal assaults from the other house or from the President.

Another unwritten standard is *civility,* or politeness. Whether debating the issues in committee or on the floor of Congress, members are careful to respect the views of others. Statements are often phrased "in all respect to the distinguished senator from California . . ." or "The distinguished representative from Alabama has a good point, but . . . ." Such courtesy contrasts strikingly with behavior in other legislatures. In the British House of Commons, for instance, booing and personal insults are commonplace.

New members of Congress quickly learn that they cannot be experts in every area. Instead each is expected to carve out an area of expertise, or *specialization.* For example, a representative might become an authority on acid rain, wheat price supports, or automobile import quotas. Being an expert is also a source of power, because other members will defer to an expert member's knowledge.

Specialized knowledge is more important in the House than in the Senate, because there are fewer senators to tackle the same range of issues.

354

Critical Thinking
● *How might civility help (or hinder) the work of Congress?* (Uncivil behavior would probably be disruptive, wasting time and energy; civility, however, could be seen as cumbersome, time-wasting, and hypocritical.)

Each senator must become familiar with a wider, more general, range of topics.

A fourth tradition is *reciprocity* (reh-sih-PROS-ih-tee) — the mutual exchange of political favors. In legislative jargon, this practice is called "log-rolling" — put simply, "If you support my bill, I'll support your bill." For example, Senator X wants to build a new dam in her state but needs the support of Senator Y. Senator Y wants an Amtrak route through his state but needs Senator X's vote. By log-rolling, both senators get what they want.

The many diverse interests represented in Congress make it necessary to *compromise*. No Congress member can get what he or she wants all the time. Rather, members must learn to bargain or compromise. A compromise usually takes this form: "I want A, you want C, so let us agree on B." As Chapter 1 discussed, compromise is what politics is all about. It is the civilized way to settle differences.

Another congressional tradition is respect for **seniority** — the length of a member's continuous service. Members with more seniority are generally given preference in office space, in major committee assignments, and in leadership positions.

Congress recognizes three types of seniority: (1) service on a committee, (2) membership in one political party, and (3) service in Congress. Though the three types are closely related, they are not necessarily the same thing. For example, a senator who switches committees may go to the bottom of committee seniority, even though he or she has been in the Senate for many years. Likewise, a member who switches political parties will almost certainly lose seniority.

The seniority system has drawn both praise and criticism. On the one hand, seniority ensures that experienced legislators occupy leadership positions. On the other hand, seniority does not guarantee competence. Experienced legislators may be out of touch with the voters or physically unable to meet the demands of office. Recent reforms have enabled members to bypass incompetent leaders, even those with seniority.

Figure 13–1 COMPARISON OF THE SENATE AND HOUSE OF REPRESENTATIVES 8G

SENATE	HOUSE
• Smaller (100 members)	• Larger (435 members)
• Longer term (6 years)	• Shorter term (2 years)
• Represents a broader constituency (entire state)	• Represents a narrower constituency (single districts)
• More flexible rules (only about 100 pages of rules)	• Less flexible rules (almost 400 pages of rules)
• Policy generalists	• Policy specialists
• Lawmaking more personal	• Lawmaking less personal
• More reliance on staff	• Less reliance on staff
• Unlimited floor debate	• Restricted floor debate (typically 5 minutes)
• Fewer committees	• More committees
• More influential in foreign affairs	• More influential in budgetary matters
• Amendments need not be germane	• Amendments must be germane
• More attention by media (TV, press coverage)	• Less attention by media (TV, press coverage)

355

Global Awareness

■ CRITICAL THINKING In the British House of Commons, booing and personal insults are commonplace. Have students hypothesize how the British tradition might have developed. (In the Middle Ages, the House of Commons consisted of merchants and others not necessarily schooled in manners. Catcalls and insults might have been standard behavior and then become a tradition.)

▲ CRITICAL THINKING *How would class discussions be affected if students were allowed to boo and insult the student speaking?* (People's feelings would be hurt; fights might break out; little would get done.)

Critical Thinking

▲ *If Congress did not resolve its conflicts through compromise, how might the nation's problems be approached?* (In uncivilized ways, where, for example, "might makes right"; or in undemocratic ways, such as a dictatorship.)

Figure 13–1

● *In your opinion, what is the most important difference between the Senate and the House? Why?*

(Possible answers include the longer term for senators or the different constituencies represented by members of the two houses. Students should explain their answers.)

The symbol ♙♙ denotes active participation strategies.

Activities are keyed for student abilities:
▲ = Basic
● = All Levels
■ = Average/Advanced

Civic Participation

● [CRITICAL THINKING] *What personal qualities are needed in the various congressional leadership positions?* (The Speaker and Majority Leader must command respect and be persuasive; the Minority Leader must be able to organize; the party whip must be able to communicate easily and to persuade in face-to-face meetings.)

Politics

▲ [CRITICAL THINKING] Only one standing committee has an equal ratio of Democrats to Republicans: the Standards of Official Conduct Committee in the House, which contains six Democrats and six Republicans. *Why might this be so?* (The issues it deals with are non-partisan.)

Congressional Leadership

Besides establishing its own rules, each house of Congress chooses its own leaders by majority vote. This vote, however, is only a formality. The real selection of officers is actually made by the political parties. Before each term begins, the parties hold caucuses in both houses to choose their leaders.

Election results determine which party will hold the majority and minority in each house. In the 99th Congress (1985–1987), for example, the Democrats were the majority party in the House, as they had been since 1955. They held a 253 to 182 edge over the Republicans. In the Senate, however, the Republicans were the majority party, outnumbering the Democrats 53 to 47. Republicans had gained a Senate majority in 1981, after nearly thirty years of being a minority party in that house.

In 1987, the Democrats regained control of the Senate, and they controlled both houses of Congress until 1995. That year, the Republicans held a majority of both houses of Congress for the first time since 1954. (Figure 13-2 shows changes in party control of Congress and the presidency.)

House leaders

The most important leaders in the House are the Speaker of the House, two **floor leaders** — the Majority Leader and Minority Leader — and two assistant leaders, or **whips**.

SPEAKER OF THE HOUSE   The Speaker is the most powerful member of the House and is always a member of the majority party. Characteristically, the Speaker is a loyal party member who ranks high in seniority and holds moderate issue positions. The Speaker has many formal powers. One is to preside over House debates. The Speaker can therefore determine which representatives will speak and for how long. The Speaker can also influence committee assignments and assign bills to committee. The committee to which a bill is assigned may ultimately determine whether it will pass or be defeated.

HOUSE MAJORITY LEADER   The Majority Leader is the chief strategist and spokesperson for the majority party. Backing up the Speaker, the Majority Leader's central role is to shepherd legislation through the House. This job requires a skilled, seasoned, and energetic person.

HOUSE MINORITY LEADER   The primary function of the Minority Leader is to organize the opposition to the majority party. If the President

Figure 13–2 PARTY CONTROL OF CONGRESS AND THE PRESIDENCY SINCE 1873   8B

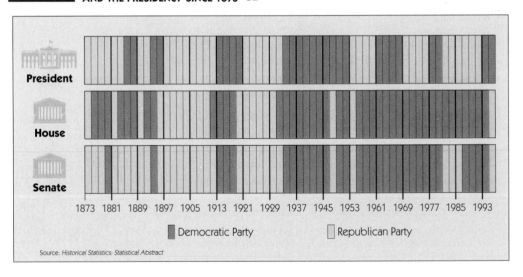

Source: *Historical Statistics: Statistical Abstract*

Figure 13–2
▲ *When have the presidency, the House, and the Senate all been controlled by a single party?* (1873–1875, 1881–1883, 1889–1891, 1893–1895, 1897–1911, 1913–1919, 1921–1931, 1933–1947, 1949–1953, 1953–1955, 1961–1969, 1977–1981, 1993–1995.)

Background: *Politics*
The Speaker's authority can be limited by the Rules Committee (described on p. 368). Over the years, control of floor debate has shifted between the House leadership and the Rules Committee. Since 1974, party leaders have gained more influence over floor debate.

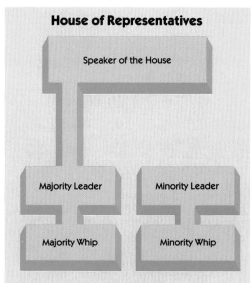

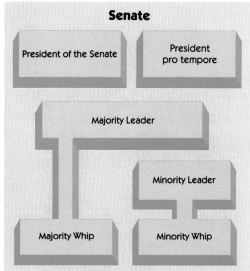

Figure 13-3 LEADERS OF CONGRESS 8G

also belongs to the minority party, the Minority Leader sometimes speaks for the administration's legislative program.

PARTY WHIPS Both parties choose whips, the assistant floor leaders, largely on the floor leaders' recommendation. ("Whip" is a term borrowed from the British House of Commons. A "whipper in" was a rider in a fox hunt whose task it was to keep the hounds together.) The whips' main duties are to find out the opinions of party members on pending legislation, get party members to the floor for important votes, and substitute in the absence of the floor leader. Whips are aided by assistant whips, or "bill managers."

OTHER HOUSE OFFICIALS The House has a number of administrative personnel who are not elected officials. The Clerk of the House is the top administrative official in the House. The Clerk maintains records concerning pending legislation, lobbying activities, and campaign spending. The House also employs a parliamentarian (a person skilled in rules of debate), a chaplain, a sergeant-at-arms (an officer appointed to keep order and arrange official ceremonies), official reporters, and a postmaster.

Senate leaders

Senate leadership is similar to that in the House, with some important differences. Principal positions are president of the Senate, president *pro tempore,* Majority Leader, Majority Whip, Minority Leader, and Minority Whip.

PRESIDENT OF THE SENATE The Vice President of the United States automatically serves as the president of the Senate. Unlike the Speaker of the House, the president of the Senate has little authority. Although one formal duty is to preside over debates, this task is typically assigned to other party members. The president of the Senate also casts the deciding vote in case of a tie, which can be crucial when senators are sharply divided on important legislation. One other responsibility is to make the official count of Electoral College votes for President.

PRESIDENT PRO TEMPORE In the absence of the president of the Senate, the president *pro tempore* or *pro tem* (meaning "temporary") presides over the Senate. This prestigious position is traditionally reserved for a senior-ranking senator of the majority party. Unlike the president of the Senate, the president *pro tempore* can sit on

Cooperative Learning
● Have groups of students devise a calendar for one typical week in the life of a member of Congress. Have them choose either a senator or a representative and use the information under the heading "Scheduled meetings of Congress" (p. 352) to begin.

Have them chart the hour-by-hour activities of the member. They should brainstorm ideas for what committee the member is working on, what issues are important to the member, and so forth.

Figure 13-3
● *In the House part of the figure, why is there a line connecting the Speaker of the House with the Majority Leader but not with the Minority Leader?* (The Speaker and the Majority Leader are both members of the majority party; the Minority Leader is not.)

Background: *Cultural Literacy* The sergeant-at-arms also takes charge of the mace, a symbol of authority made of thirteen bound ebony rods and a silver globe supporting a silver eagle. On several occasions the sergeant-at-arms has "presented" the mace before an unruly member to restore order.

The symbol ▌▌ denotes active participation strategies.

Activities are keyed for student abilities:
▲ = Basic
● = All Levels
■ = Average/Advanced

GUIDED/INDEPENDENT PRACTICE

● Have students make a three-column table, labeling the columns *House of Congress, Leadership Positions,* and *Duties.* Students should complete the table by listing all of the leadership positions for both the Senate and the House of Representatives and the duties, responsibilities, and amount of authority each has. Then have them write a brief paragraph explaining why floor leaders are needed in Congress.

Although the Library of Congress was created to serve members of Congress, the public also can use its many resources. Copies of every book copyrighted in the United States are on file in the Library. The main reading room, shown here, contains the card catalog.

committees, serve as a committee chair, and vote on all matters — not just in cases of ties. The duties of this position, however, are largely ceremonial. It does not compare in importance with Speaker of the House.

SENATE MAJORITY LEADER The Senate Majority Leader is the true leader of this house of Congress. It is up to this senator to develop a legislative "game plan" for the majority party. For many years, this coveted position was determined strictly by seniority, but today the Majority Leader is chosen by the Senate party caucus.

Because the Senate Majority Leader lacks many of the formal powers of the Speaker of the House, much of his or her success depends on leadership style. Lyndon B. Johnson, for instance, who served from 1955 to 1961, was a skilled and forceful Democratic Majority Leader. He did not hesitate to do favors for his supporters or to punish those who broke party ranks. In contrast, Mike Mansfield (1961–1977) was a low-key Majority Leader who relied mainly on personal persuasion.

SENATE MINORITY LEADER The Senate Minority Leader leads the opposition to the legislative efforts of the majority party. If an election changes the balance in the Senate, this person becomes Majority Leader, the most influential person in the Senate. For example, when the Republicans supplanted the Democrats as the majority party after the 1980 elections, Minority Leader Howard Baker, a Republican from Tennessee, suddenly became Majority Leader. Robert Byrd, a Democrat from West Virginia, changed from Majority Leader to Minority Leader. (When the Democrats regained Senate control in 1986, Byrd resumed his old job as Majority Leader.)

SENATE WHIPS Senate whips, like their House counterparts, are responsible for swaying party members, mobilizing support, and making

358

Photo

The main reading room of the Library of Congress is a Washington showplace, filled with symbolic art. Statues of historic figures from each field of knowledge stand atop pillars.

Science is flanked by Isaac Newton and Joseph Henry, law by Solon and Chancellor James Kent, poetry by Homer and Shakespeare, philosophy by Plato and Bacon, art by Michelangelo and Beethoven, history by

Herodotus and Gibbon, commerce by Columbus and Robert Fulton, religion by Moses and St. Paul.

sure party members vote. Generally speaking, Senate whips are not as successful as the House whips. The Senate tends to be more informal, and members often have a more independent attitude in voting.

OTHER SENATE OFFICERS The Senate also has a number of administrative employees. The Secretary of the Senate is the top administrator, whose duty is to keep records of lobbying activities. There are also official reporters, a parliamentarian, a chaplain, and a sergeant-at-arms. The Architect of the Capitol oversees the Capitol, the Botanic Garden, and other public buildings.

3A

Support Services

Besides its internal administrative organization, Congress relies heavily on several other agencies for help in research and in writing and monitoring laws. The most important of these agencies are the Library of Congress, the General Accounting Office, the Congressional Budget Office, and the Office of Technology Assessment. In addition, thousands of staff members help individual members of Congress with their workload.

The Library of Congress

Established in 1800 largely for the benefit of Congress, the Library of Congress is today the largest library in the world, with more than 97 million books, maps, films, records, and other items. The Congressional Research Service (CRS), with a staff of 800, provides research and information on nearly any topic. For example, if a member of Congress needs a report on rice production, a group of experts will be assigned to prepare a politically unbiased report on the topic. The CRS also uses computers to keep track of every bill in Congress.

General Accounting Office

The General Accounting Office (GAO) was established in 1921. It has been called the "eyes and ears of Congress," because it audits federal activities to determine whether money is spent according to law. Besides conducting investigations, the GAO also makes recommendations on a wide range of policies, such as Social Security, Medicare, and defense spending. The GAO is headed by the Comptroller General, who is appointed by the President (with Senate confirmation) for a 15-year term. Today, this agency employs more than 5,000 people.

Congressional Budget Office

The Congressional Budget Office (CBO) was created in 1974 to help Congress examine the federal budget. The CBO employs many economists who study budget proposals, coordinate revenue bills, make financial projections, and give advice concerning the impact of budget proposals.

Office of Technology Assessment

To help Congress keep abreast of changes and advances in science and technology, the Office of Technology Assessment was created in 1972. Among its many projects, this office has conducted studies on the long-term effects of chemicals and the reliability of lie detector tests.

Congressional staffs

Members of Congress and congressional committees are also entitled to hire staff members to help them fulfill their legislative duties. Staff members do many tasks that Congress members cannot fit into their busy schedules, such as researching bills, drafting speeches, writing letters to constituents, doing casework, and welcoming visitors from the home district to Washington, D.C. In recent years the number of staff members has grown remarkably. For example, in 1964 Congress employed roughly 8,000 persons (5,000 in the House and 3,000 in the Senate). By 1979, however, the total had grown to nearly 19,000 (about 12,000 in the House and 7,000 in the Senate).

Today, each representative is given a fixed staff allowance and may hire no more than eighteen full-time and four part-time staff members. (The average staff is about fifteen.) Senators have no fixed limits on the number of staff they can hire; they are allotted staff budgets on the basis of state population. Some senators have fewer than twenty staff members, others more than seventy.

In addition, Congress members appoint a few young people from their home districts to work as congressional pages. Pages run errands for Congress members and carry messages between the congressional chambers and the House and Senate office buildings.

359

RETEACHING/CORRECTIVES

▲ Tell students that everything in this section has something to do with Congress as an organization. ***What does it mean to organize a group of people?*** (Rules are made; leaders are chosen; tasks are assigned.)

For each subheading in the section, have students find at least one detail that contributes to the organization of Congress and explain their choice.

ENRICHMENT/EXTENSION

■ Have students look for news reports of the various leaders of Congress performing their roles. Have them categorize each activity they find according to the duties and responsibilities noted in the text.

Section 1 Review Answers
1. The two years beginning on the third day of January of odd-numbered years, such as January 3, 1991, to January 3, 1993.
2. To prevent last-minute spending sprees and the passage of self-serving laws by members who lost their re-election effort.
3. Joint sessions are held for the President's State of the Union Address and the count of Electoral College votes. Special sessions are called to handle economic emergencies, confirm appointments, or ratify treaties during recess or adjournment.
4. Loyalty, civility, specialization, reciprocity.

Background: *Civic Participation* Congressional pages are of high school age and usually serve from six months to a year. Five mornings a week, pages attend a special school on the third floor of the Library of Congress. They then work until early evening (and later for night sessions) and earn relatively high salaries for their age. Usually, only senior members of Congress receive the opportunity to appoint a page.

The symbol ⅱ denotes active participation strategies.

Activities are keyed for student abilities:
▲ = Basic
● = All Levels
■ = Average/Advanced

5. (a) The Speaker presides over House debates, influences committee assignments, assigns bills to committee. **(b)** Senate Majority Leader.

6. (a) To provide information. **(b)** To assist Congress with the federal budget. **(c)** To inform Congress of changes in science and technology. **(d)** To research bills, draft speeches, write letters, do casework.

Critical thinking New members will work successfully with other members only if they fit into the existing work patterns. This is unlike organizations run by an individual or a small group.

CLOSURE

● Have students review the section by reading the first paragraph in the Chapter Summary (p. 372). Then have them read Section 2, noting the role of the committee in making laws.

SECTION 2

Committees Play a Key Role in Lawmaking
(pp. 360–363)

Section Objectives

☐ identify the different kinds of committees in Congress
☐ explain how the members of committees are chosen

Vocabulary

standing committee, subcommittee, appropriations, select committee, conference committee

👥 FOCUS

● Have students suppose that the class had five important problems to resolve in a week's

360

SECTION 1 REVIEW

Vocabulary and key terms

lame duck (352)
floor action (352)
recess (352)
special session (353)
joint session (353)
log-rolling (355)
seniority (355)

floor leader (356)
whip (356)
Speaker of the House (356)
Majority Leader (356)
Minority Leader (356)

For review

1. What period of time makes up a congressional term, such as the 102nd Congress? **3A**
2. Why was the "lame duck amendment" passed? **6C**
3. What are some reasons for holding joint sessions or special sessions? **3A**
4. Name four of the unwritten standards of congressional conduct. **6F**
5. (a) What are the formal powers of the Speaker of the House? (b) Who is the most important Senate leader? **3A**
6. What is the job of (a) the Congressional Research Office? (b) the Congressional Budget Office? (c) the Office of Technological Assessment? (d) a member of a congressional staff? **3A**

Critical thinking

DRAWING INFERENCES Why do new members of Congress need to learn the unwritten "rules" or traditions? How are these like or unlike the unwritten "rules" of other organizations? **8A**

SECTION 2   3A, 4C, 8A, 8F, 8G

Committees Play a Key Role in Lawmaking

ACCESS | **The Main Ideas**

1 What are the different kinds of committees? *pages 360–361*

2 How are the members of committees chosen? *pages 361–362*

Anyone who has ever ordered pizza with friends knows that small groups make decisions more easily than large ones. This is one reason why bills are examined by committees before being considered by the entire Congress. The committee system represents a division of labor — an efficient way of splitting up tasks to permit members to handle their particular areas of expertise. Committee appointments also reflect members' power and influence.

3A

Types of Committees

Standing committees

The most important congressional committees are the **standing committees.** Standing committees are more or less permanent bodies that deal with bills about a particular subject area. They vary in size from 11 to 57 members. For more efficient decision-making, standing committees are further divided into smaller **subcommittees.** In the 103rd Congress, the Senate had 16 standing committees and 85 subcommittees; the House had 22 standing committees and 118 subcommittees.

Standing committees differ markedly in power, prestige, and reputation. The prized committees in the Senate are Foreign Relations, Finance, Armed Services, Judiciary, and Appropriations. The most desired committees in the House of Representatives are Rules, Ways and Means, and Appropriations.

Being appointed to any of the major standing committees gives a legislator some political leverage. For instance, a senator named to the Foreign Relations Committee will have a significant voice in ratifying treaties, confirming ambassadors, and making foreign policy. Membership in the House Rules Committee puts a representative in a position to help determine which bills will be considered on the House floor.

Background: *History*
Woodrow Wilson called congressional committees "little legislatures" and wrote: "Congress in its committee rooms is Congress at work."

The "money committees," of course, are crucial. These committees control the purse strings, determining how the government collects and spends money. Congress passes laws governing both taxation and **appropriations** — setting aside money for specific purposes. The House Ways and Means Committee, for example, deals with taxation. The Appropriations Committees and Budget Committees in both houses make decisions on government spending.

Select committees

Another set of tasks are handled by the **select committees**. These committees are created for a specific purpose and a limited time. They often consider business outside the jurisdiction of the standing committees but rarely have the authority to draft bills. Examples range from the Senate Select Committee on Watergate to the Select Committee on the House Beauty Parlor.

Conference committees

Another kind of special committee is the **conference committee**, which is made up of members from both houses of Congress. The chief function of a conference committee is to reconcile Senate and House versions of the same bill. Therefore, such conference committees are normally formed during the later stages of the lawmaking process.

"Committees on committees"

Finally, each party in the Senate and House has a committee that assigns members to the standing committees. These are known as "committees on committees." For the Democrats, the Democratic Steering Committee makes committee appointments in the Senate, and the Democratic Steering and Policy Committee does so in the House. Republicans in both chambers call theirs simply the Republican Committee on Committees.

Members of Congress, in addition to committee appointments, often belong to special-interest caucuses. One of these, the Congressional Black Caucus, is led by Kweisi Mfume (second from left), a member of the House of Representatives from Maryland.

361

time. Each solution might call for in-depth research, interviews with outside experts, and hours of debate. *What would be the most practical way to organize the class to accomplish this task?* Lead students to see that by breaking the class into groups, each of which would be responsible for one problem, each problem could be resolved more efficiently than if the entire class tried to deal with all the problems. Tell students that this is the reasoning behind the committee system.

EXPLANATION

After reviewing the content of the section, you may want to consider the following activities:

Structure of Government

▲ Discuss the reasons why certain committees have more power and prestige than others. *Why is assignment to the Finance, Commerce, or Appropriations Committee in the Senate or to the Ways and Means or Appropriations Committee in the House considered a great advantage for a member of Congress?* (These "money committees" help set fiscal policy by determining how the government will collect and spend money.)

Background: *Values* A 1975 rules change opened the once-secret conference committee meetings to the public. House rules now require open conference meetings unless the full House votes for secrecy. (The Intelligence Committee is exempt.)

The symbol ᚛ᚙ denotes active participation strategies.

Activities are keyed for student abilities:
▲ = Basic
● = All Levels
■ = Average/Advanced

362

One of the most famous Senate select committees was the one set up in 1973 to investigate questions surrounding the 1972 presidential campaign and the Watergate break-in. The committee was headed by Senator Sam Ervin of North Carolina (right), shown here talking with Senator Howard Baker. The Watergate committee hearings were broadcast nationwide over public television.

3A, 4C

Committee Assignments

The majority party in each house sets the ratio of party members on each committee. Thus, in the 99th Congress, Republicans determined the committee sizes and ratios in the Senate, while the Democrats did so in the House. In the 100th Congress, the Democrats decided for both houses. Tradition dictates that the ratio should reflect the overall party membership in each house. The majority party, however, tends to give itself a few extra seats on key committees.

Although the House has more than four times as many members as the Senate, it has only six more standing committees (22 to 16). This means that a senator must serve on more standing committees than does a representative. It also increases the likelihood that a senator will be appointed to at least one of the more important committees. To ensure fairness, recent rule changes bar senators from serving on more than three standing committees and guarantee that each representative will be assigned to at least one major standing committee.

Factors in committee assignments

Committee assignments depend on many factors. One is the member's specialized knowledge or expertise. For example, a former astronaut would likely be assigned to the House Science, Space, and Technology Committee, while an ex-banker would go on the Senate Banking Committee. Another consideration is the member's constituency. Members often lobby long and hard to get on committees that could directly benefit their home district. Senators from Iowa, for example, strive to get on the Agricultural Committee. Representatives from oil-rich Texas often seek membership on the House Energy and Commerce Committee.

Seniority and party loyalty play important roles in committee assignments. Senior members are given preference over newcomers. Members who regularly vote in agreement with their own party leaders have a decided advantage over renegades.

The case of Phil Gramm illustrates the role of both of these factors: In 1978 Gramm was elected as a Democratic representative from Texas's Sixth District. In 1981 Gramm, who holds a doctorate in economics, was assigned a seat on the powerful House Budget Committee. Fellow House Democrats, however, soon became upset over Gramm's support of Republican President Ronald Reagan's budget cuts. At the urging of Speaker Thomas P. (Tip) O'Neill, the Demo-

362

cratic Steering and Policy Committee stripped Gramm of his membership on the Budget Committee.

Upset over the demotion, Gramm resigned from Congress, returned to Texas, and then ran as a Republican in a special election for his own House seat. Seven weeks later, he was back in Congress, having won the special election over ten rivals, with 55.3 percent of the vote. In 1984, Gramm ran for the Senate and was elected. He immediately sought a seat on the Senate Budget Committee but was refused because he lacked seniority in the Senate.

Selecting committee chairpersons

The leaders, or chairpersons, of each committee wield a great deal of authority over bills sent to their committee. They delegate committee work, make subcommittee assignments, lead committee debate, and more or less determine the committee's agenda. These are powerful and highly coveted positions.

Chairpersons are always members of the majority party. Until 1975, they also were selected solely on the basis of seniority — the longest continuous service on the committee. This practice drew the same criticism as the seniority system itself. Committee chairpersons tended to be older men elected from "safe" one-party districts. This practice began to change, however, following the Watergate scandal. Public reaction to the scandal brought many new representatives into office in 1974. Unwilling to abide by the old ways, these newly elected members quickly initiated important changes in congressional rules.

Under the new rules, no senator or representative may chair more than one standing committee. Although seniority is still a factor, committee chairpersons are now elected. In the House, they are nominated by the majority party's committee on committees and then elected by party members by secret ballot. In the Senate, they are elected by secret ballot if one-fifth of the party members so request.

As a result, party members now can override seniority in the selection of committee chairpersons. In 1985, for example, House Democrats voted to oust 80-year-old Melvin Price of Illinois as head of the Armed Services Committee. Price, some members claimed, could no longer manage

the committee's affairs. His replacement was 47-year-old Les Aspin from Wisconsin — the committee member ranking seventh in seniority among Democrats.

Special-interest caucuses

Apart from their regular committee duties, Congress members also belong to a number of special-interest caucuses in both houses. These are unofficial groups who meet voluntarily to advance common economic, regional, or ideological interests. In 1960 there were just four special-interest caucuses. Today, they number around 100.

Typical caucuses in Congress have included these: Congressional Rural Caucus, Solar Coalition, Congressional Black Caucus, Congressional Caucus for Women's Issues, Arts Caucus, Mushroom Caucus, Travel and Tourism Caucus, House Footwear Caucus, Senior Citizens' Caucus, Vietnam Veterans' Caucus, Gypsy Moths (liberal Republicans from the Northeast, opposed to President Reagan's policies), and Boll Weevils (conservative southern Democrats in favor of Reagan's policies).

SECTION 2 REVIEW

Vocabulary and key terms

standing committee (360)   select committee (361)
subcommittee (360)   conference committee
appropriations (361)   (361)

For review

1. What is the difference between a standing committee and a select committee? **8G**
2. Why are the Appropriations and Ways and Means Committees important? **3A**
3. What factors play a role in committee assignments? **8F**
4. How has the selection of committee chairpersons changed? **3A**

Critical thinking

DRAWING INFERENCES Why are some standing committees more prestigious than others? Why might a member of Congress prefer to be on a committee with less prestige? **8A**

363

ENRICHMENT/EXTENSION

■ Have students find out the names of the current select committees in each house of Congress and write short reports describing the concerns of each and the actions each has taken.

Section 2 Review Answers

1. Standing committees are permanent bodies dealing with all bills on a particular topic; select committees rarely draft bills and are created for a specific purpose and a limited time.
2. They determine how the government collects and spends money.
3. The member's expertise, constituency, seniority, and party loyalty.
4. Once chosen by seniority, they are now elected.

Critical thinking Some committees, such as the Rules Committee, have greater influence and exposure, and others, such as Appropriations, control purse strings. Members may wish to be on a committee that could directly benefit their home district.

CLOSURE

● Have students review the section by reviewing the Section 2 vocabulary. Then have them read Section 3, paying special attention to the chart "How a Bill Becomes Law" (p. 365).

SECTION 3

How Does a Bill Become Law?
(pp. 364–372)

Section Objectives

☐ explain how a bill gets to be voted on by the entire legislative chamber

☐ describe what happens once a bill reaches the floor of a chamber

Vocabulary

bill, sponsor, pigeonhole, discharge petition, calendar, filibuster, cloture, table, rider, sanctions, apartheid

FOCUS

● Write the following on the board: *The process by which a bill becomes law is too complicated and too boring to be worth learning.* Ask the class how many students agree with the statement. Then ask students who disagree with the statement to explain their view.

To help students appreciate the importance of knowing how Congress works, you might ask them to imagine a situation in which Congress performed all its business in secret, revealing to the public only the legislation it passed. **How would this affect the public's perception of Congress, or confidence in government, or voting behavior?** (The public would probably become more suspicious of Congress and lose confidence in government. Because their ability to influence legislation would be greatly reduced, many people might stop voting altogether.)

SECTION 3

3A, 6B, 6F, 8D, 8G, 8H

How Does a Bill Become Law?

ACCESS | **The Main Ideas**

1 **How does a bill get to be voted on by the entire legislative chamber?** *pages 364–367*

2 **What happens once a bill reaches the floor of a chamber?** *pages 367–372*

In the 1939 film *Mr. Smith Goes to Washington,* James Stewart stars as an idealistic young senator who uses his last ounce of energy to fight corruption. The film's most dramatic scene shows Stewart, his voice broken and body bent by fatigue, pleading with his fellow senators to vote on the side of honesty. In the end, Stewart and honesty triumph.

Events in the House and Senate are rarely as "Hollywood" as this. The process by which a bill becomes a law is long and complicated. This lengthy process is intended to ensure that each law receives full consideration and truly represents the will of the people. In real life, as in the movie, this process allows the voice of the people to be heard. While the legislative process is relatively open to public scrutiny, it also includes much behind-the-scenes maneuvering.

3A, 6F

Proposing a Law

All laws begin in the form of **bills**, or proposed laws. Only members of Congress can introduce bills. The person who introduces a bill is known as its **sponsor**. More than one member can introduce, or co-sponsor, a bill. Co-sponsorship is used to indicate wide support for a bill.

Sources of bills

Although a bill can be introduced only by members of Congress, ideas for legislation often come from other sources. Most legislative proposals come from two sources — the executive branch and interest groups. Ideas are also suggested by citizens, state and local officials, college professors, or staff members. Only a small percentage of bills introduced are actually written by Congress members themselves.

364

Types of bills

Bills generally fall into one of two categories. A public bill, as its name implies, is one that applies to the general public. Bills relating to federal highways, drug control, Social Security, or appropriations are examples. According to the Constitution, appropriations bills must always originate in the House. The Senate, however, may propose increasing, decreasing, or canceling the amounts submitted by the House. Therefore, both chambers have an Appropriations Committee.

By contrast, private bills concern the affairs of individual citizens and are usually of interest only to the member who sponsors them. Roughly one-third of all bills introduced in Congress today are private bills. A private bill might, for example, confer the Congressional Medal of Honor on a war hero, cut bureaucratic red tape for a person on Social Security, or grant citizenship to specific persons.

Resolutions

In addition to bills, Congress sometimes considers resolutions. A resolution is a formal statement expressing a legislative decision or opinion. There are three types of congressional resolutions.

A *simple resolution* concerns the rules or opinions of just one chamber of Congress — for instance, changing the jurisdiction of a subcommittee or congratulating the U.S. Olympic team. Simple resolutions do not require the approval of the other house or of the President and do not have the force of law.

A *concurrent resolution* expresses opinions or rules changes agreed to by both the Senate and House. Like simple resolutions, they neither have the force of law nor require presidential approval.

Finally, a *joint resolution* must be passed by both houses of Congress and signed by the President. Like bills, joint resolutions have the force of law, but they usually deal with very special matters, such as making an invitation to a foreign

---

Background: *Politics*
Members of Congress may introduce a bill as a favor to a constituent or an interest group that has made generous campaign contributions. Congress members introduce the bill "by request," which signals colleagues that the sponsor has no real interest in the bill. Such bills have little chance of passing.

Figure 13–4 HOW A BILL BECOMES LAW 6F

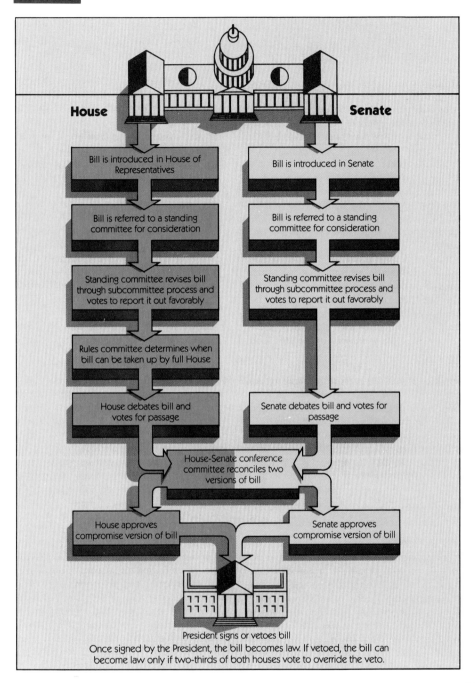

House

Senate

Bill is introduced in House of Representatives

Bill is introduced in Senate

Bill is referred to a standing committee for consideration

Bill is referred to a standing committee for consideration

Standing committee revises bill through subcommittee process and votes to report it out favorably

Standing committee revises bill through subcommittee process and votes to report it out favorably

Rules committee determines when bill can be taken up by full House

House debates bill and votes for passage

Senate debates bill and votes for passage

House-Senate conference committee reconciles two versions of bill

House approves compromise version of bill

Senate approves compromise version of bill

President signs or vetoes bill

Once signed by the President, the bill becomes law. If vetoed, the bill can become law only if two-thirds of both houses vote to override the veto.

365

EXPLANATION

After reviewing the content of the section, you may want to consider the following activities:

Controversial Issues

▲ *What is a rider?* (An amendment to a bill that has nothing to do with the bill to which it is attached.)

● CRITICAL THINKING *Why might a senator try to attach a rider to an unrelated bill?* (To slip legislation past a hostile President by attaching it to a more favored bill, to bypass unsympathetic committees, or to defeat an otherwise popular bill.)

■ Have students write a two-paragraph editorial arguing that the Senate should require all amendments to be germane.

Figure 13–4

● *True or false: Any bill receiving the support of more than half of the members of both houses will become law.* (False. If the President vetoes the bill, it must gain the support of two-thirds of both houses.)

The symbol 👥 denotes active participation strategies.

Activities are keyed for student abilities:
▲ = Basic
● = All Levels
■ = Average/Advanced

Politics

● [CRITICAL THINKING] Have students respond to the following statement: *The rules and procedures by which a bill becomes law are cumbersome and outdated. Congress should cut away some red tape and streamline procedures.* In discussing this statement, students should consider the observation made at the beginning of this section (p. 364) that the rules and obstacles of the legislative process serve a purpose, helping ensure that each law receives full consideration and represents the will of the people.

government or correcting an error in a bill previously sent to the President. Constitutional amendments are also proposed in the form of joint resolutions.

Introducing bills

The procedures for introducing bills are slightly different in each house. In the Senate, bills are introduced in the morning. A motion is made for the sponsor to introduce a bill on the floor of the Senate. There is generally no discussion. The bill is given a number, a title, and the sponsor's name. Senate bills are prefixed "S." *S.115,* for example, refers to the 115th bill introduced during a session of the Senate.

In the House, the process begins when a member places a bill in the "hopper," a wooden box on the desk of the Clerk of the House. This can be done at any time, and no motion is required. House bills are designated by number, sponsor, and title. All House bills begin "H.R."

There is no limit on the number of bills that a Congress member may introduce. Over the years, in fact, the number of bills introduced has grown. For example, the first year Congress was in session (1789), only 144 bills were introduced, about 1.6 per member. In the 90th Congress, a whopping 24,786 bills were introduced, roughly 46 for each member. During the 1980's, an average of 9,400 bills were introduced in each Congress (that is, every two years).

Not every bill introduced has an equal chance of survival. Most bills wither and die. For instance, of the 21,096 measures introduced in the 94th Congress, only 2,870 made it out of committee. Only 729, a meager 3.5 percent, eventually passed both houses.

3A

Consideration by Committee

Assigning bills to committee

After a bill or resolution has been introduced, it is sent to a standing committee for consideration. The presiding officers of the two chambers make most decisions on assigning bills to committee. When there is doubt about where to refer a bill, the Senate Majority Leader and the Speaker of the House decide for their respective chambers. The following hypothetical example shows the importance of committee referral:

H.R.1305, "A Bill Regulating Horseback Riding on Interstate Highways," has just been introduced by Congressman Jonathan M. Smith, who is a close political ally of the Speaker of the House. The Speaker of the House could refer Smith's bill to either the House Agricultural Committee (because the bill deals with horses), or the Public Works and Transportation Committee (because horseback riding is a form of transportation).

Knowing that Smith is an influential member of the Agricultural Committee, the Speaker sends *H.R.1305* there, so that it will be assured careful treatment.

Committee action

What happens after a bill is sent to the standing committee? In most cases, the committee chairperson refers the bill to a subcommittee for further study. (Subcommittees are smaller committees appointed by the head of the standing committee.) All committee and subcommittee meetings are open to the public unless the committee votes to close the meeting. Closed meetings are held when the committee is considering sensitive matters, such as national security.

Committees or subcommittees considering important proposals sometimes hold public hearings. Expert witnesses, government officials, and concerned citizens may all be given an opportunity to speak for or against the bill.

After studying a bill, the committee has several options. One is to **pigeonhole** the bill. Pigeonholing is the practice of killing a bill by simply refusing to pass it out of the committee. ("Pigeonholes" were small compartments in old-fashioned desks where members of Congress put unimportant items.) Most bills are, in fact, pigeonholed by the committee chairperson.

Another option is to "report the bill out of committee favorably," returning it to the floor with a recommendation that it be passed. Once the bill is passed out of committee, the committee chairperson remains responsible for guiding it through the floor stage. The committee may also "mark up," or amend, any or all parts of the bill. Sometimes a committee scraps the bill and writes an entirely new one, known as a "clean bill." On rare occasions, a committee "reports a bill out unfavorably." This usually involves

Background: *Civic Participation* If citizens want a bill passed but it is tied up in committee, the best thing to do is attend the public hearing on the bill. If there is no public hearing, citizens can write, call, or visit members of Congress involved with the bill.

Henry B. Gonzalez of Texas is a senior member of the Committee on Banking, Finance, and Urban Affairs in the House of Representatives.

touchy political situations in which the committee does not want to shoulder the responsibility for killing a bill.

Bypassing committees

Whenever a small group of people make decisions, there is always the possibility they will not represent the wishes of the majority. A Senate or House committee may pigeonhole a bill that the entire chamber wishes to consider. Can the full membership bypass this committee? Although there is a procedure that enables the membership to do just that, it is not very effective against the power of committees.

When a bill has been in a House committee for more than 30 days, any representative can try to dislodge it with a **discharge petition.** Such petitions must be signed by an absolute majority (218) of the members to take effect, and so are rarely successful. Since 1910, more than 900 discharge petitions have been initiated. Of those, only 26 gained the necessary signatures, and only two bills thus forced out of committee were ever passed. Because of congressional traditions, most members are reluctant to challenge the authority of the committees.

Scheduling Bills

If a bill is reported out of committee, it must then "go to the floor" of each chamber. All the members now have the chance to debate and vote on the bill. Floor action proceeds according to certain rules and procedures.

Calendars

For the sake of order, each bill is placed on a **calendar.** A calendar is merely the formal schedule of bills or resolutions to be considered. It lists bills in chronological order as they are passed out of committee. Each house has its own set of calendars.

The Senate has two calendars. The *Calendar of General Orders* contains both public and private bills. The *Executive Calendar* is reserved for nominations and treaties. Scheduling bills for floor consideration in the Senate is usually quite simple. Most bills reach the Senate floor by unanimous consent. That is, bills are taken off the calendars in the order listed, provided no member objects.

Because of its larger size, the House has five calendars and more complicated procedures.

367

Civic Participation

● [CRITICAL THINKING] Have students imagine that they have been elected to Congress and are voting on four different bills, ranging from relatively unimportant to crucial. Have students propose the substance of the four bills; write a description of each on the board. Then have students register their votes on each of the four bills, using a different voting method for each: voice vote, standing vote, teller vote, and roll-call vote. Discuss with students the reasons for using each method.

Check for Understanding
● *Is a bill that is reported out of committee unfavorably likely to pass in the full chamber?* (No. The expectation is that it will be killed on the floor.)

The symbol ⅱ denotes active participation strategies.

Activities are keyed for student abilities:
▲ = Basic
● = All Levels
■ = Average/Advanced

Politics

● ☐ CRITICAL THINKING ☐ *Is a congressional session that results in more laws better than a session that results in fewer laws? Why or why not?* (Those who believe problems are best solved at the national level may want more laws. Others may believe that local governments or private agencies can solve problems more efficiently.)

The *Private Calendar* deals only with private bills. The *Union Calendar* is reserved for public bills pertaining to revenues and appropriations, while other public bills are placed on the *House Calendar.* The *Consent Calendar* contains uncontroversial bills (for example, a resolution honoring John Wayne). Finally, there is the *Discharge Calendar* for discharge petitions.

In principle, every House bill reaches the floor in chronological order. That is, bills placed first on each calendar would be debated first. But if this rule were strictly observed, important bills placed late on a calendar might not reach the floor before Congress adjourned. This is where the Rules Committee steps in.

The Rules Committee

The Rules Committee is the "traffic cop" of the House of Representatives, because its consent is necessary for a bill to be taken from the calendar. This committee can take bills out of order, scheduling the most important bills first. It can also set the conditions for debate and amendments. To speed up action, for example, the committee can set a time limit on debate or prohibit adding amendments. This helps speed up the order of business. Some types of bills, such as those relating to taxation or crucial appropriations, are considered "privileged," meaning they have top priority. In sum, the placement of a bill on the calendar does not necessarily determine when or if it will be discussed.

In theory, there is a procedure that enables the full House to bypass even the powerful Rules Committee. On Wednesdays (except for the last two of the session), each standing committee may request the full House to consider one unprivileged bill from either the Union Calendar or the House Calendar. This procedure is called "Calendar Wednesday." A two-thirds vote may cancel Calendar Wednesday, however, and this happens frequently. Since 1950 only three laws have been enacted using this procedure.

6B, 6F

Floor Action

Conducting business

For either chamber of Congress to do official business, Article I, Section 5 of the Constitution requires that a majority of its members must be present. Given the many responsibilities of Congress, it is often difficult to get a quorum. It is especially difficult in the House.

One way the House of Representatives meets this constitutional requirement is by calling a Committee of the Whole. If at least 100 representatives are present, the House simply declares itself one giant committee. Members can then conduct business under relaxed rules of debate. Most of the House's business is transacted in this manner. Naturally, all actions taken by the Committee of the Whole must eventually be approved by the entire House. Because of its smaller membership, the Senate does not use this practice.

Rules for debate

By now it is apparent that most of the decisions in Congress are made behind the scenes, either in committees or in party caucuses. Nevertheless, floor debate is an essential part of the lawmaking process. It enables Congress members to consider the merits of the bills, air their views, and put them on record. All debate, however, must follow certain rules.

Because of its larger membership, the House has stricter rules for debate. Only one bill may be considered at a time. In addition, debate for most bills is limited. Furthermore, all debate in the House must be *germane,* that is, relevant to the bill under discussion. These limits make it unusual for the House to debate a bill more than one day.

The Senate rules contrast sharply with those of the House. Because it has fewer members, the Senate tends to be more leisurely and less rigid in its procedures. Unlike the House, the Senate may juggle three or four bills at one time. It is also a long-standing practice to allow senators unlimited speaking time. Moreover, debate does not have to be germane. That is, senators can talk on any topic they want, provided they are the recognized speaker and "have the floor."

Filibusters

Occasionally, a senator or small group of senators take advantage of unlimited debate. Using a tactic called the **filibuster**, they try to monopolize debate in an effort to block the passage of a bill. (The term *filibuster* originally meant "pirate"; in political debate, it means that someone has "captured" the floor.) To keep the floor, a senator must not sit down or stop talking. He or she may yield the floor temporarily to an-

Background: *Structure of Government* The House's *Private Calendar* deals with bills for the relief of individuals with claims against the United States. It also deals with private immigration bills.

Background: *History* The Fair Employment Practices Act (1950) and the Area Redevelopment Act (1960) were passed using the Calendar Wednesday process.

other speaker, so that group filibusters can go on for days. The hope is that supporters will finally give up on bringing the bill to a vote and call for adjournment.

One senator famous for his filibusters in the 1930's was Huey Long of Louisiana. His rambling speeches included recipes for fried oysters and corn bread and quotations from biographies of famous people. Several one-man filibusters have gone on for more than twenty hours. The record belongs to Senator Strom Thurmond of South Carolina, who spoke for 24 hours and 18 minutes on August 28–29, 1957, in an unsuccessful attempt to block passage of the 1957 Civil Rights Act.

Though such marathons are rare, filibustering has generated much criticism. The major complaint is that it violates the principle of majority rule. Senators generally endure a filibuster even though they could end it by invoking **cloture**. Cloture is a parliamentary procedure used to end debate and call for a vote. It takes one-sixth (16) of the senators to initiate a cloture petition, and three-fifths (60) of the senators must vote to pass it. If the measure is passed, then no senator may speak for more than one hour. The bill can then come to a vote. By Senate tradition, however, cloture is rarely invoked.

Action on bills

During floor action on a bill, Congress members have several options. One option is to pass the bill as it is written. This requires a simple majority vote. Once a bill is passed in one house of Congress, it must be sent to the other for consideration and passage.

A second option is to **table** the bill. Tabling is a parliamentary motion to kill a bill. If passed, this motion removes the bill from further consideration. A third option is to send the bill back to committee for further consideration. Practically speaking, these actions kill a bill's chances of passing. A fourth option is to amend the bill by adding to it, altering it, or striking out parts of it.

In the House, but not in the Senate, all amendments must be germane — related to the subject of the bill. Senators, however, frequently try to tack on a **rider**, an amendment that has nothing to do with the bill at hand. By placing a rider on an important bill, its sponsors hope that it will be passed along with the major bill. For this reason, riders are typically attached to appropriations bills.

Controversial riders are sometimes added in an effort to defeat an otherwise popular bill. This was the case with the 1964 Civil Rights Act (page 217). In an effort to kill the bill (which

Many of the individual mahogany desks in the Senate chamber have historic associations with famous senators of the past. New desks for the entire Senate were made in 1819, when the Capitol was restored after the War of 1812, and some are still in use. As new states entered the Union, similar desks were built for incoming senators.

369

Background: *History*
Riders, also called non-germane amendments, are more common in the Senate. Although House rules prohibit non-germane amendments, the House can waive the rider restriction. Odd legal combinations often result from the attachment of riders, such as in the 1980 House bill that simultaneously set new nutritional requirements for infant formulas and increased federal penalties for drug trafficking.

The symbol 👥 denotes active participation strategies.

Activities are keyed for student abilities:
▲ = Basic
● = All Levels
■ = Average/Advanced

GUIDED/INDEPENDENT PRACTICE
● Have students make a chart that uses vocabulary to compare and contrast the legislative procedures of the House and Senate. They should write the headings *House of Representatives* and *Senate* at the top of a sheet of paper and write all the vocabulary words from the section (and their definitions) down the left-hand side of the sheet. For each word, students should note differences under the proper headings. Where there is no difference, students should write *same.* Students might add other differences between the Senate and the House that are not related to vocabulary words.

Members of the technical staff check TV monitors as a Senate session is broadcast over a cable network. House sessions also are televised.

was originally intended to prohibit racial discrimination), one representative added a rider prohibiting sex discrimination in employment. Its sponsor thought the rider would weaken the bill, but, ironically, both the bill and the rider passed, putting into effect the first comprehensive policy against sex discrimination in the workplace.

Voting in Congress

Every motion, amendment, or bill must be put to a vote. There are four ways this can be done. The simplest method is by *voice vote.* Under this method the presiding officer merely asks "All in favor?" and "All opposed?" and determines whether a measure passes by the volume of response. While this method saves time, it is not very accurate. Voice votes on crucial issues are often challenged.

Another method is the *standing vote.* Members cast their votes for or against a particular measure by standing when the vote is called. This procedure allows the presiding officer to make a fairly quick and accurate tally. Neither standing nor voice votes, however, provide a record of each member's vote.

When the House wants to ensure accuracy, it sometimes uses a *teller vote.* Representatives are counted as they file past tellers (official counters) in front of the Speaker's desk. There

are two tellers — one counts votes "for" and the other counts votes "against." Once the votes are tallied, the presiding officer announces the result. According to the Legislative Reorganization Act of 1970, one-fifth of a quorum may call for a teller vote, and each member's vote is recorded. The Senate does not use the teller vote.

Both houses can use the *roll-call vote* (or "record vote") if one-fifth of the members demand it. The Constitution requires using the roll-call vote when Congress seeks to override a presidential veto. Because this method is very accurate and provides a record of members' votes, it is used for nearly all important, controversial, or closely contested legislation.

In the past, roll-call votes were used as stall tactics to permit absent members to reach the floor for a vote. It took considerable time to call all the members' names and record each vote. To expedite voting, the House installed electronic voting devices in 1973. As representatives insert plastic cards into slots, their votes are automatically recorded. Significantly more record votes have been taken since this method began. (The Senate does not use electronic voting devices.)

Sometimes members must be away from Congress during voting. On these occasions, members often try to "pair off" with legislators with opposing views who will also be absent. The members thus cancel each other out, ensuring that their absence will have no bearing on the final outcome. When a two-thirds vote is required for passage, two members "for" a measure must be paired with one "against" vote.

Political party loyalties have considerable influence on voting. It is estimated that in 30 to 50 percent of all votes, most Republicans and most Democrats are on opposite sides of an issue. The reasons for voting along party lines are clear. Members of the same party are likely to share the same views on major policy issues. Moreover, members know that committee assignments and other favors depend on their party loyalty.

Conference committees

Before a bill can become law, it must pass both the Senate and the House in identical form and then be signed by the President. Commonly there are differences between Senate and House versions of the same bill. When this happens, a conference committee is appointed to reconcile

Background: *Civic Participation* The increase in roll-call votes in recent years has been a great help to interest groups that compile vote studies. The National Farmers Union published its first study in 1919 and began an annual voting record in 1948. The AFL-CIO has been compiling voting records since 1955.

the two versions. Once agreement is reached, a conference report is issued, and the revised bill is returned to both houses for final consideration. Either chamber may reject the revised bill but rarely does so.

The members of conference committees, called conferees, come from both houses. In principle, House conferees are chosen by the Speaker, while Senate conferees are appointed by the presiding officer. In practice, however, they are chosen by the heads of the committees that reported the bill.

For example, in December 1985 the House passed a major tax reform bill. The Senate passed a different version of the bill in June 1986. A conference committee of eleven senators and eleven representatives was then appointed. It was headed by Senate Finance Committee chairperson Bob Packwood, a Republican from Oregon, and House Ways and Means Committee chairperson Dan Rostenkowski, an Illinois Democrat. In an intensive series of meetings beginning on Tuesday, August 12, Packwood and Rostenkowski forged a compromise. An agreement was finally reached around midnight on Saturday, August 16, just before Congress recessed for a three-week break.

Congress considered the revised version of the bill when it reconvened in September 1986. With little debate, first the House and then the Senate passed the new version of the bill, which was called the most fundamental change in federal income tax law since World War II.

Presidential approval

Once a bill passes both houses in identical form, it is sent to the President for final approval. The President can sign the bill, veto it, refuse to sign it, or allow it to become law without a signature. If the President vetoes a bill, Congress may still pass it. (The President's options are detailed in Chapter 15.)

Overriding a presidential veto requires a two-thirds vote in both houses. Because this action is considered a political "slap in the face," members of Congress, particularly those from the President's party, are often reluctant to vote for an override. Nonetheless, Congress sometimes feels compelled to express its strong opinions on certain subjects.

An electronic "scoreboard" behind the Speaker's rostrum makes a quick and accurate tally of the votes cast by members of the House of Representatives, who use a plastic card to cast their votes.

371

Background: *Structure of Government* Conference committees are sometimes referred to as *ad hoc joint* *committees;* conferees are often called *managers.* Rejection of a conference committee's report is rare.

Section 3 Review Answers

1. Public bills apply to the public; private bills apply to individuals.

2. (a) To pigeonhole the bill, to amend any or all parts, to report it out favorably or unfavorably. **(b)** By a discharge petition.

3. To schedule bills and to set conditions for debates and amendments.

4. (a) A majority. **(b)** A majority. **(c)** By forming a "Committee of the Whole."

5. The House considers one bill at a time; debate must be short and relevant. The Senate considers several bills at a time; debate is unlimited.

6. When the House and Senate have passed different versions of a bill.

Critical thinking Students should consider such factors as party loyalty, crowded calendars, committee assignments, procedures, the Rules Committee, the majority needed to discharge a bill from committee, and behind-the-scenes wrangling.

CLOSURE

● Have students write three "I learned . . ." statements to show what they learned in this section. Then have them read the next assigned lesson.

CHAPTER 13 CORRECTIVES

● To review the content of Chapter 13, you may want to have students complete **Study Guide/Review 13** or **Workbook Chapter 13.**

For example, in 1986 Congress passed a bill imposing economic and trade restrictions, or **sanctions,** on the Republic of South Africa. The sanctions showed U.S. disapproval of the South African government's racial policy of **apartheid** (uh-PART-hayt), the strict, legal segregation of blacks and whites. President Ronald Reagan criticized the bill as counterproductive and vetoed it. In their rejection of the administration's foreign policy, first the House, where the bill originated, and then the Senate voted to override the veto. Vice President Bush, presiding over the Senate, announced that the bill had been approved, "the objections of the President of the United States notwithstanding."

SECTION 3 REVIEW

Vocabulary and key terms

bill (364)	filibuster (368)
sponsor (364)	cloture (369)
resolution (364)	table (369)
pigeonhole (366)	rider (369)
discharge petition (367)	sanctions (372)
calendar (367)	apartheid (372)
Rules Committee (368)	

For review

1. What is the difference between a public bill and a private bill? **3A**
2. (a) What options does a committee have for acting on a bill? (b) How can a bill be forced out of committee? **3A**
3. What is the function of the House Rules Committee? **3A**
4. How many members are needed to conduct business in (a) the House? (b) the Senate? (c) How does the House do business when a quorum is not present? **3A**
5. What are some differences between the rules for debate in the House and Senate? **8G**
6. When is a conference committee necessary? **6B**

Critical thinking

DRAWING INFERENCES   Suppose you wanted to secure passage of a bill in the House. What factors would you have to consider in order to give your bill a good chance? **8H**

Chapter Summary

A congressional term lasts for two years and is made up of two regular sessions. When Congress is not in session, the President can call a special session to act on pressing legislation. Members of Congress follow both formal procedures and unwritten rules of conduct, including loyalty to one's chamber, civility, specialization, reciprocity, compromise, and seniority. The Speaker of the House and the Senate Majority Leader are the most influential members of their respective houses. Other congressional leaders include the president of the Senate (the Vice President of the United States), the Senate's president *pro tempore*, and floor leaders and whips in both chambers. Congress members are assisted by their personal staffs and by agencies such as the Library of Congress and the General Accounting Office.

Standing committees and their subcommittees, which are assigned to deal with certain areas of legislation, do much of the work of Congress. Committees that deal with money, or appropriations, are particularly influential. Committee assignments are based on members' expertise, seniority, and party loyalty.

Laws are proposed in each chamber in the form of bills. Committees research and analyze each bill and make recommendations to the rest of the chamber. Both houses also introduce and consider formal resolutions.

Once a bill has been introduced, debate on the floor follows; rules for debate in the House are much stricter than in the Senate. To become law, a bill must be passed by each house in identical form. If conflicting versions of the same bill are passed, a conference committee meets to iron out differences. Finally, bills are sent to the President for signing. If the President vetoes the bill, a two-thirds vote in both chambers will make it law over the President's objections.

Background: *History* In 1991 the sanctions against South Africa were dropped in response to government reforms within South Africa.

CRITICAL THINKING
Identifying Fact and Opinion

Which statement below is a fact?

- The Constitution of the United States was written in 1787.
- The Constitution should be changed in order to deal with modern-day problems.

The first statement is a **fact** because it can be proved as true. The second statement, however, is an **opinion**. It cannot be proved to be right or wrong. Opinions may express approval or disapproval. They often tell what should be or might be. You can often identify opinions by such words as *I think, I believe,* or *should.*

When you listen to an argument or statement about a serious topic, you need to judge whether the statement is a fact or an opinion. Are there ways to check what the speaker says? Does the speaker appeal to reason or to emotion?

It is also important to evaluate opinions when you hear them. Ask yourself: What is the experience and background of the speaker? What facts does the speaker use to support his or her opinion? An opinion that is backed by experience, supported by facts, and well thought-out is a **reasoned judgment**.

★ ISSUE: The Conflict over War Powers

The war powers of the nation are shared by Congress and the President. The President is commander-in-chief of the armed forces, but Congress has the power to declare war and to raise and finance the military. Yet, recent Presidents have sent troops to fight in "undeclared" wars without the consent of Congress. While Presidents say that such actions are necessary to protect national security, some members of Congress see such actions as violations of their constitutional powers. The War Powers Act of 1973 (page 412) attempted to restrict the President's use of military power, but the resolution has been bitterly contested and often ignored.

In an interview with *The Christian Science Monitor,* constitutional scholar Thomas Cronin offered a solution to this conflict over war powers. Cronin suggested the formation of a joint committee of Congress to oversee the President's military plans.

> We have to recognize . . . that, if a President cannot persuade the other branch of government [Congress] of the validity, legitimacy, and desirability of a given public policy — such as trading with a terrorist nation or giving military aid to *contra* rebels in Nicaragua — that the framers of the Constitution believed that *inaction,* meaning no policy, no activity, was preferable to action. . . .
>
> Now, in the late 20th century, when we have a President Johnson or a Nixon or a Carter or a Reagan saying, "This Congress isn't allowing me to do things I want to do, therefore I'm going to do them through covert [secret] operations," . . . but not letting Congress know and not winning their consent or asking for their advice — I think the framers would say that was wrong. . . .
>
> [The proposed committee] would be authorized to meet with the President and the Secretary of State and Secretary of Defense with some regularity — but particularly at a time when there was consideration for the intervention of U.S. troops or Air Force strikes in some other nation. . . . Now there is no duly authorized group that a President really must consult with.

Analyzing the Issue

1. Are Cronin's statements about the framers of the Constitution fact or opinion? How can you tell?
2. What fact is mentioned in the third paragraph? How can you confirm this fact?
3. Does Cronin's opinion fall into the category of reasoned judgment? Why or why not?
4. Before forming your own opinion about Cronin's proposal, what other information might you look for?

373

CRITICAL THINKING

Politics
Discuss with students the committee Cronin proposes.
- CRITICAL THINKING *In your opinion, what members of Congress should be on the committee?* (Students might suggest high-ranking members of relevant committees, and members of both parties.)
- CRITICAL THINKING *What would be the purpose of having the committee?* (To inform key members of Congress of military actions and their reasons.)

Analyzing the Issue Answers
1. Cronin's statements are his opinions. The statement in the first paragraph is what he assumes the framers would believe; he cites no evidence. The statement in the second paragraph begins with "I think."
2. There is no authorized congressional group that the President must consult on the use of military powers. One might check by reading the Constitution, obtaining a list of congressional committees, or asking a trusted source.
3. Cronin's opinion is a reasoned judgment. He identifies a problem, assesses what the framers might have thought, and proposes a solution.
4. One might research Cronin's qualifications, assess the pros and cons of his solution, and look for others' opinions.

The symbol ♟ denotes active participation strategies.

Activities are keyed for student abilities:
▲ = Basic
● = All Levels
■ = Average/Advanced

Answers

Vocabulary See pp. T19–T21 for suggested vocabulary activities.

Reviewing the Facts

1. Seniority ensures that experienced legislators are in positions of leadership. It may also, however, allow incompetent legislators to continue in powerful positions, hurting the legislative process.

2. The Speaker of the House; the Senate Majority Leader.

3. To provide research and information for Congress, and to keep track of every bill in Congress.

4. *House:* Ways and Means, Rules, and Appropriations. *Senate:* Foreign Relations, Finance, Armed Services, Judiciary, and Appropriations.

5. Of the simple, concurrent, and joint resolutions, only the joint resolution has the force of law.

6. If the House cannot meet the constitutional requirement that a majority of members be present to conduct business, it declares itself a giant committee so that it can conduct business.

 ★ CHAPTER REVIEW

● **Review the definitions of the following terms:**

apartheid	joint session	sanctions
appropriations	lame duck	select committee
bill	log-rolling	seniority
calendar	Majority Leader	special session
cloture	Minority Leader	Speaker of the House
conference committee	pigeonhole	sponsor
discharge petition	recess	standing committee
filibuster	resolution	subcommittee
floor action	rider	table
floor leader	Rules Committee	whip

● REVIEWING THE FACTS

1. Why is the seniority system both praised and criticized? **3A**

2. What is the top position of power in the House and in the Senate? **3A**

3. What is the function of the Congressional Research Service? **3A**

4. Which standing committees are considered the most important in each house? **3A**

5. What are the three kinds of congressional resolutions, and which one carries the force of law? **3A**

6. Why does the House sometimes call a Committee of the Whole? **6F**

▲ THINKING CRITICALLY ABOUT KEY CONCEPTS

1. How could a political party use a committee assignment to punish a disloyal member of that party? **6A**

2. Why is the step of referring a bill to committee so important to the success or failure of the bill? **8F**

3. Why might senators be reluctant to invoke cloture to end a filibuster? **8A**

4. Why might some members of Congress prefer to avoid a roll-call vote on certain issues? **8H**

374

▲ PRACTICING SKILLS

1. **Study Skills: Reading a chart.** Refer to Figure 13–1 (page 355) to answer the following questions. (a) In which chamber could a rider about highway funds be attached to a bill about education? (b) In which chamber would members have to develop a style of speaking briefly and to the point in debating a bill? (c) In which chamber would members rely more on staff and other resources rather than solely on their own expertise? (d) In which chamber of Congress would members have to pay closer attention to local politics in their home states? **8B**

2. **Critical Thinking Skills: Finding the problem.** Refer to Figure 13–4 (page 365) and Section 3 of the chapter to find the factual errors in the following passage: A bill is introduced in the Senate. It is referred to a committee, where it is pigeonholed. The Rules Committee then schedules the bill for consideration by the full Senate, which debates the bill and votes for passage. The House has passed a slightly different bill, so a House-Senate conference committee meets and reconciles the two versions. It sends the bill directly to the President, who signs it into law. **8A**

Thinking Critically About Key Concepts

1. A party could remove a member from a choice committee as a form of punishment.

2. A bill's ability to reach the floor of the chamber might depend on the choice of committee assignment. Members of a particular committee might be predisposed to oppose or favor a bill.

3. Some might be reluctant to reach out of courtesy toward the senator conducting the filibuster. Others might hope that if they respected the filibusters of other senators, their own filibusters might be respected as well.

4. On controversial issues, members might not want to

▲ PARTICIPATORY CITIZENSHIP

1. **Researching your representatives.** Identify the two senators from your state and the congressional representative from your district. Find out what committees your representative and senators serve on. What sort of work is done by those committees? Do the committees deal with issues of direct relevance to your community? **3A**
2. **Making a time line.** Select a piece of legislation that interests you. Do research on its passage through Congress and use this information to create a time line showing the events from the legislation's introduction in each house of Congress through its signing or vetoing by the President. **8F**

■ WRITING ABOUT ISSUES

1. **Composing an editorial.** Only a few discharge petitions have been successful since 1900. This shows how the power of committees can hinder majority rule. Do you agree or disagree? Why? Write an editorial explaining your position. **8C**
2. **Writing an essay.** Do you think that televising Congress in session is helpful or harmful to the government process? Why? **8C**
3. **Making a diary entry.** Imagine that you are just beginning your first term in Congress and are learning how Congress operates. Select one aspect — the committee system, for example, or how a bill becomes a law — and write a diary entry explaining what you learned and how it will affect you. **8C**

ANALYZING A POLITICAL CARTOON

In each two-year session, Congress considers thousands of bills. When Congress takes a recess, its work on many key issues must be interrupted. Look at the cartoon below and answer the following questions.

1. Whom do the people in the car represent? Where are they going? **8B**
2. Describe the condition of the kitchen as the people drive away. What does this condition represent? **8B**
3. What is the cartoonist's opinion of how successful Congress has been? **8A, 8D**

© Jerry Barnett. Courtesy, The Indianapolis News

---

from your district or state.
2. Once students have completed their time lines, you may want to compare a bill that moved smoothly through Congress with one that encountered more opposition.

Writing About Issues
1. Some students may argue that strong committees help Congress run more efficiently. Other students may argue that important legislation should not be allowed to die in committees solely for political reasons.
2. Students supporting television broadcasts may suggest that such broadcasts would increase public interest in, and understanding of, Congress. Students opposing the broadcasts might argue that Congress would spend too much time performing for the cameras and too little time doing legitimate lawmaking.
3. Volunteers could read their diary entries to the class.

Analyzing a Political Cartoon
1. Members of Congress are leaving Washington, D.C., after Congress has adjourned.
2. Many jobs have been left undone, some in a dangerous state. For example, a coffee pot is running, a kettle is boiling over on the stove. and the dog has been left unfed.
3. Many legislative issues have been left undone. Some, like the deficit, are potentially dangerous.
4. The cartoonist suggest that Congress has left the nation in bad shape.

---

go on record with a vote because they might anger voters.

Practicing Skills
1. **(a)** Senate. **(b)** House. **(c)** Senate. **(d)** House.

2. Students should find the following problems: A pigeonholed bill does not move out of committee. A Rules Committee is not part of the process in the Senate. A bill reconciled by a conference committee must be approved by each house before going to the President.

Participatory Citizenship
1. You might wish to talk with students about past representatives or senators

Chapter Review exercises are keyed for student abilities:
▲ = Basic
● = All Levels
■ = Average/Advanced

Background

This editorial was published in *The Economist*, a leading British news magazine, in March 1990. You may wish to have students refer to the text's description of the British government (pp. 756–758 and 760), especially the House of Lords. Case Study 5, on pp. 510-12 and 510-13, examines the question of congressional elections by debating the issue of limiting congressional terms.

Structure of Government

▲ *To what branch of government do members of Congress belong?* (Legislative.) *To what branch of government does the governor of a state belong?* (Executive.)

● Have student draw charts or diagrams illustrating the editorial's comparison of the effects of campaign financing on members of Congress and governors.

Constitutional Heritage

● *What is the attitude of the editorial toward the Constitution's provisions for separation of powers?* (The editorial has a negative attitude. It says that members of Congress can be bought by interest groups because members are not responsible for implementing the legislation they pass.) *Do you agree with that view?*

AS OTHERS SEE US

1C, 4B, 4C

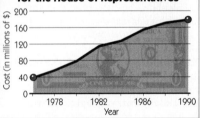

Campaign Costs of Winning Candidates for the House of Representatives

(Cost in millions of $) — 200, 160, 120, 80, 40, 0 / Years: 1978, 1982, 1986, 1990

The High Cost of Congressional Elections

Foreign observers are appalled by the increasingly expensive political campaigns in America. An editorial in the British magazine The Economist *comments on the trade-offs that members of Congress make for votes.*

London. Nothing concentrates the mind of a politician like the threat of losing his seat. That threat grows ever more remote for the typical member of Congress, who is now less likely to be defeated every two years than the average member of the House of Lords is to die over the same period. Yet, paradoxically, congressmen spend more and more of their time raising money for their next re-election. . . .

The Senate, though not yet the House, is keen to reform its system of campaign finance after some embarrassing scandals. Republicans and Democrats are coming round to a scheme . . . that would introduce "flexible spending limits." . . . Because the constitution, according to the Supreme Court, protects campaign spending as a form of free speech, limits cannot be mandatory. . . .

Remember what problem it is that needs solving. It is not the cost of campaigning *per se:* many worthwhile things cost money. Rather, it is (a) that donors—firms and individuals—favour incumbents, who then outspend their rivals so that they rarely lose; and (b) that, in seeking invincibility, incumbents sell their souls to special interests on whose behalf they distort legislation against the interests of their constituents.

Given the American constitution, it is inevitable that special interests will buy some candidates and some candidates will buy elections. For, under the constitution, congressmen have power to alter legislation but little responsibility to implement it and live by the results. So the voters elect congressmen who tell them what they want to hear and who avoid hard choices. The weakest congressmen are, and always have been, like experimental rats who get their rewards from simple acts of generosity towards their constituents. Before, they used only the pork barrel, to bring dams or defence plants to their districts. Now, increasingly, they bring regulatory loopholes and tax breaks to their wealthy donors instead.

Contrast their position with that of state governors. The governors spend just as much money getting elected . . . but . . . they are not especially beholden to lobbyists, nor are they inevitably re-elected. They are judged on their records. In short, they have both power and responsibility. Congressmen have only power. So long as that goes unreformed, all changes to America's system of campaign finance will just be so much tinkering.

From "America's money politics" in *The Economist*, March 31, 1990. Copyright © 1990 The Economist Newspaper, Inc., Ltd. Reprinted by permission of *The Economist.*

CRITICAL THINKING

1. Why are limits on campaign spending illegal in the United States?
2. What points might you make in response to the article?
3. What reforms do you think *The Economist*'s writer would suggest for financing election campaigns?
4. According to the chart, by about what ratio did incumbents outspend challengers in recent campaigns for the House?

Critical Thinking Answers
1. Because, according to the Supreme Court, they are protected as free speech.
2. Students might suggest that voters do not vote for incumbents who represent interest groups and ignore the needs of their constituents. Members of Congress have a record, just as governors do, because their votes on issues are recorded.
3. Answers may include limiting or reducing the amounts that may be spent or giving free television advertising time.
4. About three to one.

UNIT
★ 5 ★

NATIONAL GOVERNMENT: The Executive Branch

CHAPTER

14 The OFFICE of PRESIDENT

15 The POWERS of the PRESIDENT

16 GOVERNMENT at WORK

377

National Government: The Executive Branch
(pp. 377–460)

Unit Overview
Unit Five discusses the functions and organization of the executive branch of the national government. In Chapters 14 and 15, the various roles and responsibilities of the President and Vice President are discussed, and procedures are outlined for the transfer of presidential power. The history and operations of the Electoral College are also examined. Other elements of government administration are covered in Chapter 16, including the Executive Office, Cabinet, independent agencies, and civil service system.

CHAPTER 14
THE OFFICE OF PRESIDENT
(pp. 378–395)

	Section Objectives	Section Resources
Section 1 **The American Presidency Is Unique**	☐ distinguish between the President's roles as chief executive and chief of state ☐ identify the written and unwritten qualifications for holding the office of President ☐ describe the salary and fringe benefits the President receives	▲ TRANSPARENCY **33**
Section 2 **Presidential Power Is Transferred Smoothly**	☐ explain how tradition, acts of Congress, and constitutional amendments have affected the President's term, succession to the presidency, and procedures for removing the President from office ☐ cite ways in which the vice presidency has changed over time	
Section 3 **The Constitution Sets Up the Electoral College**	☐ explain the origin and history of the Electoral College ☐ evaluate proposals for reform of the Electoral College	▲ SKILLS PRACTICE WORKSHEET **14** ■ SKILLS CHALLENGE WORKSHEET **14** ▲ TRANSPARENCY **34**

Essential Elements

The list below shows Essential Elements relevant to this chapter.
(The complete list of Essential Elements appears in the introductory
pages of this Teacher's Edition.)

Section 1: 1C, 2A, 2C, 3A, 6A

Section 2: 1D, 2A, 2C, 3A, 6H

Section 3: 1B, 1D, 2A, 2E, 4B, 6C, 6F, 6H, 8B

Chapter Review: 1B, 1C, 1D, 2A, 2C, 3A, 4B,
4C, 4D, 6C, 8A, 8B, 8C, 8F

Section Resources are keyed
for student abilities:
▲ = Basic
● = All Levels
■ = Average/Advanced

Homework Options

Each section contains activities labeled "Guided/Independent Practice," "Reteaching/Correctives," and "Enrichment/Extension." You may wish to choose from among these activities when assigning homework.

Students Acquiring English Activities

Have students consult Figure 14–2 (p. 388) and Figure 14–3 (p. 390) and then make a chart showing which candidate your state supported in the presidential election of each of the following years: 1888, 1980, 1984, and 1992. Ask students also to show in their charts which party that candidate belonged to as well as the number of electoral votes that your state cast.

LISTENING/SPEAKING: Read aloud the excerpts from John F. Kennedy's Inaugural Address on p. 385 to the class. Have students listen for the major issues raised by the President. (You may prefer to read from a different inaugural address, such as that of Thomas Jefferson on p. 277, or you may prefer to read selections from several presidential addresses and have students compare them.)

Teacher Bibliography

Edwards, George C. III, Steven A. Chull, and Norman C. Thomas. *The Presidency and Public Policy Making.* University of Pittsburgh Press, 1985. Essays on the ability of the President to affect the making of public policy and the various means by which he does so.

Germond, Jack and Jules Witcover. *Whose Broad Stripes and Bright Stars?: The Trivial Pursuit of the Presidency 1988.* Warner Books, 1990. Two experienced political journalists analyze the 1988 presidential campaign.

White, Theodore H. *The Making of the President, 1960–1972.* 4 vols. Macmillan, 1961–1973. An inside view of the four presidential campaigns from 1960 to 1972.

Student Bibliography

Caroli, Betty Boyd. *First Ladies.* Oxford University Press, 1988. Examines the role of presidential wives as it has been interpreted by different first ladies.

DeGregorio, William A. *The Complete Book of U.S. Presidents.* 3rd ed. Dembner, 1991. Valuable facts about the lives and administrations of past Presidents.

Robinson, Donald L. *"To the Best of My Ability:" The President and the Constitution.* Norton, 1987. How Presidents have succeeded in fulfilling their oath to "preserve, protect, and defend the Constitution of the United States."

Literature

Carter, Jimmy. *Keeping Faith: Memoirs of a President.* Bantam, 1983. Jimmy Carter recounts his presidency.

Serling, Robert. *The President's Plane Is Missing.* Doubleday, 1967. When the President's plane vanishes from the radar screen, government investigators, the Vice President, members of the Cabinet, and White House reporters are affected.

Wallace, Irving. *The Man.* Simon & Schuster, 1964. A senator becomes the first black President.

Knebel, Fletcher. *Night of Camp David.* Harper & Row, 1965. A young senator discovers the President is a dangerous paranoiac.

Films and Videotapes*

The Electoral College. (Series title: *Our Election Day Illusions: The Beat Majority, Part 2.*) 25 min. Carousel, 1961. f. An older film that covers the functions, procedures, safeguards, and inadequacies of the electoral college. Alternative plans are discussed, concluding with a strong statement by former President Truman to leave the system as it is.

Software*

MECC Dataquest: The Presidents (Apple). MECC. Presents the historical context and major contributions of the 41 Presidents. Students learn to form and answer questions by searching the database and learn to formulate hypotheses based upon the search results.

---

* For a complete guide to audiovisual sources, see page T22.

The Office of President *(pp. 378–395)*

Chapter 14 begins by looking at the ways in which the American presidency is unique, then describes the qualifications for the job and the ways in which tradition, congressional acts, and constitutional amendments have influenced the presidency and vice presidency, and concludes with a study of the Electoral College system.

Chapter Objectives

After students complete this chapter, they will be able to:

1. Distinguish between the President's roles as chief executive and chief of state.

2. Identify the written and unwritten qualifications for holding the office of President.

3. Describe the salary and fringe benefits the President receives.

4. Explain how tradition, acts of Congress, and constitutional amendments have affected the President's term, succession to the presidency, and procedures for removing the President from office.

5. Cite ways in which the vice presidency has changed over time.

6. Explain the origin and history of the Electoral College.

7. Evaluate proposals for reform of the Electoral College.

CHAPTER

14

The OFFICE of PRESIDENT

I do solemnly swear (or affirm) that I will faithfully execute the office of President of the United States, and will to the best of my ability, preserve, protect, and defend the Constitution of the United States.

The Constitution
(Article II, Section 1, Clause 7)

378

Photo
Oval Office (the White House).

The Constitutional Convention had been meeting for one week on June 1, 1787, when James Wilson rose to speak. A Scot who had come to the United States as a young man, Wilson was a great believer in democracy and a strong national government. Now he proposed that the executive powers — mentioned only vaguely in the Virginia Plan, a working draft of a new constitution — be controlled by a single person.

An embarrassed silence followed. The memory of the tyranny of a king's rule was fresh in the minds of the delegates. Yet they also recalled the weak and ineffectual committee that had served as the executive under the Articles of Confederation. Finally Benjamin Franklin spoke up. This is a point of great importance, he said, asking delegates to "deliver their sentiments on it." And so discussion of a chief executive began.

Through public debate and private committee work, the Constitutional Convention came up with Article II of the Constitution: the executive branch. In that article, they created the office of the President, a new kind of official for a new nation. This chapter examines the ways that office has developed through our history.

CHAPTER OUTLINE

1 The American Presidency Is Unique

Presidential Roles
The Job of President

2 Presidential Power Is Transferred Smoothly

Term of Office
Presidential Succession
The Vice Presidency

3 The Constitution Sets Up the Electoral College

History of the Electoral College
The Electoral College Today
Flaws in the Electoral College
Electoral College Reforms

379

CHAPTER SUPPORT MATERIAL

Skills Practice Worksheet 14

Skills Challenge Worksheet 14

Transparencies 33–34

Study Guide/Review 14

Workbook Chapter 14

Chapter 14 Test, Forms A-C

 VIDEOTAPE SERIES

This would be an appropriate place to use Houghton Mifflin's videotape, *Public Opinion and the Presidency.*

The American Presidency Is Unique

Theodore Roosevelt called it "a bully [splendid] pulpit." John F. Kennedy believed it to be "a formidable, exposed, and somewhat mysterious institution." Harry Truman said, "No one who has not had the responsibility can really understand what it is like . . . not even his closest aides or members of his immediate family."

These three men were all talking about the same office: serving as President of the United States. As their descriptions suggest, the American presidency is like no other job in the world.

Today the President is leader of the most powerful nation on earth, a nation that is home to a quarter of a billion people of a great variety of races and religions. The job carries with it immense powers and responsibilities, for the American President fills a number of important roles.

1C, 2A, 3A

Presidential Roles

The framers of the Constitution gave the President dual roles, making the office both unique and powerful. In addition to having constitutional powers, the President today is also head of a political party and a leader of public opinion.

The President as chief executive

Because of the powers conferred by Article II of the Constitution, the President is the **chief executive** of the United States. This title is given to the official who actually runs or administers a government. As chief executive, the President may call out the armed forces, grant reprieves

and pardons, negotiate treaties, appoint ambassadors and judges, recognize foreign governments, and see that the law is carried out.

The President as chief of state

A nation needs more than just an efficient administrator, however. It also needs a symbolic leader, a **chief of state**. In the United States, the President has this role as well. As chief of state, the President entertains foreign leaders, speaks to charitable organizations, tosses out the first baseball of the major league season, bestows medals on military heroes, unveils monuments to war veterans, and hosts the White House Easter egg hunt.

By contrast, in almost all other modern political systems, the roles of chief of state and chief executive are separate and are taken by different people. In Great Britain, for example, the Queen is the ceremonial head of state, but the Prime Minister and Cabinet run the government. In Japan, the Emperor symbolizes the nation, while the Prime Minister executes government policy.

2C, 3A, 6A

The Job of President

Constitutional requirements

The Constitution places only three restrictions on those holding the office of President. First, the President must be a "natural-born citizen" — anyone born on United States territory. Persons born in foreign countries who later become citizens by naturalization are not eligible.

Second, the President must be at least 35 years old. The youngest President ever *elected* was John F. Kennedy, at age 43. The youngest President, however, was Theodore Roosevelt, who took office at age 42 upon the death of William McKinley. The oldest President was Ronald Reagan, elected in 1980 at the age of 69 and re-elected in 1984 at the age of 73.

Third, the President must have lived in the United States for at least fourteen years. The fourteen years do not have to be consecutive; both

380

Herbert Hoover and Dwight Eisenhower had lived overseas for several years prior to their election as President.

Traditional qualifications

In addition to these simple requirements, there appear to be some unwritten qualifications for becoming President. These "qualifications," however, are merely historical traditions, not constitutional provisions.

For example, all Presidents so far have been men. The Democratic Party's nomination of Geraldine Ferraro for Vice President in 1984 may have been the first step toward a future woman President.

All Presidents have also been white, though recently that qualification has been challenged. Jesse Jackson and Governor Douglas Wilder of Virginia made bids for the Democratic nomination in 1988 and 1992 respectively. In addition, all but one President — John Kennedy, a Roman Catholic — have been Protestants. A non-Christian has never been nominated by a major party.

Although presidential candidates like to refer to their humble beginnings, most Presidents were raised in well-to-do families. Less than half a dozen were born in poverty. A few Presidents, such as George Washington, Franklin D. Roosevelt, and John F. Kennedy, were extremely wealthy. In addition, all but nine Presidents have had college educations. Harry S Truman is the only President since 1900 who never attended college.

Nearly all Presidents were born and raised in small towns or rural areas. Theodore Roosevelt (New York City), William Howard Taft (Cincinnati, Ohio), and John Kennedy (Boston, Massachusetts) are the only exceptions. All Presidents but one have been married, though some were widowed when they took office. James Buchanan was the only bachelor, while Ronald Reagan was the first to have been divorced. Finally, most Presidents have had military experience. Indeed, ten had been army generals.

Salary and benefits

The President's salary is established by Congress. To guarantee the President's independence, the Constitution provides that presidential compensation may not be increased or decreased during a President's term. Since 1969, the President's yearly salary has been fixed at $200,000. It is subject to taxation.

In addition, the President also receives a number of perquisites ("perks"), or fringe benefits. These benefits, like the President's salary, are also set by Congress. Presidential "perks" include the following:

As chief executive, the President negotiates treaties with leaders of foreign states. In 1978, President Jimmy Carter mediated an agreement between Egyptian President Anwar Sadat (left) and Israeli Prime Minister Menachem Begin (right).

381

Presidential "perks" include residence in the White House and a staff of cooks and butlers. Here, former First Lady Nancy Reagan samples confectioneries in the White House kitchen.

- A travel account of $100,000 per year (which is non-taxable).
- An expense account of $50,000 per year (which is taxable).
- Residence at the White House, the presidential mansion. Its facilities include a private gym, swimming pool, library, bowling alley, and movie room.
- An Executive Residence Staff of roughly 100 people, including chefs, butlers, carpenters, electricians, and floral designers, to perform various functions around the White House.
- A 180-acre vacation estate in Maryland called Camp David, complete with tennis courts, skeet range, heated pool, and 150 Navy personnel.
- A team of medical doctors, dentists, and other health care experts readily available.
- A dozen jets, eight helicopters, and the presidential jet, *Air Force One*.
- A retirement package that includes $138,900 per year (taxable), plus support staff and Secret Service protection.

Against the President's "perks" must be set the pressures and stresses of the job, coupled with the threat of assassination attempts and other dangers. In addition, Presidents have little privacy. Everything the President does, publicly or privately, is subject to radio, television, and press coverage.

SECTION 1 REVIEW

Vocabulary and key terms

chief executive (380)   chief of state (380)

For review

1. What are some of the President's duties (a) as chief executive? (b) as chief of state? **3A**
2. What are the three constitutional requirements for the office of President? **3A**
3. What are some "unwritten" qualifications that most Presidents have met? **3A**

Critical thinking

DRAWING INFERENCES Why are the roles of chief executive and chief of state separate in most countries but not in the United States? **1C**

382

SECTION 2
Presidential Power Is Transferred Smoothly

The Main Ideas

1 How have tradition, acts of Congress, and constitutional amendments affected the President's term, succession to the presidency, and procedures for removal from office? *pages 383–385*

2 How has the vice presidency changed over time? *pages 385–386*

In 1964 François Duvalier, leader of Haiti since 1957, had himself declared "president for life." When he died in 1971, his son — only 19 years old — took over. Like his father, Jean-Claude Duvalier relied on the armed forces and a ruthless secret police to stay in power. In 1986 Haitians revolted against his corruption and cruelty, forcing him to flee the country. From 1987 to 1991, the military continually disrupted attempts to establish a democratic government. Finally, in 1994, the United States used military intervention to restore democratically elected President Jean-Bertrand Aristide to power in Haiti.

Haiti's tragedy of unstable government and violent overthrow is not uncommon in the world. By contrast, the American people have always been able to count on Presidents handing over the office in a smooth and orderly way. Though the Constitution is vague about presidential succession and length of service, these questions have, for the most part, been resolved through tradition, acts of Congress, and constitutional amendments.

2A, 2C, 3A

Term of Office

During the Constitutional Convention, there was heated debate over the length of the President's term in office. Some delegates wanted a three-year term allowing for re-election. Others supported a six- or seven-year term with no possibility of re-election. A few even favored electing a President for life. The delegates finally compromised on a four-year term with the possibility of re-election.

The two-term tradition

George Washington decided not to seek a third term in 1796, beginning a tradition that Presidents would serve only two terms. This tradition rested partly on respect for Washington and partly on the principle that frequent changes in officeholders keep a government more democratic. Although several Presidents considered seeking a third term, it was Franklin D. Roosevelt who broke the tradition, winning a third term in 1940 and a fourth in 1944.

The Twenty-Second Amendment

When the Republicans gained control of Congress after the war ended in 1945, they quickly proposed a constitutional amendment to restrict the number of years a President can remain in office. This proposal became the 22nd Amendment in 1951 after it was ratified by the required three-fourths of the state legislatures. It provides (1) that no one can be elected President more than twice (a maximum of eight years), and (2) that no one who serves more than two years of another President's term can be elected more than once.

To see how this amendment works, consider this example. When President Nixon resigned in August 1974, Vice President Gerald Ford became President. Two years later, in 1976, Ford ran for President but lost to Jimmy Carter. If Ford had *won* in 1976, he could not have run again in 1980, because he had served more than two years of Nixon's term.

The Twentieth Amendment

Another constitutional amendment dealing with the presidential term is the Twentieth, or "lame duck," amendment, passed in 1933 (page 352). Originally, the President and Vice President began their terms on March 4, as did members of Congress. This meant that Presidents who were defeated or did not seek office in November of the previous year still served four months. The Twentieth Amendment changes the date so that the President and Vice President are sworn in at noon on January 20.

383

SECTION 2

Presidential Power Is Transferred Smoothly
(pp. 383–387)

Section Objectives
☐ explain how tradition, acts of Congress, and constitutional amendments have affected the President's term, succession to the presidency, and procedures for removing the President from office
☐ cite ways in which the vice presidency has changed over time

Vocabulary
presidential succession

FOCUS
● Have students consider the following statement by Woodrow Wilson: "There is very little to be said about the Vice President. . . . His importance consists in the fact that he may cease to be Vice President." Have them explain what Wilson meant. (The Vice President's only important job is that he or she may become President.)

Have students compare Wilson's statement with the remark by John Nance Garner on p. 385. Then ask them to characterize the vice presidency in one or two sentences.

Background: *History* In *The Federalist* (Nos. 71 and 72), Alexander Hamilton defended the four-year term. A term of this length, he argued, provided the President with enough time to acquire experience, exhibit leadership skills, and develop stable policies.

Check for Understanding
● *What is the longest amount of time one person can serve as President today?* (Ten years.)

The symbol 👥 denotes active participation strategies.

Activities are keyed for student abilities:
▲ = Basic
● = All Levels
■ = Average/Advanced

EXPLANATION

After reviewing the content of the section, you may want to consider the following activities:

Controversial Issues

● CRITICAL THINKING Have students debate the following question: ***Should the President be limited to one six-year term?*** (Students supporting the idea might argue that Presidents, freed from re-election duties, would have more time to govern and would be more inclined to take tough, unpopular stands. Students arguing against the idea might claim that it would make Presidents less accountable to the voters.)

Politics

▲ CRITICAL THINKING To help students understand the problems associated with being a lame duck President, have them consider what would happen if you were required to give students a final grade for this course one month before the term ended. ***Would students' productivity increase or decrease in the month following the release of grades?*** (Probably decrease.)

Structure of Government

▲ ***What law established the line of presidential succession in use today?*** (The Presidential Succession Act of 1947.)

● ***Review Figure 14–1. Which branches of the federal government are represented?*** (The executive and legislative branches.)

● CRITICAL THINKING ***Why is orderly transition in government important in a democracy?*** (Uncertainty about political succession can lead to political instability, possibly encouraging the seizure of power by unelected and unaccountable persons.)

Presidential Succession

Eight American Presidents have died in office: four of natural causes and four by assassins' bullets. Another four have been the targets of unsuccessful assassination attempts. Clearly, there must be a method for filling a vacant presidency quickly and smoothly. Congress has passed several **presidential succession** laws, the most recent of which was adopted in 1947.

The line of succession

The Presidential Succession Act of 1947 establishes the line of succession beyond the Vice President: Speaker of the House, president *pro tempore* of the Senate, then members of the President's Cabinet according to the seniority of their department. That is, the first Cabinet officers in line for the presidency are those who head the oldest departments — the Secretaries of State, Treasury, and Defense — followed in order by the heads of newer departments.

The Twenty-Fifth Amendment

Sometimes Presidents still in office have been too ill to perform their duties. In 1881, James A. Garfield lingered for 80 days before he died from a gunshot wound. Woodrow Wilson was paralyzed for months following a stroke in 1919. Dwight Eisenhower suffered two heart attacks while he was in office. When Lyndon Johnson became President in 1963 after Kennedy's assassination, the vice presidency was vacant.

Figure 14–1 LINE OF PRESIDENTIAL SUCCESSION The following are in line to assume the office of President. 3A

The Vice President *(1)*
Speaker of the House *(2)*
President *pro tempore* of the Senate *(3)*
Secretary of State *(4)*
Secretary of the Treasury *(5)*
Secretary of Defense *(6)*
Attorney General *(7)*
Secretary of the Interior *(8)*
Secretary of Agriculture *(9)*
Secretary of Commerce *(10)*
Secretary of Labor *(11)*
Secretary of Health and Human Services *(12)*
Secretary of Housing and Urban Development *(13)*
Secretary of Transportation *(14)*
Secretary of Energy *(15)*
Secretary of Education *(16)*
Secretary of Veterans Affairs *(17)*

Each of these situations raised serious questions that neither the Constitution nor the Presidential Succession Act could answer. Who, for example, determines whether a President is too ill to serve? Does the Vice President become "acting" President or "actual" President? What happens when there is no Vice President?

The 25th Amendment established procedures for dealing with presidential disability and filling the vice presidency. The amendment, ratified in 1967, has four main provisions:

1. If the President resigns, is impeached, or dies in office, the Vice President becomes the "actual" President.
2. If a vacancy occurs in the vice presidency, the President nominates a new Vice President, who takes office after being approved by a majority of both houses of Congress.
3. If the President or the Vice President and a majority of the Cabinet declare the President unable to serve, then the Vice President becomes "acting" President.
4. If the President declares himself fit, he may resume the duties of President, unless the Vice President and a majority of the Cabinet disagree, in which case Congress must decide. A two-thirds vote by both houses of Congress is required for the Vice President to remain as acting President.

The 25th Amendment was put to use for the first time in October 1973, when Vice President Spiro Agnew resigned. President Richard Nixon nominated House Minority Leader Gerald R. Ford to be Vice President, and he was confirmed by Congress. In August 1974, Nixon resigned and Ford became President. To fill the office of Vice President, Ford nominated Nelson R. Rockefeller of New York.

Removing a President from office

Under the Constitution, any federal government official — including the President — can be impeached and removed from office for treason, bribery, or serious misconduct. Impeachment is the process of bringing formal charges against a public official. Impeachment does not

Figure 14–1

■ ***Why are the Speaker of the House and the president* pro tempore *of the Senate placed before the members of the Cabinet in the order of succession?*** (They are elected officials and therefore have more authority than appointed officials.)

Background: *History* The Presidents who died in office of natural causes were William Henry Harrison, Zachary Taylor, Warren G. Harding, and Franklin D. Roosevelt. Assassinated Presidents were Abraham Lincoln, James Garfield, William McKinley, and John F. Kennedy.

mean removal from office but is the first step toward it. Only the House of Representatives can impeach a federal official, and only the Senate can remove him or her from office.

The process begins when the House of Representatives, by majority vote, passes "articles of impeachment." The Senate, with the Chief Justice of the United States presiding, then acts as the court to try the case. A two-thirds vote is necessary to remove an official from office.

Andrew Johnson, the seventeenth President, was the only President ever to be impeached. In 1868, the House charged Johnson with violating the Tenure of Office Act, which prohibited the President from removing a public official without the Senate's consent. Johnson, however, was *not* removed from office. The Senate fell one vote short of the necessary two-thirds majority.

The only President ever to resign from office was Richard M. Nixon, on August 9, 1974. His resignation followed public outcry and an investigation by the House Judiciary Committee into Nixon's involvement in the Watergate scandal. Evidence indicated that he had taken part in a criminal conspiracy to cover up the 1972 burglary of Democratic national headquarters in the Watergate building in Washington, D.C. Faced with certain impeachment, Nixon resigned. Although some people feared that Watergate might cause a crisis in American government, even this painful transition was carried out smoothly.

3A

The Vice Presidency

Vice Presidents are often the forgotten men of history. Who, for example, has ever heard of Schuyler Colfax, Levi P. Morton, Hannibal Hamlin, or Charles W. Fairbanks? Many former Vice Presidents considered the job meaningless. John Nance Garner, Franklin D. Roosevelt's first Vice President, is remembered chiefly for having said that the vice presidency "isn't worth a pitcher of warm spit!"

The role of the Vice President

A brief look at the powers and duties of the Vice President explains the office's lack of prestige. Under the Constitution, the Vice President's main formal duty is to act as president of the Senate. This job carries little authority, except the power to vote in case of a tie.

LANDMARKS in LIBERTY

Kennedy's Inaugural Address (1961)

The election of John F. Kennedy in 1960, after a hard-fought campaign against Richard Nixon, marked the beginning of an idealistic political era. In his inaugural speech, the young President called on Americans to rise above party differences and unite behind the principles on which the country was founded.

" We observe today not a victory of party but a celebration of freedom . . . signifying renewal as well as change. For I have sworn before you and Almighty God the same solemn oath our forebearers prescribed nearly a century and three-quarters ago. . . .

The world is very different now. For man holds in his mortal hands the power to abolish all forms of human poverty and all forms of human life. And yet the same revolutionary beliefs for which our forebearers fought are still at issue. . . .

We dare not forget today that we are the heirs of that first revolution. Let the word go forth from this time and place, to friend and foe alike, that the torch has been passed to a new generation of Americans. . . .

Let every nation know, whether it wishes us well or ill, that we shall pay any price, bear any burden, meet any hardship, support any friend, oppose any foe to assure the survival and the success of liberty. . . .

And so, my fellow Americans: ask not what your country can do for you — ask what you can do for your country. "

1. To what, according to Kennedy, has the United States always been committed?
2. What might have been Kennedy's reason for repeatedly referring to "our forebearers"?
3. In concluding his speech, what does Kennedy ask the American people to do?

385

Politics

● Have students choose a presidential campaign and determine the ways in which the vice-presidential candidates balanced their party's ticket.

👥 Cooperative Learning

● Divide the class into small groups and have each group brainstorm ways that the vice presidency could be enhanced. Each group should compile a list of suggestions that includes at least one idea from each student. Have each group trade its list with another group and then evaluate the suggestions of the other group.

GUIDED/INDEPENDENT PRACTICE

● Have students write a newspaper editorial dealing with the 20th, 22nd, or 25th Amendment. The editorial should either explain why the amendment is well conceived or explain why it should be revised or repealed.

RETEACHING/CORRECTIVES

▲ Have students write three short paragraphs. Each paragraph should summarize the main idea of one of the headings in the section.

Landmarks in Liberty Answers
1. The preservation of liberty in the United States and around the world.
2. He might have hoped to instill in Americans a common purpose or to encourage the idea that his aims were part of a historical American mission.
3. He asks them to participate in society by working for the good of the country rather than working only to their own advantage.

The symbol 👥 denotes active participation strategies.

Activities are keyed for student abilities:
▲ = Basic
● = All Levels
■ = Average/Advanced

386

ENRICHMENT/EXTENSION

■ Have students read the newspaper and watch the TV news for four days, keeping count of the number of times the President is mentioned and the number of times the Vice President is mentioned. At the end of the four days, students should bring their tabulations to class and use them to draw conclusions about the relative importance of the two positions.

Section 2 Review Answers

1. (a) It moved the inauguration date from March 4 to January 20. **(b)** It limited election terms to two, and only one for anyone serving more than two years of another President's term.
2. Speaker of the House, president *pro tempore* of the Senate, then Cabinet members in order of seniority of the departments.
3. (a) Vice President. **(b)** President. If the Vice President and Congress disagree with the President, Congress decides.
4. The President nominates a candidate, whom Congress must confirm.

Following the assassination of John F. Kennedy on November 22, 1963, Federal District Judge Sarah T. Hughes administered the presidential oath to Vice President Lyndon Johnson aboard a presidential jet.

It could be argued, in fact, that the Vice President is most important *before* taking office. During the election campaign, he or she is supposed to help balance the party ticket and gain support from certain regions or groups of voters. For example, George Bush, a Texas resident born in Massachusetts, chose Indianan Dan Quayle.

Once the election is won, however, the Vice President must wait to be given tasks by the President. Historically, most Presidents have given little responsibility to their Vice Presidents for fear that they might upstage the President or interfere with policy-making.

Changes in the vice presidency

Assassinations and other events, however, have forced Americans to recognize that the Vice President is "only a heartbeat away" from the presidency. Therefore, it is important to choose a qualified person. Furthermore, beginning with Harry Truman, most recent Presidents have given their Vice Presidents additional responsibilities, such as chairing commissions, meeting foreign dignitaries, representing the nation abroad, and advising the President.

Al Gore, President Clinton's Vice President, confers with the President regularly and has taken an active role in managing the federal government. A former senator, Gore drew upon his expertise to lobby Congress on environmental and health-care issues. Gore also spearheaded the President's plan to "reinvent government." The plan aimed at making government more efficient and eliminating wasteful spending.

386

Background: *History* John Adams, the first Vice President, called it "the most insignificant office that ever the invention of man contrived or his imagination conceived." When he was Vice President under Franklin Roosevelt, John Nance Garner described his office as "a spare tire on the automobile of government."

SECTION 2 REVIEW

Vocabulary and key terms

"lame duck" amendment (383) presidential succession (384)

For review

1. How was the President's term affected by the provisions of (a) the 20th Amendment? (b) the 22nd Amendment? **3A**
2. After the Vice President, what officials are in the line of succession to the presidency? **3A**

3. (a) According to the provisions of the 25th Amendment, who takes the President's place in case of temporary disability? (b) Who determines whether the President is able to resume office? **2A**
4. What happens when the office of Vice President is vacant? **3A**
5. Why have former Vice Presidents criticized the office as being meaningless and lacking prestige? **3A**

Critical thinking

FORMING AN OPINION   What are the pros and cons of limiting the President to two terms? **3A**

1B, 1D, 2A, 2E, 4B, 6C, 6F, 6H, 8B

SECTION 3 The Constitution Sets Up the Electoral College

ACCESS The Main Ideas

1 **What is the origin and history of the Electoral College?** *pages 387–391*
2 **How might the Electoral College be reformed?** *pages 391–393*

When voters went to the polls on Election Day, 1992, most people thought they were voting for a presidential candidate. They were not. In reality, each person voted in his or her state for a slate of electors who were pledged to vote for one of the candidates.

This is the Electoral College system, a unique way of choosing a President. It is also a system that has resulted in controversy. Electors have cast their ballots for someone other than the candidate to whom they were pledged. Campaigns may bypass smaller states in favor of those with the most electoral votes. Candidates have even won elections with fewer popular votes than their opponents.

Is the Electoral College out of date, out of touch, and undemocratic? Or is it an excellent way to allow for clear victors and to maintain a two-party system?

1B, 1D, 2A, 2E, 4B

History of the Electoral College

Perhaps the longest debate at the Constitutional Convention concerned the method for selecting the President. Giving this power to Congress — one early suggestion — would destroy the idea of separation of powers. Most of the delegates also opposed direct election of the President by the voters at large. After several weeks of arguing, the delegates arrived at a compromise called the **Electoral College**, allowing *indirect* popular participation.

The original Electoral College plan

The original plan for the Electoral College system is found in Article II of the Constitution. (Some modifications in the original plan later proved necessary.) Each state is to choose a group, or **slate**, of **electors** as directed by the state legislature. The number of electors to which each state is entitled equals the total number of senators and representatives it has in Congress. (This formula is still in use.) No elector may be a member of Congress or hold any other federal office.

387

5. The Constitution gives the Vice President little authority except to act as president of the Senate. Presidents tend to give Vice Presidents little responsibility out of fear that they might be upstaged.

Critical thinking Students should discuss such issues as the need for experienced leadership, concentration of power, demands of the office, needs of constituents, continuity of government, and any "lame duck" disadvantages.

CLOSURE
● Have students identify the following: 20th Amendment, 22nd Amendment, 25th Amendment, impeachment. Then have them read Section 3, noting how the election maps illustrate the main points of the section.

SECTION 3

The Constitution Sets Up the Electoral College *(pp. 387–393)*

Section Objectives
☐ explain the origin and history of the Electoral College
☐ evaluate proposals for reform of the Electoral College

Vocabulary
Electoral College, slate, electors, electoral vote

Background: *History* Most of the delegates to the Constitutional Convention did not trust ordinary voters to vote directly for the President.

The symbol 👥 denotes active participation strategies.

Activities are keyed for student abilities:
▲ = Basic
● = All Levels
■ = Average/Advanced

FOCUS

● Present the class with the following scenario: a presidential candidate wins a majority of votes yet is not elected President. *What are two different possible explanations for this?* (The candidate might have received a majority of popular votes but not a majority of electoral votes, or some of the electors pledged to the candidate might have voted for a different candidate.)

EXPLANATION

After reviewing the content of the section, you may want to consider the following activities:

Constitutional Heritage

● Have students reread the original text of Article II, Section 1, Clause 2 of the Constitution (pp. 120–121). Then have volunteers draw a chart on the board to show how the original Electoral College worked.

● *Why did the rise of political parties make this plan hard to follow?* (The original plan did not take into account the fact that a running mate would probably get the same number of votes as the presidential candidate of his or her party. Nor did it account for the possibility that the two candidates receiving the largest number of votes might belong to different parties.)

● *How did the Twelfth Amendment correct this problem?* (It required electors to cast separate ballots for President and Vice President.)

Under the original plan, the electors would meet in their own states, and each one would vote for two candidates. The results were sealed and sent to the nation's capital, where they were to be opened and tallied by the president of the Senate (the Vice President) before a joint session of Congress. The candidate receiving the most **electoral votes**, provided it was a majority, would become President; the runner-up would become Vice President. If there were a tie, or if no candidate received a majority of the electoral votes, the House of Representatives was to choose the President. Each state would cast one vote; the winner needed a majority.

In the beginning, the Electoral College plan appeared to work quite well: George Washington won the first two elections by unanimous votes. What the original plan did not anticipate was the rise of political parties. By the end of Washington's second term, the Federalist and Democratic-Republican parties were well established. This created a difficult situation in 1797, when the President and Vice President were of different parties — John Adams, a Federalist, and Thomas Jefferson, a Democratic-Republican. Although troublesome, this problem was minor compared with the election of 1800.

The election of 1800

In 1800 a tie occurred in the Electoral College, because each elector cast his two votes for his party's two candidates, without specifying

Figure 14–2 ELECTORAL VOTES IN FOUR PRESIDENTIAL ELECTIONS The Electoral College results usually exaggerate the popular vote. 8B

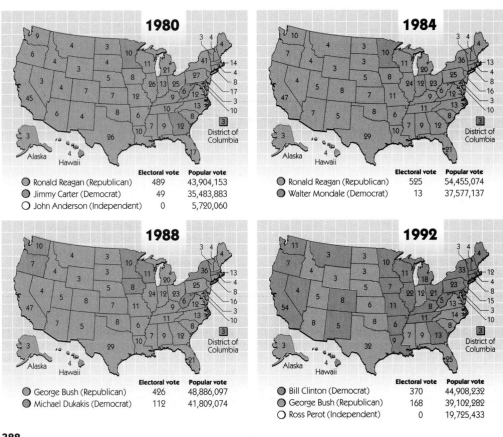

1980	Electoral vote	Popular vote
● Ronald Reagan (Republican)	489	43,904,153
● Jimmy Carter (Democrat)	49	35,483,883
○ John Anderson (Independent)	0	5,720,060

1984	Electoral vote	Popular vote
● Ronald Reagan (Republican)	525	54,455,074
● Walter Mondale (Democrat)	13	37,577,137

1988	Electoral vote	Popular vote
● George Bush (Republican)	426	48,886,097
● Michael Dukakis (Democrat)	112	41,809,074

1992	Electoral vote	Popular vote
● Bill Clinton (Democrat)	370	44,908,232
● George Bush (Republican)	168	39,102,282
○ Ross Perot (Independent)	0	19,725,433

388

Background: *Constitutional Heritage* The 23rd Amendment, which took effect in 1961, granted three electors to Washington, D.C.

Figure 14–2
▲ *Which of the elections was most one-sided in terms of electoral votes?* (Reagan's election in 1984.) *In these four elections, has any state or region consistently supported the Democratic candidate?* (Yes: Minnesota and the District of Columbia.)

which one was to be President and which Vice President. The two Democratic-Republicans, Thomas Jefferson and Aaron Burr, each got 73 votes. The two Federalists, John Adams and Charles C. Pinckney, received 65 and 64 votes respectively. Because of the deadlock, the election was thrown into the House of Representatives.

The Democratic-Republicans clearly intended Jefferson, the party leader, to be President, but the Federalist-dominated House at first backed Burr. Even though Jefferson and he had long been rivals, Alexander Hamilton, the Federalist legislative leader, was even more dismayed at the thought of Burr as President. After 35 ballots, Hamilton was able to persuade enough Federalist members to elect Jefferson President, making Burr Vice President.

The Twelfth Amendment
The election of 1800 showed clearly the growing role of political parties in selecting presidential and vice presidential candidates. More important, the bitterly fought election led to the passage of the Twelfth Amendment in 1804. Among its several provisions, the Twelfth Amendment altered the original Electoral College system to require electors to cast separate ballots for President and Vice President. The Jefferson-Burr problem could not occur again.

4B, 6F

The Electoral College Today

Every four years, presidential elections are held on the Tuesday after the first Monday in November. But to be exact, this is actually the day for selecting *electors*. Many Americans are not aware of this step; in three-fourths of the states, the electors' names do not even appear on the ballot. In those states, a vote for a presidential candidate is assumed to be a vote for the corresponding electors.

Choosing the electors
The Constitution does not specify how electors are to be nominated, but since 1800, political parties have chosen them. As a result, presidential electors are not truly independent, as the delegates to the Constitutional Convention intended, but closely tied to a political party.

Once the voters have cast their ballots, it is up to each state to determine how the electoral vote is to be distributed. Today, every state except Maine and Nebraska awards its electors on an at-large, "winner-take-all" basis. The presidential candidate who receives a plurality of the state's popular vote wins the entire slate of electors. That is, to win a state, a candidate needs more votes than any other candidate (a plurality), but not necessarily a majority.

Technically, these popular votes do not count — and the President is not elected — until the first Monday following the second Wednesday in December. This is the date set by Congress for the electors to meet in their respective state capitals, sign their ballots, and send them to Washington for counting by the president of the Senate. A candidate must have a majority of the electoral votes to become President. Today there are 538 electoral votes (based on 435 representatives and 100 senators, plus 3 votes for the District of Columbia), and so 270 electoral votes are needed to become President. Otherwise, the election is decided in the House of Representatives, where each state has one vote, regardless of size.

6F, 6H

Flaws in the Electoral College

Even in the early years of American government under the Constitution, the Electoral College system was a source of controversy. It is still criticized today for a number of reasons.

The problem of representation
One major criticism of the Electoral College system is that it violates the principle of "one person, one vote." Each state, no matter how small its population, is guaranteed a minimum of three electoral votes. Voters in the smallest states therefore tend to be overrepresented, while voters in the largest states are underrepresented. For example, Wyoming, a state with about 470,000 people, has three electoral votes. With only .18 percent of the total U.S. population, it has .55 percent of the Electoral College vote.

On the other hand, some critics argue that the larger states have too much importance. A candidate could be elected President by carrying only the eleven most populous states.

The "unpopular" Presidents
Another serious flaw in the Electoral College system is the continuing possibility of electing a

---

Civic Participation
● Have students trace the map of the United States on p. 339 and use the information on the number of representatives from each state to figure out the number of electoral votes each state has. (Remind them that the number of electoral votes is equal to the sum of representatives and senators. Also remind them to include the District of Columbia, with three votes.)

Geography
● Explain to students that delegates to the Constitutional Convention from smaller states worried that the more populous states would dominate the presidency. Ask students to consider if that is still a cause for concern. (Yes, since a candidate can be elected by carrying only the eleven most populous states.)

▲ CRITICAL THINKING **Why might the Electoral College system discourage a candidate from campaigning in all fifty states?** (Candidates would want to concentrate their time on the most populous states.)

● CRITICAL THINKING **Why would the direct vote plan encourage presidential campaigning in all fifty states?** (Winning the most populous states would no longer guarantee winning the election.)

Background: *History* Four years after Hamilton helped Jefferson defeat Burr for President, Burr mortally wounded Hamilton in a duel.

Check for Understanding
▲ *Why, under the current Electoral College system, is even the smallest state guaranteed three votes?* (Because each state has two senators and at least one representative, and electoral votes are based on this number.)

The symbol 👥 denotes active participation strategies.

Activities are keyed for student abilities:
▲ = Basic
● = All Levels
■ = Average/Advanced

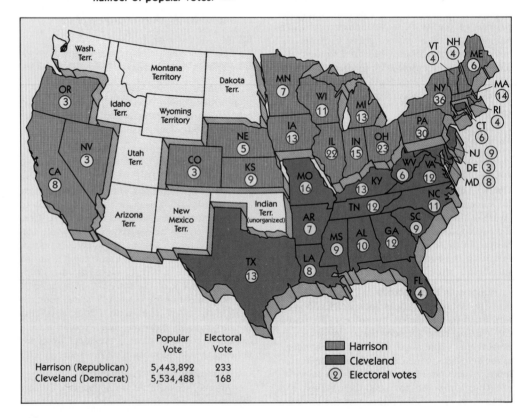

Cooperative Learning

● Divide the class into groups and have each group imagine that its members belong to a Senate select committee formed to study proposals for reforming the Electoral College system. Groups should choose to examine one of the plans discussed in the text, summarizing it and indicating the advantages and disadvantages of the plan.

President who loses the popular vote. John Quincy Adams in 1824, Rutherford B. Hayes in 1876, and Benjamin Harrison in 1888 all received fewer votes than their opponents but won the presidency in the Electoral College or in the House of Representatives.

In other presidential elections, a switch of a few thousand votes could have changed the results. Although Harry Truman defeated Thomas E. Dewey by more than 2 million votes in 1948, a change of about 12,000 Truman votes in Ohio and California would have thrown the election into the House. Similarly, if just 9,000 votes in Missouri and Illinois had switched from Kennedy to Nixon in 1960, the House again would have determined the presidency.

Independent electors

The original intent of the Electoral College was to allow fair and independent electors actually to decide on candidates. Time and party politics have changed this. Nevertheless, electors are not legally bound to cast their votes for the candidate who won their state's popular vote. Although most electors are "pledged" to vote for their state's preference, there have been occasions when so-called "faithless" electors have broken this pledge. Electors have also occasionally violated their state's winner-take-all rule. In 1960, for example, fifteen electors from Alabama, Mississippi, and Oklahoma voted for Senator Harry Byrd of Virginia for President, instead of either John Kennedy or Richard Nixon. Such

Figure 14–3 THE ELECTION OF 1888 Benjamin Harrison was elected President by the Electoral College in 1888 even though Grover Cleveland, the incumbent, received a greater number of popular votes. **8B**

	Popular Vote	Electoral Vote
Harrison (Republican)	5,443,892	233
Cleveland (Democrat)	5,534,488	168

Harrison
Cleveland
② Electoral votes

Background: *History* In the 1876 presidential election Samuel J. Tilden (D) won 184 electoral votes; Rutherford B. Hayes (R) won 165. Twenty votes were in dispute. The commission created by Congress to decide how these votes should be awarded contained eight Republicans and seven Democrats. It voted strictly along party lines, giving the disputed votes and the presidency to Hayes.

Figure 14–3
▲ *What region of the country voted for Cleveland?* (South.) *What regions of the country voted for Harrison?* (North and West.)

votes have never been numerous enough to affect the outcome.

4B, 6C

Electoral College Reforms

For all these reasons, some Americans have long been unhappy with the Electoral College system. A proposed constitutional amendment to change the system has been introduced in nearly every session of Congress since 1789. Proposals for reforms fall into three main types.

Proportional vote plan

The Lodge-Gossett proposal, introduced in 1948, would make the relationship between the popular vote and the electoral vote in each state exactly proportional. Instead of winner-take-all voting, electoral votes in each state would be given to the presidential candidates in proportion to the number of popular votes they received. (Electoral votes would be carried to three decimal places.) If no candidate received a total of at least 40 percent of all the states' electoral votes, a joint session of Congress would be held to select the President between the top two vote-getters.

The proportional vote plan had wide support at first but has since been criticized. The proposal does not balance the votes of large and small states. Each state still receives at least three electoral votes, no matter how small its population. A candidate who loses the popular vote but wins in the "right" states can still win the election. For example, had the proportional vote plan been employed in 1960, John Kennedy, who had 113,000 more popular votes than Richard Nixon, would have lost the presidency by a margin of 263.632 electoral votes to 262.671 electoral votes.

Another consideration is that the plan might encourage the formation of third parties. Under the present system, a third party candidate gets no electoral credit for individual votes unless he or she wins the popular vote in a state. Under the proportional plan, all votes count.

District vote plan

Many reform plans have suggested distributing electoral votes by congressional districts. Under this system, electors would be chosen in the same way as U.S. representatives and sena-

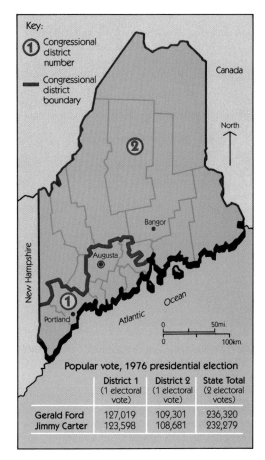

Key:
① Congressional district number
— Congressional district boundary

Canada

North

②

Bangor

Augusta

New Hampshire

① Portland

Atlantic Ocean

Popular vote, 1976 presidential election

	District 1 (1 electoral vote)	District 2 (1 electoral vote)	State Total (2 electoral votes)
Gerald Ford	127,019	109,301	236,320
Jimmy Carter	123,598	108,681	232,279

Figure 14–4 THE DISTRICT VOTE PLAN The state of Maine is an example of the district vote plan in action. 8B

tors. That is, one elector would be chosen from each congressional district (as members of the House are). His or her vote would go to the presidential candidate with a plurality of the popular vote in that district. Two more electors would be chosen at large from the entire state (as senators are). Their votes would go to the candidate with a plurality of the popular vote statewide. The district vote plan is used in Maine, as Figure 14–4 shows. In 1976, Gerald Ford won a plurality statewide and in both districts, taking all four electoral votes. A switch of just 311 votes in District 2, however, would have given Jimmy Carter that district's vote.

391

Background: *Cultural Literacy* Bills are usually named after their congressional sponsors. The Lodge–Gossett proposal described above got its name from its two sponsors, Senator Henry Cabot Lodge (R, MA) and Representative Ed Gossett (D, Texas).

Figure 14–4
▲ Ask students to consider what would happen under Maine's district vote plan if one candidate won by a large majority in District 1, while the other candidate barely won in District 2. *Would the electoral vote of Maine represent the popular vote under those circumstances?* (No.)

GUIDED/INDEPENDENT PRACTICE
● Have students create their own political cartoons expressing their opinions on the Electoral College system.

The symbol 👥 denotes active participation strategies.

Activities are keyed for student abilities:
▲ = Basic
● = All Levels
■ = Average/Advanced

Bill Clinton reaches out to a crowd of supporters in Little Rock, Arkansas, following his Election Night victory speech in November 1992.

Under the district plan, the candidate with a majority of the electoral votes nationwide would become President. If no candidate received a majority, then the newly elected representatives and senators, voting individually, would select the President from among the three highest vote-getters.

Critics of the district plan argue that it still allows the election of a President who has not won the popular vote. Equally important, the plan might increase the temptation for the majority parties in the state legislatures to gerrymander congressional districts to favor their party in the Electoral College.

Direct vote plan

The most popular proposal to replace the Electoral College is the direct vote plan. Under this plan, electors would be eliminated and the President would be chosen by a nationwide popular vote. This proposal offers four main advantages: (1) It is simple to understand. (2) It treats every vote equally, affirming the democratic principle of "one person, one vote." (3) Presidential candidates would be encouraged to campaign in all states, including small states and one-party states. Finally, (4) the person elected President would have to have more popular votes than any other candidate.

Nevertheless, critics find at least one major problem in a direct popular election of the President. The present winner-take-all system strengthens the two-party system and makes it difficult for third-party candidates to succeed. But, like the proportional vote plan, the direct vote would encourage third-party candidates. As more candidates emerge, the chances of the winning candidate getting a majority decreases. Thus, a direct election could result in a President with only a plurality of the vote — perhaps as low as 35 percent. The options then would be to have a run-off election, to allow Congress to decide, or to put up with a President who does not represent a majority of the voters.

Although many Americans favor the direct election plan, the chances of it or other reforms

392

being adopted in the near future appear slim. Any change in the Electoral College requires a constitutional amendment, and it is unlikely that three-fourths of the states would ratify such a proposal. Both large and small states enjoy certain advantages under the present system. Moreover, many leaders of minority groups oppose direct election of the President. Under the present system, electoral votes in competitive two-party states often are swung by cohesive bloc voting. For example, a high voter turnout among Hispanic voters in Dallas or black voters in Philadelphia could decide the winner of Texas's 32 electoral votes or Pennsylvania's 23. Under the direct election plan, the impact of bloc voting in national elections would be minimized.

Finally, like the Electoral College itself, none of the reform plans solves all the problems. Many Americans would prefer not to tamper with the existing system.

SECTION 3 REVIEW

Vocabulary and key terms

Electoral College (387) electoral vote (388)
slate (387) "faithless" electors
electors (387) (390)

For review

1. (a) How are electoral votes divided among the states? (b) If no candidate receives a majority of the electoral votes, who chooses the President? **2A**
2. What change was made in the Electoral College system by the Twelfth Amendment? **2A**
3. What was unusual about the elections of 1824, 1876, and 1888? **6F**
4. What are the two major criticisms of the Electoral College? **6F**
5. What three general plans to reform the Electoral College have been suggested? **6C**

Critical thinking

ORGANIZING AN ARGUMENT List several reasons for changing the Electoral College system. On the basis of these arguments, defend one of the proposals explained in this section, or come up with a proposal of your own. **6C**

Chapter Summary

The President is both the chief of state and the chief executive of the United States. Thus, the President performs ceremonial duties and also runs the government. The Constitution requires the President to be a natural-born citizen, at least thirty-five years old, and to have lived in the U.S. for at least fourteen years. The President's salary and fringe benefits are set by Congress.

The President serves a four-year term beginning on January 20 after the November election. George Washington established the two-term tradition, which became the legal limit with the passage of the 22nd Amendment. The order of presidential succession is set by Congress, while the 25th Amendment provides procedures for cases of presidential disability or the necessity of replacing a Vice President who succeeds to the presidency or leaves office in the middle of a term. The House of Representatives can impeach the President for misconduct; the Senate votes whether to remove the President from office.

The vice presidency has long been considered an insignificant office, even by former Vice Presidents. The Vice President's only official role is to preside over the Senate. In recent years, however, Presidents have assigned their Vice Presidents greater responsibility.

The President and Vice President are chosen by the Electoral College. Each state receives a number of electoral votes equal to its total representation in Congress. In November, voters in each state choose a slate of electors pledged to vote for a pair of candidates. After the controversial election of 1800, the Twelfth Amendment was adopted, requiring electors to cast separate ballots for President and Vice President.

Some flaws in the Electoral College include the possibility of electing a President who loses the popular vote, the problem of "faithless" electors, and the criticism that the system is undemocratic. Proposals to replace the Electoral College have included a proportional vote plan, voting by congressional district, and direct election of the President.

393

Section 3 Review Answers

1. (a) The number of electoral votes for each state equals the total number of its representatives and senators. **(b)** The House of Representatives.
2. Electors were required to cast separate ballots for President and Vice President.
3. The candidate who won the popular vote lost the electoral vote and therefore the election.
4. It violates the principle of "one person, one vote" and allows the election of a President who has not won the popular vote.
5. The proportional vote plan, the district vote plan, and the direct vote plan.

Critical thinking Students may point to the danger of having a President not popularly elected, or to the disparity in importance of large and small states in an election. They may argue for one of the plans described in the text or propose one of their own.

CLOSURE
● Remind students of the pre-reading objectives at the beginning of the section. Pose one or both of these questions again. Then have them read the next assigned lesson.

CHAPTER 14 CORRECTIVES
● To review the content of Chapter 14, you may want to have students complete **Study Guide/Review 14** or **Workbook Chapter 14.**

The symbol ♦♦ denotes active participation strategies.

Activities are keyed for student abilities:
▲ = Basic
● = All Levels
■ = Average/Advanced

CHAPTER 14 REVIEW

Answers

Vocabulary See pages T19–T21 for suggested vocabulary activities.

Reviewing the Facts

1. *Chief executive*—Calls out armed forces, grants pardons, negotiates treaties, appoints ambassadors and judges, recognizes foreign governments, sees that the law is executed. *Chief of state*—Entertains foreign leaders, speaks to charitable organizations.

2. In most other nations, the roles of chief executive and chief of state are separate.

3. A three-year term allowing for re-election; a six- or seven-year term with no opportunity of re-election; election for life; a four-year term allowing for re-election. The last was accepted.

4. After Kennedy was killed, Johnson became President, leaving the vice presidency vacant. The 25th Amendment provides a way of choosing the Vice President if the office becomes vacant.

5. The House. The Senate.

6. The number of electors for each state equals the total number of representatives and senators that the state has in Congress.

7. Members of Congress and holders of any other federal office.

8. Political parties.

9. If one party dominated the state legislature, it could redistrict the state to its own advantage and thereby improve the prospects of its presidential candidate.

10. A constitutional amendment.

Thinking Critically About Key Concepts

1. No. There were no precedents for the office. Ideas varied regarding how much power the President should have.

2. (a) Republicans had opposed FDR's four consecutive terms. After gaining control of Congress after World War II, they proposed

---

● **Review the definitions of the following terms:**

chief executive	electoral vote	"lame duck" amendment
chief of state	electors	presidential succession
Electoral College	"faithless" electors	slate

● REVIEWING THE FACTS

1. Give two examples of the duties of the President as chief executive and the duties as chief of state. **3A**

2. How is the position of President different from the leadership positions in most other modern nations? **1C**

3. During the Constitutional Convention, what were the four different proposals concerning the length of the President's term in office, and which proposal was finally accepted? **2A**

4. How did the assassination of President Kennedy lead to the passage of the 25th Amendment? **8F**

5. Who has the power to impeach federal officials, and who can remove them from office? **3A**

6. How is the number of electors for each state determined? **1D**

7. Who are specifically prohibited from being electors? **3A**

8. What important characteristic of American politics did the original plan for the Electoral College fail to anticipate? **4B**

9. Why is gerrymandering a potential problem with the district vote plan? **4B**

10. What would be required to change the Electoral College system? **6C**

▲ THINKING CRITICALLY ABOUT KEY CONCEPTS

1. Was creation of the office of President easy for the framers of the Constitution? Explain your answer. **2A**

---

2. (a) What role did party rivalry play in the creation of the 22nd Amendment? **(b)** Does the 22nd Amendment help protect rule by the people, or is it an infringement on rule by the people? Present *both* sides of this argument. **3A**

3. Is ensuring a quick and smooth presidential succession more important, or less important, now than it was in past centuries? Explain your answer. **2A**

4. Why did the framers of the Constitution require that both houses of Congress participate in the impeachment and removal from office of a federal official? **3A**

5. (a) Why does the Vice President usually exercise very little power? **(b)** Should the office of Vice President be dissolved? Explain your answer. **3A**

6. (a) How does the Electoral College system serve to strengthen the two-party system? **(b)** Should preservation of the two-party system be a goal of any Electoral College reform? Explain. **3A**

▲ PRACTICING SKILLS

1. Study Skills: Reading a special-purpose map. Refer to Figure 14–2 (page 388) to answer the following questions. (a) Which electoral votes did Walter Mondale win in 1984? (b) In which election did the winner beat the challenger by a margin of 314 votes? (c) Did Ross Perot win the popular vote in any states in 1992? How do you know? (To review map skills, see Study Skill 4 on page 780.) **8B**

---

the 22nd Amendment.
(b) Some claim that the amendment protects rule by the people by preventing the emergence of an overly powerful President. Others claim that by restricting voters' choices, it interferes

with popular rule.
3. Students should note that the power of the federal government has grown and the President now has control over nuclear weapons.
4. It helps ensure that an official will not be removed

from office for purely political reasons.
5. (a) The Vice President has little formal authority except to preside over the Senate. **(b)** Students should explain their answers.

2. **Critical Thinking Skills: Finding the main idea.** Reread the subsection "Proportional vote plan" on page 391. Does the author believe that this plan is likely to replace the Electoral College system? Explain your answer by writing one sentence that represents the main idea of that three-paragraph subsection. **8A**

3. **Critical Thinking Skills: Interpreting a speech.** Refer to President John F. Kennedy's Inaugural Address (page 385). Read the second paragraph of the speech, beginning "The world is very different now." For each of the three sentences in this paragraph, describe or give examples of what you think President Kennedy meant. **4C**

▲ PARTICIPATORY CITIZENSHIP

1. **Examining local history.** Find out more about a President who was born in or near your state. (The birthplaces of the Presidents are listed on pages 810–813.) Do research to discover where he grew up and went to school, what jobs he held before entering politics, and what political offices he held before being elected President. Also find out if there are any schools, memorials, or museums in his name near your community. **2C**

2. **Expressing your views.** Study the Electoral College system and the reform proposals described in Section 3, and decide which method of electing the President you prefer. Then write a letter to your representatives in Congress advocating your view. **8C**

■ WRITING ABOUT ISSUES

1. **Writing a dialogue.** Imagine an argument between two persons on the issue of whether the presidency has become too "imperial" an office, and write down statements and responses of this argument. Refer to the President's salary and benefits, described on pages 381–382, as necessary. **3A**

2. **Expressing your opinion.** The direct vote was not favored by many delegates to the Constitutional Convention, who thought the ordinary voter "was not in a position to judge the candidates' qualifications." Is this still true today? Write a brief essay explaining your opinion. **4D**

3. **Creating a skit.** Write a brief play of the meeting of the Electoral College after the most recent presidential elections. **1B**

▲ ANALYZING A POLITICAL CARTOON

The electoral college system has been criticized by those who favor the direct popular election of the President and Vice President. Its defenders claim the system protects small states and minorities. Look at the cartoon below and answer the following questions.

1. What is the "suggestion box" referred to in the caption? **8B**
2. What is the significance of the age of the figure in the cartoon? **8B**
3. Based on the cartoon, what can you infer about the cartoonists' view of the role of the popular vote in presidential elections? **8A**

"NOW TO GO THROUGH THE SUGGESTION BOX"

Copyright © 1976 by Herblock, The Washington Post.

but also the power to destroy all of human life. And yet, despite our vast power, all people are not free.

Participatory Citizenship

1. You might give students the address of the presidential library of the President under research.
2. Students' letters should justify their views.

Writing About Issues

1. One may say that the trappings of the presidency are inconsistent with the values of a democratic society. The other might argue that the benefits are in keeping with the President's roles as chief executive and chief of state.
2. Students should note that advances in communication have given candidates more exposure, allowing voters to judge their qualifications. Others may argue that even today, voters do not pay close enough attention to candidates, especially in an age when image is given so much attention.
3. Students may choose to have the skit involve an informal meeting of electors from different states before the actual balloting begins.

Analyzing a Political Cartoon

1. The U.S. public vote.
2. The figure is very old, suggesting that the Electoral College is out of date.
3. The cartoonist feels that the popular vote is not considered important by the Electoral College, and that the electoral vote does not reflect the popular vote.

6. **(a)** In most states, it awards all of the electoral votes to one candidate. **(b)** Some will argue that the two-party system provides stability. Others may say that third parties should not be discriminated against.

Practicing Skills

1. **(a)** Minnesota and Washington, D.C. **(b)** 1988. **(c)** No; he did not win the electoral votes of any state.
2. No. The proportional vote plan had wide support at first, but since then sev-

eral valid criticisms of the plan have emerged.
3. *Example:* The world has greatly changed since the first Inaugural Address. We now have the economic power to eliminate poverty

Chapter Review exercises are keyed for student abilities:
▲ = Basic
● = All Levels
■ = Average/Advanced

CHAPTER 15
THE POWERS OF THE PRESIDENT
(pp. 396–419)

	Section Objectives	Section Resources
Section 1 **The President Is a Leader at Home**	☐ identify the powers Presidents exercise in domestic affairs ☐ describe the limits the Constitution places on the President's power to make domestic policy	■ SUPREME COURT DECISION **56**
Section 2 **The President Guides America's Foreign Policy**	☐ distinguish between treaties and executive agreements ☐ describe the President's military powers	▲ SKILLS PRACTICE WORKSHEET **15** ■ CONSTITUTIONAL ISSUES WORKSHEET **11** ● PRIMARY SOURCE WORKSHEET **18** ▲ TRANSPARENCY **35**
Section 3 **Presidential Style Affects Performance**	☐ explain how presidential style influences presidential performance ☐ list the factors that affect presidential popularity	■ SKILLS CHALLENGE WORKSHEET **15** ● SIMULATION **2** ▲ TRANSPARENCY **36**

Essential Elements

The list below shows Essential Elements relevant to this chapter. (The complete list of Essential Elements appears in the introductory pages of this Teacher's Edition.)

Section 1: 2D, 3A, 3B, 3C, 6A, 6F, 7B, 8E, 8F

Section 2: 3A, 3B, 4B, 6H

Section 3: 2C, 3A, 4A, 4B, 5C, 7A, 8B

Chapter Review: 2C, 3A, 3B, 3C, 4A, 4B, 4D, 6A, 8A, 8B, 8C, 8G

Section Resources are keyed for student abilities:
▲ = Basic
● = All Levels
■ = Average/Advanced

Homework Options

Each section contains activities labeled "Guided/Independent Practice," "Reteaching/Correctives," and "Enrichment/Extension." You may wish to choose from among these activities when assigning homework.

Students Acquiring English Activities

Write the following categories on the board: *Executive Powers, Legislative Powers, Judicial Powers, Spending Powers, Diplomatic Powers, Military Powers.* Divide the class into six groups and assign a category to each. Each group should write six examples of specific presidential powers for its category. Collect these items. Then have students create their own bingo boards, choosing four of the categories as column heads. (Each column should have five rows.) Call items out one at a time. Students should decide if the power falls under one of the categories listed on their boards, and if it does, write the power in a square in that column. When a student has filled a row or column with powers, he or she should call out *Powers!*

LISTENING/SPEAKING: Obtain a copy of a presidential address on a military matter, such as Franklin Roosevelt's request for a declaration of war against Japan in December 1941, and read it to the class.

Case Studies

When teaching this chapter, you may use Case Study 6, which addresses the issue of defense budget cuts, or Case Study 11, which debates the question of gun control. (Case Studies may be found following p. 510.)

Teacher Bibliography

Berman, Larry. *The New American Presidency.* Scott, Foresman, 1987. Features case studies of American Presidents since FDR.

Kellerman, Barbara. *The Political Presidency: Practice of Leadership from Kennedy Through Reagan.* Oxford University Press, 1986. An analysis of successful presidential leadership.

Neustadt, Richard E. *Presidential Power and the Modern Presidents: The Politics of Leadership from Roosevelt to Reagan.* Free Press, 1990. How a President obtains and wields power.

Student Bibliography

Bernstein, Carl and Bob Woodward. *All the President's Men.* Simon & Schuster, 1987. The step-by-step story of Watergate as told by the reporters most responsible for uncovering the scandal.

Cunliffe, Marcus. *The Presidency.* 3rd ed. Houghton Mifflin, 1987. An in-depth look at presidential powers.

Plischke, Elmer. *Presidential Diplomacy: A Chronology of Summit Visits, Trips, and Meetings.* Oceana, 1986. The history of presidential diplomacy through a chronology of the Presidents' journeys abroad.

Literature

Donaldson, Sam. *Hold On, Mr. President!* Random House, 1987. Donaldson, a White House correspondent, describes his experiences covering Presidents and American politics in the nation's capital.

Vidal, Gore. *Lincoln.* Random House, 1984. Emphasizes Lincoln's crisis leadership during the Civil War.

CHAPTER RESOURCES

Study Guide/Review 15
Workbook Chapter 15
Chapter 15 Test, Forms A–C

Films and Videotapes*

President of the United States: Too Much Power? 25 min. EBEC, 1972. f. Hubert Humphrey examines presidential power and its checks, analyzing the use of power by Jefferson, Lincoln, the Roosevelts, Truman, Kennedy, and others.

Truman and the Uses of Power. (Series title: *The Truman Years.*) 19 min. LCA (Coronet), 1969. f, v. Illustrates how President Truman enlarged the power of the President. Questions the extent to which national attitudes are influenced by the personality and convictions of the President.

Software*

MECC Dataquest: The Presidents (Apple). MECC. Presents the major contributions and historical context of the 41 Presidents. Students learn to form and answer questions by searching the database and learn to formulate hypotheses based upon the search results.

The Presidency Series (Apple). Focus. This interactive program illustrates how the roles and powers of the modern presidency have evolved beyond the brief description provided in the Constitution. The five programs include: The Nature of the Office, Presidential Roles and Uses of Power, Organization of the Presidency, Who Can Be President?, and Evaluating Presidential Leadership.

* For a complete guide to audiovisual sources, see page T22.

CHAPTER 15

The Powers of the President *(pp. 396–419)*

This chapter examines the powers of the President, both domestic powers and diplomatic and military powers, and discusses the factors that contribute to the success of a President.

Chapter Objectives
After students complete this chapter, they will be able to:

1. Identify the powers Presidents exercise in domestic affairs.
2. Describe the limits the Constitution places on the President's power to make domestic policy.
3. Distinguish between treaties and executive agreements.
4. Describe the President's military powers.
5. Explain how presidential style influences presidential performance.
6. List the factors that affect presidential popularity.

CHAPTER

15

The POWERS of the PRESIDENT

The Buck Stops Here.

Sign on the desk of
President Harry S Truman

396

Photo
Inauguration of
Ronald Reagan.

President Truman had the reputation of being a man who said what he thought — and he was very clear about the presidency. "Being President is like riding a tiger," he said. "A man has to keep riding or be swallowed."

The President is "chief" of just about everything in American politics: chief executive, chief of state, chief legislator, commander-in-chief, chief diplomat, chief politician. Wearing all these political "hats," the President may appear to be the most powerful man on earth. Yet presidential power is limited by the Constitution, Congress, Supreme Court decisions, international crises, economic conditions, political promises, time constraints, and public opinion.

Nevertheless, the President is still held responsible for keeping peace, maintaining economic stability, and establishing coherent policies. Harry Truman was clear about that, too. A sign on his desk declared "The Buck Stops Here." Chapter 15 examines the decisions and responsibilities that land on the President's desk, and how different Presidents have handled them.

CHAPTER OUTLINE

1 The President Is a Leader at Home

Executive Powers
Legislative Powers
Judicial Powers
Spending Powers

2 The President Guides America's Foreign Policy

Diplomatic Powers
Military Powers

3 Presidential Style Affects Performance

Presidential Style
Popularity and Public Opinion

 VIDEOTAPE SERIES

This would be an appropriate place to use Houghton Mifflin's videotape, *Public Opinion and the Presidency.*

SECTION 1

The President Is a
Leader at Home
(pp. 398–406)

Section Objectives
☐ identify the powers Presidents exercise in domestic affairs
☐ describe the limits the Constitution places on the President's power to make domestic policy

Vocabulary
executive order, civil service, executive privilege, pocket veto, item veto, reprieve, pardon, amnesty, impoundment

FOCUS
● Write the word *President* on the board and give students one minute to write down on a sheet of paper all the words, phrases, and images that come to mind in connection with that word. Then ask students to circle the three things on their paper they believe most descriptive and write them on the board. When all students have contributed to the list, ask the class to come up with one or two generalizations that describe their view of the presidency.

2D, 3A, 3B, 3C, 6A, 6F, 7B, 8E, 8F

SECTION 1
The President Is a Leader at Home

> **ACCESS** The Main Ideas
>
> **1** What powers do Presidents exercise in domestic affairs? *pages 398–406*
> **2** What are the constitutional limits on the President's power to make domestic policy? *pages 399–400*

On March 4, 1933, one out of every four American workers was out of a job. Thousands of banks had failed in the previous year, causing millions to lose their life savings. About one million Americans lived in shacks made of old crates without heat or running water. Families struggled to buy food, and the Children's Bureau reported that one out of every five children in the United States was not getting enough of the right things to eat.

March 4 was the day a new President took office. Franklin D. Roosevelt began his term with words of encouragement and strength. "This great nation will endure as it has endured, will revive and will prosper," he reassured Americans. "The only thing we have to fear is fear itself."

Roosevelt followed those words with actions. He declared a bank holiday, called Congress into special session, and pushed for passage of relief and recovery programs.

Roosevelt's actions illustrate the wide scope of presidential power. Roosevelt worked to end the Great Depression by relying on his *domestic* powers, the powers that give the President authority over what happens inside the United States. This section examines both the domestic powers and limitations of the presidency.

2D, 3A, 3B

Executive Powers

The President of the United States, in a sense, acts as the chief executive officer of the largest company in the world. The President is in charge of millions of employees and a yearly budget of more than a trillion dollars. The President has the responsibility for running the vast machinery of American government to carry out the laws and policies of the United States. The executive powers, then, are those that give the President the powers needed to run the country.

Enforcing the law
Just as Congress's principal duties involve lawmaking, the President's chief responsibility is to "take care that the laws be faithfully executed" (Article II, Section 3). Does this provision mean that the President must enforce *every* law? Practically speaking, this is impossible. Presidents have neither the time, money, nor staff to enforce every law strictly. Given these limitations, the President must set priorities. Some Presidents, for example, have placed emphasis on civil rights laws; others have cracked down on crime. Each President's priorities have a great influence on the direction of national policy.

To see that a particular law is carried out, the President can issue an **executive order**. An executive order is a rule issued by the President or the executive branch to help enforce a treaty, a law, a court ruling, or the Constitution. President Lyndon Johnson, for example, used an executive order to begin federal affirmative action plans in 1965. Executive orders do not require congressional approval but have the force of law.

Appointing federal officials
The Constitution grants the President authority to appoint people to fill federal government offices and positions. Presidential appointments to most major government positions must be approved by a majority vote of the Senate. Appointments that require the Senate's "advice and consent" include ambassadors, Supreme Court justices, other federal judges, heads of Cabinet departments and regulatory commissions, federal marshals, and high-ranking White House officials such as the Budget Director. In addition, Congress may permit the President to appoint "inferior officers" without Senate approval. Examples are bureau chiefs, military officers, and most White House staff members.

The power to make appointments is very important. To run the government effectively, the

---

Cross-reference
Thousands of executive orders have been issued and are numbered sequentially in the Federal Register. Chapter 7, pp. 198 and 209, discusses executive orders dealing with civil rights.

Background: *Constitutional Heritage* The Constitution, Article II, Section 2, Clause 2, specifies that the President "shall nominate and . . . with the advice and consent of the Senate shall appoint" ambassadors, diplomats,

judges of the Supreme Court, and other federal officers.

Congressional leaders watch as President Lyndon Johnson signs the bill establishing the Department of Housing and Urban Development in 1965. HUD is concerned with such issues as housing needs, fair housing, and community development. (Presidents often use many different pens to sign major bills, giving them to key people as souvenirs.)

President must be able to choose persons in whom he has confidence and trust. In addition, this power allows the President to reward loyal friends and party members with government jobs. The appointment power thus helps ensure that the President will be surrounded by people who are sympathetic to administration policies.

Limits on the appointment power

There are some constraints on the President's power of appointment. Although most appointments are quickly confirmed, the Senate occasionally rejects the President's choice. For example, in 1832 the Senate refused President Andrew Jackson's nomination of Martin Van Buren to be minister to Great Britain. Two of President Nixon's nominees to the Supreme Court were turned down in 1969 and 1970. After a rejection, the President nominates another person, and the process begins anew.

The number of positions the President may appoint has steadily diminished. Most federal jobs today are filled through the civil service. Under this system, public employees are hired and promoted on the basis of their qualifications rather than their political party affiliation. In 1984, there were more than 1.8 million civilian employees in the executive branch of the federal government (outside the Defense Department).

Of those workers, only about two-fifths of 1 percent were presidential appointees.

The power of removal

The Constitution protects the jobs of federal judges (except in cases of misconduct) but says nothing about the President's power to dismiss other appointed officials. Can the President fire officials because they criticize the administration? Should the Senate have a say in removing an official whose appointment it had to approve? This issue was faced for the first time by the Supreme Court in the 1926 case of *Myers v. United States.*

In 1917 President Woodrow Wilson appointed Frank S. Myers to a four-year term as postmaster of Portland, Oregon. Three years later, Wilson decided to fire Myers. Citing an 1876 statute that said the President could not remove postmasters without the Senate's consent, Myers challenged his removal.

The decision in the *Myers* case was finally handed down in 1926, after both Myers and Wilson had died. The Supreme Court ruled 6–3 that the President does have the authority to remove anyone he has appointed. Chief Justice William Howard Taft, who had once been President, delivered the majority opinion. According to Taft, the power of removal was implied by both the

399

Background: *History* The United States did not appoint its first *ambassadors* until 1893. Until that time, the United States appointed *ministers,* a lower rung on the diplomatic scale.

Background: *Constitutional Heritage* Chief Justice Taft based his opinion in the *Myers* case on "the decision of 1789," a congressional action defining the executive department.

Civic Participation

● Ask groups of students to produce skits on "A Day in the Life of the President." Tell the groups that their skits must include examples of at least five different kinds of presidential powers.

Economics

● *Why would a President want an item veto?* (It would give him more control over the budget.) *Why would Congress oppose giving the President that power?* (It would reduce Congress's control over the budget.)

● CRITICAL THINKING *Do you think the President should have an item veto? Explain.* (Students should balance the potential gain in spending efficiency against the potential loss of congressional power.)

● Have students find out if the governor of your state has item veto power.

President's power to appoint and the authority to see that the laws are faithfully executed. Taft's own experience suggested that Presidents needed this power in order to be fully responsible for their own administrations.

The *Myers* decision appeared to give the President unlimited power to fire officials (except for judges). Nine years later, however, the Court qualified its ruling in a case involving William E. Humphrey, a member of the Federal Trade Commission (FTC). President Franklin D. Roosevelt sought to remove the conservative Humphrey and choose someone more agreeable to his policies. Under the law creating the FTC, however, the President could remove commissioners only for "inefficiency, neglect of duty, or malfeasance in office." Because Roosevelt had failed to show such causes, Humphrey sued for a year's salary. (When Humphrey died, the case was carried out by the executor of his estate.)

The Supreme Court held that the President had overstepped his authority (*Humphrey's Executor v. United States*, 1935). In its decision, the Court distinguished between executive agencies and independent regulatory commissions, such as the FTC. Executive agencies come under the direct control of the President. Control over independent regulatory commissions, however, is shared by Congress and the President. While the President can dismiss officials in other executive agencies, commissioners can be removed only for causes specified in the law.

Executive privilege

Since George Washington, Presidents and top executive officials have claimed the right to withhold information from Congress and the courts. This is known as **executive privilege** (sometimes called "executive immunity"). The Constitution says nothing about this practice. It has been justified under the principle of separation of powers, and because of the need for secrecy in high-level communications. Critics, however, charge that executive privilege can be used to hide questionable executive actions.

The most serious challenge to the practice of executive privilege was the celebrated case of *U.S. v. Nixon* (1974). In October 1973, during the Senate investigation of the Watergate affair, a federal court ruled that President Richard Nixon must turn over his secret White House tape recordings to Special Prosecutor Archibald Cox. Nixon, claiming executive privilege, refused to surrender the actual tapes, and ordered that Cox be fired. "No President could function," Nixon contended, "if the private papers of his office, prepared by his personal staff, were open to public scrutiny."

The question of the White House tapes finally went to the Supreme Court. In July 1974 the Court ruled unanimously against the President. Executive privilege, it said, could not be used to withhold evidence needed in criminal proceedings. The evidence in the tapes — showing that Nixon had in fact ordered the Watergate cover-up — brought about his resignation.

3A, 3B, 6F

Legislative Powers

In addition to carrying out the laws, the President also takes a leadership role in making them. Although only members of Congress may actually introduce and pass laws, in practice the executive branch participates in every stage of the lawmaking process.

Recommending legislation

Many bills introduced in Congress actually originate in the executive branch. The President has several ways of making the administration's lawmaking plans known to Congress. One way is through formal messages and reports. The President is required by law to deliver three legislative messages to Congress.

STATE OF THE UNION ADDRESS The Constitution (Article II, Section 3) provides that the President "shall from time to time give to the Congress information of the state of the Union, and recommend to their consideration such measures as he shall judge necessary and expedient." By custom, the State of the Union Address is given yearly at the beginning of each session of Congress. This gives the President an opportunity to set clear legislative priorities.

From 1801 to 1913, Presidents sent Congress a State of the Union message in writing. In 1913 President Wilson established the current practice of delivering the address personally before a joint session of Congress. Today, the State of the Union message is broadcast nationally over major television and radio networks.

Background: *History* What was termed the "Saturday Night Massacre" began when President Nixon ordered Attorney General Elliot Richardson to fire Special Prosecutor Archibald Cox. Richardson resigned in protest. Richardson's deputy, William Ruckelshaus, also resigned after refusing to dismiss Cox. The White House tapes were eventually turned over to Leon Jaworski, Cox's successor.

Background: *Constitutional Heritage* In *U.S. v. Nixon,* the Court also ruled that executive privilege is absolute for presidential communications regarding military, diplomatic, or sensitive national security matters.

CRITICAL THINKING

Determining Relationships

What happens if you place your hand on a hot burner? You get a burn.

This situation is an example of a **cause-and-effect** relationship. The cause (putting your hand on a hot burner) results in an effect (getting burned). One way to clarify a cause-and-effect relationship is to ask *Why?* Why did something (the effect) happen? The answer to *why* tells the cause.

Look for the cause-and-effect relationship in this sentence: "The President vetoed the bill because he objected to its cost." Why did the President veto the bill (the effect)? He did so because he objected to its cost (the cause).

A cause-and-effect relationship can describe what has happened or what always happens. The prediction of an effect that *may* result from a particular cause is called a **contingency**. A contingency relationship shows the likelihood of one thing causing another. This is an example: "If the rain continues, people will be flooded out of their homes."

★ ISSUE: A Presidential Line-Item Veto?

The line-item veto is a power held by many state governors that allows them to reject part of a bill, particularly an appropriations bill, without rejecting the whole bill. Many people have proposed giving the President the same power over money bills. President Ronald Reagan, for instance, has called the line-item veto "a powerful tool against wasteful or extravagant spending."

Those who oppose the presidential line-item veto say that the issue is not a budget issue but a constitutional issue. They argue that a line-item veto will take power from Congress, thus upsetting the system of checks and balances.

The following excerpts are taken from speeches made in Congress in a 1985 debate over the line-item veto. Read them, looking for cause-and-effect and contingency relationships.

Edward M. Kennedy, U.S. Senator, Massachusetts

Growing support for the line-item veto in the Senate and the House of Representatives is a reflection of the inability of Congress to extricate [remove] itself from the massive federal budget deficit. The budget process is in shambles, the deficit is out of control, and Congress is part of the problem. Our system of checks and balances, which functions adequately, even brilliantly in most areas, is out of kilter in the area of the budget. Congress has too much power over the purse, and the President has too little. The line-item veto . . . is one of the few available tools to redress the balance.

Carl M. Levin, U.S. Senator, Michigan

The line-item veto threatens a significant shift in the balance of power from the legislative branch to the executive branch. Right now . . . members of Congress are presented with bills which frequently have some elements in them which they like and some which they oppose. When asked to vote on a bill, they have to balance the pros and cons. Under current law, the President must do exactly the same analysis in deciding when to sign a bill. With the line-item veto, the President . . . would not have to compromise. He, alone, could pick and choose what would be enacted into law.

Analyzing the Issue

1. According to Kennedy, what is the cause for the growing support in Congress of the line-item veto?
2. What does Kennedy think the contingent effect(s) of a line-item veto would be?
3. According to Levin, what is the effect of having Congress and the President consider bills, parts of which they favor and parts of which they oppose?
4. What does Levin see as a contingent effect of a line-item veto?

401

Analyzing the Issue Answers

1. Congress's difficulties in dealing with the budget deficit.
2. Kennedy thinks a line-item veto would strengthen the system of checks and balances in budget matters.
3. It forces them to assess the pros and cons of a bill and make compromises.

4. Levin thinks a line-item veto would give the President too much power over making laws.

CRITICAL THINKING

Structure of Government
▲ If students are unfamiliar with the concept of a veto, you might have them review the discussion of vetoes on pp. 402–404.

Politics
Point out to the class that both Senator Kennedy and Senator Levin are Democrats, and that the speeches they gave date from Ronald Reagan's presidency.
● CRITICAL THINKING *Why would Kennedy favor a line-item veto when this would give more power to a Republican President?* (His position on the line-item veto was based on constitutional considerations, not political ones.)

The symbol ⅱ denotes active participation strategies.

Activities are keyed for student abilities:
▲ = Basic
● = All Levels
■ = Average/Advanced

Controversial Issues

● CRITICAL THINKING *Do you agree with President Ford's decision to pardon Nixon? Explain.* (Students supporting the decision might claim that it allowed the nation to turn its attention to other issues. Students opposing the decision might argue that it prevented a full disclosure of the events surrounding Watergate.)

Cooperative Learning

● Divide the class into groups and tell the groups to imagine that they are advisers to a newly elected President. Have each group create a short list of priorities for the administration. Each member of the group should contribute at least one idea to the list. Then have the groups present their lists to the class, asking students after each presentation if they would have voted for a candidate who declared those priorities.

President Gerald Ford delivers the State of the Union Message to a joint session of Congress, as the Constitution requires.

ECONOMIC REPORT The Employment Act of 1946 requires each President to submit an Economic Report to Congress each January. This report is prepared by the Council of Economic Advisers, a part of the Executive Office of the President. In it, the President informs Congress about the nation's unemployment, inflation, and economic trends, and makes economic policy recommendations for Congress to consider.

BUDGET MESSAGE The provisions of the Budget and Accounting Act of 1921 place the responsibility for the federal government's financial plans squarely on the shoulders of the President. The President is required to send Congress a written Budget Message no later than fifteen days into each regular session. The Budget Message spells out actual and expected income and expenditures for the federal government. It is prepared by the Office of Management and Budget (OMB), part of the Executive Office.

The President is not limited to these formal messages about legislation. Modern Presidents have used public appearances and press conferences to push for specific measures being considered by Congress. In addition, Presidents and their staff members frequently meet in private with key senators and representatives, urging

them to vote for the President's position on a particular bill.

Approving legislation

Once a bill passes the Senate and the House in identical form, it is sent to the President. To approve legislation, the President has several options: The President may sign the bill, thus making it law. The President may also choose to do nothing. If ten days (excluding Sundays) pass without any action by the President, the bill becomes law without his formal consent.

The veto power

If the President is opposed to a bill passed by Congress, he may choose to veto it. (*Veto* is the Latin word for "I forbid.") The President must then send the bill back to the house where it originated, along with a message explaining the objections. (For example, if the bill was first drafted in the Senate, the President's remarks would be sent there.) Congress, however, may still pass the bill over the President's veto. Overriding a presidential veto requires a two-thirds vote in each house of Congress.

Before the Civil War, Presidents used their veto power sparingly. In fact, from 1789 to 1865, only 36 regular vetoes were issued. (Of these, only six were overridden by Congress.) Some Presidents, such as Thomas Jefferson, John Adams, and John Quincy Adams, vetoed no bills. Beginning with President Andrew Johnson, however, the veto power became a potent presidential weapon. Regular vetoes were used most extensively by Presidents Cleveland and Franklin Roosevelt. (See Figure 15–1.)

Interestingly, very few vetoes are overridden. Through 1990, only about 7 percent of the over 1,400 total regular vetoes were overridden. It is obviously difficult for Congress to muster the two-thirds vote necessary to override a veto. Therefore, the mere *threat* of a presidential veto is often enough to kill a bill.

The pocket veto

One other legislative option is available to the President — the **pocket veto**. Usually, a bill becomes law if the President neither signs nor vetoes it within ten days. But if Congress adjourns during this ten-day period, the President can kill a bill merely by failing to act. This is known as a "pocket" veto.

402

Background: *Politics* The effectiveness of the President's power of persuasion is critical when it comes to sustaining vetoes. With phone calls, invitations to the White House, or promises of help on future campaigns, Presidents can gain support for their position.

8E

Figure 15–1 PRESIDENTIAL VETOES AND OVERRIDES

PRESIDENT	PERIOD	REGULAR VETOES	POCKET VETOES	VETOES OVERRIDDEN
George Washington	1789–1797	2		
John Adams	1797–1801			
Thomas Jefferson	1801–1809			
James Madison	1809–1817	5	2	
James Monroe	1817–1825	1		
John Quincy Adams	1825–1829			
Andrew Jackson	1829–1837	5	7	
Martin Van Buren	1837–1841		1	
William Henry Harrison	1841			
John Tyler	1841–1845	6	4	1
James K. Polk	1845–1849	2	1	
Zachary Taylor	1849–1850			
Millard Fillmore	1850–1853			
Franklin Pierce	1853–1857	9		5
James Buchanan	1857–1861	4	3	
Abraham Lincoln	1861–1865	2	5	
Andrew Johnson	1865–1869	21	8	15
Ulysses S. Grant	1869–1877	45	48	4
Rutherford B. Hayes	1877–1881	12	1	1
James A. Garfield	1881			
Chester A. Arthur	1881–1885	4	8	1
Grover Cleveland	1885–1889	304	110	2
Benjamin Harrison	1889–1893	19	25	1
Grover Cleveland	1893–1897	42	128	5
William McKinley	1897–1901	6	36	
Theodore Roosevelt	1901–1909	42	40	1
William H. Taft	1909–1913	30	9	1
Woodrow Wilson	1913–1921	33	11	6
Warren G. Harding	1921–1923	5	1	
Calvin Coolidge	1923–1929	20	30	4
Herbert C. Hoover	1929–1933	21	16	3
Franklin D. Roosevelt	1933–1945	372	263	9
Harry S Truman	1945–1953	180	70	12
Dwight D. Eisenhower	1953–1961	73	108	2
John F. Kennedy	1961–1963	12	9	
Lyndon B. Johnson	1963–1969	16	14	
Richard M. Nixon	1969–1974	26	17	7
Gerald R. Ford, Jr.	1974–1977	48	18	12
Jimmy Carter	1977–1981	13	18	2
Ronald Reagan	1981–1989	39	39	9
George Bush	1989–1993	29	15	1
Bill Clinton	1993–	*		
Total		1448	1065	104

SOURCE: U.S. Senate Library   *no vetoes as of the end of 1994

403

GUIDED/INDEPENDENT PRACTICE

● Have students draw up a list of presidential powers, arranging the powers in order from the most important to the least important.

RETEACHING/CORRECTIVES

▲ Have students distinguish among the terms in each of the following sets: (a) executive order, executive privilege; (b) regular veto, pocket veto, item veto; (c) reprieve, pardon, amnesty.

Figure 15–1
■ *Is a President who makes and sustains many vetoes necessarily more powerful than one who makes few vetoes? Explain.* (Not necessarily. If a President has consistent majority support in Congress for his policies, relatively few bills opposed by the President will come out of Congress in the first place.)

The symbol 👥 denotes active participation strategies.

Activities are keyed for student abilities:
▲ = Basic
● = All Levels
■ = Average/Advanced

A pocket veto differs from a regular veto in two important ways. First, a pocket veto does not require a presidential explanation, letting the President avoid touchy political issues. More important, Congress has no chance to override a pocket veto (since it has adjourned). A bill cannot be carried over from one Congress to the next.

The item veto

A legislative power enjoyed by most state governors, but not the President, is the **item veto** (sometimes called a "line" or "line-item" veto). An item veto lets an executive cancel parts of a bill while signing the rest into law. Governors usually use item vetoes only for appropriations bills. Advocates of a presidential item veto believe it would help the President balance the federal budget, cutting out riders and "pork-barrel" legislation. Opponents argue that giving the President such power would seriously undermine Congress's legislative powers and its responsibility for federal spending.

Special sessions of Congress

As Chapter 13 discussed, the Constitution allows the President to call either or both houses of Congress into special session. The President has no authority, however, to determine the legislative agenda for this session. Nonetheless, a timely call for a special session can work to the President's advantage.

In the summer of 1948, the Republican National Convention nominated Governor Thomas Dewey of New York to be its presidential standard-bearer. The Republicans also endorsed a platform calling for sweeping governmental reform. Soon after the convention, President Harry Truman, a Democrat, called a special session and challenged the Republican-controlled 80th Congress to fulfill its promises. When Congress failed to act, Truman made the "Do-Nothing Congress" an issue in his successful campaign for re-election.

3A, 3B, 3C, 6A

Judicial Powers

Although the courts, particularly the Supreme Court, hold the judicial power of the United States, the President also has some powers in the judicial system. For example, it is the President who appoints most federal judges. In addition, the President has some powers that allow him to negate federal court decisions.

Under Article II, Section 2, the President has the power to grant **reprieves** and **pardons** for crimes against federal (but not state) laws. A reprieve is a delay in carrying out a punishment. Such a postponement might enable persons convicted of a crime time to find evidence to prove their innocence. A pardon is a release from punishment, either "absolute" or "conditional." An absolute pardon wipes out all charges. A conditional pardon requires a person to complete some obligation (such as paying a fine) before the charges are dropped.

Pardons are granted for a variety of reasons. The President might believe that someone has been wrongly convicted or has already paid his or her debt to society. A striking illustration was President Reagan's conditional pardon of Marvin Mandel, former Democratic governor of Maryland. In 1977 Mandel and five others were sentenced to federal prison for mail fraud and racketeering. In 1981, after Mandel had spent nineteen months in jail, Reagan ordered his release. The President pointed out that Mandel had already served a longer sentence than his co-defendants. Reagan also pardoned one of Mandel's co-defendants.

The most controversial presidential pardon was given by one President to a former President. After Richard Nixon resigned the presidency in 1974 to avoid impeachment for his role in the Watergate scandal, his successor, Gerald Ford, issued a pardon. Ford's action prevented Nixon from being charged with criminal misconduct relating to Watergate. The new President hoped this would, in effect, bring Watergate to an end and heal the divisions in the country.

Amnesty

Sometimes Presidents confer a general or blanket pardon on a group of people, usually for political offenses. This is known as **amnesty**. President Thomas Jefferson granted amnesty to those convicted of violating the Alien and Sedition Acts passed by the previous administration. (These acts prohibited "false, scandalous, and malicious" remarks about the government and called for the deportation of dangerous aliens.) President Andrew Johnson in 1867 extended am-

Democratic presidential candidate Bill Clinton visits a relief distribution area in Florida, following Hurricane Andrew. The August 1992 storm devastated the southern region of the state. Congress approved over $9 billion in relief funds to parts of Florida declared disaster areas.

nesty to former Confederate soldiers. More recently, in 1977 President Carter gave amnesty to all Vietnam War draft evaders.

Presidential pardons and amnesties have occasionally been challenged. Congress tried to block President Johnson's amnesty proclamation after the Civil War. The Supreme Court ruled, however, that Congress lacked such authority (*Ex parte Garland,* 1867).

There are some legal restrictions on the President's pardoning power. The Constitution specifies that pardons do not extend to cases of impeachment. In addition, the President may not pardon those convicted of *state* crimes. For instance, only the governor of a state — not the President — may stop the execution of a person given the death penalty under state law.

3A, 3B, 7B

Spending Powers

In principle, Congress controls the national government's purse strings, holding the exclusive power to appropriate money (Article I, Sec-

tion 9). In practice, though, the President has a great deal of control over government spending.

Emergency funding

Congress cannot possibly anticipate every emergency that might occur in the nation. To deal with unexpected crises, Congress has established a number of emergency funds. These are "lump-sum" appropriations that the President can spend in national emergencies. A typical example is the Federal Disaster Act of 1950, which allows the President to declare a "national disaster" following a flood, earthquake, drought, tornado, or similar emergency. For example, in the summer of 1993, torrential rains caused record flooding and destruction along the Mississippi and Missouri rivers. In response, President Clinton declared Iowa and parts of Missouri, Illinois, and Arkansas disaster areas, making billions in federal funds available to help flood victims.

The power not to spend

Nowhere in the Constitution does it say that the President must spend money appropriated by Congress. Beginning with Thomas Jefferson in

405

Background: *Constitutional Heritage* The President's inability to grant pardons to those convicted of state crimes is a good example of the federal system, since state and national executive powers are here clearly separated.

The symbol 👥 denotes active participation strategies.

Activities are keyed for student abilities:
▲ = Basic
● = All Levels
■ = Average/Advanced

5. The President cannot pardon impeached officials or those convicted of state crimes.

Critical thinking Impoundment threatens the separation of powers by giving the President, rather than Congress, control over spending.

CLOSURE

● Summarize the main ideas of the lesson by having students read the first paragraph of the Chapter Summary on p. 417. Then have students read Section 2, noting the many diplomatic and military powers of the President.

SECTION 2

The President Guides America's Foreign Policy *(pp. 406–412)*

Section Objectives
☐ distinguish between treaties and executive agreements
☐ describe the President's military powers

Vocabulary
ambassador, diplomatic recognition, treaty, executive agreement

FOCUS
● Ask students to suggest a story in today's news that is about foreign affairs or military policy. Have them identify the role of the President in these current events. *Do you approve of the job the President is doing in setting foreign policy? Explain your answer.*

406

1803, Presidents have occasionally refused to spend money Congress has authorized. This practice is called **impoundment**. For the most part, impoundment has been confined to military spending. Using their authority as commander-in-chief, Presidents Truman, Eisenhower, Kennedy, and Johnson all refused to spend money for what they thought were unnecessary weapons.

President Nixon, however, used the impoundment power to drastically cut domestic spending. During his first term, Nixon impounded nearly $40 billion in non-military funding, cutting back programs in agriculture, highway construction, education, welfare, and the environment. Some of these appropriations had been passed by Congress over Nixon's veto. The President contended his action was necessary to control inflation. Congress, however, saw impoundment as a threat to its authority.

To regain its control over government spending, Congress enacted the Budget and Impoundment Control Act of 1974. This act provides, in part, that the President must notify Congress if he intends to withhold funds. Either house of Congress can then vote to force the President to spend the funds in question. Opponents have charged that this act contains a legislative veto, but it has not been tested in court.

SECTION 1 **REVIEW**

Vocabulary and key terms

executive order (398)   item veto (404)
civil service (399)   reprieve (404)
executive privilege (400) pardon (404)
State of the Union   amnesty (404)
  Address (400)   impoundment (406)
pocket veto (402)

For review

1. What are some limits on the President's power to appoint and remove federal officials? **3B**
2. Why was executive privilege denied in the case of the White House tapes? **3A**
3. What are the President's four options for action on a bill? **3B**
4. What are the arguments for and against the item veto? **3B**
5. What limits are there on presidential pardons? **3A**

Critical thinking

EXAMINING BASIC PRINCIPLES Explain how the President's use of impoundment creates a conflict between the principles of separation of powers and of checks and balances. **3B**

3A, 3B, 4B, 6H

SECTION 2 The President Guides America's Foreign Policy

┌─ **ACCESS** ─ The Main Ideas
1 What are the President's diplomatic powers? *pages 406–410*
2 What is the President's role as commander-in-chief of the military? *pages 410–412*

At 2 AM on the morning of August 2, 1990, 100,000 Iraqi troops crossed into Kuwait, marching toward its capital. By the end of the day, Iraqi soldiers controlled the oil-rich country and stood poised on the border of Saudi Arabia, a nation with even larger petroleum reserves.

406

American officials believed that Iraq's actions posed a great threat to United States interests. Within days President George Bush had frozen Iraqi and Kuwaiti assets in the United States, imposed economic sanctions against Iraq, ordered U.S. military forces to Saudi Arabia, and spoken with the leaders of such nations as Japan, Britain, the Soviet Union, Saudi Arabia, and Turkey, to organize an international response to Iraq's aggression.

President Bush was fulfilling his constitutional responsibilities. It is the President's job to serve as top diplomat and commander-in-chief.

Cross-reference
Chapter 12, p. 334, discusses the 1983 *Chadha* case, in which legislative vetoes were found unconstitutional.

Cross-reference
Sovereignty is defined and discussed in Chapter 1, pp. 6–7.

President and Mrs. Nixon's trip to China in 1972 was an important step in the establishment of diplomatic relations with the People's Republic.

3A, 3B

Diplomatic Powers

To most of the world, the President represents the United States — its people and its policies. The diplomatic powers give the President the authority to speak for the United States.

Appointing diplomatic representatives

Overseas, the United States is represented by thousands of diplomatic and consular personnel, who are members of the Foreign Service (a branch of the State Department). Under the Constitution, the President appoints diplomatic representatives with Senate approval.

Ambassadors are the highest-ranking diplomats. The President appoints an ambassador to most foreign countries recognized by the United States. These men and women are the President's personal representatives, with full responsibility for carrying out U.S. foreign policy in the country to which they are assigned. Some ambassadors are friends or political supporters of the President, but most are "career diplomats" who have spent many years in the Foreign Service.

A number of other Foreign Service officers serve in U.S. embassies and consulates abroad. Depending on their rank, they monitor foreign events, convey messages, protect American citizens abroad, safeguard American economic interests, issue visas, and conduct negotiations.

Recognizing foreign governments

In addition to naming diplomatic personnel, the President has the authority to recognize foreign governments by receiving their diplomatic representatives. This power belongs solely to the President and does not require the consent of Congress. Thus, President Harry Truman was able to extend official diplomatic recognition to Israel on May 14, 1948, the day it declared its independence.

On the other hand, the President can use this power to refuse to recognize a government. Following the Russian Revolution of 1917, Presidents Wilson, Harding, Coolidge, and Hoover all refused to recognize the legitimacy of the Soviet Union. Not until 1933 did President Franklin Roosevelt extend diplomatic recognition to the

407

Politics

● **Why might Presidents want to make executive agreements rather than negotiate treaties?** (Executive agreements do not require the President to go through the time-consuming process of winning Senate approval.)

Constitutional Heritage

Read students the following statement by Harry Truman: "If there is one basic element in our Constitution, it is civilian control of the military."

▲ **How did the framers of the Constitution seek to ensure civilian control of the military?** (They made the President commander-in-chief of the armed forces.)

● CRITICAL THINKING **Why would it not be practical to place the armed forces under the joint command of the President and Congress?** (Congress is too large a body to make the quick decisions sometimes necessary in military affairs. Also, joint command would create the potential for stalemate between the President and Congress; this could endanger national security.)

President Bill Clinton joined six other leaders at a 1994 economic summit in Naples, Italy. The 1994 "Group of Seven" summit also included Russian President Boris Yeltsin.

Soviet Union. Similarly, after the Chinese Communists took control of mainland China in 1949, American Presidents refused to recognize the People's Republic of China. Instead, recognition was extended to the government of Nationalist China (Taiwan). In 1972, however, President Nixon made overtures, including an exchange of ping-pong teams, that gradually led to diplomatic relations. In 1979, President Jimmy Carter formally recognized the People's Republic.

Demonstrating other uses of diplomatic powers, Carter in 1979 broke off diplomatic relations with the government of Iran. He acted after Americans in Iran were taken hostage by Iranian students backed by the Khomeini government. In 1991, when hard-line conservatives took power in the Soviet Union, President Bush instructed the new United States ambassador, Robert Strauss, not to present his credentials. After coup leaders were overthrown a few days later, Strauss made his official presentation in Moscow.

Treaty-making

In addition to heading America's diplomatic corps, the President has the sole authority to enter into formal agreements, or **treaties**, with foreign nations. The treaty-making powers give the President authority to negotiate with foreign leaders on behalf of the United States and to make treaties, which must be ratified by two-thirds of the Senate. Since independence, the United States has been involved in roughly 1,300 treaties. Two notable examples are the Partial Nuclear Test Ban Treaty of 1963 and the Panama Canal Treaty of 1978.

The treaty-making process involves a number of steps:

1. The President begins negotiations with the leaders of foreign governments. Actual arrangements are usually worked out by the State Department.
2. The President talks with the foreign leaders. Before such meetings, Presidents usually find it wise to consult with key senators, especially members of the Senate Foreign Relations Committee.
3. Once an agreement is reached, the proposed treaty is sent to the Senate for approval. The Senate can accept the treaty (by a two-thirds vote), reject it, or impose conditions on it. Few treaties are rejected outright by the Senate. More often, the Senate kills a treaty by imposing unacceptable conditions.
4. If the Senate imposes conditions, the President may either try to get the other parties to agree or drop negotiations altogether.
5. Once the Senate approves the treaty, and it is signed by the President and foreign leaders, it becomes law. Article VI of the Constitution (the "supremacy clause") provides that "all treaties made . . . under the authority of the United States, shall be the supreme law of the land." This means that treaties take precedence over state constitutions, state laws, or even acts of Congress.

Executive agreements

Perhaps even more important than negotiating treaties is the President's power to engage in **executive agreements**. An executive agreement is an agreement between the President and a head of a foreign government that does not require the Senate's approval. The Constitution does not mention such agreements, but the Supreme Court has made it clear that they command a dignity and status similar to that of treaties (*U.S. v. Pink,* 1942). To date, American Presidents have engaged in about 11,000 executive agreements—more than 9,500 since 1940.

408

Background: *History* In the Partial Nuclear Test Ban Treaty, the United States and other nations agreed to stop testing nuclear weapons in the atmosphere and under water.

Background: *History* An example of Senate response to a treaty (#4 above) is the Treaty of Versailles ending World War I. The Senate refused to ratify it unless President Wilson agreed to change the provision calling for a League of Nations. Wilson refused, and the United States did not sign the treaty.

S omeone unfamiliar with American politics might assume that every four years, candidates fight an honest, civilized battle for the right to become President. Andrew Jackson would disagree. During the election of 1828, his opponents unfairly called him an adulterer, slave-trader, gambler, drunk, and murderer. Jackson's opponents were engaging in **mudslinging**—using wild, unsubstantiated charges to attack a political opponent.

The History of Mudslinging

Presidential campaigns throughout American history are filled with colorful examples of mudslinging. In 1796 Thomas Jefferson's opponents called him a trickster, coward, and anarchist. They called his followers, "cut-throats who walk in rags and sleep amidst filth and vermin." In the election of 1844 Henry Clay's opponents claimed that Clay had systematically violated every one of the Ten Commandments!

The campaign of 1860 was particularly noteworthy because of the intense emotions generated by the fight over slavery. Some newspapers were extremely hostile to the candidates, especially Abraham Lincoln. The *Houston Telegraph* remarked that:

> Lincoln is the leanest, lankest, most ungainly mass of legs and arms and hatchet face ever strung on a single frame. He has most unwarrantably abused the privilege, which all politicians have, of being ugly.

Mudslinging did not stop in the twentieth century, although it gradually lessened in severity. In 1916 Woodrow Wilson was accused of carrying on two affairs that caused his wife Ellen to die of a broken heart. In 1928 rumors circulated that if Democrat Al Smith, a Catholic, were elected, Protestant marriages would be annulled. Lyndon Johnson's supporters produced a television commercial in 1964 implying that a vote for opponent Barry Goldwater was a vote for nuclear war. In 1980 Jimmy Carter raised eyebrows by suggesting that if Ronald Reagan won the election, "Americans might be separated, black from white, Jew from Christian, North from South, rural from urban." Bush supporters were accused of racism during the 1988 election when they produced commercials implying that Michael Dukakis's support of prison furlough programs in Massachussetts had led to the death of a Maryland man. (One of the prisoners released under the furlough program, an African American named Willie Horton, had killed the man, who was white.)

Mudslinging will likely continue to be part of the American political landscape. Sometimes the mud "sticks" to those who sling it as well as to the victims. As Adlai Stevenson said with tongue-in-cheek in 1954, "He who slings mud generally loses ground."

CRITICAL THINKING

1. Why might the vicious personal attacks that characterized elections in the 1800's be less frequent today?
2. What was Adlai Stevenson's view of mudslinging? Do you agree with it or not? Explain your answer.

CIVIC LITERACY

6G

Political Mudslinging in Presidential Campaigns

CIVIC LITERACY

Values

Explain to students that just as a division can be made between attacks on a person and attacks on his or her political views, it is possible to divide personal attacks into different categories.

▲ CRITICAL THINKING *What kind of personal criticism was made of Lincoln?* (That he was ugly.) *What kind of personal criticism was made of Wilson?* (That he was unfaithful and cruel to his wife.)

● CRITICAL THINKING Ask students whether attacks on a person's appearance are a legitimate part of a campaign, and to what degree voters should consider a candidate's character flaws when voting.

Critical Thinking Answers

1. Extensive media coverage of public figures gives voters a great deal of information about those figures. Personal attacks are less effective on candidates already known to the public.

2. Stevenson believed that mudslinging harmed those who practiced it, rather than its intended victims. Students should defend their opinions.

The symbol 👥 denotes active participation strategies.

Activities are keyed for student abilities:
▲ = Basic
● = All Levels
■ = Average/Advanced

Controversial Issues

● Have students work in pairs to draw political cartoons expressing their opinion of the War Powers Act.

Cooperative Learning

● Divide the class into groups and have the groups create charts listing the diplomatic and military powers of the President, as well as some examples of those powers. Groups may choose to write out the examples or illustrate them with photographs or drawings. Each member of the group must take responsibility for at least one specific power included in the chart.

U.S. Army tanks advance across the Saudi Arabian desert into Kuwait. For five months Iraqi forces occupied Kuwait, before a multinational armed force directed by the United States drove them out in early 1991.

There is no logical dividing point between treaties and executive agreements. Like treaties, executive agreements have been used for a wide variety of foreign-policy issues. They have been used to settle boundary disputes, establish fishing rights, annex territory, regulate trade, and create military bases, to list just a few. Executive agreements can be concluded quickly and secretly. Moreover, they do not require the President to consult the Senate.

Understandably, some senators have voiced concern over the widespread use of executive agreements. They complain that most treaties sent to the Senate deal with trivial matters, while important issues are settled by executive agreements. The practice is restricted somewhat by the Case Act of 1972, which requires the President to report all executive agreements to Congress within 60 days. All things considered, executive agreements give the President almost unlimited power to conduct foreign policy.

3A, 3B, 6H

Military Powers

The President as commander-in-chief

The President's military powers are spelled out in the Constitution: the President shall be "commander-in-chief of the Army and Navy of the United States, and of the militia of the several states, when called into the actual service of the United States." This clause ensures that the President, a civilian, has supreme command over the military. It is the basis for many of the President's powers over foreign affairs. The President also has command of the U.S. Coast Guard, Marines, and Air Force.

The National Guard (the state militia) is normally under the jurisdiction of the state governor, though it is trained by the national government. But the President can use his power as commander-in-chief to press the Guard into action — even over the objections of a governor. This was the case, for example, at Little Rock (Arkansas) Central High School in 1957 (page 201).

Although Presidents rarely overrule military decisions, a dramatic use of this presidential power took place during the Korean War in 1951. General Douglas MacArthur, a popular hero of World War II, commanded United Nations forces helping the South Koreans resist an invasion by Communist-held North Korea. When Chinese troops crossed the border to reinforce the North Koreans, MacArthur called for an all-out attack on China. President Truman and UN officials, however, did not want to expand the war. When MacArthur persisted in demands for the bombing of China, Truman fired him as commander. Despite outcries from Congress and the public, the President's decision was final.

410

Background: *History* While commanding forces in Korea, General MacArthur had been highly critical of President Truman, publicly voicing his criticisms of the commander-in-chief.

Though many Americans saw MacArthur as a military hero and were angered by his firing, there was also widespread support for the principle that the general must obey his commander.

There are limits on the President's power as commander-in-chief. For example, in the early 1950's a dispute broke out between the steel workers and their employers. The United Steel Workers of America called a nationwide strike in April 1952. Believing that a halt in steel production would hurt the war effort in Korea, President Truman ordered his Secretary of Commerce, Charles Sawyer, to seize and operate the steel plants. The owners of the steel companies reluctantly cooperated with Sawyer, but decided to take him to court in the meantime. They claimed that the President's action was illegal interference with their business.

In *Youngstown Sheet and Tube Company v. Sawyer* (1952), the Supreme Court agreed that the President's power as commander-in-chief did not include the power to end labor disputes. "This is a job for the nation's lawmakers," said Justice Black, "not for its military authorities."

Conflicts over military powers

In principle, Congress appears to have the greatest power over military operations. Only Congress can declare war and appropriate money for the armed forces. In practice, however, determined Presidents can usually get what they want militarily.

For example, in 1907 President Theodore Roosevelt wanted to send the U.S. Navy on a world tour. Congress disliked the idea and threatened to withhold necessary funding. "Very well," said Roosevelt. "The existing appropriation will carry the Navy halfway around the world, and if Congress chooses to leave it on the other side, all right!" Congress quickly supplied the money.

A more serious problem is "undeclared wars." Senator Barry Goldwater once remarked, "We have been in only five declared wars out of over 150 that we have fought." This may be an exaggeration. Still, throughout American history, Presidents have used their authority as commander-in-chief to order military operations without a congressional declaration of war. For example, in 1801 President Jefferson sent ships to fight North African pirates without consulting Congress. President Theodore Roosevelt took military action in Panama and the Dominican Republic in 1903 and 1904, while President Wilson sent troops into Mexico several times.

The most serious "undeclared wars" were those in Korea, Vietnam, and the Persian Gulf. Although all are appropriately called "wars," none was fought under a formal declaration.

THE WAR IN KOREA The Korean War began in 1950 when Communist North Korean forces invaded South Korea. Without seeking Congress's approval, President Truman sent U.S. troops to join United Nations forces aiding South Korea. Before a truce was finally declared in 1953, over 54,000 Americans had died. Over 100,000 other Americans were wounded.

THE WAR IN VIETNAM American involvement in Vietnam developed more slowly and was more complex. During World War II, many nationalist movements against colonial rule took root in Southeast Asia. In 1950, Truman sent 35 military advisers to help the French maintain their colonial rule. In 1954 the French withdrew, and Vietnam was divided. The government in South Vietnam was friendly to the United States. A Communist government under Ho Chi Minh ruled the north and sought to reunite the country. To assist South Vietnam, Presidents Eisenhower and Kennedy sent military advisers and economic aid. By 1963 there were about 15,000 advisers in Vietnam without any act of Congress.

In 1964 events took a dramatic turn. U.S. destroyers were reportedly attacked by North Vietnamese ships in the Gulf of Tonkin. President Johnson asked Congress for authority to fight back. Congress overwhelmingly passed the Gulf of Tonkin Resolution, which, short of a formal declaration of war, allowed the President to take the steps necessary to protect American troops.

When the nation's longest war officially ended in 1973, American losses were some 58,000 killed, more than 153,000 wounded, and many others reported as prisoners or missing in action. At home, controversy over the war had caused deep and bitter divisions among Americans.

THE PERSIAN GULF WAR In August 1990, Iraqi forces invaded and annexed neighboring Kuwait. Despite an international uproar, Iraq's President Saddam Hussein refused to withdraw and even threatened to invade Saudi Arabia. Protesting this aggression, the U.N. passed a resolution imposing a trade embargo against Iraq. The United States' initial involvement was to protect Saudi Arabia. Without seeking approval from Congress, President Bush sent 200,000 U.S.

411

Background: *Constitutional Heritage* Justice Robert H. Jackson wrote in a concurring opinion to *Youngstown Sheet and Tube Co. v. Sawyer,* "The Constitution did not contemplate that the title commander-in-chief of the Army and Navy will constitute him also commander-in-chief of the country, its industries, and its inhabitants. He has no monopoly of 'war powers,' whatever they are."

GUIDED/INDEPENDENT PRACTICE
● Have students complete **Primary Source Worksheet 18,** which examines President Eisenhower's address on the military-industrial complex.

RETEACHING/CORRECTIVES
▲ Have students identify the type of presidential power being illustrated in each of the pictures in this section.

Have students complete **Skills Practice Worksheet 15,** which reviews the domestic and foreign powers of the President.

You may also want to use **Transparency 35,** a political cartoon on President Nixon's trip to China.

ENRICHMENT/EXTENSION
■ Have students complete **Constitutional Issues Worksheet 11,** which analyzes presidential power in foreign affairs.

The symbol ⅱ denotes active participation strategies.

Activities are keyed for student abilities:
▲ = Basic
● = All Levels
■ = Average/Advanced

Section 2 Review Answers

1. Recognizing a foreign government by receiving its diplomatic representatives.

2. The President negotiates with foreign leaders. If an agreement is reached, the proposed treaty is sent to the Senate, where it is either approved by a two-thirds vote, rejected, or altered. If approved and signed by both nations, it becomes law.

3. **(a)** Because they can be implemented quickly and secretly, without the approval of the Senate. **(b)** Because it does not follow the constitutional call for Congress to be consulted.

4. Under their power as commander-in-chief.

5. The President may not dispatch troops unless there is a national emergency, Congress declares war, or a specific law authorizes such an action.

Critical thinking *For*—The President's power to send troops is too broad; the heavy losses and social upheaval caused by undeclared wars in the past have shown the need for congressional involvement. *Against*—The President needs the freedom to be able to take swift military action if necessary.

CLOSURE

● Ask students to consider the various presidential powers described in this section and suggest the power they consider most important. Students should explain their choice. Then have students read Section 3, comparing the style and popularity of past and present Presidents.

---

troops to Saudi Arabia to deter an Iraqi invasion and enforce UN sanctions.

When the sanctions did not have the desired effect, Bush sent more troops and equipment to Saudi Arabia, but Hussein refused to budge from Kuwait. The UN granted the allied coalition the authorization to use "all necessary means" to force the Iraqis to withdraw. In the coming weeks, a divided Congress debated the issue of using American forces to liberate Kuwait. On January 12, 1991, both the House and Senate voted to support the use of force.

On January 16, 1991, the allied forces began air assaults on Iraqi military targets. These air assaults continued for several weeks before the ground troops were dispatched to drive the Iraqis out of Kuwait. Once the ground assault began, the conflict was ended in short order and Kuwait was liberated. Estimates of casualties were fewer than 150 Americans and more than 100,000 Iraqis killed in combat.

The War Powers Act

The heavy losses in Korea and Vietnam raised serious questions about the President's power to engage American troops in undeclared wars. To limit such wars, Congress passed the War Powers Act of 1973. This law, which was passed over President Nixon's veto, restricts the President's use of American troops abroad. Specifically, the President may not send troops unless (1) Congress declares war, (2) a law authorizes such action, or (3) there is a national emergency.

If there is a national emergency, the President can send troops without consulting Congress but must notify Congress within 48 hours. Thereafter, American troops may not remain abroad longer than 60 days without congressional approval. At any time, Congress can require the President to withdraw American forces by passing a concurrent resolution.

The War Powers Act has been invoked several times. For instance, in 1983 President Reagan sent troops to Beirut, Lebanon, as part of the United Nations peacekeeping forces. When the 60-day limit expired, Congress granted the President an 18-month extension. Shortly thereafter, terrorists bombed the American military installation, killing 241 sailors and marines. The remaining troops were soon withdrawn.

The War Powers Act does not forbid the Presi-

---

dent from taking military action. For example, in 1980 President Carter launched an unsuccessful mission to rescue American hostages in Iran. In 1989 President Bush ordered U.S. troops into Panama to protect Americans there and to apprehend dictator General Manuel Noriega for trial on federal drug-trafficking charges. Two years later President Bush sent 4,000 U.S. troops to provide food relief for starving people in the African country of Somalia. In 1993 President Clinton ordered additional forces to Somalia to protect American soldiers attacked by rebel fighters.

In each of these cases, the President notified Congress within the War Powers Act's two-day limit, *after* taking action. In some cases, the President told congressional leaders shortly before the action. Still, some said Congress as a whole should have been notified in advance.

The War Powers Act has not been challenged in the courts, but it is controversial. Some believe it puts too many restrictions on a President's military powers, amounting to a legislative veto. Others say it restores to Congress the right to declare war. Others believe the term "national emergency" is so ambiguous it lets the President send troops anywhere, anytime.

SECTION 2 REVIEW

Vocabulary and key terms

Foreign Service (407)
ambassador (407)
diplomatic recognition (407)

treaty (408)
executive agreement (408)
commander-in-chief (410)
War Powers Act (412)

For review

1. What is "diplomatic recognition"? **3A**
2. What are the steps in negotiating a treaty? **3A**
3. (a) Why might a President prefer executive agreements to treaties? (b) Why would Congress object? **3B**
4. Under what power have Presidents engaged American troops in undeclared wars? **6H**
5. What limits does the War Powers Act place on the President? **3A**

Critical thinking

ORGANIZING AN ARGUMENT Should the President's military powers be limited? List several arguments for and against this point of view. **3A**

Background: *History* The coalition forces' ground attack on Iraqi-held Kuwait, known as Operation Desert Storm, began on February 24, 1991. (Because of differences in the time zones, it was still February 23 in the United States.) Though allied forces liberated Kuwait City and President Bush announced the suspension of offensive actions on February 27, the cease-fire did not formally take effect until April 6.

Presidential Style Affects Performance

ACCESS | The Main Ideas

1 How does presidential style influence presidential performance?
pages 413–415

2 What factors affect presidential popularity?
pages 415–417

In your opinion, who was the greatest President of the United States? Who was the worst? How did you determine your choices?

People have been evaluating Presidents ever since George Washington took the first oath of office in 1789. They have examined presidential priorities, actions, and decisions. Most evaluations — including probably your own — also take into account the personal style of the Presidents, as well as the public's response to that style. Often it has been the President's personality and presentation that determined how successful he was.
2C, 4A, 4B, 5C

Presidential Style

The personal approach that characterizes each President can be termed *style*. Style results from an overlapping combination of personality traits, political philosophy, background, and past experiences. Political scientists have studied the presidency from each of these different standpoints.

Attitudes toward power

The Constitution gives Presidents considerable leeway in taking and using the powers of the office. Some Presidents interpret the Constitution very strictly, and are unlikely to take any powers that previous Presidents have not used. They take history as their roadmap for future actions. Such Presidents use power sparingly and are willing to let Congress take policy initiatives. Historical examples include James Madison, James Buchanan, William Howard Taft, and Dwight Eisenhower (in his first term).

At the other end of the spectrum are Presidents who interpret their powers broadly. Presi-

dents with this philosophy break with tradition and chart their own courses by taking bold, decisive actions. Most flourish during times of crisis — war or economic hardship. Examples include George Washington, Andrew Jackson, Abraham Lincoln, Theodore Roosevelt, and Franklin Roosevelt.

Character traits

Another way of looking at Presidents as people was developed in the 1970's by political scientist James David Barber. Barber believed that it is possible to predict how Presidents will perform in office by understanding what kind of person they are and the patterns of their childhoods and early careers. These are an indication, at least, of how they will look at issues and make decisions in office.

From his study of past Presidents, Barber came up with four character types. These depend on different combinations of two factors: energy level and attitude toward one's work.

Basing his judgment on how much energy Presidents put into their job, Barber classified them as *active* or *passive*. Active Presidents not only put in long hours of intense action, but also exert strong leadership, chart new directions, and devise innovative policies. Presidents with passive personalities, on the other hand, are more relaxed and devote less time and energy to being President. They are inclined to let Congress take charge.

Presidents' personalities (according to Barber) can also be judged by how much they enjoy politics in general and their job as President in particular. *Positive* Presidents enjoy the power and responsibilities of the office. They like the challenge and are confident of meeting it. *Negative* Presidents, on the other hand, serve out of a sense of civic duty or a wish to prove themselves. They find the job burdensome but think they should do it.

Presidents, like people in general, are too complex to fit these classifications absolutely. Yet each one tends toward one end of the active/passive, positive/negative scales. Figure 15–2

Section Objectives
☐ explain how presidential style influences presidential performance
☐ list the factors that affect presidential popularity

 FOCUS

● Take a quick poll of the class to determine students' approval rating of the present President. Ask if they highly approve, somewhat approve, somewhat disapprove, or highly disapprove of the President's performance. Have students calculate the percentage of the class approving of the President.

Background: *History*
Students should note that many observers disagree with Barber's way of classifying Presidents. For example, critics have argued that Eisenhower was not a passive-negative President. These critics have cited evidence that behind the scenes Eisenhower was a very active politician.

The symbol denotes active participation strategies.

Activities are keyed for student abilities:
▲ = Basic
● = All Levels
■ = Average/Advanced

EXPLANATION

After reviewing the content of the section, you may want to consider the following activities:

👥 Civic Participation

● CRITICAL THINKING Find a large, recent photograph of the President in a newspaper or magazine and cut it into an oval shape to resemble the pictures on this page. Attach the photo to a large posterboard or to the chalkboard and underneath the photo write *Characteristics* and *Examples*.

Have students suggest adjectives that describe the President, and fill those in next to *Characteristics*. Then have students give examples of actions the President has taken that illustrate those adjectives, and write those next to *Examples*.

■ CRITICAL THINKING Finally, have the class determine if the President's character traits are positive or negative and if the President's style is passive or active.

Science and Technology

● CRITICAL THINKING *Why have effective communication skills become more important to Presidents?* (With the invention of radio and television, it has become possible for the President to reach the entire nation.)

■ CRITICAL THINKING *How do the skills helpful for holding a press conference differ from those helpful for making televised speeches?* (Press conferences require a firm knowledge of the issues and the ability to think quickly. Speeches require good eye contact, timing, and expressiveness of tone.)

Figure 15–2 PRESIDENTIAL CHARACTER TRAITS One way of describing Presidents' personalities is to look at the ways they approach this demanding job. 8B

POSITIVE

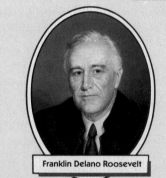

Active

Franklin Delano Roosevelt

- **Characteristics:** highly energetic, self-confident, flexible, dynamic
- These Presidents aim for results and want to make significant contributions to the art of government.
- **Examples:** Franklin Roosevelt, Harry Truman, John Kennedy

Passive

Warren Harding

- **Characteristics:** likable, agreeable, cooperative
- These Presidents want to be loved and respected by others.
- **Examples:** William Taft, Warren Harding

NEGATIVE

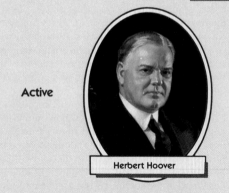

Active

Herbert Hoover

- **Characteristics:** ambitious, aggressive, inflexible, eager for power
- These Presidents take criticism personally and are hurt and angered by it.
- **Examples:** Woodrow Wilson, Herbert Hoover, Lyndon Johnson, Richard Nixon

Passive

Calvin Coolidge

- **Characteristics:** virtuous, principled
- These Presidents enter political life out of a sense of duty but often try to remain "above politics," avoiding political conflict.
- **Examples:** Calvin Coolidge, Dwight Eisenhower

414

Figure 15–2
■ *What is a problem with using categories this general to analyze presidential personalities?* (They are subjective; most Presidents' personalities are too complex to fit neatly into one category.)

shows how some 20th-century Presidents have combined these characteristics.

Powers of persuasion

Harry S Truman once said, "The principal power that the President has is to bring people in and try to persuade them to do what they ought to do *without* persuasion. That's what I spend my time doing. That's what the powers of the President amount to." Not all Presidents, however, are equally skilled at persuading others. This, too, is a question of style.

Modern Presidents have many ways of persuading others. Some are skilled in using one-on-one discussions to influence legislators to support administration policies. For example, the President might invite key committee chairpersons to breakfast at the White House. Presidents Lyndon Johnson and Gerald Ford, both of whom served years as party leaders in Congress, were very successful with this technique.

Perhaps the most influential tool of persuasion available to modern Presidents is the mass media. Gifted Presidents, for instance, know just when to call a press conference and how to answer questions posed by newspaper and TV reporters. Presidents Kennedy and Reagan both used the media skillfully. Both were witty and charming and usually maintained good relationships with news correspondents. Other Presidents have been less at ease, stumbling over their replies or losing their tempers.

Live broadcasts on television and radio enable Presidents to bypass reporters and speak directly to the people. President Franklin Roosevelt was particularly effective in using the radio. During the Great Depression, his famous "fireside chats" helped reassure the nation in warm, comforting tones. President Reagan, an experienced actor, became known as the "great communicator" for his mastery of television. The relaxed, confident image Reagan projected helped him to gain public support for many of his policies.

2C, 3A, 4A

Popularity and Public Opinion

While presidential style influences performance, the President's performance also depends on what people expect and on the circumstances and crises of the time. To perform well in office, one thing that Presidents need is the support of the American people. But Americans are not always clear or consistent about what we expect from the President.

Public expectations

One political scientist has identified the following as some of the contradictory ideas Americans have about the presidency:

- Americans desire a common person to be President, but expect uncommon leadership. That is, we want the President to be "one of us," but we also want our President to be someone of whom America can be proud. The President is supposed to symbolize America's best.

- Americans want the President to be bold and decisive yet moderate. If a President acts too boldly, he may be accused of acting like a dictator. But if he fails to take decisive action, he may be accused of being "weak."

- Americans expect the President to represent the majority but protect minority rights.

- Americans expect the President to stand "above politics," yet any presidential candidate must be a skillful political leader.

- Americans want the President to be strong and tough-minded, but also concerned and caring.

Presidential popularity

How well a President meets these expectations is reflected in public opinion of his performance. Since 1945 the Gallup Poll has periodically asked Americans: "Do you approve or disapprove of the way (the incumbent) is handling his job as President?" The results are published as presidential approval ratings.

A study of these ratings reveals several patterns (see Figure 15–3). For example, when the economy is slumping, the President's approval rating tends to drop. Presidents are nearly always blamed for problems of high unemployment, inflation, and recession. For example, President Reagan's lowest approval rating in his first term (35 percent) was recorded in January 1983. Not surprisingly, this occurred when unemployment reached 10.4 percent and the economy appeared stagnant.

415

History
● Have students examine Figure 15–3 and identify the more popular and less popular Presidents. (For example, Kennedy, Reagan, and Bush were more popular; Ford and Carter were less popular.)
● CRITICAL THINKING **Would it be possible for a President who was not popular while in office to be judged later a "great President"? Explain.** (Yes, if the President's policies involved short-term sacrifices for long-term gains or if the President understood better than most people of the time what policies would best benefit the nation.)

Values
● CRITICAL THINKING Have students examine the chart of the Presidents on pp. 810-813. Have them use the chart and their own knowledge to choose the five greatest and five worst Presidents. (You might want to refer to **Transparency 36** to compare their choices with those of historians.) Then ask them to determine where on the scale of greatness the current President would fall. If there is strong disagreement among students, you could hold a class debate on this issue.

Background: *History*
Lyndon Johnson was Senate Majority Leader before being elected Vice President in 1960. Gerald Ford was House Minority Leader before being appointed Vice President in 1973.

Background: *Cultural Literacy* The political scientist who identified the contradictory ideas Americans hold about the presidency is Thomas Cronin.

The symbol 👥 denotes active participation strategies.

Activities are keyed for student abilities:
▲ = Basic
● = All Levels
■ = Average/Advanced

Cooperative Learning
● Have students perform **Simulation 2,** which deals with a presidential news conference.

GUIDED/INDEPENDENT PRACTICE
● Have students review the subsection "Public expectations" on p. 415 and write a short essay explaining why each of the five ideas Americans have about the presidency contains a contradiction.

RETEACHING/CORRECTIVES
▲ Have students write thesis statements expressing the main idea of each of the subheadings of the section.

You may want to use **Transparency 36,** which provides a rating system for Presidents.

ENRICHMENT/EXTENSION
■ Have students complete **Skills Challenge Worksheet 15,** which asks them to interpret an excerpt from a biography of Harry Truman.

During crises, however, the President's popularity almost always increases. In times of crisis, Americans put aside their differences to support the President. Some observers call this the "rally round the flag" phenomenon. For example, in 1985 President Reagan was diagnosed as having colon cancer, and his approval ratings rose sharply. Likewise, after Iraq's 1990 invasion of Kuwait led President Bush to order troops into the Persian Gulf, his popularity shot up.

Every President's approval rating tends to decline over time, however. Even international crises cannot guarantee a President's popularity indefinitely. Although President Bush's popularity skyrocketed during the Persian Gulf crisis, it declined steadily thereafter. This was due largely to the public's perception that the economy was stagnant and showing no signs of improvement. The only exception to the crisis trend was President Eisenhower, whose popularity rating remained fairly high and stable during his eight years in office.

Rating the President
A President's popularity while in office is not necessarily reflected in the way history judges his performance. Over the past decades, historians and political scientists have made several lists of "best" and "worst" Presidents. All surveys have consistently named Abraham Lincoln as our "best" President. Washington, the two Roosevelts, and Jefferson round out the top five. Other

Figure 15–3 PRESIDENTIAL POPULARITY POLLS, 1981–1994 A President's popularity is affected by economic conditions at home, events abroad, and the administration's actions. 8B

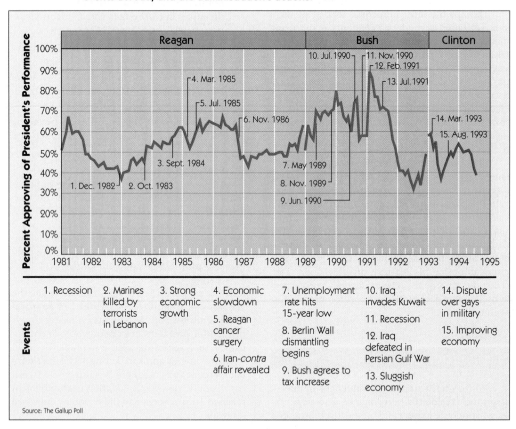

Source: The Gallup Poll

Figure 15–3
● **Based on the chart, what type of event leads to a decline in a President's approval rating?** (An economic slowdown.) **What type** of event leads to an increase in a President's approval rating? (An upswing in the economy, a crisis.)

Presidents often rated in the top ten are Wilson, Jackson, and Truman.

The surveys' unanimous choice for ''worst'' President is Warren G. Harding. Nonetheless, Harding was very popular in the 1920's. When he died in office, thousands of grief-stricken Americans waited along the route of his funeral train. The experts are less unified in choosing the other ''ten worst'' Presidents. Two 1982 surveys included in this category Presidents Richard Nixon, U.S. Grant, James Buchanan, Andrew Johnson, Franklin Pierce, and Calvin Coolidge.

The presidential dilemma

In essence, Presidents are often caught in a ''no-win'' situation. What the public expects tends to exceed what is humanly possible. The President cannot be all things to all people. Perhaps this is why Thomas Jefferson once remarked, ''No man will ever bring out of the presidency the reputation which carries him into it.''

This is not to suggest that the President is powerless. As we have seen, the office is vested with vast powers. The President, to be successful, must learn when and how to use power — wisely and within the limits of the Constitution. As Clinton Rossiter puts it, ''There is virtually no limit to what the President can do if he does it for democratic ends and by democratic means.''

SECTION 3 REVIEW

For review

1. Why can a President's personality have such a great effect on the office itself? **4A**
2. What are two contrasting approaches to presidential power? **3A**
3. How do ''positive'' and ''negative'' Presidents differ in the way they regard being President? **4A**
4. What national problems almost always lower a President's popularity rating? **7A**

Critical thinking

DRAWING INFERENCES   Looking at the active/passive, positive/negative profiles of the Presidents in Figure 15–2, which of the four types do you think would make the best Presidents? Why? Are there times in history when Americans might prefer a different type? Why? **4A**

Chapter Summary

The President shares power over American domestic policy with Congress and the courts. As chief executive, the President carries out the laws passed by Congress and appoints federal officials not covered by the civil service. The President also takes part in the lawmaking process by recommending legislation to Congress, approving it or using the veto power, and using executive orders to set policy. The President can also grant reprieves, pardons, and amnesty to individuals or groups who have broken federal laws. The President has emergency spending powers and in some cases may use impoundment to stop the spending of funds allocated by Congress.

The President has almost exclusive power over foreign affairs. The President, with senatorial consent, appoints all diplomatic personnel and alone decides whether to grant diplomatic recognition to other governments. The President can negotiate treaties, which require the Senate's consent, or enter into executive agreements with the heads of other states, without congressional approval. Although Congress has the power to declare war and provide for the armed forces, President as commander-in-chief has almost complete control over the military and can even engage in ''undeclared wars.'' With the War Powers Act Congress attempted to regain its control over making war; some critics, however, believe this law may be unconstitutional.

How Presidents use their powers can depend on personal factors such as their view of presidential power, the level of energy they bring to the job, and whether they enjoy their duties. Presidents' use of persuasion may also determine how they achieve their policy goals. The American people often have conflicting expectations of Presidents, which, despite all their powers, Presidents can rarely fill. How well a President meets the public's expectations is measured in presidential popularity polls. History's view of a President may be very different from contemporary opinion, however.

Section 3 Review Answers

1. Since the Constitution does not specify how the office should be run, each President's individual style affects how powerful the office will be.
2. Some Presidents interpret their powers strictly and use them sparingly, while others interpret those powers broadly and take decisive actions.
3. "Positive" Presidents enjoy the office; "negative" Presidents serve out of a sense of duty or a need to prove themselves.
4. High unemployment, inflation, and recession.

Critical thinking Students should explain why one type makes a better President, using past or present Presidents as examples. At specific times in history, such as wars or domestic crises, Americans are likely to prefer a more assertive and decisive President than at calmer times.

CLOSURE

● Remind students of the pre-reading questions at the beginning of the section. Pose one or both of these questions again. Then have students read the next assigned lesson.

CHAPTER 15 CORRECTIVES

● To review the content of Chapter 15, you may want to have students complete **Study Guide/Review 15** or **Workbook Chapter 15.**

Background: *History*   Much of Warren Harding's poor reputation as a President stems from the scandals caused by his associates while he was in office. The most famous case of corruption during Harding's administration—the Teapot Dome scandal—resulted in the imprisonment of the Secretary of the Interior for accepting bribes.

The symbol **ïï** denotes active participation strategies.

Activities are keyed for student abilities:
▲ = Basic
● = All Levels
■ = Average/Advanced

CHAPTER 15 REVIEW

Answers

Vocabulary See pp. T19–T21 for suggested vocabulary activities.

Reviewing the Facts

1. The Senate may reject an appointment; the growth of the civil service system has limited the number of presidential appointees.
2. State of the Union, Economic Report, and Budget Message.
3. *Approve*—Sign the bill or do not do anything for ten days. *Kill*—Veto the bill or do not do anything if it is within ten days of Congress's adjournment.
4. The federal government extends diplomatic recognition. The President.
5. The Senate must approve the treaty for it to become law. The Senate can reject a treaty or impose conditions on it, forcing the President to renegotiate it.
6. Besides authorizing money to pay for the wars, Congress passed the Gulf of Tonkin Resolution in 1964 authorizing President Johnson to escalate U.S. involvement in Vietnam, and Congress voted to support the use of force against Iraq in 1991.
7. The President may not send troops unless Congress has declared war, there is a specific law authorizing the action, or there is a national emergency.
8. Such crises almost always send the approval rating up.

Thinking Critically About Key Concepts

1. **(a)** The regular veto, unlike the pocket veto, calls for specific action and an explanation.
(b) Students may argue against eliminating the pocket veto, because without it bills would have to be carried over to the next legislative session.
2. **(a)** Since the 1940's executive agreements have become a substitute for treaties in many cases.
(b) This has allowed the President

● **Review the definitions of the following terms:**

ambassador	executive order	pocket veto
amnesty	executive privilege	reprieve
civil service	Foreign Service	State of the Union Address
commander-in-chief	impoundment	treaty
diplomatic recognition	item veto	War Powers Act
executive agreement	pardon	

● **REVIEWING THE FACTS**

1. What are the two major constraints on the President's power to appoint federal officials? **3B**
2. What three official messages is the President required to present to Congress? **3A**
3. Which two options may a President use to approve legislation? Which two may be used to kill legislation? **3B**
4. Is diplomatic recognition extended by the federal or state governments? Which official is responsible? **3C**
5. What is the Senate's role in making treaties with foreign nations? **3B**
6. What actions did Congress take to support the wars in Vietnam and the Persian Gulf? **3A**
7. What are the main restrictions on a President's use of American troops according to the War Powers Act of 1973? **3B**
8. What is the usual effect of an international crisis on the President's approval rating, or popularity? **4A**

▲ **THINKING CRITICALLY ABOUT KEY CONCEPTS**

1. **(a)** Which of the two types of presidential veto is the more honest and responsible action? Why? **(b)** If you were in Congress, would you vote to eliminate the pocket veto by allowing bills to be carried over to the next Congress? Why or why not? **3B**

418

---

2. **(a)** How has the use of executive agreements changed over time? **(b)** What does this indicate about the powers of the President today regarding foreign affairs, as opposed to his position in earlier times? **3A**
3. How do the Constitution, custom, and acts of Congress affect presidential messages to Congress regarding the administration's legislative wishes? **3A**
4. How can the use of executive agreement and executive privilege give the President the power to wage hidden wars? **3A**
5. What skills does a President need in order to use the mass media as an effective tool for changing public opinion? **4B**
6. **(a)** To what degree do you think television has altered the way in which the U.S. public views a President or presidential candidate? **(b)** What are the advantages and dangers of vastly increased presidential access to the public through television and other mass media? **4B**

▲ **PRACTICING SKILLS**

1. **Study Skills: Reading a table.** Refer to Figure 15–1 (page 403) to answer the following questions. **(a)** Which three Presidents issued the greatest total number of vetoes? **(b)** Which two Presidents served with a Congress that overrode more than half of their regular vetoes? **8B**
2. **Study Skills: Analyzing a photograph.** **(a)** How does the photo on page 405 illus-

---

to increase his power and independence in foreign affairs.
3. The Constitution calls only for a State of the Union Address, customarily given orally at the start of each session of Congress; legisla-

tion calls for the Economic Report and Budget Message.
4. The President could make an executive agreement with the head of a foreign country to supply arms or money for a foreign war, and then refuse to

release information about such actions, citing executive privilege.
5. It helps to be witty, charming, relaxed, and confident, especially on television.

trate Bill Clinton's leadership style? (b) Do you think this photograph helped Clinton's popularity or harmed it? Why? **8B**

3. **Critical Thinking Skills: Comparing and contrasting.** Refer to Figure 15–3 (page 416). Prepare a table to compare and contrast the effect of crises in foreign affairs on presidential approval ratings. In the first column, write each President's name. In the second column, write each foreign crisis (some Presidents had none; some had more than one). The heading for the third column should be "Approval Rating." Put either an arrow pointing up or an arrow pointing down in this column, depending on whether the crisis sent the approval rating up or down. **8G**

▲ PARTICIPATORY CITIZENSHIP

1. **Writing to the President.** Write a letter to the President on a domestic or foreign policy issue that you feel strongly about. **4D**
2. **Polling public opinion.** Perform the Gallup Poll's public opinion survey on presidential popularity (page 415) among the members of your grade or school. Compare your findings with the results of the national survey. **4A**

■ WRITING ABOUT ISSUES

1. **Writing an essay.** President Lincoln said of making presidential appointments: "Filling a patronage job creates nine enemies and one ingrate." Write an essay explaining his quote and addressing the question of whether most Presidents would prefer not to have to make such appointments. **2C**
2. **Composing a speech.** Write a five-minute speech for the President on the issue of foreign aid. Remember that you are not writing for yourself, and try to take the President's personal style into account. **8C**
3. **Summarizing information.** Look up print material that deals with a recent presidential military action. Examples include the war

with Iraq and the sending of U.S. forces to Somalia. Write a summary of a news story or an editorial on the action. **4B**

▲ ANALYZING A POLITICAL CARTOON

Although the concept of executive privilege is mentioned nowhere in the Constitution, the President and other executive department officials have occasionally claimed that it means that they are not obligated to give documents or testimony to Congress. This was one of the defenses used by President Nixon during the Watergate investigation. Look at the cartoon below and answer the following questions.

1. What legendary event is being recalled in the cartoon? **8B**
2. In the original version of the story, what did George Washington say? **6A**
3. In comparison with Washington's response, how does the cartoonist view President Nixon's response? **6A**
4. Is the cartoon effective? Why, or why not? **8A**

I claim executive privilege.

Cartoon by Bill Mauldin. Reprinted with permission from the Chicago Sun-Times.

3. Check students' tables against the information in Figure 15–3.

Participatory Citizenship

1. Students may wish to choose a current issue.
2. Students should be consistent in their questioning and should double-check the figures.

Writing About Issues

1. Lincoln may have meant that the people he did not appoint were upset and turned against him, while those he did appoint tended to be disloyal. Still, most Presidents enjoy the right to make appointments to ensure that their administration is run by people they know and trust.
2. Students should do some research to find out the President's stand on this issue.
3. Summaries should include the main points of the article.

Analyzing a Political Cartoon

1. George Washington chopping down the cherry tree.
2. "I cannot tell a lie." He admitted cutting down the tree.
3. The cartoonist suggests that by claiming executive privilege, Nixon has tainted the image of the presidency.
4. By comparing Nixon to Washington, the cartoon emphasizes the sense of lying and betrayal surrounding Nixon's involvement in the Watergate scandal.

---

6. (a) Students may note that individual personality has become more important than political party affiliation. (b) *Advantages*—Direct appeal to voters, increased information available to voters. *Dangers*—Appeal is

much more emotional, possibility for demagoguery increased.

Practicing Skills

1. (a) Presidents Cleveland, F. Roosevelt, and Truman. (b) Pierce and A. Johnson.

2. (a) He is shown as involved, active, informal (by the way he is dressed), and accessible. (b) Probably helped his image, since he is shown as active, aware, and involved in a time of crisis.

Chapter Review exercises are keyed for student abilities:
▲ = Basic
● = All Levels
■ = Average/Advanced

CHAPTER 16
GOVERNMENT AT WORK
(pp. 420–445)

	Section Objectives	Section Resources
Section 1 **The Executive Office Advises the President**	☐ identify the agencies that make up the Executive Office of the President and state their functions ☐ distinguish between the pyramid and circular styles of presidential management	
Section 2 **Cabinet Departments Carry Out Policies**	☐ explain how Cabinet departments are organized ☐ trace the changing role of Cabinet members	■ SKILLS CHALLENGE WORKSHEET **16**
Section 3 **The Government Works Through Independent Agencies**	☐ distinguish among independent regulatory commissions, government corporations, and executive agencies ☐ explain how federal agencies work with outside contractors	▲ SKILLS PRACTICE WORKSHEET **16** ▲ TRANSPARENCY **37**
Section 4 **The Civil Service System Controls Government Jobs**	☐ give reasons for the growth of the merit system in the federal government ☐ describe the benefits and drawbacks of working under the civil service system	● CITIZENSHIP WORKSHEET **6**

Essential Elements

The list below shows Essential Elements relevant to this chapter. (The complete list of Essential Elements appears in the introductory pages of this Teacher's Edition.)

Section 1: 2C, 3A, 5C, 8B

Section 2: 2C, 3A, 4B, 4C, 6A, 8B, 8H

Section 3: 3A, 3B, 4B, 7C, 7D

Section 4: 2C, 2E, 3A, 4A, 4C, 8B

Chapter Review: 3A, 4A, 4C, 4D, 7C, 8A, 8B, 8C, 8H

Section Resources are keyed for student abilities:
▲ = Basic
● = All Levels
■ = Average/Advanced

Homework Options

Each section contains activities labeled "Guided/Independent Practice," "Reteaching/Correctives," and "Enrichment/Extension." You may wish to choose from among these activities when assigning homework.

Students Acquiring English Activities

Divide the class into groups and have each group create an illustrated time line on butcher paper showing the fourteen executive departments, starting with the first department created (Treasury in 1789) and ending with the last one established (Veterans Affairs in 1989). Students should look through magazines to find appropriate pictures, write to the departments for informational brochures, and/or draw their own illustrations.

LISTENING/SPEAKING: Have students check the telephone directory for the names of any federal agencies that are of interest to them. Ask the class to choose one of these agencies and then have volunteers invite a speaker from that agency to address the class.

Case Studies

When teaching this chapter, you may use Case Study 10, which examines the issue of required national service for all eighteen-year-olds. (Case Studies may be found following p. 510.)

Teacher Bibliography

Acheson, Dean. *Present at the Creation: My Years in the State Department*. Norton, 1987. An inside look at the Department of State.

Mackenzie, G. Calvin, ed. *The In-And-Outers: Presidential Appointees and Transient Government in Washington*. Johns Hopkins University Press, 1987. Spotlights the drawbacks of the presidential appointment system.

Rosen, Howard. *Servants of the People: The Uncertain Future of the Federal Civil Service*. Olympus, 1985. Defends the federal civil service as an institution, while pointing out its deficiencies.

Student Bibliography

Alexander, Kent. *Countdown to Glory: NASA's Trials and Triumphs in Space*. Price/Stern/Sloan, 1989. This history of the American space program is richly illustrated.

McCarthy, Dennis V. and Philip W. Smith. *Protecting the President: The Inside Story of a Secret Service Agent*. Dell, 1987. One man's story of protecting Presidents from Johnson to Reagan.

Literature

Clancy, Tom. *Clear and Present Danger*. Putnam, 1989. A special operation is set up to stop drug smuggling by the Colombian cartel. The novel analyzes the legal and ethical issues involved in this covert military campaign.

Knebel, Fletcher and Charles W. Bailey. *Seven Days in May*. Bantam, 1988. The President and six trusted men attempt to foil a government takeover.

Lewis, Sinclair. *Arrowsmith*. Harcourt Brace Jovanovich, 1990. An ambitious doctor who finds he is unable to work in public health because of its political aspects examines the issues of medical ethics and success. Pulitzer Prize winner.

CHAPTER RESOURCES

Study Guide/Review 16
Workbook Chapter 16
Chapter 16 Test, Forms A–C

Films and Videotapes*

Diplomatic Channels. (Series title: *Inside Story*.) 29 min. PBS, 1984. v. Hodding Carter discusses how the professional work of reporters has changed from the days of closed-door diplomacy to today's current informal chats via satellite with diplomats, speculating on the effect on government officials.

The Executive Branch. (Series title: *Branches of Government*.) 22 min. NGS, 1982. f, v. Shows how actions of the executive branch affect people's lives.

Software*

American Government V (Apple, IBM, Macintosh). Queue. Students learn about the development and processes of American government using three interactive tutorials. The programs cover the judiciary, federal and state courts, the Supreme Court, the civil service, the federal bureaucracy, and the executive branch.

* For a complete guide to audiovisual sources, see page T22.

419B

CHAPTER 16

Government at Work *(pp. 420–445)*

This chapter examines the organizations that are responsible for the day-to-day operation of the federal government, including the Executive Office of the President, the Cabinet departments, the many independent commissions and agencies that work outside the Cabinet departments, and the civil service system.

Chapter Objectives
After students complete this chapter, they will be able to:

1. Identify the agencies that make up the Executive Office of the President and state their functions.
2. Distinguish between the pyramid and circular styles of presidential management.
3. Explain how Cabinet departments are organized.
4. Trace the changing role of Cabinet members.
5. Distinguish among independent regulatory commissions, government corporations, and executive agencies.
6. Explain how federal agencies work with outside contractors.
7. Give reasons for the growth of the merit system in the federal government.
8. Describe the benefits and drawbacks of working under the civil service system.

CHAPTER
16

GOVERNMENT
at WORK

The very essence of a free government consists in considering offices as public trusts, bestowed for the good of the country, and not for the benefit of an individual or a party.

John C. Calhoun
U.S. Senator (1835)

Photo
Pennsylvania Avenue, Washington, D.C.

On an average day, the United States Postal Service handles about 226 million first class letters. The Department of Veterans Affairs spends $26 million on medical services for the nation's more than 27 million veterans. About 154,000 visitors enter national parks, 701 young people enlist in the armed forces, and 4,637 illegal aliens are caught by the U.S. Border Patrol. In a day, the U.S. government takes in about $44.5 million in customs duties and $15.6 million in excise taxes on alcohol. In the same 24 hour period, it spends about $3 billion, $416 million of that on interest on the national debt.

All this collecting, spending, processing, handling, administering, and helping are done by employees of the executive branch of government. This chapter examines the structure and organization of this bureaucracy.

CHAPTER OUTLINE

421

The statistics cited in the chapter introduction are from *On an Average Day* by Tom Heymann (Fawcett Columbine, 1989) and *Statistical Abstract of the United States, 1990*.

CHAPTER SUPPORT MATERIAL

Skills Practice Worksheet 16

Skills Challenge Worksheet 16

Citizenship Worksheet 6

Transparency 37

Study Guide/Review 16

Workbook Chapter 16

Chapter 16 Test, Forms A-C

SECTION 1

The Executive Office Advises the President *(pp. 422–426)*

Section Objectives
☐ identify the agencies that make up the Executive Office of the President and state their functions
☐ distinguish between the pyramid and circular styles of presidential management

Vocabulary
bureaucracy, administration

👥 FOCUS

● Tell the class that for this class you have designated yourself President and they are all Cabinet members, executive agency heads, or members of Congress. Have them jot down an important question or problem they feel they must discuss with you in your capacity as President. Then ask them to consider how you could best deal with all these questions and problems, given that you have only this class period in which to deal with them. **Should the President deal with people on a first come, first served basis? Should the President limit meetings to two minutes? Should the President appoint a Chief of Staff to prioritize the requests for help?** Have students discuss the pros and cons of different methods of management.

SECTION 1 — The Executive Office Advises the President

ACCESS The Main Ideas

1 **Which agencies make up the Executive Office of the President and what are their functions?** *pages 422–424*

2 **What is the difference between the pyramid and the circular style of presidential management?** *pages 425–426*

If you visit Washington, D.C., and take a tour of the White House, you will see the State Dining Room, several beautifully decorated reception rooms, and a few old-fashioned parlors. Your tour guide will not, however, lead you through the press facilities, past the President's Oval Office, and into the bustling executive wing. This is the working White House, the nerve center of the executive branch. Here hundreds of government workers prepare for news briefings and interviews with reporters, schedule presidential meetings, confer with Congress and the Cabinet, answer letters, and keep track of events in this country and abroad.

The majority of the executive branch employees do not work in the White House, however, or even in Washington. The approximately three million people employed by the federal government work in office complexes, bases, and stations around the United States and the world. They are the federal **bureaucracy**, the nonelected officials who carry out specific government functions. These officials, or bureaucrats, work within a highly structured system of offices, or bureaus. Under the civil service system, most of them keep their jobs no matter who the President is.

For the most part, that is not true of the people who work in the White House. Along with Cabinet members, they are directly responsible to the President. Together with the Chief Executive, they make up what is called the **administration**. When news stories refer to "administration policies," they mean the President and these many close assistants, staff, and advisers.

The Presidential Staff

Before World War II, American Presidents managed to carry out their duties with very little administrative staff. James Buchanan, in 1857, was the first President to have a government-paid secretary. President Lincoln had three secretaries, yet he handwrote many of his own letters. Presidents Cleveland and McKinley answered the White House telephone personally, and President Wilson often typed his own speeches.

The need for a larger presidential staff became clear in the mid-1930's. During the Great Depression, Congress created hundreds of New Deal programs to meet America's serious social and economic problems. Each new program required more people to run it. President Franklin D. Roosevelt did not have enough staff to handle these new administrative demands.

In 1936, Roosevelt appointed a special commission, headed by Louis Brownlow, to study the problem of understaffing. The Brownlow commission, known officially as the President's Committee on Administrative Management, made its recommendation one year later. Part of the report read:

> The President needs help. His immediate staff assistance is entirely inadequate. He should be given a small number of executive assistants who would be his direct aides in dealing with the managerial agencies and administrative departments. . . . These aides would have no power to make decisions or issue instructions in their own right. They would not be interposed between the President and the heads of his departments. They would not be assistant Presidents in any sense. . . .
>
> Their effectiveness in assisting the President will, we think, be directly proportional to their ability to discharge their functions with restraint. They would remain in the background, issue no orders, make no decisions, emit no public statements.

Background: *Structure of Government* Though most of the employees of the Department of Education and the U.S. Information Agency work in the Washington, D.C., area, fewer than 3 percent of the employees of the Postal Service do. Internal Revenue Service agents, federal court personnel, and FBI agents are examples of federal employees who are based in regional and local federal offices.

Check for Understanding
▲ *How did the Depression affect the President's need for staff?* (Congress created programs to deal with the Depression, thereby increasing the burden on the presidential staff.)

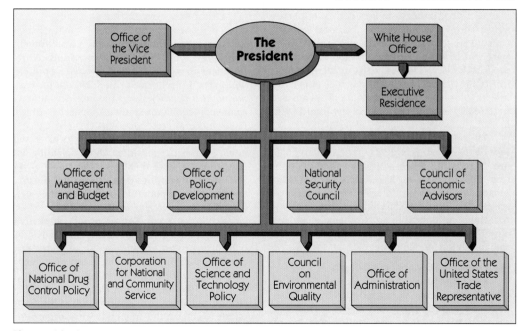

Figure 16–1 THE EXECUTIVE OFFICE OF THE PRESIDENT 8B

Following this report, Congress enacted the Reorganization Act of 1939, which brought several agencies together to form the Executive Office of the President. Roosevelt himself issued an executive order creating the White House Office.

The Executive Office

The Executive Office of the President (EOP) has been reorganized frequently over the years, with new branches added to meet new needs. Every President has tailored the EOP to fit his own particular style. Figure 16–1 shows the current structure of the EOP, which today includes the White House Office, several specialized administrative units, and their staff members.

The White House Office

The White House Office is the "command post" of the executive branch. This "inner circle" includes the President's most trusted personal friends and political allies. Theodore Sorensen, one of President Kennedy's closest aides, described his job at the White House: "staff members are chosen . . . for their ability to serve the President's needs and to talk the President's language." Staff members advise the President on such important matters as congressional relations, foreign affairs, and public relations.

The most important members of the White House staff are the President's Chief of Staff, Deputy Chief of Staff, Counsel, and Press Secretary. In addition to these top advisers, the White House Office employs legions of "deputy assistants," "special assistants," secretaries, social secretaries who arrange official dinners and receptions, and many others. Most of these aides work in the West Wing of the White House, near the President's Oval Office.

Over the years the White House Office has grown significantly. In 1943, President Roosevelt had a staff of about 50 people. By 1971, under President Nixon, staff numbered more than 580. Despite some cuts, the staff remains at more than 500 people.

National Security Council

The National Security Council (NSC), established in 1947, gives advice to the President on matters relating to domestic, military, and for-

423

eign security. Besides the President, who serves as its chairman, members of the National Security Council are the Vice President, the Secretaries of State and Defense, and the President's National Security Adviser. The NSC also directs the operation of the Central Intelligence Agency (CIA). By law, the director of the CIA is an official adviser to the NSC, as is the chairman of the Joint Chiefs of Staff.

The role of the NSC varies, depending on the President. Some Presidents have held regular meetings, while others consulted the NSC only from time to time. All have called the NSC into session during serious domestic or international crises. The 1986 scandal involving arms trading with Iran and donations to Nicaragua's *contras* raised some serious questions about the NSC's role in making foreign policy.

Council of Economic Advisers

The Council of Economic Advisers consists of three noted economists appointed by the President and confirmed by the Senate. This staff agency was created by the Employment Act of 1946 for the purpose of making proposals "to maintain employment, production, and purchasing power." The Council analyzes the nation's economic situation and provides information and recommendations that go into the President's annual economic report to Congress. The Council is assisted by a staff of about 35, most of whom are economists.

Office of Management and Budget

As the federal budget has grown, the Office of Management and Budget (OMB) has become one of the most important units in the entire federal bureaucracy. Its many duties include collecting and analyzing estimates for the federal budget, preparing a budget proposal for the President to submit to Congress, evaluating the organization and operations of the entire executive branch, reviewing legislative proposals submitted by the Cabinet departments, and coordinating the different executive agencies.

The OMB is headed by the Budget Director, who is appointed by the President with Senate approval. In principle, this 600-person agency is independent of party politics. In practice, however, the OMB head usually supports White House economic policies.

Other Executive Office agencies

There are eight other agencies in the Executive Office, plus the Office of the Vice President. The *Office of Policy Development* advises the President on issues relating to events and policies within the United States. The *Council on Environmental Quality* assists the President in environmental problems and works closely with the Environmental Protection Agency. The *Office of Science and Technology Policy,* as its name suggests, advises the President about scientific and technological developments. The *Office of Administration* supplies data processing, research assistance, transportation, and secretarial help for other units in the EOP. The *Office of the United States Trade Representative* advises on matters relating to foreign trade. The head of this office has the status of ambassador and represents the President in negotiating trade agreements with other nations.

The *Office of National Drug Control Policy* is responsible for managing the administration's efforts to combat the drug trade. The *Corporation for National and Community Service* operates AmeriCorps, an agency that provides people age 17 and older the opportunity to perform community service in exchange for college financial aid or for vocational training. AmeriCorps is intended to be an alternative to military service.

2C, 3A, 5C

Managing the Executive Office

The way the Executive Office is used depends on the person who occupies the White House. Each new President develops a style of working with his staff that reflects individual personality, skills, and knowledge.

There are two general styles of managing the EOP, which can be compared to a circle and a pyramid. As Figure 16–2 shows, the circular style is like a bicycle wheel, with the President at the hub. The Executive Office advisers (on the "rim" of the wheel) are connected directly to the President. In the pyramid structure, by contrast, the President is at the top of the EOP. Below the President are widening layers of administrative assistants who filter information on its way to the top of the pyramid. Only the very top advisers have direct access to the President.

424

"Circular" management

President Franklin D. Roosevelt's administration was a good example of the circular style of managing the EOP. Roosevelt's staff was small, informal, and often disorderly. He liked to pit one aide against another by assigning the same task to different assistants. Conflict was common among staff members, but it served several purposes. First, the President never had to rely on the advice of just one staff member. The opportunity to see information from several perspectives helped him make better decisions. In addition, no staff member could become too powerful by gaining a monopoly either on information or on access to the President.

Presidents John Kennedy, Gerald Ford, and Jimmy Carter also took a circular approach to managing the White House staff. Unlike Roosevelt, however, these Presidents encouraged cooperation rather than conflict among their aides. Each tried to surround himself with trusted friends and loyal political associates. For Kennedy, this meant "Ivy League" college friends and family members. (For example, his brother Robert Kennedy served as his Attorney General.) Ford brought in friends from Congress and his home state of Michigan. Carter relied upon many of his campaign staffers from Georgia.

There are drawbacks to the circular method. For example, at the beginning of his term, Carter permitted all his advisers ready access to the Oval Office because he wanted to acquire as much information as possible. But as time went on, Carter became swamped with detail. Eventually, Carter had to assign more and more work to his top assistant, Hamilton Jordan.

The "pyramid" style

The pyramid style of managing is much like the organization of a business corporation or military unit. Not surprisingly, President Dwight Eisenhower, a former army general, preferred this structure. Each staff member in his administration had a particular task, with few overlapping functions. Eisenhower relied on his Chief of Staff, Sherman Adams. Adams served as a "gatekeeper" to screen senators, Cabinet members, and others before they could see the President.

Figure 16–2 PRESIDENTIAL MANAGEMENT STYLES The access that close advisers have to the President depends largely on whether the Executive Office of the President is managed in the pyramid (left) or the circular (right) style. 8B

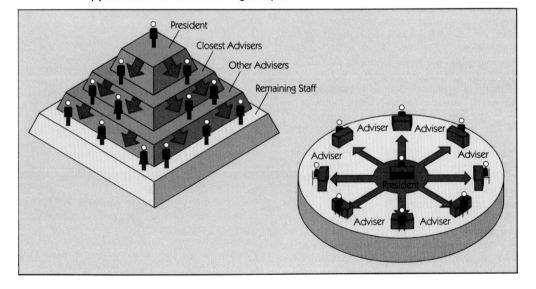

Figure 16–2
● *With which management style would you feel most comfortable? Why?*

GUIDED/INDEPENDENT PRACTICE
● Have students paraphrase the excerpt from the Brownlow report on p. 422 and then write a brief paragraph presenting their opinion of the report's recommendations.

RETEACHING/CORRECTIVES
▲ Have students create their own versions of Figure 16–1 by copying the organization of the chart and then annotating it with information from the text.

ENRICHMENT/EXTENSION
■ Have students do research to find out about the professional background of the present President's Chief of Staff, Deputy Chief of Staff, Counsel, and Press Secretary. Have them present their information in the form of oral reports and include photographs of the individuals researched. The class might then compare the backgrounds of the officials.

The symbol denotes active participation strategies.

Activities are keyed for student abilities:
▲ = Basic
● = All Levels
■ = Average/Advanced

Section 1 Review Answers

1. The White House Office.

2. The National Security Council.

3. The Office of Management and Budget.

4. (a) The President receives information from many Executive Office advisers. **(b)** Information is passed through increasingly smaller layers of assistants. Only the very top advisers have direct access to the President.

Critical thinking Students should weigh the President's need for assistance in handling a highly complex job against the problem of unelected officials making decisions that affect the public.

CLOSURE

● Have students work in pairs to write questions dealing with information in the section. Have the pairs take turns quizzing the class. Then have students read Section 2, noting how the role of the Cabinet has varied in different administrations.

Vice President Al Gore has had a greater role in the Clinton White House than vice presidents in earlier administrations. Gore led the task force that developed a plan to cut government waste. Clinton announced the plan at a ceremony where stacks of federal rules and regulations were displayed, symbolizing red tape to be cut by the government-streamlining plan.

President Richard Nixon's administration was even more structured than Eisenhower's. His Chief of Staff, H. R. Haldeman, was accused of erecting a "Berlin Wall" around the White House. As a result, the President was isolated, a fact that may help explain his alleged unawareness of many Watergate-related activities.

President Bush developed a hybrid management style. On some issues, Bush relied heavily on his first chief of staff, John Sununu, to screen information and restrict access to the Oval Office. On the other hand, Bush maintained an "open-door" policy with some officials. Close friends, such as Treasury Secretary Nicholas Brady and Secretary of State James Baker, had direct access to the President, along with such key advisers as National Security Adviser Brent Scowcroft and Budget Director Richard Darman.

The Clinton style

President Clinton's style is a modified circular approach. At the outset of his administration, Clinton favored an "open door." He surrounded himself with many of the youthful advisers who helped him get elected. However, in time Clinton came to rely more on "Washington insiders" for advice. One innovation in presidential appointments was Clinton's formal naming of his wife, Hillary Rodham Clinton, to chair an interagency task force on national health care reform.

SECTION 1 REVIEW

Vocabulary and key terms

bureaucracy (422)
administration (422)
Executive Office of the
  President (EOP) (423)
White House Office (423)

National Security
  Council (423)
Office of Management
  and Budget (OMB)
  (424)

For review

1. What group is the central "command post" of the Executive Office of the President? 3A
2. Which group in the EOP oversees security and intelligence-gathering? 3A
3. Which EOP unit is in charge of organizing and financing the executive branch of the government? 3A
4. What is the relationship between the President and his advisers in (a) the circular style of management? (b) the pyramid style? 3A

Critical thinking

TRACING HISTORICAL DEVELOPMENTS The 1937 report suggesting an Executive Office recommended that assistants "remain in the background, issue no orders, make no decisions." Looking at the EOP today, do you think this advice is realistic or even desirable? Why? 3A

Cabinet Departments Carry Out Policies

ACCESS — The Main Ideas

1 How are Cabinet departments organized?
pages 427–428

2 How has the role of Cabinet members changed?
pages 428–431

If you were asked to make recommendations on updating the executive branch, what new Cabinet departments would you suggest? Does the country need a Department of Space Exploration, a Department of Environmental Protection, or possibly a Department of Ethics?

Cabinet departments play a vital role in the administration of government, but they also reflect the nation's priorities. That is one reason why the number of departments has grown from just three in 1789 to fourteen today.

2C, 3A, 4B

Development of the Cabinet

Early executive departments

The heads of the fourteen executive departments make up the **Cabinet**, an informal advisory group chosen by the President to assist in making decisions. Though the Constitution mentions "executive departments," it does not set up a Cabinet as it exists today. Congress established the first three executive departments — State, Treasury, and War — in 1789. President George Washington began the practice of seeking advice from the Secretaries, or heads, of each department: Thomas Jefferson (State), Alexander Hamilton (Treasury), and Henry Knox (War). Edmund Randolph, the Attorney General, also met with Washington's Cabinet but did not head a department.

Although the President may make recommendations, only Congress can create or abolish a Cabinet department. Beginning in 1798, Congress has established, combined, modified, or eliminated a number of departments as the need for government action arose. The growth of the Cabinet in a way parallels changes in national

concerns and priorities. Some of the newer departments, for instance, reveal the federal government's concern with issues such as energy, urban development, education, and veterans' affairs. The Guide to Executive Departments on pages 447–460 outlines the history and operations of each present-day department.

Each department is headed by a Secretary, except for the Justice Department, which the Attorney General runs. Cabinet heads are directly accountable to the President. Below the Secretaries are layers of undersecretaries, deputy secretaries, assistant secretaries, bureau chiefs, agency directors, and so on. Cabinet Secretaries and some higher officials are appointed by the President with Senate approval. Traditionally, each new President names new Cabinet members as part of the incoming administration.

YOU DECIDE

8H

Cabinet members are often caught between conflicting interests: the needs of the group they serve, versus the aims of the President who appointed them. Consider this situation. Due to the huge influx of Japanese automobiles, many American autoworkers have been laid off. Senators from Michigan and employees in the Department of Labor want the Secretary of Labor to urge the President to impose strict quotas on Japanese automobiles. The President, however, believes that import quotas will result in harmful retaliation.

What advice should the Secretary of Labor give the President?

Section Objectives

☐ explain how Cabinet departments are organized
☐ trace the changing role of Cabinet members

Vocabulary
Cabinet

FOCUS

● Ask students to name as many executive departments as they can without looking in their books. Write the names of those departments on the board. Then ask students if they know the names of any of the current secretaries, and write those on the board as well. After referring to an almanac or to the Guide to Executive Departments on pp. 447–460, fill in the missing departments. You may want to refer to this list for the rest of the lesson.

You Decide Answer
Students should defend their answers. Students might suggest a compromise proposal, combining temporary limitations on Japanese imports with government efforts to help American automobile manufacturers become more competitive.

The symbol 🕇 denotes active participation strategies.

Activities are keyed for student abilities:
▲ = Basic
● = All Levels
■ = Average/Advanced

3A, 4B, 4C, 6A

EXPLANATION

After reviewing the content of the section, you may want to consider the following activities:

Structure of Government

● Have volunteers take on the roles of specific department secretaries. Encourage them to study the description of their departments found in the Guide to Executive Departments on pp. 447–460. Then have the "secretaries" stand in front of the class and arrange themselves in the order of the founding of their department.

● [CRITICAL THINKING] Have the "secretaries," in consultation with other students, rearrange themselves in order of importance. Have students explain their priorities.

Civic Participation

▲ **What two roles do Cabinet secretaries serve?** (They advise the President and administer their departments.) **How might these two roles conflict?** (Cabinet secretaries might be torn between a desire to serve the President and a desire to back the interests of their departments.)

The size, budgets, influence, and activities of the Cabinet departments differ widely. By far the largest is the Department of Defense, with about a million civilian employees. The smallest is the Department of Education, with about 5,000 workers. The departments' budgets in a recent year ranged from under $3 billion for the Commerce Department to over $500 billion for the Department of Health and Human Services (about three-fourths in Social Security and Medicare payments). For many years the Department of Defense alone spent more than a fifth of the entire federal budget.

Choosing Cabinet members

Since Washington's administration, the Cabinet has consisted of all department Secretaries, the Vice President, and any other officials that the President names. Several factors go into the President's choice of Cabinet members. Naturally, the President seeks competent and trustworthy people to fill Cabinet posts. Often they are not politicians but come instead from universities, law firms, private foundations, state government, labor unions, or business. They are usually college-educated, many with doctorates and law degrees. Many are willing to take a severe cut in pay to join the Cabinet because of the honor and prestige associated with this position.

Besides experience, political and symbolic factors also figure in selecting a Cabinet. Most Cabinet members are of the President's political party. Some are appointed to please a particular element or wing within the party. From time to time, a President appoints someone from the opposition party to symbolize that the administration represents all the people. For instance, President Kennedy, a Democrat, appointed Republicans C. Douglas Dillon and Robert McNamara as Secretaries of Treasury and Defense. In making such appointments, the President still looks for a person who shares the same political philosophy.

Cabinet members are also chosen to represent certain regions of the country and specific interest groups. Traditionally, the Secretary of the Interior comes from a western state, while the Secretary of Agriculture is from a midwestern farm-belt state and has some farming background. The Secretary of Housing and Urban Development, a newer post, usually is from one of the nation's big cities. Custom also dictates that the Secretary of Commerce must come from the business community, the Secretary of Labor must be acceptable to organized labor, and the Secretary of the Treasury should have a background in banking or finance.

As in other parts of government, recent Presidents have deliberately tried to make the Cabinet more representative of the people and have named more women, blacks, and other minorities. The first woman member of the Cabinet was Frances Perkins, named Secretary of Labor by Franklin D. Roosevelt in 1933. Women Cabinet members were rare, however, until the 1970's. President Ford appointed Carla Hills to head HUD, and President Carter named several women Cabinet Secretaries. Robert C. Weaver, who was named to lead HUD in 1966, was the first black Cabinet member, while Lauro Cavazos, chosen by President Reagan as Secretary of Education in 1988, was the first Hispanic American to serve in a Cabinet. Presidents Bush and Clinton both included women, African Americans, and Hispanics in their Cabinets.

The modern Cabinet, then, tends to reflect the diversity of America while still meeting a President's requirements for background, experience, interest-group support, and political harmony. There is seldom any significant congressional opposition to Cabinet appointees.

3A, 4B, 4C, 6A

The Role of the Cabinet

The Cabinet's influence in the administration depends largely on what the President wants it to be. Several Presidents — notably Buchanan, Harding, and Coolidge — have given their Cabinets a very important role. Coolidge especially believed that most of his administrative duties could be handled by the Cabinet.

Other Presidents have used the Cabinet sparingly. President Andrew Jackson disliked Cabinet meetings. Instead, he met in the White House with a small group of friends, who included several journalists and Treasury officials. Because they often met in the back rooms of the White House, the group was nicknamed the "Kitchen Cabinet." Presidents Lincoln, Wilson,

---

Cross-reference
Frances Perkins, the first woman member of the Cabinet, is the subject of "Speaking Out" on p. 803.

Background: *History* Six rejections of Cabinet appointees occurred in Tyler's administration (three were of the same man on the same day); two occurred in Coolidge's administration; Jackson, Eisenhower, and Andrew Johnson each had one rejection.

President Clinton, in selecting members of his Cabinet, sought to reflect the diversity of America while also seeking people of experience and achievement. Sitting beside Clinton in this Cabinet meeting are (left) Donna Shalala, Secretary of Health and Human Services, and Henry Cisneros, Secretary of Housing and Urban Development. Shalala, an expert on urban finance, had served as Chancellor of the University of Wisconsin. Cisneros was the first Hispanic mayor of an American city—San Antonio.

Theodore Roosevelt, Truman, and Kennedy also gave their Cabinets a fairly minor role. On the other hand, Presidents Eisenhower, Lyndon Johnson, Ford, Carter, Reagan, and Bush used the Cabinet as a sounding board to test opinions.

President Bush relied more heavily on his Cabinet for advice than did his recent predecessors. This greater reliance may have been due to the fact that his Cabinet included several of Bush's long-time friends, along with seasoned "Washington insiders" and innovative newcomers. Cabinet meetings were also attended by the Vice President, budget director, and chief of staff. Furthermore, the Bush Cabinet appeared to be somewhat more collegial and consensual than previous Cabinets.

Presidents, of course, are free to disregard the Cabinet's advice. President Lincoln once submitted an idea to his seven Cabinet members.

When they unanimously rejected his proposal, Lincoln exclaimed, "Seven nays, one aye — the ayes have it!"

Cabinet members' influence

In each administration, some Cabinet members have greater influence and more access to the President than others. In President Truman's administration, this was true of George Marshall, Secretary of State and, later, Defense. Other influential Cabinet members were John Foster Dulles, Eisenhower's Secretary of State, and Robert McNamara, Secretary of Defense for both Kennedy and Johnson. In the Reagan administration, Secretary of State George Shultz, Secretary of Defense Caspar Weinberger, and Attorney General Edwin Meese met frequently with the President. By contrast, some of Nixon's Cabinet members had to wait months to see the Chief Executive.

429

Background: *History* The Constitutional Convention debated the need for a "Privy Council," or Cabinet. The actual proposal (which was never voted on) called for a council that would "advise [the President] in matters respecting the execution of his office, which he shall think proper to lay before them; but their advice shall not conclude [bind] him, nor affect his responsibility for the measure which he shall adopt."

Cross-reference
George Marshall is the subject of "Speaking Out" on p. 802.

Controversial Issues
● Have students prepare a debate on the following statement: *Cozy triangles are harmful to the democratic process, and Congress should pass legislation to prevent their development.* Students supporting such legislation should suggest specific measures to be taken.

Cooperative Learning
● Divide the class into groups and have each group choose a different executive department. Have the groups create posters illustrating the work of each department. Groups should design an emblem (for example, a gavel or scales of justice for the Justice Department, a dollar sign for the Treasury) and use illustrations or clippings to suggest the activities of the department.

GUIDED/INDEPENDENT PRACTICE
● Have each student prepare a list of questions for the Cabinet member he or she would most like to interview. Students may write a cover letter and send their questions to the Cabinet official. A list of the addresses of all Executive Departments can be found in most almanacs and in the *United States Government Manual.*

The symbol ᴪ denotes active participation strategies.

Activities are keyed for student abilities:
▲ = Basic
● = All Levels
■ = Average/Advanced

Typically, the Cabinet members who work most closely with the President are the Attorney General and the Secretaries of State, Defense, and Treasury. These departments are sometimes called the "Inner Cabinet." Not only are these the oldest departments, but their Secretaries also tend to share the goals and outlook of the President. The remaining departments, the "Outer Cabinet," have been established to represent particular interests, such as agriculture and labor. The goals of these departments, therefore, may differ from the President's.

Conflicting loyalties

Cabinet members — particularly those in the "Outer Cabinet" — serve two important, but often conflicting, roles. As advisers to the President, they are supposed to fulfill the wishes of the President. But they are also administrators of their departments. After a time, Secretaries tend to become spokespersons for the programs of their department and the people whose interests they represent.

For instance, Robert Finch was a long-time friend and California political ally of Richard Nixon. In 1969, Nixon appointed Finch to be his first Secretary of Health, Education, and Welfare (HEW). Nixon immediately gave Finch directives to be tough and cut the HEW budget. In just a few months, however, Finch became an advocate of HEW programs and resisted the President's demands for cuts. Caught in this dilemma, Finch resigned in 1970. Such intense cross-pressures are one reason why many Cabinet members leave their office before the end of the President's term.

Conflicts over policy may also lead Cabinet members to leave their posts. For example, in April 1980, President Carter's Secretary of State, Cyrus Vance, resigned because he disagreed with Carter's decision to take military action against Iran to secure the release of American hostages. Vance's resignation came days after an attempted raid on Iran ended with a helicopter crash, killing eight Americans. No Secretary of State had resigned over a policy dispute since William

Figure 16–3 THE "COZY TRIANGLE" Executive departments have close relationships with the congressional committees and interest groups in their field. 8B

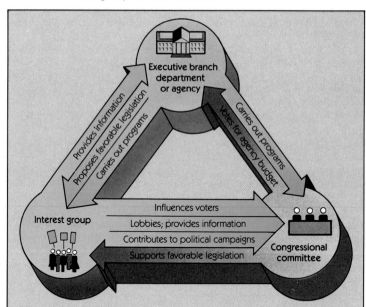

430

Figure 16–3

▲ *How do interest groups influence the executive and legislative branches?* (They provide information to executive departments and agencies and to congressional committees. They also contribute to congressional campaigns, influence voters, and lobby members of Congress.)

Jennings Bryan in 1915. Bryan had objected to a letter written by President Woodrow Wilson protesting the sinking of the *Lusitania*.

Internal disagreements

Conflicts over loyalty and policy are not the only reasons why Cabinet members resign or are fired by the President. Like other officials, Cabinet secretaries may embarrass the President by their actions or remarks. For example, in 1970, Secretary of the Interior Walter Hickel publicly disagreed with President Nixon on the decision to invade Cambodia. Hickel also criticized Nixon for not allowing him greater access to the White House. Nixon quickly fired Hickel. Similarly, Joseph Califano, President Carter's Secretary of Health, Education, and Welfare, became critical of President Carter's policies, especially subsidies given to tobacco growers. Carter asked Califano to resign.

Perhaps the best illustration of "foot-in-mouth disease" was President Reagan's first Secretary of the Interior, James Watt. When first appointed, Watt was strongly opposed by environmental groups, such as the Sierra Club and the National Wildlife Federation. From Watt's background and earlier career, they feared he would sell federal lands and commercialize the national parks. Watt's statements and behavior while running the Interior Department continued to upset these groups. Watt next caused Reagan embarrassment when he labeled the Beach Boys' music "distasteful" and canceled their scheduled Fourth of July show on the Washington Mall. Millions of Beach Boys' fans, including the Reagans, disagreed with Watt's judgment. Watt finally was forced to resign from his Cabinet post after making a tasteless joke that offended many minorities and women.

Ethical questions

Administration officials also leave government service to take jobs in private industry. The relationships of government officials and agencies with outside businesses and interest groups has long been a touchy question. Some observers point to a "revolving door" between government jobs and jobs in related fields of business. As a result, they say, a "triangle" develops between an executive branch department or agency, congressional committees, and outside associations or interest groups in the same area. Political observers call these "cozy triangles," "subgovernments," or "iron triangles." Figure 16-3 illustrates this relationship.

In such a triangle, all the members exchange favors. The lobby or interest group gives information to the agency and, perhaps, campaign contributions to members of a congressional committee. Congress, of course, votes on funding for the agency. The agency, in turn, carries out programs and performs services that benefit both the interest group and the Congress members' constituents at home.

Critics of "cozy triangle" relationships worry about the amount of influence they give to those who represent small, special-interest groups. Others point out that within any field there are only a limited number of people with the knowledge and experience to head a government agency or manage a private corporation. These men and women are likely to know each other, to have worked together, and to share a common interest in advancing their industry or profession.

SECTION 2 REVIEW

Vocabulary and key terms

Cabinet (427)　　　　　　"cozy triangle" (431)

For review

1. (a) What part did George Washington play in the development of the Cabinet? (b) In what ways are new Cabinet departments established? 2C
2. What factors does a President consider in naming Cabinet members? 4B
3. (a) Why are the heads of "Inner Cabinet" departments likely to be closest to the President? (b) Why are other Cabinet members likely to face conflicting loyalties? 4C

Critical thinking

MAKING A DECISION If you were the President, what qualities would you look for in choosing Cabinet members? 3A

Section 2 Review Answers
1. **(a)** He began the practice of seeking advice from the heads of the executive departments. **(b)** Congress creates new Cabinet departments.
2. Experience, political affiliation, relationship to a specific region or interest group.
3. **(a)** These departments are the oldest, their responsibilities are essential, and their heads most closely share the goals and outlook of the President. **(b)** As advisers to the President, they represent his viewpoint, but as administrators of departments, they come to represent the programs and interests of their departments.

Critical thinking Students' answers should show an understanding of Cabinet members' functions—to advise the President, to administer an agency, and to represent the needs of a segment of the population.

CLOSURE

● Have each student write a question dealing with the information in the section. Have students take turns asking the class their questions. Then have students read Section 3, noting the differences among the various administrative units of the executive branch.

Background:
Multiculturalism Watt's offensive comments (column 1, par. 2) were about the broad range of people he had appointed. He noted that the group included "a woman, two Jews, and a cripple."

The symbol ▮▮ denotes active participation strategies.

Activities are keyed for student abilities:
▲ = Basic
● = All Levels
■ = Average/Advanced

SECTION 3

The Government Works Through Independent Agencies *(pp. 432–437)*

Section Objectives

☐ distinguish among independent regulatory commissions, government corporations, and executive agencies

☐ explain how federal agencies work with outside contractors

Vocabulary

independent regulatory commission, commissioners, deregulation, government corporation, executive agency

👥 FOCUS

● Write the term *bureaucracy* on the board. Have students come to the board and write the word or phrase that occurs to them when they see that term. Ask volunteers to describe their experiences in dealing with the federal bureaucracy. (For example: filing taxes, applying for a social security card, going through immigration, applying for a passport, dealing with customs officials.)

SECTION 3

The Government Works Through Independent Agencies

ACCESS The Main Ideas

1 What are the functions of independent regulatory commissions, government corporations, and executive agencies?
pages 432–437

2 How do federal agencies work with outside contractors?
page 437

Think about the activities of the following agencies: Federal Election Commission, Farm Credit Administration, Selective Service System, Pennsylvania Avenue Development Corporation, National Foundation of the Arts and Humanities, ACTION, and Office of Government Ethics.

Their reponsibilities are varied, yet these agencies are just a few of the roughly 200 federal administrative units that work outside the Cabinet departments. Until the 1880's, the Cabinet departments carried on most of the federal government's business. Since then, the government has taken on more responsibilities. To help cope with these, Congress has created a host of "independent agencies." They can generally be divided into three categories: (1) independent regulatory commissions, (2) government corporations, and (3) independent executive agencies.

3A, 3B, 4B, 7C

Regulatory Commissions

Independent regulatory commissions are agencies that make rules and regulations to protect the public interest. Most are concerned with establishing rates and rules for fair practices in various aspects of the economy, such as preventing unfair business dealings, false advertising, employment discrimination, and the like. Others protect the public from defective or dangerous products, ranging from toys to nuclear reactors.

Reasons for commissions

Most of the commissions were originally created in response to social or economic conditions that brought public demands for regulation. For example, America's first regulatory commission

432

was the Interstate Commerce Commission (ICC), created in 1887. The ICC was set up to regulate interstate shipping and commerce after irate farmers protested that the railroads' practices were unfair and monopolistic.

Another reason for commissions is that members of Congress have neither the time nor expertise to deal with the technical aspects of regulation. Instead, Congress sets broad policy guidelines. The commissions' job is to fill in the details and carry out policies on a day-to-day basis.

Certain periods in history have been notable for the creation of commissions. The Federal Reserve System ("the Fed") and Federal Trade Commission (FTC), which regulate the nation's economy, were created in 1913 and 1914 as outgrowths of the Progressive Movement. The problems of the Great Depression inspired the creation of numerous regulatory commissions still in existence today. These include the Securities and Exchange Commission (SEC), Federal Communications Commission (FCC), and National Labor Relations Board (NLRB). In the 1970's, new commissions appeared in response to the consumer movement and the energy crisis — the Consumer Product Safety Commission (CPSC), was created in 1972; the Nuclear Regulatory Commission (NRC) in 1975; and the Federal Energy Regulatory Commission (FERC) came into existence in 1977.

The independence of commissions

The word *independent* in the name for these agencies emphasizes that Congress wanted regulation to be politically neutral. Whereas each Cabinet department or similar federal agency is headed by a single individual, an independent regulatory commission is headed by a group of five to eleven **commissioners**. Commissioners are appointed by the President and confirmed by the Senate. After that, the President has no direct control over commissioners.

Several factors ensure commissions' independence. First, the law requires each commission to be bipartisan, consisting of commissioners from both major political parties. That helps ensure that neither party will be able to "pack" a commission and thereby gain control over its policies. (Of course, the President is still free to appoint members who share his political outlook and attitudes.)

Finally, Presidents do not have the opportunity to appoint all the members of any commission. Commissioners serve longer terms than the President — from 5 to 14 years. Moreover, their terms are staggered so that in any President's administration, only a few commissioners' jobs will become available. No matter what political disagreements exist, the President cannot dismiss commissioners except for good cause. This limitation on the President's removal power, discussed on page 400, is designed to protect the independence of the commissioners.

The status of commissions

Even though they are part of the executive branch, independent regulatory commissions enjoy a unique status in the federal bureaucracy. In fact, their functions are also partly legislative and partly judicial.

The commissions take a legislative role because, under Congress's broad guidelines, they establish rules and regulations that have the force of law. At the same time, commissions are partly executive, because they can enforce or implement these rules. And they are partly judicial because they can settle questions of the application of the regulations and impose penalties on those who disobey. Since they clearly do not follow the principle of separation of powers, independent regulatory commissions have sometimes been called the "fourth branch" of government.

Cutting back on regulation

The spurt of new commissions in the 1970's brought complaints that overregulation was hurting free competition. The government's response was **deregulation**, reducing or removing regulations in some industries. Presidents Carter, Reagan, and Bush took steps in the deregulation of

The Federal Energy Regulatory Commission sets rates for the transportation of energy, including oil carried by the Trans-Alaska pipeline, shown here.

Cross-reference
The Supreme Court decision that determined that Presidents cannot dismiss commissioners without good cause is *Humphrey's Executor v. U.S.* (1935), discussed in Chapter 15, p. 400.

Background: *Cultural Literacy* The functions of independent regulatory commissions are often described as *quasi-legislative, quasi-executive,* and *quasi-judicial. Quasi* is a Latin prefix that means "resembling" or "seemingly."

EXPLANATION

After reviewing the content of the section, you may want to consider the following activities:

👥 Structure of Government

▲ *Why are independent regulatory commissions sometimes called the "fourth branch of government"?* (They combine executive, legislative, and judicial responsibilities.)

● Have the class create on one side of the board a chart showing the separation of powers of the federal government. On the other side, have them create a chart illustrating the ways in which independent regulatory commissions do not follow the principle of separation of powers.

■ *How might the fact that independent regulatory commissions possess executive, legislative, and judicial powers allow them to function more efficiently?* (The commissions can ensure that their regulations will be interpreted in the ways they want them to be interpreted, and can create new regulations when necessary to deal with new situations.)

The symbol 👥 denotes active participation strategies.

Activities are keyed for student abilities:
▲ = Basic
● = All Levels
■ = Average/Advanced

Structure of Government

● Have students find out the responsibilities of the regulatory commissions listed in column 2 of p. 432. (The SEC is responsible for monitoring the stock and bond markets. The FCC licenses television and radio stations and approves interstate rate increases for telephones and telegraph systems. The NLRB works to correct or prevent unfair labor practices committed by employers or unions. The CSPC works to protect consumers from unsafe products. The NRC licenses and oversees the construction of nuclear power plants. The FERC sets rates for the transportation and sale of natural gas, the transmission and sale of electricity, and the pipeline transportation of oil; it also licenses hydroelectric projects.)

Economics

▲ **Why was the Airline Deregulation Act of 1978 passed?** (Airlines complained of unnecessary paperwork; passengers complained of high fares. The government believed that over-regulation was hurting free enterprise.) **How did deregulation affect the airline industry?** (Many airlines closed down or merged because of lower profits; employees lost their jobs.)

● **Has airline deregulation affected you? How?** (Students might cite lower fares or reductions in the number of flights.)

Although their money is insured by the federal government, concerned customers gather outside a failed savings and loan.

trucking, railroads, banking, telecommunications, and airlines.

For example, the Airline Deregulation Act of 1978 gradually phased out and then ended the Civil Aeronautics Board (CAB). For years the CAB had regulated domestic airline routes and airfares. The airline industry, however, complained about unnecessary paperwork. Passengers complained that some rates were too high.

The results of deregulation in the airline industry were mixed. Free competition led to price wars and bargain airfares for travelers. On the other hand, airline profits fell, forcing some airlines to merge or close down. Many employees either lost their jobs or took cuts in pay. Another drawback, for some passengers, was that major airlines were no longer required to fly certain routes. They cut back or stopped service to over 130 cities on the less profitable routes. In

434

addition, there was concern about airline safety standards and pilot training.

The Motor Carrier Act of 1980 helped deregulate the trucking industry. It reduced the power of the Interstate Commerce Commission over trucking, promoted competition among truckers, and thus reduced freight rates — perhaps by as much as 40 percent. Some critics, however, feared that truck safety standards also had been lowered.

The savings and loan crisis

The most severe consequence of deregulation occurred in the savings and loan industry. Traditionally, savings and loans (S&Ls) had been limited to two main activities: receiving savings deposits from individual investors and loaning out that money in the form of home mortgages. S&Ls were prohibited from engaging in activities common to commercial banks, such as most commercial loans, real estate development, or other high-risk investments. These regulations made S&Ls a slow-growing but stable industry.

In the early 1980's, however, many of the regulations on S&Ls were removed. They were allowed to operate more like commercial banks and with much less supervision by federal regulators. Many S&Ls began to make risky, high-interest loans, and to engage in fraudulent practices. By 1988, over 500 S&Ls had collapsed, and many more were near bankruptcy.

Because S&L deposits are federally insured, with each account guaranteed up to $100,000, the government stepped in to bail out the industry. The Resolution Trust Corporation (RTC) was formed to oversee the operations of failing S&Ls, and to sell them off if necessary. In the 1990's, government estimates put the cost of the S&L bailout at about $200 billion, a cost that ultimately will be paid by the American public.

3A, 7C

Government Corporations

Another type of organization in the federal bureaucracy is the **government corporation**. As the name implies, government corporations combine features of both public (government) and private (corporation) organizations. They provide certain commercial or business-like serv-

---

Check for Understanding
● **What are the arguments for and against the deregulation of the trucking industry?** (*For*—Deregulation would reduce freight prices. *Against*—Safety standards might be lowered.)

Background: *Economics*
The Resolution Trust Corporation itself came under fire in 1991 when it was accused of poor accounting and bad management.

ices, often the kind of public services that private industry is unable or unwilling to undertake.

Private and public corporations

A private business corporation issues shares of stock, which are bought by investors called shareholders. Shareholders elect a board of directors who, in turn, choose corporate officers or managers to run day-to-day operations. The purpose of a private corporation is to make a profit for its shareholders.

Like a private corporation, a government corporation has a board of directors and managers. They are appointed by the President with Senate approval. Government corporations, however, do not issue stock or have shareholders. They are given long-term funding by Congress but also hope to make profits, which are plowed back into the corporation itself. Like private corporations, government corporations — particularly the Post Office and AMTRAK — sometimes lose money. In this case, the government makes up the loss, usually by charging higher rates for services or through taxation.

Government corporations can be more flexible and sometimes more efficient in handling pressing economic problems than other government agencies. They are relatively independent of both Congress and the President.

Services of public corporations

America's first government corporation was the First Bank of the United States, chartered in 1791. There were few federal government corporations, however, until the Great Depression of the 1930's. Then Congress set up dozens, such as the Commodity Credit Corporation (CCC), the Federal Deposit Insurance Corporation (FDIC), and the Tennessee Valley Authority (TVA). There are now more than sixty government corporations. Three examples give an idea of their variety:

TENNESSEE VALLEY AUTHORITY (TVA) The TVA was created in 1933 and is considered the "granddaddy" of government corporations. The TVA helps control the waters of the Tennessee River, generates relatively inexpensive electricity for a seven-state area, and serves as a "yardstick" by which to measure electrical rates for private electric companies.

U.S. POSTAL SERVICE The office of Postmaster General was established in 1789, but at that time the Post Office offered few services. There was no home delivery of mail, and the person who received a letter paid the postage. In the 1840's, the Post Office Department was reorganized and, for the first time, issued national postage stamps for sending letters. It became a Cabinet department in 1829.

In 1970, the Postal Reorganization Act made the Post Office a government corporation. The U.S. Postal Service is now run by a bipartisan board appointed by the President with Senate approval. The Board, in turn, chooses a Postmaster General. The U.S. Postal Service is the nation's largest government corporation, with close to 700,000 workers and about 40,000 post offices and branches.

AMTRAK The nationwide rail service, administered by the National Railroad Passenger Corporation, is AMTRAK. It was created in 1970 with the goal of replacing outdated trains, renovating tracks, and stimulating passenger train service, which private rail lines were abandoning. Today AMTRAK maintains about 23,000 miles of track, serves over 500 stations, and carries more than 20 million people yearly.

Scores of other government corporations carry out a wide range of functions. For instance, the Export-Import Bank loans money for foreign trade, while the Federal Deposit Insurance Corporation insures bank deposits. COMSAT sells time-sharing on satellites, while CONRAIL provides railway freight service.

3A

Executive Agencies

By far the most numerous administrative units in the federal government are the independent **executive agencies**. An independent executive agency is headed by one person (not a governing board) and typically oversees a single area within the executive branch.

Independent executive agencies do not have as much freedom as independent regulatory commissions. In a sense, they are much like Cabinet departments, except that agency heads are not members of the President's Cabinet. Some executive agencies are, in fact, larger than some Cabinet departments. The National Aeronautics and Space Administration (NASA), for example, employs about 26,000 workers. That is more than

435

Multiculturalism
● CRITICAL THINKING Tell students that the federal government has guidelines for its contractors, encouraging minority contractors and requiring that all government contractors be equal opportunity employers. Ask students if they think it is fair for the government to use its enormous economic power to press for social change in this way.

ii Cooperative Learning
● Many of the executive agencies were created in response to the specific needs of Americans in the 20th century. Divide the class into small groups and ask each group to write a short paper describing an agency that they think might be needed in the next century. (For example: an Office of Space Colonization, a Genetic Engineering Regulatory Agency, a Solar Regulatory Commission.)

Background: *Geography*
The TVA affects Tennessee, North Carolina, Virginia, Georgia, Alabama, Kentucky, and Mississippi. Flooding on the Tennessee River was eliminated, soil erosion was slowed, hydroelectric power was generated, and navigation was improved. Farm practices were bettered and living standards were raised in a 40,000 square-mile area.

The symbol ii denotes active participation strategies.

Activities are keyed for student abilities:
▲ = Basic
● = All Levels
■ = Average/Advanced

all the workers in the Departments of Education and Energy combined.

The independent executive agencies perform a variety of functions within the government. Here are some significant examples:

NATIONAL SCIENCE FOUNDATION (NSF) Founded in 1950, NSF works to stimulate scientific research and education. For example, it awards research grants to students in colleges and universities, funds seminars, and distributes information to scientists.

NATIONAL AERONAUTICS AND SPACE ADMINISTRATION (NASA) NASA was created in 1958 to explore outer space for peaceful purposes. NASA is charged with building, launching, and maintaining space vehicles, plus conducting scientific research. Its accomplishments include putting the first person on the moon and building the space shuttle. The space shuttle program came to a sudden halt, however, after the *Challenger* disaster in January 1986. Seven Americans, including Sharon Christa McAuliffe, a New Hampshire school teacher, were killed as the shuttle burst into flames during the first minutes of flight.

Following the *Challenger* disaster, NASA came under fire for its failure to notice flaws in the shuttle's rocket boosters, as well as for the decisions that permitted the *Challenger* to lift off under less than ideal conditions. After a 32-month review and testing period, the shuttle program resumed. The space shuttle *Discovery* was

NASA, one of the best-known executive agencies, explores outer space for the United States. In 1984, astronauts aboard the space shuttle *Discovery* successfully retrieved satellites orbiting the earth.

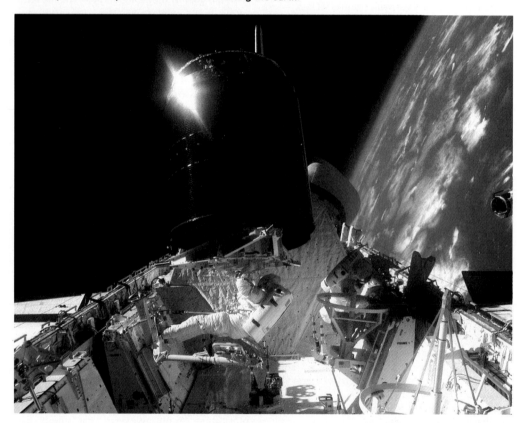

436

launched in September 1988 carrying five astronauts into space. Two months later, *Atlantis* successfully completed the 27th shuttle mission. In January 1990, *Columbia* succeeded in retrieving an 11-ton scientific satellite that had begun falling from its orbit.

GENERAL SERVICES ADMINISTRATION (GSA) The GSA was established in 1949 to serve as a "housekeeping" agency for the entire federal government. Currently, it employs more than 20,000 workers. Its various duties include (1) preventing fraud and abuse in government purchasing and contracts, (2) overseeing the construction and upkeep of federal buildings, (3) maintaining federal transportation and communications, (4) purchasing and selling federal properties, and (5) serving as a clearing house for government information.

3A, 7D

Government Contractors

Even though the various independent agencies of the executive branch carry out thousands of tasks, there is still more work in administering the federal government. The federal agencies must often call on independent contractors, private businesses hired by the government to fulfill specific duties.

Many important government operations are carried out by private government contractors. The number of people who work for private firms under government contracts exceeds even those who work directly for the national government. For example, in 1990 the Defense Department made close to 250,000 contracts worth almost $130 billion.

Government contracts can take many forms. They may go to private medical clinics, major corporations (Westinghouse, Boeing, or DuPont, for example), law firms, accounting firms, or universities. Services contracted cover everything from providing cafeteria and janitorial services to making weapons, conducting medical research, building highways, and supplying goods from paper clips to computer chips.

Outside contractors are needed because, despite its size, the federal government does not have enough workers to go around. Moreover, government personnel may lack the training to do certain types of technical jobs. Often private contractors can provide services at lower cost. Contracting also allows for greater flexibility, because there are fewer rules and regulations. Nevertheless, all contractors, subcontractors, and labor unions dealing with the federal government must follow guidelines for equal employment opportunity and not discriminate in hiring. They are also subject to audits by the General Accounting Office. Contractors who violate these rules will lose their government contracts.

On the other hand, outside contractors, particularly defense contractors, have been criticized even more sharply than government agencies for waste, inefficiency, and overcharges. In 1984, for example, a Senate investigating committee found that the Air Force had paid private suppliers $7,600 for a coffee maker, $436 for a hammer, and $748 for a pair of pliers. Both Congress and the executive agencies have tried to set up methods to catch and halt wasteful overcharges by outside suppliers.

SECTION 3 REVIEW

Vocabulary and key terms

independent regulatory commission (432)
commissioners (432)
deregulation (433)
government corporation (434)
executive agency (435)

For review

1. Why are independent regulatory commissions sometimes called a "fourth branch" of government? 3A
2. What is a government corporation? 3A
3. What are some examples of the types of services provided by government corporations? 3A
4. In general, what is the job of an independent executive agency? Give two examples. 3A

Critical thinking

DRAWING INFERENCES What are the advantages of setting up government corporations? What might happen if, for instance, the government did not run the Postal Service? 7C

437

Section 3 Review Answers
1. They do not follow the principle of separation of powers.
2. A business that combines features of public and private corporations and provides certain commercial services.
3. Electricity by the TVA, mail delivery by the Postal Service, train transportation by AMTRAK.
4. To oversee a single area within the executive branch, such as NASA or the GSA.

Critical thinking The government takes on the kinds of public services that private industry is unable or unwilling to do, either because providing the service is not very profitable or because the initial costs are too high. Students might note that without the government, many rural customers might not be able to get mail, yet competition for urban postal customers might be chaotic.

CLOSURE
● Ask students to explain the following statement from p. 433: "Even though they are part of the executive branch, independent regulatory commissions enjoy a unique status in the federal bureaucracy." Then have students read Section 4 and write a short definition of each vocabulary term as they come across it.

Background: *Politics* The President's power over government jobs has declined over the years, but presidential power over federal contracts has remained strong. One observer noted that a President can use this power "to reward and punish congressional friends and foes quite vigorously. . . ."

The symbol 👥 denotes active participation strategies.

Activities are keyed for student abilities:
▲ = Basic
● = All Levels
■ = Average/Advanced

SECTION 4

The Civil Service System Controls Government Jobs

(pp. 438–443)

Section Objectives

☐ give reasons for the growth of the merit system in the federal government

☐ describe the benefits and drawbacks of working under the civil service system

Vocabulary

civil service, patronage, spoils system, veterans' preference, GS rating

FOCUS

● Ask students if any family members, neighbors, or friends work in the federal civil service. Ask those students to describe what they know about the duties, benefits, and working conditions that are a part of those civil service jobs. ***Do you think you would like a federal civil service job? Why or why not?***

2C, 2E, 3A, 4A, 4C, 8B

The Civil Service System Controls Government Jobs

| ACCESS | **The Main Ideas** |

1 Why has the merit system in the federal government grown over time?
pages 438–441

2 What are the benefits and drawbacks of working under the civil service system?
pages 441–443

James Polk, President from 1845 to 1849, kept a diary throughout his term. Near the end of those four years, he made this entry: "There is no class of our population by whom I am annoyed so much, or for whom I entertain a more sovereign contempt, than for the professed office-seekers who have besieged me ever since I have been in the Presidential office."

Polk's complaints were echoed by other Presidents, for in the nineteenth century most federal positions were filled by the President. Today only the top administrators are chosen that way. The rest of the federal work force — not counting people in military service — are protected by some form of the **civil service** or merit system. They are considered "classified workers," as opposed to presidential appointees who are commonly referred to as "unprotected" or "unclassified."

2C, 2E, 3A, 4C

Growth of the Merit System

Political patronage

When the federal government began in 1789, President Washington set out to hire the most qualified persons, regardless of their political beliefs. In the next decade, however, most of the roughly 2,000 administrative positions came to be filled by members of the Federalist Party. After taking office in 1801, Thomas Jefferson dismissed a number of Federalist administrators and replaced them with qualified members of his own Democratic-Republican Party. This was the start of the **patronage** system, the practice of rewarding political friends by giving them government jobs.

Patronage became solidly established when President Andrew Jackson assumed office in 1829. By then there were more than 10,000 workers in the federal bureaucracy. Jackson fired more than 1,000 federal employees who had been appointed by his predecessors — more than all of the Presidents before him combined.

Jackson, a rugged frontiersman, cared little about the qualifications of his appointees. He believed that the job of administrator was so routine and simple that almost any person could handle it, no matter how little education he had. Jackson's main concern was with rewarding loyal political allies. The winning party, he thought, was entitled to fill the federal bureaucracy with party members. In other words, "to the victor belong the spoils." Henceforth, the term **spoils system** became synonymous with Jackson and political patronage.

Jackson also believed in shifting federal workers frequently from one job to another. Bureaucrats who stayed in the same job, he thought, became powerful, complacent, and unresponsive to elected officials. Jackson's administration had a profound effect, and the spoils system dominated presidential appointments for the next fifty years.

Under this system, however, the government was not able to meet the demands of rapid industrialization and the Civil War. Between 1861 and 1880, the federal bureaucracy nearly tripled, to more than 100,000 workers, many of them incompetent. Presidents complained that filling patronage positions took too much time. Citizens denounced the corruption and dishonesty in government.

At last, in the election of 1880, the spoils system became a hot campaign issue. Within the Republican Party, the "Stalwarts" backed the spoils system and bitterly opposed reform. Still, the Republican convention nominated James A. Garfield, a moderate reformer, for President. To balance the ticket, Chester A. Arthur, a "Stalwart," was nominated as his vice-presidential running mate.

438

Background: *History* The Radical Republicans, to which the Stalwarts (column 2, par. 5) belonged, dominated Congress after 1866. Radical Republicans were staunch Reconstructionists; they divided the South into five military districts, disenfranchised former Confederate soldiers, and gave the vote to former slaves. Later, they opposed civil service reform.

Getting Information from the Government

CITIZENSHIP SKILLS

439

Can you think of *one* place where you could get information about making pickles, buying a used car, exploring Mars, being a better babysitter, camping in national parks, and raising livestock? That one place is the U.S. Government Printing Office, or GPO, which publishes about 3,000 books and pamphlets every year on subjects ranging from astronomy to zoology. These publications come from many different government agencies and departments.

Because the information put out by government departments and agencies actually belongs to you and all other Americans, the government has tried to make it easy to obtain. Many government publications are free; many others are inexpensive (often less than a dollar). Your best guides to finding these materials are your local library and your telephone book.

Ten times a year, the GPO issues a catalog of all its new publications; many libraries receive this catalog. If you live in or near a large city, you may find a GPO bookstore near you. (Look under "U.S. Government" in your telephone book.) It has copies of the government publications that people most often ask for, along with books or pamphlets of special interest in your region. Otherwise, you can order by mail from this address: Superintendent of Documents, U.S. Government Printing Office, Washington, D.C. 20402.

If you want specific information from a certain government agency — for instance, the National Park Service or the Consumer Products Safety Commission — you can usually obtain it by getting in touch with a local office. If there is no local office listed in your phone book, write to the agency in Washington, using the address listed in *The United States Government Manual* (also in your library).

In 1970 the federal government set up the Consumer Information Center to encourage people to take advantage of all the information available to them. The Center issues a free catalog listing current publications of special interest. You can get your own copy by writing to the Consumer Information Center, Pueblo, Colorado 81009.

Follow-up

1. Check with the librarian in your school or public library to see whether a copy of the GPO catalog is available, or write to the Consumer Information Center for its current publications. What kind of information is available?

2. Look under the heading "U.S. Government" in your telephone directory. Think of a question you might ask one of the agencies listed; then call and ask. Report to the class about your call. Who did you talk to? What information did you find out? How helpful was it?

CITIZENSHIP SKILLS

Controversial Issues

● CRITICAL THINKING *Is providing information on such topics as making pickles and buying a used car a legitimate function of the federal government? Explain.* (Some students will argue that providing such information serves the public and therefore is useful. Other students will argue that the federal government should confine itself to more important tasks.)

● Have students complete **Citizenship Worksheet 6,** which helps students to direct government agency inquiries.

Follow-up Answers
1. Students should note the variety of topics and the varying levels of information available.

2. Student questions may deal with topics in this chapter, such as civil service positions or government corporations. Remind students of telephone courtesy when making telephone calls. Students should identify themselves and the school, state the purpose of the call, and be sure to thank the person they speak with for his or her time.

The symbol ⅱ denotes active participation strategies.

Activities are keyed for student abilities:
▲ = Basic
● = All Levels
■ = Average/Advanced

EXPLANATION

After reviewing the content of the section, you may want to consider the following activities:

History

▲ *What is the patronage system?* (The practice of rewarding political friends by giving them government jobs.) *When and how did it begin?* (In 1801, when Thomas Jefferson fired Federalist administrators and replaced them with qualified members of his own party.)

▲ *How did the term "spoils system" come into use?* (Andrew Jackson, believing that the winning party deserved the spoils of victory, used patronage to reward his friends with government jobs, regardless of their qualifications.)

▲ *What 1883 law sought to replace the spoils system?* (The Civil Service Reform Act, or Pendleton Act.) *What replaced party loyalty as the basis for government employment?* (Merit.)

● CRITICAL THINKING *How might the replacement of the spoils system with the merit system have affected political parties?* (It hurt them by reducing their ability to reward loyal members with government jobs.)

👥 Civic Participation

● Call or write your nearest Federal Job Information Center for an application for a civil service job, preferably GS1–3. (If you cannot find a phone number or address in the government listings of the local directory under *Office of Personnel Management,* write or call: Office of Personnel Management, 1900 E Street N.W., Washington, D.C. 20415; 202–606–2424.) Copy the form and distribute copies to students. Then have the class

Garfield won the election, but only a few months later he was shot and killed. His assassin, Charles Guiteau, was a disgruntled office seeker whom Garfield had denied a position in the diplomatic service. Upon his arrest, Guiteau shouted, "I am a Stalwart, and Arthur is President now!" Despite his earlier loyalties, Arthur as President immediately pressed Congress for civil service reform.

The Civil Service Act

With President Arthur's backing, Congress in 1883 enacted the Civil Service Reform Act, usually called the Pendleton Act. The goal of this act was to appoint persons to government positions on the basis of their ability rather than party politics. Ability was to be judged by a competitive examination given to all applicants for government jobs. This is the *merit system* principle. To administer the act, Congress established a three-person Civil Service Commission.

At first, only about 10 percent of all federal employees were protected by the Civil Service Act. Through various amendments, laws, and executive orders, well over 90 percent of all federal workers now are covered by civil service.

Recent civil service changes

Although the number of workers covered by civil service increased dramatically, the Civil Service Commission's underlying purpose and organization remained generally unchanged until 1978. Meanwhile, the tasks involved in running the system had grown far too complex for a single agency to handle. To improve the system, Congress passed the Civil Service Reform Act of 1978. It replaced the Civil Service Commission with three new independent agencies.

The Office of Personnel Management (OPM) is the largest of the three units, with 6,900 workers and five regional offices. This agency is responsible for recruiting, examining, training, and promoting most federal civil servants.

To look out for federal workers' interests, the Merit Systems Protection Board (MSPB) was set up to see that the system is applied fairly. The board is a three-person bipartisan panel chosen by the President and confirmed by the Senate. It is responsible for investigating cases of wrongdoing and hearing appeals from employees who have been fired or have other complaints.

The third agency is the Federal Labor Relations Authority (FLRA). This three-person board

Figure 16–4 GETTING A GOVERNMENT JOB   8B

1 **Find announcements of job openings.** Check newspapers, the post office, libraries, or write to the nearest Federal Job Information Center for available jobs.

2 **Apply for a job.** Request, complete, and return a job application. You will be notified when and where the next examination will be given.

3 **Take the civil service examination.** If you pass the exam (usually by a score of 70 or better), your name is placed on a list of qualified applicants (the register) in order of your grade.

4 **Wait for notification.** When there is an opening, the top three applicants in the appropriate job category are interviewed.

5 **Interview for the job.** If you are hired, you will be given a GS rating according to your job, skill, and experience. If you are not hired, your name remains on the register and you may be called for future openings.

440

Figure 16–4
■ *How does the process of getting a government job differ from getting a job in the private sector?* (Few private jobs require a standardized test; the top three applicants are not necessarily interviewed; the process is often less formal.)

Background: *Structure of Government* The 10 percent of government employees not covered by the Civil Service Act are said to work in the "excepted service." The Foreign Service, for example, operates entirely on its own merit system.

protects the right of federal workers to organize unions and bargain collectively.

Two other independent agencies play a role in regulating the civil service. Questions that involve discrimination are turned over to the Equal Employment Opportunity Commission (EEOC). The Office of Government Ethics is in charge of ethical issues, such as conflict of interest. **3A, 4A**

Inside the Civil Service

More than 2,000 different job categories fall under the civil service system. They include nurses, janitors, typists, chemists, forestry experts, construction workers, computer programmers, engineers, truck drivers, and lawyers. The rules and regulations governing these jobs are quite elaborate. Figure 16–4 diagrams the typical steps from the time a job is announced until an employee is hired.

Civil service examinations

As the diagram shows, every applicant is required to take some type of examination. Most positions require written examinations several hours long. For certain specialized jobs, however, applicants may be judged on education or prior experience. Veterans of military service are given a special status in the civil service system. Any honorably discharged veteran is given a bonus of 5 points on his or her test score. Veterans who are at least 30 percent disabled are given 10 points and a high position on the eligibility list.

This practice, called **veterans' preference** has generated considerable debate. Supporters believe that veterans deserve special consideration for giving their time and jeopardizing their lives to protect the United States. Critics do not dispute the need to reward veterans, but feel that job preference is not the proper way to do it.

People who pass the civil service exam (usually with a score of at least 70) are placed on a list, or register, by the OPM. When a federal agency wants to hire someone, the OPM generally furnishes the names of the three top-ranking applicants. Of those three, the agency usually hires one, and the other two names are returned to the register. When the next job opening occurs, these two names, plus the next person on the register, are submitted, and so on.

Figure 16–5 GS RATINGS AND SALARIES 8B

GRADE	ANNUAL SALARY	TYPICAL JOB
GS-1	$11,903–14,891	Beginning file clerk
GS-2	13,382–16,843	Messenger
GS-3	14,603–18,986	Clerk-typist
GS-4	16,393–21,307	Nursing assistant
GS-5	18,340–23,839	Forestry technician
GS-6	20,443–26,572	Beginning computer operator
GS-7	22,717–29,530	Sports specialist
GS-8	25,159–32,710	Border patrol agent
GS-9	27,789–36,123	Customs inspector
GS-10	30,603–39,783	Librarian
GS-11	33,623–43,712	Internal revenue agent
GS-12	40,298–52,385	Aerospace engineer
GS-13	47,920–62,293	Meteorologist
GS-14	56,627–73,619	Patent attorney
GS-15	66,609–86,589	Physician
ES-1	92,900	Highly skilled manager or supervisor
ES-2	97,400	
ES-3	101,800	
ES-4	107,300	
ES-5	111,800	
ES-6	115,700	

Source: U.S. Office of Personnel Management

GS ratings

Most federal civil servants hold a **GS rating** (for *G*eneral *S*chedule rating) based on a system of classes and ranks. There are fifteen GS classes, ranging from GS-1 (the lowest) to GS-15. Each class includes jobs that are comparable in qualifications, difficulty, and pay. There are several pay rates within each class. Promotions and pay raises are based upon competitive examinations and seniority. The system gives veterans preferential treatment.

Figure 16–5 shows examples of the kinds of jobs and salary ranges in the civil service. Recent college graduates could expect to begin at GS-5 to GS-7. Those with master's degrees may start at GS-9 or higher.

work together to identify the information requested and fill in the form.

Prejudice Reduction
● Have the class review the concept of comparable worth, discussed on pp. 217–218. Have them consider how GS ratings attempt to classify positions into categories of comparable jobs. *What criteria should be used to compare jobs?* (The skills, background, experience, and education necessary for the job; the difficulty and responsibilities of the job; the competition and desirability of the job.)

👥 Politics
● Have students work individually or in small groups to create political cartoons expressing opinions on one of the following: the replacement of the spoils system with the merit system, the Hatch Acts, the decision of the Supreme Court to uphold the constitutionality of the Hatch Acts, the firing of PATCO members following their illegal strike, the benefits or drawbacks of working for the federal government.

👥 Cooperative Learning
● Divide the class into groups and have each group create a skit acting out the steps involved in getting a government job, as illustrated by Figure 16–4.

441

Background: *Structure of Government* Civil Service examinations vary with the type of job. Some exams are written, while others are oral. Some include performance tests, but for many jobs the examiner simply evaluates applications on the basis of education, training, and experience in that field.

Figure 16–5
● *About how much education would you need to qualify for a GS-3 position?* (High school diploma.) *A GS–11 position?* (College degree.) *GS–15?* (Professional or graduate school degree.)

The symbol 👥 denotes active participation strategies.

Activities are keyed for student abilities:
▲ = Basic
● = All Levels
■ = Average/Advanced

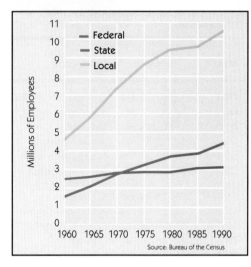

Figure 16–6 GOVERNMENT EMPLOYEES SINCE 1960 8B

The Senior Executive Service

Because of complaints about this rigid class system, the Senior Executive Service (SES) was created in 1978. In 1991 it became the only category for the approximately 8,000 managers and supervisors who had once been classified as GS-16–18. The SES, the "cream of the crop," are paid higher salaries but have less security. They can be transferred within positions, agencies, or regions as the need arises and have fewer protections against poor performance reviews or demotions.

Separate merit systems

Some federal agencies where jobs require unusual specialization have their own merit systems. Among these are the Federal Bureau of Investigation (FBI), the Central Intelligence Agency (CIA), the Public Health Service, the Foreign Service, and the U.S. Postal Service.

Limits on political activities

One original goal of the civil service system was to protect government workers from political pressures. For this protection to work, however, merit workers were expected to restrict their political participation. The major laws in this area are the Hatch Acts of 1939 and 1940.

442

Under the Hatch Acts, federal merit workers are protected from being fired for belonging to the "wrong" party. In return, the original Hatch laws forbade them from taking any part in partisan political campaigns. Under the terms of a law that revised the Hatch Acts in 1993, however, federal employees may now endorse candidates and work as volunteer helpers in political campaigns, either partisan or nonpartisan. They still cannot run for public office themselves.

Workers' rights and benefits

For many years, federal government employees had only the protection of the civil service system. In 1962 President Kennedy issued an executive order that gave all federal workers the right to organize unions and bargain collectively. Since then government employee unions have flourished.

Unlike workers in the private sector, federal workers are pledged not to strike. Those who do can be fired. The most notable case was that of the Professional Air Traffic Controllers (PATCO)

Among the millions of civil service employees are highly trained lab technicians and scientists.

union. In 1981, PATCO members at airports throughout the country walked off their jobs, demanding higher pay and better working conditions. President Reagan ordered them back to work. When they refused, Reagan fired them with no chance to be rehired.

The PATCO case — an illegal strike — was unusual. Very few civil servants are fired. In fact, one criticism of the federal bureaucracy has been the difficulty and "red tape" involved in firing even incompetent or unnecessary workers.

Most federal workers leave the federal civil service voluntarily. Some resign to take higher paying positions in the private sector; others leave for personal reasons. Still others retire after reaching a certain age or serving a specified number of years. Like most workers in private firms, civil servants receive "perks" and fringe benefits — paid vacations, health insurance, and the like. Retirement benefits are generous. Each worker has 7 percent of his or her salary set aside for retirement, and those with 30 years of federal service may retire at half pay.

SECTION 4 REVIEW

Vocabulary and key terms

civil service (438)
patronage (438)
spoils system (438)
Pendleton Act (440)

veterans' preference (441)
GS rating (441)
Senior Executive
   Service (442)

For review

1. (a) Which federal government workers are appointed by the President? (b) How do others get federal government jobs? **3A**
2. When was the merit system established and why was it needed? **2E**
3. How are government jobs and pay scales standardized? **3A**
4. What limits are placed on the right of government workers to belong to labor unions and take part in politics? **3A**

Critical thinking

FORMING AN OPINION Were the Hatch Act restrictions on political activities before 1993 wise or unwise? Explain your answer. **4A**

Chapter Summary

To manage the responsibilities of the executive branch, the President depends largely on the many agencies and departments in the federal bureaucracy, or administration. The Executive Office of the President (EOP) includes the President's closest advisers and personal staff, as well as several advisory groups. Presidents have organized the EOP in either a "circular" or "pyramid" style.

The fourteen executive departments are responsible for most government operations. The heads of these departments, called Secretaries, are appointed by the President and make up the Cabinet, an advisory body to the President. Members of the "Inner Cabinet" — the Secretaries of State, Defense, and Treasury — usually share the President's views and are among his closest advisers. Other Cabinet Secretaries are more likely to concentrate on their own department's programs. Some Cabinet departments, corresponding congressional committees, and outside interest groups are said to make up a "cozy triangle" that influences policies.

The executive branch bureaucracy includes hundreds of other agencies. Independent regulatory commissions are concerned with making and enforcing regulations for specific activities and businesses. They serve legislative and judicial (as well as executive) functions. Complaints about too much regulation led to deregulation of many industries in the 1970's and 1980's. Government corporations provide certain public services under principles similar to those in private businesses. Executive agencies fulfill specialized functions outside of the Cabinet departments. The bureaucracy also hires government contractors to perform specific government-related jobs.

Most jobs in the bureaucracy are covered by the civil service system. Government jobs were formerly awarded to loyal party supporters under the spoils system. The Pendleton Act of 1883 established the merit system to award government jobs by competitive examinations. GS ratings determine the pay that workers receive. Like workers in private industry, federal employees receive a variety of fringe benefits.

443

2. In 1883, because many government employees were blatantly corrupt and/or incompetent. Presidents were also concerned about the time involved in filling patronage jobs.
3. Through the GS rating system.
4. They can organize and join unions, but they may not strike. Government workers cannot run for political office in a partisan campaign. Since the revision of the Hatch Acts, they can take part in partisan political campaigns.

Critical thinking Students may say that the restrictions were wise because the civil service should not become politicized. Others may argue that the restrictions violated the First Amendment rights of federal employees, and that it is only fair to allow these individuals to take part in political activity so long as no hiring or promotion decisions are made on a political basis.

CLOSURE
● Have students reread the quotation on p. 420 and explain how it applies to the section. Then have them read the next assigned lesson.

CHAPTER 16 CORRECTIVES
● To review the content of Chapter 16, you may want to have students complete **Study Guide/Review 16** or **Workbook Chapter 16.**

The symbol 👥 denotes active participation strategies.

Activities are keyed for student abilities:
▲ = Basic
● = All Levels
■ = Average/Advanced

Answers

Vocabulary See pp. T19–T21 for suggested vocabulary activities.

Reviewing the Facts

1. President Roosevelt needed help in administering his many New Deal programs.
2. The EOP was created by the Reorganization Act of 1939 to give administrative help to Roosevelt, whose staff was too small to implement all the New Deal programs.
3. The Attorney General and the Secretaries of State, Defense, and the Treasury are called the "Inner Cabinet" because they work most closely with the President and tend to share the President's goals and outlook.
4. In response to social and economic conditions that brought public demands for regulation.
5. Government corporation.
6. Not enough government workers to perform technical jobs, lower cost, and greater flexibility due to fewer regulations.
7. A written examination.

Thinking Critically About Key Concepts

1. The President can use advisers to screen and condense detailed information before it reaches his desk.
2. Members of the triangle might work together to advance their own interests rather than the interests of the nation. For example, pro-defense interest groups, defense-related congressional committees, and the Pentagon might join forces in support of a costly and unnecessary new weapons system.
3. Some students may argue that the former limitations on political activities violated the First Amendment. Others may say that such limitations helped to preserve workers' objectivity. For example,

444

● **Review the definitions of the following terms:**

administration	Executive Office of the	Office of Management and
bureaucracy	President	Budget
Cabinet	government corporation	patronage
civil service	GS rating	Pendleton Act
commissioners	independent regulatory	Senior Executive Service
"cozy triangle"	commission	spoils system
deregulation	National Security Council	veterans' preference
executive agency		White House Office

● **REVIEWING THE FACTS**

1. Why did the size of the presidential staff increase during the 1930's? **3A**
2. When and why was the Executive Office of the President (EOP) created? **3A**
3. Which Cabinet members are referred to as the "Inner Cabinet"? Why? **3A**
4. Why were independent regulatory commissions created? **7C**
5. The Postal Service is an example of which type of independent government agency? **3A**
6. What are three reasons why the government contracts with private businesses to perform certain tasks? **3A**
7. What process are applicants for the civil service required to complete? **3A**

▲ **THINKING CRITICALLY ABOUT KEY CONCEPTS**

1. President Carter's tendency to get bogged down in detail may have been a result of his taking President Truman's saying, "The Buck Stops Here," too seriously. How can a President overcome the problem of too much work and too little time? **4D**
2. What questionable conduct could result from the "cozy triangle" relationship involving executive agencies, congressional committees, and outside interests? Give specific examples. **4C**

444

3. Do you think the limits on the political activities of civil service employees before the revision of the Hatch Act were fair? How were these limits a restriction of civil liberties? How might an absence of limits have allowed an employee to take advantage of his or her position? Give reasons for your opinion. **4A**

▲ **PRACTICING SKILLS**

1. **Study Skills: Reading an organization chart.** Refer to Figure 16–1 (page 423) to answer the following questions. (a) Which office might address the problem of air pollution? (b) Which two elected officials are part of the EOP? (c) Which office probably handles the staffing of the President's residence? (To review charts, see Study Skill 2 in the back of the book.) **8B**
2. **Study Skills: Analyzing a photograph.** Examine the photo on page 434. (a) How can you tell that the Old Court Savings and Loan is closed? (b) Why might you assume that the people standing outside the savings and loan are customers? **8B**
3. **Critical Thinking Skills: Summarizing information.** Reread the subsection "Reasons for commissions" (page 432), and write a summary of the information presented there. Briefly restate the information in your own words, using the heading as a clue to what is important. **8C**

---

a civil service worker with ties to a presidential campaign could provide the campaign with sensitive information.

Practicing Skills
1. **(a)** The Council on Environmental Quality.
(b) President, Vice President.
(c) The White House Office.
2. **(a)** There is a notice on the front door, and people are waiting in line to get in.

(b) They are not dressed like bank employees.
3. Students should note that most commissions were created because of social or economic conditions and public demand for regula-

PARTICIPATORY CITIZENSHIP

1. **Government information.** Write a letter to a Federal Job Information Center to find specific information on the civil service. You might ask which jobs are presently available and what the requirements are for each. If you are interested in a certain career, you might ask when there may be an entry-level opening in that field. **3A**

2. **Research report.** Use the *Readers' Guide to Periodical Literature* to locate articles about AMTRAK and the Postal Service, two government corporations. Then write these corporations to obtain any other information you need. What are the problems associated with these corporations? What criticisms have been made about the way they are run, and what reforms have been suggested? Write a report detailing your findings. **3A**

WRITING ABOUT ISSUES

1. **Scripting a dialogue.** Write the dialogue of an argument between two people concerning reorganization of the Executive Office of the President. One person should propose placing all executive departments under the control of the Vice President, who then would report to the President. The other person should disagree. Have both sides explain their positions. **3A**

2. **Lobbying your representative.** Imagine that you are a federal merit worker and belong to a union. You feel that the denial to federal workers of the right to strike is an unfair restriction of your rights. Write a letter to your representative in Congress, explaining your viewpoint and advocating that the requirement that federal workers take a pledge not to strike be eliminated. **4C**

departments channeled through the Vice President.

2. Letters may argue that not being able to strike deprives a union of a basic weapon in efforts to protect members' rights.

Analyzing a Political Cartoon

1. The Pentagon and the defense industry.

2. Large defense contracts that profit corporations at taxpayers' expense.

3. They exchange places, creating a revolving door that closely links government agencies with private corporations.

4. The approach is ineffective because the two persons have simply exchanged places. Wasteful practices have not been eliminated.

ANALYZING A POLITICAL CARTOON

Advocates of ethics in government have long been concerned about the "revolving door" relationship between defense officials and corporations that make most of their profits from defense contracts. Look at the cartoon below and answer the following questions.

1. Who do the two men at the table represent? **8B**
2. What problem are they discussing? **8A**
3. What is their solution to the problem? **8B**
4. Does the cartoon suggest that their approach will be effective? Explain. **8H**

Cartoon by Dan Wasserman. Copyright, Boston Globe. Distributed by Los Angeles Times Syndicate. Reprinted with permission.

tion. They should also give a brief description of important commissions and their functions.

Participatory Citizenship

1. You may wish to invite one or more government workers from your area to visit the class and answer questions about their careers.

2. Students may work individually or in groups, and may present their reports to the class.

Writing About Issues

1. Dialogues should examine whether a President is better served by having direct contact with department heads or by having information from the

Chapter Review exercises are keyed for student abilities:
▲ = Basic
● = All Levels
■ = Average/Advanced

Background

One of the most vital issues of the 1992 presidential campaign was the future of the economy. A lingering recession had forced many businesses to close and millions of Americans were out of work. Angry voters, unhappy with the government's perceived unwillingness to tackle the issue, demanded that the candidates' focus their campaigns on their plans for economic recovery. Bill Clinton's emphasis on this issue helped him to win the election.

The newspapers quoted here express their concerns over the domestic problems facing the Clinton administration. They also express the fear that by concentrating on problems at home, the United States might neglect its role as a leader in the post-cold war world.

Geography

● On a classroom map or the world map on pp. 808–809, have students locate the different countries represented by newspapers quoted on this page. Then have students write a short summary of each editorial on a small adhesive note, and use these notes to annotate the map.

TRUTH, JUSTICE AND A SECOND TERM

AS OTHERS SEE US

1C, 5C

The World Press on President Clinton's Election

When the United States elects a President, the whole world watches. The following excerpts come from international press coverage of the 1992 presidential race between Bill Clinton and George Bush.

MUNICH, *Süddeutsche Zeitung.* It is difficult to discern a program or policy in the new President's persona. He succeeded in pleasing everyone and aggravating no one with a perfect marketing strategy.... No, Clinton was not elected, Bush was summarily fired.

NEW DELHI, *The Statesman.* A little rebellion now and then, Thomas Jefferson once wrote, is a good thing and as necessary to the political world as storms in the physical. While it may be a trifle hyperbolic to call Bill Clinton's victory a "little rebellion," ... his mandate is a ringing affirmation for change.

PARIS, *Libération.* Clinton's scenario is one of governmental activism, but it is limited by the deficit. He cannot allow himself the luxury of permitting the public debt to grow.... Making the "rich" pay will prove insufficient, given the size of the problem.

LIMA, *Expreso.* Bill Clinton's election as President of the U.S. could be the worst news of the year.... It may mean the return of the kind of advisers that surrounded the last Democratic President, Jimmy Carter.

PRAGUE, *Svobodné Slovo.* Such a decision by the most important world power is ... also a challenge for other nations. The governor of one of the poorest states in the union—Arkansas—embodies a President of a new, Kennedyesque type, next to whom European politicians undoubtedly will age in the eyes of the public.

BAGHDAD, *Al-Gomhouriya.* Bush is on his way to the dustbin of history, cursed by Iraqi children whose milk and dreams he burned.

TOKYO, *Yomiuri Shimbun.* Governor Bill Clinton's victory signals change for the United States, and we hope that the President-elect will make all out efforts to restructure the U.S. economy and display strong international leadership at this critical moment in world history.... Despite its preoccupation with domestic concerns, the U.S. must not neglect its diplomatic role in the post-cold war era.

MEXICO CITY, *La Jornada.* The election of Bill Clinton and Al Gore means the choice of a President and Vice President who are part of a young generation of North American men and women who did not participate in the second world war, who lived through the pain of Vietnam and, later, the decline of the U.S. economy and society. Without a doubt, they will know how to set new priorities and ... put their house in order.

From *World Press Review,* December, 1992.

CRITICAL THINKING

1. Which excerpt is critical of Bush? Why?
2. How would you characterize the general reactions to this election?

Critical Thinking Answers

1. The *Al-Gomhouriya* excerpt is critical of Bush. The Baghdad newspaper would be expected to criticize Bush after Iraq's defeat in the Gulf War.

2. The reactions are generally favorable toward Clinton's election, but cautious about the problems facing the United States.

GUIDE TO EXECUTIVE DEPARTMENTS

Even though the Cabinet and Executive Departments are not specifically mentioned in the Constitution, today they constitute a large part of the federal bureaucracy. Since the original three departments — State, War, Treasury — were established in 1789, other departments have been created and reorganized to meet the nation's changing needs.

DEPARTMENT	DATE ESTABLISHED	PAGE
AGRICULTURE	1889	448
COMMERCE	1903	449
DEFENSE	1949	450
EDUCATION	1979	451
ENERGY	1977	452
HEALTH and HUMAN SERVICES	1953	453
HOUSING and URBAN DEVELOPMENT	1965	454
INTERIOR	1849	455
JUSTICE	1870	456
LABOR	1913	457
STATE	1789	458
TRANSPORTATION	1966	459
TREASURY	1789	460
VETERANS AFFAIRS	1989	447

DEPARTMENT OF VETERANS AFFAIRS

The Department of Veterans Affairs was created in 1989 from what was formerly the Veterans Administration (VA). Before it was given cabinet-level status, the VA was the largest independent federal government agency, serving over 80 million Americans since its formation in 1930.

The Department of Veterans Affairs represents the interests and administers programs for the benefit of this country's veterans of military service and their dependents and beneficiaries.

The Secretary of Veterans Affairs directs the department and advises the President on issues relating to veterans.

Veterans Health Services and Research Administration Provides in-patient and out-patient medical care, as well as nursing home and home health care services to veterans and their dependents. Conducts research and aids in education in the health care professions.

Veterans Benefits Administration Offers a variety of benefits including disability and life insurance, pension plans, and other compensation packages. Provides vocational and rehabilitative training, access to employment services, and educational assistance. Provides credit assistance to prospective home-buyers, and operates a referral service informing veterans and their dependents of the rights and benefits to which they are entitled.

National Cemetery System Provides monuments for veterans' graves as well as aid to states for the creation and maintenance of veterans' cemeteries.

447

Guide to Executive Departments

This special feature section examines each of the Cabinet departments in the executive branch, listing their principal divisions and agencies. These overviews can give students an idea of the many areas in which the government acts, including activities with which they themselves may come in contact. This section also provides the starting point and background for numerous research projects and reports.

DEPARTMENT of AGRICULTURE

The Department of Agriculture (USDA) was created in 1862. In 1889 its duties were enlarged and the Secretary of Agriculture became a Cabinet member.

The department helps farmers improve and maintain their incomes and works to expand foreign markets for U.S. agricultural products. The department also works to prevent hunger and malnutrition and to help maintain the nation's soil, water, forests, and other natural resources. It also enforces standards of food quality.

The Secretary of Agriculture directs the department and advises the President on U.S. agricultural conditions and federal policies.

Agricultural Cooperative Service Assists farmers in organizing cooperatives to market farm products and purchase supplies.

Commodity Credit Corporation Protects farm income and prices by purchasing surplus products and selling them at home and abroad.

Consolidated Farm Service Agency Helps stabilize the price and production of crops and other commodities through loans, purchases, and payments to eligible farmers. Also provides income support and loans to farm families for farm operating costs, purchase or improvement of farmlands, and emergencies arising from natural disasters. Supervises Federal Crop Insurance Corporation.

Federal Crop Insurance Corporation Promotes the stability of agriculture by providing crop insurance to cover unavoidable losses caused by weather conditions, insects, crop disease, fires, floods, or earthquakes.

Food and Consumer Service Administers the Food Stamp Program, the National School Lunch Program and other child nutrition programs, and various consumer services.

Irrigating croplands in the arid West.

Food Safety and Inspection Service Inspects and ensures accurate labeling of meat and poultry products moving in interstate or foreign commerce to make sure they are safe.

Foreign Agricultural Service (FAS) Promotes the exportation of American farm products, the expansion of overseas markets, and the elimination of trade barriers. It also provides loans to countries importing U.S. agricultural products and donates food for famine relief, economic development, and school lunch programs.

Forest Service Supervises the national forests to provide a continuing flow of renewable resources and to manage the nation's nonrenewable energy and mineral resources.

Natural Resources Conservation Service Provides technical and financial assistance for soil and water conservation programs. Creates incentives for farmers to conserve wetlands and forests that lie in farming areas.

Rural Housing and Community Development Service Provides loans for construction of homes for farm families and construction of community facilities in rural areas.

Rural Utilities Service Provides financial assistance for the construction and maintenance of rural electric and telephone utilities. Also supplies grants for water and waste treatment facilities and services.

Other Services
Agricultural Marketing Service
Agricultural Research Service
Animal and Plant Health Inspection Service
Grain Inspection, Packers and Stockyards
    Administration
Human Nutrition Information Service
Office of International Cooperation and Development

DEPARTMENT of COMMERCE

The Department of Commerce and Labor was created in 1903. In 1913 all labor activities were transferred to the newly created Department of Labor.

The department promotes the nation's international trade, economic growth, and technological advancement. It carries out a number of programs to achieve these goals while maintaining a competitive free enterprise system.

The Secretary of Commerce directs the department and advises the President on federal policies and programs affecting industry and trade.

Bureau of the Census As directed by the Constitution, the bureau takes a census of U.S. population every 10 years. It collects, tabulates, and publishes a variety of statistical information about the people and economy of the United States, including agriculture, manufacturing, population trends, employment, and housing.

Bureau of Economic Analysis Provides a clear picture of the U.S. economy by preparing accounts of the gross national product (GNP), personal income, and foreign trade. Analyzes measures of business activities and forecasts economic developments.

Minority Business Development Agency Assists businesses run by minority groups to participate in the American free enterprise system and to overcome economic disadvantages that have limited their participation in the past. Provides management and technical assistance to minority firms. Coordinates federal, state, and local efforts to provide market opportunities for minority businesses.

National Institute of Standards and Technology Provides a national system of physical and chemical measurements. Coordinates with the measurement systems of other nations to ensure fair trade. Provides research in engineering, science, and technology to strengthen the productivity and competitiveness of American industry.

National Oceanic and Atmospheric Administration (NOAA) Explores, maps, and charts the world's oceans in order to manage, use, and conserve ocean resources and sea life. Forecasts the weather in the United States and its possessions and issues warnings of hurricanes, tornadoes, floods, and tidal waves. Operates a national satellite system to observe the environment.

Weather balloon at an Antarctic research station.

National Technical Information Service The central source for the public sale of U.S. government-sponsored research, development, and engineering reports in print and on computer files. Makes available scientific and technical information gathered from U.S. and foreign sources.

Patent and Trademark Office Oversees a system of patents to provide inventors with exclusive rights to the results of their creative efforts and to promote invention, investment in research and development, and the commercial use of new technology. Registers trademarks — distinctive words, names, or symbols — used by businesses to identify their products and distinguish them from products sold by others.

Other Services

Economic Development Administration
International Trade Administration
National Telecommunications and Information Administration
U.S. Travel and Tourism Administration

DEPARTMENT of DEFENSE

The United States Army, Navy, and Marine Corps were all created by the Continental Congress in 1775. The Department of War (1789) and the Department of the Navy (1798) were combined with the Air Force into a single Department of Defense (DOD) in 1949. Within the DOD, the Army, Navy, and Air Force now constitute separate departments, each with its own secretary.

The Department of Defense is responsible for providing the necessary military forces to prevent war and to protect the nation's security. The armed forces are made up of close to 2 million men and women on active duty, with about a million on reserve in case of emergency. The DOD also employs about a million civilians.

The Secretary of Defense, always a civilian, is the President's principal adviser on matters of national defense. Under the direction of the President, who is commander-in-chief of the armed forces, the Secretary directs the DOD's Operations.

Military aircraft warming up before a flight.

Joint Chiefs of Staff The Joint Chiefs of Staff are the principal military advisers to the President, the Secretary of Defense, and the National Security Council. They are the top military officers of the U.S. Army, Navy, Marine Corps, and Air Force. Commands given by the President are handed down through the Joint Chiefs to the military units. In addition, the Joint Chiefs prepare strategic plans and recommend military actions.

Department of the Air Force Provides air forces to help maintain the peace and security of the United States. Provides air transportation for personnel and cargo of all U.S. military forces worldwide. Prepares for air defense and reconnaissance in the continental U.S. as well as in Alaska, the Pacific, Europe, and in space.

Department of the Army Organizes, trains, and equips active duty and reserve forces to defend the nation. The Army trains soldiers with modern weapons and equipment to be ready to respond quickly for operations on land. It also assists federal, state, and local governments in emergencies.

The Secretary of the Army also oversees the Panama Canal Commission, the civil works program of the Corps of Engineers, and Arlington and Soldiers' Home National Cemeteries.

Department of the Navy Both the U.S. Navy and the U.S. Marine Corps are under the authority of the Department of the Navy. Their mission is to protect the United States by carrying out war at sea and to maintain freedom of the seas.

The Navy maintains seagoing forces including the Pacific Fleet, the Atlantic Fleet, and the Military Sealift Command. These fleets are composed of ships, submarines, and aircraft.

The Marine Corps is a separate service within the Department of the Navy. It provides forces to defend and seize naval bases and performs land operations that may be necessary in a naval campaign.

Service Academies A college education plus military training are offered by the U.S. Military Academy (West Point, N.Y.), the U.S. Naval Academy (Annapolis, Md.), and the U.S. Air Force Academy (Colorado Springs, Colo.).

National Security Agency Protects U.S. communications and computer systems, establishes security procedures for the U.S. government, and gathers information about foreign governments through surveillance and codebreaking.

Other Services
DOD Specialized Agencies
National Defense University (includes National War College, Armed Forces Staff College)
Strategic Defense Initiative Organization

DEPARTMENT of EDUCATION

The Department of Education was created in 1979. Its functions were previously carried out by the Department of Health, Education, and Welfare.

The department establishes policies for, administers, and coordinates most federal education programs.

The Secretary of Education directs the department and advises the President on the government's programs, policies, and plans relating to education.

Office of Bilingual Education and Minority Languages Affairs Ensures access to equal educational opportunities for students with limited ability in English. Provides assistance for the development and implementation of programs to desegregate public schools.

Office of Civil Rights Administers and enforces civil rights laws related to education and disabled students. Ensures that education programs receiving federal funding meet civil rights requirements.

Office of Elementary and Secondary Education Formulates policy for and directs activities relating to preschool, elementary, and secondary education. Administers grants to state educational agencies and local school districts for the education of Native Americans, migrants, neglected and delinquent students, and students with special needs arising from racial segregation and discrimination.

Office of Postsecondary Education Formulates policy and directs programs for assistance to colleges, universities, and their students. Administers federal programs of student financial aid, including Basic Educational Opportunity Grants (BEOG) and the Guaranteed Student Loan (GSL) program.

Office of Special Education and Rehabilitative Services Carries out special education programs designed to meet the needs and develop the full potential of children with disabilities. Programs include the training of teachers, grants for research, and media services and captioned films for the deaf.

Office of Vocational and Adult Education Administers programs of grants, contracts, and assistance for vocational and technical education, professional education, and community schools.

The office is also responsible for providing a comprehensive approach to education in rural areas of the nation.

Federally Aided Corporations The Department of Education's budget also includes funding for the following educational institutions: American Printing House for the Blind (Louisville, Ky.), Gallaudet College (Washington, D.C.), which provides higher education for hearing-impaired students, National Technical Institute for the Deaf (at the Rochester [N.Y.] Institute of Technology), and Howard University (Washington, D.C.).

Programs supported by the U.S. Department of Education offer special opportunities for students with disabilities.

DEPARTMENT of ENERGY

The Department of Energy, created in 1977, brought together the major federal energy programs previously carried out by several executive departments and agencies.

The department provides the framework for a balanced national energy plan. It is responsible for the research and development of energy technology, energy conservation, nuclear weapons, and programs that regulate energy use.

The Secretary of Energy directs the department and is the principal adviser to the President on energy policies, plans, and programs.

Office of Civilian Radioactive Waste Management Handles programs for the storage and disposal of high-level radioactive wastes from nuclear reactors and used fuel rods.

Office of Conservation and Renewable Energy Develops programs to increase the production and use of renewable energy (solar, wind, geothermal, alcohol fuels, etc.). It also researches more efficient ways of using energy for transportation, buildings, and industries. The office administers federal financial assistance programs for state energy planning and conservation.

Office of Defense Programs Directs U.S. nuclear weapons research, development, testing, and production. The office also monitors foreign nuclear weapons development and testing.

Office of Energy Research Manages the department's research programs in basic energy physics, high energy physics, and fusion. The office funds research in universities and other projects outside the department. It also conducts research to determine the environmental, health, and safety aspects of energy programs.

An offshore oil rig in the Gulf of Mexico.

Office of Fossil Energy Conducts research and development programs involving coal, petroleum, and natural gas. Its objective is to provide information that can be used to develop these sources. The office also manages federal Energy Technology Centers, the Strategic Petroleum Reserve, and the Naval Petroleum and Oil Shale Reserves.

Office of International Affairs and Energy Emergencies Develops programs relating to U.S. international energy policies. The office monitors prices and trends of world energy supplies. It also works with foreign governments and international organizations in coordinating energy programs.

Office of Nuclear Energy Conducts research and development of nuclear reactors, nuclear fuel, and space applications of nuclear energy. Evaluates proposed nuclear technologies.

Federal Energy Regulatory Commission (FERC) An independent commission of five members within the Department of Energy. It is responsible for setting the rates and charges for the transportation and sale of natural gas, the transmission and sale of electricity, and the licensing of hydroelectric plants. The commission also establishes rates for the transportation of oil by pipeline.

Other Services
Economic Regulatory Administration
Energy Information Administration
Office of Environment, Safety, and Health
Office of Minority Economic Impact
Alaska Power Administration
Bonneville Power Administration
Southeastern Power Administration
Southwestern Power Administration
Western Area Power Administration

DEPARTMENT of HEALTH and HUMAN SERVICES

The Department of Health, Education, and Welfare was created in 1953. In 1979 its responsibilities were divided between two departments — the Department of Education and the present Department of Health and Human Services.

The Department of Health and Human Services is the executive department most concerned with people and their needs. Its most important functions include making health services more widely available to the public and administering the Social Security system.

The Secretary of Health and Human Services directs the department and advises the President on health, welfare, and income security policies.

Administration for Children, Youth, and Families Supports and encourages the sound development of children, youth, and families. It also administers Head Start and oversees programs for runaway, abused, and neglected children.

Alcohol, Drug Abuse, and Mental Health Administration (Public Health Service) Conducts research on causes, treatment, and prevention of alcoholism, drug abuse, and mental illness.

Centers for Disease Control and Prevention (Public Health Service) Administers national programs for the prevention and control of communicable and other preventable diseases and implements programs for health emergencies. Develops workplace safety and health standards. Conducts research and education about smoking and health.

Food and Drug Administration (FDA) Protects the health of the nation against impure and unsafe food, drugs, cosmetics, and other potential hazards. Develops and implements standards for the safety and proper labeling of food and drugs. Conducts programs to control exposure of humans to radiation and toxic chemicals.

Health Care Financing Administration Administers Medicare and Medicaid. Medicare is a health insurance program for persons over 65 years of age and certain disabled persons. Medicaid provides medical services to those who cannot afford adequate medical care.

National Institutes of Health Conducts research into the causes, prevention, and cure of cancer, arthritis, diabetes, allergies, and other diseases. Runs the National Library of Medicine.

Medical personnel in a research laboratory.

Resources and Services Administration Administers programs to improve health services. Coordinates efforts to finance public and private health care organizations, including health maintenance organizations (HMOs). Plans and administers training programs. Provides assistance for modernizing health care facilities.

Other Services
Administration on Aging
Administration for Native Americans
Administration on Developmental Disabilities
Health Resources and Services Administration
National Center for Health Statistics
Office of Child Support Enforcement
Office of Community Services
Office of Family Assistance
Office of Refugee Settlement
Substance Abuse and Mental Health Service
   Administration

DEPARTMENT of HOUSING and URBAN DEVELOPMENT

The Department of Housing and Urban Development (HUD) was created in 1965. It is the main federal agency concerned with housing needs, fair housing opportunities, and community development.

The department helps families buy homes, provides subsidies for lower-income families to rent homes, and repairs and preserves urban centers.

The Secretary of Housing and Urban Development directs the department and advises the President on federal policy, programs, and activities relating to housing and community development.

Construction workers discussing building plans.

Office of Block Grant Assistance Assists in the development of urban communities by providing decent housing, a suitable living environment, and greater economic opportunities, primarily for persons of low or moderate income. Grants are provided for cities to revitalize neighborhoods, encourage economic development, and provide improved community services.

Office of Environment and Energy Develops policies to protect and enhance environmental quality and to conserve energy in communities. Activities include setting standards for minimum distances between housing and for sources of noise pollution; weatherizing housing; installing solar equipment; and preparing strategies for energy use.

Office of Fair Housing and Equal Opportunity Formulates policies and carries out federal laws relating to civil rights and equal opportunity in housing, community development, employment, and business.

Office of Housing Insures loans for the buying, building, or fixing of housing; for property improvement; and for housing for the elderly, nursing homes, and group medical practices. Supplies grants to communities for the development of rental housing.

Office of Policy Development and Research Conducts research, studies, and testing of existing and proposed programs and policies relating to housing and community development.

Office of Public and Indian Housing Provides technical and financial assistance in planning, developing, and managing public housing programs. Helps meet special housing and development requirements for Indian and Alaskan Native communities.

Office of Urban Development Action Grants Provides grants to encourage new or increased private investment in cities and urban communities experiencing economic difficulties.

Office of Urban Rehabilitation Provides low-interest loans to help repair family homes. Transfers federally owned residences to homesteaders who agree to repair, maintain, and live in them for at least three years.

Other Services
Government National Mortgage Association

DEPARTMENT of the INTERIOR

The Department of the Interior was created in 1849 as a general "housekeeper" for the federal government. Its chief responsibility is now the conservation of our natural resources.

The department oversees the use of most of the nationally owned public lands and natural resources in the United States. This includes ensuring wise use of land and water resources, protecting fish and wildlife, managing mineral resources, and preserving national parks and historical places. The department also administers American Indian reservations and U.S. island territories.

The Secretary of the Interior directs the department and advises the President on national policies concerning resources and governing the territories.

Bureau of Indian Affairs Seeks to encourage and train Indian and Alaskan Native people to manage their own affairs. Works to guarantee adequate educational opportunities, social and community development, economic advancement, and full use of natural resources.

Bureau of Mines Helps ensure an adequate supply of minerals for security and other nonfuel purposes. Conducts research to provide technology for the safe extraction, processing, use, and recycling of minerals.

Bureau of Reclamation Manages water projects to improve the quality of life in dry areas of the western states. Water supplies are developed for drinking, irrigation, power generation, recreation, navigation, and flood control.

Fish and Wildlife Service Works to conserve, protect, and enhance fish and wildlife and their habitats. Administers a national program for appreciation of wildlife. Works to protect and restore endangered species. Manages fisheries throughout the United States.

Geological Survey (USGS) Prepares maps, conducts research, and performs experiments to identify land, mineral, water, and energy resources. Classifies federal lands for resources and energy potential. Investigates earthquakes, volcanoes, and landslides.

National Park Service Maintains a system of more than 330 national parks, historic sites, and recreational areas for the enjoyment and education of the public. Assists state and local governments in the development of parks and protection of the natural environment.

Office of Surface Mining Reclamation and Enforcement Protects people and the environment from the effects of coal mining. Regulates strip mining activities to prevent permanent damage to land and water resources and assists the states in developing regulatory programs.

Office of Youth Programs Develops programs for employment and training of youth, including the Job Corps Civilian Conservation Centers program and the Youth Conservation Corps.

Other Services
Bureau of Land Management
Mineral Management Services

Geologists at work.

DEPARTMENT of JUSTICE

The Department of Justice was established in 1870 with the Attorney General as its head. Before 1870, the Attorney General was a member of the President's Cabinet but not the head of a department.

The department enforces the law in the interest of the American people. It protects them against crime, ensures healthy competition among businesses, and enforces naturalization and immigration laws. The department represents the United States in legal affairs and handles all Supreme Court cases concerning the United States.

The Attorney General directs the Department of Justice and gives legal advice to the President and the heads of the executive departments. The Solicitor General represents the U.S. government before the Supreme Court. In extremely important cases, the Attorney General appears personally before the Court.

Antitrust Division Promotes and maintains business competition by enforcing federal antitrust laws. These laws prohibit activities that restrain trade or are intended to gain or keep monopoly power in any industry.

Civil Rights Division Enforces federal laws that prohibit discrimination on the basis of race, national origin, religion, sex, or handicap in the areas of voting, education, employment, housing, credit, the use of public facilities and accommodations; and in programs and research receiving federal aid.

A Border Patrol officer with aerial back-up.

Criminal Division Investigates and prosecutes criminal violations, including narcotics and dangerous drug trafficking, espionage, sabotage, fraud, and white-collar crime.

Federal Bureau of Investigation (FBI) The main investigative division of the Department of Justice, it is responsible for putting together evidence, reporting facts, and locating witnesses for federal cases. The FBI also carries out fingerprint identification, laboratory examinations, and police training.

Immigration and Naturalization Service (INS) Controls and facilitates the entry of qualified persons into the United States; denies admission to unqualified aliens. Promotes and carries out naturalization of resident aliens; apprehends and removes aliens who have entered the United States illegally.

International Criminal Police Organization (INTERPOL) An international organization made up of 136 member countries. Its purpose is to prevent or suppress international crime. It investigates violent crimes, robbery, large-scale narcotics offenses, fraud and counterfeiting, as well as certain humanitarian cases such as missing persons. It also locates and arrests international fugitives and returns them to the country where they committed crimes.

Other Services
Bureau of Prisons
Civil Division
Drug Enforcement Administration
Land and Natural Resources Division
Tax Division
U.S. Marshals Service

DEPARTMENT of LABOR

The Department of Labor was created in 1913. Its responsibilities were previously carried out by the Department of Commerce and Labor, organized in 1903.

The purpose of the department is to promote the welfare of wage earners in the United States. It carries out laws guaranteeing safe working conditions, fair wages, freedom from job discrimination, unemployment insurance, and worker's compensation. It also oversees the activities of labor unions. A Bureau of International Labor Affairs represents the interests of American workers in worldwide trade agreements and policies.

The Secretary of Labor directs the department and advises the President on labor and employment policies.

Bureau of Labor-Management Relations and Cooperative Programs Assists employers and employees in meeting long-range problems caused by changing economic and technological conditions. Provides data for use in negotiations between management and labor. Helps presidential emergency boards deal with major labor disputes.

Bureau of Labor Statistics (BLS) Gathers and publishes data on employment, unemployment, prices, family expenses, wages, and other areas related to labor. Calculates the consumer price index (CPI).

Employment Standards Administration Administers minimum wage and overtime pay laws. Determines wages to be paid in government contracts. Ensures nondiscrimination and affirmative action in hiring of minorities, women, veterans, and disabled workers for government contracts.

Employment and Training Administration Manages the federal-state unemployment insurance program to provide income support for people thrown out of work. Assists states in providing job placement offices for the unemployed and recruitment services for employers. Administers the Work Incentive program (WIN) to help persons receiving welfare become self-supporting and the Job Training Partnership Act to train low-income individuals for jobs in the private sector. Oversees a number of other programs relating to employment and job training.

Occupational Safety and Health Administration (OSHA) Develops job safety and health standards and regulations. Conducts investiga-

Protective clothing to ensure workers' safety.

tions to make sure standards are met and imposes penalties on employers who fail to comply.

Office of Labor-Management Standards Regulates the handling of union funds, the election of union officers, and other internal union procedures to protect the rights of union members. Oversees the labor organizations of postal workers and other federal employees.

Other Services
Office of Pension and Welfare Benefit Programs
Mine Safety and Health Administration
Veterans' Employment and Training Service

457

DEPARTMENT of STATE

The Department of State, created in 1789, is the oldest executive department. Under the President's direction, it makes and carries out foreign policy for the United States.

The department's overall goal is to coordinate foreign policy to promote the security and well-being of the United States. It analyzes American overseas interests, recommends future actions, and takes the necessary steps to carry out established policy. The department represents the United States in foreign nations, in the United Nations, and in over fifty international organizations. It also negotiates treaties and agreements with foreign nations.

The Secretary of State directs the department and is the President's chief foreign policy adviser. The Secretary represents the President in meetings with heads of foreign nations and is a member of the National Security Council.

A U.S. passport issued by the State Department.

Undersecretary for Economic Affairs Helps make and carry out foreign economic policy, including international monetary affairs, trade, energy, and relations with developing nations.

Regional Bureaus Five regional bureaus direct foreign affairs in major geographic regions: the Bureaus of African Affairs, European and Canadian Affairs, East Asian and Pacific Affairs, Inter-American Affairs, and Near Eastern and South Asian Affairs.

Bureau of Consular Affairs Issues passports, visas, and related documents in accordance with immigration and nationality laws. It is also responsible for the welfare of American citizens and interests abroad.

Bureau of Intelligence and Research Coordinates intelligence programs and research for the department and other federal agencies. Gathers and analyzes information critical to the determination and execution of foreign policy.

Bureau of Politico-Military Affairs Develops department policies on security, military assistance, nuclear weapons, and arms control.

Bureau of Public Affairs Supervises the exchange of information between the department and the American people through media appearances, conferences, and briefings. Advises the department on public opinion. Produces publications, films, videotapes, and other educational materials on U.S. foreign policy.

Foreign Service Maintains embassies, consulates, and other offices throughout the world. These offices conduct U.S. affairs in foreign nations and keep the department and the President informed on developments that affect the welfare of the American people. Activities include negotiating agreements, explaining U.S. policy, and maintaining cordial relations with the nations in which they are located. Ambassadors represent the President and are in charge of Foreign Service operations in the country of their assignment.

Office of the Chief of Protocol Principal adviser to the U.S. government on diplomatic procedure and international laws and customs. Coordinates visits of foreign officials, operates the President's guest house, and conducts official ceremonial events.

Other Services
Bureau of International Organization Affairs
Bureau of Oceans and International Environmental and Scientific Affairs
Office of Human Rights and Humanitarian Affairs

DEPARTMENT of TRANSPORTATION

The Department of Transportation was created in 1966 to coordinate the nation's overall transportation policy. Its duties and responsibilities include highway planning, development, and construction; urban mass transit; railroads; air travel; and the safety of waterways, ports, highways, and gas and oil pipelines.

The Secretary of Transportation directs the department and is the principal adviser to the President in all matters relating to federal transportation programs.

U.S. Coast Guard The Coast Guard is a service of the Department of Transportation except when operating as part of the Navy in time of war or when the President directs. It is responsible for saving lives and property on the high seas and for enforcing federal and international laws in the navigable waters of the United States. It also administers safety standards for commercial vessels and offshore structures. Other responsibilities include protection of the marine environment, safety of ports and bridges, icebreaking, and safety of recreational boats.

Federal Aviation Administration (FAA) Regulates both commercial and military air navigation. Enforces safety standards for the manufacture and operation of aircraft. Certifies pilots. Oversees airport safety, and operates control towers to regulate air traffic.

Federal Highway Administration Oversees all aspects of the nation's highways. Provides financial assistance to the states for highway construction and maintenance and for urban roads and streets. It ensures highway safety and enforces safety laws for all vehicles involved in foreign or interstate commerce. It also conducts research concerning traffic congestion, street and highway safety, and effective highway design.

Federal Railroad Administration Administers and enforces federal laws to promote railroad safety. Administers a program of assistance for national, regional, and local railroads. Conducts research to improve safety and to develop techniques for ground transportation.

National Highway Traffic Safety Administration (NHTSA) Carries out motor vehicle safety programs to reduce highway accidents and to reduce the seriousness of injuries when crashes do occur. Sets automobile fuel economy standards. Oversees national speed limit laws.

Urban Mass Transportation Administration Provides grants and loans to state and local governments and private business to develop and operate mass transit systems. Conducts research to improve efficiency of mass transportation. Gives grants to universities for research relating to urban transportation.

Other Services
Maritime Administration
Research and Special Programs Administration
Saint Lawrence Seaway Development Corporation

Highway and traffic patterns in a crowded city.

459

DEPARTMENT of the TREASURY

The Department of the Treasury was created in 1789. It is responsible for coordinating the federal government's economic, financial, and tax policies. It also manufactures coins and currency and manages the public debt.

The Secretary of the Treasury directs the department and advises the President on domestic and international economic policy.

Customs Service officials inspecting a package.

Bureau of Alcohol, Tobacco, and Firearms Enforces and administers laws covering the production, distribution, and use of firearms, explosives, and alcohol and tobacco products. Collects excise taxes on the alcohol and tobacco industries.

Bureau of Engraving and Printing Designs, engraves, and prints U.S. paper currency, postage stamps, Treasury certificates, and other U.S. securities. Assists in the design and production of other government documents that require protection from counterfeiting.

Bureau of the Public Debt Manages the public debt and payment of interest. Does the bookkeeping for most federal borrowing.

Federal Law Enforcement Training Center Conducts training programs for 59 federal law enforcement agencies. Offers specialized training programs for state and local law enforcement officials.

Financial Management Service Manages the collection, investment, payment, and accounting of the federal government's money. Issues Treasury checks for payment of federal salaries, payments to persons who supply goods and services to the government, income tax refunds, and social security and veterans' benefits.

Internal Revenue Service (IRS) Collects nearly all federal taxes, including personal and corporate income taxes as well as social security, excise, estate, and gift taxes. It also enforces tax laws and provides information to taxpayers.

Office of the Comptroller of the Currency Administers federal laws regulating nearly 5,000 national and District of Columbia banks. Approves charters for new national banks. Conducts periodic examinations of banks to appraise their financial condition, management, and compliance with federal laws.

U.S. Customs Service Collects duties from imports and enforces customs and other related laws. Inspects goods entering and leaving the United States to prevent smuggling and other illegal practices in international trade.

U.S. Mint Manufactures coins for national commerce and proof sets for collectors. The Mint also oversees the government's reserves of gold and silver and manufactures national medals.

U.S. Savings Bond Division Promotes and sells United States savings bonds.

U.S. Secret Service Protects the President and Vice President and members of their immediate families, former Presidents and their wives or widows, presidential and vice-presidential candidates, and visiting heads of foreign states. It also enforces laws against counterfeiting.

UNIT
★ 6 ★

NATIONAL GOVERNMENT: The Judicial Branch

CHAPTER

17 The SUPREME COURT and the FEDERAL COURT SYSTEM

18 LAW and the LEGAL PROCESS

Photo
Supreme Court building.

National Government: The Judicial Branch
(pp. 461–510)

Unit Overview
Article III of the Constitution establishes the judicial branch of the federal government. It creates the Supreme Court and authorizes Congress to set up the rest of the federal courts. Congress began this process with the Judiciary Act of 1789 and over the past 200 years has expanded the system. In fashioning the nation's judicial structure the framers of the Constitution, and then Congress, carefully balanced the rights of the individual and society's need for laws. The results of this combination are outlined in Chapters 17 and 18, which review how the law has developed and how it is applied in both the civil and criminal settings.

CHAPTER 17
THE SUPREME COURT AND THE FEDERAL COURT SYSTEM
(pp. 462–487)

	Section Objectives	Section Resources
Section 1 The Federal Courts Interpret National Laws	☐ detail the different kinds and jurisdictions of federal courts ☐ describe the structure of the federal court system	▲ SKILLS PRACTICE WORKSHEET **17**
Section 2 Federal Judges Are Appointed Officials	☐ detail the rules governing the impeachment and salaries of federal judges ☐ describe the appointment process for federal judges	▲ TRANSPARENCY **38**
Section 3 The Supreme Court Decides Difficult Cases	☐ explain how cases reach the Supreme Court ☐ describe the typical procedure for a Supreme Court case	▲ TRANSPARENCY **39**
Section 4 Many Factors Influence Supreme Court Decisions	☐ describe the factors that influence Supreme Court decisions ☐ explain how the President and Congress check the powers of the Supreme Court	■ SKILLS CHALLENGE WORKSHEET **17** ● PRIMARY SOURCE WORKSHEET **19** ■ CONSTITUTIONAL ISSUES WORKSHEET **12**

Essential Elements

The list below shows Essential Elements relevant to this chapter. (The complete list of Essential Elements appears in the introductory pages of this Teacher's Edition.)

Section 1: 1D, 3A, 3C, 8B, 8H

Section 2: 3A, 3B, 4B, 8F

Section 3: 2D, 3A, 6C, 6I, 8B

Your Turn feature (p. 479): 5B, 5C

Section 4: 2A, 3B, 4B, 5C, 6I, 8B, 8D

Chapter Review: 2A, 2C, 3A, 3C, 4B, 4C, 7D, 8A, 8B

> Section Resources are keyed for student abilities:
> ▲ = Basic
> ● = All Levels
> ■ = Average/Advanced

Homework Options

Each section contains activities labeled "Guided/Independent Practice," "Reteaching/Correctives," and "Enrichment/Extension." You may wish to choose from among these activities when assigning homework.

Students Acquiring English Activities

Show the video *The Road to the Supreme Court—The Webster Case* before assigning this chapter. Play "Jeopardy" on the contents of the video by giving students names and definitions of individuals and laws discussed in the video. For example: Answer provided—Frank Susman; question supplied by students—Who was the attorney for the plaintiff? Answer provided—it declared life begins at conception; question supplied by students—What was the preamble to the Missouri law passed in 1986?

LISTENING/SPEAKING: Review with the class the following court cases that affected educational institutions: *Brown v. Board of Education* (pp. 200–201), *Engel v. Vitale* (p. 146), and *Regents of the University of California v. Bakke* (pp. 210–211). Ask students to decide whether their opinions would have been with the majority or the minority. Then ask them to explain their positions.

Case Studies

When teaching this chapter, you may use Case Study 2, which discusses the issue of preventing minors from buying albums considered obscene, or Case Study 3, which examines the role of religion in public education. (Case Studies may be found following p. 510.)

Teacher Bibliography

Cox, Archibald. *The Court and the Constitution.* Houghton Mifflin, 1988. Chronicles the issues, debates, and individuals who have kept the Constitution vital.

Steamer, Robert J. *Chief Justice: Leadership and the Supreme Court.* University of South Carolina Press, 1986. Analyzes the style and contributions of the fifteen men who have served as chief justice.

Woodward, Bob. *The Brethren: Inside the Supreme Court.* Avon, 1980. The classic exposé of the inner workings of the Supreme Court from 1969 to 1976.

Student Bibliography

Anzovin, Steven and Janet Podell, eds. *The U.S. Constitution and the Supreme Court.* Wilson, 1988. A collection of articles that explores the ways in which the Supreme Court interprets the Constitution.

Tribe, Laurence H. *God Save This Honorable Court: How the Choice of Supreme Court Justices Shapes Our History.* Random House, 1985. Emphasizing the pervasive impact of the high court's decisions, the author urges a more careful selection and approval of justices.

Literature

Douglas, William O. *The Court Years, 1939–1975; The Autobiography of William O. Douglas.* Random House, 1980. The memoirs of one of the great Supreme Court justices.

Stites, Francis N. *John Marshall: Defender of the Constitution.* Little, Brown, 1981. Describes the Court and its chief justice during the early days of the republic.

Truman, Margaret. *Murder in the Supreme Court.* Fawcett, 1985. A whodunit that delves into the public and private lives of Supreme Court justices and their staffs.

CHAPTER RESOURCES

Study Guide/Review 17
Workbook Chapter 17
Chapter 17 Test, Forms A–C

Films and Videotapes*

The Judicial Branch. (Series title: *Government As It Is.*) 26 min. Pyramid, 1980. f, v. An analysis of the evolution of the powers and functions of the federal judiciary. Looks at the district courts, Circuit Court of Appeals, and the Supreme Court.

The United States Supreme Court: Guardian of the Constitution. 2nd ed. 23 min. EBEC, 1973. f. The history of the U.S. Supreme Court, including synopses of some landmark cases.

Software*

Law in American History I and *Law in American History II* (Apple, IBM). Queue. Students are presented with the facts of Supreme Court landmark cases through the case study method and must identify legal issues, relate them to the Constitution, examine precedents, and render an opinion.

The Research Companion: Supreme Court Decisions (Apple). Focus. Students become legal assistants to a Supreme Court justice who has access to landmark cases.

* For a complete guide to audiovisual sources, see page T22.

CHAPTER 17

**The Supreme Court
and the Federal Court
System** *(pp. 462–487)*

Chapter 17 examines the role of
the Supreme Court and other
federal courts, including their
jurisdictions, the organization of
the federal court system, and the
manner in which judges are
appointed.

Chapter Objectives

After students complete this
chapter, they will be able to:

1. Detail the different kinds and
jurisdictions of federal courts.
2. Describe the structure of the
federal court system.
3. Detail the rules governing
the impeachment and salaries of
federal judges.
4. Describe the appointment
process for federal judges.
5. Explain how cases reach the
Supreme Court.
6. Describe the typical procedure for a Supreme Court case.
7. Describe the factors that
influence Supreme Court
decisions.
8. Explain how the President
and Congress check the powers
of the Supreme Court.

CHAPTER

17

The SUPREME COURT and the FEDERAL COURT SYSTEM

It is the body to which all Americans
look for the ultimate protection of
their rights. It is to the U.S. Supreme
Court that we all turn when we seek
that which we want most from our
government: equal justice under the
law.

Justice Sandra Day O'Connor
Confirmation hearing, 1981

462

Photo
Supreme Court chambers.

When Sandra Day O'Connor graduated from Stanford University Law School in 1952, she was ranked number three in her class. The top student that year, William Rehnquist, got a job in Washington, D.C., clerking for a Supreme Court justice. O'Connor looked around for a position in a private law firm. "I interviewed with law firms in Los Angeles and San Francisco," she recalled years later. "But none had ever hired a woman before as a lawyer and they were not prepared to do so." She did get one offer—to work as a legal secretary.

Eventually Sandra Day O'Connor got quite a different job in the legal profession. She became a Supreme Court justice, the first woman to serve in that capacity.

Justices and other federal judges play an important role in our government. Though the President and Congress shape the policies and laws of the United States, the courts are where these laws are ultimately tested. This chapter examines the Supreme Court and the federal court system.

CHAPTER OUTLINE

1 The Federal Courts Interpret National Laws

Federal Court Jurisdiction
Federal Court Structure
Special Courts

2 Federal Judges Are Appointed Officials

Constitutional Provisions
Selecting Federal Judges
Who Becomes a Federal Judge?

3 The Supreme Court Decides Difficult Cases

Selecting Supreme Court Cases
The Supreme Court in Action

4 Many Factors Influence Supreme Court Decisions

Legal Precedents
Judicial Philosophies
Public Opinion
Checks and Balances

463

SECTION 1

The Federal Courts Interpret National Laws *(pp. 464–469)*

Section Objectives

☐ detail the different kinds and jurisdictions of federal courts
☐ describe the structure of the federal court system

Vocabulary

jurisdiction, admiralty law, maritime law, original jurisdiction, appellate jurisdiction, constitutional court, legislative court, district court, court of appeals, circuit court, territorial court, sovereign immunity, court-martial

FOCUS

● Write the following statement on the board: *If I could spend a day watching one branch of the federal government in operation, I would choose . . . .* Poll the class to see how many students would choose the judiciary, and ask those who would choose the judiciary to explain their reasons why. (Judges deal with specific cases involving real people and issues; courtroom scenes are often dramatic confrontations.)

SECTION 1 — The Federal Courts Interpret National Laws

The Main Ideas

1 **What are the different kinds and jurisdictions of federal courts?**
pages 464–467

2 **What is the structure of the federal court system?**
pages 467–469

You are the owner of a sailing boat, floating lazily in the Gulf of Mexico. All of a sudden a large fishing vessel slams into you, ripping your boat in half. Where should you file a lawsuit against the owner of the fishing vessel?

You are the manager of a bank that has just experienced an armed hold-up. Can you call the FBI for help?

These questions arise because the United States has a *dual* court system. Both the states and the federal government investigate and try cases.

Federal Court Jurisdiction

A court's authority to hear cases is called its **jurisdiction**. Some courts have authority to hear certain types of cases. Others have jurisdiction in a certain geographic region or district. Article III of the Constitution gives the federal courts specific jurisdiction over several types of cases.

Types of federal cases

All cases that involve national laws — the Constitution, laws passed by Congress, or treaties — are "federal questions." These are clearly cases in which state courts could not act effectively, and so they must be heard in a federal court. In addition, federal courts hear cases involving **admiralty** or **maritime law**. This branch of law covers navigation, shipping, and commerce on the high seas or on the Great Lakes

Questions involving ships at sea or on the Great Lakes and major rivers are judged by federal courts according to the principles of maritime law. These fishing boats are in the Bering Sea off the coast of Alaska.

464

Background: *Cultural Literacy* The word *jurisdiction* comes from Latin—*juris* (law) and *dictio* (declaration). It literally means, "to say what the law is."

and major rivers within the United States. For example, federal courts decide cases of piracy, ship collisions, merchant ship regulations, ocean routes, fishing rights, or dockside contracts.

Federal jurisdiction also extends to all cases in which foreign citizens or governments are involved. The parties in such cases may be foreign ambassadors or other diplomatic personnel; a U.S. citizen and a foreign citizen or government; or a state and a foreign citizen or government. The federal courts also rule in cases concerning U.S. government officials or agencies and in disputes between two or more state governments or between citizens of two different states.

The Eleventh Amendment

When the Constitution was first written, Article III also gave the federal courts jurisdiction over suits "between a state and citizens of another state." This provision was challenged almost immediately when, in 1793, a South Carolina man sued the government of Georgia over a land claim. Georgia naturally wanted the case to be decided in its own state courts, but the Supreme Court ruled that the federal courts had jurisdiction (*Chisholm v. Georgia,* 1793). All the states protested this decision as a violation of their sovereignty, and the Eleventh Amendment was quickly ratified (1798). Under this amendment, a state government cannot be sued by a nonresident in federal court.

Federal and state jurisdiction

In the types of cases assigned specifically by the Constitution, the federal courts have *exclusive* jurisdiction. That is, no other courts can hear cases involving national law, the federal government itself, or other governments (state or foreign). Because bankruptcy, copyrights, and patents are all under federal law, federal courts also have exclusive jurisdiction in those cases.

Some cases, however, can be decided in either federal or state courts. The two court systems have *concurrent* jurisdiction over these cases. For example, concurrent jurisdiction exists when someone breaks both state and federal criminal law. A person who robs a federally insured bank, for example, can be prosecuted in *both* federal and state courts. Careful legal strategy is involved in determining which court system will hear such cases, for both the law and the penalties may differ.

LANDMARKS in **LIBERTY**

Marbury v. Madison (1803)

Chief Justice John Marshall's opinion in *Marbury v. Madison* upheld the supremacy of the Constitution over Congress. In this case, the Court for the first time declared an act of Congress — a clause of the 1789 Judiciary Act — unconstitutional. The Court's action established the principle of judicial review, providing a check on the power of the legislative branch.

     The powers of the legislature are defined and limited; and that those limits may not be mistaken or forgotten, the Constitution is written. To what purpose are powers limited, and to what purpose is that limitation committed to writing, if these limits may, at any time, be passed by those intended to be restrained? . . .

It is emphatically the province and duty of the judicial department to say what the law is. Those who apply the rule to particular cases must of necessity expound and interpret that rule. . . .

So if a law be in opposition to the Constitution; if both the law and the Constitution apply to a particular case, so that the court must either decide that case conformably to the law, disregarding the Constitution, or conformably to the Constitution, disregarding the law, the court must determine which of these conflicting rules governs the case. . . .

If, then, the courts are to regard the Constitution, and the Constitution is superior to any ordinary act of the legislature, the Constitution, and not such ordinary act, must govern the case to which they both apply.

1. According to Marshall, what is the purpose of a written constitution?
2. Why is it appropriate for the judicial branch to interpret the law?
3. Why, does Marshall say, must the courts uphold the Constitution over other laws?

465

EXPLANATION

After reviewing the content of the section, you may want to consider the following activities:

Controversial Issues

Tell students that the states reacted with anger and disbelief to the ruling in *Chisholm v. Georgia*. The Georgia House of Representatives, for example, passed a bill prescribing that any official who followed the ruling would be judged "guilty of felony and shall suffer death, without benefit of clergy, by being hanged."

● CRITICAL THINKING *Why did the issue provoke such anger?* (The states had recently joined to form the United States and did not want the federal government to diminish their sovereignty.)

Landmarks in Liberty Answers

1. To define the powers of the legislature.
2. Because the judiciary applies the law to different cases and must interpret it in different contexts.

3. The Constitution is superior to legislative acts.

The symbol ♙♙ denotes active participation strategies.

Activities are keyed for student abilities:
▲ = Basic
● = All Levels
■ = Average/Advanced

Constitutional Heritage

● Refer students to the text of the Constitution on pp. 112–138 and ask them to find the section that mentions federal jurisdiction over bankruptcy, copyrights, and patents. (Article I, Section 8, Clauses 4 and 8.)

● Have them read Article I, Section 8 and suggest other crimes that would come under federal jurisdiction. (Crimes involving international trade, Indian tribes, immigration law, and counterfeiting; postal crimes, piracy and maritime crimes, crimes in the District of Columbia, and crimes on military bases.)

Structure of Government

▲ Ask students to describe the relationship between a district court and a court of appeals. (The district court tries federal cases. Most appeals of those cases go to the court of appeals.)

Does the court of appeals retry the case? (No. The judges review the case.)

▲ ***From what federal court is there no appeal?*** (The Supreme Court.)

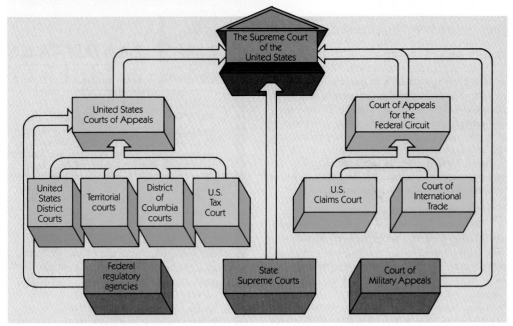

Figure 17–1 **THE FEDERAL COURT SYSTEM** The structure of the federal court system determines the route by which cases may be appealed. The Supreme Court is the highest court for all federal and some state cases. **8B**

Concurrent jurisdiction also exists if the parties in a civil case are citizens or businesses from two different states. Laws passed by Congress determine the requirements for bringing such a case to federal court.

Other questions of jurisdiction

Courts with the authority to hear and decide cases for the first time are said to have **original jurisdiction**. If the losing party feels that the law has been applied incorrectly or unfairly, it may appeal the case to a higher court. Courts that hear appeals from lower courts are said to have **appellate** (ah-PELL-ut) **jurisdiction**. Appellate courts may uphold, reverse, or modify lower court decisions, or they can send the case back to be tried again.

The Supreme Court has *both* original and appellate jurisdiction, depending on the case. From its power to review other cases derives the Court's very important power of *judicial review*. This power lets the Court judge whether acts of the other branches are or are not constitu-

tional. The Court's position as the final interpreter of the Constitution was firmly established in the case of *Marbury v. Madison*. Lower courts can also exercise judicial review, but the Supreme Court makes the final decision.

Establishment of the federal courts

The Supreme Court is the only federal court actually mentioned in the Constitution. All other federal courts have been created by Congress as necessary. This power comes from Article III of the Constitution: "The judicial power of the United States shall be vested in one Supreme Court and in such inferior courts as the Congress may from time to time ordain and establish."

Under this provision, Congress has established what are called **constitutional courts**. The first Congress, in fact, saw the need for a national court system and set it up through the Judiciary Act of 1789. The federal district courts are the mainstay of this system.

Judges in constitutional courts are appointed to serve "during good behavior" — they remain

466

Cross-reference
Marbury v. Madison is discussed in Chapter 3, pp. 67–68, and is excerpted in the "Landmarks in Liberty" feature on p. 465.

Figure 17–1
▲ ***Cases from which courts are appealed to the Court of Appeals for the Federal Circuit?*** (U.S. Claims Court and the Court of International Trade.) ***To which court***

would you appeal a case decided by a federal regulatory agency? (U.S. Court of Appeals.)

in office for life, unless they resign or commit a crime. Their salaries cannot be reduced during their service on the court. These provisions ensure the independence of the judicial branch from Congress and the President.

Congress has also created federal courts to help carry out the legislative powers in Article I, such as the power to lay taxes, to govern U.S. territories and the District of Columbia, and to regulate the armed forces. These **legislative courts** do not have to follow the same rules as constitutional courts. Congress can, for example, set the salaries of judges. Congress may also assign these courts duties other than hearing cases.

3A

Federal Court Structure

Most cases, civil and criminal, that arise under federal law are tried in the regular federal court system created by Congress under Article III. As Figure 17–1 shows, the federal court system has several levels of courts and several routes by which cases may be appealed. The Supreme Court is the "highest" court.

Federal district courts

Most federal cases are handled by federal **district courts**. (This includes bankruptcy courts, which are separate units of district courts.) There are currently 94 federal district courts, with at least one in every state, plus one in the District of Columbia and one in Puerto Rico. (See Figure 17–2.) Most district courts have two judges, although the number can range from one to more than twenty. Altogether more than 500 judges serve in the district courts.

Federal district courts have original jurisdiction over most questions of federal law, both criminal and civil. Cases may range from stolen vehicles and kidnapping charges to employment discrimination and school desegregation suits.

In federal criminal cases, a federal grand jury determines whether the prosecuting attorney has shown enough evidence against a suspect to justify a trial in district court. If a trial is held, a trial (petit) jury decides whether the accused person is guilty or innocent.

In civil cases, a petit jury may be called to decide whether damages should be awarded. If both parties in a civil suit agree, they can waive, or give up, the right to a jury trial. The case is then decided by a district court judge (or a panel of judges). In most cases, district court decisions are final; however, they may be appealed to a higher court.

Courts of appeals

Most appeals from federal district courts are handled by the **courts of appeals**. This level of courts was first established in 1891 to help lessen the workload of the Supreme Court and serve as an intermediate stage of appeal. Today the courts of appeals are divided into twelve "circuits," or regions, and so are sometimes called **circuit courts**. The circuit courts have from 6 to 28 judgeships, headed by a chief judge. In addition, a Supreme Court justice is assigned as circuit justice. (Figure 17–2 shows the locations of the twelve circuits.)

As the name indicates, courts of appeals have *only* appellate jurisdiction. About 40,000 cases are filed each year, mainly from the federal district courts. The courts of appeals also rule on decisions of the independent regulatory commissions, such as the Federal Trade Commission.

Appealing a case does not mean that a new trial is held. Instead, a panel of judges, usually three, reviews the case by examining the written records of the lower court. Sometimes the panel asks to hear oral arguments. The decisions in these courts are usually final, but cases may be appealed once more—to the Supreme Court.

8H

YOU DECIDE

Danny Smith was approached by two plain-clothes police officers in an unmarked vehicle. Without identifying himself, one officer asked Smith to "come here a minute." Smith kept walking to his own car. When the officer identified himself, Smith threw the bag he was carrying onto his car. The officer asked Smith what the bag contained. Smith did not answer. The officer opened the bag and found drug paraphernalia. Smith was arrested.

Is the evidence admissible?

Cross-reference
Grand and petit juries are discussed in Chapter 6, pp. 176 and 181. Chapter 16, Section 3 (pp. 432–437), deals with independent agencies.

You Decide Answer
Students should defend their answers. The United States Supreme Court ruled that the evidence was not admissible (*Danny Smith v. Ohio*, 1990).

Geography
● CRITICAL THINKING Have students examine Figure 17–2 and compare the size of the judicial circuits in the eastern part of the United States with the size of the western circuits. *Why might western circuits cover more territory than eastern circuits?* (Because when the circuits were established, there were many more people living in the East than the West.)

Cooperative Learning
● Have students find the circuit and district courts for your community on the map on p. 468. Then divide the class into groups and have the groups use the route of appeal shown in Figure 17–1 to make a flow chart showing the actual path that a case arising in your district would follow if it were appealed all the way to the Supreme Court.

The symbol 👥 denotes active participation strategies.

Activities are keyed for student abilities:
▲ = Basic
● = All Levels
■ = Average/Advanced

GUIDED/INDEPENDENT PRACTICE

● Have students create Venn diagrams illustrating the concurrent and exclusive jurisdictions of state and federal courts.

RETEACHING/CORRECTIVES

▲ Have students define the vocabulary words and then use each of them in a sentence.

Have students complete **Skills Practice Worksheet 17,** which reviews the structure of the federal court system.

👥 ENRICHMENT/EXTENSION

■ Have students find information about the courts in your community and, working in groups, create large charts showing that system.

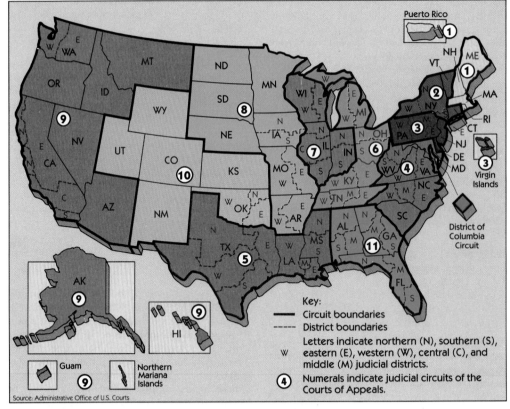

Figure 17–2 U.S. JUDICIAL CIRCUITS AND DISTRICTS The federal appeals courts are divided into eleven regional circuits, which hear appeals from the district courts in their jurisdiction. The District of Columbia is a twelfth circuit. 8B

The Supreme Court

The Supreme Court is the apex of the judicial system in the United States. It is the nation's "court of last resort," the final interpreter of the Constitution. It normally hears appeals from the twelve circuit courts of appeals, but may also hear appeals directly from the federal district courts or from any other federal court. The Supreme Court may also review decisions made by the highest state courts if federal questions are raised. (See Section 4 of this chapter.)

Territorial courts

Under its authority to govern U.S. territories, Congress has established **territorial courts** in the Virgin Islands, the Northern Mariana Islands, and Guam. These courts correspond closely to the federal district courts but also deal with some local questions. Appeals from territorial courts are heard by the federal courts of appeals.

District of Columbia courts

Congress has likewise created a system of courts for our nation's capital, the District of Columbia. The District of Columbia has its own federal district court and one of the twelve courts of appeals. In addition, Congress (as administrator of the District) has set up two courts to hear local cases. These are the Superior Court, which acts as a trial court, and a Court of Appeals.

468

Background: *Geography*
A territory is a region controlled by the U.S. government. Territories have an unequal status with the states because they do not have voting representatives in the national government.

Guam and the Virgin Islands are self-governing territories; and the Northern Mariana Islands are a commonwealth.

Figure 17–2
▲ *How many judicial districts does Texas have?* (Four.) *Which circuit is Texas in?* (The Fifth Circuit.)

Special Courts

While most federal courts hear civil and criminal cases about many issues, some courts are authorized to deal only in specialized areas.

The Court of International Trade

Civil cases involving foreign business dealings are handled by the Court of International Trade (once the Customs Court). This court settles disputes over unfair practices by international firms, questions about import duties, and lawsuits against foreign trading companies. It is headed by a chief judge who presides over eight associate justices. Trials are normally conducted at such port cities as Boston, New Orleans, San Francisco, and New York City.

The U.S. Claims Court

It is a long-standing principle of law that the United States — or any sovereign government — cannot be sued. This is known as the doctrine of **sovereign immunity**. There are, however, two basic exceptions to this rule: Public *officials* can be sued for wrongful and illegal acts. It is also possible for Congress to rule that the government will let itself be sued.

For many years, a person with a claim against the United States could be "redressed," or compensated, only if Congress passed special legislation. In 1855, however, Congress established the Court of Claims to handle certain cases. The court was reorganized in 1982 as the United States Claims Court. Cases handled by the Claims Court may involve payments for land taken by the federal government, disputes over government pensions, or claims for income tax refunds.

The U.S. Tax Court

With its power "to lay and collect taxes," Congress created the United States Tax Court in 1924. This court handles disputes between taxpayers and the Internal Revenue Service (IRS). It also makes rulings on tax-related issues, such as the status of tax-exempt organizations or questions about retirement plans. Cases appealed from this court go to the courts of appeal.

Special appeals

In certain kinds of civil cases, the Court of Appeals for the Federal Circuit takes the place of the regular courts of appeals. For example, patent and copyright cases from any district court or territorial court can be heard here. This twelve-judge court also hears appeals from two specialized courts — the Court of International Trade and the United States Claims Court — and reviews rulings made by some executive agencies.

The Court of Military Appeals

Trials of men and women in military service are conducted outside the ordinary justice system. A **court-martial** is a military court that tries members of the armed forces accused of violating military laws. (The same term is also used for a ruling by one of these courts.) Congress established the Court of Military Appeals in 1950 to review court-martial decisions. The court consists of five civilian judges appointed by the President. Because it has the last word in deciding nearly all military appeals, it is popularly called the "GI Supreme Court."

SECTION 1 REVIEW

Vocabulary and key terms

jurisdiction (464)	legislative court (467)
"federal question" (464)	district court (467)
admiralty law (464)	court of appeals (467)
maritime law (464)	circuit court (467)
original jurisdiction (466)	territorial court (468)
appellate jurisdiction (466)	sovereign immunity (469)
constitutional court (466)	court-martial (469)

For review

1. Why must federal courts hear cases about treaties or laws passed by Congress? **3C**
2. What is the difference between constitutional and legislative courts? **3A**
3. Which courts hear the bulk of federal cases? **3A**
4. Under what authority did Congress create (a) the territorial courts? (b) the District of Columbia courts? (c) the U.S. Tax Court? **3A**
5. (a) What is the doctrine of sovereign immunity? (b) What exceptions can be made? **3A**

Critical thinking

DRAWING INFERENCES Why is it important to have a federal court system that is independent of the executive and legislative branches? **3A**

469

Section Objectives

☐ detail the rules governing the
impeachment and salaries of
federal judges

☐ describe the appointment
process for federal judges

FOCUS

● Write the following phrase on
the board: *A good federal judge
is. . . .* Have students come to
the board and write adjectives
or phrases to complete the
sentence.

Have students consider the
following question as they study
the section: **Do you think the
current process of appointing
federal judges encourages the
appointment of good judges?**

EXPLANATION

After reviewing the content of
the section, you may want to
consider the following activities:

Politics

Discuss the issues involved in
securing Senate approval for
presidential appointees to federal
judgeships.

● **What part does senatorial
courtesy play in the approval
process?** (An important one: by
failing to return the Judiciary
Committee's "blue slip," even
senators who are not on the
Judiciary Committee can influence the choice of judges for
judicial districts in their state.)
How important is party loyalty?
(Party loyalty influences the
President's appointments and
almost always influences the
actions of Congress.) **How**

470

ACCESS The Main Ideas

1 **What are the rules governing the
impeachment and salaries of federal
judges?**   *pages 470–471*
2 **How are federal judges appointed?**
pages 471–473

Because laws are only as just as the people who
interpret them, judges are the lifeblood of any judicial system. William Blackstone, a respected
18th-century English legal scholar, said: "They
are the depositaries of the laws; the living ora-
cles, who must decide in all cases of doubt, and
who are bound by an oath to decide according to
the law of the land."

This section looks at the selection of the federal judges, who must assume for the United
States the responsibilities Blackstone described.
It also discusses recent controversies over the
confirmation of federal judges.

3A

Constitutional Provisions

The Constitution (Article II, Section 2) provides that the President "shall nominate, and, by
and with the advice and consent of the Senate,
shall appoint . . . judges of the Supreme Court."
Congress has extended the same procedure to
other judges in the federal court system. Most
federal judges, including Supreme Court justices,
are appointed by the President and must be confirmed by a majority of the Senate.

To make the judiciary as powerful as the
other two branches, the framers of the Constitution wanted federal courts to be independent of
Congress and the President. Therefore, most federal judges are appointed for life — provided
they do not quit, retire, or commit crimes.
Judges in some legislative courts (page 467)
have shorter terms.

Impeachment

Like other federal officials, federal judges
can be removed from office through the im-

peachment process. Congress may charge them
with "treason, bribery, or other high crimes and
misdemeanors." In all of American history, thirteen federal judges have been impeached by the
House of Representatives. Only seven were actually removed from office by the Senate. (No
other federal officials have ever been both impeached and removed.)

Only one Supreme Court justice has ever
been subjected to impeachment proceedings. In
1804 Samuel Chase, a Federalist appointed by
George Washington, was impeached by the
House (where Democratic-Republicans were
a majority) for his alleged unfairness to
Democratic-Republicans in trials under the Alien
and Sedition Acts. The Senate did not convict
Chase, however. These proceedings began a tradition that partisan political activities should not
be a reason for impeachment.

On October 9, 1986, the chief judge for the
U.S. district court of Nevada, Harry E. Claiborne,
became the first federal official in fifty years to be
impeached by the House and removed from office by the Senate. Since then two other district
court judges, Alcee L. Hastings and Walter L.
Nixon, Jr., have been removed from office for
such crimes as perjury and bribery.

Compensation

Congress sets the pay for all federal judges.
According to Article III, judges' compensation
"shall not be diminished during their continuance in office." This is just another way to ensure
judges' independence from Congress. Members
of the Supreme Court are, naturally, the highest
paid federal judges. Associate justices of the Supreme Court are paid over $160,000, while the
Chief Justice receives over $170,000.

Federal judges are also entitled to generous
retirement benefits. The amount of benefits depends on two factors — age and length of service. Judges who retire at the age of 65 after at
least fifteen years on the bench receive their full
salary for the rest of their lives. Judges who turn

Background: *History* Two
Supreme Court justices have
faced serious threats of
impeachment for alleged
improprieties. Abe Fortas,
whom President Johnson
had nominated for Chief
Justice in 1968, eventually

resigned in 1969. William O.
Douglas, investigated by the
House in 1953 and again in
1970, continued to serve
until 1975.

Federal courts, like the one above in Indianapolis, handle cases that involve the application of federal laws. Santiago E. Campos (inset), judge of the United States District Court, District of New Mexico, is one of the many judges in the federal system.

70 and have served ten years on the court also get full pay until they die. The Chief Justice may, however, call on retired judges to serve in the lower courts if they are needed. There is no mandatory retirement age for judges, and several Supreme Court justices have served well into their eighties.

Many observers of the courts claim that federal judges are not paid enough. In recent years a number of federal judges have resigned and returned to private legal practice, where they may easily earn twice as much.

3B, 4B

Selecting Federal Judges

Because most federal judges serve for life, judicial appointments offer the President a chance to have a lasting influence on public policy. After all, there have been forty-two Presidents, but only sixteen Chief Justices. Whenever judicial vacancies occur, Presidents take great care in appointing new federal judges.

Screening candidates

In selecting nominees for federal judgeships, Presidents first consult with their top advisers, particularly the Attorney General, who heads the Justice Department. The Attorney General, with help from the department staff, prepares a list of top candidates — usually judges in state courts, law professors, or outstanding lawyers. The FBI conducts intensive background checks on each prospective candidate.

The Attorney General looks also for candidates whose philosophies and political party ties are compatible with the President's. Justice Hugo Black once observed, "Presidents have always appointed people who believed a great deal in the same things that the President who appoints them believes in." Critics charge, however, that this practice can sometimes be carried too far. During George Bush's presidency, for example, some legal scholars contended that the President and the Attorney General were giving more weight to conservative political views than to merit and ability when choosing new judges.

471

important is ideology? (Extremely important, especially in the case of a Supreme Court nomination.)

Multiculturalism

● CRITICAL THINKING Have students consider the increasing diversity of the federal judiciary. *Do you think it is important for federal judges to reflect the different ethnic groups that live in the United States? Why or why not?* (Some students may feel that ethnic balance within the judiciary would make the judiciary more even-handed in its treatment of all citizens. Other students may argue that competence, rather than ethnicity, should be the primary criterion in choosing judges.)

👥 Cooperative Learning

● Divide the class into groups and ask each group to function as the Senate Judiciary Committee as it considers a nominee to the Supreme Court. Have the groups draw up a list of questions they want the nominee to answer. Then call the class together and have a representative from each group present the group's questions to the class.

Cross-reference
A chart on p. 476 lists the sixteen Chief Justices and the Presidents who appointed them.

Background: *Values*
Personal philosophies often evolve, even for Supreme Court justices. When asked whether a judge changes his views after reaching the Court, Justice Felix Frankfurter replied, "If he is any good, he does."

The symbol 👥 denotes active participation strategies.

Activities are keyed for student abilities:
▲ = Basic
● = All Levels
■ = Average/Advanced

American Bar Association influence

Once the list of top candidates is announced, the American Bar Association (ABA) becomes involved. The ABA is a nationwide voluntary organization of lawyers. Since 1956, the ABA's Committee on the Federal Judiciary has ranked all federal judicial appointees. Each potential judge is given a rating, ranging from "exceptionally well qualified" to "not qualified." Members of the Senate, many of whom are lawyers, give serious attention to the ABA ratings.

Other interest group opinions

Because court decisions frequently affect interest groups, their members are deeply concerned with the selection of federal judges — particularly Supreme Court justices. While interest groups may have little impact on the President's nominations, they can try to influence the Senate vote of confirmation.

For example, the NAACP successfully fought President Richard Nixon's nomination of G. Harrold Carswell in 1970 because of Carswell's racial views. In 1971 William Rehnquist was confirmed as an associate justice, despite the American Civil Liberties Union's protests over his conservative positions on civil rights issues. The National Organization for Women unsuccessfully opposed Gerald Ford's nomination of John Paul Stevens because of his earlier lower court decisions on women's issues.

Recently, a number of interest groups have opposed Supreme Court decisions of the 1960's and 1970's that extended the rights of accused criminals and the right to privacy. These groups, therefore, have tried to influence judicial appointments. They include the Education Foundation, Inc., the Center for Judicial Studies, and the Washington Legal Foundation.

Supreme Court Justices themselves may try to influence the selection of their potential colleagues. For example, in 1922 Chief Justice William H. Taft, himself a former President, pushed unabashedly for the appointment of Justice Pierce Butler. Justice Harlan Stone campaigned openly for the appointment of a New York judge, Benjamin Cardozo, who joined the Court in 1932. Chief Justice Warren Burger convinced President Nixon to appoint Burger's life-long friend, Harry Blackmun, to the Court. Not sur-

prisingly, most justices want a colleague who is compatible, hard-working, competent, and dependable.

Senate scrutiny

After the Senate receives the President's nomination, it is up to the Senate Judiciary Committee to recommend whether the Senate should confirm or reject this choice. The Committee usually holds public hearings as well as weighing the recommendations of the Attorney General, the American Bar Association, and other interested parties.

In appointments for federal district judges, the Judiciary Committee observes senatorial courtesy and sends a "blue slip" to the senators

Before her appointment to the Supreme Court, Justice Sandra Day O'Connor was first an Arizona state legislator and then a state court judge.

Critical Thinking
▲ *What are the arguments for and against the involvement of interest groups in the confirmation process?*
(*For*—They may uncover important background information about a nominee. *Against*—They may try to destroy the reputation of a nominee whose views they oppose.)

from the judicial district. If the senator of the President's party does not return the "blue slip," this means that the senator finds the nominee personally unacceptable. In such a case, other senators are likely to reject the nomination.

After the Judiciary Committee makes its recommendation, the full Senate votes on the nomination. The full Senate rarely rejects the nomination of federal district judges. Supreme Court nominations, however, are a different story. About one-fifth of all nominees to the Court have failed to win confirmation.

The confirmation process came under fire in recent years. In 1987, conservative legal scholar Robert Bork was rejected by the Senate after bitter hearings. Four years later, President Bush nominated Judge Clarence Thomas to the Court. The Judiciary Committee sent Thomas' name to the full Senate without recommendation. Before the vote, however, law professor Anita Hill charged Thomas with sexual harassment. The Judiciary Committee met again in televised hearings, and for four days Americans were riveted by the testimony. Thomas was confirmed, but many had been angered by the proceedings. Thomas' supporters charged Democrats with character assassination, while Hill's supporters contended that the all-male Judiciary Committee was insensitive to women's issues.

In 1993, President Clinton nominated Judge Ruth Bader Ginsburg to replace retiring Justice Byron White. The Senate's hearings on this nomination involved little controversy. In 1994, Justice Harry Blackmun retired. Judge Stephen Breyer was nominated to succeed Blackmun. Like Ginsburg, Breyer was approved by the Senate with little opposition.

3A

Who Becomes a Federal Judge?

Lower court judges

Most federal district court and appellate court judges are graduates of top colleges and law schools. Most were successful lawyers or state judges and were about 45 years old when appointed. Most have been white, male, and Protestant. Since the civil rights movement of the 1960's, more women, African Americans, and Hispanics have been chosen for federal judgeships.

Presidents overwhelmingly choose judges of their own political party. For example, 94 percent of Jimmy Carter's appointees were Democrats, while 94 percent of George Bush's were Republicans. Carter, however, named a higher percentage of women and minorities to judgeships than did Bush. About 4 percent of Bush's appointees were African American or Hispanic.

Supreme Court justices

The backgrounds of Supreme Court justices are also quite distinctive. At the time of their appointment, most were either practicing attorneys or federal or state judges. The average age of justices, when appointed, was 53. Most have been college-educated. A great many have come from a few prestigious law schools, notably Harvard, Yale, and Columbia. In 1967 Thurgood Marshall became the first black justice, and in 1981 Sandra Day O'Connor became the first woman on the Supreme Court.

About 90 percent of Supreme Court justices have been Protestants, mainly Presbyterians, Episcopalians, and Methodists. Roman Catholics have served on the Court since 1836, beginning with Chief Justice Roger B. Taney. The first Jewish justice was Louis D. Brandeis, appointed in 1916.

SECTION 2 REVIEW

For review

1. How are most federal judges appointed? (b) How long do they serve? (c) How can they be removed? **3A**
2. What constitutional provisions keep federal judges independent of the executive and legislative branches? **3B**
3. Describe the role of each of the following in the selection of judges: (a) Attorney General, (b) American Bar Association, (c) Senate Judiciary Committee, (d) Senate. **3B**

Critical thinking

DRAWING INFERENCES How have the characteristics of federal judges changed since the civil rights movement of the 1960's? What difference might this make? **8F**

473

Section 2 Review Answers
1. (a) By the President, with approval by a majority of the Senate. **(b)** For life. **(c)** Through impeachment proceedings in the House, followed by conviction in the Senate.
2. Federal judges are appointed for life and their salaries cannot be lowered by Congress.
3. (a) Prepares a list of top candidates. **(b)** Rates potential judges. **(c)** Recommends confirmation or rejection. **(d)** Votes to confirm or reject the nomination.

Critical thinking Students should note that more women, African Americans, and Hispanics have been appointed since the 1960's. This trend might affect those groups' perceptions of the judicial system and of social progress in general.

CLOSURE
● Remind students of the pre-reading objectives at the beginning of the section. Pose one or both of these questions again. Then have them read Section 3, identifying the steps involved in determining a Supreme Court case.

Cross-reference
Louis Brandeis, the first Jewish justice (column 2, par. 3), is quoted in "Speaking Out," p. 801.

The symbol 👥 denotes active participation strategies.

Activities are keyed for student abilities:
▲ = Basic
● = All Levels
■ = Average/Advanced

The Supreme Court Decides Difficult Cases *(pp. 474–478)*

Section Objectives

☐ explain how cases reach the Supreme Court

☐ describe the typical procedure for a Supreme Court case

Vocabulary

writ of *certiorari,* moot question, brief, docket, law clerk, conference, opinion, majority opinion, concurring opinion, dissenting opinion

FOCUS

● Explain to students that the Supreme Court, like any court, can only handle a limited number of cases each year. Ask students for their opinions on the following proposal: *To ease the Supreme Court's workload, the federal government should replace the single Court with eleven regional supreme courts modeled on the federal appeals courts.* (Students should recognize from this exercise that there must be a *single* federal court to resolve disputes arising at lower levels.)

2D, 3A, 6C, 6I, 8B

SECTION 3

The Supreme Court Decides Difficult Cases

ACCESS **The Main Ideas**

1 How do cases reach the Supreme Court?
  pages 474–476

2 What is the typical procedure for a Supreme Court case?
  pages 476–478

William O. Douglas was on the Supreme Court 36 years, longer than any other justice. He served from 1939 to 1975, through World War II, the start of the cold war, the social upheaval of the 1960's, and Watergate. Douglas saw the Court as "a storm of controversial issues. For to it come the most troublesome, contentious problems of each age, problems that mirror the tensions, fears, and aggressiveness of the people." This section examines the complex process by which the Supreme Court accepts and decides cases.

3A, 6C

Selecting Supreme Court Cases

Frustrated by a legal problem, people sometimes exclaim, "I'll take my case to the Supreme Court!" The chances of taking a case all the way to the Supreme Court, however, are less than one in 10,000. Each year, about 10 million cases are tried in the United States, but only about 5,000 cases are appealed to the Supreme Court. Of those 5,000 cases, the Court will decide only about 150. Of those 150 cases, the Court usually renders signed opinions on roughly 125. How, then, do cases reach the Supreme Court?

The Court's jurisdiction

Like any other court, the Supreme Court must have proper jurisdiction to hear a case. The High Court (as the Supreme Court is also known) has original jurisdiction in only a few types of cases. Generally these are cases involving two or more states, the United States and a state government, or foreign ambassadors and diplomats. On the average, the Supreme Court hears fewer than fifteen original jurisdiction cases each year.

474

The bulk of the Supreme Court's cases stem from its appellate jurisdiction. In the early years of the Republic, cases could be appealed directly from the federal district courts to the Supreme Court. Because the Court was soon swamped with cases, Congress set up the circuit courts (page 467) and let the Supreme Court strictly limit its cases. Today, there are two main routes to reach the Supreme Court: (1) on appeal and (2) by a writ of *certiorari.*

Only about 10 percent of the Court's cases come "on appeal." Most commonly, they are questions of a law's constitutionality. For example, if a state supreme court or a lower federal court rules a federal law unconstitutional, the case might reach the Supreme Court on appeal. For a case to be heard "on appeal," however, four of the nine justices usually must agree. (This is called the "rule of four.")

Most cases come to the Supreme Court through **writs of** *certiorari* (sir-shee-uh-RARE-ee). This writ is an order from the Supreme Court to a lower court to prepare and send records of a case for review. (The Latin word *certiorari* means "to be made more certain.")

Either party in a lower court case can petition the Supreme Court for *certiorari* (which lawyers call "certs"). The petition must cite some error in the lower court or raise a serious constitutional issue. All petitions sent to the Court are screened by the law clerks. The Chief Justice compiles a "discuss list" for the justices to study during their regular conferences. Once again, the "rule of four" applies. If four justices approve the petition, a writ is sent to the lower court asking for the records. Otherwise, the lower court decision stands. Most petitions for *certiorari* are denied.

Reasons for denial

Over the years, the Supreme Court has developed many practices that sharply limit the types of cases it will hear. In a 1936 case (*Ashwander v. TVA*), Justice Louis Brandeis listed some of the Court's rules, which are paraphrased here:

Background: *Structure of Government* Citing the large number of cases that reach the Supreme Court every year, former Chief Justice Warren Burger and others have called for the establishment of a National Court of Appeals to help lessen the caseload.

- The Supreme Court will not rule on the constitutionality of any law unless the person challenging the law is actually harmed. Persons cannot challenge laws merely because they believe them to be wrong or unfair.

- The Supreme Court will not give "advisory opinions" — that is, rule on whether a proposed law *would be* constitutional.

- The Supreme Court will not decide questions that make no difference. These are called **moot questions.** For example, the Court did not decide whether Idaho could reverse its ratification of the Equal Rights Amendment (page 73). Because the amendment was not ratified by enough states before the deadline expired, Idaho's action had no real effect. The question was moot.

- The Supreme Court will not decide "political questions." That is, it will not decide any issue that it believes should be resolved by the executive or legislative branch.

Legal costs

Getting a case to the Supreme Court is not only extremely rare; it can also be very expensive. If people are too poor to absorb such costs, however, the Supreme Court often allows them free petitions for *certiorari* and pays an attorney to represent them. This is called *in forma pauperis* — meaning, "in the manner of a pauper [poor person]." About half of all certiorari petitions the Court receives are *in forma pauperis.* Most come from convicts in federal or state prisons. This was the procedure used by the penniless Clarence Earl Gideon when he sent his handwritten appeal to the Court (page 182).

Filing briefs

Once the Supreme Court accepts a case, lawyers for both sides file a **brief.** A brief is a written document arguing one side of the case. Briefs normally cite relevant facts, legal principles, and previous cases that support the argument. Contrary to their name, briefs are not always "brief."

Members of the Supreme Court are (from left): Justices Clarence Thomas, Antonin Scalia, Sandra Day O'Connor, Anthony Kennedy, David Souter, Stephen Breyer, John Paul Stevens, William Rehnquist (Chief Justice), and Ruth Bader Ginsburg.

475

EXPLANATION

After reviewing the content of the section, you may want to consider the following activities:

Economics

Inform students of the high cost of bringing a case before the Supreme Court. There are application fees; petitioners must make 40 copies of the writ of *certiorari* and pay the cost of furnishing the records of the lower court; lawyers may charge hundreds of dollars an hour.

● *Why are petitions* **in forma pauperis** *important?* (They make the Court accessible to all citizens.) *How is the provision for this kind of a petition consistent with the inscription on the Court building, "Equal Justice Under Law"?* (All people, regardless of wealth, have the same legal rights.)

Civic Participation

● Ask students to identify an issue of concern to them in school, such as dress code changes, regulations governing the use of school buildings, rules about absences, or academic requirements. Have students imagine that they are going to appear before a "Supreme Court of Schools" to argue their case. Ask them to work in pairs to prepare one- or two-page briefs stating their main argument and summarizing why the court should make a ruling in support of that argument.

Cross-reference
Some state supreme courts render advisory opinions on whether a proposed law would be constitutional. See Chapter 24, p. 657.

The symbol 👥 denotes active participation strategies.

Activities are keyed for student abilities:
▲ = Basic
● = All Levels
■ = Average/Advanced

Cooperative Learning

● Divide the class into groups and have each group write ten questions dealing with information in this section. Then have the groups compete as teams in a "Supreme Court bowl," with teams gaining points by stumping the other teams or answering questions correctly, and losing points by answering incorrectly.

GUIDED/INDEPENDENT PRACTICE

● Have students make a flow chart showing what happens to a case once it reaches the Supreme Court. Note that the flow chart should have at least two outcomes—one for cases denied a hearing and one for cases in which an opinion is handed down.

Many run several hundred pages. Because judges often rely upon briefs, lawyers strive to make them as logical and convincing as possible.

As Chapter 9 discussed, concerned interest groups who are not actually parties in the case often file *amicus curiae* ("friend of the court") briefs supporting one side of a case. In the *Bakke* case (1978), for example, more than fifty *amicus* briefs were submitted to the Supreme Court.

Once briefs are filed, cases are put on the Supreme Court's **docket**, or schedule. The Court notifies all parties when their case is scheduled to be heard.

2D, 3A

The Supreme Court in Action

The Supreme Court meets in a magnificent building, a symbol of American justice. Built in 1935, this five-story marble "palace" occupies a full square block directly across from the Capi-

tol. It is supported by 24 huge marble columns, modeled after the Greek temple of Artemis at Ephesus. Its gigantic bronze doors weigh six and one-half tons each. Above the doors are inscribed the words "Equal Justice Under Law."

The Court begins its regular yearly term on the first Monday in October and normally adjourns in late June or early July. Each term is designated by the year in which it starts.

Supreme Court staff

The Supreme Court itself includes the Chief Justice of the United States and eight associate justices. Congress determines how many justices there will be, but the number has remained at nine since 1869. (Before that, membership varied between six and ten.)

Many people assist the justices. The Clerk of the Supreme Court handles much of the paperwork on cases. The Supreme Court Marshal maintains security. Each justice has his or her

Figure 17–3 CHIEF JUSTICES OF THE UNITED STATES 8B

NAME	PRESIDENT APPOINTED BY	AGE ON TAKING OATH	TERM OF SERVICE	REASON FOR ENDING SERVICE
John Jay	Washington	44	1789–1795	resigned
John Rutledge	Washington	55	1795	rejected*
Oliver Ellsworth	Washington	50	1796–1800	resigned
John Marshall	John Adams	45	1801–1835	death
Roger B. Taney	Jackson	59	1836–1864	death
Salmon P. Chase	Lincoln	56	1864–1873	death
Morrison R. Waite	Grant	57	1874–1888	death
Melville W. Fuller	Cleveland	55	1888–1910	death
Edward D. White	Taft	65	1910–1921	death
William H. Taft	Harding	63	1921–1930	retired
Charles E. Hughes	Hoover	67	1930–1941	retired
Harlan F. Stone	F. D. Roosevelt	68	1941–1946	death
Frederick M. Vinson	Truman	56	1946–1953	death
Earl Warren	Eisenhower	62	1953–1969	retired
Warren E. Burger	Nixon	61	1969–1986	retired
William H. Rehnquist	Reagan	62	1986–	—

* Appointed while Congress was not in session, Rutledge served briefly, but the Senate refused to confirm his appointment.

Cross-reference
The case of *Regents of the University of California v. Bakke* is discussed in Chapter 7, pp. 210–211.

Background: *Cultural Literacy* The temple of Artemis (column 2, top), who is known as Diana in Roman mythology, is listed as one of the Seven Wonders of the World, famous for its decoration and extensive use of marble.

Figure 17–3
▲ *Which President chose the most Chief Justices?* (Washington.) *Which Chief Justice served the longest time on the Supreme Court?* (John Marshall, 34 years.)

own personal secretaries. Perhaps the most important support comes from the **law clerks**.

Law clerks are recent law school graduates with excellent records, who help the justices in a variety of ways. They conduct research, summarize cases, and even help draft opinions. Other judges and lawyers also use clerks, but clerking for the Supreme Court is a special opportunity.

Law clerks often go on to distinguished careers. Indeed, three current Supreme Court justices were once clerks. Justice Stevens clerked for Justice Wiley Rutledge in the 1947–1948 session; Chief Justice Rehnquist served as a law clerk for Justice Robert H. Jackson in 1952–1953; and Justice Breyer clerked for Justice Arthur J. Goldberg in 1963–1964.

Hearing the case

After the lawyers' briefs are filed, oral arguments before the Court are scheduled in seven "sittings," each two weeks long. After hearing cases for a two-week sitting, the Court recesses to decide cases. These sessions, which are open to the public, are held in the high-ceilinged first-floor courtroom of the Supreme Court building.

A Supreme Court session begins as the Marshal of the Court raps his gavel on a wood block and cries, "The honorable, the Chief Justice and the associate justices of the Supreme Court of the United States." The audience stands as the nine black-robed justices emerge, in order of seniority, through the purple velvet curtains and take their seats. The Marshal's voice again rings out:

> Oyez! Oyez! Oyez! All persons having business before the honorable, the Supreme Court of the United States, are admonished to draw near and give their attention, for the Court is now sitting. God save the United States and this Honorable Court!

Following the formal preliminaries, the lawyers for each side are given 30 minutes to present the oral arguments for their case. The justices often interrupt to ask questions or even to help the lawyers with their arguments. Red and white lights on the lawyers' lectern warn when their time is short or has ended.

Conferences

At the end of the week, after reading the briefs and listening to oral arguments, the jus-

In 1967 Thurgood Marshall became the first African American justice on the Supreme Court. He served from 1967 to 1991.

tices meet in **conference**. Conferences are regularly scheduled Friday meetings to discuss and decide cases. Meetings may last from six to eight hours and are absolutely secret.

Since 1888, tradition dictates that the justices shake hands as they file into the oak-paneled conference room behind the courtroom. The Chief Justice, presiding over the conference, begins by summarizing the case under consideration. Each justice is then called upon, in order of seniority, to present his or her own view.

Discussion follows, and then the justices vote. Six justices constitute a quorum (the minimum needed to vote), and each vote counts equally. Since John Marshall's day it has been tradition for the justices to vote in reverse order of seniority, with the Chief Justice voting last.

In most cases, all nine justices vote. Occasionally, justices are absent or disqualify themselves because of a conflict of interest. Justice Thurgood Marshall, for example, disqualified himself from all cases that he had previously handled as Solicitor General. About one-third of Supreme Court decisions are unanimous. In a tie, the lower court decision stands.

477

Background: *Constitutional Heritage* Law clerks come primarily from prestigious law schools and serve a single justice for one or two years.

Background: *Cultural Literacy* The Marshal's call "Oyez" is from Norman French, meaning "Hear ye." It is pronounced oh-YEZ or oh-YAY.

RETEACHING/CORRECTIVES

▲ Ask students to identify the main responsibilities of the following Supreme Court positions: associate justice (decides on cases to hear, hears cases, writes majority or minority opinion); Chief Justice (hears cases, presides over conferences, decides who will write up decisions); law clerk (reviews petitions, conducts research, summarizes cases, helps draft opinions); Marshal (keeps security, announces justices).

You may want to use **Transparency 39,** which shows the layout of the Supreme Court building.

👥 ENRICHMENT/EXTENSION

■ Have individual students or groups of students do library research to find news reports or articles on recent cases that the Supreme Court has refused to hear. Have them describe those cases to the class. Then have the class discuss which of the four reasons for denial listed on p. 475 applied in each case.

You may also want to have students complete **Supreme Court Decision 58,** which involves *amicus curiae* briefs.

The symbol 👥 denotes active participation strategies.

Activities are keyed for student abilities:
▲ = Basic
● = All Levels
■ = Average/Advanced

Section 3 Review Answers

1. (a) Cases involving two or more states, the federal government and a state government, or foreign diplomats. **(b)** Cases involving the constitutionality of a law.

2. Either party in a lower court case petitions the Supreme Court for *certiorari,* the petitions are screened by law clerks, a "discuss list" is compiled by the Chief Justice, and if four justices approve the petition, a writ asking for records of the case is sent to the lower courts.

3. (a) To argue one side of a case in writing, citing relevant facts, legal principles, and previous cases. **(b)** To allow concerned parties to show support for one side of a case.

4. (a) The Chief Justice, if he or she votes with the majority; otherwise, the most senior associate justice in the majority. **(b)** A concurring opinion offers different reasons in support of the majority. A dissenting opinion is the "minority opinion."

Critical thinking Students might note that secrecy allows justices to feel free to say what they truly think. Students who agree with the principle of secrecy may argue that it is the only way to guarantee fairness and privacy for the defendant; those opposed may argue that there is no place for secrecy in a democracy.

CLOSURE

● Ask students to choose which aspect of a Supreme Court justice's responsibilities they believe is most important, and have them explain their choice. Then have students read Section 4, noting the ways in which public opinion affects the Supreme Court.

478

Written opinions

After the vote, the justices issue a short statement of their decision or a more lengthy written **opinion**. An opinion summarizes the case and presents the questions of law, the ruling, and the reasoning of the Court. Throughout this book, you have read numerous excerpts and quotations from these opinions. Written opinions have two basic purposes. First, they help instruct lawyers and lower court judges about what to do in similar situations. That is, opinions establish precedents. Second, opinions communicate the Court's ideas to the executive and legislative branches of government, to the state courts and governments, and to the American people.

The **majority opinion** presents the view of the justices who supported a decision. Majority opinions become precedents for future cases. Sometimes one or more of the justices offer a **concurring opinion**. This is an opinion that supports the majority decision but offers different reasons for reaching that decision.

Finally, one or more of the justices may issue a **dissenting opinion** (or "minority opinion"), disagreeing with the majority. Dissenting opinions have no legal force but can indicate an important point of view. For example, Justice Harlan's lone dissent in the 1896 case of *Plessy v. Ferguson* helped lay the foundation for *Brown v. Board of Education* in 1954. (See page 197.)

Writing the majority opinion

Because the majority opinion represents the "law of the land," much care goes into selecting the person to write it. When the Chief Justice votes with the majority, he or she may write the opinion personally or assign it to an associate justice whose views are similar. This gives the Chief Justice tremendous influence over the direction of the Court. When the Chief Justice votes with the minority, the most senior associate justice on the majority side assigns the writing of the opinion. (Historically, this has seldom occurred.)

Much care goes into writing opinions. Some justices rely upon their law clerks to help them draft opinions. Others write the entire document themselves. The essential part of the opinion explains the vital constitutional issues involved in the decision. The opinion may also include other remarks that are relevant to the case but have no legal force.

Once the first draft of the opinion is completed, it is circulated among the justices, who make comments and criticisms and exchange memos and telephone calls. To ensure complete secrecy, the Supreme Court justices have a private telephone system that is not connected to the main switchboard. Significant portions of the opinion may be revised or deleted. Justices have even been known to switch their votes after reading an opinion.

This bargaining process may take days, weeks, or months. When the final document is ready, the Supreme Court publicly announces its decision. Majority decisions are usually read aloud on Mondays at the start of a sitting. Finally, the decision is officially recorded in the *United States Reports,* kept in most large public libraries.

SECTION 3 REVIEW

Vocabulary and key terms

"rule of four" (474)	conference (477)
writ of *certiorari* (474)	opinion (478)
moot question (475)	majority opinion (478)
brief (475)	concurring opinion (478)
docket (476)	dissenting opinion (478)
law clerk (477)	

For review

1. (a) Over what sorts of cases does the Supreme Court have original jurisdiction? (b) What kinds of cases generally reach the Supreme Court "on appeal"? **3A**
2. What is the procedure followed for requesting and issuing writs of *certiorari*? **3A**
3. What is the purpose of (a) a lawyer's brief? (b) an *amicus* brief? **3A**
4. (a) Who decides which justice will write the majority opinion? (b) What other kinds of opinions can be written, and what purposes do they serve? **3A**

Critical thinking

EXAMINING BASIC PRINCIPLES For what reasons are Supreme Court conferences held in absolute secrecy? Do you agree or disagree with this policy? Explain your answer. **6I**

Check for Understanding
● *How do the justices communicate their decision on a case?* (Through written opinions.)

Background: *Constitutional Heritage* The choice of who writes the majority opinion is based on workload, expertise, public opinion, and also the ability to hold the majority together, since the vote is still only tentative at the drafting stage.

I n the United States, the responsibilities of governing are shared by the national, state, and local authorities. Salina Franklin, a Navajo high school student, can turn to another government, however. Salina lives on the Navajo reservation. With a population of 185,000, the reservation is 25,000 square miles—about the size of West Virginia—and includes parts of Arizona, New Mexico, and Utah. State boundaries are not that important, though, since the Navajo have their own police force, firefighters, and utilities. They also face serious problems: reservation land is eroded, and Navajo families are among the poorest in the country. Salina explains the organization, strengths, and weaknesses of the Navajo government.

Salina Franklin, Newcomb High School, New Mexico

The Navajo nation is divided up into agencies, and from those agencies there are smaller chapters. In each community there are chapter houses for the people, and they have at least two meetings each month. There is a councilman from each chapter house and a chapter president. What the people want, they tell the council. Then the councilman goes to Window Rock, which is the Navajo capital. The councilmen from all chapters meet there and they tell the Navajo nation president what their people want.

Chapter meetings mostly consist of senior citizens. Younger people aren't interested in the Navajo government, I guess. They are not really doing important issues, like unemployment and alcoholism. Those aren't really talked about at the meetings.

I have gone to chapter meetings. Our school wanted some money to send my cross-country team to Chicago so we asked the chapter. We had to go to the meeting and tell the people what we wanted. Then they made a motion, and they gave us some money. We asked the councilman to ask the capital. Both the chapter and the capital gave us money.

There's no taxes here on the reservation. No sales tax, nothing. The money comes from the federal government.

The Navajo government helps people who really need help. If a house burned down, the chapter would get money from the capital to help build a new house. During the winter they will give out free food to anybody who needs food, like sugar, coffee, and stuff.

STUDENT PARTICIPATION

1. Do you think it is important for the Navajo to have their own government? Explain.
2. Attend a local government meeting—school board, town council, etc.—and compare your experience with Salina's.

Salina Franklin (top); Navajo tribal council chamber in Window Rock, Arizona.

Background

The Navajo, the largest Indian nation in the United States, were moved onto their reservation by the U.S. Army in 1868. About 100 years later, the Navajo took over responsibility for the reservation from the Bureau of Indian Affairs. Navajo Community College, founded in 1968, is the first college owned and operated by Indians in the United States. The Navajo have a tradition of local public meetings attended by both men and women, but a general tribal organization was not established until the 1920's.

Multiculturalism

● Ask for volunteers to do research on the American Indians who lived in your area 500 years ago to find out what has happened to the descendants of that group. Have the volunteers report the information to the class.

Cultural Literacy

● Students may be interested in reading mystery novels by Tony Hillerman, which discuss Navajo culture and have tribal policemen as their protagonists.

479

Student Participation Answers

1. Students who feel it is important may note that the Navajo should be able to control their lands and future; those who disagree may point to the existence of local government in the states in which the Navajo live as sufficient to represent their interests.

2. Students should describe the meeting's procedures, as well as the make-up of those in attendance, in their comparisons.

The symbol ii denotes active participation strategies.

Activities are keyed for student abilities:
▲ = Basic
● = All Levels
■ = Average/Advanced

SECTION 4 — Many Factors Influence Supreme Court Decisions

Section Objectives

☐ describe the factors that influence Supreme Court decisions

☐ explain how the President and Congress check the powers of the Supreme Court

Vocabulary

stare decisis, judicial restraint, judicial activism

FOCUS

● Ask students to imagine for a moment that they are a Supreme Court justice. A case has been argued before them, and now they are free to make their own decision. No other court can overrule their decision, and they cannot be voted out of office. Have students suggest what thoughts might be going through their minds.

ACCESS	The Main Ideas

1 What factors influence Supreme Court decisions? *pages 480–482*

2 How do the President and Congress check the powers of the Supreme Court? *pages 482–485*

In 1857 the Supreme Court ruled that African Americans were not citizens *(Dred Scott v. Sanford).* The outcry against the Court in northern states was immediate. Newspapers declared *Dred Scott* a "wicked and false judgment." By 1863, Chief Justice Roger B. Taney, the author of the *Dred Scott* ruling, was doubtful that the Court would "ever again be restored to the authority and rank which the Constitution intended to confer upon it."

Faith in the Supreme Court was restored, but the justices had learned that public opinion must be respected when considering cases. Several other factors also influence the Supreme Court's decisions.

6I

Legal Precedents

Perhaps the most important legal principle affecting judicial decisions is *stare decisis* (STAH-ray dih-SIGH-sis), which is Latin for "to let the decision stand." According to this principle, once the Supreme Court makes a ruling on one case, it normally takes that ruling as a precedent, or model, to decide similar cases.

The principle of *stare decisis* is important for several reasons. First, *stare decisis* makes for fair, uniform decisions. Because all judges try to follow precedents, a ruling in one court is likely to be followed in another court. As a result, *stare decisis* also makes the law more predictable. Finally, following precedent enables the courts to be more efficient. Judges do not have to establish new rulings for every case they hear.

Still, Supreme Court decisions are not cast in concrete. Justices sometimes depart from a precedent when they believe it is no longer correct. As Justice Felix Frankfurter observed, "Wisdom too often never comes, and so one ought not to reject it merely because it comes late." In *Brown v. Board of Education,* for example, the Supreme Court overturned the "separate but equal" doctrine it had established 58 years earlier in *Plessy v. Ferguson.* The *Brown* decision then became the new precedent for later cases.

5C

Judicial Philosophies

It is no secret that judges' legal and personal philosophies play a part in their decisions. One of the most controversial aspects of legal philosophy is what role the justices should take in applying the Constitution. Should the Court simply act as referee, making sure that Congress and the President play by the constitutional rules? Or should the Court be an active player, taking a vigorous role in setting policies?

One view is that judicial decisions should not contradict the wishes of the elected members of government (the President and Congress) unless their actions clearly violate specific provisions of the Constitution. This philosophy is known as **judicial restraint**. Judicial restraint is often associated with Justices Louis D. Brandeis, Oliver Wendell Holmes, Jr., and Felix Frankfurter. Frankfurter emphasized that "one's own opinion about the wisdom or evil of a law should be excluded altogether when one is doing one's duty on the bench."

By contrast, the philosophy called **judicial activism** holds that Supreme Court justices should take an active role in making policy, even if it means going beyond the actions of the elected branches. Chief Justice Charles Evans Hughes once said, in fact, that "the Constitution is what the judges say it is." More recently, the Court under Chief Justice Earl Warren (1953–1969) was often associated with judicial activism. It was the Warren Court, for example, that called for integrated public schools in *Brown v. Board of Education* and expanded the rights of accused persons in *Miranda v. Arizona.*

480

Cross-reference
Chapter 7, p. 194, discusses the Dred Scott case in more detail. *Precedent* is introduced as vocabulary in Chapter 2, p. 33.

Background: *History*
President Nixon named Warren Burger, a conservative, to succeed Earl Warren as Chief Justice in 1969. The Burger Court did not, however, practice judicial restraint as often as Nixon would have liked.

Figure 17-4 GREAT SUPREME COURT DECISIONS 8B

DATE	CASE	RULING
1803	Marbury v. Madison	First Supreme Court decision to declare an act of Congress unconstitutional. Established the courts' power of judicial review.
1819	McCulloch v. Maryland	Allowed a broad interpretation of the Constitution in determining the implied powers.
1824	Gibbons v. Ogden	Federal laws take priority over state laws in regulating interstate commerce. Broadened the definition of commerce.
1877	Munn v. Illinois	The states may regulate privately owned businesses in the interest of the public.
1919	Schenck v. United States	The government may abridge free speech only if it creates a "clear and present danger."
1954	Brown v. Board of Education	Separate facilities for black and white students in public schools are unconstitutional and inherently unequal.
1962	Engel v. Vitale	Public schools cannot require students to recite prayers.
1963	Gideon v. Wainwright	The states must provide free legal counsel to defendants accused of felonies who cannot afford a lawyer.
1964	Reynolds v. Sims	Seats in the U.S. House of Representatives and in both houses of state legislatures must be apportioned on the basis of "one person, one vote."
1964	Escobedo v. Illinois	An accused person has a right to counsel when being questioned by police (as well as at a trial).
1966	Miranda v. Arizona	Accused persons must be informed of their rights to remain silent and to have a lawyer before they are questioned.
1978	Regents of the University of California v. Bakke	Colleges and universities may consider a person's race as one condition of admissions policy.

4B

Public Opinion

Because Supreme Court justices are appointed for life terms, many Americans have the impression that justices are isolated from the stresses of politics. They do escape much of the pressure that elected officials face. When asked to compare his earlier experience in Congress with his days on the Supreme Court, Justice Harold Burton jokingly replied, "Have you ever gone direct from a circus to a monastery?"

Supreme Court justices nevertheless face public pressure. They are supposed to remain independent, unbiased protectors of the Constitution. Yet, they are also human beings who read newspapers, watch television, receive mail, and converse with friends. Moreover, they can never totally ignore public opinion. Public opinion is a reflection of legitimacy — the people's acceptance of authority as being right, correct, or appropriate. Without legitimacy the Supreme Court's decisions would be meaningless.

481

EXPLANATION

After reviewing the content of the section, you may want to consider the following activities:

Law

▲ *What is the principle of stare decisis?* (The Supreme Court uses prior decisions to help it decide current cases.)

● CRITICAL THINKING *Imagine that you are a Supreme Court justice. Under what circumstances would you depart from precedent?* (Students might suggest that they would depart from precedent if they disagreed with the Court's reasoning in the original case, or if they believed that conditions had dramatically changed since that original case was decided.)

Controversial Issues

● CRITICAL THINKING *How are public attitudes toward the Supreme Court affected by Court decisions that reverse earlier decisions?* (Reversals can remind the public that the justices are human and that their decisions may reflect changing events and attitudes. On the other hand, reversals can also shake public faith in the institution, making the law look impermanent.)

Background: *Politics*
Twenty-seven members of Congress, six governors, and one President (Taft) have served on the Court.

Figure 17-4
● *What makes a decision "great"?* (It might reverse a long-standing precedent, establish an important new precedent, or deal with an issue central to American government or society.)

The symbol 👥 denotes active participation strategies.

Activities are keyed for student abilities:
▲ = Basic
● = All Levels
■ = Average/Advanced

Civic Participation

▲ Have students examine the political cartoon on p. 482 and identify the symbols used to represent the President (the captain), Congress (a sailor), and the Supreme Court (a compass). Remind them that the government is often known as the "ship of state."

● Have students consider the role of public opinion in the decisions of the Supreme Court and create a political cartoon illustrating that role.

Constitutional Heritage

● Review the system of checks and balances (Chapter 3, pp. 65–66) with the class, asking students to give examples of the executive and legislative branches' ability to check each other. (Congress's power to impeach, the President's power to veto, Congress's power to override a presidential veto.)

● *What checks do the executive and legislative branches have on the Supreme Court?* (The President chooses justices; the Senate confirms them; Congress can propose constitutional amendments to reverse Court decisions; Congress can pass laws affecting the size of the Court.) Ask students to suggest recent events that illustrate the influence of checks and balances on the Court.

Commenting on the "court-packing" plan, a 1937 newspaper cartoon pictured Roosevelt as someone who insisted on having things his own way.

For example, public opinion played a key role in the "flag-salute" cases of the early 1940's (page 147). The Supreme Court upheld compulsory flag-salute laws in *Minersville School District v. Gobitis* (1940). This decision touched off a storm of public criticism. Just three years later, in *West Virginia Board of Education v. Barnette* (1943), the Supreme Court made a complete turnaround, ruling that such laws violated the free exercise clause of the First Amendment.

One of the justices who switched his vote was Hugo Black. When Justice Douglas informed Justice Frankfurter that Black had switched his vote, Frankfurter asked, "Why, has he reread the Constitution?" Douglas replied, "No, but he has read the papers!"

Public opinion also has had an impact on judicial decisions concerning the death penalty. In 1972 the Supreme Court held in *Furman v. Georgia* (page 186) that the death penalty, as it was then applied, violated the Eighth Amendment. This decision was widely criticized. More than thirty states soon enacted new death penalty

laws. In 1976, in *Gregg v. Georgia,* the Supreme Court held that the death penalty was sometimes constitutional. In its decision, the High Court referred to public opinion polls.

3B

Checks and Balances

Finally, the Court also responds to the actions and influence of the other branches of the government — the President and Congress.

Presidential appointments

Clearly the most important influence the President has on the Supreme Court is the power of appointment. Presidents tend to appoint justices whose views mirror their own. For example, President Lyndon Johnson appointed liberal justices like Thurgood Marshall and Abe Fortas, who agreed with his civil rights policies. Likewise, President Reagan appointed conservative Justices O'Connor and Scalia and named Justice Rehnquist to be Chief Justice.

Still, the President's influence is usually confined to the justices he actually appoints. At any given time, the President faces a Supreme Court composed in part of justices appointed by previous Presidents. Moreover, once on the bench, justices sometimes make decisions contrary to the wishes of the President who appointed them. For example, President Dwight Eisenhower, a moderately conservative Republican, in 1953 chose Earl Warren to be Chief Justice. Much to Eisenhower's surprise, Warren led possibly the most liberal Court in U.S. history.

Roosevelt's "court-packing" scheme

Some Presidents have attempted to expand their influence on the Court. Under President Franklin D. Roosevelt's New Deal program, Congress passed many laws designed to get America out of the Depression. In 1935 and 1936, however, the Supreme Court ruled many of these programs unconstitutional. Roosevelt feared that the Court would strike down other New Deal legislation, particularly the Social Security Act.

After his landslide re-election in 1936, Roosevelt set out to change the composition of the Court — which he termed the "nine old men." The average age of the justices in 1937 was 72 — the oldest in Court history. All but two had been named by Republican Presidents.

Cross-reference
The flag-salute cases are discussed in Chapter 5, pp. 147–148.

Background: *History*
Noting Earl Warren's liberal record as Chief Justice, Eisenhower said that choosing Warren to be Chief Justice was the worst mistake of his life. Similarly,

President Nixon appointed four of the justices on the Court that ruled unanimously against him during Watergate (*U.S. v. Nixon*).

⭐ CRITICAL THINKING
Identifying Assumptions

Try to solve this riddle:

A man and his son were driving in an automobile that was hit by a truck. The man was killed instantly, and the boy was rushed to the hospital. In the emergency room the surgeon announced, "I can't operate on this boy. He is my son." How can this be explained?

Did you guess that the surgeon was the boy's mother? Although this is the obvious answer, it never occurs to many people because they assume that the surgeon must be a man. This riddle shows the power of **assumptions**, the things people expect to be true or take for granted.

Identifying assumptions is important not only to solving the riddle, but to evaluating arguments. Whenever you are presented with an argument, you need to examine not only what is said, but also the assumptions behind it.

★ ISSUE: The Thomas Nomination

In 1991 President George Bush nominated United States District Court Judge Clarence Thomas to the Supreme Court. Thomas, an African American, was named to replace Justice Thurgood Marshall, the first African American on the Court. This nomination was approved by the Senate, but only after bitter debate.

From the outset, Thomas's nomination was controversial. Opponents felt that Thomas, 43, was too inexperienced and too unfamiliar with constitutional issues. They also criticized his conservative stance on civil rights issues. Supporters pointed to the strength of character and intelligence that allowed Thomas to rise from a childhood of poverty to graduation from a prestigious law school and a career in public service. Last minute charges of sexual harassment further complicated the debate.

Below are two excerpts from editorials in the *Houston Post* published around the time of the Senate Judiciary Committee's confirmation hearings on Judge Thomas's nomination. Read each carefully, looking for obvious and hidden assumptions.

Birdia M. Churchwell, Houston Independent School District administrator and consultant

No black man in America who has come through the toughness of a poor black upbringing and has been educated in a sane state of mind should be allowed to forget his past, deny his present, or refrain from forecasting the future possibilities of himself and his people . . . .

Surely it is his intent to work within the system to ensure that the masses of his race receive the same blessings as he did. . . .

We, as blacks, . . . must serve notice on Thomas that, in supporting his confirmation, we demand his total commitment to work to deliver his race by gaining the support of the President, entire Supreme Court, and other powers that be. . . .

Thomas Kleven, professor of law, Texas Southern University

Thomas is no doubt very learned and very smart. But his career, while a successful one, is hardly stellar. . . . Overall, his career doesn't even begin to compare to Thurgood Marshall's prior to his appointment to the Court. While Marshall's background would be hard to match, there are many people in the country more qualified than Thomas.

Then why did President Bush pick him? Did the fact that Thomas is black, as well as conservative, enter in? Clearly. By all accounts only minorities and women were considered at all. Ah, but here's the rub. For taking ethnicity, along with other relevant factors, into account is essentially what affirmative action is all about. Yet the conservative agenda today opposes affirmative action, and it is obvious that President Bush picked Thomas largely because of his outspoken opposition.

Analyzing the Issue

1. Did Ms. Churchwell favor or oppose Thomas's confirmation? On what grounds?
2. What assumptions did Professor Kleven make about why President Bush appointed Thomas?
3. Did Professor Kleven favor or oppose Thomas's confirmation? How can you tell?

483

Cooperative Learning

● Divide the class in half. Have one side prepare arguments in favor of judicial restraint, while the other side prepares arguments in favor of judicial activism. Then hold a formal debate on the following question: **Did the framers of the Constitution intend for the Supreme Court to follow a policy of judicial restraint or judicial activism?**

GUIDED/INDEPENDENT PRACTICE

● Have students complete **Primary Source Worksheet 19,** which examines the Supreme Court's decision in *Brown v. Board of Education.*

RETEACHING/CORRECTIVES

▲ Have students change the headings in the section into questions covering the main idea of each subsection. Then have them answer the questions.

ENRICHMENT/EXTENSION

■ Have students complete **Skills Challenge Worksheet 17,** which examines the way the Supreme Court made its decision in the 1987 case *Johnson v. Joyce.*

Assign **Constitutional Issues Worksheet 12** to the class to help students analyze the role of the judicial branch.

Section 4 Review Answers

1. (a) Decisions tend to be fairer and more uniform, the law is more predictable, and the courts are more efficient. **(b)** When it feels a decision is no longer correct.

The glare of publicity surrounded controversial Supreme Court nominee Clarence Thomas, who was confirmed by one of the narrowest margins in the Court's history.

Establishing a mandatory retirement age for Supreme Court justices would have required a constitutional amendment, so Roosevelt sent to Congress a plan to enlarge the Court.

The plan allowed the President to appoint an additional judge to the Court if a justice did not retire by the age of 70½. Though the plan limited the Court to fifteen, it still would have let Roosevelt appoint six new justices. While many Americans disliked the Court's anti-New Deal rulings, they disliked Roosevelt's "court-packing" plan even more. Public opinion was strongly against Roosevelt's plan, and Congress rejected the proposal outright.

Although he disagreed with Roosevelt's remedy, Chief Justice Charles Evans Hughes did realize that the Court was out of step with the times. Hughes, a former New York governor and presidential candidate, used his political skills to forge a new direction for the Court. In 1937 the Court heard two important New Deal cases — including a minimum wage law similar to one it had earlier declared unconstitutional. This time, the Court voted 5 to 4 to uphold the law. The switch came from Justice Owen Roberts. Of Justice Roberts's sudden reversal it was commonly said that, "A switch in time saved nine!"

484

The role of Congress

Congress also has some opportunities to influence the Supreme Court. Most importantly, the Senate must confirm the appointment of all federal judges. Congress also sets the pay of federal judges. While Congress is forbidden to reduce judges' pay, it has been known to refuse to give pay raises during times of inflation.

In addition, Congress can alter the size of the Supreme Court, as it did frequently until 1869. Tradition now dictates that nine justices sit on the Supreme Court. Any attempts to change the size of the Court would likely meet the same response as Roosevelt's court-packing plan. Furthermore, Congress can change the type of cases over which the Court has jurisdiction.

Over the years, Congress has considered more than 150 proposed laws restricting the power of the Court. In 1923, for example, Senator William E. Borah proposed a law that would require concurrence by seven of nine justices to invalidate an act of Congress. In 1956, about 100 southern Congress members signed a "Declaration of Constitutional Principles" protesting *Brown v. Board of Education* and other Court decisions on school desegregation. In 1958 the Jenner-Butler Bill sought to deprive the Supreme

Background: *History* The Senate Judiciary Committee concluded its statement on President Roosevelt's court-packing plan with these words: "It is a measure which should be so emphatically rejected that its parallel will never again be presented to the free representatives of the free people of America."

Court of its authority to review certain types of cases, such as those relating to contempt of Congress and national security. Like the vast majority of court-curbing bills, these attempts failed.

Constitutional amendments

Finally, Congress can propose constitutional amendments to overturn Supreme Court decisions. The Eleventh Amendment was initiated by Congress following the case of *Chisholm v. Georgia* (1793). The Thirteenth and Fourteenth Amendments stemmed, in part, from the Supreme Court's invalidation of the Missouri Compromise and the denial of Dred Scott's citizenship in *Dred Scott v. Sanford* (1857). The Sixteenth Amendment resulted from the Court's nullification of a federal income tax law in *Pollock v. Farmers' Loan and Trust Co.* (1895). Nevertheless, most proposed amendments aimed at reversing Supreme Court decisions have failed.

SECTION 4 REVIEW

Vocabulary and key terms

stare decisis (480)   judicial activism (480)
precedent (480)   "court-packing"
judicial restraint (480)   plan (484)

For review

1. (a) What are the advantages of following precedent? (b) Under what conditions would the Supreme Court depart from *stare decisis*? **6I**
2. What role does the Supreme Court play under the philosophy of (a) judicial restraint? (b) judicial activism? **5C**
3. What was the effect of public opinion in (a) the "flag-salute" cases? (b) the death penalty controversy? **4B**
4. Why did President Roosevelt's court-packing plan fail? **3B**
5. What are some ways Congress can influence the Supreme Court? **3B**

Critical thinking

ANALYZING AN ISSUE   Some people think the Supreme Court should interpret the Constitution by considering the intent of its writers. What are the strengths and weaknesses of this approach? **2A**

Chapter Summary

The United States has two separate judicial systems of federal and state courts. The federal courts have jurisdiction over all cases that involve national laws or foreign governments or citizens, state governments, U.S. officials, or citizens of different states. Courts that hear cases for the first time are said to have original jurisdiction; courts with appellate jurisdiction hear appeals from lower courts. The constitutional courts are set up by Congress under the authority of Article III of the Constitution. Courts created by Congress to carry out its other powers are called legislative courts. The Justice Department administers the law for the executive branch.

The federal district courts handle most federal cases. Decisions by the district courts may be reviewed by the courts of appeals, also called circuit courts. The Supreme Court can review decisions by the courts of appeals or any other court in the land. Congress has created many special courts for specific kinds of cases.

Most federal judges are appointed by the President with Senate consent, and most serve for life. They can be removed only if impeached by the House and convicted by the Senate. The Attorney General usually recommends nominees for federal judgeships. Presidents and the Senate also consider the opinions of the American Bar Association and other groups. The Senate Judiciary Committee holds hearings on nominees and makes recommendations to the full Senate.

Most cases heard by the Supreme Court concern important constitutional questions. People who wish to have the Supreme Court review their cases petition for writs of *certiorari*. Lawyers for both sides state their arguments in briefs, and other interested parties may file *amicus curiae* briefs. Lawyers present oral arguments before the Supreme Court, and the nine justices reach their decisions in conference. One justice writes the majority opinion, while others may file concurring or dissenting opinions.

The Supreme Court justices usually follow precedent in deciding cases, but may break with precedents if they believe they are no longer correct. Different Courts have followed philosophies of judicial restraint or judicial activism in making rulings.

485

2. (a) The Court acts as a referee, making sure that the President and Congress do not go against the Constitution. (b) The Court plays an active role in making policy.
3. (a) and (b) Public opinion helped reverse a previous ruling.
4. The public and Congress strongly opposed it.
5. Congress can stop giving pay raises, alter the size of the Court, change the types of cases over which the Court has jurisdiction, and propose constitutional amendments to overturn Court decisions. The Senate confirms appointments to the Court.

Critical thinking *Strengths*— Rulings would be more consistent with each other and more true to the original spirit of the Constitution. *Weaknesses*—The Court would have less flexibility and would not be as responsive to modern ideas and issues; regarding some issues, there is disagreement over the framers' intent.

CLOSURE

● Have students suggest major factors that influence the way the Supreme Court interprets the Constitution. Then have them read the next assigned lesson.

CHAPTER 17 CORRECTIVES

● To review the content of Chapter 17, you may want to have students complete **Study Guide/Review 17** or **Workbook Chapter 17.**

Cross-reference
Chisholm v. Georgia is discussed on p. 465.

Background: *Values*
Robert Cushman, an authority on the Constitution, wrote in 1925, "The Supreme Court does not work in a vacuum. Its decisions upon important constitutional questions can be fully understood only when viewed against the background of history, politics, and economics out of which they grew."

The symbol 👥 denotes active participation strategies.

Activities are keyed for student abilities:
▲ = Basic
● = All Levels
■ = Average/Advanced

CHAPTER REVIEW

Answers

Vocabulary See pp. T19–T21 for suggested vocabulary activities.

Reviewing the Facts

1. The United States has a system of federal courts and a system of state courts.

2. To be the guardian of the Constitution and of the rights it ensures the people.

3. Federal court.

4. Cases involving the federal government or federal officials.

5. They can lobby senators who will vote on judicial confirmations. They can also influence public opinion, which may influence judicial decisions.

6. The Court will not rule on a law's constitutionality unless the person challenging the law has been harmed; it will not give an advisory opinion; and it will not decide moot or political questions.

7. They establish precedents and communicate the Court's ideas to the other branches, to the states, and to the people.

8. The sitting Supreme Court, comprised almost entirely of conservatives, had struck down much of his New Deal legislation.

Thinking Critically About Key Concepts

1. Some students might say that competitive salaries would expand the pool of potential judges. Others might suggest that the honor of serving as a federal judge is a major reward, and that the government does not have the resources of private law firms.

2. Students should note that interest groups represent a point of view that should be heard. Also, they may uncover important background information about a nominee. However, they may manipulate the media to further their own interests.

● **Review the definitions of the following terms:**

admiralty law	dissenting opinion	maritime law
appellate jurisdiction	district court	moot question
brief	docket	opinion
circuit court	"federal question"	original jurisdiction
concurring opinion	judicial activism	precedent
conference	judicial restraint	"rule of four"
constitutional court	jurisdiction	sovereign immunity
court-martial	law clerk	*stare decisis*
court of appeals	legislative court	territorial court
"court-packing" plan	majority opinion	writ of *certiorari*

● **REVIEWING THE FACTS**

1. What is meant by the statement that the United States has a dual court system? **3A**

2. For what major purpose did the framers of the Constitution create the federal court system? **2A**

3. Which court, federal or state, would hear a case involving citizens of two different states? **3C**

4. What sorts of cases does the United States Claims Court decide? **3A**

5. How can interest groups influence the federal judiciary? **4B**

6. Name two limitations the Supreme Court has placed on the kinds of cases it will hear. **3A**

7. What two purposes do the written opinions of the Supreme Court serve? **3A**

8. Why did President Franklin Roosevelt propose to enlarge the Supreme Court? **2C**

▲ **THINKING CRITICALLY ABOUT KEY CONCEPTS**

1. Some people believe that federal judges are not paid enough and that the judicial system loses many good judges to private practice. Do you think the salaries of federal judges should be raised in order to be competitive

486

with those in the private sector? Explain your reasoning. **7D**

2. Should interest groups have the ability to influence the process of choosing federal judges, including Supreme Court justices? Explain your answer. **4C**

3. Judicial restraint calls for Supreme Court justices to follow the wishes of elected officials when making decisions. Judicial activism calls for them to take an active role in making policy. Do you agree with the philosophy of judicial restraint or that of judicial activism? Why? **3A**

▲ **PRACTICING SKILLS**

1. **Study Skills: Reading a special-purpose map.** Refer to Figure 17–2 (page 468) to answer the following questions. (a) How many circuits of federal appeals courts are there in the United States? (b) In which circuit would an appeal from a district court in southern Ohio be heard? (c) Which states are included in the Tenth Circuit? (d) How many district courts are there in the state of Florida? Alabama? Idaho? (To review map skills, see Study Skill 4 in the back of the book.) **8B**

2. **Critical Thinking Skills: Interpreting a document.** Review Chief Justice John Marshall's opinion in *Marbury v. Madison*

---

3. Students might suggest that judicial restraint is usually called for, but that judicial activism has, in the past, served to advance the good of society.

Practicing Skills

1. **(a)** Twelve. **(b)** Sixth Circuit. **(c)** Wyoming, Utah, Colorado, New Mexico, Kansas, Oklahoma. **(d)** Three in Florida; three in Alabama; one in Idaho.

2. A rhetorical question is one to which no answer is expected, or there is only one answer. By asking a rhetorical question, Marshall makes it clear that his opinion is incorrect only if the

(page 465). The first paragraph ends with a rhetorical question. Find the meaning of "rhetorical question" in a dictionary. Then explain what Marshall's point was and how a rhetorical question helped him make that point. **8A**

▲ PARTICIPATORY CITIZENSHIP

1. **Identify the federal judiciary.** Find out where the U.S. district court for your district meets and the names of the district court judges. Then locate the seat of the court of appeals for your circuit and the appeals court judges. You may wish to identify the President who appointed these judges. Construct an organization chart using this information. **3A**

2. **Writing for information.** Choose an interest group which has aims that you support and write or call the group's local office, asking if the group took a stand on the last Supreme Court nominee, and if so, what the stand was and the reasons for it. **4B**

■ WRITING ABOUT ISSUES

1. **Research report.** Find information on three important cases the Supreme Court heard in the past year. What were the issues? What were the decisions? What was the public response, if any, to the decisions? Were any opinions unanimous? Which rulings contained dissenting opinions? Write a report that answers these questions and presents any other information you find. **3A**

2. **Biography.** Write a biographical sketch of a famous Supreme Court justice. Focus on the justice's career, including any particularly well-known decisions and any lasting impact the justice had on the Court. **2C**

▲ ANALYZING A POLITICAL CARTOON

In 1987, Supreme Court nominee Robert Bork was rejected by the Senate — in part because of his outspoken claim that there was no constitutionally protected right to privacy. Since Bork, nominees have refused to discuss their views on controversial topics, such as abortion rights. Often the reason given is unwillingness to voice an opinion on still-pending issues. Look at the cartoon below and answer the following questions.

1. Why is the cartoon character's response inappropriate for the question on the quiz? **8A**

2. What does the cartoon suggest is the real reason for the character's reluctance to answer the question? **8B**

3. What point is the cartoonist trying to make? Is he successful? Why, or why not? **8A**

Cartoon by Jeff MacNelly, 1991. Reprinted by permission: Tribune Media Services.

487

CHAPTER 18
LAW AND THE LEGAL PROCESS
(pp. 488–509)

	Section Objectives	Section Resources
Section 1 **The American Legal System Has Many Branches**	☐ describe the sources of American law ☐ distinguish between private law and public law ☐ describe the function and organization of the Justice Department	● PRIMARY SOURCE WORKSHEET **20**
Section 2 **The Criminal Justice System Enforces the Law**	☐ list and explain pre-trial procedures	● CITIZENSHIP WORKSHEET **7**
Section 3 **Trials Determine Guilt or Innocence**	☐ list and explain the steps in a typical trial ☐ explain what forms imprisonment may take and on what grounds a prisoner may be released	▲ SKILLS PRACTICE WORKSHEET **18** ■ SKILLS CHALLENGE WORKSHEET **18** ● SIMULATION **3** ▲ TRANSPARENCY **40**

Essential Elements

The list below shows Essential Elements relevant to this chapter.
(The complete list of Essential Elements appears in the introductory
pages of this Teacher's Edition.)

Section 1: 1C, 1D, 2A, 3A, 6E, 8B

Section 2: 3A, 6E, 8B

Citizenship Skills feature (p. 5C1): 4D

Section 3: 3A, 6A, 6D, 6E, 6G, 8B

Chapter Review: 3A, 4D, 5C, 6C, 6D,
6E, 6I, 8A, 8B, 8C, 8H

> Section Resources are keyed
> for student abilities:
> ▲ = Basic
> ● = All Levels
> ■ = Average/Advanced

Homework Options

Each section contains activities labeled "Guided/Independent Practice," "Reteaching/Correctives," and "Enrichment/Extension." You may wish to choose from among these activities when assigning homework.

Students Acquiring English Activities

Divide the class into four teams. Play a word game in which you read aloud words or phrases as clues until one of the teams guesses the type of tort or felony crime being described. For example, describe the tort of *assault* by first stating, "intentional." If a team guesses correctly, it gets five points. If no team guesses correctly, the second clue is "fearful." A correct guess wins four points. The last clue for this answer is "his or her life," and the correct response is worth three points. Other possible crimes are *kidnapping:* "carrying away" (five points); "person" (four points); "no permission" (three points). *Forgery:* "unlawful gain" (five points; "false information" (four points); "providing" (three points).

LISTENING/SPEAKING: With the class, review p. 499 on the juvenile justice system and how it affects young people in your community.

Case Studies

When teaching this chapter, you may use Case Study 4, which discusses mandatory drug testing, or Case Study 7, which addresses the issue of local curfews. (Case Studies may be found following p. 510.)

Teacher Bibliography

Bender, David L. and Bruno Leone, eds. *Criminal Justice.* Greenhaven, 1987. Presents authoritative articles on key criminal justice issues.

DiPerna, Paula. *Juries on Trial: Faces of American Justice.* Dembner, 1984. Relates the history of the American jury system and explores jury-related controversies.

Student Bibliography

Gustafson, Anita. *Guilty or Innocent?* Holt, 1985. Absorbing accounts of ten of the most famous criminal trials in history give the reader the opportunity to reach a verdict.

Wishman, Seymour. *Anatomy of a Jury.* Times Books, 1986. A criminal lawyer gives an insider's view of the jury system.

Zerman, Melvyn Bernard. *Beyond a Reasonable Doubt.* Crowell, 1981. A lively, yet authoritative, account of how the jury system works.

Literature

Cozzens, James Gould. *The Just and the Unjust.* Harcourt Brace Jovanovich, 1965. Day-by-day events in a small town murder trial illustrate much about the life of lawyers and the vagaries of the law.

Turow, Scott. *Presumed Innocent.* Farrar, Straus & Giroux, 1987. The murder of a prosecuting attorney at election time in a large Midwestern city presents political problems for the attorney in charge of the investigation.

Uhnak, Dorothy. *False Witness.* Fawcett, 1982. A New York District Attorney must decide whether to prosecute the man actually responsible for a vicious crime.

CHAPTER
RESOURCES

Study Guide/Review 18
Workbook Chapter 18
Chapter 18 Test, Forms A–C

Films and Videotapes*

The Judicial Branch. (Series title: *Branches of Government.*) 26 min. NGS, 1982. f, v. Follows a case involving the State of Alaska that started in the state court system and eventually reached the U.S. Supreme Court. Provides an excellent review of how our judicial system works.

Law: A System of Order. (Series title: *Humanities.*) 17 min. McGraw-Hill (CRM), 1971. f, v. Traces the development of laws in many countries from the time the laws were part of an oral tradition to the present. Concludes by considering questions raised by international law.

Software*

American Government V (Apple, IBM, Macintosh). Queue. Students learn about the development and processes of American government using three interactive tutorials. The programs cover the judiciary, federal and state courts, the Supreme Court, the civil service, federal bureaucracy, and the executive branch.

Supreme Court Decision (Apple, IBM). Queue. Students become attorneys who must prepare and argue a civil or criminal law case through the pre-trial level, the trial, an appeal in a state or federal court, and finally to the Supreme Court.

---

* For a complete guide to audiovisual sources, see page T22.

Chapter 18 looks at the American legal system, tracing the history of American legal principles, contrasting the private and public branches of American law, explaining the responsibilities and organization of the Justice Department, and outlining the procedures followed by the criminal justice system.

Chapter Outline

After students complete this chapter, they will be able to:

1. Describe the sources of American law.
2. Distinguish between private law and public law.
3. Describe the function and organization of the Justice Department.
4. List and explain pre-trial procedures.
5. List and explain the steps in a typical trial.
6. Explain what forms imprisonment may take and on what grounds a prisoner may be released.

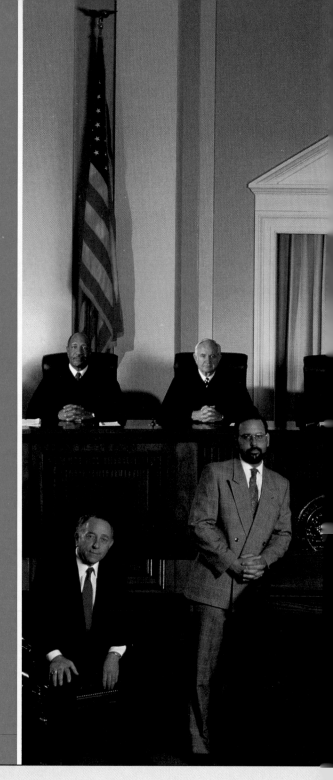

CHAPTER

18

LAW and the LEGAL PROCESS

The law is the last result of human wisdom acting upon human experience for the benefit of the public.

Dr. Samuel Johnson
English scholar (1709–1784)

488

Photo
Florida State Supreme Court.

here is a classic trial scene in movies, plays, and television programs. It comes after the case has been going badly for the defense. A witness is called to the stand. The courtroom is large and gloomy, the judge looks down from the high wooden bench, and the lawyer asking questions paces before the witness stand.

"So you were there when the victim was attacked; you did see who killed her!" the defense lawyer cries. "Who was the murderer?"

Crying, the witness points to a face in the back of the courtroom. "It was that man. He did it."

This scene may be your image of how the law works in the United States. In reality, the dramatic moment in a trial when all is revealed is rare. Instead, the legal process is a slow and careful set of procedures, rooted in a system of laws that govern many aspects of our lives. When those laws are violated, the process that may bring a person to trial is triggered.

This chapter examines the American legal system and the procedures that the government must follow in carrying out the law.

CHAPTER OUTLINE

1 The American Legal System Has Many Branches

Sources of American Law
Private Law
Public Law
The Justice Department

2 The Criminal Justice System Enforces the Law

Investigating a Crime
Pre-Trial Court Procedures

3 Trials Determine Guilt or Innocence

The Trial Setting
The Trial
Imprisonment and Release

489

CHAPTER SUPPORT MATERIAL

Skills Practice Worksheet 18

Skills Challenge Worksheet 18

Citizenship Worksheet 7

Primary Source Worksheet 20

Simulation 3

Transparency 40

Study Guide/Review 18

Workbook Chapter 18

Chapter 18 Test, Forms A-C

SECTION 1

The American Legal System Has Many Branches (pp. 490–497)

Section Objectives

☐ describe the sources of American law

☐ distinguish between private law and public law

☐ describe the function and organization of the Justice Department

Vocabulary

ordinance, equity, private law, civil law, real property, contract, tort, public law, administrative law, international law, criminal law, Solicitor General

FOCUS

● Have students suggest activities they perform in the course of an average day that are governed by laws. (Drive a car, attend school, pay for purchases, etc.) Have them consider what would happen if there were no laws governing these activities. *Why might people have developed legal codes?* (To bring order to society and to make human interactions more predictable.)

SECTION 1
The American Legal System Has Many Branches

| ACCESS | The Main Ideas |

1 **What are the sources of American law?**
pages 490–492

2 **What is the difference between private and public law?**
pages 492–496

3 **What is the function and organization of the Justice Department?**
page 496

In 1850 an Englishman named W. K. Loftus noted four large mounds in the south of present-day Iran. The mounds, Loftus determined, marked the site of an ancient city. Archeologists dug up the largest, which rose almost 125 feet in the air, uncovering a fortress thousands of years old. Within the fortress, a French archeologist discovered a block of stone with Babylonian writing on it. Experts deciphered the writing, enabling them to read a list of laws issued by Hammurabi, ruler of Babylonia about 3,750 years ago. This Code of Hammurabi, one of the world's oldest sets of written laws, addresses a host of issues including religion, family relations, business, and crime.

The roots of American law can be traced back to the Code of Hammurabi. In the United States, as in ancient Babylonia, law is intended to provide a way to settle disputes peacefully and fairly, so that a person receives justice. Laws reflect what people in a society at a given time believe is appropriate ethical and moral conduct.

American law also draws on the Bible, which originally served as the law for the Hebrew civilization in early Palestine. Principles of American law can be traced to the legal systems of the Roman Empire, medieval England, and the colonial period. This section examines the most important sources and branches of the American legal system.

This mosaic from Ravenna, Italy, shows the 6th-century Byzantine emperor Justinian, who had his scholars collect and codify the laws of ancient Rome. Justinian's Code is one of the models for today's systems of statutory law.

Background: *Cultural Literacy* The roots of American law are depicted in the Supreme Court chambers. Above the bench, for example, is a carving of the Ten Commandments flanked by two carved figures— "majesty of the law" and "power of government."

Figure 18-1

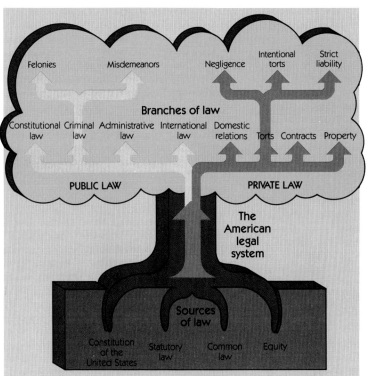

THE AMERICAN LEGAL SYSTEM The two main branches of American law — public law and private law — divide into many different categories. The legal system traces its roots to four sources. 8B

1C, 1D, 2A, 6E

Sources of American Law

As Figure 18-1 illustrates, it may be useful to think of the American legal system as a tree. The many types of matters decided in American courts can be thought of as "branches" of the legal system. To understand the development of the branches, it is important to look first at the "roots," or sources, of American law.

The Constitution

The most important source of American law is the Constitution of the United States, the "supreme law of the land." The Constitution describes both the powers of government and the rights of individuals. Its provisions are applied by both the federal and the state court systems, with final authority resting in the Supreme Court of the United States. The Constitution can be amended only by a joint action of Congress and the states.

Each state in the United States also has its own constitution. State constitutions represent the final legal authority in each state; only the national Constitution can overrule them. Each state also has a supreme court with final say over the meaning of its constitution. Like the Constitution, state constitutions may be amended. They may also be revised by a vote of the people.

Statutory law

American law is also based on the thousands of statutes, or written laws, passed by legislatures or other lawmaking bodies. These make up statutory law. Most statutes are detailed and precise and must be frequently revised.

Statutory law can be traced to ancient Rome where, in about 450 B.C., the "Twelve Tables" gave the Roman people a written set, or code, of laws. For the next thousand years, Roman rulers added to, revised, and reorganized these written codes, which formed the basis of the Roman legal system. As the Roman Empire stretched from

491

EXPLANATION
After reviewing the content of the section, you may want to consider the following activities:

Cultural Literacy
● CRITICAL THINKING The "Twelve Tables" of ancient Rome were cast in bronze and attached to the "rostrum," or orator's platform, in the Roman Forum. This way, all Roman citizens could read and understand the law. *How does everyone benefit from the publication of laws?* (Knowledge of laws protects people from arbitrary rule.)

Background: *Constitutional Heritage* The Declaration of Independence and Constitution were both written by men trained in English common law.

Cross-reference
State constitutions are discussed in Chapter 24, Section 1 (pp. 634–638).

Figure 18-1
▲ *What are the two subdivisions of criminal law?* (Felonies and misdemeanors.)

The symbol ⅱ denotes active participation strategies.

Activities are keyed for student abilities:
▲ = Basic
● = All Levels
■ = Average/Advanced

Values

● Read to the class the following statement by Hubert H. Humphrey: "There are not enough jails, not enough policemen, not enough courts to enforce a law not supported by the people." Have students paraphrase the statement. (If most people do not support a law, the government will be unable to make them obey it.) Ask students if they can think of any laws that are not obeyed by most people. (Possible examples include speed limits and pedestrian laws such as jaywalking.)

● CRITICAL THINKING **Should the government do away with laws that most people refuse to obey? Explain.** (Some students may argue, citing Humphrey, that there is no point in trying to force a law on an unwilling public. Other students may argue that if the public disapproves of a law, it should seek its repeal through legal means, not simply ignore it, and that a law may serve a necessary function despite being unpopular.)

Egypt to England, it influenced law throughout the Western world. For this reason, statutory law is sometimes called "Roman law."

Today many countries have legal systems based on written codes of law. The most influential was that established in France by Napoleon Bonaparte in 1804. This body of statutes, the Napoleonic Code, with some revision, is still in force today. It was the model for the legal systems set up in most of Europe, in parts of Africa, throughout Latin America, and in Japan. The Napoleonic Code also provides the foundation for the laws of the state of Louisiana and the Canadian province of Quebec, both of which were once French colonies. Louisiana's civil code of 1825 (revised in 1870) is still in force today.

The United States government and the remaining 49 states rely a good deal, but not exclusively, upon statutory law. Statutes are enacted both by Congress and the state legislatures. Local legislative bodies, such as city councils, also enact statutes, called **ordinances**. All statutory law in the United States, of course, must comply with state and national constitutions.

Common law

While statutory law is a written code of laws made by legislatures, common law is made by judges. As Chapter 2 discussed (page 33), the common-law system dates back to 11th-century England, where important court decisions were gathered and recorded in yearbooks. Judges consulted these books to see what rulings were "common" in other courts throughout England. In cases similar to those already on the books, judges followed previous rulings. This was the origin of *stare decisis* (page 480). In unique cases, judges would make their own decisions based on custom and tradition. These decisions became precedents for later cases. For this reason, common law is also called "case law."

English colonists brought the common-law tradition with them to America. It is the basis, for example, of libel and slander rulings. Common law continued to develop in all of the states except Louisiana. It was the main source of American law till the mid-1800's.

Merging the two legal systems

Common law and statutory law both still play an important role in the American legal system. Because statutes are passed by the people's

elected representatives, they can override or change common law. But when no conflict exists, common law is as effective legally as statutory law. The California Civil Code, for example, states that the "common law of England, so far as it is not repugnant to or inconsistent with the Constitution of the United States, and the constitution or laws of this state, is the rule of decision in all the courts of this state."

Moreover, courts are continually asked to interpret the meaning of new statutes. Rulings in such cases then serve as the precedents, or case law, for similar cases in the future. In this way the common law continues to develop.

Equity

Another inheritance from English law is **equity** — meaning "fairness" or "justice." While the common law brought order to the English legal system, it gradually became quite rigid. People could not use the law courts unless they followed precise procedures. They therefore complained directly to the king. Eventually, a separate system of courts was set up for cases not covered by common law. These were called "courts of equity" or "courts of chancery."

Cases in equity differ from common-law cases. There are no juries, and judges settle the issues. Most importantly, equity can be used to *prevent* wrongs from being done, not merely to deal with wrongs that have already been committed. As a result, the most common form of relief in an equity case is an injunction, a court order that forbids a certain act. Injunctions might be used to stop a factory from polluting the air, prevent highway construction in a residential area, or compel a baseball team to honor the provisions of a player's contract. Since the 19th century, the same courts generally handle both law and equity cases in the United States.

6E

Private Law

As Figure 18–1 illustrates, the American legal system "tree" has two main branches — private law and public law — which further divide into smaller branches. The relations between people in society fall into the branch known as **private law** or **civil law**. Private law generally deals with disputes between individ-

Background: *Law*
Legislatures continually pass statutes and ordinances but rarely repeal any after they have served their purpose. For example, in the town of Robinson, Illinois, an ordinance requires people entering town with a motor vehicle to call first at City Hall.

uals, businesses, or other organizations. The outcome of a civil case is usually a fine or an award of money, not a jail sentence. Private law has four important branches, dealing with property, contracts, family relations, and *torts,* or injuries.

Property

One branch of private law covers people's ownership and use of property. Land and everything attached to it, such as houses and barns, is called **real property**. Movable property, like cars or jewelry, is called *personal* property. Personal property can also include intangible items such as stocks, bonds, copyrights, and patents.

Under American law, the right to own property is guaranteed and protected by the government. Ownership involves not only having property, but also using it, preventing others from using it, and selling it. There are some limits on property rights, however. For example, zoning laws may forbid a landowner from building a factory in a residential area. Owners of buildings may not discriminate in renting or selling their property. Likewise, property cannot be used for illegal activities such as gambling or drug dealing. In such cases, public welfare outweighs the rights of private ownership.

Contracts

The law of **contracts** is a second branch of private law. A contract is a formal legal agreement between two or more individuals, businesses, or other organizations. For example, the federal government may hire a construction company to build a bridge. The contract may spell out many details, such as minimum standards for the bridge, how long it will take to be built, how much the company will be paid, and even the number of minority workers that must be hired.

Family relations

A third branch of private law concerns domestic relations, the relationships among family members. Marriages, divorces, and child custody cases are covered by this branch of law. Domestic relations cases make up a major portion of cases heard in state courts.

Torts

The last branch of private law is the law of **torts**. A tort is a wrongful act that injures a person or someone's property. (*Tort* was the medieval Latin word for "wrong.") Under the law of torts, the wronged person may sue the person responsible for the injury. The injured party in

The British legal system today follows customs that began centuries ago. American law is also influenced by British tradition.

Background: *Cultural Literacy* Students unfamiliar with the term *real property* may be more familiar with the term *real estate.* The term has acquired an extended meaning through statutes and judicial decisions. An oil and gas lease, for instance, was held to be real estate in *U.S. v. Texas Eastern Transmission Corp.*

Background: *Constitutional Heritage* Contracts are mentioned in the United States Constitution. Article I, Section 10, Clause 1 bars any state from "impairing the obligation of contracts."

Civic Participation
● Hold a mock civil trial, choosing students to play the role of defendant, plaintiff, counsels, judge, jury, and witnesses. Start by having the class decide the subject of the litigation, identifying the branch of private law that is involved. (For example, one student could be suing another for damages caused by a traffic accident. This would be a negligence tort.)

The symbol 👥 denotes active participation strategies.

Activities are keyed for student abilities:
▲ = Basic
● = All Levels
■ = Average/Advanced

Law

● Have students suggest questions they would like to ask your local U.S. Attorney if he or she were to visit your class. If your school is near the seat of a federal judicial district, you might have students invite the U.S. Attorney or a representative of the office to speak to the class, at which time the students could ask their questions.

Cooperative Learning

● Have students work in groups to create charts illustrating specific examples of the four types of public law. You may want to assign each member of the group responsibility for one category: administrative, constitutional, international, or criminal.

such lawsuits usually seeks money, or damages, to compensate for the wrong or injury. Sometimes the injured party also seeks extra compensation as a way of punishing the wrongdoer.

There are three main categories of torts. An *intentional tort* is a willful act done with the purpose of harming someone, such as assault, battery, or defamation. Some of these actions are also crimes. For example, someone who beats up another person (battery) might be sued in civil court for damages and also tried in criminal court. (See Figure 18–2 for a list of common terms for torts.)

Another kind of tort is *negligence*. A person is negligent if he or she fails to do something that a reasonably careful person would do — such as cleaning ice from a slippery sidewalk in front of a store. Negligence can also be some act that a reasonable person, exercising ordinary care, would not do — such as driving a car with faulty brakes or leaving a loaded gun in one's yard.

A third category of torts is called *strict liability*. There are certain accidents for which someone can be held liable, or legally responsible, even if the accident is not intentional and not the result of negligence. Such accidents usually involve things that are basically dangerous, such as explosives, wild animals, or faulty products. For example, the owner of a pet lion that escapes and bites someone's leg is responsible for the lion's action, even if the owner was being careful and did not let the lion escape on purpose.

Figure 18–2 COMMON TORTS AND FELONY CRIMES *The following are illegal activities you have probably heard mentioned. They fall into categories described in this chapter.* 8B

	Intentional torts
ASSAULT	Intentionally causing someone to be fearful for his or her life.
BATTERY	Physically harming someone.
CONVERSION	Using or possessing another's property without permission.
DEFAMATION	Intentionally injuring someone's good name or reputation (includes libel and slander).
FALSE IMPRISONMENT	Intentionally preventing someone from going where they have a legal right to go.
TRESPASS	Illegally entering another's real property.

	Crimes against persons (felonies)
HOMICIDE	Killing someone. *First-degree murder* is intentional and planned killing; *manslaughter* is intentional but unplanned.
KIDNAPPING	Taking and carrying away a person without permission. (May also constitute the tort of false imprisonment.)
MAYHEM	Intentionally maiming or disfiguring another.
ROBBERY	Taking property from another by violence or fear.

	Crimes against property (felonies)
ARSON	Burning another's property.
BURGLARY	Breaking and entering into another's dwelling or property with the intent of committing a crime.
FORGERY	Providing false information to secure unfair or unlawful gain.
LARCENY	Taking another's property without permission.

494

Critical Thinking
▲ *What factors might affect the amount of compensation a jury might set for punishing a defendant in a lawsuit?* (The jury's feelings about the plaintiff and the defendant, the seriousness of the crime.)

Figure 18–2
● *What is the difference between* assault *and* battery? (*Battery* is actually harming someone; *assault* is causing a person to be fearful of harm.)

The World Court building, located in The Hague, Netherlands, is a focal point of international law.

6E

Public Law

The second major branch of the American legal system is **public law**. Public law concerns the relationship between the government and citizens. It usually involves legal actions initiated by the government to benefit the people as a whole. It has four categories — administrative, constitutional, international, and criminal law.

Administrative law

Congress and the state legislatures have established various governmental agencies — such as commissions and executive agencies — to carry out public policy. The rules and regulations issued by these agencies make up the body of **administrative law**.

Constitutional law

The Constitution is the most important source of the American legal system. Constitutional law, therefore, is one of the most important branches of law. It derives from the text of the Constitution and its amendments and also includes thousands of Supreme Court rulings. These clarify and interpret the meaning of such concepts as "cruel and unusual punishment" and "due process." Each state also has a body of law based on its state constitution.

International law

The principles and rules that guide relations among nations, called **international law**, make up the third branch of public law. Sources of international law include customs, treaties, executive agreements, and rulings of the International Court of Justice, or World Court. The World Court was created in 1945, as part of the United Nations, to help settle disputes among nations. Nations are not bound to follow international law but abide by its provisions voluntarily.

In October 1985, the United States announced it would no longer automatically abide by World Court decisions. The World Court at the time was hearing charges by the Nicaraguan government that the United States was supporting military actions against Nicaragua. The Court ruled in June 1986 that the United States had violated international law, but the Reagan administration denounced this decision.

Criminal law

The largest, and probably the most familiar, branch of public law is **criminal law**. Criminal laws and the penalties for breaking them are usually spelled out in statutes passed by state legislatures. The main functions of criminal law are to protect the public from wrongful acts, to punish wrongdoers, and to prevent future crimes.

495

Cross-references
Commissions and executive agencies are discussed in Chapter 16, pp. 432–437. The United Nations is discussed in Chapter 20, Section 4 (pp. 556–559).

Background: *Global Awareness* The World Court's most important contributions have involved the law of the sea, boundaries, nationality, human rights, treaties, procedures for arbitration, and international constitutional law.

GUIDED/INDEPENDENT PRACTICE
● Have students complete **Primary Source Worksheet 20,** which examines the Code of Hammurabi and the Ten Commandments.

RETEACHING/CORRECTIVES
▲ Have students create an annotated version of Figure 18–1, either copying the tree structure or creating their own kind of chart.

The symbol ♟ denotes active participation strategies.

Activities are keyed for student abilities:
▲ = Basic
● = All Levels
■ = Average/Advanced

This marshal, who was responsible for maintaining law and order in the old West, was a forerunner of the modern-day federal marshal.

The most serious offenses in criminal law are felonies, which are crimes punishable by imprisonment for more than one year (or even by death). Felonies are classified as either "crimes against persons" or "crimes against property." Figure 18–2 includes common examples.

A misdemeanor is a less serious criminal offense that carries lesser penalties than a felony. A misdemeanor conviction may thus result in a fine (say $1,000), a prison sentence of 30 days or several months, or both. Examples of misdemeanors include jaywalking and shoplifting.

A person who has committed a crime is considered to have harmed society as a whole. Therefore, the government takes action against the accused. (Individuals who are wronged as the result of crimes also may seek damages or compensation through private law.) The government, acting on the people's behalf, brings the charges, and the courts see that justice is done.

3A

The Justice Department

The Department of Justice is responsible for seeing that federal laws are carried out and that violators are punished. Sometimes called "the largest law firm in the nation," the Justice Department has been a Cabinet department since 1870.

496

The department is, in a sense, the lawyer for the American people as a whole. It investigates federal crimes, enforces federal laws, supervises federal prisons, and represents the federal government (and the people) in legal matters.

Justice Department officials

The Justice Department is headed by the Attorney General, who is the chief legal officer of the United States and a member of the President's Cabinet. Most actual legal work involving the United States government is undertaken by the **Solicitor General**. The Solicitor General decides which cases the federal government will appeal to the Supreme Court and represents the government before the Court. The Solicitor General often submits *amicus curiae* (page 261) briefs to the Supreme Court to express the President's opinions on key cases.

In each federal judicial district, the chief lawyer for the Justice Department is the United States Attorney. These lawyers are responsible for prosecuting people charged with federal crimes. They also represent the United States in civil cases. U.S. Attorneys are appointed for four-year terms by the President, with the consent of the Senate.

A United States marshal is also appointed for every federal judicial district. The duties of a federal marshal closely resemble those of a county sheriff. Marshals may arrest criminals, carry out federal court orders, deliver warrants, summon jurors, and take custody of criminals.

Every district court also has at least one U.S. magistrate. Magistrates handle many duties once done by the federal district court judges, such as setting bail, issuing warrants, and trying those charged with minor offenses.

Department divisions

Thousands of lawyers also work for the many divisions and bureaus of the Justice Department, described in the Guide to Executive Departments on pages 447–460. The Law Enforcement Assistance Administration (LEAA), for example, works with local police to fight crime. The Civil Rights Division enforces civil rights laws. The Drug Enforcement Administration (DEA) works against the sale and use of illegal narcotics and dangerous drugs. Finally, the Federal Bureau of Investigation (FBI) investigates federal crimes and pursues dangerous criminals.

SECTION 1 REVIEW

Vocabulary and key terms

ordinance (492)   public law (495)
equity (492)   administrative law (495)
private law (492)   international law (495)
civil law (492)   criminal law (495)
real property (493)   Solicitor General (496)
contract (493)
tort (493)

For review

1. What are the four sources of the legal system in the United States? **1D**
2. What can equity achieve that common law cannot? **6E**

3. What kinds of cases are settled by private law? **6E**
4. Would each of the following tort situations be considered intentional, negligent, or strict liability? (a) A bully gives someone a black eye during a fight. (b) Gasoline stored in your garage explodes and starts a fire. (c) A neighbor hitting golf balls in his backyard breaks your window. **6E**
5. Who is always responsible for bringing charges in criminal cases? **6E**
6. What official represents the federal government in (a) Supreme Court cases? (b) district court cases? **3A**

Critical thinking

IDENTIFYING BASIC PRINCIPLES   Which of the four sources described has contributed the most to the American legal system? Explain your answer. **1D**

---

4. **(a)** Intentional. **(b)** Strict liability. **(c)** Negligence.
5. The government.
6. **(a)** Solicitor General. **(b)** U.S. Attorney.

Critical thinking Students may choose the Constitution, because it is the "supreme law of the land"; statutory law, because it is so old; common law, because it was the main source of American law in the nation's earliest years; or equity, because it can be used to issue injunctions.

CLOSURE

● Have students suggest the most important idea they learned in the class period. Then have them read Section 2, noting the steps a suspect passes through from arrest to trial.

SECTION 2

3A, 6E, 8B

The Criminal Justice System Enforces the Law

ACCESS	The Main Idea

What are the legal steps taken to bring a suspect to trial?   *pages 497–500*

In his 1903 address to Congress, President Theodore Roosevelt declared, "No man is above the law, and no man is below it." By this, Roosevelt meant that every person who breaks the law must pay the penalty. Enforcing criminal law is the function of the criminal justice system. At each step in the system, however, the accused person is presumed innocent until proven guilty. Thus, even lawbreakers receive the protections of due process guaranteed in the Bill of Rights.

Many steps in the criminal justice system may seem familiar to you from fictional stories on television or reports of real cases in the newspapers. This section examines how the criminal justice system in the United States attempts both to enforce criminal law and to protect the rights of citizens.

6E

Investigating a Crime

The first step in the criminal justice system is finding and arresting suspected criminals. Once a crime has been committed, law enforcement officials — police, sheriffs' departments, or state highway patrols — begin an investigation. They look for witnesses and interview them, examine the scene of the crime, take fingerprints, check records, and look for information in many other ways. Chief suspects may be questioned at length. The goal of the investigation is, obviously, to determine who may have committed the crime.

Arrest

If police believe that they have sufficient evidence, or probable cause, to link a suspect to a crime, the next step is usually obtaining a warrant from a judge or magistrate. A valid arrest warrant must specify the suspect's name and the alleged crime. In some cases — for example,

497

SECTION 2

The Criminal Justice System Enforces the Law *(pp. 497–500)*

Section Objective

☐ list and explain pre-trial procedures

Vocabulary

juvenile justice system, bondsman, information, arraignment, plea bargaining

---

Check for Understanding

● *What initial steps are taken to investigate a crime?*
(Law enforcement officials find and question witnesses, examine the scene of the crime, and check records.)

The symbol 🎁 denotes active participation strategies.

Activities are keyed for student abilities:
▲ = Basic
● = All Levels
■ = Average/Advanced

FOCUS

● Ask the class if they have already heard such terms as *booked, bondsman, indictment, arraignment,* and *plea bargaining.* **Why are so many people who have had no direct contact with the criminal justice system familiar with these terms?** (The news media report criminal justice cases; also, many television shows are centered on the criminal justice system.)

EXPLANATION

After reviewing the content of the section, you may want to consider the following activities:

Cultural Literacy

▲ Ask students to suggest television programs or movies they have seen that include scenes of arrest or pre-trial proceedings. Ask them to compare the way those proceedings are shown in the media with the description in the text.

● CRITICAL THINKING **Why might the media's portrayal of criminal proceedings differ from reality?** (Because producers of movies and television programs aim to entertain viewers, they may eliminate the parts of the proceedings they consider complicated or boring.)

Law

● Have a representative of the juvenile justice system speak to the class about the goals and procedures of the system. Encourage students to ask questions.

The juvenile justice system deals with youths accused of committing crimes. Here, a police officer reads a young man his rights.

when police catch a suspect in the act of committing a crime — an arrest warrant is not required. Occasionally a suspect may surrender to authorities, making a warrant unnecessary

With their warrant, police can take the suspect into custody, transporting him or her to the police station. Under the rules set up by the *Miranda* decision (page 184), they must warn the accused person of the right to remain silent and to have a lawyer present during questioning. This warning must be given before the suspect is questioned or has a chance to make any incriminating statements.

At the police station, the suspect is first "booked," meaning that the charges are recorded in the police register. Then he or she may be photographed, fingerprinted, or placed in a line-up for identification by witnesses. For drunk-driving charges, the accused is given a test to determine the amount of alcohol in the blood.

Conducted properly, such procedures do not violate a person's rights. Attorneys do not have to be present, though a suspect has the right to ask for a lawyer before giving a statement or answering questions.

498

Pre-Trial Court Procedures

To protect the rights of citizens in police custody, the courts step in immediately after arrest. The courts are the guardians of due process for those suspected of crimes.

The courts treat accused persons under 18 differently from others. Young suspects are handled in a separate **juvenile justice system.** Although juveniles are entitled to most of the protections of due process, the proceedings in the juvenile justice system are generally fewer and less formal than in the criminal justice system. Figure 18–3 illustrates these procedures. The remainder of this chapter discusses the steps in the adult criminal justice system.

Initial appearance

Following arrest, charges against the suspect are filed in the court having the appropriate jurisdiction. Usually within 24 hours, the accused, now called the defendant, is brought before a judge. At this time, the defendant's lawyer (or a public defender named by the court) usually is present. During this initial, or first, appearance, the judge tells the defendant the charges. The judge also repeats the *Miranda* warnings.

If the charge is a misdemeanor, the defendant has two options. He or she may plead "guilty" and let the judge decide on a penalty. Or the plea may be "not guilty," in which case a trial date is set. If the charge is a felony, the defendant usually does not enter a plea. Instead, the judge sets a date for a preliminary hearing. If the defendant chooses to give up the right to a hearing, the judge sets a trial date.

Setting bail

At the initial appearance, the judge may also set bail, a sum of money that the defendant must leave with the court until he or she returns for trial. It may be in cash or property. If necessary, the defendant may borrow from a professional lender, or **bondsman**. The judge may give the defendant one of many options concerning the payment of bail.

Defendants are sometimes released "on recognizance," or without actually putting up bail. More commonly the judge requires the defendant to deposit only a percentage of the bail. When the defendant appears in court, the deposit

Cross-reference
See Chapter 6, Section 2 (pp. 170–175), for a full discussion of warrants and searches. The constitutional provisions for bail are discussed on p. 185.

is returned. If the defendant does not appear, the deposit is forfeited and the entire amount must be paid. Judges sometimes require a defendant to post the full amount of bail. With particularly dangerous suspects, the judge may not allow release on bail at all.

Preliminary hearing

The next step in a felony case is usually a brief preliminary hearing before a judge. The purpose of this hearing is to determine whether there is probable cause to believe that the defendant committed the crime. The prosecuting

Figure 18–3 THE JUVENILE JUSTICE SYSTEM The goal of the juvenile justice system is to rehabilitate young offenders and return them to the community, not to punish them. 8B

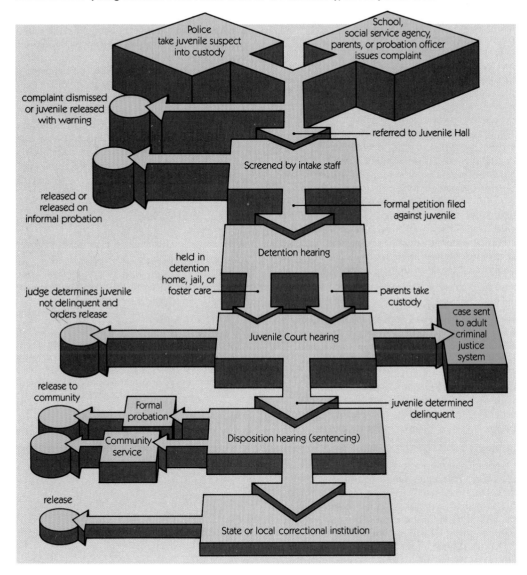

Police take juvenile suspect into custody

School, social service agency, parents, or probation officer issues complaint

complaint dismissed or juvenile released with warning

referred to Juvenile Hall

Screened by intake staff

released or released on informal probation

formal petition filed against juvenile

held in detention home, jail, or foster care

Detention hearing

parents take custody

judge determines juvenile not delinquent and orders release

Juvenile Court hearing

case sent to adult criminal justice system

release to community

Formal probation

juvenile determined delinquent

Community service

Disposition hearing (sentencing)

release

State or local correctional institution

499

Figure 18–3
▲ *What are the three possible outcomes of a Juvenile Court hearing?* (The case can be sent to the adult criminal justice system; the juvenile can be determined not delinquent and released; or the juvenile can be determined delinquent and sent to a disposition hearing.)

Section 2 Review Answers

1. Investigation by law enforcement officials, issuing of a warrant by a judge or magistrate, arrest, and reading of *Miranda* rights.

2. **(a)** A judge repeats the charges and *Miranda* warnings and then, if the defendant pleads guilty to a misdemeanor, imposes a penalty. If the defendant pleads not guilty, the judge sets a trial date. If the charge is a felony, the judge sets the bail and date for the preliminary hearing. **(b)** A judge determines if probable cause exists.

3. The state prosecutor files an "information."

4. **(a)** At arraignment.
(b) Guilty, not guilty, not guilty by reason of insanity, *nolo contendere.*

Critical thinking Each step helps assure that the rights of the accused are protected. The courts, in their role as guardians of due process, act quickly to protect those rights.

CLOSURE

● Ask students to identify the step in the pre-trial proceedings that *follows* each of these steps: arrest (suspect is booked, initial appearance); preliminary hearing (case is dismissed or continued to a grand jury or information); arraignment (defendant pleads). Then have students read Section 3, distinguishing between the steps that precede the trial and the trial itself.

---

attorney, a government official, presents the government's (or "the people's") evidence against the defendant. Upon hearing the evidence, the judge determines whether the prosecution has a case. If the judge decides the government lacks legal evidence, he or she dismisses the case. Otherwise, the case proceeds to the next stage.

Decisions for a trial

The next step in the process varies. In federal courts, and in many state courts, felony cases go to grand jury hearings. (This is a constitutional right in federal crimes.) The grand jury hears the prosecution's charges (the *indictment*) and decides whether a trial is justified. Grand jury hearings are secret, and neither the defendant nor the defense attorney is present. In addition, grand juries can consider kinds of evidence not usually allowed in trials.

The case may be dropped at this stage if a majority of the grand jury decides there is not enough evidence. If the grand jury believes that a trial should be held, it issues a "true bill" supporting the prosecutor's indictment.

Although many state constitutions allow for grand jury hearings, most states, especially those west of the Mississippi River, use a different procedure. After the preliminary hearing, the state prosecutor files an **information**, a sworn statement that there is enough evidence to go to trial.

Arraignment

The next step in the criminal justice process is the **arraignment** (uh-RAIN-ment), where the formal charge (indictment or information) is read to the defendant in an open courtroom. At this time, the judge makes sure the defendant is represented by counsel. The judge may also question the defendant to determine if he or she understands the process. If everything is in order, the judge reads the charges. A copy of the charges is also presented to the defendant.

Pleas

After hearing the official charge, the defendant must enter a plea answering the charge. The defendant may enter one of four possible pleas: (1) not guilty; (2) not guilty by reason of insanity; (3) guilty; or in some cases, (4) *nolo contendere,* meaning, "I will not contest it."

If the defendant pleads "not guilty" or "not guilty by reason of insanity," there must be a

---

trial. If the plea is "guilty" or "*nolo contendere,*" there is no trial and the judge decides the punishment. (A nolo plea is an indirect way of admitting guilt, but does not go on the records as a guilty plea.)

Even before arraignment, the prosecutor and defense attorney often have already engaged in **plea bargaining**. Plea bargaining is a pre-trial negotiation in which the prosecutor seeks to dispose of the case without going to trial. Most commonly, the prosecutor agrees to charge the defendant with a less serious crime if the defendant agrees to plead guilty. All such negotiations must be approved by the judge.

Plea bargaining has become quite popular in recent years. Because most state courts are overburdened with cases and trials can be very costly, the states often prefer to dispose of cases without a trial. On the other hand, critics charge that plea bargaining allows criminals to escape the full consequences of their actions, thus making the criminal justice system less effective in preventing future crimes.

SECTION 2 REVIEW

Vocabulary and key terms

juvenile justice system (498)	information (500)
bondsman (498)	arraignment (500)
	plea bargaining (500)

For review

1. What steps are normally necessary to arrest a person suspected of a crime? **6E**
2. What occurs at (a) the initial appearance? (b) the preliminary hearing? **6E**
3. In places where grand juries are not used, how are accused persons brought to trial? **6E**
4. (a) When are the official charges read to a defendant? (b) What options do defendants have in answering the charges? **6E**

Critical thinking

EXAMINING BASIC PRINCIPLES Why are there so many steps involved in bringing an accused criminal to trial? Why do the courts step in long before the trial is held? **6E**

Background: *Law* Grand juries were intended to act as a check on the power of the prosecutor. The average grand jury, however, spends only five to ten minutes reviewing a case and almost always follows the prosecutor's recommendations.

Background: *Constitutional Heritage* Students should note that presenting a copy of the charges to the defendant is one of the provisions of the Sixth Amendment.

Participating in the Legal System

4D

501

What kind of crime is committed every day on the streets of practically every city by otherwise law-abiding people? Possible answers include parking violations, jaywalking, and minor driving offenses. For many people, the tickets given for these minor crimes represent their only real contact with the U.S. legal system. They pay their fine by mail or perhaps argue their case in a local traffic court. Money that is collected as fines goes into the city or county treasury and helps support local government.

Another part of the legal system that you might encounter deals with minor disputes, or "small claims," between individuals. Small claims courts handle lawsuits involving relatively small sums quickly and at minimal cost. If you buy something that does not work, and the seller refuses to refund your money or replace the product, you can take the seller to small claims court. There are no lawyers allowed here. You (the plaintiff) and the seller (the defendant) must both present your own case. You should have all the facts of the case with you, including receipts and any other records of your contacts with the seller. After you each tell your side of the story, the judge makes a ruling.

Another way that you might one day take part directly in the legal system is to perform jury duty. You would be one of a group of citizens (usually twelve) chosen to attend a trial and decide whether a defendant is guilty or innocent, or which of two parties in a dispute is right. Jurors may be chosen from lists of local taxpayers, registered voters, or licensed drivers. They may even be chosen from the telephone directory.

Qualifications for serving on a jury vary among the state and federal court systems. Generally a juror must be a U.S. citizen of voting age, have no serious criminal record, be able to read and write English, and be mentally and physically capable of serving. The right to a jury trial is guaranteed by the Constitution, and serving on a jury is one of the duties of citizenship.

Follow-up

1. In the Constitution (pages 111–138), locate the three amendments that deal specifically with the right to a jury trial. Write a paragraph in which you summarize the main points of these three amendments.
2. Create a classroom version of small claims court. Students should play the parts of plaintiff, the defendant, and the judge. First think of a problem, such as a faulty product or a broken contract. Have one group of students think of arguments to support the plaintiff, while another group develops arguments for the defendant. After each person's testimony is given, the judge should make a ruling.

Civic Participation

▲ CRITICAL THINKING **Suppose that every person convicted of a crime, even a parking violation, were required to spend at least one night in jail. What effects might this have?** (People might observe laws more faithfully. On the other hand, the problem of prison overcrowding would increase tremendously.)

Values

● CRITICAL THINKING **Why, do you suppose, are persons with serious criminal records barred from jury duty?** (People who have not shown respect for the law in their own lives are not good judges of others' activities.)

● Have students complete **Citizenship Worksheet 7,** which involves mock claims courts.

Follow-up Answers
1. Students should summarize the Fifth, Sixth, and Seventh Amendments.
2. Students should identify the kinds of witnesses they would call to make their points.

The symbol ⅈⅈ denotes active participation strategies.

Activities are keyed for student abilities:
▲ = Basic
● = All Levels
■ = Average/Advanced

501

SECTION 3

Trials Determine Guilt or Innocence

(pp. 502–507)

Section Objectives

☐ list and explain the steps in a typical trial

☐ explain what forms imprisonment may take and on what grounds a prisoner may be released

Vocabulary

bench trial, litigant, adversary proceeding, plaintiff, deposition, venue, peremptory challenge, sequester, cross-examination, verdict, acquittal, mistrial, sentence, probation, parole

FOCUS

● Have students suggest TV shows or movies they have seen that included scenes of a criminal trial. Have them describe how the trial was depicted and what their reaction to the scene was. **Why are trial scenes shown so frequently in the popular media?** (They can be exciting, dramatic confrontations.)

Trials Determine Guilt or Innocence

> **ACCESS** The Main Ideas
>
> 1 What are the steps of a typical trial?
> *pages 502–506*
>
> 2 What are the forms of imprisonment and on what grounds are prisoners released?
> *pages 506–507*

Before testifying in court, witnesses are asked the following question: "Do you swear that the testimony you shall give this court will be the truth, the whole truth, and nothing but the truth, so help you God?"

Trials are the most important stage in the criminal justice process. Anyone charged with a crime punishable by a jail sentence has the constitutional right to a trial by jury. In many jurisdictions, there is also the option of a **bench trial**, trial by a judge.

The American legal system is based on the principle that every defendant who walks into the courtroom is considered innocent. Guilt must be proven.

3A, 6D, 6E

The Trial Setting

A trial is often compared to a boxing match. Both are contests between *adversaries,* persons who oppose or fight one another. In a trial, the adversaries are called **litigants**, and rather than hitting each other, they challenge each other's evidence and testimony. For this reason, an American trial is often labeled an **adversary proceeding**. The judge acts as a referee and interprets the rules of the "match."

The litigant who files suit in a civil case is called the **plaintiff**. In a criminal trial, the prosecution brings the charges. The United States Attorney (page 496) is the prosecutor in federal cases. In state trials, the prosecutor may be known as the state's attorney, county prosecutor, or district attorney. The litigant being sued or charged with the crime is the defendant.

Every trial has two purposes: to establish the facts of the case, and to find the law that applies. The role of the jury is to decide questions of fact.

For example, did the defendant actually rob the victim? Is a witness lying or telling the truth? The job of the judge is to determine questions of law. If the jury decides that the defendant did, in fact, commit the robbery, then the judge must determine the penalty prescribed by law.

Preparing for the trial

Many legal steps take place before the trial begins. To give each side ample opportunity to prepare for the case, trials are usually scheduled six to eight weeks after the arraignment.

Both sides are entitled to issue subpoenas. These are court orders commanding witnesses to appear or evidence to be supplied at any time during a judicial proceeding. Those who fail to comply with the subpoena are held in "contempt of court," a serious criminal charge.

Both the prosecution and the defense also take part in "pre-trial discovery." That is, each side allows the other to examine any evidence they intend to use. This includes physical evidence (such as the murder weapon) and the results of scientific tests (ballistics tests, blood samples) or medical examinations (such as psychiatric evaluations). In addition, each side must provide the names and addresses of their witnesses.

At this time also, witnesses are asked to give **depositions**. A deposition is a formal interview given under oath before the trial. Both sides may ask questions, and all responses are transcribed by a court reporter.

Depositions serve many functions. For example, they preserve the witnesses' testimony. If a witness dies before the trial, his or her testimony can still be read to the jury. Depositions also provide attorneys with useful information and enable them to test how each witness responds to questioning. Furthermore, they can be used during the trial to discredit a witness's testimony.

Finally, both sides are allowed to enter pretrial motions to set the ground rules for courtroom procedures. For instance, the defense attorney may move to keep any illegally obtained

502

Background: *Law* See that students understand the judge's role as a referee to interpret the rules of the "match." If, for example, the prosecuting attorney makes a statement violating procedure, the judge does not comment *unless* the defendant's attorney challenges the statement. Only then does the judge rule.

SUBPOENA

ORDER TO APPEAR AND PRODUCE DOCUMENTS
IN THE CIRCUIT COURT OF
BOONE COUNTY STATE OF MISSOURI
Boone County Court House
8th and Walnut Streets, Columbia, Missouri

PLAINTIFF The State of Missouri
VS.
DEFENDANT   John Doe

THE STATE OF MISSOURI TO: Jane Q. Public
YOU ARE COMMANDED TO APPEAR AT:
      DATE: January 4, 1993
      TIME: 9.00 A.M.
      DIVISION: 1

MAXINE OWENS, CIRCUIT CLERK, BOONE COUNTY, MO

By _____
DATE OF ISSUE: October 16, 1992   DEPUTY CIRCUIT CLERK

SHERIFF'S RETURN

I hereby certify that I served this writ, in the County of _____,
State of Missouri by: Reading/delivering a copy to _____

Date: _____

A sheriff or police officer serves a subpoena, like the one shown here, to persons who are requested to be witnesses at a trial. Witnesses may be commanded to testify, produce evidence, or both.

EXPLANATION
After reviewing the content of the section, you may want to consider the following activities:

Law
● Have students consider the differences between what the prosecution wants in a juror and what the defense wants. Describe a hypothetical criminal case to the class—the burglary of a house, for example.

Divide the board into three columns. Ask students to suggest questions the defense lawyer and the prosecutor might ask prospective jurors. List the questions in the first column. Then have students speculate on how a juror the prosecution liked might answer the questions. Write those answers in the second column. In the third column, list suggestions of how jurors preferred by the defense might answer.

evidence out of the trial. The prosecutor may move to have the defendant examined by a psychiatrist. Occasionally, the defense will ask to move the trial to a different court because of harmful local publicity. This is called a change of **venue** (VEN-yoo), or location. These motions often serve as the basis for later appeals.

Choosing jurors
Just before the trial begins, a trial jury is selected from citizens residing within the court's jurisdiction. Although procedures vary from place to place, Figure 18–4 shows the general steps involved in calling a jury.

Prospective jurors must first go through pretrial questioning to determine their qualifications to serve. In federal courts, the judge does most of the questioning. In many states, it is largely in the hands of the lawyers for both sides. They might ask such questions as, "Do you know either of the litigants? Do you know anything about the case at hand?"

Any potential juror can be challenged and disqualified "for cause" if he or she is considered prejudiced for or against one of the litigants. A limited number of jurors can also be dismissed by **peremptory challenge**. A peremptory challenge enables either side to disqualify a potential juror without stating a reason. The number of peremptory challenges allowed depends on the jurisdiction and the crime. Most courts allow each side five or six. Peremptory challenges are not intended to be used to discriminate against jurors of one sex, race, or ethnic background.

503

Background: *Cultural Literacy* The process of pre-trial questioning of jurors is called *voir dire* (VWAR DEER), meaning "to speak the truth" (Old French).

The symbol 👥 denotes active participation strategies.

Activities are keyed for student abilities:
▲ = Basic
● = All Levels
■ = Average/Advanced

Controversial Issues

▲ *In a jury trial, whose job is it, the judge's or the jury's, to determine the guilt or innocence of the accused?* (The jury's.)

Explain to students that in many countries in the world, judges rather than juries determine guilt or innocence.

● CRITICAL THINKING *Some people in the United States argue that jury trials are an amateurish, inefficient means of determining a legal issue. What are the arguments against that point of view? With which side do you agree?* (Students may suggest that trial by one's peers is an essential element of American democracy.)

Law

● Divide the class into groups and have each group write an account of a fictional trial involving the steps described in this section. When the accounts are complete, a representative from each group should read that group's account to the class. Class members should then ask questions of other members of the group regarding the steps involved in the trial.

Figure 18–4

STEPS IN THE PROCESS OF JURY SELECTION
This chart shows the five steps that lead up to jury duty. 8B

1 Lists are compiled In each jurisdiction a court officer, usually the Clerk of the Court, prepares a list of potential jurors. In most cases, lists are drawn from voter registration rolls. A few jurisdictions draw names from motor vehicle registration, driver's licenses, or telephone company listings.

2 Questionnaires are sent Persons whose names appear on the juror's list are sent questionnaires. The purpose of the questionnaire is to determine whether the persons are qualified for jury duty. Persons may be disqualified for many reasons, including being too young, being mentally impaired, or lacking citizenship.

3 Names are drawn The names of qualified citizens are then printed on separate cards, and the cards are placed in a *jury wheel*. A jury wheel is usually a drum from which the cards are drawn randomly, much like a lottery.

4 Summonses are issued Persons whose names are drawn are issued a *summons*. A summons is a writ or court order commanding prospective jurors to appear in court. The technical name for this writ is *venire* (vihn-EYE-ree). Hence, potential jurors are called veniremen.

5 Jurors appear in court Every person summoned must appear in court on the date and time indicated. Those who fail to do so face punishment. Persons summoned for grand jury duty may be required to serve about twenty days. Persons chosen for petit jury duty may serve from one day to two weeks. Pay usually ranges from $10 to $20 a day.

504

Once twelve persons, plus alternates, have been accepted, jury selection is completed. The judge then instructs the jurors on trial procedures. In some sensitive cases, jurors may be **sequestered**. This means that they are not permitted to return home until the trial is over.

3A, 6E, 6G

The Trial

Only a small percentage of real-life trials are as dramatic or exciting as those in television or films. Nonetheless, anyone on trial has much at stake — freedom, money, perhaps life itself.

The trial begins with an opening statement by the prosecuting attorney. In it, the prosecutor outlines the evidence to be presented as proof that the defendant did commit the crime. The defense attorney then makes an opening statement in support of the defendant.

Presenting evidence

Because the defendant is presumed "innocent until proven guilty," it is the prosecutor's duty to prove both that there was a crime and that the defendant committed it. He or she may present supporting evidence such as written documents, photographs, fingerprints, or weapons. The prosecutor may call and question witnesses, who are sworn to tell the truth. This is called direct examination. The defense then has its turn at **cross-examination**, questioning the opposing side's witnesses in an effort to discredit their testimony.

At any time during the presentation of evidence, either side may raise objections. An objection is a claim that a particular piece of evidence or line of questioning should not be allowed. Common objections might be that the evidence was obtained illegally or that a question is not relevant to the case. The judge may sustain, or uphold, the objection and forbid the admission of the evidence in question. On the other hand, the judge may overrule, or reject, the objection and allow the attorney being challenged to proceed.

At the end of this first round of examination, the defense may ask the judge to dismiss the case. If the judge agrees that the prosecution has failed to establish evidence, then the case is dismissed. If the motion to dismiss is denied, the

Background: *Civic Participation* Valid excuses from jury duty are (1) those not qualified because of age (under 18), illiteracy, illness, or criminal record; (2) those employed in an occupation "vital to the public interest" (physicians, pharmacists, teachers, firefighters); and (3) those for whom service would mean real hardship.

Figure 18–4
● Ask students if, in their opinion, persons summoned for jury duty should be required to appear or should have the option of refusing.

trial moves on to a second round of testimony. This time the defense attorney begins with the direct examination of the defense witnesses. The prosecution is then permitted to cross-examine these witnesses.

According to the Fifth Amendment, a defendant does not have to be a witness in her or his own trial. This rule protects a defendant from giving testimony that may be self-incriminating. If the defendant does decide to testify, however, he or she must answer all questions during direct and cross-examination.

Finally, each side is given equal time to make a closing statement. The prosecutor argues first, then the defense presents its final rebuttal. Closing statements are not considered evidence, but attorneys frequently use them to try to sway the jury's feelings and opinions.

The verdict

At the conclusion of the trial, the judge reads a set of instructions ("the charge") to the jury. These instructions remind the jurors what constitutes a crime, what the law is, and what they must find to render a **verdict**, or decision. Most judges in state courts have specific instructions they must read to the jury, for state laws set the rules. Federal judges, however, have considerable freedom in giving instructions.

Jury deliberations, in which the jurors weigh the evidence and discuss the case, mark the final stage of the trial. All deliberations are secret, and there is no set length for discussion. Some juries reach a verdict in a matter of minutes. Others may deliberate for days.

To find the defendant "guilty" the jury must agree that the case has been proved "beyond a reasonable doubt." The jury may likewise find the defendant "not guilty" and vote for his or her **acquittal**, in which case all charges are dropped. If the jury cannot agree on a verdict, they are called a "hung jury." In this case, or if the judge believes that the fairness of the trial has been jeopardized, a **mistrial** is declared. Another trial with a new jury usually is held at a later date.

Sentencing

If the defendant is found guilty, the next step in the process is sentencing. A **sentence** is a punishment decided by the court. The sentence is usually determined by the judge. In a few states, the jury decides the sentence.

In felony cases, there is usually a delay between conviction and sentencing. This enables the judge to investigate the defendant's background and consider all "mitigating circumstances" — factors surrounding the crime that may be considered in giving a lesser penalty.

Although state and federal statutes specify the penalties for each offense, judges (or juries) usually have considerable leeway in imposing sentences. A first-time offender might receive a suspended sentence for a minor crime. He or she

Courtroom confrontations have been the subject of many popular films and television programs. Gregory Peck won the Academy Award for Best Actor for his portrayal of a trial attorney in the 1962 film, *To Kill a Mockingbird.*

505

Cooperative Learning
● Have the class perform **Simulation 3,** which contains material that can be used for a class simulation of a trial.

GUIDED/INDEPENDENT PRACTICE
● Have students create a political cartoon or write a letter to the editor of your local newspaper expressing their views on the juvenile justice system.

Background: *Law* If the judge instructs the jury incorrectly or in a prejudicial way, the case could probably be successfully appealed.

Photo
To Kill a Mockingbird is based on the Pulitzer Prize-winning novel by Harper Lee. The story, told by the daughter of a lawyer in a small Alabama town, centers on the lawyer's defense of an African American man falsely accused of raping a white woman.

The symbol ▪▪ denotes active participation strategies.

Activities are keyed for student abilities:
▲ = Basic
● = All Levels
■ = Average/Advanced

San Quentin, a state penitentiary located on San Pablo Bay in northern California, is one of the nation's best-known maximum-security prisons.

would not spend any time in jail but would be on **probation**, remaining free but following certain restrictions. Persons with criminal records are likely to get harsher sentences.

Persons convicted of felonies and most misdemeanors have the right to appeal their cases to a higher court. A death sentence is almost always appealed to the state's supreme court. If the defendant is acquitted, however, the prosecution (in most cases) has no right to appeal. Such an appeal would place the defendant in double jeopardy (page 177).

3A, 6A

Imprisonment and Release

Imprisonment

The judge's sentence states both the length and the place of a jail or prison sentence. Just as there are separate federal and state courts, there are both federal and state prisons or penitentiaries, where those convicted of felonies serve time. People who commit misdemeanors are likely to be sent to a city or county jail.

Imprisonment (or "incarceration") also depends on the seriousness of the crime. Most felons — especially those who have committed violent crimes — are sent to maximum-security prisons. These are high-walled, tightly guarded facilities that afford the prisoner little freedom.

These prisons are also where criminals await execution on "death row."

Other felony convictions, especially "white-collar" crimes such as embezzlement or tax evasion, may bring sentences to minimum-security prisons, such as prison farms or work camps. Younger felons, between 18 and 21, are often sent to reformatories. Reformatories place greater emphasis on education and rehabilitation than do regular prisons.

The length of a prison term also depends on the crime and person who commits it. Those convicted of misdemeanors typically serve relatively short, fixed sentences — say, 60 days in jail. Those imprisoned for felonies, however, are normally given a minimum and maximum sentence, and may be released at any point in between. For example, a convicted criminal may be sentenced to 15 to 20 years. The goal of such a sentence is to provide incentives for good behavior, which can bring early release. Most felons do not serve the maximum sentence.

The prison system has come under intense criticism in recent years. Prisons are often overcrowded, poorly supervised, and expensive to run. Moreover, many criminals are set free or given suspended sentences because of lack of prison space. Other critics doubt whether the threat of imprisonment or even execution does in fact deter people from committing crimes.

506

Release

A prisoner may be released from prison after he or she either completes the full term of the sentence, is pardoned by the state governor or the President, or is freed on **parole**. Parole is the conditional early release of a prisoner who has served the minimum sentence. It is granted by a parole board, which reviews the prisoner's case and prison behavior.

If parole is granted, the prisoner is released under supervision of a parole officer. The person on parole must meet various conditions, such as not associating with certain people and not gambling or drinking alcohol. Parole violators must return to prison. Those who keep their parole are discharged from their sentence and return to normal life. This is the final step in the criminal justice process.

SECTION 3 REVIEW

Vocabulary and key terms

bench trial (502)	cross-examination (504)
litigant (502)	verdict (505)
adversary proceeding (502)	acquittal (505)
plaintiff (502)	hung jury (505)
deposition (502)	mistrial (505)
venue (503)	sentence (505)
peremptory challenge (503)	probation (506)
sequester (504)	parole (507)

For review

1. (a) Who are the "adversaries" in a trial? (b) Who acts as the "referee"? **3A**
2. (a) Which parties in a case may call witnesses? (b) How is this done? **3A**
3. In what two ways can lawyers dismiss prospective jurors? **6E**
4. (a) In the trial itself, which side of the case is presented first? (b) Why? **6E**
5. Where is a criminal who has committed a serious felony likely to spend his or her prison sentence? **6A**
6. When can a prisoner be released on parole? **6A**

Critical thinking

MAKING INFERENCES Why might juvenile hearings be designed to shelter young offenders from the exposure of a public trial? **6E**

Chapter Summary

The American legal system has developed from many sources and has many different branches. American laws stem from the national and state constitutions, statutory law passed by Congress and state legislatures, common law decisions made by judges, and the concept of equity. Disputes among citizens over property, contracts, family relations, and torts are settled by private law. The government is involved in public law cases, which include criminal law as well as administrative, constitutional, and international law. The Justice Department also works on the people's behalf by prosecuting criminals accused under federal law.

Many steps in the criminal justice system ensure that the rights of those accused of crimes are upheld. A person under arrest first has an initial appearance before a judge and may be released on bail. A preliminary hearing is scheduled to determine whether there is probable cause that the defendant committed the crime. For a felony case to go to trial, either a grand jury must decide there is sufficient evidence, or the state prosecuting attorney must file an information. If a trial is necessary, the defendant is read the charges at the arraignment and enters a plea. If the defendant pleads "not guilty," a trial is held. Sometimes plea bargaining is used to reduce the charges and avoid going to trial if the defendant agrees to plead "guilty."

A trial in the American criminal justice system is often described as an adversary proceeding between two litigants, with a judge acting as a referee. Evidence is gathered by subpoenas to witnesses, pre-trial discovery, and depositions. Jurors are chosen, but can be challenged by either side. Using a peremptory challenge, either side can dismiss a juror without stating a reason. During the trial, each litigant is allowed to present witnesses and cross-examine the opponent's witnesses. The jury delivers a verdict, either convicting or acquitting the accused. The judge, or in some cases the jury, decides the sentence for convicted criminals.

Section 3 Review Answers

1. (a) The litigants. (b) The judge.
2. (a) The plaintiff, prosecution, and defense. (b) By issuing subpoenas.
3. "For cause" and the peremptory challenge.
4. (a) The prosecution. (b) He or she must establish that there was a crime and that the defendant committed it.
5. At a maximum-security prison.
6. After serving the minimum sentence on good behavior.

Critical thinking To provide young people with the opportunity of starting all over again, without the handicap of publicity or a criminal record.

CLOSURE

● Remind students of the pre-reading objectives at the beginning of the section. Pose one or both of these questions again. Then have students read the next assigned lesson.

CHAPTER 18 CORRECTIVES

● To review the content of Chapter 18, you may want to have students complete **Study Guide/Review 18** or **Workbook Chapter 18.**

The symbol **ii** denotes active participation strategies.

Activities are keyed for student abilities:
▲ = Basic
● = All Levels
■ = Average/Advanced

CHAPTER 18 REVIEW

Answers

Vocabulary See pp. T19–T21 for suggested vocabulary activities.

Reviewing the Facts

1. Common law is made by judges, whose decisions serve as precedents for later cases.
2. Fines or money awards, not imprisonment.
3. Examples of negligence include driving with faulty brakes, failing to clean a slippery walk, and leaving a gun in a public place.
4. It investigates federal crimes, enforces federal laws, runs federal prisons, and represents the federal government in legal matters.
5. Juveniles have most of the same protections of their rights as adults, but the proceedings are less formal.
6. Anyone charged with a crime carrying a potential jail sentence.
7. The jury considers facts and determines guilt or innocence; the judge decides questions of law. The sentence may be determined by either the judge or the jury.
8. Felonies, the most serious offenses in criminal law, are punishable by imprisonment for more than one year. Misdemeanors are less serious crimes and carry lesser penalties.

Thinking Critically About Key Concepts

1. The person who has committed a criminal act is considered to have harmed society as a whole; government is responsible for protecting the people. Emotional motivations such as revenge might take the place of fairness in trials if victims were to prosecute offenders.
2. Some students may contend that the benefits of unclogging the courts outweigh any problems, while others may argue that the rights of both the suspect and

---

● **Review the definitions of the following terms:**

acquittal	equity	plea bargaining
administrative law	hung jury	private law
adversary proceeding	information	probation
arraignment	international law	public law
bench trial	juvenile justice system	real property
bondsman	litigant	sentence
civil law	mistrial	sequester
contract	ordinance	Solicitor General
criminal law	parole	tort
cross-examination	peremptory challenge	venue
deposition	plaintiff	verdict

● **REVIEWING THE FACTS**

1. How is common law made? **6C**
2. What is the usual outcome of civil cases? **6E**
3. Give an example of negligence, as it is defined by law. **6E**
4. What are the responsibilities of the U.S. Department of Justice? **3A**
5. How is the juvenile justice system similar to the adult criminal justice system? How is it different? **6E**
6. Who has a constitutional right to a trial by jury? **6E**
7. What is the role of a jury in a trial? What is the role of the judge? **6I**
8. What is the difference between a misdemeanor and a felony in criminal law? **3A**

▲ **THINKING CRITICALLY ABOUT KEY CONCEPTS**

1. What principle is illustrated by always having the government bring charges in a criminal case? What problems might arise if individuals or companies were to prosecute criminal cases? **6I**
2. Is the increasing reliance on plea bargaining justified, considering that it helps avoid lengthy and costly trials? Whose rights could

---

be violated by the misuse of this process? **6D**
3. You may have read or heard about trials in which a lawyer who is a persuasive speaker has a very strong effect on a jury. What might happen to the legal points in such a trial? Could the evidence become less important than the lawyer's speaking skills? What special responsibility would a jury have in such a situation? **6I**

▲ **PRACTICING SKILLS**

1. **Study Skills: Reading a diagram.** Refer to Figure 18–1 (page 491) to answer the following questions. (a) What are the four sources of law in the American legal system? (b) Which main branch of American law deals with contracts? (c) Does negligence involve criminal law or the law of torts? **8B**
2. **Study Skills: Reading a form.** Examine the copy of a subpoena shown on page 503. (a) Who is on trial in this case? Who is being ordered to be a witness in this trial? (b) Where and when should this witness report? (c) What might happen to the witness if she did not appear at the correct time and place? **8B**
3. **Critical Thinking Skills: Making judgments.** Review Section 3, "Trials Determine Guilt or Innocence" (pages 502–507). Suppose a jury at a criminal trial must come

---

the accuser can be violated by this truncated justice.
3. Students may conclude that a good orator can influence juries to pay more attention to emotions than facts and that they therefore must focus more strongly on

the evidence when it comes time to deliberate.

Practicing Skills
1. **(a)** The Constitution, statutory law, common law, equity. **(b)** Private law. **(c)** Law of torts.

2. **(a)** John Doe is on trial; Jane Q. Public is the witness. **(b)** The witness should report to the Boone County Court House on January 4, 1993. **(c)** She could be held in contempt of court.

to a unanimous verdict to convict the defendant. One of the twelve jurors is convinced the defendant is innocent, but the others believe the defendant is guilty. Do you think the one juror should agree to go along with the others so they can avoid having a "hung jury"? Explain your reasoning. **8H**

▲ PARTICIPATORY CITIZENSHIP

1. **Mass media.** Read newspaper or magazine accounts of a criminal trial, and take notes on the details. Note all interesting points, including the specific crime, the names of those involved, important pieces of evidence, the verdict, and the sentence, if any. **6I**
2. **Careers.** Interview a lawyer, either in person or by phone. Write out your questions ahead of time. You might tape-record the lawyer's answers or take notes during the interview. Sample questions: What skills are needed to

be a good lawyer? What has been your most interesting case? What do you like best about being a lawyer? **4D**

■ WRITING ABOUT ISSUES

1. **Analyzing arguments.** Many individuals and businesses have criticized the large amounts awarded by juries in some strict liability suits against corporations. Write a short essay presenting the arguments in favor and against awarding such large amounts. **8C**
2. **Composing a response.** Read "As Others See Us" on page 510, which describes the stand of Amnesty International, a human rights organization, on the use of the death penalty for juvenile offenders in the United States. Write a response to Amnesty International's leadership, explaining your opinion on this issue. **5C**

▲ ANALYZING A POLITICAL CARTOON

The prison system of the United States is overcrowded. In fact, the U.S. has a larger share of its citizens in jail than any industrial nation except South Africa. Severe overcrowding has led to early releases to make room for new convicts. Look at the cartoon below and answer the following questions.

1. What is the point of the cartoon? **8B**
2. Is the cartoon effective? Explain. **8A**
3. What suggestions, if any, would you make in order to improve the way the criminal justice system works in the United States? Explain your answer. **8H**

Cartoon by Rob Rogers. Reprinted by permission of UFS, Inc.

Writing About Issues

1. *For*—Pays for the suffering of individuals, may serve to prevent future negligence. *Against*—An enormous cost to the economy, may prevent services and products that are risky but desirable from being introduced to the market.
2. Letters should make clear why the student agrees or disagrees with Amnesty International's stand.

Analyzing a Political Cartoon

1. Crime sentences are growing shorter.
2. The cartoon uses exaggeration to make an effective point: Criminals are serving ridiculously short prison terms.
3. Students may suggest building more prisons, funding more rehabilitation programs, or passing harsher laws concerning sentences. Yet they should also remember the rights of the accused and the protection from cruel and unusual punishment guaranteed by the Constitution.

3. Students should consider the principle of "innocent until *proven* guilty" as well as the rule that jurors must agree that the case has been proved "beyond a reasonable doubt." They should also realize that the one

juror's opinion is just as valid as those of the other jurors.

Participatory Citizenship

1. Students may choose an ongoing case, or one that occurred in the past.

2. Students may wish to evaluate the answers based on their own personal interests to see if the field of law is of interest to them.

Chapter Review exercises are keyed for student abilities:
▲ = Basic
● = All Levels
■ = Average/Advanced

AS OTHERS SEE US

Vocabulary

instruments—treaties.

Background

Amnesty International, a London-based human rights organization that won the Nobel Prize for Peace in 1977, is opposed to the death penalty. In 1991, some 24 states allowed the death penalty to be imposed on persons who were under age 18 at the time of the crime. The graph on this page shows only the top seven states for the imposition of the death penalty on juveniles.

Global Awareness

● ***According to this report, what countries presently impose the death penalty on criminals under the age of 18?*** (The United States, Iran, Iraq, Nigeria, Pakistan, and Bangladesh.) Ask students to volunteer their impressions of the governments of these countries, other than the United States. (Students may note that the armed forces rule or are very powerful in those countries; that Iraq is ruled by a dictator and Iran by a theocracy.)

● CRITICAL THINKING ***What point is Amnesty International trying to make by linking the policy of the United States with that of these other countries?*** (It is trying to make capital punishment for juveniles appear undemocratic and cruel by pointing to undemocratic and cruel governments that enforce that policy.)

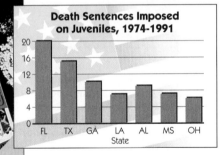

Death Sentences Imposed on Juveniles, 1974-1991

Amnesty International Criticizes the Death Penalty for American Juveniles

Although the United States often bases its foreign policies on considerations of human rights, some international observers believe that America itself violates human rights standards.

More than 90 juveniles have been sentenced to death in the USA since the death penalty was reinstated in the 1970s; all were aged between 15 and 17 at the time of the offense. Although many have had their sentences vacated on appeal, four were executed between 1985 and 1990, and 31 remained on death row as of 1 July 1991. Although they represent only a small proportion of the more than 2,400 prisoners under sentence of death in the USA, there are more juvenile offenders on death row in the USA than in any other country known to Amnesty International.

The imposition of death sentences on juvenile offenders is in clear contravention of international human rights standards contained in numerous international instruments.... In 1984 the UN Economic and Social Council adopted a series of Safeguards guaranteeing the rights of those facing the death penalty which also provides a minimum age limit of 18.

The execution of juvenile offenders is extremely rare. More than 70 countries which retain the death penalty by law have abolished it for people under 18 at the time of the crime. The USA is one of only seven countries known to have carried out such executions in the last decade (the other countries are Barbados, which has since raised the minimum age to 18, Iran, Iraq, Nigeria, and Pakistan; one such execution was also reported in Bangladesh).

All those sentenced to death in the USA have been convicted of murder. Amnesty International does not argue that juveniles should not be held criminally liable or subjected to severe penalties where appropriate. However, international standards were developed in recognition of the fact that the death penalty—which denies any possibility of rehabilitation or reform—is a wholly inappropriate penalty for individuals who have not attained fully physical or emotional maturity at the time of their actions. . . .

U.S. capital punishment laws contain safeguards intended to ensure that the death penalty is applied fairly and imposed only for the worst crimes and most culpable offenders. The evidence in the cases examined suggests that these safeguards have not been met in practice.

From "Amnesty International Publications—United States of America: The Death Penalty and Juvenile Offenders" (AI Index: AMR 51/23/91). Reprinted by permission of Amnesty International.

CRITICAL THINKING

1. How does the United States compare to other nations in its use of the death penalty for juveniles?
2. What reasons does Amnesty International give for saying the death penalty is inappropiate for those under 18?
3. Generally, what are the international standards for the death penalty?
4. According to the chart, in what region of the country have most juvenile death sentences been imposed?

Critical Thinking Answers
1. According to Amnesty International, very few other countries impose the death penalty on juveniles, and the United States has more juveniles on death row than any other country.

2. The death penalty denies any possibility of rehabilitation; juvenile offenders have not attained physical or emotional maturity at the time of their actions.

3. International human rights standards have set a minimum age of 18 for the death penalty.

4. The South.

CASE STUDIES OF CONTROVERSIAL ISSUES

This book examines the fundamental structure of American government. In the previous units, you have learned about the basic principles under which we live: the provisions of the Constitution, the guarantee of civil rights and liberties, the expression of democracy, and the organization of our national government. To participate as a citizen, you must apply those principles, as well as your personal values, to current issues. The following pages examine controversial issues and ask for your opinion. There are no right or wrong answers. As with many decisions, the key is to analyze the choices you face—and to participate.

CONTENTS

510-1

Case Studies of Controversial Issues
(pp. 510-1 to 510-32)

Feature Overview

This feature presents a discussion of fourteen controversial issues in a pro/con debate format. Though each Case Study includes an even-handed presentation of both sides of the issue, they have been written in a colorful and forceful style in order to stimulate debate and analysis by your students. Despite this style, this book takes no editorial stand on any of these issues.

Short quotations from students across the country have also been included to stimulate discussion. You may wish to explain to your students that these are *real* students who were asked to express their opinions on the Case Study questions. Volunteers in your classroom may write their own statements, pro or con, to illustrate the Case Study.

Chapter References
This case study may be used with Chapters 2, 3, and 7.

●● INTRODUCING THE
▮▮ CASE STUDY

● Ask volunteers to come up to the board and list ethnic groups that lived in the area that is now the United States in 1787. You may wish to add *women* to the list. Then ask another student to circle those groups that were represented at the Constitutional Convention.

How has the Constitution been amended to include groups not represented at the Constitutional Convention? (The 13th, 14th, 15th, 19th, and 24th Amendments.)

TEACHING THE ISSUE

Multiculturalism
● *What do Arredondo and Tapia mean when they write that Mexican Americans do not want to be "just another spicy seasoning in the American melting pot"?* (They want their special identity and contributions to be acknowledged.) *How does Wilkins's description of himself contrast with his description of those who wrote the Constitution?* (Wilkins identifies himself as an African American born in the 20th century, as opposed to a white man who might have owned slaves.)

How Is the Constitution Relevant in Today's Multicultural Society?

THE U.S. POPULATION IN THE NEXT CENTURY

This classroom reflects the growing diversity of American society. As the graph shows, experts predict that within a century about half of all Americans will be non-Hispanic whites.

The United States is one of the most diverse societies on Earth—and it is getting more diverse every year. Yet although Americans come from a variety of ethnic groups, the country has one basic set of laws, the Constitution. This document was written more than 200 years ago. Amendments have been added to the Constitution to bring all races and both sexes into the political system.

Does the Constitution speak to all members of today's cultural mix? The following excerpts reflect the experiences of Mexican Americans, African Americans, and women.

Lorenzo Arredondo and Donato Tapia
The authors are attorneys. This article was first published as "El Chicano y la Constitution."
Today an old voice with a new sound is being heard throughout the

land. Millions of Mexican Americans . . . are demanding equality under the law. . . .

The nation's Mexican Americans are tired of being stereotyped as sleeping under a big sombrero. They do not want to eat corn "cheeps" or look through the "jello" pages. They no longer want to be task-forced to death by various government agencies and ignored by "promising" politicians. . . .

The sleeping bandido has stirred and awakened—the siesta is over. He does not want to walk the earth an alien in his own land. He does not want to be just a spicy seasoning in the American melting pot. He is demanding attention, recognition and redress. . . .

The signing of the Treaty of Guadalupe Hidalgo on February 2, 1848, marked the end of the [Mexican] war. . . . The treaty guaranteed civil and property

rights to those who became American citizens. Many argue that the prejudice and discrimination against Mexican Americans stems from this treaty. It identified those who came with the conquered lands as a defeated people and turned them into strangers in their own land. . . .

The charge of the Chicano attorney and the profession which he professes is clear. We must strive to secure for all, their constitutional birthright—a place in the sun and a voice in their destiny.

Roger Wilkins
The author, a professor of history, had this to say on the 200th anniversary of the Constitution.
When I tell people that I began my education in a one-room segregated schoolhouse in Kansas City, I feel like a fraud, not because the fact is wrong (it is not), but because the emotional image it conveys—of a

poor little four-year-old black child having his spirit crushed by segregation in the State of Missouri—is wrong. I was an optimistic and very

lucky child who had an unshakable faith that America would keep her constitutional promise to us. . . .

The celebration of the 200th anniversary of the Constitution is, on one level, about pictures and memories. The dominant pictures are those of a group of contemplative people dressed in eighteenth-century clothing in a room in Philadelphia 200 summers ago. . . .

Those are powerful images. But even in youthful innocence, a black American born in the

Roger Wilkins

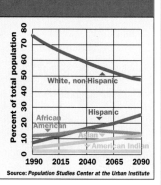

twentieth century cannot avoid noticing that all the people in the pictures are white and male. . . . After all, his American memory contains the possibility that one or more of the men in the picture actually owned one or more of his black ancestors. . . .

I viewed the Constitution as a Promise, a basket . . . of things I'd heard about: . . . "We the people" and the commands of the First, Thirteenth, Fourteenth, and Fifteenth Amendments. All of that added up, in my young mind, to promises of freedom and equality and justice to all of us "We the people," in a country great enough to dream up those promises in the first place.

Rose Bird

Rose Bird was Chief Justice of the California Supreme Court from 1977 to 1986.

In Sacramento, there is a men's club that had a long tradition of giving honorary memberships to newly appointed members of the California Supreme Court. That court had a long tradition of its own. For 127 years, its members had all been white men.

In March 1977, both traditions ended. Simultaneously, I became the first woman appointed to the court and the first justice not to receive an honorary club membership. As a result, the only way I could join the court at lunch was to wait to be personally invited by one of my male colleagues who had been made a member.

That was not all. Although my colleagues were addressed in public as "Justice," I was often called "Rose." . . .

My experiences only mirrored a harsh national reality. . . . The ringing declaration that "all men

Rose Bird

are created equal" did not apply to women by its very terms. . . .

Although we have not yet achieved equal rights within our society, we have come a long way since 1787. But it will take a vigilant eye and a resolute will to make certain that the last century of achievement for women is only the starting point for an even better future—a future in which the words of our Constitution will truly speak for "We the people," and a future in which all men and all women will be seen as truly "created equal."

Take a Stand

8H

1. Do the authors quoted here see the Constitution as protecting or restricting their rights? How can you tell?
2. Write an essay explaining your view of whether the Constitution speaks to all Americans equally.

510-3

Chapter References

This case study may be used with Chapters 5, 17, and 24.

●● INTRODUCING THE ▮▮ CASE STUDY

You may wish to share the following background information with your class: The practice of labeling albums containing explicit lyrics was begun voluntarily by record companies in the mid-1980's, prompted by Senate hearings in 1985. The rap group 2 Live Crew has been particularly controversial. It was their album, *As Nasty As They Wanna Be,* that led to the conviction of record-store owner Charles Freeman in Broward County, Florida, on obscenity charges. Recording artists have also been attacked for songs on suicide. Performer Ozzy Osbourne has been sued two separate times by parents alleging that his song, "Suicide Solution," resulted in their children's suicides.

▲ CRITICAL THINKING Refer students to pp. 156–157 for the Supreme Court's definition of obscenity. *According to that definition, can song lyrics be considered obscene? Explain your answer.* (Yes, because even though they are not visual illustrations, they can lack artistic merit and describe things that appeal to prurient interest and are offensive.) *Do you agree with the Court's definition of obscenity? Why or why not?*

CASE STUDY 2

6G

Heavy metal bands, such as Mötley Crüe (right), are criticized for the negative message of their songs.

Should Minors Be Banned from Buying Albums Considered Obscene?

In some record stores today, teenagers are asked to prove that they are over eighteen before they can buy certain albums. In fact, in the early 1990's, lawmakers in nearly twenty states introduced bills that would make it a criminal offense to sell certain records without a warning label.

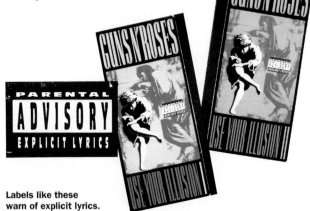

Labels like these warn of explicit lyrics.

510-4

These actions were in response to parents and church leaders who are concerned about the message of songs by certain musicians—especially rap artists and heavy metal bands. The recording industry has tried to answer these concerns. It voluntarily agreed to put warning stickers on albums that use graphic language. Many musi-

cians object to stickers, however, claiming that labels amount to censorship. Yet critics argue that voluntary labeling does not go far enough. They want young people to be unable to buy these albums.

Is a ban on sales to minors an acceptable way to uphold community standards?

 **This music is harmful to young people.** The songs are laced with obscenities, often contain graphic descriptions of sex and drug use, and sometimes degrade women or ethnic groups. Tipper Gore, the co-founder of the Parents' Music Resource Center (PMRC) and wife of Vice President Albert Gore, says that young people today are at risk because of the "graphic brutality marketed to these kids through music and television." New York's Roman Catholic archbishop, John Cardinal O'Connor, has publicly

510-4

accused some rock songs of encouraging teenagers to commit suicide. Minors should not be allowed to buy these albums.

> "If you're under eighteen, you shouldn't be allowed to buy those albums."
>
> *—Sean Mahoney,*
> *Peabody Veterans Memorial High*
> *School, Massachusetts*

Labeling is not enough. In 1986 the Recording Industry Association of America (RIAA) volunteered to put stickers on albums containing explicit language. Even recording executives agreed that this music is obscene and destructive. Joe Smith, chairman of Capitol/EMI, has told an interviewer, "It's hard to defend some of our records." If that is true, isn't it necessary to go further and ban sales to minors?

Demonstrators, like these in Austin, Texas (below), charge that young people who attend heavy metal and rap concerts are being exposed to pornography.

Parents cannot be everywhere. Labels serve as important warnings, but they only work if parents are present to determine whether their children are ready to listen to the albums. Few teenagers go shopping for music with their parents, however. As with alcohol and cigarettes, parents should be able to rely on government regulations to prevent their children from buying things that are harmful to their physical and emotional health.

This music is obscene, and obscenity should be banned. The Supreme Court has consistently ruled that free speech protections do not cover obscenity. Jack Thompson, a Florida attorney, has a simple answer for people who argue that such bans will have a chilling effect on free speech. "It's supposed to have a chilling effect," he declares. "Chilling to criminal activity, not the First Amendment."

> "If all kids hear is negativity, it shows in their actions."
>
> *—David Odoms, William*
> *McKinley High School,*
> *Washington, D.C.*

510-5

● Have students consider the argument that music reflects different cultures. Divide the class into groups and have each group create a chart listing styles of music and the culture from which that style originated. (Examples: *salsa*—Latino; *country western*—British Isles; *jazz and rock and roll*—African American.) Students may wish to do further research and to present examples of the different kinds of music to the class.

CASE STUDY 2 *continued*

Banning music is an assault on free expression. The First Amendment protects rock music just as it protects literature and political speeches. Even if the lyrics are offensive, we do not have the right to restrict them. Jeff Ayeroff, co-managing director of Virgin Records, admits that he doesn't like the message of some rap music. "But this is America," he adds. "Supporting the Bill of Rights doesn't mean you're in favor of pornography. It means that you live in a country that must . . . tolerate obnoxious things."

Deciding what teenagers listen to is parents' responsibility. Critics claim some music is immoral and obscene, and that's a good reason not to make selling certain albums to minors illegal. Morality and personal values should not be determined by the government. Parents are the people best able to judge whether their children should or should not listen to certain music.

"Censoring and banning the music we like to listen to is taking away our rights."

—*Autumn Hoffman,*
Bullitt Central High School,
Shepherdsville, Kentucky

510-6

(Above) Demonstrators support a concert by rap group 2 Live Crew (shown below), whose album, *As Nasty As They Wanna Be,* was ruled obscene by a federal judge in 1990. Three band members were arrested following their performance at a concert in Florida.

Banning certain music ignores cultural differences. Music, such as rap music, reflects the nation's cultural diversity. Charles Freeman, a Florida record store owner, was convicted for selling a rap album judged obscene. The album was by the controversial rap group 2 Live Crew. Freeman believes that rap music is an important expression of African American culture and experience. His lawyer argued that the music's form and message may seem unacceptable only to those who do not share in that culture.

> "I don't think it's government's job to decide these things."
>
> —*Stella Liu,*
> *Plano Senior High School,*
> *Texas*

Charles Freeman, owner of a record store in Fort Lauderdale, Florida, protests his conviction on obscenity charges for selling a rap album.

Music cannot be blamed for the problems teenagers face. People are right to be concerned about drug and alcohol addiction, violence, and suicide among teenagers, but blaming these tragedies on rock albums is absurd. No song lyric is going to convince a young person who does not already have problems to act in a destructive way. Instead of banning record albums, concerned parents should lobby for programs that help young people stay in school and stay off drugs. Society must take responsibility for helping teenagers, without looking for scapegoats.

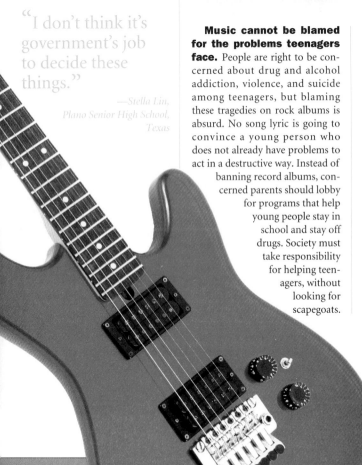

Take a Stand

8H

1. What are the main arguments in favor of labeling albums with explicit lyrics and preventing the sale of those albums to minors? What are the main arguments against such restrictions?
2. Write an essay expressing and supporting your opinion on this issue.

510-7

Chapter References

This case study may be used with Chapters 5, 9, and 17.

INTRODUCING THE CASE STUDY

▲ You may wish to share the following background information with your class. A *Time/CNN* poll published in December 1991 found that 78 percent of respondents favored prayer in public schools and only 9 percent opposed a moment of silent meditation for public school students. About three-quarters of those polled supported voluntary Bible classes on school grounds and prayers before athletic games. More than 50 percent of those polled felt there was too little religious influence on American life.

Ask students their opinions on those questions and compare the class's response to the *Time*/CNN poll.

TEACHING THE ISSUE

Multiculturalism

● Divide the class into groups and provide each group with a copy of the local yellow pages directory. Ask them to list the different religious groups in your community. These should be listed under the headings *Churches, Temples, Synagogues, Mosques,* etc. Have representatives of each group work together to create a class list. Then ask the class to suggest types of religious practices that these groups might agree should be allowed in public schools.

2D

CASE STUDY 3

Is There Any Role for Religion in Public Schools?

Football players at Yorktown High School in Virginia pray silently.

In 1947, Justice Hugo Black presented the classic interpretation of the opening phrase of the First Amendment. "The First Amendment has erected a wall between church and state," he wrote. "That wall must be kept high and impregnable." What does that mean when it comes to religion in government-run public schools? Does it mean no prayers or moments of silence of any sort at any school function? Or are there situations when students should be able to worship?

The Supreme Court has had to examine those question in many cases over the years, and yet the issue remains unresolved. (See the time table on this page.) Is there a role for religion in public schools?

 **Religion is an important part of our lives.** Polls show that the vast majority of Americans believe in God. The Declaration of Independence speaks of a "Creator," and even our currency includes the phrase "In God We Trust." The First

510-8

Amendment bans the establishment of a particular religion, but a moment of silent prayer at the start of school or a general blessing at an important and solemn occasion such as graduation does not support a specific religion. If anything, preventing students from expressing such a central part of their lives during school functions or on school property goes against the First Amendment's call for "the free exercise" of religion.

Over the past 50 years, the Supreme Court has limited, but not excluded, religion in public education.

SELECTED SUPREME COURT CASES ON RELIGION AND PUBLIC SCHOOLS		
YEAR	**CASE**	**DECISION**
1948	McCollum v. Board of Education	Religious education in public schools violates establishment clause.
1952	Zorach v. Clauson	Religious education during school time, but off public school property, is constitutional.
1962	Engel v. Vitale	Prayer in public schools is unconstitutional.
1963	Abington School District v. Schempp	Bible reading in public schools violates the establishment clause.
1985	Wallace v. Jaffree	Law allowing moments of silent prayer in class is overturned.
1990	Board of Education of Westside Community Schools v. Mergens	Extracurricular religious clubs are allowed on school property.
1992	Lee v. Weisman	Prayer at public school graduations is unconstitutional.

> "They complain about morals falling apart in schools, yet they won't let you take time to think about God."

> —John Garza,
> Pharr-San Juan-Alamo
> Upper Level High School, Texas

Religious activities are not mandatory. Students do not have to attend graduations, be involved in sports, or belong to religious clubs. Thus, if they find prayers said during those events offensive, they can avoid them. Even if an atheist does belong to a sports team that prays before a game, he or she can just keep quiet and not participate. A moment of silence can be used for meditation or even daydreaming as easily as for prayer. The minority of students who are not involved in a religion of any sort should not penalize the majority of students for whom it is important.

Texas public school students hold a morning prayer session.

Religious activities do not need to be in schools. Students have many opportunities to express their faith outside of official school time or school functions: at home, in church, even quietly during lunch or study hall. A blessing for graduates or a religious club meeting is more appropriately done in church. A school cannot possibly represent all religions in its speakers and after-school clubs. It is better to keep all religion out of school than to offend one group.

> "Religion is for the church, it's for the families. It has no place in school."

> —Lazonni Gates,
> Paul Laurence Dunbar
> Community High
> School, Baltimore

The Weisman family of Rhode Island objected to prayer during graduation ceremonies. Their case went to the Supreme Court.

Personal feelings need to be protected. The Supreme Court may begin its sessions with "God save the United States and this honorable court," but justices are older and not as affected by the peer pressure which influences teenagers. Even if prayer is not required, students may feel uncomfortable not bowing their heads in worship with everyone else. Justice Anthony Kennedy has noted that students who are told they can avoid hearing prayers by not attending graduation have a "very, very substantial burden" put on them.

Take a Stand

8H

1. What are the main arguments in favor of religion playing a role in public schools? What are the main arguments against it?
2. Write an essay expressing and supporting your point of view.

510-9

CASE STUDY 4

6D

Should Drug Testing Be Mandatory?

Random drug tests have begun for airline employees.

For many Americans, illegal drugs are the number one problem in the United States. They note that the destructiveness of drugs goes beyond increased gang violence and crime. Drug use causes health problems, hurts the economy, and is a threat to public safety.

To combat drug abuse, more and more organizations now require drug tests. In 1991 Congress passed a bill ordering random drug and alcohol testing of certain transportation workers. Olympic competitors and football players are among those athletes who must submit to drug tests. A drug test is also required of job applicants by some private businesses. Some high schools have even begun testing athletes for the presence of steroids and other drugs.

Critics object to mandatory drug tests, arguing that such tests allow the government, private companies, and athletic organizations to invade people's private lives.

Is mandatory testing necessary to control the drug abuse problem in the United States?

510-10

YES **We must do everything possible to limit drug abuse.** The use of illegal drugs by workers costs businesses billions of dollars each year in absenteeism, employee turnover, and property losses. Athletes' use of steroids to artificially build muscles undermines the credibility of their performance. Athletes also serve as role models for many young people, and their use of illegal drugs and steroids sends the wrong message. Mandatory tests would prevent many athletes and workers from taking a chance on using drugs, as well as identifying those who are harming their teams and employers.

> "Would you want a pilot that's on drugs?"
> —*Irineo Cruz,*
> *Pharr-San Juan-Alamo Upper*
> *Level High School, Texas*

In 1988 sprinter Ben Johnson lost his Olympic gold medal after testing positive for steroids.

Public safety is more important than privacy. Substance abuse by transportation workers has led to fatal train and subway accidents. Factory workers under the influence of drugs can cause accidents that hurt others. As the former surgeon general, C. Everett Koop, has said, "When the privacy rights of an individual threaten the health and the safety of others, then those rights end."

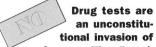 **Drug tests are an unconstitutional invasion of privacy.** The Fourth Amendment guarantees protection against unreasonable searches. If an individual shows no sign of being under the influence of drugs, then there is no reason to search him or her with a drug test. Mandatory tests of all workers or athletes violates their constitutional rights.

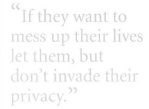

"If they want to mess up their lives let them, but don't invade their privacy."

—Donté Green,
Chatsworth High School,
Los Angeles

Drug testing will not solve the problem. Mandatory tests may cause some individuals to take more care not to be caught, but such tests would do little to help those people who are identified as drug abusers. Workers could lose their jobs and athletes would face public humiliation, yet they would still be dependent on drugs. Instead of mandatory drug tests, individuals should be encouraged to voluntarily seek professional help.

Take a Stand

8H

1. What are the main arguments in favor of mandatory drug testing? What are the main arguments against it?
2. Write an essay expressing and supporting your opinion on this issue.

The control tower operator on duty during this derailment, in which 25 people were injured, fled the scene. Three days later he voluntarily submitted to tests that showed traces of narcotics in his system.

510-11

Chapter References

This case study may be used with Chapters 10, 11, and 12.

●● INTRODUCING THE
▊▊ CASE STUDY

▲ On the board, create a chart. Label the columns *Senators and Representatives, First Elected,* and *Number of Years Served.* Ask students to fill in the chart with information on your local members of Congress. You may want to provide an almanac or other reference book for the class so that students can look up information they do not know.

TEACHING THE ISSUE

●● Civic Participation

● Explain to students that laws to limit terms of officeholders have been introduced through voter *initiatives.* Ask a small group of volunteers to find out what is necessary to get such an initiative on the ballot in your state and report that information to the class. Divide the class into groups and ask each group to devise a strategy for getting an initiative on limiting congressional terms on the ballot.

CASE STUDY

3A

5

Should the Number of Congressional Terms Be Limited?

Robert Byrd of West Virginia has been a member of the United States Senate since 1959. He has served as Senate president *pro tempore* and Senate Majority Leader.

Many Americans believe Congress is doing a poor job of solving the nation's problems. They want congressional reform, yet in election after election, voters return their senators and representatives to the Capitol. This worries many people, who want to limit the number of terms a member of Congress can serve. That idea has caught on, and almost every western state has either imposed or is considering imposing term limits on state and federal legislators. Is it time for a national law limiting length of service in Congress?

Colorado's Patricia Schroeder has been a member of the House of Representatives since 1973.

YES **Long-term lawmakers are out of touch.** Some have lived away from their home districts for decades. According to Mary Ann Best, executive director of Citizens for Congressional Reform, "Your typical congressman no longer represents the people who elected him."

"If they didn't have to worry about getting re-elected, they could actually do their job.**"**

—Bolivar Fraga, Bellaire High School, Texas

Members of Congress spend all their time running for office. Under the present system, an estimated one-half of representatives' and senators' time is devoted to fund-raising. This increases the power of one-issue political action committees (PACs), which make sizable campaign contributions. If lawmakers did not worry about re-election, they could turn their attention to the country's problems—and say no to lobbyists' requests.

Perpetual candidates won't make tough decisions. Right now, lawmakers find it easy to support pork-barrel projects that win them votes but cost taxpayers millions. On the other hand, important but politically painful issues—cutting the deficit or reforming the health care system, for example—are often tabled. If serving in Congress were not a career but one stage of a professional life, representatives and senators might be free to take unpopular stands that are good for the country, not their re-election campaigns.

510-12

NO **Less experience in Congress will mean chaos.** Legislators gain experience and seniority the longer they stay in office. Limiting congressional terms would force skilled lawmakers out of office and make Congress even less efficient than it is today.

"We already have term limitation. It's called the vote."

—*Satish Rao, Plano Senior High School, Texas*

Power will transfer to congressional staffs. Members of Congress might have to leave office, but congressional staffers would remain. These officials are not elected and would not be responsive to constituents. The Continental Congress had three-year term limits. When it came time to write the Constitution, however, delegates rejected term limits, believing that the need to run for re-election would force legislators to keep their constituents' interests in mind.

Charles Grassley (left), Strom Thurmond (center), and Robert Dole (right) together have more than half a century of experience in the Senate. Dole has been in office since 1969, and Thurmond was first elected in 1954.

Voters lose the right to choose. As Margaret Colony of the League of Women Voters says, "This type of measure is so drastic. . . . If you want somebody out of office, vote them out."

Most congressional incumbents win their bid for re-election.

Take a Stand

8H

1. What are the main arguments in favor of limiting the number of congressional terms? What are the main arguments against it?

2. Write an essay expressing and supporting your point of view.

510-13

Politics

● Ask students to suggest the advantages an incumbent has over his or her challenger in an election. (Voter familiarity, the ability to get on the news in connection with official activities, advantages in raising money.) ***What disadvantages does an incumbent have to overcome?*** (A record that voters may dislike, the appearance of being a political "insider.")

Take a Stand Answers

1. *In favor*—Members of Congress get out of touch with their constituents; they spend too much time running for re-election; they are afraid to do anything that will jeopardize their re-election. *Against*—We need experience in Congress; congressional staffers can gain too much power if they are the only long-term people in Congress; takes away voters' freedom of choice.

2. Students should present and defend their arguments, using examples to illustrate them.

The symbol 👥 denotes active participation strategies.

Activities are keyed for student abilities:
▲ = Basic
● = All Levels
■ = Average/Advanced

Chapter References

This case study may be used with Chapters 4, 15, 19, and 29.

INTRODUCING THE CASE STUDY

▲ Ask students to suggest specific events that have occurred in recent years that might influence U.S. defense policy. (Examples: collapse of Soviet Union, Persian Gulf War, tightening of government controls in China, peace talks in the Middle East.)

TEACHING THE LESSON

Global Awareness

▲ Have students annotate a classroom map of the world with adhesive notes marking the following information on U.S. defenses around the world in 1993: Pacific Ocean—3rd and 7th fleets; Japan—46,000 troops; Guam—7,800 troops; South Korea—36,000 troops; Diego Garcia in Indian Ocean—1,200 troops; Mediterranean Sea—6th Fleet; Europe—160,000 troops; Iceland—3,000 troops; Atlantic Ocean—2nd Fleet; Cuba—2,300 troops; Panama—11,000 troops.

● CRITICAL THINKING **In which areas of the world might the United States cut back its military presence? Explain your answer.** (Students may suggest troop cuts in Europe because of the break-up of the Soviet Union; they may also argue that there is less need for troops in Japan.)

Should the United States Cut Back Its Defense Budget?

The destruction of the Berlin Wall symbolized the end of Communist domination of Eastern Europe. The break-up of the Soviet Union has led to a planned decrease in American troops and weapons in Europe.

Following the close of the cold war the United States government began to re-examine its defense spending. The Clinton administration ordered drastic cuts in the military budget, including the closing of bases around the country.

Some Americans felt the defense cuts did not go far enough, saying even more cuts were needed to reduce the federal deficit. Others worried that the reductions would harm the nation's economy and weaken its defenses. Is it time for the country to reduce the level of its military spending?

YES

The world today is a safer place. In the early 1980's, when President Reagan increased defense spending, the Soviet Union threatened American security. Today that nation no longer exists. The United States is unquestionably the most powerful country in the world—and we don't need more arms to prove our strength.

We already have enough weapons. Some threats to world peace and security remain, but the United States already has a large stockpile of nuclear and conventional weapons. The navy planned to buy several Seawolf submarines—$2 billion apiece—that were developed to sink Soviet subs. That is a perfect example of wasteful Pentagon spending.

> "There is too much waste in military spending."
>
> —*Mary Hardin,*
> *Bullitt Central High School,*
> *Shepherdsville, Kentucky*

There are better things to do with the money. The price-tag of just one B-2 bomber airplane, $865 million, would more than pay for the entire cost of a proposed Healthy Start program that would lower the nation's high infant mortality rate. Money cut from defense could go to help schools, the homeless, and the poor. Or the cuts could be used to help balance the budget and lower the national debt, which is over $3 trillion.

NO **We have to prepare for the future.** New weapons depend on sophisticated technology and take years to develop. Large cuts in research and development today will mean weak defenses in the next century—when a new threat may arise.

"Do you want some other country to see that the United States is getting weak?"

—*Sarah Silver, Highland Park High School, Illinois*

Defense cuts will hurt the economy. Defense industries employ thousands of workers, and military bases are vital to the economies of many communities.

Despite the large number of weapons stockpiled by the military, the army has ordered thousands more rockets for its Multiple Launch Rocket System (left).

PROJECTED LOSS OF DEFENSE-RELATED JOBS, 1991 - 1997	
Industry	Jobs Lost, in Thousands
Aerospace/guided missiles	195.7
Computer/electronic equipment	71.9
Broadcast/communication equipment	55.3
Shipbuilding and repairing	35.2
Steel mills/metal products	23.3
Ordnance and accessories	18.1

Source: *Bureau of Labor Statistics*

Estimates show that over half a million jobs will be lost through defense cuts (see chart above), and deeper cuts could mean more unemployment. Besides, research performed for defense can often be applied to civilian industries. Computers, jet engines, and radar were improved and developed through Pentagon spending.

There are still threats to U.S. security. Despite the end of the cold war, the United States must be prepared to deal with outbreaks of aggression and to protect its interests. Wars and civil conflicts continue today to rage in many different areas of the world. Clearly it is the national interest of the United States to develop modern weapons and to maintain fully supplied armed forces.

As the chart above shows, cuts in defense spending could mean the loss of thousands of highly skilled and well-paid jobs in defense industries.

Take a Stand

8H

1. What are the main arguments in favor of cutting the defense budget? What are the main arguments against it?
2. Write an essay expressing and supporting your point of view.

510-15

CASE STUDY 7

Chapter References
This case study may be used with Chapters 6, 18, and 27.

INTRODUCING THE CASE STUDY
▲ Ask students if your community—and/or any of the towns or cities nearby—has a curfew for young people. If the answer is yes, have them describe the curfew's regulations. (Time span of curfew on weeknights and weekends, age limit, and the penalties for breaking curfew.)

Do you think that the curfew is strictly enforced? Is it strictly observed?

If your community does not have a curfew, you may wish to ask students to suggest reasons why a city or town would impose a curfew on young people. (Possible answers: to fight crime, gang violence, because there have been complaints against teenagers "hanging out" in certain areas.)

TEACHING THE ISSUE

Civic Participation
● Ask for two volunteers to play the role of teenagers "hanging out" past curfew in a community that has a curfew. Then ask for two more volunteers to play the role of police officers in that community. With the rest of the class watching, have the volunteers act out a short scene in which the police confront the teenagers about being out after curfew. Afterwards, ask the other students to comment on the way the police and teenagers acted, making suggestions for alternative approaches and responses. You may wish to have another

510-16

CASE STUDY 7

6C

Should Curfews for Young People Be Illegal?

Teenagers congregate in front of an apartment building in Brooklyn, New York. New York City does not have a curfew.

Hundreds of communities across the country are trying to control the problem of juvenile crime by imposing curfews on young people. These laws require minors to be off the streets after ten or eleven at night. Penalties can be stiff. Under a Dallas curfew, minors who broke curfew could be detained, and their parents could be fined up to $500.

Critics charge that these penalties are unfair and that curfews do little to stop crime. Should these curfews be made illegal?

 **Curfews are the responsibility of parents, not the government.** Laws lump all young people together, ignoring differing levels of maturity. Parents, on the other hand, are best able to determine when and under what circumstances their children should be out at night.

Police already have the authority to arrest law-breakers. Officers do not need a curfew law to arrest young people who are selling drugs or playing loud music late at night. Teenagers who commit crimes are not going to rush inside when curfew starts. Curfews only affect law-abiding young people, by making the innocent action of being outside after a certain hour a crime.

Driving around is a popular activity for young people.

Officers have better things to do with their time. Police in such cities as Dallas and Atlanta are struggling to control high murder rates, drug trafficking, and property crimes. They should not waste their energies making sure that teenagers are at home at night.

"It is a waste of the police's time to pick up kids for not doing anything wrong."

—Louis Schillace, Chatsworth High School, Los Angeles

510-16

These former gang members participate in activities at a Los Angeles Buddhist temple. Supervised programs encourage teenagers not to violate curfews.

While there is no proof that curfews lower crime, they do limit freedom. In Atlanta, juvenile crime actually went up after the curfew law was enacted. Police officers in other communities with curfews admit that the laws are rarely enforced. The laws can be used to harass certain teenagers, however, such as members of minority groups. The Dallas curfew, challenged by a group of teenagers and the American Civil Liberties Union, was struck down in mid-1992 by a U.S. district judge who argued that it amounted to "house arrest" for innocent, law-abiding juveniles.

NO **Curfews cut crime.** Curfews will not stop deliberate lawbreakers, but young people hanging out at night without supervision are more likely to get into trouble than those who are at home. If curfews were strictly enforced, there would be far fewer opportunities for juvenile crime.

The streets are not a safe place for young people at night. Curfews not only prevent teenagers from committing crimes, they protect them from being victims of late-night robberies and assaults. With the growing threat of gang violence, innocent young people are better off inside their homes, away from the threat of confrontation.

"Why should kids be able to be out causing trouble?"

—*Trace Major, Plano Senior High School, Texas*

These laws strengthen parental authority. Government curfews don't replace family rules, they make it easier for parents to enforce them. Glenda Lock, a spokeswoman for the Atlanta police department, has described the reaction in her city this way: "Parents see it as something that reinforces what they are trying to teach their children at home."

Curfew laws are not inflexible. In California, curfews do not affect young people who are accompanied by an adult; returning from a meeting, performance, or school activity; running an errand; or at work. The Dallas law excused teenagers exercising their right to free speech or assembly. These laws take into account the legitimate reasons why young people might be out at night. On the other hand, teenagers who are hanging out and looking for trouble can be sent home. Curfews serve as useful tools for the police in their attempt to control juvenile crime.

Take a Stand

8H

1. What are the main arguments in favor of making curfew laws illegal? What are the main arguments in favor of curfews?
2. Write an essay expressing and supporting your opinion on this issue.

510-17

group of volunteers enact a scene incorporating the class's suggestions.

Law
● Have students suggest other laws, besides curfews, that may be used to prevent young people from gathering in groups late at night. (Possible answers: laws prohibiting loitering, unlawful assembly, disturbing the peace, trespassing.)

Take a Stand Answers
1. *In favor*—Parents, not the government, should set curfews; curfews are unnecessary and a waste of police time; curfews limit personal freedom. *Against*—Curfews control crime, keep young people safe, enforce parental authority, and can be written to take individual situations into account.
2. Students should present and defend their arguments, using examples to illustrate them.

The symbol 👥 denotes active participation strategies.

Activities are keyed for student abilities:
▲ = Basic
● = All Levels
■ = Average/Advanced

Chapter References

This case study may be used with Chapters 3, 7, and 20.

INTRODUCING THE CASE STUDY

Have students refer to the graph on p. 510-19 while you tell them the following limitations that applied to women in the U.S. forces in 1991, during the Gulf War: Women could fly helicopters ferrying troops and supplies into enemy territory and evacuating the wounded, but they could not fly gunships or scout helicopters. They could not serve on carriers, battleships, destroyers, or submarines, nor could they serve in the infantry, paratroops, Ranger battalions, or commando units such as the Special Forces. They were banned from service in tanks, armed personnel carriers, field artillery, and mobile antiaircraft that led ground assaults. In addition, women were barred from service as combat engineers. (In 1993 the Secretary of Defense lifted restrictions on women's participation in aerial combat.)

● CRITICAL THINKING **Why might these regulations exist?** (Tradition, the services may not want to put women in the direct line of fire where they can be killed or captured, etc.)

5C

CASE STUDY 8

Should Women Be Allowed to Hold Combat Positions?

Women can now fly combat airplanes in all the services.

Women are officially banned from serving in most ground combat positions in the U.S. armed forces. This ban, supported by law and military policy, keeps women out of many military units.

In 1993 the Defense Department ended a ban that had kept women from flying in combat. Yet the ban on women in other combat roles continued.

Some people believe that women should be excluded from combat units and ships. Others argue that women are as capable of combat action as men. Do you think women should be allowed to serve in combat?

YES **The military needs intelligence, not brute strength.** Combat pilots fire their weapons by pushing buttons, and battleships and carriers are highly mechanized. Women have the same right to serve in those positions as men. As for the more physically demanding jobs, experts say that the strongest 20 percent of women are

as strong as the weakest 20 percent of men. Why not let those women serve in infantry and commando units?

"Females should be given their chance to fight."

— *Kimberly Gunn, Bullitt Central High School, Shepherdsville, Kentucky*

Banning women from combat positions hurts their careers. These positions are important stepping stones in advancement in the military. Female naval officers who cannot serve on combat ships, for example, have a hard time proving themselves capable of higher command. Keeping women out of combat positions prevents them from getting promotions.

No place is safe during war. Women are already piloting military airplanes, serving on supply ships, and filling support positions. Regulations and laws keep them out of the front lines, but in modern warfare there is no safe role. Though U.S. servicewomen were barred from combat in the Gulf War, two were captured by the enemy, and five were killed in action. Trying to protect women by keeping them in the back lines is absurd.

Women in the military fill technical as well as administrative positions.

 **Physical strength still matters.** Being in the infantry means carrying up to 110 pounds of weapons and supplies, while artillery crews have to load four 100-pound shells a minute. The only way to open those jobs to women is to lower standards, and that means making those units less safe for everyone.

Women have different needs from men. These needs would complicate their serving in combat units. Submarines, for example, have open toilets and no privacy. Pregnancy may force women soldiers to leave crucial jobs unfilled.

"Women should not be allowed to hold combat positions because they are built differently from men."

—*Bohra Arwa, Chatsworth High School, Los Angeles, California*

Women in combat units would be bad for military morale. Men might feel the need to protect the women in their units and therefore take unneccessary risks to prevent female soldiers from harm. Feeling comfortable and trusting other soldiers is essential for troops under fire. As Brigadier General Ed

Captain Linda Bray, standing second from right, commanded a platoon in a firefight during the U.S. invasion of Panama in 1989—the first time American women soldiers fought hostile troops in modern combat.

Scholes, who commanded troops in Saudi Arabia, explained, "I want people on my right and on my left who will take the pressure when the shooting starts. Men simply cannot treat women like other men."

These female troops are a few of the 35,000 servicewomen who took part in the Persian Gulf War. Though none served on the front lines of combat, five women were killed by the enemy.

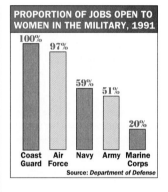

PROPORTION OF JOBS OPEN TO WOMEN IN THE MILITARY, 1991

Coast Guard	Air Force	Navy	Army	Marine Corps
100%	97%	59%	51%	20%

Source: *Department of Defense*

Take a Stand

8H

1. What are the main arguments in favor of allowing women to fill combat positions? What are the main arguments against it?

2. Write an essay expressing and supporting your view.

510-19

TEACHING THE ISSUE

Civic Participation
● Have students invite a representative of your local armed forces recruiting center to come to class and speak about the role of women in the military today. Have students prepare a short list of questions to ask the representative on this issue.

History
■ *In what ways did women serve in the military in the United States before 1975?* (Mostly as nurses in wars from the Civil War to Vietnam. In this century, they also have acted as drivers and held clerical positions. Students may note that in the Revolution and Civil War, some women disguised themselves as men and fought and others served as spies.)

Take a Stand Answers
1. *In favor*—Many combat positions do not require great physical strength; keeping women from holding combat positions hurts their careers; women already serve in risky positions. *Against*—Physical strength is still important; women have special requirements that would affect military efficiency; women's presence would hurt morale.
2. Students should present and defend their arguments, using examples to illustrate them.

The symbol 👥 denotes active participation strategies.

Activities are keyed for student abilities:
▲ = Basic
● = All Levels
■ = Average/Advanced

Chapter References

This case study may be used with Chapters 9, 13, 21, and 28.

INTRODUCING THE CASE STUDY

● Conduct an informal poll, asking students if they have ever (1) had an after-school job; (2) had a summer job; (3) looked for a job. Ask volunteers to tell the class about their experiences. Then ask students how difficult they think it is for teenagers to find employment in your community.

TEACHING THE ISSUE

Values

● Ask students to suggest ways that being employed might conflict with school. (The job might take time away from schoolwork, force a student to miss classes, prevent involvement in extracurricular activities.) *Could an after-school job help a student improve his or her school performance?* (Possible answers include: Yes, if it teaches the student to be responsible; no, it would always interfere with schoolwork.) Discuss with students what is more important, having the money they could make from an after-school job or doing well in school.

Economics

● Ask students if they can explain the law of supply and demand. (As the price of a good goes up, more people are willing to sell it, so supply increases. Fewer people are willing to pay the higher price, so the demand decreases.)

CASE STUDY 9

7C

Should There Be a Special Minimum Wage for Teenagers?

Most young people look for jobs that require few skills or special training. This teenager works in the deli counter of a supermarket.

Unemployment levels have gone up and down in the last ten years, but for some groups it is always hard times. In 1990, when 5.5 percent of American workers overall were out of a job, 15.5 percent of teenagers in the labor force were unemployed. Those figures were particularly bad for African American teenagers, who suffered from a 31 percent unemployment rate.

Summer jobs are particularly important to young people.

510-20

To combat those ugly statistics, Congress created a special, lower minimum wage for entry-level workers. This subminimum wage was designed to open more positions to teenagers. Yet opponents say a subminimum wage means a subminimum job. Will a lower minimum wage help teenagers?

YES **A lower minimum wage will open up jobs to young people.** Teenagers are the least experienced, most untested workers, and employers are often doubtful about hiring them. Paying younger workers slightly less, however, would be the incentive businesses need. A survey done in the 1980's by the U.S. Chamber of Commerce showed that 49 percent of employers said they would hire teenagers at a subminimum wage. That translates to many more opportunities for teenagers looking for work.

Teenagers can afford lower wages. Some people in their late teens are supporting themselves, but for most teenagers a job is a way to earn spending money or to pay for education. No one wants to earn less money, but that is better than being unemployed and earning no money at all.

> "I think it makes good sense. You spend time training new workers, getting them to where they can do as well as others."
>
> —*Scott Kimpel,*
> *Plano Senior High School, Texas*

Young workers can get training and experience. Ask most executives and professionals about their first work experience, and you will probably hear about a low-paying position. The importance of that first job was not the money, but the experience of

---

Ask students to consider supply and demand in terms of employment. *What is being supplied?* (Labor.) *Who supplies it?* (Workers.) *What is demand in this case?* (The need of em-

ployers for workers to make a product or perform a service.) *What is another word for price in this situation?* (Wages.) *What is the quantity?* (The number of workers.)

Help students understand how the law of supply and demand applies in the case of a minimum wage by drawing the graph, shown here, on the board.

being accountable and responsible, and of learning a skill. Once a teenager has work experience to put on his or her resumé, the possibility of finding a better-paying job in the future increases.

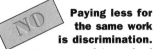

Paying less for the same work is discrimination. Teenagers work just as hard as other workers. A subminimum wage based on age is no more fair than paying people less because of their sex or race. All deny the fundamental right to equal protection.

"Why should an adult get more money for the same amount of work done?"

—Minh Le,
Chatsworth High School,
Los Angeles, California

Leaders of the fast food industry, which employs many young people, have long called for a subminimum wage for teenagers.

Lower pay for teenagers will hurt adult workers. In hard times, businesses look for any way to cut costs. They may lay off less-skilled adult workers to hire teenagers at the subminimum wage. The newly unemployed adults will be willing to accept low salaries because they need work. That means higher unemployment and lower wages for everybody in the labor force.

A subminimum wage doesn't address the true cause of teenage unemployment. In today's economy there are fewer and fewer unskilled jobs. Lack of schooling is the real reason teenagers cannot find work. In inner cities, where teenage unemployment is particularly high, there are not many positions available for workers regardless of their age. Lowering wages may open some dead-end jobs to teenagers, but a more permanent solution to teenage unemployment will come from improvements in education and a revitalized urban economy.

WAGES OF TEENAGERS, 1990

Above minimum wage
4,457,000
(81.1%)

Below minimum wage
675,000
(12.3%)

At minimum wage
364,000
(6.6%)

Total Teenagers Employed at Hourly Rates = 5,496,000

Source: U.S. Bureau of Labor Statistics

The majority of teenagers earn more than the minimum wage.

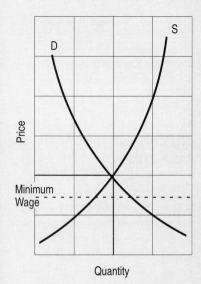

Quantity

Have a volunteer draw a dotted line on the chart signifying where a lower minimum wage for teenagers would fall. (The line should be parallel and below the minimum wage line.)

Take a Stand Answers

1. *In favor*—Provides more jobs and training opportunities; teenagers can afford lower wages. *Against*—Teenagers should not be discriminated against; lowering their wages lowers all wages; teenage unemployment has deeper roots.
2. Students should present and defend their arguments, using examples to illustrate them.

Take a Stand

8H

1. What are the main arguments in favor of a lower minimum wage for teenagers? What are the main arguments against it?
2. Write an essay expressing and supporting your view.

510-21

Ask a volunteer to relabel the chart to reflect the fact that it is being applied to employment. ("Price" should be "Wage," "D" is "Employers," and "S" is "Workers.")

Point to the portions of the supply and demand lines that lie below the minimum wage horizontal. **What do these portions signify?** (They show the number of employers who

would be willing to hire workers for below minimum wage and the number of workers who would be willing to work for those wages.)

INTRODUCING THE CASE STUDY

● Ask students if any of them are planning on joining the military after completing school. Ask for volunteers among those students to explain why they want to serve in the armed forces. Then ask students if they have ever thought of joining the Peace Corps, VISTA, or a religious service organization.

● CRITICAL THINKING **What is your personal definition of "service to the nation"?** (Students may suggest the military, volunteer work, being a law-abiding citizen.)

CASE STUDY 10

6D

Should Eighteen-Year-Olds Be Made to Perform National Service?

These marine pilots and crews voluntarily joined the military. A national service requirement would give young men and women the option of entering the armed forces to fulfill their obligation.

In 1993 Congress passed the National and Community Service Trust Act. This program, requested by President Bill Clinton, enables young people to earn money for college or technical training in return for community service. The service can involve work in education, environmental restoration, or other useful public programs sponsored by government agencies or colleges and universities. These work programs are voluntary. Similar proposals have called for national service as a requirement for all eighteen-year olds.

Is it time to launch a program requiring national service by all eighteen-year-olds?

YES

Young people owe their country a debt of gratitude. The United States guarantees its citizens universal education, enormous personal freedom, and equal protection under the law. The country also provides young people with many opportunities for their future. One year of national service is not much to ask in return. As former representative Paul McCloskey has explained, "The privilege of being an American justifies a duty to serve the country a year or two in one's youth."

"It's a good idea. You can contribute to the country."

—*Matthew Russell, Henry M. Gunn High School, Palo Alto, California*

A strong military and improved social services would be guaranteed. Many eighteen-year-olds would choose to fulfill their obligation by serving in the armed forces. This would enlarge the standing army and make it more representative of the population as a whole. Young people who choose to work in hospitals, schools, public land, and with the disadvantaged would help maintain important social and environmental programs.

Young people will have a greater stake in their country. Devoting a year of your life to serving the nation will lead to a greater interest in its public policies. In later life, citizens who have performed this service may be more inclined to vote and to be active in political and civic affairs. National service, argues William F. Buckley, will transform a young person into a "morally awakened citizen."

510-22

Serving one's country should be a matter of free choice. You cannot legislate a sense of gratitude or obligation. If a young person wants to serve the United States, many opportunities already exist. Requiring eighteen-year-olds to serve, however, limits their personal freedom.

> "If they require you, then they are taking away your right to make your own decisions."
>
> —*Traci Wabbington, William McKinley High School, Washington, D.C.*

Mandatory national service is unnecessary. Right now, the Defense Department is cutting back the number of military personnel, which should go down 25 percent between 1990

High school graduates could serve as teachers' aides and tutors to young children.

An outreach worker helps a homeless person, one of the types of jobs young people could fill to perform their national service.

and 1995. The armed forces do not need more recruits. Social services require skilled professionals such as doctors and teachers, not high school graduates. Requiring all eighteen-year-olds to serve would add about three million people to the government's payroll, with little gain in return.

Young people can better serve their country in other ways. Since an educated population is vital to economic success,

the United States would be better off if young people went to college instead of joining the military or a civic works corps. Teenagers who get jobs and do not go to college also contribute to the country with their taxes and productivity. It is through education and employment that young people become committed to this country, not through government programs.

Take a Stand

8H

1. What are the main arguments in favor of mandatory national service? What are the main arguments against it?
2. Write an essay expressing and supporting your opinion on this issue.

510-23

CASE STUDY 11

6D

Should There Be Strong Gun Control Laws?

A policeman exhibits a confiscated firearm in Washington, D.C.

In 1968 Congress passed the Gun Control Act, which banned the mail-order shipment of firearms and required dealers to keep records on handgun purchasers. In 1993 Congress, after years of effort from handgun control advocates, passed the Brady bill. This law was named for Ronald Reagan's press secretary, James Brady, who was disabled by a gunshot wound during an attempt on President Reagan's life. The Brady law requires a five-day waiting period before a handgun purchase. In 1994, President Clinton signed into law an anti-crime bill. Among the bill's provisions was a ban on 19 types of assault weapons.

Even after the passage of these bills, gun-control advocates called for more legislation. Local gun-control laws do exist, but some people say more national gun-control laws should be passed. Others object not only to new laws but to many of the existing regulations.

Does the nation need strong gun-control laws?

James Brady, Ronald Reagan's press secretary, was shot (inset) during the 1981 attempted assassination of the President. He and his wife, Sarah Brady (center), worked hard for passage of national handgun legislation.

Guns lead to crime and violence in the United States. Firearms account for about 30,000 deaths a year in the United States and are involved in approximately one-third of all robberies. In 1988, 80 percent of all law-enforcement officers killed in the line of duty were murdered with handguns. In

1991, 23 innocent people were slain in Killeen, Texas, by one heavily armed man. Five elementary school children died in Stockton, California, in 1989 because an unbalanced man was able to buy an assault weapon. Limiting gun ownership would control this violence.

"I'm for laws like waiting periods and checks."

—Derek Kupper,
Plano Senior High School, Texas

Even honest citizens should not have easy access to guns. A family quarrel can become a fatal tragedy if there is a gun in the house, and accidental shootings left some 1,500 people dead in 1988. Law-abiding gun owners are an important source of firearms for criminals, since an estimated 40 to 70 percent of firearms used in crimes are stolen. A national registry of gun owners would enable law enforcement officials to track these weapons.

Gun control laws are effective. Cities and states have had good results from strong laws. A background check requirement in New Jersey has prevented more than 10,000 convicted felons from purchasing handguns. A study published in the *New England Journal of Medicine* reported that a tough handgun control law passed in 1976 in Washington, D.C., led to a 25 percent drop in the homicide-by-firearm rate by 1987. The law probably prevented 47 deaths a year.

Gun control is constitutional. The Supreme Court has consistently ruled that the Second Amendment, which speaks of the "right to bear arms," allows for gun control laws. The amendment begins with the words, "A well-regulated militia being necessary to the security of a free state. . . ." Many constitutional scholars interpret the amendment as referring only to arming organized militias, not to individuals.

Gun control does not mean a total ban on all firearms. The law could be written so that hunting rifles and other recreational guns could still be purchased. Certain weapons—assault rifles and small revolvers, for example—clearly have no recreational purpose. Those weapons should not be available to individuals. They were designed to be used against other human beings.

"It is far too easy for anyone to obtain a gun."

—Teo Kljaic,
Bullitt Central High School, Shepherdsville, Kentucky

A weapons dealer displays two assault rifles at a Miami, Florida, gun show. Though some states and cities have limited the sale of these weapons, they may be purchased with few restrictions in many places.

510-25

TEACHING THE ISSUE

Science and Technology

● Explain to students that there have been proposals to make guns safer by mandating indicators that would show whether or not a gun was loaded, making them child-proof with hard-to-pull triggers, building in combination locks for triggers that would make it hard for thieves to use stolen guns, and lengthening handgun barrels to make guns harder to conceal. Ask volunteers to draw a "safer" gun on the board, using the above suggestions and/or adding their own.

Civic Participation

● Have students do research, working with partners, to find state and local laws that restrict or regulate firearm ownership. Have them use that information to create posters showing the relationship between state and local gun control laws, restrictions on the sale of firearms, or the procedure required for the purchase of a firearm in your community.

Law

● Ask a volunteer to paraphrase the quote by J. Warren Cassidy, found at the end of the arguments against gun control. (Instead of limiting gun ownership, which would limit individual liberty, we should strengthen laws against those who use guns illegally.) Ask other students to respond to Cassidy's words.

👥 Cooperative Learning

● Divide the class into groups and have the members of each group imagine that they are Supreme Court justices considering a gun control case in which an individual is appealing a state law banning the sale or purchase of small-caliber handguns on the basis of the Second Amendment. Have the "Courts" come to a decision and assign members to write the majority and dissenting opinions. They may wish to refer to Supreme Court procedures on pp. 477–478.

CASE STUDY 11 *continued*

NO **Gun control hurts honest people, not criminals.** According to one study, only 17 percent of guns used by criminals were bought from licensed dealers. That means that laws regulating firearm purchases would not affect about 83 percent of all crimes committed with guns. On the other hand, hunters and homeowners who wanted weapons for protection would have to cope with red tape and restrictions. That is not only silly, but it leaves law-abiding citizens vulnerable.

Most gun owners are good citizens. There are approximately 70 million gun owners in the United States, and about one in four households has some kind of handgun. For the vast majority of these Americans, firearms are used only for target practice, hunting, and protection.

They follow in the tradition of gun ownership in this country, from the Revolution when armed individuals fought the British for independence, to the settlers who hunted and trapped in the West.

> "People who use guns responsibly should not be punished for the irresponsible acts of others."
>
> —*Nooshi Romezi, Chatsworth High School, Los Angeles, California*

Gun ownership is a constitutional right. The Second Amendment clearly states that "the right of the people to keep and bear arms shall not be infringed." Laws banning some weapons and regulating sales of others are a clear violation of that right.

Registration laws threaten personal liberty. Background checks for gun purchasers are an invasion of privacy. Even worse would be a requirement that all firearms purchasers be registered. Such a law would increase the power of government officials to keep track of millions of honest Americans.

510-26

> "A law to keep criminals from getting guns is not going to do any good."
>
> —*Aisha Griffith, William McKinley High School, Washington, D.C.*

These laws do not stop crime. New York City has very tough gun control laws, yet it is far from safe and peaceful. Saying gun control works in Washington, D.C., is absurd, since it has one of the highest murder rates in the country. The way to stop the criminal use of firearms is through harsh punishment of those convicted of using a weapon to commit a crime. As J. Warren Cassidy, executive vice president of the National Rifle Association, has written, "Tough laws designed to incarcerate violent offenders offer something gun control cannot: swift, sure justice meted out with no accompanying erosion of individual liberty."

Goose hunters in a blind aim their weapons. In a recent poll, half of all firearm owners gave hunting as the main reason for having a gun.

Women at a firing range practice their aim (left). About one quarter of all gun owners are women. A Florida gun store owner (right) exhibits a few of the handguns he has for sale.

Take a Stand

8H

1. What are the main arguments in favor of strong gun control laws? What are the main arguments against it?
2. Write an essay expressing and supporting your opinion on this issue.

510-27

Chapter References

This Case Study may be used with Chapters 7 and 15.

INTRODUCING THE CASE STUDY

You may wish to share these statistics with the class: the leading cause of death of black males between the ages of 15 and 24 is homicide; though African American men are only 6 percent of the U.S. population, they are 46 percent of the state prison population; close to one in four black men in their twenties is either in prison, on parole, or on probation.

● CRITICAL THINKING Ask students to consider the problems faced by African American males in the United States and suggest how prejudice may have led to the high unemployment and low college enrollment rate of this group. (Students may note that discrimination may prevent young black males from believing that they can get jobs, even if they get high school or college diplomas.)

TEACHING THE ISSUE

Values

● CRITICAL THINKING Divide the board into two columns, one labeled *Benefits* and the other labeled *Drawbacks*. Ask students to suggest the plusses and minuses of single-sex education and put their suggestions in the appropriate column. (*Benefits*— Fewer social distractions in school, can concentrate on the needs of one group. *Drawbacks*—Students do not get the chance to learn certain social skills, discriminatory.)

Should There Be Special Public Schools for African American Males?

T he statistics are alarming. Fewer than two-thirds of African American males graduate from high school. Only about a quarter go on to college. Jawanza Kunjufu, a Chicago educator who has studied the issue, notes that though African American males are only 8.5 percent of the public school population, they are 37 percent of all students suspended.

For some people, the solution to this crisis lies in the establishment of special all-male academies where African American men will teach an Afrocentric curriculum. Such academies have been proposed in New York, Milwaukee, Detroit, Miami, and other cities. Not everyone approves of the idea, however, and a federal judge in Detroit declared a proposed male academy unconstitutional.

Should all-male schools for African Americans be established?

510-28

 Special academies will keep African American males in school.

Many black children live in areas where there are few positive male role models. Special schools, staffed mainly by African American males and teaching courses in African culture and history, will promote pride and self-confidence. In Dade County, Florida, for example, special kindergarten and first-grade classes for black boys resulted in increased attendance and higher test scores. Those are the kinds of results that need to be repeated across the country.

"Speaking as an African American, we really have a need for these schools in our community."
—*Chandra Boyd, Plano Senior High School, Texas*

Jawanza Kunjufu is an educational consultant and author.

This would be a positive use of segregation. Jawanza Kunjufu notes that many African American boys are already segregated, because they are disproportionately found in special education classes and detention schools. "They remind me of a negative male academy," writes Kunjufu of these special classes. On the other hand, special schools would be a positive experience. "So long as the class is already segregated, why not turn it into a class for winners?" asks Kunjufu.

Advocates want special schools to be staffed by African American men.

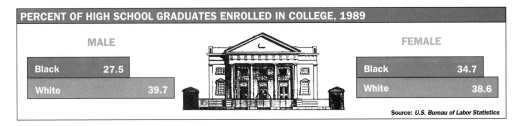

PERCENT OF HIGH SCHOOL GRADUATES ENROLLED IN COLLEGE, 1989

MALE		FEMALE	
Black	27.5	Black	34.7
White	39.7	White	38.6

Source: U.S. Bureau of Labor Statistics

While African American women are closing the gap in college enrollment, black men lag behind their white counterparts.

NO

Segregation is never a good solution. Americans live in a diverse society, and children need to be exposed to more cultures, not fewer. Kenneth Clark's

Kenneth Clark is a noted educator and psychologist.

research played a role in the famous desegregation case, *Brown v. Board of Education* (1954). He argues that the *Brown* decision still expresses the basic argument against segregation, for any reason. As Chief Justice Earl Warren wrote, "To separate [black children]. . . solely because of their race generates a feeling of inferiority. . . ." Those words are still true today.

" Isn't that segregation? "

—*Cecilia Ramírez, Pharr-San Juan-Alamo Upper Level High School, Texas*

All students—not just black males—might benefit from special schools. African American females must also cope with crime and discrimination. Though fewer go to jail, many end up living in poverty. Why prevent them from attending these academies? Besides, all students should learn about the contributions of African Americans—just as African Americans should learn about the contributions of other groups. To divide up students and curriculum based on sex, race, or religion, goes against the basic principles of this country.

Take a Stand

8H

1. What are the main arguments for creating separate schools for African American males? What are the main arguments against it?
2. Write an essay expressing and supporting your point of view.

510-29

Chapter References

This Case Study may be used with Chapters 5 and 27.

INTRODUCING THE CASE STUDY

▲ Ask students to describe the official restrictions on dress that exist in your school, if any.

● CRITICAL THINKING **Do you think these restrictions are acceptable? What other restrictions might you add?**

TEACHING THE ISSUE

Values

● Have a volunteer read aloud Cynthia Freeman's quote, and ask students to suggest dress restrictions that apply in "real life." (Many people have to dress a certain way on the job; certain professions wear uniforms; even in your social life you often have to dress a certain way to be acceptable.)

History

● Assign students an oral history project on dress codes. Students should interview their parents, grandparents, and/or older friends and relatives about high school dress restrictions in the past. Have students present the information they collect to the class. Encourage them to be creative in their presentations.

CASE STUDY 13

6C

Should Public Schools Enforce Strict Dress Codes?

In schools in Bastrop and Spring Branch, Texas, boys with long hair have been ordered to detention centers. In Brooklyn, New York, Boys and Girls High School has required male students to wear ties on Mondays, Tuesdays, and Wednesdays. In Detroit, Michigan, the Board of Education has asked all schools to develop dress codes for students.

More and more public schools are imposing dress codes or strengthening those codes that already exist. Students have been sent home or to detention centers for hair that is too long or for wearing shorts that are too short. Some public schools have even mandated uniforms, a requirement traditionally limited to parochial school students. Feelings run deep on both sides of the question: Do public schools need strict dress codes?

Some administrators say that outfits like this undercut discipline.

510-30

YES **Dress codes protect students from crime.** Teenagers in Chicago have been killed for their fashionable jackets, and a student was murdered in Detroit for his high-priced sneakers. Girls and boys have had their gold jewelry stolen. Dress codes barring expensive and trendy items make schools safer. For example, when schools in Baltimore, Maryland, banned certain fashions, student crime dropped.

Dress codes are necessary to school discipline. Frank Mickens, the principal of Boys and Girls High in Brooklyn, imposed the dress code because he believed it would promote civil behavior.

Caps with tags (above) and top-of-the-line sneakers (right) are some of the fashion fads that are prohibited by strict dress codes.

Young men at several schools have been asked to cut their hair for reasons of discipline as well as for hygiene. Helping students learn to respect rules is an important part of educating them to become good citizens.

> "School is a place for learning, not a fashion show."
>
> —Denise Chu,
> Chatsworth High School,
> Los Angeles

Students need to concentrate on education, not fashion. Young people often spend too much time and money trying to dress in the latest styles. Students from poorer families may suffer a loss of self-esteem because they cannot dress as fashionably as others. Rena Wilcox, vice president of the Nassau-Suffolk (New York) School Boards Association, has commented that a dress code improves education in a variety

mentary student in detention for his ponytail. "We are dealing with a constitutional issue," Beall has said.

"*Students should be able to wear what they want because in real life you wear what you want.*"

—*Cynthia Freeman, Belmont High School, Massachusetts*

Requiring this kind of conformity is undemocratic. American society values individu-

of ways. "It eliminates peer competition, reduces financial stress, instills pride in self, and encourages parent participation," she said.

NO **To tell students that they cannot wear certain fashions denies them their First Amendment rights.** Requiring boys to cut their hair is sex discrimination, claims Charles Beall, the attorney for a Texas ele-

alism, and dress codes deny that value. Restricting young people's ability to dress as they wish does not enhance their education as citizens, but limits it.

Dress codes do little to solve the real problems students face. Blaming murders and thefts on clothing denies reality. Drugs and violence cannot be controlled by dress codes, and students with few skills and limited chances for future employment will not feel better about themselves because they wear ties or skirts to schools. Instead of imposing dress codes, educators should concentrate on real solutions to today's issues.

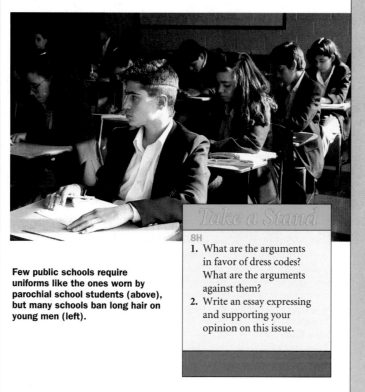

Few public schools require uniforms like the ones worn by parochial school students (above), but many schools ban long hair on young men (left).

Take a Stand

8H

1. What are the arguments in favor of dress codes? What are the arguments against them?
2. Write an essay expressing and supporting your opinion on this issue.

510-31

CASE STUDY 14

5C

Should the United States Adopt English as the Official Language?

A former senator from California, S.I. Hayakawa (above), always spoke to his mother in Japanese because she never learned English. Hayakawa, however, believed that speaking English in this country is essential. In 1981 he made an unsuccessful attempt to pass a constitutional amendment to make English the official language. The issue mains controversial. Sixteen states have official-language laws.

Should English be made the United States' official language?

510-32

YES **A common language preserves national unity.** In the 1980's, more than six million legal immigrants arrived in the United States. Bilingual education and translation of documents into foreign languages discourages immigrants and their children from learning English. If this trend continues for generations, we may end up like Canada, where French-speakers are demanding independence from the English-speaking majority.

Those without English skills are at a great disadvantage. To get a well-paying job, to understand a political campaign, or to be involved in the cultural mainstream of the United States, you need to know English. Declaring it the official language makes that point clear.

NO **Most immigrants learn English anyway.** No one knows better than a person who cannot speak English, how important English is in this country. A recent survey in South Florida found that 98 percent of

Bilingual signs can be found in many neighborhoods.

Hispanic parents want their children to read and write perfect English.

Official-English laws reflect prejudice against immigrants. The call for an official language stems from fear over the growing diversity of this country. Rich Castro, of the Mayor's Office of Human Rights and Community Relations in Denver, says that there is nothing wrong with defining English as our common language. "It's the mean-spiritedness of the idea of needing such an amendment that we disagree with," he adds.

Take a Stand

8H

1. What are the arguments in favor and against declaring English as the official language?
2. Write an essay expressing and supporting your opinion on this issue.

UNIT
★ 7 ★

GOVERNMENT in ACTION: American Public Policy

CHAPTER

19 TAXING, SPENDING, and ECONOMIC POLICIES

20 FOREIGN POLICY and NATIONAL DEFENSE

21 POLICIES TOWARD BUSINESS, LABOR, and AGRICULTURE

22 POLICIES for ENERGY and the ENVIRONMENT

23 SOCIAL POLICIES and PROGRAMS

511

Government in Action: American Public Policy
(pp. 511–630)

Unit Overview

The United States government determines that certain public policies will best serve the needs of the country. These policies, which generally issue from the executive branch, include both domestic and foreign plans of action. Chapter 19 discusses taxing, spending, and economic policies, including sources of revenue, areas of expenditure, and details about the government's influence on the nation's economy. Chapter 20 examines the goals and results of American foreign policy and looks at the officials who make and carry out this policy. Chapter 21 explores the role of business in the free enterprise system and details government policies toward business, labor, and agriculture. Chapter 22 describes government attempts to protect the environment and regulate energy use. Chapter 23 examines social policies and programs, including social insurance, Medicare, and public assistance.

CHAPTER 19
TAXING, SPENDING, AND ECONOMIC POLICIES
(pp. 512–535)

	Section Objectives	Section Resources
Section 1 **The Government Raises Money Through Taxing and Borrowing**	☐ explain the basic mechanism of the personal income tax ☐ list the major sources of federal tax revenue	● CITIZENSHIP WORKSHEET **8** ▲ TRANSPARENCY **41**
Section 2 **How Is Federal Spending Decided?**	☐ list the largest categories of federal spending ☐ trace the steps followed in making the federal budget	▲ SKILLS PRACTICE WORKSHEET **19** ▲ TRANSPARENCIES **42–44**
Section 3 **The Federal Government Influences the Nation's Economy**	☐ distinguish among Keynesian economics, supply-side economics, and fiscal conservatism ☐ compare and contrast the purposes of fiscal policy and monetary policy and describe the effects of each	■ SKILLS CHALLENGE WORKSHEET **19** ▲ TRANSPARENCIES **45–46**

Essential Elements

The list below shows Essential Elements relevant to this chapter. (The complete list of Essential Elements appears in the introductory pages of this Teacher's Edition.)

Section 1: 6G, 6H, 7B, 7C, 7D, 8A

Section 2: 6B, 7B, 8D, 8H

Section 3: 6G, 6H, 7A, 7B, 7C, 7E, 8A, 8G

Chapter Review: 3A, 7B, 7C, 7E, 8A, 8B, 8C, 8F, 8H

> Section Resources are keyed for student abilities:
> ▲ = Basic
> ● = All Levels
> ■ = Average/Advanced

Homework Options

Each section contains activities labeled "Guided/Independent Practice," "Reteaching/Correctives," and "Enrichment/Extension." You may wish to choose from among these activities when assigning homework.

Students Acquiring English Activities

Ask students to get copies of Internal Revenue Service tax forms from the post office or federal building in your community. Give different students different forms and have them work in groups to fill out all the forms, using any figures they would like.

LISTENING/SPEAKING: Have volunteers invite an accountant, tax representative, or employee of the IRS to the class to describe his or her job. Ask students to prepare a list of questions to ask the speaker.

Case Studies

When teaching this chapter, you may use Case Study 6, which deals with defense budget cuts. (Case Studies may be found following p. 510.)

Teacher Bibliography

Cranford, John. *Budgeting for America*. 2nd ed. CQ Press, 1989. Analyzes and discusses changes in the federal budget process from the 1930's to the present.

Gilder, George F. *The Spirit of Enterprise*. Simon & Schuster, 1984. Advocating the free market system, this book mixes economic philosophy with biographies of great entrepreneurs.

Woll, Peter. *Public Policy*. University Press of America, 1982. Evaluates the role of interest groups, political parties, the three branches of government, and the bureaucracy in forming public policy.

Student Bibliography

Friedman, Milton and Rose Friedman. *Free to Choose*. Harcourt Brace Jovanovich, 1980. Presents the case for less government involvement in the financial life of the nation.

Kimmens, Andrew C., ed. *The Federal Deficit*. Wilson, 1985. A history of deficit spending that concentrates on issues such as the huge deficits of the 1980's and the reasoning behind deficit spending.

Malkin, Lawrence. *The National Debt: How America Crashed into a Black Hole and How We Can Crawl Out*. Rev. and updated ed. New American Library, 1988. A readable account of why and how the U.S. debt has grown so large, with an overview of national and international finances.

Films and Videotapes*

The Military Budget: Dollars and Defense. 28 min. CGuild, 1984. v. Hodding Carter questions Pentagon spending as it affects national policy and economic well-being, using footage of news conferences, congressional hearings, and budget reports.

Taxes Raise Revenue. 15 min. AIT, 1984. v. Explains how taxation transfers resources from use by private persons to use by various levels of government.

Software*

The Budget Process (Apple, IBM, Macintosh). TS. Students participate in a congressional effort to produce a balanced budget. As sponsors of a budget bill before the House of Representatives, students must consider economics, inflation, unemployment, and legislative maneuvering as they try to win support for their bill.

Economics: What, How, and for Whom? (Apple). Focus. Using simulations, tutorials, analysis, graph interpretations, and decision-making skills, students learn and use the basic principles of economics. Consists of five programs: What Is Economics?; Economics: Definition and Laws; Economic Systems: Traditional, Command, and Market; Capitalism, Communism, and Socialism; and Teacher's Classroom Demonstrations: Economic Models.

* For a complete guide to audiovisual sources, see page T22.

511B

CHAPTER 19

Taxing, Spending, and Economic Policies
(pp. 512–535)

Chapter 19 explains how the government raises money, how government spending policies are formulated and implemented, and how the government uses fiscal policy and monetary policy to regulate the economy.

Chapter Outline
After students complete this chapter, they will be able to:

1. Explain the basic mechanism of the personal income tax.
2. List the major sources of federal tax revenue.
3. List the largest categories of federal spending.
4. Trace the steps followed in making the federal budget.
5. Distinguish among Keynesian economics, supply-side economics, and fiscal conservatism.
6. Compare and contrast the purposes of fiscal policy and monetary policy and describe the effects of each.

CHAPTER
19

TAXING, SPENDING, and ECONOMIC POLICIES

Money is, with propriety, considered as the vital principle of the body politic; as that which sustains its life and motion, and enables it to perform its most essential functions.

Alexander Hamilton
The Federalist (1787–1788)

512

Photo
Security guard, bank vault.

Western Pennsylvania, 1794 — Farmers fed up with taxes and tax collectors attack government officials. President Washington himself leads troops to suppress the rebellion.

California, 1978 — Proposition 13, a citizens' movement, succeeds in pushing property tax rates down. The modern-day drive for lower taxes is born.

Most Americans dislike paying taxes. From the time of the Whiskey Rebellion to the present, tax burdens have appeared excessive. What would happen, however, if there were no taxes? Since the federal government gets nearly all its money from taxes of one sort or another, the government would soon stop functioning. Schools, courts, the military, and national parks would all close down. Consumer and environmental protection programs, crime prevention programs, highway repair, farm subsidies, and the space program would also disappear. Even if you consider some of these programs wasteful, you probably see others as essential. This chapter looks at how the federal government uses its power to tax, spend, and regulate the economy.

CHAPTER OUTLINE

1 The Government Raises Money Through Taxing and Borrowing

Federal Income Taxes
Other Tax Revenues
Government Borrowing

2 How Is Federal Spending Decided?

Federal Spending
Making the Federal Budget

3 The Federal Government Influences the Nation's Economy

Government and the Economy
Fiscal Policy
Monetary Policy

513

SECTION 1

The Government Raises Money Through Taxing and Borrowing
(pp. 514–520)

Section Objectives

☐ explain the basic mechanism of the personal income tax

☐ list the major sources of federal tax revenue

Vocabulary

revenue, income tax, direct tax, progressive tax, withholding, capital gains, deduction, exemption, social insurance, payroll tax, regressive tax, excise tax, estate tax, gift tax, customs duty, national debt

FOCUS

● To begin a discussion of government finances, particularly taxes and borrowing, ask students to list as many government services as they can. (*Examples:* interstate highways, national parks, veterans' hospitals.) Then have students give examples of ways in which the government helps ensure public welfare. (*Examples:* national defense, social security.)

Where does the government obtain money to pay for its programs? (From the people, through taxes.) Close by reading to students the famous comment by Benjamin Franklin, "In this world nothing is certain but death and taxes."

SECTION 1 — The Government Raises Money Through Taxing and Borrowing

ACCESS — **The Main Ideas**

1 How does the personal income tax work?
pages 514–518

2 What are the major sources of federal tax revenue?
pages 518–520

In 1961 President John F. Kennedy advised Americans, "Ask not what your country can do for you — ask what you can do for your country." Kennedy was speaking mainly of the voluntary services that citizens might provide. However, the chief way in which most individuals help the government is through paying taxes. Americans more often ask, therefore, what their country can do for them, and especially what services they are getting for their tax dollars. Most Americans agree that government should provide services to the public and ensure public welfare. To carry out the tasks expected of them, governments need money, or **revenue**. In 1992 the United States collected a record $1,165 billion (excluding borrowing) in revenue. This revenue came mostly from taxes: individual and corporate income taxes, social insurance taxes, excise taxes, and customs duties.

No one enjoys paying taxes, but as Justice Oliver Wendell Holmes, Jr., once said, "Taxes are what we pay for a civilized society."

Federal Income Taxes

The tax that people are most aware of is the individual **income tax**. As its name suggests, this is a tax on a person's yearly income. The individual income tax is the largest single source of federal revenue. (See Figure 19–1.)

Steps toward the income tax

The first federal income tax was imposed in 1861 to help finance the Civil War. This tax expired in 1872. Twenty-two years later, in 1894, Congress passed another income tax act, which placed a 2 percent tax on all personal income over $4,000.

Figure 19–1 FEDERAL GOVERNMENT FINANCES 7B

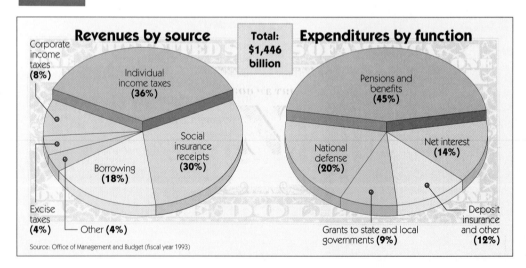

Revenues by source — Total: $1,446 billion — **Expenditures by function**

Corporate income taxes (8%)
Individual income taxes (36%)
Social insurance receipts (30%)
Borrowing (18%)
Excise taxes (4%)
Other (4%)

Pensions and benefits (45%)
Net interest (14%)
National defense (20%)
Grants to state and local governments (9%)
Deposit insurance and other (12%)

Source: Office of Management and Budget (fiscal year 1993)

514

Figure 19–1
● *About how many times as much revenue comes from individual income taxes as from corporate income taxes?* (About five times as much.)

This tax, however, was quickly declared unconstitutional by the Supreme Court. In *Pollock v. Farmers' Loan and Trust Co.* (1895), the Court ruled (5–4) that an income tax is a **direct tax**, a tax on individuals. The Constitution specifically prohibits direct taxes unless they are based on population (Article I, Section 9). This limitation was probably not intended to prohibit a tax on individuals' incomes. Rather, the writers of the Constitution were fearful that Congress, dominated by the larger states, might tax each state a certain amount without considering its population.

Nevertheless, to allow an individual income tax, it was necessary to pass the Sixteenth Amendment, adopted in 1913. Several months after the amendment had passed, Congress enacted another income tax. This tax, like the 1894 tax, was very modest. It was not until World War II that the income tax became a major source of federal revenue.

The federal income tax historically has been a **progressive tax**. A progressive tax is one that assigns higher tax rates to people with higher incomes. The idea of a progressive tax is that the wealthy, who can better afford it, should carry more of the "tax burden" than the poor. The reasoning is that, even after paying a higher percentage of their income in taxes, the wealthy will still have much more money left to spend.

During World War II, for example, tax rates started at 23 percent at lower levels of income and rose to a staggering 94 percent for the highest incomes. In the 1970's, tax rates ranged from 14 to 70 percent. A major tax reform in 1981 provided for fourteen tax "brackets," or income categories, ranging from 11 to 50 percent. People in the lowest bracket paid the 11 percent rate. Those in each higher bracket paid at a higher rate, up to the maximum.

Paying federal taxes

According to law, you must pay federal taxes on your earnings throughout the year. Most American workers pre-pay their taxes through **withholding** — employers automatically deduct taxes from each paycheck and send them to the Internal Revenue Service (IRS) in the Treasury Department. People whose taxes are not withheld must estimate their income and make payments to the federal government four times a

Americans' federal income tax returns are processed by computer operators in hundreds of IRS offices throughout the country.

year. Profits made from the selling of real estate, stocks, or other assets — which are called **capital gains** — must also be reported.

Each year, you must submit a tax form to the IRS, stating your earnings, other income, and taxes you have already paid. A tax form must be sent to the IRS on or before "Tax Day," April 15 of the following year. When computing your taxes, you may subtract certain **deductions** and **exemptions**. *Deductions* are expenses (such as medical expenses or interest payments) that you can subtract from your total income. An *exemption* is a fixed amount that individuals are allowed to subtract for themselves and their dependents.

Deductions and exemptions thus reduce your "taxable income," the amount on which you must pay taxes. Once you have calculated this amount, the tax form tells you how much you must pay. At this time, you may find that your employer has withheld more taxes than you owe. In this case, the IRS will send you a refund. On the other hand, you may discover that you

515

Background: *History*
Tariffs were the major source of government revenue until the early 1900's. In 1910, customs duties brought in close to 50 percent of all federal revenue; by the 1980's, customs duties brought in only 2 percent.

EXPLANATION
After students have read the section, you may want to consider the following activities:

Economics
● Have students translate the data in Figure 19–1 into two horizontal bar graphs, one for revenue and one for expenditures. When they have completed the bar graphs, ask students whether the circle graphs or the bar graphs present the material with greater impact.

History
● CRITICAL THINKING *Why was the maximum tax rate as high as 94 percent during the early 1940's?* (The government needed extra revenue to pay for the war effort.) *What specific costs does the government have during wartime?* (It must regularly buy new stocks of weapons and ammunition; it must pay soldiers and provide medical care for wounded soldiers and civilians; it must give emergency aid to allies.)

Values
▲ CRITICAL THINKING Ask students how they feel about tax evaders. *What arguments could you make in response to tax evaders?* (Not paying taxes will not reduce government waste; if the tax structure is unfair it should be modified, not ignored.)

The symbol 👥 denotes active participation strategies.

Activities are keyed for student abilities:
▲ = Basic
● = All Levels
■ = Average/Advanced

Economics

Discuss the tax laws enacted in 1986 and 1993 (pp. 516, 518). Remind students that tax reform was a response to criticism of the previous tax structure.

▲ **What were the criticisms of the previous tax structure?** (Loopholes enabled too many people to avoid paying taxes. Some people argued that taxes were discouraging investment. The tax form was complicated.)

▲ **How did the 1986 tax reform try to correct these problems?** (It closed some loopholes that had been exploited by wealthy persons. It also simplified the tax structure and permitted millions of low-income Americans not to pay taxes.)

● You might want students to research the effects of recent tax legislation and report their findings to the class.

Standing outside the White House in the bright sunlight of an October day, members of Congress watch President Reagan sign the historic 1986 tax reform bill into law.

owe additional taxes. You must then send the IRS a check for the amount you owe.

The IRS, at one of its ten regional centers, runs a computer check on each tax form, or "return," that it receives. Of the more than 172 million returns filed each year, the IRS audits, or double-checks, several million. To collect unpaid taxes, the IRS has the power to seize a person's bank accounts or property and impose fines or jail sentences.

Criticism and tax reform

Questions about deductions were one major criticism of the tax structure in the early 1980's. Critics pointed out that many wealthy people were able to take unfair advantage of deductions to avoid paying taxes. While millions of people at poverty levels were paying taxes of 11 percent or higher, several hundred millionaires paid no taxes at all.

Other critics maintained that the tax scheme made the economy less productive. Individuals and corporations with money to invest looked for the investments that would reduce their taxes the most. A new tax plan, it was argued, would encourage people to make more efficient investments, stimulate the economy, and create jobs. Other critics thought that the current tax form was simply too complicated.

The tax reform of 1986

One of the first public officials to push for tax reform was Democratic Senator Bill Bradley of New Jersey. Bradley, a former basketball star for the New York Knicks, became a serious critic of the existing tax plan when he learned that the team owners had deducted him as a "property" that was losing value because it was getting older.

President Ronald Reagan also strongly supported tax reform and in 1985 proposed a radically new tax plan. He suggested a modified flat-rate plan with just three brackets — 15, 25, and 35 percent. (In a flat-rate, or proportional, tax scheme, all income is taxed at the same percentage.) Reagan also proposed ending many deductions. After months of debate, Congress in 1986 passed a new tax bill.

The 1986 tax plan included only two brackets, 15 and 28 percent. About six million low-income families no longer had to pay income tax. Congress also closed "loopholes" in the tax code that had allowed many wealthy people and businesses to avoid paying any taxes. In addition, the 1986 law transferred $120 billion of the tax burden from individuals to corporations. The maximum corporate tax rate was lowered to 34 percent. By 1992 federal revenue from corporate taxes had fallen from ten percent in 1990 to seven percent.

Background: *Economics*
The IRS often prosecutes celebrities for tax evasion, partly because the accompanying publicity serves as a deterrent to others. The IRS has investigated boxer Joe Louis and former Vice President Spiro Agnew, among others.

Paying Income Taxes

7B, 8B

What do you think when you hear the word *taxes*? Many people have negative feelings about taxes, because taxes take away some of their money. Realistically, we must pay income taxes to support our government and its programs. Taxes reflect the democratic ideal that the people control the government. Nevertheless, workers often lose sight of this ideal when they see how much money is taken out of their paycheck each week or think of the complex tax forms they must fill out every year. You may never have earned enough to fill out an income tax return, but if you have held a job, taxes were probably withheld from your paycheck.

When you receive a paycheck, there is usually a form or a stub attached. This is a record of your earnings and of any taxes that your employer has held back. A typical paycheck stub tells you how much money has been withheld for federal income taxes and for any state or local taxes that apply where you live. Another category on your paycheck stub is FICA, which stands for Federal Insurance Contributions Act. The amount listed under FICA is your contribution to Social Security, which is basically a fund to support you when you retire.

At the end of the year, your employer will send you a W-2 form, which states exactly how much you earned for the year and how much was withheld for taxes. When you calculate how much you owe in taxes, you get to subtract the amount already withheld. Withholding, then, is really an advance payment of taxes. If more money has been withheld than you owe, you will receive a refund.

If you have already filed a tax return, the proper forms — probably Form 1040A or 1040EZ — will be sent to you by mail. If you do not receive these forms, you can get them at most post offices, many banks, or at a local office of the Internal Revenue Service (IRS). Look under United States Government in your telephone directory for your local Internal Revenue Service office or for a number to call for tax forms.

As you fill out your income tax return, remember that you are helping to pay for everything your government does. If you really want to have a say in how your tax money is spent, perhaps you will become actively involved in government.

Follow-up

1. Find a copy of the latest tax forms and read the instructions. Who must file a tax return? Do you have to?
2. Get several copies of an income tax form and an instruction booklet from a post office or the IRS, or arrange with your teacher to make copies. Make up income and withholding information for an imaginary person, then practice filling out as much of the form as you can. (Do *not* send it to the IRS!)

CITIZENSHIP SKILLS

Economics

A tax amnesty program has been instituted in a number of states. This program gives delinquent taxpayers the opportunity to repay the taxes they owe (plus interest) without fines or legal penalties. The program has generated large amounts of revenue that states otherwise might not have collected. A federal amnesty program has been considered by Congress to collect the estimated $100 billion in federal taxes that go unpaid each year.

● CRITICAL THINKING *Do you favor a federal amnesty program? Why or why not?* (Some students may argue that the federal government needs the money an amnesty would raise. Other students may argue that an amnesty would reward lawbreakers.)

● Assign students **Citizenship Worksheet 8**, which reviews basic information about income taxes.

517

Follow-up Answers

1. You might select students to read the instructions aloud and then have the class put the instructions in their own words.

2. Have students suggest why the IRS needs the various kinds of information requested in income tax forms.

The symbol ♋ denotes active participation strategies.

Activities are keyed for student abilities:
▲ = Basic
● = All Levels
■ = Average/Advanced

Economics

● **List three ways in which Social Security taxes differ from federal income taxes.** (They are matched by the employer; they are not collected on incomes above a certain figure; they do not go into the federal government's general operating budget.)

● **How are the funds raised from Social Security taxes used?** (They are paid out to retired or disabled workers or dependents of deceased workers.)

■ CRITICAL THINKING **How might the purpose of Social Security funds explain why they are collected only to a yearly maximum income?** (In theory, once a person has put a certain amount of money into the system, he or she has "paid for" his or her future Social Security benefits.)

Cooperative Learning

● Divide the class into small groups. Ask each group to describe situations that involve each of these taxes: income, excise, estate, gift, customs, and duties. (*Example:* Margaret has just received her first paycheck from the retail store where she works. On her check stub she reads, "Federal *income tax* withheld.") When the groups have come up with situations involving each of the taxes, have them share them with the entire class. Have class members decide if the appropriate tax was used in each situation.

518

The tax reform act of 1993

By 1993 the federal government faced a budget deficit of more than $4 trillion. To reduce the deficit, President Clinton proposed a plan that called for tax increases and spending cuts over a five-year period. The plan won congressional approval by the narrowest of margins. It passed in the Senate only after Vice President Al Gore voted to break a 50-50 tie.

The Clinton plan aimed at generating an additional $255 billion over a five-year period. Although the plan called for increased taxes on corporations, motor fuels, Medicare, and Social Security, the bulk of the revenue was to come from increased income taxes. The new law raised the tax rate for persons earning more than $115,000 and couples earning over $140,000 in taxable income to 36 percent. Supporters of the plan said that persons making that much money could afford to pay higher taxes. Critics said greater cuts should be made in federal spending.

7B

Other Tax Revenues

Social insurance taxes

The second largest, and fastest growing, source of federal revenue is **social insurance** payments. In 1992, social insurance taxes generated 30 percent of all federal revenue, up from just 16 percent in 1960. Social insurance includes a variety of programs, including health care, unemployment compensation, and pensions for the elderly, disabled, and workers' dependents. Social Security taxes typically are withheld from each worker's paycheck and matched by the employer. Thus, they are often termed **payroll taxes**.

The bulk of social insurance taxes are paid to the Social Security Administration, which oversees the Old Age, Survivors, and Disability Insurance program (OASDI). Money from Social Security also finances Medicare. (Each of these programs is discussed in detail in Chapter 23.)

Employers and employees pay Social Security taxes at the same percentage rate on wages up to a yearly maximum. This may appear to be a flat-rate tax but in fact is a **regressive tax** (the opposite of a progressive tax). That is, people with higher incomes pay taxes at a lower rate than people with middle or low incomes. Social insurance taxes are regressive because even high-income taxpayers pay Social Security tax on only the yearly maximum. They therefore are paying a lower percentage of their total income.

Unlike other federal taxes, Social Security contributions do not go into the federal government's general operating budget but into a special trust fund under the direction of the Treasury Department. When people retire, become disabled, or die, they or their dependents receive benefits from social insurance.

Excise taxes

Approximately 3 percent of federal revenues are generated by **excise taxes.** An excise tax is paid on specific activities, services, or goods that are produced, manufactured, sold, transported, or used within the United States. Because most excise taxes are included in the price of an item, they are sometimes called "hidden taxes."

The tax on gasoline brings in the largest federal excise tax revenue. Taxes on beer, wine, and distilled liquors are the second largest source. Many goods — such as firearms, ammunition, and gasoline — are taxed when they are sold by the manufacturer. Others are taxed at the time of sale, including airline tickets, tires, oil, and long-distance telephone service. Taxes on items such as diamond rings and sporting goods are frequently referred to as "luxury taxes."

The Constitution specifies, "Excises shall be uniform throughout the United States." This prevents the federal government from imposing different excise tax rates on the same items in different states. For example, Congress could not levy a gasoline tax of 10 cents per gallon in California and 15 cents per gallon in Florida.

Estate and gift taxes

An **estate tax**, also called an "estate duty," is a tax on the money or property of a person who has died. A person's estate might include houses, cars, furniture, jewelry, life insurance, stocks, bonds, savings, or pensions. Estate taxes were established in 1916 to keep money from being concentrated in the hands of a few wealthy families. They are progressive taxes: in 1989, for example, rates ranged from 39 percent for estates valued at $750,000 up to 55 percent for estates worth $3 million or more.

A **gift tax** is levied on the transfer of money or property between living persons. The federal

518

Critical Thinking

● **Despite claims that fraud and waste abound in social insurance programs, very few legislators call for cutbacks in these programs. Why is this the case?** (Doing so could prove very unpopular with constituents who receive payments from these programs.)

Background: *Economics*
Excise taxes are very convenient for the government and much of the public because (1) they are usually not applied to "essentials" and (2) they help discourage "undesirable" types of consumption.

gift tax was established in 1924, mainly to prevent persons from giving away their estates *before* they died and avoiding estate taxes. The federal gift tax is also progressive. A person can give away up to $10,000 per year tax-free. Thereafter, the rates range from 18 percent to a maximum of 55 percent on gifts over $3 million. Together, estate and gift taxes bring in only about 1 percent of federal revenues.

Taxes on imports

Taxes on goods imported into the United States are called **customs duties**. (They are also called tariffs, imposts, or import duties.) Today they make up about 1 or 2 percent of total federal revenue, but before Congress enacted the income tax in 1913, they were the federal government's largest source of revenue.

The primary purpose of customs duties is to protect American-made goods from lower-priced foreign competition. By taxing foreign goods and making them more expensive, the federal government encourages citizens to buy American goods. This is called a "protective" tariff.

Not all imports are subject to customs duties. Coffee, bananas, and Bibles, for example, are not taxed. Americans who travel abroad also may bring back personal items "duty-free," up to a certain value. Thousands of other foreign articles, however, are taxed in varying degrees. The President, by executive order, can raise or lower customs duty rates by as much as 50 percent. Among the most highly taxed imports are wool, wheat, and tobacco, for these are valuable American products. Tariffs on some kinds of imports — shoes, steel, automobiles, electronics — which also are important to American businesses, remain a hotly debated issue.

7B

Government Borrowing

Taxation is not the only source of federal revenue. In the recent past, a portion of the federal government's money came from borrowing. Governments, like individuals and businesses, need to borrow when government expenditures are greater than the revenue generated through

Like most goods sent to the United States from other countries, the cargo of this Japanese ship is subject to import taxes, or tariffs.

519

Check for Understanding
● *How do customs duties protect American companies?* (By making foreign goods more expensive and therefore less competitive.)

3. They reduce "taxable income" and allow the wealthy to pay less tax.

4. Two tax brackets—15 and 28 percent—were instituted, many low-income families were no longer taxed, "loopholes" were closed, and corporations were taxed more.

5. Employers use withholding to deduct taxes from workers' paychecks.

6. (a) They fund social insurance programs, including social security, unemployment compensation, and health care. **(b)** They prevent the concentration of money in a few wealthy families.

7. Foreign goods become more expensive and less attractive. This encourages the purchase of American goods.

8. It sells securities to private citizens, corporations, banks, and other institutions.

Critical thinking Supporters of progressive taxes believe that, as one's income increases, so should one's share of the tax burden. Supporters of regressive taxes believe that the people who benefit from federal programs should pay for them. Supporters of flat-rate taxes believe that taxing everyone at an equal percentage is the most equitable plan. Students should support their view as to which method is fairest.

CLOSURE

● Remind students of the pre-reading objectives at the beginning of the section. Pose one or all of these questions again. Then have students read Section 2, noting the roles played by the President and Congress in the budget-making process.

520

---

taxes. The Constitution (Article 1, Section 8) gives Congress the power to "borrow money on the credit of the United States." Only Congress, with the President's approval, can determine when to borrow, how much to borrow, and how much interest to pay. Congress, however, almost always consults with experts in the Treasury Department before borrowing.

The government borrows money by selling securities to private citizens, corporations, banks, or other institutions. Securities are pieces of paper that represent ownership or credit. Government securities include savings bonds, Treasury certificates, and Treasury notes ("T-notes"). The government promises to pay back these loans within a specified period and also to pay investors a certain amount of interest.

Government securities usually offer a lower rate of return than does investing in the private sector, such as buying and selling stocks. On the other hand, government securities are less risky than many other investments because they are backed by the "full faith and credit" of the United States government. Moreover, profits made from government securities are not subject to state taxes. *McCulloch v. Maryland* (p. 88) established the principle that states cannot tax the federal government.

The national debt

Unfortunately, government borrowing increases the **national debt**. The national, or "public," debt is the total sum of money owed by the federal government to investors. Historically, the greatest increases in our national debt have been due to wars and economic depressions. For instance, the federal government incurred debts of $23 billion during World War I and $200 billion to finance World War II. Over $100 billion was raised in World War II by selling "war bonds" to private citizens.

In recent years, the national debt has reached astronomical proportions. Between 1980 and 1985 the federal debt nearly doubled, from more than $900 billion to $1.8 trillion. The increase alone was larger than the combined debts of every presidential administration from George Washington through Gerald Ford. Expenditures on the Gulf War and the Savings and Loan industry have added to the national debt. In 1994 it was nearly $4.5 trillion. The interest paid

520

---

on the federal debt in 1994 exceeded the total federal budget for 1972.

It is difficult to comprehend just how much money this really is. In 1981, President Reagan offered this illustration to show the value of one trillion dollars: "If you had a stack of $1,000 bills in your hand only four inches high, you'd be a millionaire. A trillion dollars would be a stack of $1,000 bills 67 miles high." Or, as the magazine *U.S. News and World Report* put it, "Two trillion $1 bills placed end to end would stretch 186 million miles — from the earth to the sun and back." As we will see in the next section, such a massive national debt has a profound impact on federal spending and the overall management of the economy.

SECTION 1 **REVIEW**

Vocabulary and key terms

revenue (514)	social insurance (518)
income tax (514)	payroll tax (518)
direct tax (515)	regressive tax (518)
progressive tax (515)	excise tax (518)
withholding (515)	estate tax (518)
capital gains (515)	gift tax (518)
deduction (515)	customs duty (519)
exemption (515)	national debt (520)

For review

1. What are the main sources of federal government revenue? 7B
2. Why was the Sixteenth Amendment necessary? 7B
3. How do deductions make income taxes less progressive? 7D
4. What were the major provisions of the 1986 tax reform bill? 7B
5. How are most federal income taxes collected? 7B
6. What is the purpose of (a) social insurance taxes? (b) estate taxes? 7B
7. How do customs duties protect American businesses? 7C
8. How does the government borrow money? 7B

Critical thinking

ORGANIZING AN ARGUMENT What are the arguments for progressive, flat-rate, and regressive taxes? Which is the fairest way to distribute the tax "burden"? 8A

SECTION 2

6B, 7B, 8D, 8H

How Is Federal Spending Decided?

ACCESS

The Main Ideas

1 **Which are the largest categories of federal spending?** *pages 521–522*

2 **What steps are followed in making the federal budget?** *pages 523–525*

Unless you have either a lot of money or very few expenses, you need to be aware of how much money you spend. If you want to spend money for new clothes, you might have to cut back in other areas, such as movies, so as to have enough. Families, too, must decide whether to spend money on, say, more expensive food or an air conditioner, new furniture or a vacation. In other words, people routinely make decisions about spending priorities.

One way people can make these decisions in an organized way is by planning their incomes and expenses for a month or a year in advance. This plan is called a *budget*. Not all individuals take the time and effort to plan a budget (or to stick to it). The federal government, however, is required to do so under the Constitution. Each year the President submits a **federal budget** for the approval of Congress. The federal budget is as thick as a big-city telephone directory. It is a detailed estimate of federal expenditures and revenues for the year to come.

Figure 19–2 A DOLLAR OF GOVERNMENT SPENDING: 1791, 1876, 1993

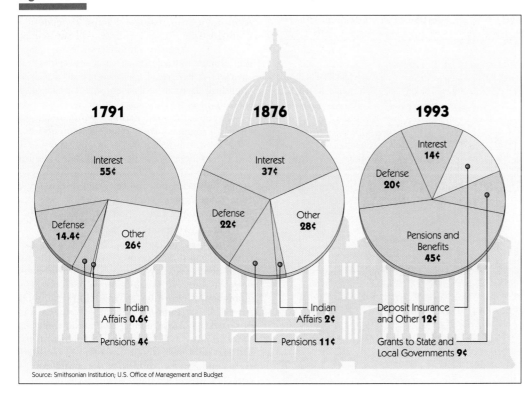

Source: Smithsonian Institution; U.S. Office of Management and Budget

521

Figure 19–2

● **If the federal government had spent a total of $1 billion in 1992, how much of that would it have spent on defense?** ($200 million.)

Interest? ($140 million.) **Pensions and benefits?** ($410 million.) **Grants to state and local governments?** ($120 million.)

Sidebar

SECTION 2

How Is Federal Spending Decided? *(pp. 521–526)*

Section Objectives

☐ list the largest categories of federal spending

☐ trace the steps followed in making the federal budget

Vocabulary

federal budget, entitlements, fiscal year

👥 FOCUS

● Write the following on the board: *A federal budget is necessary because . . . .* Have students come to the board and complete the statement. (Possible answers include: The Constitution requires it; the government does not have unlimited money; government agencies need to know how much they can spend; it forces the government to assign spending priorities.)

The symbol 👥 denotes active participation strategies.

Activities are keyed for student abilities:

▲ = Basic
● = All Levels
■ = Average/Advanced

EXPLANATION

After students have read the section, you may want to consider the following activities:

Economics

● CRITICAL THINKING Point out to students that many families and individuals also operate under a budget. *What might be some drawbacks to a budget?* (Unforeseen expenses often arise; individuals or agencies sometimes spend all the money allotted to them, even if such spending is wasteful.)

Politics

Discuss the division of labor between Congress and the President in the budget-making process, and have the class determine the steps in that process for which each branch of government is responsible.

● *How does the budget-making process exemplify the principle of separation of powers?* (One branch—the executive—proposes and signs the budget, while another branch—the legislative—reviews and approves it.)

Federal Spending

During the half-century between the presidencies of George Washington and William Henry Harrison, the federal government spent a total of nearly one billion dollars. While this is certainly an extraordinary sum of money, some more recent figures put it in perspective. In 1993 alone, the federal government spent over $1,400 billion — roughly $3.9 billion a day.

Current spending

The second graph in Figure 19-1 (on page 514) shows how the federal government spent $1,446 billion in 1993. The largest share, about $658 billion, went in direct payments to individuals, called **entitlements.** Entitlements are payments required by law for people who meet certain eligiblity requirements. For example, many people are "entitled" to Social Security,

Medicare, or Medicaid payments; veterans' benefits; or federal retirement pensions.

The next largest category of federal spending in 1993 was national defense, about $291 billion. This includes contracts for building tanks, ships, and airplanes; research on new weapons technology; and salaries for the armed forces. Interest payments on the national debt were the third largest federal expenditure. Next came grants to state and local governments.

Spending trends

Federal spending patterns are to a great extent a reflection of national policies. These changed significantly in the 1970's and 1980's. For example, direct payments to individuals (entitlements) increased dramatically during the 1970's and continue to rise. Between 1970 and 1980, entitlements rose from 28 to 42 percent of total federal spending. In 1993 entitlements accounted for 46 percent of the total (See Figure 19-3.)

Defense spending has also changed. From 1970 to 1980, following the end of U.S. involvement in Vietnam, national defense expenditures dropped from 42 to 23 percent of the federal budget. The Reagan administration increased the military budget after it took office in 1981. By 1987 it had reached 28 percent of federal spending. It dropped to about 20 percent in 1992 and has remained at that level.

At the same time, national policy regarding civilian programs (other than entitlements) was heading in a different direction. Between 1970 and 1980, federal spending in areas such as education, community development, anti-poverty programs, transportation, and scientific research rose from 22 to 26 percent of the budget. By 1993, that figure had dropped to 13 percent.

The growing national debt

The most dramatic increase in federal government spending, however, was due to the national debt. Like any borrower, the government must pay interest on all money it borrows. The more money it borrows, the more interest it must pay. The last time the federal government did *not* have to borrow to meet its expenditures was 1969. Thus, in 1970 interest payments on the national debt were about 7 percent of total federal spending. By 1992 they accounted for 14 percent and seemed likely to go on rising.

Figure 19–3 FEDERAL SPENDING Spending on entitlements consumes a large portion of the federal budget. 7B

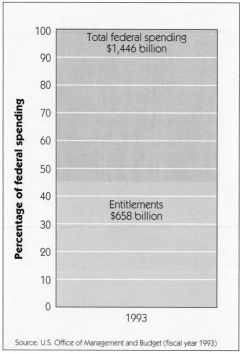

Total federal spending
$1,446 billion

Percentage of federal spending

Entitlements
$658 billion

1993

Source: U.S. Office of Management and Budget (fiscal year 1993)

522

Figure 19–3
● *What percentage of federal spending did entitlements comprise in 1993?* (46 percent.) *Do you think entitlements make up too high a percentage of federal spending? Explain your answer.*

(Some students may say the government should not be responsible for so many social programs. Others may note that entitlements are necessary to help needy citizens.)

Making the Federal Budget

The Constitution specifies that "no money shall be drawn from the Treasury, but in consequence of appropriations made by law." This means that Congress must pass an act to authorize any and all federal spending. Yet if Congress had to pass a bill every time the government needed to build a highway, conduct an investigation, or pay an employee, it would have time for nothing else. Instead, once a year Congress passes a set of appropriations bills, which authorize each government agency to spend a certain amount of money for the year. The federal budget is the combination of all these appropriations.

Federal budgets are calculated for a **fiscal year**. A fiscal year is any twelve-month period (not always a calendar year) during which a government or a business keeps accounts. The federal government's fiscal year runs from October 1 to September 30. Each fiscal year is named after the year in which it ends. Hence, "fiscal 1993" (or "FY 93"), is the twelve-month period ending September 30, 1993.

The federal budget is the government's most important statement on public policy — the actions it will take to solve social and economic problems. By giving some agencies and programs more funds than others, the government is setting the nation's policy priorities. Most obviously, perhaps, choices must be made between military spending and civilian programs — sometimes described as "guns or butter." If the administration wants to develop a new weapon or increase military salaries, it usually means cuts must be made in civilian programs. If the current policy is to increase scientific research, transportation, education, or grants to local governments, military spending must be cut.

The federal budget is also an important political document. It reflects a long and complex bargaining process involving Congress, the President, interest groups, political parties, and government employees. The entire budgetary process takes more than three years. As one year's budget is in operation, another is being planned, and a third is being reviewed.

The President and the budget

The responsibility for making the budget is shared by the President and Congress. It is the

YOU DECIDE 8H

In 1992, the Fish and Wildlife Service declared 6.9 million acres of Pacific Northwest forest off limits to logging because some of it is habitat for the spotted owl, an endangered species. The Bureau of Land Management (BLM) wants to harvest a tract of that land, maintaining that the timber industry is vital to the economy, providing thousands of jobs. The BLM has offered to relocate some of the owls.

Should the Fish and Wildlife Service change its policy?

President's job to prepare the budget, while Congress must check, alter, and pass the budget bill into law.

Many changes have taken place since President Washington jotted down the nation's first budget on a single piece of paper. For many years, the Secretary of Treasury was responsible for submitting a budget to Congress for approval. Increased federal spending during and after World War I, however, created a need for tighter control over the budget-making process. The Budget and Accounting Act of 1921 placed responsibility for preparing the budget squarely on the President. It created the Bureau of the Budget (BOB) in the Treasury Department to assist the President in coordinating all federal expenditures and required the President to submit an annual Budget Message to Congress each January. Finally, the act established the General Accounting Office (GAO), an independent agency under Congress, to audit federal expenditures.

In 1939 the BOB was transferred to the Executive Office of the President, giving the President even tighter control over the budget. In 1970 it was renamed the Office of Management and Budget (OMB). The director of the OMB (appointed by the President) and the OMB staff are charged with the day-to-day task of preparing the federal budget and overseeing government spending.

523

Economics
● CRITICAL THINKING Have students agree or disagree with the following statement and explain their position: *People can learn everything they need to know about a President's political philosophy just by looking at the federal budget.* Students may note that spending priorities do tell a great deal about a President's political philosophy. However, if Congress does not share the President's philosophy, the final budget will probably reflect a compromise between the two branches.

Cooperative Learning
● Divide the class into groups and have each group write the transcript of a debate dealing with the information presented in Figure 19–2. Each group should decide the specific topic of the debate—current spending priorities, the evolution of spending priorities, etc.

Background: *Cultural Literacy* The slogan "guns or butter" probably comes from a speech made in Berlin in 1936 by Nazi leader Goebbels: "We can do without butter, but, despite all our love of peace, not without arms. One cannot shoot with butter but with guns."

You Decide Answer
Students should defend their answers.

The symbol 👥 denotes active participation strategies.

Activities are keyed for student abilities:
▲ = Basic
● = All Levels
■ = Average/Advanced

524

GUIDED/INDEPENDENT PRACTICE

● Have students review the categories of government spending and select one. Then have students describe how they would be affected if Congress drastically cut the allocation of funds in this category.

RETEACHING/CORRECTIVES

▲ Have students make a chart listing the steps in the budget-making process.

Have students complete **Skills Practice Worksheet 19,** which reviews the budget-making process.

You may also want to use **Transparency 42,** a graph depicting national government outlays from 1940–1993, and **Transparencies 43–44,** which present political cartoons dealing with the deficit and defense spending.

Preparing the budget

Work on the budget begins at least a year and a half before the date it goes into effect. For example, preparation of the budget for fiscal 1996 (effective October 1, 1995) began in March 1994. The OMB begins the process by making preliminary budget recommendations to the President. The President considers the OMB proposal along with economic forecasts provided by the Council of Economic Advisers, the Secretary of the Treasury, and other Cabinet officials. The President's policy priorities are then returned to the OMB, where they are translated into budget guidelines and sent to all the government agencies.

The agencies have about three months to make their preliminary requests for funding to the OMB. They typically base their requests on past expenses, current appropriations, and estimated future needs. Agencies usually pad their requests, knowing that the President, the OMB, or Congress will almost certainly make cuts. The agency requests are scrutinized by the OMB, which compares them with previous requests, double-checks all calculations, and discusses changes with the agencies. The OMB next compiles the agency requests and provides the President with a revised budget estimate. Once again the President consults with economic advisers and makes changes.

The revised budget is returned to the agencies. Each agency is permitted a public hearing to defend its requests and protest any cuts. Interest groups and political party leaders also become involved, all seeking to expand or preserve their favorite programs.

Decision-making factors

Two main factors influence the way decisions are made about the federal budget. The first is that federal agencies, the OMB, and Congress almost always use the previous year's budget as the "base" for determining the next year's budget. From year to year, budgets change by small steps, or "increments." Budget-makers, therefore, do not have to reconsider the entire appropriation for every program or agency each year. They need argue only over the amount of increase or decrease for each department.

"Uncontrollable" expenditures are another important factor influencing budget decisions.

Uncontrollable expenditures are the results of past policies that commit present-day lawmakers to future spending. For example, about 60 million Americans receive payments from long-established entitlements. They include the elderly and retired; war veterans and their families; and the disabled, sick, and poor. Lawmakers clearly would become very unpopular with their constituents for cutting such programs. Nor can budget-makers reduce interest payments on the national debt, defense contracts, or non-defense contracts (highway construction, for example). All of these must be paid because the federal government is legally obligated to do so.

Altogether, well over half of the federal budget is made up of "uncontrollable" expenditures. Thus, the current President and Congress do not have complete freedom to control federal spending. Only in the portion of the budget that does not deal with existing obligations can they make their choices — primarily between military and civilian programs.

Presenting the budget

In December or January, the President and OMB director confer over the nearly completed budget. Last-minute adjustments are made, and the budget is whisked off to the printer. Altogether the printed document is over 1,000 pages long, roughly the size of the "yellow pages" directory for a major city.

Finally, by early February the President presents to Congress the *Budget of the United States Government* for the fiscal year beginning the following October 1. In it the President assesses the overall economy, makes recommendations for expenditures, and forecasts the budget's impact. The budget also contains an estimate of revenues, which is largely the work of the Treasury Department. Passing the federal budget is now up to the two houses of Congress.

The role of Congress

Congress debates spending after the President's proposed budget is delivered to it. The Budget Committees in both the House and the Senate study the President's proposals and obtain information from the Congressional Budget Office (CBO), which furnishes Congress with reports about the economy made independently of the OMB. Working together, the House and Senate committees propose a concurrent resolution

524

Critical Thinking
▲ *Why would a member of Congress find it easier to support cuts in the military budget than cuts in entitlements?* (Many constituents would be adversely affected by an entitlement cut. They would be less affected by a decrease in defense, unless their district housed a number of defense-related industries.)

Congressional budget-makers' decisions on spending for certain programs may be influenced by the actions of citizen interest groups. Here, members of the Gray Panthers protest suggested cuts in Social Security payments.

that sets targets for overall revenues and expenditures and serves as a guideline for the standing committees. This concurrent budget resolution must be approved before April 15.

After this has been done, the various congressional standing committees (page 360) hammer out taxing and spending bills. For example, the Armed Services Committees are responsible for defense spending; the Agriculture Committees investigate appropriations for the Department of Agriculture. Committees often hold public hearings, and interest groups are given ample opportunity to respond. Altogether there are thirteen separate appropriations bills, each covering broad categories of spending.

The appropriations bills are then combined into reconciliation bills, which make the actual changes in law and establish binding spending limits on the entire federal government. From that point on, no appropriations may exceed these limits. After each appropriation bill passes both houses of Congress and is signed by the President, the budget is completed. On October 1, the federal government may begin spending the money appropriated by Congress.

Often there are deep disagreements between the House and Senate, or between Congress and the President. On occasion they have not been able to agree on appropriations before the fiscal year begins. The risk of this happening is especially great when different parties control Congress and the White House.

Without an appropriation, the federal government, by law, may not spend any more money. For government employees, this means that they will not receive their paychecks until Congress and the President can agree on the budget. To avoid this problem, Congress usually passes a last-minute emergency spending bill, which allows the government to continue operations temporarily. In fact, on Friday, October 17, 1986, the federal government shut down because it had run out of money. Congress quickly passed appropriations bills, and government employees were back at work the following Monday.

Checking expenses

The final stage of the budget-making process is the audit, or review. Between the close of the fiscal year (September 30) and November 15, the General Accounting Office, under the direction of Congress, checks the books of all government agencies to determine whether their funds were spent in accordance with the law. This completes one budget cycle, with the next budget already well underway and a third being planned.

525

SECTION 3

The Federal Government Influences the Nation's Economy *(pp. 526–533)*

Section Objectives

☐ distinguish among Keynesian economics, supply-side economics, and fiscal conservatism

☐ compare and contrast the purposes of fiscal policy and monetary policy and describe the effects of each

Vocabulary

capitalism, free enterprise, inflation, depression, deficit spending, recession, fiscal policy, monetary policy, discount rate

---

4. Military and civilian programs.

5. Long-established entitlements, interest payments on the national debt, defense contracts, and non-defense contracts.

Critical thinking Students should defend their answers. Difficulties may include interest group pressure, constituent priorities, the "guns or butter" dilemma, and administration pressure.

CLOSURE

● Have students write three "I learned . . ." statements describing what they learned in class today. Then have students read Section 3, noting the difference between monetary policy and fiscal policy.

SECTION 2 REVIEW

Vocabulary and key terms

federal budget (521) "uncontrollable"
entitlements (522)   expenditures (524)
fiscal year (523)

For review

1. What were the federal government's three largest expenditures in 1992? **7B**
2. How do administration policies affect the making of the budget? **7C**
3. What is the role in the budget-making process of (a) the Office of Management and Budget? (b) government agencies? (c) Congress? **7B**
4. What are the two main areas of spending over which the government has the most control? **7B**
5. What are the federal government's main "uncontrollable" expenditures? **7B**

Critical thinking

FORMING AN OPINION Which of the government expenditures mentioned in this section do you think are most important? Give reasons for your answers. What difficulties might budget-makers encounter in making such decisions? **8D**

6G, 6H, 7A, 7B, 7C, 7E, 8A, 8G

SECTION 3

The Federal Government Influences the Nation's Economy

6G, 7A, 7E

ACCESS

The Main Ideas

1 What are the different ideas behind Keynesian economics, supply-side economics, and fiscal conservatism?
pages 526–530

2 What are the purposes of fiscal policy and monetary policy and how does each affect the economy?
pages 530–533

Imagine that you are President. The country is in economic trouble. Domestic industries are failing and unemployment is high. How can you address these problems? You meet with your economic advisers. One may remind you that you can use the power of government to aid industry. For example, in the late 1800's, the government gave railroads land on which to build. Another adviser may suggest that the government undertake construction projects that will employ people. Another advises lowering taxes on businesses to free up money for hiring.

The federal government can use a variety of means to regulate and influence the nation's economy. Tax policies and government expenditures can create jobs and stimulate industries. They can also have the opposite effect.

526

Government and the Economy

Americans expect a great deal of economic freedom. From the very beginning, our nation has operated under **capitalism**, or the **free enterprise** system. In a free enterprise system, factories, businesses, property, and money — capital — are owned and controlled by private individuals or corporations. People have the right to invest their money freely, to start their own businesses, and to change jobs without government interference.

The free market

Our nation's earliest economic policy was designed to encourage manufacturing and make the country prosperous. Most leaders believed in the ideas stated in the influential book *The Wealth of Nations*, published by Scottish economist Adam Smith in 1776. Smith contended that if the government stayed out of economic decisions, the "invisible hand" of free competition would improve the lot of everyone in society. This policy is known as *laissez faire* (LESS-ay FAIR). (*Laissez faire* is a French term that means "leave things alone.")

Check for Understanding
▲ *In what year did Adam Smith's* **Wealth of Nations** *appear?* (1776.) *What other important document appeared in that year?* (The Declaration of Independence.)

According to Smith, the workings of the market, where goods are bought and sold freely, should dictate the price and production of goods. When people's desire (*demand*) for a certain product outstrips the availability (*supply*) of that product, the price goes up. Seeing an opportunity to make a profit, new investors will begin to produce that product. Conversely, when the supply of a product exceeds the demand, the price for that product goes down. This process is known in economics as the "law of supply and demand."

Free enterprise is not free of economic problems. "Supply and demand" may not work perfectly. When the supply of some commodities is too large, or the demand too small, some workers must be laid off and some companies will fail. Prices for some goods may rise too rapidly, a situation called **inflation**, and consumers will not be able to afford them. Smith recognized that there would be periods of economic slump as well as prosperity. He believed these were a minor inconvenience compared with the advantages of a free market.

Government involvement

The government's economic policy began to change somewhat beginning in the late 1880's. Reacting to public outcry over the railroad monopolies, which were preventing free competition, Congress passed the Interstate Commerce Act in 1887. This was followed by the Sherman Antitrust Act of 1890 and other laws that sought to limit the unrestricted power of business monopolies. (Antitrust policies are discussed further in Chapter 21.) Some people objected to this kind of government interference in the economy, but public opinion in general approved of protecting people against the unfair and often corrupt practices of big business in that era.

Depression era policies

It was not until the Great Depression of the 1930's, however, that the government became intimately involved in the economy. In economic terms, a **depression** is a condition in which widespread unemployment, idle factories, business stagnation, farm foreclosures, bank failures, and other problems continue for a year or more. The Depression of the 1930's was the most serious economic crisis the United States had ever faced, with unemployment reaching nearly 25 percent in 1932.

To help get America out of the Great Depression, President Franklin D. Roosevelt embarked on a new economic policy — **deficit spending** Deficit spending means that the government's expenditures exceed its revenues. The theoretical

FOCUS

● Draw the diagram below on the board but do not label it. Ask students if any of them can identify the diagram. Explain that it represents the phases of the business cycle—an economy's fluctuation between growth and contraction. Then explain that through the fiscal and monetary policies discussed in the section, the federal government can influence the cycle.

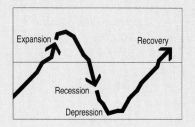

For many desperate people in 1930, even selling apples on the street seemed better than being unemployed. More than one-quarter of the nation's workers were jobless at one point during the Depression.

527

Background: *History* The federal government had run deficits prior to the 1930's, most notably during the Civil War and World War I.

The symbol 👥 denotes active participation strategies.

Activities are keyed for student abilities:
▲ = Basic
● = All Levels
■ = Average/Advanced

EXPLANATION

After students have read the section, you may want to consider the following activities:

Economics

Draw a basic supply-demand graph, such as the one below, on the board. Have students copy it on a sheet of paper.

● ⬚CRITICAL THINKING⬚ **Why does the supply increase when the price increases?** (The higher price encourages people to produce more.) **Why does the demand fall when the price increases?** (Fewer people can afford to buy the product.)

■ ⬚CRITICAL THINKING⬚ Explain that the point at which the supply and demand curves meet is called the *equilibrium price.* Have students explain why a higher or lower price would not produce equilibrium, or balance. (At a higher price, supply would exceed demand, and the price would drop. At a lower price, demand would exceed supply, and the price would rise.)

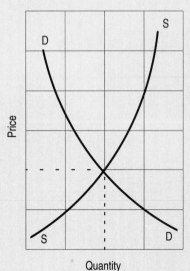

Film star Joan Crawford poses for photographers to publicize a World War II "bond drive," with the goal of raising $38 billion in defense bonds for the government's wartime spending needs.

cornerstone of deficit spending was laid by British economist John Maynard Keynes (pronounced KAINZ) in his *General Theory of Employment, Interest, and Money* (1936). Keynes argued that, in time of depression, the government should not worry about trying to balance its budget — spending only as much as it brings in. Rather, it should spend more money to help stimulate the economy. To finance deficit spending, according to Keynes, the government must borrow money.

Government spending did increase significantly during the late 1930's, but federal deficits remained fairly modest. It was not until World War II that deficit spending skyrocketed. Government spending from 1941 to 1945 was double that for all the years between 1789 and 1941 combined. With the rapid production of war goods, industries ran at full capacity, people found jobs, and the economy bounced back. To finance the massive war effort, the federal government borrowed nearly $200 billion from banks, businesses, and individuals.

Postwar changes

After the war ended in 1945, policy-makers began to worry about the transition to a peacetime economy. Many remembered the difficul-

ties America had experienced after World War I, when many workers lost their jobs as the nation switched from making war goods to peacetime goods. The fear of mass unemployment led to the passage of the Employment Act of 1946.

The Employment Act marked a milestone in federal economic policy. Its goal was cooperation between the federal government and business, labor, agriculture, and state and local governments to maintain "maximum employment, production, and purchasing power." The law required the President to present to Congress an annual Economic Report, outlining the nation's economic conditions and suggesting appropriate policies. This law also established the Council of Economic Advisers (page 424). The Employment Act symbolized a new attitude among the American people — that it is the federal government's responsibility to exert some control over the health and stability of the country's economy.

Although private ownership, economic freedom, and competition are still the driving forces of the American economy, Americans today also expect the federal government to prevent inflation, keep unemployment down, and protect against **recessions**. (A recession is a mild, short-term economic slump.)

528

Background: *Controversial Issues* Deficit spending is a controversial practice. A Yale professor named Donald G. Ogilvie believed that deficit spending "stimulated spending by allowing the federal government to avoid the pain of directly imposing the cost of new programs on the people through higher taxes."

Background: *Economics* The difference between a recession and a depression is merely one of severity.

7B, 7C

Fiscal Policy

One important tool the federal government uses to manage the economy is **fiscal policy.** Fiscal policy is a way of influencing the economy by deliberately changing levels of taxing and spending. Neither economists nor government officials, however, agree on *how* this should be done. Three important theories of fiscal policy have influenced the American economy in recent times: Keynesian economics, "supply-side" economics, and fiscal conservatism.

Keynesian economics

Keynesian (KAIN-zee-un) economic theory is named after John Maynard Keynes. According to Keynes, the best way to manage the economy is to influence the *demand* for goods and services. If consumers are not buying enough goods, so that production slows down and unemployment rises, Keynesians believe that the government should increase public expenditures. If consumers' demand increases too much and causes inflation, the government should take money out of the economy. This can be done by cutting federal spending or increasing taxes. Keynesians maintain that it is not necessary to balance the federal budget every year, as long as the economy is healthy.

Supply-side economics

Supply-side economics is a more recent theory, named by economist Herbert Stein in 1976. As the name implies, supply-siders believe that government policy should concentrate on increasing the *supply* of goods and services. To do so, they maintain that government should cut tax rates, giving individuals and businesses an incentive to work harder and earn more, without paying higher taxes. Money that would have gone for taxes can instead be invested in new businesses, creating new jobs. Moreover, according to this theory, increased economic activity in the long run will "trickle down" and raise the income of all individuals and businesses, generating more taxes and offsetting revenues lost by the original tax cut.

During the late 1970's, other economists began to advocate supply-side theory. Representative Jack Kemp and Senator Warren Roth (both Republicans) supported the idea and proposed

Hundreds of economic decisions are made each day on the busy trading floor of the Chicago Mercantile Exchange, where commodities are traded.

529

Economics

Have students review pp. 527–528 and then ask them the following questions:

▲ *How did the Great Depression affect government involvement in the economy?* (To fight the Great Depression, the federal government became intimately involved in the economy for the first time.)

▲ *How did United States entry into World War II affect the federal deficit?* (The deficit increased greatly.)

▲ *What was the aim of the Employment Act of 1946?* (To maintain maximum employment, production, and purchasing power.)

● *What was the long-term significance of the Employment Act of 1946?* (It showed that the American people looked to the federal government to exert some control over the national economy.)

Background: *Economics*
Many supply-siders support the theory of the "Laffer curve," named after economist Arthur Laffer. It advocates cutting federal income taxes to increase government revenues.

Background: *Economics*
Students should be aware that economics is an inexact science, in part because there are so many variables. Every theory depends a great deal on the peculiar circumstances of the time.

Two wryly defined economic absolutes are attributed to President Coolidge: "When a great many people are unable to find work, unemployment results"; and "Business will be better or worse."

The symbol 👥 denotes active participation strategies.

Activities are keyed for student abilities:
▲ = Basic
● = All Levels
■ = Average/Advanced

Economics

● Write *Fiscal Policy* at the top of the board and beneath it create three columns, each containing two terms. In the first column write *Keynesian economics* and *Supply-side economics*. In the second column write *supply* and *demand*. In the third column write *tax rates* and *government spending*. Have volunteers come to the board and use a term from each of the three columns to create a sentence. (*Keynesian economics* tries to influence the *demand* for goods through changes in *government spending*. *Supply-side economics* seeks to influence the *supply* of goods through changes in *tax rates*.)

Then have a volunteer come to the board and write a sentence explaining how fiscal conservatism differs from the two theories outlined above. (Fiscal conservatism argues that balancing the budget, rather than using fiscal policy to tinker with the economy, will produce a sound economy.)

Controversial Issues

● *According to Keynes, why should government spending be increased in times of economic trouble?* (This would make more money available to businesses and consumers to invest in the economy. As more money is invested, demand will increase, spurring economic growth.)

● *According to supply-side economists, how will tax cuts for the rich eventually benefit the poor?* (If the rich have more money, they will invest in business, thereby creating jobs.)

legislation for tax cuts. During the 1980 presidential campaign, Ronald Reagan endorsed the "supply-side" idea and the tax cuts.

Fiscal conservatism

The goal of fiscal conservatism is a balanced federal budget, that is, keeping government spending at the same level as tax revenues. Fiscal conservatives object to government's using fiscal policy to tinker with the economy. Rather, they argue that a balanced budget would assure private investors that the economy is sound. It would also stop government borrowing, which drains money from investments in business and industry. To balance the budget, of course, government must increase taxes, decrease federal spending, or both.

Congress and the balanced budget

The huge national debt and its interest costs brought many demands to balance the federal budget, including a proposed constitutional amendment. To head off such action, Congress in 1985 passed the Gramm-Rudman Act. Named after its sponsors, Republican senators Phil Gramm (Texas) and Warren Rudman (New Hampshire), this law called for an end to budget deficits by 1991. To reach that goal, the law sets strict timetables for yearly budget cuts. Moreover, it provided that if Congress and the President could not agree on how to cut the deficit, automatic cuts would be imposed.

The first deadline under Gramm-Rudman was an $11.7 billion reduction by March 1, 1986. When the President and Congress could not agree what to cut, the automatic reductions took effect: 4.3 percent for all domestic programs and 4.9 percent for all military spending. Some programs, such as Social Security and interest payments on the national debt, were exempt.

Twelve members of Congress challenged the Gramm-Rudman Act in court, contending that Congress could not turn over its constitutional responsibility for spending decisions to non-elected federal agencies. In *Bowsher v. Synar* (1986), the Supreme Court overturned the law on the grounds that it violated separation of powers by having a legislative official advise the President on budget cuts.

In 1987 the Gramm-Rudman Act was rewritten. The budget deficit target for 1989 was

raised, and the deadline for balancing the budget was put off to 1993. But the deficit continued to increase.

By 1993 both the President and Congress recognized that action had to be taken to deal with the deficit. After much debate and compromise, Congress passed President Clinton's deficit-reduction plan (page 518). Under this plan, the government will generate an additional $255 billion over the period 1993–1998 by raising a variety of taxes. The plan also calls for cuts in government spending over the same period.

The success of the plan hinged on several assumptions: growth of the national economy (to generate increased tax revenues), no spending increases for unforeseen emergencies, and Congress's willingness actually to cut federal spending in the future.

7B, 7C

Monetary Policy

Taxing and spending policies — fiscal policy — are familiar parts of government policy. People in general are less aware of **monetary policy**, the government's second tool for managing the economy. This policy affects the amount of money in circulation and people's ability to borrow money. As noted earlier, Article I, Section 8 gives Congress the exclusive power "to coin money [and] regulate the value thereof."

A primitive form of monetary policy was simply for the government to print more money. Putting more money in circulation, it was believed, would stimulate the economy. Even when it did, the true effect of printing money was to cause inflation and make the dollar worth less. Recognizing the need for a more sophisticated monetary policy, Congress in 1913 created the Federal Reserve System.

The "Fed"

The Federal Reserve System, or the "Fed," as it is usually called, comprises twelve Federal Reserve Banks in major cities across the United States, as shown in Figure 19–4. The Federal Reserve Banks are really the "bankers' bank." Just as people borrow from banks, banks borrow from the Federal Reserve Banks. All federally chartered banks are required to join the system. State banks may also join if they meet certain require-

530

Background: *Law* The case of *Bowsher v. Synar* (1986) revolved around a 1921 law that gave Congress the power to remove the Comptroller General. The Supreme Court found that this statute violated the separation of powers. Chief Justice Warren Burger wrote, "To permit an officer controlled by Congress to execute the law would be, in essence, to permit a congressional veto."

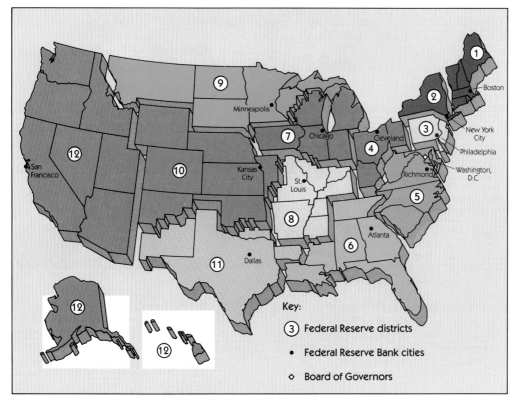

Figure 19–4 **THE FEDERAL RESERVE SYSTEM** Federal Reserve Banks in each of twelve regional districts make loans to member banks. **7C**

Key:
③ Federal Reserve districts
• Federal Reserve Bank cities
◇ Board of Governors

Cultural Literacy
Direct students' attention to the heading "Monetary policy options" (this page) and the text following it. Have students read the first sentence silently.

▲ *What clue words in that sentence indicate the kind of information that will appear in the next few paragraphs?* (The words *four basic ways.*) Have students skim the rest of the material following this heading to identify the four basic ways of creating monetary policy. (Buying and selling government securities, regulating the discount rate, altering the reserve requirement, and altering the margin requirement.) Point out that noticing such clue words prepares them for what is coming by suggesting how the following material is organized. This can help them better understand what they are reading.

ⅱ **Cooperative Learning**
● Have students work in teams to prepare oral reports (including graphic aids) to explain one of these important economic concepts: supply and demand; inflation, depression, and recession; Keynesian economics; supply-side economics; the Federal Reserve System. Assign a different topic to each team. Have teams present their reports to the class.

ments. Roughly 6,500 of the nation's 14,000 banks belong to the Federal Reserve System. Member banks hold over 90 percent of the nation's bank deposits.

The Fed is managed by a Board of Governors, whose members are appointed by the President with Senate confirmation. They serve for fourteen years, with one seat becoming vacant every two years. One board member is appointed by the President to act as chairperson for four years. Although board members are appointed, they are independent of both the President and Congress.

The Federal Reserve Board of Governors convenes in Washington, D.C., at least four times yearly to analyze the economy and to set monetary policy. The seven board members, plus five of the twelve Federal Reserve Bank presidents, also meet as the Open Market Committee. This committee supervises the buying and selling of government securities.

Monetary policy options
The Fed has four basic ways to create monetary policy. First, it can buy and sell government securities — such as U.S. savings bonds and Treasury notes — on the open market. When the Fed *sells* government securities, it takes money out of circulation. That is, investors are putting their money into the government rather than into private enterprise. Less money is in circulation, so that private borrowing becomes more difficult and economic activity slows down. Conversely,

Figure 19–4
▲ *In which regional district does your area belong? Which district contains the fewest states?* (Region 2 contains only New York State.)

Background: *History* The Fed chairperson tends to dominate both the institution and the course of the national economy. Paul Volcker, chairperson from 1979 to 1987, was often called "the second most powerful man in the United States."

The symbol ⅱ denotes active participation strategies.

Activities are keyed for student abilities:
▲ = Basic
● = All Levels
■ = Average/Advanced

Democratic presidential candidate Bill Clinton holds up a copy of his book *Putting People First* while speaking at a campaign rally in Michigan. The book outlined his plans for the economy, one of the most important issues of the 1992 campaign.

when the Fed *buys* government securities — that is, when it gives people cash in return for their bonds and notes — it injects money into the economy. More money in circulation makes it easier for people to borrow and invest.

Second, the Fed can regulate the **discount rate**. When member banks borrow money from Federal Reserve Banks, they are charged interest. The rate of interest they are charged is called the discount rate. By raising or lowering the discount rate, the Fed can affect the amount of money in circulation. High discount rates mean that member banks will borrow less money from the Federal Reserve Banks. They will have less money to lend their customers and will charge higher interest rates. Low discount rates, on the other hand, encourage member banks to borrow money from the Fed. With more money available in the banks, it is easier and less costly for their customers to borrow.

Third, the Fed can alter the *reserve requirement.* Member banks lend out most of the money that their customers deposit in them. The Fed, however, requires member banks to keep a certain amount of money (reserves) in Federal Reserve Banks to back up their customers' deposits. The percentage ratio of reserves to loans is the reserve requirement.

If the Fed *raises* the reserve requirement, member banks have less money to lend. If the Fed *lowers* the reserve requirement, banks have more money to lend. To illustrate, if the reserve requirement is 20 percent, a bank can loan out $80 for every $100 deposited. If the reserve requirement is reduced to 10 percent, then the bank can loan out $90 for every $100 it has on deposit.

Finally, the Fed sets *margin requirements* for people buying stock on credit. The margin requirement is the percentage of money people can legally borrow to buy stock. Raising the margin requirement makes it more difficult for people to buy stock. Thus, less money circulates in the economy. Lowering the margin requirement produces the opposite effect. It makes it easier for people to buy stock and so pumps money into the economy.

"Tight money" versus "easy money"

The Fed can use its four monetary tools to help fight inflation and recession. During periods of inflation, the Fed typically wants to "cool down" the economy and discourage spending. It does so by *selling* government securities, *raising* the discount rate, and raising both the reserve requirements and the margin requirements. These

532

actions take money out of circulation and create a "tight money" policy.

In recessions, on the other hand, the Fed usually seeks to stimulate the economy with more money. Hence, it *buys* government securities, *lowers* the discount rate, and lowers requirements for reserves and margin. This is referred to as an "easy money" or "loose money" policy.

Economists are far from agreement over whether it is possible, or even desirable, to "fine-tune" the economy using tight money and easy money policies. Others argue about whether fiscal or monetary policy is the most effective way to influence the economy, or whether government should try to influence the economy at all. The debate is likely to continue.

SECTION 3 REVIEW

Vocabulary and key terms

capitalism (526)	fiscal policy (529)
free enterprise (526)	monetary policy (530)
laissez faire (526)	Federal Reserve System (530)
inflation (527)	discount rate (532)
depression (527)	tight money (533)
deficit spending (527)	easy money (533)
recession (528)	

For review

1. What is the basic principle behind *laissez-faire* economic policy? **6G**
2. How has the role of government in the U.S. economy changed over the years? **7C**
3. What should be the use of fiscal policy according to (a) Keynesian economics? (b) supply-side economics? **8G**
4. Why was the Gramm-Rudman Act ruled unconstitutional? **6H**
5. What four actions can the Fed take in making monetary policy? **7C**

Critical thinking

EXAMINING BASIC PRINCIPLES   How does the use of fiscal and monetary policy conflict with the principles of free enterprise? Under what circumstances should the government interfere in the economy? **8A**

Chapter Summary

The federal government raises revenue by taxing and borrowing. Individual income taxes are the largest single source of federal revenue. Criticism that many deductions made the income tax less progressive led to major tax reform in 1986. Most people pay their taxes through withholding from their paychecks. Income tax on corporate profits is another source of tax revenue. Other taxes include social insurance taxes, excise taxes, estate and gift taxes, and customs duties. Government raises additional revenues from borrowing, by selling securities to individuals and businesses. Increased borrowing has led to a massive national debt.

The federal budget details the government's income and expenditures. The largest government expenditures go for entitlements, which are direct payments of benefits to individuals. Defense spending and interest on the national debt are the next largest categories of spending. The budget for each fiscal year is prepared by the Office of Management and Budget, with the President's approval. Congress must then approve the budget in a series of appropriations bills. Agency budgets are based on the previous year's budget plus or minus small changes. "Uncontrollable" expenditures force Congress and the President to make choices between military spending and civilian programs.

The United States economy is capitalism, or a free enterprise system. The federal government, which once generally followed a laissez-faire policy, now plays a vital role in keeping the economy healthy and stable. Manipulating levels of taxing and spending, called fiscal policy, is one way of exerting an influence on the economy. Experts disagree about whether the government should try to stimulate supply or demand; fiscal conservatives argue that the most important thing is to maintain a balanced budget. The Federal Reserve System regulates the economy through the use of monetary policy, which affects the amount of money in circulation.

3. **(a)** It should influence the *demand* for goods and services. **(b)** It should increase the *supply* of goods and services.
4. It violated separation of powers by having a legislative official advise the President on what cuts to make.
5. The Fed can buy and sell government securities on the open market, regulate the discount rate, alter the reserve requirement, and alter the margin requirement.

Critical thinking Students should understand that fiscal and monetary policy attempt to manage the economy and that free enterprise ideally keeps government out of the economy. Students then should consider what kinds of situations (depressions, recessions, war) call for government intervention.

CLOSURE

● Remind students of the pre-reading objectives at the beginning of the section. Pose one or all of these questions again. Then have students read the next assigned lesson.

CHAPTER 19 CORRECTIVES

● To review the content of Chapter 19, you may want to have students complete **Study Guide/Review 19** or **Workbook Chapter 19.**

The symbol ⅱ denotes active participation strategies.

Activities are keyed for student abilities:
▲ = Basic
● = All Levels
■ = Average/Advanced

CHAPTER 19 REVIEW

Answers

Vocabulary See pp. T19–T21 for suggested vocabulary activities.

Reviewing the Facts

1. *Revenue:* income taxes, social insurance taxes and contributions, excise taxes, estate and gift taxes, customs duties, borrowing. *Expenditures:* entitlements, national defense, interest payments on the national debt, grants to state and local governments.
2. A progressive tax.
3. The legislative branch.
4. Fiscal policy and monetary policy.
5. If national policies favor programs in one area over those in another, government spending will increase for the first area and decrease for the second.
6. They promoted deficit spending to stimulate the economy and suggested that a balanced budget was not necessary.
7. To fight inflation it sells government securities and raises the discount rate, reserve requirement, and margin requirement. These moves take money out of circulation and cool down the economy. To fight a recession, it stimulates the economy by buying securities and lowering the discount rate, reserve requirement, and margin requirement.

Thinking Critically About Key Concepts

1. Students favoring regulation may argue that it helps ensure fairness in business practices. Students opposed may suggest that it hinders economic growth.
2. Students may note that since each year's budget request is based on the previous year's, which was padded, the agency would "lose ground" if it stopped padding requests. Tighter auditing procedures might help eliminate padding.

534

● **Review the definitions of the following terms:**

capital gains	exemption	payroll tax
capitalism	federal budget	progressive tax
customs duty	Federal Reserve System	recession
deduction	fiscal policy	regressive tax
deficit spending	fiscal year	revenue
depression	free enterprise	social insurance
direct tax	gift tax	tight money
discount rate	income tax	"uncontrollable"
easy money	inflation	expenditures
entitlements	*laissez faire*	withholding
estate tax	monetary policy	
excise tax	national debt	

● **REVIEWING THE FACTS**

1. Name two sources of revenue and two areas of expenditure for the federal government. **7B**
2. Which would a lower-income worker likely favor, a regressive tax or a progressive tax? **8H**
3. Which branch of government has the constitutional authority to borrow money? **3A**
4. What are the two main tools that the government uses to regulate the economy? **7C**
5. How do trends in government spending reflect national policies? **7B**
6. How did Keynesian theories influence the economy during the Depression? **7E**
7. How does the Fed use tight-money policies to fight inflation and easy-money policies to fight recession? **7C**

▲ **THINKING CRITICALLY ABOUT KEY CONCEPTS**

1. Do you believe that government should attempt to regulate the nation's economy? If so, in what ways and with what goals in mind? If not, why not? **7C**
2. The author suggests that agencies pad their budget requests, asking for more money than they really need because they know

534

their requests will be cut. Do you think that all agencies should be required to make accurate requests? Why? How could the government enforce such a rule? **8H**

▲ **PRACTICING SKILLS**

1. **Study Skills: Reading a circle graph.** Refer to Figure 19–1 (page 514) to answer the following questions. (a) From which two sources does the government raise most of its revenue? (b) Which two areas each comprises more than 15 percent of expenditures? (c) From which source does the government gain more revenue, corporate income taxes or borrowing? (d) Which three functions comprise the smallest government expenditures? (To review graph skills, see Study Skill 3 in the back of the book.) **8B**
2. **Critical Thinking Skills: Predicting consequences.** Review the subsection "Paying federal taxes" (pages 515–516). Consider the following situation: Last year you had no medical bills and paid no interest on any debts. You filed your tax return and received a small refund from the Internal Revenue Service. This year you are working at the same salary, but you had some very large

---

Practicing Skills

1. **(a)** Social insurance receipts and individual income taxes. **(b)** National defense and entitlements. **(c)** Borrowing. **(d)** Deposit insurance, grants to state

and local governments, and other federal operations.
2. Students should expect to receive a larger refund because medical and interest payments can be deducted from income, thus lowering

the amount of taxable income.

medical bills, most of which your insurance did not cover. You also paid interest on a loan you took out for your new house. When you file your tax return for this year, would you expect to pay additional taxes or receive a refund? Why? **8H**

PARTICIPATORY CITIZENSHIP

1. **Debate.** Debate with your classmates the merits and the drawbacks of Keynesian economics, supply-side economics, and fiscal conservatism. Discuss the effects of each of these fiscal policies on the economy. **7C**
2. **Awareness of issues.** Through newspaper articles or other media sources, find out about a budgetary debate currently going on in Congress. What are the programs being debated? What are the differences between the various sides in the debate? Where does the President stand on the issue? Present your analysis to the class. **8A**

WRITING ABOUT ISSUES

1. **Writing an editorial.** Gather information about a regressive tax, such as a tax on gasoline or cigarettes, or a general sales tax, and write an editorial expressing your opinion about it. Explain why you think such a tax is fair or unfair. **8C**
2. **Reporting an interview.** Interview a local business person about the effects of recent tax reform on his or her business. Write a report of the results of your interview. **8C**

ANALYZING A POLITICAL CARTOON

Government spending is always controversial. Some people argue that a nation's problems can be fixed by increased government spending. Others feel that such spending only results in higher taxes. Look at the cartoon below and answer the following questions.

1. What problem affects the patient? Who is the patient? **8B**
2. Whom does the doctor represent? **8B**
3. What solution does the doctor suggest? **8B**
4. What is the cartoonist's opinion about the government's usual solution to problems? Do you agree? Explain. **8A, 8D**

© Michael Ramirez. Courtesy, Copley News Service, San Diego.

535

Analyzing a Political Cartoon
1. Congressional spending, in the form of an octopus, is attacking the patient. The patient is the average American citizen or the whole nation.
2. The doctor represents a government official.
3. The solution is to remove the patient's wallet—that is, take money from, or tax, the patient.
4. The cartoonist's opinion is that the government's solution to problems is to raise taxes, whereas a more obvious solution would be to cut government spending. Students should explain why they agree or disagree with the cartoonist.

Participatory Citizenship
1. Students should consult the library to gather information to support their arguments.
2. Students should consult newspapers and news magazines to gather information.

Writing About Issues
1. Before forming their arguments, students may want to visit local businesses to see how regressive taxes affect them.
2. After the reports have been made, you might have students compare and contrast the effects of tax reform on a variety of businesses.

Chapter Review exercises are keyed for student abilities:
▲ = Basic
● = All Levels
■ = Average/Advanced

	Section Objectives	**Section Resources**
Section 1 **U.S. Foreign Policy Meets Several Goals**	☐ explain the four main goals of U.S. foreign policy ☐ describe and explain the major trends and changes in U.S. foreign policy	▲ SKILLS PRACTICE WORKSHEET **20** ■ PRIMARY SOURCE WORKSHEETS **21–25** ▲ TRANSPARENCIES **47–48**
Section 2 **The Executive Branch Guides Foreign Policy**	☐ describe the roles of the Central Intelligence Agency and the National Security Council ☐ explain how the Departments of State and Defense help create and carry out foreign policy	■ SKILLS CHALLENGE WORKSHEET **20**
Section 3 **The United States Maintains Many Foreign Policy Options**	☐ describe the ways the United States seeks to influence other nations ☐ explain the issues raised by the emphasis on nuclear weapons for defense	
Section 4 **The United States Is a UN Member**	☐ describe how votes are allotted in the UN General Assembly ☐ explain the functions of the Security Council and other major branches of the UN	

Essential Elements

The list below shows Essential Elements relevant to this chapter. (The complete list of Essential Elements appears in the introductory pages of this Teacher's Edition.)

Section 1: 1C, 1D, 6F, 6G, 8A, 8F, 8G

Section 2: 3A, 3B, 8A, 8G, 8H

Section 3: 1D, 6G, 7D, 8A, 8C

Section 4: 1A, 1C, 1D, 3A, 6B, 8C, 8F

Chapter Review: 1D, 3A, 4D, 5C, 8A, 8B, 8C

Section Resources are keyed for student abilities:
▲ = Basic
● = All Levels
■ = Average/Advanced

Homework Options

Each section contains activities labeled "Guided/Independent Practice," "Reteaching/Correctives," and "Enrichment/Extension." You may wish to choose from among these activities when assigning homework.

Students Acquiring English Activities

Assign seven pairs of students to pretend to be veterans of the following wars: Mexican War, Spanish-American War, World War I, World War II, Korean War, Vietnam War, or Persian Gulf War. Have the rest of the class ask them questions about the conflict, for example, its duration, difficulties and outcome. For added depth, have one student in the pair represent the United States and the other student represent the opposition.

LISTENING/SPEAKING: Ask students how the map on p. 542 would be redrawn if it were to reflect the world today.

Case Studies

When teaching this chapter, you may use Case Study 8, which examines the issue of women serving in combat positions. (Case Studies may be found following p. 510.)

Teacher Bibliography

Hunt, Michael H. *Ideology and U.S. Foreign Policy.* Yale University Press, 1987. Studies the course of American diplomacy from its inception to the present.

Kissinger, Henry. *Years of Upheaval.* Little, Brown, 1982. The memoirs of the former Secretary of State, including his views on Vietnam and the Middle East.

Rubin, Barry. *Secrets of State: The State Department and the Struggle over U.S. Foreign Policy.* Oxford University Press, 1987. Describes the clash of different branches and departments of government in the making of foreign policy.

Student Bibliography

Barnet, Richard J. *The Giants: Russia and America.* Simon & Schuster, 1977. Surveys relations between the two superpowers from 1945 to 1976.

Franck, Thomas M. *Nation Against Nation: What Happened to the U.N. Dream and What the U.S. Can Do About It.* Oxford University Press, 1985. Discusses the strengths and the flaws of the United Nations and details the roles the United States has played in relation to this institution.

Turner, Stansfield. *Secrecy and Democracy: The CIA in Transition.* Harper & Row, 1986. An insider's overview of the recent history of U.S. intelligence work.

Literature

Lederer, William J. and Eugene Burdick. *The Ugly American.* Norton, 1958. Stories of Americans in Southeast Asia, some of whom understand the culture and customs of the people and others who are insensitive and patronizing.

Michener, James. *Legacy.* Random House, 1987. An army officer involved in aiding the Nicaraguan *contras* is called before a Senate investigation committee. This novel examines the influence of the Constitution on the country and its citizens.

Wibberley, Leonard. *The Mouse That Roared.* Bantam, 1971. A tiny country declares war on the United States so that when it is defeated it can receive foreign aid.

CHAPTER RESOURCES

Study Guide/Review 20
Workbook Chapter 20
Chapter 20 Test, Forms A–C

Films and Videotapes*

Anatomy of an Embargo. (Series title: *Enterprise.*) 29 min. MTI (Coronet), 1986. v. An examination of economic sanctions that also examines the ramifications of the 1985 U.S. embargo on banana imports from Nicaragua. Narrated by Eric Severeid.

Security Council. 18 min. FRI, 1982. f, v. Outlines the role, functions, composition, and activities of the U.N. Security Council.

Software*

American Foreign Policy (Apple). Focus. Covers the development of America's foreign policy from colonial times to the 1980's. The four programs include: The Emerging Nation Period; From Isolationism to Imperialism; From World War to Cold War; and Super Powers in the Nuclear Age.

Foreign Policy (Apple, IBM, Macintosh). TS. A king of a strategically important nation needs help in suppressing a popular uprising. Students, guided by examples of U.S. foreign policy, must confront the kinds of international relation dilemmas our country has struggled with throughout its history.

---

* For a complete guide to audiovisual sources, see page T22.

Chapter 20 outlines the history of
United States foreign policy,
discusses the role of the executive branch in foreign policy, and
explores the purpose, structure,
and operation of the United
Nations.

Chapter Objectives

After students complete this
chapter, they will be able to:

1. Explain the four main goals
of U.S. foreign policy.

2. Describe and explain the
major trends and changes in U.S.
foreign policy.

3. Describe the roles of the
Central Intelligence Agency and
the National Security Council.

4. Explain how the Departments of State and Defense help
create and carry out foreign
policy.

5. Describe the ways the United
States seeks to influence other
nations.

6. Explain the issues raised by
the emphasis on nuclear weapons for defense.

7. Describe how votes are
allotted in the UN General
Assembly.

8. Explain the functions of the
Security Council and other major
branches of the UN.

CHAPTER

20

FOREIGN POLICY and NATIONAL DEFENSE

We yet realize that America's leadership and prestige depend, not
merely upon our unmatched material progress, riches, and military
strength, but on how we use our
power in the interests of world
peace and human betterment.

Dwight D. Eisenhower
Farewell Address (January 17, 1961)

Photo
Nelson Mandela and President
Clinton at an appearance in
Philadelphia in 1993.

We live in an interdependent world. Events in foreign countries can have profound effects in the United States. War in the Middle East disrupts our vital supply of oil. Terrorism in Western Europe affects American investment and travel abroad. A change in the value of foreign currency, such as the Japanese yen or German mark, alters the value of the American dollar. The deployment of nuclear weapons anywhere affects our national security. Similarly, events in the United States have far-reaching effects in other parts of the world.

American foreign policy — the actions we take in international affairs — is of great importance not only to Americans but to other nations as well. Foreign policy involves a wide range of activities, including diplomacy, trade, participation in international organizations, cultural exchanges, and military action. As President Eisenhower, quoted on the opposite page, suggested, America's foreign-policy makers must determine what policies will best accomplish "world peace and human betterment."

Chapter 20 examines the goals, issues, and achievements of American foreign policy, as well as the individuals who make this policy.

CHAPTER OUTLINE

537

CHAPTER SUPPORT MATERIAL

Skills Practice Worksheet 20

Skills Challenge Worksheet 20

Transparencies 47–48

Primary Source Worksheets 21–25

Study Guide/Review 20

Workbook Chapter 20

Chapter 20 Test, Forms A-C

U.S. Foreign Policy Meets Several Goals

ACCESS

The Main Ideas

1 What have been four main goals of U.S. foreign policy? *pages 538–539*

2 What have been some of the major trends and changes in U.S. foreign policy? *pages 539–544*

How much money should the United States spend for national defense? Should we build more nuclear weapons, or should we negotiate to eliminate them? How can the United States keep a favorable balance of trade and ensure the supply of important resources from abroad? Should we continue to give aid to developing nations? Which ones? Should the government continue to support a political ally in spite of that country's record of human rights violations? These are the kinds of decisions that the President, members of Congress, and their advisers must make in planning and carrying out foreign policy.

1C, 1D, 6F, 6G

Foreign Policy Goals

Throughout history, the United States has sought certain goals in its dealings with foreign nations. These goals influence the direction that the nation's leaders take in making foreign policy decisions.

Protecting the country

The overriding goal of American foreign policy, or any nation's foreign policy, is national security. National security clearly means defending ourselves against foreign invasion. It also means creating an international climate in which the United States can freely carry on its business and govern itself without threats from the outside. National security therefore involves not only maintaining military forces for national defense, but also negotiating with other countries to make the world less dangerous.

Carrying out foreign trade

Since the early days of the Republic, the United States has sought to trade with countries around the globe. Foreign trade provides the United States with many indispensable resources, such as oil, raw materials, and precious metals. Likewise, American business depends heavily on foreign markets. Many countries buy weapons, technology, manufactured goods, and food from the United States. Therefore, an important goal of American foreign policy has been to maintain favorable trade relations worldwide.

Maintaining the balance of power

After World War II, international politics changed drastically with the emergence of two **superpowers**, the United States and the Soviet Union. Each superpower pressured other nations to join its side. Intense superpower competition made it difficult for smaller nations to remain neutral, or **nonaligned**, and fueled potentially explosive conflicts around the world.

Given these developments, a goal of American foreign policy after World War II was to maintain a **balance of power** with the Soviet Union — to prevent sudden shifts in alliances that could lead to war. The major tools the United States used in preserving the balance of power were (1) foreign aid, both economic and military, to governments it considered allies, and (2) military force to defend allies and overthrow governments it considered hostile.

The development of nuclear weapons increased superpower tensions. Nuclear weapons threaten not only global security but human existence as well. Following the invention and use of the atom bomb by the United States in 1945, the superpowers began an **arms race**, each seeking to gain military advantage by developing new and more powerful weapons. Despite progress in arms control, there are still thousands of deadly nuclear weapons left in the world. The vast majority of them belong to the United States or to the former Soviet Union.

Promoting democracy

Finally, the United States has long sought to promote democracy and human rights throughout the world. As President Kennedy said in his

538

Inaugural Address (page 385), "We shall pay any price, bear any burden, meet any hardship, support any friend, oppose any foe to assure the survival and success of liberty." Carrying out this policy may mean providing economic assistance or military aid to certain countries. Several times in this century American troops have been sent to defend a country from invasion or against a revolution. On a few occasions, the United States has taken part in the overthrow of an unfriendly government.

The United States also uses foreign policy to reach humanitarian goals. Both government agencies and private groups have provided relief for victims of earthquakes in Mexico, volcanoes in Colombia, and famine in Ethiopia. Another foreign policy goal of the United States is to protect human rights. We tried, for example, to help Jewish citizens leave the Soviet Union, where they were denied religious freedom; and have withheld aid from countries that are known to abuse human rights.

History of American Policy

President Gerald Ford once observed that "America has had a unique role in the world since the day of our independence two hundred years ago. And ever since the end of World War II, we have borne successfully a heavy responsibility for ensuring a stable world order and hope for human progress." The history of America's foreign policy reveals how different policies have achieved particular goals.

Isolationism

The United States in 1789 was sparsely populated, financially strapped, and lacking a strong army or navy. Recognizing that it would take time for the fledgling nation to become strong, President Washington pursued a policy of **neutrality** and advised against foreign alliances. Separated from most other nations by wide oceans, the United States followed a policy of **isolationism** for most of the 1800's, avoiding

Maintaining international trade has long been an important goal of U.S. foreign policy. In the late 1700's, the Chinese artist Youqua showed both American and European trading ships in the harbor at Canton, China.

539

EXPLANATION

After students have read the section, you may want to consider the following activities:

History

● *What have been the four main foreign policy goals of the United States?* (Protecting the country, carrying out foreign trade, maintaining the balance of power, and promoting democracy.)

● CRITICAL THINKING *Give one example of how any two of these goals might conflict with one another, and one example of how they might work together.* (*Conflict:* The United States might decide to limit trade with a nation that did not practice democracy or respect its citizens' rights. *Work together:* By defeating an aggressor, the United States might simultaneously protect itself and maintain the world balance of power.)

Background: *Civic Participation* Many humanitarian aid campaigns were organized by private-sector groups in the 1980's for such causes as Ethiopian famine relief. Two successful efforts were U.S.A. for Africa, which raised $45 million, and the Live Aid concert, which raised more than $70 million.

The symbol 👥 denotes active participation strategies.

Activities are keyed for student abilities:
▲ = Basic
● = All Levels
■ = Average/Advanced

Global Awareness

● CRITICAL THINKING Ask students to use inferential reasoning to respond to the following questions: **Why was the United States, unlike European nations, not economically ravaged by World War II?** (The war did not take place on American soil.) **What were the similarities and differences between the conflicts in Korea and Vietnam?** (Both were civil wars in Asia in which the United States fought against Communist forces. The United States preserved South Korean independence, but South Vietnam fell to the Communists.)

unnecessary involvement in world affairs. This policy let the country grow strong internally, avoid international confrontations, and maintain its independence.

The Monroe Doctrine

In the early 1800's, many Spanish and Portuguese colonies in Latin America revolted and declared their independence. The United States feared that other European powers would try to take control of these newly independent nations. In addition, Russia, which controlled Alaska, was extending its North American settlements.

Fearing that European involvement in the Americas would endanger the security of the United States, President James Monroe issued a bold proclamation on December 2, 1823. The Monroe Doctrine, as it became known, warned European powers to stay out of the internal affairs of all independent nations in the Western Hemisphere. In return, the United States promised not to interfere in the internal concerns of any European state (which it was not likely to do). The Monroe Doctrine became the cornerstone of American isolationist policy for the rest of the 19th century.

Invoking the Monroe Doctrine to defend its interests in the Panama Canal, the United States "lion" blocks the path of European investors.

540

Interventionism

By the late 1890's, the United States had a formidable navy. In addition, it had expanded its overseas markets and was searching for new sources of raw materials. Accordingly, the United States adopted a foreign policy of intervention. This meant stepping into the internal affairs of foreign nations to ensure a favorable situation or outcome for the United States.

The Spanish-American War in 1898 was the first major demonstration of this policy. The war began as a conflict between harsh Spanish rulers and their subjects in Cuba and other Caribbean island colonies. When an American battleship, the *U.S.S. Maine,* was mysteriously blown up in Havana harbor, the United States became involved in Cuba's affairs. Newspapers warned Americans to "Remember the Maine!" and stirred up public opinion against the Spanish. Congress soon declared war, and in just four months the United States had soundly defeated Spain. With victory, the United States gained possession of Puerto Rico, Guam, and the Philippines. (The Philippines gained full independence in 1946.)

The Roosevelt Corollary

The United States became further involved in Latin American affairs during President Theodore Roosevelt's administration (1901–1909). Roosevelt summed up his foreign policy in one sentence: "Speak softly and carry a big stick." Roosevelt believed that the United States should not be afraid to take military action to accomplish its goals in world affairs. Accordingly, the United States backed a 1903 revolution in Panama, then controlled by Colombia. Colombia had refused to grant the United States permission to build a canal in Panama. With the help of the U.S. Navy, Panama gained independence and then gave permission to build the canal.

In 1904 Roosevelt issued the "Roosevelt Corollary" to the Monroe Doctrine. According to this policy, the United States would intervene in the internal affairs of any Latin American nation that could not pay its foreign debts or maintain order. In 1912, for example, the United States sent Marines to quell a revolution in Nicaragua that threatened property owned by American citizens. Such intervention stirred resentment among Latin American people, who called this U.S. policy "gunboat diplomacy."

Background: *History* The Monroe Doctrine made four key points: (1) the Americas were "not to be considered as subjects for future colonization by any European powers"; (2) the European system of monarchy was not to be imposed on these countries; (3) the United States would not interfere with existing European colonies in the Americas; (4) the United States would continue not to interfere in the internal affairs of European nations.

On D-Day — June 6, 1944 — American troops stormed the beaches of Normandy, beginning the campaign to free Europe from Nazi occupation.

World War I

In 1914 World War I broke out in Europe. At first, the United States remained neutral, reflecting the customary policy of steering clear of European affairs. In 1917, however, after German submarines attacked American ships carrying military supplies to England, President Wilson asked Congress for a declaration of war. World War I, which Wilson hoped would make the world "safe for democracy," marked the first time American soldiers were sent to fight on European soil.

In 1919 President Wilson personally participated in framing the Treaty of Versailles, which formally ended World War I. He offered a plan known as the "Fourteen Points," which called for freedom of the seas, open diplomacy, elimination of economic trade barriers, and most importantly, the creation of a League of Nations as an international peacekeeping body. The U.S. Senate, however, refused to ratify the treaty. Clinging to isolationism, the Senate objected to U.S. participation in the League of Nations.

Good Neighbor Policy

Beginning with President Herbert Hoover in the early 1930's, the United States tried to cultivate better relations with its neighbors in Latin America. Diplomacy replaced military intervention as the United States tried to convince Latin Americans that it had no intention of conquering them. The so-called Good Neighbor Policy was continued by President Franklin Roosevelt into the 1940's.

World War II

While the United States retreated from international affairs during the 1920's and 1930's, major changes were taking place in Europe and Asia. Ruthless dictators rose to power in Germany, Italy, and Japan. Known as the Axis powers, these dictatorships launched invasions of nearby countries. Italy invaded Ethiopia. Germany took control of Czechoslovakia and Austria. Japan invaded China, claiming Asia as its sphere of influence. When Germany invaded Poland in 1939, France and Great Britain declared

541

Values

● CRITICAL THINKING Does morality have any place in international relations? Statesmen from Machiavelli to Henry Kissinger have answered "no." Others, such as President Jimmy Carter, have said "yes." Have class members debate this question, using specific examples to support their points of view.

Background: *History*
Woodrow Wilson, a fervent proponent of American neutrality, once said, "There is such a thing as a man being too proud to fight." After American shipping and lives were threatened, Wilson changed his view: "America cannot be an ostrich with its head in the sand."

Background: *History*
Franklin Roosevelt first used the term *Good Neighbor Policy* in his 1933 Inaugural Address: "In the field of world policy I would dedicate this nation to the policy of the good neighbor."

The symbol ▮▮ denotes active participation strategies.

Activities are keyed for student abilities:
▲ = Basic
● = All Levels
■ = Average/Advanced

Cooperative Learning

● Explain to students that the United States has aided and supported some non-democratic governments for such reasons as stopping the spread of communism or encouraging reform in those nations. Have students pretend they are advisers to the President. Have them work in small groups to create a set of standards to be applied in deciding whether to aid a nation that has requested economic or military assistance from the United States. Groups should share their criteria with the class.

war. The Soviet Union joined when it, too, was attacked. German forces, however, quickly over-ran and occupied France and northern Europe.

When fighting broke out in Europe, Americans had great sympathy for France, Great Britain, and other victims of Axis aggression. Still, the United States stayed out of the war, for public opinion opposed foreign involvement. But on December 7, 1941, when Japanese forces bombed the U.S. naval base at Pearl Harbor, Hawaii, an outraged President asked Congress to declare war immediately. With firm public support, the United States joined the Allied forces — Britain, France, the Soviet Union, China, and others — to challenge the Axis powers.

America's entry into World War II tipped the balance in favor of the Allies. American aid went beyond military power. Our farms, factories, and workers provided the food, equipment, and ar-maments necessary to wage war successfully. Germany surrendered in May 1945. War in the Pacific ended abruptly in August 1945, soon after President Harry Truman ordered the use of the atomic bomb against Japan.

The costs of World War II were devastating. At least 45 million people — including some 400,000 Americans — lost their lives. The United States emerged as the only major nation not economically ravaged by war. American farms and factories remained intact and operating at full capacity. We were the only nation to possess nuclear weapons. The United States was, without question, the most powerful nation in the world.

World affairs would henceforth rank high on America's policy agenda. U.S. foreign policy became international, as the nation took an active part in foreign affairs for the purpose of maintaining peace and stability.

Figure 20–1 A DIVIDED EUROPE The membership of NATO and the Warsaw Pact reflected the split between East and West after World War II. The Warsaw Pact disbanded in 1991. 1D

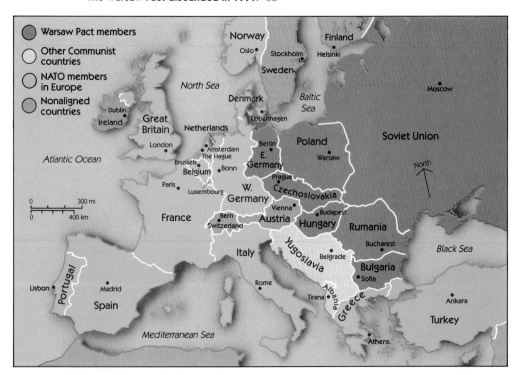

Figure 20–1
▲ *Which countries on the map are shown as non-aligned?* (Ireland, Switzerland, Austria, Sweden, Finland.)

Background: *History*
Truman's purpose in using the atomic bomb was to force a Japanese surrender without an invasion of Japan. Truman and his advisers believed that an invasion of Japan would cost a million Allied lives. Some historians have also suggested that Truman hoped the atomic bomb would intimidate the Soviet Union into making concessions to the United States after the war.

The United Nations

Toward the close of World War II, President Roosevelt began talks with Soviet Premier Joseph Stalin, British Prime Minister Winston Churchill, and other leaders about creating an international peacekeeping organization. In April 1945, representatives from fifty nations gathered in San Francisco to form the United Nations (UN). The goal of this multinational organization is to provide a forum for peacefully settling disputes among nations. Unlike the League of Nations, the UN was overwhelmingly accepted by the U.S. Senate. Participation in the United Nations has been an integral part of U.S. foreign policy. (The UN is described in Section 4.)

Containment and cold war

The Soviet Union suffered the greatest losses in World War II — more than 7 million soldiers and 10 million civilians dead, and another 14 million wounded. Despite this, the Soviet Union emerged from the war as the dominant power in Eastern Europe. It immediately set out to extend its territory and spread the Communist ideology. By 1949, Poland, Hungary, Czechoslovakia, Rumania, and Bulgaria had become Soviet "satellites," collectively known as the **Soviet bloc** (see Figure 20–1). When Germany was divided in two by the peace treaty, East Germany became a Communist state under Soviet influence.

In a speech at Fulton, Missouri, Winston Churchill warned Americans that the Soviet Union had dropped an "iron curtain" over Eastern Europe that would threaten the free world. **Containment**, or limitation of Communist expansion, became America's foreign policy goal.

On March 12, 1947, President Truman announced to Congress that the United States would support any free nation resisting Communist takeover. This declaration, known as the "Truman Doctrine," was aimed against Soviet efforts to take over Greece and Turkey. With United States aid, both countries remained free. Similar efforts prevented the Soviet Union from gaining control of West Berlin.

The growing hostility in U.S.-Soviet relations following World War II became known as the **cold war**. The cold war was not a direct confrontation on the battlefield; rather, it was a battle of diplomacy, economic policy, propaganda, ideologies, espionage, and nerves.

The Korean War

There were times after World War II when cold war tensions became quite "hot." For example, in June 1950 troops from Communist North Korea (the Democratic People's Republic of Korea) invaded non-Communist South Korea (the Republic of Korea).

U.S. soldiers were drawn into the confrontation as part of a United Nations force sent to defend South Korea. The North Koreans had Soviet backing and help from the Chinese Communists. After three years the war ended in a stalemate. American losses included 54,246 dead and more than 100,000 wounded. Korean losses, both North and South, ran even higher. The United States has kept troops in South Korea ever since to help avert future North Korean assaults.

The Cuban missile crisis

The two superpowers themselves nearly came to blows during the Cuban missile crisis in October 1962. A Communist government led by Fidel Castro had come to power in Cuba in 1959 and allied itself with the Soviet Union. In 1961 the United States severed diplomatic relations with Cuba. A year later, U.S. aerial photographs revealed the unmistakable presence of Soviet missiles in Cuba, just 90 miles south of Florida. On October 22, 1962, President Kennedy went on national television to inform the American people and the world that the United States would not tolerate any missiles in Cuba. Kennedy demanded that the Soviet Union withdraw all missiles from Cuba and ordered the Navy to search and seize any Cuban-bound Soviet ships.

Tension mounted as Soviet vessels steamed toward Cuba. A showdown — possibly World War III — appeared imminent. At the last minute, Soviet Premier Nikita Khrushchev offered to call off Soviet ships and withdraw the missiles in exchange for a U.S. promise not to invade Cuba. The U.S. also promised to remove missiles that it had earlier installed in Turkey near the Soviet Union. Kennedy asked the Soviets not to publicize this part of the agreement. The Soviet ships then turned around and the crisis ended.

The Vietnam War

Like Korea, the Vietnam War involved Americans in a distant civil war. Vietnam, once a French colony, had been divided in 1954. The Communist government in the north, headed by

543

Background: *Global Awareness* South Korea's economy has expanded tremendously since the 1950's because of its ability to produce and export at low cost such products as clothing, electronics, and steel.

RETEACHING/CORRECTIVES

▲ Have students outline the section by writing down both of the red headings in the section, followed by each of the black subheadings. Next to each subheading should be a short definition or description of that subheading.

Have students complete **Skills Practice Worksheet 20,** which asks them to create a time line of major events in the history of U.S. foreign policy.

You may also want to use **Transparency 47,** which shows causes and effects of the cold war, and **Transparency 48,** which presents a time line of United States involvement in world affairs.

ENRICHMENT/EXTENSION

■ Have students complete **Primary Source Worksheets 21-25,** which provide excerpts from major presidential statements on foreign policy.

You may also want students to complete **Supreme Court Decision 57,** which deals with the rights of refugees seeking asylum in the United States.

Section 1 Review Answers

1. Protecting the country, carrying out foreign trade, maintaining the balance of power, and promoting democracy.
2. It maintained no alliances; its situation between the Atlantic and Pacific oceans allowed it to remain physically isolated.
3. To ensure a favorable situation or outcome for the United States by intervening in the internal affairs of foreign nations.
4. The nation continued its active role, begun during the war, of working to maintain peace and stability.

The United States' involvement in the Vietnam War sharply divided the American people. The picture above shows U.S. Marines in combat.

Ho Chi Minh, sought to reunite the country under its rule. The United States supported the non-Communist government in the south.

The prevailing view among American policymakers was the **domino theory.** If one country fell to communism, the neighboring countries would also fall, like a stack of dominoes. Americans feared that the fall of South Vietnam would lead to a Communist takeover of all Southeast Asia. Beginning with President Eisenhower in the mid-1950's, the United States sent a steady stream of economic and military aid to the South Vietnamese. By 1968, some 525,000 American troops were engaged in Vietnam.

Public opinion at first supported the effort, but as U.S. casualties mounted, the war grew increasingly unpopular at home. In 1969 President Nixon decided to phase American troops out of Vietnam over the next four years. By the time a peace treaty was finally signed in 1973, more than 57,700 Americans had died. Two years after the withdrawal of American troops, South Vietnam fell to the Communists. The two Vietnams were joined to form the Socialist Republic of Vietnam. The neighboring countries of Laos and Cambodia also soon came under Communist rule.

544

The loosening of tensions

Despite the conflicts over Korea, Cuba, and Vietnam, world leaders continued to meet and negotiate. In 1955 President Eisenhower, Soviet Premier Nikolai Bulganin, and other heads of state met in Geneva, Switzerland, in the first **summit meeting.**

World leaders, realizing that a war between the superpowers could result in nuclear war, worked to improve relations. The result was a new foreign policy called **détente** (day-TAHNT), a French word meaning "loosening." This policy sought a relaxation of international tensions. Certain incidents, like the Soviet invasion of Afghanistan in 1979, strained détente. In the late 1980's, however, improved superpower relations produced agreements to reduce nuclear stockpiles and build economic and cultural ties.

The break-up of the Soviet Union and the end of the cold war altered American foreign policy. The Clinton administration's goals are to boost economic aid for Russia and other former Soviet republics, and to support international peacekeeping activities. The aim is to stem regional conflicts and assist fledgling democracies in efforts to build stable governments.

SECTION 1 REVIEW

Vocabulary and key terms

superpower (538)
nonaligned (538)
balance of power (538)
arms race (538)
neutrality (539)
isolationism (539)
Monroe Doctrine (540)

Roosevelt Corollary (540)
Soviet bloc (543)
containment (543)
cold war (543)
domino theory (544)
summit meeting (544)
détente (544)

For review

1. What are the major goals of American foreign policy today? **6G**

2. Why could the United States maintain an isolationist policy until the early 1900's? **8F**
3. What is the goal of interventionist policy? **8A**
4. How did World War II affect the United States' participation in foreign affairs? **8F**
5. In what ways did the Truman Doctrine, the Korean War, and the Vietnam War reflect the goal of containment? **1D**

Critical thinking

ANALYZING POLICIES   Have American foreign policy positions since World War II (Truman Doctrine, containment, détente, etc.) remained basically consistent, or have they changed significantly? Cite specific examples to support your point of view. **8G**

3A, 3B, 8A, 8G, 8H

SECTION 2

The Executive Branch Guides Foreign Policy

ACCESS

The Main Ideas

1 What are the roles of the Central Intelligence Agency and the National Security Council?
pages 545–546

2 How do the Departments of State and Defense help carry out foreign policy?
pages 547–549

During the Cuban missile crisis (page 543), President Kennedy faced a problem: how to get the Soviet Union to remove its missiles from Cuba without starting a war. Kennedy met with his Cabinet. Robert Kennedy described the decision-making process: "We split into groups to write our recommendations. . . . We exchanged papers, each group dissected and criticized the other, and then the papers were all returned to the original group to develop further answers. Gradually, from all this came the outline of definitive plans."

Although most foreign policy decisions are less pressured than this, they often require Presidents to meet with top advisers to analyze courses of action and their consequences.

3A, 3B

The President's Advisers

Cabinet members

Traditionally, the Secretary of State is the most important presidential adviser in matters of foreign policy. The Secretary often negotiates with the top officials of other nations in place of the President. The Secretary of Defense is often a key adviser to the President on military matters. In some administrations, Vice Presidents have also played leading foreign policy roles.

The CIA

The Central Intelligence Agency (CIA) is an executive agency created in 1947 to gather **intelligence** — information about foreign governments. The Director of Central Intelligence is appointed by the President, with Senate approval.

The CIA gathers social, political, economic, and military information, which is essential for making decisions on foreign policy. CIA agents read foreign government documents, monitor overseas newspapers, listen to broadcasts, and

545

Background: *History*   The CIA replaced the Office of Strategic Services (OSS), the World War II spy agency.

---

5. All three were aimed at keeping Communist countries from expanding their influence.

Critical thinking Some students may suggest that such general goals as maintaining free trade and spreading democracy throughout the world have remained consistent. Other students may argue that the end of the cold war will produce important changes in American foreign policy.

CLOSURE

● Remind students of the pre-reading objectives at the beginning of the section. Pose one or both of these questions again. Then have students read Section 2, paying special attention to the different agencies involved in helping the President in foreign policy.

SECTION 2

The Executive Branch Guides Foreign Policy
(pp. 545–550)

Section Objectives

☐ describe the roles of the Central Intelligence Agency and the National Security Council

☐ explain how the Departments of State and Defense help create and carry out foreign policy

---

The symbol 🎁 denotes active participation strategies.

Activities are keyed for student abilities:
▲ = Basic
● = All Levels
■ = Average/Advanced

Vocabulary

intelligence, counterintelligence, protocol, chargé d'affaires, consul, diplomatic immunity, Pentagon, conscription

👀 FOCUS

● Write the following acronyms on the board: *CIA, NSC, DOD, JCS*. Ask volunteers to come to the board and write below each acronym the name of the organization and a brief description of its role.

Have any of these organizations been in the news lately? In what context? You might have students bring to class newspaper articles concerning these organizations.

EXPLANATION

After students have read the section, you may want to consider the following activities:

👥 Controversial Issues

● Tell students that in the mid-1970's a Senate investigation revealed secret, illegal operations by the CIA, including spying on thousands of Americans who opposed the Vietnam War, assassination attempts against foreign politicians, and mind-control experiments at prisons and hospitals.

You may want to hold a class debate on the CIA. Questions for debate could include: *Since the CIA is part of the executive branch, what role should Congress play in overseeing CIA activities? Does the American public have a right to know about CIA activities abroad? Should the CIA collect intelligence in "friendly" as well as "unfriendly" countries?*

talk to experts. Other information is obtained secretly by electronic eavesdropping, spy satellites, and undercover activities. The CIA also carries on **counterintelligence** — attempting to monitor and counter the activities of other nations' intelligence-gathering agencies.

The CIA has also toppled "unfriendly" governments and aided ones considered "friendly." In the 1980's, for example, it helped rebels, known as *contras*, fight the Sandinistas — the revolutionary government of Nicaragua. The Sandinistas had previously overthrown a U.S.-backed dictatorship.

As a result, the CIA has often been the center of controversy. There is always concern that such a secret or semi-secret agency will go too far and do something unwise, illegal, or embarrassing to the nation. Questions arise about whether certain undercover activities are legal and how much control the President has over them. Concern also rose during the 1991 Senate confirmation of CIA chief Robert Gates, that the agency had deliberately exaggerated the Soviet threat.

National Security Council

The National Security Council, or NSC, was also created in 1947. It is part of the Executive Office of the President (page 423). The NSC's main job is to monitor, coordinate, and sift through the masses of information collected by the CIA and other intelligence-gathering agencies. The NSC then makes that information available to the President, emphasizing the foreign policy choices the President has and what the likely consequences of those choices are.

The NSC director, the National Security Adviser, has often played a key role in advising the President, sometimes overshadowing the Secretary of State. For example, President Kennedy's top foreign-policy adviser was McGeorge Bundy, his National Security Adviser. Henry Kissinger, who headed the NSC before becoming Secretary of State, was Richard Nixon's most influential adviser. Because National Security Advisers are not approved by the Senate, reliance on them has drawn some criticism.

The Iran-*contra* affair

Late in 1986, it was disclosed that staff members of the National Security Council had arranged the sale of weapons to the Iranian government. It was hoped that this sale would

bring the release of American hostages kidnapped in Lebanon by Muslim terrorists linked to Iran. The secret arms sale was embarrassing to President Reagan, who had often stressed that the United States would never bargain with terrorists.

The situation became even worse when it was discovered that millions of dollars from the arms sale had been channeled to the *contras* in Nicaragua. This secret funding was illegal. Congress had prohibited such aid. At first, the Reagan administration strongly denied that it was funding the *contras*. However, after an American pilot employed by the CIA was shot down inside Nicaragua in the fall of 1986, the administration was forced to change its story. It admitted that aid had been sent, but claimed that it was unauthorized. Meanwhile, National Security Adviser John Poindexter and his deputy, Oliver North, destroyed and altered documents to cover up the illegal operation.

As Congress began an investigation, President Reagan asked a panel headed by John Tower, a former Texas senator, to report. The Tower Commission criticized the President for not keeping closer track of NSC activities. It also blamed Cabinet and White House staff members for not using the NSC correctly.

In the course of the trial of former National Security Adviser Poindexter, Ronald Reagan agreed to testify on videotape. The ex-President appeared confused and claimed several times not to remember key events and dates. Poindexter was convicted of five felony charges, including making false statements to Congress. A federal appeals court in Washington, D.C., later overturned Poindexter's conviction.

How well did the constitutional system of checks and balances work in the Iran-*contra* affair? To some observers, the system appeared to have failed. Reagan administration officials pursued a foreign policy that contradicted the clear intent of Congress. High-ranking members of the CIA and the State Department conspired to keep Congress and the public in the dark. Justice Department officials allowed important evidence to be destroyed.

In 1991 President Bush and Congress agreed on new rules to govern covert (secret) intelligence activities. The new rules, a reaction to the Iran-*contra* affair, required that the President keep Congress more closely informed.

546

Background: *Law* Within the United States, CIA activities are limited by law and must be coordinated with the FBI.

Background: *Law* In 1991 Elliott Abrams, an Assistant Secretary of State at the time of the Iran-*contra* affair, pleaded guilty to charges that he had misled Congress as part of the cover-up of American aid to the *contras*. Abrams admitted that he had also lied to Congress about his efforts to solicit a $10 million gift for the *contras* from the sultan of Brunei.

Prime Minister Rabin of Israel and PLO Chairman Arafat signed a historic agreement in Washington in 1993 as President Clinton looked on. The handshake photo reflected the President's active role in supporting the Israeli-Palestinian negotiations that resulted in the agreement.

3A

State Department Personnel

The State Department, the oldest executive department, is charged with carrying out America's foreign policy. Its main duties are to negotiate treaties and executive agreements, keep the President informed of international developments, maintain diplomatic relations, promote cultural exchanges between the United States and other countries, guard American investments and protect American citizens overseas, and plan international conferences. (See the Guide to Executive Departments, page 458.)

State Department organization

The State Department is the smallest executive department, in both budget and personnel. Its head is, of course, the Secretary of State.

The State Department's work is largely administered by its bureaus. Five State Department bureaus are organized along regional lines: the bureaus of African Affairs; European and Canadian Affairs; East Asian and Pacific Affairs; Near Eastern and South Asian Affairs; and Inter-American Affairs. There is also a bureau for international organizations. Each is headed by an Assistant Secretary. Some bureaus are responsible for specific functional duties, such as intelligence, research, or planning.

The Foreign Service

State Department personnel who represent the United States overseas are part of the Foreign Service. Members of the Foreign Service are selected carefully through competitive examinations, personal interviews, and background checks. Those selected typically are college graduates with specialized skills; most speak one or more foreign languages well.

Once selected, Foreign Service personnel are put through rigorous State Department training. They must be thoroughly familiar with the culture and government of their host country. They must be equally well versed in **protocol**. Protocol refers to the set of customs and courtesies that foreign officials observe in dealing with one another. After training, Foreign Service personnel may stay in the United States or be stationed in offices overseas.

The United States has about 140 embassies throughout the world. An embassy is a country's

547

Constitutional Heritage
Ask students to reread the description of the Iran-*contra* affair on p. 546.

▲ *What was the purpose of weapons sales to Iran?* (To gain the release of American hostages in Lebanon.) *Why were the sales embarrassing to President Reagan?* (He had vowed that the United States would not bargain with terrorists.) *What happened to profits from the arms sales?* (They went to support *contra* rebels in Nicaragua.) *How did American aid to the* contras *become public?* (A pilot employed by the CIA was shot down inside Nicaragua in 1986.)

● CRITICAL THINKING *In what way was the Iran-contra affair a breakdown of checks and balances?* (The executive branch pursued a policy despite Congress's opposition and kept that policy secret from Congress and the public.)

■ CRITICAL THINKING *What lessons can you draw from the Iran-contra affair regarding Congress's role in foreign policy?* (*Example:* Because the agencies that carry out foreign policy are part of the executive branch, Congress is at a disadvantage when confronting the President over foreign policy issues.)

Critical Thinking
▲ *What are the advantages and disadvantages of following protocol?* (Students might note that the advantages and disadvantages of protocol are similar to those of congressional courtesy, discussed in Chapter 13, p. 354.)

The symbol ♦♦ denotes active participation strategies.

Activities are keyed for student abilities:
▲ = Basic
● = All Levels
■ = Average/Advanced

548

Cooperative Learning

● Divide the class into three groups and have each research the CIA's role and the role of American corporations in one of the following: the overthrow of the Mossadegh government in Iran in 1953, the overthrow of the Arbenz government in Guatemala in 1954, and the overthrow of the Allende government in Chile in 1973. Have each group present its findings to the class.

diplomatic headquarters in a foreign nation and is, in fact, considered to be a part of the home country's territory, subject to its laws. The primary functions of U.S. embassies are to help negotiate agreements between the United States and the host country, and to protect U.S. citizens living abroad. To make communications easier between the State Department and foreign leaders, embassies are almost always set up in the host country's capital city. Thus, the State Department maintains embassies in cities such as London, Moscow, Cairo, Beijing, Buenos Aires, and Nairobi.

Each embassy is headed by an ambassador. Ambassadors are charged with carrying out American foreign policy in the country to which they are assigned; they are the President's personal representatives to heads of foreign states. Although ambassadors are appointed by the President, most come up through the ranks of the Foreign Service. In the absence of the ambassador, the **chargé d'affaires** (shahr-ZHAY dah-FAIR) takes over. Other embassy personnel include military, economic, and political specialists; interpreters; staff members, such as secretaries and clerks (often local people); and a Marine Corps security guard unit.

Another type of Foreign Service office is a consulate, which is headed by a Foreign Service officer, the **consul**. Consulates are usually located in major foreign commercial or tourist centers rather than in foreign capitals. Their main purpose is to help American tourists and encourage American business interests abroad, rather than to engage in diplomatic negotiations. They often assist foreign citizens who wish to visit the United States in obtaining travel visas. There are about 120 American consulates.

Treatment of diplomatic personnel

Following international law, all State Department personnel and their families, as well as foreign diplomats in this country, enjoy **diplomatic immunity** while in the host country. They are not governed by the laws of the nation-state in which they serve. Thus, they cannot be taxed or jailed by the host country. Nor can the host country intercept their mail or interfere with diplomatic operations. Such immunity gives diplomats the necessary freedom to carry out their business.

548

The Military Establishment

Department of Defense

Another important part of U.S. foreign policy is maintaining national security. This responsibility rests with the Department of Defense (DOD). The DOD was established in 1949 by combining the Departments of War and Navy. In keeping with the principle of civilian control over the military, federal law mandates that the Secretary of Defense must be a civilian. The Secretary may, and usually does, have military experience but must have been away from active duty for at least ten years.

The Department of the Army, Department of the Navy, and Department of the Air Force are the three basic divisions of the DOD. (The U.S. Marine Corps falls under the jurisdiction of the Navy, but has separate officers, uniforms, and regulations.) Like the Secretary of Defense, the Secretaries of the Army, Navy, and Air Force must be civilians. Today the DOD employs about three million Americans — two million military personnel and one million civilians.

The **Pentagon** in Arlington, Virginia (across the Potomac River from Washington, D.C.), is headquarters for the Department of Defense. (In fact, the DOD is often popularly referred to as "the Pentagon.") This massive five-sided structure, completed in 1943, is one of the world's largest office buildings. It covers 34 acres and has offices for more than 20,000 personnel. Within its walls are four inner pentagons or "rings," linked by ten web-like corridors. The Pentagon contains not only offices but also shops, clinics, a bank, a drugstore, and a florist. In many respects, the Pentagon is a self-contained city.

Joint Chiefs of Staff

The Joint Chiefs of Staff (JCS) are the Defense Department's most important military advisers. This five-member body assesses U.S. military strength, monitors weapons technology, and advises the President on military strategy. Its members include the nation's highest-ranking military personnel: the Chief of Staff of the Army, Chief of Naval Operations, the Commandant of the Marines, and the Chief of Staff of the Air Force. The President selects the Chairman of the Joint Chiefs, who serves for two years.

Background: *History* The seizure of the U.S. embassy in Iran in 1979 illustrated just how powerless diplomats can be when the host country does not recognize an embassy as foreign territory. Over 50 Americans were held hostage for more than 14 months. The Iranian government took little action except to inform the United States that it would secure the release of the hostages if the United States returned the former shah to Iran for trial.

Recruiting the armed forces

The military cannot function without well-trained personnel. Historically, America has relied upon two methods to recruit members of the armed services: (1) by enlisting, or signing up volunteers; and (2) by military **conscription**. Conscription, better known as the draft, is the forced enrollment of young men into the armed forces for a specified period of mandatory service.

For many years the national government relied entirely on volunteers to staff the Army and Navy. Help also came from the state militias. During the Civil War, World War I, World War II, the Korean War, and the Vietnam War, however, so many soldiers were needed that thousands of young men had to be drafted.

Authority for a military draft is found in Article I, Section 8 of the Constitution, which gives Congress the power to "raise and support armies" and to "provide and maintain a navy." In 1918 the Supreme Court upheld the draft over objections that it was a violation of the protection against "involuntary servitude" in the Thirteenth Amendment.

Selective Service System

The Selective Service System, an independent agency in the executive branch, administers the draft. When that agency was established in 1948, all males between the ages of 18 and 26 were required to sign up for the draft. College students, fathers, and handicapped men, however, commonly were excused from being drafted to serve in the military.

At the end of the Vietnam War in 1973, President Nixon abolished the draft. Two years later, all Selective Service registration ended and the United States returned to an all-volunteer army. Threats of an international crisis, however, caused President Carter to reinstate compulsory *registration* — but not the draft — in 1980. Today, all males must register their name and address with the Selective Service System within thirty days of their eighteenth birthday. This may be done at any U.S. post office. Should a national emergency require the reinstatement of the draft, the government would then have a pool of names from which to draw. Women are excluded from draft registration.

The Pentagon in Arlington, Virginia, is headquarters for the Department of Defense and the office for thousands of its civilian employees.

549

Background: *Values*
Individuals who refuse on moral grounds to fight in war are known as *conscientious objectors*.

Background: *Values* In its 1918 upholding of the draft, the Court ruled that conscription was not "involuntary servitude," but rather "supreme and noble duty."

Background: *History* The first peacetime draft was established in 1940.

GUIDED/INDEPENDENT PRACTICE

● Ask students to make a chart of the various government departments and agencies involved in making foreign policy and identify the responsibilities of each.

RETEACHING/CORRECTIVES

▲ Have students scan the section for answers to the following questions: ***What are the functions of the CIA?*** (pp. 545–546.) ***What are the main duties of the State Department?*** (p. 547.) ***Who belongs to the Joint Chiefs of Staff?*** (p. 548.) ***What two methods has the United States used to recruit members of the armed forces?*** (p. 549.)

ENRICHMENT/EXTENSION

■ Have students complete **Skills Challenge Worksheet 20,** which asks them to analyze a speech by President Lyndon Johnson concerning Vietnam.

Section 2 Review Answers

1. **(a)** The CIA and the National Security Council. **(b)** Both have been criticized for undertaking illegal, unwise, and embarrassing actions beyond the bounds of their authority.

2. Embassies, located in foreign capitals, engage in diplomatic negotiations and protect U.S. citizens living abroad; consulates, located in foreign trade and tourist centers, assist American tourists and encourage American business abroad.

The symbol 👥 denotes active participation strategies.

Activities are keyed for student abilities:
▲ = Basic
● = All Levels
■ = Average/Advanced

3. The Joint Chiefs of Staff.
4. By a draft of all registered males.

Critical thinking Advantages include providing an inexpensive labor force to accomplish national goals and giving young people training and experience. Disadvantages include the cost of administering such a program, the loss of freedom of choice for those required to participate, and the harm that could result from participation in a war.

CLOSURE

● Review the vocabulary with students to help reinforce key concepts from the section. Then have students read Section 3, noting the extent and variety of United States defense policies.

SECTION 3

The United States Maintains Many Foreign Policy Options (pp. 550–555)

Section Objectives

☐ describe the ways the United States seeks to influence other nations

☐ explain the issues raised by the emphasis on nuclear weapons for defense

Vocabulary

foreign aid, embargo, collective security, deterrence, proliferation, arms control

---

SECTION 2 REVIEW

Vocabulary and key terms

intelligence (545)   consul (548)
counterintelligence (546)   diplomatic immunity (548)
protocol (547)   Pentagon (548)
chargé d'affaires (548)   conscription (549)

For review

1. (a) What are the two major non-Cabinet agencies that give the President foreign-policy advice? (b) Why have they been criticized? **3A**

2. What are the main differences between embassies and consulates? **8G**

3. Who are the President's most important military advisers? **3A**

4. How would members of the armed forces be recruited in case of a national emergency? **8H**

Critical thinking

FORMING AN OPINION Some nations require all young men and women to perform one or two years of "national service." This service is usually, but not necessarily, in the military. What are some advantages or drawbacks of this system? **8A**

1D, 6G, 7D, 8A, 8C

SECTION 3 The United States Maintains Many Foreign Policy Options

ACCESS

The Main Ideas

1 In what ways does the United States seek to influence other nations? *pages 550–553*

2 What issues are raised by the emphasis on nuclear weapons for defense? *pages 553–555*

August, 1991 — Democratic forces in the Soviet Union reverse an attempted coup by hardline Communists. The Communist Party falls from power. One of the world's superpowers is undergoing a revolution. How should the United States act as these events unfold? How can the country best pursue its goals of world peace, democracy, and markets for trade (Section 1)? How should it aid the democratic forces? As a world leader, the United States must grapple with these and many other foreign policy questions.
1D, 7D

Diplomatic Policies

By maintaining diplomatic relations with foreign countries, the United States encourages other nations to act favorably toward us. Diplomacy is also sometimes used as a protest against hostile acts of other nations.

550

Foreign aid

One way the United States maintains good diplomatic relations is by providing assistance to other nations. **Foreign aid**, as such assistance is called, may include military weapons, technological advice, medical care, engineering, low-cost loans, and food. Foreign aid has several interrelated goals. It carries out Americans' ideals of sharing and helping to fight disease and feed the hungry. It also has political goals, to cultivate better relations and so create closer ties and alliances against aggression.

The most striking example of American foreign aid was the assistance provided to Western Europe and Japan after World War II. This aid went both to our allies and to the enemies we had just defeated. Not only were these war-torn nations vulnerable to communism, but they also were important to the U.S. economy. Europe especially had been a major source of trade and raw materials for the United States.

In June 1947, Secretary of State George Marshall unveiled a proposal to offer massive economic aid to our allies. (See the "Speaking Out" feature on page 802.) The so-called Marshall Plan, which was soon adopted by Congress,

---

The defense of the United States is a topic debated day in and day out at government agencies in Washington, D.C. Each year, defense personnel write thousands of reports, design computer models, and hold meetings to analyze the trends and changes that could affect American defense strategy.

At the same time that this work is taking place, a different type of analysis is going on. Authors, using their knowledge of advanced military technology, are writing political thrillers or novels. The following excerpt is from *The Hunt for Red October*, the best-selling novel about a Soviet submarine, by Tom Clancy. Although *The Hunt for Red October* is a work of fiction, Clancy combines his extensive knowledge of U.S. and Soviet military technology with his imagination to create a dramatic yet believable story. Clancy's novel is one example of how authors can use the workings of American government—in this case defense systems—to create realistic, dramatic literature.

While reading the excerpt, note Clancy's references to technology that is unfamiliar to most people: "688-class attack submarine," "ELINT," "reactor plant noise." You will discover that this technical information can be understood in the context of the story.

The Hunt for Red October

Thirty miles to the northeast, the USS *Bremerton* was on a heading of two-two-five, just emerging from under the icepack. A 688-class attack submarine, she had been on an ELINT—electronic intelligence gathering—mission in the Kara Sea when she was ordered west to the Kola Peninsula. The Russian missile boat wasn't supposed to have sailed for another week, and the *Bremerton's* skipper was annoyed at this latest intelligence screw-up. He would have been in place to track the *Red October* if she had sailed as scheduled. Even so, the American sonarmen had picked up on the Soviet sub a few minutes earlier, despite the fact that they were traveling at fourteen knots.

"Conn, sonar."

Commander Wilson lifted the phone. "Conn, aye."

"Contact lost, sir. . . ."

"Very well. He's probably settling down to a slow drift. We'll be creeping up on him. Stay awake, Chief." Commander Wilson thought this over as he took two steps to the chart table. . . .

"If it was me, I'd go down near the bottom and circle slowly right about here." Wilson traced a rough circle on the chart that enclosed the *Red October's* position. "So let's creep up on him. We'll reduce speed to five knots and see if we can move in and reacquire him from his reactor plant noise."

CRITICAL THINKING

1. What was the job of the American sonarmen? For what reasons might the USS *Bremerton* be tracking the *Red October*?
2. How can novels such as *The Hunt for Red October* help readers enrich their knowledge of American government?

Connecting Literature and Government

Cultural Literacy

● CRITICAL THINKING *Why, in your opinion, did Clancy make wide use of detailed, technical terms in* **The Hunt for Red October?** (The use of such details makes the story more believable and more interesting to readers.)

Ask students to name other examples of fiction writing dealing with government. (Spy novels, political thrillers, fictionalized biographies of famous persons.)

551

Critical Thinking Answers
1. To track the Soviet submarine. To analyze its capabilities or to discover the purpose of its mission.

2. Such novels provide readers with a picture of how different parts of the United States government operate.

The symbol ▓ denotes active participation strategies.

Activities are keyed for student abilities:
- ▲ = Basic
- ● = All Levels
- ■ = Average/Advanced

The United States provides foreign aid in many ways. Members of the Peace Corps, for example, work side-by-side with people in developing countries. Here, a volunteer instructs a group of students in Costa Rica.

FOCUS

● Ask students to review the four basic foreign policy goals outlined in Section 1. (Protecting the country, carrying out foreign trade, maintaining the balance of power, promoting democracy.) Explain that this section will describe the different ways in which the United States pursues these goals.

EXPLANATION

After students have read the section, you may want to consider the following activities:

Geography

● The top ten U.S. foreign aid recipients in 1990 and their total aid figure (in millions of dollars) were Egypt ($4,977), Israel ($4,377), Pakistan ($522), Poland ($383), Turkey ($367), El Salvador ($300), Greece ($282), Zaire ($241), Brazil ($235), and Honduras ($218). Have students locate these countries on a world map or globe. Ask them why each country is considered important to the United States.

Global Awareness

● Have interested students obtain information on the Peace Corps by writing to Peace Corps, 1990 K Street NW, Washington, D.C. 20526. The following are some questions students may wish to pose in their letters: *What kind of training does a Peace Corps volunteer receive? What countries participate in the Peace Corps program? What jobs do Peace Corps volunteers carry out in the countries to which they are sent? How does Peace Corps work benefit those countries?*

provided $13 billion in loans, grants, and supplies to sixteen Western European nations between 1948 and 1952. Europe's dramatic economic recovery in the 1950's was due largely to the Marshall Plan.

Since World War II, the United States has provided billions of dollars in aid to more than 100 foreign nations. American foreign aid to developing countries is administered by the Agency for International Development (AID), which acts in cooperation with the State Department.

Peace Corps

A very special type of foreign aid is provided by the Peace Corps. The Peace Corps is a program created by President Kennedy in 1961 to foster friendship between the United States and developing nations. Under this program, American volunteers are sent abroad to help others improve their standards of living. Kennedy believed that person-to-person contact would accomplish more than just sending money to developing nations.

Peace Corps volunteers can be from 18 to 80 years old. They are screened and trained before they are sent to needy communities, usually for a two-year stay. There they teach language courses and such skills as carpentry, masonry, plumbing, welding, farming, and health care. Thousands of

Peace Corps volunteers have gone to Latin America, Asia, Africa, and other parts of the world. Originally part of the State Department, today the Peace Corps is an independent agency.

Providing information

Another way the United States fosters favorable relations is by giving out information through the United States Information Agency (USIA). The mission of USIA is to cultivate better images of Americans abroad. Among its activities, the USIA promotes American movies, television shows, and magazines. It also advises the President on how foreign opinion abroad is reacting to current or proposed policies.

USIA's most important contribution is perhaps the *Voice of America,* a shortwave radio broadcast that spotlights American life. Broadcasting in 47 languages, the *Voice of America* reaches some 127 million listeners each week.

Sanctions

While foreign aid encourages friendly nations, sanctions show disapproval of other nations' policies or acts. Sanctions often involve withdrawing economic privileges, but they may be political or military actions as well. A common sanction is the **embargo**, a ban on trade.

552

Critical Thinking

▲ *How might the Peace Corps affect other nations' ideas about the United States?* (It shows them that Americans are a generous people who want others around the world to enjoy the advantages that so many Americans have.)

Under the conditions of an embargo, foreign ships may be prohibited from entering U.S. ports, or the United States may stop shipping certain goods to foreign ports. For example, the United States might prohibit the sale of computer chips or tanks to a particular nation, until it changes its policies. In the 1980's, the United States imposed embargoes on Iran (for taking U.S. hostages) and on South Africa (for its policies of racial segregation).

Another type of sanction is the boycott, a refusal to take part in some international event. For example, in 1980 the United States refused to participate in the Olympic games held in Moscow. President Carter ordered the boycott to protest the presence of Soviet troops in Afghanistan. In 1984, the Soviet Union and fourteen Soviet-bloc nations boycotted the Olympics in Los Angeles, complaining that security was inadequate.

1D

Defense Policies

Diplomatic policies can be effective in maintaining stable foreign relations. When diplomacy breaks down, however, the United States must be ready to use other means to defend its interests and its allies from aggression. Like diplomatic policies, defense policies meet a variety of foreign policy goals.

Collective security

An important way in which the United States maintains the balance of power and secures peace is through **collective security**. To establish collective security, two or more nations agree that an attack on one of them will be considered an attack on all. They will assist each other if any of them is attacked by enemy forces. These agreements or alliances are thought to make a foreign attack less likely.

Since World War II, the United States has been a firm advocate of collective security pacts, or agreements. The United States is a party to about 45 pacts. Many involve the United States and only one other nation. Such agreements are termed *bilateral* treaties. The Japanese Pact of 1951, the Philippines Pact of 1951, and the South Korean Pact of 1953 are examples. In each instance, the United States pledged to lend military support should the other country be attacked. In return, the United States is permitted to maintain military bases in that country. International agreements between three or more nation-states are called *multilateral* treaties.

NATO

In 1949 the United States, Canada, and ten western European nations formed NATO — the North Atlantic Treaty Organization. (See the map on page 542.) NATO is a military alliance that was designed to protect Western Europe against invasion by the Soviet Union and its East European allies. The Soviet Union, in turn, feared invasion by the West. It formed its own security alliance, the Warsaw Pact, in 1955.

NATO forces possessed both nuclear and conventional (non-nuclear) weapons. They were typically headed by a U.S. general and included tens of thousands of American troops. The late 1980's and early 1990's saw dramatic changes in Eastern Europe — the reunification of Germany, the disbandment of the Warsaw Pact, and the break-up of the Soviet Union. These changes also raised new questions about NATO's future. Should NATO expand its role, for example, beyond Europe? And should Eastern European countries be allowed to join the organization? Meanwhile, the United States began reducing its troop levels in Europe.

Other collective security pacts

In 1951 the United States joined in a multilateral defense alliance with Australia and New Zealand, called ANZUS. Its original purpose was to prevent future Japanese aggression, but as U.S. ties with Japan grew closer, the objective became to prevent the spread of communism.

In 1947 the United States and 21 Latin American nations signed the Rio Pact, pledging to support one another in the event of attack. A year later, the United States and twenty of these same nations established the Organization of American States (OAS). The purpose of the OAS is to help settle disputes peacefully, foster cultural exchanges, and promote economic development in the Americas. Both the Rio Pact and the OAS backed the U.S. blockade of Cuba during the Cuban missile crisis.

Preventing attacks

Another foundation of America's defense policy is **deterrence** — the attempt to deter, or

553

Background: *History* In 1966, during the presidency of Charles de Gaulle, France announced that it would take over all NATO bases on its territory and withdraw its troops from NATO forces by April 1969.

Cooperative Learning

● Divide the class into groups and have the groups look for recent accounts of foreign policy issues in newspapers, magazines, and television. Have them follow these stories for several days. Ask them to prepare reports answering the following questions: *What government agencies and departments were involved? Was it a diplomatic or military policy or both? How was the policy formulated and adopted? Did the policy change, and if so, why? Was the issue resolved, and if so, how?*

GUIDED/INDEPENDENT PRACTICE

● Have students create two categories, *Independent policies* and *Cooperative policies,* and place each of the diplomatic and defense policies outlined in the section into one of the categories. Students should then make a general statement about the advantages and disadvantages of independent and cooperative policies.

RETEACHING/CORRECTIVES

▲ Have students write a paragraph summarizing the diplomatic policies and defense policies that together make up U.S. foreign policy. Have students compare their summaries with the third paragraph of the Chapter Summary on p. 559.

ENRICHMENT/EXTENSION

■ Have students research the history of U.S. sanctions against the government of South Africa. *Why were sanctions instituted and what did they consist of? Why did the United States lift sanctions in 1991? What is the current state of relations between the United States and South Africa?* You may wish to have students present

prevent, an enemy attack. Deterrence is based on the notion that if the U.S. military is very strong, then no enemy will dare attack. For many years, the United States relied solely on ground, air, and naval forces — so-called conventional forces — to deter potential aggressors. Since World War II, however, strategic nuclear weapons have become the building blocks of U.S. deterrence.

The arms race

Immediately after World War II, the United States was the world's sole possessor of nuclear weapons. This monopoly was short-lived, as the Soviet Union exploded its first atomic bomb in 1949. Three years later, the United States developed the new, more powerful hydrogen bomb. Not to be outdone, the Soviet Union developed its own hydrogen bomb in 1953. This was the start of the arms race.

Next, the superpowers began competing on delivery systems, ways of getting these bombs to their targets. In 1957 the Soviet Union devel-

oped the first ICBMs (short for "*i*ntercontinental *b*allistic *m*issiles"). These are long-range nuclear warheads that are capable of striking targets some 4,000 miles away. The United States deployed its own ICBMs in 1959. The arms race became more complicated with the development of MIRVs ("*m*ultiple *i*ndependently-targeted *r*een-try *v*ehicles"). These are individual missiles that carry many bombs, each of which can be directed to a different target. The United States installed the MIRVs in 1970, and the Soviets followed suit in 1975.

Today the nations of the world have enough nuclear weapons to cause vast amounts of destruction. Some observers argue that this very fact decreases the likelihood of nuclear war. That is, the mere threat of mutual destruction is enough to keep the peace. Others say that the spread, or **proliferation**, of nuclear weapons only enhances the possibility that these weapons will be used. Therefore, they urge a halt, or "freeze," in making any new weaponry.

The United States maintains a well-equipped, modern air force as a part of its national defense. In 1991, during the Persian Gulf War, the Stealth Fighter (below) was used successfully to oust Iraqi forces from Kuwait.

554

Background: *Science and Technology* Atomic bombs get their explosive power from the fission (splitting) of atoms. Hydrogen bombs, which have vastly greater destructive potential than atomic bombs, get their power from the fusion (joining together) of atoms.

Background: *Global Awareness* Nuclear deterrence has traditionally been based on the concept of MAD, "mutual assured destruction." The theory is that if one nation attacked another, the victim would still be able to retaliate in a horribly destructive way. Thus, neither nation will attempt a "first strike."

Efforts to limit nuclear weapons

During the cold war, the United States and the Soviet Union attempted to reduce the risk of nuclear war through **arms control** — placing limits on building and testing nuclear devices. In 1963 the Nuclear Test Ban Treaty prohibited tests in the atmosphere, under water, and in space. (Limits later were placed on underground tests as well.)

In 1972 a milestone was reached with the signing of the first Strategic Arms Limitation Treaty (SALT I). Under the terms of SALT I, both sides agreed to limit the number of ICBMs, missile-carrying submarines, and antiballistic missiles (defensive weapons designed to destroy incoming missiles before they reach their targets). In 1968 the two superpowers and over fifty other nations had signed the Nuclear Non-Proliferation Treaty, a pact intended to limit the spread of nuclear weapons.

In 1979 the superpowers agreed to further arms limitations in SALT II. President Carter and Soviet Premier Brezhnev signed the treaty, but Congress refused to ratify it.

President Reagan and the new Soviet leader, Mikhail Gorbachev, attempted in vain to reach agreement at a summit meeting in Reykjavik, Iceland, in 1986. One stumbling block was Reagan's plan for the Strategic Defense Initiative (SDI). Reagan claimed that this system of space-based lasers would create an impenetrable shield over the United States. Many scientists, however, doubted the program's effectiveness.

The next major U.S.-Soviet arms control accord came in 1987, with the Intermediate-Range Nuclear Forces Treaty (INF). It called for the destruction of missiles with a range of up to 3,400 miles as well as inspection of weapons sites. With the close of the cold war, President George Bush announced in 1991 that the United States would eliminate nuclear warheads on thousands of short-range missiles in Western Europe. In 1992 Bush and President Boris Yeltsin of Russia agreed in principle to drastic cuts in long-range nuclear weapons.

Nuclear issues that concern the United States now include (1) the safety of nuclear weapons that remain in Eastern Europe; and (2) the potential of some Third World countries — for example, North Korea, Iraq, Iran, and Pakistan — to develop nuclear arsenals.

Military force

As a last resort, the United States, or any nation, may use military action to achieve its policy goals. Since World War II American troops have been sent to counter Communist aggression in South Korea and South Vietnam. In December 1989, President Bush ordered a military invasion of Panama, called "Operation Just Cause," in an effort to capture Panama's dictator Noriega and bring him to trial in the U.S. on drug charges. In August 1990, Iraqi forces invaded and occupied Kuwait. To deter further Iraqi aggression, President Bush sent over 400,000 troops to Saudi Arabia and the Persian Gulf. In early 1991 an American-led coalition launched an air and ground battle, driving Iraqi troops out of Kuwait.

Using military actions requires the utmost care. Policy-makers must consider whether force will accomplish their goals or be an unnecessary risk of American lives. They must be careful to ensure that a small conflict does not escalate into a major war involving the major powers and nuclear weapons.

SECTION 3 REVIEW

Vocabulary and key terms

foreign aid (550)   NATO (553)
Marshall Plan (550)   deterrence (553)
embargo (552)   proliferation (554)
collective security (553) arms control (555)

For review

1. What are some of the reasons why the United States provides foreign aid? **1D**
2. Why does the American government impose sanctions on other nations? **6G**
3. Why does the United States participate in collective security agreements? **1D**
4. What is the goal of deterrence? **8C**

Critical thinking

FORMING AN OPINION Supporters of deterrence say that a large stock of nuclear weapons discourages enemy attacks. Critics hold that nuclear weapons are more likely to *cause* nuclear war. What are some arguments that might be used to support or oppose these positions? **8A**

555

their findings to the class or stage a debate on what U.S. policy toward South Africa should be.

You may also want students to complete worksheets for **Supreme Court Decision 57.** This case deals with the rights of Haitian refugees.

Section 3 Review Answers

1. To cultivate better relations with foreign nations, to create alliances against aggression, to carry out the American ideal of sharing, and to help fight disease and feed the hungry.
2. To show disapproval of other nations' policies or acts.
3. To maintain the balance of power and to secure the peace.
4. To prevent an enemy attack by maintaining a strong defense.

Critical thinking Supporting arguments include the idea that a large worldwide stock of weapons prevents any nation from winning a nuclear war. This, in turn, discourages any nation from starting a nuclear war. Opposing arguments include the idea that some nation could accidentally (or deliberately) trigger an all-out nuclear world war.

CLOSURE

● Remind students of the pre-reading objectives at the beginning of the section. Pose one or both of these questions again. Then have students read Section 4, noting the different parts of the United Nations.

The symbol ᠄᠄ denotes active participation strategies.

Activities are keyed for student abilities:
▲ = Basic
● = All Levels
■ = Average/Advanced

The United States Is a UN Member

(pp. 556–559)

Section Objectives

☐ describe how votes are allotted in the UN General Assembly

☐ explain the functions of the Security Council and other major branches of the UN

Vocabulary

General Assembly, Security Council, Secretariat

 FOCUS

● Have volunteers come to the board and list issues and problems that involve more than one nation. (Wars, pollution, international travel and communication, migration and refugees, disputes over resources or territory, etc.)

When can an international organization like the UN be of help? When will it probably not be effective? (Students may suggest that the UN may be effective in cases where a third party is needed to aid in negotiations, or where there is widespread international agreement on an issue. The organization will probably not be effective if international opinion is sharply divided, or if a powerful nation opposes action on an issue.)

1A, 1C, 1D, 3A, 6B, 8C, 8F

SECTION 4

The United States Is a UN Member

ACCESS **The Main Ideas**

1 How are votes allotted in the UN General Assembly? *page 556*

2 What are the functions of the Security Council and other major branches of the UN? *pages 556–559*

World War II left the world with two superpowers: the U.S. and the Soviet Union. In the early 1990's the collapse of communism in Eastern Europe and the end of the Soviet Union left the United States as the world's sole military superpower. How would this dramatic shift affect international relations? President George Bush called for a "new world order" that would give a wider role to the United Nations.

1D, 3A

UN Organization

The United Nations Charter, in a sense, resembles the American Articles of Confederation of 1781, because each member nation retains its sovereignty. The Charter sets forth the basic components of the United Nations' peacekeeping organization.

The General Assembly

The **General Assembly** is the largest organizational body of the UN. It is a forum where member nations may air their differences, debate issues, and suggest possible solutions. The General Assembly meets annually in its headquarters in New York City. Each member nation is entitled to send five delegates to the General Assembly. Each nation is allowed just one vote, however, regardless of size or population. Most measures before the General Assembly require a simple majority vote. On "important" questions, as defined by the Charter, a two-thirds vote of those nations present and voting is required.

Because so many different nations are represented, all the proceedings of the General Assembly are translated simultaneously into the UN's six official langages — Arabic, Chinese, English, French, Russian, and Spanish. Although meet-

556

ings of the General Assembly sometimes produce significant agreements, certain countries use them primarily as a chance to vent their hostilities. The United States in particular has criticized the General Assembly for being a forum for small countries to berate the United States. Still, decisions made by the General Assembly carry little real authority. All the Assembly's recommendations must be referred to the Security Council before any action can be taken.

The Security Council

The **Security Council** is the most important body of the UN. It determines whether the peace has been violated and what action, if any, will be taken. The Council consists of five permanent and ten temporary member nations that meet continuously at UN headquarters. Permanent members are the United States, Russia, Great Britain, China, and France. Temporary members are elected by the General Assembly for two-year terms. Terms are staggered, however, so that five new members are chosen each year.

The Security Council's voting rules are quite complex. Each member nation is entitled to one vote. A vote of nine of the fifteen members is needed to take any action. All five permanent members, however, have the power of veto. That is, any permanent member nation can prevent the Security Council from taking an action that it opposes, even if the vote is fourteen to one. During the cold war, the Soviet Union used its veto frequently. Security Council voting, therefore, often resulted in stalemate.

The Security Council may use a variety of options to maintain peace. One option is to end formal relations with belligerent nations. Another possible sanction is to cut off trade with aggressor nations. Still another option is to send UN peacekeeping troops. A good example is Cyprus, where UN forces have been stationed since 1964 to keep the peace between the Greek majority and Turkish minority.

The Security Council had no success in resolving conflicts among the superpowers. Since

---

Background: *Global Awareness* The General Assembly holds one regular session each year, beginning in September and lasting about three months. A special session may be called if either the Security Council or a majority of the member states request it. An emergency special session may be called on 24 hours' notice if peace is threatened anywhere in the world and the Security Council has not acted. Such sessions have been held to deal with serious situations in the Middle East and elsewhere.

Figure 20-2 ORGANIZATION OF THE UNITED NATIONS

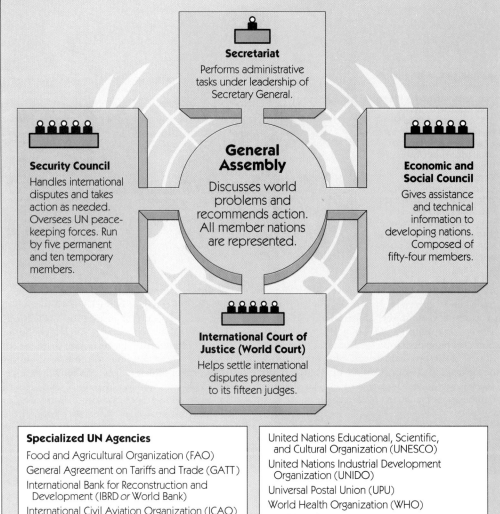

Secretariat
Performs administrative tasks under leadership of Secretary General.

Security Council
Handles international disputes and takes action as needed. Oversees UN peace-keeping forces. Run by five permanent and ten temporary members.

General Assembly
Discusses world problems and recommends action. All member nations are represented.

Economic and Social Council
Gives assistance and technical information to developing nations. Composed of fifty-four members.

International Court of Justice (World Court)
Helps settle international disputes presented to its fifteen judges.

Specialized UN Agencies

Food and Agricultural Organization (FAO)
General Agreement on Tariffs and Trade (GATT)
International Bank for Reconstruction and Development (IBRD *or* World Bank)
International Civil Aviation Organization (ICAO)
International Development Association (IDA)
International Finance Corporation (IFC)
International Fund for Agricultural Development (IFAD)
International Labor Organization (ILO)
International Maritime Organization (IMO)
International Monetary Fund (IMF)
International Telecommunication Union (ITU)

United Nations Educational, Scientific, and Cultural Organization (UNESCO)
United Nations Industrial Development Organization (UNIDO)
Universal Postal Union (UPU)
World Health Organization (WHO)
World Intellectual Property Organization (WIPO)

Other UN Organizations

International Atomic Energy Agency (IAEA)
United Nations Children's Fund (UNICEF)
United Nations High Commission for Refugees (UNHCR)
United Nations Relief and Works Agency (UNRWA)

557

EXPLANATION

After students have read the section, you may want to consider the following activities:

Historic Documents

● Have students obtain a copy of the Charter of the United Nations and read the preamble. *What events provided the impetus for forming the United Nations?* (The two world wars.) *What "ends" or goals are described in the preamble?* (Tolerance, international peace and security, an end to the unjust use of force, and the economic and social advancement of all peoples.)

■ CRITICAL THINKING *The nations belonging to the United Nations have widely different forms of government. How were they able to agree on the goals listed in the preamble?* (The goals are very broad and do not mention specific political or economic approaches.)

Global Awareness

● Ask students to list some of the advantages and disadvantages of using the UN to solve international problems. (*Advantages*—The UN has prestige, resources, and nearly worldwide membership. *Disadvantages*—If a member of the Security Council objects, the UN cannot act; the International Court of Justice has no enforcement powers.

Figure 20-2
▲ *In which body shown on the chart are all UN member nations represented?* (The General Assembly.)

Background: *Global Awareness* Some of the territories that were not self-governing at the end of World War II were the colonies of Italy and Japan. Others were German colonies that had become

mandates of the League of Nations after World War I. There were originally eleven trust territories, administered by Great Britain, France, Australia, the United States, Belgium, Italy, and New Zealand.

The symbol 👥 denotes active participation strategies.

Activities are keyed for student abilities:
▲ = Basic
● = All Levels
■ = Average/Advanced

Cooperative Learning

● Have students work in groups to research and create bulletin board displays of UN achievements. Have them include the organizational bodies as well as appropriate agencies. You may wish to refer students to Figure 20–2 for a chart of UN branches and agencies. Students may use pictures from magazines or original drawings for their displays.

GUIDED/INDEPENDENT PRACTICE

● Have students compare the UN General Assembly to the UN Security Council. Have students list at least five differences between the two.

RETEACHING/CORRECTIVES

▲ Have students review the organization of the United Nations by copying Figure 20–2 on a sheet of paper.

ENRICHMENT/EXTENSION

■ Have students debate the question of national sovereignty versus the authority of the United Nations. *Under what circumstances should UN personnel be used in a country against the wishes of its government?*

Section 4 Review Answers

1. (a) To provide a forum to debate issues and to produce agreements. **(b)** The United States feels that the Assembly sometimes acts as a forum for small countries to criticize the United States.
2. Five permanent and ten temporary member nations. The United States, Russia, Great Britain, China, and France are permanent members.

558

Madeleine K. Albright, shown here in her UN office, was named by President Clinton to serve as U.S. Ambassador to the United Nations. Daughter of a Czech diplomat who brought his family to the United States after the Communist take-over of Czechoslovakia in 1948, Albright is a scholar in international studies and has long advised Democratic leaders, especially in Russian and Eastern European affairs.

the end of the cold war, however, the Council has taken an aggressive role in dealing with areas of conflict around the globe. From 1988 to 1992, for example, the Council approved 14 peacekeeping operations — one more than in the previous forty-year period. Places where UN peacekeeping forces were sent in the early 1990's included Kuwait, Angola, the Balkans, Cambodia, Somalia, and Mozambique.

Secretariat

Administrative duties for the UN are handled by the **Secretariat**, the "executive branch" of the UN. The Secretariat consists of about 18,000 persons selected from member nations. The chief administrator is the Secretary General, who is appointed for a five-year term by the General Assembly in consultation with the Security Council. Among other things, the Secretary General helps set the UN agenda, mediates conflicts, and oversees peace settlements. Obviously, the position requires a competent person who is acceptable to the major nations. Throughout the cold war the Secretary General was generally from a nation not allied too closely with either the United States or the Soviet Union. Past Secretaries General have been citizens of Norway, Sweden, Burma, Austria, and Peru.

558

International Court of Justice

The judicial body of the United Nations is the International Court of Justice, or World Court. This tribunal, which meets at The Hague, Netherlands, helps settle international disputes and renders advisory opinions to the United Nations. It consists of fifteen judges, elected for nine-year terms by the General Assembly and Security Council. Nine judges constitute a quorum, and all decisions are made by majority vote. To ensure neutrality, no two judges may be from the same country.

In reality, the World Court plays a rather limited role in preserving the peace. Its authority is restricted to disputes in which the parties have agreed to abide by the World Court's decisions. Some nations simply choose to ignore decisions they disagree with. In 1984, for example, when Nicaragua accused the United States of aggression, President Reagan announced that this nation would not participate in World Court proceedings. Because the Court depends on the Security Council to enforce its decisions, there is nothing it can do without U.S. approval.

Other UN agencies

The United Nations has many other specialized bodies. The Economic and Social Council, for instance, furnishes aid and technical informa-

Background: *Global Awareness* In the case involving Nicaragua, the World Court ruled that the United States had violated international law by placing explosive mines in Nicaragua's harbors and ordered the United States to pay damages. The United States refused.

tion to developing nations. The World Food Council helps deliver millions of tons of food to underdeveloped countries, and the World Health Organizations fights disease worldwide. The United Nations Children's Fund (UNICEF) is well known for helping needy children around the world.

The UN and the United States

The end of the cold war raised issues about the United States' relationship with the United Nations. Viewed now as the world's only superpower, the United States has increasingly been called on to help settle conflicts throughout the world. Should this country take on a more active role as a global police force, or should the UN alone carry out that role? Is the United States willing to relinquish some of its authority to the UN in international affairs? And should the United States break with tradition and allow its armed forces to serve under UN command? These are among the serious issues facing the United States in rethinking its UN relationship in the 1990's.

SECTION 4 REVIEW

Vocabulary and key terms

General Assembly (556)   Secretariat (558)
Security Council (556)

For review

1. (a) What is the purpose of General Assembly meetings? (b) Why have they been criticized by the U.S.? 6B
2. What is the composition of the Security Council? 1A
3. What has sometimes made it difficult for the Security Council to take action on conflicts? 8F
4. What are some of the weaknesses of the World Court? 8C

Critical thinking

ORGANIZING AN ARGUMENT   Is the UN an effective way of preventing world conflicts? Why or why not? What might make it more effective? What alternative to the UN exists? 8C

Chapter Summary

The goals of American foreign policy are to maintain national security, carry out foreign trade, defend democracy, and, recently, uphold the balance of power. The United States followed a policy of neutrality or isolationism for most of the 1800's. With the development of military forces and foreign trade, America assumed an interventionist role. Since World War II the United States has followed an internationalist policy. During the cold war period, containment of Communist expansion became the overriding foreign-policy goal. The détente policies of the 1970's allowed a temporary relaxation of tensions between the superpowers.

The Secretaries of State and of Defense, along with the National Security Council and the CIA, are the President's top foreign-policy advisers. The State Department, with embassies and consulates throughout the world, carries out United States diplomatic policy. The Department of Defense, with headquarters in the Pentagon, is responsible for national defense. In a national emergency, military personnel can be drafted by the Selective Service System.

American diplomatic policies include providing foreign aid to our allies, sending Peace Corps volunteers to developing nations, and maintaining a positive image abroad. Sanctions can be used against other nations to protest policies we oppose. Collective security agreements, such as NATO, and deterrence became important components of America's defense policies during the cold war. Proliferation of nuclear weapons, however, poses a threat to all humanity.

The United Nations is a worldwide organization that attempts to maintain world peace. All member nations are represented in the General Assembly, but the Security Council makes important decisions. The veto power held by the permanent members of the Security Council made it difficult for that body to take action during the cold war. The Secretariat is the UN's administrative wing, and the World Court its judicial branch. Other UN organizations carry out specific tasks.

3. All five permanent members have veto power, which often prevents any action from being taken.
4. Some nations ignore World Court decisions with which they disagree. The Security Council is empowered to enforce court decisions, but it is often stymied by the permanent members' veto power.

Critical thinking Student answers might address the challenges of strengthening the Security Council's power to enforce international law, promoting peaceful resolution of conflicts, and maintaining a world governing body whose members have such diverse policy goals and economic, political, and social systems.

CLOSURE
● Have students write three "I learned . . ." statements about the section. Then have students read the next assigned lesson.

CHAPTER 20 CORRECTIVES
● To review the content of Chapter 20, you may want to have students complete **Study Guide/Review 20** or **Workbook Chapter 20.**

The symbol 👥 denotes active participation strategies.

Activities are keyed for student abilities:
▲ = Basic
● = All Levels
■ = Average/Advanced

CHAPTER 20 REVIEW

Answers

Vocabulary See pp. T19–T21 for suggested vocabulary activities.

Reviewing the Facts

1. It means defending this nation against foreign invasion as well as attempting to make the world more stable and peaceful.

2. It was issued to keep European powers out of Latin America and to keep Russia from extending its settlement beyond Alaska. It proclaimed that European powers were to stay out of the internal affairs of all independent nations in the Western Hemisphere. In return, the United States would not interfere in the internal concerns of any European state.

3. Isolationism allowed the United States to grow strong internally, avoid international confrontations, and maintain its independence.

4. The domino theory held that if one country fell to communism, neighboring countries would also fall. The United States feared that a Communist takeover of Vietnam would lead to a Communist takeover of all Southeast Asia.

5. The CIA gathers social, political, economic, and military information about other nations; such information is used to make foreign policy decisions. The NSC assembles information gathered by the CIA and other organizations and makes it available to the President.

6. The State Department.

7. The Security Council makes the important decisions in the UN, and the five permanent members have veto power over all decisions.

Thinking Critically About Key Concepts

1. **(a)** When the United States was economically and militarily weak, it had to remain neutral in

---

● **Review the definitions of the following terms:**

arms control	deterrence	neutrality
arms race	diplomatic immunity	nonaligned
balance of power	domino theory	Pentagon
chargé d'affaires	embargo	proliferation
cold war	foreign aid	protocol
collective security	General Assembly	Roosevelt Corollary
conscription	intelligence	Secretariat
consul	isolationism	Security Council
containment	Marshall Plan	Soviet bloc
counterintelligence	Monroe Doctrine	summit meeting
détente	NATO	superpower

● **REVIEWING THE FACTS**

1. What does national security mean in terms of American foreign policy? **1D**

2. Why was the Monroe Doctrine issued, and what did it proclaim? **1D**

3. How did the policy of isolationism help the United States in the 1800's? **1D**

4. Explain the theory that helped get the United States involved in the Vietnam War. **1D**

5. What are the roles of the Central Intelligence Agency and the National Security Council in making foreign policy? **3A**

6. Which executive department carries out America's foreign policy? **3A**

7. What makes the permanent members of the Security Council so powerful in the United Nations? **3A**

▲ **THINKING CRITICALLY ABOUT KEY CONCEPTS**

1. **(a)** How did the growth of U.S. military and economic power contribute to a shift in foreign policy? **(b)** Why are aggressive policies potentially more dangerous today than they were before World War II? **1D**

2. In what ways does the United States pursue **(a)** diplomatic policy? **(b)** defense policy? **8A**

3. How does participation in the United Nations help the United States meet a foreign policy goal? **3A**

▲ **PRACTICING SKILLS**

1. **Study Skills: Reading a map.** Refer to Figure 20–1 (page 542) to answer the following questions. **(a)** Were there more members of NATO or the Warsaw Pact as shown on the map? **(b)** Which countries on the map were nonaligned? **(c)** Which Communist countries were not members of the Warsaw Pact? **8B**

2. **Study Skills: Making an outline.** Outline the subsection "History of American Policy" (pages 539–544). Note the policies that prevailed in different periods and the events and declarations that characterized each period. Also note which Presidents' administrations were responsible for which policies. **1D**

3. **Critical Thinking Skills: Analyzing a political cartoon.** Refer to the political cartoon on page 540. Think of three questions you might ask yourself about this cartoon if you were trying to determine its meaning. (To review the skill of reading political cartoons, see Study Skill 5 in the back of the book.) **8B**

560

---

foreign disputes. As the country grew, its military forces were expanded, and the United States began to seek foreign markets more aggressively. Foreign policy became more aggressive as well, as the United States

became involved in the internal affairs of foreign nations to protect its interests. **(b)** Nuclear weapons, which did not exist before World War II, create the potential for a disastrous war.

2. **(a)** Through foreign aid, the Peace Corps, distribution of information, sanctions, and boycotts. **(b)** Through collective security agreements, deterrence, and military actions.

▲ PARTICIPATORY CITIZENSHIP

1. **Interview.** Ask someone who was a soldier, or who was in high school or college during the Vietnam War about attitudes or events that they remember from that time. How did the war affect their life, and what did they think about government policies? Report your findings to the class. **5C**
2. **Careers.** Find information about careers in the U.S. Foreign Service. What kind of education and skills would you need to become a member of the Service? What kinds of positions would be open to you? Write a description of a Foreign Service position that interests you. **4D**

■ WRITING ABOUT ISSUES

1. **Writing an essay.** Secret CIA operations, including assassinations and attempted coups, were revealed in Senate investigations during the mid-1970's. Do you believe the CIA should be free to pursue such activities, or do you favor strict controls on its operations? Write an essay explaining your answer. **8C**
2. **Biography.** Research one of the following Secretaries General of the United Nations: Trygve Lie, Dag Hammarskjöld, U Thant, Kurt Waldheim, Javier Pérez de Cuéllar, or Boutros Boutros-Ghali. Write a biographical sketch, including any important contributions he made to world peace. **8C**

▲ ANALYZING A POLITICAL CARTOON

As the cold war ended in the late 1980's and early 1990's, the United States government no longer viewed the Soviet Union and the other former Communist nations of Eastern Europe as the enemy. Instead, President George Bush called for a "new world order." Look at the cartoon and answer the following questions.

1. Describe the cartoonist's map of the old world order. **8B**
2. Describe how the cartoonist portrays the new world order. **8B**
3. How does the expression on the man's face suggest the message of the cartoon? **8B**

© Signe Wilkinson, Philadelphia Daily News. Courtesy, Cartoonists & Writers Syndicate, New York.

561

Practicing Skills

1. **(a)** NATO. **(b)** Finland, Sweden, Ireland, Switzerland, Austria. **(c)** Yugoslavia and Albania.
2. Students should include isolationism, the Monroe Doctrine, interventionism, the Roosevelt Corollary, World War I, the Good Neighbor Policy, World War II, the United Nations, containment, the cold war, the Korean War, the Cuban missile crisis, and the Vietnam War, as well as the appropriate Presidents, in their outlines.
3. Possible questions include: What is the setting? Who is represented by the lion? Who are the four other characters? What does the shovel signify?

Participatory Citizenship

1. Students may want to talk to people who served in the Persian Gulf War to compare and contrast attitudes, policies, and events.
2. You might invite a present or former member of the Foreign Service to visit the class, or encourage students to write letters to members whose careers they find interesting.

Writing About Issues

1. Students may want to consult newspapers and news magazines for articles on the CIA. They should support their arguments with specific details.
2. Students could work in groups and present reports to the class.

Analyzing a Political Cartoon

1. In the old-world-order map, the world was split between "good" and "evil" countries.
2. The new-world-order map is a patchwork of countries characterized by degrees of good or evil.
3. His expression shows uncertainty about the new world order.

3. The UN helps the United States meet its foreign policy goal of encouraging world peace and stability by giving nations a forum for settling disputes and encouraging cooperation among nations.

Chapter Review exercises are keyed for student abilities:
▲ = Basic
● = All Levels
■ = Average/Advanced

CHAPTER 21
POLICIES TOWARD BUSINESS, LABOR, AND AGRICULTURE
(pp. 562–587)

	Section Objectives	Section Resources
Section 1 **America Depends on Free Enterprise**	☐ explain the legal advantages of incorporating a business ☐ describe the types of economic assistance national and state governments provide to business	
Section 2 **The Government Regulates Business Practices**	☐ explain why the government is interested in maintaining competition ☐ describe how and why the government has acted to regulate big business	■ CONSTITUTIONAL ISSUES WORKSHEET **13** ▲ TRANSPARENCY **49**
Section 3 **Government Policies Affect Workers**	☐ describe legislation affecting labor unions ☐ describe government services that protect workers	▲ SKILLS PRACTICE WORKSHEET **21** ▲ TRANSPARENCY **50**
Section 4 **Agriculture Receives Government Support**	☐ describe how farm productivity has changed since World War II ☐ explain how the government uses direct price supports and other policies to help farmers	■ SKILLS CHALLENGE WORKSHEET **21** ▲ TRANSPARENCY **51**

Essential Elements

The list below shows Essential Elements relevant to this chapter. (The complete list of Essential Elements appears in the introductory pages of this Teacher's Edition.)

Section 1: 6G, 7C, 8A

Section 2: 3A, 4B, 6G, 7A, 7C, 8A

Section 3: 4B, 6B, 6C, 6E, 6G, 7A, 7C

Section 4: 7C, 8A, 8B, 8C, 8H

Chapter Review: 6G, 7C, 7D, 8A, 8B, 8C, 8D, 8E, 8F

> Section Resources are keyed for student abilities:
> ▲ = Basic
> ● = All Levels
> ■ = Average/Advanced

Homework Options

Each section contains activities labeled "Guided/Independent Practice," "Reteaching/Correctives," and "Enrichment/Extension." You may wish to choose from among these activities when assigning homework.

Students Acquiring English Activities

Have students read excerpts from the novel *The Grapes of Wrath* by John Steinbeck and/or watch the movie before studying Sections 3 and 4. Ask groups of students to dramatize sections of the book. Then discuss the effects of the Dust Bowl and President Roosevelt's New Deal farm programs.

LISTENING/SPEAKING: Have students debate the advantages and disadvantages of belonging to a labor union. Ask them to find out about the unions that exist in your community.

Case Studies

When teaching this chapter, you may use Case Study 4, which examines the issue of mandatory drug testing, or Case Study 9, which discusses the question of a special minimum wage for teenagers. (Case Studies may be found following p. 510.)

Teacher Bibliography

Farm Policy: The Politics of Soil, Surpluses, and Subsidies. CQ Press, 1984. Offers a general survey of United States food and agricultural politics and policies.

Seligman, Joel. *The Transformation of Wall Street: A History of the Securities and Exchange Commission and Modern Corporate Finance.* Houghton Mifflin, 1982. Traces the history of the SEC and analyzes the impact of the commission on the financial world.

Strickland, Allyn D. *Government Regulation and Business.* Houghton Mifflin, 1980. Looks at the relationship between American business and government. Covers antitrust policy, public utility regulation, and social regulation.

Student Bibliography

Schwartz, Alvin. *The Unions: What They Are, How They Came to Be, How They Affect Each of Us.* Viking, 1972. An overview of labor union history, its operations and organization, and a discussion of the interactions among unions, government, management, and the public.

Terkel, Studs. *The Great Divide: Second Thoughts on the American Dream.* Pantheon, 1988. The author reports and comments on interviews with 96 Americans who speak out on the major political, economic, and social issues of the 1980's.

Literature

Hailey, Arthur. *The Moneychangers.* Doubleday, 1975. A fast-paced novel about the world of banking and high finance.

Levy, Jacques E. *Cesar Chavez; Autobiography of La Causa.* Norton, 1975. This biography of Chavez is also a record of the founding and growth of the United Farm Workers.

Steinbeck, John. *The Grapes of Wrath.* Viking, 1977. The story of an Oklahoma farm family during the Great Depression forced to move to California in search of work.

Thomas, Michael M. *Hanover Place.* Warner Books, 1991. A novel about the rise and fall of a brokerage house from the Depression to the modern age of junk bonds and takeovers.

Films and Videotapes*

Government. (Series title: *American Enterprise.*) 29 min. MTPS, 1976. f, v. A middle management government employee tells how the government has contributed to America's economic growth as employer, borrower, and consumer.

The New Deal. (Series title: *American History.*) 25 min. McGraw-Hill (CRM), 1971. f, v. Uses photographs and newsreels to reconstruct the Depression and the New Deal policies of FDR. The hardships of the period are described as well as specific New Deal programs, many of which still exist today.

Software*

Industrialism in America: An Economic History (Apple). Focus. Students examine economic events from the rise of the factory system to the twentieth century. They learn the vocabulary and concepts necessary for understanding current economic events. Programs include: The Industrial Revolution Comes to the U.S.; The Age of Big Business; and Industrial America in the Twentieth Century.

---

* For a complete guide to audiovisual sources, see page T22.

CHAPTER 21

Policies Toward Business, Labor, and Agriculture *(pp. 562–587)*

Chapter 21 explains how business, labor, and agriculture operate under the United States economic system.

Chapter Objectives
After students complete this chapter, they will be able to:

1. Explain the legal advantages of incorporating a business.
2. Describe the types of economic assistance national and state governments provide to business.
3. Explain why the government is interested in maintaining competition.
4. Describe how and why the government has acted to regulate big business.
5. Describe legislation affecting labor unions.
6. Describe government services that protect workers.
7. Describe how farm productivity has changed since World War II.
8. Explain how the government uses direct price supports and other policies to help farmers.

CHAPTER

21

POLICIES TOWARD BUSINESS, LABOR, and AGRICULTURE

What we seek is balance in our economic system — balance between agriculture and industry and balance between the wage earner, the employer, and the consumer.

Franklin D. Roosevelt
(March 5, 1934)

Photo
Farmer feeding cattle.

homas Jefferson distrusted business. "The selfish spirit of commerce," Jefferson said, "knows no country, and feels no passions or principles but that of gain." However, without the quest for economic growth and the rewards of free enterprise there might well be no American nation. This quest motivated Americans to push back the country's frontiers, start farms and plantations, found business empires, and invent new technologies.

Advances in business changed the traditional roles of labor and agriculture. Labor unions grew in size and number in response to industrialization and the growth of factories in the late 19th century. Agriculture became more efficient, and the United States began exporting food around the world.

As American business expanded, so did government's regulatory role. This chapter examines how the federal government both promotes and regulates business, labor, and agriculture.

CHAPTER OUTLINE

1 America Depends on Free Enterprise

Assistance to Business

2 The Government Regulates Business Practices

Maintaining Competition
Protecting the Public

3 Government Policies Affect Workers

Policies Toward Unions
Protecting Workers

4 Agriculture Receives Government Support

Roots of Agricultural Policy
New Deal Farm Programs
Today's "Farm Problem"

563

CHAPTER SUPPORT MATERIAL

Skills Practice Worksheet 21

Skills Challenge Worksheet 21

Constitutional Issues Worksheet 13

Transparencies 49–51

Study Guide/Review 21

Workbook Chapter 21

Chapter 21 Test, Forms A-C

SECTION 1

America Depends on Free Enterprise
(pp. 564–567)

Section Objectives

☐ explain the legal advantages of incorporating a business

☐ describe the types of economic assistance national and state governments provide to business

Vocabulary

capital, corporate charter, underwriting, subsidy, merchant marine

ⅱ FOCUS

● Have one volunteer play the part of an owner of a small business and another volunteer play the part of an executive of a major corporation. Each of the volunteers should ask the class, which represents the federal government, for assistance in running his or her business. Both volunteers should also describe the consequences if help is not given. Have class members discuss their reactions. (The corporate executive, unlike the small business owner, can claim that failure to help his or her firm would directly harm the national economy.)

EXPLANATION

After students have read the section, you may want to consider the following activities:

Values

● CRITICAL THINKING Tell students that Ambrose Bierce defined a corporation as "an ingenious device for obtaining individual profit without individual responsibility." *What did Bierce mean?* (Individuals receive

---

6G, 7C, 8A

America Depends on Free Enterprise

ACCESS The Main Ideas

1 What are the legal advantages of incorporating a business? *page 564*

2 What are some types of economic assistance that national and state governments provide to business? *pages 565–566*

During the course of a day you might buy a newspaper from a newsstand, buy your lunch, fill up at a gas station, and go to a movie. Or you may watch a ballgame (and plenty of ads) broadcast by a television network on a set made by an electronics company. In each case you are in contact with a variety of business — money-making activities. In each case people have put **capital**, or invested money, in the business.

President Calvin Coolidge believed that "The business of America is business." Coolidge meant to emphasize the key role business plays in America's economic system.

6G, 7C

Assistance to Business

A healthy economy is necessary for a government to be stable and for a nation to prosper. For this reason, government often acts to promote our economic system. The Constitution links Congress with business in several ways: the power to set protective tariffs; to establish laws for bankruptcy; to coin money; to fix standards of weights and measures; and to issue copyrights, patents, and trademarks. Together, these federal powers create a climate in which business can function smoothly.

Charters and licenses

State governments also interact with business. Perhaps the most important state power is the chartering of corporations. Before a corporation can operate, it must receive a **corporate charter** from the state. A charter is a legal document that grants a corporation the right to operate. When a business receives a charter, it is said to be "incorporated."

564

In legal terms, a corporation is treated much like a "real" person. It can buy and sell property, enter into contracts, file lawsuits, and be sued. It must also follow laws and pay taxes. Corporations enjoy two distinct legal advantages in conducting business. First, they have perpetual life. That is, a corporation can exist after its original owners have left the business or died. Second, a corporation's stockholders cannot be held legally responsible for the company's losses. All they can lose is the amount of their investment. For instance, if a stockholder owns $1,000 of stock in Company Y, and Company Y goes $2 million into debt, the stockholder can lose only $1,000. Both of these features make it attractive for people to invest their money in corporations.

State governments also promote a favorable climate for business by requiring licenses for many professionals. For example, teachers, doctors, lawyers, stockbrokers, morticians, dentists, barbers, beauticians, and architects all must be licensed by the state in which they work.

Licensing serves two distinct purposes. First, it protects the public from untrained or unqualified operators. Furthermore, it protects the business interests of professionals by limiting the number of people who can practice a certain profession. Less competition means more business for those who hold licenses.

Public facilities

The government also provides many public facilities that make it easier for businesses to operate. Federal and state governments maintain an immense system of roads and highways, for example. All Americans benefit from using the roads, including businesses that transport their goods by truck. Airports, built with tax money, benefit not only passengers but also commercial airline companies. Barge and shipping companies benefit from government-supported river dredging, flood control, and navigation aids. The Saint Lawrence Seaway, for instance, is maintained and operated by a U.S. government corporation and its counterpart in Canada.

Critical Thinking
● *What groups other than airline companies and passengers benefit from airports? Why?* (The local community, because the construction and operation of an airport generate many types of jobs and because visitors who pass through airports help support service industries.)

Technical information and services

Businesses need up-to-date information about markets, competition, economic trends, science, technology, natural resources, and many other subjects. With this in mind, Congress created the Department of Commerce in 1903. Its primary purpose is to "foster, promote, and develop foreign and domestic commerce of the United States." Today, numerous bureaus and agencies in this department offer a wide assortment of free business information and services. (See page 449 of the Guide to Executive Departments for a detailed description of the Commerce Department's activities.)

Other federal agencies also provide free information and services to business. For example, the Federal Reserve Board publishes economic trends and forecasts in the *Federal Reserve Bulletin*. The U.S. Coast Guard (part of the Department of Transportation) patrols thousands of miles of American coastal waters to assist shipping and fishing vessels. The U.S. Forest Service (Department of Agriculture) and the Bureau of Mines (Department of the Interior) conduct research and publish technical data to aid the lumber and mining industries.

Tax breaks

As Chapter 19 describes, businesses are required to pay federal income taxes on their profits. Federal tax laws, however, also permit businesses to deduct many of their expenses. For instance, corporations may "write off" the cost of new machinery, business losses, and some new investments. Similarly, business persons are permitted to deduct the cost of many business-related activities, such as lunches, airplane tickets, and hotel accommodations. Although the tax reform of 1986 (page 516) significantly reduced the tax deductions available to business, there are still many ways that the business community can save tax dollars.

Loans to businesses

The federal government offers several kinds of financial help to encourage those who want to start and run businesses. One of the first programs to offer low-interest business loans was the Reconstruction Finance Corporation (RFC).

The St. Lawrence Seaway, a canal operated jointly by the governments of the United States and Canada, provides the Great Lakes region with a water passage to the Atlantic Ocean.

dividends from corporate profits, but no individual must pay the full cost of corporate losses.)

Economics

■ CRITICAL THINKING Discuss with the class the government's multibillion bailout of the savings and loan industry (p. 434). Have students find out why the bailout was necessary and who will pay for it. Ask students to evaluate the government's policy toward the banking industry and suggest ways in which it might be improved.

👥 Cooperative Learning

● Divide the class into groups and ask each group to choose the type of business that it would like to start. Using the text and any appropriate government publications, groups should create lists of the government programs and policies that might assist the enterprises and the ways in which they would help.

GUIDED/INDEPENDENT PRACTICE

● Have students create a table, based on the information presented on pp. 564–566, that shows how government assists business. Have students distinguish between state and federal assistance. Discuss the organization of the table before students begin.

565

Background: *Geography*
Some major cities that are served by the St. Lawrence Seaway are Toronto, Cleveland, Toledo, Detroit, Chicago, Milwaukee, Duluth, and Buffalo.

Background: *Economics*
The corporate income tax, which provides about 9 to 10 percent of the government's income, is a tax on a corporation's net income, or profits. Dividends paid out of already-taxed corporate profits are considered personal income for those receiving them, and are in effect taxed twice.

The symbol 👥 denotes active participation strategies.

Activities are keyed for student abilities:
▲ = Basic
● = All Levels
■ = Average/Advanced

Several government agencies help citizens get loans to buy or repair homes. Such policies not only help homeowners, but also strengthen real estate and construction businesses.

Founded in 1932 during the Depression, the RFC loaned out some $13 billion to business ventures in an effort to revive the economy. The program was ended in 1953 as part of an effort to cut federal spending. Since 1953, the Small Business Administration has provided loans and advice to small businesses.

Other federal loan programs aid business indirectly. The Department of Veterans Affairs and the Federal Housing Administration underwrite millions of dollars in home mortgage loans to qualified home buyers. **Underwriting** means that the federal government guarantees the loan and will take responsibility if the borrowers fail to pay it back. Such policies help not only new homeowners but also banks, builders, construction companies, and real estate firms.

In recent years, the federal government has given massive loans to several giant corporations that were on the verge of bankruptcy. Such "bailouts" saved the Penn Central Railroad, Chrysler Corporation, and the Continental Illinois National Bank and Trust Company. The government grants such loans to prevent widespread unemployment and to restore confidence in the business community. Critics of such loans, however, argue that such failures are due to company mismanagement and that the federal government cannot afford to bail out every troubled business.

566

Subsidies to businesses

In addition, the federal government provides **subsidies** (SUB-sih-deez) to businesses. A subsidy is any grant given by the government to reduce the cost of something. For example, during the 19th century, the federal government wanted to encourage settlement in the West. It gave railroad companies free land and provided services and grants to help lay miles of track. In the early days of air travel, the U.S. Post Office provided funds for private airlines to transport the mail. Moreover, postal rates for business mail — magazines, catalogs, and other mailings — have long been cheaper than those for personal letters.

One of the best examples of federal subsidies helps maintain the **merchant marine**, the private ships used in international trade. (Merchant ships are also used to carry supplies during war.) In recent years it has become increasingly difficult for American shipbuilders to compete with foreign companies, whose ships are built with cheaper labor and often supported by their governments. To offset these differences and maintain a strong shipping industry, the United States government subsidizes America's merchant fleet at the cost of roughly $200 million per year. The federal government also runs the U.S. Merchant Marine Academy, which trains people who want to work in the merchant fleet.

Background: *Economics* In 1983 Chrysler Corporation repaid the federal government loans in full—seven years before they were due.

SECTION 1 REVIEW

Vocabulary and key terms

capital (564)   subsidy (566)
corporate charter (564)   merchant marine (566)
underwriting (566)

For review

1. What two legal advantages do corporations have? **7C**

2. How do public facilities help businesses as well as private citizens? **7C**
3. What are some Cabinet departments that assist businesses? **7C**
4. In what ways does the federal government give businesses direct financial help? **7C**

Critical thinking

ORGANIZING AN ARGUMENT What are some reasons for government assistance to private business? What are some arguments against such government support? **8A**

3A, 4B, 6G, 7A, 7C, 8A

SECTION 2 · The Government Regulates Business Practices

| ACCESS | The Main Ideas |

1 **Why is the government interested in maintaining free competition?**
pages 567–570

2 **How and why has the government acted to regulate big business?** *pages 570–573*

In 1917 Theodore Roosevelt remarked, "The corporation has come to stay, just as the trade [labor] union has come to stay." Roosevelt also warned, "Each should be favored as long as it does good, but each should be sharply checked where it acts against law and justice." President Roosevelt believed, and the American public has long agreed, that there are circumstances under which government regulation of business is necessary.

The national government's power to regulate business stems primarily from Article I, Section 8, Clause 3 — the commerce clause. The power to regulate interstate commerce gives the federal government some authority over manufacturing, insurance, transportation, communications, public accommodations, and sales. In 1877 the Supreme Court ruled that a state government also had the right to regulate grain elevators and other businesses that were "affected with a public interest" (*Munn v. Illinois*).

7C

Maintaining Competition

Until the late 1800's, federal government policy encouraged the growth of giant industries and corporations that eventually acquired immense economic and political power. The government's first restrictions on business were intended to halt these corporations' uncontrolled growth, combat unfair business practices, and restore healthy competition in the economy.

The Interstate Commerce Act

By the 1880's, the rapidly expanding nation had become dependent on the railroads. Farmers in particular relied on the railroads to transport their products to market. Seizing an opportunity to make higher profits, the railroad companies agreed to divide their territory and eliminate competition on certain routes. Free from competition, railroad companies in each area could then charge customers whatever they desired. It was not uncommon for railroads to charge different customers different rates for hauling the same goods. Farmers often paid more for short hauls than long hauls. Upset over such abuses, angry farmers pressured the federal government to regulate the railroads. The result was the Interstate Commerce Act of 1887.

567

Critical thinking Supporting arguments should stress the interdependence of a healthy economy, a stable government, and a prosperous nation. Students might also cite instances in which the needs of society outweigh the importance of corporate profits. Opposing arguments should discuss the importance and incentives of the free enterprise system.

CLOSURE

● Remind students of the pre-reading objectives at the beginning of the section. Pose one or both of these questions again. Then have students read Section 2, noting the reasons why government regulates business.

SECTION 2

The Government Regulates Business Practices (pp. 567–573)

Section Objectives

☐ explain why the government is interested in maintaining competition
☐ describe how and why the government has acted to regulate big business

Vocabulary

trust, monopoly, divest, merger, takeover, conglomerate, public utility

---

The symbol 👥 denotes active participation strategies.

Activities are keyed for student abilities:
▲ = Basic
● = All Levels
■ = Average/Advanced

The Interstate Commerce Act requires railroads to charge "reasonable and just" rates to all its customers. The Act also created the Interstate Commerce Commission (ICC), an independent regulatory commission. The ICC's original function was to regulate railroad rates. Today the ICC regulates all common carriers, including interstate trucking companies, bus lines, motor carriers, boat lines, and ferry services. It also oversees mergers, sales, accounting practices, and rates of such companies.

The Sherman Antitrust Act

The railroads were not the only businesses involved in unfair practices in the 1880's. The **trusts** were another serious problem. A trust was a business combination formed to limit competition and fix prices. Stockholders of competing corporations would get together and "entrust" their stocks to a small board of "trustees," in effect creating one giant corporation. The trustees made all business decisions — how to divide up markets, place limits on production, fix prices, and split profits. The result was a **monopoly**,

A cartoon of the time shows the Standard Oil trust as an octopus whose tentacles grip oil, railroads, banks, shipping, and even the government.

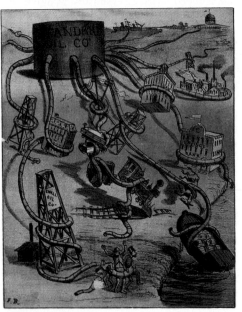

568

a situation in which a single business or firm controls an entire market.

Trusts came to dominate many industries, such as tobacco, sugar, matches, coal, whiskey, steel, gunpowder, lead, meat-packing, and fruit-canning. The best-known, and most unpopular, was the Standard Oil trust, formed by John D. Rockefeller and his associates in 1882. Standard Oil soon controlled over 90 percent of the nation's oil business. Oil prices rose, and by 1892, the shrewd Rockefeller had amassed a personal fortune worth more than $800 million (several billion by today's standards).

Public outrage over trusts led Congress to pass the Sherman Antitrust Act of 1890. The goal of this act was to maintain competition. It made illegal any "combination in the form of trust . . . in restraint of trade or commerce." It also made it a crime to "monopolize, or attempt to monopolize . . . any part of the trade or commerce." The law, however, failed to define such key terms as "trust," "monopoly," and "restraint of trade." The vagueness of the Sherman Act, plus Supreme Court decisions that limited its scope, made enforcement difficult and did little to halt abuses by big business.

The Clayton Act

Congress fought back in 1914, passing the Clayton Antitrust Act. This law prohibited specific business practices, including unfair or discriminatory pricing, "interlocking" boards of directors, and contracts that reduced competition. Unlike the Sherman Antitrust Act, the Clayton Act clearly spelled out what was illegal.

Also in 1914, Congress established the Federal Trade Commission (FTC) to carry out these provisions. The FTC's main duties are to establish rules for fair trade, investigate unfair trade practices, and issue "cease and desist" orders to stop unfair practices. The FTC's functions were later enlarged to include regulating advertising and protecting consumers.

Trends in antitrust policy

Today antitrust policy is carried out by some twenty federal agencies. Most antitrust enforcement, though, rests with the FTC and the Antitrust Division of the Justice Department.

The 1982 breakup of AT&T (American Telephone and Telegraph) — the world's largest corporation — was the most striking example of

Figure 21–1 STRUCTURE OF A CONGLOMERATE A typical conglomerate includes a diversity of companies and products.

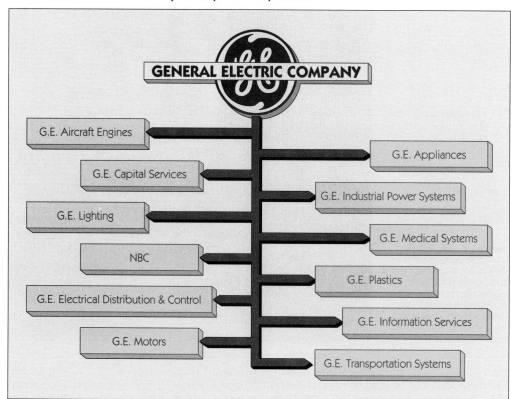

GENERAL ELECTRIC COMPANY

G.E. Aircraft Engines

G.E. Capital Services

G.E. Lighting

NBC

G.E. Electrical Distribution & Control

G.E. Motors

G.E. Appliances

G.E. Industrial Power Systems

G.E. Medical Systems

G.E. Plastics

G.E. Information Services

G.E. Transportation Systems

Economics

Refer students to Figure 21–1, which shows the organization of a conglomerate. Have students note the many different fields of manufacturing and production represented there.

● CRITICAL THINKING *Why might a corporation choose to expand into many different fields?* (To increase sources of sales revenue after old markets are saturated, to make use of existing sales and financial networks to sell multiple products.)

■ CRITICAL THINKING If a large corporation is headquartered nearby, you might want to have some students obtain a copy of its annual report and prepare a similar organizational chart of its corporate holdings.

modern antitrust activity. Following a seven-year lawsuit initiated by the Justice Department, AT&T was forced to **divest** — to give up ownership of 22 regional telephone companies. Out of this action, seven new telephone companies emerged: BellSouth, NYNEX, Bell Atlantic, Ameritech, Pacific Telesis, Southwest Bell, and U.S. West. The breakup ended AT&T's near-monopoly over U.S. communications and made the industry much more competitive. A number of competitors were encouraged also to challenge AT&T's control of long-distance phone service.

Maintaining free competition is still a difficult task. Although federal and state laws forbid trusts and most monopolies, there has been a growing trend toward a concentration of industries. Government has been cautious in taking action to stop corporate **mergers** — two companies combining — or to prevent **takeovers** —

one company buying another, even against its wishes (a "hostile takeover").

A number of markets are dominated by a few huge companies. The American automobile manufacturing industry, for example, is dominated by three very large companies — General Motors, Ford, and Chrysler. These corporations, of course, do compete among themselves. Moreover, they face stiff competition from foreign imports, particularly automobiles from Japan, West Germany, and Korea.

Oil companies, airlines, food manufacturers, and communications companies are other areas where mergers have become common. Of the roughly 200,000 industrial corporations in the United States today, the 100 largest now control over 58 percent of the wealth. Many of these are **conglomerates** — corporations with many companies in different fields (see Figure 21–1).

Figure 21–1

■ *Suppose one of the divisions listed were to lose a great deal of money in a given year. How might the executives at General Electric respond?* (They might sell that division or transfer profits from other General Electric divisions in order to make the troubled division more competitive.)

Background: *Global Awareness* Many European firms have merged to compete with U.S. and Japanese firms.

The symbol ⅈⅈ denotes active participation strategies.

Activities are keyed for student abilities:

▲ = Basic
● = All Levels
■ = Average/Advanced

Mandatory inspection protects consumers from diseased or unwholesome food products. Here, an inspector from the Food and Drug Administration checks fresh vegetables that are being imported into the United States.

Figure 21–2 shows America's ten largest industrial corporations as listed by *Fortune* magazine. These companies own between 30 and 40 percent of the corporate assets of the 500 largest companies.

6G, 7A, 7C

Protecting the Public

In addition to ensuring competition and fair business practices, the federal government is active in many other areas of business. The government's primary concern is to protect the general welfare of the American public.

Regulating the sale of stocks

The federal government sets rules for selling corporate stocks to the public. These regulations are in part designed to avoid the kinds of unscrupulous business practices that had helped cause the stock market crash of 1929 and bring on the Depression. To restore investors' confidence, Congress in 1934 established the Securities and Exchange Commission (SEC). The SEC requires

570

detailed financial reports from all corporations issuing stocks. These reports include data regarding profits, sales, and debts, which are then passed on to potential investors so that they can make informed decisions about buying and selling stocks.

Regulating public utilities

Both national and state governments closely monitor the **public utilities** — companies that provide a community with vital services such as gas, electricity, water, or telephone services. Some of these services may be provided by local governments. Otherwise, public utilities frequently are granted monopolies over the areas they serve. The reason is that competition among, say, electric companies could be impractical, inefficient, and dangerous.

In exchange for being granted a monopoly, public utilities must submit to more government regulation than other businesses. The government may set rates, determine services, or limit profits. Public utilities that operate within state boundaries are governed by various state regulatory commissions. The federal government regulates interstate utilities. Natural gas pipelines, for example, are regulated by the Federal Energy Regulatory Commission.

Regulating transportation

Transportation, another public service, is also regulated by the government. As mentioned earlier, interstate trucking, railroad lines, and bus companies are regulated by the Interstate Commerce Commission. The ICC has the power to impose safety standards and set reasonable rates. Highway safety is the responsibility of the National Highway Traffic and Safety Administration (NHTSA). For example, the NHTSA tests seat belts and monitors nationwide speed limits. Transportation within a state, such as local bus and taxi service, is supervised by state or local governing boards.

Airline safety falls under the jurisdiction of the Federal Aviation Administration (FAA). The FAA issues and enforces safety standards for air-

craft; trains and assigns air traffic controllers; certifies pilots, crew, and ground personnel; maintains airport security to prevent hijackings; investigates plane crashes; and conducts research to improve air safety.

Food and drug regulation

The rapid growth of industry after the Civil War had a profound impact on manufacturers of food and medical products. Mass production and distribution of canned goods and commercial medicines gradually began to replace home canning and home remedies for illness. Although these changes frequently were improvements, they sometimes created health problems. Some processed foods were contaminated, and drug companies often made false claims about their products. Consumers had little protection from useless and even dangerous products.

In the early 1900's, a group of crusading journalists, known as the "muckrakers," began reporting on social conditions and problems, especially in the food and drug industries. In

Figure 21-2 THE TEN LARGEST U.S. INDUSTRIAL CORPORATIONS, RANKED BY SALES (from The *Fortune* 500) 7C

1992 RANK	COMPANY (HEADQUARTERS)	1992 SALES (BILLIONS OF DOLLARS)	PROFITS
1	General Motors (Detroit)	132.8	7.3
2	Exxon (Irving, TX)	103.5	0.3
3	Ford Motor (Dearborn, MI)	100.8	13.3
4	International Business Machines (Armonk, NY)	65.1	−0.5
5	General Electric (Fairfield, CT)	62.2	3.3
6	Mobil (Fairfax, VA)	57.4	0.8
7	Philip Morris (New York City)	50.2	4.3
8	E.I. du Pont de Nemours (Wilmington, DE)	37.6	−3.1
9	Chevron (San Francisco)	37.5	1.8
10	Texaco (White Plains, NY)	37.1	−1.1

571

Figure 21-2
● *If most automobiles were replaced by public transportation, how many of the top ten U.S. corporations would be dramatically affected? Which ones?* (Six—all of the automobile manufacturers and oil companies.)

Background: *Economics* When Standard Oil was dissolved by the Supreme Court in 1911, 33 separate companies were formed. Today, the five largest of the old Standard Oil companies are Exxon (the largest petroleum company in the world), Mobil, Amoco, Chevron, and Atlantic Richfield.

Cooperative Learning
● Have groups of students prepare bulletin board displays showing examples of misleading and deceptive advertising. Students should analyze the techniques that the ads employ to sell products. Students may create their own examples or find them in print.

GUIDED/INDEPENDENT PRACTICE
● Have students use information in this section to compare the government's role in business during the 1800's with its role during the 1900's. Students should write essays describing government's changing policy toward business.

The symbol ᵦ denotes active participation strategies.

Activities are keyed for student abilities:
▲ = Basic
● = All Levels
■ = Average/Advanced

The Jungle (1906), novelist Upton Sinclair described in brutal detail the unsanitary conditions in the meat-packing industry. After reading *The Jungle,* President Theodore Roosevelt ordered an investigation of Chicago's meat-packing plants. The report confirmed Sinclair's shocking account. With pressure from Roosevelt, Congress immediately passed the Pure Food and Drug Act and the Meat Inspection Act (both in 1906).

The Pure Food and Drug Act prohibited the manufacture or sale of falsely labeled or "adulterated" foods or drugs. (Adulteration means that some vital ingredients have been removed, or that some harmful or poisonous matter has been added.) To enforce the provisions of the law, Congress created the Food and Drug Administration (FDA).

The Meat Inspection Act banned the shipment and marketing of diseased or unwholesome meat in interstate commerce. The law authorized the Department of Agriculture (USDA) to inspect and label all meat before it is sold. In the 1950's, USDA inspections were expanded to include poultry (chicken, turkey, duck).

The Food, Drug, and Cosmetic Act of 1938 strengthened food and drug laws and expanded coverage to cosmetics and health devices. For example, certain dyes may not be used in lipstick or hair coloring. Food package labels must list all the ingredients in order of quantity. In addition, all new medicines and food additives must be tested and approved as safe by the FDA before being put on the market. For example, Nutra-Sweet®, a sugar substitute used in diet foods and beverages, underwent years of testing before the FDA approved its use.

Regulations on advertising
Congress has also passed laws to ban the advertising of harmful foods, drugs, cosmetics, and therapeutic devices. The Federal Trade Commission (FTC) is charged with enforcing these regulations. Perhaps the most controversial of these laws have concerned cigarette advertising. In the early 1960's, the Surgeon General (an official of the Public Health Service) released a report linking cigarette smoking to lung cancer. In 1965 Congress required the following warning to be printed on all cigarette packages and ads: "Caution: Cigarette smoking may be hazardous

Because of the health risks linked with smoking, Congress in 1984 required the warnings now printed on cigarette packages.

to your health." In 1984 Congress required cigarette manufacturers to print several stronger warnings.

Additionally, in 1971 Congress banned all cigarette advertising on television and radio. Cigarette advertising on billboards and in newspapers and magazines was still permitted, but all ads had to carry the Surgeon General's warning. The future of tobacco advertising is still a subject of heated debate. The American Medical Association has taken the position that all forms of tobacco advertising should be prohibited. The American Tobacco Institute, however, maintains that such a ban would violate the First Amendment guarantee of free speech.

The FTC is also authorized to prohibit any false or misleading advertising, including radio, television, billboard, magazine, newspaper, or mail ads. Here are some examples of FTC crackdowns:

- In a television advertisement for Campbell's Soup, marbles were placed in the soup to make the vegetables rise to the top. The advertising agency was ordered to remove the marbles.

- The makers of Listerine mouthwash were prohibited from claiming Listerine could prevent or cure colds.
- The makers of Wonder Bread were ordered to stop advertising that "Wonder Bread helps build strong bodies twelve ways" because they were unable to prove the claim.
- To demonstrate how Rapid Shave could soften beards, a handful of the shaving cream was placed on a piece of "sandpaper," which was then shaved clean. The "sandpaper" was really a piece of glass with sand sprinkled over it. Rapid Shave was ordered to stop running the TV ad.

Consumer protection

Since the 1930's, consumers unhappy with shoddy, defective, and unsafe goods have formed private groups to test and rate products. In the early 1960's the movement known as "consumerism" brought about many new government policies aimed at consumer protection. One early consumer advocate was a young lawyer, Ralph Nader, who in 1965 published a book called *Unsafe at Any Speed*. The book attacked the design and safety record of General Motors' Corvair, a compact rear-engine car. Although General Motors tried to discredit Nader, Congress began an investigation of automobile safety.

In 1966 Congress passed two important automobile safety acts — the Highway Safety Act and the National Traffic and Motor Vehicle Safety Act. The first law required states to set up federally approved safety programs or risk losing 10 percent of their federal highway construction funds. The second law required automobile manufacturers to meet federal standards for automobile and tire safety.

The public and Congress also pushed for government action in other areas of consumer protection. Also in 1966, Congress enacted the "truth-in-packaging" act, which required manufacturers to label their products more clearly and accurately. Two years later, a "truth-in-lending" law required clear statements of loan or credit card terms and penalties. For instance, a borrower who agrees to pay "just 2 percent interest per month" must be told that this amounts to a rate of 24 percent *yearly* interest. The FTC enforces both these laws.

Another consumer issue faced by Congress was product safety. It was estimated that each year 20 million Americans are injured, and 30,000 die, as a result of using common household products. To help eliminate hazardous products, the Consumer Product Safety Commission (CPSC) was established in 1972. The function of this independent agency is to evaluate consumer products and develop uniform safety standards. Among the products the CPSC has investigated are lawnmowers, baby toys, bicycles, and kitchen appliances.

SECTION 2 REVIEW

Vocabulary and key terms

Interstate Commerce Act (567)
trust (568)
monopoly (568)
Sherman Antitrust Act (568)
Clayton Antitrust Act (568)
divest (569)
merger (569)
takeover (569)
conglomerate (569)
public utility (570)
muckraker (571)

For review

1. Under what constitutional power did Congress enact the Interstate Commerce Act and other laws regulating business? **3A**
2. What was the purpose of the Sherman Antitrust Act? **7C**
3. How did the Clayton Act correct the problems of the Sherman Act? **7C**
4. Why are public utilities subject to strict government regulation? **7C**
5. What are some federal agencies that regulate transportation? **7C**
6. (a) Why did some people call for a ban on cigarette advertising? (b) What do opponents of the ban argue? **8A**

Critical thinking

THINKING ABOUT BASIC IDEAS What was the role of public opinion in calling government attention to food and drugs, advertising, and consumer protection? Would government have acted in these areas without the pressures of public opinion? Can you think of any current government policies in which public opinion has played a similar role? **4B**

5. Interstate Commerce Commission, National Highway Traffic and Safety Administration, Federal Aviation Administration.
6. (a) Cigarettes were found to be harmful. (b) A ban on all cigarette advertising violates the First Amendment guarantee of free speech.

Critical thinking Students should note the pressure brought about by the public—especially journalists and organized groups—and speculate about the impact this pressure has had on the government. They might also discuss current issues, such as food contamination or hazardous conditions in the workplace, that reflect public concerns and generate public pressure on the government.

CLOSURE
● Review the Section 2 vocabulary with students to help reinforce key concepts from the section. Then have students read Section 3, noting the ways in which government regulation helps workers.

573

The symbol ⅱ denotes active participation strategies.

Activities are keyed for student abilities:
▲ = Basic
● = All Levels
■ = Average/Advanced

SECTION 3

Government Policies
Affect Workers

(pp. 574–579)

Section Objectives

☐ describe legislation affecting
labor unions

☐ describe government services
that protect workers

Vocabulary

collective bargaining, closed
shop, union shop, right-to-work
law, mediator, consumer price
index, minimum wage, worker's
compensation, unemployment
compensation

FOCUS

● Ask students why workers
might want to organize unions.
(To have more power in dealings
with management.) Then ask
how the government might
become involved in conflicts
between labor and management.
(If one or both sides used bargaining tactics that threatened
the public interest.)

Finally, ask students if they
know of any current issues
involving laws or government
policies that affect workers.
(Students may suggest civil rights
legislation or court cases deciding whether to allow employers
to bar women from certain
occupations.)

SECTION 3

Government Policies
Affect Workers

> **ACCESS** The Main Ideas
>
> **1** In what ways have business owners and
> management opposed labor unions?
> *pages 574–576*
>
> **2** What are some government services that
> protect workers?
> *pages 576–579*

To workers at the Pullman Palace Car Company,
George M. Pullman was both the landlord and the
boss. They were required to live in the company-
owned town of Pullman, Illinois. When the
economic depression of the 1890's hit, many
Pullman workers lost their jobs. The rest found
their wages cut, but the rent and fees they paid
Pullman stayed at the same high levels. A
workers' committee tried to meet with Pullman,
but he refused and their leaders were fired.

A young labor leader, Eugene V. Debs, called
a strike against the Pullman Company, but Pullman and other railway executives conspired to
thwart it. They called in strikebreakers from
Canada and linked mail cars to the Pullman
trains. When strikers tried to block the trains,
they were accused of interfering with the mail.
The government under President Grover Cleveland supported the railway owners, and Debs was
imprisoned. The union was forced to concede.

The American labor movement grew in response to the Industrial Revolution. Government policies initially worked against the labor
movement. As unions gained political strength,
government began to protect workers.

6B, 6G, 7A, 7C

Policies Toward Unions

The growth of unions

The first nationally organized unions in the
United States brought together skilled workers in
one craft — the National Typographical Union in
1852 and the Brotherhood of Engineers in 1863.
The first major union for all workers, skilled and
unskilled, was the Knights of Labor, founded in
1869. (Even some cowboys in the West were
members of this union.) The Knights grew to

more than 600,000 members before internal disputes led to its downfall in 1886. In that same
year, a group of craft unions under the leadership
of Samuel Gompers combined to form the American Federation of Labor (AFL). The AFL's primary
goals were to gain higher wages and better working conditions for union members.

One of the main tools used by labor unions is
collective bargaining. Collective bargaining is
the process in which a group of workers, represented by their union, negotiate with employers.
By banding together, workers have greater power
in bargaining for wages and working conditions.
The union's major weapon is the threat that members will strike, walking off the job until their demands are met.

Early labor unions met with stiff opposition
from company owners and managers. Both the
government and the courts generally took the
company's side in labor disputes. Business
owners could usually secure court injunctions to
prevent strikes, for many states viewed union
practices as illegal violations of property rights.
Some employers would not hire union workers,
while others forced new workers to sign yellow-
dog contracts, in which they agreed not to
join the union. Management would sometimes
blacklist known union supporters; that is, they
publicly singled out these workers as "trouble-
makers," making it difficult for them to find
jobs. Finally, management could hire "strikebreakers," thugs who used strong-arm tactics to
intimidate union workers.

Early labor legislation

Facing such obstacles, labor leaders decided
on a new course — political action. Union members, after all, were also voters. Beginning in the
early 1900's, many public officials sympathetic
to labor were elected.

Pro-labor politicians gradually began to have
an impact on legislation. The first major breakthrough was the Clayton Antitrust Act of 1914
(page 568). The Sherman Antitrust Act had been
used against labor unions, declaring them to be

Background: *Politics*
Eugene Debs's experiences
during the Pullman strike
converted him to socialism.
He ran for President five
times as the Socialist candidate, gaining nearly a million votes in 1920.

Background: *Economics*
Collective bargaining was
also called "bread and butter" unionism, as opposed to
socialist or revolutionary
unionism, the purpose of
which was to transform
society.

in illegal "restraint of trade." The Clayton Act, however, exempted labor unions from antitrust laws and recognized them as legitimate organizations. The Clayton Act was hailed by Samuel Gompers as the "Magna Charta of labor." In 1932 Congress passed the Norris-LaGuardia Act, which prevented federal courts from issuing injunctions against peaceful labor strikes. It also made yellow-dog contracts unenforceable in federal courts.

The Wagner Act

If the Clayton Act was labor's "Magna Charta," then the National Labor Relations Act of 1935, or Wagner Act, was labor's "bill of rights." The Wagner Act guaranteed workers the right to organize, join unions, and bargain collectively. In addition, it prohibited employers from discriminating against union workers, firing union workers for filing complaints, or setting up "company unions," which were unions controlled by management. To administer the law and settle disputes, the act also created the National Labor Relations Board (NLRB).

With government protection assured by the Wagner Act, labor union membership rose dramatically. Between 1935 and 1947, union membership increased from 3.6 million to nearly 15 million. Still, unions represented only about one-third of the labor force. Membership was especially low in the South.

After World War II, the Wagner Act began to draw criticism. Management denounced what it felt were unfair labor practices, such as being forced to adopt **closed shops** in order to avert strikes. A closed shop means that employers can hire only union members. Many Americans also became impatient over the growing number of strikes. In 1946 and 1947, strikes in the coal, steel, railroad, and automobile industries caused severe shortages and rising prices. Public sentiment favored some form of restraint on "big labor," just as it had earlier on "big business."

The Taft-Hartley Act

In 1946, Republicans won a majority in both houses of Congress for the first time since 1929. The election brought an about-face in federal

Federal regulations protect laborers by establishing maximum working hours and minimum wages. Employers are responsible for maintaining a safe working environment.

EXPLANATION
After students have read the section, you may want to consider the following activities:

Economics
Read the following statement, attributed to Theodore Roosevelt, to the class: "The corporation has come to stay, just as the trade union has come to stay. Each can do and has done great good. Each should be favored as long as it does good, but each should be sharply checked where it acts against law and justice."

● CRITICAL THINKING *Consider the use of the terms* good, law, *and* justice. *What potential source of controversy exists in these terms?* (Different people have different interpretations of *good* and *justice*. Also, while everyone agrees that no person or organization should break the law, not everyone agrees about what the law should say.)

Background: *Economics*
Union membership showed some increase in the early 1960's, largely because of the growth of public employee unions. Since 1980, however, the percentage of all workers enrolled in unions has been declining. This decline is largely due to the shift of the labor force from manufacturing and manual work (areas in which unions have always been strong) into service organizations.

The symbol 👥 denotes active participation strategies.

Activities are keyed for student abilities:
▲ = Basic
● = All Levels
■ = Average/Advanced

History

● Ask volunteers to come to the board and create a time line showing the major pieces of labor legislation discussed on pp. 574–576.

▲ **Why was the Clayton Anti-trust Act of 1914 important to workers?** (It recognized labor unions as legitimate organizations.)

▲ **What additional protections did workers receive from the Wagner Act of 1935?** (It guaranteed workers the right to organize, join unions, and bargain collectively.)

● CRITICAL THINKING **How did the Taft–Hartley Act of 1947 and the Landrum–Griffin Act of 1959 mark a new direction in the federal government's policy toward unions?** (While earlier legislation had focused on giving workers more rights, these later laws limited unions' ability to demand the use of union labor and sought to ensure that unions were run honestly.)

Controversial Issues

● Have students look in recent newspapers and magazines for articles, editorials, or letters from readers supporting or opposing a raise in the minimum-wage level. Then hold a class debate on the issue, with students presenting arguments for and against a higher minimum wage. Encourage students to consider the issue from the viewpoints of both employers and employees.

labor policy. In 1947 Congress passed the Labor-Management Relations Act, or Taft-Hartley Act, over Democratic President Harry Truman's veto. Named after its sponsors, Senator Robert Taft of Ohio and Representative Fred Hartley of New Jersey, this act limited union activities.

Among its many provisions, the Taft-Hartley Act outlawed closed shops, although it permitted **union shops**. In a union shop, workers do not have to be union members but must join a union after being hired. The law did allow states to adopt **right-to-work laws**, which prohibit using union membership as a condition for employment at all. Under right-to-work laws, workers may join unions, but they cannot be compelled to do so. Labor leaders feel that such laws undermine unions, because workers can benefit from union negotiations without joining. Business leaders, on the other hand, maintain that right-to-work laws protect the freedom of workers to choose the conditions of their employment. Today a number of states around the nation have right-to-work laws.

Figure 21-3 LABOR UNION MEMBERSHIP The number of workers belonging to labor unions has tapered off in recent years. **7A**

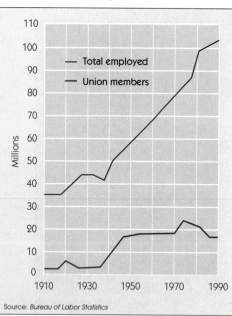

Source: Bureau of Labor Statistics

576

Perhaps the most controversial Taft-Hartley provisions concern the right to strike. The law forbids strikes by federal government employee unions. Other labor unions are required to give management 60 days notice before striking, providing a period to iron out their differences.

Taft-Hartley also allows government to intervene in labor disputes. It created the Federal Mediation and Conciliation Service, which supplies federal **mediators** to work out compromises when talks have failed. It also lets the President delay a strike for up to 80 days by securing an injunction. Presidents most often use this power during crises, when a prolonged strike in a vital industry could cripple the nation. Both workers and employers, however, usually prefer to settle disputes without government intervention.

The Landrum-Griffin Act

During the 1950's, public attention was drawn to corruption in labor unions by a special Senate committee investigation of union racketeering. The committee found that Dave Beck and Jimmy Hoffa, both presidents of the Teamsters Union, had not only misused union funds but also used violence to intimidate union members. The investigation also tied Teamsters leaders to organized crime and illegal gambling. To curb such practices and ensure democracy within unions, Congress in 1959 passed the Landrum-Griffin Act (officially called the Labor-Management Reporting and Disclosure Act).

The Landrum-Griffin Act set standards to make union elections fairer and more honest. It guarantees members the right to nominate and elect their leaders by secret ballot, to speak freely, and to sue their unions for unfair practices. The act also requires labor unions to file annual reports with the Department of Labor. Furthermore, it bars individuals with criminal records or conflicting business interests from holding union offices. In sum, the goal of labor policy is to strike a balance between management and labor, while protecting the public interest. **7A, 7C**

Protecting Workers

In addition to regulating relations between unions and employers, the federal government also protects working people. In 1913 Congress added a Department of Labor to the Cabinet, with

Figure 21-3
● **What might have caused the sharp rise in the number of union members beginning in the late 1930's?** (The passage of the Wagner Act in 1935, which guaranteed workers the right to join unions.)

Like any labor union, the United Farm Workers—shown here at a San Juan, Texas, convention—is subject to federal supervision of its elections and finances.

the goals: "To foster, promote, and develop the welfare of wage earners of the United States." Congress also passes laws to ensure fair wages, reasonable working hours, and safe workplaces. Many of these regulations are the result of union activity, though they benefit all working people.

Providing data on labor

One of the many services provided by the Labor Department is the collection, evaluation, and publication of data. This function is handled by the Bureau of Labor Statistics (BLS).

One useful statistic compiled by the BLS is the **consumer price index** (CPI), also called the "cost of living" index. It measures the costs of goods and services usually purchased by consumers, such as food, clothing, transportation, housing, and entertainment. The CPI provides one way of measuring the consumer's actual buying power — how much his or her paycheck will buy. For instance, if workers are offered a 5 percent raise, but the cost of living has increased by 10 percent, they are actually taking a cut in real wages. Thus, the CPI is often used by labor in negotiating contracts and adjusting salaries and benefits to keep up with the cost of living.

Policies on wages and hours

Except for allowing union contracts, the federal government had no federal policy regarding employee wages or hours until the 1930's. In 1936 Congress passed the Walsh-Healey Public Contracts Act, which prohibited the federal government from buying more than $10,000 worth of supplies from firms whose employees had to work more than eight hours a day or 40 hours a week. If employees worked overtime, they had to be paid time-and-a-half, that is, their hourly wage plus 50 percent.

A more important and far-reaching hours and wage law was the Fair Labor Standards Act of 1938. Its sponsor was Senator Hugo Black of Alabama. The law established a "floor under wages" and a "ceiling over hours" for workers engaged in interstate commerce. The **minimum wage** that workers could be paid was set at 25 cents per hour, and the maximum number of hours was set at 40 per week. For anything over 40 hours, workers had to be paid time-and-a-half.

About three million Americans are paid the minimum wage, which rises periodically to keep up with inflation. In 1991, Congress raised the minimum wage from $3.80 to $4.25 per hour. Labor leaders supported greater increases, while business leaders claimed these were unnecessary. Most, but not all, workers are covered by the Fair Labor Standards Act. Exceptions include part-time employees, salespersons, babysitters, and people employed in agriculture and fishing.

Restrictions on child labor

Even in the early 1900's it was common for children and women to work in sweatshops — crowded, airless factories where people toiled long hours for very low wages. Many states passed laws restricting child labor, but the Fair Labor Standards Act of 1938 was the first statement of a national policy on the issue. This law set minimum age requirements for certain types of jobs: 14 years for non-manufacturing jobs outside of school hours, 16 years for those employed in interstate commerce during school hours, and 18 years for those employed in hazardous occupations.

Prohibiting job discrimination

Discrimination is another problem that has long plagued many American workers. A number of federal laws now prohibit job discrimination. The Civil Rights Act of 1964 is the best example. Title VII of this act prohibits discrimination in hiring or promotion because of race, sex, religion, or color. It also set up the Equal Employment Opportunity Commission (EEOC). More recent laws also protect older workers, the disabled, and veterans. Finally, affirmative action programs have been implemented to make up for past discrimination. (Chapter 7 discusses laws against job discrimination in greater detail.)

Workplace safety

Until 1970, the responsibility for health and safety in the workplace fell largely on state governments. The few federal safety laws on the books applied only to dangerous industries such as railroads and coal mining and were poorly enforced. In 1970 a House committee investigating work-related accidents noted these figures for one year: "14,500 workers killed, 2,200,000 workers injured, 390,000 cases of occupational disease (lung cancer, asbestosis, etc.); 250 million man-days of work lost (ten times as many as by strikes). More than $1.5 billion in lost wages. More than $8 billion loss to GNP."

Faced with such strong evidence of dangers in the workplace, Congress enacted the Occupational Safety and Health Act of 1970. The law was to be administered by the Occupational Safety and Health Administration (OSHA), an agency of the Labor Department. OSHA's main duties are to (1) set industrial safety standards; (2) identify and eliminate cancer-causing sub-

Many children, like this mill worker, labored under unhealthful conditions until the federal government limited child labor.

Background: *Economics* According to the Bureau of Labor Statistics, the occupational injury and illness rate rose from 7.9 cases per 100 full-time private sector employees in 1986 to 8.3 per 100 in 1987.

Background: *History* The first scheme to insure workers against unemployment appeared in a Wisconsin law passed in 1932. States alone were unable to carry the burden, and in 1935, with the passage of the Social Security Act, the federal and state governments formed a partnership to ease the burden of unemployment.

stances (carcinogens) found in the workplace; (3) investigate charges of safety violations; and (4) enforce federal safety standards. OSHA has been criticized by business leaders for being too picky and trivial and by labor for not doing enough. Nevertheless, it appears that OSHA has had a significant impact on reducing work-related accidents.

In addition, every state requires employers to compensate workers who are injured or become ill on the job. This is known as **worker's compensation** (often called "worker's comp"). Most states require employers to reimburse workers for lost earnings and to pay for medical expenses and rehabilitation. The federal government provides worker's compensation to federal employees, maritime workers, railroad workers, and others not covered by state laws.

Employment services

Unemployment is a problem that affects the entire economy. But neither the federal government nor the states offered any complete employment services before the Great Depression of the 1930's. When the national unemployment rate reached a record high of 23.6 percent in 1932, the federal government took action. The Wagner-Peyser Act (1933) created the first nationally coordinated employment service. Under this act, the federal government agreed to pay each state three-quarters of the cost of operating state employment agencies. Soon each state provided employment services, making it possible for unemployed workers to secure information about possible job openings.

Another important development was the establishment of **unemployment compensation** under the Social Security Act. Unemployment compensation is paid to persons who lose their jobs through no fault of their own. States run the programs following federal guidelines.

Money for unemployment compensation comes from a tax on employers. The amount of tax varies, depending on the state and the employer. Employers with records of stable employment pay less than employers with high turnover. The money is collected by the states and placed in the Federal Unemployment Trust Fund, from which it is distributed as needed.

Eligible workers who lose their jobs must wait one or two weeks, then register with the appropriate state employment agency. To receive benefits, the person must agree to look for work and take a suitable job if it is found. Unemployment benefits vary from state to state.

Family emergency rights

Should employees be allowed time off from their jobs when family members become ill? Until recently the United States was one of the few industrialized nations that had no national policy concerning this kind of employment issue. In 1993, Congress enacted, at President Clinton's request, the Family and Medical Leave Act. Under its terms a worker may take up to 12 weeks of unpaid leave for the birth or adoption of a child, the illness of a child or other close relative, or the worker's own illness. The act covers all employers with more than 50 workers.

SECTION 3 REVIEW

Vocabulary and key terms

collective bargaining (574)
closed shop (575)
union shop (576)
right-to-work law (576)
mediator (576)
consumer price index (577)
minimum wage (577)
worker's compensation (579)
unemployment compensation (579)

For review

1. (a) What is the advantage of collective bargaining for workers? (b) What is labor's most useful weapon in negotiating with management? 6B
2. What were the two early breakthroughs in pro-labor legislation? 6C
3. What changes in public opinion led to passage of the Taft-Hartley Act? 4B
4. Why is the consumer price index important to labor in collective bargaining? 6B
5. What programs are available for people who are hurt at work or who lose their jobs? 6E

Critical thinking

ANALYZING AN ISSUE How do government policies try to balance the interests of management and labor? 7C

Section 3 Review Answers

1. (a) Together, the workers have greater bargaining power. **(b)** Threatening to walk off the job until its demands are met.
2. Clayton Antitrust Act of 1914; Wagner Act of 1935.
3. Many Americans began to favor restraints on "big labor" because of the growing number of strikes.
4. This figure is used in labor negotiations to adjust salaries and benefits in relation to the cost of living.
5. Worker's compensation and unemployment compensation.

Critical thinking On the one hand, the government has allowed states to adopt right-to-work laws, which management supports, and has set standards to ensure that unions are fairly run. On the other hand, the government has guaranteed workers the right to strike; it has also set a minimum wage, worked to prevent job discrimination, and taken other actions to benefit labor.

CLOSURE

● Have students write three "I learned . . ." statements to show what they learned in this section. Then have them read Section 4, paying special attention to the historical origins of today's farm policies.

The symbol ⅱ denotes active participation strategies.

Activities are keyed for student abilities:
▲ = Basic
● = All Levels
■ = Average/Advanced

SECTION 4 — Agriculture Receives Government Support

> **ACCESS The Main Ideas**
>
> **1** In what ways has farm productivity changed since World War II? *pages 580–581*
>
> **2** How does the government use direct price supports and other policies to help farmers? *pages 581–585*

What do you think of when you think of agriculture in America? Many people think of a family living on a small farm. In the past, this was more true than it is today. In 1790, for example, about 95 percent of all Americans lived on family farms. Today, only about 2 percent do. However, the United States still grows enough food to feed its population and to export food overseas.

Farms in America today are much larger and more efficient than ever before. Government policies reflect this dramatic shift.

Roots of Agricultural Policy

Encouraging agriculture

In the early 1800's, the federal government's policies supported westward expansion and settlement. By 1862, the government began actively to encourage farming and raising livestock, especially in the West and Midwest. Soon after the Civil War began, President Lincoln signed the Homestead Act to encourage food production for the Union and for export. Under this act, Congress offered 160 acres of public land to any settler or family who paid a registration fee and lived on the land for five years. By 1900, millions of acres of farmland had been parceled out to these pioneers, called "homesteaders."

Also in 1862, Congress created the Department of Agriculture to provide information and

Families such as this one in Custer County, Nebraska, were able to acquire farmland with the incentives of the federal government's Homestead Act.

Background: *History* As late as the mid-1930's, almost one-fourth of all Americans lived in rural areas.

assistance to farmers. (It was not given Cabinet status until 1889.) Congress also passed the Morrill Act, which granted funds from public lands in each state still in the Union to establish agricultural and mechanical colleges. These schools, known as **land-grant colleges**, were to teach agriculture, veterinary medicine, engineering, and other subjects vital to farming.

Many of today's large state universities developed from land-grant colleges, including Iowa State, Michigan State, Texas A&M, Purdue, the University of Illinois, and the University of Missouri. A second Morrill Act, in 1890, continued the program. Today there are about 75 land-grant colleges. The federal government continues to provide funds for these institutions.

The land-grant colleges also experimented with better crops and farming methods. In addition, in 1914, Congress granted funds to states to establish agricultural extension programs. These educational programs are cooperative efforts by the Department of Agriculture, the land-grant colleges, and county agents to improve farming.

"Boom and bust" years

The early years of the 20th century are often called the "golden years" of American agriculture. With the help of new techniques, farm production increased and profits rose. The federal government promoted soil conservation. The outbreak of World War I in 1914 increased the demand for exports, especially in Europe. In addition, Congress created a system of federal Farm Loan Banks, which helped farmers purchase additional land and equipment. This agricultural boom, however, was short-lived.

The end of World War I in 1918 had a devastating effect on American farmers. Postwar poverty in Europe halted the great demand for agricultural exports, so that American farmers were producing far more than they could sell. Prices for wheat, corn, and cotton fell to record lows. In addition, many farmers were heavily in debt from borrowing during the war.

When the Depression struck the United States in the early 1930's, farm problems grew worse. The price of agricultural goods continued to drop. Scores of farmers could not make payments on their farms and lost their land. The final blow was a severe drought in 1934, which coupled with overworked land to create a "Dust

YOU DECIDE

8H

Minnesota law requires all slow-moving vehicles to display a sign. Jacob Hershberger was ticketed for failing to display the sign on his horse-drawn buggy. A member of the Amish community, Hershberger does not use modern conveniences and says that his beliefs emblem conflicts with his beliefs because it means he puts faith in a "worldly" symbol instead of God.

Does Hershberger have a case?

Bowl." The Southwest was particularly hard hit, as millions of acres of topsoil blew away from farms in Texas, Oklahoma, and other states.

7C
New Deal Farm Programs

To meet this emergency, President Franklin Roosevelt's New Deal program made dramatic changes in federal farm policies.

Agricultural Adjustment Act

The first major legislation was the Agricultural Adjustment Act (AAA) of 1933. Under this act, the federal government set limits on the production of crops and livestock, such as wheat, corn, hogs, and cattle. Farmers were then paid *not* to produce at full capacity. A smaller supply of agricultural products meant higher prices and greater profits for farmers.

To further protect farmers, the AAA called for the federal government to pay farmers **parity**. Parity, meaning equality, is a method of **price supports** that helps farmers maintain their purchasing power and standard of living. For example, in a good year a farmer can sell one bushel of corn for enough money to buy a pair of shoes. Later the price of shoes doubles. To maintain purchasing power, the farmer would have to charge twice as much for a bushel of corn. The AAA required the government to make up the difference by paying parity.

581

EXPLANATION
After students have read the section, you may want to consider the following activities:

History
▲ *Why did the federal government encourage people to move west and begin farming during the Civil War?* (To raise food production for domestic use and for export.)

▲ *What was the purpose behind the creation of the Department of Agriculture?* (To provide information and assistance to farmers.)

▲ *How did the Morrill Act affect agriculture in the United States?* (It provided for the creation of land-grant colleges, which would teach subjects related to farming.)

▲ *What events during the 1930's led to a more active federal role in agriculture?* (The Depression caused farm prices to drop and drove many farmers off their land; the Dust Bowl physically destroyed many farms.)

Background: *Economics*
Parity is based on a year in which farmers did well economically. The AAA used the "boom" years of 1910–1914 as its base.

You Decide Answer
Students should defend their answers. Minnesota's state supreme court ruled that the state could not force Hershberger to display the sign.

The symbol 👥 denotes active participation strategies.

Activities are keyed for student abilities:
▲ = Basic
● = All Levels
■ = Average/Advanced

Politics

■ Tell students that one of the ways the government supports agriculture in arid western lands is to sell farmers water from government-built dams at prices well below cost. Ask students to research the sources of water used by farmers in your state. *Where would farmers get water if this source were more expensive or unavailable?*

Economics

● Hold a class debate on the issue of price supports for agricultural products. One side in the debate should call for the complete elimination of price supports. The other side should argue that the nation is better off with supports than without them. Explain that opponents of price supports must be able to explain how they will deal with the economic effects of ending price supports and that backers of price supports must be able to explain why price supports are not inconsistent with a free market economy.

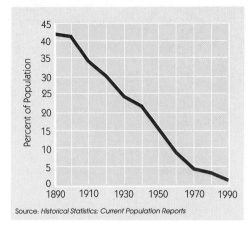

Source: *Historical Statistics; Current Population Reports*

Figure 21–4 PERCENTAGE OF AMERICANS LIVING ON FARMS 8B

The Supreme Court, however, ruled the AAA unconstitutional in 1936 on grounds that regulating farm production was a power reserved for the states. Congress revised the law and enacted another Agricultural Adjustment Act in 1938. It was again challenged, but this time the High Court upheld it. The AAA became the model for present-day agricultural policies.

Utilities for rural areas

Another important New Deal creation was the Rural Electrification Administration (REA), established in 1935 to bring electrical service to rural areas. By providing long-term, low-interest loans, it helped local governments and farm cooperatives purchase and build electrical lines and equipment. In 1949 the REA was authorized to help bring telephone service to rural America. When the REA was formed, less than 10 percent of America's farms had electricity. Today nearly 99 percent have electricity and telephones.

Soil conservation

By 1935, soil erosion by wind and water had seriously damaged an estimated 300 million acres of American farmland. The Soil Conservation Act of 1935 established a joint federal-state program to assist farmers in learning and practicing soil conservation techniques. Today there are over 2,900 soil conservation districts to assist farmers in these techniques.

582

Farm Security Administration

Still another New Deal farm innovation was the Bankhead-Jones Tenant Act of 1937. During the Depression over 20 percent of American farmers lost their own farms and became tenants who worked on an owner's land. This act offered long-term, low-interest loans to help these farmers buy their own farms. The Farm Security Administration was created to administer the program and was later replaced by the Farmers Home Administration.
7C

Today's "Farm Problem"

Since World War II, changes in technology and in world conditions have created a new set of issues in American agriculture. For the government, the continuing "farm problem" has been to keep the farm economy stable and prosperous but, at the same time, to keep food prices low for consumers in the rest of the economy.

Postwar changes in agriculture

Advances in technology following World War II led to greater and more efficient farm production. Scientific research produced better fertilizers, high-yield crops, and chemicals to control plant and animal diseases. Machines took over many farm chores. On the other hand, increased efficiency and productivity meant that fewer farmers were needed. In 1940, for example, one farm worker could produce enough food to feed ten people. Today a single farmer is capable of feeding more than eighty people.

The number of farms and farmers has continued to diminish steadily. Moreover, during that same period, the average size of farms has swelled from 167 acres to 462 acres. While some small family farms remain, many "farms" are actually large commercial enterprises, "food factories" producing a single crop. They are part of **agribusiness**, a network of food production, processing, and marketing organizations.

While farm productivity rose sharply because of technology, so did the costs of running a farm. New equipment, fertilizers, and even land became more expensive. Interest rates also were high for mortgages and loans. Again, these costs were a greater burden for the small family farm.

Another result of high farm productivity was a **surplus** — an extra supply — of agricultural

Figure 21–4
The percentage of Americans living on farms was how many times greater in 1900 than in 1970? (About eight times—42 percent in 1900 versus 5 percent in 1970.)

Background: *Constitutional Heritage* The Court upheld the second AAA's constitutionality in *Mulford v. Smith* (1939).

Background: *History* Lyndon Johnson credited much of his congressional election success to bringing electricity to his district. One Texan explained: "He brought the lights. No matter what Lyndon was like, we loved him because he brought the lights."

goods. Farmers were caught in a vicious circle. They needed large harvests to make good use of their expensive land and equipment. Yet surplus crops caused farm prices to fall and so reduced the farmers' profits.

Postwar farm policies

Government policies have tried to address these complications of the "farm problem." They have focused mainly on keeping prices stable and limiting production through purchases, payments, or subsidies.

One approach is setting acreage allotments. Researchers in the U.S. Department of Agriculture (USDA) estimate world demand for various agricultural products, then calculate how many acres of crops are needed to meet this demand. Farmers are then assigned an allotment, a limited number of acres they can cultivate. Farmers who plant more acres than their allotment become ineligible for other federal help. Under other federal programs, farmers can voluntarily leave some of their land idle, in return for crops or cash.

Another program designed to control the supply of agricultural products depends on farmers' voluntarily keeping back some of their crops. This program, run by the USDA's Agricultural Marketing Service, establishes marketing quotas that set the amount to be sold or kept in storage till demand increases.

Direct price supports are another tactic of farm policy. Since 1973, the USDA has established **target prices** for basic commodities, such as wheat, rice, peanuts, milk, wool, and cotton. Under this program, the federal government pays farmers cash if prices on the open market fall below the target prices. In 1985, for example, the target price for wheat was set at $4.38 per bushel. If the market price fell below $4.38 per bushel, the federal government made up the difference. A limit of $50,000 a year was set on payments to a single farmer.

Crops acquired by the government become the responsibility of the Commodity Credit Corporation (CCC), an agency created in 1933, now part of the USDA. Some surplus commodities are

The increasing use of farm machinery, such as this harvester in an Idaho wheat field, has made American agriculture more productive and encouraged the development of agribusiness.

583

Check for Understanding
● *How and why does the government influence the prices of farm products?* (By limiting production through purchases, payments, or subsidies. This increases the price of these products, thereby keeping farmers in business.)

Cooperative Learning
● Divide the class into groups and have each group research one of the following sets of questions and present a report to the class.

What percentage of land farmed in America belongs to agribusiness (corporations) as opposed to family-owned farms? How has this percentage changed in the past twenty years? In the past fifty years?

Which companies are the most important in agribusiness? Identify the eight largest corporate farmers. Identify some advantages and disadvantages of agribusiness as opposed to family farming.

What crops grown in your state receive price supports? How do these price supports work? What other government agricultural policies affect farming in your state?

The symbol ▮▮ denotes active participation strategies.

Activities are keyed for student abilities:
▲ = Basic
● = All Levels
■ = Average/Advanced

stored until the market prices rise and the goods can be sold for a profit. Surplus crops may also be donated to school lunch programs, child day-care centers, and welfare programs. Some are sold overseas or used for famine relief.

Loans and insurance

While much farm policy is aimed at stabilizing prices, other policies simply provide aid. Farming is risky, for an entire year's crop can be wiped out by drought, flood, storm or wind damage, insects, or disease. The Federal Crop Insurance Corporation (FCIC) was another New Deal program, instituted to help insure farmers against such unavoidable losses. Farmers can choose a variety of insurance programs, at varying costs. Although not all crops are covered by federal insurance, the program's coverage was expanded in 1980. In 1990, it applied to 52 different crops.

Because the cost of farming is staggering and the risks are high, farmers have difficulty borrowing money to keep going. The government's program of giving or guaranteeing low-cost farm loans, which began in the New Deal, is now run by the Consolidated Farm Service Agency. Other loans come through the federal land banks, a cooperative system administered by the Farm Credit Administration, an independent agency.

New problems for farmers

Farm policies from the 1950's through the 1970's were affected by political changes. Nevertheless, price supports kept farm profits up, while demand overseas kept American agricultural exports high. Encouraged by the federal government, many farmers took out loans to buy new land and increase production. By the beginning of the 1980's, agricultural exports had reached record levels.

Then foreign demand decreased sharply. Countries such as China and India, which had once had to buy American grain, improved their own agriculture. They began to export farm products. European farmers, helped by government subsidies, could also compete successfully with American growers. In addition, the value of the dollar abroad increased, making the prices of American farm products seem very high.

An **embargo** called by President Jimmy Carter in January 1980 also hurt exports. The

Despite the problems faced by many farmers, small family enterprises like this dairy farm remain an important part of the American scene.

584

embargo halted wheat shipments to the Soviet Union to protest the Soviet invasion of Afghanistan. It was lifted in 1981, but many farmers blamed it for causing foreign buyers to lose confidence in the United States as a steady source of food supplies. By 1986, farm exports had dropped by more than 30 percent, from $43.3 billion in 1981 to less than $30 billion. Farmers once again faced surpluses, as government storehouses filled with grain and dairy products.

Hardest hit by the decline were the small family farmers, who could not raise enough money to make payments on the loans taken out during the times of expansion. Family farms simply could not compete with the larger agribusiness firms. While many farms were auctioned off and families left their land, farmers pushed Congress and the President to find new policies and new markets for exports.

SECTION 4 REVIEW

Vocabulary and key terms

land-grant college (581) agribusiness (582)
Agricultural Adjustment surplus (582)
  Act (581) target price (583)
parity (581) embargo (584)
price support (581)

For review

1. What was the purpose of (a) the Homestead Act? (b) the Morrill Act? **7C**
2. What were the major provisions of the Agricultural Adjustment Act of 1933? **7C**
3. How have advances in technology both benefited farmers and caused them problems? **8A**
4. What methods does the government use to limit farm production? **7C**
5. What factors lowered farm exports in the 1980's? **8C**

Critical thinking

ANALYZING A PROBLEM To better understand the "farm problem," list some factors that may influence a farmer's success or failure. For each factor on your list, propose a policy that might assist farmers. Do the policies work together or contradict one another? **8H**

Chapter Summary

Federal policy tries to maintain a healthy balance between business, labor, and agriculture. By chartering corporations, licensing professionals, and maintaining public facilities, government creates a favorable climate for business to operate. Tax advantages, low-interest loans, and subsidies are also intended to encourage business.

Government regulation of business began with the Interstate Commerce Act, aimed against unfair practices by the railroads. To put an end to trusts and monopolies, Congress passed the Sherman and Clayton Antitrust Acts. Government policy toward business also involves protecting the public. For instance, public utilities and transportation are subject to strict regulations. The FDA (Food and Drug Administration) inspects, tests, and sets standards for food and drugs, while the FTC (Federal Trade Commission) prohibits false advertising.

Unions developed to bargain collectively for workers. The Clayton Act made unions legal, and the Wagner Act included many provisions that supported labor. Criticism of labor practices eventually led to the Taft-Hartley Act, which placed limits on union activities. The federal government also assists labor by providing statistics such as the consumer price index (CPI), setting the minimum wage and maximum working hours, restricting child labor, preventing job discrimination, and eliminating hazards in the workplace. In addition, the states ensure worker's compensation for those injured at work and unemployment compensation for those who lose their jobs through no fault of their own.

Federal agricultural policy began with the Homestead Act, to encourage settlement of the West, and the Morrill Act, to promote agricultural education. During the Depression, the Agricultural Adjustment Act kept farm prices high by paying farmers not to grow crops and offering parity to maintain farmers' purchasing power. Federal programs also brought electricity and telephone services to rural areas, helped conserve the soil, provided loans to farmers, and provided crop insurance. Today, to prevent over-supply of farm products, the federal government uses acreage allotments, carefully monitors the market, and maintains target prices.

3. Technology has made greater and more efficient farm production possible. On the other hand, it has reduced the number of farmers needed.
4. Purchases, payments, and subsidies.
5. Improved farm methods decreased world demand for U.S. products; the value of the dollar increased; an embargo of the Soviet Union shook the confidence of foreign buyers.

Critical thinking Students should recognize the following factors: the growing role of technology, the inherent risks and high costs of farming, the growth of agribusiness, farmers' dependence on government support, the vicious circle of surplus and debt, and the changing domestic and world markets.

CLOSURE
● Remind students of the pre-reading objectives at the beginning of the section. Pose one or all of these questions again. Then have students read the next assigned lesson.

CHAPTER 21 CORRECTIVES
● To review the content of Chapter 21, you may want to have students complete **Study Guide/Review 21** or **Workbook Chapter 21.**

585

Background: *Economics* In 1991 the Department of Agriculture reported that despite a decline in wheat shipments, U.S. farm exports had risen to $40 billion— nearly the 1981 level.

The symbol **ii** denotes active participation strategies.

Activities are keyed for student abilities:
▲ = Basic
● = All Levels
■ = Average/Advanced

CHAPTER 21 REVIEW

Answers

Vocabulary   See pp. T19-T21 for suggested vocabulary activities.

Reviewing the Facts

1. The government provides public facilities, technical information and services, loans, tax breaks, and subsidies.
2. A healthy economy is vital to government stability and national prosperity.
3. Areas include the stock market, public utilities, transportation, food and drugs, advertising, product labeling, and product safety.
4. It outlaws strikes by federal government employee unions, makes other unions give management 60 days notice before striking, provides for a mediator to work out a compromise if talks fail, and permits the President to delay a strike for up to 80 days.
5. The Occupational Safety and Health Administration (OSHA).
6. Production was high, but postwar poverty in Europe lowered the demand for agricultural exports. Thus, prices fell dramatically at a time when many farmers were heavily in debt.
7. The Commodity Credit Corporation, part of the USDA, stores some surplus crops until they can be sold for a profit. It donates some for domestic use and sells some overseas. It may also send crops overseas to aid famine relief efforts.

Thinking Critically About Key Concepts

1. The free enterprise system depends on the ability of businesses to compete for their share of a given market. Regulation has helped maintain healthy competition by curbing trusts and monopolies.
2. In the early 1800's the government played no role in relations

586

● **Review the definitions of the following terms:**

agribusiness	Interstate Commerce Act	Sherman Antitrust Act
Agricultural Adjustment Act	land-grant college	subsidy
capital	mediator	surplus
Clayton Antitrust Act	merchant marine	takeover
closed shop	merger	target price
collective bargaining	minimum wage	trust
conglomerate	monopoly	underwriting
consumer price index	muckraker	unemployment compensation
corporate charter	parity	union shop
divest	price support	worker's compensation
embargo	public utility	
	right-to-work law	

● **REVIEWING THE FACTS**

1. Name two ways in which the federal government helps business. **7C**
2. Why does the federal government help business? **6G**
3. Name two areas in which government regulates business in order to protect the public. **7C**
4. How does the Taft-Hartley Act affect workers' right to strike? **7C**
5. What government agency is responsible for safety in the workplace? **6G**
6. Why was the period after World War I an unprofitable time for American farmers? **8F**
7. What agency is responsible for surplus crops acquired by the government, and what does it do with them? **7C**

▲ **THINKING CRITICALLY ABOUT KEY CONCEPTS**

1. How has the regulation of business practices helped the free enterprise system? **7C**
2. How has government policy toward labor changed from the early 1800's to today? **7C**

586

3. Name three ways in which government has acted to protect American workers. **7C**
4. How has high productivity contributed to today's "farm problem"? **7D**

▲ **PRACTICING SKILLS**

1. **Study Skills: Reading a line graph.** Refer to Figure 21–4 (page 582) to answer the following questions. (a) During which decade did more than 40 percent of Americans live on farms? (b) What percentage of Americans lived on farms in 1980? (c) In one sentence, summarize the data presented in this graph. (To review graph skills, see Study Skill 3 in the back of the book.) **8B**
2. **Critical Thinking Skills: Predicting consequences.** Reread the subsection "Regulations on advertising" (pages 572–573). Write a list of questions that you might ask the American Medical Association and the American Tobacco Institute concerning their positions on cigarette advertising. **8A**
3. **Critical Thinking Skills: Identifying cause and effect.** Refer to the subsection "Maintaining Competition" (pages 567–570) to answer the following questions

---

between workers and employers. In 1914, 1932, and 1935, Congress passed laws favorable to unions. In 1947 and 1959, however, Congress passed laws restricting unions. The government has also established policies on wages, safety, working conditions, equal opportunities, and civil rights.
3. It has placed restrictions on child labor and has established laws to prohibit job discrimination and fight dangers in the workplace.

4. High productivity has meant that fewer farmers are needed to produce the same amount of goods. Surpluses of goods have caused prices (and farmers' profits) to fall.

concerning the history of trust regulation in the United States. **(a)** What was the series of events that resulted in the Interstate Commerce Act of 1887? **(b)** What was the effect of the public outrage over trusts in the late 1800's? **(c)** What was the direct cause of the breakup of AT&T in 1982? **8F**

▲ PARTICIPATORY CITIZENSHIP

1. **Interview.** Interview at least one person who is or has been a member of a labor union. Find out about why and how the union was organized. Did the person think the union was a help? If so, in what ways? If not, how was it inadequate? Report your findings to the class. **8A**
2. **Bulletin board.** Find newspaper and magazine clippings to illustrate the government's efforts to protect U.S. industry from foreign competition. Arrange them, with a title, on a bulletin board. **8E**

■ WRITING ABOUT ISSUES

1. **Writing an essay.** Give reasons supporting or opposing the formation of conglomerates through mergers and takeovers. What do you think should be the government's policy toward this concentration of industry? **8C**
2. **Writing a screenplay.** The future of the family farm in America is in doubt. Research the problems facing farm families and write a screenplay based on what you find. You may wish to explore the question of whether the government should do more to help the family farm, or increase its support of agribusiness. **8C**

▲ ANALYZING A POLITICAL CARTOON

Government subsidies affect most people engaged in agriculture from small farmers to agribusiness. The cost of these subsidies is, of course, borne by the nation's taxpayers. Look at the cartoon below and answer the following questions.

1. Who does the man in the car represent? Who is the man outside the car? **8B**
2. What analogy is the cartoonist making? **8B**
3. Do you think the cartoon is effective? Why, or why not? **8D**

By Dana Summers © 1986, Washington Post Writers Group. Reprinted with permission.

stop these abuses. **(b)** The Sherman Antitrust Act of 1890. **(c)** A lawsuit initiated by the Justice Department.

Participatory Citizenship
1. You might invite members of different labor unions to speak to the class.
2. Students may want to discuss whether they approve or disapprove of specific efforts to protect U.S. industries from foreign competition.

Writing About Issues
1. *Supporting*—Conglomerates are more efficient and keep prices more stable. *Opposing*—Conglomerates limit competition, concentrate too much power in too few hands, and stifle the development of other companies.
2. Students may want to work in groups and then read their screenplays to the class to show different aspects of the tensions between family farms and agribusiness, as well as the role of the government in the problem.

Analyzing a Political Cartoon
1. The U.S. government. The agriculture industry.
2. According to the cartoonist, the relationship between the government and recipients of farm subsidies is similar to the relationship between a drug dealer and an addict.
3. Students should support their answers with evidence from the cartoon.

Practicing Skills
1. **(a)** 1890's. **(b)** About 2 or 3 percent. **(c)** The farm population as a percentage of total population has steadily decreased since 1890.

2. Students should try to find out why the American Medical Association opposes cigarette advertising and why the American Tobacco Institute contends that a ban on advertising violates the First Amendment.

3. **(a)** Railroad companies, on which farmers relied to transport their products, cooperated to eliminate competition on certain routes in order to make higher profits. Angry farmers pressured the government to

Chapter Review exercises are keyed for student abilities:
▲ = Basic
● = All Levels
■ = Average/Advanced

CHAPTER 22
POLICIES FOR ENERGY AND THE ENVIRONMENT
(pp. 588–611)

	Section Objectives	Section Resources
Section 1 **Government Attempts to Protect the Environment**	☐ describe the history of government involvement in environmental protection ☐ describe recent environmental legislation	▲ SKILLS PRACTICE WORKSHEET **22** ▲ TRANSPARENCIES **52–53**
Section 2 **Federal Policies Regulate Energy Use**	☐ contrast fossil fuels with renewable sources of energy ☐ describe energy policies in recent administrations	■ SKILLS CHALLENGE WORKSHEET **22** ▲ TRANSPARENCY **54**

Essential Elements

The list below shows Essential Elements relevant to this chapter.
(The complete list of Essential Elements appears in the introductory
pages of this Teacher's Edition.)

Section 1: 4C, 6A, 6D, 6G, 7C, 7D, 8A, 8B, 8C,
8F, 8H

Section 2: 6A, 7A, 7C, 8A, 8C, 8D, 8F, 8G

Chapter Review: 3A, 5C, 6G, 7A, 8A, 8B, 8C, 8F,
8G, 8H

> Section Resources are keyed
> for student abilities:
> ▲ = Basic
> ● = All Levels
> ■ = Average/Advanced

Homework Options

Each section contains activities labeled "Guided/Independent Practice," "Reteaching/Correctives," and "Enrichment/Extension." You may wish to choose from among these activities when assigning homework.

Students Acquiring English Activities

Have students carefully trace the U.S. map (including state boundaries) on p. 601. Students should locate and label your state and determine whether it has a nuclear reactor. Ask students to write in the names of states containing nuclear reactors, using Figure 22–3 as a guide.

LISTENING/SPEAKING: Have the class watch the movie *China Syndrome* and ask students to compare the events in the movie with the actual nuclear accident at Three-Mile Island near Harrisburg, Pennsylvania.

Teacher Bibliography

Kelman, Steven. *Making Public Policy: A Hopeful View of American Government*. Basic, 1988. Looks at how the government bureaucracy makes effective public policy.

Rosenbaum, Walter A. *Energy, Politics, and Public Policy*. 2nd ed. CQ Press, 1987. Investigates the formulation of an energy policy.

Simon, David J., ed. *Our Common Lands: Defending the National Parks*. Island Press, 1988. A collection of essays on legislation pertinent to national parks such as the Clear Water Act, the Clean Air Act, and the Endangered Species Act.

Student Bibliography

Carson, Rachel. *Silent Spring*. Houghton Mifflin, 1962. Discusses the widespread use of pesticides and their effect on the balance of nature.

Gay, Kathlyn. *Silent Killers: Radon and Other Hazards*. Watts, 1988. The author explains health hazards such as pesticides and herbicides, carbon monoxide, mercury, lead, radioactive wastes, and asbestos as well as prevention measures and clean-up.

Middleton, Nick. *Atlas of Environmental Issues*. Facts on File, 1989. Informative discussion of environmental issues such as nuclear power, acid rain, deforestation, and air and water pollution.

Literature

MacDonald, John. *Barrier Island*. Fawcett, 1987. A developer who wants to turn an ecologically important area into a posh resort bribes an official to influence a hearing.

Zumwalt, Elmo, Jr., and Elmo Zumwalt, III. *My Father, My Son*. Dell, 1987. Admiral Zumwalt, who ordered the spraying of Agent Orange in Vietnam, lives with the fact that his son suffers from cancer and a grandson has multiple learning disabilities, as the result of his exposure to the deadly chemical.

Films and Videotapes*

Energy Supply. (Series title: *The Power Struggle*.) 34 min. Bullfrog, 1986. v. Energy consumption in the United States indicates the need to conserve through product design and the use of renewable energy sources. The role of government in promoting both is explored.

Population Story: Collision with the Future? 23 min. EBEC, 1984. f. Animation and live footage are combined in a look at the future of a dangerously overpopulated earth.

CHAPTER RESOURCES

Study Guide/Review 22
Workbook Chapter 22
Chapter 22 Test, Forms A–C

Sludge: Spreading Trouble. 29 min. PSUAVS, 1982. v. Lack of trust in government, experts, and company officials is shown in this depiction of a township which objected to the spreading of sludge on local strip-mined land for safety and other reasons. People wanted assurances which those in charge could not give. Discussion guide included.

Software*

Refinery (Apple, IBM, Commodore). PSC. Students become operations managers of a modern refinery who must maximize company profits, yet consider the refinery's impact on the environment.

Balance of the Planet (IBM, Macintosh). Accolade. Students act as the High Commissioner of the Environment with the power to levy taxes and grant subsidies for issues that affect the environment. This game dramatically displays the interdependence among economic systems and the environment.

Pollution Control (Apple, IBM). Focus. Students act as the head of the Pollution Patrol of a city. They must control or eliminate a pollutant and identify its sources. Students examine the causes and effects of pollution as well as the economic and social costs of control.

---

* For a complete guide to audiovisual sources, see page T22.

Policies for Energy and the Environment
(pp. 588–611)

This chapter outlines federal government efforts to protect federal land, explains how environmental policy is developed, and describes federal policies concerning energy use and conservation.

Chapter Objectives

After students complete this chapter, they will be able to:

1. Describe the history of government involvement in environmental protection.
2. Describe recent environmental legislation.
3. Contrast fossil fuels with renewable sources of energy.
4. Describe energy policies in recent administrations.

CHAPTER

22

POLICIES for ENERGY and the ENVIRONMENT

If the Bill of Rights contains no guarantee that a citizen shall be secure against lethal poisons distributed either by private individuals or by public officials, it is surely only because our forefathers . . . could conceive of no such problem.

Rachel Carson
Silent Spring (1962)

588

Photo
Park ranger, Grand Canyon National Park.

Christopher Columbus recorded his first impressions of the Caribbean islands and the lands that came to be known as the Americas as follows: "There are many harbors on the sea coast, beyond comparison with others which I know in Christendom, and numerous rivers, good and large, which is marvelous. Its lands are lofty and in it there are many sierras and very high mountains. . . . All are most beautiful, of a thousand shapes, and all accessible, and filled with trees of a thousand kinds. . . . There are marvelous pine groves, and extensive meadow country; and there is honey, and there are many kinds of birds and a great variety of fruits. Upcountry there are many mines of metals. . . ."

Five hundred years after Columbus, many of America's vast natural resources still exist. Others, however, have disappeared or are seriously threatened. Toxic wastes pollute rivers and lakes. Factories and automobiles pollute the air. Mounting numbers of plant and animal species are threatened with extinction. Americans depend on foreign sources to meet their increasing demand for energy. Chapter 22 addresses the question of how national policies attempt to protect our environment while meeting the nation's energy demands.

CHAPTER OUTLINE

1 Government Attempts to Protect the Environment

Preserving Natural Resources
Making Environmental Policy
Anti-Pollution Policies

2 Federal Policies Regulate Energy Use

Fossil Fuels
Other Sources of Energy
Recent Energy Policies

589

SECTION 1
Government Attempts to Protect the Environment

> **ACCESS** The Main Ideas
>
> **1** Describe the history of government involvement in environmental protection. *pages 590–595*
>
> **2** Describe recent environmental legislation. *pages 595–599*

March, 1989 — The supertanker *Exxon Valdez* runs aground. Eleven million gallons of crude oil spill near the south coast of Alaska. The spilled oil destroys fish and other animals, and contaminates beaches. David Kelso, Alaska's environmental commissioner, says, "Every time people here go to a favorite fishing hole, they will think of the spill and they will be angry." Red Swanson, who has worked for the oil industry, disagrees. "The environmentalists have stopped Alaska from being great," he complains. "They say hundreds of birds have been killed by the spill. But we have millions of birds. These things happen." The oil spill highlights a basic policy dilemma: government can allow industry to exploit natural resources such as oil and forests to the fullest. Alternatively, it can protect resources by declaring them off-limits to industry.

6D, 6G

Preserving Natural Resources

Nearly one-third of the land and coastal areas of the United States belongs to the federal government. This property includes military bases, weapons test sites, mineral deposits, and government offices. Much federal land also has been set aside for preservation and conservation.

The national parks
For more than a hundred years, many areas in the United States have been preserved and protected as part of a system of national parks, monuments, and historic sites. As Figure 22–1 shows, national parks are found in many states, including Alaska and Hawaii. In addition, the states have set aside historic sites and wilderness areas of their own.

The idea of a "national" park system began during the exploration of the West. Early in the 1800's, trappers and explorers in what is now Wyoming discovered a remarkable area of canyons, valleys, geysers, hot springs, and bubbling mud volcanoes. Some of the explorers suggested that a place of such natural beauty and scientific wonder should belong to all the people. Officially named Yellowstone, the area became the first national park in 1872. President Ulysses S. Grant signed the bill declaring Yellowstone under federal government protection as "a public park or pleasuring ground for the benefit and enjoyment of the people."

President Theodore Roosevelt gave both personal and official support to the conservation of natural resources and wilderness areas. (Some of his ideas are quoted in "Landmarks in Liberty" on page 593.) In the early 1900's, other remote areas in the West were designated as public lands. These included the desert rock formations of Zion Canyon, the spectacular Grand Canyon, and the ancient Indian cliff dwellings at Mesa Verde in Colorado. Hawaii was not yet a state, but its active volcanoes were made part of a national park. To manage the parks, the National Park Service was set up in 1916 as part of the Department of the Interior.

Today, many national parks preserve the natural landscape in isolated parts of the nation. Many others, however, are near densely populated areas and draw huge crowds of visitors. Heavy use of the national parks sometimes conflicts with the goal of preserving wilderness, but the ideal of keeping the land available for all the people is still carried out.

The national forests
The U.S. Forest Service (part of the Department of Agriculture) is responsible for maintaining the public forest lands across the country. All together, the national forests are much larger than the states of California and Nevada combined. Unlike the national parks, which are preserved intact, parts of the national forests are open for

590

Figure 22–1 THE NATIONAL PARK SYSTEM National parks across the United States preserve areas of natural beauty and scientific curiosity for the public's education and enjoyment. 8B

EXPLANATION

After students have read the section, you may want to consider the following activities:

Geography

● Ask students if they know of any national parks, national monuments, historic sites, or wilderness areas near your community. Have students find out more about the history of these parklands and inquire about current policies for their use.

Figure 22–1
● **Which region has the most national parks? Why might this be the case?** (The West; when the park system was created, large areas of the West were still undeveloped.) Ask students whether they have visited any of the national parks shown on the map and what they remember about them.

The symbol 👥 denotes active participation strategies.

Activities are keyed for student abilities:
▲ = Basic
● = All Levels
■ = Average/Advanced

Controversial Issues

● Tell students that many environmental groups object to legal industrial activity (such as lumbering and mining) in U.S. national forests and have resorted to drastic, illegal tactics. For instance, protesters have sabotaged logging equipment and climbed to the tops of trees about to be felled.

Ask for three volunteers from the class. One will act as a reporter doing a story on this issue. Another will play the part of one of the radical environmentalists, and the third will play the part of a U.S. Forest Service official. Have the reporter interview the two persons in front of the class. Then ask class members for their reaction to the opposing arguments.

recreation and for commercial use by lumber, paper, and other wood product manufacturers. Grazing livestock and mining are also allowed. Commercial users must lease the land from the Forest Service and follow regulations in their use of the forests. The goal of Forest Service policy is to ensure that forest growth is greater than the amount of forest destroyed and that animal life and water sources are protected.

Protecting wildlife

The federal government has long been committed to preserving wildlife for the benefit of the American people. Today the U.S. Fish and Wildlife Service (in the Department of the Interior) protects migratory birds, endangered species, and marine mammals such as whales, seals, and dolphins. It is also responsible for keeping America's fisheries stocked.

The Fish and Wildlife Service conducts studies of wildlife, educates the public, and manages the environment to enhance fish and wildlife. It also seeks to balance public demand for recreational fishing and hunting with the survival of animal life. Finally, it works to restore dwindling animal populations and protect other species from becoming endangered.

Land use policy

There are many pressures on the national government to allow commercial use of the lands it protects. Business and industry see federal lands as a valuable source of minerals and other resources. Moreover, the leasing of such land can generate billions of dollars in revenues for the federal government. On the other hand, environmentalists and concerned citizens believe that such lands should be left unspoiled. In recent years, the potential uses of the Alaskan tundra, the western deserts and plains, and coastal waters have stirred heated debate. One of the federal government's most difficult tasks is to establish a land use policy that is widely acceptable to the American people.

Water conservation

Providing a reliable, safe supply of water is an important concern of state and local governments. Many experts in the 1990's predicted that Americans would soon face serious shortages of water. Homes, farms, and industries were using up water faster than rainfall could replenish the supply.

People in the Southwest had the most immediate problems. Their water supplies depend on

In addition to the federal government, the states have set aside land for preservation and conservation. This beautiful lake is part of Matthiessen State Park, in Illinois.

the Ogallala **aquifer** (AH-kwih-fur), a huge natural area of groundwater storage stretching from Nebraska to Texas. At the rate water was being used, however, it was estimated that this supply would be gone in 40 years. Other parts of the country faced water problems nearly as serious, if not as urgent. Understanding and solving the water problem became a new issue facing policy-makers.

4C, 7A

Making Environmental Policy

Though the government long followed a policy of preserving natural resources and wildlife on federal lands, private industry was not so careful. By the 1960's, thick smog covered the nation's cities, oil spills and toxic chemicals were killing fish and wildlife, and once-clear water had turned to sludge. The polluted Cuyahoga River near Cleveland, Ohio, actually caught fire in the 1960's. Most importantly, human health was endangered. **Pollutants** — chemicals and other damaging substances in the water and air — were increasingly linked to skin rashes, allergies, heart and lung disease, birth defects, and some kinds of cancer.

Ecology — the study of the relationship of living organisms to their environment — became the watchword of the 1960's and 1970's. Groups like the Sierra Club, the National Wildlife Federation, and the Audubon Society were successful in drawing public attention to environmental problems. *Silent Spring,* a book written in 1962 by biologist Rachel Carson, brought national attention to the long-term damage caused by chemical pesticides. (A quotation from Carson opens this chapter.) Other writers and scientists addressed different ecological issues.

Formulating environmental policy

Congress began passing laws to limit pollution and protect the environment as early as the 1950's, but these early efforts were uncoordinated and poorly funded. The first major step toward a coherent national policy was the National Environmental Policy Act, which President Nixon signed into law on January 1, 1970. This law established the Council on Environmental Quality, a panel of three noted environmentalists appointed by the President to give advice on environmental issues.

PRIMARY SOURCE

6G

LANDMARKS in LIBERTY

Theodore Roosevelt on Conservation (1907)

Theodore Roosevelt's concern for the environment prompted him, in his Seventh Annual Message to Congress, to outline an ambitious conservation program. Through his actions and through speeches such as this, Roosevelt made the American people aware of the serious consequences of environmental problems already surfacing in the early 1900's.

"The conservation of our natural resources and their proper use constitute the fundamental problem which underlies almost every other problem of our national life. . . . But there must be the look ahead, there must be a realization of the fact that to waste, to destroy our natural resources, to skin and exhaust the land instead of using it so as to increase its usefulness, will result in undermining in the days of our children the very prosperity which we ought by right to hand down to them amplified and developed. . . .

Optimism is a good characteristic, but if carried to an excess it becomes foolishness. We are prone to speak of the resources of this country as inexhaustible; this is not so. The mineral wealth of this country, the coal, iron, oil, gas, and the like, does not reproduce itself, and therefore is certain to be exhausted ultimately; and wastefulness in dealing with it today means that our descendants will feel the exhaustion a generation or two before they otherwise would. . . . "

1. What kind of "optimism" did Roosevelt warn against?
2. Why did Roosevelt particularly seek to conserve mineral resources?
3. What did he say would happen if natural resources were wasted?

593

Politics

■ Help students select a significant example of a public policy that has influenced the outcome of an environmental issue. Possible examples include the policies leading to the National Environmental Policy Act, the establishment of the Environmental Protection Agency, the Water Pollution Control Act and the 1986 Clean Water Act, the Clean Air Act of 1970, and the establishment of "Superfund" in 1980.

Have students research and present a report describing the public policy that established the act or agency they selected.

Background: *Cultural Literacy* The title *Silent Spring* refers to the absence of birds and other creatures in a countryside devastated by the use of pesticides.

Landmarks in Liberty Answers
1. Roosevelt warned against optimism carried to such an extent that it becomes foolish. Seeing the country's resources as inexhaustible is an example of that kind of optimism.
2. Because they are nonrenewable and will ultimately be exhausted.
3. Future generations would be deprived.

The symbol ♋ denotes active participation strategies.

Activities are keyed for student abilities:
▲ = Basic
● = All Levels
■ = Average/Advanced

Politics

● Have students monitor news-papers, magazines, and TV news for information on current products or practices that damage the environment and that the federal government is trying to regulate. Students should report to the class on the issues they have analyzed and should end by presenting their own views on those issues.

The law also required all federal agencies beginning new projects to file "environmental impact statements" (EIS) with the Council 90 days before starting work. These reports had to describe the project's likely effects on its surroundings — air, water, land, and plant and animal life. For example, before the Trans-Alaska Pipeline could be built, the Department of the Interior had to file a seventeen-volume, 9,750-page study detailing the effects the pipeline construction would have on the Alaskan tundra and on deer and other wildlife. While critics object to the details and delays of such reports, others believe they are necessary to prevent careless abuse of the environment.

The EPA

Also established in 1970 was the Environmental Protection Agency (EPA), which determines mileage ratings, issues permits for waste disposal, and administers grants to state and local governments for cleanup programs. It enforces policies on water and air pollution, solid and toxic waste, pesticides, and radiation. In 1989 some government and environmental leaders sought to elevate the EPA to Cabinet-level status, thereby giving environmental issues the same importance as economic and defense issues.

Environmental controversies

Since its inception, the EPA has been a target of criticism and controversy. Even though pollution affects the quality of everyone's life, public opinion frequently is divided on a particular environmental issue. It may take a major, highly publicized disaster, such as an oil spill or chemical accident, for public opinion strongly to favor governmental action.

The harshest critics of regulatory policies are those who bear the brunt of anti-pollution laws — major industrial or chemical firms, oil companies, automobile manufacturers, and some workers in these industries. They argue that environmental regulations create tiresome red tape for industries to follow, require costly programs that do little to protect the environment and endanger workers' jobs. Well-organized lobbies and interest groups back this point of view.

A volunteer mops up oil that washed ashore after the *Exxon Valdez* ran aground off the Alaskan coast in March 1989. A second ship was sent to pump the remaining oil from the *Valdez*'s holding tanks.

Background: *Science and Technology* Students may be most familiar with the EPA from automobile advertisements in which EPA mileage ratings are cited.

Critical Thinking
▲ *Why do highly publicized disasters increase the chance of government action on an environmental issue?*
(Media coverage increases public awareness and discussion of a problem. This, in turn, can often force the government to take action.)

Environmental interest groups supporting tougher government policies also lobby actively. Although they have consistent public support, these groups tend to be smaller and less well funded.

6A, 7D

Anti-Pollution Policies

Water pollution

For years, industries, city governments, and private citizens have dumped garbage, sewage, oil, industrial wastes, and agricultural run-off into the nation's streams, lakes, rivers, and coastal areas. Such pollutants kill fish and plants, contaminate the food chain, make the shorelines and beaches unsafe, and cause cancer and other diseases.

As early as the Refuse Act of 1899, the federal government tried to prevent industries and cities from dumping waste into navigable waters. The law did little to stop water pollution at the time, though in the late 1960's several environmental groups used it to bring lawsuits against water polluters.

In 1956 the Water Pollution Control Act made federal grants available to state and local governments to help finance sewage-treatment plants. Under the act, conferences alerted public officials to the problem of water pollution. The Water Quality Act of 1965 was an effort to set standards for water quality. Both laws left the responsibility for setting standards up to the individual states. Because states feared that strict regulations might discourage industry, their standards tended to be very lax. Neither of these laws, therefore, did much to stop pollution.

Recent water legislation

The environmental movement of the 1970's brought the first significant efforts to end water pollution. Between 1970 and 1974, Congress passed laws to prevent oil spills by tankers, refineries, and off-shore drilling rigs; to restrict the disposal of municipal and industrial wastes at sea; and to set minimum standards for drinking water throughout the nation.

The Water Pollution Control Act of 1972 (amended in 1977) established the federal government's basic water pollution policies. The two major goals of this act were (1) to make all of the nation's streams safe for fishing and swim-

Chemicals spilled from factories fill a river with streaks of polluted foam.

ming, and (2) to end all discharges of pollutants into navigable waters. To achieve these goals, the act gave the EPA the power to set limits on the amount of waste water, chemicals, and other pollutants that factories can discharge into rivers and streams. To dump wastes into streams, an industry now must first obtain a permit from the EPA and then follow the standards it sets. The Water Pollution Control Act also required cities to install better waste-treatment plants.

A follow-up law, the 1986 Clean Water Act, authorized spending some $20 billion on cleaning up lakes and rivers, reducing pollution from run-off, and constructing modern sewer systems. Though President Reagan pocket-vetoed the bill, Congress in 1987 voted to override his veto.

As a result of such legislation, lakes and rivers are now much cleaner, and much fish and plant life has returned. Still, the nation has a long way to go to make waterways safe for fish and recreational swimming. Because the cost of cleaning up water and treating waste is staggering, industries remain reluctant to comply with EPA regulations. For policy-makers, the challenge is to find ways of preserving our precious water that business will support.

595

Economics

▲ CRITICAL THINKING **Why is there often a trade-off between a cleaner environment and economic growth?** (It is usually cheaper for companies to ignore environmental concerns. Cleaning up existing pollution and preventing future pollution cost money.)

● CRITICAL THINKING **Should the government's role in environmental policy be to protect the environment as much as possible or to balance protecting the environment and encouraging economic growth?** (Students should defend their answers.)

■ CRITICAL THINKING Suppose that a candidate for governor of your state promised to make your state's pollution standards stricter than those of any other state and to pay whatever costs were necessary to eliminate water and air pollution, even if that meant raising taxes. **How would you react to these promises?** (Students will probably applaud the desire for a cleaner environment but should realize that stricter pollution standards might discourage firms from settling in the state. They should also realize that pollution travels across state boundaries; therefore, fighting pollution requires cooperation among states.)

Background: *Law* The laws passed between 1970 and 1974 (column 1, par. 5) included the Water Quality Improvement Act (1970) and the Safe Drinking Water Act (1974).

Background: *Politics* The 1986 Clean Water Act also called for the construction of sewage treatment plants and a concerted effort to clean up water containing high concentrations of toxic chemicals.

The symbol 👥 denotes active participation strategies.

Activities are keyed for student abilities:
▲ = Basic
● = All Levels
■ = Average/Advanced

Figure 22–2 MAJOR AIR POLLUTANTS AND THEIR EFFECTS 8F

★ **Particles** Particles include smoke, dust, or soot that floats in the air. Particles can harm the lungs and enable toxic metals and cancer-causing agents to enter the bloodstream.

★ **Lead** Lead (Pb) can accumulate in bones and can harm blood formation, kidneys, and the nervous system.

★ **Sulfur dioxide** Sulfur dioxide (SO_2) is a poisonous gas that is linked to coughs, asthma, and bronchitis. When combined with water, it contributes to acid rain, which destroys trees, plants, fish, and wildlife.

★ **Carbon monoxide** Carbon monoxide (CO) is a colorless, odorless, tasteless, but poisonous gas. It deprives the body of oxygen, causing drowsiness, headaches, poor vision, impaired coordination, and even death.

★ **Nitrogen oxide** Nitrogen oxide (NO_2) irritates the eyes, nose, and throat, and damages the lungs. It also damages plants, buildings, monuments, and other structures. It contributes to acid rain and smog.

★ **Hydrocarbons** Hydrocarbons result from the incomplete burning of gasoline and the evaporation of paints and solvents; they contribute to smog.

★ **Ozone** Ozone (O_3) is the primary component of smog. It is the by-product of nitrogen oxide and hydrocarbons. Ozone irritates the eyes, nose, and lungs. It also causes coughing and is associated with asthma, bronchitis, and other breathing disorders.

Air pollution

Clean air consists of about four-fifths nitrogen, one-fifth oxygen, plus traces of other gases and water vapor. In recent years, our air, like our water, has become polluted by many other substances. The major air pollutants and the effects they can have on the human body are shown in Figure 22–2.

Roughly half of all air pollution comes from gasoline-powered internal-combustion engines, such as those in cars, trucks, buses, and lawnmowers. It is estimated that **emissions** from motor vehicles send over 700 million tons of pollutants into the air each year, including carbon monoxide, hydrocarbons, lead, nitrogen dioxide, and particles. Other major sources of air pollution are electrical power plants, particularly coal-burning plants; industries processing iron, copper, lead, zinc, aluminum, and petroleum; and burning garbage dumps, forest fires, wood stoves, and fireplaces.

Weather and geography, too, play an important part in determining the severity of air pollution. Wind often blows pollution from one location to another. For instance, chemicals sent into the air by coal-burning power plants in the Midwest combine with water in the air to become **acid rain**, which falls throughout the eastern United States and Canada.

Another climatic problem is **inversion**, which occurs when warm air traps a layer of cool air near the ground. Pollutants then build up in the cool air but have nowhere to go. The result is smog. Such air inversions are especially troublesome in Los Angeles and Denver, where the surrounding mountains tend to trap the smog.

Clean air legislation

In 1955 the federal government passed legislation providing funding to help study air pollution. The Clean Air Act of 1963 provided funding for state and local governments to call

596

Figure 22–2
● *What groups of people are especially vulnerable to air pollution?* (Very young children, elderly persons, and those with breathing difficulties.)

Background: *Science and Technology* Most research has concluded that acid rain is caused by sulfur-based emissions from industry. When the sulfur is released into the air, it joins with

water droplets and forms sulfuric acid, which then falls as rain. Lakes become "dead," or unable to support marine life; trees and plants are killed; buildings and monuments are scarred.

Civic Participation

● Have students find out about your state's or community's recycling efforts. They might invite an official to speak to the class about the state's or community's recycling policy.

If your school does not have a recycling program, encourage students to begin one. Discuss with the class the various tasks involved in starting one, such as gaining permission from school authorities, publicizing the program, encouraging students and others to participate, and providing for the transportation of recycled materials.

Cooperative Learning

● Divide the class into small groups and have group members quiz each other on the vocabulary words for the section.

conferences to deal with air pollution. Both acts relied upon voluntary compliance by the states and proved ineffective.

The first significant federal effort in fighting air pollution was the Motor Vehicle Air Pollution Control Act of 1965. It provided additional funds for research and gave the federal government authority to set standards for automobile emissions (the pollutants released from car engines). In 1970 a second Clean Air Act authorized the EPA to set standards for reducing air pollutants to levels less harmful both to humans and to trees, buildings, and other structures.

Anti-pollution measures drew sharp criticism. People complained that they reduced gasoline mileage and energy efficiency in industry. When the price of oil skyrocketed in the mid-1970's, pressure mounted to relax the 1970 standards. Congress responded by lowering emission standards for automobiles and trucks and extending deadlines for compliance.

A 1990 Clean Air Act called for sharp cuts in acid rain pollutants, smog, and toxic emissions by the year 2000. Still, air pollution is a signifi-cant problem. Using coal to replace more expensive but cleaner fuels adds a new threat to clean air. As long as Americans depend on cars, planes, and electricity, air pollution will be a problem.

Toxic waste

Since World War II, Americans have relied increasingly on chemicals for making thousands of useful products — soap, dye, medicines, fertilizer, tape, paint, plastic, records, glue, clothing, bottles, and eyeglasses. Unfortunately, many by-products of chemical manufacturing are poisonous substances, called **toxic wastes**. Each year the United States generates about one ton of toxic waste per person — enough to fill a large stadium, like the Los Angeles Coliseum, every day for a year!

For many years, industries disposed of toxic wastes carelessly, with little concern for the environment. Toxic chemicals were spilled into streams, dumped at sea, burned, or buried. There were few government regulations, and only about 10 percent of all toxic wastes were disposed of safely.

Air pollutants travel many miles before acid rain returns them to earth. This water specialist is testing for acid rain at a lake near Grand Marais, Minnesota.

GUIDED/INDEPENDENT PRACTICE
● Have students make a chart with columns for the following types of pollution: water pollution, air pollution, toxic waste, and solid waste. The chart should have two rows: in one, students should explain how each type of pollution is produced; in the other they should list any laws that attempt to limit that type of pollution.

Background: *Global Awareness* Most of the industrialized world suffers from waste disposal problems. In the 1970's, for example, many of the beaches on the Mediterranean Sea were declared unsafe for bathers because sewage from 120 coastal cities was being dumped untreated into the sea.

The symbol 👥 denotes active participation strategies.

Activities are keyed for student abilities:
▲ = Basic
● = All Levels
■ = Average/Advanced

The Love Canal incident

Then public concern over toxic wastes began to grow as a result of several events. The Love Canal is a mile-long trench, fifteen yards across, located near Niagara Falls, New York. The canal was dug in the late 1800's by William T. Love to transport goods but was never used. In the 1940's, the Hooker Chemicals and Plastics Corporation used the abandoned canal to bury some 20,000 tons of toxic wastes, stored mainly in 55-gallon drums. In 1953 the Niagara Falls Board of Education bought the land and built a school. Houses soon sprang up near the canal.

In time, Love Canal residents began to notice some disturbing things. The dump site seemed to glow at night. Thick sludge oozed into basements and clogged sewers. Children swimming in a nearby pond developed ugly skin rashes. Residents complained of headaches and strange odors. Worst of all, they began to notice an increase in miscarriages, birth defects, and cancer. Complaints led to an EPA investigation, which uncovered the leaking drums of toxic chemicals.

In 1978 Love Canal was declared a disaster area. More than 200 families had to be evacuated.

Love Canal was not an isolated example. Between 1983 and 1985, more than 4,600 similar incidents were reported to the federal government. The EPA estimates that there may be more than 50,000 unknown toxic waste dumps throughout the nation. As some experts say, America is sitting on an "ecological time bomb." The question remains — how do we locate and clean up these toxic dumps?

Toxic waste legislation

There are two major federal laws dealing with toxic wastes. The Resource Conservation and Recovery Act of 1976 (amended in 1980) authorized the EPA to determine what chemicals are hazardous and the best methods for disposing of them. Under this act, those wishing to dispose of toxic wastes must get a permit from the EPA.

The second major toxic waste policy — known as "Superfund" — was started in 1980 in response to the Love Canal disaster. Superfund

To guard against the hazards of handling drums full of toxic materials, workers wear special protective masks and coveralls.

made $1.6 billion available over a five-year period to clean up toxic dumps and accidents. For example, in 1982 the entire town of Times Beach, Missouri, had to be permanently evacuated after a contractor accidentally spread dioxin-contaminated oil on its streets. (Dioxin is one of the most deadly chemicals known.) Superfund paid for the evacuation and resettlement of the residents of Times Beach.

Money for Superfund is generated primarily from taxes on oil and chemical companies, which are the major producers of toxic wastes. These companies object to the tax, saying that consumers who use chemical products should share the burden. In 1986 Congress allocated $9 billion to Superfund for another five-year period. While Superfund is a step in the right direction, experts estimate that it may cost from $22 to $100 billion to clean up existing dump sites.

Solid waste

Yet another source of pollution is **solid waste** — garbage and trash. It is estimated that the typical American throws away four to five pounds of solid waste each day. On a yearly basis, this adds up to about 30 million tons of paper, 487 billion cans, 26 billion bottles and jars, and some 4 million automobiles. Altogether, our "throw-away society" generates about 6 billion tons of solid waste per year.

Many problems are associated with the continued accumulation of solid wastes. Open dumps and automobile graveyards are eyesores and present health hazards. The costs of disposing of solid wastes are huge, and many cities are running out of space for dumping. Burning dumps also contribute to air pollution.

There are several ways to deal with solid waste. One way is to bury it in sanitary landfills, which later can be built on. The EPA suggests that cities spread the solid waste in thin layers and cover it with dirt daily. Some communities burn solid wastes to produce steam for heating. To reduce waste, many communities have begun recycling paper, glass, aluminum, and other reusable products. Several states now require deposits on soft drink bottles and cans. Deposits encourage consumers to return their bottles for recycling. Such measures have chipped away at the mountains of trash we create each year, but they have not yet made them disappear.

YOU DECIDE

8H

North Carolina has an Adopt-a-Highway program, under which the state puts up road signs naming a group or business that has pledged to clean a stretch of road. The Rockingham County chapter of the Ku Klux Klan wants to adopt 3.4 miles of road that go through a predominantly African American neighborhood, but the state has denied the group's request.

Is the state's denial fair?

SECTION 1 REVIEW

Vocabulary and key terms

aquifer (593)
pollutant (593)
ecology (593)
Environmental
   Protection Agency
   (EPA) (594)

emissions (596)
acid rain (596)
inversion (596)
toxic waste (597)
solid waste (599)

For review

1. What are the purposes of (a) the national parks and (b) the national forests? **7C**
2. What were two steps taken by the federal government in 1970 toward a national environmental policy? **7C**
3. What were the goals of the Water Pollution Control Act? **8C**
4. What are the major sources of air pollution? **8C**
5. (a) What causes toxic waste? (b) What is the most important federal program for cleaning up toxic waste? **8A**

Critical thinking

ANALYZING AN ISSUE What can individuals and businesses do to limit pollution? What prevents them from taking such actions? Is governmental regulation more effective than individual action in stopping pollution? **4C**

599

4. Motor vehicles, coal-burning power plants, metal-processing industries, burning garbage dumps, forest fires, wood stoves, and fireplaces.
5. (a) Some kinds of chemical manufacturing. (b) Superfund.

Critical thinking Students should mention actions that they can take (recycling, walking) and that industry can adopt (using less coal, discharging cleaner water, controlling emissions) and then discuss the problems of cost and convenience. Finally, students should note that historically government has acted (or forced industry to act) because of the size and cost of the problem.

CLOSURE

● Ask students to sum up the lesson by imagining that they are making environmental policy for the federal government. Have them state the major dilemmas they would face on the job. Then have students read Section 2, keeping track of the different kinds of energy used today.

Background: *Science and Technology* There *is* a difference between garbage and trash. Garbage is generally considered to be food wastes, while trash can be any discarded material.

You Decide Answer
Students should defend their answers. The state refused the Ku Klux Klan's request. The American Civil Liberties Union criticized the decision.

The symbol ⚹ denotes active participation strategies.

Activities are keyed for student abilities:
▲ = Basic
● = All Levels
■ = Average/Advanced

SECTION 2

Federal Policies Regulate Energy Use *(pp. 600–609)*

Section Objectives
☐ contrast fossil fuels with renewable sources of energy
☐ describe energy policies in recent administrations

Vocabulary
fossil fuel, nonrenewable, strip mining, nuclear power, renewable, hydroelectric power, geothermal power, solar power

👥 FOCUS

● Write *Daily Energy Use* on the board. Have each student come to the board and write down one way in which people consume energy during a typical day. (If students begin to run out of ideas, you might remind them that energy is used in cooking, cleaning, transportation, entertainment, and other activities.)

As a supplementary activity, you could ask each student to suggest ways in which the energy-using activity he or she listed on the board could be made more energy-efficient.

SECTION 2 — Federal Policies Regulate Energy Use

ACCESS The Main Ideas

1 What are the differences between fossil fuels and renewable sources of energy? *pages 600–608*

2 What energy policies have recent administrations pursued? *pages 608–609*

What would happen if you woke up one day to find that there was no electricity and all the oil had run out? It might feel very cold or very hot since many of us rely on these forms of energy to heat and cool our homes. Without oil, you and your family might have a harder time getting to schools and workplaces. Once you arrived, buildings would be without light, air conditioning, or heat. Think about all the items we use daily that rely on electric power — refrigerators, ovens, factories, televisions, and computers.

All in all, America uses enormous amounts of energy — more than any other nation. Although we make up only 5 percent of the world's population, Americans consume 23 percent of all the energy used on earth. Moreover, our energy needs keep growing. Where does this energy come from, and how much longer will it last? The major sources of energy now available include coal, oil, natural gas, water power, nuclear power, and sun and wind power. Government policies can promote the use of one energy source or another. These policies aim to find the mix of energy sources (and energy conservation) that meets the nation's needs.

6A, 8G

Fossil Fuels

Most of America's energy comes from plant and animal materials that were formed millions of years ago and stored in the earth's crust. These **fossil fuels** — coal, oil, and natural gas — still fill the great majority of our energy needs. The greatest drawback is that these energy sources are **nonrenewable** — no new supplies are being formed. One day the supply of fossil fuels will run out.

Coal

Coal is America's most abundant energy source. Coal provides only about 22 percent of America's total energy consumption today, but it accounts for nearly 90 percent of our total fossil fuel reserves. It is estimated that the United States has at least a 500-year supply of coal. Most of these reserves are located in three regions — the Appalachian Mountain states, pockets of the Midwest, and the western plains and deserts. About one-third of these reserves are located on federal lands, as shown in Figure 22–3.

Coal as an energy source poses several major problems. First, burning coal pollutes the air. Much of North American coal has high sulfur content. It gives off sulfur dioxide when burned, which combines with water to produce sulfuric acid, a major component of acid rain. Although sulfur can be removed from coal with "scrubbers," the process is very expensive.

A second problem is getting at the coal. Underground mining in shafts is both dangerous and costly in terms of labor. The most economical way to dig coal is by surface, or **strip mining,** especially in the West, where coal reserves lie close to the surface. Strip mining, however, scars the land and destroys vegetation and wildlife. In 1977 Congress required the coal industry to restore all land used for strip mining as closely as possible to its original shape. This includes rebuilding hills, replacing topsoil, and replanting native vegetation.

Finally, coal has rather limited uses. Eighty-five percent of coal is used in power plants to produce electricity. The rest is used mainly by industry or exported. Coal cannot currently be used to fuel automobiles, trucks, buses, or airplanes. Technology to convert coal into a clean-burning, efficient liquid fuel exists but is complex and expensive.

Oil

Oil, or petroleum, was first drilled in the United States in 1859. Before 1900, it made up only about 2 percent of the nation's total energy

600

Background: *Science and Technology* "Scrubbers" actually wash the smoke produced by burning coal. Installed in smokestacks, scrubbers spray a mixture of chemicals at the discharged smoke to wash the sulfur particles out.

Background: *History* The first oil well was drilled in Titusville, Pennsylvania, by a railroad conductor named Edwin Drake.

consumption. Gradually, however, oil began to replace coal as the nation's most important energy source. Easier to transport, cleaner burning, and more versatile than coal, oil was soon dubbed "black gold."

Before World War II, the United States produced enough oil both to meet our own needs and to export overseas. Industrial expansion during and after the war, however, stimulated demand. The United States began to import foreign oil and, by the early 1950's, was using about 10 percent imported oil.

The 1960's and 1970's sparked even more demand for imported oil. Industrial production had increased markedly, in part because of the Vietnam War effort. Americans purchased more automobiles and drove more miles. Between 1960 and 1965, demand for gasoline increased nearly 17 percent. Moreover, many utility companies had begun to switch from coal to cleaner burning oil as part of a national policy to clean up the environment. By 1973, the United States was importing roughly 35 percent of its oil.

The OPEC oil embargo

The winter of 1973–1974 marked a turning point in American oil policy. It was then that OPEC (the Organization of Petroleum-Exporting Countries) began exerting significant influence on world oil prices. OPEC was formed in 1960 to stabilize oil production and increase profits among oil-producing nations. Its membership includes seven Arab countries (Algeria, Iraq, Kuwait, Libya, Qatar, Saudi Arabia, and the United

Figure 22–3 ENERGY RESOURCES IN THE UNITED STATES The map shows major reserves of coal and oil/natural gas and the locations of nuclear power plants. 8A

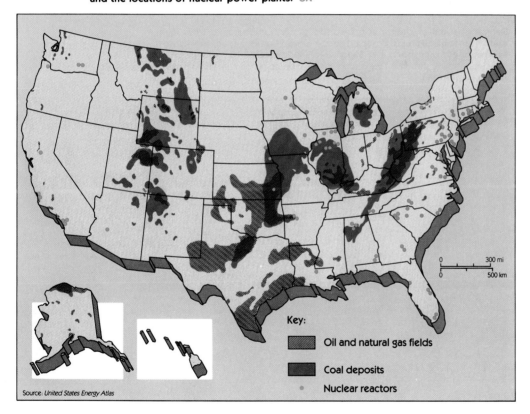

Source: United States Energy Atlas

601

EXPLANATION
After students have read the section, you may want to consider the following activities:

Science and Technology
● Refer students to the vocabulary listed in the Section 2 Review (p. 609). Have students discuss the terms, using the following classifications:

1. comparing similarities and differences: *renewable* and *nonrenewable; nuclear power, hydroelectric power,* and *geothermal power.*
2. explaining word roots: *hydroelectric, nuclear, solar, geothermal.*
3. identifying extended meanings: *fossil fuel; strip mining.*

Have students find the words in their books and use them in context.

Figure 22–3
● *What three regions contain the most U.S. coal reserves?* (The Appalachian states, the Midwest, and the western plains and mountains.) *What state has the greatest area of oil and natural gas fields?* (Texas.) *Where are most of the nuclear reactors located?* (The East and the Midwest.)

The symbol 👥 denotes active participation strategies.

Activities are keyed for student abilities:
▲ = Basic
● = All Levels
■ = Average/Advanced

Science and Technology

▲ **What is America's most abundant energy source?** (Coal.) **How large are this nation's coal reserves?** (They make up 90 percent of our total fossil fuel reserves and constitute a 500-year supply.)

● **What three problems limit the desirability of coal as an energy source?** (Burning coal pollutes the air; digging for coal harms the landscape; coal cannot be used as a fuel for vehicles.)

● CRITICAL THINKING Have students consider their answers to the two questions above and then draw conclusions about the future of coal in U.S. energy policy. (Students will probably conclude that because the United States possesses such large coal reserves, efforts should continue to make coal easier to obtain and cleaner to burn.)

Arab Emirates) and six others (Ecuador, Gabon, Indonesia, Iran, Nigeria, and Venezuela).

Initially, disagreement among OPEC members led to overproduction and lower oil prices. In 1973, however, the United States supported Israel in its war with the Arab states. Furious Arab leaders called for a meeting of the OPEC oil ministers, who voted an embargo on sales of oil to the United States and other "unfriendly nations."

The embargo shocked energy users in the United States. The price of imported oil quadrupled between October 1973 and January 1974. Although the embargo was soon lifted, the price of oil continued to skyrocket. Not only were there gasoline shortages, but prices rose from about 35 cents a gallon in the early 1970's to over $1.36 a gallon in 1980. Utility companies, which had earlier converted from coal to oil, were forced to raise their electrical rates. Home heating costs soared. Americans came to the harsh realization that they could no longer afford to be dependent on foreign sources of oil.

Changing conditions

Oil remains the major source of energy for the United States, accounting for 41 percent of all energy used in 1990. (Figure 22–4 shows Americans' use of different energy sources.) After the crises of the 1970's, however, the use of imported oil dropped. Imports fell from 43 percent of the total in 1979 to about 27 percent in 1985.

Changing conditions in the later 1980's reversed this trend. Increased production of American oil, along with disharmony among OPEC nations, brought lower OPEC prices. By 1986, the price of imported oil fell as low as $9 a barrel (down from well over $30 in 1981). Imports began to rise again, while domestic oil production declined.

While lower oil prices were good news for consumers, they were devastating for people in oil-producing states such as Texas, Louisiana, and Oklahoma. When Texas crude oil reached a record high of $39 a barrel in 1980, the healthy

Each year, about one-tenth of the world's oil production comes from Saudi Arabia. Most of this oil is exported to the United States, Japan, or western Europe. These oil exports give Saudi Arabia influence on the foreign policies of many nations. This photo shows workers at an oil refinery near Jiddah, Saudi Arabia.

602

Background: *Economics* OPEC has been troubled by internal disagreements throughout its existence. One of its main problems is how to control members' production levels. OPEC tries to keep oil production low enough that oil prices remain high.

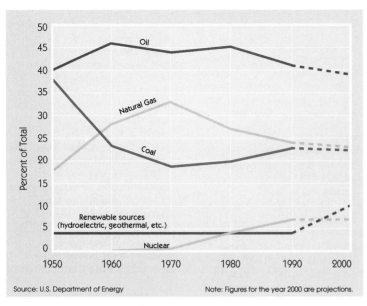

Figure 22–4 U.S. ENERGY CONSUMPTION Americans' use of different energy sources depends not only on availability and price but also on federal energy policies. 8A

Texas economy attracted business from across the nation. In 1986, however, oil prices fell to $15 a barrel, and Texas was racked by economic decline and high unemployment. Newly built skyscrapers stood empty; banks and hotels closed down. Understandably, these states have pushed Congress to place high taxes on foreign oil to keep prices up. Clearly, political considerations both at home and abroad influence legislators in making policy about oil.

Natural gas

Natural gas is an odorless, colorless, poisonous, and explosive gas that is found below the earth's crust. It is usually found with oil deposits and pumped from oil wells. For many years, few realized the energy potential of natural gas. Moreover, gas pipes leaked badly, making it impossible to transport natural gas very far. In the 1920's, however, new pipeline technology made it possible to pump natural gas over great distances. Today natural gas from Texas and Louisiana travels in pipelines thousands of miles to the Midwest and Northeast.

Because the interstate distribution of natural gas was considered a natural monopoly, the federal government believed regulation was necessary to protect consumers. In 1938 Congress passed the Natural Gas Act. This act gave the Federal Power Commission (FPC) authority to oversee pipeline construction and maintenance and to ensure that prices for natural gas shipped in interstate commerce were "just and reasonable." (In 1977 the FPC became the Federal Energy Regulatory Commission [FERC].) These regulations kept the price of natural gas artificially low, thus encouraging usage — and waste.

All segments of the American economy now rely on natural gas. In many respects it is the ideal fuel. It is convenient, clean burning, and efficient. It can be used to cook food, heat homes, make plastics, and power factories, to name just a few uses. Currently, natural gas supplies roughly one-fourth of America's energy use. Unfortunately, supplies are limited, and it is estimated that the United States has only a few decades of natural gas reserves. Already gas is being imported from Canada and Mexico.

603

Economics

Explain to students that the oil embargo of 1973 produced intense frustration among many Americans. The long lines at gasoline pumps were unbelievable to most Americans. Anger sometimes resulted in shouting matches and fighting at gas stations. To ease the crisis, some states allowed the purchase of gasoline only on certain days, depending on whether one's license plate ended in an odd or even number. Another idea—which was not used—was to distribute gas rationing coupons like those issued during World War II.

● Tell students to imagine that they were President during the embargo. Have them write a statement, two or three paragraphs long, that they would make to present and explain a gas rationing system. Then select a few students to read their statements to the class.

Background: *Economics*
During the early 1980's, Texas officials estimated that every dollar drop in the price of a barrel of "crude" caused the state to lose $40 million in oil severance taxes. Including franchise and sales taxes, a single dollar drop caused a $70 million loss.

Figure 22–4
▲ *What is the trend shown in the use of oil?* (Its use is decreasing.)

Background: *Geography*
Natural gas is located in the holes of sandstone, limestone, and other porous rocks. It can be released only by drilling or by a shift in the earth's surface that cracks the rock.

The symbol ▌▌ denotes active participation strategies.

Activities are keyed for student abilities:
▲ = Basic
● = All Levels
■ = Average/Advanced

Other Sources of Energy

Realizing that the supply of fossil fuels is finite and likely to become more costly, Americans have begun to look for other sources of energy. Businesses, scientists, and the government continue to search for new ideas and technology to give America reliable energy for the future.

Nuclear power

Development of atomic energy began during World War II. After the first atomic bombs were dropped on Japan in 1945, Americans began to ponder the potential uses of atomic energy, or **nuclear power**. In the 1946 Atomic Energy Act, Congress put the development of all nuclear programs under the supervision of the Atomic Energy Commission (AEC), a regulatory agency.

At first the AEC was concerned only with the military uses of the atom, but soon it began to explore the peaceful uses of nuclear energy. In 1951 a government experimental plant in Arco, Idaho, produced the first nuclear-generated electricity. Many began to speculate that nuclear power would be the energy of the future.

Such speculation proved unsettling to private utility companies, who feared that a federal monopoly over nuclear power plants would put them out of business. Yielding to mounting pressure, Congress voted in 1954 to permit private companies to develop nuclear power plants. The AEC, however, continued to monitor nuclear power closely through licensing, rate regulation, and safety inspection. Regulation, plus high building costs, slowed development.

After the OPEC oil embargo, however, many utility companies wanted to convert to nuclear power as quickly as possible. To facilitate this conversion, the AEC was abolished and replaced by two new agencies. The Nuclear Regulatory Commission (NRC) regulates nuclear power, and the Energy Research and Development Administration (ERDA) conducts research.

How nuclear power works

Most electrical power plants run on steam, produced by water and intense heat and pressure. The steam turns large turbines, which in turn power generators that produce electricity. In a nuclear reactor, heat is produced by the splitting of atoms (nuclear fission) in uranium-filled rods. Water is circulated between several hundred of these rods, producing steam and cooling the reactor rods. The rods also produce poisonous nuclear wastes, which must be removed periodically. One such by-product is plutonium, one of the most dangerous substances known.

How to dispose of used fuel rods and other nuclear wastes is a serious problem. Nuclear waste is so radioactive that it must be stored thousands of feet underground for at least 10,000 years. Today, nuclear waste products generally are stored in concrete ponds near the plants. In 1985 there were an estimated 11,000 metric tons of such waste in temporary storage.

A law enacted by Congress requires the federal government to select sites for long-term storage of nuclear waste. But while everyone agrees that nuclear waste must be stored securely, nobody wants it buried in their "backyard." The search for a site raised heated local controversies.

Nuclear safety

During the early 1970's, many scientists and other concerned citizens voiced their fears about the safety of nuclear energy. Besides the problem of nuclear waste, they warned of the potential danger of a nuclear accident or "meltdown" at one of the plants. In response, the AEC in 1972 commissioned a detailed study of the nuclear power industry, which concluded that the chances of a disaster were small. By 1979, 72 nuclear plants were producing roughly 12.5 percent of the nation's electricity.

One of these was the Three-Mile Island plant at Harrisburg, Pennsylvania. On March 28, 1979, the core of the reactor overheated, causing a partial meltdown and releasing some radioactive material into the atmosphere. Nobody was killed, but a $2 billion investment was rendered worthless in 30 seconds. By a coincidence, the movie *China Syndrome,* a fictional account of a nuclear disaster, was showing around the nation at the same time. Suddenly the issue of nuclear safety leaped high on the public agenda.

Immediately, President Jimmy Carter appointed a twelve-member commission to study the disaster. Its report blamed many factors, including the plant's construction, federal regulations, and human error. The report touched off renewed debate, delays in licensing, and the cancellation of many proposed plants.

604

☆☆ CRITICAL THINKING
Recognizing Point of View

Imagine this conversation:

"I'm voting for Alvarez again because I approve of her support for education."

"I'm not voting for her. She didn't work to keep the army base open, and as a result I lost my job."

Each of these persons was expressing a **point of view** toward a political candidate. A point of view is like a pair of glasses through which one sees issues. Many things affect a person's point of view, including experience, information, values, occupation, and even the opinions of others. Emotions also can affect point of view. Emotional feelings such as fear, anger, and sympathy can influence how we think.

★ ISSUE: Disposal of Nuclear Waste

Forty years into the nuclear age, the United States faces a crucial problem: What should we do with the radioactive waste that is a by-product of nuclear energy? Radioactive waste, which can remain dangerously potent for centuries, can cause cancer, birth defects, and even death.

In 1982 Congress authorized the Department of Energy to develop a plan for two sites to bury and store the waste. In determining a site, the department was to consider primarily the geology, or structure of the earth, in the area. The geology of a site is of vital importance because over time storage containers might disintegrate, allowing radioactive waste to contaminate nearby water supplies.

Department of Energy scientists chose several potential sites across the country. Each site, the department said, had the kind of rock that would prevent leakage of radioactivity. The announcement of the sites, however, created a furor. Not one of the states chosen wanted a nuclear-waste dump within its borders.

What is the point of view of each of the persons quoted in the next column?

Landowner, Deaf Smith County, Texas

We're worried about our water. How are we going to sell our crops when people find out there's a dump under the ground?

Anti-nuclear activist, northern Idaho

These guys (at the Department of Energy) go to school for eight years to learn how to reassure everyone. They accuse people like me of being emotional. But that's why we're in this, because they have no emotion . . . we need some high-powered, raw emotion to turn this thing around. We need to see people crying.

Lawyer, Asheville, North Carolina

We come not asking anything of you. . . . We do not beg. We come, rather, to tell you. And we tell you. Ye shall not. Ye shall not desecrate our land. . . . We are united. We shall fight you to the last breath and to the last drop of blood. We shall not fail. We shall overcome.

Member of Congress

I hope very much that we can begin to sort out the real issues from the emotion that has engulfed this program. It is absolutely essential that we determine the circumstances under which the program can go forward.

Analyzing the Issue

1. Which views are primarily emotional in their opposition to a proposed dump? Explain your answer.
2. Which point of view expresses economic concerns? Explain.
3. How does the point of view of the member of Congress differ from the others?
4. What effects, both positive and negative, can an emotional point of view have on public policy decisions?
5. If you were a public official, would you pay more attention to the landowner, the activist, or the lawyer? Why?

605

Politics

Tell students that the 55 m.p.h. speed limit imposed following the oil embargo of 1973 is still in use in many areas. In 1987, however, Congress allowed states to raise highway speed limits to a maximum of 65 m.p.h.

● Have students consider the speed limit issue from the viewpoint of several different people (for example, an Energy Department official, a state legislator, a person who commutes by car, a hospital worker). Students should write brief, first-person accounts in which each of the persons explains his or her view on the issue.

The most widely used energy alternatives to fossil fuels are nuclear power from reactors like these at Rancho Seco, California, and hydroelectric power, generated by dams like Hoover Dam on the Colorado River. Other possibilities are solar cells that gather the sun's energy and turbines powered by the force of the wind.

606

In 1981 the construction of a nuclear power plant at Diablo Canyon, California, raised further doubts. Widespread local protests and civil disobedience drew attention to the fact that the plant was built near an earthquake fault and led to the discovery that its earthquake protection system had been installed incorrectly. (After years of hearings before the NRC, Diablo Canyon quietly began operations in 1984.)

The Chernobyl disaster

In April 1986, the cooling system failed in a reactor at the Chernobyl nuclear plant near Kiev, in the western part of the Soviet Union. The core heated to over 5,000 degrees Fahrenheit, causing a massive explosion and releasing clouds of radioactivity over much of Europe. The initial blast reportedly killed only two workers, but hundreds of Soviet citizens were exposed to deadly radiation, and many later died of radiation sickness. Drinking water and crops were contaminated, and more than 100,000 people were evacuated. Radioactivity 100 times greater than normal was detected as far away as Sweden.

Because Soviet officials were at first very secretive about the incident, the full extent of the damage was difficult to assess. The official Soviet report blamed incompetent plant managers for the disaster. Western experts pointed to faulty reactor design. Whatever the cause, the Chernobyl disaster raised further doubts about the safety of nuclear energy.

The future of nuclear power

By the late 1980's, the United States had nearly 100 operating reactors, with over 30 under construction or on order. The possibility of accidents, the disposal of wastes, and the costs of building plants continue to be stumbling blocks for the future of nuclear power. Security and public opposition are other problems. People worry about a terrorist bombing of a nuclear plant, or the possibility that terrorists might steal the deadly plutonium produced in the plants. There is also public concern about health dangers and plant safety. The closing of nuclear power plants has been a referendum issue in several places.

Finally, nuclear power uses nonrenewable sources. Just like fossil fuels, the supply of uranium ore in the earth's crust is finite. One possible solution to this problem is the "breeder" reactor. Unlike conventional nuclear plants, breeder reactors use the by-products of nuclear power generation to create more fuel. This process offers a potentially unlimited source of energy. On the other hand, the chances of a catastrophic accident are far greater at a breeder reactor than at a conventional plant.

Tapping the elements

Some alternative ways of generating electricity rely on ongoing processes that occur in nature. Because these processes are never-ending, such energy sources are said to be **renewable**.

Hydroelectric power is produced by the energy of falling water channeled through dams. It has been used in America since the late 1800's, and there are dozens of hydroelectric plants in operation in the United States. Some of the largest are Hoover Dam on the Arizona-Nevada border and Grand Coulee Dam in Washington.

While hydroelectric power is an inexpensive, non-polluting, dependable, and renewable source of energy, it is practical only for rivers in certain kinds of terrain. (Some experimental hydroelectric plants draw on tidal power.) Moreover, building a dam on a river can disrupt people's lives and harm plant and animal life.

Another potential energy source is wind. Although windmills have long been used for power, the amount of energy they generate is quite limited. Wind power is unlikely ever to be a major energy source but can help save energy.

Geothermal power is produced by tapping into the great amounts of heat stored in the earth's interior. Such "hot spots" are typically found near volcanoes and hot springs. Water can be injected into the earth where there is high thermal activity, converted to steam, and returned to the surface, where it powers a generator. The only major geothermal project in the United States today is The Geysers in northern California. A few areas in the Rocky Mountains and Alaska are considered potential sources for geothermal power.

The sun's rays generate enough energy, or **solar power**, in a half hour to satisfy America's energy needs for a year. Methods for collecting, distributing, and using solar energy, however, are still quite primitive. Small solar units are now available to help heat homes and hot water, but these depend largely on climate. (Solar units

Background: *Global Awareness* The nuclear fallout from the Chernobyl disaster harmed Laplanders —the people living in the northern regions of Sweden, Finland, and the Soviet Union. Reindeer, which supply most of their basic needs, were contaminated by radiation through the plants they ate. Reindeer meat will not be safe to eat for many years.

Background: *Science and Technology* The Chernobyl reactor apparently lacked a "containment structure," a large, reinforced concrete dome designed to prevent the release of radioactive materials in an accident.

RETEACHING/CORRECTIVES

▲ Have students list the advantages and disadvantages of each of the following sources of energy: coal, oil, natural gas, nuclear power, hydroelectric power, solar power.

You may want to use **Transparency 54,** which shows a political cartoon dealing with Three-Mile Island.

ENRICHMENT/EXTENSION

■ Have students complete **Skills Challenge Worksheet 22,** which asks them to predict consequences of environmental policy decisions.

Section 2 Review Answers

1. Coal uses are limited; burning coal pollutes the air; mining coal is dangerous, costly, and destructive to land and wildlife.
2. The United States stopped relying as heavily on foreign oil; conservation measures were increased.
3. Radioactive wastes, the possibility of accidents or terrorist acts, and potential health hazards.
4. Water, wind, the heat stored in the earth, and the sun.

work better in southern states where there are many sunny days.) Large-scale solar plants to run factories and produce electricity for cities have yet to be developed. If such techniques can be perfected, solar power may be a promising solution to some future energy needs.

Other potential sources

There are many other possible energy sources. Biomass, for example, is organic material, such as garbage or wood, that can be burned and converted into energy. Another potential source is oil shale. Shale, a type of rock found in Colorado and Wyoming, often contains oil. The oil can be extracted, but only by a very costly process. "Synfuels," gas or liquid fuels made from coal, offer another possibility. Researchers have also had some success running automobiles with "gasohol," a fuel made from grain. Thus, a variety of potential energy sources, each with its own advantages and disadvantages, are available to meet the world's growing energy needs. Their development depends in part on whether businesses and governments think it is worthwhile and necessary to spend money on research.

7C

Recent Energy Policies

No single source is likely to satisfy America's long-term energy needs. Which energy policies the United States should pursue, however, is a question that policy-makers must try to answer now. Five recent Presidents — Nixon, Ford, Carter, Reagan, and Bush — have all taken somewhat different approaches.

Nixon's energy policies

Following the 1973 OPEC oil embargo, President Richard Nixon set a goal for America — to become energy independent. During Nixon's presidency, construction began on the Trans-Alaska Pipeline, which would carry oil from the oil-rich North Slope to ports in southern Alaska. In addition, environmental standards were relaxed to permit more burning of coal. To conserve energy, Congress extended nationwide daylight savings time. Congress also imposed a nationwide 55 miles-per-hour speed limit. (Before this, each state set its own speed limit.) Slower driving was estimated to save 130,000 barrels of oil per day, in addition to reducing

accidents. The Nixon administration also emphasized voluntary conservation, such as using less heat or air-conditioning in homes and offices.

Ford's energy policies

Gerald Ford's administration (1974–1977) continued the policies begun by Nixon but made some major changes. A law passed in 1975 required automobile makers to improve gasoline mileage. To comply, many companies began new lines of small cars, which soon gained popularity. Congress also approved grants to states to encourage conservation and to help people insulate their homes against cold weather. Utility companies were allowed to switch back from oil to coal, and a $2 per barrel tax was placed on foreign oil to help discourage imports.

Carter's energy policies

One of Jimmy Carter's top goals as President was the development of a complete energy policy. In his words, it was the "moral equivalent of war." The first major step was the creation of the Cabinet-level Department of Energy (DOE) in 1977. The DOE consolidated energy programs previously carried out by the Departments of the Treasury, Defense, State, Commerce, and Interior. Nuclear energy was also encouraged.

The cornerstone of Carter's energy policy was the National Energy Act of 1978. This act had many provisions. Most new utility companies were required to burn coal rather than oil. A tax was placed on inefficient "gas-guzzling" cars, beginning with the 1980 models. The prices of oil and natural gas were gradually deregulated. It was thought that rising prices of domestic oil and natural gas would force consumers to conserve energy. Moreover, homeowners were given tax credits for insulating their dwellings and using solar energy.

Reagan's energy policy

While Carter's view was that America was running out of energy, President Ronald Reagan took the position that America had an abundance of energy. All that was needed, according to Reagan, was to give private industry the right incentives to discover and develop it.

To that end, the Reagan administration called for increased deregulation of domestic oil and natural gas, the relaxation of rules for oil drilling offshore and on federal lands, continued

Background: *Economics*
Because oil and coal are still relatively plentiful, money and attention will probably not be diverted to researching alternate sources of energy. Business, especially, has little incentive if the result is to be a $5.00 gallon of "synfuel." However, proponents of alternative sources point out that oil prices do not reflect the real costs of oil, which include oil spills and foreign aid to oil-producing countries.

use of nuclear energy, and cuts in funding of solar energy research. Reagan vetoed the Clean Water Act, saying it was too expensive.

Bush's energy goals

President George Bush sought to revitalize nuclear power as an energy source. He approved funding for continued research on clean coal technology. He favored drilling off-shore and in Alaska's National Wildlife Refuge, if oil reserves could be tapped safely.

Energy policy under Clinton

President Clinton indicated that he opposed increased reliance on nuclear power, and he urged greater emphasis on conservation. In 1993 legislation increased the federal fuel tax, for example, in part to encourage Americans to conserve in their use of gasoline.

SECTION 2 REVIEW

Vocabulary and key terms

fossil fuel (600)	Nuclear Regulatory
nonrenewable (600)	Commission (NRC) (604)
strip mining (600)	renewable (607)
OPEC (601)	hydroelectric power (607)
nuclear power (604)	geothermal power (607)
Atomic Energy	solar power (607)
Commission (AEC) (604)	

For review

1. What are the major disadvantages of using coal as a source of energy? **8C**
2. How did the OPEC oil embargo affect U.S. energy policy and use? **8F**
3. What are some of the dangers associated with nuclear power plants? **8C**
4. What are some natural sources of renewable energy? **8C**
5. (a) What were the main components of President Carter's energy policy? (b) How did Reagan's energy policy differ from Carter's? **8G**

Critical thinking

ANALYZING AN ISSUE What are the trade-offs between energy and the environment regarding coal, oil, and nuclear power? Which should take precedence, energy needs or safety concerns? **8A**

Chapter Summary

The federal government has long maintained a policy of preserving the environment and natural resources of the United States. The national parks, operated by a part of the Interior Department, protect areas of wilderness and scientific importance. The national forests, maintained under the Department of Agriculture, allow commercial use while preserving the land and water. Programs have also been put in place to protect wildlife for the benefit of all Americans. Land use policy and water conservation, finally, have also been concerns of the federal government.

Efforts to protect the environment from pollution began in the 1950's and were fully organized under the Environmental Protection Agency (EPA) in 1970. Water pollution, air pollution, toxic wastes, and solid wastes continue to be pressing environmental problems for the American people and government policy-makers.

Closely related to environmental policy is energy policy. Fossil fuels — coal, oil, and natural gas — are the most important sources of energy today, and the United States has long depended on them; however, their supply is finite and they are *nonrenewable*. In addition, the OPEC embargo of 1973 pointed out the danger of relying too heavily on foreign sources of oil.

Nuclear power offers an alternative to fossil fuels but carries the problem of nuclear wastes and the threat of nuclear accidents. Energy sources that tap the earth's ongoing natural processes, such as geothermal, hydroelectric, and wind power, offer potential renewable sources of energy. Solar power may prove to be one answer to future energy, particularly in states that enjoy many sunny days, but development costs for any alternative source are likely to be high.

Recent Presidents have taken different approaches to solving the nation's energy problems. Most have given greater weight when formulating energy policy to the concerns of industry than to the problems of pollution, resource conservation, and safety.

5. **(a)** Carter's energy policy created the Department of Energy, ordered the burning of coal in new utility companies, taxed "gas-guzzling" cars, deregulated oil and natural gas prices, gave tax credits to energy-saving homeowners, provided federal money for alternative energy research. **(b)** Reagan thought there were ample sources of energy and that private industry should develop them.

Critical thinking Students should note that although coal and oil are nonrenewable resources and their extraction damages the environment, the United States is dependent on the energy these fuels provide. They should understand that nuclear power is reliable but potentially hazardous.

CLOSURE
● Have students write three "I learned. . ." statements explaining what they learned in the section. Then have students read the next assigned lesson.

CHAPTER 22 CORRECTIVES
● To review the content of Chapter 22, you may want to have students complete **Study Guide/Review 22** or **Workbook Chapter 22**.

The symbol ⅱ denotes active participation strategies.

Activities are keyed for student abilities:
▲ = Basic
● = All Levels
■ = Average/Advanced

CHAPTER 22 REVIEW

Answers

Vocabulary See pp. T19–T21 for suggested vocabulary activities.

Reviewing the Facts

1. National parks are preserved intact for public enjoyment, while national forests are open for commercial use as well as recreation.

2. The EPA issues permits for waste disposal, administers grants to state and local governments, and enforces government policies concerning pollution, wastes, pesticides, and radiation.

3. To make all the nation's streams safe for fishing and swimming and to end all discharges of pollutants into navigable waters.

4. Coal is America's most abundant energy source.

5. Prices can fluctuate and oil output can be manipulated by oil-producing countries.

6. A commission was appointed to study the disaster; the debate about nuclear safety was renewed; delays in further licensing occurred; many proposed nuclear plants were canceled.

7. The possibility of accidents, the disposal of waste, and the high cost of building more plants.

8. A new goal was set—energy independence. Effects included the construction of the Trans-Alaska Pipeline, increased use of coal, and energy conservation programs.

Thinking Critically About Key Concepts

1. **(a)** Early efforts were poorly funded and uncoordinated. **(b)** Later legislation established the Environmental Protection Agency to enforce federal policies.

2. Because of the existence of some 50,000 toxic waste dumps, which must be located and cleaned up.

610

● **Review the definitions of the following terms:**

acid rain	fossil fuel	OPEC
aquifer	geothermal power	pollutant
Atomic Energy	hydroelectric power	renewable
Commission	inversion	solar power
ecology	nonrenewable	solid waste
emissions	nuclear power	strip mining
Environmental Protection	Nuclear Regulatory	toxic waste
Agency	Commission	

● **REVIEWING THE FACTS**

1. What is the difference between a national park and a national forest in terms of how it is used? **8G**

2. How does the Environmental Protection Agency protect the environment? **3A**

3. What major goals were established by the Water Pollution Control Act of 1972? **8E**

4. Why is coal, despite its problems, an attractive energy source in the United States? **8A**

5. What are some dangers of relying on foreign oil supplies? **8H**

6. What were some effects of the nuclear accident at the Three-Mile Island power plant in Pennsylvania? **8F**

7. What are some major obstacles to the future development of nuclear power? **8H**

8. How did the OPEC oil embargo of 1973 affect U.S. energy policy? **8F**

▲ **THINKING CRITICALLY ABOUT KEY CONCEPTS**

1. (a) Why was federal water and air pollution legislation in the 1950's and early 1960's largely ineffective? (b) How did later legislation try to deal with this problem? **7A**

2. Why do some experts say that America is sitting on an "ecological time bomb"? **8A**

3. Why did the United States come to depend

610

---

so heavily on foreign oil following World War II? **8F**

4. Name some advantages and disadvantages of hydroelectric, geothermal, and solar power. **8A**

▲ **PRACTICING SKILLS**

1. **Study Skills: Reading a line graph.** Refer to Figure 22–4 (page 603) to answer the following questions. (a) In 1950, what were the three major energy sources in the United States? (b) According to the graph, what will be the three major energy sources in the year 2000? (c) When did the consumption of natural gas reach its peak? (d) By the year 2000, which sources of energy are expected to be increasing in consumption? (To review graph skills, see Study Skill 3 in the back of the book.) **8B**

2. **Critical Thinking Skills: Comparing and contrasting.** Reread the subsection "Recent Energy Policies" (pages 608–609). Make a chart to compare and contrast the policies of each President. You might write the names of the Presidents along the top of the chart and list different energy policies down the left-hand side. Then you could put a check mark under the name of each President who followed a certain policy. Policies might include voluntary conservation, burning of coal, grants and tax credits to consumers, deregulation, research, and nuclear energy. **8G**

---

3. Industrial production increased, more people bought cars, and many utility companies switched from coal to oil.

4. *Advantages*: hydroelectric—inexpensive, dependable, non-polluting,

renewable; geothermal—renewable; solar—renewable, generates tremendous amounts of energy. *Disadvantages:* hydroelectric—practical only on certain kinds of terrain, can disrupt the lives of nearby residents

and harm wildlife when dams are built; geothermal—limited number of potential sources in the United States; solar—techniques not yet far enough advanced.

■ WRITING ABOUT ISSUES

1. **Research report.** Research a current pollution problem in your community or state. Determine the extent of the problem and what is being done to solve it. Write a report detailing your findings. **8C**
2. **Writing an essay.** Groundwater contamination is an important environmental issue. Should local and state governments be responsible for solving this problem, or should the federal government handle it through a national groundwater policy? Argue for and against a national groundwater policy. **8C**
3. **Position paper.** Some experts argue that the money spent on nuclear power plants could be better used to develop alternative, renewable sources of energy. Provide arguments for and against this view. **8C**

▲ PARTICIPATORY CITIZENSHIP

1. **Getting involved.** Find out about local environmental groups in your area. What types of projects are they working on? Ask a volunteer coordinator at one of the groups about ways that you and your classmates can assist in the groups' efforts. **6G**
2. **Debate.** Gather information from newspapers, magazines, or other library resources to prepare an argument either for or against allowing oil exploration in the Arctic National Wildlife Refuge in Alaska. **5C**

▲ ANALYZING A POLITICAL CARTOON

Critics hold certain corporations responsible for environmental damage that affects the health and safety of millions of Americans. Many corporations have traditionally resisted pollution control laws as meddlesome and expensive. Look at the cartoon below and answer the following questions.

1. How does the cartoonist portray corporate attitudes toward environmental legislation? **8B**
2. What does the cartoonist see happening in the 1990's? Do you agree? Why, or why not? **8B**

Reprinted by permission of Joe Heller, Green Bay Press-Gazette.

Writing About Issues
1. Students may want to research problems of air or water pollution or toxic waste. They may also want to write letters to local officials to determine how the problems are being addressed.
2. In their arguments, students might refer to states' inability to solve earlier water pollution problems when they were given that responsibility under the Water Pollution Control Act and the Water Quality Act.
3. Students should evaluate the factors of cost, environmental impact, and technical feasibility.

Participatory Citizenship
1. You may want to invite a local environmental activist to speak to students about how environmental issues affect their lives and how they can become involved.
2. Students might split up into teams to debate the issue.

Analyzing a Political Cartoon
1. As resistant to pollution control laws because of expense.
2. The cartoonist portrays corporations as using environmentalism as a public relations tool.

Practicing Skills
1. **(a)** Oil, natural gas, coal.
(b) Oil, natural gas, coal.
(c) 1970. **(d)** Coal, renewable sources.
2. Nixon, Ford, Carter, and Clinton encouraged conservation. Carter, Reagan, and Bush encouraged nuclear energy. Ford and Carter encouraged conservation through grants and tax credits. Nixon, Ford, Carter, and Bush favored the use of coal. Carter and Reagan carried out deregulation. Carter provided more money for research and development. Reagan reduced federal involvement in energy programs. Bush favored drilling off-shore and in Alaska. Clinton favored a higher fuel tax.

Chapter Review exercises are keyed for student abilities:
▲ = Basic
● = All Levels
■ = Average/Advanced

CHAPTER 23
SOCIAL POLICIES AND PROGRAMS
(pp. 612–629)

	Section Objectives	**Section Resources**
Section 1 **Most Americans Benefit from Social Programs**	☐ describe the origins and functions of the major social insurance programs ☐ describe other major public health issues	▲ SKILLS PRACTICE WORKSHEET **23** ■ SKILLS CHALLENGE WORKSHEET **23** ▲ TRANSPARENCY **55**
Section 2 **Public Assistance Programs Help Those in Need**	☐ explain the benefits and criticisms of the AFDC program ☐ describe the Medicaid and food stamp programs	

Essential Elements

The list below shows Essential Elements relevant to this chapter.
(The complete list of Essential Elements appears in the introductory
pages of this Teacher's Edition.)

Section 1: 4C, 6B, 6E, 7A, 7B, 8A, 8E, 8F

Section 2: 6E, 6G, 7B, 8G, 8H

Chapter Review: 3A, 5B, 5C, 6E, 6G, 7A, 7B, 8A, 8B, 8C, 8D

Section Resources are keyed
for student abilities:
▲ = Basic
● = All Levels
■ = Average/Advanced

Homework Options

Each section contains activities labeled "Guided/Independent Practice," "Reteaching/Correctives," and "Enrichment/Extension." You may wish to choose from among these activities when assigning homework.

Students Acquiring English Activities

Divide the class into groups and have each group fill out a chart on the following social policies and programs: Social Security, Medicare, Medicaid, Aid to Families with Dependent Children, and food stamps. Tell the groups that their charts must answer the following questions: Who qualifies? When was the program initiated? What are the benefits? How is the program funded? What problems with the program exist?

LISTENING/SPEAKING: After completing its chart, each group should propose a new social program aimed at solving a particular problem. The groups should provide a complete description of their programs.

Case Studies

When teaching this chapter, you may use Case Study 10, which addresses the issue of required national service for all eighteen-year-olds. (Case Studies may be found following p. 510.)

Teacher Bibliography

Bernstein, Merton C. and Joan B. Bernstein. *Social Security: The System that Works.* Basic, 1989. A surprising analysis of a much-derided monolith.

Boskin, Michael J. *Too Many Promises: The Uncertain Future of Social Security.* Kraus, 1986. Exposes weaknesses in the Social Security system and suggests a closer correlation between benefits and contributions.

Kozol, Jonathan. *Rachel and Her Children: Homeless Families in America.* Fawcett, 1988. Powerful account of homelessness, using a case study approach.

Student Bibliography

Dudley, William, ed. *Poverty: Opposing Viewpoints.* Greenhaven, 1988. A stimulating debate on the causes of poverty, how to end it, the relationship of poverty to homelessness, and the welfare system.

Fisher, David Hackett. *Growing Old in America.* Oxford University Press, 1978. A discussion of the impact of the growing proportion of older citizens in the nation's population.

Szumski, Bonnie, ed. *The Health Crisis: Opposing Viewpoints.* Greenhaven Press, 1988. Examines such public health issues as AIDS, health care for the elderly, and rising medical costs.

Literature

Armstrong, William H. *Sounder.* Harper, 1969. The tragic story of a black sharecropper who steals food to feed his hungry family.

Martin, George. *Madam Secretary, Frances Perkins.* Houghton Mifflin, 1976. A biography of the first woman to hold a Cabinet post in the U.S. government.

Rossner, Judith. *Emmeline.* Simon & Schuster, 1980. A novel about a young girl who leaves her family's farm in 1839 to work in the cotton mills of Lowell, Massachusetts, and the ensuing tragedy of her life.

Films and Videotapes*

Bread, Butter and Politics. 60 min. PBS, 1984. v. Questions whether increases in federal food programs have had an effect on hunger in America.

Living Below the Line. 60 min. PBS, 1984. v. An examination of the welfare system through the experience of an older African American man trying to survive on government assistance.

Social Security (How Secure). 52 min. Films, 1976. f. A study of the Social Security system and its future.

CHAPTER RESOURCES

Study Guide/Review 23
Workbook Chapter 23
Chapter 23 Test, Forms A–C

* For a complete guide to audiovisual sources, see page T22.

611B

CHAPTER 23

Social Policies and Programs (pp. 612–629)

This chapter begins by tracing the history of government involvement in social assistance programs, then outlines the various kinds of social insurance programs available today, and concludes by examining public assistance programs.

Chapter Outline

After students complete this chapter, they will be able to:

1. Describe the origins and functions of the major social insurance programs.

2. Describe other major public health issues.

3. Explain the benefits and criticisms of the AFDC program.

4. Describe the Medicaid and food stamp programs.

CHAPTER

23

SOCIAL POLICIES and PROGRAMS

We have pledged our common resources to help one another in the hazards and struggles of individual life.

Harry S Truman
State of the Union Address (1949)

612

Photo
Special insurance payments help Americans of retirement age.

U ntil the 1930's, government assumed little responsibility for the well-being of society. Then, during the Depression, President Franklin Roosevelt committed the government to a broad array of social programs. "One of the duties of the state," Roosevelt declared, "is that of caring for those of its citizens who find themselves . . . unable to obtain even the necessities of mere existence. . . . To these unfortunate citizens aid must be extended by the government — not as a matter of charity but as a matter of *social duty*."

More recently, Ronald Reagan offered a very different perspective on government's role. America's problems, Reagan declared, "all stem from a single source: the belief that government, particularly the federal government, has the answer to our ills and that the proper method of dealing with social problems is to transfer power from the private to the public sector. . . . Federal authority has clearly failed to do the job. Indeed, it has created more problems." Do the responsibilities of government include the well-being of its citizens? If so, what forms should that responsibility take?

CHAPTER OUTLINE

1 Most Americans Benefit from Social Programs

Changing Social Concerns
Social Security Today
Medicare
Other Health Care Issues

2 Public Assistance Programs Help Those in Need

Aid to Families
Other Assistance Programs

613

SECTION 1

Most Americans Benefit from Social Programs (pp. 614–622)

Section Objectives
- ☐ describe the origins and functions of the major social insurance programs
- ☐ describe other major public health issues

Vocabulary

social insurance, public assistance, Medicare, epidemic

 FOCUS

● Have each student write the following on a sheet of paper: *When I see a homeless person on the street or on television, my immediate reaction is. . . .* Have students complete the statement. Then ask volunteers to read their statements to the class.

You may at this point want to discuss the issue of homelessness with students. If you prefer to move directly to the content of the section, ask students what their reaction to homelessness tells them about their views about social programs in general.

SECTION 1 — Most Americans Benefit from Social Programs

ACCESS | The Main Ideas

1 What are the origins and functions of the major social insurance programs?
pages 614–621

2 What are some major public health issues?
pages 621–622

How and why did the government become involved in the business of providing such services as school lunches, legal assistance, college loans and work-study programs, unemployment benefits, and benefits and health care for the elderly? All of these are government social programs. This section examines how the major programs work.

6B, 6E, 7B

Changing Social Concerns

Most federal government social programs in effect today are a legacy from the policies of the New Deal. Until the Great Depression of the 1930's, there were virtually no federal social programs, nor did most Americans think there should be. Families, churches, and private charities had the responsibility of caring for the elderly, the poor, and the homeless.

Some local governments — counties and towns — set up "poorhouses" or "workhouses" for people with no other resources or no place to go. Conditions there were often deplorable — overcrowded, unsanitary, and demeaning. By the early 1900's, many states also took some responsibility for the needy. Some set minimum health care standards for local governments or provided modest financial aid to orphans, the blind, and the homeless.

The Great Depression of the 1930's changed this situation dramatically. People who had worked hard, saved money, and tried to plan wisely suddenly faced economic ruin. One out of four workers was unemployed. Millions were homeless and hungry. President Franklin D. Roosevelt said, "I see one-third of a nation ill-housed, ill-clad, ill-nourished."

Many Americans now clamored for federal assistance because there seemed to be nowhere else to turn. Such government help takes two basic forms — programs of **social insurance** that depend on personal contributions, and programs of **public assistance** that are supported by tax dollars.

New federal assistance programs

Roosevelt launched many new programs in the effort to pull America out of the Depression. One, the Social Security Act of 1935, marked a turning point in America's social policies. Entitled "an act to provide for the general welfare," it was America's first federal social insurance program. Social insurance programs do not give direct aid. People who can draw benefits are those who have already paid into the program. Later, they or their families can collect from the program's funds.

The Social Security Act actually set up two social insurance programs — the retirement plan that most people think of as "Social Security" and the program for unemployment compensation (page 579). Other social programs, known as public assistance or welfare, were also established by the act. These programs, paid for with state and federal funds, are available only to those who can prove that they need help.

Many people at first opposed the Social Security program. Both employers and employees challenged the legality of imposing a tax to finance the program, but the Supreme Court upheld the law. (In the "Speaking Out" feature on page 803, Labor Secretary Frances Perkins points out other reasons behind Social Security.)

The war on poverty

The next era of widespread government action in social programs came in the 1960's. While the nation as a whole was prospering, poverty stubbornly persisted among many groups, both urban and rural.

"If a free society cannot help the many who are poor," President John Kennedy said, "it cannot save the few who are rich." Kennedy's suc-

---

Background: *Constitutional Heritage* The cases in which the Supreme Court upheld Social Security were *Steward Machine Co. v. Davis* and *Helvering v. Davis* (both 1937). Justice Benjamin N. Cardozo wrote,

"Needs that were narrow or parochial a century ago may be interwoven in our day with the well-being of the nation."

cessor, Lyndon Johnson, started or expanded many federal social programs. Johnson had the support of a liberal Democratic Congress in this "war on poverty." Some programs gave direct aid; others aimed at preventing poverty. Federal aid went to education, public-housing programs, job training, mass transit, and community development.

Reducing government's role

A major shift occurred in federal social programs in the 1980's, when the Reagan administration took office. To lower spending and reduce the growing budget deficit, Reagan cut back funds for most public assistance programs. The stated policy was to provide a "safety net" that would give benefits only to the "truly needy." Eligibility rules were tightened, eliminating many of the working poor from welfare programs and reducing benefits for others.

Public opinion on the Reagan policies was sharply divided. Supporters of the budget cuts argued that jobs and economic expansion would be more help than welfare programs. Opponents charged that the President was trying to "balance the budget on the backs of the poor." Almost no one argued that either approach offered a perfect solution to the problems of poverty in America. **4C, 6E, 7A**

Social Security Today

The central core of Social Security today is Old Age, Survivors, and Disability Insurance (OASDI). As its name suggests, OASDI provides monthly benefits to retired persons, to survivors of wage-earners, and to persons too disabled to work. This makes it a broad expansion of the original act, which was an old-age retirement fund. In the mid-1990's, over 42 million people — roughly 16 percent of all Americans — receive some form of Social Security benefits. After defense spending, OASDI is the largest single expense in the federal budget.

For social insurance to protect all members of the society, all must take part. Most working Americans, therefore, are required to participate in the Social Security program. Today, about 95 percent of the American work force contributes to and may benefit from Social Security.

Since the Depression, Americans have looked toward their government to play a greater role in helping people meet economic difficulties. Here, people wait in line at a government assistance office in Michigan.

615

Background: *Economics*
In 1993 there were over 36 million Americans below the poverty level. About 27 million received food stamps and almost 14 million received AFDC benefits. (AFDC is described on pp. 623–625.) Those not receiving welfare were the "working poor"—those ineligible for welfare assistance because they hold jobs, even though those jobs pay very little.

EXPLANATION
After students have read the section, you may want to consider the following activities:

History
Review with students the history of federal efforts to aid the needy.

▲ *Prior to the 1930's, who chiefly cared for the elderly, the poor, and the homeless?* (Families, churches, and private charities.) *What event brought about federal involvement in this area?* (The Great Depression.) *Why?* (The Depression created a tremendous need for social assistance, and people felt that only the federal government could help.)

▲ *When was the next era of widespread government action in social programs?* (The 1960's.) *What sorts of programs were involved?* (Direct aid to needy persons, aid to education, public-housing programs, mass transit, community development.)

▲ *How and why did government social programs change during the 1980's?* (President Reagan cut funding for most programs in an effort to reduce spending and lower the budget deficit.) *What criticism was made of the new policy?* (That poor people were being forced to bear the brunt of spending cuts.)

The symbol 👥 denotes active participation strategies.

Activities are keyed for student abilities:
▲ = Basic
● = All Levels
■ = Average/Advanced

Economics

▲ Ask students to recall the definition of a regressive tax given in Chapter 19 (p. 518). **Why is FICA called a regressive tax?** (People pay tax only up to a certain level of income. Therefore, people with higher incomes pay a smaller percentage of their total income.)

Refer students to Figure 23–1 (this page), showing FICA tax rates and income ceilings over time.

● **Which person would pay more FICA tax under current rules, one earning $75,000 or one earning ten times that amount?** (Each would pay the same amount.) **Who would pay more FICA tax if it were a progressive tax?** (The person who earned $750,000.)

● CRITICAL THINKING **What might have been legislators' reasons for making FICA a regressive tax?** (Students may suggest that because the purpose of Social Security is to provide a safety net rather than simply to raise revenue, there was a limit to the amount of money needed from each contributor. Others may suggest that a regressive tax was seen as more politically acceptable.)

Financing Social Security

The Social Security system is financed by a compulsory payroll tax on employees and employers. This tax is listed on one's paycheck as FICA: Federal Insurance Contributions Act. Every payday, a specified percentage of a worker's earnings, up to a maximum yearly amount, is deducted for FICA. This amount is then matched by the employer. In 1994, the FICA payroll tax rate was 7.65 percent. Self-employed persons pay all their own contributions when they file their federal income tax returns.

Most of the FICA tax is imposed only on income up to a maximum limit. As Figure 23-1 shows, these limits change frequently to account for inflation and other factors. Because of the ceiling, FICA is a regressive tax. Persons earning far more than the maximum pay a smaller percentage of their income than those with incomes below the limit.

Social Security benefits

RETIREMENT Supplementing retired people's savings and pension income was the original goal of the Social Security Act. American workers covered by Social Security are entitled to collect full retirement benefits when they are 65, 66, or 67, depending upon when they were born. They may choose to retire as early as age 62, but their benefits will be permanently reduced if they do. Workers who go on working after reaching retirement age receive slightly higher benefits when they do retire.

To qualify for retirement benefits, a worker must have worked and contributed to the system for a specified length of time. The actual benefits depend on a complex formula, which includes a worker's earnings and length of working time. The average monthly retirement benefit has risen from $341 in 1980 to $693 in 1995.

When a retired person's husband or wife reaches retirement age, he or she is also entitled to monthly benefits equal to one-half the spouse's benefits. Thus, if a retiree received $674 per month, his or her spouse would get $337 per month. If the spouse is also entitled to retirement benefits based upon separate contributions, he or she may draw whichever amount is higher.

SURVIVOR'S BENEFITS A second feature, survivors' benefits, was added to Social Security in 1939. If the family's main income-provider dies, his or her family receives money for burial costs,

Figure 23–1 SOCIAL SECURITY CONTRIBUTIONS: RATES AND LIMITS, 1970–1994 7B

	MAXIMUM TAXABLE INCOME	TAX RATE ON EMPLOYER AND EMPLOYEE	MAXIMUM ANNUAL TAX
1970	$ 7,800	4.80%	$ 374
1975	$14,100	5.85%	$ 825
1980	$25,900	6.13%	$1,588
1981	$29,700	6.65%	$1,975
1982	$32,400	6.70%	$2,171
1984	$37,800	7.00%	$2,533
1985	$39,600	7.05%	$2,792
1986	$42,000	7.15%	$3,003
1988	$45,000	7.51%	$3,380
1990	$51,300	7.65%	$3,856
1992	$55,500	7.65%	$4,246
1994*	$60,600	7.65%	$4,636

*An additional tax of 1.45% had to be paid on earnings over $60,600.
Source: U.S. Social Security Administration

Figure 23–1
▲ *By about how much did the maximum taxable income for Social Security increase from 1990 to 1994?* ($9,300.)

H ave you ever been to a museum or listened to a symphony orchestra? Are there any murals or paintings in your local post office or a similar public building? If your answer to either question is yes, you have probably benefited from government support for the arts. A brief history of that support in the United States follows.

Government Ponders Its Role in the Arts

At the time of the nation's founding, American leaders had a large number of important issues to deal with, including the construction of a new government. On a list of national priorities, the arts fell toward the bottom. John Adams, in a letter to his wife Abigail, wrote "I must study politics and war that my sons may have liberty to study mathematics and philosophy . . . in order to give their children a right to study painting, poetry, music, [and] architecture."

The federal government gave little money to the arts in the 1800's. Wealthy families increased American interest in art in the late 1800's, however. They began to build up great private collections and donated money and art to growing museums.

The Arts in the Twentieth Century

Franklin Roosevelt radically changed the relationship between government and the arts by forming the Works Progress Administration (WPA) during the New Deal. Between 1935 and 1938, the WPA became the largest public arts program in the world, at one point employing over 40,000 people. Actors performed plays, musicians played in symphonies, and artists painted murals in public buildings. In 1943, however, with World War II at its peak, the federal arts program came to an end.

In 1965 Congress created the National Endowment for the Arts (NEA). Its goal was to give money to art projects around the country. The NEA's budget grew from $16 million in 1970 to $180 million in 1979. Congress maintained a strong level of funding through the 1980's.

The relationship between government and the arts became embroiled in controversy in 1989 when NEA funds helped support exhibits by the artists Robert Mapplethorpe and Andres Serrano. Some members of Congress, led by Jesse Helms, denounced some of these artists' works as obscene. They claimed that most taxpayers would not want their money spent on such exhibits. Opponents argued that censoring art that some people might find offensive restricted artistic freedom. After months of wrangling, Congress decided in 1990 to continue to fund the NEA, but not for any art considered "obscene."

Government support for the arts has grown remarkably in the last thirty years. Despite the recent battles, artists should be able to count on continued support in the future.

CRITICAL THINKING

1. Why could FDR's New Deal arts program be called "radical"?
2. What factors might cause Congress to increase NEA funding in the future? Decrease funding?

CIVIC LITERACY
6B

Government Support of the Arts

617

Controversial Issues

▲ *What were the parts of the 1983 reform of Social Security?* (Payroll taxes and taxable wages were increased, Social Security participation was widened, benefits over $25,000 were made taxable, changes were made in benefit payment increases, and the age for receiving benefits was raised.) *What was the primary goal of the 1983 reform?* (To restore the Social Security system's financial stability.)

▲ *What was the result of the 1983 reform?* (The system built up a huge surplus.) *What happened to part of the surplus?* (The federal government borrowed from it to reduce the federal deficit.)

■ CRITICAL THINKING *When word of government borrowing from the Social Security fund became public, some administration critics complained that the practice harmed the working class. Explain their argument.* (The surplus in that fund had been created by raising rates on a regressive tax, the Social Security tax. Borrowing from that fund meant that the government was being funded not only through the income tax, which is progressive, but also through the Social Security tax, which is regressive and therefore places a greater burden on lower-income taxpayers.)

plus monthly allowances for each child under 18, and other benefits.

DISABILITY BENEFITS Another Social Security provision, added to the program in 1956, is disability insurance. *Disability* is defined as any long-term physical or mental condition that prevents a person from working to earn money. A physician must determine disability. The amount of benefits depends, in part, upon one's contributions, age, and family status. For example, if a worker became disabled in 1994 at age 55 and had been earning $40,000 a year for a family of four, the worker would receive a monthly benefit of $1,735. If the worker were single, the monthly benefit would be $1,157.

A troubled system

Social and economic changes in the United States have caused many problems in the Social Security system, however. Most of the tax money goes into two trust funds, one for retirement and survivors' benefits, the other for disability. (The rest finances Medicare.) The original plan was

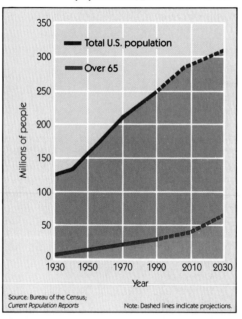

Figure 23–2 AMERICANS OVER 65 Americans over the age of 65 make up a rapidly increasing segment of the population. 8B

350

300

Millions of people
250

200 ■ Total U.S. population

150 ■ Over 65

100

50

0

1930 1950 1970 1990 2010 2030
Year

Source: Bureau of the Census; *Current Population Reports*   Note: Dashed lines indicate projections.

618

that the interest on money in the trust fund, or reserve, would be used to pay benefits to those who retired. The first benefits from the 1935 law were not to be paid until 1942, when the interest had built up. But this plan gradually became unworkable, bringing the Social Security system to a point of crisis.

One added strain on the system is that Americans are living longer today, collecting benefits for many more years. Figure 23–2 shows the increase in Americans over 65 years old since 1930. When Social Security began in 1935, Americans could expect to live just 61 years — below the age when they could collect retirement benefits. Today life expectancy is about 74 years and still increasing.

This shift in population has dramatically changed the ratio between the number of active workers and the number of people collecting benefits. In 1935 about seventeen persons were paying into the system for every person who collected benefits. Because of expanded coverage, more retired persons, and longer lifespans, relatively fewer people are now paying into the system. In 1983 there were three workers for each retired person. By the year 2010, it is estimated that the ratio will be only two to one, endangering benefits for those who will retire then.

A second problem is that more people are getting benefits than in the original plan, which provided only a retirement fund. In addition, economic inflation over the years seriously eroded the trust fund and the income it provided for retirees. To keep up with inflation, Congress in 1972 added Cost of Living Adjustments, known as COLAs. These are automatic increases in benefits, based on the rate of inflation.

As a result, Social Security did not build up a self-supporting reserve of money, but worked on a "pay-as-you-go" basis. Money paid into the system by payroll taxes was immediately paid out to recipients. In effect, one generation paid for the benefits of the generation before it. With rising costs, the system was running at a deficit.

Reforming Social Security

By 1982, part of the Social Security system was on the verge of bankruptcy. One of the trust funds had to borrow $17.5 billion in order to send retired people their monthly checks. President Reagan established a bipartisan commission

---

Background: *Economics* A trust (column 1, bottom) is a form of property ownership in which one person agrees to hold property for the benefit of another.

Figure 23–2
▲ *According to the chart, about how many Americans will there be in the year 2000?* (About 275 million.)

Background: *Economics* The life expectancy figure

(column 2, par. 1) is an average of male and female life expectancies. An average female born in 1989 has a life expectancy of 78.5 years. An average male born in 1989 can expect to live 71.8 years.

Bill Clinton speaks to senior citizens in New Hampshire during a campaign stop in 1992. Most political candidates maintain a "hands-off" policy toward Social Security for fear of alienating older voters.

to study the problem. In 1983, Congress adopted many of the commission's suggestions for change. Both workers' and Social Security recipients' pocketbooks were hit by the changes. First, to bring in more revenue, payroll taxes and taxable wages were to increase gradually. Social Security participation also was extended to include all new federal employees. Employees of churches, hospitals, and other nonprofit organizations also had to participate.

People had never before had to pay income tax on their Social Security benefits. Under the new law, however, a retired individual with an income over $25,000 per year could be taxed on half of his or her federal benefits. Finally, the age for receiving benefits was to increase very gradually to 67, beginning in the year 2003.

The future of Social Security

Additional changes came in 1993. As part of a plan to help reduce the federal deficit, Congress increased taxes for more affluent Social Security recipients. The law raised the taxable amount of Social Security income from 50 percent to 85 percent. The increase, however, only applies to annual incomes over $34,000 for single persons and $44,000 for married couples.

The 1983 changes assured the survival of the Social Security system but did not solve all its problems. The system was now building up a huge surplus, which would be needed early in the next century when the "baby boom" generation began to retire. Nevertheless, in 1990 it was revealed that the federal government was borrowing from this surplus to pay operating costs and reduce the federal deficit, thus depleting the reserve.

In 1994 Congress passed a bill that made the Social Security Administration an independent agency. The agency was separated from the Department of Health and Human Services to make it less susceptible to political pressures. **6E**

Health Care Costs

The newest major social insurance program is **Medicare**, a national health insurance program mainly for people over 65. (Younger disabled persons and those with kidney problems also take part.) Medicare was established in 1965 after President Johnson made it one of the main priorities of his program to create a "Great Society."

Economics
Tell students that in 1960 about 40 percent of the nation's senior citizens were officially considered poor. After Medicare was established in 1965, that figure dropped to below 20 percent.

● CRITICAL THINKING *Suppose you were a legislator considering a proposal to abolish Medicare. How would the above information help you make your decision?* (It indicates that Medicare has succeeded in reducing poverty among senior citizens. Knowing this, you would be reluctant to abolish Medicare.) *What further information would you want before making a final decision?* (Whether a different program might prove as effective, or more effective, and at lower cost.)

Critical Thinking
■ *Why is raising the age at which people can receive Social Security benefits an appropriate reform of the system?* (People are living longer than before.)

Background: *History* The phrase "Great Society" was first used in May 1964 when Lyndon Johnson declared, "We have the opportunity to move not only toward the rich society and the powerful society, but upward to the Great Society."

The symbol ♟ denotes active participation strategies.

Activities are keyed for student abilities:
▲ = Basic
● = All Levels
■ = Average/Advanced

Until that time, the American Medical Association, the insurance companies, and many Americans had vigorously and successfully opposed any such federal health care program. Medicare was a compromise. It did not supply national health care but extended the existing social insurance of Social Security to help older Americans pay for their special medical needs without being driven into poverty.

Funding for Medicare comes from FICA payroll taxes, general government revenues, and fees paid by persons receiving Medicare. Up until 1994, Medicare payroll taxes had to be paid only on income below a certain level. That year, the income ceiling was removed. Medicare is managed by the Health Care Financing Administration, an agency of the Department of Health and Human Services.

Medicare coverage

Basic Medicare (known as "Part A") is a medical insurance plan to help pay for hospital care and for nursing home or home care after hospitalization. Medicare patients still pay some of the costs. Before the coverage begins, the patient must pay a "deductible" ($696 in 1994). This means that the Medicare recipient pays the first $696 of hospital costs. The deductible is intended to discourage unnecessary hospital visits.

Once the deductible is paid, Medicare pays the remaining hospitalization costs for up to 60 days. If the patient must remain in the hospital after the 60 days are up, Medicare will pay part of the bill for up to 30 more days. The patient must make a "co-payment" during this time. The patient has a lifetime reserve of 60 more co-payment days to use as needed. Some types of nursing-home care are covered by Medicare.

The other part of Medicare is a voluntary supplemental medical insurance plan for people over 65. It helps pay for medical expenses not covered by hospital insurance, such as physicians' and surgeons' services and the cost of x-rays. Those wishing to enroll in "Medicare B," and almost all do, pay a monthly premium of about $45 for the insurance. The federal government supplements this amount.

Rising health care costs

Most people agree that Medicare has succeeded in giving older Americans the basic health care they might not otherwise have. Nevertheless, putting the program into effect proved more complicated and more expensive than expected. In 1966, the program's first year, total Medicare costs were $3.2 billion. By 1993 total Medicare costs had ballooned to over $143 billion!

Despite its immense costs, many Americans argue that Medicare does not go far enough in helping the elderly meet medical bills. Medicare, for instance, does not cover dental care, eyeglasses, or prescription drugs. Doctors may charge more than the "allowable" charges and patients must make up the difference. Nor does Medicare offer protection against "catastrophic" or long-term illness. Extra medical expenses can use up savings and income, sending elderly people into poverty. A 1988 law to provide "catastrophic" coverage, financed by a new tax on the elderly, was repealed by Congress in 1989.

Some of Medicare's problems are due to the same factors that trouble Social Security. First (as Figure 23-2 shows), more and more Americans are living longer and using Medicare. In addition, the program was extended in 1972 to cover disabled persons and kidney patients. Today some 36 million Americans, or about 13 percent of the population, receive Medicare benefits.

Finally, health care costs — hospital charges and doctors' fees — have soared. Some critics maintain that Medicare itself has been one cause of this. They claim that it offers no incentives to cut health care costs, because hospitals and doctors are assured of payment.

Changes in Medicare

To check the skyrocketing cost of Medicare, the federal government made several changes in the early 1990's. It increased the patients' share of the cost of medical procedures to 20 percent. The government also began evaluating doctors' charges based on the average cost of each type of medical procedure. If a doctor charged a patient more than the average amount, Medicare would not pay for the amount above the average. The government also began allowing doctors to charge Medicare recipients for costs not covered by Medicare. Despite these changes, medical costs continue to soar. Many experts have warned that without more reforms Medicare will go bankrupt early in the 21st century.

620

A health-care reform plan

Following up on a campaign promise, President Clinton made enactment of a comprehensive universal health-care plan the top priority of his administration. He began by appointing his wife, Hillary Rodham Clinton, to chair a special task force appointed to develop such a plan. After months of hearings, the President and Mrs. Clinton submitted a 1,300-page proposal to Congress in 1993.

The Clinton plan contained many complex provisions. It provided that all citizens would be entitled to insurance for doctors' fees, hospitalization, and prescription drugs. The plan would be financed mostly by employers who would be responsible for 80 percent of the cost, with employees paying the balance. Subsidies would be available to small companies for whom this expense would be a hardship. Higher cigarette taxes would also help with the cost. To reduce the costs of health care, the federal government would require uniform billing procedures and malpractice reform.

Finally, to stimulate competition and reduce costs, the government would create regional health-care alliances and would set up a National Health Board to oversee their operations.

The Clinton health plan proposal generated a great deal of debate. On whether reform was needed, public sentiment seemed clear. A survey showed that the proportion of Americans believing the system needed either "fundamental change or complete rebuilding" jumped from 57 percent in 1992 to 84 percent in 1993

The Clinton proposal met with strong opposition when it was introduced in Congress. Several legislators introduced alternative plans, and by the time the 103rd Congress adjourned in October 1994, no significant health care reform had been passed. The administration had to abandon its goal of universal coverage.

6E

Other Health Care Issues

Besides providing people with assistance in meeting the expenses of health care, all levels of government take an active role in protecting public health. Public health considerations, for instance, are reasons for government concern over

As well as helping to pay medical bills, the government also sponsors programs to detect and prevent diseases. Blood pressure readings, as shown here, help identify health risks.

Background: *Economics*
A "catastrophic" illness has been defined by a government official as being either "a short-term condition requiring intensive care services or a lingering illness requiring years of care."

GUIDED/INDEPENDENT PRACTICE

● Have students write essays contrasting the approaches taken to the problem of poverty during the administrations of Lyndon Johnson and Ronald Reagan. Have them analyze the philosophy underlying each approach and indicate which features they agree or disagree with and why.

RETEACHING/CORRECTIVES

▲ Have students write down the basic facts about Social Security and Medicare: when each program was established, its aims, how it is funded, and current issues facing the program.

Have students complete **Skills Practice Worksheet 23,** which asks them to analyze a graph of Social Security contributions and payments.

You may also want to use **Transparency 55,** which presents a cause-and-effect chart on the Great Depression.

ENRICHMENT/EXTENSION

■ Have students complete **Skills Challenge Worksheet 23,** which asks them to analyze a cartoon on the politics of Social Security.

The symbol 👥 denotes active participation strategies.

Activities are keyed for student abilities:
▲ = Basic
● = All Levels
■ = Average/Advanced

Section 1 Review Answers

1. Because the widespread problems brought on by the Depression caused Americans to favor government involvement.
2. (a) Retirees. **(b)** It now includes disabled persons and survivors of wage-earners.
3. By a compulsory payroll tax on employees and employers.
4. One part is an insurance plan that helps pay for hospital care and some types of nursing home care. The second part is a voluntary, supplemental insurance plan for people over 65.
5. Longer life spans have increased the number of people receiving benefits and the number of years benefits are collected, thus putting a financial strain on both programs.

Critical thinking Students should consider the economic and social costs and benefits, as well as the "proper" roles of federal and state governments.

CLOSURE

● Have students write three "I learned. . ." statements to show what they learned in this section. Then have them read Section 2, noting the many different kinds of public assistance programs in existence.

---

clean water and air and safe disposal of wastes. Another concern is the prevention, control, and cure of disease, particularly communicable diseases that can affect hundreds or thousands of people. Promoting good health for all citizens is another goal.

The U.S. government's first move to guard the public health came in 1798, when Congress authorized the building of hospitals to care for American merchant sailors. From this grew the Public Health Service and many other federal government agencies.

The Public Health Service

The Public Health Service (PHS) is a major section of the Department of Health and Human Services. Today it serves as an "umbrella" for government agencies and institutes devoted to a great variety of health concerns, including drug and alcohol abuse, cancer research, allergies, and aging. The Food and Drug Administration (page 572) is part of the PHS, as are the National Institutes of Health (NIH) and the Centers for Disease Control.

The head of the Public Health Service is the Surgeon General. Federal government health research led in 1964 to the *Surgeon General's Report* that linked smoking with heart disease, lung cancer, and other health problems. Later the government required cigarette manufacturers to print warnings by the Surgeon General on all cigarette packs.

Controlling communicable diseases

The PHS agency chiefly concerned with preventing the spread of communicable diseases is the Centers for Disease Control and Prevention (CDC), located in Atlanta. One of the Centers' primary concerns is investigating and controlling **epidemics** — the rapid spread of diseases. Since the early 1900's, public health measures have greatly reduced the death rates from such infectious diseases as tuberculosis and influenza (flu). In the 1970's, CDC researchers found the cause and prevention for a mysterious new illness know as "Legionnaire's disease."

In the late 1970's another new and deadly illness first appeared in the United States and began to spread rapidly. It attacked people's immune systems, fatally damaging their bodies' ability to fight off disease or infection. It was

called *Acquired Immune Deficiency Syndrome,* or AIDS. Because of its deadliness and rapid spread, AIDS quickly became a serious public health concern.

When the first AIDS cases were diagnosed in the United States in 1981, Public Health Service researchers immediately began to study the nature of the disease. By 1985, researchers at the National Institutes of Health, as well as scientists at the Pasteur Institute in France, identified the virus that causes AIDS. Researchers also developed methods of testing donated blood, so as to protect the nation's blood supply.

As scientists searched for a cure or a vaccine against AIDS itself, public health officials concluded that education was the best available means for halting the spread of the disease. AIDS education proved controversial, however, as some religious and government officials objected to it on moral grounds. By the early 1990's AIDS had killed over 100,000 Americans (about twice as many as died in Vietnam).

SECTION 1 **REVIEW**

Vocabulary and key terms

social insurance (614)	FICA (616)
public assistance (614)	Medicare (619)
Social Security (614)	epidemic (622)

For review

1. Why did most of today's social programs begin during the Depression? **8E**
2. (a) Who originally benefited from Social Security? (b) How has the program been broadened? **6E**
3. How is Social Security financed? **7B**
4. What kinds of protection are given by the two parts of Medicare? **6E**
5. How have changes in the American population caused problems for both Social Security and Medicare? **8F**

Critical thinking

FORMING AN OPINION   Some people favor a federal health insurance program for everyone. What arguments can be made on each side of this question? **8A**

SECTION 2
Public Assistance Programs Help Those in Need

ACCESS | The Main Ideas

1 Explain the benefits and criticisms of the AFDC program. *pages 623–625*
2 Describe the Medicaid and food stamp programs. *pages 625–627*

Should tax money be used to provide citizens in need with food, housing, and medical care? Do such programs help reduce poverty or do they perpetuate it? Unlike other social insurance, public assistance benefits are based on need, not prior contributions. Tax revenues finance these benefits, which are often called "welfare." This section examines only the major public assistance programs — aid to families, medical help, and food stamps.

Aid to Families

One provision of the Social Security Act of 1935 set up a joint federal–state program to provide income for families with dependent children when the breadwinner dies, is disabled, or abandons the family. *Aid to Families with Dependent Children*, or AFDC, is now administered by an agency in the Department of Health and Human Services. In recent years approximately five million American families have received AFDC payments.

State regulations

AFDC is actually a federal program administered by the states. It is the states that determine

The Head Start program, administered by the Department of Health and Human Services, prepares underprivileged children for school by offering a variety of play and learning activities.

623

Background: *Economics*
The 12.8 million people receiving AFDC in 1991 represented about 5 percent of the total U.S. population.

Critical Thinking
● *Why does it make sense for income levels of AFDC recipients to vary from state to state?* (The cost of living varies from one state to another.)

SECTION 2

Public Assistance Programs Help Those in Need *(pp. 623–627)*

Section Objectives
☐ explain the benefits and criticisms of the AFDC program
☐ describe the Medicaid and food stamp programs

Vocabulary
Medicaid, food stamps

FOCUS
● Write the following statements on the board: "We shall soon, with the help of God, be within sight of the day when poverty shall be banished from this nation."—Herbert Hoover, 1928. "This administration today, here and now, declares unconditional war on poverty in America." —Lyndon Johnson, 1964.

Ask students for their reactions to the two statements. (Possible reactions include: the wish to eliminate poverty is persistent; eliminating poverty is more difficult than is sometimes thought.) Ask students what events during the years immediately following 1928 and 1964 damaged the two Presidents' hopes for ending poverty. (The Great Depression, the Vietnam War.) Close by asking students to consider what government can do, and what government cannot do, to fight poverty.

The symbol ⅱ denotes active participation strategies.

Activities are keyed for student abilities:
▲ = Basic
● = All Levels
■ = Average/Advanced

EXPLANATION

After students have read the section, you may want to consider the following activities:

Controversial Issues

Have students reread the subsection "Criticisms of AFDC" on pp. 624–625. Then explain that in some states, if a welfare recipient takes a full-time job, assistance checks are reduced or stopped. If the recipient is then laid off, weeks may pass before welfare payments resume. In other words, employment is uncertain, while assistance is not. Furthermore, the jobs available to most recipients do not produce much more income than does assistance, especially when transportation and child care are considered. Typical day-care costs, for example, exceeded $2,000 a year per child in 1990.

● CRITICAL THINKING Have students imagine that they are members of a commission created to suggest reforms in AFDC. *How would you begin this process?* (Suggest that a proper place to begin would be to examine basic questions, such as: What are the goals of AFDC? How does the program currently seek to meet these goals? Is it effective? Are there any ways in which the program worsens the problems it is trying to solve? If so, how can this situation be resolved?) Write on the board these and other questions suggested by students. Then have students discuss the questions.

Economics

▲ Have students analyze Figure 23–3, particularly the column showing the percentage of the total population living below the poverty level. *Which years saw the smallest percentage of Americans living in poverty?* (1973, then

the income level required to maintain families of different sizes. Depending upon a state's economic condition, the federal government provides 50 to 65 percent of the costs of AFDC. If a state pays $200 per month, for example, the federal government would give at least $100.

To be eligible for AFDC, a family must meet several guidelines. A "dependent" child is generally one who is under 13 years old, lives with a single parent or relative, and cannot be fully supported by his or her parents. The states set income levels for families, depending on the number of children.

Because states administer AFDC, income limits and benefits vary greatly from state to state. In 1991, for example, monthly AFDC benefits for a family of four in Alaska were $990 per month. By contrast, a family of four in Mississippi received $144 per month. The median monthly payment for a family of four in 1991 was $432.

Criticisms of AFDC

Although social insurance programs are politically popular, most public assistance programs are not. AFDC is perhaps the most controversial of these programs. Many critics charge that AFDC actually weakens the family, leading to the breakup of poor families and even encouraging unmarried women to have children so as to get benefits.

AFDC was intended to provide support for children whose fathers died or became incapacitated. It also provided benefits to children whose fathers had deserted the family. As a result, in some cases men have left home in order to make their families eligible for AFDC benefits. Today, about 80 percent of AFDC families are headed by a woman.

Other critics of "welfare" believe that government benefits discourage people from looking for work to support themselves. People who grow up in such families, they say, also tend to go on welfare when they are adults. They carry on a "culture of poverty."

Welfare recipients themselves are unhappy with AFDC. To qualify for benefits, recipients must fill out numerous forms and answer embarrassing questions. Many people contend that benefit levels are too low, keeping them below the poverty level. Moreover, most recipients would rather work if they could.

Figure 23–3 AMERICANS BELOW THE POVERTY LEVEL   Each year, the "poverty level" for a family of four is redefined to account for inflation. 6E

YEAR	INCOME AT POVERTY LEVEL (family of 4)	BELOW POVERTY LEVEL NUMBER OF PEOPLE	% OF TOTAL POPULATION
1960	$ 3,022	39,851,000	22.2
1965	$ 3,223	33,185,000	17.3
1969	$ 3,721	24,147,000	12.1
1973	$ 4,540	22,973,000	11.1
1975	$ 5,500	25,877,000	12.3
1977	$ 6,191	24,720,000	11.6
1979	$ 7,412	26,072,000	11.7
1981	$ 9,287	31,822,000	14.0
1983	$10,178	35,303,000	15.2
1985	$10,989	33,064,000	14.0
1987	$11,611	32,221,000	13.4
1990	$13,359	33,585,000	13.5
1992	$14,335	36,880,000	14.5

Source: *Current Population Reports*

Figure 23–3
■ *Why has the poverty level income, which is set by the government, risen so dramatically since 1960?* (To reflect the effects of inflation.)

Background: *Economics*
The poverty index is based solely on money income; it does not include non-cash benefits such as food stamps, Medicaid, or public housing.

The Reagan administration, along with several states, supported the idea of "workfare." Such programs required welfare recipients to take jobs in order to get benefits. Both this idea and compulsory job-training programs had mixed results, however. Many participants lacked the education to do well in the programs or to earn more than the minimum wage. Often jobs were not available. Many who wished to work could not afford day care for their children, particularly after day-care funds were cut back in the federal budget. The AFDC program remained a troubling problem for both the poor and the nation as a whole.

7B

Other Assistance Programs

Supplemental Security Income

Before 1974, the states aided elderly, blind, or disabled people who needed aid and were not covered by Social Security. Because programs and benefits varied greatly from state to state, the federal government set up Supplemental Security Income, or SSI. Its aim was to provide uniform benefits to needy persons by giving them a minimum income.

Although the program is administered by the Social Security Administration, it is funded out of general tax revenues. The monthly cash payments depend on income and other resources. About 3.5 million Americans, or 1.4 percent of the population, now receive SSI. Many states still supplement SSI benefits.

Medicaid

Because both Medicare and Medicaid were established in 1965 under the Social Security Act, many people confuse these similar-sounding programs. Medicaid is a joint, federal-state program to aid the poor in paying for medical expenses. Patients do not make prior contributions or pay premiums. Money is provided to participating states through the Health Care Financing Administration in the Department of Health and Human Services. All states have chosen to take part in Medicaid.

The amount of federal money each state gets depends on its per capita (per person) income. To qualify for federal funds, states must offer specified medical benefits without cost to the

patients. These basic health care services include hospitalization, skilled nursing, home health care, early screening and treatment of physical and mental defects, and family planning services. States can also choose to cover other medical services, such as physical therapy, nursing home care, dental care, and eyeglasses. The federal government reimburses between 50 and 83 percent of the states' Medicaid expenses.

Eligibility for Medicaid varies considerably. Each state generally is required to extend coverage to persons who receive SSI and AFDC. (It is up to each state, though, to determine eligibility for AFDC.) Beyond that, each state can extend Medicaid to any needy person it desires to help. About thirty states now provide Medicaid to people who do not receive other welfare help but still cannot pay for medical expenses. In all, some 33 million Americans receive Medicaid benefits.

Problems with Medicaid

Most observers agree that Medicaid has dramatically improved health care for many Americans. Nevertheless, the program has many critics. As with Medicare, one major problem is fast-growing costs. From 1974 to 1993, for example, Medicaid payments jumped from $10 billion to over $100 billion. Some attribute this to the states extending coverage to more people. Others point out that many elderly people must

625

1977 and 1979.) **What happened during the 1980's?** (The percentage living in poverty grew sharply, then began declining.)

Economics
● CRITICAL THINKING Tell students that in recent years, cuts in federally run social programs have shifted much of the responsibility for those programs to the states. Ask the class to suggest some advantages and disadvantages of having states, rather than the federal government, pay for and administer such programs. (*Advantages*—State governments may tailor programs to meet the specific needs of their citizens. *Disadvantages*—Some states may not have either the funds to pay for the programs or the political will to raise taxes. It may be more efficient to administer the programs through one large bureaucracy than through fifty smaller ones.)

Cooperative Learning
● Read to the class the statement on p. 627: "Millions of Americans suffer from hunger and malnutrition. Many are homeless." Ask students to work in small groups to analyze the roots of poverty in the United States. Groups should identify several causes of poverty. Then ask groups to discuss ways in which the government might address these causes. Have groups share their ideas with the class.

You Decide Answer
Students should defend their answers. Students should consider the desirability of expanding medical coverage to poor Americans, as well as the costs involved and the possible decline in quality of care.

The symbol ♙♙ denotes active participation strategies.

Activities are keyed for student abilities:
▲ = Basic
● = All Levels
■ = Average/Advanced

GUIDED/INDEPENDENT PRACTICE

● Ask students to write an essay describing the goals of the AFDC program. Ask them under what kinds of circumstances most families enter the program. *What are some of the problems with the program? What remedies have been proposed? Can you suggest other approaches?*

RETEACHING/CORRECTIVES

▲ Have students find answers on pp. 623–624 to the following questions: *How are social insurance benefits (discussed in the previous section) and public-assistance benefits different?* (Social insurance benefits are based on prior contributions; public assistance benefits are based on need and come from general tax revenues.) *How are both the federal and state governments involved in AFDC?* (It is a federal program administered by the states.) *Why is AFDC controversial?* (Critics charge that it breaks up families and encourages dependence on the government.)

ꙮ ENRICHMENT/EXTENSION

■ Invite a worker at a local shelter for the homeless to come to class to speak about the shelter's work. (If there is no homeless shelter, you may wish to invite a representative from a government agency that serves people in poverty.) Students may want to ask questions about how the shelter is funded, what its goals are, and what kinds of people depend on the shelter's services. Students may also wish to inquire about volunteer opportunities at the shelter.

Section 2 Review Answers

1. **(a)** A typical recipient is under age 13, lives with a single

Food stamps are made available so that individuals and families with insufficient incomes can still buy healthful, nutritious food products.

eventually turn to Medicaid because of high nursing home costs and limited Medicare coverage. Another criticism is that (as with Medicare) there are no incentives to cut costs, because the government will pay the bill. Still others cite fraud and mismanagement in the administration of the program.

During the 1980's, at the urging of the Reagan administration, several changes were made to Medicaid to bring down costs. The growth in federal contributions to Medicaid was slowed and states were given more power to carry out cost-cutting reforms. The cost of the program continues to rise, however.

Food stamps

A variety of federal programs aim at helping ensure that Americans will have enough food to eat. For instance, surplus food bought under Agriculture Department programs (page 448) has been made available free or at low cost. Some federal funds also support or subsidize programs such as school lunches, infant nutrition, and meals for the elderly.

In 1964 the **food stamp** program was established. This program offers stamps, or coupons, that can be used to purchase food in retail grocery stores. The amount of food stamps one receives depends on many factors, including

626

income, family size, the cost of living, and the price of a nutritionally balanced diet. In 1991 a record 23 million Americans (about ten percent of the population) received food stamps, at a cost to the government of about $19.6 billion. The average food stamp benefit per person, per meal was only about 65 cents in 1991. Food stamps can be used only for food, not for items such as tobacco, alcohol, magazines, or soap.

The food stamp program is administered by the Department of Agriculture, which sets the guidelines and pays nearly the entire cost of food stamps. County governments, however, usually put the program into action.

Changes in the program

The food stamp program grew slowly between 1964 and 1974, partly because county governments could refuse to join. Moreover, many eligible persons were discouraged from participating because they had to purchase the food stamps in advance out of their own pockets. The lower their income, the less they paid for food stamps.

Several changes in the 1970's spurred the growth of food stamps. In 1974 the program became available nationwide. Because unemployment was high in the mid-1970's, many more people applied. In 1977 the requirement of

Background: *Economics*
Many elderly people must pay all their medical bills until they are poor enough to qualify for Medicaid, a process known as "spending down."

Cross-reference
County governments are discussed in Chapter 26, Section 1 (pp. 690–694).

buying the stamps was dropped. Eligibility standards were broadened to make stamps available to people on strike and their families. In 1980 more than 21 million people used food stamps.

In an effort to cut costs and curb possible abuses, the Reagan administration also cut back the food stamp program. Congress limited spending and tightened eligibility, removing about one million persons from the program. Still, the number of people *eligible* for food stamps is more than double those who actually receive them.

The problems of the food stamp program are part of the overall dilemma of public assistance programs. Millions of Americans suffer from hunger and malnutrition. Many are homeless. Most Americans realize that poverty is a persistent problem — even in a nation as prosperous as the United States. In addition to government programs, many private volunteer charitable and religious organizations work hard to try to solve the problem of poverty. But neither policy-makers nor the public have fully agreed on approaches or solutions.

SECTION 2 REVIEW

Vocabulary and key terms

AFDC (623)

"workfare" (625)

Supplemental Security
Income (SSI) (625)

Medicaid (625)

food stamps (626)

For review

1. (a) What are the general guidelines for AFDC eligibility? (b) Who sets these limits? 6E
2. (a) How does Medicaid differ from Medicare? (b) What problems do these programs share? 8G
3. What is the aim of the food stamp program? 6E
4. Why did the food stamp program grow rapidly in the 1970's, and why was it later cut back? 7B

Critical thinking

DRAWING INFERENCES In a situation requiring budget cuts, why would a politician be more likely to cut funds for public assistance programs rather than for Social Security? 8H

Chapter Summary

In response to widespread economic hardship caused by the Great Depression, the Social Security Act of 1935 created America's first federal programs to help elderly, poor, or otherwise needy people. Federal government programs include both social insurance, based on personal contributions, and public assistance, based on need and financed by tax revenues. Social programs were expanded during the 1960's as part of President Lyndon Johnson's "war on poverty." In the 1980's, many public assistance programs were cut back as budget deficits rose.

Social Security, the basic social insurance program in the United States, is financed by deductions from employees' paychecks, which are matched by employers. Social Security was originally intended to be a retirement plan but was expanded to include those who become disabled and families whose main income provider dies. Longer life expectancy, an increased number of people receiving benefits, and inflation have put a strain on Social Security reserves, however. Medicare, also a social insurance program, was introduced in 1965 to help pay the hospital and medical bills for older Americans. Medicare costs have risen sharply, creating a problem for policy-makers.

Public assistance programs, or welfare, provide direct aid to those in need. The Aid to Families with Dependent Children program, better known as AFDC, provides money for single parents who need help supporting dependent children. Supplemental Security Income (SSI) provides uniform benefits to elderly, disabled, or blind people who are not covered by Social Security. Medicaid coverage is a joint federal-state program that provides aid for the poor in paying their medical expenses. The food stamp program provides families and individuals with help in buying food. Each of these policies has been heavily criticized; while Americans agree that poverty is a serious problem, they are far from agreement on the solution.

627

parent or relative, and cannot be fully supported by his or her parents. **(b)** Each state.
2. (a) Medicaid is a federal-state program to help the poor pay medical expenses; patients do not make contributions. **(b)** Fast-growing costs, larger population.
3. To help ensure that Americans have enough food to eat.
4. It became available nationwide, unemployment was high, eligibility standards were broadened, and more people applied. The Reagan administration cut back the program to cut costs and curb abuse.

Critical thinking Students may suggest that politicians might cut public assistance first. Social Security programs are more popular since, in theory, people are getting back what they themselves have contributed. Public assistance programs are often less popular because taxpayers generally do not imagine that such programs will benefit them personally.

CLOSURE
● Review the Section 2 vocabulary with students to help reinforce key concepts from the section. Then have students read the next assigned lesson.

CHAPTER 23 CORRECTIVES
● To review the content of Chapter 23, you may want to have students complete **Study Guide/Review 23** or **Workbook Chapter 23.**

The symbol 👥 denotes active participation strategies.

Activities are keyed for student abilities:
▲ = Basic
● = All Levels
■ = Average/Advanced

Answers

Vocabulary See pp. T19–T21 for suggested vocabulary activities.

Reviewing the Facts

1. Most people believed that those who worked hard enough could survive. People in need could turn to families, churches, and private charities for help.
2. From personal contributions by individuals.
3. From general tax revenues.
4. 95 percent.
5. Retired persons and their dependents, survivors of wage-earners, and disabled persons.
6. The person must have worked and contributed to the system for a specified length of time.
7. A COLA, or Cost of Living Adjustment, was added to Social Security payments to adjust them for inflation. It provides automatic increases in benefits.
8. The Surgeon General.

Thinking Critically About Key Concepts

1. **(a)** During the Great Depression and during the "war on poverty" in the 1960's. **(b)** During the Depression, millions were homeless and hungry. In the 1960's, it was realized that many groups were still living in poverty in spite of national prosperity.
2. **(a)** Medicare does not go far enough in meeting high medical bills; it does not cover dental care, eyeglasses, or prescription drugs; it does not offer protection against catastrophic illness. **(b)** Because hospitals and doctors know they will be paid, there is little competition and scant motivation to keep medical costs at a reasonable level. **(c)** Efforts to expand Medicare benefits include catastrophic coverage. Efforts to reduce Medicare costs include an increase in patients' share of costs and a fixed scale of allowable costs.

Review the definitions of the following terms:

AFDC	Medicaid	Social Security
epidemic	Medicare	Supplemental Security
FICA	public assistance	Income
food stamps	social insurance	"workfare"

● REVIEWING THE FACTS

1. Why were there no federal social programs in the United States before the Depression? **6E**
2. Where do the funds come from to pay for social insurance programs? **7B**
3. Where do the funds come from to pay for public assistance programs? **7B**
4. What percentage of the work force in the United States contributes to the Social Security program? **7B**
5. What three categories of persons receive Social Security benefits? **6E**
6. What does a worker have to do, in general, to qualify for retirement benefits under the Social Security Act? **7B**
7. Explain what a COLA is and its purpose. **6E**
8. What is the top position in the Public Health Service? **3A**

▲ THINKING CRITICALLY ABOUT KEY CONCEPTS

1. (a) During which two periods in the 20th century have a large number of federal social programs been created? (b) In each case, why was there such a flood of legislation? **7A**
2. (a) What are some criticisms of Medicare from people who claim it does not go far enough? (b) What is the basis for the criticism that Medicare causes higher medical fees? (c) What solutions have been offered to address the criticisms on both sides of the

628

Medicare question? **8A**
3. What are the criticisms of AFDC, both from recipients of benefits and others? **5B**
4. Social Security is a politically sensitive issue. For this reason, according to the author, government policymakers have tried to keep benefit levels high and at the same time keep Social Security taxes low. What is the problem with such a policy? Do you think it should be changed? If so, how? **5C**

▲ PRACTICING SKILLS

1. **Study Skills: Reading a line graph.** Refer to Figure 23–2 (page 618) to answer the following questions. (a) In 1930, was the number of Americans over the age of 65 less or more than 10 million? (b) What was the total population, approximately, in 1980? (c) According to the projection, what will the total population be in the year 2030? (d) According to the projection, how many Americans will be over 65 in the year 2030? (e) In which 20-year period do you see the fastest rise in the number of Americans over the age of 65? **8B**
2. **Critical Thinking Skills: Drawing conclusions.** Refer to Figure 23–3 (page 624). Read the caption and the column headings of this table. Then examine the figures in each column, year by year. Use the figures to answer the following question: What trend, if any, is represented by the data in this table? In other words, is there either a steady rise or a steady decline that would allow you to predict the figures for future years? Explain your reasoning. **8B**

---

3. *Nonrecipients*—Welfare discourages people from looking for work; fathers leave home in order to make their families eligible for AFDC. *Recipients*— Numerous forms must be filled out and embarrassing questions answered; benefit levels are too low; people would rather work if they could.

4. The combination of high payments and low taxes could bankrupt the system. Students should explain and defend their opinions.

▲ PARTICIPATORY CITIZENSHIP

1. **Interviews.** Find out about how your community views the problem of homelessness. Interview the staff of local agencies that provide services to the homeless. What services do they provide? Where does funding come from? You may also wish to interview homeless people to find out what they consider the best type of help to be, or members of the community who oppose providing shelters or other services. **6G**

2. **Current events.** Look through recent newspapers and magazines for articles concerning a major social insurance or public assistance program. Summarize the articles by stating what the specific issue is and providing details to show what actions are being taken regarding the issue. **6G**

■ WRITING ABOUT ISSUES

1. **Contrasting positions.** Write a dialogue between a supporter of government programs that give assistance to the poor and unemployed and an opponent of such programs. Try to think of the best arguments each side could present. **8C**

2. **Writing an essay.** The Surgeon General of the United States has determined that smoking cigarettes is dangerous to human health and requires that tobacco companies put a variety of warnings on their products. The federal government regularly subsidizes the large growers of tobacco. Do you see a conflict of interest here? What, if anything, should be done when different agencies or areas of the federal government take contradictory actions? **8C**

▲ ANALYZING A POLITICAL CARTOON

The Social Security system depends on contributions from working men and women to pay for benefits for retirees. Look at the cartoon below and answer the following questions.

1. What is the cartoonist's view of today's Social Security recipients and their expectations? **8D**

2. How does the cartoonist view the future of Social Security? **8B**

Cartoon by Dick Locher, Chicago Tribune. Reprinted by permission: Tribune Media Services.

629

Practicing Skills

1. **(a)** Less than 10 million.
(b) Approximately 230 million.
(c) Approximately 305 million.
(d) About 65 million. **(e)** In the period 2010–2030.
2. The percentage of Americans below the poverty level fell dramatically, then rose somewhat, and then began falling again. The rise may indicate that further reductions in poverty are not likely or may simply have been a temporary setback.

Participatory Citizenship

1. Students might want to consult local politicians to determine their positions on the issue of homelessness.
2. You might have students read their summaries to the class.

Writing About Issues

1. You may want to have students work in pairs and present their dialogues to the class.
2. Some students may argue that the government should not simultaneously encourage the production of tobacco and discourage its consumption. Other students may argue that consumption is a personal matter and should not be a concern of government. Students should then discuss the merits and the difficulties of preventing policy conflicts within the federal government.

Analyzing a Political Cartoon

1. The cartoonist suggests that Social Security recipients put an unfair burden on the rest of the nation by expecting to be carried through life.
2. The cartoonist fears that the high cost of Social Security endangers the program.

Chapter Review exercises are keyed for student abilities:
▲ = Basic
● = All Levels
■ = Average/Advanced

Vocabulary

dole—welfare. *SEC*—Securities and Exchange Commission. *FTC*—Federal Trade Commission.

Background

Japan, with a population not quite half as large as that of the United States, has the second highest gross national product in the world. At more than $23,000, its per capita GNP is higher than the per capita GNP of the United States. The Sony Corporation, a consumer electronics company, employs more than 95,000 people and has annual sales of over $18 billion. Founded after World War II, the company introduced the world's first pocket transistor radio in 1957 and in 1969 produced a color videocassette recorder for homes and businesses. In the late 1980's, Sony purchased the world's largest record company, CBS Records, and Columbia Pictures Entertainment, Inc.

Economics

● Ask for volunteers to play the roles of a Japanese business executive, stockholder, and government official. Give the "business executive" twenty pennies, explaining that the money is the profit for the year. Ask the class to suggest how the money should be distributed and have the "executive" follow the suggestions.

Akio Morita

Contrasting American and Japanese Business Styles

Government policies toward business and the economy vary greatly from country to country and can affect international trade. A leading Japanese businessman, Akio Morita, chairman of Sony Corporation, analyzes differences between Japanese and American government policies toward business.

Tokyo. Many Americans seem proud of the adversarial relationship between government and business, as though their aims are naturally antagonistic. In Japan we do not see it that way. To put it bluntly, whether we like it or not, the government is a partner in our business without owning a single share of Sony stock or running any risk. And the American government is a partner of American business, too, in the same way. The Japanese government takes away more than 50 percent of our profits, and that in a sense makes it a majority partner. So from our government's viewpoint, it wants its partner to work hard and make a profit. By doing so, business is able to keep people employed, enabling the company and its employees to pay taxes rather than to go on the public dole. This is done with a long-range viewpoint. So while we often have our disagreements with the government and its bureaucracy, which actually runs the government, and while I often criticize specific government programs or policies, I know the relationship is basically supportive.

The American system of management, in my opinion, also relies too much on outsiders to help make business decisions, and this is because of the insecurity that American decision makers feel in their jobs, as compared with most top Japanese corporate executives. The legal requirement for disclosure puts the manager's performance on show every quarter and the main evaluation of an executive too often is done in this shortsighted way. Obviously after the Great Crash of 1929 the reasons for regulation and/or constant public reporting were evident to everyone, and the objective of protecting the shareholders was a worthy one. But the SEC and the FTC became like policemen. And maybe that is justified in the United States, where there have been so many cases of executives being arrested for economic crimes.

In Japan a person who holds an executive position of trust and who violates it is really disgraced, and because of our closed-circle society, it would be impossible for him to continue to do damage to company after company, as some have done in the U.S. and even in Europe. Often if some major failure or illegality takes place somewhere within the company, or if there is a breach of trust with the consumers, it is the president who resigns.

From *Made in Japan* by Akio Morita with Edwin M. Reingold and Mitsuko Shimomura. Copyright © 1986 by E. P. Dutton. Used by permission of the publisher, Dutton, an imprint of New American Library, a division of Penguin Books USA Inc.

CRITICAL THINKING

1. Give an example of how government and business are "adversarial" in the U.S. Do you agree with Morita's idea that they should be partners instead? Why?
2. How does Morita view U.S. regulatory agencies like the SEC? Why does he think policing may be neccessary?

630

Critical Thinking Answers
1. Answers may cite environmental regulations, limits on stock trading, rules against price fixing, etc. Students should support their opinions.

2. As "policemen." Morita seems to regard American executives as more likely to commit crimes than Japanese executives.

UNIT
★ 8 ★

STATE GOVERNMENT

CHAPTER

24 The STRUCTURE of STATE GOVERNMENTS

25 STATE POLICIES and FINANCES

631

State Government
(pp. 631–686)

Unit Overview

Each of the fifty states has its own state government. Unit Eight explains what these governmental units have in common and how they operate. Chapter 24 examines the basic features of state constitutions and the amendment process. Then it considers the organization of the legislative, executive, and judicial branches of state government. Chapter 25 traces the policy-making process as it takes place at the state level. It also looks at the ways states make budgets and finance state spending.

Photo
Iowa State Capitol,
Des Moines.

CHAPTER 24
THE STRUCTURE OF STATE GOVERNMENTS
(pp. 632–661)

	Section Objectives	Section Resources
Section 1 **State Constitutions Establish Government Structure**	☐ describe the features of state constitutions ☐ explain how state constitutions can be amended ☐ list some criticisms of state constitutions	
Section 2 **Legislatures Make State Law**	☐ explain how state legislatures are structured ☐ describe how state legislatures operate ☐ explain how citizens can directly participate in lawmaking	
Section 3 **Governors Administer State Governments**	☐ list the qualifications and powers of governors ☐ describe the other parts of the state executive branch	▲ SKILLS PRACTICE WORKSHEET **24** ■ SKILLS CHALLENGE WORKSHEET **24** ● CITIZENSHIP WORKSHEET **9**
Section 4 **State Court Systems Interpret State Law**	☐ describe the different levels of state courts ☐ explain how state judges are selected and removed	▲ TRANSPARENCY **56**

Essential Elements

The list below shows Essential Elements relevant to this chapter.
(The complete list of Essential Elements appears in the introductory
pages of this Teacher's Edition.)

Section 1: 3A, 3B, 6C, 6H, 8B

Section 2: 2D, 3A, 4A, 4B, 4C, 4D, 6C, 6F

Section 3: 3A, 3B, 6D

Section 4: 3A, 3B, 6D, 6E, 6F, 6I, 8H

Chapter Review: 3A, 3B, 3C, 4A, 4B, 4C, 6C, 6E, 6F,
6H, 8B, 8D

> Section Resources are keyed
> for student abilities:
> ▲ = Basic
> ● = All Levels
> ■ = Average/Advanced

Homework Options

Each section contains activities labeled "Guided/Independent Practice," "Reteaching/Correctives," and "Enrichment/Extension." You may wish to choose from among these activities when assigning homework.

Students Acquiring English Activities

Using Figure 24–2 on p. 642, dictate the seven steps by which a bill becomes a state law, asking students to skip a line between each step. Do not number the steps. After dictation, students should check Figure 24–2 to correct spelling and grammar. Then have students cut their lists into strips of paper, so that each step appears on a separate strip. Have students work with partners, and hand out an envelope to each pair. Students should close their textbooks and place the strips of paper into the envelopes. At your command, have them empty the envelopes onto their desks and sequence the steps as quickly as possible. Award prizes to the students who finish fastest.

LISTENING/SPEAKING: Have students refer to the state information at the back of the text to create posters that show your state's representation.

Case Studies

When teaching this chapter, you may use Case Study 2, which examines the issue of banning minors from buying albums considered obscene. (Case Studies may be found following p. 510.)

Teacher Bibliography

Dye, Thomas R. *Politics in States and Communities.* 7th ed. Prentice Hall, 1990. A view of the machinery of state and local politics.

Gona, Deborah A. *Lieutenant Governor: The Office and Its Powers.* Rev. ed. Council of State Governments, 1983. An analysis of the responsibilities of an office often viewed as a political sinecure.

Martin, David L. *Capitol, Courthouse, and City Hall.* 7th ed. Longman, 1988. A classic collection of articles by public officials, journalists, and lobbyists that offers a practical introduction to state and local government.

Student Bibliography

The Book of the States. The Council of State Governments, biennial in even-numbered years. Information on constitutions, elections, legislatures, legislation, the judiciary, administrative organization, finance, intergovernmental relations, and state services.

Sabato, Larry. *Goodbye to Good-time Charlie: The American Governor Transformed, 1950–1975.* Lexington, 1978. Describes a major improvement in the quality of state governorship from the ineffectual "Good-time Charlie" to responsible and dynamic leadership.

Literature

O'Connor, Edwin. *All in the Family.* Little, Brown, 1966. A wealthy Irish father insists his sons enter politics; one becomes Governor, but instead of routing out corruption becomes prey to it.

CHAPTER RESOURCES

Study Guide/Review 24
Workbook Chapter 24
Chapter 24 Test, Forms A–C

Warren, Robert Penn. *All the King's Men.* Harcourt Brace Jovanovich, 1983. Pulitzer Prize-winning story of a young journalist involved in Willie Stark's bid to be elected governor, who becomes disillusioned with the exploitation, deceit, and violence of the campaign.

Williams, Ben Ames, Jr. *The Unconquered.* Houghton Mifflin, 1953. A saga of an old southern family and Louisiana politics during the period of Reconstruction.

Films and Videotapes*

Legislator. (Series title: *Inside Government.*) 26 min. Churchill, 1976. f, v. Examines the mechanics of state government by showing the efforts of one state legislator to get a controversial bill passed.

Politics, Power and the Public Good. (Series title: *Searching for Values.*) 20 min. LCA (Coronet), 1972. f. Broderick Crawford portrays a clever, ruthless, and wheeling-dealing state governor in this dramatization of the abuse of power.

* For a complete guide to audiovisual sources, see page T22.

631B

CHAPTER 24

The Structure of State Governments

(pp. 632–661)

This chapter examines state constitutions and the three branches of state government.

Chapter Objectives

After students complete this chapter, they will be able to:

1. Describe the features of state constitutions.
2. Explain how state constitutions can be amended.
3. List some criticisms of state constitutions.
4. Explain how state legislatures are structured.
5. Describe how state legislatures operate.
6. Explain how citizens can directly participate in lawmaking.
7. List the qualifications and powers of governors.
8. Describe the other parts of the state executive branch.
9. Describe the different levels of state courts.
10. Explain how state judges are selected and removed.

CHAPTER

24

The STRUCTURE of STATE GOVERNMENTS

To create a nation while preserving the states was the main reason for the grant of powers which the national government received. . . . The several states have changed greatly since 1789, but they are still commonwealths whose wide authority and jurisdiction practical men are agreed in desiring to maintain.

James Bryce
The American Commonwealth (1888)

Photo
John Waihee (yellow lei), following his inauguration as governor of Hawaii.

The slogan, "Me for Ma, And I Ain't Got a Dern Thing Against Pa" may seem odd for a political campaign, but it helped Miriam ("Ma") Ferguson become Texas's first woman governor in 1925. Eight years earlier the state legislature had removed her husband, Governor James ("Pa") Ferguson, from office on corruption charges. "Pa" had won points among rural Texans for his populist policies, but "Ma's" administration was dogged by charges that she pardoned criminals too easily and too often. (Some people called the executive mansion "the House of a Thousand Pardons.") Defeated in 1926 by her own attorney general, "Ma" was elected six years later for one more term as governor before the Fergusons' political careers ended.

Colorful characters and bitter political battles are only two of the things that state governments have in common with the federal government. States, like the federal government, have written constitutions and three-branch governments. This chapter compares and contrasts the basic structures of state governments today.

CHAPTER OUTLINE

1 State Constitutions Establish Government Structure

State Constitution Features
Amending State Constitutions
Constitutional Reform

2 Legislatures Make State Law

Legislative Structure
Legislatures in Action
Direct Legislation

3 Governors Administer State Governments

The Office of Governor
The Governor's Powers
Other Executive Officers

4 State Court Systems Interpret State Law

State Court Organization
Selecting State Judges

633

3A, 3B, 6C, 6H, 8B

SECTION 1
State Constitutions Establish Government Structure

If your teacher asked you to stand in front of the class and give a five-minute talk on the United States Constitution, could you do it? Could you give a five-minute talk on your *state's* constitution? Each state has a written constitution. Many Americans are unaware of their state's constitution beyond the simple fact that it exists. Some people do not know even that much.

Constitutions vary from state to state, but they do have much in common. For one thing, they are all fundamental law. State constitutions embody the "supreme law of the state." This section discusses the general features of state constitutions, as well as criticisms that have been made of them.

3A, 3B, 6H

State Constitution Features

The thirteen original states adopted their first constitutions around the time of the Declaration of Independence in 1776. Connecticut and Rhode Island merely reworded their original colonial charters. Other states drafted new constitutions, either at special conventions or in the state legislatures.

These early state constitutions were quite short, ranging from 3,000 to 6,000 words. Each incorporated the principles of popular sovereignty, separation of powers, and checks and balances. Seven state constitutions contained a bill of rights, but voting in every state was restricted to property-holders. Finally, each of these early state constitutions was ratified by the legislature, not by the people directly. The first state constitution submitted to the citizens for approval was Massachusetts's *second* constitution, in 1780.

Modern state constitutions

Each of the original thirteen state constitutions was eventually scrapped in favor of a new document. Only two constitutions still in effect today predate the federal Constitution — the revised constitutions of Massachusetts (1780) and New Hampshire (1784). Since 1780, more than 130 state constitutions have been written and ratified. New states have drafted constitutions before entering the Union. Other states have revised their earlier constitutions. Louisiana holds the record, with eleven different constitutions since 1812. Georgia has had ten (since 1777), and South Carolina seven (since 1776). Figure 24–1 on page 637 lists a variety of facts about state constitutions.

Like the earlier versions, modern constitutions incorporate the principles of popular sovereignty, separation of powers, and checks and balances. Governors generally possess more power than before. Modern constitutions are also much more democratic. All constitutions in effect today were ratified by popular vote. Universal suffrage is guaranteed, and most state and local officials are elected directly. In addition, each contains a bill of rights.

Structure of state constitutions

While state constitutions differ greatly in specific provisions, their basic organization is quite similar. Nearly all contain a preamble, a bill of rights, a body of articles, and provisions for amendments.

PREAMBLE Most preambles are patterned after that of the federal Constitution. They typically begin with a statement of popular sovereignty, such as "We the people. . . ." Unlike the federal Constitution, many state constitutions refer to God or a "Supreme Being" in their preamble. Preambles are generally not regarded as part of a state's constitutional law.

BILL OF RIGHTS A bill of rights is part of the main text of each state constitution. Carrying out the principle of limited government, these bills list fundamental civil rights and civil liberties

634

upon which the state government may not infringe. The importance of these protections is shown clearly by their placement near the beginning of most state constitutions, just after the preamble. State bills of rights contain essentially the same protections found in the federal Constitution and Bill of Rights. In addition (as Chapter 6 explains), the Fourteenth Amendment guarantees the protections in the national Bill of Rights to citizens in every state.

State constitutions also typically list other, more detailed, rights. Some provisions, for example, forbid discrimination against disabled persons, guarantee the right to collective bargaining, prohibit imprisonment for debt, and call for equal rights for women and men. A few of the more unusual provisions include the rights to fish in public places, migrate to other states, and start a revolution. Protections in the state constitutions can go beyond — but not limit — those in the federal Constitution.

ARTICLES The framework and powers of the state government are outlined in several articles, or sections. The exact number and content of these articles vary. All state constitutions have separate articles for the legislative, executive, and judicial branches, in that order. These articles set forth the structure, powers, and limitations of each branch. They also spell out the qualifications, method of selection, length of term, and specific duties of officials in each branch.

Nearly all state constitutions contain an article detailing the structure and operation of local governments, such as counties, townships, and cities. Other articles commonly deal with finance, elections and suffrage, education, social services, corporations, and agriculture. Specific articles may pertain to regional concerns — for instance, levees in Mississippi, irrigation in Colorado, or canals in New York.

Following the articles, each state constitution sets out a **schedule**, stating how the document will go into effect. The schedule specifies the time and method of ratification and, frequently, the location of the state capital.

Early state constitutions were difficult, sometimes impossible, to amend. All modern state constitutions, however, include an amending article. Usually at the end of the document, it describes the ways in which the constitution can be formally amended.

As each new state entered the Union, it drafted a constitution to set up a government structure and meet the state's special needs. In this woodcut, members of the Texas legislature meet at the capital, Austin.

EXPLANATION
After reviewing the content of the section, you may want to consider the following activities:

History
▲ *What documents formed the basis of the first state constitutions of Connecticut, Rhode Island, and Massachusetts?* (Their colonial charters.)
● CRITICAL THINKING *What is the significance of this fact?* (It demonstrates that many of the structures and principles of government adopted after independence had their roots in colonial-era government.)

Constitutional Heritage
▲ *Can state constitutions grant citizens rights not guaranteed by the federal Constitution?* (Yes.)
▲ *Can state constitutions deny citizens rights guaranteed by the federal Constitution?* (No.)
● CRITICAL THINKING *Explain your answers to the above questions.* (Because the federal Constitution is the supreme law of the land, a state constitution cannot contradict it—for example, by denying a right guaranteed by the federal Constitution. A state constitution can, however, go beyond the federal Constitution and guarantee a right not protected there.)

Background: *Constitutional Heritage* State constitutions, like the United States Constitution, are fundamental law (p. 78). Yet state constitutions list many detailed rights in addition to the basic principles of government. This is because state constitutions reflect more specific regional concerns and because state governments historically have been influenced by special interests.

Cross-reference
The structure and operation of local governments are discussed in Chapter 27.

The symbol ïï denotes active participation strategies.

Activities are keyed for student abilities:
▲ = Basic
● = All Levels
■ = Average/Advanced

Cooperative Learning

● Divide the class into small groups. Have each group prepare a short pamphlet entitled, "A Guide to State Constitutions." The purpose of the pamphlet is to help people unfamiliar with state constitutions gain a general understanding of the organization of such documents, the topics they cover, and the procedures they contain for proposing and ratifying constitutional amendments. Groups might illustrate their pamphlets with cartoon figures, tables, or diagrams.

GUIDED/INDEPENDENT PRACTICE

● Have students compare state constitutions with the United States Constitution, listing at least three similarities and three differences.

Amending State Constitutions

As with the federal Constitution, there are two basic steps involved in the formal amending process — proposing and ratifying amendments.

Proposing constitutional amendments

Among the fifty states, there are four formal methods of proposing constitutional amendments: (1) legislative proposal, (2) popular initiative, (3) constitutional convention, and (4) constitutional commission.

LEGISLATIVE PROPOSAL   The most common method of initiating constitutional amendments is a proposal by the legislature. Most states require a two-thirds or three-fifths majority of both houses to propose an amendment.

POPULAR INITIATIVE   Some seventeen states allow their citizens to propose constitutional amendments via the initiative. An initiative is a method by which the voters can propose a constitutional amendment directly, without waiting for the state legislature. The first state to allow initiatives was Oregon in 1902. (The initiative process is described in detail later in this chapter, page 645.)

CONSTITUTIONAL CONVENTION   In 41 states, a constitutional convention can be called to propose changes. Such conventions usually develop or revise the entire document, rather than deal with single amendments. More than 200 state constitutional conventions have been called since 1787.

Normally, the state legislature calls for a convention, and a majority of the voters must then approve. In fourteen states, the question of calling a constitutional convention is automatically put before the voters at specified intervals — say, every 10 or 20 years. (Voters generally reject the opportunity.)

Convention delegates are usually popularly elected, either by district, at large, or both. Once the convention completes its work, the proposed new constitution is submitted to the voters for final approval.

CONSTITUTIONAL COMMISSION   A state legislature or governor occasionally appoints a special commission of prominent citizens or policy-makers to study and recommend constitutional changes. This process saves lawmakers a great deal of time and effort.

636

Ratifying constitutional amendments

Before state constitutional amendments can become law, the people must vote to ratify, or approve, them. Usually only a simple majority vote is needed.

Informal methods of change

Like the federal Constitution, state constitutions change through informal methods. State courts continually interpret and clarify their provisions. State legislatures enact statutes that modify them. Likewise, governors may interpret their constitutional powers differently. In short, state constitutions are living documents that can be modified by custom and usage as well as by formal amendment.

6C

Constitutional Reform

Experts in state government agree that most state constitutions badly need reform. Although the problems differ from state to state, constitutional scholars have identified several major, often interrelated, weaknesses.

Length and detail

The most common criticism of state constitutions is that they are too long and detailed. As a result, they often are confusing, contradictory, and difficult to enforce. The average state constitution contains around 28,000 words, making it roughly four times as long as the Constitution of the United States.

State constitutions tend to be long because they are bogged down with details. They may contain provisions for such items as school courses, street names, state holidays, bingo games, and historical monuments. South Dakota's constitution specifies what vines shall grow on the walls of the state prison. California's constitution authorizes the legislature to regulate the time of wrestling matches.

Such details can go out of date and interfere with governing the state efficiently. For example, Kentucky's constitution, written in 1891, lists official salaries. A state supreme court decision was necessary to allow pay raises for state officials. North Dakota's constitution (1889) provides that the state's "debts shall not exceed the sum of $200,000," while the Ohio constitution (1851) restricts state debts to $750,000.

Background: *Structure of Government*   The seventeen states that allow initiatives are Arizona, Arkansas, California, Colorado, Florida, Illinois, Massachusetts, Michigan, Missouri, Montana, Nebraska, Nevada, North Dakota, Ohio, Oklahoma, Oregon, and South Dakota.

Background: *Structure of Government*   A convention is voted upon every nine years in Hawaii; every ten years in Alaska, Iowa, New Hampshire, and Rhode Island; every sixteen years in Michigan; and every twenty years in Connecticut, Illinois, Maryland, Missouri, Montana, New York, Ohio, and Oklahoma.

636

Figure 24–1 STATE CONSTITUTIONS The fifty states' constitutions reflect the great variety among the states themselves. 8B

STATE	NUMBER OF CONSTITUTIONS	DATE OF PRESENT CONSTITUTION	NUMBER OF WORDS*	NUMBER OF AMENDMENTS
Alabama	6	Nov. 28, 1901	174,000	556
Alaska	1	Jan. 3, 1959	16,675	23
Arizona	1	Feb. 14, 1912	28,876	119
Arkansas	5	Oct. 30, 1874	40,720	81
California	2	July 4, 1879	33,350	485
Colorado	1	Aug. 1, 1876	45,679	124
Connecticut	4	Dec. 30, 1965	9,564	28
Delaware	4	June 10, 1897	19,000	123
Florida	6	Jan. 7, 1969	25,100	65
Georgia	10	July 1, 1983	25,000	39
Hawaii	1	Aug. 21, 1959	17,453	86
Idaho	1	July 3, 1890	21,500	109
Illinois	4	July 1, 1971	13,200	8
Indiana	2	Nov. 1, 1851	9,377	38
Iowa	2	Sept. 3, 1857	12,500	49
Kansas	1	Jan. 29, 1861	11,865	90
Kentucky	4	Sept. 28, 1891	23,500	32
Louisiana	11	Jan. 1, 1975	51,488	54
Maine	1	March 15, 1820	13,500	162
Maryland	4	Oct. 5, 1867	41,349	205
Massachusetts	1	Oct. 25, 1780	36,690	117
Michigan	4	Jan. 1, 1964	20,000	17
Minnesota	1	May 11, 1858	9,500	113
Mississippi	4	Nov. 1, 1890	24,000	116
Missouri	4	March 30, 1945	42,000	81
Montana	2	July 1, 1973	11,866	18
Nebraska	2	Oct. 12, 1875	20,048	197
Nevada	1	Oct. 31, 1864	20,770	113
New Hampshire	2	June 2, 1784	9,200	143
New Jersey	3	Jan. 1, 1948	17,086	44
New Mexico	1	Jan. 6, 1912	27,200	123
New York	4	Jan. 1, 1895	80,000	213
North Carolina	3	July 1, 1971	11,000	27
North Dakota	1	Nov. 2, 1889	20,564	129
Ohio	2	Sept. 1, 1851	36,900	151
Oklahoma	1	Nov. 16, 1907	68,800	146
Oregon	1	Feb. 14, 1859	26,090	188
Pennsylvania	5	1968†	21,675	56
Rhode Island	2	May 2, 1843	19,026	36
South Carolina	7	Jan. 1, 1896	22,500	463
South Dakota	1	Nov. 2, 1889	23,300	99
Tennessee	3	Feb. 23, 1870	15,300	32
Texas	5	Feb. 15, 1876	76,000	353
Utah	1	Jan. 4, 1896	11,000	82
Vermont	3	July 9, 1793	6,600	50
Virginia	6	July 1, 1971	18,500	23
Washington	1	Nov. 11, 1889	29,400	88
West Virginia	2	April 9, 1872	25,600	64
Wisconsin	1	May 29, 1848	13,500	129
Wyoming	1	July 10, 1890	31,800	61

* Estimated. †1874 constitution partially revised, 1967–1968.   Source: *The Book of the States*

RETEACHING/CORRECTIVES

▲ Have students outline the section, using both headings and subheadings as entries and including significant details.

ENRICHMENT/EXTENSION

■ Have students examine a copy of your state's constitution to see whether the major criticisms of state constitutions (excessive length and detail, poor wording, unwise amendments) apply to it. (Copies of the constitution can be obtained from your state's secretary of state.)

Figure 24–1

▲ *Which constitution is the longest?* (Alabama's, with 174,000 words.) *Which is the shortest?* (Vermont's, with 6,600 words.)

Background: *Structure of Government* Before its revision in 1982, Georgia's constitution contained nearly 600,000 words, rivaling *Gone With the Wind* in length.

The symbol ⅱ denotes active participation strategies.

Activities are keyed for student abilities:
▲ = Basic
● = All Levels
■ = Average/Advanced

Section 1 Review Answers

1. Modern constitutions are more democratic and are ratified by popular vote; governors generally have more power; universal suffrage is guaranteed; state and local officials are directly elected; and bills of rights are included. They tend to be longer and more detailed than earlier constitutions.

2. Preamble, bill of rights, and articles.

3. Popular initiative, legislative proposal, constitutional convention, and constitutional commission.

4. Excessive length and detail often make them contradictory, confusing, and difficult to enforce.

Critical thinking One advantage would be that citizens could have a direct effect on the state's constitution; a disadvantage would be that interest groups could unduly influence the process. Students should describe fundamental law and state whether they think constitutional conventions are important in a democracy.

CLOSURE

● Have students list five important facts about state constitutions from the section. Then have students read Section 2, noting similarities and differences between the state and federal lawmaking processes.

State governments are often housed in impressive buildings in the state's capital city. This picture shows the Georgia state capitol building, located in the heart of downtown Atlanta.

Wording

Compared with the federal Constitution, state constitutions are often poorly written. They also tend to be so laden with legal jargon that even lawyers have difficulty comprehending them. The Missouri Constitution, for example, contains a single sentence that is 392 words long. In it are seven semicolons, nine *provided*'s, nine *herein*'s, and two *thereon*'s.

Abuse of amendments

Generally speaking, the older a constitution is, and the easier it is to amend, the more amendments it will have. State constitutions that are easy to amend often become targets for interest groups seeking special treatment. If an interest group fails to get what it wants from the legislature or the courts, it may call for a state constitutional amendment.

Despite such criticisms, most citizens are inclined to tolerate their state's constitution. Voters tend to turn down automatic chances for a constitutional convention and to resist other proposals for change.

638

SECTION 1 REVIEW

Vocabulary and key terms

schedule (635)
initiative (636)

For review

1. In what ways do modern state constitutions differ from earlier ones? **6H**
2. What are the three main elements of state constitutions? **6H**
3. What are four ways that changes in state constitutions can be proposed? **6C**
4. Why have some state constitutions been criticized for their length and amount of detail? **6C**

Critical thinking

DRAWING CONCLUSIONS What are the advantages and disadvantages of making state constitutions easy to amend? Should citizens be able to change fundamental law? **6C**

2D, 3A, 4A, 4B, 4C, 4D, 6C, 6F

Legislatures Make State Law

The Main Ideas

1 How are state legislatures structured?
pages 639–640

2 How do state legislatures operate?
pages 641–643

3 How can citizens directly participate in lawmaking?
pages 644–645

You have probably noticed cars sporting bumper stickers labeled something like "NO ON 9." The number refers to a particular ballot question — an issue to be decided by the voters on Election Day.

Ballot questions allow citizens to participate directly in the state lawmaking process. However, it is the state legislature, called the *General Assembly* or the *General Court* (in Massachusetts and New Hampshire) or simply the *Legislature*, that performs the bulk of the lawmaking tasks for the state.

3A, 4C, 4D, 6F

Legislative Structure

Bicameral legislatures

As Chapter 2 points out, most of the legislatures in colonial America followed the English parliamentary pattern and set up two-house, or bicameral, legislatures. By the end of the Revolutionary War, every state but Georgia and Pennsylvania had a bicameral legislature. Today, every state except Nebraska has a two-house legislature. The upper house in every state (as well as Nebraska's single chamber) is called the Senate. The lower house in most states is called the House of Representatives.

In the national government, bicameralism reflects the principle of federalism. The U.S. Senate gives each state equal representation, while the U.S. House represents the people. In the states, bicameralism ensures that legislative power is not concentrated in a single chamber. Bicameralism permits each house to check the other and makes it harder for lobbyists and interest groups to influence the legislative process.

Most state legislatures have a total membership of between 100 and 200. In each state, the lower house outnumbers the upper house. The smallest bicameral legislature is Alaska, with 20 members in the upper house and 40 in the lower. The largest is New Hampshire, with 24 in the upper house and 400 in the lower. Nebraska, with 49 senators in its single chamber, has the fewest state legislators.

Unicameralism

Although Nebraska, since 1934, has had the only unicameral legislature, this plan has numerous supporters. They argue that bicameralism has no practical purpose in state governments, which are not federal systems. Futhermore, they say, unicameralism is more efficient and economical. There are fewer legislators and staff members to pay and less duplication of effort in committees.

Legislative apportionment

All state legislators are elected by districts, and every state constitution specifies how those districts are to be apportioned, or divided, within the state. Until 1964, state legislators were chosen in much the same way as members of Congress. State senators usually represented *geographic* areas such as counties. Members of the lower house, on the other hand, represented population.

This arrangement caused many inequities. Because counties varied considerably in population, persons in highly populated urban counties were underrepresented in many state senates. People from sparsely populated counties were often overrepresented.

In addition, state legislatures are supposed to redistrict — or redraw district boundaries — every 10 years, following the federal census. Many states failed to do so; some states went as long as 60 years without redistricting. Meanwhile, the U.S. population shifted dramatically from rural to urban areas. This meant that rural voters were greatly overrepresented relative to city-dwellers in state legislatures.

639

Background: *Structure of Government* In Maryland, Virginia, and West Virginia, the lower house is named the House of Delegates; in California, New York, Nevada, and Wisconsin, it is known simply as the Assembly. In New Jersey, the lower house is called the General Assembly.

Check for Understanding
● *Who represents your district in the state legislature? In the state senate?*

Section Objectives
☐ explain how state legislatures are structured
☐ describe how state legislatures operate
☐ explain how citizens can directly participate in lawmaking

Vocabulary
pre-file, referendum, recall

FOCUS
● Ask students to describe current or recent issues involving your state's legislature. Have them consider what sorts of issues commonly come before the legislature and which of these issues are the most controversial.

If your state legislature is currently in session, you might ask each student to bring in a newspaper article describing some legislative action. The articles could be discussed individually or placed together in a display.

The symbol ☷ denotes active participation strategies.

Activities are keyed for student abilities:
▲ = Basic
● = All Levels
■ = Average/Advanced

EXPLANATION

After reviewing the content of the section, you may want to consider the following activities:

Constitutional Heritage

Justice John Marshall Harlan— the lone dissenter in *Reynolds v. Sims* (pp. 70–71)—criticized the view that "every major social ill in this country can find its cure in some constitutional 'principle,' and that this Court should take the lead in promoting reform when other branches of government fail to act. The Constitution is not a panacea for every blot upon the public welfare, nor should this Court, ordained as a judicial body, be thought of as a general haven for reform movements. . . ."

Harlan's statement can be used as the basis of a discussion concerning judicial activism and judicial restraint (p. 480).

● CRITICAL THINKING **What danger, if any, is posed by the Supreme Court's involvement in a wide range of reform issues?** (Some students may argue that resolution of important issues should be the task of elected representatives, not unelected judges, and that leaving issues up to the judiciary could endanger democratic government.)

● CRITICAL THINKING **How might members of the Court majority have responded to Harlan's comment?** (They might have said that since the state legislature was the cause of the problem, one could not wait for the legislature to solve it; another branch of government had to intervene. Also, a basic constitutional principle was at stake.)

California in 1962 offered a stunning example. Los Angeles County, with a population of more than 6 million, had only one state senator — the same as a county in the Sierra Nevada with just over 14,000 people. Altogether, 11 percent of California's population could elect a majority of the state senators. Many other states suffered similar electoral imbalances.

"One person, one vote"

This problem was finally addressed in a landmark Supreme Court case, *Reynolds v. Sims* (1964). The issue in this case was whether Alabama's failure to reapportion its state senate violated the "equal protection" clause of the Fourteenth Amendment. Alabama's 35 state senators each represented one county. The counties, however, ranged in population from 15,000 to 635,000. Citizens in some populous counties were underrepresented by more than 40 to 1.

In the *Reynolds* decision (quoted on the facing page), the Supreme Court ruled that such imbalances were unconstitutional. According to Chief Justice Earl Warren, "as a basic constitutional standard, the Equal Protection Clause requires that the seats in both houses of a bicameral state legislature must be apportioned on a basis of population."

Few cases have provoked such strong reactions as *Reynolds*. People in urban areas, who stood to gain more representation, hailed the decision. Representatives from rural areas, on the other hand, feared that big cities would now dominate the lawmaking process. Despite protests, by 1968 every state legislature had been reapportioned to conform to the "one person, one vote" principle.

Legislators' qualifications

State constitutions also set the legal qualifications for being a state legislator. In several states, people may serve as legislators when they are 18 years old; a few have age requirements as high as 25 or 30 years. States also require legislators to have lived for a certain length of time in the state and district they represent. All states require legislators to be U.S. citizens.

Like other political candidates, a potential legislator also needs many "informal" qualifications. A lawmaker must have considerable time and energy to give to the job. A full-time doctor, student, homemaker, or factory worker would

640

find it difficult to serve. Lawyers, farmers, and people who run their own businesses are more likely to have the necessary time and flexibility for public service.

Belonging to the "right" political party is essential to a candidate for state legislatures. In solidly Republican districts, a Democratic candidate stands very little chance of winning, and vice versa. Moreover, districts are often gerrymandered to preserve a party's representation in the legislature. (The only state where party labels do not matter is Nebraska, where state legislators are elected on nonpartisan ballots.)

Length of term

In most states, representatives serve two-year terms. State senators in 38 states serve four-year terms, while senators in the remaining states serve two-year terms. In Alabama, Louisiana, Maryland, and Mississippi, members of both chambers serve four-year terms. In 1990, Oklahoma, California, and Colorado set limits on the number of terms legislators could serve, the first states to do so.

Turnover among state legislators is high. Normally, one-fourth of any state legislature is made up of first-term members. Many legislators simply decline to serve another term because what starts out as a part-time job quickly turns into a never-ending series of meetings and committee work, disrupting family and professional life. Also, turnover is generally higher in the lower house than in the upper house, presumably because representatives serve shorter terms and consider their position less prestigious than that of senators.

Compensation

Most citizens realize that a legislator's job is pressure-packed and time-consuming. Nevertheless, in few states are lawmakers paid enough to support themselves without another source of income. Low pay may be another important reason for the high turnover among state legislators.

State legislators may be entitled to other benefits in addition to their salaries, however, such as travel allowances, postage, insurance policies, and retirement plans. Legislators usually determine their own salaries. They may often be reluctant to vote themselves a pay raise because they will surely draw criticism from their constituents and the media.

Background: *Geography* The Sierra Nevada is a rugged mountain range in eastern California that extends about 400 miles from north to south and rises above 14,000 feet. Population density is quite low, from 2 to 25 people per square mile.

Cross-reference Gerrymandering is discussed in Chapter 12, p. 338.

Legislatures in Action

Legislative sessions

In the early days of the United States, most Americans lived on farms. Most state legislators were also farmers. Legislative sessions, therefore, were held from January through March — between the fall harvest and spring planting.

Before World War II, only four states held sessions every year. Now, however, to meet increasing demands on state government, more than 40 states hold annual sessions. In some states, every other session deals only with budgetary matters.

Many states set strict limits on how long their legislatures meet. Texas, for example, limits its sessions to 140 days every other year. North Dakota's legislature is limited to 80-day sessions, and Wyoming is confined to 40 days in odd-numbered years and 20 days in even-numbered years. Some states refuse to pay their legislators beyond a specified number of days. At the other extreme, California's legislative session runs continuously for two years. By and large, the more populous the state, the fewer the restrictions.

To deal with emergencies between regular sessions, all states provide for special sessions. These may be called by the governor, or, in a number of states, by the legislature itself.

Presiding officers

Like the U.S. Congress, every state legislature has a set of leaders. The lieutenant governor presides over the state senate in 28 states. In the remaining states, senators choose their own president. The lieutenant governor's role closely resembles that of the U.S. Vice President as president of the U.S. Senate. Lieutenant governors usually are allowed to vote only in case of a tie, and they are not permitted to take part in floor debate or make committee assignments. In states where the presiding officer is chosen by the senate, he or she may possess such powers.

In the absence of the lieutenant governor or senate president, the president *pro tempore* takes over. The president *pro tem* is chosen by the membership of the senate and is always a member of the majority party. In addition, all state senates have majority and minority leaders and assistant leaders, known as whips. These leaders function much like their counterparts in the U.S. Senate (page 357).

PRIMARY SOURCE

LANDMARKS in LIBERTY

2D, 6C

Reynolds v. Sims (1964)

In *Reynolds v. Sims*, the Supreme Court took up the question of voter equality in state elections in Alabama, where districts were divided by geography, not population. Following the "one person, one vote" principle, earlier High Court decisions had already required many states to redistrict for elections to the U.S. House of Representatives. This principle was now extended to the state legislatures, based on the Fourteenth Amendment's promise of equal protection. Chief Justice Earl Warren expressed the majority opinion.

Legislators represent people, not trees or acres. Legislators are elected by voters, not farms or cities or economic interests. As long as ours is a representative form of government, . . . the right to elect legislators in a free and unimpaired fashion is a bedrock of our political system. . . . Overweighting and overvaluation of the votes of those living here has the certain effect of the dilution and undervaluation of the votes of those living there. The resulting discrimination against those individual voters living in disfavored areas is easily demonstrable mathematically. Their right to vote is simply not the same right as that of those living in a favored part of the State.

. . . We conclude that the Equal Protection Clause guarantees the opportunity for equal participation by all voters in the election of state legislators. Diluting the weight of votes because of place of residence impairs basic constitutional rights under the Fourteenth Amendment.

1. How is apportionment based on geographic area likely to affect voting rights for people in areas with high population?
2. To what legislatures does the ruling apply?
3. On what constitutional grounds was this ruling based?

641

Structure of Government

● Have students redraw Figure 24–2, using as their model Figure 13–4 (p. 365), which shows how a bill becomes a law at the federal level.

Landmarks in Liberty Answers

1. Voters in highly populated areas will be underrepresented in comparison with voters in sparsely populated regions. In areas of high population concentration, each representative will represent a greater number of constituents.
2. The ruling applies to state legislatures.
3. The Equal Protection Clause of the Fourteenth Amendment guarantees all voters the right to equal participation in the election of state legislators.

The symbol 👥 denotes active participation strategies.

Activities are keyed for student abilities:
▲ = Basic
● = All Levels
■ = Average/Advanced

Values

● Write the terms *Referendum, Initiative,* and *Recall* on the board and have students come to the board and write the definition below each term, along with the different forms of each. Then divide the class into two groups and hold a debate on the question of whether referendum, initiative, and recall procedures make state government *more* democratic or *less* democratic.

In the lower house of each state legislature, the presiding officer is called the speaker of the house. Like the Speaker of the U.S. House of Representatives, the speaker is elected by the state representatives and is always a member of the majority party. Speakers generally have the power to refer bills to committee, recognize members during floor debate, and interpret legislative rules. Most state speakers also have the authority to make committee assignments and appoint committee chairpersons. Each lower house also has majority and minority leaders and whips.

Committee system

Most of the work in state legislatures is done by committees, which review bills and make recommendations to the legislature as a whole. Most states have standing, or permanent, committees on matters such as education, appropriations, transportation, finance, local government, and welfare. Subcommittees help distribute the workload of the permanent committees.

State legislators commonly serve on three or four standing committees. Committee membership reflects party strength in the chamber. For example, if Republicans control the lower house by a 60 to 40 percent margin over Democrats, Republicans would chair each of the standing committees. In addition, the ratio of Republicans to Democrats on each committee would be roughly 6 to 4. Legislative leaders usually consider their colleagues' seniority, expertise, and party loyalty when making committee assignments.

Many states establish joint committees, permanent bodies composed of members from both houses of a legislature. Such committees save legislators time, money, and duplication of effort. (In Connecticut and Maine, all standing committees are joint committees.)

There is also a growing trend toward interim committees, which meet between sessions. Regular legislative sessions often are short, and legislatures seldom meet year-round. Interim committees investigate problems between sessions and offer their recommendations to the legislature at its next regular session.

The lawmaking process

The primary function of state legislatures is to make laws for the state. Although the precise rules and procedures vary from state to state, the process in general is much like the way bills are passed in Congress (pages 364–372). Figure 24–2 provides a summary of the lawmaking process at the state level. Its main steps are as follows:

INTRODUCTION OF BILLS Only legislators may formally introduce bills into their own chamber, usually at the beginning of the session. Many states allow their members to **pre-file** bills before the regular session officially begins, so that the legislators can begin considering bills immediately.

Some bills reflect the ideas of legislators themselves. Many originate with the executive branch, particularly the governor or the attorney general. Many come from agencies, interest

Figure 24–2 HOW A BILL BECOMES STATE LAW This chart shows the basic steps by which a bill becomes law in a typical state. 3A

LOWER HOUSE	UPPER HOUSE
1. Bill is introduced.	1. Bill is introduced.
2. Bill is referred to a standing committee.	2. Bill is referred to a standing committee.
3. Committee holds hearings, revises bill, and votes to recommend passage.	3. Committee holds hearings, revises bill, and votes to recommend passage.
4. Lower house debates bill and votes for passage.	4. Upper house debates bill and votes for passage.
5. Conference committee, composed of members from each house, reconciles the two versions of bill.	
6. Lower house approves compromise version of bill.	6. Upper house approves compromise version of bill.
7. Governor signs or vetoes bill.	

Critical Thinking
▲ *Why, from the standpoint of the committee system, is it important for a party to win a majority of the seats in a state legislature?* (All committee chairpersons come from the majority party, and committee membership is based on the relative strengths of the parties in the chamber.)

Figure 24–2
● *How does the state bill-making process exemplify* *the system of checks and balances?* (A conference committee must reconcile House and Senate versions of the bill; both houses must approve the final version; the governor can sign or veto it.)

The Nebraska legislature, shown here in session, is the only unicameral state legislature in the United States. In 1990, Ben Nelson (inset) was elected governor, succeeding Kay Orr, Nebraska's first woman governor.

groups, local governments, or concerned private citizens. In many states, a thousand or more bills are likely to be introduced during each regular session. In New York, 20,000 bills in a session is not uncommon. The next highest is typically Massachusetts, with about 9,000 bills. Idaho, South Dakota, Utah, Vermont, and Wyoming usually have the fewest bills introduced — around 700 per session.

COMMITTEE CONSIDERATION After a bill is introduced, it is sent to the appropriate standing committee for scrutiny. All committee and subcommittee meetings to discuss legislation are open to the public. A bill that is approved by a standing committee is then placed on a calendar. Many states use a "consent" calendar to dispense with relatively minor bills, such as congratulating the state university basketball team for winning a national title.

FLOOR ACTION Once a bill reaches the floor, the entire chamber has an opportunity to debate, amend, and vote on it. Often the legislative chambers meet as a "committee of the whole" (page 368) to consider the bill under informal rules of debate before it comes to a vote. As in Congress, legislators may vote by voice, teller, or roll-call. Many states now have electronic voting systems, which flash results on a large "scoreboard" immediately after the vote is taken.

In bicameral legislatures, as in Congress, a bill must pass both houses in identical form. To reconcile differences in two versions of a bill, members from both houses meet in a conference committee.

EXECUTIVE ACTION If a bill passes both houses by a majority vote, it is submitted to the governor. The governor can either sign the bill into law or (in every state except in North Carolina) veto it. Generally, he or she is given a reasonable time to act on a bill, usually 30 days. (Nebraska gives the governor only 5 days to act, but other states, like Illinois, allow up to 60 days.) Most state legislatures can override the governor's veto, usually by a two-thirds vote in both chambers.

643

ii Cooperative Learning
● Divide the class into small groups. Have each group write a three-minute editorial for a local television news show. The editorials should support or oppose one of the following: (1) making the state legislature unicameral; (2) making all committees of the legislature joint committees; (3) abolishing recall, initiative, and referendum procedures.

GUIDED/INDEPENDENT PRACTICE
● Have students compare Figure 13–4, "How a Bill Becomes Law" (p. 365), with Figure 24–2, "How a Bill Becomes State Law" (p. 642). Each student should identify four similarities and two differences in the legislative process at the state and national levels.

Background: *Structure of Government* Joint committees perform the functions of conference committees in some states.

The symbol **ii** denotes active participation strategies.

Activities are keyed for student abilities:
▲ = Basic
● = All Levels
■ = Average/Advanced

Direct Legislation

In the early 1900's, a reform movement known as the "Progressive movement" spread across the United States. Its goal was to stop government corruption and make public officials more responsive to the people. To this end, a number of states, especially in the West and Midwest, passed measures to allow citizens direct participation in state lawmaking.

Referendum

The **referendum** allows voters to approve or disapprove of a statute or constitutional amendment proposed by the state legislature. In other words, state legislative proposals are "referred" to the people. The first state to adopt the referendum was South Dakota in 1898. Today, most states have some form of referendum.

COMPULSORY REFERENDUM Most state constitutions specify that certain measures proposed by the state legislature *must* be submitted to the voters. These measures are called compulsory, or mandatory, referendums. For example, in many states a proposed state constitutional amendment must be approved by the voters. Certain types of statutes, questions of state debt, and state bond issues are other measures that voters often must approve.

ADVISORY REFERENDUM Under an advisory, or optional, referendum, the legislature may decide to submit measures to the voters. An advisory referendum usually involves a highly sensitive issue that legislators are reluctant to decide by themselves. For example, the legislature might call for an advisory referendum on whether to allow the death penalty or increase taxes. Using this method, voters make important policy choices, and legislators escape the blame for the decision.

POPULAR REFERENDUM A number of states use the popular (or protest) referendum. It

Angry taxpayers in California placed the initiative called "Proposition 13" on the ballot in 1978 (page 718). Its passage led to lower taxes.

644

allows the voters to prevent a statute passed by the legislature from taking effect. In states with popular referendums, there is usually a 30- to 90-day lag between the legislature's passage of a law and the time it takes effect. During this time, citizens who object to the law may circulate a petition for a popular referendum. A specified percentage of registered voters must sign the petition within a given time period. If the petition drive is successful, the issue will be placed on the ballot, either in a special election or the next general election. A majority vote keeps the law from going into effect.

Initiative

Voters in 21 states can propose laws through initiative petitions. The initiative enables the people to bypass legislators who ignore or fail to enact desired measures. Depending on the state, voters may be permitted to propose statutes, constitutional amendments, or both.

DIRECT INITIATIVE A *direct* initiative allows the voters to place an issue directly on the ballot. This is the method generally used for proposing constitutional amendments (page 636). Those wishing to propose a law or amendment must first circulate a petition describing it. The petition must be signed by a specified number of registered voters, usually between 8 and 15 percent of the number of people who voted in the last general election. If the petition is in order, the proposal appears on the ballot at the next election. If approved by a majority of voters, it becomes law.

INDIRECT INITIATIVE In an *indirect* initiative, citizens' proposals for laws go to the state legislature first. Again, to start the proposal citizens must circulate a petition and acquire the necessary signatures. The proposal then goes to the state legislature. If the legislature does not pass the measure, it is put before the voters at the next election. If approved by a majority vote, it becomes law.

Recall

In fifteen states, voters can remove legislators, the governor, and sometimes judges from office with a **recall**. Once again, a petition drive starts the process. Typically, the number of signatures must equal 25 percent of the votes cast for that office in the last general election. If the petition is successful, a special recall election is held. A majority vote is needed to remove the official.

A successful move for recall took place in Michigan in 1983, when two state senators were removed for voting to increase taxes. This was the first time any legislator had been recalled since two California state senators were ousted in 1913 and 1914.

Since their creation, the referendum, initiative, and recall have stirred much debate. Supporters maintain that these methods represent the purest form of democracy and stimulate public interest in government. Critics, however, argue that direct legislation undermines confidence in elected officials, lengthens ballots, confuses the public, and increases the influence of interest groups. It almost always takes a well-organized, well-funded group to get such issues on the ballot.

SECTION 2 REVIEW

Vocabulary and key terms

Reynolds v. Sims (640)
pre-file (642)
referendum (644)
direct initiative (645)
indirect initiative (645)
recall (645)

For review

1. What are the advantages of bicameralism for state legislatures? 3A
2. What arguments have been made in favor of unicameral state legislatures? 3A
3. (a) What problems of representation did the Supreme Court try to correct in *Reynolds v. Sims*? (b) What was the result of the *Reynolds* decision? 6F
4. What is the reason for the high turnover in state legislatures? 4D
5. What is the purpose of the (a) referendum? (b) initiative? (c) recall? 4C

Critical thinking

FORMING AN OPINION Many doctors, lawyers, and business executives earn more money than state lawmakers. Why, then, do citizens and the media often harshly criticize any attempt to raise lawmakers' salaries? 4D

3. (a) Legislative apportionment. **(b)** By 1968, all state legislatures conformed to the "one person, one vote" principle.
4. The main reason is that the demands of office become time-consuming, often disrupting a legislator's family and professional life.
5. (a) A referendum allows voters to accept or reject a constitutional amendment or statute proposed by a state legislature. **(b)** An initiative enables voters to propose constitutional amendments and/or statutes. **(c)** A recall can remove legislators, governors, and judges from office.

Critical thinking Public anger may reflect the fact that lawmakers award themselves the pay increase or the fact that lawmakers' pay comes from tax revenues.

CLOSURE

● Remind students of the pre-reading objectives at the beginning of the section. Pose one or all of these questions again. Then have students read Section 3, noting the executive, legislative, and judicial powers of the governor.

The symbol denotes active participation strategies.

Activities are keyed for student abilities:
▲ = Basic
● = All Levels
■ = Average/Advanced

Governors Administer State Governments
(pp. 646–653)

Section Objectives
☐ list the qualifications and powers of governors
☐ describe the other parts of the state executive branch

Vocabulary
executive clemency, commute, attorney general, advisory opinion, auditor, comptroller

👥 FOCUS

● Tell students to imagine the following situation. They are the head of some organization—a business or sports team, for example. Every time they leave town on business, their second-in-command takes over and does things in a completely different way. Yet they have no power to fire this subordinate.

Explain that this is the situation some governors confront and that it results from having a governor and a lieutenant governor of different parties in power at the same time. Note that because of the governor's importance, such disputes can create serious problems for state governments.

3A, 3B, 6D

SECTION 3 Governors Administer State Governments

┌─────────┐
│ ACCESS │ **The Main Ideas**
└─────────┘
1 **What are the qualifications and powers of governors?**   *pages 646–652*
2 **What are the other parts of the state executive branch?**   *pages 652–653*

Among this century's most powerful governors was Huey Long of Louisiana. Called a dictator by some for his strong-arm tactics, Long was loved by others for his attention to the needs of the poor. Long provided free textbooks to all students, built many new roads and bridges, and repealed the poll tax. He also made many enemies, one of whom shot and killed him in 1935. Huey Long demonstrated in an extreme form a governor's unique ability to shape state policies and events.

3A

The Office of Governor

Qualifications

In most states, governors must meet certain age, residency, and citizenship requirements. The usual minimum age is 30 years, but requirements range from 18 years in California and Washington to 31 in Oklahoma. Most states require the governor to be a United States citizen and to have lived in the state for at least five years.

There is much more to becoming governor than just satisfying the minimum legal requirements. A quick summary of governors' backgrounds reveals some of the "informal" requirements for office, although no single set of characteristics applies in every state.

RACE Nearly every governor has been white. There have been four Hispanic governors. In 1989, Douglas Wilder of Virginia became the nation's first African American to be elected governor.

SEX Up until 1980, only five women had been elected governor. Several women were elected governor during the 1980's. In 1990 alone, three women were elected to their state's top office: Joan Finney (Kansas), Barbara Roberts (Oregon), and

Ann Richards (Texas). From 1991 to 1994, only one woman — Christine Todd Whitman of New Jersey — was elected governor.

AGE It appears that governors are getting younger. During the 1970's only six governors were over age 60, while 23 were younger than 40. By contrast, in the 1940's, 33 were older than 60 and only ten under 40. The median age for governors today is in the mid-50's. Experts attribute some of this trend to television, with its accent on youth.

RELIGION Religion may play a significant role in the election of governors, depending on the state. Being a Roman Catholic in Rhode Island or a Mormon in Utah, for example, might be an electoral advantage.

OCCUPATION AND INCOME Governors represent a wide range of occupations. There have been restaurant owners (Lester Maddox, Georgia), peanut farmers (Jimmy Carter, Georgia), business leaders (George Romney, Michigan), truck drivers (Harold Hughes, Iowa), and marine zoologists (Dixy Lee Ray, Washington). Over half, however, were lawyers, and 90 percent had previously held public office. Governors have come from both poor and wealthy backgrounds.

Term and compensation

The governors of New Hampshire and Vermont serve two-year terms. In other states, the term is four years. About half the states restrict the number of terms a governor may serve.

Governors' salaries vary considerably. The average among all governors is about $86,000. Most states provide an official state residence, popularly called "the governor's mansion." Most states also provide additional benefits, such as an automobile, an airplane, travel allowances, health care, and pension plans.

The lieutenant governor

Forty-three states have lieutenant governors. In 42 of these states, the lieutenant governor is popularly elected; the exception is Tennessee, where the presiding officer elected by the senate

646

Background: *Structure of Government* Kansas has no formal qualifications for the office of governor.

Background: *History* The four Hispanic governors were Jerry Apodaca and Toney Anaya, both of New Mexico, Raul Castro of Arizona, and Bob Martinez of Florida.

Background: *History* The five woman governors were Nellie Tayloe Ross of Wyoming, Miriam Ferguson of Texas, Lurleen Wallace of Alabama, Ella Grasso of Connecticut, and Dixy Lee Ray of Washington.

doubles as lieutenant governor. The role of lieutenant governor is somewhat like the office of the Vice President of the United States. He or she is in direct line to succeed the governor and is the presiding officer in the state senate. Besides these two responsibilities, the lieutenant governor has few formal duties.

In 22 states, the governor and lieutenant governor run as a political team. In the others, lieutenant governors are elected separately from the governor. If the two belong to different political parties, problems can arise. For example, in 1979 California Governor Jerry Brown was often out of the state campaigning for the Democratic presidential nomination. During Brown's absence, his Republican lieutenant governor, Mike Curb, assumed the duties of governor and threatened to veto bills that Brown supported.

Filling vacancies

Succession to the governor's office differs from state to state. If there is a lieutenant governor, he or she becomes governor when the office falls vacant because of death, disability, or resignation. In Arizona, Oregon, and Wyoming, the secretary of state takes the office. In Maine, New Hampshire, New Jersey, and West Virginia, the president of the senate succeeds the governor.

Where governors and lieutenant governors are elected separately, a governor may be succeeded by a lieutenant governor who belongs to the opposition political party. In states where governors and lieutenant governors run as a team, a different problem can arise. Because the governor has the power to fill vacancies in the U.S. Senate, governors have on occasion resigned so that their successor can appoint them to the Senate. For example, soon after Senator Walter Mondale of Minnesota resigned in 1976 to become Vice President, Governor Wendell Anderson also resigned. His replacement, former Lieutenant Governor Rudy Perpich, then appointed Anderson to the Senate. Partly because of this "self-appointment" ploy, Anderson lost when he ran for senator in the next election.

Removal from office

There are two ways in which governors can be removed from office during a term. In every state but Oregon, the governor can be im-

Most states provide their governor with a residence for the duration of his or her term. This picture shows the governor's mansion in Montgomery, Alabama.

Politics

● CRITICAL THINKING Bill Clinton was the incumbent governor of Arkansas during his 1992 presidential campaign. **What are the pros and cons of an incumbent governor running for President?** (*Pros*—He or she has had recent experience managing a large bureaucracy and commands more power, influence, and publicity while still in office. *Cons*—He or she has less time to handle state duties and will be held responsible for problems affecting the state.)

Structure of Government

Have students compare the powers of governors (pp. 648–652) with the powers of the President (pp. 398–411) and answer the following questions:

● **What powers does the President have that governors do not have?** (Powers related to foreign affairs.) **Do governors have any powers that the President does not have?** (The power to stop an execution for a state crime.) **Why is the veto a more powerful tool for many governors than it is for the President?** (Many governors have item vetoes.)

---

peached. This process parallels the system used by Congress to remove federal officials. Governors are impeached by the lower house of the state legislature and tried by the state senate. The last governor to be removed by impeachment was Evan Mecham of Arizona in 1988.

In fifteen states, governors may be recalled by the voters (page 645). Only one governor has ever been recalled — Lynn J. Frazier of North Dakota in 1921.

3A, 3B

The Governor's Powers

State constitutions outline the governor's major powers, while other powers derive from statutes and custom. The legislative and judicial branches of state government generally have some checks on the governor's powers.

Executive powers

The executive powers give the governor the authority to carry out state law and manage the state government.

Often the most powerful governors are those of the largest states. George W. Bush, elected governor of Texas in 1994, is the son of a President and grandson of a U.S. Senator.

648

APPOINTMENT POWER Governors must have dependable, trustworthy administrators and assistants to carry out their policies. Every state gives its governor the power to appoint staff members, department heads, and members of various state commissions.

There are limits on the appointment power. Major appointments in nearly every state require approval of the state senate. In addition, many high-ranking state administrators — such as lieutenant governor, secretary of state, and attorney general — are elected independently of the governor. Thus, the governor often has no formal control over the choice of his or her most important assistants.

State laws place other constraints on the appointment power. For example, many commissions and boards appointed by the governor are required by law to have bipartisan membership. The governor must, therefore, appoint some members of the other party.

Most states also have some form of merit system (page 438). This means that civil servants are hired and promoted on the basis of competence, not chosen by the governor.

REMOVAL POWER Sometimes subordinates ignore or defy a governor's orders. It has long been argued that governors, like the President, should be able to remove any person they appoint. This is not always the case. Most states allow the governor to remove appointed officials only for specific actions spelled out in law. Others require the state senate to approve of any removal by the governor.

COMMANDER-IN-CHIEF Every governor is the commander-in-chief of the state militia, or National Guard. Governors often call the National Guard into service during state emergencies — for instance, to help flood victims, to bring water to drought-stricken areas, or to break up riots. Many state governors also direct the state police or highway patrol.

The governor's control of the National Guard may come into conflict with the President's power to "nationalize" the militia. This happened on several occasions during the civil rights movement. Under a 1986 law, the President can mobilize the National Guard for training missions outside the country even if the governor objects.

BUDGET-MAKING The budget shows the state's priorities in carrying out public policy by

---

Background: *History* Frazier (column 1, par. 1) was recalled in a special election because of controversial state bank policies. It was only a temporary setback, however; he went on to win three terms in the U.S. Senate.

Background: *Controversial Issues* The 1986 law concerning the National Guard was a response to efforts by some governors to prevent the deployment of National Guard troops in Latin America for training exercises. In 1990 the Supreme Court unanimously upheld the 1986 law in the case *Perpich v. Department of Defense.*

Interacting with Government

6D

Most people your age are gradually becoming less dependent on their parents. You may already have learned to drive, found a job, bought a car, or otherwise begun to prepare yourself for life as an adult. If so, you may be aware of certain government requirements associated with driving, working, and other activities. You are responsible for following these laws.

All drivers must have a state driver's license. To get a license, you must pass certain tests, usually a written test on the "rules of the road" and an actual driving test. You can get information about tests and licenses from your state's motor vehicle department or from your school if it offers a course in driver education. When you sign your driver's license, you are making a contract with the government. You promise to obey all state laws, and the state allows you to drive on state roads.

Most likely, you already have a social security number. Anyone who works must have one, and as of 1991, anyone over 1 year old who is claimed as a dependent on a parent or guardian's tax form must have one. Social security is basically an insurance policy to provide money for people whose earnings have been reduced because of retirement, death, or disability. For information about social security, look in the U.S. Government pages of your telephone book for the number of the Social Security Administration (perhaps listed under Department of Health and Human Services in older directories). If there is no local listing, write to Office of Public Inquiry, Social Security Administration, 6401 Security Blvd., Baltimore, MD 20235.

One more important law affecting teenagers is draft registration. All male U.S. citizens and most resident aliens (non-U.S. citizens) between the ages of 18 and 26 must be registered with the Selective Service System. You must register within 30 days of your eighteenth birthday. Registration forms are available at U.S. post offices and at U.S. embassies in foreign countries. Penalties for not registering may be severe. For more information, you can write to this address: Public Affairs, Selective Service System, 1023 31st St. N.W., Washington, D.C. 20435.

Follow-up

1. Find the address of your state's motor vehicle department. Write a business letter to the department, requesting a copy of the state's motor vehicle laws.
2. Discuss with your classmates personal experiences with obtaining a driver's license or social security number. If you do not have a driver's license or social security number, how would you go about getting one?

CITIZENSHIP SKILLS

649

CITIZENSHIP SKILLS

Values

▲ CRITICAL THINKING **Why do states require that all drivers be licensed?** (Passing the tests shows that a driver can safely operate a vehicle and knows state driving regulations.)

● CRITICAL THINKING **How would you respond to the argument that since state roads are built with taxpayer dollars, each taxpayer has the right to use them, regardless of whether he or she has a license?** (Most students should respond that no one should have the right to do something that endangers the lives of others.)

Civic Participation

Mention to students that failing to register for the draft carries a stiff penalty: the maximum is five years in prison and a $10,000 fine.

▲ CRITICAL THINKING You might ask students for their opinion about Selective Service registration.

● Have students complete **Citizenship Worksheet 9,** which quizzes students on interacting with the government.

Follow-up Answers
1. Those laws might serve as the basis of a class discussion.

2. You might want to remind students that the Social Security Administration used to be part of the Department of Health and Human Services and is now an independent agency.

The symbol ⅱ denotes active participation strategies.

Activities are keyed for student abilities:
▲ = Basic
● = All Levels
■ = Average/Advanced

■■
▮ Controversial Issues
● Have students write the transcript of an imaginary debate between a governor and a member of the state legislature over the issue of the governor's item veto. The governor should defend the item veto, arguing that it is a useful tool for controlling state spending. The legislator should criticize the veto as an unfair limitation on the legislature's "power of the purse." Students may, if they wish, discuss the item veto for non-appropriation bills or refer to specific spending issues affected by the item veto.

deciding how much money each state agency and program will get. In 42 states, the governor has complete responsibility for preparing the budget and so has an important voice in setting the state's priorities. (State budget-making is detailed in Chapter 25.)

In other states, however, the governor's role is quite limited. Some governors must share budget-making duties with a state finance or budget director whom he or she has not appointed. In addition, state legislatures often cut or alter the governor's requests. In some states, such as Michigan, California, and Missouri, the constitution places restrictions on overall taxing and spending.

Legislative powers

Governors, like the President, also play a role in lawmaking. They may recommend legislation, call special sessions of the legislature, adjourn the legislature, and veto bills.

LEGISLATIVE PROPOSALS Governors often seek to fulfill promises made during their campaign by introducing legislation. Through their annual speeches before the legislature, such as the "state of the state" address and the yearly budget message, governors make their agenda known to state lawmakers. Such messages also arouse public awareness and spur legislators into action.

The governor's staff also work diligently, often in cooperation with legislators, to draft bills and suggest laws. Although only state legislators may formally introduce bills, it is no secret that many bills are introduced on behalf of the governor. Moreover, every keen legislator knows which are the "governor's bills."

SPECIAL SESSIONS In all fifty states the governor has the power to call the legislature into special session. Special sessions may be called to deal with emergency situations or to finish legislation left over from the regular session. In about one-third of the states, governors can determine what bills the legislature must consider.

VETO POWER The governor's most important legislative power is the veto, which prevents a bill from becoming law. The threat of a veto often enables a governor to prevent a bill from

Christine Todd Whitman of New Jersey was the only woman to be elected governor during the four-year period 1991–1994. Here she speaks to a delegate at a state NAACP convention.

650

Background: *Structure of Government* The governor has veto power in every state but North Carolina.

being passed. Legislators do not like to waste time on bills that have little chance of passing.

The veto is a more powerful tool for many governors than it is for the President of the United States. In 43 states, governors possess an item veto, sometimes called a line, or line-item, veto. An item veto allows the governor to strike a single provision (item, or line) from a bill while accepting the rest.

Item vetoes are almost always used for appropriations bills. The governor can thus eliminate money for a specific agency program while keeping the rest of the budget intact. About ten states also permit the governor to reduce appropriations. A few states allow their governors to strike items in any bill, not just an appropriation.

Governors have a "pocket veto" in fifteen states. In these states, if the legislature adjourns before the governor has acted on a bill, the bill is considered dead.

In most states, the legislature can pass a bill despite the governor's regular or item veto. (Pocket vetoes cannot be overridden.) Seven states have special "veto sessions" at the end of the regular session to consider overriding vetoes. Most state constitutions require a two-thirds or three-fifths vote in both houses to override a veto. If enough legislators vote to override the veto, the bill becomes law. (Fewer than 5 percent of all governors' vetoes are overridden.)

Judicial powers

Governors also have a number of judicial powers. For example, nearly one-fourth of all state judges are appointed by the governor. Additionally, most governors possess the power of granting **executive clemency**. Executive clemency is the governor's ability to reduce or end a convicted criminal's sentence. Governors of most states can grant reprieves, pardons (page 404), and parole (page 507) for state prisoners. They can also **commute**, or reduce, jail sentences — from life to 15 years, for example. Executive clemency is an especially significant power in the 36 states with the death penalty. (Only governors — not even the President — can stop an execution for a state crime.)

Decisions to grant pardons are often highly controversial. In many states, the governor shares this power with state boards or commis-

Douglas Wilder won Virginia's gubernatorial race in 1989 to become the first African American to be elected governor in U.S. history.

sions. Often the governor can grant executive clemency only with the recommendation or approval of such a board or commission.

The governor's informal roles

Besides their formal powers and duties in administering the state's government, governors have a number of other responsibilities. Much of a governor's time is taken up with ceremonial duties such as meeting foreign dignitaries, leading parades, attending state high school tournaments, cutting ribbons, and breaking ground for new buildings.

As ceremonial leaders, governors must be careful to project the right image. In 1985, Missouri Governor John Ashcroft faced a dilemma when two Missouri baseball teams — the St. Louis Cardinals and the Kansas City Royals — faced each other in the World Series. To avoid offending either side, Ashcroft wore a double-billed baseball cap with the Cardinals on one side and the Royals on the other.

The governor also serves as kind of a diplomat in dealing with other levels of government. At the local level, the governor often helps city and county officials in developing and carrying

GUIDED/INDEPENDENT PRACTICE

● Have students make a chart listing the powers of the governor. The chart should separate the governor's executive, legislative, and judicial powers and also list the governor's informal roles.

RETEACHING/CORRECTIVES

▲ Have students transform the three headings in this section into questions and then supply answers to the questions.

Have students complete **Skills Practice Worksheet 24,** which deals with the powers of the branches of state government.

ENRICHMENT/EXTENSION

■ Have students complete **Skills Challenge Worksheet 24,** which compares the high school graduation requirements of ten states.

out programs. Similarly, the governor works closely with governors of other states to deal with shared problems such as flood control, pollution, and law enforcement. Governors also lobby Congress to see that their state gets its fair share of federal funds for education, highways, social services, and defense contracts. Recently, many governors have traveled abroad to generate interest about their state among foreign businesses and tourists.

Governors are usually the leaders of their state political party. They campaign for local candidates, help with fundraising, and work closely with their party's legislative leaders. The governor is also a leader of public opinion. His or her actions are front-page news, and public appearances usually make the evening television news. Such media coverage enables the governor to bring statewide attention to pressing problems and to marshal public support for his or her policies and programs.

3A

Other Executive Officers

The governor is the only elected member of the executive branch in three states — Maine, New Jersey, and Tennessee. In the other 47 states, the governor shares the administration of government with other independently elected officials.

Among the most important state executive officials are the so-called "constitutional officers" — lieutenant governor, attorney general, secretary of state, treasurer, auditor, comptroller, and superintendent of education. These officers are called "constitutional" because their positions are usually established by state constitutions.

Attorney general

Every state has an **attorney general**, who is the state's chief lawyer. He or she is elected in 43 states and appointed, usually by the governor, in the others. As lawyer for the state, the attorney general gives legal advice to the governor and represents the state in lawsuits — as the prosecutor in criminal cases and as the defense attorney in cases against the state. In some states the attorney general is responsible for supervising statewide law-enforcement efforts.

March Fong Eu was elected California secretary of state five times. She served from 1975 to 1993.

In addition, attorneys general often render **advisory opinions**. An advisory opinion is a judgment whether a planned action conforms to the state constitution or state law. For instance, the governor may wish to fire a state official but wonders if the action is legal. He or she may ask the attorney general for an advisory opinion. The attorney general's ruling serves as a guideline and is considered law unless overruled by the courts.

Secretary of state

All but three states — Alaska, Hawaii, and Utah — have a secretary of state. He or she is elected in 36 states, appointed by the governor in eight, and chosen by the legislature in three. The secretary of state is, in essence, the chief clerk and record-keeper for the state. Duties com-

Background: *Global Awareness* Although it is not a state, Puerto Rico is a self-governing commonwealth voluntarily associated with the United States. It has a popularly elected Legislative Assembly and governor who appoints his or her executive officers. Puerto Rico also has a supreme court and an elected resident commissioner to the U.S. House of Representatives, who has a voice but no vote.

Check for Understanding
● *Does a state secretary of state perform the same functions as the U.S. secretary of state?* (No.)

monly include overseeing voter registration, preparing state ballots, supervising elections, certifying election results, verifying petition drives, maintaining state records, issuing corporation charters, and keeping the state's "Great Seal" — the state symbol that is affixed to official documents. In some states, the secretary of state also handles motor vehicle registration.

Finance officials

The state treasurer is the custodian of the state's money. He or she collects and invests state revenues, dispenses payroll checks to state employees, and pays the state's bills. In essence, the treasurer is the state's banker. The treasurer is elected in 38 states and appointed, either by the governor or the legislature, in the others.

At the end of each budget year, the **auditor** reviews the records of each agency and department to ensure it has used its allotted budget according to law. Auditors are independently elected in about half the states; they come under the jurisdiction of the legislature in others. Experts generally agree that auditors should be elected apart from either the legislature or the governor, so that they will be free from partisan politics and able to make unbiased judgments.

Many states also have a **comptroller**, or controller. In ten states, this official is elected. Whereas auditors normally check the books after funds have been spent, comptrollers keep track of funds *while* they are being spent. Today, more than half the states have both an auditor and a comptroller.

Superintendent of education

Each state has a chief school administrator, commonly called the superintendent of education, superintendent of public instruction, or commissioner of education. In sixteen states, the superintendent is elected. In the remaining states, either the governor or the state board of education appoints the superintendent. His or her main function is to administer state education laws regarding courses of instruction, requirements for graduation, textbook selection, teacher qualifications, and educational testing.

The governor's staff

In addition to the state constitutional officers, all governors need a staff to assist them.

Staff duties include answering letters, screening phone calls, drafting speeches, preparing budgets, reviewing bills for signature, and keeping track of the governor's busy schedule.

Perhaps the two most important qualities a staff member must have are loyalty and competence. Many staff members are picked from the governor's campaign team. These people naturally share the governor's views on issues and tend to be very loyal. Campaign experience, however, may not be enough. Governors also need people who have training in law, journalism, public relations, economics, or agriculture.

Staff sizes differ from state to state. Usually, the more populous the state, the larger the staff. In small states, the staff might consist of an administrative assistant and a few secretaries. In large states, such as New York or California, it is not uncommon to see a staff of a hundred or more. A "typical" staff might include administrative assistants, a press secretary, a receptionist, secretaries, legislative advisers, legal counselors, and file clerks.

SECTION 3 REVIEW

Vocabulary and key terms

executive clemency (651)   advisory opinion (652)
commute (651)   auditor (653)
constitutional officer (652)   comptroller (653)
attorney general (652)

For review

1. What are the governor's main executive powers? **3A**
2. How do governors use the item veto? **3B**
3. What are the duties of the lieutenant governor? **3A**
4. Briefly describe the duties of the (a) attorney general, (b) secretary of state, (c) comptroller, (d) auditor. **3A**

Critical thinking

DRAWING INFERENCES   How might the independent election of constitutional officers make the governor's job more difficult? In what ways might it make for better state government? **3B**

653

SECTION 4

State Court Systems
Interpret State Law
(pp. 654–659)

Section Objectives

☐ describe the different levels of state courts

☐ explain how state judges are selected and removed

Vocabulary

justice of the peace, magistrate, municipal court, small claims court, will, probate, juvenile court, domestic relations court, court of record, Missouri Plan

FOCUS

● Ask if any students have seen the television program, *The People's Court.* Ask students familiar with the program to explain how it works and the kinds of cases that appear on it. Tell students that it represents small-claims court, one of the kinds of state courts described in this section.

State Court Systems Interpret State Law

ACCESS The Main Ideas

1 What are the different levels of state courts? *pages 654–657*

2 How are state judges selected and removed? *pages 657–659*

What do the following situations have in common? A husband and wife agree to get a divorce, but cannot agree on how to divide their property and which parent shall have custody of their child. A man convicted of robbery believes that the judge in his trial was not impartial. One tenant in an apartment building insists on playing her stereo at top volume, night and day.

All of these situations could involve the state courts. Each state has its own court system, and together the state courts handle some 90 million cases yearly. By contrast, the federal courts only hear roughly 250,000 cases each year. State courts have jurisdiction over questions involving the state constitution, state laws, and local ordinances.

3A, 6D, 6E, 6I

State Court Organization

Like snowflakes, no two state court systems are exactly alike. Some states have few courts, while others have so many courts that they nearly defy classification. Still, it is possible to divide most state court systems into four basic levels: (1) minor courts, (2) major trial courts, (3) intermediate courts of appeal, and (4) state supreme courts.

Minor courts

Minor courts handle the state's least serious cases. Their jurisdiction typically is limited to misdemeanor cases (especially traffic and parking violations) and civil suits involving less than $1,000. Generally, minor courts are staffed by a single judge, lawyers are not present, and few formal rules are observed. The judge usually disposes of cases quickly, although decisions may sometimes be appealed to a higher court.

654

JUSTICE OF THE PEACE A **justice of the peace** (called a *squire* in some places) is a minor court official in many small towns and rural areas. Justices of the peace, or "JPs," typically handle minor civil and criminal cases, such as disturbing the peace and speeding. They also may perform marriage ceremonies, issue search warrants, and conduct preliminary hearings.

Most JPs are elected by the citizens in their area and serve only on a part-time basis. They may lack formal legal training and are often paid by the case or receive a portion of the fines they collect. The office has been the target of judicial reform. Many states now have training schools for JPs, and a few require them to be lawyers. Some states have replaced the fee system with salaries. Many states have eliminated the position altogether. Only about half the states still have justices of the peace.

MAGISTRATE COURT Magistrate courts, sometimes called *police courts,* are found mainly in urban areas. Their chief officer, the **magistrate**, is roughly the city equivalent of a justice of the peace. Magistrate courts handle a city's minor civil and criminal cases, mostly traffic cases. Like JPs, many magistrates are not well trained in the law.

MUNICIPAL COURT In many states, magistrates and justices of the peace have been replaced by **municipal courts**. These courts are established by a city or a town to enforce local ordinances — laws passed by city and town councils. Most municipal court time is taken up handling misdemeanors, particularly parking violations, speeding tickets, disturbing the peace, and public intoxication. Municipal courts are often overcrowded. To accommodate as many persons as possible, many hold sessions at night and so are known as "night courts."

SMALL CLAIMS COURT Civil cases involving relatively small sums, usually under $1,000, are heard in **small claims courts**. Most cases heard in small claims court fall into one of three categories — tenant-landlord claims, vehicle damage suits, and unpaid accounts. Other cases might

Background: *Law* Small claims courts hear a wide variety of cases. For instance, a boy sued his mother for $100 in babysitting fees. A former pizza shop owner sued the new owner, claiming the new owner reneged on a deal to provide him with 150 pizzas a week. One woman sued her former fiancé for all the collect calls he had made to her residence; he countersued for the engagement ring.

involve disputes over an engagement ring, a run-away pet, or a garden fence.

There are generally no formal rules of procedure in small claims courts. Each side presents its evidence and witnesses, in most cases without the help of a lawyer. (Some states, in fact, prohibit lawyers from appearing in small claims courts.) There is no jury. After questioning both sides, the judge renders a decision. The entire process usually takes less than 30 minutes. (The Citizenship Skills lesson on page 501 discusses bringing a case to small claims court.)

PROBATE COURT To direct what they want done with their property after they die, people make out a legal document known as a **will**. Although most wills go uncontested, heirs or creditors sometimes question the authenticity of a will or dispute its provisions. Some state courts, therefore, specialize in **probate**, verifying the validity of a will. Besides settling inheritances, probate courts also choose guardians for orphans and oversee the management of estates (property, bank accounts, investments).

JUVENILE COURT Cases involving persons under 18 years old go to **juvenile courts**. These courts are not designed to punish but to provide guidance and rehabilitation for young persons in need of education, care, or protection. Cases heard in juvenile courts typically involve children who are habitually truant from school, exhibit criminal tendencies, or have been physically or emotionally abused. Juveniles who continually run afoul of the law may be sent to reform school, or in rare cases may be tried as adults in regular courts. (The figure on page 499 outlines juvenile court procedures.)

DOMESTIC RELATIONS COURT The **domestic relations courts**, or *family courts,* settle disputes among husbands, wives, children, and other family members. The bulk of their cases concern divorce settlements and reconciliations. They may also deal with adoptions, child support, and neglected children. In some respects, domestic relations courts resemble counseling centers more than courts.

Appealing minor court decisions

Decisions in minor courts are almost always final. Nevertheless, either party can usually appeal to a higher court. Minor courts are not **courts of record**; that is, there are no written transcripts, or records, of the proceedings. When a minor court case is appealed, an entirely new trial must be held, as if the minor court trial had never happened. Because of this right to a new trial, it is constitutionally permissible for minor courts to skip some guarantees of procedural due process, such as the right to an attorney or a jury trial.

Major trial courts

Most cases related to state constitutions, statutes, and common law are heard in the major trial courts. The courtrooms seen in television dramas, for example, are usually state trial courts. Civil cases (involving more than $1,000) and felony cases (such as murder, rape, or robbery) are heard in these courts.

There are roughly 1,500 major trial courts throughout the fifty states. These courts usually serve two or more counties and are located in a major city or a county seat. They have many different names: "district courts," "circuit courts," "county courts," or "superior courts." They are called "courts of common pleas" in Pennsylvania and Ohio, "trial courts" in Massachusetts, and "supreme courts" in New York.

Disputes between neighbors over barking dogs or property lines are among the kinds of cases that may be heard in small claims courts.

EXPLANATION
After reviewing the content of the section, you may want to consider the following activities:

 Values

● Conduct a class debate on the topic of juvenile justice, centering on the following questions: *Should courts treat juveniles any differently than adults? Why or why not?* Factors to consider include the effectiveness of punishment in deterring future crime; the potential danger of exposing juveniles to older, "hardened" criminals; the question of the age at which persons should be held accountable for their actions; the role of the family and/or state agencies in reforming juveniles.

Background: *Cultural Literacy* The retrial of a minor court case is termed *de novo,* which means "anew."

The symbol denotes active participation strategies.

Activities are keyed for student abilities:
▲ = Basic
● = All Levels
■ = Average/Advanced

Law

Use the following questions to review the concept of appeal:

▲ *What is an appeal?* (A request made by the losing side in a court case for a reconsideration of the decision.)

▲ *Can minor court decisions be appealed?* (Yes, usually.) *What happens if an appeal is granted?* (An entirely new trial begins.)

▲ *On what grounds might an appellate court reverse a lower court's decision?* (If it decided that the lower court did not apply the law correctly.) *What is the highest appellate court in a state?* (The state supreme court.)

● CRITICAL THINKING *What might account for the fact that few minor court decisions are appealed?* (Many minor court decisions involve only small sums of money.)

Global Awareness

▲ *Does every country grant its citizens the right of appeal?* (No.)

● CRITICAL THINKING *Why might this not be a universal right?* (The right of appeal may not be traditional in some societies; an authoritarian regime may deny its citizens the right of appeal in order to keep tighter control of the populace; court costs in some countries may be too high to sustain an appeals process.)

Unless overruled by the U.S. Supreme Court, the state supreme courts have the ultimate authority to decide questions of state constitutional law. This picture shows the Idaho supreme court building.

Major trial courts differ from minor courts in three ways. First, judges in these courts generally are lawyers or have sound legal training. Second, major trial courts follow strict rules of procedure, with provisions for both grand jury hearings and trial juries. Finally, they are courts of record, where a court reporter records all proceedings word for word. These records can later be used for appeals.

Intermediate courts of appeals

Intermediate appellate courts, most commonly called "courts of appeals," are found in 37 states. Courts of appeals review cases decided by major trial courts and so reduce the workload of the state supreme court. A typical appellate court has five to seven judges, although some have many more.

Following a decision by a major trial court, the losing side may file an appeal with the appellate court. If the appeal is granted, lawyers for both sides present their case. They may offer oral arguments, written briefs, or both. Appellate courts do not decide questions of fact, consider new evidence, or hear witnesses. They determine only whether the lower court applied the law correctly. For example, an appellate court may find that inadmissible evidence was introduced, or that jurors were given the wrong instructions. Appellate courts can either uphold the lower court's decision, reverse it, or send the case back for a new trial. Their decisions are almost always final.

State supreme courts

Each state has a court of last resort, which makes final decisions on questions of state law. In most states, it is simply called the "supreme court." In New York and Maryland, however, it is called the "Court of Appeals." In Massachusetts and Maine, it is the "Supreme Judicial Court." In West Virginia, it is known as the "Supreme Court of Appeals." The number of supreme court judges varies, from three to nine. Texas and Oklahoma have two supreme courts — one to rule on criminal law and one to rule on civil law.

State supreme courts are headed by a chief justice, who presides over the court much as the

656

Check for Understanding
● *What is the difference between a state supreme court and the U.S. Supreme Court?* (State supreme courts are the final arbiters of *state* law; the Supreme Court is the court of last resort on questions of *federal* law, that is, the Constitution.)

Chief Justice of the United States presides over the Supreme Court. Most state supreme courts hear cases *en banc,* meaning all the justices sit together. In some states, judges divide up the cases to reduce the workload.

State supreme court rulings are final. This court is the ultimate voice on the state constitution and state laws. Decisions are made by majority vote among the judges. In some states, the supreme court is also required to give advisory opinions on pending legislation at the request of the legislature or the governor.

3A, 3B, 6F

Selecting State Judges

Courts are no better than the judges who staff them. Judges preside over trials, supervise jury selection, grant or deny motions, interpret laws, and determine punishments.

Qualifications

Despite the important role of judges, many state constitutions are virtually silent about their qualifications. About half to two-thirds of the states mention nothing about U.S. citizenship, minimum residency requirements, or minimum age limits for judges. States that do set qualifications usually require a judge to be a U.S. citizen, a resident of the state for five years, and at least 30 years old.

State judges may not be required to have formal legal training. Many state constitutions say that judges must be "learned in the law," but this phrase is ambiguous. Some state supreme courts have interpreted this to mean a law degree, but only six states require all state judges to be lawyers. Because as many as half of all state judges are non-lawyers, many states provide legal training programs for judges.

Judicial terms

Judges serve different terms throughout the 50 states. Terms usually range from 2 to 15 years, with the most common being 6 years. In Massachusetts and New Hampshire, major trial judges may serve to age 70. Only in Rhode Island are trial court judges allowed to serve for life (unless removed for misbehavior). In general, the higher the court, the longer the term. That is, supreme court judges serve longer than trial court judges.

Compensation

Judges' salaries usually are set by state law. Salaries for municipal judges may be set by local ordinances following state guidelines. Some minor court judges are paid per case or by the hour. In Missouri, for example, some are paid $2.50 per case, while others are paid an hourly wage of $40.

On major trial courts and higher courts, judges are paid salaries. Annual salaries for major trial judges range from about $60,000 to $115,000. State supreme court judges receive the highest pay among state judges. Their salaries range from $60,000 to as high as $115,000 in a few states.

Selection of state judges

There are five basic methods of selecting state judges. Many of the states use a combination of these methods when it comes to selecting their judges.

APPOINTMENT BY THE GOVERNOR During the colonial period, most judges were appointed by the governor. Today only three states — Delaware, Massachusetts, and New Hampshire — give their governor exclusive power to appoint all state judges. In numerous states the governor may appoint some or all judges. The governor may only do so, however, if the state senate approves his or her recommendations.

YOU DECIDE

8H

A woman in Illinois told police that she had been assaulted by Edward Rodriguez in an apartment. She referred to it as "our" apartment, and said she had clothes and furniture there. The woman unlocked the door and gave the officers permission to enter. They found drugs and arrested Rodriguez. His attorney maintains that the evidence was illegally obtained because the woman had moved earlier and had no authority to consent to the officers' entry. **Is the evidence permissible?**

657

Depending on the state, judges can be appointed by the governor or the legislature or elected by the voters (inset). Here, new municipal judges in Austin, Texas, are being sworn in.

SELECTION BY THE LEGISLATURE   Three states — Connecticut, South Carolina, and Virginia — let the legislature appoint all state judges. In Rhode Island, appellate judges are selected by the legislature.

PARTISAN ELECTION   Thirteen states elect some or all of their judges on partisan ballots. To become a judge in these states, a candidate must first receive his or her political party's nomination, usually in a primary election. The nominees then meet in the general election like other political candidates.

NONPARTISAN ELECTION   By far the most common method of selecting state judges is by nonpartisan ballot. Nineteen states currently employ nonpartisan elections to choose some or all of their state judges. Under this plan, judges' names appear on the ballot without party labels. This method makes judicial selection less political but favors candidates who are well known in the community.

MISSOURI PLAN   The **Missouri Plan** for selecting state judges combines appointment by the governor with popular election. Sponsored by the American Bar Association, this plan was first used in California in 1934. It did not gain national attention until it was adopted by Missouri in 1940. A dozen states now employ the Missouri Plan to select some or all judges.

Under the Missouri Plan, judicial candidates are first screened by a nonpartisan commission. The commission typically consists of lawyers, private citizens, and a judge. The commission recommends its top prospects to the governor, who then picks one of them to be judge.

After one year, the newly appointed judge must be approved by a majority of the voters. The judge's name appears on the ballot without opposition, and voters are asked whether he or she should be retained in office. If a majority vote "yes," the judge is entitled to a full term. If the vote is "no," the judge is removed, and the process begins anew.

Each of these ways of choosing judges has drawbacks. Appointments by the governor or the legislature often reflect political considerations rather than judges' competence. Although popular elections appear most democratic, there is some doubt whether voters are fully aware of judges' qualifications. Moreover, popularly elected judges may let public opinion and the desire for re-election affect their decisions.

658

Removal of judges

While most state judges are conscientious and reliable public servants, some (as in any profession) may be incompetent or dishonest. There are several methods for removing such judges from their jobs. Judges can be defeated at the polls, either in a regular or Missouri Plan election. In five states, they can also be recalled. In most states, judges can be impeached.

Most recently, many states have established disciplinary commissions and boards to oversee the behavior and actions of state judges. These bodies, often composed of lawyers, judges, and members of the general public, investigate alleged misconduct or incompetence, then recommend action to the state supreme court. The state supreme court can then suspend or remove the judge in question.

SECTION 4 REVIEW

Vocabulary and key terms

minor court (654)
justice of the peace (654)
magistrate (654)
municipal court (654)
small claims court (654)
will (655)
probate (655)
juvenile court (655)
domestic relations
court (655)
court of record (655)
Missouri Plan (658)

For review

1. What is the function of (a) small claims, (b) probate, (c) juvenile, and (d) domestic relations courts? **3A**
2. Why are minor courts allowed to skip formal rules of procedure? **6E**
3. What types of cases are heard in state major trial courts? **3A**
4. What is the role of the state supreme courts? **3A**
5. What are the five basic methods of selecting state judges? **6F**

Critical thinking

ORGANIZING AN ARGUMENT What are the advantages and disadvantages of popular election of state judges? How do these compare with the advantages and disadvantages of other methods of selecting judges? **6F**

Chapter Summary

Every state has a constitution, which embodies its fundamental law. Each contains a preamble, a bill of rights, and a body of articles. State constitutions can be amended by legislative proposals, initiatives from the voters, constitutional conventions, or commissions. In most cases, amendments must be ratified by a majority of the voters. State constitutions have been criticized for being too long, detailed, and restrictive. Those that are easy to amend may be targets for interest groups.

The legislature makes laws for the state. All states but Nebraska have bicameral legislatures. All seats in both houses must be apportioned according to population. Most legislatures meet yearly for a specified time. Each chamber has its presiding officers and committees, with interim committees to meet when the legislature is not in session. Bills must pass both houses in identical form, and be signed by the governor, to become law. Many states allow citizens to propose laws directly through the referendum and initiative, and to remove officials by recall.

The governor is the chief executive of the state. Governors have executive, legislative, and judicial powers. The item veto allows the governor to reject single parts of bills, and executive clemency gives him or her the power to reduce the sentences of convicted criminals. If the office becomes vacant, the lieutenant governor succeeds in most states. Other elected officials also help the governor carry out state policies.

Each state also has a judiciary to settle disputes and interpret state law. Justices of the peace and magistrates handle minor civil cases and misdemeanors, while other minor courts hear specific types of cases. Minor courts are not courts of record; if their decisions are appealed, a new trial must be held. Major trial courts hear felony cases or civil suits involving large sums. Their decisions can be appealed to intermediate appeals courts, and the state supreme courts have the final word on questions of state law. Judges typically serve for fixed terms. They can be appointed by the governor or the legislature, elected by partisan or nonpartisan ballot, or chosen by the Missouri Plan.

Section 4 Review Answers

1. **(a)** To hear civil cases involving small sums of money. **(b)** To verify the validity of wills. **(c)** To try cases involving persons under the age of 18. **(d)** To settle family disputes.
2. Because if the case is appealed, an entirely new trial is held.
3. Cases related to state constitutions, statutes, and common law.
4. They are courts of last resort that make final decisions on questions of state law.
5. Appointment by the governor, selection by the legislature, bipartisan election, nonpartisan election, the Missouri Plan.

Critical thinking Students should note that popular election gives citizens the power to select judges but may prevent lesser-known candidates from winning elections. Students can then compare popular election with other methods, discussing the role public opinion plays in an election and the effect political pressure can have on a governor who appoints judges.

CLOSURE

● Have students outline the section. Then have students read the next assigned lesson.

CHAPTER 24 CORRECTIVES

● To review the content of Chapter 24, you may want to have students complete **Study Guide/Review 24** or **Workbook Chapter 24**.

Background: *Law* A California case raised many questions about the popular election of judges. Voters chose not to reconfirm Chief Justice Rose Bird at the polls in 1986. Her opponents raised $5 million to defeat her, charging she was "soft" on crime. (Bird had overturned all 61 death sentences that had come before her.) Her supporters argued that qualifications and competency—not unpopular decisions—should be the standard against which judges are measured.

Answers

Vocabulary See pp. T19–T21 for suggested vocabulary activities.

Reviewing the Facts

1. Bill of rights.
2. They are too long and too detailed; they are often poorly and confusingly written; and many are too easy to amend, thus becoming targets for interest groups seeking special treatment.
3. Referendum, initiative, recall.
4. Governors may be impeached in every state except Oregon, and in fifteen states may be recalled. They may also be defeated at the polls.
5. Lieutenant governor, attorney general, secretary of state, treasurer, auditor, comptroller, and superintendent of education.
6. The state's supreme court.
7. Depending on the state, judges may be defeated at the polls, recalled, or impeached.

● **Review the definitions of the following terms:**

advisory opinion	executive clemency	pre-file
attorney general	indirect initiative	probate
auditor	initiative	recall
commute	justice of the peace	referendum
comptroller	juvenile court	*Reynolds v. Sims*
constitutional officer	magistrate	schedule
court of record	minor court	small claims court
direct initiative	Missouri Plan	will
domestic relations court	municipal court	

● **REVIEWING THE FACTS**

1. Which part of a state constitution contains a list of the fundamental liberties guaranteed to citizens? **6H**
2. What are some common weaknesses of state constitutions, according to constitutional scholars? **6H**
3. What are the three basic tools that allow citizens to participate directly in the making of state laws? **6C**
4. How may governors be removed from office? **3B**
5. Who are the seven "constitutional officers" of a state's executive branch? **3A**
6. What is a state's court of last resort? **3A**
7. How may judges be removed from their jobs? **3B**

▲ **THINKING CRITICALLY ABOUT KEY CONCEPTS**

1. Explain why the issue of redistricting is (a) important, and (b) controversial. **6F**
2. Give one argument supporting, and one argument opposing, the governor's item veto. **3B**
3. Why might some states prohibit lawyers from appearing in small claims court? **6E**

▲ **PRACTICING SKILLS**

1. **Study Skills: Reading a chart.** Refer to Figure 24–2 (page 642) to answer the following questions. (a) Are the basic steps in the passage of a bill the same in the upper and lower houses? (b) Is a bill revised before or after it is referred to a standing committee? (c) Which step in the process involves both houses? (d) Which branch of government is involved in the final step of a bill's becoming law? **8B**
2. **Study Skills: Analyzing a photograph.** Look at the photographs on page 644. Why did supporters of Proposition 13 include such slogans as "Save the American Dream" and "Don't Take It, Do Something" on their signs, rather than simply stating, "Vote Yes on 13"? **8B**
3. **Critical Thinking Skills: Distinguishing fact from opinion.** Refer to the third paragraph in the subsection "Recall" (page 645). Determine whether each of the following statements is a fact or an opinion. (a) The referendum, initiative, and recall have stirred much debate. (b) These methods of removing officials represent the purest form of democracy. (c) Direct legislation undermines confidence in elected officials and confuses the public. (d) It usually takes a well-funded group to get such issues on the ballot. **8D**

Thinking Critically About Key Concepts

1. **(a)** How a state draws its legislative boundaries will help determine which party and which interest groups control the legislature and thereby affect the flow of state funds to different parts of the state. **(b)** People in rural areas fear a loss of influence to urban areas; also, the minority party fears a loss of influence to the majority party.

2. *Supporting*—It allows the governor to eliminate unnecessary spending without rejecting the entire budget. *Opposing*—It undermines the legislature's authority over spending.

▲ PARTICIPATORY CITIZENSHIP

1. **Creating a petition.** The referendum, initiative, and recall processes all start with the circulation of a petition. Think of an issue, either real or fictional, that might cause you to begin a petition drive. Create a petition that expresses the change you would like to make. You may wish to research the proper form of a petition before you create your own. Circulate your completed petition among friends and relatives. What would be the next steps in the process? **4A**

2. **Contacting your representative.** Write a letter that you might send to your state representative or senator to ask for information about recent initiatives or referenda in your state (if any). Find out the issue and outcome in each case. **4B**

■ WRITING ABOUT ISSUES

1. **Composing a speech.** Review the "informal" requirements for the office of governor listed on page 646. Then imagine that you are a candidate for governor and that you do not match most or all of these requirements. Write a speech arguing that voters should not consider your lack of these factors in deciding whom to support. **4A**

2. **Writing an essay.** Because states can write their own laws, laws may vary from state to state. Write an essay explaining why this is good or bad, for the country. **3C**

3. **Writing an editorial.** Write a newspaper editorial proposing that the pay of state legislators be tied to inflation—that is, it would rise automatically with the cost of living. Then write a letter opposing this idea. **4C**

▲ ANALYZING A POLITICAL CARTOON

During the early 1990's most states faced cutbacks in their education budgets because of higher costs and lower revenues. Look at the cartoon below, which discusses the situation in Tennessee during the governorship of Ned Ray McWherter and answer the following questions.

1. Who, according to the cartoon, is responsible for the school budget crisis? **8B**
2. What is the governor's goal? **8B**
3. How would you describe the cartoonist's view of the situation? **8D**

Bruce Plante/The Chattanooga Times.

661

Participatory Citizenship

1. The class as a whole might brainstorm to produce ideas for petitions. The next steps would be to obtain the necessary number of signatures and submit the petition either to be placed on the ballot or to the state legislature to be considered.

2. Students may already be aware of the titles and issues of some recent referendums.

Writing About Issues

1. Speeches should explain that the "informal" qualifications are not measures of fitness for office.

2. *Good*—Differences in laws reflect the differences among states. *Bad*—People will be encouraged to take advantage of states with more lenient laws.

3. Editorials should argue that this measure would make legislative pay less controversial. Letters should reply that pay should be tied to the health of the state's economy.

Analyzing a Political Cartoon

1. Governor McWherter.
2. To gain support for his legislative proposals.
3. The governor is manipulating the people for his own benefit.

---

3. This lowers the cost of bringing a suit, thereby giving common persons access to the legal system.

Practicing Skills

1. **(a)** Yes. **(b)** After. **(c)** The meeting of the conference committee. **(d)** The executive branch, when the governor signs or vetoes the bill.

2. Some voters might not know the issue covered by Proposition 13. Also, the slogan helps explain why voters should back the referendum.

3. **(a)** Fact. **(b)** Opinion. **(c)** Opinion. **(d)** Fact.

Chapter Review exercises are keyed for student abilities:
▲ = Basic
● = All Levels
■ = Average/Advanced

CHAPTER 25
STATE POLICIES AND FINANCES
(pp. 662–685)

	Section Objectives	Section Resources
Section 1 **The States Make Public Policy**	☐ explain how state characteristics affect state policies ☐ list the four categories of state policies	▲ PRIMARY SOURCE WORKSHEET **26**
Section 2 **The States Plan Their Spending**	☐ explain how state budgets are formulated ☐ explain how state spending has changed	▲ SKILLS PRACTICE WORKSHEET **25**
Section 3 **State Revenues Come from Many Sources**	☐ list the different taxes that states collect ☐ describe the other sources of revenue available to states	■ SKILLS CHALLENGE WORKSHEET **25** ▲ TRANSPARENCY **57**

Essential Elements

The list below shows Essential Elements relevant to this chapter. (The complete list of Essential Elements appears in the introductory pages of this Teacher's Edition.)

Section 1: 1A, 2E, 3A, 4A, 5C, 6C, 7C, 8F, 8H

Section 2: 3A, 3B, 4B, 7A, 7B

Civic Literacy feature (p. 675): 8F

Section 3: 3C, 6A, 6G, 7A, 7B, 7D

Chapter Review: 2E, 3A, 7B, 7C, 7D, 8B, 8C, 8F

> Section Resources are keyed for student abilities:
> ▲ = Basic
> ● = All Levels
> ■ = Average/Advanced

Homework Options

Each section contains activities labeled "Guided/Independent Practice," "Reteaching/Correctives," and "Enrichment/Extension." You may wish to choose from among these activities when assigning homework.

Students Acquiring English Activities

Divide the class into four groups and assign each group to be responsible for one of the following categories of state policy: education, public safety, public health and welfare, and regulation. Ask students to pretend that they work for an advertising agency and have been asked by their state government to create advertisements on state policies for industries interested in relocating to the state. Each group should concentrate on advertising information on the particular category of state policy to which that group has been assigned. Videotape the advertisements. Encourage the groups to make charts and use photos or diagrams to make their videos attractive.

LISTENING/SPEAKING: Have the class watch the videos and critique them.

Case Studies

When teaching this chapter, you may use Case Study 11, which examines the issue of gun control. (Case Studies may be found following p. 510.)

Teacher Bibliography

Bingham, Richard D. *State and Local Government in an Urban Society.* McGraw-Hill, 1986. Discusses the effect of the continued urbanization of the United States on the way state and local governments do business.

Gittell, Marilyn, ed. *State Politics and the New Federalism.* Longman, 1986. The shock wave of the shift in the federal attitude toward the states travels through state government.

Ransone, Coleman B., Jr. *The American Governorship.* Greenwood, 1982. An evaluation of the three functions of American governors: public relations, policy formation, and management.

Student Bibliography

Allen, James Paul and Eugene James Turner. *We the People: An Atlas of America's Ethnic Diversity.* Macmillan, 1987. A wide variety of information, including settlement patterns, is given on different ethnic, immigrant, and racial groups using text and colorful maps.

Ravitch, Diane. *The Schools We Deserve: Reflections on the Educational Crisis of Our Times.* Basic, 1985. A compendium of critical essays including such topics as tuition tax credits and the role of the government in education.

Szumski, Bonnie, ed. *America's Prisons: Opposing Viewpoints.* Greenhaven, 1985. A wide range of opinions on the types and effectiveness of prisons in the United States is presented.

CHAPTER RESOURCES

Study Guide/Review 25
Workbook Chapter 25
Chapter 25 Test, Forms A–C

Films and Videotapes*

State Government: Resurgence of Power. 21 minutes. EBEC, 1976. f, v. Outlines the changing roles of state governments as they take on responsibilities once reserved for the federal government.

Software*

PC USA (IBM). PC Globe. An "electronic atlas" with information on the political demographics of the 50 states and Puerto Rico. The program includes information on the states in nineteen separate categories, including population, age distribution, ethnic groups, average annual pay, and crime statistics.

---

* For a complete guide to audiovisual sources, see page T22.

CHAPTER 25

State Policies and Finances *(pp. 662–685)*

This chapter explores the factors that influence state policies, the policies themselves, and how states spend and raise money.

Chapter Objectives
After students complete this chapter, they will be able to:

1. Explain how state characteristics affect state policies.
2. List the four categories of state policies.
3. Explain how state budgets are formulated.
4. Explain how state spending has changed.
5. List the different taxes that states collect.
6. Describe the other sources of revenue available to states.

CHAPTER
25

STATE POLICIES and FINANCES

. . . The debate about the proper role of government, which was lively at the time our Constitution was framed, has in fact become more vigorous today.

How much are we our brother and sister's keeper?

It is a question which we must ask of ourselves and then answer through our public policy decisions.

Governor Madeleine Kunin
Inaugural Address, 1985

Photo
Commencement ceremony, University of Wisconsin, Madison.

In West Virginia it is illegal to sneeze on a train. California's State Housing Act of 1923 forbids sleeping in the kitchen. In Oklahoma it is against the law to rob a bird's nest in a public cemetery. In Kansas you may not catch fish with your bare hands.

Some state laws are outdated, and a few — such as those listed above — even appear a bit silly. Yet they, like other actions by state governments, are attempts to ensure the well-being of state residents. From birth to death, the state we live in affects nearly every aspect of our lives. It is the states that keep birth certificates, issue marriage licenses, regulate divorces, supervise child support, and issue death certificates. State governments license drivers and register motor vehicles. It is the states that have the main responsibility for setting up our educational system. Finally, it is up to the states to raise most of the money needed to pay for these services.

This chapter describes how state governments make, finance, and carry out policies.

CHAPTER OUTLINE

1 The States Make Public Policy

State Characteristics
State Policies

2 The States Plan Their Spending

Making State Budgets
State Spending

3 State Revenues Come from Many Sources

State Taxes
Other Revenue Sources

SECTION 1

The States Make Public Policy (pp. 664–671)

Section Objectives
☐ explain how state characteristics affect state policies
☐ list the four categories of state policies

Vocabulary
density, urbanization, per capita income, highway patrol, corrections

FOCUS
● Students seldom think of state government as playing an important part in their lives. To focus their attention on state government, ask them to identify a service they have received from the state or contact they have had with a state employee. Examples include drivers' licenses, hunting or fishing licenses, state-maintained highways, and licensing of doctors or other professionals. Finish by reminding students of the most obvious example—state educational requirements.

The States Make Public Policy

> **ACCESS** The Main Ideas
>
> 1 What state characteristics affect state policies? *pages 664–668*
>
> 2 What are the four categories of state policies? *pages 668–671*

It is easy to understand why snow removal is a bigger issue in Minnesota than in Texas, or why more Vermonters than Floridians concern themselves with the health of the maple syrup industry. States differ in their geography, their population, their economic base, and their political make-up. State social and economic policies, which reflect each state's individual character, differ as well. In this section we will briefly look at some of the differences among the states and the different policy issues that arise out of each state's particular conditions.

2E, 5C

State Characteristics

Geography

The fifty states vary greatly in size, physical features, and climate. By far the largest state is Alaska, followed by Texas, California, and Montana. The smallest state is Rhode Island. Delaware, Connecticut, and Hawaii are the next smallest.

Twenty-four states have seacoasts, and eight border on the Great Lakes. In these states, shipping and fishing play vital economic roles. In other states mighty rivers, such as the Mississippi, Missouri, Ohio, and Colorado, provide both transportation and jobs. The vast plains of Kansas, Nebraska, and other midwestern states offer fertile land for farming and grazing livestock. Huge mountain ranges, like the Rockies and the Appalachians, furnish vital minerals as well as recreation for millions of Americans.

Part of Oregon, in the wet Pacific Northwest, gets from 60 to 120 inches of rain each year. By contrast, part of Arizona receives only about 3 inches. People living in Florida almost never see snow, while Minnesota averages 40 to 70 inches

every year. The chances of sunshine during the daytime are over 85 percent in Arizona but only about 53 percent in Illinois. Such physical differences influence a state's economy, agriculture, energy use, and its citizens' lifestyles.

Population

The United States' 260 million people are distributed unevenly throughout the country. California has the largest population, with over 31 million residents, followed by New York and Texas. Wyoming has the smallest population—with about 470,000 people. Vermont and Alaska are next smallest in population.

Perhaps a truer indication of a state's population is its **density** — the number of people concentrated in a given area. New Jersey is the most densely populated state, with about 1,000 persons per square mile, followed by Rhode Island, Massachusetts, and Connecticut. At the low end of the scale, Alaska averages less than one person per square mile. Of the 48 contiguous states, Wyoming has the fewest people per square mile — about 5. For the United States as a whole, there are about 70 persons per square mile.

An important trend in recent years has been a shift in population from the northeastern and midwestern "snowbelt" states to the western and southern states, popularly called the "sunbelt." In the 1970's, population in the South and West grew about 20 percent, while population in the Northeast and Midwest grew by less than 5 percent. This trend continued through the 1980's.

One reason for this change is that the sunbelt's warmer climate has attracted millions of people, particularly retired persons. Many businesses and industries have also relocated to the sunbelt to take advantage of cheaper land and energy, lower corporate taxes, and less unionization. In addition, the sunbelt states have encouraged the so-called "sunrise" industries — those involving new fields such as computers and aerospace technology. The snowbelt, on the other hand, has been tied to older industries, such as automobiles and steel, which depend on

664

Background: *Geography*
Density is a measure of the *average* number of people per square mile. Averaging is used because some areas of a state (i.e., cities) are much more heavily populated than other areas.

heavy raw materials, such as iron ore and coal. This regional migration has meant a loss of tax revenue and employment for the snowbelt. Economic growth in the sunbelt, meanwhile, has created a demand for new housing, electricity, roads, sewers, water, schools, police protection, and other necessities.

Another way of looking at a state's population is through its degree of **urbanization**. The Bureau of the Census defines urbanization as the percentage of a state's population living either in cities of more than 2,500 people or in the suburbs of cities of 50,000 or more. California, New Jersey, and Rhode Island, all with about 90 percent urban dwellers, rank highest in the country. The least urbanized states are Vermont and West Virginia, with roughly 35 percent of the population living in cities.

Policy issues in each state are also influenced by the ethnic, racial, and religious backgrounds of its people. For example, African Americans make up more than 25 percent of the population of Mississippi, South Carolina, Louisiana, Georgia, and Alabama. School integration and affirma-tive action are important issues in these states. Similarly, persons of Spanish origin make up a significant percentage of the population in New Mexico, Texas, California, Arizona, Colorado, and parts of Florida and New York. As a result, the issue of bilingual education has received a great deal of attention in these states.

Economics

The states also differ in their economic development. One way to measure a state's wealth is by **per capita income,** the average yearly income per person. In 1992, per capita income among all Americans was $20,139. This average varied considerably from state to state. Connecticut, at $26,979, topped the list, fol-lowed by New Jersey ($26,457) and Mas-sachusetts ($24,059). At the bottom end of the income scale were Mississippi ($14,088), West Virginia ($15,065), and Utah ($15,325). These figures must be considered in relation to the cost of living in the states. Although Connecti-cut and New Jersey have high per capita incomes, they are also expensive to live in.

Typical of the sunbelt states, Florida enjoys a warm climate and an expanding economy, which have brought a rapid rise in population.

665

Cross-reference
See Chapter 26, p. 699, for a graph depicting the growth of urban America.

Background: *Economics*
The comparatively low per capita incomes in Mississippi and West Virginia are due to the primarily rural economies in those states.

EXPLANATION
After reviewing the content of the section, you may want to consider the following activities:

👥 Geography

● Ask volunteers to point out the sunbelt and the snowbelt on a classroom map. Then ask:

▲ *Which of these regions has been growing more quickly in recent years?* (The sunbelt.) *Why?* (Many people are attracted to the sunbelt's warmer climate; busi-nesses want to take advantage of cheaper land and energy, lower taxes, and less unionization.) *How has this rapid growth affected the sunbelt?* (It has increased the demand for housing, electricity, roads, and police and other public services.)

● CRITICAL THINKING Ask students how the migration to the sunbelt has affected the make-up of Congress. (The sunbelt states have gained representatives in the House of Representatives at the expense of the snowbelt states.) Students can review these changes by studying Figure 12–2 on p. 339.

● If your state is part of the sunbelt or snowbelt, you might ask if students know of any current issues in your state relating to the population shift.

The symbol 👥 denotes active participation strategies.

Activities are keyed for student abilities:
▲ = Basic
● = All Levels
■ = Average/Advanced

Economics

The following questions could be used as the basis of class discussion or as subjects for student research:

■ *What are the largest revenue-producing industries in your state? Are they growing industries (e.g., high technology)? Are they dependent on uncontrollable conditions (e.g., farming, which is dependent on weather, or oil production, which is dependent on world oil prices)? Have imports hurt those industries (e.g., automobiles, shoes, or textiles)? Is your state economically dependent on the well-being of only one or two industries?*

Cultural Literacy

● Have students name public colleges and universities in your area. Ask if students have friends or family members who have attended these institutions and if any students plan to attend these institutions themselves.

The vast plains of Texas, which provide plentiful pasture land for grazing, are one reason why Texas leads the nation in cattle-raising. The livestock business is an essential part of the Texas economy.

The economic development of the states depends largely on the occupations of the people who live there. Michigan is the nation's automobile capital, for example, while Texas, Oklahoma, and Louisiana are rich in oil and natural gas. California is a leader in the computer and entertainment industries, while Massachusetts is a center for high technology. North Carolina is famous for textiles, Illinois for meat-packing, Pennsylvania for its steel and iron foundries, West Virginia for coal, and New York for banking.

Agriculture plays a major role in many states. Texas leads the nation in cattle and cotton. North Carolina is the largest producer of tobacco, while Kansas and North Dakota are the nation's leading wheat producers. Idaho is noted for its potatoes; Iowa and Illinois are synonymous with corn and hogs. Louisiana is known for soybeans, Wisconsin for dairy products, California and Florida for oranges, Oregon for timber, Washington for apples, Kentucky for thoroughbred horses, and Georgia for peanuts. The ups and downs of business and agriculture affect every state's income and employment levels.

Political forces

Each state has its own approach to American political culture — attitudes and beliefs concerning citizenship and government. People in Minnesota, for example, apparently place a high value on political participation, with consistently high voter turnout. In the 1992 presidential election, an estimated 70 percent of Minnesota voters turned out, compared with the national average of about 55 percent.

The degree of political party competition also varies among the states. For example, Massachusetts is considered a strongly Democratic state because the Democrats usually control the state legislature. Democrats used to dominate state elections in over twenty other states, but that number is probably decreasing due to increased competition from Republicans. Republicans are traditionally stronger in some states,

666

Critical Thinking
● *What does it mean when one party "controls" a state legislature?* (That the party has a solid majority and can thus influence legislation and state policies.)

CRITICAL THINKING
Predicting Consequences

Consider the following situation: Gloria needs to save $1,000 for her first college tuition payment, which is due in three months. She has already saved $200. From earnings at her summer job, she is able to place $50 in her savings account each week.

What might result from these circumstances? To answer this question, you need to predict consequences.

To predict consequences, you must draw on your own knowledge and experience. For instance, if you were to predict consequences from only the information given above, you might say that Gloria will not be able to meet her tuition requirement. If you draw on other information or on your own knowledge, however, you might predict that Gloria will try to increase her savings by reducing spending or that she will ask her parents for a loan.

★ ISSUE: Water Shortages

In the arid West, water is a key concern, and has been since the 1800's. Large-scale irrigation has made farming possible in areas that receive little rainfall. Rivers have been dammed and underground water sources called aquifers have been tapped on a massive scale. Yet in recent years some experts have warned that the West is using up its water far too quickly. A related problem is the buildup of salt in soil that is heavily irrigated. Most irrigation water contains small amounts of salts, which remain in the soil after the water has been absorbed or evaporated. In time the buildup of salt makes the soil less fertile.

Read the following excerpt from a book about the water issue and then answer the questions.

Cadillac Desert, by Marc Reisner

The vanishing groundwater in Texas, Kansas, Colorado, Oklahoma, New Mexico, and Nebraska is all part of the Ogallala aquifer, which holds two distinctions: one of being the largest discrete aquifer in the world, the other of being the fastest-disappearing aquifer in the world. This was the region called the Dust Bowl, the one devastated by the Great Drought; that was back before anyone knew there was so much water underfoot, and before the invention of the centrifugal pump. The prospect that a region so plagued by catastrophe could become rich and fertile was far too tantalizing to resist; the more irrigation, everyone thought, the better.

. . . In the portions of New Mexico that overlie the Ogallala, . . . some farmers withdraw as much as five feet of water a year, while nature puts back a quarter of an inch. What will happen to the economy of [New Mexico] when its major agricultural region turns to dust?

. . . Without Uncle Sam masquerading from the 1930s to the 1970s as a godfather of limitless ambition and means, the seven Ogallala states might never have chosen to exhaust their groundwater as precipitously as they have; they let themselves be convinced that the government would rescue them when the water ran out. . . . But now the desert is encroaching on the islands of green that have risen within it, . . . the government is broke, the cost of rescue is mind-boggling, and the rest of the country, its infrastructure in varying degrees of collapse, thinks the West has already had too much of a good thing.

. . . It was through the federal government that millions of acres of poorly drained land not only were opened to farming but were sold dirt-cheap water; the farmers flooded their fields with their cheap water and made the waterlogging and salt problems even worse; now that the lands are beginning to succumb to salt it looks as if the farmers will, in many cases, have to solve things on their own, and a lot of land that cost a fortune to bring into production is going to be left to die.

From Cadillac Desert *by Marc Reisner. © 1986 by Marc Reisner. Reprinted by permission of Viking Penguin, a division of Penguin Books USA Inc.*

Analyzing the Issue

1. What has been the consequence of irrigation on the Ogallala aquifer?
2. Why might the federal government be unable to solve the region's agricultural problems?
3. According to Reisner, how will farmers be affected by salt damage?
4. List three different possible consequences for western states of the growing water shortage.

CRITICAL THINKING

Cultural Literacy
Some of the terms in the selection may not be familiar to students, such as *discrete* (single, separate), *replenishment* (renewal), *centrifugal pump* (a pump that uses a rotating, propeller-like blade to create suction and draw fluid through a pipe), *precipitously* (rapidly), *infrastructure* (basic framework, e.g., roads and bridges).

● You might take this opportunity to discuss with students the use of context clues to understand unfamiliar terms.

Analyzing the Issue Answers
1. It has become the fastest-disappearing aquifer in the world.
2. The government encouraged large irrigation projects earlier, but now the government does not want to pay the cost of repairing the damage.
3. Lacking government help, they will be forced to stop farming some lands.
4. Western states will develop effective water conservation programs; new sources of fresh water will be found; the amount of land devoted to farming will substantially decrease.

The symbol ii denotes active participation strategies.

Activities are keyed for student abilities:
▲ = Basic
● = All Levels
■ = Average/Advanced

Civic Participation

● *Where are your state's parks? Do you know of any historical landmarks preserved by your state? Where are they?* (You might have students point out parks and landmarks on a wall map of your state.)

Cooperative Learning

● Divide the class into four groups and assign each group one of the following categories—geography, population, economics, and political forces. Have each group find out your state's characteristics in its assigned category and then suggest how these characteristics might affect policy in your state. (For example, the geography of Texas includes vast plains that are useful for cattle ranching. State policies are geared to aid ranchers.)

including Utah, New Hampshire, and Wyoming. Over twenty states are usually considered "two-party" states because the political influence of Democrats and Republicans is about even.

1A, 3A, 7C

State Policies

The great variety among the states is reflected in their policies. It would be impossible to list every state's policies. State policies can, however, be grouped into four basic categories: education, public safety, public health and welfare, and regulation. There is considerable overlap among these categories — environmental laws, for example, involve both public health and regulatory policies.

Educational policies

As early as 1785, land was set aside for public schools in new states. The Northwest Ordinance of 1787 stated: "Religion, morality, and knowledge being necessary to good government and the happiness of mankind, schools and the means for education shall be forever encouraged." Today, public education is the fundamental responsibility and the greatest expense of state governments.

State governments determine the overall educational policies under which local schools must operate. For example, states set the number of days students must attend school each year (usually 180). State laws determine teacher qualifications and salaries, minimum and maximum ages for public school children, and basic courses of instruction. States also impose limits on local school taxing, spending, and borrowing. Nearly all states require students to pass competency exams in mathematics and reading, and a number of states now test teacher competency as well. In most states, a superintendent of public education (page 653) sees that these policies are carried out.

Every state provides local schools with financial assistance to supplement local revenues. State policy-makers commonly try to balance funding among school districts within the state, giving poorer districts a higher proportion of state funds than wealthier ones. State funding can be used to influence standards in local school districts, because schools that fail to comply with state standards may lose essential funds.

In 1900, state governments supplied only 17 percent of public school spending in the nation as a whole. Local revenues supplied the

Supporting state-funded colleges and universities is one important goal of state government education policies. The University of Arizona at Tucson, for example, is one of several Arizona schools financed by state tax dollars.

Background: *History* The Northwest Ordinance (p. 44) provided for the government of the Old Northwest (the region east of the Mississippi and north of the Ohio River). The Ordinance set forth certain requirements that the territory (and all future territories) had to meet before applying for statehood. It also laid the foundation for social and political democracy in the West by prohibiting slavery, encouraging education, and protecting civil liberties.

rest. Today, states provide about half of total funding for U.S. elementary and secondary education; the federal government also contributes a small percentage (6 to 7 percent). The amount contributed within individual states, however, varies considerably. The highest percentages of state contributions are found in Hawaii (87.1 percent), New Mexico (73.5 percent), and Washington (70.8 percent). New Hampshire ranks lowest, contributing just 8.5 percent of funding for local schools.

Higher education

Recognizing the need for well-trained and highly educated citizens, all states provide aid to colleges and universities. Every state operates at least one state university. California leads the country with some 135 public colleges and universities.

Most states provide four types of public colleges. Many of these schools were originally created with the help of federal land grants. First, there are the "flagship" universities, prestigious institutions with high standards for admissions and impressive research facilities. Examples include Ohio State University (Columbus), the University of Texas (Austin), the University of Michigan (Ann Arbor), the University of Nebraska (Lincoln), and the University of California (Berkeley). Second are the agricultural and technical universities, such as Iowa State, Kansas State, and Texas A & M ("Agricultural and Mechanical"). Third, most states provide four-year teacher's colleges for general courses of instruction (though many of these have now become part of state university systems). Finally, many states have community colleges offering two-year programs in liberal arts or vocational training; students earn an associate degree. Students who complete two years at community college often transfer to four-year institutions to earn a bachelor's degree.

Public safety

State police play a vital role in carrying out the state's responsibility for protecting the general public. The first state police unit was the famous Texas Rangers, created as a border patrol in 1835. Other states did not establish state police units until the early 1900's, when the spread of automobiles made state police forces neces-

The Connecticut state trooper shown here uses a radio to patrol a state highway. The state police, or highway patrol, work to ensure safety on state roads and to enforce state laws.

sary. Local police and sheriffs' departments had neither the resources nor the authority to handle statewide highway travel.

To enforce traffic laws on the state's highways, every state (except Hawaii) has a state police force. It is commonly called the **highway patrol**. Some states also have special units to investigate arson and drug cases. Additionally, state crime labs often assist city and county local law-enforcement agencies in conducting ballistics (weapons) tests and analyzing blood and fingerprints.

Each state also maintains a **corrections** system, which includes several types of correctional institutions to handle persons convicted of state crimes. Depending on the seriousness of the crime, prisoners may be sent to "work farms," penitentiaries, or maximum-security prisons. Young offenders may go to "reform school" or "reformatories."

Building and maintaining highways is one of the state's most expensive responsibilities. Of the roughly 4 million miles of roadways across the United States, roughly 80 percent are state or

Cross-reference
Federal land-grant colleges are discussed in Chapter 21, p. 581.

Background: *Cultural Literacy* An associate degree signifies completion of two years of college work; a bachelor's degree indicates successful completion of four years of college work. The most common associate degrees are the Associate in Arts and the Associate in Science; the most common bachelor's degrees are the Bachelor of Arts and the Bachelor of Science.

● Have students bring to class articles that show state government policy decisions or actions in the areas of education, public safety, public health and welfare, and regulation. Ask students to summarize their articles for the class. Students could then use the assembled articles to make a bulletin-board display or a collage showing state government in action.

You might also want students to complete **Primary Source Worksheet 26,** which presents an excerpt from the Northwest Ordinance.

RETEACHING/CORRECTIVES

▲ Have students outline the material under the heading, "State Policies," listing under each subheading all the examples provided of that type of policy.

The symbol 👥 denotes active participation strategies.

Activities are keyed for student abilities:
▲ = Basic
● = All Levels
■ = Average/Advanced

ENRICHMENT/EXTENSION

■ Have students use the following statistics to construct a graph showing changes in population density in the United States since 1790.

Persons per square mile:	
1790:	4.5
1840:	9.8
1890:	21.2
1940:	44.2
1990:	70.3

Ask students to draw conclusions from the data, including the extent of the population density increase, the time period of the greatest increase, and the causes of the increase at different points in United States history.

local roads. Even federal highways — the U.S. and interstate highways — are built with the help of state contributions.

States also try to make their highways safe. All roadways must be carefully engineered and properly sloped. Traffic lights and highway signs control the speed and flow of cars and trucks, and state regulations set licensing and weight restrictions. State maintenance crews repair bridges, fill potholes, and remove snow.

Health and welfare

States promote their citizens' health in a variety of ways. State health authorities inspect food, monitor contagious diseases, issue quarantines, and require certain immunizations. Publicly supported hospitals and clinics provide emergency treatment, infant care, diagnostic testing, physical therapy, and treatment for the chronically ill and mentally disabled. State universities conduct research and train medical personnel. Nursing homes and hospices are subject to state standards. Finally, the states license health care professionals, including physicians, nurses, hygienists, chiropractors, psychologists, pharmacists, and physical therapists.

Recently the states have become concerned with environmental influences on public health. In conjunction with the federal Environmental Protection Agency (page 594), states monitor the use of pesticides and insecticides and test for water and air purity. The states must ensure a supply of safe water for homes, farms, and industry. In some parts of the country, they also must solve serious problems with scarce water resources. All states now regulate the disposal of toxic wastes and radioactive materials. Environmental standards in many states, such as Oregon and California, are tougher than those enforced by the EPA.

As Chapter 23 discusses, many federal assistance programs, such as AFDC and Medicaid, are joint federal-state programs. The states run the programs, determine who is eligible for benefits, and provide some of the funding. In addition, the states provide relief or welfare for needy persons, such as orphans or the homeless, who may not qualify for federal programs. Finally, many states now have "workfare" programs, in which able-bodied welfare recipients are required to perform some public service in exchange for their monthly benefits.

State agencies play an important role in emergency situations. Here, state workers clear a snow-bound highway to allow safe travel and to keep local businesses from closing.

670

Background: *Constitutional Heritage* Federal contributions are crucial to the construction of state highways and can be used as a bargaining tool by the federal government to change state policies, such as the legal drinking age.

8H

YOU DECIDE

A student at the University of Missouri, George Gruenewald, was evicted from his dormitory because he had displayed anti-Semitic messages in his window. Gruenewald was banned from living on campus based on university policy that prohibits "offensive decorations" outside of dorm rooms. Gruenewald insists, "I'm not anti-Semitic. The whole thing was a joke, and now it's blowing up in my face."

Is the university justified in evicting Gruenewald?

Conservation and recreation

As another way of ensuring people's welfare, states set aside public lands for both conservation and recreation. State forests and state parks preserve natural scenery and give people places to camp, hike, picnic, or enjoy water sports.

Most states have also preserved a number of important historical buildings and landmarks. Through universities and other institutions, states may establish museums, supply funds for music and art programs, and in many other ways try to improve the quality of life.

Regulatory policies

The states also have a wide variety of regulatory policies. Many overlap the state's responsibility to protect its people, natural resources, and environment. For example, every state maintains wildlife conservation programs. State licenses are required to hunt and fish. Endangered animals, birds, and plant life may be protected by state law.

To preserve the land and water, strip-mining is regulated, and both state and federal governments prohibit dumping chemicals in lakes and streams. Campfires are restricted in state forests. To reduce litter, a number of states have "bottle bills" requiring deposits on disposable bottles and cans. Many states have programs for both soil and water conservation.

Consumer protection has become an essential responsibility of state government. To protect the public, all states require doctors, lawyers, real estate agents, teachers, and other professionals to be licensed. Most states protect consumers from defective automobiles, high interest rates, and deceptive advertising. Many states now have consumer protection agencies that investigate complaints of unfair trade practices.

Finally, states also regulate businesses. States grant charters permitting the formation of corporations. State banks are scrutinized by bank examiners to ensure that loan limits and interest rates conform to state law. Insurance companies are also closely regulated by state officials. State public service or utility commissions commonly set rates for public utilities, including telephone, gas, and electric companies, as well as bus lines and railroads. Most states also regulate labor unions and have laws to ensure safe working conditions. Thus, state policies touch nearly every aspect of people's lives.

SECTION 1 REVIEW

Vocabulary and key terms

density (664)   highway patrol (669)
urbanization (665)   corrections (669)
per capita income (665)

For review

1. Why has there been a shift in population from the snowbelt to the sunbelt? **8F**
2. Why might comparisons of state wealth based on per capita income be inaccurate? **4A**
3. What is the role of the states in education? **3A**
4. What is the main function of state police forces? **6C**
5. What sorts of business activity are regulated by the state? **7C**

Critical thinking

APPLYING KEY CONCEPTS How would you describe the geography, population, economy, and political character of your state? Can you trace any of your state government's policies to these factors? **4A**

671

Section 1 Review Answers

1. The warmer climate and the expanding number of businesses in the sunbelt have drawn people from the snowbelt.
2. The cost of living may vary greatly from state to state.
3. States determine the overall education policies for public schools and provide financial assistance to public schools and colleges.
4. To enforce traffic laws on state highways.
5. The activities of corporations, state banks, insurance companies, public utilities and transportation systems, and labor unions.

Critical thinking Students should consider the state policies listed in this chapter (education, public safety, health and welfare) in discussing the special characteristics of your state.

CLOSURE

● Have students list five different state policies that affect the average citizen. Then have students read Section 2, noting especially the chart of state revenue and expenditures on p. 672.

You Decide Answer
Students should defend their answers. Gruenewald did not re-enroll in the university.

The symbol ♟ denotes active participation strategies.

Activities are keyed for student abilities:
▲ = Basic
● = All Levels
■ = Average/Advanced

SECTION 2

The States Plan Their Spending *(pp. 672–674)*

Section Objectives
☐ explain how state budgets are formulated
☐ explain how state spending has changed

Vocabulary
executive budget

FOCUS
● Begin by reminding students of Chapter 19, Section 2, which discusses spending at the national level. Ask students how state spending issues compare with federal spending issues. (States have much less money to distribute than does the federal government. States do not have to spend money on foreign aid. State and federal governments both spend money on education, public safety, health and welfare, and regulation.)

EXPLANATION
After reviewing the content of the section, you may want to consider the following activities:

👥 Economics
● To check students' understanding of the effect of inflation on state budgets, assign each student a base spending figure and a steady yearly inflation rate. Have students calculate the amount that the budget would have to rise each year simply to keep pace with inflation. (For example, starting at a base spending figure of $30 billion and with an inflation rate of 5 percent, a state would have to spend $31.5 billion the following year, $33.1 billion the year after that, and so on.)

SECTION 2

3A, 3B, 4B, 7A, 7B, 8F

The States Plan Their Spending

ACCESS | **The Main Ideas**

1 How are state budgets formulated? *pages 672–673*

2 How has state spending changed? *pages 673–674*

The idea behind a budget, as you learned in Chapter 19, is to *plan* the kinds and amounts of future spending so that money will go where it can do the most good. Before the early 1900's, states generally did not do this. State agencies would simply use whatever influence they had with the legislature to obtain as much money as possible. Beginning in California and Wisconsin in 1911, the states developed systematic ways to plan their budgets in order to spend money wisely and fairly. However, budgetary battles over taxes and spending are a fact of political life.

Figure 25–1 STATE GOVERNMENT FINANCES **7B**

3A, 3B, 4B, 7A, 7B

Making State Budgets

Like the federal government, each state government has a budget. Each state budget contains an estimate of proposed spending and anticipated revenues for a given time period. To most people, the term *budget* brings to mind a boring, detailed document filled with lots of numbers. State budgets, however, serve as blueprints of how their governments will operate — where the state's money will come from and how it will be spent. In short, the budget is a state's most important statement on public policy and state priorities.

In 47 states, the budget is prepared under the direct supervision of the governor and is therefore called an **executive budget**. The governor makes the initial proposals, and the state

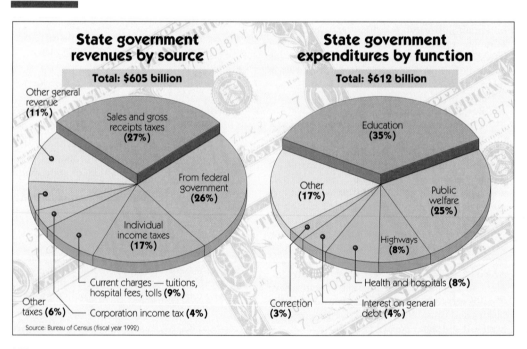

State government revenues by source — Total: $605 billion
- Other general revenue (11%)
- Sales and gross receipts taxes (27%)
- From federal government (26%)
- Individual income taxes (17%)
- Current charges — tuitions, hospital fees, tolls (9%)
- Other taxes (6%)
- Corporation income tax (4%)

State government expenditures by function — Total: $612 billion
- Education (35%)
- Other (17%)
- Public welfare (25%)
- Highways (8%)
- Health and hospitals (8%)
- Correction (3%)
- Interest on general debt (4%)

Source: Bureau of Census (fiscal year 1992)

Background: *Economics*
When expenditures exceed revenues, this is known as being "in the red." When revenues exceed expenditures, this is known as being "in the black." These are based on the colors of ink used on balance sheets.

Figure 25–1
● Explain that the category *Correction* includes police and prison expenditures. Also point out that the figures shown represent totals for all fifty states. Ask students what kinds of factors would determine each state's spending percentages. (Number of school-age children, crime situation, need for social welfare programs.)

legislature acts on them. The governor then has the power to approve, and sometimes change, the legislature's decisions.

In the other three states, the governor has only partial control over the state budget. In Texas and South Carolina, the budget is prepared by a joint executive-legislative board. Mississippi has a Commission of Budget and Accounting to prepare its budget.

Budgets are made yearly in 32 states. The other eighteen states adopt a budget every two years. In all but four states, the fiscal year — the period for which the budget is made — begins on July 1 and ends on June 30 (either 12 or 24 months later). In Alabama and Michigan the fiscal year starts on October 1, like that of the national government. The fiscal year begins on September 1 in Texas and April 1 in New York. Whatever the period, state agencies and officials must make do with the monies appropriated for that particular fiscal year.

Specific procedures for budget-making vary from state to state. Nevertheless, the process of making an executive budget follows the same general pattern. It involves both the executive branch and the state legislature.

The executive branch

Months before the start of the fiscal year, the governor's budget director sends each state agency a set of guidelines. Using these guidelines, each agency then estimates its financial needs and supplies data to support its requests. The agencies almost always ask for the amount of their current budget, plus a little bit more. This "little bit more" makes up for inflation and indicates that the program is growing. It also gives the budget director, governor, and legislature something to cut from the request without diminishing the original funding.

The budget director then reviews all requests. After comparing previous budgets with new requests, the budget director may conduct hearings at which department heads can explain their new programs and the funding they will need. Revised budget estimates are then consolidated and presented to the governor.

The governor examines the preliminary budget and adjusts it according to his or her policy priorities. With the governor's approval, the proposed budget is submitted to the legislature.

The legislature's role

The proposal is usually taken up by appropriations committees in both houses of the legislature. They often hold public hearings, in which the budget director, agency heads, interest groups, and concerned citizens have a chance to protest or defend parts of the proposed budget. The appropriations committees then make their recommendations, which are submitted to the entire legislature. Both houses must approve the document.

The final appropriations, often combined in a single budget bill, are then sent to the governor. He or she may sign the budget or reject it. Governors who possess the item (or line-item) veto may strike out portions or individual lines of the bill. Once the governor has acted, the new budget takes effect.

When the budget has been approved, departments and agencies are authorized to spend money. At the end of the fiscal year, the state auditor (if there is one) or an independent accounting group determines whether funds were spent in accordance with the law. While this is taking place, proposals for the next fiscal year are well under way.

7B

State Spending

Increases in state expenditures

The cost of operating state governments has accelerated greatly in recent years. In 1960 the combined expenditures for all fifty states were about $27 billion. By 1992 total state expenditures had increased nearly twentyfold, reaching $612 billion. Indeed, California and New York each spent more money than all 50 states together had spent 25 years earlier. California's expenditures were over $83 billion in 1992, while New York's amounted to more than $60 billion.

Much of this increase is due to inflation. Another factor has been the increase in population. More people require more schools, highways, sewers, and other government services. Finally, it seems that Americans are demanding more and more from their state governments — better roads, improved health care, increased police protection, and other services. All these things cost money.

673

♊ Cooperative Learning

● Divide the class into groups of five and have each group act out the budget-making process. The parts are: budget director, agency head, governor, interest group representative, and legislator (acting on behalf of the entire legislature). Students should follow the procedure outlined on this page.

GUIDED/INDEPENDENT PRACTICE

● Have students use the information on pp. 672–673 to create a flow chart showing the steps in the budget-making process. When students have completed their charts, have them compare the process of making a budget at the state level to the same process at the federal level. (Students will need to review pp. 523–525 of Chapter 19.)

RETEACHING/CORRECTIVES

▲ Write the following statement from p. 672 on the board: "the budget is a state's most important statement on public policy." Have students write short essays explaining this statement, using examples from the text to support their explanations.

Have students complete **Skills Practice Worksheet 25,** which shows revenue sources for one state.

The symbol ♊ denotes active participation strategies.

Activities are keyed for student abilities:
▲ = Basic
● = All Levels
■ = Average/Advanced

ENRICHMENT/EXTENSION

■ Obtain a copy of the most recent state budget from the budget director's office. Have students, alone or in groups, prepare a circle graph showing spending in your state by category. Then have students write a paragraph explaining how spending in your state varies from the general spending pattern shown in Figure 25–1.

Section 2 Review Answers

1. The governor makes the initial proposal for the legislature to act upon. The governor then approves, rejects, or suggests changes in the legislature's proposal.
2. **(a)** The budget director sends state agencies budget guidelines, reviews all agency requests, and then presents revised budget estimates to the governor. **(b)** State agencies estimate their financial needs and supply data to support their requests. **(c)** The legislature— through its appropriations committees—holds public hearings. Both houses approve the budget before sending it to the governor.
3. Education and social services.

Critical thinking Students should read newspapers, listen to radio programs, or watch local news programs to learn about important state budget issues.

CLOSURE

● Remind students of the pre-reading questions at the beginning of the section. Pose one or both of these questions again. Then have students read Section 3, noting the differences among taxes collected by states.

This scenic stretch of road in Colorado, financed by the state government, serves the needs of residents, businesses, and tourists alike.

Breakdown of state spending

Just as states vary in geography, resources, and population, no two states have exactly the same expenditures. Nevertheless, it is possible to trace some general spending patterns among the fifty states. The first graph in Figure 25–1 provides a breakdown of state spending by broad categories.

Education stands out as the largest expenditure among the states: 35 percent of total state spending in 1992. Of that money, over half went to public elementary and secondary schools, while about one-third went to higher education. Public welfare programs, such as Aid to Families with Dependent Children (AFDC), Medicaid, and other general assistance programs, constituted the second largest expenditure with 25 percent of the total state spending. Other expenditures, including unemployment payments, worker's compensation, and retirement benefits for former state employees, were third, making up close to 17 percent.

674

SECTION 2 REVIEW

Vocabulary and key terms

executive budget (672)

For review

1. What is the role of the governor in preparing the executive budget? **3A**
2. In a typical budget-making process, what is the role of (a) the budget director? (b) state agencies? (c) the legislature? **3B**
3. What are the two largest spending categories for state governments? **7B**

Critical thinking

DRAWING INFERENCES From what you know about your state's economy, geography, and people, what issues are likely to be most important in making your state budget? **7B**

How does your state government plan its spending? Does it just write blank checks for its programs? That is, does it give all of its agencies as much money as they request each year? The answer is no—your state government would go broke! Rather, all states plan their finances by preparing a **budget**, which estimates spending and revenues over a certain time period. A budget acts as a blueprint for a state's public policy or spending goals. You may be surprised to learn that a budget can help *you* in the same way.

A Personal Budget

Drawing up and following a budget will allow you to set your personal spending goals and save money. There are three steps to follow in setting up a budget:

1. Estimate your income. If you presently work and earn a paycheck, you know what your take-home pay, or **disposable income** is. If you haven't worked, the idea of **deductions** may be new to you. Deductions are money taken out of a paycheck to pay for taxes and insurance. So, for example, if your total pay, or **gross income**, is $1,000 each month, your disposable income may only be $750 after deductions. When estimating your income for your budget, make sure you know your disposable income.

2. Figure out your expenses. What do you buy or have to pay for every month? Many people, especially after graduating from high school, have both **fixed expenses** and **variable expenses**. Fixed expenses are those items that cost the same each month. Rent, mortgage, or loan payments are good examples. Variable expenses tend to vary from month to month. They might include clothing, movie tickets, trips, or car repairs. When you are trying to save money, concentrate on reducing your variable expenses. Using coupons in a grocery store or buying a less expensive pair of sneakers are two examples.

3. Keep good financial records. Begin by keeping an **expense record**. Write down what you spend money on every day, using categories such as transportation, entertainment, and clothing. At the end of the month, tabulate the totals in each column. This will show you how you spend your money each month, and will help you decide where you can save. (Some people may want to total their expenses weekly.)

You should also maintain a **budget form**, a list of your income, fixed expenses, and variable expenses. The form should include how much you want to save each month. Try to make saving a priority, especially for your long-term spending goals.

CRITICAL THINKING

1. Why does the government automatically take taxes out of workers' paychecks, rather than letting workers compute them and pay when they file their tax returns?
2. When following a budget, why do most people try to reduce their variable expenses rather than their fixed expenses?

CIVIC LITERACY

8F

Use a Budget to Achieve Your Spending Goals

675

Economics
● *Why is keeping good financial records a critical part of meeting spending goals?* (Without such records, you would not be able to see where your money goes each month.)

Structure of Government
■ CRITICAL THINKING *What are some examples of a government's fixed expenses?* (Salaries and pensions of government employees; rent, utilities, and other operating expenses.) *What are some examples of a government's variable expenses?* (Social welfare programs, aid to private organizations or other governmental organizations.)

Critical Thinking Answers
1. By taking the money out of paychecks, the government gains access to the money sooner.

2. Fixed expenses are by their nature difficult to reduce because they are outside an individual's control.

The symbol ☰ denotes active participation strategies.

Activities are keyed for student abilities:
▲ = Basic
● = All Levels
■ = Average/Advanced

SECTION 3 — State Revenues Come from Many Sources

ACCESS The Main Ideas

1 What different taxes do states collect?
pages 676–680

2 What other sources of revenue do states have?
pages 680–683

In the previous section, we discussed state government *expenditures,* the money the states spend in order to provide services for their citizens. Of course, for every dollar the states spend, they must collect another dollar from somewhere else. In this section we look at the various sources that provide the states with income, or *revenues.*
3C, 6G, 7B, 7D

State Taxes

About half of all state revenues come from taxes. A tax is a compulsory payment made by individuals or corporations to support a government. Like the taxes imposed by the federal government, there are many types of state taxes. The kinds of taxes used by the states, however, are restricted by both the federal Constitution and the states' own constitutions.

Federal limits on state taxes

To preserve the balance of power between the states and the national government, the Constitution places certain restrictions on state and local taxation. Thus, states cannot impose taxes that interfere with foreign or interstate commerce. Article 1, Section 10 specifically prohibits the states from laying duties on imports or exports. Nor may the states tax federal activities or property. For example, the states cannot place taxes on post offices and military bases, nor on income from U.S. savings bonds or Treasury notes.

Furthermore, the states can neither place taxes on religious organizations nor use tax money to support religion. This restriction stems from the First Amendment, which has been held to apply to the states through the "due process" clause of the Fourteenth Amendment. Finally, the Fourteenth Amendment's "equal protection" clause forbids taxes that make unreasonable distinctions between people.

General sales taxes are added to the price of many goods at the time of purchase. The state later collects the tax revenues from retailers.

676

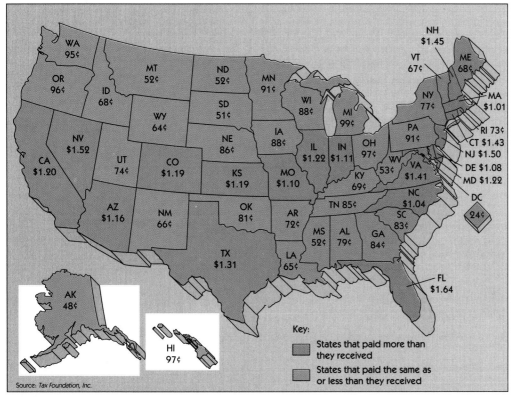

Figure 25–2 THE TAX BURDEN BY STATE This map shows how much the taxpayers in each state paid in 1988 for every dollar of federal aid that their state received. 7B

State constitutional restrictions

State constitutions likewise place limits on taxation. A few state constitutions prohibit certain types of taxes, such as income taxes or sales taxes. Many states require voter approval before increasing property taxes. Many state constitutions set maximum tax rates, and nearly all require taxes to be uniform throughout the state. In addition, churches and temples, nonprofit organizations, and charities are generally exempt from paying taxes.

Sales tax

The largest single source of revenue among the states is the **general sales tax**. A general sales tax is simply an extra charge on items purchased within the state. Consumers pay the tax as an extra whenever they purchase a taxable item. The first state to adopt a statewide general sales tax was West Virginia in 1921. Today, almost every state has a sales tax. Together, sales taxes account for about one-fourth of all state revenues (see Figure 25–1).

State sales taxes vary both in rates and in the items that are not taxed (exemptions). Most commonly, states exempt some basic necessities from sales taxes. Oklahoma, for example, exempts prescription drugs. Texas and California exclude both food and prescription drugs. Some states allow exemptions for other items. In Missouri, for example, consumers do not have to pay sales taxes on feed for livestock, fertilizers, farm machinery, newsprint, orthopedic devices, and other materials.

677

EXPLANATION

After reviewing the content of the section, you may want to consider the following activities:

Constitutional Heritage

Remind students that the principle that states may not tax federal activities or property was established in *McCulloch v. Maryland* (p. 88). In an attempt to protect its own banks from competition, Maryland levied a tax on the national bank. McCulloch, a cashier at the Baltimore branch of the Bank of the United States, was convicted of refusing to pay the tax. The Supreme Court reversed the decision after considering two key questions: Did Congress have the power to charter the bank? (Yes.) If so, did the states have the power to tax an instrument of the federal government? (No.)

● CRITICAL THINKING *How would the relationship between the states and the federal government be affected if states had the power to tax the federal government?* (States would become much more powerful than they are now and would be able to tax out of existence any federal activity they opposed.)

Figure 25–2
▲ *How much did your state pay for every dollar of federal aid received?*

The symbol ▓ denotes active participation strategies.

Activities are keyed for student abilities:
▲ = Basic
● = All Levels
■ = Average/Advanced

In some states, local governments are allowed to levy an additional sales tax. This practice is known as "piggybacking." The retailer, or seller, collects all the sales taxes and submits them to the state government. If there is a local sales tax, the state returns a portion of its receipts to local authorities. For example, if the state rate is 4 percent and the city rate 1 percent, the customer pays 5 cents in sales taxes on every dollar's worth of goods. The state would keep 4 cents and return 1 cent to the city.

Excise taxes

All fifty states collect **excise taxes**, selective sales taxes on the manufacture or sale of specific items. States may, for example, tax insurance policies, motels, automobiles, and amusement parks. The most common excise taxes are levied on gasoline, tobacco, and alcoholic beverages.

In 1992, state gasoline taxes ranged from 7.5 cents per gallon in Georgia to 28 cents per gallon in Connecticut. (This is in addition to the federal excise tax of about 14 cents.) Because more than two-thirds of the states set aside gasoline tax revenues for highway construction and maintenance, they are often called **highway user taxes.** The principle behind this tax is simple: those who use the highways the most should pay for them.

Cigarette taxes range from a low of 2.5 cents per pack in Virginia and 3 cents in Kentucky to 43 cents in Minnesota and 41 cents in Texas. Most states also levy a tax on every gallon of alcohol, while Georgia taxes 11 cents per liter of table wine and a dollar per liter of distilled spirits. These taxes are usually paid by the manufacturer or the distributor, who places an official tax stamp on the seal of the package or bottle. The amount of tax is passed on to the consumer in the form of higher prices. Revenues from such taxes may be set aside for special purposes. In many states, revenues from cigarette excise taxes are earmarked for education.

In this picture, loggers in Coos Bay, Oregon, prepare timber for export to Japan. Lumber and paper companies in Oregon must pay a severance tax for the trees they use.

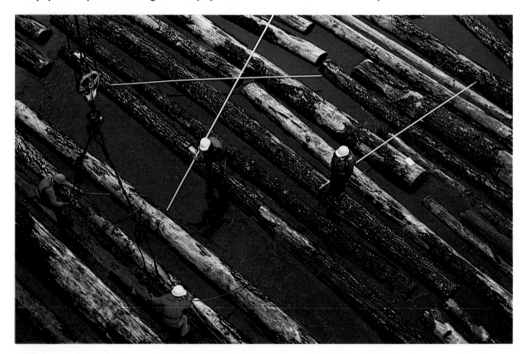

678

Taxes on tobacco and alcoholic beverages are sometimes called **sumptuary** (SUHMP-choo-air-ee) **taxes**. These are taxes on things that are considered extravagant or unnecessary. Historically, sumptuary taxes were enacted for moral or religious reasons, to discourage people from buying certain kinds of clothing, food, or other items. Such taxes, therefore, are used not only to generate revenue, but to regulate people's behavior as well.

Individual income taxes

The individual income tax is the most important source of revenue for the federal government (page 514). In 43 states, people must pay the state an additional tax on their personal income. These taxes account for about 15 percent of all state revenues. Two states — Tennessee and New Hampshire — tax only interest and dividends, not earned income (wages and salaries). Alaska, Florida, Nevada, South Dakota, Texas, Washington, and Wyoming tax neither income nor dividends.

Tax rates and the ways they are applied vary greatly among the states. Five states — Illinois, Indiana, Massachusetts, Michigan, and Pennsylvania — have a flat-rate income tax; that is, all individuals pay the same percentage rate. In a few states, all taxpayers pay an amount equal to a certain percentage of their federal income tax; for example, state income tax may be 25 percent of the federal tax. Most states have progressive rates, which vary with income levels. A typical state may have five tax brackets, with rates ranging from 1 percent of the first $1,000 to 15 percent of anything in excess of $50,000.

Corporate income taxes

Forty-six states levy taxes on the incomes of corporations. In many states the corporate tax is set at a fixed rate — usually between 2 and 10 percent. Many states have progressive corporate taxes, charging higher rates on businesses with higher incomes. Again, a typical state may have multiple tax brackets, with rates ranging from 6 percent tax on the first $25,000 of earnings up to 12 percent on earnings over $250,000.

Severance tax

About two-thirds of the states impose a tax on the extraction of natural resources from the state's land or water. These taxes are called **severance taxes**. For example, Alabama has a 3-cent tax on every ton of iron ore extracted. Alaska taxes fisheries 3–5 percent of the value of the fish they catch. Oregon imposes a tax of about 5 percent of the value of lumber harvests. Mississippi has a salt severance tax, Minnesota has a copper-nickel tax, and Washington taxes uranium milling.

Severance taxes have become especially important to the states where oil, coal, and natural gas are produced. In Alaska, Texas, Oklahoma, Louisiana, Montana, New Mexico, and Wyoming, severance taxes make up a large percentage of total state revenues. Energy-poor "consumer" states, like Massachusetts and Connecticut, have complained that such taxes have allowed some states to get rich at other states' expense. With the international drop in oil prices in 1986, however, energy-producing states suffered tremendous losses in revenues from severance taxes. Oklahoma, Texas, and Louisiana were particularly hard hit.

Property taxes

States may also impose a **property tax** on real property — buildings and land — or even on personal property, such as jewelry, automobiles, and boats. Before World War II, the property tax generated a sizable portion of state revenues. Although 42 states still have property taxes, today they generate less than 1 percent of total state revenues.

The main reason for the decline in state property taxes is that state governments have relinquished this tax to local governments. Today, the property tax is the largest single source of revenue for local governments. (Local government taxing and spending policies are discussed in Chapter 27.) Moreover, these taxes became too difficult and costly to administer on a statewide basis.

What is an "ideal" tax?

State governments, which use a variety of taxes to raise money, must consider many factors in setting tax policy. Most policymakers agree that taxes should be fair, taking into account people's ability to pay. This is why many state income taxes are progressive, with higher rates at higher levels of income. On the other hand,

Background: *History* In some countries, sumptuary taxes were levied in order to preserve a class system. One method was to force people to buy domestically manufactured products. In England, for example, a law in the 1600's required lower-class men to wear English-made woolen caps. Upper-class men, on the other hand, could wear the more expensive French or Italian velvet hats.

Cross-reference
Chapter 19, Section 2, explains progressive and regressive taxes. See pp. 515 and 518.

The symbol ⅱ denotes active participation strategies.

Activities are keyed for student abilities:
▲ = Basic
● = All Levels
■ = Average/Advanced

679

many states do not tax unearned income, such as dividends from stock and interest on investments. Excluding this type of income from taxation benefits the wealthy over the poor, who are unlikely to own stock or have valuable investments.

The sales tax has also been criticized as regressive, because it does not take into account people's ability to pay. All people, rich and poor, pay the same sales taxes on the same goods, regardless of the fact that the rich can more easily afford it. This is why states frequently exempt necessary items, such as food and medicine, from sales taxes.

A tax can also be considered "fair" if the people who benefit from it pay a larger share. One good example is the highway user tax, which derives money for highways from gasoline taxes. Excise and severance taxes, however, have been criticized because they place the burden on the wrong party. Although the seller or manufacturer of the good initially pays the tax, it is eventually passed on to the buyer in the form of higher prices. For example, the severance tax that the coal-mining company had to pay to extract the coal is included in the consumer's monthly heating bill.

Taxes also should be simple and convenient to collect. The sales tax, for example, is paid in small amounts and is easy for the state government to collect. Income taxes, on the other hand, create large amounts of paperwork for both taxpayers and the government. If a tax is too difficult or costly for the state government to administer, it defeats the main purpose of taxes — to raise money.

Finally, taxes should be dependable. The states must be assured of a stable tax source in order to plan budgets and expenses in good years as well as bad. Taxpayers also need to know well in advance how much they will have to pay so they can plan their personal budgets.

6A, 7B

Other Revenue Sources

Taxes are not the only source of state revenues. The most common other sources of income include the federal government, gambling and lotteries, licenses and fees, state-owned business, and borrowing.

680

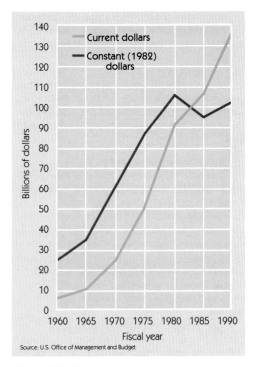

Source: U.S. Office of Management and Budget

Figure 25–3 **FEDERAL AID TO THE STATES**
Federal grants-in-aid are shown in current and constant dollars. 7B

Federal government support

About one-fourth of all state revenue is provided by the federal government. Most of this money comes as grants-in-aid (page 101). Federal government funds must be spent in accordance with guidelines set by Congress. They are often used for such purposes as highway construction, public health, or conservation of natural resources. As Figure 25–2 on page 677 shows, some states benefit more from federal funding than others, depending on the particular federal program and the state's special needs.

Federal aid to the states decreased significantly in the 1980's. In 1972, for example, 27.2 percent of all state funding came from the federal government. By 1985, that figure was reduced to 20.9 percent, and by 1987, it was below 20 percent of total state revenues. This reduction was due primarily to the Reagan administration's efforts to reduce state dependence on the federal government. President Reagan's 1982 budget was the first in recent years in which aid to the states decreased in dollar amount (see Figure 25–3).

Gambling and lotteries

Many states derive some income from state-regulated gambling. For example, racetrack betting on horse racing and dog racing is allowed in a number of states. In such "pari-mutuel" gambling, people bet against each other, but the government takes a portion of all bets. Nevada is the only state that permits statewide casino gambling, which generates nearly one-half of the state's revenues. New Jersey allows casino gambling only in Atlantic City, a tourist spot. Most states tax people's winnings from gambling.

In recent years many states have set up lotteries. Lotteries are not new to Americans: all thirteen original states, at one time or another, had lotteries. The state's share of lottery money was used to build bridges, canals, roads, and schools. Some of our nation's oldest universities — Harvard, Yale, Brown, Columbia, Dartmouth, and William and Mary — were supported with the help of lottery receipts. Corruption and scandals, however, caused all states to abandon lotteries by the 1890's.

New Hampshire revived the state lottery in 1963. Its success in generating revenue for education quickly drew attention from other states. Today more than half the states have lotteries. The most common version is the "instant" lottery game. Adults can buy lottery tickets at designated places, such as local supermarkets or gasoline stations. Tickets typically cost $1 or $2, and prizes range from free tickets to thousands of dollars. The chances of getting a winning ticket, however, decrease with the dollar amount. That is, while the odds of winning $5 may be 1 in 200, the odds of winning $100,000 may be 1 in 3 million. The "big winner" is the state.

Many states also have daily or weekly drawings. Players buy tickets and select a combination of numbers, usually four or six. Players who choose the exact combination are entitled to the amount in the jackpot.

Although popular, lotteries are also a controversial source of revenue. Critics call lotteries

Lotteries are a source of revenue for many states. Here, people wait in line to buy lottery tickets.

Background: *Cultural Literacy* The term *pari-mutuel* comes from the French *pari,* meaning "wager," and *mutuel,* meaning "mutual" or "shared." In this system, winners divide the total amount of the bet (after management expenses are deducted) in proportion to the sums wagered individually.

Background: *Global Awareness* The earliest recorded lottery was held in France in 1520. Ireland started the internationally famous Irish Sweepstakes in 1930 to benefit its hospitals.

Section 3 Review Answers

1. States cannot impose taxes that impede commerce, support religion, or distinguish between groups of people. States cannot tax federal property or religious organizations.

2. (a) A general sales tax is an extra charge on taxable items; an excise tax is a selective sales tax on the manufacture or sale of specific items. **(b)** The consumer.

3. States should be compensated for the extraction of resources.

Many states collect tolls for travel on certain highways and bridges. Such charges place the burden of paying for public facilities on the people who use them.

regressive, because lower-income people buy most of the tickets. The glimmer of "striking it rich," they argue, lures poor people into throwing away their money. Moreover, adminstrative costs are high, reducing the state's profits.

Lottery supporters, however, maintain that unlike paying taxes, nobody is forced to play the lottery. They also argue that people are likely to gamble whether or not it is legal. It is better for their gambling losses to go to the state (as in the lottery) than to organized crime. State lottery funds support worthwhile causes such as education, the arts, care for the elderly, building projects, and local government operations.

Licenses, fees, and fines

All states generate money from issuing licenses. A license gives its holder government authorization to conduct a business or carry out some activity. Although states collect revenues from licensing fees, the main purpose of a license is to protect the public. Thus, in every doctor's office or restaurant you enter, you will see a state license displayed on the wall.

Besides requiring licenses for many professions and businesses, states also require licenses to hunt, fish, drive, or get married. Of these, driver's licenses produce the greatest income for the states. Some license fees are set aside for special purposes. For example, hunting and fishing license fees are often used to support wildlife

conservation, while driver's license fees frequently go for highway safety projects.

States also raise money through special fees and fines. Nonresident students, for example, generally pay higher tuition at state colleges and universities. States also charge money for recording and transferring legal documents, such as mortgages and birth certificates. Registration fees must be paid for motorcycles, automobiles, trucks, trailers, and other vehicles. Finally, states also raise money by fining certain illegal acts, such as speeding, littering, and cheating on taxes.

State-operated businesses

States also generate money from a wide assortment of business enterprises. One-third of the states are involved in selling alcoholic beverages through state-run stores. South Dakota operates a cement plant. North Dakota runs a state-owned bank and mills "Dakota-Maid" flour. Many states raise money by operating ferry services, toll roads, and toll bridges.

Borrowing

State revenues often are not great enough to meet emergencies or finance large projects such as new highways or universities. Such projects simply cannot be built little by little as funds become available. It would be unreasonable to build a 100-mile highway in 5-mile stretches each year. To undertake large projects, state governments must borrow money.

682

Critical Thinking
▲ *How does licensing protect the public?* (Licensing ensures that acceptable, uniform standards are upheld. For example, doctors and lawyers must pass written exams; restaurants must meet cleanliness standards.)

State governments borrow money by selling **bonds**. A bond is basically a loan by private persons or corporations to the government. When a government sells a bond, it agrees to repay the entire loan, plus interest, by a specified date. State governments usually have no difficulty selling bonds. They are considered safe investments, and, more importantly, the interest from these bonds is not subject to taxation by the federal government.

State governments must be careful not to borrow too much. During the 1930's, many state and local governments had so much debt that they were unable to repay those who held their bonds. To prevent this from happening again, many state constitutions were amended to limit the amount and the purposes for which the state could borrow. In many states, voters must approve debt over a certain amount. In California, for example, a bond issue must be approved by a two-thirds popular vote.

SECTION 3 REVIEW

Vocabulary and key terms

general sales tax (677)	severance tax (679)
excise tax (678)	property tax (679)
highway user tax (678)	bond (683)
sumptuary tax (679)	

For review

1. How is the states' taxing power restricted by the U.S. Constitution? **3C**
2. (a) What is the difference between a general sales tax and an excise tax? (b) Who ultimately pays both taxes? **7B**
3. What is the reasoning behind the collection of severance taxes? **7B**
4. Why do sales taxes often exempt food and prescription drugs? **7B**
5. (a) Why have state lotteries been criticized? (b) What arguments have been made in their defense? **6A**

Critical thinking

ORGANIZING AN ARGUMENT Should the voters be consulted whenever a state wants to borrow money? Why or why not? **7A**

Chapter Summary

The states vary widely in geography, population, economic development, and political forces. Consequently, policies and priorities differ from state to state. In general, states carry out programs in four broad areas — education, public safety, public health and welfare, and regulatory policies.

The states determine guidelines for local schools to follow, and they also help finance elementary, secondary, and higher education. They provide for public safety through their highway patrols and corrections systems. A number of state-sponsored programs and policies protect citizens from health hazards, while regulatory policies protect the public in other ways.

To allocate funds among these programs, each state makes a budget. Most states use an executive budget, which is prepared by the budget director under the supervision of the governor. Agencies make requests, the governor submits a proposed budget to the legislature, and the legislature authorizes appropriations in a budget act. In many states, the governor can use the item veto to strike or reduce individual appropriations. The largest state expenditures are for education, social services, and transportation.

State taxes account for about half of state revenues. The largest source of tax revenue is the general sales tax, collected on most goods sold within the state, generally excluding food and prescription drugs. Excise taxes are levied on particular items, such as gasoline, tobacco, and alcoholic beverages. Individual and corporate income taxes are an important source of revenue for many states. Most states also charge a severance tax on the extraction of natural resources. Nontax sources of state revenues include grants-in-aid from the federal government, gambling and lotteries, license fees, and fines. States sometimes borrow money by selling bonds, often requiring the approval of the voters.

4. Food and drugs are exempted because they are basic necessities.
5. **(a)** Lower-income people tend to play the most; administrative costs are high. **(b)** No one is forced to play; gambling losses go to the state, not to organized crime; worthy causes are supported with lottery-generated income.

Critical thinking Students should discuss the benefits of having the public act as a "watchdog" on the state's debt, as well as the drawbacks of public supervision of a complex financial process.

CLOSURE

● Have students list and describe two tax sources and two non-tax sources of state revenue. Then have students read the next assigned lesson.

CHAPTER 25 CORRECTIVES

● To review the content of Chapter 25, you may want to have students complete **Study Guide/Review 25** or **Workbook Chapter 25.**

The symbol 👥 denotes active participation strategies.

Activities are keyed for student abilities:
▲ = Basic
● = All Levels
■ = Average/Advanced

Answers

Vocabulary See pp. T19–T21 for suggested vocabulary activities.

Reviewing the Facts

1. The "sunrise" industries are newer, stronger industries, such as those involving computers and aerospace technology; they are generally found in the sunbelt states. The "sunset" industries are older, more troubled industries, such as automobiles and steel; they are generally in the snowbelt.
2. Health-care professionals such as physicians, nurses, hygienists, chiropractors, psychologists, pharmacists, and physical therapists.
3. The widespread use of the automobile, which led to increases in state highway travel that local police and sheriffs were not authorized to handle.
4. Budgets allow states to make the careful financial plans necessary for carrying out state policies.
5. Education.
6. Sources include the federal government, gambling, lotteries, licences, fees, fines, state-owned businesses, and borrowing.
7. All individuals pay at the same rate, or percentage of income.
8. It does not take into account people's ability to pay; everyone pays the same sales tax on the same goods, even though the rich can afford it more than the poor.

Thinking Critically About Key Concepts

1. *Possible advantages*—More efficient lawmaking process; fewer conflicts among state leaders. *Possible disadvantages*—Corruption; less government sensitivity to people's needs.
2. Migration of people into a state increases the demand for state services. Cuts in federal aid to states require the state to cut its own spending or increase revenues. National economic trends,

★ CHAPTER 25 REVIEW ★

● **Review the definitions of the following terms:**

bond	general sales tax	severance tax
corrections	highway patrol	sumptuary tax
density	highway user tax	urbanization
excise tax	per capita income	
executive budget	property tax	

▲ REVIEWING THE FACTS

1. What are the "sunrise" industries and the "sunset" industries, and where are they generally located? **7B**
2. What types of occupations are licensed by state health authorities? **7C**
3. What was the main reason for establishing state police forces in the early 1900's? **3A**
4. Why do state governments prepare a budget? **7B**
5. What is the largest category of spending among state governments? **7B**
6. Name three sources of state revenue other than taxes? **7B**
7. What is a flat-rate income tax? **7B**
8. Why is the general sales tax considered to be regressive? **7B**

▲ THINKING CRITICALLY ABOUT KEY CONCEPTS

1. What are the potential advantages and disadvantages of having one political party dominate a state? **2E**
2. How can events outside a state increase the cost of government within the state? **7B**
3. In what way do sumptuary taxes support John Marshall's statement, "The power to tax involves the power to destroy"? **7B**
4. Why would it be impractical to fund all state services solely by taxing those who use those services? **7B**

684

▲ PRACTICING SKILLS

1. **Study Skills: Reading a circle graph.** Refer to Figure 25–1 (page 672) to answer the following questions. (a) Which kind of tax provided the most revenue to the states? (b) Into which revenue category would a student's college tuition payment fall? (c) What was the smallest category of revenue? (d) What percentage of the states' budget was spent on such items as Aid to Families with Dependent Children? (e) Into which expenditure category would teachers' salaries fall? **8B**
2. **Study Skills: Reading a line graph.** Look again at Figure 25–3 (page 680). Use the data in the graph to present two arguments: (a) one claiming that the federal government is backing away from its financial commitment to the states, and (b) the other one claiming that the federal government is maintaining that commitment. **8B**
3. **Critical Thinking Skills: Identifying cause and effect.** Refer to the subsections "Geography" (page 664) and "Population" (pages 664–665). Read the following sentences, each of which states a cause. Write one or more effects that might result from each of these causes. (a) Twenty-four states have seacoasts, and eight border on the Great Lakes. (b) African Americans make up more than 25 percent of the population of Mississippi, South Carolina, Louisiana, Georgia, and Alabama. **8F**

such as rising inflation or unemployment, can raise state government costs and increase the demand for services.
3. Sumptuary taxes not only raise revenue but also

try to discourage certain kinds of behavior.
4. Many state services are aimed at poor people, who would not be able to afford high taxes. Also, services such as police protection

benefit all citizens, directly or indirectly.

▲ PARTICIPATORY CITIZENSHIP

1. **Creating a chart.** Obtain, from the state or your school, information about state-run colleges and universities. Use this information to create a chart showing these institutions and the different programs and degrees they offer. **8C**
2. **Creating a bulletin board.** Use library resources to determine how the geography of your state has affected your state's resources. Research both modern industries and those that were important in the past. Work with other students to create a bulletin board showing the link between geography and industry in your state. If applicable, note how this connection has changed over the years. You may also wish to include climate or other factors in your report. **7D**

■ WRITING ABOUT ISSUES

1. **Writing an editorial.** A news columnist once made this remark about a state's lottery: "The lottery people like to tell you that seven people have won the million-dollar lottery this past year. I'd like to tell you that the people of this state have lost $60 million to the lottery this past year." Explain and expand upon that comment as part of a newspaper column. Then write another column rebutting the first. **8C**
2. **Composing a speech.** Imagine that you are the governor of a state that does not have an individual income tax. Write a speech in which you recommend the institution of such a tax and a corresponding reduction in the state sales tax. Explain the benefits you think this plan would bring. **8C**

▲ ANALYZING A POLITICAL CARTOON

During the early 1990's opponents of taxes and government spending gained political power in many states. Some observers worried that crucial public services would suffer cutbacks as a result. Look at the cartoon below and answer the following questions.

1. Why did Smithers meet an early death? **8B**
2. How does Smithers react to his fate? **8B**
3. How does the cartoonist view the issue of state tax rates and state services? **8B**

Bruce Plante/The Chattanooga Times.

685

Participatory Citizenship
1. This would be a good opportunity to discuss with students their plans for college.
2. Bulletin boards could contain photographs, drawings, newspaper articles, and drawings.

Writing About Issues
1. The first column should explain that lotteries take in more money than they give out in winnings and that most of this money comes from poorer people. The second column should point out that a portion of lottery revenues is used for worthwhile public services, many of which benefit the poor.
2. The speech should point out that, unlike a sales tax, an income tax can be made progressive. A state, by depending more on income taxes and less on sales taxes, could shift the tax burden to those better able to afford it.

Analyzing a Political Cartoon
1. There were no emergency services to save his life.
2. He is happy that he did not have to pay more taxes to provide services.
3. The cartoonist seems to feel that tax increases are necessary to support vital public services.

Practicing Skills
1. (a) Sales and gross receipt taxes. **(b)** Current charges. **(c)** Corporation income taxes. **(d)** 25 percent. **(e)** Education.

2. (a) Students should note the severe drop in federal aid during the early 1980's. **(b)** Students should note the long-term increase in federal aid over the past three decades.

3. (a) Shipping and fishing play important economic roles in these states. **(b)** School integration and affirmative action are important issues in these states.

Chapter Review exercises are keyed for student abilities:
▲ = Basic
● = All Levels
■ = Average/Advanced

AS OTHERS SEE US

Vocabulary

Verdun and the Somme—two World War I battles fought in France in 1916. Total casualities in these battles exceeded 1.5 million.

Background

Since the end of World War II, many barriers to travel and trade among countries in western and central Europe have gradually been eliminated. In recent years 13 nations have begun to form an economic union called the European Union (EU). The EU's plan is to issue a common passport and to introduce a common currency that would rival the U.S. dollar in influence. The individual countries will still maintain their own political systems and conduct their own foreign policies.

👥 Economics

● To clarify the difference between state and federal government roles, list some economic functions that the U.S. government controls and the states do not. For example, in the United States, the federal government controls the currency and establishes foreign trade regulations. Discuss whether European countries should allow a central EU government to control their economic policies.

Geography

● Have students research and list the countries or states that belong or belonged to the following unions:
(A) the European Union (EU)
(B) the North American Free Trade Agreement (NAFTA)
(C) the Confederacy (American Civil War)

686

The flag of the European Union (EU) flies in front of the flags of the EU's member nations.

AS OTHERS SEE US

3C, 7B

What Can Europeans Learn from American History?

How strong should a nation's central government be? What powers should individual states keep? Should states be able to secede from the nation? Today, the European Union, an economic union of nations, is facing these questions. The following excerpt from the British magazine The Economist *considers the lessons about states' rights that Europeans can learn from United States history.*

London. [The Revolutionary War] had been prosecuted by 13 states, not one; and it did not forge anything that, to modern eyes, looks like a nation-state. Indeed, this absence of unity was made explicit by the articles of confederation.... Article 2 said that the states retained their "sovereignty, freedom and independence." They merely (article 3) entered into a "firm league of friendship with each other."

After only six years, the articles of 1781 were deemed unsatisfactory enough to warrant revision. The result—today's constitution — provided a system of government that was federal in form, but with a much stronger central government than had existed before....

But one awkward lesson from America is permanent....America did not take its final political shape in 1787: three-quarters of a century later, the founding fathers' structure blew up.

Most non-Americans do not realise how large the civil war of 1861–65 looms in American's collective memory. It killed more than 600,000 people, foreshadowing the efficient slaughter that Europe did not experience until Verdun and the Somme 50 years later. In its last year, when the North's armies under Grant and Sherman marched into the South's heartland, it became unbearably brutal. If you are going to have a constitution linking several states that cherish their sovereignty, it is worth making sure in advance that it does not lead to the kind of war America's constitution led to....

Nobody knows what explosive arguments the future of Europe will bring. Some countries may see relations with Russia as the right centrepiece for Europe's foreign policy; others may put relations with America in that place; still others will focus on the Arab world to Europe's south. Some Europeans may want far more restrictive immigration policies than others, which could lead to some sharp intra-European border tensions. Country X will favour fewer controls on arms sales abroad than Country Y. Europe's capacity to speak and act as one is still almost entirely theoretical. If Europeans are genuinely interested in learning from the American experience, this lesson should be taken to heart: make it clear in advance that, whatever union is to be forged, states can leave it, unhindered, at will.

From "If you sincerely want to be a United States ..." in *The Economist*, March 23, 1991. Copyright © 1991 The Economist Newspaper, Inc., Ltd. Reprinted by permission of *The Economist*.

1. Why did Americans in the 1780's find the Articles of Confederation to be an unsatisfactory basis for a government?
2. What "awkward lesson" regarding the power of states does *The Economist* think Europeans should learn from U.S. history?
3. Explain whether or not you would support an amendment to the United States Constitution allowing states to leave the Union.

686

Critical Thinking Answers
1. Americans found the Articles of Confederation to be unsatisfactory because the central government was so weak that trade and national defense suffered.

2. The "awkward lesson" pertained to America's devastating Civil War. If Europeans form a union, they should make clear that any country can leave the union whenever it wants.

3. Students might cite historical examples or Constitutional principles to support their opinions. Some students may feel such an amendment is necessary to avoid another civil war.

UNIT
★ **9** ★

LOCAL GOVERNMENT

687

Unit Overview

Unit Nine describes the various forms of local government and their functions. Chapter 26 examines the differences among counties, townships, municipalities, and special districts. The chapter explains how each is organized and identifies the political leaders in each. Chapter 27 considers the policy-making process at the local level, focusing on the challenges towns and cities face in providing services and planning for growth.

Photo
Los Angeles City Hall.

CHAPTER 26
THE STRUCTURE OF LOCAL GOVERNMENTS
(pp. 688–707)

	Section Objectives	Section Resources
Section 1 **County Governments Carry Out State Policies**	☐ explain the functions of counties ☐ explain how counties are governed	■ SKILLS CHALLENGE WORKSHEET **26** ▲ TRANSPARENCY **58**
Section 2 **Local Government Has Many Smaller Units**	☐ explain how towns and townships are governed ☐ describe the functions performed by school districts and special districts	● SIMULATION **4**
Section 3 **Municipal Governments Have Grown in Importance**	☐ explain how municipalities are formed ☐ describe the different forms of city government	▲ SKILLS PRACTICE WORKSHEET **26**

Essential Elements

The list below shows Essential Elements relevant to this chapter. (The complete list of Essential Elements appears in the introductory pages of this Teacher's Edition.)

Section 1: 1D, 3A, 3B, 4A, 7B, 8H

Section 2: 1B, 3A, 4A, 7B, 8A

Section 3: 3A, 3B, 4D, 8B

Chapter Review: 3A, 3B, 3C, 4A, 5C, 6A, 6F, 8A, 8B

> Section Resources are keyed for student abilities:
> ▲ = Basic
> ● = All Levels
> ■ = Average/Advanced

Homework Options

Each section contains activities labeled "Guided/Independent Practice," "Reteaching/Correctives," and "Enrichment/Extension." You may wish to choose from among these activities when assigning homework.

Students Acquiring English Activities

Invite a local government official or Chamber of Commerce officer to describe your community's government to the class. Have students prepare a list of questions about budgets, important issues, and plans for the future.

LISTENING/SPEAKING: Ask for a volunteer to read aloud the quote on p. 688. Ask students to suggest what they think they will remember about your community when they are 50 years old. Then have students interview their parents and/or grandparents about the community where they grew up and compare those descriptions with the community the students live in today.

Teacher Bibliography

Holli, Melvin G. and Paul M. Green. *The Making of the Mayor, Chicago, 1983.* Eerdmans, 1984. Recreates, through the words of nine essayists, the election of Chicago's first African American mayor.

Martin, David L. *Running City Hall: Municipal Administration in America.* 2nd ed. University of Alabama Press, 1990. An examination of the work of the people who make America's cities work.

Stewart, Debra W., ed. *Women in Local Politics.* Scarecrow, 1980. Studies the impact of women at the grassroots level.

Student Bibliography

Broder, David S. *Changing of the Guard: Power and Leadership in America.* Penguin, 1981. Short biographies of young political leaders in the United States at all levels of government.

Literature

O'Connor, Edwin. *The Last Hurrah.* Little, Brown, 1985. A revealing study of the rise and fall of an Irish political boss in Boston.

Royko, Mike. *Boss: Richard J. Daley of Chicago.* NAL-Dutton, 1988. Focuses on the career of the man who was mayor of Chicago from 1955 to 1976.

Films and Videotapes*

City Government in the United States. 18 min. Phoenix, 1977. f, v. Introduces and examines two basic forms of city government—the city manager form and the mayor-council form—using Santa Monica and Los Angeles as examples.

A Local Conflict. (Series title: *Inside Government.*) 25 min. Churchill, 1976. f. Controversy over a land development and the subsequent pressure from citizen groups on a councilwoman show the workings of city government.

CHAPTER RESOURCES

Study Guide/Review 26
Workbook Chapter 26
Chapter 26 Test, Forms A–C

Software*

Our Town Meeting (Apple, IBM). TS. Students learn how community government works by participating in a town's planning and budgeting process. Armed with town surveys, revenue projections, and cost estimates, they discuss vital community issues and compete for the town's limited budget dollars, which they then agree to spend in the most effective way possible.

SimCity (Commodore, IBM, Macintosh). BS. Students design and manage a city with the aid of statistics, maps, polls, and an on-screen budget. They provide services, manage a budget, and make decisions about pollution, traffic, and disasters.

---

* For a complete guide to audiovisual sources, see page T22.

The Structure of Local Governments
(pp. 688–707)

This chapter examines local government, beginning with a look at the relationship between state and county government and then exploring the smaller units of local government, such as towns, townships, and municipalities.

Chapter Objectives
After students complete this chapter, they will be able to:

1. Explain the functions of counties.
2. Explain how counties are governed.
3. Explain how towns and townships are governed.
4. Describe the functions performed by school districts and special districts.
5. Explain how municipalities are formed.
6. Describe the different forms of city government.

CHAPTER

26

THE STRUCTURE of LOCAL GOVERNMENTS

Everyone has deep in their heart the old town or community where they first went barefooted, got their first licking, traded their first pocket knife, grew up, and finally went away thinking you were too big for that Burg. But that's where your old heart is.

Will Rogers
American humorist (1879–1935)

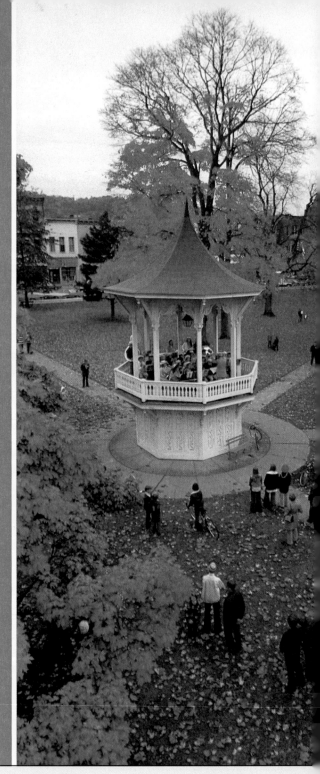

Photo
Town center, Gallipolis, Ohio.

W
hen you turn eighteen, you will register to vote. Someday you may want to get a marriage license or need to show a birth certificate. Perhaps you will need a permit to remodel your house. In an emergency, you may need to call an ambulance, the fire station, or the police. In all of these situations, you are likely to call on your local government.

In many ways, community governments are closer to their residents than either the national or state governments. Humorist Will Rogers, quoted on the facing page, points out that home towns are "where your old heart is." Local communities — large or small — are also where you live day by day. Therefore, it is local governments that take care of most everyday needs — roads, bridges, hospitals, street lights, transportation, sewer and water service. This chapter explains what the various units of local government are, how they are organized, and what they do.

CHAPTER OUTLINE

1 County Governments Carry Out State Policies

The Role of Counties
Governing the Counties

2 Local Government Has Many Smaller Units

Towns and Townships
"District" Governments

3 Municipal Governments Have Grown in Importance

Municipal Corporations
Forms of City Government

689

CHAPTER SUPPORT MATERIAL

Skills Practice Worksheet 26

Skills Challenge Worksheet 26

Simulation 4

Transparency 58

Study Guide/Review 26

Workbook Chapter 26

Chapter 26 Test, Forms A-C

County Governments Carry Out State Policies (pp. 690–694)

Section Objectives

☐ explain the functions of counties

☐ explain how counties are governed

Vocabulary

county, county seat, home rule, county manager, consolidation

FOCUS

● Begin by asking students to name three responsibilities or powers they think local governments have. (Possibilities include police and fire protection, garbage removal, recreation facilities, property tax assessment.)

Students may have difficulty describing local government functions, since the services provided by these government units, being a part of everyday life, are often taken for granted. Point out that awareness of these services increases greatly when they are impeded, as by a strike or natural disaster.

Tell students that in this chapter they will look at the structure and powers of local government; the services provided by local government will be explored in Chapter 27.

1D, 3A, 3B, 4A, 7B, 8H

SECTION 1

County Governments Carry Out State Policies

ACCESS **The Main Ideas**

1 What are the functions of counties?
pages 690–692

2 How are counties governed? *pages 692–694*

In the federal system, the national government and the fifty states are equal partners, their respective powers divided by the Constitution. State and local governments in the United States, however, are not equal partners. The relationship between state and local governments is unitary (see Chapter 1). The only authority local governments possess is that given to them by the state.

This relationship holds true for the more than 83,000 different local governments that exist in the United States today. They include more than 3,000 counties, 16,000 townships, 19,000 municipalities, and almost 15,000 school districts and 30,000 special districts. The basic unit of local government in the United States is the **county**.

1D, 3A

The Role of Counties

Counties are another part of American government's heritage from English law. In medieval England, rulers divided their kingdoms into smaller units to make them easier to rule. These units were called "shires," and the king appointed officials called "reeves" to oversee them. (The word *shire-reeve* eventually came to be pronounced "sheriff.") After the Norman Conquest of England in 1066, the shire was called by a French-based word, *county*. County officials — the sheriff, coroner, and others — gradually came to be elected, not appointed by the king.

English colonists in America soon established a similar government organization. In 1634, Virginia was divided into eight counties. Massachusetts adopted a county system nine years later, and most other colonies followed suit.

Each county's official center is known as the **county seat**. Because people used to travel

The county courthouse for Queen Annes County in eastern Maryland is this handsome Federal-style building in Centreville, built in 1792.

690

Cross-reference
Unitary government is discussed in Chapter 1, p. 12.

Background: *History*
William the Conqueror strengthened royal authority in England by setting up an efficient administration based on the Anglo-Saxon shire system; it allowed him to gain control over local government and to subdue the Anglo-Saxon people.

Background: *Cultural Literacy* The term *county* comes from the Norman French *counté*, a word derived from the Latin *comitatus* meaning "territory of a count."

mainly by horse and buggy or on foot, it was essential for the county seat to be located within a day's travel from anywhere in the county. The showpiece of the county seat was the county courthouse, the building that housed county government offices. County courthouses were almost always built on large, park-like blocks or "squares" in the very center of town, surrounded by markets and shops. Besides being a center of political life, county seats were also important places for trade and social gatherings.

Modern counties

Counties are still the major territorial and political units of the states. There are 3,042 counties in the United States today. All fifty states have counties; however, they are called *parishes* in Louisiana and *boroughs* (BUR-ohz) in Alaska. Counties are especially important in rural areas in the South and Midwest. In New England, towns, rather than counties, are the most active units of local government. In Rhode Island and Connecticut, counties are only territorial divisions; there are no county governments. Major cities also provide many services that counties perform in more rural areas.

The number of counties varies greatly from state to state. Texas leads all states with 254 counties, followed by Georgia with 158, Kentucky with 119, and Missouri with 114. Delaware has the fewest — just three. The average number is about sixty counties.

The largest county in the United States is San Bernardino County in southeastern California. It covers 20,062 square miles, greater than the area of Rhode Island, Massachusetts, Connecticut, and Delaware combined. (Alaska has one borough that is larger than every state in the Union except Texas and California.) The smallest county is Arlington County, Virginia, with an area of 26 square miles. It would take 772 Arlington counties to equal one San Bernardino County.

California also has the most populous county — Los Angeles County, with 8.9 million people. Next are Cook County (Chicago), Illinois; Harris County (Houston), Texas; San Diego County, California; Orange County, California; and Kings County (Brooklyn), New York. Each has more than 2 million people. Altogether, more than two-thirds of the U.S. population is concentrated in fewer than 400 counties. At

Figure 26–1 UNITS OF GOVERNMENT   3A

TYPE OF GOVERNMENT	NUMBER OF UNITS
National	1
State	50
County	3,042
Municipal	19,200
Township	16,691
School district	14,721
Special district	29,532
Total	83,237

Source: Bureau of the Census

the other end of the scale, Kalawao County, Hawaii, had only 85 residents in 1990. Most of the nation's counties have between 10,000 and 50,000 people.

Functions of counties

The primary purpose of counties is to carry out state government functions in one local area. Although the specifics vary from county to county and state to state, county governments commonly act in the following areas:

ELECTIONS Counties are largely responsible for registering voters, preparing ballots, supervising elections, and counting votes for local, state, and national elections.

RECORDS All types of important documents, such as birth certificates, marriage licenses, wills, mortgages, police records, and health permits are kept by county governments.

SOCIAL SERVICES Counties provide vital social services, such as care for orphans and homeless people. They also administer a wide range of health and welfare programs for both the state and national governments, including food stamps, aid to the blind, and vaccinations.

PUBLIC FACILITIES Counties supervise hospitals, airports, public utilities, libraries, and recreation centers. They are also responsible for the construction and upkeep of many roads and bridges within their boundaries.

LAW ENFORCEMENT State laws are enforced at the county level by minor courts, county prosecutors, and law-enforcement officers such as the

691

EXPLANATION
After students have read the section, you may want to consider the following activities:

Geography
▲ **Do all states have the same number of counties?** (No.)
● CRITICAL THINKING Tell students that a California county averages 2,823 square miles, compared to about 1,057 square miles for a Texas county and 879 square miles for a New York county. Most western counties are much larger than eastern counties. **Why might this be so?** (Many western areas have smaller population density than eastern areas.)

Civic Participation
▲ **Why must all election districts within a county (page 692) have equal population?** (To ensure that each voter's vote counts equally.)
● CRITICAL THINKING **Which voters would suffer if election districts were not of equal population?** (Those in the more populous districts.)

Figure 26–1
● **Which one of the figures in the chart is least likely to change? Why?** (National. A change in that figure would only happen after the dissolution of the United States.)

The symbol ♙ denotes active participation strategies.

Activities are keyed for student abilities:
▲ = Basic
● = All Levels
■ = Average/Advanced

● Divide the class into six groups. Assign each group one of the following areas: elections, records, social services, public facilities, law enforcement, and land use regulation. Have each group prepare a short report describing the types of services their county provides in the area assigned. The report can also include examples of ways residents make use of these services and of specific places in the community where these services or further information can be obtained. As a starting point, students can consult the county listings in a local telephone directory.

GUIDED/INDEPENDENT PRACTICE

● Have students list and explain the six proposed reforms in county government described on pp. 693–694. (Home rule, fewer elected officials, county merit system, county manager, consolidation of counties, functional consolidation.)

sheriff and coroner. Counties also maintain jails and other correctional facilities for both adult and juvenile offenders.

LAND USE REGULATION Counties adopt and implement planning and zoning laws to regulate local building and growth.

3A, 3B, 7B

Governing the Counties

County governments are usually run by a popularly elected board or committee. Throughout the fifty states, these governing boards have many different titles, such as "county board," "county commission," or "board of supervisors." Some boards have judicial-sounding names, like "county judges," "quorum court," or "county court," though they often have nothing to do with the judicial branch.

Governing boards

Most county governing boards can be described in terms of their size. Large boards, often called *boards of supervisors,* may have anywhere from 15 to 100 members. They are common in heavily populated counties that include a large city. Board members are usually elected officials from regional subdivisions of the county. Counties in New York, Michigan, Wisconsin, and portions of Illinois tend to have such large boards.

Small county boards, often called *boards of commissioners,* typically have three to seven members. Most small boards are elected at large from the county as a whole. (That is, if there are five seats on the board, each county resident votes for five candidates.) Some counties, however, are divided into election districts. According to the Supreme Court ruling in *Avery v. Midland County* (1968), all districts within a county must be of equal population, conforming to the "one person, one vote" principle. Small boards are found mainly in Ohio, Indiana, Pennsylvania, and the states in the South and West.

County board members serve from one to eight years, with four-year terms being the most common. Most boards hold regular public meetings either weekly or monthly.

Duties of county boards

County boards have both legislative and executive powers. Their lawmaking powers, how-

ever, are often limited strictly by the state constitution and statutes. County laws generally deal only with financial and regulatory matters, such as requiring vaccinations for animals, setting speed limits on county roads, approving zoning changes, establishing county tax rates, appropriating funds, and borrowing money.

The primary function of the county board is executive — to oversee the operation of the county. As administrator, the board may issue liquor licenses, maintain buildings, buy and sell county property, contract for building bridges, and make the county budget. The board usually appoints a planning commission and a budget commission, but board members may split these duties among themselves.

Other county workers

Carrying out the county government's functions takes many other officials, both elected and appointed. Some of the more common posts are listed in Figure 26–2. In addition to those listed, there may be county nurses, inspectors, dogcatchers, and so on. Most of these officials serve for two or four years.

In addition to the governing board, counties typically have a vast array of minor boards and commissions with authority over one particular area. For example, there may be a hospital board, a sanitation board, a county fair commission, a civil service board, a parks commission, and so on. Some of these commissioners are appointed, while others are elected. Members of the governing board commonly head the minor boards.

Finally, county governments depend on a host of employees. Across the United States there are about 2 million workers handling the counties' daily operations. These workers include nurses, janitors, secretaries, painters, carpenters, deputies, receptionists, file clerks, mechanics, librarians, truck drivers, and managers. Many are selected through some sort of merit system, while others are appointed.

Problems and reforms in the counties

Despite the importance of counties in providing services, they are often an almost invisible level of government. Few citizens understand the workings of county governments; many are not even aware they exist. Counties have sometimes been criticized for their inefficiency in providing services. Many of the problems of county

692

Background: *Civic Participation* Another common official is the county agricultural extension agent, an official employed by nearly every county in the nation. Extension agents help people solve agricultural and family-living problems. Agents receive assistance from federal, state, and county offices. In both rural and urban areas, agents advise 4-H leaders and provide information about gardening and pest control.

Figure 26-2 COUNTY OFFICIALS Below are descriptions of some of the elected officials who serve in county governments. 3A

PROSECUTING ATTORNEY	also called "state's attorney," "county attorney," or "district attorney (DA)." Prosecutes accused criminals, defends the county in lawsuits, gives legal advice to county officials.
SHERIFF	keeps law and order, operates the county jail, delivers warrants and subpoenas, apprehends suspects.
RECORDER OF DEEDS	registers legal transactions, including real estate sales, mortgages, articles of incorporation, birth certificates, and marriage licenses.
ASSESSOR	determines the value of all real and personal property for tax purposes.
COUNTY CLERK	supervises elections, including voter registration, ballots, and polling places; records proceedings of the county board; makes up tax rolls. Serves as recorder of deeds in some counties.
COLLECTOR	receives tax payments; conducts sale of property confiscated for tax penalties.
TREASURER	responsible for all county funds; invests them in local banks and makes authorized payments.
AUDITOR	checks county's financial records; may also serve as bookkeeper and assessor. Many are certified public accountants (CPAs).
CORONER	also called "medical examiner." Investigates suspicious deaths, identifies bodies, maintains county morgue. Some states require coroners to be licensed doctors.
SURVEYOR	determines boundaries and property lines, settles disputes between landowners.
COUNTY ENGINEER	oversees construction projects; sometimes serves as surveyor.
PUBLIC ADMINISTRATOR	manages the property and finances of orphans and people unable to take care of themselves.
CLERK OF COURTS	keeps records of the local courts.

RETEACHING/CORRECTIVES

▲ Have students make a chart of county functions. At the top of the chart should be the words *State Government*. Below that should be *County Government*. Below that should be the six functions of counties listed on pp. 691–692. Students should write a brief explanation next to each of the six functions.

You may also want to use **Transparency 58,** which shows causes and effects of the urbanization of America.

ENRICHMENT/EXTENSION

■ Have students complete **Skills Challenge Worksheet 26,** which deals with the changing number of governmental units in the United States.

governments stem from poor organization or from legal or physical constraints. To improve county government, a number of reforms have been suggested.

HOME RULE Because of restrictions set by state constitutions and statutes, county officials often are powerless to deal with pressing social and economic problems. A frequent suggestion for improving county government is for the state to allow **home rule**. Under home rule, a county government, with the approval of its voters, has the power to design its own structure and institu-

tions. Home rule, its supporters stress, gives county officials the flexibility and power they need to be more effective. Although thirty states now permit home rule, only about a hundred counties have adopted it.

ELECTION REFORM Many suggestions for improving county government deal with the ways that county officials and employees are selected. As Figure 26–2 indicates, there are a great many elected county officials. To shorten election ballots and make voters' choices easier, many reformers have suggested that only officials who

693

Background: *History* An early example of home rule began in 1875, when Missouri adopted a constitutional measure for home-rule government; the movement reached its peak at the turn of the 20th century. Interest then declined until the 1950's, when several states—among them Tennessee, Georgia, Louisiana, Maryland, and Rhode Island—permitted home rule in their cities.

Figure 26–2
● *Since the treasurer and auditor both deal with county funds, why should they not be the same person?* (There would be no check on the improper use of funds by the treasurer.)

The symbol ♟ denotes active participation strategies.

Activities are keyed for student abilities:
▲ = Basic
● = All Levels
■ = Average/Advanced

Section 1 Review Answers

1. Run elections, keep records, administer social services, maintain public facilities, provide law enforcement, and regulate land use.

2. Lawmaking powers are restricted to finance and regulation; executive powers come from their role as overseers of county operations.

3. Certain social and economic problems. Counties without home rule are often powerless to deal with such problems.

4. Those with administrative or technical jobs.

5. By combining counties with little tax revenue, counties can provide better services more efficiently.

Critical thinking Students should recognize that county governments have both legislative and executive powers. County lawmaking powers, however, are very limited; counties generally carry out the wishes of the *state* legislature.

CLOSURE

● Remind students of the pre-reading questions at the beginning of the section. Pose one or both of these questions again. Then have students read Section 2, noting the difference between towns and townships and the different kinds of district governments.

YOU DECIDE

8H

Jamie Carroll, a seventeen-year-old high school senior from Polo, Missouri, received failing grades because of unexcused absences. Jamie alleged that she was discriminated against for her religious beliefs since school officials refused to excuse her absences from class so that she could attend numerous religious observances relating to her membership in the Remnant Church of God. The unexcused absences jeopardized Jamie's position on the cheerleading squad and membership in the National Honor Society.

Advise the school board.

---

actually make public policy should be elected. Those who have technical or administrative jobs, such as surveyors and collectors, would then be appointed on the basis of their professional qualifications.

Moreover, many county officials are selected on the basis of party politics. Reformers think that such partisan appointments could in many cases be replaced by a county merit system. This would allow the most qualified people, not necessarily those with political connections, to be hired and promoted.

In addition, county government often is overloaded with minor boards and commissions. Although many serve necessary functions, others are wasteful and inefficient. Their sheer numbers also make it difficult to pinpoint responsibility for decisions or inaction. To clarify lines of responsibility and make government more efficient, some counties now hire professionally trained **county managers**. The county manager is appointed by the governing board to oversee the day-to-day operations of the county. Ideally, the governing board makes policy, and the county manager carries it out.

694

CONSOLIDATION Counties with small populations and few industries face a serious problem because their tax revenues are also very small. Without enough income, counties cannot provide all the services that people need. One possible solution to this problem is **consolidation**, the combining of sparsely populated counties. By pooling their resources, counties can provide better services more efficiently. Because of tradition and local pride, however, many counties resist consolidation.

As a less drastic step, a number of counties have tried *functional* consolidation, in which two or more counties share a particular government service. The service may be a hospital, a library, or a water system. In some areas, large cities have consolidated with their host county to provide services. This is called "city-county consolidation."

SECTION 1 REVIEW

Vocabulary and key terms

county (690)   county manager (694)
county seat (690)   consolidation (694)
home rule (693)

For review

1. What are the six main functions of county governments? **4A**
2. What are some of the legislative and executive powers possessed by county governing boards? **3A**
3. What problems of county government is home rule intended to solve? **3A**
4. According to county government reformers, which officials should be appointed rather than elected? **3A**
5. How can consolidation help a county that is short of funds? **7B**

Critical thinking

COMPARING AND CONTRASTING In general, how are the powers of county governments described in this section like and unlike the powers of the legislative and executive branches of the national government? **3A**

You Decide Answer
Students should defend their answers. A U.S. district judge granted a request by Carroll's parents and ordered her reinstated as a student in the school and as a member of the cheerleading squad.

SECTION 2

Local Government Has Many Smaller Units

ACCESS | **The Main Ideas**

1 **How are towns and townships governed?**
pages 695–697

2 **What functions do school districts and special districts perform?**
pages 697–698

Waxahachie, Texas; Muddy, Illinois; Embarrass, Minnesota; Newcomerstown, Ohio; Frostproof, Florida — the colorful names of some American communities are stories in themselves. In many of these smaller communities, especially those in the West and South, most local government functions are the responsibility of the county government. However, in other parts of the country, such as New England and the Midwest, towns and townships have important governing tasks. School districts and other special districts also exist in every state to handle specific functions.

1B, 3A

Towns and Townships

New England towns

In colonial New England the primary unit of local government was the **town**, and town government is still significant today. Towns were established first by the Pilgrim and Puritan settlers of Massachusetts in the early 1600's. Each of these small communities included a village, the

Section Objectives

☐ explain how towns and townships are governed

☐ describe the functions performed by school districts and special districts

Vocabulary

town, town meeting, selectmen, town manager, township, school district, special district, school board

FOCUS

● Ask if any students are familiar with the term *town meeting* from this course or from some other source. (The term is mentioned in the last sentence on p. 15 as part of the discussion of direct democracy.) Then ask if any students are familiar with the terms *school district, school board,* and *superintendent of schools.* Explain that all terms deal with forms of local government discussed in this section.

Throughout New England, as in this Vermont town, a white-spired church stands at the heart of the community.

695

Background: *Politics* The cities of Denver, Honolulu, and San Francisco comprise entire counties; Baltimore and St. Louis are municipalities outside any county.

The symbol ᎥᎥ denotes active participation strategies.

Activities are keyed for student abilities:
▲ = Basic
● = All Levels
■ = Average/Advanced

EXPLANATION

After students have read the section, you may want to consider the following activities:

👥 Structure of Government

● Divide the class into groups of two. Have each group make a five-column table. The columns should be labeled *Unit of Local Government, Officeholders, How Selected, Duties,* and *Where Found in United States.* In the first column, students should list the following units of local government: town, township, school district, and special district. Then have students complete the tables.

Politics

▲ *Why has the number of school districts decreased in recent years?* (Improved transportation and communication have made it possible to consolidate many school districts.)

● *Why has the number of special districts increased in recent years?* (Forming special districts is a useful way to deal with problems that spread beyond existing government boundaries or to get around local limits on taxing and spending.)

central "common" or "green," a church, and the surrounding farms and forests. The church played a central role both in colonial daily life and in the town governments. In time, towns spread from Massachusetts across the rest of New England.

Today, the six New England states are still divided into towns. (Government units called "towns" also exist in Minnesota, New York, and Wisconsin, where New Englanders migrated.) "Towns" now may include large cities as well as small communities. Although towns may physically be part of a county, town governments assume many of the responsibilities taken by counties and cities elsewhere.

Town meetings and officials

The **town meeting** is one of the features that distinguish New England towns from other local governments. Once a year, usually in the spring, citizens in each New England town meet officially to decide the basic policies of the town. These meetings, which are open to all qualified town voters, are the best example of direct democracy in the United States today. Here the townspeople debate and decide the town's

New England communities still hold town meetings, just as they did in colonial days.

budget, taxes, laws, and any other pressing local issues. They also elect officials to handle the day-to-day operations of the town between meetings.

Although all qualified town voters have the right to attend town meetings, voice their opinions, and cast their ballots, not every person exercises this right. Moreover, in larger towns, it is impractical for every person to attend and participate in the town meeting. In these cases, towns are divided into districts. Citizens in each district elect a person to represent them at the town meeting. These towns, then, are actually practicing representative, not direct, democracy.

A number of officials are elected at the town meeting. First is the board of **selectmen** — three to five men and women who supervise the town's affairs. The selectmen are roughly equivalent to the members of county governing boards. Other elected officials may include an assessor, tax collector, treasurer, surveyor, town clerk, justice of the peace, constable, dog-catcher, school board members, and road commissioner. To cope with growing populations and complex administrative duties, many larger towns now employ a full-time, professionally trained **town manager** to oversee daily operations. The town manager is hired by the board of selectmen.

Townships and their governments

County subdivisions called **townships** also date back to colonial times. Townships first were organized in New Jersey, New York, and Pennsylvania in the late 1600's and are still the basic unit of local government there. The Land Ordinance of 1785 divided the Northwest Territory (north of the Ohio River and west of Pennsylvania to the Mississippi River) into townships six miles square, with one square mile set aside to support schools. Because of this, township organization is common in midwestern states.

Some townships today are nothing more than lines on the map, used for administrative and statistical purposes. Other townships perform many of the grassroots functions of the counties. Township governments may enforce the law, administer elections, supply water, collect taxes, and maintain roads. In some urban and suburban areas of Pennsylvania, New Jersey, and Michigan, townships assume many of the functions of cities, such as fire and police protection.

Background: *Geography* By the time the frontier closed in the 1890's, much of the rural population (except the thirteen original states and Texas) was distributed across the land in the checkerboard pattern of the township land division system. This system was devised in the Ordinance of 1785 to survey properties easily and avoid confusion over boundaries in the newly opened lands. The nationwide system represents the largest area of planned rural settlement in the world.

Township governments typically are run by popularly elected governing boards called *boards of supervisors* or *trustees*. These boards usually consist of three or five members who serve four-year terms. The board's principal duties are to supervise township elections, assess and collect property taxes, and oversee road construction and maintenance. Some townships elect a treasurer, assessor, or constable.

3A, 7B

"District" Governments

Counties, towns, and townships all perform a variety of government functions. Other local political units have more limited tasks. One type is the **school district**. A newer type of local political unit, the **special district**, is set up to provide a few specialized services.

School districts

Because education is probably the most important function of state and local government, the states have created thousands of school districts. There are nearly 15,000 school districts in the United States. There were once more than 100,000, but roads, school buses, and improved communications have made it practical in many places to consolidate two or more districts. Consolidation lets communities pool their funds for salaries, books, and equipment.

Most school districts are governed by an elected **school board**, or *board of education*. These boards are usually composed of three to fifteen citizens who serve for two or four years without pay. The board's main function is to set local school policy. This may include making the budget, determining school requirements and courses, and hiring teachers. Because board members serve part-time, they usually hire a professionally trained superintendent of schools to run the school district's day-to-day operations.

Special districts

Special districts are the fastest growing type of government in the United States. In 1962, there were about 18,000 special districts (not including school districts). By 1982, that figure had increased by 10,000. Special districts have been described as phantom governments: they are all around us, but few people know where they are or what they do.

8A

LANDMARKS in LIBERTY

"Articles of Agreement,"
Springfield, MA(1636)

Within two years of the founding of the Massachusetts Bay Colony, settlers began spreading westward. One group, led by William Pynchon, left the town of Roxbury and started Springfield. The group wrote a plan for governing the new settlement that was copied in towns throughout New England. It illustrates the practical, day-to-day decisions made by local governments even in colonial times.

" [ARTICLE 1] We intend by God's grace, as soon as we can, with all convenient speed, to procure some Godly and faithful minister with whom we purpose to join in church covenant to walk in all the ways of Christ.
[2] We intend that our town shall be composed of forty families, or, if we think meet after[ward] to alter our purpose, yet not to exceed the number of fifty families, rich and poor.
[3] That every inhabitant shall have a convenient proportion for a house lot, as we shall see meet for everyone's quality and estate.
[4] That everyone that hath a house lot shall have a proportion of the cow pasture to the north of End Brook lying northward from the town; and also that everyone shall have a share of . . . all the woodland.
[5] That everyone shall have a share of the meadow or planting ground over against them, as nigh as may be on Agawam side. "

1. What was the first priority for the town planners?
2. How were basic resources, such as land for pasture and crops, to be used?
3. On what basis were house lots allocated?
4. What is meant by the expression "if we think meet"?

Cooperative Learning
● Have students perform **Simulation 4,** which recreates a town meeting.

GUIDED/INDEPENDENT PRACTICE
● Have students write one brief paragraph for each subheading in the section, summarizing the information contained under that subheading.

RETEACHING/ CORRECTIVES
▲ Write on the board the terms *Town, Township, School District,* and *Special District.* Have students list on the board at least three similarities and three differences among these units of local government.

ENRICHMENT/EXTENSION
■ Have students find out information about your school district—how it is organized, whether it was consolidated, and so on. Students should write a brief report on their findings.

Section 2 Review Answers
1. They are unusual because some towns still practice direct democracy rather than representative democracy.
2. **(a)** Selectmen supervise town affairs. **(b)** Town managers oversee the town's day-to-day operations.
3. Townships are most common in the Midwest.

Landmarks in Liberty Answers
1. To find a town minister.
2. Land for pasture and crops would be divided among the town's inhabitants, each to have a share of the land near his or her house lot.
3. House lots were to be given to each inhabitant according to that person's needs as determined by the signers of the agreement.
4. "If we think it proper or suitable."

The symbol ii denotes active participation strategies.

Activities are keyed for student abilities:
▲ = Basic
● = All Levels
■ = Average/Advanced

4. Special districts are needed to provide services that local governments cannot or do not handle.

Critical thinking Students should discuss the additional services that smaller units of government are able to provide as well as the bureaucratic problems that can arise from having many government units. Students should recognize that having more units of government creates additional opportunities for citizens to participate.

CLOSURE

● Have students review the vocabulary terms listed on this page, defining each and then using it in a sentence. Then have students read Section 3, noting differences among types of municipal governments.

SECTION 3

Municipal Governments Have Grown in Importance
(pp. 698–705)

Section Objectives
☐ explain how municipalities are formed
☐ describe the different forms of city government

Vocabulary
municipality, incorporation, charter, municipal corporation, mayor-council form, code, council-manager form, city manager, commission form

Special districts provide services that other local governments do not or cannot handle. Among the most common are districts for fire protection, water supply, soil conservation, sanitation, and irrigation. Some of the more unusual special districts include noxious weed districts, mosquito control districts, and parking facility districts.

Special districts are useful for problems that spread beyond existing governmental boundaries. Minnesota, for example, has thousands of lakes where mosquitoes breed. Mosquitoes obviously do not pay any attention to county lines. To control these pests, the state of Minnesota has established "mosquito control districts."

Special districts also provide a way around local government limits on taxing and spending. By establishing a special district, citizens are better able to raise and spend money to deal with a particular problem. Most special districts are governed by a board of three to seven elected members. (Some boards are appointed.) The board is responsible for determining tax rates or user's fees, borrowing money, and supervising the special district's operations.

SECTION 2 REVIEW

Vocabulary and key terms

town (695)   township (696)
town meeting (696)   school district (697)
selectmen (696)   special district (697)
town manager (696)   school board (697)

For review

1. Why are some New England town meetings unusual? **1B**
2. What are the duties of (a) selectmen? (b) a town manager? **3A**
3. Where are townships most common as a form of government? **3A**
4. Why are special districts needed? **3A**

Critical thinking

EXAMINING BASIC PRINCIPLES   What are some advantages or disadvantages of having many small local units of government? How might they enable more people to take part in government? **4A**

3A, 3B, 4D, 8B

SECTION 3
Municipal Governments Have Grown in Importance

ACCESS   **The Main Ideas**

1 **How are municipalities formed?**
pages 698–700

2 **What are the different forms of city government?**
pages 702–705

For most of its early history, the United States was primarily a rural nation. The vast majority of Americans lived on farms. As Figure 26–3 on the opposite page indicates, when the first census was taken in 1790, only a small percentage of the population lived in cities. County governments could provide most of the services people needed and carry out state functions in their areas.

As cities grew, county governments were less able to meet the changing needs of fast-growing urban populations. Today, with about three-fourths of the American population living close together in urban areas, the tasks of local government have become much more numerous and complex.

Accordingly, units of government called **municipalities** now provide many local government services for city dwellers. A municipality is any local community that enjoys self-government — it may be called a city, town, or village, depending on its population and history. There are more than 19,000 municipalities throughout the United States today.

698

Municipal Corporations

In looking at local governments, it is important to keep in mind that the states have unitary forms of government. State legislatures usually establish counties and townships without the approval of the residents within them. Municipalities, by contrast, are created at the request of the residents of the community. For this reason, these governments differ in their legal status, powers, and functions.

Incorporation

The process of becoming a municipality is called **incorporation**. It begins when the community meets a minimum population requirement and gathers enough signatures on a referendum petition. If the voters approve the referendum at the next election, the state issues a **charter**, which officially recognizes the community as a **municipal corporation**. A municipal corporation, much like a business corporation, has the legal status of an artificial person. This status makes the municipality more independent, but also gives it added responsibility.

Municipal corporations have broad legislative powers as well as administrative responsibilities. Counties, as Section 1 points out, are primarily administrative and make few laws. City government officials, such as mayors and

Figure 26–3 URBAN AND RURAL POPULATION The number of Americans living in cities and their suburbs make up an ever-increasing percentage of the population. 8B

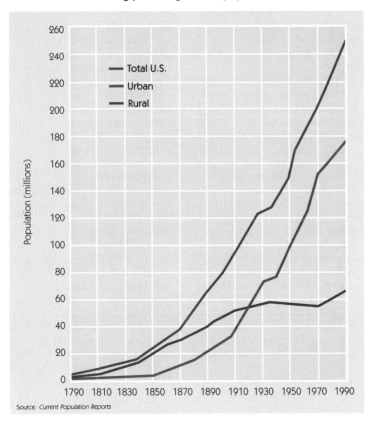

Source: Current Population Reports

699

Background: *Structure of Government* State legislatures can also establish quasi-municipal corporations (which are primarily administrative bodies that include counties, townships, and special districts) without community approval. They perform *governmental functions* (activities carried out on behalf of the state, such as police protection, education, public health, libraries) but few *proprietary functions* (activities conducted for a profit, such as public utilities, transportation, golf courses, liquor stores).

Figure 26–3
● *When did the tremendous increase in the urban population begin?* (1850.)

 FOCUS

● Divide the class into two groups. Have each member of one group write on the board one image of the United States of 1790. Have each member of the other group write one image of the United States of today. Then have the class compare the two images, keeping this question in mind as they do so: *How do these images show the transformation of the United States from a rural society into an urban one?*

EXPLANATION

After students have read the section, you may want to consider the following activities:

History

▲ *Was the United States mostly rural or mostly urban at the time of its creation?* (Mostly rural.) *When did this change?* (According to Figure 26–3, the number of urban residents passed the number of rural residents around 1920.)

▲ *Has the number of people living in urban areas ever decreased since this nation's founding?* (No.) *Has the number of people living in rural areas ever decreased?* (Yes: between the 1930's and 1970.)

● CRITICAL THINKING Have students suggest causes of the rise in urban population. (Causes include immigrants moving to cities, the growth of industry, and the mechanization of farming.)

The symbol denotes active participation strategies.

Activities are keyed for student abilities:
▲ = Basic
● = All Levels
■ = Average/Advanced

Structure of Government

Remind students of the role that state governments play in the creation of corporations (Chapter 21, p. 564). Communities, like companies, can request and be granted incorporation.

▲ *What role do the citizens of a community play in its incorporation?* (First, a certain number of people must sign a referendum petition. Then the voters must approve the referendum at the next election before the state will issue a charter.)

● CRITICAL THINKING *Why might residents not want their community to be incorporated?* (They might be satisfied with their current levels of taxation and government service.)

council members, have greater power than most county governing boards.

Acting on behalf of the state, municipal corporations carry out governmental functions such as police and fire protection, education, traffic regulation, and public health. They also may run businesses such as electric and water companies, as well as bus and subway services, golf courses, and swimming pools.

The doctrine of sovereign immunity (page 469) protects states against private lawsuits. As creations of the states, cities generally are protected from lawsuits when performing governmental functions, such as running schools and enforcing traffic laws. On the other hand, a municipal corporation can be sued for injuries that take place on a city-operated bus or around a city-owned swimming pool. Many cities have been besieged by lawsuits in recent years. To avoid being sued, or to avoid paying high liability insurance fees, some cities have been forced to close playgrounds and other recreational areas in which injuries may occur.

City charters

As with all local governments, a municipality's powers and limitations are decided by the state. A city's fundamental law is set forth in its charter. The charter specifies the city's official name, defines its boundaries, grants it powers, stipulates the form of government it may have, outlines the duties of its officials, and specifies its financial and lawmaking powers. There are three general types of municipal charters.

SPECIAL CHARTERS   The oldest type of charter is the *special charter,* dating back to the Declaration of Independence. At that time, each city's charter was specially tailored by the state legislature to apply only to that community. Charters for two similar cities might vary widely.

City leaders complained that state legislators had too much control over local affairs. State legislators, in turn, disliked having to spend so much time dealing with specific local problems. Although most states abandoned special charters, they are still found in Maine, New Hampshire, Delaware, and Vermont.

CLASSIFICATION CHARTERS   To simplify the charter system, more than half the states adopted *classification charters.* The state first classifies

each city according to population, then devises a uniform charter for each class. For example, there may be one type of charter for cities with 25,000 to 50,000 people, and another type of charter for cities with more than 50,000 residents.

Though simple, this charter system is by no means perfect. Cities that are equal in population do not necessarily have the same needs. A resort area with 25,000 residents would have different concerns than would an industrial area with the same population. Moreover, classification charters are sometimes nothing more than disguises for special charters. For example, a state may mandate a charter specifically for "all cities with more than a million residents," when in fact there is only one city in the state with a population that large. The effect, therefore, is to create a special charter.

A modification of the classification charter is the *optional charter* system, now used in sixteen states. Under this arrangement, the state legislature classifies each city according to population. Every city within each group, however, has the option of adopting one of several forms of government.

HOME RULE CHARTERS   Many states now permit their cities to draft and adopt any form of government they please, without interference from the state legislature. This self-government arrangement is called municipal home rule (as distinct from county home rule, page 693). Thirty-four states now provide for home rule in their constitutions, while seven states have passed statutes to allow it. Most of the largest cities in the United States now operate under home rule — about two-thirds of all cities with 200,000 or more residents.

Home rule does not give cities complete independence from the state. On the contrary, states frequently impose strict limitations on city governments, especially on local taxing and spending policies. Home rule does give cities flexibility to use all the powers not specifically prohibited by state constitutions or laws. In some respects, then, home rule is to the cities what the reserved powers are to the states. Should a conflict arise between the city and state, however, most state courts would rule in favor of the state.

700

Background: *Constitutional Heritage* In *Smith v. Wade* (1983), the Court ruled that prison and jail guards could be sued for heavy punitive damages if they allowed the assault or rape of inmates. The Court further ruled that any governmental official could be prosecuted under the Ku Klux Klan Act of 1871, which made it a crime to deny any citizen equal protection under the law by means of "force, intimidation, or threat."

R *ight now, your life is probably filled with school activities. You may not realize that there are ways you can be involved in your community. Ricardo Gonzalez, a senior at Hialeah–Miami Lakes High School in Florida, worked for a community leader, Alexander Penelas, for several years. In 1990 Penelas became the first Cuban American elected to the Metro Dade County Commission and Ricky began to work in Penelas's office. This is what Ricky has to say about what he does and why he does it.*

Ricardo Gonzalez

Most of the times I answer the calls that come in and deal with concerns of constituents. For example, there's a lady who says a tree's leaves are causing flooding on her street. She wants to see if we can do anything. We call the different departments in the county. Then we tell her, "Okay, ma'am, the parks and recreation will attend to that Monday." It's how a democracy works. Someone with a problem should go to their local representative. That's their source of representation. They elected these people, these people should serve them to the best of their abilities.

In the office, most of the calls we have are in Spanish, so it's valuable that I can speak both Spanish and English. Our community down here is very diverse in terms of ethnic background. I think Hialeah is the most Cuban city, most Hispanic city in the nation. Our leaders are often Hispanic. But you have to maintain a kind of balance between Hispanics and Anglos and blacks. You have to try to reach out and bring different ethnic groups together.

I find political events pretty exciting. The worst part is having to go after a long day at school. After I'm there I feel good, but sometimes I think, "Oh no, I have to go all the way downtown." No matter how silly the questions may be or the problems people have, at least I'm answering them. Sometimes I have to turn them away. Still, I think I do make a difference. Not a big one—I'm not the commissioner— but I think I do make a difference.

Voters nowadays are disenchanted with politics, they don't have faith in the system. They say, "This is wrong with our community, and this is wrong with our state." You're really not doing anything by complaining. You have to get out there and be active. I think every citizen has a responsibility to play a role in their community.

STUDENT PARTICIPATION

1. Find out who your representatives are on the municipal and/or county level.
2. Identify a local issue that is important to you. Write a letter to your local representative stating your opinion, or call or visit his or her office and explain your point of view.

YOUR TURN

4D

A Cuban American Student Serves His Community

Ricardo Gonzalez (top); Alexander Penelas, Metro Dade County Commissioner (center), visiting a school in his community.

701

Geography

■ Standing next to a wall map, ask volunteers to come forward and point out cities whose mayors they can name. Then ask what the cities mentioned have in common. (Most should be large cities or ones located near your community.)

Cooperative Learning

● Divide the class into four groups. Have each group prepare a short written summary of one of the following types of city government: mayor-council with a weak mayor, mayor-council with a strong mayor, council-manager, commission. Reports should identify the key decision-makers or governing bodies, the powers of the mayor or other chief executive, the groups or individuals who have legislative or executive powers, the types of cities most likely to use that type of plan, and the weaknesses and strengths of that form of government. Each group might also prepare a chart showing how the government is organized under each type of plan.

Forms of City Government

Each municipal charter specifies the form of government a city may have. Although there are many variations, most municipalities are organized in one of three ways.

Mayor-council form

The oldest and a very common form of municipal government is the **mayor-council form**. Residents elect both a city council and a mayor as their governing officials. Before 1900, most city councils and mayors were elected on a partisan basis. Corruption in many city halls in the early 1900's, however, led reformers to adopt nonpartisan elections. Most cities now elect their city councils and mayors on nonpartisan ballots.

Although councils were once bicameral, nearly every city now has a unicameral council. Most have five or seven members who serve two- or four-year terms. (Chicago's fifty-member city council is the nation's largest.) Council members in most cities are elected at large; some,

however, are selected by wards, or city districts. Some city councils have a combination of at-large and ward representatives.

A city council's powers are mostly legislative. One of its basic responsibilities is to manage the city's finances. This includes enacting the city's annual budget, setting tax rates, authorizing spending, and borrowing money if necessary. The council's second basic function is to pass ordinances, or city laws. Many ordinances specify standards, called **codes**, for certain activities. Building codes, for example, set safety standards for buildings under construction.

The mayor is the city's chief executive or administrator. He or she may preside over city council meetings and supervises the city's operations on a day-to-day basis. The mayor is also the city's ceremonial leader. Symbolic duties of the office include breaking ground for new buildings, leading parades, representing the city at conferences, and speaking at schools and civic luncheons. Most mayors are elected at large for the same length of term as the council members.

Figure 26–4 MAYOR-COUNCIL FORMS OF GOVERNMENT **The powers held by the mayor can vary in different city governments.** 3A

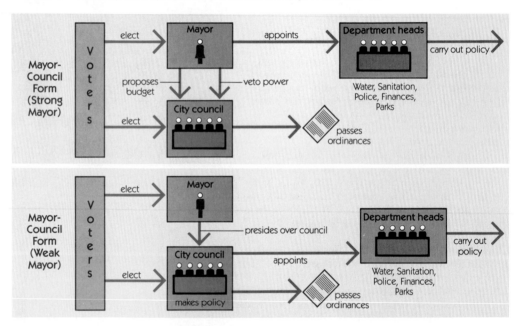

Cross-reference
A ward map of Boston is provided in Chapter 11, p. 310.

Figure 26–4
● *Why is a "strong mayor" stronger than a "weak mayor"?* (A strong mayor has veto power over the city council and appoints department heads.)

Weak mayors and strong mayors

Mayor-council systems vary from city to city, depending on the powers given to the mayor or kept by members of the council. Figure 26–4 shows the two basic ways powers are divided.

In the "weak-mayor" form, the mayor presides over council meetings, but has few other powers. He or she has little or no veto power and in some cities can vote only in case of ties. The mayor's power to hire and fire department heads and other city officials is also quite restricted. The weak-mayor form is found usually in small-to medium-sized cities.

By contrast, the "strong-mayor" form allows the mayor the power both to propose the city's budget and to veto the council's ordinances. The mayor also possesses the sole authority to appoint and remove department heads, such as the chief of police or the public works director. The concentration of authority in one person tends to make city government more efficient. The strong-mayor form is found in most of the nation's largest cities.

Council-manager form

The **council-manager form** of municipal government originated in Staunton, Virginia, in 1908, but was popularized by Dayton, Ohio, which adopted the system in 1913. The council-manager system — diagrammed in Figure 26–5 — is patterned after the management techniques of private corporations. In a business corporation, stockholders elect a board of directors to set company policy. The directors, in turn, choose a president to run the company.

Similarly, in a council-manager city, the voters first elect a city council to make the city's policy. The council typically has five or seven nonpartisan members, elected at large for two-year terms. The mayor may be chosen by the city council but has no independent powers. He or she merely presides over the council meetings and serves as the city's ceremonial head.

The city's chief executive is not the mayor but a professionally trained manager appointed by the city council. It is the **city manager** who must oversee the city's operations. He or she

GUIDED/INDEPENDENT PRACTICE

● Have students write four-paragraph essays restating the information presented in Figure 26–4 and Figure 26–5. One paragraph should be devoted to each of the four forms of city government shown.

RETEACHING/CORRECTIVES

▲ Have students outline the section, using the headings and subheadings as entries and supplying necessary details.

Have students complete **Skills Practice Worksheet 26,** which contains a chart showing the different forms of city government.

Figure 26–5 COUNCIL-MANAGER AND COMMISSION FORMS OF MUNICIPAL GOVERNMENT 3A

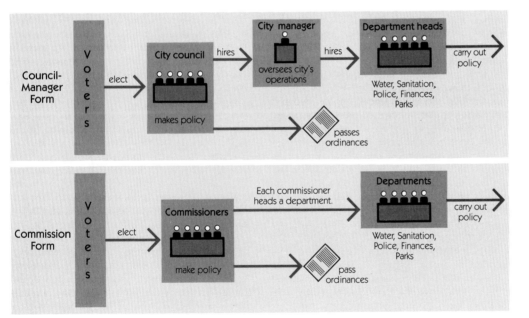

703

Background: *History* As in Galveston (p. 704), a natural disaster prompted Dayton to change its form of local government. Heavy rains in 1913 caused three rivers to flood Dayton, killing more than 300 people and causing about $100 million in damage. Later that year the city adopted the council-manager form of government, with a professional city manager hired to handle the problems caused by the flood.

Figure 26–5
● *What is the role of the city manager in the council-manager form of municipal government?* (The city manager, hired by the city council, hires and oversees the department heads.)

The symbol 👥 denotes active participation strategies.

Activities are keyed for student abilities:
▲ = Basic
● = All Levels
■ = Average/Advanced

Richard Riordan (center) won election as mayor of Los Angeles in 1993. Los Angeles has a mayor-council form of city government.

prepares the city budget, hires and fires city employees, and carries out policies made by the council. The manager, having been hired by the council, can also be fired.

Well over 2,000 municipalities use the council-manager system, making it the most popular form of city government. It has become especially popular among medium-sized cities in the South and West. The advantages of this form are that it provides for professional management, frees council members to concentrate on policy matters, and separates legislative and executive powers. Critics sometimes complain that managers often make policy even though they are not democratically elected.

Commission form

The **commission form** of municipal government began in Galveston, Texas, in 1900. Galveston had been devastated by a giant hurricane and tidal wave that killed 6,000 people, and the city's mayor-council government was unable to handle the disaster. With permission from the Texas legislature, Galveston's leading citizens created a special commission to rebuild the city. Each commissioner was responsible for a different operation, such as water or housing. The plan worked, and order was soon restored. Because the plan proved so successful, Galveston opted to continue it.

The next city to adopt the commission form was Des Moines, Iowa, in 1907. The plan spread rapidly. By 1920, more than 500 cities utilized the plan. Thereafter, its popularity slowly diminished. Today, fewer than 200 cities use the commission form — even Galveston and Des Moines have abandoned it. Among the largest cities still using this plan are Portland, Oregon and Tulsa, Oklahoma.

Under the commission form, the people elect a small commission, usually with five, seven, or nine members. Commissioners are typically elected at large on nonpartisan ballots and serve for two- or four-year terms. One commissioner is selected as mayor, but he or she merely presides at meetings and special functions.

704

Together, the commissioners approve the city's budget, enact ordinances, and set overall policy — just like a regular city council. In addition, each commissioner is also the head of a particular department. For example, there may be a finance commissioner, a parks commissioner, or a public works commissioner. In other words, commissioners are both policy-makers and administrators. There is no separation of powers. (See Figure 26–5.)

The advantages of the commission plan are that it is simple to understand, shortens the ballot, makes decision-makers highly visible, and reduces the number of administrative departments to a manageable size. Opponents argue that the commission form lacks leadership and coordination, makes it difficult to pinpoint responsibility, and allows amateurs who lack sufficient knowledge to run a complex operation.

SECTION 3 REVIEW

Vocabulary and key terms

municipality (698)	code (702)
incorporation (699)	council-manager
charter (699)	form (703)
municipal corporation (699)	city manager (703)
mayor-council form (702)	commission form (704)

For review

1. What is the difference in the way municipal and county governments are created? **3A**
2. Briefly describe three main types of municipal charters. **3A**
3. (a) How is power divided under the mayor-council form of municipal government? (b) How does the position of mayor differ in the weak- and strong-mayor variations of the mayor-council form? **3B**
4. How is power divided in the council-manager form? **3B**
5. How is the commission form organized? **3A**

Critical thinking

ANALYZING AN ISSUE What are the advantages of having a mayor with a good deal of authority? What are some reasons for having other administrators in municipal governments? **3B**

Chapter Summary

The county is the basic unit of local government in the United States. Counties carry out functions of the state at the local level, such as administering elections, keeping records, providing social services and public facilities, enforcing the law, and regulating land use. Elected governing boards in each county have limited lawmaking and wide administrative powers. Other elected officials, commissions, and county employees also perform essential functions. Many states have adopted home rule to give county governments more powers. Some counties have hired county managers to carry out the policies made by governing boards. To provide services to greater numbers more efficiently, many counties have adopted forms of consolidation.

In New England, the town is the basic unit of local government. All the town's citizens decide on local policies at the town meeting and elect a board of selectmen to oversee the town government between meetings. Townships are an important unit of government in New Jersey, New York, and Pennsylvania, and many midwestern states. School districts are established to set and carry out local school policy. Special districts are single-purpose governments giving specific services that other local governments do not or cannot provide.

A municipality is any local community or city that enjoys self-government. Municipal corporations differ from counties in that they are created at the request of their residents, have greater lawmaking powers, and carry out nongovernmental activities. Charters outline the powers of a municipal government; depending on the state, a city may have a special charter, classification charter, or home rule charter.

City governments are most often organized under the mayor-council, council-manager, or commission form. Mayor-council forms vary depending on the way powers are divided between the council and a weak or strong mayor.

4. The council is popularly elected; one council member is selected to serve as ceremonial mayor. The council appoints a professional city manager to oversee city operations.
5. Commissioners are elected on a nonpartisan ballot; one commissioner is selected to serve as mayor.

Critical thinking Students should note that the concentration of authority in a strong mayor tends to make big-city government more efficient. However, the separation of powers in the council-manager form frees council members to concentrate on policy and allows them the freedom to remove the city manager when necessary.

CLOSURE

● Have students write three "I learned. . ." statements describing what they learned in this section. Then have students read the next assigned lesson.

CHAPTER 26 CORRECTIVES

● To review the content of Chapter 26, you may want to have students complete **Study Guide/Review 26** or **Workbook Chapter 26.**

The symbol ♨ denotes active participation strategies.

Activities are keyed for student abilities:
▲ = Basic
● = All Levels
■ = Average/Advanced

705

CHAPTER 26 REVIEW

Answers

Vocabulary See pp. T19–T21 for suggested vocabulary activities.

Reviewing the Facts

1. It is especially important in rural areas in the South and Midwest; it is not so important in New England, where town governments are more important; in urban areas, cities provide many services that counties perform in rural areas.

2. To carry out state government functions in one local area.

3. To oversee county operations—issue licenses, maintain buildings, buy and sell county property, contract for building bridges, make the county budget.

4. Because it is impractical for all people to attend a town meeting, voters in a district can instead elect someone to represent them.

5. Communities can pool their funds for buildings, teacher salaries, books, and equipment.

6. A community meets the minimum population requirement; enough signatures are gathered on a referendum petition; voters approve the referendum; and the state issues a charter.

7. The municipality can adopt any form of government it wants. It can use all the powers not specifically prohibited by the state's constitution or laws.

8. The mayor is the city's chief executive as well as ceremonial leader. A "strong" mayor's powers include the right to propose the budget, veto the council's ordinances, and appoint and remove department heads.

Thinking Critically About Key Concepts

1. First, the Constitution was designed to deal with issues involving the nation as a whole. Second, all powers given to local government come from the state,

● **Review the definitions of the following terms:**

charter	county seat	selectmen
city manager	home rule	special district
code	incorporation	town
commission form	mayor-council form	town manager
consolidation	municipal corporation	town meeting
council-manager form	municipality	township
county	school board	
county manager	school district	

● **REVIEWING THE FACTS**

1. How does the importance of the county vary in different areas of the United States? **3A**

2. What is the primary purpose of counties? **3A**

3. What are the main duties of county governing boards? **3A**

4. Why are some larger towns divided into districts? **3A**

5. What is the practical advantage of consolidating school districts? **7B**

6. How is a municipality created? **3A**

7. What powers does a home rule charter give to a municipality? **3A**

8. In the mayor-council form of government, what is the role of a "strong" mayor? **3B**

▲ **THINKING CRITICALLY ABOUT KEY CONCEPTS**

1. Why does the Constitution not refer to local government? **3C**

2. How does the national government's relationship to the states differ from the states' relationship to local governments? **3C**

3. Some of the reform proposals for county government involve making county posts less "political." List the possible advantages and disadvantages of replacing elected officials with appointed ones. **6F**

706

4. Do you think that municipal corporations should be protected from lawsuits, as states are? Explain your view. **6A**

▲ **PRACTICING SKILLS**

1. **Study Skills: Reading a diagram.** Refer to Figures 26–4 and 26–5 (pages 702, 703) to answer the following questions. (a) To whom are department heads responsible under the commission form of government? (b) To whom are department heads responsible under the council-manager form? (c) Under which form of government does one group both make policy and carry it out? (d) Who appoints department heads under the mayor-council form of government when there is a "weak mayor"? (e) Under the mayor-council form with a "strong mayor," does the city council or the mayor seem to have more power? Explain. **8B**

2. **Critical Thinking Skills: Drawing conclusions.** Refer to Figure 26–3 (page 699). The graph suggests that total U.S. population will continue to rise steadily into the future. What conclusions can you draw concerning the future direction of the urban population and the rural population? Based on the graph, predict what the total, the urban, and the rural populations will be in the year 2000. How certain can you be about these figures? Explain your answer. **8B**

not the national government.

2. The national government is an equal partner with the states through the federal system, while state government is unitary—local authority comes from the state.

3. Possible advantages include emphasizing merit instead of political connections. Possible disadvantages include weakening the accountability of these officials to the public.

4. Some students will argue that municipal corporations should be protected in order to enable them to perform necessary public functions, such as transportation and education. Other students will argue that the ability to

▲ PARTICIPATORY CITIZENSHIP

1. **Attending a meeting.** Attend a public meeting of your county, city, or town government. Take notes on the proceedings, and make an oral report to your class summarizing what took place. **5C**
2. **Learning about your community.** Gather information on the founding of your community, and trace its form of government. Write a report to explain how and why your community's government has changed. **3A**
3. **Researching a special district.** Find out about a special district in or near your community. Prepare an oral report on the purpose of the district, how it carries out its functions, and whether or not it has been successful in accomplishing its purpose. **3A**

■ WRITING ABOUT ISSUES

1. **Writing a letter.** Write a letter to your county's governing board, asking for information about the specific powers it has. **3A**
2. **Writing a letter to the editor.** Imagine that you live in a city that has one of the forms of government shown in Figure 26–4 and Figure 26–5. Write a letter to the editor pointing out the weaknesses of that form and calling for a different form. **4A**

▲ ANALYZING A POLITICAL CARTOON

In 1991, police officers in Los Angeles were filmed severely beating an unarmed motorist. Following the incident, calls poured forth for the resignation of police chief Darryl Gates. Mayor Tom Bradley wished to fire Gates, but only the city council had the authority to do so. Look at the cartoon below and answer the following questions.

1. Which parties are fighting in the cartoon? **8B**
2. How does the cartoonist portray fighting among the city officials as affecting Gates? **8B**
3. Is the cartoon effective? Why, or why not? **8A**

Cartoon by Paul Conrad, 5/15/91. Copyright, 1991, Los Angeles Times. Reprinted by permission.

absolute certainty about these figures, especially since the rural population shows a definite rise after 1970. Yet barring drastic social or economic changes, such projections, based on reliable data, should not be too far off.

Participatory Citizenship
1. Issues raised at a public meeting could be used for class debates.
2. An appropriate classroom activity would be for students to construct a time line of your community's history for display.
3. Students might be asked to explain how the special district in your area reflects your community's special conditions or needs.

Writing About Issues
1. It might be useful to review the style of a business letter with students.
2. Letters should outline the drawbacks of the present form of government and the advantages of the chosen alternative.

Analyzing a Political Cartoon
1. The Police Commission, Mayor Tom Bradley, and the City Council.
2. He is getting away while city officials fight with each other.
3. Students who feel that the cartoon is effective may suggest that its imagery recalls the film of the actual beating.

707

sue is citizens' best protection against harmful actions by government officials.

Practicing Skills
1. **(a)** As department heads, the commissioners are responsible only to themselves and the voters. **(b)** The city manager. **(c)** Commission form. **(d)** The city council. **(e)** The mayor. He or she proposes the budget, appoints department heads, and has veto power over the council.

2. The urban population will continue to rise steadily with the total population. The rural population may not change dramatically. *Total*—260 million. *Urban*—200 million. *Rural*—70 million. There is no

Chapter Review exercises are keyed for student abilities:
▲ = Basic
● = All Levels
■ = Average/Advanced

CHAPTER 27
LOCAL GOVERNMENT POLICIES AND FINANCES
(pp. 708–729)

	Section Objectives	Section Resources
Section 1 **Local Governments Provide Needed Services**	☐ explain how local governments protect their citizens ☐ explain how local governments can improve the quality of life in the community	▲ TRANSPARENCY **59** ● CITIZENSHIP WORKSHEET **10**
Section 2 **Local Governments Must Pay for Community Services**	☐ list the taxes that local governments collect ☐ describe other sources of money that local governments have ☐ explain how local governments spend money	▲ SKILLS PRACTICE WORKSHEET **27** ■ SKILLS CHALLENGE WORKSHEET **27**
Section 3 **Cities and Counties Plan for the Future**	☐ explain how local governments regulate land use ☐ explain how local governments regulate urban growth	

Essential Elements

The list below shows Essential Elements relevant to this chapter. (The complete list of Essential Elements appears in the introductory pages of this Teacher's Edition.)

Section 1: 1A, 3A, 4A, 4B, 4C, 4D, 6C, 7B, 8B

Section 2: 3B, 4A, 4B, 4C, 7B

Section 3: 3A, 4A, 8A, 8H

Chapter Review: 1A, 3A, 4D, 5C, 6C, 6D, 6G, 7A, 7B, 7D, 8A, 8B, 8D

> Section Resources are keyed for student abilities:
> ▲ = Basic
> ● = All Levels
> ■ = Average/Advanced

Homework Options

Each section contains activities labeled "Guided/Independent Practice," "Reteaching/Correctives," and "Enrichment/Extension." You may wish to choose from among these activities when assigning homework.

Students Acquiring English Activities

Have students work individually or in groups to prepare brochures advertising your community that could be sent to students in another country. Encourage them to write a slogan that would describe your area.

LISTENING/SPEAKING: Ask students to present their brochures to the class, and then have the class vote on the three best brochures.

Case Studies

When teaching this chapter, you may use Case Study 7, which discusses curfews for young people, or Case Study 13, which addresses the issue of dress codes in public schools. (Case Studies may be found following p. 510.)

Teacher Bibliography

Chicoine, David L. and Norman Walzer. *Governmental Structure and Local Public Finance.* Oelgeschlager, Gunn & Hain, 1985. A case study of a local government, detailing how it finances and provides services.

Harrigan, John J. *Political Change in the Metropolis.* 4th ed. Scott, Foresman, 1989. A consideration of the changes in metropolitan and municipal government and their effect on urban policy.

Owen, C. James and York Willbern. *Governing Metropolitan Indianapolis: The Politics of Unigov.* University of California Press, 1985. A case history of local government consolidation that resulted in increased efficiency.

Student Bibliography

Dolan, Edward F. and Margaret M. Scariano. *The Police in American Society.* Watts, 1988. An overview of the function and impact on society of law enforcement as well as the role of the police in preventing crime and keeping the peace.

Gerard, Karen. *American Survivors: Cities and Other Scenes.* Harcourt Brace Jovanovich, 1984. A study of city government, using New York City as an example.

Klebanow, Diana. *Urban Legacy: The Story of America's Cities.* NAL, 1977. A look at the historic role of American cities and their socioeconomic, ethnic, and racial conflicts.

Films and Videotapes*

The Albatross, Parts I and II. (Series title: *Powers That Be.*) 30 min. each. PSUAVS, 1985. v. The first video presents a dilemma for three county commissioners in rural Pennsylvania when bankruptcy threatens a nursing home. The second video illustrates the confusion and misapprehension which are typical in intergovernmental affairs when the commissioners meet with state officials.

The Numbers Nightmare. (Series title: *Powers That Be.*) 30 min. PSUAVS, 1985. v. Tension arises between the incoming and outgoing boards of commissioners in a rural Pennsylvania county over the development of an annual budget and a proposed tax increase.

CHAPTER RESOURCES

Study Guide/Review 27
Workbook Chapter 27
Chapter 27 Test, Forms A–C

A Tale of Five Cities: Tax Revolt Pennsylvania Style. 27 min. CENFPD, 1984. f. Shows how five cities pioneered a graduated tax rate which increased the rates on land while decreasing those on buildings, having a positive effect on city revenues and growth.

Software*

Our Town Meeting (Apple, IBM). TS. Students learn how community government works by participating in a town's planning and budgeting process. Armed with town surveys, revenue projections, and cost estimates, they discuss vital community issues and compete for the town's limited budget dollars, which they then agree to spend in the most effective way possible.

The Environment (Apple, IBM, Macintosh). TS. Acting as a town's mayor, students consider the roles of individuals, communities, and government in a variety of local and global environmental problems. Students must weigh conflicting viewpoints and information, make decisions, and analyze the implications of their actions.

Urbanization: Growth of the Cities (Apple, IBM). TS. Students act as the mayor of a small town on the verge of an economic windfall. They must decide whether to trade the town's quiet life style for that of a boomtown. Students learn about the tradeoffs and responsibilities of rapid industrial growth.

* For a complete guide to audiovisual sources, see page T22.

707B

Local Government Policies and Finances
(pp. 708–729)

This chapter describes the duties of local governments toward their citizens, the ways in which local governments raise revenue, and the methods by which local governments regulate land use and urban growth.

Chapter Objectives
After students complete this chapter, they will be able to:

1. Explain how local governments protect their citizens.
2. Explain how local governments can improve the quality of life in the community.
3. List the taxes that local governments collect.
4. Describe other sources of money that local governments have.
5. Explain how local governments spend money.
6. Explain how local governments regulate land use.
7. Explain how local governments regulate urban growth.

CHAPTER

27

LOCAL GOVERNMENT POLICIES and FINANCES

A strong America depends on its cities — America's glory and sometimes America's shame.

John F. Kennedy
State of the Union Address (1962)

708

Photo
The Gateway Arch in St. Louis is a symbol of the city and its role as a gateway to the West.

November 6, 1990 — Today the voters of Staten Island took a giant step toward independence . . . from New York City. By a four-to-one margin they approved a referendum calling for the creation of a commission to look at ways in which the borough might leave New York City. The vote reflects a widespread belief among the island's 400,000 residents that city services are inadequate. "Living on Staten Island is like getting a phone bill without having a phone," said one resident. Supporters of independence argue that leaving New York City will allow Staten Islanders to provide local services more effectively.

Providing adequate services is a critical challenge for every local government. Local officials try to protect residents from crime, fire, and disease, and to improve the lives of residents through public housing and other forms of assistance. Local governments must obtain funding to pay for these efforts, as well as plan for the orderly growth of the community. In this chapter you will read how local governments deal with these tasks.

CHAPTER OUTLINE

1 Local Governments Provide Needed Services

Protecting Citizens
Improving Citizens' Lives

2 Local Governments Must Pay for Community Services

Tax Revenues
Nontax Revenues
Local Government Spending

3 Cities and Counties Plan for the Future

Planning and Zoning
Regulating Urban Growth

709

SECTION 1

Local Governments Provide Needed Services (pp. 710–715)

Section Objectives
☐ explain how local governments protect their citizens
☐ explain how local governments can improve the quality of life in the community

Vocabulary
urban renewal, homesteading, mass transit

👥 FOCUS

● Have class members identify various government services that improve the quality of life for citizens. Then have groups of students write short scenarios describing what life would be like if local governments suddenly stopped providing these services. For example, groups might speculate that illnesses resulting from food poisoning would increase if restaurants and food stores were no longer inspected to ensure cleanliness. Groups might develop worst-case scenarios in which individual families had to provide services for themselves or go without, and best-case scenarios in which these services were provided privately. In their scenarios, students should take cost implications into account. Have each group present its scenarios to the class.

SECTION 1

Local Governments Provide Needed Services

ACCESS **The Main Ideas**

1 In what different ways do local governments protect their citizens?
pages 710–711

2 How can local governments improve the quality of life in the community?
pages 711–714

Every time you drink tap water, cross a street, or stroll through a park you are relying in some way on local government. It is your local government that ensures the purity of the water, and maintains the streets and parks in good repair. Local governments have a host of other responsibilities as well, from police and fire protection to providing the needy with food and shelter. Local government policies are generally aimed at protecting citizens and improving the quality of life in the community.

1A, 3A, 6C, 7B

Protecting Citizens

Police protection
Almost every community in the United States is served by a local police force. Police protection involves at least three basic activities. First, local police try to prevent crime. Crime prevention may include patrolling streets on foot or in squad cars, locating runaways, organizing neighborhood "crime watches," or talking to schoolchildren about the dangers of drugs.

Second, police enforce the laws. This is no simple task. Crime is a serious problem across America, especially in larger cities. Among the crimes the police must deal with frequently are home burglaries, auto thefts, family disturbances, child abuse, illegal gambling, violent crimes, and scores of drug-related offenses. (Figure 27–1 shows some recent crime statistics.) Following the legal procedures that assure citizens due process, local police investigate these crimes and make necessary arrests.

The third major job of the police is traffic control. Every year, thousands of people are

killed or seriously injured in traffic accidents. To help prevent such tragedies, police officers crack down on speeding motorists, arrest drunk drivers, and enforce safety laws. Police also give out tickets for parking violations, assist ambulance drivers and firefighters, and direct the flow of traffic on busy streets and near stadiums and arenas after games or concerts.

Fire protection
Each year thousands of Americans perish in fires. In addition, fires cause billions of dollars in damage to homes, businesses, and personal property. Fire protection clearly is important for the safety of a community. Major cities have full-time professional fire departments, while many small towns rely on volunteer fire brigades staffed by townspeople.

Firefighters, like police, perform a number of different functions. First, firefighters try to prevent fires from starting. They educate schoolchildren about the causes of fire, inspect buildings, check fire hydrants, and enforce local fire codes for electrical wiring and smoke detectors. When fires do occur, firefighters risk their lives controlling them. Many firefighters also double as paramedics to help accident victims.

Public health
Protecting the health of the community is one of the essential functions of local government. To reduce the spread of disease, local health officials may isolate or quarantine persons with certain illnesses or require immunization against contagious diseases such as influenza, measles, or polio. Officials regularly inspect restaurants and food stores to ensure cleanliness. Hundreds of communities maintain hospitals and clinics, and many operate emergency ambulance services.

Public health also demands a reliable supply of clean water. Local governments — often special water districts — establish plants to treat and purify drinking water. They also set up tanks and reservoirs to store water until it is pumped to homes, buildings, parks, or fire hydrants.

710

Cross-reference
Due process is discussed in Chapter 6, p. 168.

Background: *Law* In the United States in 1990 an average of 5,820 crimes were committed for every 100,000 people. Atlanta, with an average of 19,236 crimes per 100,000 people, ranked highest among major

U.S. cities. Despite its reputation, New York was outdistanced by Newark (New Jersey), Dallas (Texas), and Seattle (Washington), among others, in incidents of crime per 100,000 population.

The proper disposal of waste is also essential to public health. Communities build sewer systems to carry away chemicals and human wastes, as well as water-treatment plants to purify polluted water. Sanitation departments are needed to haul garbage, dispose of trash, and operate sanitary landfills and dumps. Many communities also operate recycling centers to re-use glass, metal, and paper. Sanitation may not be the most glamorous function of local governments, but it is certainly one of the most important.

1A, 3A, 7B

Improving Citizens' Lives

Public assistance

Despite America's richness as a nation, many families and individuals still live in poverty. As Chapter 23 explains, helping the needy was for many years left up to local communities, private individuals, and church-supported charities. Today some local governments provide cash assistance when state and federal aid is either not available or not adequate. Other local governments run free medical and dental clinics for those who cannot afford health care. Most cities and counties maintain programs to help abused and homeless women and children. They may also provide "soup kitchens" and shelters for the homeless. To assist the elderly or disabled, many cities offer free transportation and "meals on wheels." Private contributions and volunteer help play an important part in these welfare programs at the local level.

Public housing

Obtaining safe, comfortable, and affordable housing has become a problem in many American communities. Low-cost homes and apartments quite often lack adequate heating, water, or plumbing. Single-family houses are becoming too expensive for many Americans to afford, while apartment rentals are also high.

Providing housing is a shared federal-local function. One way the federal government assists local governments is through public housing

Figure 27–1 CRIME RATES IN THE UNITED STATES 8B

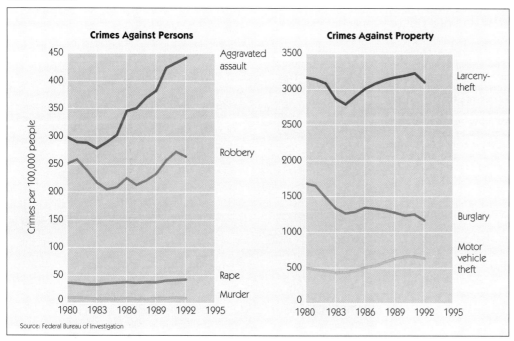

Crimes Against Persons
- Aggravated assault
- Robbery
- Rape
- Murder

Crimes per 100,000 people
450, 400, 350, 300, 250, 200, 150, 100, 50, 0
1980 1983 1986 1989 1992 1995

Crimes Against Property
- Larceny-theft
- Burglary
- Motor vehicle theft

3500, 3000, 2500, 2000, 1500, 1000, 500, 0
1980 1983 1986 1989 1992 1995

Source: Federal Bureau of Investigation

711

EXPLANATION
After reviewing the content of the section, you may want to consider the following activities:

Economics
In such large cities as Boston and New York, housing and apartment rental prices skyrocketed in the 1980's. The price of a house in Boston rose more than 15 percent annually for several consecutive years in the 1980's.
● CRITICAL THINKING *An influx of young professionals is one cause of fast-rising housing costs. Explain the link between these two trends.* (Young professionals are able and willing to pay higher prices for houses and rent. This demand drives up all housing prices.)

👥
🏛 **Civic Participation**
● Most communities have some form of public assistance to the needy. *Does your community have free medical or dental clinics? Soup kitchens? Homeless shelters? "Meals on wheels"? What are some other volunteer programs in your area?* Ask students how they might go about finding such programs. You might also ask if any students are interested in volunteering for such programs.

Cross-reference
Figure 18–2, p. 494, illustrates some common torts and felonies.

Cross-reference
The Citizenship Skills lesson on p. 713 discusses volunteer work.

Figure 27–1
● *Which type of crime has decreased most significantly since the early 1980's?* (Burglary.) *Which crime has increased most significantly since the early 1980's?* (Aggravated assault.)

The symbol 🏛 denotes active participation strategies.

Activities are keyed for student abilities:
▲ = Basic
● = All Levels
■ = Average/Advanced

Controversial Issues

● *What sorts of politically controversial issues would arise in the construction of a mass transit system?* (The areas the system would service and the schedule of service, who would pay to build and maintain the system, how land would be obtained for the system.)

▊▊ Cooperative Learning

● Ask each student to keep a log of the community services he or she uses over a three-day period. Remind the class to include such items as traffic lights and stop signs, public transportation, water from public water supplies, elevators with inspection stickers, and public libraries, parks, and swimming pools. Have the class discuss the logs and the extent to which public services figure in students' lives.

GUIDED/INDEPENDENT PRACTICE

● Have each student make two lists, one detailing the ways in which local governments protect citizens and the other detailing the ways in which local governments improve citizens' lives. Then discuss with students whether any of these government activities can be considered more or less important than the others.

projects. The federal housing program was established by the Housing Act of 1937. This act offered funds to local governments to build, own, and manage public housing developments for low-income families and individuals.

Local governments that wish to participate in a housing project apply to the Department of Housing and Urban Development (HUD). HUD makes loans available to local authorities to construct and manage the buildings (often called "projects"). In return, local authorities must comply with federal guidelines. For instance, they cannot discriminate on the basis of race in selecting residents, and monthly payments must be based on a tenant's ability to pay. If the cost of the program exceeds the payments received, HUD makes up the difference.

Public housing programs have helped millions of low-income persons who would otherwise be unable to afford adequate housing. On the other hand, the "projects" have created new problems. Many early housing projects were clusters of high-rise buildings in run-down urban areas. The buildings were often impersonal, dangerous, and hard to maintain. Crime and drug abuse were common. To avoid these problems, builders have designed recent projects as lower buildings scattered throughout residential neighborhoods. This is called "scatter-site" housing.

Urban improvement

Another way local governments seek to improve the lives of many citizens is through **urban renewal**, the improvement or rebuilding of declining downtown areas. Beginning with the Housing Act of 1949, the federal government has provided financial aid to cities for renovation. Results have been mixed. In some communities, urban renewal meant the replacement of deteriorating apartment buildings with public buildings or parking lots. New or renovated buildings and improved neighborhoods also meant higher rents. Little effort was made to provide housing for displaced former residents. But for some communities, like Boston, Philadelphia, Pittsburgh, and Chicago, urban renewal has meant better housing, more attractive downtown areas, and a return of business and tourism.

One innovative housing policy is urban **homesteading**. Under this arrangement, a local government sells abandoned houses and apartments to interested buyers for small sums of money, sometimes as little as one dollar. The buyer must agree to make any necessary repairs in compliance with local building codes and to live in the building for a specified number of years. These programs provide a way for cities to revitalize urban areas without spending any local tax or federal revenues.

The renovation of downtown Pittsburgh, as seen in this open area facing the city's planetarium, is an example of urban renewal. Largely because of these improvements, Pittsburgh was rated one of the nation's most "livable" cities in the 1980's.

712

Background: *Civic Participation* Former President Jimmy Carter has helped publicize the plight of many public housing projects by personally working on project renovations together with other concerned citizens.

Volunteering for a Cause

4B, 4C, 4D

You have probably read in newspapers or seen on television many stories about people who have banded together to protest something. These people have decided to do more than just complain privately about a problem. They have chosen to exercise their rights of free speech and assembly to bring attention to an issue that is important to them.

Can you picture *yourself* volunteering to support a cause? Imagine that one day seepage from a toxic waste dump is found leaking from the ground in your neighborhood. Some of your neighbors call the local environmental agency and even your state legislator, but they are told that nothing can be done right away. You know how dangerous toxic wastes can be, and you are concerned. If a neighbor comes to you with a petition to send to the governor, will you sign it? If a local group decides to march, with protest signs, in front of the city hall, will you participate? Suppose that one of your neighbors decides to oppose your state legislator in the upcoming election and promises to clean up the toxic waste if elected. Will you offer your support? Will you work in your neighbor's political campaign?

These are questions that you may not be able to answer without actually being in such a situation. They may, however, lead you to understand how "ordinary" people can become involved with community issues.

Many people, for a variety of reasons, volunteer to help other people win elections. They may go door-to-door trying to interest voters in their candidate, or they may work out of a campaign office, mailing letters and answering telephones. Other people may be more inclined to help out in a hospital or health clinic, to work in a church fund-raiser, to recycle newspapers, or to collect food and clothing for the homeless. Usually these people are not paid for what they do. Their reward is the reward of all people who do volunteer work — the satisfaction of having taken a personal role in an important cause.

Follow-up

1. In the school or public library, examine back issues of a newspaper to find three examples of people protesting something in public. For each example, list who is protesting, what they are protesting, and why.
2. Think of a cause for which you might volunteer your time. Then try to think of all the possible things you and others might do to help convince the government, the public, and the media of the importance of your cause. Write a short report outlining all your possible actions.

CITIZENSHIP SKILLS

713

Follow-up Answers

1. You might want to discuss with students the various methods of protest (street marches, sit-ins, etc.).

2. Ask students how and when they first became interested in their causes.

The METRO subway system connects downtown Washington, D.C., with surrounding suburbs in Maryland and Virginia, bringing thousands of commuters to work in the nation's capital each day.

Transportation

In urbanized America, millions of individuals and businesses depend on the daily movement of automobiles, motorcycles, buses, and trucks. Local governments therefore have built a vast transportation and communication network that includes paved streets, expressways, tunnels, bridges, traffic signals, and street signs. The costs of building such structures are astronomical, and so are the costs of maintaining them.

Town and city road crews repair cracks and potholes in streets and roads. Maintenance workers also must handle street cleaning and snow removal. Most major cities have some form of **mass transit**, a system of moving large numbers of people from place to place. These systems may be run by the local government or operated with government subsidies. City buses are the most common method of mass transit. Government-provided buses also transport millions of elementary and secondary students to school. Many cities have a network of commuter trains that transport thousands of workers from the suburbs to the city and back each day. A large number of urban areas also have subways. These include new systems like Atlanta's MARTA, San Francisco's BART, and Washington, D.C.'s, METRO, as well as older lines in Boston, New York, and Chicago.

Mass transit has many advantages over the individual automobile. Mass transit systems can carry more people more efficiently, using less energy and causing less pollution per passenger. Nevertheless, many Americans prefer the freedom and convenience of their automobiles. But as urban populations increase, traffic jams worsen, and pollution becomes a bigger problem, mass transit may appear more appealing or necessary to many communities.

Recreation

Finally, local governments offer a wide range of recreational and cultural activities for their citizens' leisure time. Nearly all cities have free public libraries and parks. Many large cities also maintain public museums, zoos, swimming pools, and sports arenas. There also may be local baseball, softball, hockey, volleyball, and other sports programs. Some communities offer courses in art, swimming, auto mechanics, dancing, and aerobics, plus a wide range of adult education courses.

714

Background: *History* The world's first subway was constructed in London in 1863. The first U.S. subway was in Boston, which built a 1.5–mile subway in 1897. New York City operates the world's largest system: A passenger can travel from the New Jersey shore, under the city, beneath two rivers to Long Island without ever going above ground.

SECTION 1 REVIEW

Vocabulary and key terms

urban renewal (712)   mass transit (714)
homesteading (712)

For review

1. What kinds of protection do most local governments provide their citizens? **3A**
2. What are the three major jobs of local police? **6C**

3. How do the federal and local governments work together to provide housing and to improve cities? **7B**
4. What are some conveniences and recreational activities that local governments provide for their citizens? **7B**

Critical thinking

APPLYING KEY CONCEPTS   Local government services, as discussed in this section, touch our lives daily. Since you got up this morning, how many local government services have you used? **4A**

3B, 4A, 4B, 4C, 7B

SECTION 2 Local Governments Must Pay for Community Services

ACCESS | The Main Ideas

1 What taxes do local governments collect?
pages 715–719

2 What other sources of money do local governments have?
pages 719–720

3 How do local governments spend money?
pages 720–721

Who pays the salaries of your teachers? Who pays the costs of maintaining your school building and buying new books and equipment? Public education, as well as the other community services you read about in Section 1, has traditionally been funded by local governments, mainly through property taxes. The ways in which local governments collect and spend money is one of the most important, and controversial, issues in local politics.

3B, 4A, 4B, 4C, 7B

Tax Revenues

Much local government revenue comes from taxation. The taxes that support local governments are primarily property, sales, excise, and income taxes. These taxes can be collected with state taxes or separately, depending on the state and the type of tax.

Property taxes

Property taxes are one of the oldest and largest sources of local revenue. They account for about 23 percent of all city government revenues and 28 percent of county revenues. Although some local governments tax personal property — such as boats, automobiles, and jewelry — property taxes are typically levied on real property, such as land and buildings.

Property taxes depend on both property value and local tax rates. Before property can be taxed, an **assessment**, or estimate of its value, must be made. The assessed value usually equals what the property would be worth if the owner were to sell it.

A few localities depend on self-assessment. Under this arrangement, each property owner estimates his or her own property value. Because this method often is inaccurate, local governments more commonly employ an **assessor**. This official, either elected or appointed, personally inspects each property and sets its value. Real property is typically assessed every two to four years. In some areas, real property is assessed only when it is sold. With this method, however, two identical houses built at the same time may end up being taxed at different rates, depending on when they are sold. Many local

715

---

4. Local governments maintain roads, provide mass transit, and provide libraries, parks, museums, and adult education courses.

Critical thinking Students might mention taking a shower (clean water), putting out the trash (waste disposal), and riding on a school bus (educational assistance).

CLOSURE

● Remind students of the pre-reading objectives at the beginning of the section. Pose one or both of these questions again. Then have students read Section 2, noting the ways in which local governments pay for community services.

SECTION 2

Local Governments Must Pay for Community Services
(pp. 715–721)

Section Objectives

☐ list the taxes that local governments collect
☐ describe other sources of money that local governments have
☐ explain how local governments spend money

The symbol **ii** denotes active participation strategies.

Activities are keyed for student abilities:
▲ = Basic
● = All Levels
■ = Average/Advanced

Vocabulary

assessment, assessor, mill, board of equalization, tax base, municipal bond, user's fee

FOCUS

● If your community has recently experienced a controversy over property taxes, ask students to recall the controversy and its effects on their lives.

If there has been no controversy, ask students how your community obtains money to pay for education. Then ask: **Should property owners who do not have school-age children be given property tax breaks? Why or why not?**

EXPLANATION

After reviewing the content of the section, you may want to consider the following activities:

Economics

▲ *How might property taxes serve to discourage people from making improvements on their houses?* (Improvements increase the value of a house. Because taxes are based on the assessed value of a house, the taxes of a homeowner who makes improvements will usually increase.)

Point out to students that the value of a piece of property is also affected by the relative economic prosperity of the area. If the area as a whole becomes more attractive to outside buyers, property values will increase, bringing about higher property taxes.

716

governments have adopted regular reassessment to avoid this problem.

Property is usually taxed at only a fraction (typically one-third or one-half) of its assessed value. The amount each property owner is taxed depends, finally, on the tax rate set by the local government. Property tax rates are given in **mills**, which are equal to one-tenth of a penny ($.001). A tax rate of 25 mills, for example, is 2.5 percent. Figure 27–2 shows how property taxes are calculated.

Criticisms of property taxes

The property tax has been criticized for many reasons. One complaint is that assessment practices are often unfair. Some tax assessors are not adequately trained to determine the true value of property; others have been accused of doing personal or political favors by setting low values. In some places, property value is assessed solely on the basis of size in square feet, no matter what its condition or location. To make property taxes fairer, many local governments have established **boards of equalization**. Citizens who feel their property has been assessed unfairly can often appeal to this board, which is authorized to make adjustments.

A second common criticism is that property taxes are unfairly regressive because they do not take into consideration a person's present ability to pay — only the value of property that may have been bought long ago. For example, an elderly couple whose only income is now Social Security benefits of about $7,500 a year and a single person earning $75,000 a year may live in identical houses. Both households pay the same property tax, but it is a much larger portion of the elderly couple's income.

To ease this situation, many states and local governments have set limits on the amount of property taxes that low-income persons, particularly the elderly, must pay. Under this system, property taxes may not exceed a certain percentage of a person's or family's income. Many local governments also permit low-income persons certain exemptions from their property taxes. For example, if a homeowner makes repairs on his or her house, these improvements would normally increase the value of the house and the property taxes as well. Because the tax increase might discourage people from making improvements, local governments sometimes let poor or elderly homeowners make repairs without an increase in taxes.

Property taxes and education

Local property taxes provide close to half of all of the funds for most school districts. The

Figure 27–2 CALCULATING PROPERTY TAX Property taxes are determined by assessing a property's value and applying local tax rates. 7B

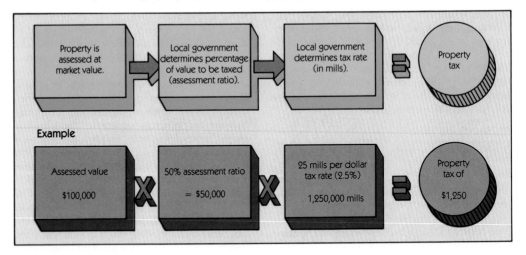

716

Cross-reference
Regressive taxes are explained in Chapter 19, p. 518.

Figure 27–2
● *In the box showing property assessment, what does the phrase "at market value" mean?* (The assessed value of property usually equals

what the property would be worth if the owner were to sell it.)

716

Much of the funding for public school programs and facilities, including this basketball court, comes from local property taxes.

amount of money a school district gets, therefore, depends upon its **tax base** — the thing or value on which taxes are levied. If a school district's tax base is small, it has less to spend on buildings, teachers, books, new programs, and classroom or sports equipment. As a result, the quality of public schools varies widely from community to community.

In 1971, parents from a predominantly black and Hispanic neighborhood in Baldwin Park, California, challenged the funding of schools exclusively through property taxes. The parents showed that while per pupil expenditures in Baldwin Park were just $577, the wealthy Beverly Hills district nearby spent $1,232 per pupil, more than twice as much. The California Supreme Court ruled that this difference violated the guarantee of equal protection in the California constitution (*Serrano v. Priest*). California soon adopted a revised method for funding schools. Under the new system, a greater share of state taxes was set aside for schools in communities with lower tax bases.

When a similar case from Texas reached the U.S. Supreme Court two years later, however, the Court upheld funding public education through local property taxes. In *San Antonio Independent School District v. Rodriguez* (1973), the sharply divided Court ruled 5 to 4 that this practice did not violate the Fourteenth Amendment's equal protection clause. Justice Lewis F. Powell, Jr., stated, "the ultimate solutions must come from the lawmakers and from the democratic pressures of those who elect them." In other words, state laws that govern funding for public schools are not bound by the federal Constitution. Nevertheless, state supreme courts in both New Jersey and Connecticut followed California's example in later cases.

Tax revolts

In the late 1970's, property taxes became a target of many discontented citizens. They felt that their taxes were too high, that state and local programs were poorly run, and that government was becoming too intrusive in their lives. In an effort to reduce their taxes and limit government spending, citizens in many states organized so-called "taxpayers' revolts." The first to gain national attention was a controversial initiative

Politics

Have students reread Justice Powell's statement on this page regarding *San Antonio Independent School District v. Rodriguez.* Then discuss with students the issues raised by the use of property taxes to support public education.

▲ *Why do poorer communities tend to have poorer schools?* (Their tax base is smaller, and therefore there is less money available for education.) *How might this situation be changed?* (School districts could pool their resources and distribute them evenly; minimum spending requirements for public education could be agreed upon; schools in poorer areas could be improved indirectly through efforts to bring economic prosperity to depressed areas.)

● *Give at least one reason why unequal spending on education should be changed, and at least one reason why it should not be changed.* (*For change*—The present situation is unfair to students in poorer areas; society as a whole has an interest in seeing that all children receive a good education. *Against change*—The present situation is not unconstitutional; it allows economically successful parents to pass on advantages to their children; any changes in the system would dilute local control over public education.)

717

The symbol ⅱ denotes active participation strategies.

Activities are keyed for student abilities:
▲ = Basic
● = All Levels
■ = Average/Advanced

History

● CRITICAL THINKING Tell students that Howard Jarvis, one of the sponsors of California's Proposition 13, believed that "the only way to cut the cost of government is not to give them money in the first place." *What other ways to cut the cost of government can you think of?* (Examining programs for spending reductions *before* cutting revenues.) *Why was the tax-cut referendum method popular among voters?* (By backing such referendums, voters guaranteed themselves lower taxes.)

Economics

Discuss with students the difference between payroll taxes and other taxes, as well as the importance of payroll taxes to large cities as a way of gaining tax revenue from suburban residents.

● *What city services do suburban commuters probably take advantage of?* (Mass transit, city-licensed taxis, sanitation, drinking water, municipal parks.)

👥 Cooperative Learning

● Divide the class into small groups (two or three people). Have each group review the criticisms of property taxes on p. 716. Have them also review the criteria for judging taxes, as presented in the subsection "What is an 'ideal' tax?" (Chapter 25, pp. 679–680).

People of all ages enjoy themselves at city zoos. Zoos are one of many recreational activities that are supported by local taxes.

called "Proposition 13," placed on the ballot and passed by California voters in the summer of 1978.

Proposition 13 limited property taxes and reduced property assessments statewide. The overall result was a 57 percent cut in property taxes, causing a $7 billion loss in local revenues. A large surplus in the California state budget, along with booming business, helped offset the loss in revenue. Nevertheless, school budgets still had to be reduced. Many state employees lost their jobs, and many services were curtailed or cut completely. On the other hand, property owners, especially those with large holdings, enjoyed a significant savings in taxes.

California's tax revolt touched off similar movements in other states. In 1980, Massachusetts's "Proposition $2\frac{1}{2}$" reduced property taxes and evened out the rates charged across the state. The loss in revenues, however, affected nearly every state service. Cities had to reduce fire and

police protection. Budgets for snow removal and street cleaning were slashed. Schools had to cut many programs, fire teachers, and overcrowd classrooms.

While everyone wants to pay lower taxes, not everyone agrees which state programs can and should be cut. Moreover, it is often high- or middle-income property owners who gain from property tax cuts. Low-income people who do not own property often are the ones who suffer from cuts in government programs.

Other local taxes

In general, state laws place strict limits on taxation by local governments. Still, local governments make limited use of sales, excise, and income taxes.

SALES TAX About half of the states permit their local governments to levy a general sales tax on purchases made within local boundaries. As Chapter 25 explains (page 678), the local tax is placed on top of the state tax, a practice called "piggybacking." Store owners send the entire tax amount to the state, which then returns a portion to the local government.

Sales taxes generate about 7 percent of all city revenue and 6 percent of all county income. Local governments must be careful in charging sales tax, however. If the local sales tax is too high, consumers will travel to nearby cities or counties to make their purchases and thus harm local businesses.

EXCISE TAXES Some local governments also impose excise taxes on selected goods and services. Local excise taxes are commonly charged on cigarettes, alcoholic beverages, gasoline, movies, amusement parks, restaurants, and hotels.

INCOME TAXES Local income taxes are allowed in several states, mainly in the East. Income taxes are more widely used in cities than in counties. They generate about 6 percent of total city revenues, but only 1 percent of total county revenues.

Local income taxes can be a percentage of either business profits or individual incomes. Local individual income taxes are usually payroll taxes; they are withheld from each worker's paycheck and then submitted to the local government. Payroll taxes are especially important for large central cities, like New York City. Because many people who work in central cities live in suburbs, it is the suburbs that receive commuters' property taxes and most of their sales taxes. Without payroll taxes, commuters would be able to take advantage of city services without paying for them.

7B

Nontax Revenues

Federal aid

Local governments receive a small portion of their revenue from the federal government. About 5 percent of all city revenues and 2 percent of county revenues come in the form of federal aid. Most of this money comes from grants-in-aid. Federal funds are used for a wide range of local government services, such as housing, transportation, urban renewal, waste treatment, and health care.

State aid

States supply more aid to local government than the federal government does. Nationwide, state aid accounts for roughly 20 percent of all city revenues and 32 percent of all county revenues, several times the percentage supplied by the federal government. The state collects the tax revenues, then redistributes them to local governments. Most states have complex formulas to distribute funds for schools fairly between wealthier and poorer districts. Many states also share state gasoline taxes with local governments for local road building and repair.

Borrowing

Like other levels of government, local governments must at some time borrow money to finance major projects, such as sports arenas and school buildings. To borrow money, local governments sell **municipal bonds**. These bonds represent a city's promise to repay the buyer the amount paid for the bond plus interest. Municipal bonds are considered fairly safe, conservative

City governments often borrow money by selling municipal bonds. Investors often prefer to buy municipal bonds because the interest payments are exempted from federal income taxes.

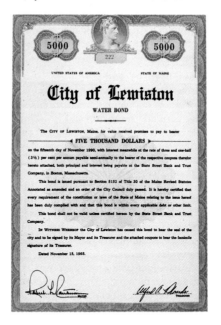

● Then have groups evaluate the property tax in terms of those criteria. *Which criterion do critics say the property tax fails to meet?* (Fairness, because of the variation in assessment practices and the regressive nature of the tax.) *Which criteria does this tax clearly meet?* (Ease of collection, dependability.) Conclude the discussion by having students describe the ways in which local governments have tried to deal with the problems cited by critics of property taxes.

GUIDED/INDEPENDENT PRACTICE

● Have students write brief essays answering the following questions: *What is the property tax? How is it calculated? Why is it controversial?*

RETEACHING/CORRECTIVES

▲ Have students outline the section, using the headings and subheadings as entries and adding other information as necessary.

Have students complete **Skills Practice Worksheet 27,** which provides an example of a city's spending priorities.

719

Background: *Economics* A grant-in-aid (p. 101) is a sum of money appropriated by one level of government, given to a lower level of government, and spent for a specified purpose.

Grants-in-aid are based on the "deep pockets theory" that larger or higher levels of government are more able to pay for social programs than local communities or individuals.

The symbol ⚏ denotes active participation strategies.

Activities are keyed for student abilities:
▲ = Basic
● = All Levels
■ = Average/Advanced

ENRICHMENT/EXTENSION

■ Ask students to research and report to the class on the so-called "taxpayers' revolts" in various states. Reports can focus on the methods used to organize and influence voters and the effects of the revolts on local services in the selected state.

Have students complete **Skills Challenge Worksheet 27,** which deals with *San Antonio Independent School District v. Rodriguez.*

Section 2 Review Answers

1. (a) Estimated property value. **(b)** Assessments are used to determine property taxes.
2. Many have limited the taxes these groups have to pay, and some local governments allow certain exemptions.
3. Inequalities in education result from unequal tax bases. Districts with small tax bases have smaller amounts of revenue available for education than districts with large tax bases.
4. They are sold by local governments to raise revenue.

Fines for traffic violations provide revenue for many communities. Here, a parking enforcement officer tickets an illegally parked vehicle.

investments. Local governments are likely to repay their debts, and the interest paid by municipal bonds is free from state and federal taxation. Cities cannot, however, issue bonds whenever they want. Most state constitutions place limits on how much local governments can borrow. In addition, taxpayers often have the right to vote on major bond issues.

Fines, licenses, and fees

A small portion of local revenue comes from fines paid by people who violate local ordinances, particularly traffic and parking laws. Many local governments also charge license fees for certain businesses. Local licenses may be required, for example, to run taxi services, restaurants, hotels, movie theaters, grocery stores, or gasoline stations.

User's fees are a fast-growing source of local revenue. As the name implies, user's fees are charged for the "use" or consumption of some service. Examples of user's fees include admission to city zoos or museums, fees to play in a city softball league or attend a park district camp, and charges for metered water and electricity.

These fees are especially important to many special districts. Their supporters praise user's fees because those who use services are required

to pay for them. Critics argue that such fees are regressive because they do not consider a person's ability to pay.

Other revenue sources

Finally, there are several miscellaneous sources of local governmental revenue. Some local governments maintain money-making operations, such as parking garages, bus lines, warehouses, farmer's markets, utilities, liquor stores, and housing projects. Some income is also derived from special assessments. Special assessments are additional fees paid by property owners for services or improvements that benefit them directly. For example, a group of neighbors might be assessed extra taxes for the addition of new sidewalks, trees, or streetlights to their block.

7B

Local Government Spending

Local budgets

Like any other government unit, local governments must prepare budgets to balance spending with income. Local budgets are prepared yearly by the appropriate governing body — a county commission, township board, city council, mayor, or city manager.

Budget-making is no easy task. Demand for local governmental services nearly always exceeds the available resources. Therefore, elected local officials must make difficult choices on how funds will be spent. For example, should the city install new streetlights or build a new sewer system?

City spending

Figure 27–3 summarizes spending patterns for the nation's cities and counties. Among all the nation's cities, the largest expenditures are for police protection and education. Cities spend about 12 percent of their budgets on police protection, and nearly 12 percent on education. The next highest expenditures, in order, are for highways, interest on debt, sewers, fire protection, public welfare, housing, parks and recreation, and hospitals.

County spending

Spending patterns for counties are somewhat different from those of cities. Among the nation's

720

Figure 27-3 LOCAL GOVERNMENT FINANCES
7B

Revenues of city governments by source

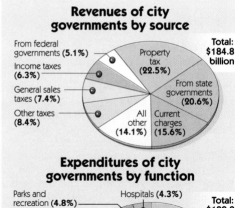

From federal governments (5.1%)
Income taxes (6.3%)
General sales taxes (7.4%)
Other taxes (8.4%)
All other (14.1%)
Current charges (15.6%)
From state governments (20.6%)
Property tax (22.5%)
Total: $184.8 billion

Expenditures of city governments by function

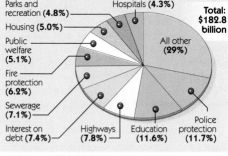

Parks and recreation (4.8%)
Housing (5.0%)
Public welfare (5.1%)
Fire protection (6.2%)
Sewerage (7.1%)
Interest on debt (7.4%)
Highways (7.8%)
Education (11.6%)
Police protection (11.7%)
Hospitals (4.3%)
All other (29%)
Total: $182.8 billion

Revenues of county governments by source

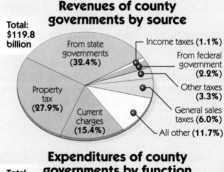

Total: $119.8 billion
From state governments (32.4%)
Property tax (27.9%)
Current charges (15.4%)
Income taxes (1.1%)
From federal government (2.2%)
Other taxes (3.3%)
General sales taxes (6.0%)
All other (11.7%)

Expenditures of county governments by function

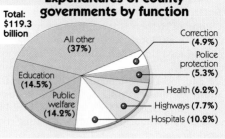

Total: $119.3 billion
All other (37%)
Education (14.5%)
Public welfare (14.2%)
Correction (4.9%)
Police protection (5.3%)
Health (6.2%)
Highways (7.7%)
Hospitals (10.2%)

Source: U.S. Department of Commerce, Bureau of the Census. Data published 1991.

---

counties, three areas stand out with the highest percentages of total spending: public welfare, education, and hospitals. Other significant areas of spending are county highways and roads, health care, and law enforcement.

When looking at overall local government spending, it is important to remember that spending patterns vary from city to city, county to county, and region to region. For example, large cities may spend proportionally more on police and fire protection than small cities. Small cities may spend relatively more on public health and recreation. Urban counties, with more people to educate or help, are likely to spend more money on schools and welfare than rural counties would spend. The fact that county governments have greater importance in the South and West makes their spending totals higher than the national average.

SECTION 2 REVIEW

Vocabulary and key terms

assessment (715)
assessor (715)
mill (716)
board of equalization (716)
tax base (717)
municipal bond (719)
user's fee (720)

For review

1. (a) What do assessments determine? (b) What are they used for? **7B**
2. How have state and local governments tried to make property taxes fairer for the poor and elderly? **7B**
3. How does using property taxes for education sometimes produce inequalities? **7B**
4. What are municipal bonds used for? **7B**
5. How do city and county spending patterns differ? **7B**

Critical thinking

ORGANIZING AN ARGUMENT "Taxpayers' revolts" demonstrate the trade-off between taxes and government services. If you were a city or county official, would you vote to lower property taxes if it meant cutting some local services? Of the services described in this chapter, which would you cut? **4A**

---

5. Cities' largest expenditures are for education and police protection; counties spend the highest percentages of their funds on public welfare, education, and hospitals.

Critical thinking Students should discuss why property tax cuts are regressive, which groups are most affected by service cuts, and whether tax revenue losses can force government to use funds more efficiently.

CLOSURE

● Have students complete the following statements, using information in the section and especially Figure 27–3: *Local governments spend money on.... Local governments obtain money through....* Then have students read Section 3, noting the ways in which cities and counties plan for the future.

Figure 27–3
● Have students make a general statement regarding city and county revenues and expenditures. (Cities and counties gain revenue from a combination of taxes, aid, and charges; they spend money on such services as education, police protection, and public welfare.)

The symbol ⅱ denotes active participation strategies.

Activities are keyed for student abilities:
▲ = Basic
● = All Levels
■ = Average/Advanced

SECTION 3

Cities and Counties Plan for the Future
(pp. 722–727)

Section Objectives

☐ explain how local governments regulate land use

☐ explain how local governments regulate urban growth

Vocabulary

planning, zoning, variance, subdivision, plat, annexation

 FOCUS

● Draw on the board a rough outline of the school building and school grounds. Ask for volunteers to come to the board and show (perhaps with colored chalk) how the different parts of school property might be "zoned." (The cafeteria could be zoned for eating, the playing fields and gymnasium for recreation, etc.)

 SECTION 3

Cities and Counties Plan for the Future

> **ACCESS** **The Main Ideas**
>
> **1** How do local governments regulate land use? *pages 722–724*
>
> **2** How do local governments regulate urban growth? *pages 724–727*

Before 1900, cities grew like weeds, sprawling and uncontrollable. Planning was practically nonexistent. Property owners could use their land in whatever way they wanted without government interference. City dwellers, for example, could raise chickens and hogs in their backyards. A landowner might build a factory in a residential neighborhood. Another might construct a barn just two feet from the street. Housing was constructed without regard for safety.

As cities grew, conditions worsened. One person's misuse of property immediately affected others. Raising livestock in the city created a stench. Factories spewed smoke and soot over the entire city. Poorly constructed buildings placed too close together allowed fires to sweep through whole neighborhoods. Unsanitary dumps and insufficient sewers spread disease. Groups of concerned citizens and political leaders realized that some sort of land-use regulation was necessary.

3A

Planning and Zoning

Local governments have two basic, closely related ways to regulate land use. **Planning** refers to setting long-range overall guidelines for community development. The goal of planning might be to revitalize a business district, to attract new factories, to build a new football stadium, or to make room for new houses.

Zoning — making regulations for the use or occupancy of land — is local government's tool for carrying out its plans. Zoning laws divide an area into districts or zones that are set aside for specific uses, such as residences, business, or farming. Within each zone, all buildings and land use must conform to specific regulations.

722

Early planning efforts

Before 1900, very few American communities were planned. One notable exception is Washington, D.C. Planning for the seat of government began in 1791 after President Washington had personally selected the site on the Potomac River. Washington then hired the French engineer and architect Pierre Charles L'Enfant to design the new city.

L'Enfant's plan provided wide avenues radiating from the White House and the Capitol building, intersecting a rectangular grid of streets. An aerial view reveals a pleasant mix of circles and parks throughout the entire city. While L'Enfant's plan was not actually carried out in full until the early 1900's, Washington, D. C., remains a beautiful, planned city with strict zoning laws. For example, no building can be taller than the Capitol building.

Legal foundations of zoning laws

In 1916, New York City enacted the nation's first zoning ordinance. This ordinance was soon struck down by New York's Court of Appeals. The court believed that zoning restrictions amounted to taking private property for public use without giving just compensation.

In 1926, however, the United States Supreme Court upheld the practice of zoning in an Ohio case, *Village of Euclid v. Ambler Realty Company*. The Court declared that local governments can regulate the use of private property to prevent fire hazards, traffic congestion, health problems, and crime.

Following the Supreme Court ruling, the U.S. Department of Commerce, then under the direction of Herbert Hoover, took an active role in promoting local planning and zoning. In 1928 an advisory board known as the Hoover Commission drafted two model laws to assist state and local governments. (These were the Standard Zoning Enabling Act and the Standard City Planning Enabling Act.) Both acts served as the basis for most local planning and zoning laws passed thereafter.

Background: *History* Savannah (Georgia), Charleston (South Carolina), and Philadelphia were also early planned cities.

Background: *History* The Washington Monument is taller than the Capitol; it is not considered a building or a detraction from the Capitol.

CRITICAL THINKING

Making Decisions

Imagine that you are a member of your city council. Your community has high unemployment. Property values and income from property taxes have both declined. A large company has offered to open offices in your city if you will excuse it from paying local property taxes for ten years. What should you and the other city council members do?

Making such a decision can be made easier if you follow a problem-solving technique. Problem-solving should include each of the following steps:

- Define the problem. State clearly the problem you seek to answer.
- Decide on the basis, or criteria, for judging possible solutions. Criteria may include cost, benefits, fairness to the most people, public opinion, and any identifiable contingent effects.
- Gather and analyze information. This should include facts that are appropriate to the established criteria.
- Develop alternative solutions to the problem. Evaluate each solution according to the criteria.
- Make a tentative decision.
- Review the decision in terms of the problem, the criteria, and the information you have analyzed. If everything "fits," then proceed with the decision.

★ ISSUE: Placement of Group Homes

Throughout the nation, communities have had to take increasing responsibility for the care of the homeless, the poor, and those who are mentally retarded. The need for community-based facilities has increased in part because states have been closing down large institutions that once took care of numbers of these disadvantaged people. Many now end up in group homes where they can live with others in a similar situation. In group homes they receive help and counseling, and learn skills.

A community as a whole usually recognizes the need for low-income housing or group homes. "But not in my neighborhood," many people say. Most often, they fear the effect of such outsiders on their neighborhood.

Read the following summary of an actual case and then answer the questions that follow.

Case study of a community decision

Two women in a Texas community asked the city to give them a permit to house in their four-bedroom home persons with mental retardation. State inspectors said the house was large enough for thirteen residents. If the house were to be turned into a nursing home or boarding house, no city permit was necessary. The house was across the street from a junior high school.

Neighbors urged the city to turn down the request. In their statements they expressed fear about the consequences of allowing retarded persons in their community. In such statements, people argued that the house was too small or that the street traffic too dangerous. Some pointed out that the house was located on a flood plain, thus making it an unsafe location. Other locations in town were more appropriate, people said. The two women were even called "greedy capitalists" who wanted to make money off people who need their help.

Analyzing the Issue

1. Define the problem described in this case.
2. What criteria might be followed in making a decision?
3. Which neighborhood complaints deserve further investigation? Why?
4. What additional information would be helpful in making a decision?
5. List three alternate solutions to this problem. Evaluate each solution in terms of the criteria you developed in Question #2 to determine the best decision.

723

EXPLANATION

After reviewing the content of the section, you may want to consider the following activities:

History

● Tell students that historians believe Hippodamus, an architect in ancient Greece, developed the first systematic theories about comprehensive city planning. The ancient Greek city of Miletus, designed by Hippodamus, was one of the first cities to arrange city blocks in the grid pattern. *Does your community follow such a pattern?*

● Then ask students if your city (or the closest major city) has the characteristics of a newer city, where business and residential areas are separated, or the characteristics of an older city, where these areas are integrated.

Economics

▲ CRITICAL THINKING *Why might the federal government require local governments seeking federal aid to submit a comprehensive plan for future growth?* (Having such a plan should help local governments spend funds, including federal aid, more wisely.)

● CRITICAL THINKING *What evidence is there that planning does not always work?* (Planners have tended to put all buildings of a given function in the same area, which has resulted in the creation of deserted and dangerous neighborhoods.)

The federal government became further involved in local planning and zoning after World War II. To deal with the severe housing shortage caused by the return of millions of American soldiers, Congress enacted the Housing Act of 1949. Its goal was to provide "a decent home and a suitable living environment for every American family."

The Housing Act provided generous grants for local housing projects. To receive these funds, local governments were required to submit a general plan for city development. The federal Housing Act of 1954 required even more detailed plans. As a result of such housing laws, nearly every American community now has an overall plan to regulate expansion.

3A, 4A

Regulating Urban Growth

Local governments have a wide choice of legal tools to regulate urban growth. These include (1) master plans, (2) zoning laws, (3) subdivision regulations, (4) building permits and codes, and (5) annexation.

Master plans

Each local government seeking federal aid must have a comprehensive "master plan" for development, a blueprint for community growth. Master plans usually include several items. A series of maps show physical features, such as hills and rivers; community boundaries, including streets and property lines; the locations of various types of buildings, such as single-family dwellings, apartments, factories, and offices; and primary and secondary roads and highways. The plan also shows population trends and characteristics such as age, race, family incomes, birth rates, and migration patterns.

Based on these statistics, the plan makes forecasts of future land needs — how much land will be needed for housing and how much for industry. Finally, the plan contains detailed information about major industries, services, and agricultural development in the community. It also estimates financial resources, including the community's total property tax base, tax rates, and outstanding bonds and debts.

Although planning may seem like a perfectly sensible thing to do, the results of planning have

not always been happy. Critics have pointed out that planners, especially in the 1950's and 1960's, tended to design cities that look fine on paper but quickly turn into unused or even dangerous places. Planners tended to put all shopping malls in one place, office buildings in another, and houses somewhere else. Large areas were deserted at night, making easy targets for vandals and dangerous places for people on foot.

On the other hand, critics noted that the safest, liveliest parts of older cities were those that had many different kinds of people working and living together at all times of the day. In such places, shops, movie theaters, and apartments were mixed together. There were always neighbors and passers-by to keep an eye on things. This old, haphazard natural development seemed to fit human nature better than modern planning.

Zoning laws

Zoning regulates a community's growth by placing certain restrictions on the use of land. Naturally, the types of zones differ greatly in each community, depending upon its geography, economy, and particular needs. Typically, zoning laws divide communities into residential, commercial, industrial, and recreational areas. Figure 27–4 shows an example of some common zoning classifications and a zoning map.

Zoning laws are usually enforced by the city council, the county governing board, or a special zoning commission. To make zoning more flexible, many zoning boards are authorized to grant **variances**, which free property owners from zoning restrictions under certain circumstances. For example, a variance might allow a developer to build an apartment complex in a neighborhood zoned for single-family houses.

Zoning has many defenders. Supporters argue that zoning brings about orderly, attractive, and manageable growth in a community. In addition, they say, zoning protects property values and preserves the character of residential neighborhoods. By preventing a chemical factory from being built near people's homes, for example, zoning laws make it possible for homeowners to sell their property at a fair price.

Critics, however, believe that zoning can be discriminatory. For example, low- and middle-income families probably could not afford to live in a residential area where lots must be at least

724

Figure 27–4 ZONING CLASSIFICATIONS This chart shows some zoning regulations from Boone County, Missouri. The map suggests how those regulations might be used. **3A**

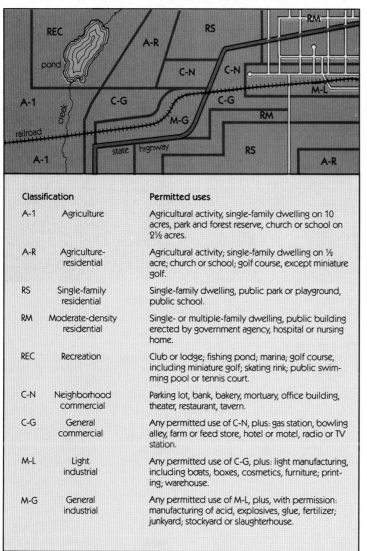

Classification		Permitted uses
A-1	Agriculture	Agricultural activity, single-family dwelling on 10 acres, park and forest reserve, church or school on 2½ acres.
A-R	Agriculture-residential	Agricultural activity; single-family dwelling on ½ acre; church or school; golf course, except miniature golf.
RS	Single-family residential	Single-family dwelling, public park or playground, public school.
RM	Moderate-density residential	Single- or multiple-family dwelling, public building erected by government agency, hospital or nursing home.
REC	Recreation	Club or lodge; fishing pond; marina; golf course, including miniature golf; skating rink; public swimming pool or tennis court.
C-N	Neighborhood commercial	Parking lot, bank, bakery, mortuary, office building, theater, restaurant, tavern.
C-G	General commercial	Any permitted use of C-N, plus: gas station, bowling alley, farm or feed store, hotel or motel, radio or TV station.
M-L	Light industrial	Any permitted use of C-G, plus: light manufacturing, including boats, boxes, cosmetics, furniture; printing; warehouse.
M-G	General industrial	Any permitted use of M-L, plus, with permission: manufacturing of acid, explosives, glue, fertilizer; junkyard; stockyard or slaughterhouse.

five acres or homes must follow a certain architectural style. Zoning practices that indirectly favor the wealthy are sometimes called "snob zoning." Critics also complain that zoning boards and city councils sometimes grant variances as political favors.

Subdivision regulations

Another way local governments control land use is through regulating **subdivisions**. The term *subdivision* refers to the way land is divided and prepared for sale and occupancy. For instance, a developer may buy 250 acres of land

725

Background: *Cultural Literacy* A political favor takes place when someone in a position of political authority uses his or her power to help a person or a business, either as a reward for past support or as an incentive for future support.

Suburban subdivisions must comply with certain local regulations. This aerial view shows a recently developed subdivision.

and want to divide it into smaller lots for single-family houses. Before doing so, the developer must satisfy certain subdivision regulations.

Subdivision regulations usually include three requirements. First, developers must set aside a specified percentage of their land to the city or county for public use. The law might require, for example, that 12 percent of the land be used for parks, schools, streets, or fire stations. Second, developers are usually required to lay out new streets, curbs, and sidewalks; install sewers, water mains, and streetlights; or even plant trees and shrubs. Third, developers must submit a plan for dividing their property into **plats**, which are small parcels of land. Each plat must satisfy certain requirements. For instance, each plat in a residential zone might have to be at least 5,000 square feet. The local zoning commission generally enforces these regulations.

Building permits and codes
For public safety, nearly every local government requires property owners to have a permit

to construct a new house or garage, install a swimming pool, build a porch, or remodel a house. Building permits specify how close such structures can be built to streets and neighboring property. In addition, most local governments also have building codes governing new construction or repairs. Building codes are usually quite detailed. They may specify proper wall construction, door heights, electrical wiring, heating, ventilation, insulation, and fire alarms. Most communities employ building inspectors to enforce building codes.

Annexation
As a city's population grows, people tend to move to areas outside the city limits. One way cities can regulate this type of growth is through **annexation**. Annexation allows a city to expand its boundaries to include a nearby "unincorporated" area that has not yet become part of another municipality. Procedures for annexation are governed by state laws and vary considerably. In general, two methods are used.

Cross-reference
Municipal corporations are discussed in Chapter 26, p. 699.

In most cases, people living both inside and outside the city limits must agree on annexation. This is called *bilateral* annexation. Either the city council or the city's population may vote on the city's consent. A majority of the people living outside the city in the new area must also vote for annexation.

A few states permit a city to annex a neighboring area without the consent of its inhabitants. This is *unilateral* annexation. Unilateral annexation can be accomplished by either a vote of the city council, a vote of city residents, or a court order. Many people criticize unilateral annexation as a completely undemocratic method of regulating city growth. On the other hand, it is one way to make sure that citizens in outlying areas will receive necessary local government services and at the same time pay for them as part of a local tax base.

SECTION 3 REVIEW

Vocabulary and key terms

planning (722) subdivision (725)
zoning (722) plat (726)
variance (724) annexation (726)

For review

1. What is the relationship between planning and zoning? **3A**
2. How did the Supreme Court and the federal executive branch encourage planning and zoning in the 1920's? **3A**
3. What are some typical zoning classifications? **3A**
4. What are three general requirements set forth in subdivision regulations? **3A**
5. Briefly describe the two basic methods of annexation. **3A**

Critical thinking

APPLYING BASIC PRINCIPLES Why do cities plan for future growth? Is such planning an unfair interference with such principles as the right to own property or the freedom to make choices? Do planners always do a better job than ordinary people making individual choices? **3A**

Chapter Summary

Local government policies touch citizens' daily lives in many different ways. To protect citizens, local governments maintain police and fire departments and provide clean water and sanitation services. Local governments also give assistance to the needy and, with the help of the federal government, sponsor housing projects and urban renewal. For the public's convenience, local governments provide a transportation and communications network, mass transit within most major cities, and a variety of educational and recreational facilities.

To provide these many services, local governments must raise money. Property taxes make up a large portion of local government funds. Property tax is based on an assessment of a property's value. The total assessed value of property in a community is its tax base, which is important in determining local school funding. In many communities, the use of property taxes has been the target of widespread criticism and so-called "taxpayers' revolts."

Sales, excise, and payroll taxes are other sources of local tax revenues. In addition, state and federal aid are significant nontax sources of revenue. Local governments can also borrow money by selling municipal bonds. Spending patterns differ somewhat between cities and counties. Cities spend the most money on police protection and education, while the biggest expenses of counties are public welfare, education, and hospitals.

By the early 1900's, worsened conditions in cities led to efforts to regulate growth. Planning and zoning are two tools that allow cities and counties to plan for the future. Comprehensive plans provide detailed descriptions of a community's growth, and zoning laws classify areas for residential, commercial, and other uses. Local governments may allow variances for exceptions to zoning laws under certain conditions. Communities also regulate growth through subdivision regulations, building codes, and annexation.

3. Residential, commercial, industrial, recreational.
4. Most developers must (a) set aside part of their land for public use; (b) lay out new streets, curbs, and sidewalks and install sewers, water mains, and street lights; and (c) submit a plan for dividing their property into plats.
5. *Bilateral annexation* requires the consent of the people living inside and outside city limits. *Unilateral annexation* permits a city to annex an area without the consent of the inhabitants.

Critical thinking Students should discuss the conditions in many cities before planning was undertaken, the trade-off between freedom of choice and the public good, and the criticism that planning and zoning laws are sometimes discriminatory and not thought through.

CLOSURE
● Remind students of the pre-reading objectives at the beginning of the section. Pose one or both of these questions again. Then have students read the next assigned lesson.

CHAPTER 27 CORRECTIVES
● To review the content of Chapter 27, you may want to have students complete **Study Guide/Review 27** or **Workbook Chapter 27.**

The symbol 👥 denotes active participation strategies.

Activities are keyed for student abilities:
▲ = Basic
● = All Levels
■ = Average/Advanced

CHAPTER 27 REVIEW

Answers

Vocabulary   See pp. T19–T21 for suggested vocabulary activities.

Reviewing the Facts

1. Local governments provide police protection, fire protection, and public health protection.
2. The Department of Housing and Urban Development lends money for construction and management in return for compliance with federal guidelines.
3. It carries people more efficiently, using less energy and making less pollution per passenger.
4. Property, sales, excise, and income taxes.
5. Local property taxes.
6. Without such income taxes, suburban commuters could take advantage of city services without having to pay for them.
7. Police protection, education.
8. It drafted two model laws to help state and local governments plan land use. These laws became the basis for most local planning and zoning laws.
9. To ensure public safety.
10. They must set aside a certain percentage of land for public use. They must lay out new streets, curbs, and sidewalks; install sewers, water mains, and street-lights; and in some cases, plant trees and shrubs. They must submit a plan for dividing the property into units (called plats).

Thinking Critically About Key Concepts

1. If no effort is made to improve the community that surrounds a housing project, the community's problems will infect the project as well.
2. To prevent people from buying a large number of buildings at little cost, and to ensure that owners show a commitment to the area.

728

● **Review the definitions of the following terms:**

annexation	mill	urban renewal
assessment	municipal bond	user's fee
assessor	planning	variance
board of equalization	plat	zoning
homesteading	subdivision	
mass transit	tax base	

● REVIEWING THE FACTS

1. Name three ways in which local governments provide protection for their citizens. **1A**
2. How does the federal government participate in local public housing projects? **3A**
3. What are the advantages of mass transit over the individual automobile? **5C**
4. What are the major taxes that support local governments? **7B**
5. What provides close to half of the funds for most school districts? **7B**
6. Why are payroll taxes important to large central cities, much of whose work force lives in the suburbs? **7B**
7. What are the two largest expenditures among all the nation's cities? **7B**
8. How did the Hoover Commission help regulate land use? **7B**
9. What is the basic purpose of building codes and permits? **3A**
10. What are the three steps developers must take to meet subdivision regulations? **3A**

▲ THINKING CRITICALLY ABOUT KEY CONCEPTS

1. What might account for the problems, such as crime and drug abuse, that plague many housing projects? **6D**
2. Why might homesteading regulations require a buyer of a building to live in that building for a certain number of years? **6D**

728

3. Why is it in a property owner's interest to have as low an assessment as possible? **7B**
4. (a) Which groups would you expect to back "taxpayers' revolts"? (b) Which groups would you expect to oppose them? **7B**
5. What evidence is there that the development of cities might be better accomplished by market forces than by comprehensive plans? **7D**
6. Explain why the entire community has an interest in seeing that new structures meet building code standards. **6C**

▲ PRACTICING SKILLS

1. **Study Skills: Reading a chart and a map.** Refer to Figure 27–4 (page 725) to answer the following questions. (a) What are the five general zones in Boone County? (b) Under which zoning classification might you find a feed store near a printing plant? (c) In which zone is the pond located? (d) Would a warehouse likely be located next to the railroad or next to the creek? Why? (e) Would more people likely live in the zones represented on the left-hand side of this map or on the right-hand side? Why? **8B**
2. **Critical Thinking Skills: Finding the problem.** Reread the subsection "Property taxes and education" (pages 716–717). Identify the basic problem involved in the relationship between education and property taxes. State the problem in your own words, and tell why the problem can lead to discrimination in education. **8A**

3. Because the lower the assessment, the lower the property tax paid by the property owner.
4. (a) People with highly valued property. (b) People who own little or no property or who depend on state services likely to be reduced to compensate for lower tax revenues.
5. Comprehensive plans often create single-purpose neighborhoods that are empty and dangerous at times, whereas in unplanned cities more mixed neighborhoods emerge.
6. Most structures are used by people other than their owners. Also, unsafe structures are more likely to collapse or catch fire.

1. **Hearing from a police representative.** Invite a representative from your local police force to speak to your class about the department, its duties, and any special law enforcement problems your community faces. Is the department currently implementing any new policies? **3A**
2. **Drawing a zoning map.** Divide into groups and have each group work together to draw a zoning map of your community, using information gathered from the library or from your local government offices. Be sure to include a list of classifications and any abbreviations you use on your map. (You may wish to refer to Figure 27–4 on page 725 for help in designing a zoning map.) When the maps have been completed, compare your group's map with the maps of other groups in your class. **3A**

1. **Creating a poster.** Imagine that you belong to an organization in need of volunteers, such as a political campaign, citizens' lobbying group, or social service organization. Create a poster urging people to volunteer. Explain in the poster the organization's goals and why people should join it. **4D**
2. **Writing a letter to the editor.** Imagine that you are a homeowner whose property value— and therefore property taxes— have skyrocketed in recent years. Write a letter to the editor explaining your situation and offering a solution. **7A**
3. **Writing an essay.** Review the local government policies and programs discussed in this chapter from the standpoint of the homeless. What are their special needs? What unique problems do they pose for local governments? **6G**

▲ ANALYZING A POLITICAL CARTOON

Economic problems such as unemployment and deficits in the 1980's and 1990's created a strain on government finances. As a result, all levels of government looked for new sources of revenue. Look at the cartoon below and answer the following questions.

1. How are all of the characters in this cartoon alike? **8B**
2. Describe the expression on the faces of the taxpayer. **8B**
3. Summarize the problem in government financing that this cartoon conveys. **8A**

© Rob Rogers. Reprinted by permission of UFS, Inc., New York.

Participatory Citizenship

1. Students may want to look through local newspapers to brush up on law enforcement issues..
2. If information on local zoning is difficult to obtain, students might draw zoning maps of an ideal community instead.

Writing About Issues

1. Students might be advised that posters are most effective when they contain a few catchy slogans rather than extended statements.
2. Letters should point out that increases in property value raise a person's property taxes without raising his or her income. Solutions might include lowering property tax rates or assessment ratios or providing tax breaks to certain property owners.
3. Homeless persons are especially vulnerable to crime and health problems and therefore require special efforts at protection. In terms of housing, attempts must be made to provide adequate short-term emergency shelters and opportunities for more permanent low-income apartments.

Analyzing a Political Cartoon

1. Each one is holding out a cup, indicating that he or she needs money.
2. Of the four characters, he looks the most unhappy and confused.
3. Federal, state, and local governments, as well as taxpayers, are begging for financial help; there is little the four can do to help one another financially.

Practicing Skills

1. **(a)** Agriculture, residential, recreation, commercial, industrial. **(b)** Light industrial. **(c)** Recreation. **(d)** Next to the railroad. Warehouses are zoned M-L for light industrial. **(e)** The right side. Most of the residential zones are there.
2. *Problem:* Since property taxes are a major funding source for school districts, a district with a small tax base has less money for education. In many low-income neighborhoods, residents do not own property or their property is worth little, resulting in a small tax base and less money per pupil. Hence, families with low incomes receive a poorer education.

Chapter Review exercises are keyed for student abilities:
▲ = Basic
● = All Levels
■ = Average/Advanced

Background

Vladimir Nikolayev first visited the United States in 1958 and has reported on the American people in later visits. The Soviet Union itself had a tradition of powerful centralized government and weak local government. Since the breakup of the country, the republics have been free to redefine their systems of national and local government.

Economics

● Write the word *taxes* on the board and ask students to suggest words or phrases that come to mind. Have students compare their response to Nikolayev's description of Soviet feelings about taxes.

● CRITICAL THINKING **Why might taxes not seem very significant to Soviet citizens?** (Under communism the entire economy was controlled by the government, so it was not necessary to tax individuals directly to raise money.)

Civic Participation

● Have students attend a meeting of your local government and take notes on what occurred. Then have them write a description of the meeting as though they were reporting on local government for people in another country.

Values

● Ask a volunteer to read aloud the last paragraph of the feature. Ask students to suggest why homelessness is a problem in a prosperous nation like the United States.

A Soviet Journalist Looks at the United States

Under glasnost, *the Moscow weekly magazine* Ogonyok *led the struggle for greater freedom of the press. In 1989,* Ogonyok *sent journalist Vladimir Nikolayev to the United States. Nikolayev looked mainly at local government.*

Moscow. After three days at Duke [University], I spent time with the City Council in Durham [NC]. . . .

I began to study the City Council's work by attending one of its regular sessions. . . . The issues discussed were of the most mundane kind. For example, in one of the city districts there were plans to build a shopping center. . . . Two residents, who said they represented the interests of 150 of their neighbors, were protesting against the projects. Their argument: The district involved is one that people moved to precisely because it is quiet. The new centers would cause a great deal of traffic and ruin the air. Advocates of the construction contended that these fears were exaggerated. The issue was left for further study.

Durham's financial management . . . depends mostly on funds collected from local taxpayers. This subject is very complicated, especially for us Soviet people, since we do not have such procedures. The very concept of "tax" does not arouse in any special emotions or thoughts in us, but [Durham's finance and budget chief] spoke to me about it with [great] reverence and anxiety. . . .

Interest in the most diverse aspects of local administration and public life is characteristic of the American provinces. As I mentioned earlier, Durham has a population of 130,000. But the local weekly, the *Independent,* contains hundreds of notices on various events during the week, in both the city and its environs: meetings, lectures, encounters, exhibitions. . . . Clearly, such a range of activ-

ities can be provided only through enthusiasm to volunteer. The roots of this enthusiasm, in my opinion, can be traced to the authority of local government, which stems from its self-administration and the participation in it of interested residents.

The U.S. is a nation on wheels. . . . Without getting out of his car, an American can withdraw money from a bank, see a movie, and so forth. On the other hand, vehicles and roads cause an incalculable number of problems, starting with pollution. . . .

When you travel around the U.S., you never cease to be amazed at the diversity of voluntary activities. In San Francisco, I spent several hours in a shelter for the homeless. It exists only through volunteer efforts. The problem of the homeless is an acute one in the U.S.: Tattered people with bags and cartons in their hands . . . are to be found in every U.S. city. Such a quantity of them against the backdrop of prosperous America produces an especially painful impression.

CRITICAL THINKING

1. What are some features of life and government here that impressed Nikolayev?

2. How does the Soviet journalist explain the large number of activities in Durham? From his reaction, what can you deduce about the Soviet Union at that time?

3. If a foreign journalist visited your city, what would you show him or her? Why?

730

Critical Thinking Answers

1. The importance of local government and local tax issues, the importance of the automobile, the diversity of activities, contrasts between rich and poor.

2. He believes that Americans are very willing to volunteer to be involved in activities, implying that Soviet citizens were not.

3. Students might suggest local museums, parks, entertainment, or social activities.

UNIT
★10★

COMPARATIVE GOVERNMENT

731

UNIT 10

Comparative Government
(pp. 731–776)

Unit Overview

Unlike earlier units, which focus on American political life, Unit Ten examines the political and economic systems of other nations. In this unit students are given an opportunity to compare the American political system with those of other countries. Chapter 28 describes the basic features of capitalist, Communist, and Socialist economic systems and considers the role of government in economic life under each type of system. Chapter 29 examines several types of democratic governments and then describes efforts by people in many different nations to achieve greater political freedom.

Photo
Chinese Summer Palace, Beijing.

CHAPTER 28
THE ROLE OF GOVERNMENT IN ECONOMIC SYSTEMS
(pp. 732–753)

	Section Objectives	**Section Resources**
Section 1 **Capitalism Allows Personal Freedom**	☐ list and describe the four factors of production ☐ identify the characteristics and principles of capitalist economic systems ☐ explain the role of government in a capitalist system	■ SKILLS CHALLENGE WORKSHEET **28** ● CITIZENSHIP WORKSHEET **11** ▲ TRANSPARENCY **60**
Section 2 **What Are the Characteristics of Communist Economies?**	☐ explain how Lenin and Stalin applied the theories of Karl Marx to the economic system of the Soviet Union ☐ give reasons for recent changes in Communist economic policy	▲ TRANSPARENCY **61**
Section 3 **What Are the Characteristics of Socialist Economies?**	☐ list differences among the early forms of socialism ☐ identify principles common to most modern Socialist economies	▲ SKILLS PRACTICE WORKSHEET **28**

Essential Elements

The list below shows Essential Elements relevant to this chapter. (The complete list of Essential Elements appears in the introductory pages of this Teacher's Edition.)

Section 1: 6G, 7C, 7D, 7E, 8B

Critical Thinking feature (p. 741): 8A, 8B

Section 2: 1C, 5A, 5B, 5C, 6G, 7E, 8H

Section 3: 5A, 5B, 5C, 7E, 8G

Chapter Review: 6G, 7D, 7E, 8B, 8C, 8G, 8H

> Section Resources are keyed for student abilities:
> ▲ = Basic
> ● = All Levels
> ■ = Average/Advanced

Homework Options

Each section contains activities labeled "Guided/Independent Practice," "Reteaching/Correctives," and "Enrichment/Extension." You may wish to choose from among these activities when assigning homework.

Students Acquiring English Activities

On the chalkboard, draw a Venn diagram with three overlapping circles. (A discussion of Venn diagrams can be found in the essay on "Varying the Means of Instruction" in the Teacher's Professional Handbook.) Label one circle *Capitalism,* one circle *Communism,* and the third circle *Socialism.* Ask students to list the critical attributes for each economic system, and write them in the circles, taking care to fill in the overlapping section with attributes shared by all systems. You may want to form three groups to cite attributes for each system and note the overlapping attributes when they report their lists to the class.

LISTENING/SPEAKING: Ask students to suggest reasons why capitalism might have advantages over the other two systems. Students may wish to invite a businessperson to explain capitalism from a day-to-day point of view.

Case Studies

When teaching this chapter, you may use Case Study 9, which examines the issue of a special minimum wage for teenagers. (Case Studies may be found following p. 510.)

Teacher Bibliography

Galbraith, John Kenneth. *The Affluent Society.* 4th ed. Houghton Mifflin, 1984. Attacks the prevailing theories of economics and demonstrates that they are based on a negative world view that should not guide economic policy in the future.

Lee, Susan. *Susan Lee's ABZs of Economics.* Poseidon Press, 1987. Defines and clearly explains basic economic terms and concepts.

Randall, Vicky and Robin Theobald. *Political Change and Underdevelopment.* Duke University Press, 1985. A look at politics in the Third World.

Student Bibliography

Clapham, Christopher, Ian Campbell, and George Philip, eds. *The Political Dilemmas of Military Regimes.* Barnes and Noble, 1985. Considers problems faced by various military regimes.

Ebenstein, William and Edwin Fogelman. *Today's Isms: Communism, Fascism, Capitalism, Socialism.* 9th ed. Prentice-Hall, 1985. A classic study of types of governments and the economic systems associated with them.

Sobel, Robert and David B. Sicilia. *The Entrepreneurs.* Houghton Mifflin, 1986. Dramatic stories about the lives of America's most successful entrepreneurs.

Literature

Guareschi, Giovanni. *The Little World of Don Camillo.* Translated by Una Vincenzo Troubridge. Pellegrini & Cudahy, 1950. Anecdotes based on the adversarial relationship between the Communist mayor and the parish priest of a small village in Italy.

Han, Suyin. *Till Morning Comes.* Bantam Books, 1982. A love story which takes place in China during the Cultural Revolution.

Solzhenitsyn, Aleksandr. *One Day in the Life of Ivan Denisovich.* Translated by H. T. Willetts. Farrar, Straus & Giroux, 1991. One day in the life of an innocent man sentenced to ten years in one of Stalin's prison camps.

Films and Videotapes*

Capitalism. (Series title: *Capitalism, Socialism, Communism.*) 24 min. NGS, 1986. f, v. Examines the origins and philosophy of a market economy. Covers the period from the Industrial Revolution in England to the regulated economy of the United States today.

Socialism. (Series title: *Capitalism, Socialism, Communism.*) 25 min. NGS, 1986. f, v. Examines the origin and philosophy of socialism. Describes the economic/political system at work in present-day Sweden, using a shipbuilding company and the Swedish medical system as examples.

Software*

Nationalism: Past and Present (Apple). Focus. Students explore the roots of nationalism and related concepts. Contains five programs: Nationalism: Its European Roots; Nation-Building; Graphing the Nation-Building Process; Destructive Nationalism; and Nationalism Today: The Soviet Union.

* For a complete guide to audiovisual sources, see page T22.

The Role of Government in Economic Systems

(pp. 732–753)

Chapter 28 examines three basic types of economic systems—capitalism, communism, and socialism—and discusses the role of government in each system.

Chapter Outline

After students complete this chapter, they will be able to:

1. List and describe the four factors of production.

2. Identify the characteristics and principles of capitalist economic systems.

3. Explain the role of government in a capitalist system.

4. Explain how Lenin and Stalin applied the theories of Karl Marx to the economic system of the Soviet Union.

5. Give reasons for recent changes in Communist economic policy.

6. List differences among the early forms of socialism.

7. Identify principles common to most modern Socialist economies.

CHAPTER 28

THE ROLE of GOVERNMENT in ECONOMIC SYSTEMS

Fundamentally, there are only two ways of coordinating the economic activities of millions. One is central direction involving the use of coercion — the technique of the army and of the modern totalitarian state. The other is voluntary cooperation of individuals — the technique of the marketplace.

Milton Friedman
Capitalism and Freedom (1962)

732

Photo
Market scene, Soviet Union.

I n 1950 Roberto Goizueta came to the United States from Cuba as a student bound for Yale University. Eleven years later he arrived again, this time as a refugee fleeing Fidel Castro's Communist dictatorship. Goizueta's family had lost all their money in Castro's 1959 takeover of Cuba. Because Goizueta had worked for the Coca-Cola Company in Cuba, the company hired him upon his arrival in the United States. Twenty years later, in 1981, Goizueta became head of the $10 billion soft drink giant.

The life of Roberto Goizueta illustrates the stark contrasts between two kinds of economic systems, capitalism and communism. In the Communist system Goizueta left behind, the *government* owned the resources and made the economic decisions. In the capitalist system Goizueta found in the United States, *individuals* owned the resources and made the decisions. This chapter describes these two economic systems, as well as a third system called socialism, and the role that government plays in each.

CHAPTER OUTLINE

1 Capitalism Allows Personal Freedom

Government and Economics
Principles of Capitalism
Capitalism in Action

2 What Are the Characteristics of Communist Economies?

Development of Communism
Communism Today

3 What Are the Characteristics of Socialist Economies?

Development of Socialism
Modern Socialism

733

CHAPTER SUPPORT MATERIAL

Skills Practice Worksheet 28

Skills Challenge Worksheet 28

Citizenship Worksheet 11

Transparencies 60–61

Study Guide/Review 28

Workbook Chapter 28

Chapter 28 Test, Forms A-C

SECTION 1

Capitalism Allows Personal Freedom

(pp. 734–740)

Section Objectives

☐ list and describe the four factors of production

☐ identify the characteristics and principles of capitalist economic systems

☐ explain the role of government in a capitalist system

Vocabulary

economic system, factors of production, land, labor, capital, management, capitalism, free enterprise system, market economy, profit, entrepreneur

FOCUS

● Tell the class, *The shoes I am wearing are a sign of capitalism in action.* Have students explain what you mean by that statement. If students need help, ask them who made the shoes and why and how you obtained the shoes and why. (The shoes were made by a group of private individuals for the purpose of making a profit. You compared shoes made by several different companies to search for the best combination of price and quality. Then you used your own resources—money—to purchase the shoes.)

Make sure that students understand the importance of such basic capitalist principles as private ownership, freedom of choice, competition, and individual initiative. (These principles are outlined on pp. 736 and 738.)

6G, 7C, 7D, 7E, 8B

SECTION 1 — Capitalism Allows Personal Freedom

> **ACCESS** | **The Main Ideas**
>
> 1 **What is capitalism?** *pages 734–738*
> 2 **What role does the government play in a capitalist system?** *pages 738–740*

What does freedom have to do with economics? When we hear the word *freedom*, we usually think of political freedoms, such as voting and free speech. Yet freedom has an economic side as well. How "free" would you be if the government could seize your property any time it wished? How "free" would you be if you were prevented from changing jobs or starting a business?

In this section we will look at capitalism, an economic system that stresses an individual's freedom to make choices. We will also look at the role that government plays in a capitalist system.

7E

Government and Economics

An **economic system** refers to the way in which a nation organizes the production, distribution, and exchange of goods and services. The type of economic system a nation has depends on the government's role in this process.

Factors of production

The term **factors of production** is used to refer to the resources that any economy needs to produce its goods and services. As Figure 28–1 shows, the four factors of land, labor, capital, and management flow together to make the final product.

Land refers to all natural resources. It includes soil, water, and everything found underneath and within them. Land includes a river's swiftly flowing water, rich soils for agriculture, and minerals such as copper, iron, and petroleum.

Labor has to do with the human resources that are needed to produce goods and services. Labor includes people and their knowledge,

734

experience, and skills. Assembly-line workers, engineers, barbers, nurses, teachers, and even the unemployed — anyone who is capable of working — are part of an economy's labor force.

Capital is anything that can be used to produce goods; therefore, it is also called the *means of production.* Factories, machinery, transportation equipment, power plants, mines, even telephones are capital. A bakery oven is capital because the baker uses it to make bread or pastries. Money itself is capital because it can be invested to produce goods.

Management refers to the people who organize and develop the other three factors of production. Management is needed to obtain raw materials in proper amounts and to apply labor to produce goods efficiently. Able managers are also crucial in the skills of creating, acquiring, and using capital.

Government, economics, and politics

The relationship between government and the factors of production raises some interesting questions. What role, if any, should a government play in giving out resources? Who should own the means of production — government (the public sector) or individuals (the private sector)? Should a state produce more military goods or consumer goods? How should disputes between labor and management or between consumers and producers be settled? Capitalist, Communist, and Socialist systems tackle these questions differently.

A nation's economic system is also closely related to its political system. Countries that allow their citizens a good deal of political freedom usually allow a good deal of economic freedom as well. In countries where the government exercises strict control over people's political choices and allows little in the way of freedom, it usually plays a similar role in economic life. As President Franklin D. Roosevelt once said, "If the average citizen is guaranteed equal opportunity in the polling place, he must have equal opportunity in the market place."

Check for Understanding

▲ *What are the factors of production?* (Land, labor, capital, management.) *What is the means of production?* (Capital, one of the four factors of production.)

Figure 28-1 THE FACTORS OF PRODUCTION Land, labor, capital, and
management are needed to make final products. 8B

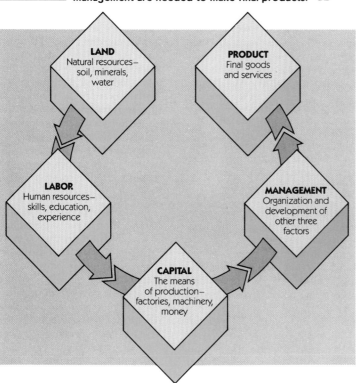

LAND
Natural resources—
soil, minerals,
water

PRODUCT
Final goods
and services

LABOR
Human resources—
skills, education,
experience

MANAGEMENT
Organization and
development of
other three
factors

CAPITAL
The means
of production—
factories, machinery,
money

6G, 7D, 7E

Principles of Capitalism

Capitalism is an economic system in which the means of production are privately owned, either by individuals or corporations. Government does not interfere with people's economic decisions. Because the owners of the means of production are free to do with them what they please, capitalism is frequently called the **free enterprise system.** Thus, all Americans are free to buy and sell property, start a business, or change careers at any time. We may purchase our own automobile, whether a bright red sports car or a blue station wagon. This freedom to pick and choose from among a vast array of goods and services is what capitalism is all about.

In a capitalist system, the price, quantity, and types of goods that are produced are determined by the independent actions of individuals. Producers make goods that they think consumers will buy. Prices are determined by how much of an item is available (supply) and how much people are willing to pay for it (demand). Because these decisions are made in a free market, capitalism is also called the **market economy.**

Origins of capitalism

One of the places where capitalism first developed was in Italy over 800 years ago. Because of their strategic location on the Mediterranean Sea, Italian towns such as Venice and Genoa were meeting places for merchants who traveled on land and for sea traders who brought goods from Asia. Gradually Italian bankers and merchants began to accumulate money, or capital, from interest on loans and profits on trade.

Another important step in the development of capitalism was the Industrial Revolution. As

735

EXPLANATION

After reviewing the content of the section, you may want to consider the following activities:

Economics

● CRITICAL THINKING Use the example of a steel mill to help students understand why all four factors of production are needed to make a finished product. Tell students to think of the classroom as the factory, themselves as the workers, and you as the manager. *A breakthrough in technology has produced a great demand for steel. What do we need to meet that demand?* (A supply of raw materials.) *Could we make a competitive product without a factory? Without workers? Without a manager?* (No. Each of these factors is vital.)

Cultural Literacy

▲ Remind students that the term *laissez faire* was introduced in Chapter 19 (p. 526). To help students remember the term, write it on the board and explain it in two parts. *The first word, laissez, is an imperative—it gives a command, "leave" or "allow." The second word, faire, means "to do" or "to make." Literally translated, then, what does the phrase mean?* ("Allow [us or them] to do.") *Broadly interpreted, the phrase means "Let us do as we choose." What basic American right does this phrase remind you of?* (Freedom of choice.)

Figure 28-1
■ *To make it easier to read, this figure is shown with only one set of arrows. What other arrows could have been drawn? Explain.* (The factors are all connected. For example, capital is needed to purchase land and labor, and management is needed to organize land, labor, and capital.)

Critical Thinking
● *What are some ways in which producers try to determine whether consumers will buy their product?* (They may conduct a survey; they may test-market the product first.)

The symbol ⅱ denotes active participation strategies.

Activities are keyed for student abilities:
▲ = Basic
● = All Levels
■ = Average/Advanced

Controversial Issues

● Write the following on the board: **Should government prevent the emergence of monopolies? Should government protect domestic manufacturers from foreign competition? Should government bail out domestic manufacturers that are in danger of failing?**

Have each student select one of the statements and write a brief essay. Students should give their opinions on the issue and state whether they would reconsider their positions under certain circumstances. (For example, someone might oppose protecting domestic manufacturers from foreign competition, yet favor such protection if the foreign competitors were engaged in unfair trading practices.)

Then have each student read his or her essay to the class. (Organize the readings by topic.) After all the essays for a given topic have been read, poll the class to determine its views on the issue.

You might also have students do research on their chosen topic and write a second essay explaining whether the research changed their opinion on the issue.

---

new agricultural techniques developed, fewer farmers were needed to tend the land. Large landowners forced small farmers and peasants to leave the land. At the same time, wealthy merchants and landowners were investing their money in the newly-developing industries, such as textiles, steel, and mining. These individuals were the first modern capitalists. The farmers forced from the land found jobs in the factories and mines.

Laissez faire

Closely associated with capitalism is the idea that government should stay out of business affairs — called the doctrine of *laissez faire* (page 526). It is said that Jean Baptiste Colbert, finance minister for France's King Louis XIV in the 1600's, once asked a group of businesspersons what the government could do to help them. One of them quickly replied, *"Laissez-nous faire!"* — "Let us alone!"

The principal function of government in a capitalist system is to keep peace and maintain order. The government's activities are supposed to be limited to such traditional services as providing an army and a navy, protecting private property, and enforcing contracts.

The theoretical basis of capitalism was put together by Scottish philosopher Adam Smith in *The Wealth of Nations*. In this book, Smith explained the theory of supply and demand (discussed in Chapter 19) and showed that government interference in the economy was both inefficient and counterproductive.

Smith's theories form the cornerstone of capitalist economics. Since its earliest days, the United States has embraced the basic ideas of capitalism. Other modern states, such as Japan and Canada, have also adopted capitalism. Four basic features common to all capitalist economies are (1) private ownership, (2) freedom of choice, (3) competition, and (4) individual initiative.

Private ownership

Capitalism encourages and respects the ownership of personal property. Every person has the right to own such things as houses, automobiles, televisions, boats, musical instruments, books, typewriters, and records. Individuals can also own businesses or parts of corporations — millions of Americans own shares of stock in at least one company.

Freedom of choice

A second important principle of capitalism is freedom of choice for producers, workers, and consumers alike. Producers have the right to manufacture and sell whatever goods they believe the public will buy. Workers have the freedom to select their own occupations and places of employment. Consumers may shop around to find the best products at the lowest prices.

In addition, the Constitution of the United States forbids the states from "impairing the obligation of contracts" (Article I, Section 10). In other words, the government may not interfere with business agreements. What any individual or corporation agrees to do is its own business.

Competition

Another important principle of capitalism is competition. Every day producers compete with one another for **profits**. Profits are the income a business has left after paying its expenses. Because successful producers are able to make big profits in a capitalistic system, economists often refer to the "profit motive."

Of course, producers cannot earn profits if their goods or services are not desired or purchased. Producers must manufacture, advertise, and sell well-made products at competitive prices. Producers that do not satisfy consumer wants or fail to make a profit will go out of business. In capitalism, the freedom to compete carries with it the risk of failure.

Individual initiative

The fourth principle of capitalism is individual initiative. Every person has the right to strive for improvement. For some, individual initiative might mean entering a trade school, going to college, or seeking a higher paying job.

For others, individual initiative means the opportunity to organize, manage, and assume responsibility for a business. Such risk-takers are called **entrepreneurs**. Each year, thousands of Americans go into business for themselves. In 1987 alone, 233,710 new ventures were launched. Among these businesses were new recording studios, construction companies, restaurants, house-cleaning services, and cookie stores. In the United States, wherever there is a need, there is usually an entrepreneur.

For example, Debbi Fields, better known as Mrs. Fields, founded a cookie shop that has be-

736

Background: *Constitutional Heritage* The ownership of personal property is encouraged and respected in the Constitution of the United States. Specifically, the Fourth Amendment prohibits "unreasonable searches and seizures" of property; the Fifth and Fourteenth state that no person shall be deprived of property "without due process of law"; and the Fifth also requires "just compensation" to be paid if property is seized.

736

Starting a Small Business 7D

You probably pass by a number of stores or offices on your way to school. You could probably list many of them by name. Your list might include a sandwich shop, a hardware store, a record store, an accountant's office, a real estate office, or a clothing store. What do these places have in common? They are small businesses, sometimes called the "backbone of the free enterprise system." Generally, small businesses are local operations owned and managed by one person or family. Compared with other businesses, their sales and staff are small.

The people who start small businesses must be willing to work hard and take risks. A very large number of new businesses fail within the first two years. Why, then, would you want to start a small business? You may have a dream, an idea for a product or service that you are certain will sell. You know you are taking a gamble, but you are positive that the opportunities for personal and financial rewards outweigh the risks.

To turn your dream into a reality, you must make a plan — a business plan. You will use this written plan to convince a bank or another lender to provide you with the money you will need to cover the expenses of starting your business. Your plan should explain why your business will be a success. It should describe your product or service, how you plan to let people know about it, and what is special about it. You also should list your qualifications to manage this business and tell exactly how you plan to spend the money you borrow.

The United States government helps small businesses through the Small Business Administration (SBA), which prints a variety of business publications. It also offers management counseling, financial assistance, and training programs.

Even if you are able to get your business started, there is no guarantee that it will be successful. In the free enterprise system, you must stay competitive through sound management practices and responsiveness to changes and trends in your business. The next time you walk into a small business, think about what it takes to be successful.

Follow-up

1. Find the address of the nearest SBA office. You may find it in the U.S. Government listings of your telephone directory or through your local Chamber of Commerce. Write a business letter requesting the kind of information available.
2. Write a brief business plan for starting your own small business. First choose a product or service. Then describe it, explain who will buy it and why, and list your qualifications to manage the business.

CITIZENSHIP SKILLS

737

come one of the most successful in the nation. Although she had held several jobs by the time she was 20 (her first job was chasing foul balls for the Oakland A's), she was undecided about a career. She decided to put her cookie-baking experience to work for her. "I didn't know anything about inventory control, labor laws, or health requirements," remembers Debbi Fields. "But I had learned early in life that if I wanted something, I had to earn it." Today, her shops can be found across the United States.

Of course, not every entrepreneur succeeds. About 50,000 businesses in the United States fail each year. Nevertheless, those who fail are free to try again.

6G, 7C

Capitalism in Action

Though capitalism is defined by private ownership and lack of government interference, governments do not sit idly by in capitalist systems. Government's role includes protecting private property rights, providing certain services, regulating businesses to protect society, ensuring competition, and helping those who for some reason are unable to share in the benefits of the free enterprise system.

Protecting private property

In the United States, private ownership is protected by the Constitution. For example, the Fourth Amendment guards against "unreasonable searches and seizures" of personal property. The Fifth and Fourteenth amendments stipulate that no person shall be deprived of property "without due process of law." The Fifth Amendment also prohibits the taking of private property "without just compensation." Similar provisions are found in nearly every state constitution.

Government services

Although the United States has a free enterprise system, the government does own some property and enterprises. The national government has set aside land for national parks and interstate highways. State governments operate toll highways and liquor stores. Almost all large cities run their own water companies.

Besides carrying out some business-like activities, government also provides national

Under capitalism, anyone is free to take a risk and start his or her own business. One successful entrepreneur is Texas businessman Antonio Sanchez. Though he came from a poor family, Sanchez helped found a bank and a petroleum company on the way to forming a multimillion dollar financial empire.

An example of private enterprise at work, Harbor Place, Baltimore, displays a variety of shops and businesses.

GUIDED/INDEPENDENT
PRACTICE
● Have students redraw Figure
28–1, labeling the four factors of
production but replacing the
definitions of these factors with
examples from a specific industry of their choice.

RETEACHING/CORRECTIVES
▲ Write the terms *Land, Labor,
Capital,* and *Management* on the
board. Have students name
businesses within your community and give examples of the
factors of production involved in
each. Note differences in land,
labor, and capital needs among
businesses and have class members speculate about the roles
played by management in each
type of business discussed.
You may also want to use
Transparency 60, which shows
the origins and features of
mercantilism and capitalism.

ENRICHMENT/EXTENSION
■ Have students complete
**Skills Challenge Worksheet
28,** in which they read an opinion and find the facts that support it.

defense, keeps law and order, and maintains
court systems. By providing these services, government enables individuals and corporations to
go about their business safely and confidently.

In addition, government is the largest single
consumer in the United States, purchasing vast
amounts of domestic goods and services, from
paper clips and paint to trucks and tanks. In fact
local, state, and national governments buy about
20 percent of all American goods and services.

Government regulation

In capitalism, individuals and businesses
have a great deal of freedom in deciding what
they will do. This freedom to choose, however,
does have some limits. Businesses may not employ illegal aliens, produce illegal or faulty products, or make false claims in advertisements. The
role of government is to guard against fraud, deception, and unfair practices.

The government therefore maintains regulations to protect society. The federal government
regulates such vital areas as nuclear power, airports, pipelines, and broadcasting. Local governments often regulate land use through planning
and zoning, deciding where restaurants, offices,
homes, or factories should be located. Govern-

ments at all levels can tax corporations, personal
income, and property.

Many business owners may complain that
government regulation reduces their ability to
provide goods efficiently and profitably. Still,
some degree of regulation is generally considered necessary to promote the public interest.

Ensuring competition

In a free enterprise system, the potential for
monopolies is a constant threat. Sometimes producers are so large that they are able to put all of
their competitors out of business. This might
occur simply because they are more efficient.
On the other hand, they might pursue unfair tactics to reduce competition. Either way, the result is complete control over a particular good or
service.

Governments can take steps to eliminate this
problem. To prevent monopolies, the government can pursue antitrust policies. The Sherman
and Clayton Antitrust Acts deter monopolies and
encourage free competition. In cases where a
monopoly is the most efficient way to run a business, such as a water utility, the government may
place restrictions on prices. (Chapter 21 discusses government regulation of business.)

739

Background: *Economics*
Government control in
many areas of business
tightened during the 1980's.
For example, under the
Immigration Reform Act of
1986, employers can be

jailed for up to six months
and fined up to $3,000 for
each illegal alien they hire.

Cross-reference
Zoning is explained in
Chapter 27, p. 722.

The symbol 👥 denotes
active participation strategies.

Activities are keyed for
student abilities:
▲ = Basic
● = All Levels
■ = Average/Advanced

Section 1 Review Answers

1. Land, labor, capital, and management.

2. They are related by the amount of freedom allowed. Countries allowing political freedom usually permit a similar amount of economic freedom; those that restrict political freedom usually control economic activity strictly.

3. (a) Individuals and corporations. **(b)** Individuals or businesses produce goods; supply and demand determine prices.

4. To keep peace and maintain order.

5. (a) Private property is constitutionally protected. **(b)** The U.S. government antitrust policies ensure competition.

Critical thinking Students should recognize that government does perform necessary tasks in a free market—providing for national defense and domestic order, for example, and enforcing contracts.

CLOSURE

● Remind students of the pre-reading objectives at the beginning of the section. Pose one or all of these questions again. Then have them read Section 2, keeping in mind the upheaval in the Communist world during the late 1980's and early 1990's.

Foreign competition

One kind of competition that presents different problems is foreign competition. The automobile, shoe, and steel industries in the United States today face intense foreign competition. Because the price of labor abroad is usually low, American manufacturers cannot afford to offer the best product at the lowest price. When cheaper imports flood the market, domestic producers find it difficult to compete. Layoffs, plant closings, and bankruptcy can result.

The shoe industry is a good example. The typical American shoemaker earns about $7.00 an hour, while a Brazilian shoemaker averages 85¢ an hour. American-made shoes are therefore more expensive than imported shoes. As a result, the American shoe industry faces collapse.

One step the government can take to help domestic manufacturers compete is to impose tariffs. This raises the price of imports and makes domestic goods more attractive to consumers. The government can also provide subsidies and tax breaks to certain troubled or vital industries. The milk, steel, and shipbuilding industries have all benefited from federal subsidies.

Tampering with foreign competition can cause more problems than it solves, though. Such tampering can weaken related industries (a tariff on steel, for instance, makes cars more expensive). Relations with trading partners may be harmed too. Some economists oppose any restrictions on foreign trade. They believe, in fact, that foreign competition is helpful because it forces American companies to be more efficient. A steel industry representative said of free trade, "At least it's a fair fight, and if you can't win you shouldn't be in the game."

Helping the unsuccessful

In a purely capitalistic economy, only competitive companies would survive. In most capitalist countries today, however, the national government intervenes when a loss of jobs or of a vital industry threatens the national interest. Government intervention, for instance, kept the Chrysler Corporation from failing in 1980, saving thousands of jobs across the country. Chrysler bounced back to become one of the most competitive American automobile manufacturers. The U.S. government also steps in to prevent major bank failures.

Furthermore, not every individual is able to compete. There are many who because of illness, discrimination, or other circumstances need help. In a purely capitalistic economy, assistance for the needy would be left entirely to churches and private charities. The U.S. government, however, has assumed a large role in caring for the needy. Social Security, Medicare, Medicaid, school lunches, and food stamps are just some of the social programs run by the national government.

Capitalism may not be perfect, but all things considered, it is a remarkable system that closely corresponds to democratic principles of government. Perhaps Winston Churchill said it best: "Some people regard private enterprise as a predatory tiger to be shot. Others look on it as a cow they can milk. Not enough people see it as a healthy horse pulling a sturdy wagon."

SECTION 1 **REVIEW**

Vocabulary and key terms

economic system (734)	capitalism (735)
factors of production (734)	free enterprise
land (734)	system (735)
labor (734)	market economy (735)
capital (734)	profit (736)
management (734)	entrepreneur (736)

For review

1. What are the four factors of production? 7E
2. How are economic systems and political systems related? 7E
3. (a) Who controls the means of production in a capitalist economy? (b) How are goods produced and their prices determined? 7E
4. According to the doctrine of *laissez faire,* what is the proper role of government in the economic system? 7E
5. In the United States, what is the role of government with regard to (a) private property? (b) competition? 7C

Critical thinking

ANALYZING AN ARGUMENT How would you respond to the argument that a free market works best when government does not exist at all? 7C

Check for Understanding
▲ *How do tariffs help domestic manufacturers?* (They add to the cost of products made outside the country, making domestic goods more attractive to consumers.)

CRITICAL THINKING
Drawing Conclusions

Imagine how different life in the United States would be without such Japanese products as cars, CD players, and cameras. Similarly, Japanese consumers would miss such U.S. items as blue jeans, soda pop, and movies. Japan and the United States are important trade partners.

However, trade relations can lead to conflicts. Government leaders from Japan and the United States often draw conflicting **conclusions** about how to resolve trade problems. A conclusion is a response—sometimes an answer—to a stated problem or development. To draw conclusions, you must identify the problem, describe the facts, analyze the relevant information, and consider the arguments of others.

★ ISSUE: Trade with Japan

Tension results from an imbalance in trade between the United States and Japan. The United States buys roughly 100 billion dollars worth of Japanese products each year. Japan buys roughly 50 billion dollars in products from the United States. The large difference—50 billion dollars—angers many American politicians. They blame the trade imbalance for the loss of jobs in the United States. Every dollar sent overseas, they say, is one less dollar spent hiring U.S. workers.

The two governments view the causes of the trade imbalance differently. The United States government blames Japanese business customs and government regulations for keeping foreign products out of Japan. In a report issued in 1994, the U.S. government charged, "As compared to other industrialized economies, Japan's domestic market still remains significantly less open to imports." The Gallup Poll results shown suggest that many U.S. citizens agree.

In contrast, the Japanese government argues that the trade imbalance results from decisions made by consumers, not the government. According to the Japanese ambassador to the United States, Takakazu Kuriyama, "Trade imbalances are mainly reflections of the savings/investment patterns of our two economies and have little to do with the relative openness of the mar-

kets." Because Japanese consumers save much more of their income than do U.S. consumers, they have little money to spend on U.S. products.

The U.S. government could take actions to reduce the trade imbalance. First, Japan could be pressured to change laws and customs that make selling foreign products in Japan difficult. While such changes could increase U.S. sales in Japan, they might also anger the Japanese. Second, the United States government could make Japanese products more expensive by adding more tariffs, quotas, or other barriers to imports. The resulting increase in cost could anger both Japanese exporters and consumers in the United States. No simple solution exists.

Analyzing the Issue

1. Identify and give three facts about the trade problems between the United States and Japan.
2. What do you think is the most important issue about trade with Japan?
3. Explain how the Japanese view the trade problem with the United States.
4. Draw a conclusion about the trade problem. What position on trade between the United States and Japan would you take if you were a member of Congress? Explain your position.

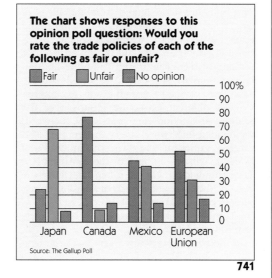

The chart shows responses to this opinion poll question: Would you rate the trade policies of each of the following as fair or unfair?

■ Fair ■ Unfair ■ No opinion

Japan   Canada   Mexico   European Union

Source: The Gallup Poll

741

SECTION 2

What Are the Characteristics of Communist Economies?

(pp. 742–747)

Section Objectives

☐ explain how Lenin and Stalin applied the theories of Karl Marx to the economic system of the Soviet Union

☐ give reasons for recent changes in Communist economic policy

Vocabulary

communism, command economy, planned economy, bourgeoisie, proletariat, Marxism, Five-Year Plan, collective farming, commune

 FOCUS

● Write the following statements on the board: (1) "Capitalist production begets, with the inexorability of a law of nature, its own negation." (2) "One morning I shot an elephant in my pajamas. How he got in my pajamas, I'll never know."

Ask students if they can identify the author of either statement. (The first is Karl Marx; the second is Groucho Marx of the Marx Brothers.) Then read them a birthday message sent by Irving Berlin to Groucho Marx: "The world would not be in such a snarl/If Marx had been Groucho instead of Karl." **What did Berlin mean?** (Karl Marx's economic theories, when acted upon by government leaders, created hardship, whereas the wit of Groucho Marx entertained people.)

What Are the Characteristics of Communist Economies?

> **ACCESS** The Main Ideas
>
> **1** How did Communist governments come to power in the Soviet Union and China?
> *pages 742–745*
>
> **2** How did communism change?
> *pages 745–747*

In the economic system known as **communism**, the government controls economic life. Thus, in Communist countries the factors of production — such as land, factories, utilities, mines, and farms — are generally state-owned and state-operated. Even the price of rental housing and wage levels are set by government economic planners.

In Communist systems, the government also plays a leading role in determining the type, quantity, and price of goods that the economy will produce. Because these decisions are the result of government planning — and not the free market — Communist economic systems are also known as **command economies** or **planned economies**.

1C, 5A, 5C, 7E

Development of Communism

The theories of Karl Marx

Communism originated from the ideas of Karl Marx, a German-born philosopher and writer. In 1848 Marx, with the assistance of his friend Friedrich Engels, laid the foundation for Communist theory in a brief pamphlet entitled the *Communist Manifesto*. In the *Manifesto* Marx stated his theory that all history is a conflict between different economic groups over the means of production. In Marx's view, the world was divided into two classes. On the one hand were the capitalists, the owners of industry and property, whom he called the **bourgeoisie** (boor-zhwah-ZEE). On the other hand were the workers, the class who could not afford property, called the **proletariat** (proh-lih-TAIR-ee-at).

The bourgeoisie, according to Marx, grew rich from the labor of the proletariat. In return, the proletariat received low wages that kept them

742

on the brink of poverty and constantly in need of work. At the time of Marx's writing, this appeared to be true. Many workers in Europe and even in the United States worked long hours and lived in squalid conditions. Marx predicted that, because they were more numerous than the bourgeoisie, the proletariat would eventually overthrow the capitalists and take over the means of production. As Marx and Engels declare in the closing lines of the *Communist Manifesto,*

> Let the ruling classes tremble at a communist revolution. The proletarians have nothing to lose but their chains. They have a world to win. Workers of the world, unite!

Marx believed that the proletariat would be unable to govern itself at first. To guide the revolution, a small group (the Communist Party) would establish a government. Marx called this stage the "dictatorship of the proletariat." In time, there would be no need for government, and the state would gradually disappear, or "wither away."

Forced to leave Germany in 1849 because of his radical beliefs, Marx spent the rest of his days in London. He and his family lived in poverty, supported largely by money from Engels. Marx spent his time in the public library working on *Das Kapital,* the first volume of which appeared in 1867. In this work, Marx laid out an economic theory of communism.

Since his death, many people have applied Marx's writings to form a large body of economic and political thought known as **Marxism**. Marxism has had a profound effect on economic thought, not only in Communist countries, but throughout the world.

Lenin and the Bolshevik revolution

Some thirty years after Marx's death in 1883, Russia became the first country to put his theory into practice. Severe shortages of food and housing, combined with heavy losses suffered by the Russian army in the first years of World War I, brought about the fall of the Russian emperor,

---

Background: *Cultural Literacy Proletariat* comes from the Latin *proletarius,* the term for a Roman citizen of the lowest class. The root *proles* means "offspring." The Roman constitution deemed that citizens without property could serve the state only by having children.

Czar Nicholas II. In October 1917, a Communist revolutionary group called the Bolsheviks gained control of the government.

The Bolsheviks were led by Vladimir Ilyich Ulyanov, better known as Lenin. Lenin had developed his own economic theory, based on Marxism but adapted to Russian conditions. Lenin proclaimed the "dictatorship of the proletariat," and took control of all economic activity. Industry, banks, and foreign trade came under government control. All men under 50 were drafted for labor or for the armed services. Women were mobilized to work in factories and on construction projects. Strikes were forbidden. To feed the people in the cities and in the army, soldiers seized food from the peasants.

Along with its control over the Russian economy, the Bolshevik government took control of other aspects of people's lives. All political opposition was suppressed. The czar, his family, and other members of the ruling class were killed. Freedom of speech and of the press were outlawed, and only one political party, the Communist Party, was allowed to exist.

By 1921, the Bolsheviks' emergency measures had failed to revive the economy. Production fell disastrously, and hundreds of thousands of people died from hunger, cold, and disease. To strengthen the country, Lenin proposed the New Economic Policy. Some small-scale manufacturing, trade, and agriculture were allowed to return to private ownership. The government kept control of major industries, banks, and means of communication.

Soviet life under Stalin

After Lenin's death in 1924, Joseph Stalin gained absolute power in Russia — now called the Union of Soviet Socialist Republics (USSR). In place of the slow changes of the New Economic Policy, Stalin imposed a policy of rapid industrialization. A series of **Five-Year Plans** established goals for the production of steel, coal, oil, transportation, and hydroelectric power, as well as for consumer goods. The State Planning Commission, the *Gosplan,* determined all the necessary supplies and raw materials. It set up specific schedules for the use of materials, machines, and for the workers to run them.

The first and most drastic Five-Year Plan began in 1928. All private business came to an end. The state was responsible for producing all goods, buying and selling all products, and hiring and firing workers.

In the October Revolution of 1917, the Bolsheviks, after violent street fighting, seized control of the Russian government. Years of upheaval followed as a Communist economic system was imposed on the Russian people.

743

EXPLANATION

After reviewing the content of the section, you may want to consider the following activities:

Economics

▲ *According to Karl Marx, what are the two main social classes?* (The bourgeoisie and the proletariat.) *What is the relationship between them?* (The bourgeoisie grow rich from the labor of the proletariat.)

▲ *What did Marx believe would result from inequality between the classes?* (The proletariat would overthrow the bourgeoisie.) *What would happen then?* (The Communist Party would establish a government in the name of the proletariat.) *What would happen to the government in the end?* (It would no longer be necessary, so it would fade away.)

👥 History

● Divide the class into groups of three. Each group should make three time lines—one showing the stages of history as predicted by Marx, a second showing the events in the Soviet Union from 1917 to the 1930's, and the third showing the events in China from 1949 to the 1960's. Ask students if events in the Soviet Union and China conformed to Marx's predictions. (Students should recognize that the regimes set up after the revolutions did not benefit the common people, nor did the state "wither away.")

Critical Thinking
● *What was there in Marx's idea of a "dictatorship of the proletariat" that Lenin used to justify the harsh measures he imposed?* (Marx believed that the people would be unable to rule themselves immediately after a revolution and that a strong centralized party would have to step in to achieve Communist goals.)

The symbol 👥 denotes active participation strategies.

Activities are keyed for student abilities:
▲ = Basic
● = All Levels
■ = Average/Advanced

Global Awareness

● Examine with the class the drawbacks of Communist economic systems. One major drawback is that government planning often fails to produce the right amounts of goods (p. 745). This results in the oversupply of certain goods and the need to ration scarce goods. An equally serious problem is the low productivity of workers. **Why are these two problems less likely to occur in a capitalist economic system?** (Under capitalism, the market determines how many and what kinds of goods are produced. The market can determine what goods are required more efficiently than can government bureaucrats, who make such decisions in Communist economies. Productivity is tied to incentive. Productivity is higher in free market economies because people benefit personally from higher output.)

YOU DECIDE

8H

In 1989, the Communist government of China ruthlessly repressed a national movement toward greater freedom. Though President Bush criticized China, he did not suspend its most-favored-nation trading status. Since then, China has jailed dissidents, exported products made by prisoners, and sold arms in violation of international treaties.

Did Bush make the right decision? Explain.

Sweeping changes took place in Soviet agriculture as well. Stalin found that the peasants would not voluntarily produce the harvests required under the first Five-Year Plan. With shops empty of goods to buy, peasants had no incentive to produce more. He was determined, however, not to let the peasants stand in the way of his plan. Stalin decided to bring agriculture forcibly under state control.

Stalin's plan called for **collective farming** — the bringing together on large tracts of land of the livestock, tools, and buildings of many small, scattered farms. The larger farms were expected to use machinery, introduce scientific farming methods, and produce food more efficiently.

Stalin was ruthless in meeting his goals. In the winter of 1929–1930, he began using armed force to collectivize the peasants' farms. In 1932 and 1933, a famine, worsened by Stalin's agricultural policies, took the lives of millions of Ukrainian peasants. By the mid-1930's collective farms, each composed of hundreds of households, were the rule in the Soviet Union.

Stalin made one concession in agriculture. He allowed the peasants to keep small plots of land for their private use. Food grown on these plots could be sold on the open market for whatever price it would bring. Much of the food on Soviet tables came from these private plots.

Stalin's harsh economic policies were unpopular, both within the government and in the countryside. To crush his opposition, he ordered

the arrest of millions of people in what was called the Great Purge. Throughout the 1930's, those accused or even merely suspected of disloyalty were either shot, put in labor camps, or sent into exile. Millions — no one knows exactly how many — were killed outright or died from mistreatment during Stalin's rule.

Communism in China

Another leader to apply Marxist ideas to his country was "Chairman" Mao Zedong (MAH-oh dzuh-DOONG). In 1949, Communists led by Mao took control of China and established the People's Republic. The problems facing China, which had been involved in wars for twenty years, were colossal. Industries were producing at low levels, and railroads, bridges, ports, and roads were in collapse. Furthermore, trade had come to a halt.

Under Mao, the Communist government took over large factories and began land reforms. In 1953, Mao imposed a strict economic program on the nation, the first of a number of Five-Year Plans aimed at increasing industrial and agricultural production.

Under the first Five-Year Plan, the government took land away from landlords and distributed it among the peasants. In time, large collective farms were started, much like those in Russia. Collectivization moved more slowly than in the USSR, but by 1957 all of China's farms were collectives.

In 1958 Communist leaders began a second Five-Year Plan, called the Great Leap Forward. The government established many small industries in the countryside. Hoping to make agriculture more efficient, the government combined the collective farms into still larger groups called **communes**. Five thousand families worked 10,000 acres on one commune, often without the help of farm machinery. The Great Leap Forward, however, failed disastrously.

Just as in the Soviet Union, Communist control of the economy spilled over into other areas of life. The most drastic measure was the Cultural Revolution, which began in 1966. In an effort to spread Communist ideas throughout China, Mao sought to rid China of its traditional ways. Privileged people, such as government officials and students, were forced to work on the communes or in factories. Much of China's tradi-

You Decide Answer
Students should defend their answers. Students should consider such questions as whether restricting economic relations with China would help or harm the cause of freedom there.

Background: *History* The disappearance of Chinese intellectuals and professionals was often explained as follows: "The doctor (professor, writer, etc.) has gone to

the countryside to receive re-education through physical labor."

tional arts and literature was destroyed, along with scores of religious shrines. Fanatic supporters of the Cultural Revolution violently attacked officials, managers, and teachers who did not show enough enthusiasm for Communist thought. Realizing his program had caused chaos, Mao called off the Cultural Revolution in 1968.

5B, 6G, 7E

Communism Today

Until recently, nearly one-third of the world's people lived under Communist rule in such nations as the Soviet Union, China, East Germany, Poland, Hungary, Czechoslovakia, Bulgaria, Romania, Cuba, North Korea, Vietnam, Laos, Cambodia, Afghanistan, Mongolia, and Ethiopia. Nearly all of these countries, including those in Eastern Europe, have since moved away from communism.

Although the remaining Communist countries practice the theory in different ways, they still have many features in common.

Central planning

The main characteristic of Communist rule, of course, is government control of the economy, coupled with rigid control over political life. Most economic decisions are made through central planning. The government and its agencies determine the levels of productivity, the resources that will be used, the kinds of goods to be produced, and the wages to be paid. For example, it is up to the government to see that a factory has the spare parts it needs, that a market receives enough fruit or meat, and that a collective farm meets its quota of wheat production.

In theory, central planning allows the government to see that people get the goods they need at prices they can afford. The government can guarantee everyone a job and can set low prices for such necessities as food, housing, medical care, and education.

Drawbacks of communism

In reality, however, Communist economies have numerous drawbacks. Government planning generally fails to produce the right kinds and amounts of certain goods. For instance, stores might be overstocked with cross-country skis but go months without dishwashing soap.

The necessities of life may be inexpensive, but they usually are also in short supply. People must spend hours in line waiting for the few goods that are available.

At the heart of the problem of shortages is the fact that Communist economies tend to be less productive than capitalist economies. In Communist economies, people work for the state, not for their personal gain. Therefore, the profit motive does not exist. If factory workers raised their output, either by working harder or through greater efficiency, their "reward" might be higher production quotas next year.

When people have an incentive to work, productivity is higher. Black markets (illegal private markets), common in Communist countries, provide goods that government planning cannot supply. Another example is the small private plots that Soviet farmers were allowed to tend in their spare time. These plots took up only 2 percent of the total farmland, yet they produced around 30 percent of the nation's meat, milk, and vegetables.

In December 1990 Solidarity leader Lech Walesa was elected Polish president. His trip to the U.S. in early 1991 included a visit to Ellis Island.

745

In November, 1989, thousands of East and West Berliners flooded through the Brandenburg Gate to celebrate the collapse of the Berlin Wall.

ENRICHMENT/EXTENSION

■ Have students write a newspaper obituary for one of the following people: Karl Marx, Lenin, Joseph Stalin, Mao Zedong. Students should do some research into the personal lives of these men but concentrate on their political records. The obituaries should close by suggesting how the person's death is likely to affect world events.

Section 2 Review Answers

1. (a) The government.
(b) By the government.
2. All history is a conflict between economic groups over the means of production.
3. (a) He directed a government takeover of industry, banks, and foreign trade; forbade strikes; drafted all men under age 50 for labor or the armed forces; mobilized women to work in industry; redistributed food. **(b)** He instituted Five-Year Plans, collectivized farming, and accelerated industrialization.
4. A period when Mao tried to spread Communist ideals by destroying traditional ways and forcing the privileged to work in factories and on collectives.

Moving away from communism

Command economies are not able to provide many necessary goods and services or to compete with capitalist economies. This was one reason why many Communist governments fell from power in the late 1980's. One of the most dramatic changes occurred in 1990, when the former Communist state of East Germany united with West Germany under a capitalist system.

Other Eastern European nations also are attempting to introduce free-market policies into their economies. Entrepreneurs are encouraged to open small businesses. Farmers are allowed to sell crops on the open market. Factory managers have been given a greater say in production decisions, and some state-run factories have been sold to private owners. Foreign companies have opened new offices and factories. In the short run, these changes have given rise to such economic problems as inflation and unemployment. Economic growth will likely be slow in the immediate future. Nevertheless, in nations such as Hungary and Poland, many people hope that capitalism will succeed.

China, too, has relied more and more on private enterprise. In 1978, China did away with the massive, unsuccessful rural communes, restored family farms, and set up free markets in agricultural and consumer goods. Since then, economic reforms have allowed free-market enterprises to boom in China. China's economy has become the world's third largest, and living standards have sharply improved.

The experience of the Soviet Union in the late 1980's showed how difficult it can be to reform a Communist economy. Mikhail Gorbachev, who took power in 1985, promised to revive the stagnant Soviet economy through a policy of *perestroika*, or "restructuring."

Gorbachev tried to tinker with the existing system to make it more efficient — giving workers incentives to produce more, for example, or allowing a few private businesses to open. Yet the Soviet economy continued to slide. More and more people decided that the Communist system had to be abandoned entirely.

The breakup of the Soviet Union in 1991 freed the individual republics to attempt their own economic reforms. Leaders in Europe and the United States urged the republics to turn toward market economies by lifting controls on prices and by restoring private property rights.

746

Background: *Economics*
Chinese leader Deng Xiaoping called the disbanding of communes in favor of freer markets "perfecting communism through capitalism."

Failures of communism

Overall, history has shown the flaws in Marxist theory. Marx predicted that workers under capitalism would be kept in poverty and would be moved to overthrow the government. Instead, workers in capitalist nations have been paid higher and higher wages. The average American worker has enough money to buy food, housing, and clothing, with enough left for an automobile, a TV set, and a vacation.

Marx's prediction that workers of the world would unite has not come to pass. Communists in Vietnam, China, and Cuba think of themselves first as Vietnamese, Chinese, and Cubans. Moreover, relations between Communist nations were often marked by conflict. In the 1960's, the Soviet Union and China came close to war. In the 1970's, relations between Vietnam and China worsened.

Finally, in Communist countries the state did not "wither away," as Marx predicted. In fact, the state became even more powerful, as the government established totalitarian rule over the people. Instead of the "dictatorship of the proletariat" that Marx had predicted, there was a dictatorship *over* the proletariat.

SECTION 2 REVIEW

Vocabulary and key terms

communism (742)   Marxism (742)
command economy (742)   Five-Year Plan (743)
planned economy (742)   collective farming (744)
bourgeoisie (742)   commune (744)
proletariat (742)

For review

1. (a) Who controls the factors of production in a Communist economy? (b) How are goods produced and their prices determined? **7E**
2. What was Karl Marx's theory of history? **5A**
3. (a) How did Lenin change Russia's economy? (b) What changes were brought on by Stalin? **7E**
4. What was the Cultural Revolution? **7E**
5. What are some of the drawbacks of Communist economies? **6G**

Critical thinking

EXAMINING BASIC PRINCIPLES Why are Communist economic systems usually accompanied by reduced political freedom? **1C**

5A, 5B, 5C, 7E, 8G

SECTION 3

What Are the Characteristics of Socialist Economies?

ACCESS The Main Ideas

1 **What were some early forms of socialism?**
pages 747–748

2 **What forms of socialism exist today?**
pages 749–751

In an economic system known as **socialism**, many of the basic means of production are owned and managed by the government. However, private enterprise also plays a major economic role. Individuals have a great deal of both economic and political freedom. Socialist economies use some central planning methods. Economic plan-ners set overall goals and targets for production of goods and distribution of wealth. Individuals, however, are allowed to start their own businesses, and the market plays a limited role in determining the prices of goods.

5A, 5B, 7E

Development of Socialism

Socialism developed as a reaction to the conditions caused by the Industrial Revolution in Europe. Socialist thinkers blamed the capitalist system for allowing some people to become wealthy while others suffered.

747

5. Central planning fails to produce sufficient goods; Communist economies are less productive than capitalist economies.

Critical thinking Students should discuss the authoritative nature of Communist governments and the immense power needed to direct a planned economy, power that spills over into politics.

CLOSURE

● Have students write three "I learned. . ." statements to show what they learned in this section. Then have them read Section 3, noting socialism's similarities to and differences from capitalism and communism.

SECTION 3

What Are the Characteristics of Socialist Economies?
(pp. 747–751)

Section Objectives

☐ list differences among the early forms of socialism
☐ identify principles common to most Socialist economies of the present day

Vocabulary

socialism, utopian, syndicalism, Christian socialism, nationalization, welfare state

Critical Thinking
● *What is the state of communism in the world today? Is it a system with a future in the world economy?* (Students should point out that its reliance on rigid central planning and unmotivated producers have brought it to the brink of extinction.)

The symbol 👥 denotes active participation strategies.

Activities are keyed for student abilities:
▲ = Basic
● = All Levels
■ = Average/Advanced

Early Socialists

During the early 1800's, the plight of working people became a popular issue among writers and reformers. Such men as Robert Owen of Great Britain and Charles Fourier (foor-YAY) of France believed that people ought to live and work in better social and economic conditions. These Socialists were called **utopians**, after the book *Utopia,* written by English statesman Sir Thomas More in 1516. *Utopia* is an account of an ideal society that eliminates private property and provides employment and equality for all.

Among the early Socialists, Robert Owen achieved international fame. He was born in poverty but by his early twenties had become owner and manager of a huge cotton mill in New Lanark, Scotland. Upset over the mill's working conditions, Owen created a model community. He gave neat houses and garden plots to his workers, provided free education for adults and children, paid high wages, reduced working hours, and furnished food and clothing at reasonable prices. After a visit, the czar of Russia was so impressed that he invited Owen to set up a model in Russia. While Owen declined the offer, he did establish communities outside of Scotland, including one in New Harmony, Indiana, in 1825. All of his utopian communities, however, proved to be financial failures.

Marxist socialism

Karl Marx developed a theory of socialism in the *Communist Manifesto* (page 742). Marx referred to his theory as "scientific" socialism to distinguish it from utopian socialism. In his *Das Kapital,* he outlined a Socialist state ruled by the proletariat. This state, Marx said, was merely a transition on the journey to communism.

Syndicalism

Another form of socialism is **syndicalism**. The syndicalist movement called on labor unions to replace the capitalist economic system and take over the state. A network of trade associations, or syndicates, of workers were to use boycotts, strikes, or even sabotage to gain control of the means of production.

In the early 1900's, the syndicalist movement became strong in Italy, France, and Spain. In the United States, Eugene V. Debs was a syndicalist leader. Debs ran as the Socialist candidate for President five times from 1900 to 1920.

In 1905, American syndicalists founded a union, the Industrial Workers of the World (IWW), popularly called the "wobblies." Before World War I, the IWW claimed 100,000 members and led 150 major strikes. After the war the IWW fell apart because of internal disagreements and government pressure.

Christian socialism

Yet another form of socialism that arose in Western Europe during the 1800's was **Christian socialism**. Christian socialism advocated a moderate social movement based upon Christian teachings. As with most other brands of socialism, oppressive working conditions and the wide gap between rich and poor gave rise to this movement. Christian Socialists sought to secure spiritual dignity and material well-being for individuals living in capitalist economies.

Today Christian socialism is most often coupled with democratic practices. Christian Democratic parties can be found in many countries throughout Europe and Latin America. The Christian Democratic Union of Germany, for example, proclaims the social duties of the state, but relies on private enterprise.

Karl Marx, author of the *Communist Manifesto* and *Das Kapital,* is considered the father of modern communism.

748

British Railways, owned and operated by the government of Great Britain since 1947, is an example of a nationalized industry. Here, passengers at London's Liverpool Street Station board a Cambridge-bound train.

5A, 5B, 5C, 7E

Modern Socialism

Among the nations that have Socialist economic systems today are Sweden, Norway, the Netherlands, France, Italy, India, and Israel. Additionally, many Socialist political parties can be found in many nations throughout the world, including the United States. The Socialist Party, the Socialist Labor Party, and the Democratic Socialists of America are all registered political groups in the United States.

Socialism is difficult to describe in precise terms because each Socialist nation has its own unique economy. Still, certain principles are common in most Socialist economic systems: (1) government ownership of certain productive resources, (2) central planning, (3) income redistribution, (4) extensive welfare programs, and (5) peaceful and evolutionary change.

Government ownership

Socialists believe that the basic means of production should be owned by the government. The process by which the government takes over private industry is nationalization. In this respect, socialism is much closer to communism than to capitalism. It is different from communism, however, because in most Socialist countries people can have a voice in deciding which industries are nationalized, and the industry owners are usually compensated. Just which industries are nationalized depends on the particular country. In France, for instance, the shipbuilding industry is almost entirely owned by private individuals, whereas in Great Britain this industry is nearly all publicly owned.

In theory, government ownership is easy to establish. A government needs simply to substitute government officials for the top management of existing corporations. It might also choose to keep the same managers but make them government officials. In either case, nationalized corporations continue to operate much like private firms, producing and selling what consumers will buy, trying to make a profit. This kind of governmentally regulated capitalism is termed "market socialism." The market is still the basic mechanism of the economy, but the government does not practice *laissez faire.*

749

Cooperative Learning
● Have groups of students create a Venn diagram to show how a typical Socialist economic system compares to a Communist system. Then have them make a Venn diagram to compare socialism and capitalism. Each group should present its work to the class, and two large Venn diagrams should be drawn on the board to incorporate appropriate results of all the groups' work.

GUIDED/INDEPENDENT PRACTICE
● Have students write one sentence summarizing each of the forms of socialism described in the section: utopianism, Marxist socialism, syndicalism, Christian socialism, and modern socialism. Each sentence should convey the essence of what that form of socialism attempted to accomplish. Remind students that the general goal of Socialists has been to improve society, but each form approaches that goal in a different way.

Background: *History*
Britain, under Prime Minister Margaret Thatcher, became less of a welfare state in the 1980's. When Thatcher came to power in 1979, she promised to reinvigorate the economy "by reducing the burden of direct taxation and restricting the claims of the public sector on the nation's resources."

Background: *Cultural Literacy* The reverse of nationalization is privatization, a trend that has been gaining momentum in many European nations.

The symbol denotes active participation strategies.

Activities are keyed for student abilities:
▲ = Basic
● = All Levels
■ = Average/Advanced

RETEACHING/CORRECTIVES

▲ Have students make a drawing or a political cartoon to show either income redistribution in a Socialist state or the "cradle-to-grave" benefits generally available in a Socialist state.

Have students complete **Skills Practice Worksheet 28,** which has them distinguish among communism, socialism, and capitalism.

ENRICHMENT/EXTENSION

■ Have students prepare reports on the economic system of a country not mentioned in the chapter. Among the countries students might research are Argentina, Brazil, Denmark, Cuba, Egypt, Greece, Japan, Kenya, and Tanzania. Students should decide whether their assigned country most closely fits the model of a capitalist, Socialist, or Communist country and be prepared to give reasons for their opinions. Students should also examine the recent history of their assigned country and report on changes or trends in its economic system.

Section 3 Review Answers

1. **(a)** The government controls many of the means of production, but private enterprise is allowed as well. **(b)** Partly through central planning and partly through the market.
2. **(a)** People should live and work in better social and economic conditions. **(b)** Labor unions should replace capitalism and take over the state. **(c)** The spiritual dignity and material well-being of individuals should be advanced through a Christian-based social movement within a capitalist economy.

Education is one of the many services the Swedish government provides free to citizens as part of its "welfare state" policies. Moreover, the government pays families an allowance for each child under 16 years of age.

Central planning

Socialist nations nearly always have some sort of plan to guide the economy. These plans range from very detailed economic tasks to broad, sweeping goals. Manufacturers, farmers, laborers, and government officials work together to meet the overall economic goals. Socialists hope that planning will meet all the needs of the people. While supply and demand have some influence on prices, targets for what to produce are made mainly by political authorities. Unlike Communist systems, Socialist economic systems usually permit protests of economic policies. Citizens can also vote to reduce or increase governmental control over the economy.

Income redistribution

One of the driving forces behind socialism is the desire to close the gap between rich and poor people. To do this, Socialists seek to distribute wealth more equally. A Socialist government redistributes wealth through two basic policies.

First, government levies heavy taxes upon the wealthy. These taxes, which can reach as high as 98 percent, discourage the concentration of wealth. A bumper sticker in Stockholm, Sweden, shows evidence of the heavy tax burden. It reads, "Born free, taxed to death."

The "welfare state"

Another reason that taxes are so high in Socialist countries is that they provide a vast array of "cradle-to-grave" benefits. "Cradle-to-grave" is more than a figure of speech. For instance, Socialist countries typically provide pregnant women with free hospital care, as well as cash grants or free baby clothes, cribs, and bottles. As the child grows, free medical care and free education are available. Workers in Socialist economies are guaranteed an annual income, sick leave, and workers' compensation. Old-age pensions and, finally, funeral costs are paid by the government. Because the government takes major responsibility for the social welfare of its people, Socialist countries are sometimes called **welfare states**.

Critics of the welfare state say that the security it provides makes life empty and boring. They add that the heavy taxes and redistribution of income that accompany welfare policies hinder individual initiative.

Peaceful and evolutionary change

Most modern Socialists believe that social and economic change must take place gradually through peaceful means and within existing political frameworks. For instance, when Great

750

Critical Thinking
● *What do heavy taxes discourage, besides concentration of wealth?* (The profit motive and individual initiative.)

Britain nationalized about one-fourth of its industry after World War II, owners were fully compensated, and most citizens noticed few day-to-day differences. Communist theory, on the other hand, calls for violent, revolutionary change in all aspects of society.

Socialism and capitalism

Socialism has had some success in reducing the gaps between the rich and the poor and providing services at low costs. However, socialism has been less successful in creating healthy economies. In France, for example, many of the industries that were once nationalized have been returned to private hands, where it is thought they will be more efficient.

Perhaps the main problem with socialism is that it is based on the idea that the government, not the people, knows what is best. Capitalism, on the other hand, holds that each individual should have the choice to decide what is best for himself or herself. This principle of individual worth is the driving force in capitalism. Though not free of problems, capitalism has produced the world's largest and strongest economies.

SECTION 3 REVIEW

Vocabulary and key terms

socialism (747)	Christian socialism (748)
utopian (748)	nationalization (749)
syndicalism (748)	welfare state (750)

For review

1. (a) Who controls the means of production in a Socialist economy? (b) How are goods produced and their prices determined? **7E**
2. What are the principal beliefs of (a) utopian socialism? (b) syndicalism? (c) Christian socialism? **8G**
3. How does central planning under socialism differ from planning under communism? **8G**
4. Why are taxes so high in Socialist countries? **7E**

Critical thinking

FORMING AN OPINION Should the government be responsible for the social welfare of citizens? Why or why not? **5C**

Chapter Summary

Economic systems can be classified according to how the factors of production — land, labor, capital, and management — are organized. In capitalism, private individuals control the factors of production and make economic decisions. Capitalism is also known as a market economy or the free enterprise system.

In capitalism, individuals are free to own property and spend their money as they choose. Competition for profits motivates entrepreneurs to start and run businesses. The government stands by to protect private property, provide needed services, regulate business practices, ensure fair competition, and help those who cannot compete.

Communism is characterized by strict government control over economic and political life. Because the government makes most economic decisions, Communist systems are called planned, or command, economies. Communism began with the ideas of Karl Marx, called Marxism, which were adapted by Lenin in Russia and Mao Zedong in China. In these countries, Five-Year Plans set goals for industry and agriculture, while individual farmers were forced to work together in collective farming. These policies were accompanied by the violent silencing of opposition. Failure of communism to provide basic goods and services has caused many Communist countries in recent years to adopt some aspects of capitalism.

Socialism describes an economic system in which the government owns basic industries but in which individuals have some economic freedom. Utopian socialism, syndicalism, and Christian socialism all attempted to correct inequalities that had developed in the early days of the Industrial Revolution. Modern socialism is characterized by nationalization, central planning, redistribution of wealth, and large welfare programs. A major drawback of socialism is that it requires high taxes, which may stifle individual initiative.

3. Unlike Communist systems, Socialist governments permit protests of economic policies and allow citizens to vote on the amount of economic control.
4. Taxes are high to redistribute wealth and to finance the vast array of "cradle-to-grave" benefits furnished by the government.

Critical thinking Some students will argue that government's only responsibility is to protect citizens and their property and that to do anything more would diminish individual freedom. Other students will argue that the quality of life for many citizens will be unacceptably poor unless government provides such benefits as health care and education.

CLOSURE

● Have students read the first sentence in the last text paragraph of the section and tell how it applies to the section. Then have them read the next assigned lesson.

CHAPTER 28 CORRECTIVES

● To review the content of Chapter 28, you may want to have students complete **Study Guide/Review 28** or **Workbook Chapter 28.**

Critical Thinking
● *What is the difference between evolutionary change and revolutionary change?* (Evolutionary change is slow and gradual, whereas revolutionary change is sudden and radical. In other words, evolutionary change is usually through ballots, not bullets.)

The symbol ⅱ denotes active participation strategies.

Activities are keyed for student abilities:
▲ = Basic
● = All Levels
■ = Average/Advanced

Answers

Vocabulary See pp. T19–T21 for suggested vocabulary activities.

Reviewing the Facts

1. *Land:* farm soils, copper, oil, water. *Labor:* engineers, teachers, nurses. *Capital:* factories, power plants, money, machinery.
2. The Fourth Amendment guards against "unreasonable searches and seizures." The Fifth and Fourteenth Amendments state that no person shall be deprived of property "without due process of law." The Fifth Amendment also prohibits taking private property "without just compensation." State constitutions usually protect private property in similar ways.
3. Private ownership, freedom of choice, competition, and individual initiative.
4. Through central planning.
5. An effort by Mao Zedong to spread Communist ideas throughout China while eliminating China's traditional ways.
6. Oppressive working conditions that arose as a result of the Industrial Revolution, the wide gap between rich and poor.
7. Government ownership of certain productive resources, central planning, income redistribution, welfare programs, peaceful and evolutionary change.

Thinking Critically About Key Concepts

1. Competition among producers weeds out inefficient firms. Freedom of choice allows people to enter different fields if their businesses collapse.
2. In both countries, the Communist regime took control of the economy, established agricultural collectives, and eliminated all political opposition. Violence occurred in both countries on a massive scale.

● **Review the definitions of the following terms:**

bourgeoisie	entrepreneur	nationalization
capital	factors of production	planned economy
capitalism	Five-Year Plan	profit
Christian socialism	free enterprise system	proletariat
collective farming	labor	socialism
command economy	land	syndicalism
commune	management	utopian
communism	market economy	welfare state
economic system	Marxism	

● **REVIEWING THE FACTS**

1. Identify the following as examples of *land, labor,* or *capital:* factories, farm soils, power plants, engineers, teachers, copper, oil, money, nurses, machinery, water. **7E**
2. What are the constitutional safeguards that protect private property in the United States? **6G**
3. What are the four basic features common to all capitalist economies? **7E**
4. How are economic decisions made in Communist economies? **7E**
5. What was the Cultural Revolution that took place in the People's Republic of China? **7E**
6. What historical conditions led to the development of the Socialist movement? **7E**
7. What are the basic principles of a Socialist economy? **7E**

▲ **THINKING CRITICALLY ABOUT KEY CONCEPTS**

1. How can capitalism be considered an efficient economic system when so many businesses fail each year? **7D**
2. Briefly compare the effects of Communist revolutions on the Soviet Union and China. **8G**
3. Describe some of the difficulties nations

might encounter in moving from communism to a free market. **7E**
4. In what way were the historical origins of socialism similar to those of communism? **8G**
5. What might account for the failure of utopian communities such as those founded by Robert Owen? **7D**

▲ **PRACTICING SKILLS**

1. **Study Skills: Reading a flow chart.** Refer to Figure 28–1 (page 735) to answer the following questions. (a) Which factor of production would include a carpenter? (b) Which factor would include the people who decide where a coal mine should be dug, who should dig it, and what equipment should be used? (c) What is the end result of this process? **8B**
2. **Study Skills: Analyzing a photograph.** Look at the photograph on page 746. Keeping in mind that for decades the wall served to divide East and West Berlin, explain the symbolism of what the people in the center of the photograph are doing. **8B**
3. **Critical Thinking Skills: Drawing conclusions.** Determine what conclusion you could draw about a country's economic system if you knew the following facts: The people of the country receive free medical

752

3. Inefficient firms would have to be shut down, which would create unemployment. Citizens would have to adjust to paying market prices for goods. The government would have to learn to encourage the

development of private businesses.
4. Both arose as a reaction against the Industrial Revolution.
5. The combination of high wages and low prices would have put financial strains on

the communities. Also, workers would not have had incentives as powerful as those in a free market economy.

care; the managers of the country's top corporations are all government workers; citizens of the country often complain about high taxes. **8H**

▲ PARTICIPATORY CITIZENSHIP

1. **Speaking with a business leader.** Invite an owner or manager of a local business to come to the class and discuss issues related to owning a business, including government involvement in business. **7B**
2. **Conducting a poll.** Poll your classmates and other students in your school on whether government should guarantee medical services to all citizens. You may want to consult the Citizenship Skills feature on page 241 for help in writing the poll question and conducting the poll. **6G**

■ WRITING ABOUT ISSUES

1. **Writing an essay.** Some critics charge that the gap between rich and poor is too wide in the United States. They argue that the government should work to close that gap. Others argue that in a free enterprise system, it is up to the individual to break out of poverty through hard work. What role, if any, do you think the government should play in closing the gap between rich and poor? Write a brief essay explaining your reasoning. **8C**
2. **Writing a letter.** Imagine that a student in a country with a Communist or Socialist economy has written you a letter in which he or she calls capitalism "unfair" and "inefficient." Write a response, explaining the basic principles of capitalism and describing how it is practiced in the U.S. **8G**

▲ ANALYZING A POLITICAL CARTOON

The restructuring of the Soviet economy, through the process of *perestroika,* was one of the most dramatic developments of the 1980's. By the early 1990's, however, various approaches had failed to solve basic problems. Look at the cartoon below and answer the following questions.

1. Who does the mechanic in the cartoon represent? **8B**
2. How would you describe his problem? **8B**
3. What would you conclude from the cartoon about the cartoonist's view of the chances for Soviet economic recovery? Explain. **8B**

Cartoon by Jim Borgman, 1989. Cincinnati Enquirer. Reprinted with special permission of King Features Syndicate, Inc.

753

CHAPTER 29
COMPARING SYSTEMS OF GOVERNMENT
(pp. 754–775)

	Section Objectives	Section Resources
Section 1 **The People Have Power in Democratic Governments**	☐ describe the structure of the British government ☐ describe the structure of the French government ☐ describe the structure of the Mexican government	▲ SKILLS PRACTICE WORKSHEET **29** ▲ TRANSPARENCY **62**
Section 2 **People Under Non-Democratic Governments Seek Change**	☐ describe the signs of movement toward democracy in Africa, Latin America, and Eastern Europe ☐ explain the changes in China and the Soviet Union	■ SKILLS CHALLENGE WORKSHEET **29** ■ COMPARATIVE GOVERNMENT WORKSHEETS ▲ TRANSPARENCIES **63–64**

Essential Elements

The list below shows Essential Elements relevant to this chapter.
(The complete list of Essential Elements appears in the introductory
pages of this Teacher's Edition.)

Section 1: 1C, 1D, 5B, 8H

Section 2: 1C, 6G, 7D, 7E

Chapter Review: 1C, 4B, 5B, 5C, 6G, 6H, 7E, 8B, 8G

Section Resources are keyed
for student abilities:
▲ = Basic
● = All Levels
■ = Average/Advanced

Homework Options

Each section contains activities labeled "Guided/Independent Practice," "Reteaching/Correctives," and "Enrichment/Extension." You may wish to choose from among these activities when assigning homework.

Students Acquiring English Activities

Have the class create two bulletin boards, one titled *Democratic Nations* and the other titled *Undemocratic Nations*. Have them look through current news magazines and newspapers to find articles and/or photographs that could be used to illustrate one of the bulletin boards. Students may also take photos illustrating freedoms enjoyed by people in democratic nations and write captions to go with those photos before putting them on the bulletin board.

LISTENING/SPEAKING: Discuss with the class the ways that names of countries vary. Have them suggest old and new names of countries, as well as the name of countries in their native languages as opposed to their English names.

Case Studies

When teaching this chapter, you may use Case Study 6, which examines the issue of defense budget cuts. (Case Studies may be found following p. 510.)

Teacher Bibliography

Galbraith, John Kenneth. *The Anatomy of Power.* Houghton Mifflin, 1985. Examines the nature of power and how it is wielded by different organizations.

Gorbachev, Mikhail. *The August Coup: The Truth and the Lessons.* HarperCollins, 1991. The former leader of the Soviet Union gives his account of the 1991 attempted coup.

Student Bibliography

Curtis, Michael. *Introduction to Comparative Government.* Harper-Collins, 1990. A basic handbook about the varieties of governments, showing their strengths and weaknesses as exemplified around the world.

McDougall, Walter A. *The Heaven and the Earth: A Political History of the Space Age.* Basic, 1985. Analyzes and compares political decisions in the United States and the Soviet Union from 1957 to the early 1980's.

Raynor, Thomas P. *Politics, Power, and People: Four Governments in Action.* Watts, 1983. The governments of the United Kingdom, the United States, the Soviet Union, and Argentina are discussed from a historical and structural viewpoint.

Literature

Criddle, Joan D. with Teeda Butt Mam. *To Destroy You Is No Loss: The Odyssey of a Cambodian Family.* Atlantic Monthly Press, 1987. An account of 15-year-old Teeda Butt Mam's flight from Cambodia to a refugee camp in Thailand.

Didion, Joan. *A Book of Common Prayer.* Simon & Schuster, 1977. An American woman retires to a Latin American republic and becomes involved in a coup d'etat.

Gordimer, Nadine. *Something Out There.* Viking, 1986. Gordimer writes movingly about the lives of people torn apart by apartheid in South Africa.

Grey, Anthony. *Peking; A Novel of China's Revolution, 1921–1978.* Little, Brown, 1988. A young missionary is captured by the Communists and forced to go on the Long March.

Koestler, Arthur. *Darkness at Noon.* Translated by Daphne Hardy. Macmillan, 1987. A condemnation of totalitarianism expressed through the arrest, imprisonment, trial, and execution of an innocent victim.

Software*

Nationalism: Past and Present (Apple). Focus. Students explore the roots of nationalism and related concepts. Contains five programs: Nationalism: Its European Roots; Nation-Building; Graphing the Nation-Building Process; Destructive Nationalism; and Nationalism Today: The Soviet Union.

---

* For a complete guide to audiovisual sources, see page T22.

CHAPTER 29

Comparing Systems of Government

(pp. 754–775)

This chapter examines the governments of several democratic countries and then looks at recent changes in certain non-democratic countries.

Chapter Objectives

After students complete this chapter, they will be able to:

1. Describe the structure of the British government.

2. Describe the structure of the French government.

3. Describe the structure of the Mexican government.

4. Describe the signs of movement toward democracy in Africa, Latin America, and Eastern Europe.

5. Explain the changes in China and the Soviet Union.

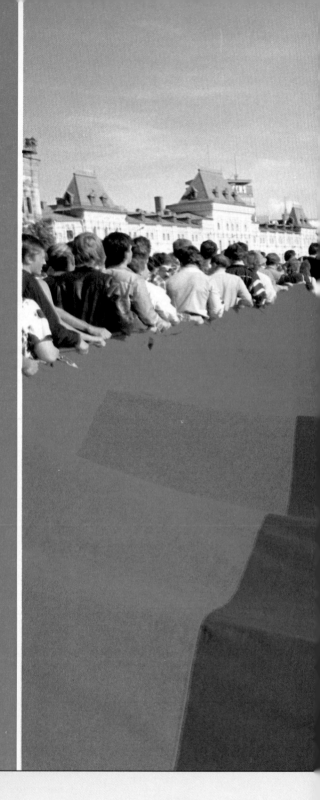

CHAPTER

29

COMPARING SYSTEMS of GOVERNMENT

I have always given it as my decided opinion that no nation had a right to intermeddle in the internal concerns of another; that everyone had a right to form and adopt whatever government they liked best to live under themselves.

George Washington
Letter to James Monroe, 1796

754

Photo
Demonstrators in Moscow, 1991.

I n Beijing, China, in June 1989, a lone man carrying a shopping bag stepped in front of a tank that was headed toward a pro-democracy demonstration. The tank turned to go around the man. He stepped to the side, continuing to block its path. Once more the tank turned, and once more the man moved to stay in front of it. Finally some onlookers pulled him away. The tank rolled on, and the demonstration was crushed.

Two years later, in the Soviet capital of Moscow, Russian President Boris Yeltsin stood on top of a tank and spoke to a nervous and angry crowd. Communist hardliners had just ousted Soviet President Gorbachev, but Yeltsin remained defiant. He urged the crowd to stand and fight the new regime. The hardliners, opposed by the people and unsure of the military's support, gave up.

This chapter will first discuss examples of democratic governments—governments controlled by, and dedicated to, the people. Then it will look at how people in non-democratic countries, such as China and the Soviet Union, have fought for freedom.

CHAPTER OUTLINE

1 The People Have Power in Democratic Governments

Government in Great Britain
The Government of France
The Government of Mexico

2 People Under Non-Democratic Governments Seek Change

Moving Toward Democracy
Reform and Reaction in China
Upheaval in the USSR

CHAPTER SUPPORT MATERIAL

Skills Practice Worksheet 29

Skills Challenge Worksheet 29

Comparative Government Worksheets

Transparencies 62–64

Study Guide/Review 29

Workbook Chapter 29

Chapter 29 Test, Forms A-C

Section Objectives

☐ describe the structure of the
British government

☐ describe the structure of the
French government

☐ describe the structure of the
Mexican government

Vocabulary

Members of Parliament,
parliamentary government,
ministry, Cabinet, shadow
Cabinet, Premier, department,
prefect

 FOCUS

● Begin by asking each student
to make a list of five or six
words or phrases that describe
the American system of government. Then write on the board
the names of the countries
whose governments will be
discussed in this chapter: Great
Britain, France, Mexico, Soviet
Union, China. Have students
offer three or four words or
phrases that describe the government of each of those nations.
Then have the class determine
whether the words or phrases
they used to describe the foreign
governments are similar to those
they used to describe the United
States.

At the conclusion of the
chapter, have the class see in
what ways their knowledge of
the governments of those countries has changed. At that time
students can be asked to change
the descriptions or offer new
ones that reflect what they have
learned.

1C, 1D, 5B, 8H

SECTION 1 — The People Have Power in Democratic Governments

ACCESS **The Main Ideas**

1 What is the structure of the British
government?   *pages 756–760*

2 What is the structure of the French
government?   *pages 760–763*

3 What is the structure of the Mexican
government?   *pages 763–765*

On November 22, 1990, headlines around the
world shouted, "THE IRON LADY FALLS!" Margaret Thatcher, Great Britain's Prime Minister for
eleven years, had announced she would resign
after losing the support of fellow Conservative
Party members. During the 1980's Thatcher had
dominated British politics like no one since Winston Churchill, leading the nation to victory in a
war against Argentina and dismantling much of
British socialism. For a time she had seemed in-
vincible. Yet public anger over a hugely unpopular poll tax finally led to her downfall.

The peaceful transfer of power in response
to popular wishes is an essential feature of democratic government. In this section we will
look at three democratic nations with different governmental structures: Great Britain, France,
and Mexico.

1C, 1D

Government in Great Britain

The United States draws many of its political
principles from British experience. Nevertheless, Great Britain has a system of government
that is quite different from our own.

The British constitution

Every modern nation has some sort of constitution, or fundamental law, upon which its government is based. Great Britain's fundamental
law is not printed in a single document but has
developed over centuries. The British constitution includes several written documents, like the
Magna Charta (1215), the Petition of Right
(1628), and the English Bill of Rights (1689). It
also includes many *unwritten* principles born
out of custom and tradition. For example, there

is no single document that describes the succession to the throne or declares that judges shall
follow common law precedents. Nevertheless,
these are practices that have been carried out for
centuries.

Because it is largely unwritten, the British
constitution is extremely flexible. A mere act of
Parliament is enough to change the constitution.
There is no formal amendment process and no supreme court to declare laws unconstitutional.
Still, because tradition is so strong and well established, major changes in the structure of British
government are highly unlikely.

The role of the monarch

For hundreds of years, Great Britain was
ruled by a monarch, the king or queen, who held
tremendous powers over the entire nation.
Today, however, the British monarchy has little
authority. The current ruler, Queen Elizabeth II,
is a constitutional monarch, limited in power by
constitutional change. She is the head of state,
and although she has a number of symbolic
duties, she does not run the British government.

Unitary government

As you know, the United States has a *federal*
form of government — that is, authority is divided between the national government and the
fifty states. By contrast, Great Britain has a *unitary* form of government. Instead of sharing
power, Britain's national government directs its
local governments.

Most of the people of Great Britain live
under a two-level form of local government,
made up of counties and districts. Forty-seven
counties enclose the non-metropolitan areas, and
six other counties enclose major cities. Each
county is further divided into districts that handle purely local issues and services. County and
district governments provide social services, education, transportation, and housing, plus fire
and police protection as directed by the national
government. Local officials are elected by the
people of the counties, but they have little power
in making policy.

Background: *Geography*
The United Kingdom, offi-
cially called the United
Kingdom of Great Britain
and Northern Ireland, con-
sists of England, Wales,
Scotland, and Northern
Ireland.

Background: *Cultural
Literacy* Britain's counties
were originally called *shires,*
a term that originated during
the time of Alfred the Great
(871–899). Many counties
incorporated the term in

their names; for example,
Cheshire, Hampshire, and
Oxfordshire.

The British Parliament

All legislative power for the United Kingdom of Great Britain is held by Parliament. Parliament is housed in Westminster Palace, located on the north bank of the River Thames (TEHMZ) in London. Parliament itself consists of two bodies — the House of Lords and the House of Commons.

HOUSE OF LORDS The House of Lords, or upper house, is one of the world's oldest legislative assemblies. It descended from the *Curia Regis,* or King's Court, in the 12th century and dominated British lawmaking for hundreds of years, gradually gaining power over the monarch. Since the 19th century, however, the House of Lords has steadily lost its authority to the House of Commons.

The House of Lords is an aristocratic body with about 1,150 members. All British nobles with inherited titles, such as duke, marquess, earl, viscount, and baron, as well as those who have been granted titles of nobility by the monarch for their lifetime only, are members of the House of Lords. The Lords also includes the archbishops of Canterbury and York, the 24 bishops of the Church of England, and about twenty appointed law lords, who hear appeals of important cases. All members of the House of Lords serve for life. Typically, only about one-fourth of the Lords attend its sessions.

Today the House of Lords has very little lawmaking authority. Its work consists mainly of reviewing bills passed by the House of Commons. The Lords can stall legislation, but they cannot prevent the House of Commons from passing a law the Commons strongly supports.

HOUSE OF COMMONS The House of Commons is the ''lower'' chamber of Parliament, although it is Britain's most important governing body. It consists of 650 representatives called **Members of Parliament,** or MPs, popularly elected from districts of approximately equal population. They serve 5 years, unless Parliament is dissolved and new elections are held. Any citizen 18 or older may vote for MPs.

All MPs can introduce bills, take part in debate, and vote, but the party leaders hold the true power in the House of Commons. MPs nearly always vote as directed by their leaders.

The House of Lords, once the more powerful of the two houses of Parliament, today exercises only limited legislative powers. Its members attend sessions in the Lord's Chamber in Westminster Palace.

757

EXPLANATION

After reviewing the content of the section, you may want to consider the following activities:

Comparative Government

Discuss with students the differences between a British Prime Minister and an American President.

● ⬜ CRITICAL THINKING *In which country is an "outsider" more likely to become chief executive? Explain.* (The United States. Because the British Prime Minister is the head of the majority party, he or she would have had experience in the House of Commons and in the running of the party. In the United States a non-politician could gain a party's nomination through the primary process and then win the presidential election.)

■ ⬜ CRITICAL THINKING Have students suggest other ways in which the different methods of selecting a chief executive might produce different kinds of leaders in the two countries. Ask students to name and describe current high-ranking members of the major American parties and then discuss how, if at all, these persons differ from recent American Presidents.

Check for Understanding
● *What are three ways in which the House of Commons differs from the House of Lords?* (Members of the House of Commons are elected; the House of Commons has most of the legislative authority; the House of Commons meets more frequently and for longer periods.)

Background: *History*
Lords formerly served without pay. Today they are allowed to collect traveling expenses if they attend sessions regularly. Members of the House of Commons have drawn salaries since 1911.

The symbol ⁞ denotes active participation strategies.

Activities are keyed for student abilities:
▲ = Basic
● = All Levels
■ = Average/Advanced

Comparative Government

■ Review with students the subsection, "The role of the President" on p. 761. Then have students select a power possessed by the French President that the American President does not possess. (Examples include suspending the normal operations of government.) Students should select an event in American history that in their opinion would have turned out differently if the American President had had this power and then write a newspaper article describing this different outcome.

Politics

● CRITICAL THINKING Have students imagine that one of the two dominant American political parties became as dominant as the PRI in Mexico. *How would such a situation affect the United States?* (Students might suggest that government would become more efficient or, conversely, that corruption and abuse of power would increase.)

■ CRITICAL THINKING *Do you think that domination by one political party endangers democracy? Explain.* (Some students will argue that if the majority of voters consistently favor one party, democracy is not threatened. Other students may suggest that lack of competition among parties could encourage the party in power to limit citizens' rights.)

The House of Commons is much more powerful than the House of Lords. It meets more frequently and for longer periods than does the House of Lords. The House of Commons also considers a wider range of problems and policies. Revenue bills, for example, must start in the Commons. Furthermore, the House of Commons can cancel or override actions taken by the House of Lords.

Lawmaking in Parliament

As in the U.S. Congress, the lawmaking process in Parliament begins with the introduction of a bill. Most bills are first introduced in the House of Commons. Although any MP may offer a bill, only bills supported by the majority party leaders or by the Prime Minister have a realistic chance of being passed. Following its introduction, a bill is debated and then sent to a committee to iron out the details.

There are eight "alphabet" standing committees in the House of Commons, designated "A" through "H." Unlike the standing committees in Congress, committees in the House of Commons are not very specialized and do not have the power to pigeonhole bills. All bills *must* be passed out of committee to the entire chamber floor, where a majority vote is needed for passage.

Bills that pass the House of Commons are sent to the House of Lords. Action in the upper chamber, however, is largely a formality. If the House of Lords fails to act upon a revenue bill within one month, it becomes law automatically. Although the House of Lords may vote down or amend bills, the House of Commons can cancel such actions.

The Prime Minister's government

Britain has a **parliamentary government**, in which the executive branch is not separated from the legislative branch. The Prime Minister, the ministry, and the Cabinet — all of whom are members of Parliament — share executive authority.

THE PRIME MINISTER Britain's chief executive is the Prime Minister. The Prime Minister is traditionally a member of the House of Commons. In principle, the Prime Minister is appointed by the monarch. In practice, however, the monarch chooses the leader of whichever party holds a majority in the House of Commons.

THE MINISTRY Once the Prime Minister is selected, he or she recommends the appointment of some 100 top "ministers," or administrators. Various positions include the Ministers of Defense, of the Home Office, and of the Foreign Office. According to custom, the Prime Minister automatically becomes First Lord of the Treasury. Together these officials form the **ministry**, also known as "the government." The term *government* (as in "the Thatcher government") is roughly the British equivalent of the American term *administration* (as in "the Reagan administration").

All ministers are chosen from among members of Parliament, and the most important ministers must be members of the House of Commons. With few exceptions, the top ministers are always leaders of the majority party in Parliament. The Prime Minister also tries to accommodate all leaders of the majority party by appointing them to some post. Technically, the monarch makes these appointments, but he or she invariably follows the recommendations of the Prime Minister.

THE CABINET The ministry is too large to serve as an advisory body. Instead, the Prime Minister personally chooses a small group of top-ranking ministers to help decide policies. This select group of party leaders is the **Cabinet**. The size of the Cabinet typically ranges from 18 to 23 members. Nearly all bills that pass Parliament are introduced by the Cabinet.

Political parties in Parliament

British politics has long been dominated by two major parties, though third parties have always played a significant role. Since World War II, the Conservative and Labour parties together have controlled more than 90 percent of the seats in Parliament. Minor parties in the House of Commons include the Social Democrats, Welsh Nationalists, Scottish Nationalists, Ulster Unionists, and other Northern Irish parties.

The Conservative Party, nicknamed the "Tories," was first organized in 1832. Conservatives are strong supporters of traditional institutions and values. Prominent Conservative Party leaders have included Benjamin Disraeli and Winston Churchill. The Labour Party began in 1906 under the leadership of Ramsay MacDonald. Its main objective has been to unify workers' political power.

758

Background: *Cultural Literacy* When a bill is "pigeonholed," it has effectively been killed because it has not been released to the full chamber for consideration. The desks of early U.S. Congress committee rooms inspired the term. These desks contained slots, or "pigeonholes," for papers.

Background: *Structure of Government* The British monarch must approve all bills passed by Parliament. The monarch does possess veto power, although no monarch has exercised this power since the early 18th century.

What does it mean to live under a different system of government? Most Americans take their political rights and freedoms for granted—as Leon Mandel is quick to point out. Leon is a high school student in Richardson, Texas, but he used to live in Kishinev, a city in Moldova. After years of waiting, his family was allowed to leave Kishinev in August 1989. This is what Leon has to say about the contrast between his old and new homes.

Leon Mandel

Why do I think Americans are lucky? The system of the country. It's the best Constitution in the world. There are elections, so that the best for the people is out there. It's not totalitarian, meaning that the President can be vetoed by Congress—that they can pass something or not pass something. They go through a long process before they do pass some bill. And there's a court which decides whether it is right or not. Again, freedom and freedom and freedom.

In the Soviet Union, to have a belief in something other than communism was a sin. It was hard for my parents. Because at home, they would try to tell me that everything they are teaching me in school about communism is not true. At the same time, if I go to school I should not say that. It would get them into big trouble.

In America, you are free to be educated. To me that is a miracle. You can become whatever you want. Over there, before you go to a good school, the first thing they look at is nationality. Then they look at how much you can pay them to get in. And then they look at, what you would say here, your SAT scores. In Kishinev most of the time you work and earn money for surviving. Making money just to go to one line to get some food, to go to another line to get some clothes—if you're lucky. Here, you earn the money, and you buy the food, and you buy the clothes, and you have more possibilities.

What do I like least? I would say the crime, and that a lot of people do not want to get educated. That very few Americans vote, that is sad. It shows lack of appreciation. In Kishinev, I remember they had elections for a deputy. They had one candidate. Who else can you elect?

One of my friends is now in Michigan. I said, "Watch out for all kinds of stuff, be careful on the streets. Also, appreciate how lucky you are." And he said, "You don't have to tell me that. I do. They—the Americans—don't."

STUDENT PARTICIPATION

1. What does Leon appreciate about America? Do you agree? Do you agree with his friend about Americans?
2. Find out how Moldova has changed since Leon left. What problems still exist?

5B

A Young Immigrant Looks at the United States

Leon Mandel (top) now lives outside Dallas, Texas.

759

YOUR TURN

Background
Leon Mandel's reference to nationality is based on Soviet identity cards, which divided Soviet citizens into national groups. In Kishinev, the "nationalities" were Romanian-speaking Moldovans, Russians, and Jews. Leon's family were Russian-speaking Jews and were discriminated against because of their religion.

Values
▲ Explain to the class that Leon's family had only one month to get ready to leave their home and that they could take only two suitcases with them. ***What might you have packed under those circumstances?*** (Students might suggest a minimum of clothing, photo albums, gifts and mementos.)

Comparative Government
● Have students use what they know about totalitarian government and what Leon says about it to create charts comparing elections and the creation of laws in a representative democracy and a totalitarian regime. Students may wish to review Chapter 1, pp. 14–15, for a discussion of totalitarianism.

Student Participation Answers
1. Leon thinks that the Constitution is excellent, that the structure allows more freedom, and that Americans have many economic and educational opportunities. Students should support their opinions with examples. **2.** Moldova became an independent republic when the Soviet Union broke up at the end of 1991. Students might research developments in Moldova since then.

The symbol ♦ denotes active participation strategies.

Activities are keyed for student abilities:
▲ = Basic
● = All Levels
■ = Average/Advanced

● Have students prepare brief oral reports on democratic nations other than those discussed in the text. Reports could cover such topics as whether the government has a one-party, two-party, or multi-party system; the role of political parties in the government; organization of the national government; powers of the chief executive and of the legislative branch; and the relationship between the executive and legislative branches. Among the countries that students might report on are Japan, Brazil, Canada, Switzerland, Sweden, Australia, and India. After each report the class can decide if the country more closely fits the model of democratic government as it is practiced in the United States or as it is practiced in Great Britain, France, or Mexico.

The domination of two parties is partly a result of Britain's electoral system. Like members of Congress in the United States, MPs are elected from single-member, winner-take-all election districts. The candidate who wins a plurality of the votes in each district wins the seat, and the losers get nothing. Minor parties can win seats only where their supporters are highly concentrated and outnumber other party supporters. This explains the handful of seats held by Welsh, Scottish, and Northern Irish parties.

In contrast to the American Democratic and Republican parties, Britain's political parties are highly disciplined. Members of Parliament almost always vote the way their leaders want them to vote. Thus, the Prime Minister and Cabinet most often get their way on important legislation.

The majority party does not go unchallenged, however. The primary function of the party out of power, officially designated "the opposition," is to debate, criticize, and offer alternative proposals. Four times every week, the opposition is permitted a "question time" to pose questions to the Prime Minister and the Cabinet. The opposition also appoints a counterpart for each Cabinet member. Together these counterparts are called the **shadow Cabinet**. The shadow Cabinet is ready to take control of the government if an election is held and the opposition wins a majority of the seats in Parliament.

Elections for the House of Commons must be held every five years. In addition, the Prime Minister may at any time dissolve Parliament and call for new elections. By this action, the Prime Minister hopes that his or her opponents in Parliament will be defeated at the polls. Sometimes, however, the opposition wins control of Parliament and takes over the government.

1C

The Government of France

Like Great Britain, France is a democracy and has many ties with the United States. Its form of government, however, is different from both Great Britain's and our own.

Despite his relative youth and inexperience as a Cabinet minister, John Major became British Prime Minister in 1990.

Critical Thinking
▲ *What are the benefits of the shadow Cabinet system?*
(It provides a smooth transition of power and offers an alternative to the Cabinet in power.)

A statue of the Duc de Sully, a famous French statesman of the late 16th and early 17th centuries, sits in front of the National Assembly, France's main house of Parliament.

The French constitution

The French political system has undergone many changes over the years. Since the French Revolution in 1789, in which the monarchy was overthrown, France has had sixteen constitutions. The most recent is the Constitution of the Fifth Republic, adopted in 1958. The government it established is a cross between a presidential and a parliamentary system.

The role of the President

Under the Fifth Republic, the leader of France is the President, elected for a seven-year term. There are no restrictions on how many times a President may serve.

The French President is chosen in a nationwide election by men and women voters over 18 years of age. Candidates from several political parties are nominated for President. If no candidate wins a majority of the votes in the first election, a run-off is held between the two candidates who received the most votes. The candidate who emerges with a majority then becomes President.

The Constitution of the Fifth Republic gives the French President enormous power. The President conducts foreign relations, ratifies treaties, appoints high government officials, nominates judges, and presides over the High Council of the Judiciary, which makes important judicial nominations. The President also commands France's military forces and has the power to suspend the government's regular operations when national security is threatened. This has happened only once, in 1961, when President Charles de Gaulle put down a military revolt in Algeria, then a French colony.

The President of France also holds some powers over lawmaking. For example, the President may submit important legislation or constitutional amendments directly to the people for a vote, thus bypassing the legislature. De Gaulle used this method in 1962 when the Constitution was amended to allow for the direct election of the President. More important, the President may dissolve the National Assembly and call for new elections. De Gaulle dissolved the Assembly twice (1962 and 1968), and François Mitterrand did so in 1981.

Premier and Cabinet

The daily operations of the French government are supervised by a Cabinet made up of about thirty ministers, or department heads. The President selects a **Premier** (the French word for

Background: *History* The First Republic was formed in 1792, three years after the French Revolution began. The Second Republic emerged after the Revolution of 1848, which deposed Louis Philippe and gave all adult French males the right to vote. The Third Republic arose after a revolt against Napoleon III in 1870; the National Assembly was formed the following year. In 1945 a new constitution, in which suffrage was extended to women, created the Fourth Republic. Charles de Gaulle, leader of the Free French in World War II, formed the Fifth (and latest) Republic in 1958.

Cooperative Learning

● Divide the class into groups of three—one person representing Great Britain, one representing France, and one representing Mexico. Tell the groups to design a clear, attractive chart comparing the three nations with each other and with the United States. The groups themselves should decide how to structure the chart and should choose the categories to be used for the comparison.

When all charts have been completed, have the class compare them.

The symbol 👥 denotes active participation strategies.

Activities are keyed for student abilities:
▲ = Basic
● = All Levels
■ = Average/Advanced

GUIDED/INDEPENDENT PRACTICE

● Write the following statement from p. 761 on the board: "The [French] government . . . is a cross between a presidential and parliamentary system." Have students write short essays explaining this statement and giving examples from the text (pp. 761–763).

As an alternate essay topic, students might explain and support the following statements from p. 763: ". . . the Mexican constitution is influenced by the Constitution of the United States. . . . In practice, though, Mexico's national government has much more power than the federal government of the United States." In preparing this essay, students should explain how the Mexican constitution is similar to the Constitution of the United States and how Mexico's government in everyday operation differs from the United States government despite the similarities in constitutions.

YOU DECIDE 8H

The North American Free Trade Agreement (NAFTA) will eliminate tariffs on almost all trade among the United States, Mexico, and Canada by the year 2000. Critics of NAFTA say the United States will lose jobs to Mexico and that increased manufacturing in Mexico will add to industrial pollution in North America.

Are free trade agreements in a nation's best interests?

"first") to head the Cabinet, and together the President and Premier select the various ministers. The Cabinet's main functions are to draft proposals for legislation and to carry out the government's policies. (Cabinet-sponsored bills are usually given priority; bills introduced by members of the legislature are generally limited to such areas as civil liberties, labor relations, and criminal punishment.) Unlike their British counterparts, French Cabinet ministers are prohibited from serving in the legislature.

The French legislature

The French legislature consists of two houses. The lower house, the National Assembly, has about 575 members, called "deputies." Deputies are popularly elected from single-member districts and serve for five years. The upper chamber, the Senate, has about 320 members who serve nine-year terms. Senators are chosen by an electoral college made up of government officials.

The National Assembly is more powerful than the Senate. All bills passed by the Senate must be approved by the National Assembly, but the National Assembly can sometimes enact bills without the Senate's consent. Bills introduced in the National Assembly are first referred to one of six standing committees, consisting of about 60 to 120 deputies. Bills reported favorably out of committee must obtain a majority vote of the en-

tire Assembly. If necessary, the bill is submitted next to the Senate for approval. If the two chambers cannot agree, the Premier appoints a joint committee to iron out the differences. If the committee cannot reach a solution, the Cabinet decides which version will prevail.

The Cabinet can sometimes bypass the National Assembly on important bills by declaring a vote on the bill a "matter of confidence." The bill then becomes law without the National Assembly's approval, unless the Assembly adopts a "motion to censure" the government. This rare action forces the Premier and Cabinet to resign. While only the President can appoint a new Premier and Cabinet, only the National Assembly can force them to resign.

The French party system

Unlike the United States and Great Britain, France has a multi-party system. Four major parties dominate French politics — two conservative, one Socialist, and the other Communist.

Between 1958 and 1961, the conservative parties dominated both the presidency and legislature. Socialist François Mitterrand won election as President in 1981 and was re-elected in 1988. In 1986, after a conservative coalition won a majority in the National Assembly, Mitterrand sought to improve government cooperation by naming a conservative as Premier. This sharing of power in the executive branch lasted until 1988, when a Socialist became Premier.

Unitary government

France, like Great Britain, has a unitary government. Thus, the central government in Paris has a great deal of control over all local governments. France has 96 basic local governmental units, called **departments**. Departments are primarily administrative subunits of the national government, but in recent years they have been given a limited degree of self-government. The General Council, the popularly elected governing body for each department, supervises the local budget, transportation, housing, census taking, welfare, health services, public employment, and cultural programs. Each department was formerly headed by a **prefect**, appointed by the national government in Paris. In 1982 the French government renamed the office of prefect the "commissioner" and transferred many of its powers to elected local officials.

762

You Decide Answer
Students should defend their answers. Some may claim that free trade benefits a nation by encouraging greater efficiency. Others may claim that free trade between unequal partners may further weaken the weaker partner.

The Government of Mexico

1C

Mexico and the United States have much in common: the two nations share a 2,000-mile border, and much of the Southwest was once Mexican land. Mexico and the United States have historically maintained close economic ties, and even our national governments have many common features.

Mexico traces its proud history back to the ancient Mayan and Aztec civilizations. In 1521 explorer Hernando Cortés conquered the Aztecs and took Mexico for Spain, beginning 300 years of Spanish rule. Mexico gained its independence from Spain in 1821 and in 1917 adopted its present form of government.

The Mexican constitution

Los Estados Unidos Mexicanos, the United Mexican States, operates under a constitution framed in 1917. As in many Latin American governments, the Mexican constitution is influenced by the Constitution of the United States. It creates a presidential system with three branches, a system of checks and balances, universal suffrage for those 18 and older, guarantees of civil liberties, and a federal form of government.

In practice, though, Mexico's national government has much more power than the federal government of the United States. The Mexican constitution allows the national government to control all natural resources and redistribute land. The national government can even limit the number of priests who can serve in Mexico.

A federal form of government

In addition to the national government, Mexico is divided into 31 states plus one federal district, which is the seat of government in Mexico City. Each state has its own constitution, modeled after the national constitution. Each state elects its own governor and legislature. Governors serve for six years, and legislators serve either three- or six-year terms.

The mighty Aztec empire is recalled in this mural by Mexican artist Diego Rivera. The mural is one of many that decorate the National Palace in Mexico City, which houses the offices of Mexico's President.

763

RETEACHING/CORRECTIVES

▲ Have each student use the information in this section to write one-paragraph summaries of the British, French, and Mexican governments. When all students have completed their summaries, have them read them to the class. Then work with the class to write final summaries using the points mentioned by students.

Have students complete **Skills Practice Worksheet 29,** which asks them to compare the governments discussed in the section.

You may also want to use **Transparency 62,** which deals with the British Parliament.

The symbol 👥 denotes active participation strategies.

Activities are keyed for student abilities:
▲ = Basic
● = All Levels
■ = Average/Advanced

ENRICHMENT/EXTENSION

■ Have students clip newspaper or magazine stories concerning the government of Great Britain, France, or Mexico and paste them on sheets of paper. Then have each student write an essay summarizing the topic of his or her story and explaining what the story reveals about that nation's system of government.

Section 1 Review Answers

1. Britain's fundamental law is not contained in a single document. Much is based on unwritten principles that have developed over the centuries.

2. The monarch appoints the Prime Minister, who is the leader of the majority party. The Prime Minister then selects approximately 100 ministers from among the MPs.

3. To debate, criticize, and offer alternative proposals to the majority party.

4. The President conducts foreign relations, ratifies treaties, appoints officials, nominates judges, presides over the High Council of the Judiciary, commands the military, has the power to suspend the government's regular operations when national security is threatened, and is able to submit legislation and dissolve the legislature.

States in Mexico may levy taxes and enact laws for their jurisdictions. As in the United States, Mexican states have reserved powers — those powers neither specifically delegated to the national government nor prohibited to the states. In reality, the powers of the states are quite limited. About 85 percent of the nation's revenues are controlled by the national government.

Mexico and the PRI

To understand Mexican politics one must understand the *Partido Revolucionario Institucional* (PRI), or Institutional Revolutionary Party. Formed in 1929, the PRI has ruled Mexico ever since. The party's control of government offices and the media has allowed it to dominate national and most local governments. When necessary, the PRI has also rigged elections.

Recent years have seen signs of a more equal competition among Mexico's political parties. The 1988 elections marked the first time an opposition party captured a seat in Mexico's Senate.

The following year, the first non-PRI governor was elected. As one PRI leader explained, "The era of what is practically a single party is ending, and we are now entering a new phase in the political life of the nation, with a majority party and very intense competition from the opposition."

The Mexican presidency

Mexico's most powerful official is the President, who is popularly elected for one six-year term. (The President may not serve two consecutive terms.) Until recently the presidential election had largely been a formality, in which the voters approved a candidate who had been selected by the outgoing President. In 1988, however, the victorious PRI candidate, Carlos Salinas de Gortari, barely captured 50 percent of the vote.

The President of Mexico has the power to appoint Cabinet members, top-level military officers, diplomats, state governors, high-ranking judges, and the heads of state-owned industries. The President also has extensive authority over

Mexico City, the world's largest city, is intersected by the wide, tree-lined Paseo de la Reforma. Along this beautiful boulevard are monuments which honor national heroes or important events. The statue Winged Victory, shown here, honors Mexico's struggle for independence from Spain.

764

Ernesto Zedillo de Ponce de León of the PRI won the 1994 presidential election in Mexico. Zedillo received 47 percent of the vote. Strong showings by two challengers reflected growing discontent with PRI domination.

Mexico's foreign affairs and dominates the national government's lawmaking process. Most policies that the President supports become law. Furthermore, the President has the power to propose constitutional amendments. Amendments require the approval of two-thirds of Congress and of the state legislatures.

Congress

Lawmaking in Mexico is carried out by a popularly elected, bicameral Congress. The lower house, called the Chamber of Deputies, consists of 500 deputies elected for 3-year terms. The upper chamber, the Senate, consists of 128 senators elected to 6-year terms. Members of Congress are not allowed to serve two successive terms. The PRI controls the presidency, three-fifths of the seats in the Chamber of Deputies, and three-fourths of the seats in the Senate.

On paper, the Congress has considerable authority. It has the power to enact laws, verify presidential election returns, set the national budget, and raise taxes. The President, however, dominates Congress. The President controls Congress through the PRI, whose leaders he appoints. Moreover, the Mexican Supreme Court has never found the President's legislation or executive orders unconstitutional. If there is substantial opposition in Congress to a presidential proposal, the proposal is usually withdrawn by the executive branch, revised, and then sent back to Congress for passage.

SECTION 1 REVIEW

Vocabulary and key terms

House of Lords (757)	ministry (758)
House of Commons (757)	Cabinet (758)
Members of Parliament (MPs) (757)	shadow Cabinet (760)
	Premier (761)
parliamentary government (758)	department (762)
	prefect (762)

For review

1. What is unusual about Britain's constitution? **1C**
2. How is the executive branch of Britain's government selected? **1C**
3. What is the role of the opposition party in Parliament? **1C**
4. What are the powers of the French President? **1C**
5. How are laws passed in the French legislature? **1C**
6. What is the relationship between Mexico's national government and its states? **1C**
7. What role do political parties play in the Mexican government? **1C**

Critical Thinking

EXAMINING BASIC PRINCIPLES How is the "will of the people" expressed in Great Britain, France, and Mexico?   **1C**

765

5. Bills originating in the National Assembly are first referred to a standing committee; if approved there, they are voted on by the full Assembly. If necessary, bills go to the Senate for approval. All Senate bills must get Assembly approval.
6. In theory, Mexican states have reserved powers. In fact, the federal government strictly limits state power.
7. One party dominates national elections; other parties win some local elections and draw government attention to national issues.

Critical thinking Students should note that all three have democratically elected legislatures. Mexico and France have popularly elected presidents, and Britain's Prime Minister is chosen from among elected representatives.

CLOSURE

● Have students write five questions (with answers) concerning the structure of the British, French, and Mexican governments. Then have students read Section 2, noting the location of the countries being described.

The symbol 👥 denotes active participation strategies.

Activities are keyed for student abilities:
▲ = Basic
● = All Levels
■ = Average/Advanced

SECTION 2

People Under Non-Democratic Governments Seek Change *(pp. 766–773)*

Section Objectives

☐ describe the signs of movement toward democracy in Africa, Latin America, and Eastern Europe

☐ explain the changes in China and the Soviet Union

Vocabulary

cadre, General Secretary

FOCUS

● Have students list on the board some of the biggest problems facing the world today. Then ask students to consider which of these problems might be lessened if every nation had a democratic form of government, and why. Also discuss with students why certain other problems might not be affected by the switch to a democratic government.

1C, 6G, 7D, 7E

SECTION 2

People Under Non-Democratic Governments Seek Change

ACCESS **The Main Ideas**

1 What signs of movement toward democracy are there in Africa, Latin America, and Eastern Europe?
pages 766–768

2 What changes took place in China and the Soviet Union?
pages 768–773

What is freedom worth to you? To preserve your freedom, or to regain it, would you step in front of a tank? Would you pass out copies of an underground newspaper? Would you protect a friend whose political views had gotten him or her in trouble with the government?

For people who live in non-democratic nations, these are very real questions. Standing up for democratic government could cost them their jobs, their freedom, even their lives. Yet people in many nations around the world have taken these risks. Their efforts have helped nations take steps on the long and difficult road toward political freedom.

1C, 7D, 7E

Moving Toward Democracy

The desire to live in a democracy is not limited to Western Europe and North America. In recent years, many non-democratic governments across Africa, Latin America, and Eastern Europe have been reformed or replaced.

New openness in Africa

In recent decades, most African governments have been controlled by the military or by a dominant single party. Because national boundaries had been drawn by the European colonial powers, each African nation contained many different ethnic groups. Some African leaders argued that only a strong, undivided central authority could maintain national unity and carry out plans for economic development.

It did not work out that way. Domination of the government by a small group of people led to tyranny and corruption. Government control over economic development was inefficient. As

Nelson Mandela (right), President of South Africa, and former South African President F.W. De Klerk (left), struggled to resolve South Africa's political crisis during a series of historic meetings that started in 1990 and culminated in approval three years later of a constitution establishing multiracial government.

a result, people in many African nations began calling for greater openness in government.

These demands came to a head in 1990. In Côte d'Ivoire in West Africa, antigovernment protests forced leaders to hold the nation's first presidential election ever. Strikes and demonstrations in Gabon led to that nation's first multiparty elections. In all, governments in *fourteen* nations were forced to accept multiparty systems.

Meanwhile, in South Africa, the white minority government legalized the African National Congress (ANC) and freed its leader, Nelson Mandela, from prison. In a series of negotiations, the government, the ANC, and other South African groups worked out a constitution for a multiracial, democratic government. Mandela was elected president of South Africa in 1994.

A lack of government became a tragic problem for Somalia. In 1992 the country suffered from corrupt warlords who intercepted food shipments intended for its starving people. In late 1992 American troops were sent to the country to make sure food reached the people safely. Whether Somalia could unite as a nation remained unclear.

Democracy in Latin America

Many nations of Latin America suffered under harsh military rule during the 1960's and 1970's. Military leaders claimed that strong government was necessary in order to fight Communists and terrorists. For many, however, it seemed that the governments themselves had turned to terrorism to stifle opposition.

One by one during the 1980's, the military dictatorships fell. In 1980 Peru held free elections. Argentina's military government, disgraced by its loss to Britain in the war over the Falkland Islands, permitted elections in 1983. Two years later Brazil and Uruguay moved from military to civilian rule. In 1989 a coup in Paraguay ended a 35-year dictatorship. Chile, under military rule since 1973, elected a civilian president at the end of 1989.

Eastern Europe rejects dictatorship

For the nations of Eastern Europe, Communist dictatorships were a legacy of World War II. Soviet troops had swept through Eastern Europe on their way to victory over Nazi Germany. The Soviet dictator Joseph Stalin set up Communist regimes throughout Eastern Europe at war's end.

Backed by Soviet tanks, these regimes held

LANDMARKS in LIBERTY

6G

Universal Declaration of Human Rights (1948)

In 1948, the General Assembly of the United Nations adopted the Universal Declaration of Human Rights, meant to be displayed and read in the schools and educational institutions of member nations. It was the hope of the General Assembly that such a statement would produce a common understanding and recognition of human rights around the world.

> ARTICLE 1. All human beings are born free and equal in dignity and rights. They are endowed with reason and conscience and should act towards one another in a spirit of brotherhood. . . .
>
> ARTICLE 3. Everyone has the right to life, liberty, and the security of person.
>
> ARTICLE 4. No one shall be held in slavery. . . .
>
> ARTICLE 5. No one shall be subjected to torture or to cruel, inhuman, or degrading treatment or punishment. . . .
>
> ARTICLE 18. Everyone has the right to freedom of thought, conscience and religion. . . .
>
> ARTICLE 21. (1) Everyone has the right to take part in the government of his country, directly or through freely chosen representatives. . . .
>
> ARTICLE 29. (1) Everyone has duties to the community in which alone the free and full development of his personality is possible.

1. According to the authors of this Declaration, where do human beings get the rights listed within it?
2. What is the relationship between Articles 21 and 29?
3. Which articles of the UN Declaration echo parts of the Declaration of Independence and Bill of Rights?

767

EXPLANATION

After students have read the section, you may want to consider the following activities:

👥 Geography

● Review with students the location of the nations discussed under the heading, "Moving Toward Democracy." Write the terms *Africa, Latin America,* and *Eastern Europe* on the board. Have volunteers point to these areas on a wall map. Then have students come to the board and write down the names of as many countries as they can recall in each of the three areas.

● Finally, call on individual students to come to the wall map, point to a country mentioned under the heading, "Moving Toward Democracy," and read the portion of the text describing events in that country.

👥 Prejudice Reduction

● Divide the class into groups and have each group write a skit about South Africa. The skit should focus on efforts by individual black South Africans and white South Africans to create a society based on the principles of equality and fairness. Groups should be encouraged to conduct library research to learn more about race relations in South Africa. Have the groups perform the skits for the class.

Landmarks in Liberty Answers

1. Human beings are born with these rights.

2. Taking part in government, whether at the national or local level, is not only a right but a duty of citizenship.

3. *Declaration of Independence*—Articles 1 and 3 specifically. *Bill of Rights*—Articles 4, 18, and 21 specifically. (Students may find other connections.)

The symbol 👥 denotes active participation strategies.

Activities are keyed for student abilities:
▲ = Basic
● = All Levels
■ = Average/Advanced

History

▲ **What was the Tiananmen Square massacre?** (In June 1989, Chinese soldiers attacked peaceful demonstrators in Tiananmen Square, Beijing, killing many of them.)

▲ **What had the protesters in Tiananmen Square been demanding?** (Democratic reforms, meetings with government leaders, and government respect for human rights.)

▲ **What happened in the months following the massacre?** (The government cracked down on dissent but did not end economic reforms.)

A lone woman runs in front of a burning vehicle along a war-torn street in Sarajevo. The once-proud city, host of the 1984 Winter Olympics, has been virtually destroyed by the ethnic violence of Yugoslavia's civil war.

power for four decades. Yet they never won the loyalty of the people. Nor could their centrally planned economies provide sustained growth. Only the threat of Soviet intervention kept the Stalinist regimes in power, and this threat faded after reformer Mikhail Gorbachev took power in the Soviet Union in 1985. In 1989, dubbed by *Time* magazine "The Year of the People," the dictatorships of Eastern Europe simply collapsed.

The first regime to fall was Poland's. In 1981 the Communist regime had declared martial law in an attempt to squash Solidarity, an independent labor movement. By 1989, facing economic crises it could not handle alone, the government was forced to permit free elections for the first time since 1945. Candidates backed by Solidarity won an astonishing 260 of 261 open seats in the legislature. In August 1989 a non-Communist prime minister took office.

Events picked up speed in the fall of 1989. Mass protests in East Germany, Czechoslovakia, and Romania forced the resignation of top Communists. The East German government opened the Berlin Wall, symbol of the division of Europe, in November 1989. The following October the

two Germanies were reunified as one non-Communist nation. One consequence of the events in Eastern Europe was a sharp rise in ethnic tensions. In mid-1991 civil war erupted in Yugoslavia when two of its republics seceded. The brutal fighting that followed killed over 100,000 people and made homeless refugees out of an estimated four million.

In the Balkans, therefore, the close of the cold war did not mean a move toward democracy but rather an eruption of ethnic violence and an end of stability in the lives of many.

1C, 7E

Reform and Reaction in China

Prospects for democracy are not bright in China. The world's most populous country, containing over one billion people, China is also among the largest in area. Approximately 55 different ethnic groups, with almost as many languages, live there. Chinese society is one of the world's oldest, with more than 4,000 years of recorded history. The driving force over the past half-century of that history has been communism.

768

Centralized power

China has a unitary form of government, dominated by the Communist Party. The central government in Beijing is the official seat of power. Below it are various levels of local government, from China's 21 provinces down to its many thousands of urban and rural districts. Each level of local government has only certain powers, which are specified by law. Furthermore, the actions of each level of government must meet with the approval of the governing body immediately above it.

At every level of government in China, skilled and educated party members, called **cadres** (KAD-reez), play an important role. The cadres hold long-term positions in the government and make many important decisions. Because they must be members of the Chinese Communist Party, the cadres form a link between the government and the party.

The structure of China's government

In China, persons 18 and older are qualified to vote. Voters elect representatives to various primary-level People's Congresses. These local bodies make laws and choose representatives to the higher People's Congresses.

The highest organ of Chinese government is the National People's Congress. It consists of about 3,000 deputies and meets for a few days once every year. On paper, the National People's Congress is the most important legislative body in China.

In reality, however, political power is in the hands of the Communist Party. A small group of Communist Party leaders, led by the **General Secretary**, make the important decisions. The General Secretary and his staff supervise and administer all committees and departments of the Communist Party and command the Chinese Army.

China under communism

The Chinese Communist Party (CCP) was begun with Soviet help in 1921, but soon developed in its own way. In the 1930's, the Chinese government began to crack down on the Communists, who by then had formed the Red Army to carry out a Communist revolution. Some 100,000 Communists, led by Mao Zedong (page 744), were forced to leave their stronghold in

After leading the revolution that made China a Communist nation in 1949, Mao Zedong tried to control all aspects of Chinese life.

southeastern China and walk 6,000 miles (9,700 km) in what became known as the Long March. Although only about 8,000 people completed the march, it provided great inspiration for the Communist Party and training for its leaders.

In 1949, the corrupt and inefficient Chinese government fled to the island of Taiwan. Mao and the Communists took power in Beijing. As Chinese communism developed, it placed emphasis on agriculture and the peasants. (By comparison, Soviet communism was more concerned with industrial development and the cities.) Chinese Communists tried to maintain close contact with the peasant masses. To teach the people the ideas of the revolution, millions of Chinese were given copies of Mao's "Little Red Book," *The Sayings of Chairman Mao*.

Many changes took place following Mao's death in 1976. The next major leader, Deng Xiaoping (DUHNG shee-ow-PING), put less emphasis on revolutionary doctrine and more on economic development, including some free market reforms. As the Chinese economy began to open up, Chinese politics did the same. Students were allowed to criticize some government policies in newspapers and in speeches.

769

Values

Read students (or copy on the board) the following statement by John Quincy Adams in 1821: "America . . . well knows that by enlisting under other banners than her own, . . . she would involve herself beyond the power of extraction, in all the wars of interest and intrigue, of individual avarice, envy, and ambition, which assume the colors and usurp the standard of freedom. The fundamental maxims of her policy would insensibly change from liberty to force. . . . She might become dictatress of the world. She would be no longer the ruler of her own spirit."

● **What did Adams mean?** (If the United States were to become involved in foreign conflicts, even those supposedly fought in the name of freedom, it might gain international power but would be tainted by those conflicts.)

● CRITICAL THINKING **What policy would Adams probably advocate toward democratic movements around the world?** (The United States should offer moral support but not become directly involved.) **Do you agree with this policy? Explain.**

The Tiananmen Square massacre

One night in June 1989, political reform came to a crashing halt. University students had gathered in Tiananmen Square in Beijing to demand democratic reforms and meetings with government leaders. The crowd, thousands strong, was peaceful. Protesters decorated the square with a replica of the Statue of Liberty and with banners calling on the government to respect human rights.

Around midnight on June 4, army troops and tanks invaded the square, ripping through the ranks of unarmed demonstrators. Hundreds of students were shot, bayoneted, or trampled to death.

In the months that followed, a government crackdown stifled all dissent. Student leaders, intellectuals, and others were jailed or executed. Chinese leaders, condemned by governments around the world for their brutality, vowed to hang on to power.

Still, China did not reverse course on economic reform. The leadership needed economic reform to keep the country strong and the people content. In other parts of the world, economic and political reform had proven to be inseparable. China's leaders were gambling that they could have one without the other.

1C, 7E

Upheaval in the USSR

In the last few years, simply by opening the daily newspaper a person could come face to face with history in the making — Nelson Mandela freed from a South African prison, the Berlin Wall tumbling, Chinese students massed in support of freedom. Yet none of these events could compare to what happened in December 1991: the Soviet Union ceased to exist as a state.

A nation covering one-sixth of the earth's land surface, the Soviet Union stretched from the Pacific to Europe. It was home to over 280 million people and dozens of different nationalities and languages. By the 1950's it and the United States were the world's two giants, the nuclear "superpowers" whose competition cast a shadow over the globe.

As President of Russia, Boris Yeltsin (waving the flag) defied a coup in August 1991. The coup, led by conservatives opposed to government reforms, failed. Four months later the Soviet Union dissolved into several independent countries.

By 1992 the Soviet Union had fallen apart and ceased to exist. In its place now were fifteen independent republics, each facing the need to overhaul a failed economic system. In Russia, the largest of the republics, the Communist Party had been outlawed. The former Soviet president, Mikhail Gorbachev, was out of a job.

The Soviet Communist system

The Soviet Union was created in 1922 by the Communists who had seized power in the old Russian Empire in 1917. On paper, the political system put in place by the Bolsheviks had much in common with those of the West. Soviet citizens 18 and older had the right to vote. Citizens were guaranteed freedom of speech, of the press, and of assembly. Each of the nation's fifteen republics had its own constitution, elected its own leaders, and selected representatives to the Soviet national legislature.

These features were meaningless. In reality the Soviet Union was ruled by the Communist Party. People could vote, but only one candidate — the party's candidate — ran for each office. Newspapers were owned and run by the party or the government. The rights of free speech and assembly applied only to pro-government activities. The central government kept the republican governments toothless. (This was partly because several republics had never wanted to be part of the Soviet Union in the first place and would secede if given the chance.)

The Communist Party was the heart of the Soviet system. While only about 5 percent of the population belonged to the party, its influence was everywhere. Small party organizations called cells were set up in farms, factories, schools, offices, and even housing complexes. Through these cells the party spread propaganda and kept watch over ordinary citizens.

In the Soviet Union, as in China, the Communist Party ran parallel to the structure of the government, with a corresponding party organization for each level of government. At the top of the party stood the General Secretary, the true head of the Soviet Union.

Turning away from communism

It was under General Secretary Mikhail Gorbachev, who took power in 1985, that the Soviet Union entered a decisive period of reform. Gorbachev hoped to revive the Soviet economy by

A Moscow family passes a toppled statue of Felix Dzerzhinsky, founder of the Soviet secret police later known as the KGB.

encouraging private producers. He hoped to reform the government by holding truly free elections for some government posts. Gorbachev also encouraged a new spirit of openness, or *glasnost*, in which public criticism of the nation's social and economic failings was permitted.

Gorbachev's aim was not to destroy the Communist Party or dismantle the Soviet Union. Rather, he wanted to make the existing system work better. This effort failed. As the nation's economy declined through the late 1980's, most citizens lost faith in Gorbachev. Party officials, fearful of losing the advantages they had under the old system, worked to block reform. Meanwhile, in virtually every republic — including Russia itself — people demanded greater independence from the central government.

Entering a new era

In August 1991 supporters and opponents of reform finally met in a showdown. In Moscow, while Gorbachev was out of town on vacation,

771

Background: *History*

Gorbachev was not the first Soviet reformer. In 1956 Nikita Khrushchev, who led the Soviet Communist Party between 1953 and 1964, stunned the Party by denouncing many of Joseph Stalin's policies. (Stalin had died in 1953.) Khrushchev also gave priority to production of consumer goods rather than weapons and heavy industry. Khrushchev's opponents within the Party forced him out of office in 1964, in part because of the humiliation he suffered during the Cuban missile crisis (p. 543).

Cooperative Learning

● Divide the class into five groups. Assign to each group one of five areas: Africa, Latin America, China, the former Soviet Union, Eastern Europe (excluding the former Soviet states). Have each group make a time line showing recent events in their area. Post the timelines around the room.

GUIDED/INDEPENDENT PRACTICE

● Have students cite five facts suggesting that democratic government will be more common in the year 2000 than it was in 1950. Then have students cite three reasons for caution regarding the likelihood of democratic change.

The symbol denotes active participation strategies.

Activities are keyed for student abilities:
▲ = Basic
● = All Levels
■ = Average/Advanced

hard-line conservatives took power. Thousands of citizens took to the streets, fearing that the hardliners would move against the freely elected Russian government also located in Moscow. Russian President Boris Yeltsin stood in front of the Russian parliament building and vowed never to give in. The order for the army to attack the building never came. Within days the coup had collapsed and Gorbachev was back in power.

The failure of the August coup was like the breaking of a dam. A torrent of changes followed. Gorbachev ended the Communist Party's monopoly on political power. (The party, discredited and losing members daily, was already in serious decline.) One by one the republics declared independence, the Baltic states of Latvia, Lithuania, and Estonia being the first. Yeltsin, as leader of the largest and most powerful republic, now rivaled Gorbachev in influence.

In December 1991, the Union of Soviet Socialist Republics was formally dissolved, as was the Soviet Constitution. Gorbachev's position was eliminated. Russian President Boris Yeltsin became the leading figure in a loose association called the Commonwealth of Independent States.

Disagreements between Russia and the other republics over such issues as military forces and border disputes soon, however, revealed deep divisions within the Commonwealth.

In Russia, President Yeltsin sought to carry out democratizing changes as well as reforms in the economic system. In 1993 he succeeded in crushing an armed rebellion by his opponents in a parliament that had survived from the Soviet break-up. But the problems facing Russia and the other former Soviet republics were huge. In some of these states, ethnic rivalries flared into violence. The economies of the region, long crippled by communism, needed massive reforms to convert to free-market systems. Meanwhile, it remained to be seen whether democracy could make headway in establishing roots in Russia.

1C, 6G

Linking Past and Present

A century ago a 13-year-old girl named Mary Antin arrived in the United States from the tiny village of Polotzk, in Russia. Like most immigrants, she had little money and knew that she

Passers-by walk by a store window displaying French perfume in Moscow's historic Red Square. The presence of this store in Russia represents a sobering reminder that in spite of the country's move to a capitalist economy, few Russians can afford to buy high-priced foreign goods.

faced a lifetime of hard work in the United States. ''Better a hard bed in the shelter of justice than a stuffed couch under the black canopy of despotism,'' she later wrote.

As we watch peoples around the world struggle for political democracy, we should recall that it was the search for freedom that brought millions of people to the shores of America. It was the search for freedom — political, economic, and religious — that motivated those who won this nation's independence and created its form of government. It was the desire to preserve freedom that motivated those who have fought and died in this nation's defense.

Do not think only of military heroes, or suppose that all our heroes have fallen on foreign soil. From the beginnings of the American nation until the present day, courageous men and women have fought and died to extend to all, the many and vast promises of American life. For each generation, the struggle has been different, but it goes on. For a people to rule themselves is the hardest thing in the world to do, and the easiest thing to give away.

SECTION 2 REVIEW

Vocabulary and key terms

cadre (769)   General Secretary (769)

For review

1. (a) What events led to Nelson Mandela becoming president of South Africa? (b) What general trend took place in Latin America during the 1980's? 1C
2. What was the significance of the opening of the Berlin Wall? 1C
3. What was the Chinese leadership's attitude toward political reform and economic reform? 1C
4. What events in 1991 led to the end of the Soviet Union? 1C

Critical thinking

EXAMINING BASIC PRINCIPLES Why did the Soviet Union and China bother with constitutions when all decisions were traditionally made by their Communist parties? 1C

Chapter Summary

Great Britain, France, and Mexico are examples of democratic nations. Parliament, made up of the House of Lords and the House of Commons, dominates the British government. Members of the House of Commons, called Members of Parliament, are popularly elected for five-year terms. The chief executive, the Prime Minister, chooses the ministry, which administers the government, and the Cabinet, whose members introduce most bills that are passed in Parliament.

The government of France is headed by a popularly elected President, who chooses a Premier and Cabinet to supervise government operations and to propose legislation. The popularly elected National Assembly and the French Senate, chosen by an electoral college, make up the legislature. France has a multi-party system, dominated by four major parties.

Mexico has a federal form of government. The people elect a President, governors, senators, and deputies, but the elections are generally dominated by a single party, the PRI. Although on paper the legislature has considerable power, the President dominates that body through party members.

Many parts of the world recently took steps toward democratic government. In Africa in 1990, the governments of more than a dozen nations moved toward acceptance of opposition parties. In Latin America, long-standing military dictatorships gave way to civilian rule during the 1980's. The Communist dictatorships of Eastern Europe, collapsed and were replaced by democratically elected governments.

In China, Communist rule remained entrenched. Led by the *General Secretary*, the head of the Communist Party, China experimented with free market reforms. When students began demanding political reforms as well, however, the army crushed them.

The most dramatic changes in recent years took place in the Soviet Union. Mikhail Gorbachev undertook political and economic reforms in the 1980's to reverse the Soviet Union's decline. However, by the end of 1991 the Communist Party had been swept out of power, communism had given way to a free-market system, and the Soviet empire had disintegrated into independent states.

773

Section 2 Review Answers

1. (a) The South African government legalized the African National Congress, freed its leader Nelson Mandela, began talks with the ANC and other groups, and held a national election. (b) Civilian governments replaced military governments in many nations.
2. The wall had symbolized the division of Europe.
3. China's leaders favored economic, not political reform.
4. A hard-line coup against Gorbachev failed; republics declared their independence; the Communist Party lost political power; the Soviet Union came to an end.

Critical thinking Elections and constitutions, even sham ones, serve as propaganda to show how "democratic" a country is to the world and to its own citizens.

CLOSURE

● Remind students of the statement by Aristotle on p. 2: "Man is by nature a political animal; it is his nature to live in a state." Ask students to consider whether it is the nature of humanity to live under representative government—whether, in other words, democracy is the only "natural" form of government.

CHAPTER 29 CORRECTIVES

● To review the content of Chapter 29, you may want to have students complete **Study Guide/Review 29** or **Workbook Chapter 29.**

The symbol ⚏ denotes active participation strategies.

Activities are keyed for student abilities:
▲ = Basic
● = All Levels
■ = Average/Advanced

Answers

Vocabulary See pp. T19–T21 for suggested vocabulary activities.

Reviewing the Facts

1. A federal form of government divides its power between the national government and smaller units, such as states. A unitary form of government puts all power in the hands of the national government.
2. The Magna Charta (1215), the Petition of Right (1628), and the English Bill of Rights (1689).
3. Committees in the British House of Commons are not very specialized and may not pigeon-hole a bill.
4. A combination presidential and parliamentary system.
5. The PRI dominates elections, chooses the President from among its own leaders, and through the President dominates the lawmaking process.
6. Control of the nomination and election of public officials; domination of government and setting of public policy; control of high military and police positions; direction of the mass media.
7. Mao Zedong.
8. During World War II, Soviet tanks swept through Eastern Europe. Later, Stalin set up Communist regimes, backed by the threat of Soviet intervention. Economic decline in the 1980's and demands for independence weakened the Communist Party in many nations, and regimes in Poland, East Germany, Czechoslovakia, and Romania collapsed.

 ★ CHAPTER REVIEW ★

● **Review the definitions of the following terms:**

Cabinet	House of Lords	prefect
cadre	Members of Parliament	Premier
department	ministry	shadow Cabinet
General Secretary	parliamentary	
House of Commons	government	

● **REVIEWING THE FACTS**

1. What is the difference between a federal and a unitary form of government? **1C**
2. What are three written documents that help make up the British Constitution? **1C**
3. Name two major differences between committees in the British House of Commons and committees in the U.S. Congress. **8G**
4. What kind of government did the Constitution of the Fifth Republic establish in France? **7E**
5. What role does the Institutional Revolutionary Party play in Mexican politics? **7E**
6. What powers did the Communist Party once have in the former Soviet Union? **7E**
7. Who was the leader of the Chinese Communists when they took control of the government of China in 1949? **7E**
8. How was Soviet influence over Eastern Europe established? What factors brought an end to that influence? **7E**

▲ **THINKING CRITICALLY ABOUT KEY CONCEPTS**

1. (a) In what way is British politics similar to politics in the United States? (b) How are political parties in Great Britain different from those in the United States? (c) What effect does this difference have on important legislation? **8G**

774

2. What major powers does the French President have that the United States President does not have regarding the legislative branch of government? **1C**
3. In Mexico, the Institutional Revolutionary Party dominates elections, especially at the national level. What are the advantages and disadvantages of a system in which one party is so powerful? **1C**
4. List major political developments that took place in the Soviet Union from 1985 to 1991. Which ones do you think were most important? Explain your choices. **5C**
5. (a) What was the early link between the Communist Party of China and that of the Soviet Union? (b) How did Chinese communism develop differently from Soviet communism? (c) How did the concerns of the Chinese government change after the death of Mao Zedong? **8G**
6. In the past, the Communist Party controlled all media in the Soviet Union. How do you think this affected the range of issues that could be covered by the media? What issues might not have been covered that would have received coverage in the U.S.? **4B**

▲ **PRACTICING SKILLS**

1. **Study Skills: Analyzing a photograph.** Look at the photograph of a woman in war-torn Sarajevo on page 768. How would living under such circumstances affect someone's day-to-day activities and future hopes? **5B**

Thinking Critically About Key Concepts

1. **(a)** It is dominated by two political parties.
(b) British political parties are highly disciplined. Members of Parliament usually vote the way their leaders want them to. **(c)** The Prime Minister and Cabinet usually get their way.
2. Unlike the United States President, the French President can ratify treaties, submit important legislation or constitutional amendments directly to the people, bypassing the legislature, and suspend the regular operations of government.
3. Students may suggest that one powerful party can get things done more efficiently. On the other hand,

2. Critical Thinking Skills: Comparing and contrasting. Create a table to compare and contrast the systems of government in Great Britain, France, and Mexico. Here are some possible categories: form of government, chief executive, upper house, lower house, local government. Include a brief description of each entry in your table. **8G**

▲ PARTICIPATORY CITIZENSHIP

1. Values. What do you think are the most important values that should be reflected in a nation's government? Write a statement of principles that you would use if you were designing a government from scratch. **6G**

2. Current events. In newspapers or news magazines, find articles about events in South Africa, the Commonwealth of Independent States, or China regarding political or social change. Be prepared to discuss the articles with the class. **1C**

■ WRITING ABOUT ISSUES

1. Research report. Research and write a report about the Magna Charta, the Petition of Right, or the English Bill of Rights. What provisions did the document make for the English people? **6H**

2. Current events. In recent years the nations of Eastern Europe have tried to move from Communist systems to free-market economies. Choose one of these countries and write a report on how new political and economic policies are affecting the people. **7E**

▲ ANALYZING A POLITICAL CARTOON

After the Soviet Union's collapse in 1991, many countries abandoned communism. For example, in Russia, President Yeltsin supported free-market reforms. Answer the following questions about the cartoon.

1. How is President Yeltsin's move to a free market economy portrayed? **8B**
2. What is the significance of the woman's statement and her facial expression? **8B**
3. What is the meaning of Yeltsin's statement? **8B**

©1992 David Horsey Seattle Post-Intelligencer. Reprinted with special permission of North American Syndicate.

775

---

6. The range of issues was probably limited. Issues of government corruption or mismanagement or any stories that might embarrass the government probably were not covered.

Practicing Skills

1. Living in a war-torn country can make a person constantly fearful. Survival itself is a challenge. Over time, people may lose hope and become demoralized.

2. When students have completed their charts, you might have them list the similarities and differences between the governments of these nations and government in the United States.

Participatory Citizenship

1. Students should compare their statements and decide what suggestions they would have made to the framers of the Constitution.

2. You might have students create a bulletin board with the theme of political and social change.

Writing About Issues

1. Students should discuss what influences these documents had on the U.S. Constitution.

2. You may want to assign groups of students to different countries and have each group present its findings to the class.

Analyzing a Political Cartoon

1. Yeltsin's move to a new economy shows him enthusiastically jumping off a cliff, dragging the Russian people with him.

2. The Russian people are terrified because they don't know how to operate in a market economy.

3. Yeltsin realizes that the biggest danger is the possibility of an economic collapse in his country.

Chapter Review exercises are keyed for student abilities:
▲ = Basic
● = All Levels
■ = Average/Advanced

---

strong opposition parties tend to ensure that the party in power stays honest.
4. Possible choices: Greater openness; creation of new, elected Congress; removal of Communist Party dominance of government, public life.

5. (a) The CCP was begun with the help of the Soviets. **(b)** It emphasized agriculture and peasants as opposed to industrial development and cities. Chinese Communists tried to maintain close contact with the

masses through the teaching of revolutionary ideas. **(c)** Less emphasis was put on revolutionary doctrine and more on economic development.

AS OTHERS SEE US

Vocabulary

ossified—became brittle. *Elbe*—river that divides Eastern and Western Europe.

Background

Carlos Fuentes, one of Mexico's leading writers, published his first novel in 1958. His work often moves back and forth in time, and *Terra Nostra* (1975) offers an alternate view of history. His 1985 novel, *The Old Gringo,* reads like a western and examines United States–Mexican relations. Fuentes has also served as Mexico's ambassador to France.

Civic Participation

● Have students write a letter to the editor in response to this article.

Economics

● CRITICAL THINKING **How did Franklin Roosevelt's actions affect the capitalist system of the United States?** (His New Deal programs expanded government involvement in the economy.) Encourage students to give examples of U.S. government actions and programs today that illustrate Fuentes's statement, "Capitalism in its pure form no longer exists anywhere in the developed world."

■ Have students write a short biography of John Maynard Keynes, John Kenneth Galbraith, or Joseph Stalin, focusing on economic philosophy.

AS OTHERS SEE US   5B

Carlos Fuentes

A Mexican Intellectual on the Future of Capitalism

As Communist governments in Eastern Europe fell in the late 1980's, it appeared that one economic system—capitalism— would soon dominate most of the world. Mexican writer and diplomat Carlos Fuentes had some words of warning— particularly for Latin Americans.

Mexico City. Every time someone proclaims the end of ideologies, I ask myself, "Which will his be?" In these times, capitalism seems to have triumphed over socialism. But since both ideologies embrace multiple realities and have undergone exchanges of thoughts and actions, the proclamations of winner and loser seem to me to be at least premature.

Let us quit beating the dead horses of the 19th century and look at the realities of the 21st. We are confronted with dynamic capitalism, because capitalism knew how to subject itself to constant self-criticism. We saw socialism stagnate because it lacked this capacity for self-criticism. Today's capitalism would be inconceivable without the political action and intellectual critiques by Franklin Roosevelt, John Maynard Keynes, and John Kenneth Galbraith. Soviet socialism ossified because it suppressed such criticism. On the other hand, socialist criticism of capitalism is what has given capitalism the ability to socialize itself.

Capitalism in its pure form no longer exists anywhere in the developed world. In Western Europe, and above all in Japan, the state reserves the right to intervene in the economy, constantly regulating, braking, and socializing private enterprise. Where capitalism has failed to exercise self-criticism—in Margaret Thatcher's Britain or in the U.S. under Ronald Reagan—the cost has been high: deficits, social imbalance, a decline in education, and eventual loss of international competitiveness. The danger of the current celebration of capitalism is that capitalism will stop criticizing itself: It may dance on Stalin's tomb and go back to its old, uncontrolled ways.

This danger affects the U.S., Western Europe, and Latin America. The rule of a single ideology, without competitors or criticism, could bring on the worst, the most implacable of dictatorships, in which . . . money alone unifies the world. . . .

The real problems of societies did not disappear with the festivities of 1989 and 1990. Whatever there is to be celebrated, there is just as much that must be examined critically, postulated as a problem, and resolved by the socialization of political life. The end of Stalinism on the other side of the Elbe does not mean the end of social injustice on either the east or west bank of that river—or on the north or south bank of the Rio Grande.

From "The Left Is Not Dead" from *World Press Review* by Carlos Fuentes in *Excélsior* of Mexico City. Copyright © 1991 by *World Press Review.* Reprinted by permission of *World Press Review* and *Excélsior.*

CRITICAL THINKING

1. Why does Fuentes say Soviet socialism "ossified" while capitalism survived?
2. What danger does Fuentes think currently confronts capitalism?
3. What might be examples of some of the problems that were not ended by the downfall of communism in Europe?

776

Critical Thinking Answers
1. Capitalism criticized itself and was criticized by Socialists; Soviet-style socialism suppressed all criticism.

2. It will stop criticizing itself and ignore social problems.

3. Answers might include hunger, pollution, civil war, poverty, and illiteracy.

REFERENCE SECTION

Study Skill 1
Practicing Skills Answers
1. The sentence in which the word appeared and the word's pronunciation go on the front of the index card; the word's meaning goes on the back.
2. Students should follow the procedure described in this lesson.

HANDBOOK of BASIC SKILLS

Study Skill 1
BUILDING YOUR VOCABULARY

A good vocabulary is helpful in studying American government or any other subject. If you acquire a broader vocabulary, all your reading and writing will become easier and more enjoyable.

Your vocabulary will grow larger naturally if you read a wide range of books. This process will be slow, however, unless you make an effort to learn and use the new words you come across. Here is one method for adding new words to your vocabulary:

- As you read, be aware of words you do not understand. Pay close attention to the words that are somewhat familiar but that you cannot define exactly. These words are easiest to learn.
- Make a list of the words you want to learn and on what page you found them.
- After you have finished your reading, make an index card for each word on your list. On the front of the card, write down the sentence in which the word appeared and underline the word. Writing the sentence will help you remember how the word is used.
- Look up each word in a dictionary. On the front of the index card, write down the pronunciation of the word. (It is easier to use and remember words that you know how to say.) On the back of the card, write down the word's meaning.
- Study your cards from time to time until you have mastered the words. Once you have

learned a set of words, make new cards for other words.
- Look for your new vocabulary words in your reading and try to use them in your writing and in conversation.

Most subjects, including American government, have a specialized vocabulary. Some of these words are unique to the subject; many are words that also have other meanings. For example, in Chapter 1 of this book you will come across the words *sovereignty, legitimacy,* and *naturalization.* All specialized government terms used in this book are listed and defined in the glossary on pages 825–842. To learn your government vocabulary thoroughly, use the method described above to make a special set of government index cards.

PRACTICING SKILLS

1. In the method taught above, what goes on the front of your vocabulary index cards? What goes on the back of each card?
2. Reread a section of this book that you have studied recently. Make a list of at least five words that are somewhat familiar but that you cannot define exactly. Make an index card for each of your words. For each of your new vocabulary words, write a sentence using the word correctly.

Study Skill 2
UNDERSTANDING CHARTS

Often the clearest way to describe a complex process or structure is by showing it in a chart. Different kinds of charts are useful for organizing, for summarizing, and for showing

relationships. In this book, for example, charts are used to show the organization of the President's staff or how a bill becomes law. They are examples of the two kinds of charts that you

SKILLS

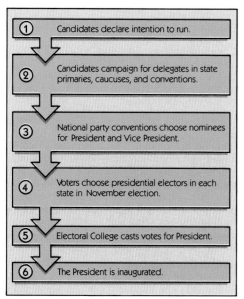

Steps in Selecting a President

1. Candidates declare intention to run.
2. Candidates campaign for delegates in state primaries, caucuses, and conventions.
3. National party conventions choose nominees for President and Vice President.
4. Voters choose presidential electors in each state in November election.
5. Electoral College casts votes for President.
6. The President is inaugurated.

will encounter frequently in studying American government — organization charts and flow charts.

An **organization chart** shows the arrangement of the parts of an organization, such as a branch of government or any agency within the government. For example, the organization chart found on page 423 shows how the Executive Office of the President is organized.

A **flow chart** shows a process, or how things happen. Flow charts are useful for outlining or simplifying the steps in a procedure. The chart on this page is typical of the flow charts found in this book.

You will be able to use a chart with confidence if you are able to recognize and understand all its parts. The first thing you should look for on a chart is the **title**. Locate the title of the chart on this page. It tells you the subject and purpose of the chart.

Next, read all the **labels** on the chart. Labels identify the different parts of a chart. In an organization chart, the labels show the major units of the organization. In a flow chart, labels identify the major steps in a process.

Lines and arrows are important symbols in both organization charts and flow charts. In an organization chart, lines or arrows show the links between units. Arrows connect different parts of a flow chart and show the order of steps in a process.

PRACTICING SKILLS

1. What kind of chart is best for showing the steps in a procedure? What kind of chart is best for showing the structure of a branch of government?
2. Read the title of the chart above. What is this chart about?
3. What is the first step in the chart on this page? What is the end result?
4. Draw an organization chart of a group or club you belong to. Show, for instance, the officers or leaders, committees, and ordinary members.
5. Think of a procedure you go through often, like studying for a test. Make a flow chart showing the important steps.

Study Skill 2
Practicing Skills Answers
1. A flow chart. An organization chart.
2. Steps in selecting a President.
3. Candidates declare intention to run; the President is inaugurated.
4. Students' charts should indicate hierarchy.
5. Students' charts should identify sequence with arrows or other indicators.

Study Skill 3
READING GRAPHS

In this and many other books, statistical information is often presented in a graph. Graphs help you see the meaning of information quickly and easily.

The most commonly used types of graphs are the line graph and the bar graph. On a **line graph,** like the one on page 780, information is plotted by dots, which are joined together by a line. A line graph is good for showing trends, or how things change over time. A **bar graph** (like the one on page 315) shows information in bars or columns. Bar graphs are useful for comparing quantities or amounts.

To get the most information, you should look at the following parts of a graph and how they are related:

- The title of a graph tells you what the graph is about.
- The **horizontal axis** runs along the bottom of the graph. On graphs that present information over time, the horizontal axis often

Study Skill 3
Practicing Skills Answers

1. Life expectancy for those born during the period 1930–1990.

2. **(a)** Year of birth. **(b)** Expected life in years. **(c)** Men, women. **(d)** Life expectancies have been increasing. **(e)** Women tend to live longer than men.

3. **(a)** Government expenditures. **(b)** Expenditures by function. **(c)** Entitlements. **(d)** $592 billion (41 percent of $1,445 billion).

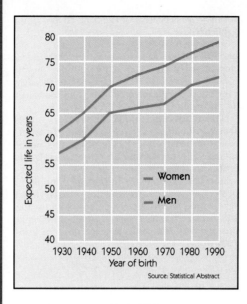

Life Expectancy, 1930–1990

shows the time period — days, months, or years.
- The **vertical axis** runs up and down on the left side of the graph. It usually shows statistical information, such as quantities or numbers. Labels are used to tell what kind of information is shown. Always look at each axis carefully.

- Graphs sometimes show two or more lines or different types of bars in order to make comparisons. When that happens, the lines or bars are usually identified by labels or in a key.
- The **source line,** sometimes found at the bottom of the graph, tells you where the information was found.

Another kind of graph used in this book is a **circle graph,** often called a **pie graph** because it is cut into sections like a pie. Each "slice" represents a portion of the whole pie. Circle graphs are especially useful for showing at a glance how something is divided. For example, the circle graph on the left on page 514 shows what percentages of all federal revenue come from various sources.

PRACTICING SKILLS

1. Study the graph on this page. What is the subject of the graph?
2. (a) What does the horizontal axis show? (b) The vertical axis? (c) What does each line stand for? (d) What overall trend does this graph show? (e) What comparison can be made?
3. Look again at the pie graphs on page 514. (a) What does the whole pie on the right represent? (b) What do the "slices" show? (c) Which slice is the biggest? (d) About how much money does it stand for?

Study Skill 4
READING MAPS

There are many different kinds of maps. **Physical maps** show the earth's physical features, such as landforms, elevation, and water bodies. **Political maps** mainly show state and national borders and major cities. **Special-purpose maps** focus on very specific kinds of information, such as election results, population densities, or the location of ancient kingdoms and civilizations.

The first step in reading a map is to look at its title. Look at the map on page 7. The title of this map, "Birthplaces of Civilization," tells you that the map shows where early civilizations developed. The caption following the title gives you further information about the purpose of this map.

Other parts of maps make analyzing and understanding them easier. Most maps have a **scale,** either in miles, kilometers, or both. The scale helps you calculate the distances between locations on the map. On the "Birthplaces of Civilization" map, for example, the scale tells you that one inch represents 1,500 miles or 2,500 kilometers.

A **compass rose,** or directional symbol, shows where north is on the map. Some compass roses show the other **cardinal directions** — south, east, and west. A detailed compass rose also shows the **intermediate directions** — northeast, northwest, southeast, and southwest. Find the compass rose on page 7. What does it show?

Many maps use **symbols** to present information. These symbols might be colors, lines, letters, numbers, or small pictures. The **key** or **legend** explains the meaning of these various symbols. According to the key, what color does the map on page 7 use for "River valley civilizations"? What other symbol is used on this map? What does it represent?

Most of the maps in this book are special-purpose maps. They show specific information about government, such as election results, representation in Congress, judicial districts, zoning classifications, and the locations of national parks.

PRACTICING SKILLS

1. What kind of map is the map of the United States on pages 806–807? What kind of map is the U.S. map on page 591?
2. What is the title of the special-purpose map on page 339? Why do you think a compass rose is not shown on this map? According to the key, what do the numbers in each state show? What do the colors signify? In one or two sentences, describe what this map shows.

Study Skill 4
Practicing Skills Answers
1. A political map. A special-purpose map.
2. "Shifts in the House of Representatives." Location is not relevant. Seats gained or lost after the 1990 census. The status of seats—gained, lost, or unchanged. The map indicates both a shift in the House and a shift in the population.

Study Skill 5
UNDERSTANDING POLITICAL CARTOONS

Cartoons have long been used to express ideas about American government. The cartoon on this page for example, was drawn by Benjamin Franklin in 1754 to urge the colonies to join together.

Cartoons that express opinions on issues and affect people's views about government are called **political cartoons.** Political cartoons today are usually created for the opinion or editorial pages of daily newspapers.

Almost all political cartoons use symbols to get their point across. Some symbols have been used so often that they could almost be considered the "vocabulary" of cartoons. Examples include Uncle Sam or an eagle to represent the United States, and the elephant and donkey to represent the Republican and Democratic parties. Other symbols are chosen by cartoonists to convey specific ideas. In Franklin's cartoon, the snake — an animal that is both respected and feared — is used as a symbol. Franklin uses this symbol to say that if the colonies join together, they too will be respected and feared.

The light socket used in the cartoon on the next page is also a symbol. To make this cartoon easier to understand, the cartoonist has labeled its parts. Because of the labels, you can tell that the light socket is being used to represent the presidency. In Franklin's cartoon, the different segments of the snake are labeled with the abbreviations for the different colonies. The **caption,** which also serves as the title, helps explain the cartoon's purpose. Captions are usually short and clear. For example, the caption "Join or Die" clearly expresses Franklin's message.

Of course, captions cannot explain everything. If you do not know what electricity or sockets are or what the labels on the second cartoon stand for, it will be meaningless to you. It takes more knowledge than you might think to understand a political cartoon.

Political cartoons express a point of view and are intended to persuade. Often cartoonists try to persuade their readers by getting them to react in a particular way — to laugh, to get angry, or to think.

Cartoonists often use humor and exaggeration to make something look ridiculous. By poking fun at an issue, however, a cartoon can also influence people to take it more seriously.

SKILLS

781

Study Skill 5
Practicing Skills Answers

1. Eight. Students might note that the New England colonies are grouped together and suggest that the cartoon was intended for a New England audience.

2. The cartoon does not specify the causes against which the colonies were to unite; however, colonists in major cities probably were aware of the general issues.

3. Students' answers should reflect what they have learned in class thus far.

Reprinted with special permission of King Features Syndicate, Inc.

Although the cartoon above shows a light socket that is obviously unrealistic, it also points out what the cartoonist thinks is a dangerous situation — that the President may have more responsibilities than one person can safely handle. Exaggeration may also be used to persuade readers to feel a certain way. Cartoonists can create different effects by drawing a character to look extremely mean, friendly, lazy, sympathetic, stupid, or intelligent.

Cartoonists also try to influence their readers through their choice of symbols. Some symbols have a generally positive effect, while others have negative effects. For instance, a dove drawn on the shoulder of a character creates a completely different effect than a hawk or a vulture drawn on the same character's shoulder. When analyzing a cartoon, you must remember that symbols, exaggeration, and humor are all techniques that cartoonists use to express their point of view and to persuade you to see things their way.

PRACTICING SKILLS

1. Cartoons often contain more information than they seem to. How many colonies are represented in Franklin's cartoon? What might this tell you about the time in which it was drawn or the audience for which it was intended?

2. What information does Franklin's cartoon leave out? For example, does it say what specific dangers the colonies were facing that would cause them to "die" if they did not "unite"? Would you know about these dangers if you were living in the colonies in 1754?

3. Examine the labels on the cartoon on this page carefully. Which labels could you clearly explain to a younger brother or sister? Which labels would you have to learn more about?

Study Skill 6
USING THE LIBRARY

At some time you may be given an assignment that requires you to do research on a particular topic. To locate information about your topic, you will need to consult several sources. Your school or public library is a neatly organized vault of information on countless topics. Having all this information available is useless, however, unless you know how to find exactly what you need.

Using reference books. A great deal of information is readily available in the **reference section** of the library. Reference books are designed to make information easy to find. Some references *contain* information on var-

ious topics; others tell you where to *find* information.

A familiar kind of reference book that contains information is the **encyclopedia.** Encyclopedias contain short articles on many subjects, usually listed alphabetically. Some encyclopedias are general; others cover a specialized topic, such as American history.

Almanacs are books of facts, published yearly. They are a useful source of up-to-date information on many subjects, especially people, places, events, and statistics. To use an almanac, consult the table of contents or the index for the topic you are looking for.

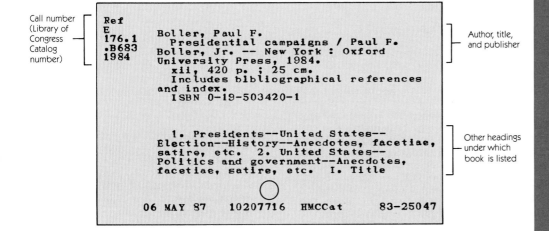

Call number (Library of Congress Catalog number)

```
Ref
E
176.1
.B683
1984
        Boller, Paul F.
          Presidential campaigns / Paul F.
        Boller, Jr. -- New York : Oxford
        University Press, 1984.
          xii, 420 p. ; 25 cm.
          Includes bibliographical references
        and index.
          ISBN 0-19-503420-1

          1. Presidents--United States--
        Election--History--Anecdotes, facetiae,
        satire, etc.  2. United States--
        Politics and government--Anecdotes,
        facetiae, satire, etc.  I. Title

        06 MAY 87   10207716  HMCCat      83-25047
```

Author, title, and publisher

Other headings under which book is listed

Almanacs and encyclopedias are just two of many types of reference books that contain information. Other examples are atlases, which are books of maps and other geographical information, and dictionaries.

Using periodical indexes. Of the reference books that tell you where to find information, **periodical indexes** are valuable for doing research. **Periodicals** are publications such as magazines and newspapers that come out periodically — usually weekly or monthly. Periodicals are the best source to use when you want to find the most recent developments in a given area. Periodical indexes help you find articles about specific subjects.

One such index is the *Readers' Guide to Periodical Literature,* which lists articles from over 150 American magazines of general interest. The *Readers' Guide* is issued several times during the year and is compiled into an annual single-volume edition.

To use the *Readers' Guide,* look up the subject that interests you. To find recent information about federal income taxes, for example, look under "Income tax." The names of several articles about income taxes and the magazine in which they appeared are listed under this heading. Other subject headings to investigate may also be listed.

Using the card catalog. In doing research, you will definitely want to look for books written about your topic. The **card catalog** lists all the books in a library. Books are listed in three ways: by author, by title, and by subject. If you know exactly which book you want, look up either the author's name or the title. If you are not sure which book you want, use the card catalog to look up subjects that interest you, just as you used the periodical index.

The card catalog will give you the book's **call number,** which tells you where you can find the book on the shelves. In the United States, two different systems are used for assigning call numbers to books according to subject matter. Libraries use either the Dewey Decimal or the Library of Congress classification system to organize the books on their shelves.

There is one other very useful source of information — the librarian. The librarian will help you use the card catalog and the indexes, find books and magazines, and think of other sources of information.

PRACTICING SKILLS

1. What kind of reference book would you use to find out about (a) the amount of corn grown in Iowa in 1985? (b) the people of China?
2. What is a periodical? What kind of information can periodicals help you find?
3. What is the call number of the book listed on the card on this page? Under what other headings would you find this book listed in the card catalog?

783

Study Skill 7

Study Skill 7
Practicing Skills Answers

1. As a study aid and as an organization tool for writing.
2. Students should incorporate headings and topic sentences in their outlines.
3. Subheadings for the three branches should be roughly parallel.

Study Skill 7
WRITING AN OUTLINE

A good way to organize and remember information you have read is to write an **outline.** Outlining is a good procedure to use in reading many kinds of books, not just textbooks. It is also a useful technique for organizing information for an essay or a report you have to write.

The first step in writing an outline is to classify all the information in the material you are reading. Look for main themes, or ideas, and separate them from the details that support these ideas. The main themes that you identify will become the main headings in your outline. The supporting details will become your subheadings.

Suppose you wanted to write an outline for the topic "Ratifying Constitutional Amendments." Your outline might look like this:

I. The role of Congress
   A. Chooses method of ratification
   B. Sets time limit for ratification
     1. Limit can be in text of amendment
     2. Limit can be in separate resolution
II. The state-legislature method
   A. Most common method
   B. Questions concerning this method
     1. Can a state change its vote?
     2. How much voice should voters have?

III. The state-convention method
   A. Used only once, for 21st Amendment
     1. Voters choose delegates in statewide election
     2. Delegates pledged to vote certain way

In this outline, notice that each main heading is listed under a roman numeral (I, II, III). Each subheading starts with a capital letter, and supporting details are numbered. If you needed more subheadings, you would use lower case letters (a, b, c . . .), then lower-case roman numerals (i, ii, iii . . .).

PRACTICING **SKILLS**

1. What are two uses of outlining?
2. Read pages 75–76 of Chapter 3. Beginning with the heading, *I. Why amendments are passed,* complete an outline of these pages with subheadings and supporting details.
3. Imagine that you are writing a paper on the three branches of government. Write an outline for your paper, using each branch as a main heading. Use subheadings to give supporting details or explanations.

Study Skill 8
TAKING NOTES/
WRITING REPORTS

Note-taking is one of the most important study skills you can master. Taking notes will help you get the most out of assigned reading and classroom lectures. It is also an invaluable skill for doing research papers and writing reports.

Taking notes while you read. Taking notes while you read helps you concentrate and identify main ideas. The following suggestions will help you take notes efficiently:

- *Finish reading each passage before making any notes.* It is usually necessary to read a complete paragraph, for instance, before you can determine its main idea.

- *Use abbreviations and symbols.* Symbols and abbreviations can help you take notes more rapidly. Keep your abbreviations simple so that they will make sense when you read them later. Examples of abbreviations are *Sen* for Senate, *HR* for House of Representatives, and *gov't* for government. Some commonly used symbols are as follows: *&* (and), *s/b* (should be), *w/* (with), and *w/o* (without).

- *Write down only the main ideas and the most important information.* Note-taking is a process of picking out the main ideas from the supporting details. Ask yourself

784

what the main ideas are. Watch for words that signal main points, such as *first, finally,* or *most important.* Also pay attention to words in **boldface** and *italic* type.

- *Write your notes in your own words.* This will force you to think about your reading. Don't just copy what is already in the textbook.

Taking notes in class. Taking notes during class lectures can help you understand and remember the important points your teacher makes. The notes you take in class are slightly different from those you take while reading.

Make your lecture notes as complete as possible. Try to capture all main points and important ideas. Use the teacher's exact words — by the time you think of your own words, the teacher will have moved on to the next point. Copy down any important terms your teacher writes on the board. Use abbreviations and symbols when you can, and be sure to write neatly.

As soon as possible after taking notes, reread them. Make sure that you can understand your symbols and abbreviations. Correct any words you can't read and fill in any spaces you may have intentionally left blank. Reviewing your notes will reinforce and help you remember what you have just read or heard. Furthermore, when it comes time to study for a test, you will have all the information you need.

Writing reports. When you are assigned to research a topic and present your findings in a well-written report, you will have to take thorough notes. Though a research assignment may seem like an awesome task, it is easier to do when you divide the task into simple steps.

Begin by choosing a subject that fits your assignment and that interests you. Narrow your topic to something that you can describe fully in the allotted number of words or pages. For example, a topic like "Programs Funded by City Governments" may be too broad for a three-page paper. A topic like "How City Governments Finance Adult Education" would be easier to cover.

Use the suggestions in Study Skill 6 to find sources of information about your topic. Keep good records about each source you find. For books, write down the author's name, the title, the publisher, and the city and year of publication. For magazine articles, list the author's name, the title, the name and date of the magazine, and the page numbers. You will need this information when you prepare the bibliography for your report or for writing footnotes.

Hardy, *Gov't in America,* pp. 63-64

Separation of powers— 3 branches of gov't to keep any 1 group from having too much power. (Idea of Montesquieu)

legislative branch— Congress— Sen. + HR— makes laws
executive branch— Pres.— carries out laws
judicial branch— S.C.— interprets laws

Using the hints explained above, take notes as you read your sources. Many students find it convenient to make notes on index cards, like the one shown on this page, using a different card for each topic. On each card, make sure to record the author and page number of the source at the top. If you find a passage you might want to quote in your report, write it down exactly as it appears.

When you feel you have taken enough notes, organize the information on your cards. Separate them into stacks that contain similar ideas. Then read through the notes in each stack and write a sentence or phrase that identifies the main point of each stack. Arrange your main points in a logical order to make an outline for your report. Look through the cards in each stack again, picking out key phrases and ideas to provide supporting details under your main headings.

Following your outline and referring to your notes when necessary, write the first draft of your report. Express your thoughts freely at this stage. After you have finished the first draft, revise your report. Make sure that your main points are clear and that your paper moves smoothly from topic to topic. Each paragraph should present a single idea, and every sentence should make sense. Before you write or type your final copy, correct all spelling, punctuation, and grammar. At the end of your report, include a bibliography. The bibliography should list, in alphabetical order (by author's last name), all the sources you used.

PRACTICING **SKILLS**

1. What are four points to remember about taking notes from your reading? How does the process differ when taking notes in class?
2. What are five separate steps involved in writing a report?

785

Study Skill 8
Practicing Skills Answers

1. Finish reading each passage before taking notes; write down only main points and important information; write notes in your own words; use abbreviations and symbols. Lecture notes should be as complete as possible and should use the teacher's exact words.

2. Choose a suitable subject; find sources of information; take notes; organize notes in an outline; write a draft and revise.

Study Skill 9
TAKING TESTS

Students who do well on tests are usually those with good study habits. Your success on a test depends greatly on how well you prepare. No matter how well you know the material, however, you must also know how to deal with different types of test questions.

Preparation for a test actually begins with the first assignment you are given. Read your assignment carefully and take good notes on your reading and during lectures.

When the day of the test arrives, remember the most important rule of test-taking, "Follow directions." Read the instructions for the test carefully. Even if you know the correct answers, you will lose points if you do not give the answer exactly as your teacher asks.

When you get the test, skim through it quickly to decide how much time you can spend on each part. If you cannot answer a question, go on to the next one so that you get credit for all the questions you can answer. When you have been through all the questions, then go back to the ones you skipped and work on them.

The most common kinds of questions in social studies classes are multiple-choice, matching, and essay questions. You need to recognize these types of questions and know how to go about answering them.

A **multiple-choice** question asks you to choose the correct answer from three or four possible answers. Read the question carefully and try to answer it before looking at the choices. If you are not certain of the right answer, eliminate those that you know are wrong. Then pick the best remaining answer. Here is an example of a multiple-choice question:

Which group favored ratification of the Constitution?
(a) Whigs (b) Tories (c) Federalists
(d) Antifederalists

In **matching** questions, you must match items in one column with items in a second column. Match first those items that you know with certainty. Look for clues in the remaining answers. Do not be fooled if one column has more items than the other. Sometimes you will be given choices that you do not need; some-times you may need to use the same answer twice. Here is an example of a matching question:

1. First written constitution in the English colonies.
2. Document limiting the powers of the British monarch.
3. Early plan for colonial unity.
4. First national constitution of the United States.

a. Magna Charta
b. Albany Plan of Union
c. Fundamental Orders of Connecticut
d. Articles of Confederation
e. Bill of Rights

An **essay** question requires you to write a short composition in a limited time. Essay questions can be more complex than other types of questions. Read the question carefully so that you will know exactly what you are being asked to do: *list, discuss, compare, contrast,* or *summarize.* If you are asked to describe the similarities between a capitalist and a socialist economy, for instance, don't waste time by listing the differences. On scratch paper, jot down the names, dates, facts, or terms required in your answer and arrange them in an appropriate order. Write an outline if you have time, listing main points and supporting details.

Be specific in your essay. An answer that is brief, detailed, and well-organized will receive more points than a long, rambling essay. After you have finished writing your essay, reread it and correct any errors in grammar, spelling, or punctuation.

PRACTICING SKILLS

1. Which students do best on tests?
2. What is the first thing you should do when you take a test?
3. What should you do if you are not certain of the answer to a multiple-choice question?
4. Write four multiple-choice questions and one matching question for a section of this book that you have recently read. Exchange papers with a partner and see if you are able to answer each other's questions.

Study Skill 10
ANALYZING THE NEWS

To make valid and effective decisions on today's important issues, you need to be informed. The most commonly used sources of current information are newspapers and television. A careful and intelligent approach to using these two sources will help you become a well-informed citizen.

The stories you find in newspapers generally fall into three groups — news, editorials, and features. **News stories** give you straight facts. These facts provide answers to six basic questions — *Who? What? Where? When? How?* and *Why?*

Editorials provide analysis and interpretation of the news. They contain opinions rather than facts. Most newspapers print their editorials on a special editorial page or on the **op-ed** page — the page *op*posite the *edi*torial.

Stories of interest that are not really news are called **features**. Articles on food, travel, fashion, and movies fall into this category.

The best way to begin reading is to take five minutes to scan through the whole newspaper. Take a look at the type size of the front page headlines. The headlines in the largest type usually accompany the day's most important stories. Next, review each page, noting headlines, pictures, and picture captions. Once you have an idea of what stories the newspaper contains, you can decide which ones you should read to get the information you need.

Television news programs also provide news stories, comments, and opinions on the news, as well as interesting feature stories. The television news is like a condensed version of a newspaper.

Television news has certain strengths. You probably have heard the old saying "a picture is worth a thousand words." This often is the case with television. A few seconds of film of famine victims, for example, has a far greater impact than a dozen newspaper stories on the same subject. A good television reporter can make you feel you are on the spot where the news is happening. It is not surprising, then, that more than 60 percent of Americans get all their news from television.

You should keep certain things in mind when watching television news. First, most national news programs last for 30 minutes. When time for the program opening and commercials is deducted, only about 22 minutes remain for the news. Thus, there is little opportunity to provide any in-depth news coverage. Second, television is made to appeal to the eyes. TV news stories, therefore, may be chosen for their visual impact rather than for their content.

Despite these reservations, watching TV news can be very useful from another point of view. The nightly network news teams include the top reporters, directors, and technicians in the country. All these people have to decide what are the most important stories to show in 22 minutes. By watching the evening news, at the least you keep in touch with what the professional TV news teams consider important.

PRACTICING SKILLS

1. What are three kinds of stories that appear in newspapers?
2. What are three things you should keep in mind when watching the news on television?
3. Choose a major news story of the moment. Follow the story in a newspaper for at least one week. Keep a scrapbook on the story by collecting news articles and editorials from the newspaper.
4. For at least one week, follow the evening news on one of the national television networks. Keep a log of the news stories included each day. Briefly describe each story. Is it news, opinion, or a feature? How much time is it given? Is it of international, national, or local interest? Share your findings with a classmate who followed the news on a different network.

Study Skill 10
Practicing Skills Answers
1. News, editorials, features.
2. TV news provides little in-depth coverage; the stories are often chosen solely on visual appeal; and the stories selected usually represent the most important news of the day.
3. Individual students might follow the same stories in different newspapers. At the end of the week they may compare levels of coverage and editorial perspectives.
4. This exercise should highlight the abbreviated nature of television news coverage.

787

CRITICAL THINKING SKILLS

You need to bring more to the study of government than just a good memory for facts. The ability to memorize is useful, but you must also be able to *think* effectively. If you can look critically at important issues and events, you will be able to make sense of the way the world is today. The critical thinking skills described here will help you look below the surface of American government or any other subject. Critical thinking makes the study of government more interesting and useful, because it enables *you* to evaluate events and policies and understand the complex decision-making processes that go on behind the scenes.

CRITICAL THINKING SKILL 1

INTERPRETATION

Interpretation is the attempt to identify a relationship between one fact, idea, or value and another fact, idea, or value. In the study of government, it often means offering an opinion as to why something happened or explaining what a group of apparently unrelated ideas has in common. You may be asked to use the skill of interpretation in any of the ways described below.

Determining cause-and-effect relationships. Identifying **cause-and-effect relationships** is essential to understanding politics and government. An action that produces an event is a *cause*. The event or development produced by an action is an *effect*. Why some things happened and others did not can be traced to causes. In other words, what made certain things happen and what kept others from happening?

During the 1920's, for example, the United States experienced a boom in productivity due to technological advances and an increased labor force. This led to the growth of advertising, as companies sought to convince Americans to buy the products they were turning out so fast. The growth of advertising led, in turn, to the expansion of credit. Offering to let people buy on credit was one method advertisers used to sell their products.

Look at the cause-and-effect relationship in the following diagram:

Boom in productivity (Cause) ⟶ Growth of advertising (Effect)

Sometimes an effect becomes the cause of another effect. This kind of cause-and-effect relationship is shown below:

Boom in productivity (Cause) ⟶ Growth of advertising (Effect/Cause) ⟶ Expansion of credit (Effect)

Some cause-and-effect relationships may not be clear until many years after the events took place. Scholars may find after studying an event that several causes led to an effect or that one cause was responsible for many effects.

Make it a habit to note the various effects of certain causes, which of those effects in turn became new causes, and whether multiple causes or multiple effects were involved.

Making and supporting generalizations. **Generalizations** are brief summaries or conclusions based on facts. You may often recognize them as topic sentences, which express the main idea of a paragraph.

In Chapter 3, page 79, for example, you will note the topic sentence, ''Over the years, Presidents have assumed many powers that are mentioned nowhere in the Constitution.'' The paragraph gives facts that support this generalization. It tells you that Presidents have sometimes called out the National Guard without an act of Congress.

Keep in mind that generalizations are general. They are used to make broad statements such as the example given above: Presidents have assumed many powers not mentioned in the Constitution. Do not assume that all Presidents have assumed powers not expressed in the Constitution, or that this practice is in violation of the law.

Inferring and drawing conclusions. The skills of inferring and drawing conclusions require you to make up your mind about something you read. **Inferring** is getting more information from reading than is actually and specifically stated. It might be described as reading between the lines. In Chapter 8 on page 228, for instance, you learn that after the bombing of Pearl Harbor in 1941, American public opinion in favor of entering World War II was strong and united. You can infer that before Pearl Harbor, opinion about the war was divided. When you infer, you make an assumption based on what you read.

When you draw **conclusions,** you make a judgment about what you have read. This judgment is based on careful thought and available information. Read this passage about Dr. Martin Luther King, Jr.'s, struggle for civil rights, from page 202:

> King's charismatic leadership gave the movement a new set of tactics—nonviolent resistance, or civil disobedience, to discriminatory laws. . . . King's followers, many of them students, held "sit-ins" at segregated lunch counters and boarded segregated buses as "Freedom Riders." Sympathizers in other parts of the country boycotted discriminatory companies and their products.

From this you can conclude that Dr. King believed that equal rights for African Americans could come through peaceful demands for change. His strategy was to increase the public's awareness of discrimination in American society through nonviolent demonstrations and thus mobilize the support of concerned citizens across the nation.

Recognizing points of view. A point of view reflects an opinion, attitude, belief, or feeling. A useful skill in studying government is the ability to recognize a point of view for what it is.

Favorable points of view are written in positive language, such as "This will benefit all people." Negative points of view will take an opposite approach, such as "The election of this candidate will lead to mass unemployment."

Detecting bias. Look carefully for **bias**—personal preference—on the part of the person whose views are being presented. If a writer or speaker wants to persuade people to act, he or she will often try to appeal to people's emotions.

Many famous public officials had strong opinions that show up in their writings and speeches. These views should be examined critically. Just because a person is famous or highly regarded does not mean that you must agree with his or her opinions. Try to be aware of bias and opinion when examining documents of the past or reading newspapers and magazine articles today.

PRACTICING SKILLS

1. Read the material on pages 43–45 of Chapter 2. What caused the Congress to adopt the Articles of Confederation? How did the effects of this decision in turn become new causes?
2. Why do generalizations make good topic sentences?
3. What is the difference between drawing a conclusion and offering an opinion?

CRITICAL THINKING SKILL 2

ANALYSIS

The purpose of **analyzing** is to show that you understand what you read. When you analyze information, you do three things:

1. Break the information into its different parts.
2. Recognize the relationship of one part to another.
3. Understand why the material has been organized as it has.

Analysis can be applied to large reading selections, such as chapters, or to single paragraphs or even sentences.

Look at Chapter 7, Section 4, pages 212–219. Read the paragraphs under the subheadings "The Right to Vote," "Discriminatory Laws," and "Ending Sex Discrimination." What is the relationship between these three parts? Why has the author chosen this organization for the material on legal aspects of women's rights?

If you look closely at "The Right to Vote" and "Discriminatory Laws," you will see that they give background information on the history of sex-based discrimination in the United States.

Critical Thinking Skill 1
Practicing Skills Answers
1. The new nation needed to establish a working central government. The Articles of Confederation, however, provided only a weak central government that could not tax, raise an army, regulate foreign commerce, or settle disputes among the states. These problems led to the calling of the Constitutional Convention.
2. They make a broad statement; the paragraph can then be used to support this statement with specific facts.
3. Conclusions are usually based on facts. Opinions are frequently based on biases.

SKILLS

They also explain the obstacles that women sought to overcome in the proposed Equal Rights Amendment. "Ending Sex Discrimination" describes the bans on sex discrimination in employment and education under the Civil Rights Act of 1964 and Title IX of the 1972 Education Amendments. You can conclude that the author wanted to describe the history of legal discrimination against women before telling you about the anti-discrimination laws that were passed during the 1960's and 1970's.

Distinguishing facts, opinions, and values. **Facts** are those things that are known to be true or to have happened. Facts are based on information that can be checked for accuracy. **Opinions** express how people feel about something, what their beliefs are, and what attitudes they take. **Values** are opinions that often involve the standards of right and wrong. All values are opinions, but not all opinions are values. You may express an opinion on a subject you know little about. You may also express an opinion about what you think will happen in a certain situation. In either example, your opinion may prove to be a fact. Values are never facts. They may be so much a part of the creed you live by that they seem like facts. If they cannot be proven to be true, however, they are not facts.

It is important that you distinguish among facts, opinions, and values. Even though opinions are not always based on fact, and values cannot be proven to be true, you can still learn from them. You can learn how people felt at a certain time, what they considered important, and what they thought about. You cannot always learn what really happened or what the facts were.

Certain words give clues that opinions are being presented—"It is my belief" or "In my view" are lead-ins to what somebody thinks. Not all opinions are easily recognized. You need to read carefully to identify what you read as fact or opinion. When people write facts, they use little emotional language. When people express opinions and values, however, they may become emotional in their choice of words.

Analyzing political cartoons. Political cartoons can effectively express opinions and points of view. Political cartoons often use symbols to get their point across. The United States, for example, is often depicted as Uncle Sam or as an eagle. In American politics, the elephant is

790

from THE HERBLOCK GALLERY (Simon and Schuster, 1964).

ESCALATION

used to represent the Republican Party, while the donkey symbolizes the Democratic Party. Knowing what the various symbols stand for is critical to understanding a political cartoon.

Cartoons in daily newspapers usually deal with contemporary issues or events. Some political cartoons are intended to call the public's attention to an important debate. Others openly convey the cartoonist's opinion as to whether something that has happened is right or wrong.

PRACTICING SKILLS

1. Read the selection from Patricio Flores's sermon on page 797. What can you identify as a fact? What can you identify as an opinion? Do you recognize any value statements?

2. Look at the political cartoon on this page. What point does the cartoonist want to make?

CRITICAL THINKING SKILL 3

TRANSLATING AND SYNTHESIZING

Translating and synthesizing are skills that require you to play an active role in the process of studying government. With these skills you can bring a fresh approach to an old subject.

Translating. Translating is presenting information in a form that is different from the way you receive it. If you tell a classmate about something you read, you are translating from the written to the oral form. You might make a chart or draw a picture instead of giving the information orally. That too would be translating.

For example, historians must translate in order to write histories. They gather as much information as they can about a historical period, from sources such as paintings, photographs, letters, and oral histories. They must then find a way of conveying in their writing what impression these things give about the time period they describe. Look at the photograph of the homesteading family on page 580. What impression does it give you of conditions on the American frontier?

Synthesizing. Synthesizing allows you to use your imagination to explain events and to speculate about what might have happened. When you synthesize, you create new ways of looking at a subject. For example, a film about the Civil War might be based on written accounts and photographs.

Take the democracy movement in China as another example. You could synthesize by writing a diary of a young Chinese student in Tiananmen Square in June, 1989, based on research about the pro-democracy student demonstrations. Another possibility might be to write a one-act play detailing the conversations among protesters before the military crackdown began.

In this type of synthesis, you should not alter known events. Rather, you should put together the pieces of knowledge you have in order to create your own interpretation of the subject.

Predicting events. Another aspect of synthesizing is **predicting**. Predicting can be separated into two categories.

The first of these asks you to speculate about what might have happened if something else had not. Suppose, for example, that the states had not demanded that a bill of rights be included in the Constitution (page 55). What kind of government might have evolved? How might the course of history have been altered?

The other form of predicting asks you to suggest the outcome of an event that is not yet resolved. Again, your prediction should be based on solid evidence and should not be guesswork. News commentators often utilize this skill when they examine recent events. For example, they may report a minor controversy in a political campaign and then predict its effect on the election.

PRACTICING SKILLS

1. Why is the ability to translate information important?

2. Choose an important event from this book, such as a debate in Congress, a Supreme Court case, or a political rally. Write an account of the event as it might have been reported by a first-hand observer.

3. Consider the present justices of the Supreme Court. Predict how vacancies and new appointments might change the character of the Court. What important laws might change if the Court changes? Why?

CRITICAL THINKING SKILL 4

PROBLEM SOLVING

When you try to solve a problem, you draw on previous experiences and on knowledge you already have. The solution you offer might be an idea, a suggestion, or an action. It is your creation, and it may or may not solve the problem. When you participate in problem solving, you are expected to come up with an answer to a problem for which no answer yet exists.

Problem solving involves making choices or **making decisions**. It can be something as simple as what to choose to eat in a restaurant or something as complex as deciding what to pursue as a career.

With difficult problems, there are steps that can be taken to help you make the right decision.

1. Clearly identify the problem.
2. Consider the various alternatives.
3. Consider the consequences and merits of each of the alternatives.
4. Make a decision.

791

Critical Thinking Skill 4
Practicing Skills Answers
1. Identifying the problem.
2. The problem of representation and taxation in those states with large slave populations. The "three-fifths" compromise determined that three-fifths of the slave population would be counted.

Critical Thinking Skill 5
Practicing Skills Answers
1. Scholars are often puzzled by large and complex questions, such as what factors caused an event to happen or how an event affected the nation. They deal with these unknowns by forming hypotheses.
2. Students should present an educated opinion and support it with facts.

Throughout the evolution of government in America, leaders have been faced with solving problems, some of which have affected the lives of thousands or even millions of people. For instance, the delegates to the Constitutional Convention in 1787 faced the difficult task of writing a Constitution acceptable to all the states. To achieve this goal, they had to address a serious problem. The first step was to identify the following problem: How to create a legislature that would fairly represent the interests of both small and large states.

After the delegates identified the main problem, they had to consider alternative ways of solving it, and the merits and consequences of each plan. After deciding that their course of action would be compromise, they put their plan for a bicameral legislature into effect.

When the problem is of the size and scope of that facing the delegates to the Constitutional Convention, the ability to define the problem clearly and to explore the alternatives can often provide a compromise and help realize the goal.

PRACTICING SKILLS

1. What is the first step in the process of making a decision?
2. Read the description of the Constitutional Convention on pages 49–54 Chapter 2. What problems still faced the delegates after they formulated the Great Compromise? How were these problems eventually resolved?

CRITICAL THINKING SKILL 5

FORMING HYPOTHESES

Many people think that the study of government consists of learning the dates and descriptions of important events, such as legislative debates, elections, and governmental processes. They assume that a textbook can tell them all there is to know about subjects such as these. That is partly true. Clear records do exist of many important events, particularly in the history of American government, which has lasted only a few

hundred years. Historical records of the workings of American government also exist, from the federal level right down to the local level.

These documents and records, however, do not tell the whole story. In addition to describing the branches of government and legislative processes, the study of government consists of questions that go beyond the facts. How can you know, for instance, why so few eligible Americans vote? How can you explain how interest groups influence the democratic process? What additional information do you need to determine the future of the two-party political system?

These are matters that can never be pinpointed exactly, but that does not mean they are not of interest. Like archeologists, historians, and scientists, you can piece together the bits of information you acquire in order to answer a puzzling question. When you feel you may know what has caused something to happen in the past, or what might occur in a given situation in the future, you form a **hypothesis**—a theory based on evidence. Hypotheses are not proven facts. They might rather be called "educated guesses."

After doing research on the history of the United States' foreign policy, for example, you might form this hypothesis: While Democrats and Republicans differ on many domestic issues, their foreign policies display more similarities than differences. You could then explain why the Cold War policy toward the Soviet Union remained basically consistent through both Democratic and Republican administrations.

Scholars often use each other's hypotheses as the basis for further discussion. They may put forward new evidence that proves an old hypothesis correct. Or, if new evidence seems to prove the hypothesis incorrect, they may propose a new hypothesis to replace it.

PRACTICING SKILLS

1. What kinds of questions are scholars unable to solve with certainty? How do they address these "unknowns"?
2. Turn to a chapter you have recently read and form a hypothesis about an event or issue in that chapter. List evidence to back up your hypothesis.

EVALUATION

When you **evaluate** you are making a judgment. It may be a judgment about an action, an event, or something you have read. You should not make a judgment without first thinking it through. You need to provide reasons that explain why you have judged something as you have.

You may find that you need to interpret, analyze, or synthesize before you are able to make an evaluation.

Developing criteria for making judgments. When you evaluate for the purpose of making a judgment, you need to do two things:

1. Set standards. That is, determine the purpose of the evaluation.
2. Decide how well your standards are met. In judging material, you might question how accurate, adequate, or biased it is.

Suppose you were asked to identify which American Presidents were good leaders and which were poor leaders. When you are faced with making that judgment, you need first to establish what constitutes a good leader. You might list such considerations as:

1. Advanced policies that brought prosperity to the country.
2. Suggested just and useful laws.
3. Managed foreign affairs successfully.
4. Gained the confidence of the people.

Once you have decided what qualities a good President should have, you can judge how well various Presidents measure up to your standards.

Evaluating historical sources. Different historical sources often provide varying accounts of the same event. When this happens, you need to evaluate the accuracy and fairness of these differing views.

When you evaluate historical documents, consider the following questions:

1. Is the information from primary or secondary sources? It is important to know whether the material is a **primary source,** written at the time the event happened, or a **secondary source,** written long after the event occurred. Primary sources are records from the past such as newspapers, diaries, letters, and government documents. Secondary sources are written by people who were not witnesses to or participants in the events they write about. Sometimes secondary sources may be more useful than primary sources even though they were written by people who did not witness the events. Secondary sources may be more accurate, more objective, or more complete. This textbook, for example, is a secondary source.

2. Is the material fact or opinion? As you know, most historical evidence includes statements of both fact and opinion.

3. Is the information accurate? A good way to check accuracy is to see how the information is presented in other sources. If you find that different sources give different data, you may wonder where your source got the information. You may also begin to question its accuracy. On the other hand, if you find that different sources give the same basic information, you may be fairly certain the material is accurate. Determining a writer's credentials is another way to check accuracy. What makes this person qualified to write about this subject?

The skills described in this Skill Review will benefit you not only in government courses but in other subjects that you study. The ability to evaluate sources of information fairly is a valuable tool that you will use throughout your life.

PRACTICING SKILLS

1. What is a primary source? What is a secondary source?
2. What methods can you use to determine whether information is accurate?
3. Choose an American President and consider the goals that he outlined at the beginning of his administration. Set standards for judging those goals and decide how close he came to meeting them.

SKILLS

Critical Thinking Skill 6
Practicing Skills Answers
1. A primary source is written at the time the event happened. A secondary source is written after the event occurred.
2. You can compare sources and check the credentials of the original source.
3. Students might make a judgment based on an evaluation of the goals set by the President they choose.

793

Speaking Out
Analyzing Primary Sources
1. Emotion. He tried to arouse colonists' anger at British actions and colonists' pride in defense of their homes and families.

2. Rebuttals should argue for continued loyalty to Britain; specifically, rebuttals might attack Paine for trying to whip up public anger and might argue that English colonists do not suffer from "oppression."

Thomas Paine
1737–1809

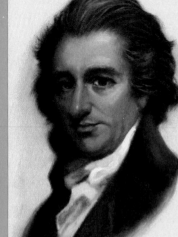

A former customs collector who became one of the most controversial people of his day, Thomas Paine wrote America's first best-seller, Common Sense. Born in England in 1737, Paine had little schooling and was unsuccessful in several jobs. After meeting Benjamin Franklin in London, Paine came to America in 1774 and began work as a journalist. His pamphlet Common Sense vigorously rejected keeping any ties with Britain. In its first three months, the pamphlet sold more than 100,000 copies. Thousands of colonists—including Washington and Jefferson—read Paine's arguments and agreed with them. Paine went to Europe in the late 1780's and, despite his radical views, was imprisoned during the French Revolution. He returned to the United States in 1802 and died there, a social outcast.

Common Sense (1776)
In the following pages I offer nothing more than simple facts, plain arguments, and common sense; . . .

The authority of Great Britain over this continent is a form of government which sooner or later must have an end. . . . Men of passive tempers look somewhat lightly over the offenses of Britain and, still hoping for the best, are apt to call out, "Come, come, we shall be friends again for all this.' But examine the passions and feelings of mankind . . . and then tell me whether you can hereafter love, honor, and faithfully serve the power that has carried fire and sword into your land. . . . But if you say you can still pass the violations over, then I ask, has your house been burned? . . . Are your wife and children destitute of a bed to lie on or bread to live on? . . . If you have, and can still shake hands with the murderers, then are you unworthy of the name of husband, father, friend, or lover, and whatever may be your rank or title in life, you have the heart of a coward. . . .

To talk of friendship with those in whom our reason forbids us to have faith, and our affections . . . instruct us to detest, is madness and folly. Every day wears out the little remains of kindred between us and them [the British]. . . .

O! ye that love mankind! Ye that dare oppose not only the tyranny but the tyrant, stand forth! Every spot of the Old World is overrun with oppression. Freedom has been hunted round the globe. Asia and Africa have long expelled her. Europe regards her like a stranger, and England has given her warning to depart. O! receive the fugitive and prepare in time an asylum [refuge] for mankind.

ANALYZING PRIMARY SOURCES
1. **CRITICAL THINKING** Was Paine's argument based more on reason or emotion? Explain your answer.
2. **WRITING ACTIVITY** Imagine that you are a pro-British colonist in 1776. Write a rebuttal to *Common Sense* that is at least three paragraphs long.

The most eloquent speaker for black civil rights in the late 1800's was Frederick Douglass, born into slavery in Maryland in 1817. Despite laws against education for African Americans, Douglass learned to read and write and, in 1838, fled to New England. He joined the movement for the abolition of slavery, becoming a noted public speaker, and later started his own abolitionist newspaper, North Star. Douglass continued to work for civil rights long past the abolition of slavery. In a speech excerpted below, which he gave to a black civil rights convention, Douglass described both his hopes and his disappointments.*

Frederick Douglass
1817–1895

Speaking Out
Analyzing Primary Sources
1. Equal voting rights for African Americans. This goal is important because any group that lacks full voting rights will not have a voice in government.
2. Possible analogies include a tumor, a disease, blindness, a water barrier, or a wall.

Address to the Louisville Convention (1883)

Though we have had war, reconstruction, and abolition as a nation, we still linger in the shadow and blight of an extinct institution. . . .

In all the relations of life and death we are met by the color line. We cannot ignore it if we would, and ought not if we could. It hunts us at midnight, it denies us accommodation in hotels and justice in the courts; excludes our children from schools, refuses our sons the chance to learn trades, and compels us to pursue only such labor as will bring the least reward. While we recognize the color line as a hurtful force, a mountain barrier to our progress, wounding our bleeding feet with its flinty rocks at every step, we do not despair. We are a hopeful people. This convention is a proof of our faith in you, in reason, in truth and justice—our belief that prejudice, with all its malign accomplishments, may yet be removed by peaceful means. . . .

This is no question of party. It is a question of law and government. It is a question whether men shall be protected by law, or be left to the mercy of cyclones of anarchy and bloodshed. It is whether the Government or the mob shall rule this land; whether the promises solemnly made to us in the Constitution be manfully kept or meanly and flagrantly broken. Upon this vital point we ask the whole people of the United States to take notice that whatever political power we have shall be exerted for no man of any party who will not, in advance of election, promise to use every power given him by the Government, State or National, to make the black man's path to the ballot-box as straight, smooth, and safe as that of any other American citizen. . . .

ANALYZING PRIMARY SOURCES
1. **CRITICAL THINKING** Toward what goal did Douglass pledge to work? Why is this goal so important?
2. **WRITING ACTIVITY** Douglass compared racism to a mountain barrier. Think of a different analogy for racism and write a paragraph explaining why that analogy is appropriate.

795

1. The reason women lack many necessary skills is that they have been denied the opportunity to use them.

2. Women's demands for suffrage must overcome the long-standing prejudice against women. Intelligent people already realize that women are qualified to vote. The weaknesses attributed to women are a result of the restrictions placed on them. Since women already enjoy freedom in non-political affairs, they deserve political freedom as well.

PRIMARY SOURCE

SPEAKING OUT

SPEAKING OUT

Carrie Lane Chapman Catt
1859–1947

*I*n more than 25 years of working for women's rights, Carrie Lane Chapman Catt changed the direction and methods of the movement. A former schoolteacher and superintendent, she became president of the National American Woman Suffrage Association in 1900. After passage of the Nineteenth Amendment in 1920, she turned the group's attention toward voter education, forming the League of Women Voters.

Address to the National American Woman Suffrage Association (1902)

The question of woman suffrage is a very simple one. The plea is dignified, calm, and logical. Yet, great as is the victory over conservatism which is represented in the accomplishment of man suffrage, infinitely greater will be the attainment of woman suffrage. . . . Woman suffrage must meet precisely the same objections which have been urged against man suffrage, but in addition, it must combat sex-prejudice, the oldest, the most unreasoning, the most stubborn of human idiosyncrasies. . . .

We need no longer argue woman's intellectual, moral, and physical qualifications for the ballot with the intelligent. The Reason of the best of our citizens has long been convinced. The justice of the argument has been admitted, but sex-prejudice is far from conquered. . . .

Four chief causes led to the subjection of women . . . obedience, ignorance, the denial of personal liberty, and the denial of right to property and wages. These forces united in cultivating a spirit of egotism and tyranny in men and weak dependence in women. . . . This world taught woman nothing skillful and then said her work was valueless. It permitted her no opinions and said she did not know how to think. It forbade her to speak in public, and said [women] had no orators. It denied her schools, and said [women] had no genius. It robbed her of every vestige of responsibility, and then called her weak. . .

. . . . The average civilized woman enjoys the right of individual liberty in the home of her father, her husband, and her son. The individual woman . . . enjoys self-government in the home and in society. The question now is . . . Shall the woman who enjoys the right of self-government in every other department of life be permitted the right of self-government in the State?

ANALYZING PRIMARY SOURCES

1. **CRITICAL THINKING** Explain the connection Catt described between discrimination against women and women's lack of skills.

2. **WRITING ACTIVITY** Write a four-sentence paragraph summarizing Catt's argument. Each sentence should be a summary of one of the paragraphs in the excerpt.

Texas-born Patricio Flores, the first Mexican American bishop to be appointed to the U.S. hierarchy of the Roman Catholic Church, is known as an outspoken leader on social as well as religious issues. The son of migrant farm workers, Flores grew up in the Houston area. Ordained a priest in 1956, Flores served as a parish priest in Houston, auxiliary bishop of San Antonio, and bishop of El Paso before being elevated to archbishop of San Antonio in 1979. A persuasive advocate of civil rights for Mexican Americans, Flores has directly involved himself in the legal defense of Mexican Americans accused of crimes and has served as the chairman of the Texas Advisory Committee of the U.S. Civil Rights Commission. Flores founded the Mexican American Cultural Center and the National Hispanic Scholarship Fund and he has also fought for farm workers' rights. The following excerpt is taken from a message to the 750,000 Catholics of the San Antonio archdiocese.

A New Pentecost (1981)

Even as I give thanks for the oneness that is being achieved through diversity, even as I glory in the beauty of the mosaic that all of us are, my heart has many times felt sadness. While our Church is rich in culture and in faith, so many of our brothers and sisters are poor. I have seen the empty gaze of families who don't have enough to eat or enough to live on. I have seen the bitterness of fathers who work and work and work and still cannot provide the necessities of life. I have felt the futility of children who go to school but who learn so little. I have seen the anger of people who feel as if life and opportunity have passed them by. I have seen the sad and hurt looks of children from broken homes, the epidemic of crime and violence, the tragic results of addiction to drugs and alcohol. We have in our midst so many people who feel isolated, oppressed, and lonely—all those who live at the edge of life, whether they be rich or poor—who will speak for them? . . .

To our children, to our young, I say simply: Be proud of who you are, of your faith, of your culture and ancestry, of your history, of the rich traditions and languages that are part of your heritage. Study the past, be aware of it, learn from it —from its good examples and its bad mistakes.

ANALYZING PRIMARY SOURCES

1. **CRITICAL THINKING** Why might religious organizations be especially effective in helping the poor and others "who live at the edge of life"?

2. **WRITING ACTIVITY** Write the dialogue of a debate between two people on the question of whether religious groups should participate in public policy issues.

Patricio Flores
1929–

Speaking Out
Analyzing Primary Sources

1. Because many religious organizations have deep roots in communities, they know which people need help and what kinds of help are needed; many religious organizations also have long-standing commitments to aid the disadvantaged.

2. Dialogues should mention the argument that religious groups have as much right as any other groups to participate in politics, as well as the argument that religion's involvement in politics threatens the separation of church and state.

SPEAKING OUT

PRIMARY SOURCE
SPEAKING OUT

Margaret Chase Smith
1897–

O ne of the first Republicans in Congress to oppose McCarthyism was a first-term senator from Maine named Margaret Chase Smith. A former businesswoman, Smith had served as official staff secretary to her husband, Clyde Smith, a Republican congressman from Maine. After his death in 1940, she ran for his seat in the House of Representatives. She served four terms in the House and then won election to the Senate, becoming the first woman to serve in both houses of Congress. Known for her firm principles but not for speechmaking, Senator Smith surprised many people with her "Declaration of Conscience," given in the Senate on June 1, 1950. In it she criticized Senator Joseph McCarthy, whose unsupported accusations of Communist subversion in the government had frightened most political leaders into silence. Smith remained in the Senate for four terms, leaving in 1973.

Declaration of Conscience (1950)

Mr. President, I speak as a Republican. I speak as a woman. I speak as a United States senator. I speak as an American.

The United States Senate has long enjoyed worldwide respect as the greatest deliberative body in the world. But recently that deliberative character has too often been debased to the level of a forum of hate and character assassination sheltered by the shield of congressional immunity. . . .

I think that it is high time for the United States Senate and its members to do some real soul-searching and to weigh our consciences as to the manner in which we are performing our duty to the people of America and the manner in which we are using or abusing our individual powers and privileges.

I think it is high time that we remembered that we have sworn to uphold and defend the Constitution. I think it is high time that we remembered that the Constitution, as amended, speaks not only of the freedom of speech but also of trial by jury instead of trial by accusation. . . .

Those of us who shout the loudest about Americanism in making character assassinations are all too frequently those who, by our own words and acts, ignore some of the basic principles of Americanism—The right to criticize, the right to hold unpopular beliefs, the right to protest, the right of independent thought. . . .

ANALYZING PRIMARY SOURCES

1. **CRITICAL THINKING** Explain what Smith meant when she contrasted "trial by jury" with "trial by accusation."

2. **WRITING ACTIVITY** Imagine that you are a senator who disagrees with Senator Smith's statement. Write a rebuttal of several paragraphs that you would give on the Senate floor.

798

One of the best-known African American women in political life is Barbara Jordan. In 1965 Jordan, then a Houston lawyer, won election to the Texas Senate, where she served until 1972. She was the first black woman member of the state senate. From 1973 to 1979 Jordan served in the United States House of Representatives. In 1976 she became the first African American keynote speaker at a national convention of the Democratic Party. While in Congress, Jordan was a member of the House Judiciary Committee, which held the famous Watergate hearings during 1974. The following remarks are taken from a statement she made during Committee meetings on July 25.

Debate on Articles of Impeachment (1974)

Earlier today we heard the beginning of the Preamble to the Constitution of the United States, We, the people. It is a very eloquent beginning. But when that document was completed on the 17th of September in 1787 I was not included in that "We, the people." I felt somehow for many years that George Washington and Alexander Hamilton just left me out by mistake. But through the process of amendment, interpretation and court decision I have finally been included in "We, the people."

Today, I am an inquisitor. . . . My faith in the Constitution is whole, it is complete, it is total. I am not going to sit here and be an idle spectator to the diminution, the subversion, the destruction of the Constitution. . . .

James Madison [said] at the Constitutional Convention: "A President is impeachable if he attempts to subvert the Constitution."

The Constitution charges the President with the task of taking care that the laws be faithfully executed, and yet the President has counseled his aides to commit perjury, willfully disregarded the secrecy of grand jury proceedings, concealed surreptitious entry, attempted to compromise a Federal judge while publicly displaying his cooperation with the processes of criminal justice. . . .

If the impeachment provision in the Constitution of the United States will not reach the offenses charged here, then perhaps that 18th century Constitution should be abandoned to a 20th century paper shredder. . . .

ANALYZING PRIMARY SOURCES

1. **CRITICAL THINKING** Why did the writers of the Constitution *not* give the House of Representatives the power to put on trial a President it had impeached?

2. **WRITING ACTIVITY** Imagine that you and a group of foreign visitors unfamiliar with American government are present for Representative Jordan's remarks. Write a brief explanation of the situation for them.

Barbara Jordan
1936–

SPEAKING OUT

799

Speaking Out
Analyzing Primary Sources

1. To help ensure that opponents of a President do not misuse the impeachment process to oust the President.

2. Explanations should describe the House's role in the impeachment process and the outlines of the Watergate scandal.

1. In choosing a President, Americans focus more on the candidates' characters than their political parties.

2. Some students may agree with Wilson, arguing that gaining the public's trust is the President's most important job. Other students may disagree with Wilson, claiming that without political skills no President could gain the accomplishments needed for public support.

SPEAKING OUT

Woodrow Wilson
1856–1924

P robably no other President has studied American government as thoroughly before *taking office as Woodrow Wilson*. For two decades Wilson wrote, taught, and lectured about American government, history, and economics at several colleges. In 1908 he published Constitutional Government in the United States, *from which this description of the presidency is taken. Entering politics in 1910, Wilson was elected governor of New Jersey. His progressive policies caught the attention of national Democratic Party leaders, and in 1912 Wilson won the presidency. Wilson guided the nation to victory in World War I, but the war interrupted his plans for reform, and his postwar hopes for peace were frustrated. He did, however, win the Nobel Prize for Peace in 1920.*

The Office of President (1908)

If the matter be looked at a little more closely, it will be seen that the office of President, as we have used and developed it, really does not demand actual experience in [political] affairs so much as particular qualities of mind and character which we are at least as likely to find outside the ranks of our public men as within them. . . . What the country will demand of the candidate will be, not that he be an astute politician, . . . but that he be a man such as it can trust, in character, in intention, in knowledge of its needs, in perception of the best means by which those needs may be met, in capacity to prevail by reason of his own weight and integrity. Sometimes the country believes in a party, but more often it believes in a man. . . .

The President is at liberty, both in law and conscience, to be as big a man as he can. . . .

How is it possible to sum up the duties and influence of such an office in such a system . . . ? In the view of the makers of the Constitution the President was to be legal executive; perhaps the leader of the nation; certainly not the leader of the party, at any rate while in office. But by the operation of forces inherent in the very nature of government he has become all three, and by inevitable consequence the most heavily burdened officer in the world. No other man's day is so full as his, so full of the responsibilities which tax mind and conscience alike and demand an inexhaustible vitality. . . .

ANALYZING PRIMARY SOURCES

1. **CRITICAL THINKING** Explain the statement "Sometimes the country believes in a party, but more often it believes in a man."

2. **WRITING ACTIVITY** Write an essay stating and defending your opinion of Wilson's claim that the presidency "really does not demand actual experience in [political] affairs."

800

*L*ouis D. Brandeis, the first Jewish justice on the Supreme Court, was one of this century's best-known jurists. After a successful career as a lawyer, during which time he championed the causes of consumers, labor unions, and small businesses against giant corporations, Brandeis was appointed to the Supreme Court by President Woodrow Wilson in 1916. In his 23 years on the Court, Brandeis spoke out against government interference with freedom of speech and of the press. His outspoken liberal views often put him in the minority against a generally conservative Court. In a landmark 1928 case, the majority of the Court ruled that wiretapping a person's telephone without a warrant was not an illegal "search and seizure." Brandeis strongly disagreed in the dissent below.

PRIMARY SOURCE
SPEAKING OUT

Louis Brandeis
1856–1941

Olmstead v. United States (1928)

The makers of our Constitution undertook to secure conditions favorable to the pursuit of happiness. They recognized the significance of man's spiritual nature, of his feelings, and of his intellect. They knew that only a part of the pain, pleasure, and satisfactions of life are to be found in material things. They sought to protect Americans in their beliefs, their thoughts. . . .

Experience should teach us to be most on our guard to protect liberty when the government's purposes are beneficent. Men born to freedom are naturally alert to repel invasion of their liberty by evil-minded rulers. The greatest dangers to liberty lurk in insidious encroachment by men of zeal, well-meaning but without understanding. . . .

Decency, security, and liberty alike demand that government officials shall be subjected to the same rules of conduct that are commands to the citizen. In a government of laws, existence of the government will be imperiled if it fails to observe the law scrupulously. Our government is the potent, the omnipresent teacher. For good or for ill, it teaches the whole people by its example. Crime is contagious. If the government becomes a lawbreaker, it breeds contempt for law; it invites every man to become a law unto himself; it invites anarchy. To declare that in the administration of the criminal law the end justifies the means—to declare that the government may commit crimes in order to secure the conviction of a private criminal—would bring terrible retribution. Against this pernicious doctrine this court should resolutely set its face.

ANALYZING PRIMARY SOURCES

1. **CRITICAL THINKING** Summarize the second paragraph in your own words.
2. **WRITING ACTIVITY** Write a brief essay explaining how the Olmstead case reflected the effects of technological change on constitutional interpretation.

801

Speaking Out
Analyzing Primary Sources
1. The most dangerous threats to liberty come not from those who oppose it, but from those who destroy liberty while trying to protect it.
2. Essays should focus on the fact that modern technology enables authorities to "search" homes without actually entering them.

PRIMARY SOURCE
SPEAKING OUT

SPEAKING OUT

George Marshall
1880–1959

I n 1947 George Marshall, a five-star army general, became the first military man ever to be named Secretary of State. Marshall had been the leading strategist for U.S. military operations during World War II. As Secretary of State (1947–1949), Marshall is best remembered for his far-reaching plan that helped rebuild Western Europe. Marshall presented the European Recovery Program (usually called the Marshall Plan) in this speech at Harvard University on June 5, 1947.

The Marshall Plan (1947)

The remedy lies in . . . restoring the confidence of the European people in the economic future of their own countries and of Europe as a whole. . . .

It is logical that the United States should do whatever it is able to do to assist in the return of normal economic health in the world, without which there can be no political stability and no assured peace. Our policy is directed not against any country or doctrine but against hunger, poverty, desperation, and chaos. Its purpose should be the revival of a working economy in the world so as to permit the emergence of political and social conditions in which free institutions can exist. Such assistance, I am convinced, must not be on a piecemeal basis as various crises develop. . . .

It is already evident that, before the United States government can proceed much further in its efforts to alleviate the situation and help start the European world on its way to recovery, there must be some agreement among the countries of Europe as to the requirements of the situation and the part those countries themselves will take. . . . The initiative, I think, must come from Europe. The role of this country should consist of friendly aid in the drafting of a European program and of later support of such a program so far as it may be practical for us to do so. The program should be a joint one. . . .

An essential part of any successful action on the part of the United States is an understanding on the part of the people of America of the character of the problem and the remedies to be applied. Political passion and prejudice should have no part. With foresight, and a willingness on the part of our people to face up to the vast responsibility which history has clearly placed upon our country, the difficulties I have outlined can and will be overcome.

ANALYZING PRIMARY SOURCES

1. **CRITICAL THINKING** Marshall claimed that free institutions depend upon a country's economic health. Explain the connection.

2. **WRITING ACTIVITY** Imagine that you are a resident of a Western European country. Write a letter to the editor explaining your attitude toward the Marshall Plan.

One of the most influential policy-makers of the New Deal was Secretary of Labor Frances Perkins, the first woman Cabinet member. A former private school teacher, Perkins had been drawn to social reform movements in the early 1900's. She joined the women's suffrage movement and spent many years working to improve factory conditions in New York. As a member of the Roosevelt Cabinet from 1933 to 1945, Perkins strengthened the Labor Department and backed policies such as the minimum wage and the 48-hour week. In this radio speech, broadcast in 1935, Perkins spoke out in favor of the controversial Social Security Act, which she helped write.

The Social Security Act (1935)

People who work for a living in the United States of America can join with all other good citizens on this forty-eighth anniversary of Labor Day in satisfaction that the Congress has passed the Social Security Act. This act establishes unemployment insurance as a substitute for haphazard methods of assistance in periods when men and women willing and able to work are without jobs. It provides for old age pensions which mark great progress over the measures upon which we have hitherto depended in caring for those who have been unable to provide for the years when they no longer can work. . . .

While it is not anticipated as a complete remedy for the abnormal conditions confronting us at the present time, it is designed to afford protection for the individual against future major economic vicissitudes. . . .

Our social security program will be a vital force working against the recurrence of severe depressions in the future. We can, as the principle of sustained purchasing power in hard times makes itself felt in every shop, store, and mill, grow old without being haunted by the spectre of a poverty-ridden old age or of being a burden on our children. . . .

The passage of this act . . . is deeply significant of the progress which the American people have made in thought in the social field and awareness of methods of using cooperation through government to overcome social hazards against which the individual alone is inadequate. . . .

ANALYZING PRIMARY SOURCES

1. **CRITICAL THINKING** What did Perkins mean by "the abnormal conditions confronting us at the present time"?

2. **CRITICAL THINKING** Perkins argued that Social Security would help avoid future depressions. How might it do this?

3. **WRITING ACTIVITY** Reread the last paragraph of the excerpt. Write a brief essay explaining Perkins' view of the government's proper role in the economy.

Frances Perkins
1882–1965

SPEAKING OUT

803

Speaking Out
Analyzing Primary Sources

1. The Great Depression.

2. By putting money in the hands of consumers, the program would help maintain business activity during economic slowdowns.

3. Essays should mention Perkins' view that government can and should take measures to protect individuals from economic downturns.

Speaking Out
Analyzing Primary Sources
1. To emphasize the gains made by African Americans since that time.

2. Problems include health issues (such as lead paint and child care), the need to care properly for senior citizens, a budget shortfall, discrimination against minority groups, and crime.

SPEAKING OUT

David Dinkins
1927–

O n January 1, 1990, David Dinkins was inaugurated as the first African American mayor in New York City's 365-year history. A graduate of Howard University and Brooklyn Law School, Dinkins won a seat in the New York State Assembly in 1966. Dinkins also served as president of the New York City Board of Elections before becoming City Clerk of New York from 1975 to 1985. He was elected Manhattan Borough President in 1985, a position he held until his election as mayor. The following excerpts from Dinkins' inaugural address show his vision for the United States' largest city.

Inaugural Address (1990)

I stand before you today as the elected leader of the greatest city of a great nation, to which my ancestors were brought, chained and whipped in the hold of a slaveship. We have not finished the journey toward liberty and justice, but surely we have come a long way. . . .

I see New York as a gorgeous mosaic of race and religious faith . . . of individuals whose families arrived yesterday and generations ago, coming through Ellis Island, or Kennedy Airport, or on Greyhound buses. . . .

This administration . . . will emphasize community-based efforts to provide prenatal care, lead screening, child care, after-school programs, and centers of culture and companionship for seniors. I recognize that we cannot do everything we should, that our finances may get worse before they get better, that for now our dreams are bigger than our budget. As a city, we cannot live beyond our means, but we will never be mean-spirited, and we must never lose sight of our dreams. . . .

We must demand the equality of women—and defend a woman's right to choose. We must oppose discrimination in any form against anyone. In dealing with AIDS, we must seek to cure the disease—and not to curse the afflicted. Most of all we must reaffirm the rule of law, fight back against the pushers and muggers, and take back our streets, our subways, and our parks. . . .

I believe that individuals can make a difference; but I also believe that there are great differences only government can make. Our city budget is complex. Yet our purpose is simple . . . to improve the standard-of-life for each and every citizen.

ANALYZING PRIMARY SOURCES

1. CRITICAL THINKING Why might Dinkins have mentioned in his speech the fact that his ancestors were slaves?

2. WRITING ACTIVITY Using the excerpt as your source, write a short essay outlining the major problems facing New York City.

804

One of the most respected world leaders of this century was Jawaharlal Nehru of India. In the 1920's Nehru became a leader of the Indian movement for independence from Britain. When independence came in 1947, Nehru was chosen as the new country's first prime minister, serving in that office until his death in 1964. In 1949, on a tour of the United States, he gave his impressions of this nation and its people.

Impressions of America (1949)

. . . How do you form impressions of countries? Certainly from what you read or hear about them. But ultimately you form impressions by the people you meet from those countries. . . .

Even a brief visit may give some insight into the ideals and objectives and the springs of action of a nation. And so I made myself receptive in order to understand somewhat the spirit of America and the sources of the inner strength that has made her great. . . .

The picture of the average American presented to the outside world is of a hardheaded, efficient, and practical businessman, intent on making money and using that money to add to his power and influence. That picture, no doubt, has some truth in it. And yet there is another picture, and, I think, a much more enduring one, of a warmhearted and very generous people, full of good will to others and with a firm belief in the basic principles on which this great republic was founded—the principles of freedom, equality, and democracy. It has been my good fortune to see this latter picture wherever I have gone, and this has made me realize wherein lies the real strength of America.

Everywhere I have found a love of freedom and a desire for peace and co-operation, and, among the people, a frankness and human approach which make a friendly understanding easier. . . .

During these wanderings of mine I have noticed the great variety of American life and at the same time the fundamental unity of it. I have been reminded again and again of my own country with its vast extent and its diversity and unity. The United States, astride between two great oceans, looks out to the east toward Europe on the one side and to the west toward Asia. So, also, India has many windows looking out at various parts of the great Asian continent. . . .

ANALYZING PRIMARY SOURCES

1. **CRITICAL THINKING** India, like the United States, is a large country containing many different ethnic groups. Why are the terms *diversity* and *unity* important concepts for such nations?

2. **WRITING ACTIVITY** Write a brief essay explaining how visiting a country helps one understand its people.

Jawaharlal Nehru
1889–1964

Speaking Out
Analyzing Primary Sources

1. Diversity can benefit a country by enriching its culture, but without an underlying unity of beliefs the nation may break apart.

2. Visiting a country allows one a chance to meet the common people—not merely the tourists and businesspersons who travel abroad—and see them in their own surroundings.

UNITED STATES: Political

ALASKA

RUSSIA

ARCTIC OCEAN

Arctic Circle

Yukon River

Alaska

Fairbanks

CANADA

Anchorage

Juneau

ALEUTIAN ISLANDS

| 0 | 300 | 600 mi. |
| 0 | 300 | 600 km |

170°E 180 170°W 160°W 150°W 140°W 130°W

65°N 60°N 55°N

PACIFIC

OCEAN

Seattle
Washington
Olympia
Columbia River
Portland
Salem
Oregon

Idaho
Boise
Pocatello
Snake River

Helena Montana
Billings

Wyomin
Casper
Che

Nevada
Carson City
San Francisco
Sacramento

Salt Lake City
Provo
Utah

Den
Colorad

California
Las Vegas

Los Angeles

San Diego

Arizona
Phoenix
Tucson

Santa Fe
Albuquerque

New Mexi

M E X I

HAWAII

KAUAI
NIIHAU
OAHU
Honolulu
MOLOKAI
LANAI MAUI
KAHOOLAWE

PACIFIC
OCEAN Hawaii

HAWAII Hilo

160°W 155°W

20°N

| 0 | 100 | 200 mi. |
| 0 | 100 | 200 km |

⊕ National capital
★ State capital
• Major city
— National boundary
— State boundary

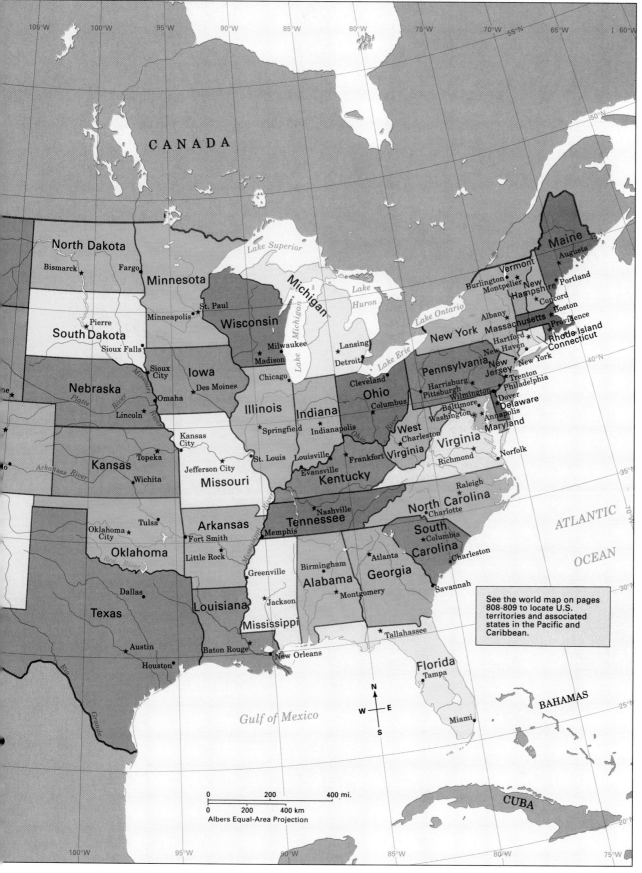

CANADA

North Dakota
Bismarck ★　★Fargo
Minnesota
Pierre ★　St. Paul ★
Minneapolis ●
South Dakota
Sioux Falls ●
Wisconsin
Milwaukee ●
Madison ★
Sioux City ●
Iowa
Nebraska
Omaha ●
Lincoln ★
Des Moines ★
Kansas City ●
Lake Superior
Michigan
Lake Huron
Lake Michigan
Lansing ★
Detroit ●
Lake Erie
Chicago ●
Illinois
Indiana
Springfield ★　Indianapolis ★
Cleveland ●
Ohio
Columbus ★
Kansas
Topeka ★
Wichita ●
Jefferson City ★
St. Louis ●
Louisville ●
Frankfort ★
Kentucky
Missouri
Evansville ●
Nashville ★
Lake Ontario
New York
Pennsylvania
Harrisburg ★
Pittsburgh ●
Albany ★
Lake Erie
West Virginia
Charleston ★
Virginia
Richmond ★
Norfolk ●
Vermont
Burlington ●
Montpelier ★
New Hampshire
Concord ★
Maine
Augusta ★
Portland ●
Boston ★
Providence ★
Massachusetts
Hartford ★
New Haven ●
Rhode Island
Connecticut
New York ●
New Jersey
Trenton ★
Philadelphia ●
Wilmington ●
Baltimore ●
Washington ●
Annapolis ★
Dover ★
Delaware
Maryland
Oklahoma
Tulsa ●
Oklahoma City ★
Fort Smith ●
Little Rock ★
Arkansas
Memphis ●
Tennessee
Greenville ●
Birmingham ●
Montgomery ★
Atlanta ★
North Carolina
Raleigh ★
Charlotte ●
South Carolina
Columbia ★
Charleston ●
Savannah ●
Georgia
Alabama
Texas
Dallas ●
Austin ★
Houston ●
Louisiana
Jackson ★
Baton Rouge ★
New Orleans ●
Mississippi
Tallahassee ★
Florida
Tampa ●
Miami ●

Nebraska
Platte River
Missouri River
Arkansas River
Red River
Rio Grande
Ohio River
Mississippi River

ATLANTIC OCEAN

See the world map on pages 808-809 to locate U.S. territories and associated states in the Pacific and Caribbean.

Gulf of Mexico

BAHAMAS

CUBA

N
W · E
S

| 0 | 200 | 400 mi. |
| 0 | 200 | 400 km |
Albers Equal-Area Projection

WORLD: Political

ABBREVIATIONS

BOS. AND HERZ.
  Bosnia and Herzegovina
CEN. AFR. REP.
  Central African Republic
DEN. Denmark
FR. France
GR. Greece
IT. Italy
N. North, Northern
NETH. Netherlands
N.Z. New Zealand
PORT. Portugal
S. South
SP. Spain
U.A.E. United Arab
  Emirates
U.K. United Kingdom
U.S. United States
W. Western

—— National boundary

World Political Map

180° 160°W 140°W 120°W 100°W 80°W 60°W

ARCTIC OCEAN

80°N

GREENLAND (Den.)

ALASKA (U.S.)

60°N

CANADA

NORTH AMERICA

UNITED STATES

40°N

PACIFIC OCEAN

AZORES (Port.)

MADE

ATLANTIC OCEAN

Area of inset

BERMUDA (U.K.)

CA

MIDWAY ISLANDS (U.S.)

Tropic of Cancer

MEXICO

20°N

HAWAII (U.S.)

CAPE VERDE G

GUINEA

VENEZUELA GUYANA SURINAME

COLOMBIA FRENCH GUIANA (Fr.)

0°

KIRIBATI

Equator

GALÁPAGOS ISLANDS (Ecuador)

ECUADOR

SOUTH AMERICA

TOKELAU (N.Z.)

W. SAMOA

AMERICAN SAMOA (U.S.)

FRENCH POLYNESIA (Fr.)

PERU

BRAZIL

20°S

COOK ISLANDS (N.Z.)

TONGA

NIUE (N.Z.)

Tropic of Capricorn

PITCAIRN ISLAND (U.K.)

BOLIVIA

PARAGUAY

EASTER ISLAND (Chile)

CHILE

URUGUAY

PACIFIC OCEAN

40°S

ARGENTINA

FALKLAND ISLANDS (U.K.)

SOUTH GEORGIA (U.K.)

60°S

Antarctic Circle

80°S

180 160°W 140°W 120°W 100°W 80°W 60°W

MEXICO, CENTRAL AMERICA, AND THE CARIBBEAN

100°W 90°W 80°W

UNITED STATES

30°W

30°N

ATLANTIC OCEAN

Gulf of Mexico

BAHAMAS

20°N

Tropic of Cancer

MEXICO

CUBA

TURKS AND CAICOS ISLANDS (U.K.)

VIRGIN ISLANDS (U.S./U.K.)

ANGUILLA (U.K.)
ST. MARTIN (Fr./Neth.)
ANTIGUA AND BARBUDA

20°N

CAYMAN ISLANDS (U.K.)

HAITI DOMINICAN REPUBLIC

JAMAICA

PUERTO RICO (U.S.)

ST. KITTS AND NEVIS

MONTSERRAT (U.K.)
GUADELOUPE (Fr.)

DOMINICA

MARTINIQUE (Fr.)

ST. LUCIA

BELIZE

GUATEMALA HONDURAS

Caribbean Sea

ST. VINCENT AND THE GRENADINES

BARBADOS

EL SALVADOR NICARAGUA

ARUBA (Neth.)

NETHERLANDS ANTILLES (Neth.)

GRENADA

TRINIDAD AND TOBAGO

10°N

PACIFIC OCEAN

Panama Canal

COSTA RICA

PANAMA

VENEZUELA

0 300 600 mi.

0 300 600 km

Azimuthal Equal-Area Projection

90°W

COLOMBIA

80°W

70°W

GUYANA

SURINAME

808

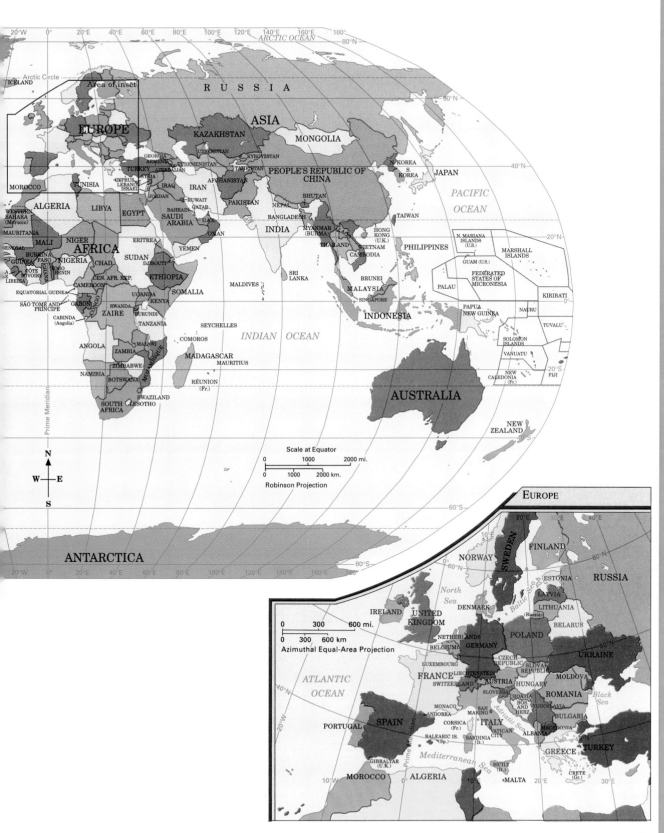

ARCTIC OCEAN

Arctic Circle
ICELAND
Area of inset

RUSSIA

EUROPE

ASIA

KAZAKHSTAN

MONGOLIA

GEORGIA
ARMENIA
UZBEKISTAN
KYRGYZSTAN
TURKEY
AZERBAIJAN
TURKMENISTAN
CYPRUS
LEBANON
SYRIA
TAJIKISTAN
ISRAEL
JORDAN
IRAQ
IRAN
AFGHANISTAN

PEOPLE'S REPUBLIC OF
CHINA

N. KOREA
S. KOREA

JAPAN

MOROCCO
TUNISIA

PACIFIC
OCEAN

ALGERIA
LIBYA
EGYPT
SAUDI
ARABIA
KUWAIT
BAHRAIN
QATAR
PAKISTAN
NEPAL
BHUTAN
BANGLADESH

TAIWAN

WESTERN
SAHARA
(Morocco)

U.A.E.

MAURITANIA

OMAN
INDIA
MYANMAR
(BURMA)
HONG KONG
(U.K.)

N. MARIANA
ISLANDS
(U.S.)

MALI
NIGER
ERITREA
YEMEN
THAILAND
VIETNAM
PHILIPPINES

MARSHALL
ISLANDS

SENEGAL
AFRICA
SUDAN
DJIBOUTI
CAMBODIA

GUAM (U.S.)

BURKINA
FASO
NIGERIA
CHAD
FEDERATED
STATES OF
MICRONESIA

GUINEA
CÔTE
D'IVOIRE
TOGO
BENIN
CEN. AFR. REP.
ETHIOPIA
SRI
LANKA
BRUNEI

PALAU

LIBERIA
CAMEROON
UGANDA
MALDIVES
MALAYSIA
KIRIBATI

EQUATORIAL GUINEA
GABON
KENYA
SOMALIA
SINGAPORE

SÃO TOMÉ AND
PRÍNCIPE
CONGO
RWANDA
ZAIRE
BURUNDI

INDONESIA

PAPUA
NEW GUINEA

NAURU

CABINDA
(Angola)
TANZANIA
SEYCHELLES

TUVALU

SOLOMON
ISLANDS

ANGOLA
MALAWI
COMOROS
INDIAN OCEAN

VANUATU

ZAMBIA
MADAGASCAR
MAURITIUS

NEW
CALEDONIA
(Fr.)
FIJI

NAMIBIA
ZIMBABWE
MOZAMBIQUE
BOTSWANA
RÉUNION
(Fr.)

AUSTRALIA

SWAZILAND
SOUTH
AFRICA
LESOTHO

N
W   E
S

Scale at Equator
0   1000   2000 mi.
0   1000   2000 km.
Robinson Projection

NEW
ZEALAND

ANTARCTICA

WORLD MAP

EUROPE

SWEDEN
FINLAND

NORWAY

ESTONIA

North
Sea
RUSSIA

IRELAND
UNITED
KINGDOM
DENMARK

Baltic Sea
LATVIA
LITHUANIA
(Russia)
BELARUS

POLAND

NETHERLANDS
BELGIUM
GERMANY
UKRAINE

0   300   600 mi.
0   300   600 km.
Azimuthal Equal-Area Projection

LUXEMBOURG
CZECH
REPUBLIC
SLOVAK
REPUBLIC
MOLDOVA

FRANCE
LIECHTENSTEIN
SWITZERLAND
AUSTRIA
HUNGARY
ROMANIA

ATLANTIC
OCEAN

SLOVENIA
CROATIA
Black
Sea

MONACO
BOS.
AND
HERZ.
YUGOSLAVIA
BULGARIA

ANDORRA
SAN
MARINO
ITALY
MACEDONIA

PORTUGAL
SPAIN
CORSICA
(Fr.)
VATICAN
CITY
ALBANIA
GREECE
TURKEY

BALEARIC IS.
(Sp.)
SARDINIA
(It.)

GIBRALTAR
(U.K.)
Mediterranean Sea
SICILY
(It.)
CRETE
(Gr.)

MOROCCO
ALGERIA
MALTA

PRESIDENTS OF THE UNITED STATES

PRESIDENT (years in office)	POLITICAL PARTY	PLACE OF BIRTH	BORN DIED	RELIGIOUS AFFILIATION	PREVIOUS OCCUPATION
1. George Washington (1789–1797)	None	Westmoreland County, VA	1732 1799	Episcopalian	Planter; Soldier
2. John Adams (1797–1801)	Federalist	Braintree (now Quincy), MA	1735 1826	Unitarian	Lawyer; Diplomat
3. Thomas Jefferson (1801–1809)	Democratic - Republican	Shadwell, VA	1743 1826	Unitarian	Planter; Lawyer
4. James Madison (1809–1817)	Democratic - Republican	Port Conway, VA	1751 1836	Episcopalian	Lawyer
5. James Monroe (1817–1825)	Democratic - Republican	Westmoreland County, VA	1758 1831	Episcopalian	Lawyer
6. John Quincy Adams (1825–1829)	Democratic - Republican	Braintree (now Quincy), MA	1767 1848	Unitarian	Lawyer; Diplomat
7. Andrew Jackson (1829–1837)	Democratic	Waxhaw, SC	1767 1845	Presbyterian	Lawyer; Soldier
8. Martin Van Buren (1837–1841)	Democratic	Kinderhook, NY	1782 1862	Dutch Reformed	Lawyer
9. William Henry Harrison[b] (1841)	Whig	Charles City County, VA	1773 1841	Episcopalian	Soldier; Farmer
10. John Tyler (1841–1845)	Whig	Charles City County, VA	1790 1862	Episcopalian	Lawyer
11. James K. Polk (1845–1849)	Democratic	Mecklenburg County, NC	1795 1849	Presbyterian	Lawyer
12. Zachary Taylor[b] (1849–1850)	Whig	Orange County, VA	1784 1850	Episcopalian	Soldier
13. Millard Fillmore (1850–1853)	Whig	Locke, NY	1800 1874	Unitarian	Lawyer; Teacher
14. Franklin Pierce (1853–1857)	Democratic	Hillsboro, NH	1804 1869	Episcopalian	Lawyer
15. James Buchanan (1857–1861)	Democratic	Mercersburg, PA	1791 1868	Presbyterian	Lawyer; Diplomat
16. Abraham Lincoln[c] (1861–1865)	Republican	Hardin (now Larue) County, KY	1809 1865	Presbyterian	Lawyer
17. Andrew Johnson (1865–1869)	Democratic[d]	Raleigh, NC	1808 1875	Methodist	Tailor
18. Ulysses S. Grant (1869–1877)	Republican	Point Pleasant, OH	1822 1885	Methodist	Soldier
19. Rutherford B. Hayes (1877–1881)	Republican	Delaware, OH	1822 1893	Methodist	Lawyer
20. James A. Garfield[c] (1881)	Republican	Orange, OH	1831 1881	Disciples of Christ	Teacher; Soldier

[a] Resigned.   [b] Died in office.   [c] Assassinated.   [d] In 1864 the Republicans, campaigning as the Union Party, chose War Democrat Andrew Johnson to be Lincoln's running mate.

DATE MARRIED/ SPOUSE'S NAME (children)	VICE PRESIDENT	IMPORTANT EVENTS
1759–Martha Dandridge Custis (none)	John Adams	Judiciary Act creates federal courts (1789); first census (1790); Bill of Rights ratified (1791).
1764–Abigail Smith (5)	Thomas Jefferson	Alien and Sedition Acts (1798); Library of Congress est.; Washington, D.C., planned as capital (1800).
1772–Martha Wayles Skelton (6)	Aaron Burr; George Clinton	*Marbury v. Madison*; Louisiana Purchase (1803); Embargo Acts (1807–1808).
1794–Dolley Payne Todd (none)	George Clinton; Elbridge Gerry	War with Great Britain begins (1812); British seize Washington, D.C.; Hartford Convention (1814).
1786–Elizabeth Kortright (3)	Daniel D. Tompkins	*McCulloch v. Maryland* (1819); Monroe Doctrine (1823); *Gibbons v. Ogden* (1824).
1797–Louisa Catherine Johnson (4)	John C. Calhoun	Erie Canal opened (1825); Noah Webster publishes *American Dictionary of the English Language* (1828).
1791–Rachel Donelson Robards (none)	John C. Calhoun[a] Martin Van Buren	Nat Turner's slave uprising in VA (1831); Whig Party organized (1834); TX declares independence (1836).
1807–Hannah Hoes (4)	Richard M. Johnson	Panic of 1837; Underground Railroad organized (1838).
1795–Anna Symmes (10)	John Tyler	First President to die in office (1841).
1813–Letitia Christian (8) 1844–Julia Gardiner (7)	None	Dorr's Rebellion (1841); Congress sets uniform presidential election day; TX annexation (1845).
1824–Sarah Childress (none)	George M. Dallas	War with Mexico begins (1846); first women's rights convention (1848); CA gold rush (1849).
1810–Margaret Mackall Smith (6)	Millard Fillmore	Department of the Interior created; Elizabeth Blackwell becomes first American woman to receive M.D. (1849).
1826–Abigail Powers 1858–Caroline McIntosh (2)	None	Compromise of 1850; Harriet Beecher Stowe's *Uncle Tom's Cabin* published (1852).
1834–Jane Means Appleton (3)	William R. King	Republican Party organized; Kansas-Nebraska Act (1854).
Never married	John C. Breckinridge	Pony Express operates mail service (1860); Confederate States of America formed (1861).
1842–Mary Todd (4)	Hannibal Hamlin; Andrew Johnson	Civil War begins; Homestead Act (1862); Emancipation Proclamation; Gettysburg Address (1863).
1827–Eliza McCardle (5)	None	13th Amendment passed (1865); Civil Rights Act (1866); Johnson impeached (1868).
1848–Julia Boggs Dent (4)	Schuyler Colfax; Henry Wilson	Transcontinental railroad completed (1869); Dept. of Justice established (1870); *Munn v. Illinois* (1877).
1852–Lucy Ware Webb (8)	William A. Wheeler	Reconstruction ends as last federal troops are withdrawn from South (1877).
1858–Lucretia Rudolph (5)	Chester A. Arthur	American Red Cross founded by Clara Barton; Tuskegee Institute founded by Booker T. Washington (1881).

PRESIDENTS OF THE
UNITED STATES (continued)

PRESIDENT (years in office)	POLITICAL PARTY	PLACE OF BIRTH	BORN DIED	RELIGIOUS AFFILIATION	PREVIOUS OCCUPATION
21. Chester A. Arthur (1881–1885)	Republican	Fairfield, VT	1829 1886	Episcopalian	Lawyer; Teacher
22. Grover Cleveland (1885–1889)	Democratic	Caldwell, NJ	1837 1908	Presbyterian	Lawyer
23. Benjamin Harrison (1889–1893)	Republican	North Bend, OH	1833 1901	Presbyterian	Lawyer; Soldier
24. Grover Cleveland (1893–1897)	Democratic	Caldwell, NJ	1837 1908	Presbyterian	Lawyer
25. William McKinley[c] (1897–1901)	Republican	Niles, OH	1843 1901	Methodist	Lawyer; Teacher
26. Theodore Roosevelt (1901–1909)	Republican	New York, NY	1858 1919	Dutch Reformed	Rancher; Soldier; Writer
27. William H. Taft (1909–1913)	Republican	Cincinnati, OH	1857 1930	Unitarian	Lawyer
28. Woodrow Wilson (1913–1921)	Democratic	Staunton, VA	1856 1924	Presbyterian	Teacher
29. Warren G. Harding[b] (1921–1923)	Republican	Corsica, OH	1865 1923	Baptist	Publisher
30. Calvin Coolidge (1923–1929)	Republican	Plymouth, VT	1872 1933	Congregational	Lawyer
31. Herbert C. Hoover (1929–1933)	Republican	West Branch, IA	1874 1964	Quaker	Engineer
32. Franklin D. Roosevelt[b] (1933–1945)	Democratic	Hyde Park, NY	1882 1945	Episcopalian	Lawyer
33. Harry S Truman (1945–1953)	Democratic	Lamar, MO	1884 1972	Baptist	Farmer; Haberdasher
34. Dwight D. Eisenhower (1953–1961)	Republican	Denison, TX	1890 1969	Presbyterian	Soldier
35. John F. Kennedy[c] (1961–1963)	Democratic	Brookline, MA	1917 1963	Roman Catholic	Writer
36. Lyndon B. Johnson (1963–1969)	Democratic	Stonewall, TX	1908 1973	Disciples of Christ	Teacher
37. Richard M. Nixon[a] (1969–1974)	Republican	Yorba Linda, CA	1913 1994	Quaker	Lawyer
38. Gerald R. Ford (1974–1977)	Republican	Omaha, NE	1913	Episcopalian	Lawyer
39. Jimmy Carter (1977–1981)	Democratic	Plains, GA	1924	Baptist	Farmer; Business person
40. Ronald Reagan (1981–1989)	Republican	Tampico, IL	1911	Disciples of Christ	Actor; Union leader
41. George Bush (1989–1993)	Republican	Milton, MA	1924	Episcopalian	Business person
42. Bill Clinton (1993–)	Democratic	Hope, AR	1946	Baptist	Lawyer

[a] Resigned.   [b] Died in office.   [c] Assassinated.

DATE MARRIED/ SPOUSE'S NAME (children)	VICE PRESIDENT	IMPORTANT EVENTS
1859–Ellen Lewis Herndon (3)	None	Standard Oil Trust organized (1882); Pendleton Act (1883); first "skyscraper" begun in Chicago (1884).
1886–Frances Folsom (5)	Thomas A. Hendricks	AFL organized (1886); Interstate Commerce Act (1887); secret ballot introduced in KY (1888).
1853–Caroline Lavinia Scott 1896–Mary Dimmick (3)	Levi P. Morton	Sherman Antitrust Act (1890); Congress establishes U.S. Courts of Appeals (1891).
1886–Frances Folsom (5)	Adlai E. Stevenson	*Plessy v. Ferguson* (1896).
1871–Ida Saxton (2)	Garrett A. Hobart Theodore Roosevelt	Spanish-American War; Hawaii annexed (1898); first direct primary held in Minnesota (1900).
1880–Alice Hathaway Lee 1886–Edith Carow (6)	Charles W. Fairbanks	Dept. of Commerce and Labor created (1903); Roosevelt Corollary (1904); Pure Food and Drug Act (1906).
1886–Helen Herron (3)	James S. Sherman	NAACP founded (1909); *Titanic* sinks (1912); 16th Amendment allows income tax (1913).
1885–Ellen Louise Axson 1915–Edith Bolling Galt (3)	Thomas R. Marshall	WW I begins in Europe (1914); 19th Amendment gives women the vote (1920).
1891–Florence Kling DeWolfe (none)	Calvin Coolidge	Teapot Dome scandal (1922).
1905–Grace Anna Goodhue (2)	Charles G. Dawes	Indian Citizenship Act (1924); Nellie Tayloe Ross (WY) is first elected woman governor; Scopes trial (1925).
1899–Lou Henry (2)	Charles Curtis	Stock market crash begins Great Depression (1929).
1905–Anna Eleanor Roosevelt (6)	Garner, Wallace, Harry S Truman	New Deal (1933–1938); World War II begins (1939); Japanese bomb Pearl Harbor (1941).
1919–Elizabeth Virginia Wallace (1)	Alben W. Barkley	UN formed; WW II ends (1945); Taft-Hartley Act (1947); NATO formed (1949); Korean War begins (1950).
1916–Mamie Geneva Doud (2)	Richard M. Nixon	*Brown v. Board of Education* (1954); Civil Rights Commission established (1957).
1953–Jacqueline Bouvier (3)	Lyndon B. Johnson	Peace Corps established (1961); Cuban missile crisis (1962); *Gideon v. Wainwright* (1963).
1934–Claudia Alta "Lady Bird" Taylor (2)	Hubert H. Humphrey	Civil Rights Act (1964); U.S. sends troops to Vietnam; Voting Rights Act (1965); *Miranda v. Arizona* (1966).
1940–Thelma Catherine "Pat" Ryan (2)	Spiro T. Agnew[a] Gerald R. Ford	U.S. astronauts land on moon (1969); Nixon visits China; Watergate break-in (1972); OPEC oil embargo.
1948–Elizabeth "Betty" Bloomer (4)	Nelson A. Rockefeller	South Vietnam falls to Communists; Apollo/Soyuz, joint U.S.-Soviet space mission (1975).
1946–Rosalynn Smith (4)	Walter F. Mondale	Dept. of Energy created (1977); Camp David accords signed (1978); U.S. hostages held in Iran (1979–1981).
1940–Jane Wyman (2) 1952–Nancy Davis (2)	George Bush	Sandra Day O'Connor named to Supreme Court (1981); *Challenger* disaster (1986); Iran-*contra* affair (1986).
1945–Barbara Pierce (6)	James Danforth Quayle	Collapse of Berlin Wall (1989); U.S. invasion of Panama (1989); Gulf War (1991); Breakup of Soviet Union (1991).
1975–Hillary Rodham (1)	Albert A. Gore	Israeli peace treaty with Jordan (1994); Black majority rule in South Africa.

FACTS ABOUT THE STATES

State (adm. to Union)	Pop. 1992 (rank)	Area (sq. miles)	Counties	Major Cities (*state capital)	Nickname
Alabama (Dec. 14, 1819)	4,136,000 (22)	52,423	67	Birmingham/Mobile/ Montgomery*	Yellowhammer State
Alaska (Jan. 3, 1959)	587,000 (48)	656,424	12	Anchorage/Fairbanks/ Juneau*	Land of the Midnight Sun
Arizona (Feb. 14, 1912)	3,832,000 (23)	114,006	15	Phoenix*/Tucson	Grand Canyon State
Arkansas (June 15, 1836)	2,399,000 (33)	53,182	75	Little Rock*/Fort Smith	Land of Opportunity
California (Sept. 9, 1850)	30,867,000 (1)	163,707	58	Los Angeles/San Diego/ San Francisco/Sacramento*	Golden State
Colorado (Aug. 1, 1876)	3,470,000 (26)	104,100	63	Denver*/Colorado Springs	Centennial State
Connecticut (Jan. 9, 1788)	3,281,000 (27)	5,544	8	Bridgeport/Hartford*/ New Haven	Nutmeg State
Delaware (Dec. 7, 1787)	689,000 (46)	2,489	3	Wilmington/Newark/ Dover*	Diamond State
Florida (March 3, 1845)	13,488,000 (4)	65,758	67	Jacksonville/Miami/ Tampa/Tallahassee*	Sunshine State
Georgia (Jan. 2, 1788)	6,751,000 (11)	59,441	159	Atlanta*/Columbus/ Savannah	Peach State
Hawaii (August 21, 1959)	1,160,000 (40)	10,932	4	Honolulu*/Pearl City	Aloha State
Idaho (July 3, 1890)	1,067,000 (42)	83,574	44	Boise*/Pocatello	Gem State
Illinois (Dec. 3, 1818)	11,631,000 (6)	57,918	102	Chicago/Rockford/ Peoria/Springfield*	Prairie State
Indiana (Dec. 11, 1816)	5,662,000 (14)	36,420	92	Indianapolis*/Fort Wayne/ Gary	Hoosier State
Iowa (Dec. 28, 1846)	2,812,000 (30)	56,276	99	Des Moines*/Cedar Rapids	Hawkeye State
Kansas (Jan. 29, 1861)	2,523,000 (32)	82,282	105	Wichita/Kansas City/ Topeka*	Sunflower State
Kentucky (June 1, 1792)	3,755,000 (24)	40,411	120	Louisville/Lexington/ Frankfort*	Bluegrass State

State (adm. to Union)	Pop. 1992 (rank)	Area (sq. miles)	Counties	Major Cities (*state capital)	Nickname
Louisiana (April 30, 1812)	4,287,000 (21)	51,843	64	New Orleans/Baton Rouge*/ Shreveport	Pelican State
Maine (March 15,1820)	1,235,000 (39)	35,387	16	Portland/Augusta*	Pine Tree State
Maryland (April 28, 1788)	4,908,000 (19)	12,407	23	Baltimore/Annapolis*	Free State
Massachusetts (Feb. 6, 1788)	5,998,000 (13)	10,555	14	Boston*/Worcester/ Springfield	Bay State
Michigan (Jan. 26, 1837)	9,437,000 (8)	96,810	83	Detroit/Grand Rapids/ Lansing*	Wolverine State
Minnesota (May 11, 1858)	4,480,000 (20)	86,943	87	Minneapolis/St. Paul*/ Duluth	North Star State
Mississippi (Dec.10, 1817)	2,614,000 (31)	48,434	82	Jackson*/Biloxi	Magnolia State
Missouri (Aug. 10, 1821)	5,193,000 (15)	69,709	114	St. Louis/Kansas City/ Jefferson City*	Show-Me State
Montana (Nov. 8, 1889)	824,000 (44)	147,046	56,	Billings/Helena*	Treasure State
Nebraska (March 1, 1867)	1,606,000 (36)	77,358	93	Omaha/Lincoln*	Cornhusker State
Nevada (Oct. 31,1864)	1,327,000 (38)	110,567	16	Las Vegas/Reno/ Carson City*	Silver State
New Hampshire (June 21, 1788)	1,111,000 (41)	9,351	10	Manchester/Concord*	Granite State
New Jersey (Dec. 18, 1787)	7,789,000 (9)	8,722	21	Newark/Jersey City/ Trenton*	Garden State
New Mexico (Jan. 6, 1912)	1,581,000 (37)	121,598	33	Albuquerque/Sante Fe*	Land of Enchantment
New York (July 26, 1788)	18,119,000 (2)	54,475	62	New York/Buffalo/ Rochester/Albany*	Empire State
North Carolina (Nov. 21,1789)	6,843,000 (10)	53,821	100	Charlotte/Raleigh*/ Greensboro	Tar Heel State
North Dakota (Nov. 2, 1889)	636,000 (47)	70,704	53	Fargo/Bismarck*	Sioux State

FACTS ABOUT THE STATES   (continued)

State (adm. to Union)	Pop. 1992 (rank)	Area (sq. miles)	Counties	Major Cities (*state capital)	Nickname
Ohio (March 1, 1803)	11,016,000 (7)	44,828	88	Cleveland/Columbus*/ Cincinnati/Toledo	Buckeye State
Oklahoma (Nov. 16, 1907)	3,212,000 (28)	69,903	77	Oklahoma City*/Tulsa	Sooner State
Oregon (Feb. 14, 1859)	2,977,000 (29)	98,386	36	Portland/Eugene/Salem*	Beaver State
Pennsylvania (Dec. 12, 1787)	12,009,000 (5)	46,058	67	Philadelphia/Pittsburgh/ Harrisburg*	Keystone State
Rhode Island (May 29, 1790)	1,005,000 (43)	1,545	5	Providence*/Warwick/ Newport	Ocean State
South Carolina (May 23, 1788)	3,603,000 (25)	32,007	46	Columbia*/Charleston/ Greenville	Palmetto State
South Dakota (Nov. 2, 1889)	711,000 (45)	77,121	67	Sioux Falls/Pierre*	Coyote State
Tennessee (June 1, 1796)	5,024,000 (17)	42,126	95	Memphis/Nashville*/ Knoxville	Volunteer State
Texas (Dec. 29, 1845)	17,656,000 (3)	268,601	254	Houston/Dallas/ San Antonio/Austin*	Lone Star State
Utah (Jan. 4, 1896)	1,813,000 (34)	84,904	29	Salt Lake City*/Provo Ogden	Beehive State
Vermont (March 4, 1791)	570,000 (49)	9,615	14	Burlington/Montpelier*	Green Mountain State
Virginia (June 25, 1788)	6,377,000 (12)	42,769	95	Norfolk/Virginia Beach/ Richmond*	The Old Dominion
Washington (Nov. 11, 1889)	5,136,000 (16)	71,303	39	Seattle/Spokane/ Olympia*	Evergreen State
West Virginia (June 20, 1863)	1,812,000 (35)	24,231	55	Charleston*/Huntington	Mountain State
Wisconsin (May 29, 1848)	5,007,000 (18)	65,503	72	Milwaukee/Madison*/ Green Bay	Badger State
Wyoming (July 10, 1890)	466,000 (50)	97,818	23	Casper/Cheyenne*	Equality State

STATES

STATE GOVERNMENT: FACTS AND FIGURES

State	GOVERNOR Term (years)[a]	GOVERNOR Annual Salary	LEGISLATURE Upper House Number of Members	LEGISLATURE Upper House Term (years)	LEGISLATURE Lower House Number of Members	LEGISLATURE Lower House Term (years)	Annual Salary[b]
Alabama	4	$81,151	35	4	105	4	$50/day
Alaska	4	$81,648	20	4	40	2	$24,012
Arizona	4	$75,000	30	2	60	2	$15,000
Arkansas	4	$60,000	35	4	100	2	$12,500
California	4	$114,826	40	4	80	2	$52,500
Colorado	4	$60,000	35	4	65	2	$17,500
Connecticut	4	$78,000	36	2	151	2	$16,760
Delaware	4	$95,000	21	4	41	2	$24,900
Florida	4	$97,850	40	4	120	2	$22,560
Georgia	4	$94,390	56	2	180	2	$10,641
Hawaii	4	$94,780	25	4	51	2	$32,000
Idaho	4	$75,000	35	2	70	2	$12,000
Illinois	4	$103,097	59	4[c]	118	2	$38,420
Indiana	4	$77,200	50	4	100	2	$11,600
Iowa	4	$76,700	50	4	100	2	$18,800
Kansas	4	$76,476	40	4	125	2	$169/day
Kentucky	4	$81,647	38	4	100	2	$100/day
Louisiana	4	$73,440	39	4	105	4	$16,800
Maine	4	$70,000	35	2	151	2	$10,500
Maryland	4	$120,000	47	4	141	4	$28,000
Massachusetts	4	$75,000	40	2	160	2	$30,000
Michigan	4	$112,025	38	4	110	2	$47,723
Minnesota	4	$109,053	67	4	134	2	$27,979
Mississippi	4	$75,600	52	4	122	4	$10,000/session
Missouri	4	$91,615	34	4	163	2	$22,862
Montana	4	$55,850	50	4[c]	100	2	$57.06/day
Nebraska	4	$65,000	49	4	—	—	$12,000
Nevada	4	$90,000	21	4	42	2	$130/day
New Hampshire	2	$82,325	24	2	400	2	$100
New Jersey	4	$85,000	40	4[c]	80	2	$35,000
New Mexico	4	$90,000	42	4	70	2	$75/day
New York	4	$130,000	61	2	150	2	$57,500
North Carolina	4	$93,777	50	2	120	2	$13,026
North Dakota	4	$68,280	49	4	98	2	$90/day
Ohio	4	$110,250	33	4	99	2	$42,426
Oklahoma	4	$70,000	48	4	101	2	$32,000
Oregon	4	$80,000	30	4	60	2	$13,104
Pennsylvania	4	$105,000	50	4	203	2	$47,000
Rhode Island	4	$69,900	50	2	100	2	$5/day
South Carolina	4	$103,998	46	4	124	2	$10,400
South Dakota	4	$72,475	35	4	70	2	$4,000
Tennessee	4	$85,000	33	4	99	2	$16,500
Texas	4	$99,122	31	4	150	2	$7,200
Utah	4	$77,250	29	4	75	2	$85/day
Vermont	2	$80,724	30	2	150	2	$8,160
Virginia	4	$110,000	40	4	100	2	$18,000
Washington	4	$121,000	49	4	98	2	$25,900
West Virginia	4	$72,000	34	4	100	2	$6,500
Wisconsin	4	$92,283	33	4	99	2	$35,070
Wyoming	4	$70,000	30	4	60	2	$75/day

[a] Limits on the number of terms governors may serve vary from state to state.
[b] Unless otherwise noted. In most states, legislators also receive expense allowances.
[c] In special cases, senators serve for only two years.
Source: *Information Please Almanac 1992; The Book of the States 1994-95*

SUGGESTED READINGS

UNIT 1 FOUNDATIONS

Bowen, Catherine Drinker. *Miracle at Philadelphia*. Rev. ed. Little, Brown, 1986. New edition of a classic account of the Constitutional Convention.

Cousins, Norman, ed. *In God We Trust: The Religious Beliefs and Ideas of the American Founding Fathers*. Harper, 1958. A clear presentation of the religion of the men who founded the nation.

Handlin, Oscar and Lillian. *Liberty and Power, 1600–1760*. Harper, 1986. A readable history that focuses on the birth and growth of liberty in colonial America.

Morris, Richard B. *Seven Who Shaped Our Destiny*. Harper, 1976. Fascinating essays on Franklin, Washington, John Adams, Jefferson, Jay, Madison, and Hamilton.

Preiss, Byron. *The Constitution Bicentennial Book*. Bantam, 1987. Contains the text of the Constitution with interpretation by well-known scholars.

UNIT 2 CIVIL RIGHTS

Brigham, John. *Civil Liberties and American Democracy*. Congressional Quarterly, 1984. Clear presentation of current themes in civil rights and liberties, with paraphrased Supreme Court decisions.

Franklin, John Hope. *From Slavery to Freedom,* 5th ed. Knopf, 1980. An award-winning history of black Americans.

King, Martin Luther, Jr. *Why We Can't Wait*. Harper, 1964. The background of the civil rights movement and a description of the strategy of the Birmingham campaign.

Lewis, Anthony. *Gideon's Trumpet*. Random House, 1964. An account of the prisoner whose letter to the Supreme Court ultimately resulted in the decision that poor people are entitled to counsel.

Lieberman, Jethro Koller. *Free Speech, Free Press and the Law*. Lothrop, 1980. The First Amendment is discussed using controversial Supreme Court cases.

Peck, Mary Gray. *Carrie Chapman Catt: A Biography*. H.W. Wilson, 1944. Reprint. Hippocrene, 1975. A biography of the suffragist by a contemporary and friend.

UNIT 3 POLITICAL PARTICIPATION

Broder, David S. *Behind the Front Page: A Candid Look at How the News Is Made*. Simon & Schuster, 1987. A critical discussion of the performance of the press by the *Washington Post* political correspondent.

Graber, Doris A. *Mass Media and American Politics*. 2d ed. Congressional Quarterly, 1984. An examination of the contribution of the media to public policy and public opinion.

Hinckley, Barbara. *Congressional Elections*. Congressional Quarterly, 1981. Analyzes the framework of congressional elections and how the voters receive and process information about candidates and issues.

McGinniss, Joe. *The Selling of the President*. Trident, 1968. A study of the role of image-making in presidential elections.

Sagstetter, Karen. *Lobbying*. Watts, 1978. A historic overview and modern account of lobbyists' influence on legislators.

UNIT 4 LEGISLATIVE BRANCH

Coffey, Wayne R. *How We Choose a Congress*. St. Martin's, 1980. Traces the events involved in running for congressional office.

How Congress Works. Congressional Quarterly, 1983. A complete survey of the dynamics of congressional action.

Members of Congress Since 1789. Congressional Quarterly, 1981. Biographical sketches of all members of Congress who served from 1789 to 1981.

Mikva, Abner J. *The American Congress; The First Branch*. Watts, 1983. A historical and current look at the two houses, including the committee system, legislative and budgetary processes, and legislators' role in representing their constituencies.

Smith, Margaret Chase. *Declaration of Conscience*. Edited by William C. Lewis, Jr. Doubleday, 1972. An autobiography presenting important speeches with appropriate capsule histories of the background and effect of each.

UNIT 5 EXECUTIVE BRANCH

Boller, Paul F. *Presidential Campaigns*. Oxford, 1984. Traces the history of presidential campaigns.

DeGregorio, William A. *The Complete Book of U.S. Presidents*. Dembner, 1984. Facts about Presidents of the United States.

Gray, Lee Learner. *How We Choose a President; The Election Year*. St. Martins, 1980. Explains the activities of the election year from naming candidates to election day.

Healy, Diana Dixon. *America's Vice-Presidents*. Atheneum, 1984. An entertaining collection of biographical sketches of America's Vice Presidents.

Roseboom, Eugene H. *A History of Presidential Elections; from George Washington to Jimmy Carter*. 4th ed. Macmillan, 1979. Portrays the personalities and issues involved in the presidential elections through 1976.

White, Theodore H. *The Making of the President, 1960–1972.* Atheneum, 4v. An inside view of the four presidential campaigns from 1960 to 1972.

Whitney, David C. *The American Presidents.* Doubleday, 1985. Biographical sketches of the Presidents through Reagan's 1985 re-election, with additional information on First Ladies, Vice Presidents, elections, historical sites.

UNIT 6   JUDICIAL BRANCH

Archer, Jules. *You and the Law.* Harcourt, 1978. Procedures of the court system are explained as they apply to jurors, witnesses, victims, defendants, and convicts.

Baum, Lawrence. *The Supreme Court.* Congressional Quarterly, 1981. Discusses the history of the Court, its effect on government and society, how judges are selected, which cases are heard by the Court, and the decision process.

Cushman, Robert F. *Leading Constitutional Decisions.* Prentice-Hall, 1982. An examination of landmark cases.

Garraty, John A., ed. *Quarrels That Have Shaped the Constitution.* Harper, 1975. Discusses sixteen historic Supreme Court decisions.

Tribe, Laurence H. *God Save This Honorable Court: How the Choice of Supreme Court Justices Shapes Our History.* Random House, 1985. Discusses the impact of Supreme Court decisions and urges careful selection and approval of justices.

Wishman, Seymour. *Anatomy of a Jury.* Times Books, 1986. A criminal lawyer gives an insider's view of the jury system.

Woodward, Bob. *The Brethren; Inside the Supreme Court.* Simon & Schuster, 1979. The classic exposé of the inner workings of the Supreme Court from 1969 to 1976.

Zerman, Melvyn Bernard. *Beyond a Reasonable Doubt.* Crowell, 1981. A lively account of how the jury system works.

UNIT 7   PUBLIC POLICY

Bemis, Samuel Flagg, ed. *The American Secretaries of State and Their Diplomacy, v15, George C. Marshall.* Cooper Sq., 1966. A well-organized biography of this Secretary of State and his foreign policy initiatives.

Foreign Policy Association. *Cartoon History of United States Foreign Policy, 1776–1976.* Morrow, 1975. Highlights U.S. foreign policy with the work of American political cartoonists.

Heilbroner, Robert L. *Five Economic Challenges.* Prentice-Hall, 1981. Covers inflation, recession, big government, the dollar's falling exchange rate, the energy crisis, and the relationship between economic and political views on these subjects.

Martin, George. *Madam Secretary, Frances Perkins.* Houghton Mifflin, 1976. A biography of the first woman to hold a Cabinet post in the U.S. government.

Spanier, John. *American Foreign Policy Since World War II.* Holt, 1982. Discusses major foreign policy issues such as the Cold War, the Third World, and détente.

UNIT 8   STATE GOVERNMENT

The Book of States. Council of State Governments. Biennial in even-numbered years. Information on constitutions and elections, legislatures and legislation, the judiciary, administrative organization, finance, intergovernmental relations, and state services.

Sabato, Larry. *Goodbye to Goodtime Charlie: The American Governor Transformed, 1950–1975.* Lexington, 1978. Describes a major improvement in the quality of state governorship, from the ineffectual "Goodtime Charlie" to responsible and dynamic leadership.

UNIT 9   LOCAL GOVERNMENT

Gay, Kathlyn. *Cities Under Stress; Can Today's City Systems Be Made to Work?* Watts, 1985. A concise and organized analysis of the problems of urban systems in the United States.

Hanmer, Trudy J. *The Growth of Cities.* Watts, 1985. Traces the growth of cities in America from colonial days to the present.

Klebanow, Diana. *Urban Legacy: The Story of America's Cities.* NAL, 1977. A look at the historic role of American cities and their socioeconomic, ethnic, and racial conflicts.

UNIT 10   COMPARATIVE GOVERNMENT

Ebenstein, William and Edwin Fogelman. *Today's Isms; Communism, Fascism, Capitalism, Socialism.* 9th ed. Prentice-Hall, 1985. An analysis of these different concepts.

Franck, Thomas M. *Nation Against Nation: What Happened to the U.N. Dream and What the U.S. Can Do About It.* Oxford, 1985. Examines the strengths and weaknesses of the U.N.

Heilbroner, Robert L. *Economics Explained.* Prentice-Hall, 1982. Covers the basics of economic theory for the beginner.

Raynor, Thomas. *Politics, Power and People; Four Governments in Action.* Watts, 1983. Discusses the governments of the United Kingdom, the United States, the Soviet Union, and Argentina.

SUPREME COURT CASES

This special index lists all the Supreme Court cases included in *Government in America.* Each entry gives the name of the case, its date, the central issue, and the page(s) on which it appears.

GLOSSARY

The glossary defines important words and terms in this book. Remember that many words have more than one meaning. The definitions given here are the ones that will be most helpful in your reading of this book. The page number in parentheses after each definition refers to the page on which each word or term is first used in the textbook.

A

absentee ballot an official ballot mailed to an election official by a voter before an election because the voter is unable to vote on election day. *(page 311)*

acid rain precipitation that carries air pollution to the ground. *(page 596)*

acquittal a Court's decision that an accused person is not guilty. *(page 505)*

administration a President, his staff, and other officials who take leadership roles in the executive branch. *(page 422)*

administrative law the rules and regulations issued by governmental agencies. *(page 495)*

admiralty law the branch of law covering navigation, shipping, and commerce on the high seas or on the Great Lakes and major rivers within the U.S.; also called *maritime law*. *(page 464)*

adversary proceeding a trial in which the two opposing sides argue before an unbiased jury and a neutral judge. *(page 502)*

advisory opinion a judgment by an attorney general as to whether a planned action conforms to a state's laws or constitution. *(page 652)*

AFDC Aid to Families with Dependent Children; a joint federal-state program to provide income for families when the breadwinner dies, is disabled, or abandons the family. *(page 623)*

affirmative action the policy of encouraging or requiring employers to recruit minorities and women in an effort to compensate for past limitations on their opportunities. *(page 209)*

agribusiness farming engaged in as a big business, embracing the production, processing, and distribution of farm products and the manufacture of farm machinery, equipment, and supplies. *(page 582)*

Agricultural Adjustment Act 1933 New Deal legislation under which the federal government set limits on the production of crops and livestock to reduce surplus and ensure greater profits for farmers. *(page 581)*

Albany Plan of Union a plan adopted in 1754 to unite the American colonies under a confederation for purposes of taxation and defense, but never carried out. *(page 37)*

alien a person who is not a citizen of the nation in which he or she lives. *(page 24)*

allegiance loyalty to one's country. *(page 5)*

ambassador the highest-ranking diplomat appointed to represent the President and carry out foreign policy in an assigned country. *(page 407)*

amicus curiae "a friend of the court"; legal arguments delivered voluntarily, often by interest groups, to give testimony for or against a decision. *(page 261)*

amnesty a general pardon given to a group of people who have broken the law. *(page 404)*

Antifederalists those who opposed the creation of the new federal system of government and the ratification of the Constitution. *(page 55)*

annexation the expansion of municipal boundaries to include a nearby area that is not part of another municipality; the addition of a territory to an existing state. *(page 726)*

apartheid (ah-PART-hite) the policy of the all-white government of South Africa by which racial groups were separated. *(page 372)*

appellate jurisdiction (ah-PELL-ut) the authority of a court to hear cases on appeal. *(page 466)*

apportionment the distribution of representatives among the states based on population. *(page 96)*

appropriations congressional grants of money set aside for a specific purpose. *(page 361)*

aquifer (AH-kwih-fur) a large natural area of groundwater storage. *(page 593)*

arms control the placing of limits on the building and testing of weapons. *(page 555)*

arms race the competition among countries seeking to gain a military advantage by developing or buying new and more sophisticated weapons. *(page 538)*

arraignment the formal reading in an open courtroom of the charges against a defendant. *(page 500)*

Articles of Confederation the original plan of unification and government of the United States. *(page 43)*

assembly a group or body of lawmakers in some state governments of the U.S. and in many foreign countries. *(page 34)*

assessment an estimate of the value of something. *(page 715)*

assessor a local government official who inspects property and estimates its value. *(page 715)*

at large a system of election by which the voters of a city, state, or country as a whole elect government officials. (*pages 273, 337*)

Atomic Energy Commission (AEC) a federal government agency formed in 1946 to supervise and regulate the development of all nuclear programs. (*page 604*)

attorney general the chief lawyer of a level of government. (*page 652*)

auditor a state's finance official who reviews the records of each agency and department at the end of each budget year to ensure that the allotted budget has been used according to law. (*page 653*)

Australian ballot originated in Australia and introduced in the U.S. in 1888, a ballot printed, paid for, and distributed by state or local governments to qualified voters at polling places established by state law; secret ballot. (*page 310*)

autocracy rule by one person. (*page 13*)

B

bail money exchanged for the release of an arrested person as a guarantee of the person's appearance for trial. (*page 185*)

Bail Reform Act law which requires federal officials to release people who cannot meet bail payments, unless they are accused of a capital crime or there is reason to believe they will fail to appear in court. (*page 185*)

balance of power a distribution of power such that no single nation is strong enough to dominate another. (*page 538*)

bench trial trial by a judge, rather than by jury. (*page 502*)

bicameral having two legislative houses. (*page 43*)

bilingual education classroom instruction in a student's native language as well as in English. (*page 205*)

bill a proposed law. (*page 364*)

bill of attainder a legislative act, prohibited by the Constitution, that declares a specific person or group guilty and inflicts punishment without a trial. (*page 89*)

bill of rights a constitutional list of the basic civil liberties of citizens. (*page 43*)

Bill of Rights the first ten amendments to the United States Constitution. (*page 75*)

bipartisan consisting of or supported by members of two major political parties. (*page 311*)

block grant a grant from the federal government channeling money to a state for general purposes. (*page 102*)

board of equalization a group of officials established by a local government to ensure fair property taxes. (*page 716*)

bond a loan by private persons or corporations to the government. (*page 683*)

bondsman a professional lender of bail money. (*page 498*)

bourgeoisie (boor-zhwah-ZEE) the term Karl Marx used for capitalists who grew rich from the labor of the proletariat. (*page 742*)

brief a written document arguing one side of a case. (*page 475*)

"broker party" a political party that is more concerned with gaining votes than with maintaining ideologies. (*page 281*)

Brown v. Board of Education the 1954 Supreme Court decision that declared racial segregation in public schools unconstitutional, rejecting the "separate but equal" doctrine. (*page 200*)

bureaucracy the agencies and offices that take part in managing the government. (*page 422*)

burgess a legislative representative. (*page 34*)

C

Cabinet the group of presidential advisers made up of the heads of the executive departments; a small group of party leaders chosen by a Prime Minister to help decide policies. (*pages 80, 427, 758*)

cadre (KAD-ree) a skilled and educated member of the Chinese Communist Party who holds a long-term position in the government and serves as a link between the government and the party. (*page 769*)

calendar a formal schedule of bills or resolutions to be considered by Congress. (*page 367*)

canvass a political survey used to determine voters' opinions. (*page 304*)

capital money or property invested in a business; the means of production. (*pages 564, 734*)

capital crime a crime for which the death sentence is a possible penalty. (*page 176*)

capital gains profits made from the selling of real estate, stocks, or other assets. (*page 515*)

capitalism the economic system based on private ownership and control of the means of production (factories, businesses, property, money); also called the *free enterprise system*. (*pages 526, 735*)

capital punishment the death penalty. (*page 186*)

casework work done by public officials to help individual constituents solve problems. (*page 346*)

categorical grant a grant-in-aid from the national government given with restrictions for a specific use to a state or local government. (*page 101*)

caucus a meeting of a political party's members to nominate candidates and decide party strategy for an election. (*page 293*)

censorship the curbing of ideas in speech or in writing before they are expressed. (*page 155*)

censure an official declaration of disapproval. (*page 344*)

census an official survey of the population. (*page 337*)

centrist a person or party with a position in the center of the ideological spectrum. *(page 281)*

chargé d'affaires (shahr-ZHAY dah-FAIR) a government official temporarily in charge of diplomatic affairs when an ambassador is absent. *(page 548)*

charter a legal document issued by a monarch to trading companies, individuals, or groups of colonists, granting permission to use land for a colony; official recognition as a municipality given by a state to a community. *(pages 34, 699)*

checks and balances a system under which each branch of government limits the power of the other branches. *(page 65)*

chief executive the official who runs or administers a government. *(page 380)*

chief of state the symbolic leader of a nation. *(page 380)*

Christian socialism a form of socialism that advocates spiritual dignity and material well-being. *(page 748)*

circuit court one of the twelve regional courts of appeals. *(page 467)*

citizenship the special status, including rights and responsibilities, given to a member of a nation. *(page 5)*

city manager the chief executive hired by a city council to oversee the city's operations. *(page 703)*

civil disobedience the refusal to obey civil laws regarded as unjust by using nonviolent, or passive, resistance. *(page 202)*

civil law the body of law that deals with the relations between people; also called *private law. (page 492)*

civil liberties the personal rights of citizens, such as freedom of speech, thought, and action, as guaranteed by the First Amendment. *(pages 19, 142)*

civil rights the right of every citizen to be treated equally under the law and to have equality of opportunity. *(page 19)*

Civil Rights Act (1964) an act that prohibited discrimination on the basis of sex, race, or religion in areas such as employment, education, and voter registration. *(page 203)*

civil service the system by which classified public employees are hired and promoted on the basis of merit rather than political party affiliation. *(pages 399, 438)*

class action suit a lawsuit brought by a person or group on behalf of all people who would benefit directly from the court's decision. *(page 261)*

Clayton Antitrust Act a 1914 law that strengthened the Sherman Antitrust Act by defining unfair business practices. *(page 568)*

"clear and present danger" a doctrine used to decide whether the danger to public welfare outweighs the right to freedom of speech. *(page 152)*

closed primary a type of direct primary in which citizens must declare their party affiliation and can vote only for their party's candidates. *(page 292)*

closed shop a place of employment in which only union members can be hired; made illegal by the Taft-Hartley Act. *(page 575)*

cloture (KLO-chur) a vote of three-fifths of the Senate to end debate and call for a vote on a bill. *(page 369)*

coalition a temporary alliance between groups with differing interests. *(page 269)*

code a system of regulations and standards. *(page 702)*

code of ethics rules and guidelines for behavior. *(page 344)*

cold war the period of growing hostility in U.S.-Soviet relations following World War II. *(page 543)*

collective bargaining talks carried on between a union and an employer to determine such things as wages, hours, and working conditions. *(page 574)*

collective farming the bringing together on large tracts of land of all the livestock, tools, and buildings of many small, scattered farms. *(page 744)*

collective security the increased protection gained when two or more nations agree to assist each other if any of them is attacked by enemy forces. *(page 553)*

comity clause clause in the Constitution (Article IV, Section 2) stating that each state must grant the residents of all other states the same rights its own residents enjoy. *(page 105)*

command economy an economic system in which the government completely controls, or commands, the nation's economy. See *communism. (page 742)*

commander-in-chief the President of the United States in his position as head of the military. *(page 410)*

commissioners a group of people appointed by the President to head an independent regulatory commission; the group of people who head a commission form of government. *(pages 432, 704)*

commission form a form of municipal government in which a small group of people is elected to perform both legislative and executive duties. *(page 704)*

common law a body of law based on custom, tradition, and past judicial decisions rather than on specific laws and statutes. *(page 33)*

commune a large group of combined collective farms. *(page 744)*

communism the economic system in which the factors of production are owned and operated by the government, which determines the type, quantity, and price of goods that will be produced; also called *command economy* or *planned economy. (page 742)*

commute to reduce (a criminal sentence). *(page 651)*

comparable worth the concept

of equal pay for men and women for jobs requiring the same, or comparable, levels of skills and responsibilities. *(page 217)*

comptroller a state's finance official who keeps track of funds while they are being spent. *(page 653)*

concurrent powers powers possessed by both national and state governments. *(page 91)*

concurring opinion an opinion that supports the majority decision of the Supreme Court but offers different reasons for reaching that decision. *(page 478)*

confederation a form of government in which two or more independent states join together to achieve a common goal, but retain their individual sovereignty in other matters. *(page 12)*

conference a regularly scheduled meeting of Supreme Court justices to discuss and decide cases. *(page 477)*

conference committee a temporary committee made up of members from both houses of Congress to reconcile Senate and House versions of the same bill. *(page 361)*

conglomerate a corporation that controls many different kinds of companies. *(page 569)*

congressional immunity freedom from arrest granted to members of Congress while they are attending or traveling to and from legislative sessions. *(page 343)*

conscientious objector a person who refuses military service because of religious or moral beliefs. *(page 147)*

conscription the forced enrollment of young men into the armed forces for a specified period of mandatory service; also called the draft. *(page 549)*

consensus general agreement. *(page 272)*

conservative a person in favor of the status quo, who is cautious about new policies,

and who generally feels that the government should stay out of the affairs of private citizens and businesses. *(page 229)*

consolidation the combining of sparsely populated counties. *(page 694)*

constituency the people to whom elected government officials are directly accountable. *(page 64)*

constitutional court a general judicial court established by Congress under Article III. *(page 466)*

constitutional monarchy a form of government in which the monarch is mainly a ceremonial head of state and shares authority with an elected legislature. *(page 13)*

constitutional officer a state executive official whose position is established by the state constitution. *(page 652)*

consul an official appointed by a government to reside in a foreign city and represent his or her government's commercial interests and give assistance to its citizens there. *(page 548)*

consumer price index (CPI) a statistic that measures the costs of goods and services purchased by consumers and provides one way of measuring the consumer's actual buying power; also called the "cost of living" index. *(page 577)*

containment the United States' post-World War II policy aimed at limiting Communist expansion. *(page 543)*

contract a formal legal agreement between two or more individuals, businesses, or other organizations. *(page 493)*

cooperative federalism system in which national and state activities are intermixed, with greater national involvement in state and local affairs. *(page 98)*

copyright the exclusive right to publish, produce, distribute, perform, display, or sell a literary or artistic work. *(page 333)*

corporate charter a legal document granted by a state to a corporation, giving it the right to operate. *(page 564)*

corrections a system of institutions (including work farms, penitentiaries, maximum-security prisons, and reform schools) where persons convicted of crimes are confined. *(page 669)*

council-manager form a form of municipal government in which the voters elect a city council to make the city's policy and the council appoints a city manager as chief executive. *(page 703)*

counsel legal advice. *(page 182)*

counterintelligence attempting to monitor and counter the activities of other nations' intelligence-gathering agencies. *(page 546)*

county the basic unit of local government in the United States. *(page 690)*

county manager a professional manager appointed by the governing board of a county to oversee day-to-day operations of the county. *(page 694)*

county seat the town or city that is the center of government in its county. *(page 690)*

court-martial a military court that tries members of the armed forces accused of violating military laws. *(page 469)*

court of appeals a court that handles appeals from a lower court. *(page 467)*

court of record a court in which written transcripts of the proceedings are kept. *(page 655)*

"court packing" plan President Franklin Roosevelt's failed attempt to enlarge the Supreme Court which would have allowed him to appoint six new justices to support his New Deal legislation. *(page 484)*

"cozy triangle" a network of

close relationships between executive departments, congressional committees, and interest groups involving exchanges of information and political favors. *(page 431)*

craft union a union made up of workers with a similar skill. *(page 254)*

criminal law the body of law that specifies offenses against the public and the penalties for committing those offenses. *(page 495)*

cross-examination one side's questioning of the opposing side's witnesses in an effort to discredit their testimony. *(page 504)*

culture a complex combination of traits that are unique to the population of a country. *(page 231)*

customs duty a tax on goods imported into a country; also called *duty,* import duty, *impost,* or tariff. *(page 519)*

D ————————————————

"dark horse" candidate a relatively unknown politician whose name is suggested for nomination and who sometimes wins when front-runners become deadlocked. *(page 299)*

deduction an expense that individuals can subtract from their taxable income. *(page 515)*

de facto existing in fact, as in racial segregation or other discrimination that exists by result of private interest. *(page 202)*

defamation false attacks on another person's character or reputation. *(page 153)*

deficit spending a policy by which government expenditures exceed revenues. *(page 527)*

de jure established by law, as in racial segregation or other discrimination that exists by government decision. *(page 201)*

delegated powers the powers specifically granted to the national government by the Constitution; also called enumerated or *expressed powers. (page 86)*

democracy rule by the people. *(page 13)*

Democratic-Republicans the political party of Thomas Jefferson which called for a strict interpretation of the Constitution and a weak central government. *(page 276)*

Democrats the political party of Andrew Jackson which was the dominant political force from 1828 until the Civil War. *(page 278)*

density the number of people concentrated in a given area. *(page 664)*

department the basic unit of local government in France. *(page 762)*

deposition a formal interview given by a witness under oath before a trial is held. *(page 502)*

depression an economic condition characterized by widespread unemployment and a decline in business activities lasting for a year or more. *(page 527)*

deregulation reducing or removing government control in an industry. *(page 433)*

détente (day-TAHNT) a relaxing of tensions between nations. *(page 544)*

deterrence the U.S. defense policy that aims at preventing enemy attack by the threat of military retaliation. *(page 553)*

dictatorship a form of autocracy in which a ruler acquires and maintains leadership through fear and force. *(page 14)*

diplomatic immunity the exemption of foreign diplomats from the laws of the nation-state in which they reside. *(page 548)*

diplomatic recognition the recognition of a foreign government by exchanging diplomatic representatives. *(page 407)*

direct democracy a form of government in which all citizens have a chance to participate on a first-hand basis. *(page 15)*

direct initiative a method of legislation that allows voters to bypass legislators and place an issue directly on the ballot. *(page 645)*

direct primary an election in which all party members may vote to choose the party's candidate. *(page 292)*

direct tax a tax, such as an income tax, levied directly on individual taxpayers. *(page 515)*

discharge petition a request by a majority of the members of the House that a bill be released by a committee to the floor. *(page 367)*

discount rate the rate of interest charged to member banks when they borrow from the Federal Reserve. *(page 532)*

discrimination treating one person or group differently from another. *(page 195)*

dissenting opinion the opinion written by a Supreme Court justice who disagrees with the majority; also called the minority opinion. *(page 478)*

district court a federal court in each of the fifty states that has original jurisdiction in most cases involving federal laws. *(page 467)*

District of Columbia Amendment a constitutional amendment, proposed in 1978, designed to give the District two senators and two representatives and thus provide its citizens with representation in Congress. *(page 74)*

divest to give up ownership. *(page 569)*

divine right the belief that royalty's right to rule comes from God. *(page 8)*

docket a schedule of cases to be argued in a court. *(page 476)*

domestic relations court a minor court that settles family disputes. *(page 655)*

domino theory the belief that if one country falls to communism, the neighboring countries will shortly follow. *(page 544)*

double jeopardy (JEH-per-dee) bringing a person to trial repeatedly for the same crime. *(page 177)*

***Dred Scott* case** the 1857 Supreme Court ruling that slaves did not have the rights of citizens and that Congress could not forbid slavery in the territories. *(page 194)*

dual federalism system in which there is a clear constitutional division between the powers of the national government and those of the states. *(page 97)*

due process of law the constitutional right of every citizen to fair treatment under the law. *(page 168)*

duty See *customs duty*. *(page 332)*

E —————————————

easy money a "loose money" policy through which the federal government seeks to stimulate the economy during a recession. *(page 533)*

ecology the study of the relationship of living organisms to their environment. *(page 593)*

economic system a nation's system for organizing the production, distribution, and exchange of goods and services. *(page 734)*

elastic clause a clause in the Constitution that permits Congress to pass laws as necessary to carry out its existing powers. *(page 86)*

electioneering publicly supporting a candidate for office. *(page 260)*

Electoral College the group of people who are elected to cast the official votes for President and Vice President. *(page 387)*

electoral vote vote cast by a member of the Electoral College. *(page 388)*

electors the people elected by the voters to represent them in the Electoral College. *(page 387)*

embargo a government order to end trade with a certain country. *(pages 552, 584)*

eminent domain the inherent power of the government to take private property for public use. *(page 90)*

emissions pollutants released into the air by an internal-combustion engine. *(page 596)*

enabling act **(1.)** a provision added to a constitutional amendment authorizing Congress to pass whatever laws are necessary to make the amendment effective. *(page 79)* **(2.)** a congressional act stating the conditions for a territory's admission to the Union. *(page 95)*

endorsement the public supporting of a candidate. *(page 304)*

English Bill of Rights the document in which Queen Mary II and King William III recognized certain basic rights of the people, some of which were later included in the United States Constitution. *(page 32)*

entitlements payments required by law for people who meet certain eligibility requirements. *(page 522)*

entrepreneur an individual who organizes, manages, and assumes the risks and responsibilities for a business. *(page 736)*

Environmental Protection Agency a federal government agency established in 1970 to enforce policies on water and air pollution, solid and toxic wastes, pesticides, and radiation. *(page 594)*

epidemic the rapid spread of disease. *(page 622)*

equal protection a guarantee of the Fourteenth Amendment whereby states may not make unfair distinctions between people. *(page 208)*

Equal Rights Amendment a constitutional amendment, first proposed in 1923, that would prohibit discrimination on the basis of sex. *(page 73)*

equity fairness, justice; a kind of law based on fairness rather than statutes or common-law precedents. *(page 492)*

establishment clause the clause of the First Amendment that forbids the government from making any law about an establishment of religion. *(page 143)*

estate tax a tax on the money or property of a person who has died; also called an estate duty. *(page 518)*

excise tax a tax paid on specific activities, services, or goods (such as alcohol, tobacco, or gasoline) that are produced, manufactured, sold, transported, or used within the U.S. *(pages 332, 518, 678)*

exclusionary rule a Supreme Court ruling stating that illegally obtained evidence cannot be used in federal court cases. *(page 173)*

executive the branch of federal, state, or local government that is responsible for putting laws into effect. *(page 63)*

executive agency an administrative unit in the federal government that oversees a single area within the executive branch. *(page 435)*

executive agreement an agreement, not requiring the Senate's approval, between the President of the U.S. and the leader of a foreign government. *(pages 79, 408)*

executive budget a state's budget that is prepared under the direct supervision of the governor. *(page 672)*

executive clemency a governor's power to reduce or end a convicted criminal's sentence. *(page 651)*

Executive Office of the President (EOP) the administrative agency of the President of the United States. *(page 423)*

executive order a rule or regulation issued by the President or another executive official to help enforce a treaty, law, or court ruling. *(page 398)*

executive privilege the theoretical right of the President and other top officials of the executive branch to withhold information from Congress and the courts. *(pages 81, 400)*

exemption a fixed amount that individuals are allowed to subtract for themselves and their dependents when they are figuring their total taxable income. *(page 515)*

expatriation the process of surrendering citizenship. *(page 23)*

ex post facto law a law, prohibited by the Constitution, that makes illegal an action that was committed before the law was passed. *(page 89)*

expressed powers See *delegated powers. (page 332)*

extradition the procedure for returning an accused person to the state or country where a crime was allegedly committed. *(page 104)*

F ————————————

factors of production the resources, including land, labor, capital, and management, that an economy needs to produce its goods and services. *(page 734)*

fairness doctrine the Federal Communications Commission's standard that requires radio and television stations to present all sides of important public issues. *(page 158)*

"faithless" electors members of the Electoral College who do not cast their states' votes for the winner of the popular vote. *(page 390)*

favorite son/daughter a candidate who is placed in nomination as a courtesy by his or her home state. *(page 299)*

federal budget a detailed plan of the federal government's expenditures and revenues for a given year. *(page 521)*

Federalists advocates of the creation of a federal system of government as outlined in the Constitution. *(page 55)*

Federal Reserve System the national banking system comprised of twelve Federal Reserve Banks in major United States cities that regulates national monetary policy. *(page 530)*

"federal question" all cases that involve national laws such as the Constitution, laws passed by Congress, or treaties. *(page 464)*

federal system a political system in which authority is divided between a national government and its political subdivisions. *(page 12)*

felony a serious crime for which the prison sentence exceeds one year. *(page 183)*

FICA the Federal Insurance Contributions Act; a compulsory payroll tax on employees and employers which funds the Social Security system. *(page 616)*

filibuster a tactic used in the Senate to monopolize debate in an effort to delay or block passage of a bill. *(page 368)*

fiscal policy a governmental tool for influencing the economy by deliberately changing levels of taxing and spending. *(page 529)*

fiscal year the twelve-month period during which a government or a business keeps accounts. *(page 523)*

Five-Year Plan a series of goals set by a Communist government for the production of goods and services. *(page 743)*

floor action discussing and voting on legislation. *(page 352)*

floor leader a party spokesperson in Congress. *(page 356)*

food stamps coupons provided free or at low cost by the federal government to the needy, that can be used to purchase food in retail grocery stores. *(page 626)*

foreign aid a government's economic or military assistance to other nations. *(page 550)*

Foreign Service a branch of the State Department which represents the United States overseas. *(page 407)*

fossil fuel an energy resource, such as coal, oil, and natural gas, formed millions of years ago from decomposed plants and animals. *(page 600)*

franchise the right to vote; also called suffrage. *(page 308)*

franking privilege free postal service for mail sent by members of Congress. *(page 344)*

freedom of assembly a constitutional guarantee included in the First Amendment which prohibits Congress from abridging the right of individuals to gather peacefully in public places. *(page 160)*

Freedom of Information Act an act of Congress requiring the government to allow journalists and other interested persons to inspect unclassified federal records. *(page 159)*

freedom of religion a constitutional guarantee included in the First Amendment that forbids Congress from passing laws to establish a religion or prohibiting the free exercise of religious beliefs. *(page 142)*

freedom of speech a constitutional guarantee included in the First Amendment prohibiting Congress from passing any laws abridging the free expression of individuals. *(page 150)*

freedom of the press a constitutional guarantee included in the First Amendment prohibiting Congress from passing censorship laws against the media. *(page 155)*

free enterprise system See *capitalism. (pages 526, 735)*

free exercise clause the part of the First Amendment that prevents the government from restricting individuals' religious practices. *(page 143)*

full faith and credit clause clause in the Constitution

GLOSSARY

(Article IV, Section 1) declaring that documents considered legal in one state must be recognized as legal by all other states. *(page 103)*

fundamental law law outlining the basic principles, powers, and structures of a government. *(page 78)*

Fundamental Orders the first written constitution in America which formed a colony from Connecticut's early towns. *(page 35)*

G

General Assembly a division of the United Nations in which every member nation has a vote. *(page 556)*

general election an election in which all voters choose the winner for each office. *(page 292)*

general sales tax a state or city tax on items or services that are sold to the public. *(page 677)*

General Secretary the person chosen by top Chinese Communist Party leaders to head the Communist Party and command the Chinese Army. *(page 769)*

geothermal power power produced by tapping into the heat stored in the earth's interior. *(page 607)*

gerrymander to draw district boundary lines in a way that favors a particular candidate or political party, or reduces the voting power of a racial or ethnic group. *(page 338)*

Gibbons v. Ogden 1824 decision in which the Supreme Court broadened the commerce clause by extending its definition to the movement of people and services. *(page 99)*

gift tax a tax on the transfer of money or property between living persons. *(page 518)*

government the people and institutions with the authority to establish and enforce laws and public policies. *(page 6)*

government corporation a government organization that combines features of both public and private organizations and that provides services that private industry is unwilling or unable to undertake. *(page 434)*

grandfather clause the provision in the laws of southern states permitting persons to vote without taking a literacy test or paying a poll tax if they or one of their ancestors had been entitled to vote in 1866. Directed against black voters, it was declared unconstitutional in 1915. *(page 309)*

grand jury a group of people who decide whether there is sufficient evidence against an accused person to justify a criminal trial. *(page 176)*

grant-in-aid money given on a matching basis to a state or local government by the national government for a particular program or project. *(page 101)*

grassroots started and carried out by people at a local level, not by professional politicians. *(page 260)*

Great Compromise a plan providing for a bicameral legislature in which the people would be represented in the House of Representatives and the states in the Senate. *(page 52)*

gross national product (GNP) the total value of all goods and services produced by a nation in a year. *(page 252)*

GS rating a General Schedule rating system for federal civil servants, based on classes and ranks for job qualifications, difficulty, and pay. *(page 441)*

H

habeas corpus (HAY-bee-us KOHR-puhs) a writ requiring that a person being held in custody be brought before a court so a judge can determine if there are legal reasons for keeping the person in jail. *(page 89)*

heckler's veto the ability of hostile onlookers to disrupt a peaceful speech or assembly. *(page 161)*

highway patrol a state's police force, which enforces traffic laws on the state's highways. *(page 669)*

highway user tax the portion of gasoline tax revenues a state sets aside for highway construction and maintenance. *(page 678)*

home rule the power of a county government, with the approval of its voters, to design its own structure and institutions. *(page 693)*

homesteading a local government's method of revitalizing urban areas, by which it sells an abandoned dwelling for a small sum of money, with the agreement that the buyer will live there for a certain number of years and make any necessary repairs to comply with building codes. *(page 712)*

hung jury a jury that cannot agree on a verdict. *(page 505)*

hydroelectric power power produced by the energy of falling water channeled through dams. *(page 607)*

I

ideology an organized pattern of looking at the political world; a systematic set of ideas that is used to justify a particular point of view. *(page 228)*

immunity the promise of legal authorities that the testimony given by witnesses will not be used to prosecute them for crimes. *(page 177)*

impeach to bring criminal charges against a government official. *(page 335)*

implied powers powers of the national government that are not specifically stated in the Constitution but that derive from the elastic clause. *(page 86)*

impost See *customs duty*. *(page 332)*

impoundment a President's refusal to spend money

appropriated by Congress. *(page 406)*

income tax a tax on a person's yearly income. *(page 514)*

incorporation the process of becoming a municipality. *(page 699)*

incumbent a person who holds a political office. *(page 346)*

independent a person who does not identify with a political party. *(page 285)*

independent regulatory commission a federal agency that makes regulations to protect the public interest. *(page 432)*

indictment (in-DYT-ment) a formal statement presented by a prosecuting attorney charging a person with committing a crime. *(page 176)*

indirect initiative a method of legislation that allows citizens' proposals to go to the state legislature before appearing on the ballot. *(page 645)*

industrial union a union that includes both skilled and unskilled workers in the same industry. *(page 254)*

inflation a rapid rise in prices. *(page 527)*

information a sworn statement, filed by a prosecutor after a preliminary hearing, that there is enough evidence to take an accused person to trial. *(page 500)*

inherent powers the powers that a national government is assumed to have because it is the government of a sovereign state. *(page 90)*

initiative a process of direct legislation that voters start by signing a petition proposing a law or constitutional amendment. *(pages 261, 636)*

injunction a court order that forbids a specific action. *(page 156)*

integration the act or process of making something open to people of all ethnic groups; desegregation. *(page 201)*

intelligence social, political, economic, and military information about foreign governments that is useful for making decisions on foreign policy. *(page 545)*

interest group an organization of people with shared ideas and attitudes who attempt to influence public policy. *(pages 236, 248)*

international law the principles and rules that guide relations among nations. *(page 495)*

Interstate Commerce Act an 1887 law that established a commission to regulate railroad rates. *(page 568)*

interstate compact an agreement between two or more states to solve a common problem. *(page 106)*

Intolerable Acts a term given to a group of new laws passed by Parliament that restricted the American colonies' self-government and invaded their privacy. *(page 39)*

inversion the situation when warm air traps a layer of cool air near the ground, preventing pollutants from rising above the cool air and thus creating smog. *(page 596)*

isolationism the policy of avoiding unnecessary involvement in world affairs. *(page 539)*

item veto an executive's power to reject part of a bill while signing the rest into law. *(page 404)*

J ──────────

"Jim Crow" laws state legislation introduced in the South after reconstruction that gave official support to segregation. *(page 196)*

joint session a congressional session in which both houses meet together. *(page 353)*

judicial the branch of federal, state, or local government that decides if laws have been broken and that punishes lawbreakers. *(page 63)*

judicial activism the philosophy that Supreme Court justices should take an active role in making policy, going beyond the actions of the elected branches if the justices think it necessary. *(page 480)*

judicial restraint the philosophy that judicial decisions should not contradict the wishes of elected members of government unless those wishes clearly violate the Constitution. *(page 480)*

judicial review the power of the courts to declare national, state, or local acts of government invalid. *(page 69)*

junta (HOON-tah) a small group of military officers who seize power and establish their own government. *(page 14)*

jurisdiction a court's authority to hear cases. *(page 464)*

jus sanguinis (yoos sang-GWY-nus) the legal principle that a child's citizenship is based on that of the child's parents. *(page 21)*

jus soli (yoos SO-lee) the principle that a child's citizenship is based on the child's place of birth. *(page 21)*

justice of the peace a court official in small towns and rural areas who handles minor civil and criminal cases. *(page 654)*

juvenile court a minor court that hears cases involving persons under 18 years. *(page 655)*

juvenile justice system the system separate from the criminal justice system that deals with persons under 18 accused of committing crimes and is intended to rehabilitate rather than punish. *(page 498)*

K ──────────

keynote speech the opening speech at a national nominating convention, which praises the party and criticizes the opposition. *(page 298)*

L ──────────

labor the human resources that are needed to produce goods and services. *(page 734)*

laissez faire the theory that government should not

interfere in economic affairs. *(page 526)*

lame duck incumbent who holds office without voter support or without seeking re-election, until the inauguration of a successor. *(page 352)*

"lame duck" amendment the Twentieth Amendment to the Constitution which changed the date of the presidential inauguration to January 20th. *(page 383)*

land all natural resources. *(page 734)*

land-grant college a school established by the Morrill Act in 1862 to teach agriculture, veterinary medicine, engineering, and other subjects vital to farming. *(page 581)*

law clerk a recent law school graduate who assists a judge by conducting research, summarizing cases, and helping to draft opinions. *(page 477)*

"left" on the political spectrum, referring to people who favor change in society. *(page 229)*

legislative the branch of federal, state, or local government that makes the laws. *(page 63)*

legislative court a court established by Congress to hear cases about and carry out the legislative powers in Article I. *(page 467)*

legislative veto the power of Congress to review or cancel an action taken by the executive branch. *(page 334)*

legitimacy governmental power and authority accepted by the people as correct, right, or appropriate. *(page 6)*

libel defamation in written form. *(page 153)*

liberal a person who believes that government should actively and peacefully promote social reform within the existing political system. *(page 229)*

limited government system in which government actions are limited to help ensure individual liberties and equality under the law. *(page 19)*

literacy test a written or oral examination, now illegal, requiring citizens to prove their ability to read, write, and understand documents before being allowed to vote. *(page 308)*

litigant an adversary in a lawsuit or trial. *(page 502)*

litigation bringing a lawsuit. *(page 260)*

lobbying organized efforts to influence legislation or public policy. *(page 258)*

log-rolling a legislative tradition of reciprocity, or the mutual exchange of political favors. *(page 355)*

loose construction an interpretation of the Constitution holding that the federal government has broad powers. *(page 87)*

"loyal opposition" in British politics, the term for opposition party; those who are loyal to the nation but oppose the policies of the party in power. *(page 269)*

M

McCulloch v. Maryland an 1819 case in which the Supreme Court favored a loose construction of the Constitution and ruled that Congress did have the power to create a bank. *(page 88)*

magistrate the chief officer of a magistrate court who hears a city's minor civil and criminal cases. *(page 654)*

Magna Charta the document in which English nobles placed limits on royal power by forcing King John to concede important rights. *(page 31)*

Majority Leader the chief strategist and spokesperson for the majority party in the House of Representatives. *(page 356)*

majority opinion the view of the Supreme Court justices who support a ruling. *(page 478)*

majority rule the principle by which people agree to abide by decisions on which more than half of them agree. *(page 20)*

management the people who organize and develop the land, labor, and capital factors of production. *(page 734)*

mandate the wishes or support of the people as expressed by their votes. *(page 237)*

Marbury v. Madison an 1803 case in which the Supreme Court asserted its right to declare laws passed by Congress unconstitutional. *(page 67)*

maritime law See *admiralty law.* *(page 464)*

market economy the capitalist economic system in which prices, quantities, and types of goods are determined in a free market by the independent actions of individuals. *(page 735)*

Marshall Plan a massive American economic aid program designed by George Marshall to help European nations recover from World War II. *(page 550)*

Marxism the body of economic and political thought formulated by Karl Marx. *(page 742)*

mass media sources of information — including radio, television, film, and the press — that influence a large number of people. *(page 157)*

mass transit a system of moving large numbers of people from place to place. *(page 714)*

Mayflower Compact the agreement in which New England settlers established their own government in 1620. *(page 34)*

mayor-council form a form of municipal government in which voters elect both a city council and a mayor as their governing officials. *(page 702)*

mediator a neutral person who helps to work out compromises between two conflicting parties. *(page 576)*

Medicaid a joint federal-state program that aids the poor in paying for medical expenses. *(page 625)*

Medicare the federal social insurance health program for people over 65. *(page 619)*

Members of Parliament (MPs) the elected representatives to the House of Commons. *(page 757)*

merchant marine the private ships used in international trade. *(page 566)*

merger the combining of two or more companies. *(page 569)*

merit employment the practice of hiring and promoting government employees on the basis of objective, competitive testing. *(page 286)*

militia (mih-LISH-uh) a volunteer civilian army. *(page 95)*

mill the monetary unit equal to one-tenth of a cent, used to calculate property tax rates. *(page 716)*

minimum wage the lowest wage an employer can legally pay an employee. *(page 577)*

ministry the administration in Great Britain, made up of the Prime Minister and his or her appointed ministers. *(page 758)*

minor court a court which handles the state's least serious cases, with jurisdiction usually limited to misdemeanor cases and small civil suits. *(page 654)*

Minority Leader the main spokesperson for the minority party in the House of Representatives who mobilizes opposition to the majority party. *(page 356)*

***Miranda* warnings** specific guidelines designed in 1966 to govern police procedure and insure due process for accused persons. *(page 184)*

misdemeanor a crime less serious than a felony. *(page 183)*

"missionary party" highly ideological political party which seeks converts or followers more than votes. *(page 281)*

Missouri Plan the method of selecting state judges that combines appointment by the governor with popular election. *(page 658)*

mistrial a trial that becomes invalid because the judge believes fairness has been jeopardized or because the jury cannot agree on a verdict. *(page 505)*

moderate a person whose attitudes and opinions are somewhere between those of a liberal and a conservative. *(page 229)*

monarchy a form of autocracy in which the ruler acquires position through inheritance or family ties. *(page 13)*

monetary policy a governmental tool for influencing the economy by varying the amount of money in circulation. *(page 530)*

monopoly a situation in which a single business or firm controls an entire market. *(page 568)*

Monroe Doctrine President Monroe's 1823 warning against new European colonization in the Western Hemisphere. *(page 540)*

moot question a question of no practical importance. *(page 475)*

muckraker a term for a journalist in the early 1900's who reported on social conditions and problems. *(page 571)*

multi-party system a political system with many rival parties competing for control of the government. *(page 271)*

municipal bond a loan by a citizen to a local government. *(page 719)*

municipal corporation a municipality as a legal body, with the right to carry out certain governmental functions. *(page 699)*

municipal court a minor court established by a city or town to enforce local ordinances. *(page 654)*

municipality any local community that enjoys self-government. *(page 698)*

N

NAACP the National Association for the Advancement of Colored People, established in 1909 to secure social and political rights for black Americans. *(page 197)*

national committee a party's leadership, fund-raising, and promotional organization. *(page 282)*

national debt the total sum of money owed by the federal government to investors; also called public debt. *(page 520)*

nationalism devotion to one's nation. *(page 97)*

nationalization the process by which the government takes over a private industry. *(page 749)*

National Security Council established in 1947, the council gives the President advice on matters of domestic, military, and foreign security, and directs the operations of the Central Intelligence Agency. *(page 423)*

NATO the North Atlantic Treaty Organization, formed in 1949 by the United States, Canada, and ten western European nations to protect Western Europe against Soviet or East European attack. *(page 553)*

naturalization the legal process of granting citizenship to someone who has not acquired it by birth. *(page 22)*

"necessary and proper" clause Article I, Section 8, Clause 18, of the Constitution (also called the elastic clause) which permits Congress to pass laws as necessary to carry out its existing powers. *(page 86)*

neutrality not favoring one side or another in a conflict. *(page 539)*

New Jersey Plan a proposal of government designed by William Paterson which favored a unicameral legislature and a plural executive branch. *(page 52)*

nominating convention the meeting of party delegates in a presidential election year to write a platform and nominate candidates. *(page 283)*

nominating petition a petition with the signatures of a required number of qualified voters who support putting a candidate's name on the ballot. *(page 293)*

nomination naming a candidate to run for election. *(page 292)*

nonaligned neutral; not in alliance with any nation. *(page 538)*

nonrenewable a kind of natural resource that is depleted with use. *(page 600)*

Northwest Ordinance a plan which outlined a governmental structure for the land north of the Ohio River and westward to the Mississippi River. *(page 44)*

nuclear power the power produced from the energy released by an atomic reaction. *(page 604)*

Nuclear Regulatory Commission (NRC) a federal government agency formed in 1974 to take over regulation of the United States' nuclear power from the abolished Atomic Energy Commission. *(page 604)*

O ————————

obscenity material not protected under the First Amendment because it is offensive and lacks serious literary, artistic, political, or scientific value. *(page 156)*

office-group ballot also called "Massachusetts" ballot; ballot which lists candidates together by the office they are seeking. *(pages 310, 326)*

Office of Management and Budget (OMB) federal office whose duties include collecting and analyzing federal budget estimates, preparing budget proposals for the President to submit to Congress, and coordinating different executive agencies. *(page 424)*

off-year election races for Congress and governor in years when there is not a presidential election. *(page 313)*

oligarchy rule by a small group. *(page 13)*

OPEC the Organization of Petroleum Exporting Countries, formed in 1960 by major oil-producing nations to set oil prices and production levels. *(page 601)*

open primary a type of direct primary in which voters do not have to declare a party preference. *(page 292)*

opinion a court's written decision that summarizes a case and presents the questions of law, the ruling, and the reasoning involved in the ruling. *(page 478)*

opposition party the party that is out of office. *(page 268)*

ordinance a statute or regulation enacted by a local legislative body. *(page 492)*

original jurisdiction the authority of a court to hear and decide a case for the first time. *(page 466)*

P ————————

pardon a legal release from punishment. *(page 404)*

parity a level for farm-product prices maintained by governmental support and intended to give farmers the same purchasing power they had during a chosen period. *(page 581)*

parliament a representative body with the power to make laws. *(page 31)*

parliamentary government a system in which legislative and executive functions are combined in an elected legislature. *(pages 65, 758)*

parole the conditional early release of a prisoner who has served the minimum sentence. *(page 507)*

party-column ballot also called "Indiana" ballot; ballot which lists all the candidates from each party in a single row or column. *(pages 310, 326)*

patent the exclusive right to produce, sell, or use an invention. *(page 333)*

patronage (PAY-truh-nij) the practice of awarding government jobs to political supporters and friends. *(pages 285, 438)*

payroll tax the Social Security tax withheld from workers' paychecks and matched by employers that is used to support social insurance programs. *(page 518)*

peers those people around us who have similar backgrounds and beliefs and may be near us in age. *(page 234)*

Pendleton Act the Civil Service Reform Act passed in 1883 to end the spoils system by appointing persons to government positions on a merit basis. *(page 440)*

Pentagon the headquarters for the Department of Defense. *(page 548)*

per capita income the average yearly income per person. *(page 665)*

peremptory challenge the disqualification, without a stated reason, of a potential juror by an attorney. *(page 503)*

perquisite ("perk") a benefit, allowance, or service in addition to a regular salary. *(page 344)*

Petition of Right a demand by Parliament in 1628 that King Charles agree to further limitations on the monarchy. *(page 32)*

petit jury a group of impartial people who evaluate the evidence presented in a trial and determine the accused person's guilt or innocence; also called a trial jury. *(page 181)*

pigeonhole to kill a bill by refusing to take action on it or pass it out of a committee. *(page 366)*

plaintiff the person who files suit in a civil case. *(page 502)*

planned economy See *communism. (page 742)*

planning setting long-range overall guidelines for community development. *(page 722)*

plat a small parcel of land. *(page 726)*

platform a statement of the goals and principles of a political party. *(page 283)*

plea bargaining pre-trial negotiations in which the

prosecutor tries to dispose of a case before going to trial by agreeing to reduce the charges if the defendant agrees to plead guilty. *(page 500)*

Plessy v. Ferguson the 1896 Supreme Court decision upholding segregation. *(page 196)*

plurality the highest number of votes. *(page 292)*

pocket veto a President's indirect veto of a bill, exercised by failing to act on it. *(page 402)*

political action committee (PAC) a legal entity set up by an interest group to collect and spend funds for political purposes. *(page 260)*

political culture those elements of a nation's culture that are related to government and politics. *(page 231)*

political party a group of like-minded citizens organized to win elections, control government, and set public policy. *(page 268)*

political socialization the process by which citizens acquire their sense of political identity. *(page 233)*

political symbol an object or expression that is part of a nation's political culture and that represents an abstract idea such as "freedom," "democracy," or the country itself. *(page 232)*

politics the process of conflict and compromise through which government works. *(page 9)*

poll tax a fee, now illegal, that a person had to pay before voting. *(page 308)*

pollutant a chemical or other harmful substance in the water or air. *(page 593)*

poll watcher a person who is present at a polling place to ensure an honest election. *(page 311)*

popular sovereignty a system in which the power to govern belongs to the people but is transferred to the government under their control. *(page 62)*

pork-barrel program a project or grant that chiefly benefits a legislator's home district. *(page 346)*

post roads routes over which the mail is carried. *(page 333)*

Preamble an introduction; specifically the introduction to the Constitution of the United States. *(page 63)*

precedent (PRESS-eh-dent) a ruling that is used as a model in deciding similar cases. *(page 33)*

precinct (PREE-sinkt) a part of a voting district set up by a state and divided by a local government; smaller than a ward. *(page 311)*

prefect now called a commissioner, the head of a French department, appointed by the national government. *(page 763)*

pre-file to file a bill before a regular legislative session officially begins. *(page 642)*

Premier the head of the French cabinet, appointed by the President to help select ministers, propose legislation, and carry out policies. *(page 761)*

presentment a formal written accusation presented by a grand jury after its investigation of a case. *(page 176)*

presidential government a system of government in which the executive branch acts independently of the legislative branch. *(page 64)*

presidential primary a primary election in which voters choose the candidate they want their convention delegates to nominate. *(page 297)*

presidential succession the order in which the office of President is to be filled if it becomes vacant before an election. *(page 384)*

price support a government program to help farmers maintain their purchasing power and standard of living. *(page 581)*

primary election a preliminary election in which voters choose the candidates who will run for office in the general election. *(page 292)*

prime minister the head of the cabinet and the chief executive of a parliamentary government. *(page 65)*

prior restraint government censorship of a work before it is published. *(page 155)*

Privacy Act law which stipulates that certain information, such as financial, health, and criminal records, about private individuals may not be made public without their consent. *(page 188)*

private law See *civil law*. *(page 492)*

probability the likelihood that something will happen. *(page 238)*

probable cause a reasonable belief that a particular crime has been or is being committed, providing grounds for a search warrant. *(page 171)*

probate verifying the validity of a will. *(page 655)*

probation a sentence in which a person convicted of a crime does not spend time in jail but must follow certain restrictions. *(page 506)*

procedural due process rules of conduct for police officers, judges, lawyers, and courts to protect persons suspected, accused, or convicted of a crime. *(page 169)*

profit the income a business has left after paying its expenses. *(page 736)*

progressive tax a tax that assigns higher tax rates to people with higher incomes. *(page 515)*

prohibited powers powers that are denied to the national government, the state government, or both; also called restricted powers. *(page 89)*

proletariat (proh-lih-TAIR-ee-at) the term Karl Marx used for the working class. *(page 742)*

proliferation spreading. *(page 554)*

propaganda any persuasive communication designed to influence people's beliefs, opinions, emotions, or actions. *(pages 15, 261)*

property tax a tax imposed on real property or personal property such as jewelry, automobiles, and boats. *(page 679)*

proportional representation the allocation of legislative seats to each political party in proportion to the votes it receives. *(page 273)*

proprietor an individual to whom a colony and a charter were granted, and who had the authority to organize the colony. *(page 34)*

prosecuting attorney the government's legal representative who brings charges and attempts to prove that a crime was committed. *(page 176)*

protocol the set of customs and courtesies that foreign officials observe in dealing with one another. *(page 547)*

public assistance federal aid programs funded by state and federal tax dollars, available to those who can prove that they are in need. *(page 614)*

public defender a lawyer employed by the state and appointed by the court to defend individuals who cannot afford legal aid. *(page 183)*

public-interest group an interest group working for the common good, rather than for benefits for specific individuals. *(page 257)*

public law the branch of the legal system that deals with the relationship between the government and citizens. *(page 495)*

public opinion the combination of many individuals' expressed feelings about government and political issues. *(page 226)*

public policy any course of government action directed toward achieving a national goal. *(page 6)*

public utility a company that provides a community with a vital service such as gas, electricity, water, or telephone service. *(page 570)*

pure speech communication by spoken word alone. *(page 150)*

Q

quorum the minimum number of people needed to conduct business. *(page 49)*

R

radical someone who favors rapid, fundamental change in the existing social, economic, or political order; on the far left. *(page 229)*

random sample a sample chosen in such a way that every member of the universe has an equal chance of being selected. *(page 239)*

ratification final approval. *(page 43)*

reactionary someone who advocates a return to a previous government or state of affairs and who may be willing to go to extremes to attain this goal; on the far right. *(page 229)*

real property land and everything attached to it, such as houses and barns. *(page 493)*

reapportionment the redistribution of legislative seats. *(page 337)*

recall the procedure by which a public official may be voted out of office. *(page 645)*

recess to take a temporary break. *(page 352)*

recession a mild, short-term economic slump; less severe than a depression. *(page 528)*

reciprocity (reh-sih-PROSS-ih-tee) the mutual exchange of respect and political favors between states or countries. *(page 107)*

redistrict to redraw the boundaries of legislative districts. *(pages 96, 337)*

referendum a form of direct legislation allowing voters to approve or disapprove a proposed amendment to the state constitution or a law already passed by the legislature. *(pages 261, 644)*

registration the act of signing up with election officials in order to be able to vote. *(page 310)*

regressive tax a tax that assigns lower tax rates to people with higher incomes. *(page 518)*

renewable a kind of natural resource that is not expected to run out or that can be replaced. *(page 607)*

representative democracy a form of government in which people elect a group of citizens to represent them in making laws and establishing public policies. *(page 16)*

reprieve a delay in carrying out a punishment. *(page 404)*

republic any government in which the people exercise their political power through elected representatives and in which no public offices are inherited. *(page 16)*

Republicans a political party formed by a coalition of antislavery forces in 1854 and which later seated Abraham Lincoln in the presidency. *(page 278)*

reserved powers powers set aside for the state governments by the Constitution. *(page 90)*

residency a requirement that voters must have lived in a state for a certain amount of time before they are allowed to vote there. *(page 310)*

resolution a formal statement expressing a legislative decision or opinion. *(page 364)*

restrictive covenant made illegal by the Civil Rights Act of 1968, an agreement in a lease or deed that prevented minorities from buying or renting homes. *(page 204)*

revenue income; the money a government collects from taxes and other sources in order to pay its expenses. *(page 514)*

revenue sharing a form of government financing by which a portion of the money collected in federal income taxes is given to state and local governments. *(page 102)*

reverse discrimination the situation in which affirmative action conflicts with equal protection and leads to loss of opportunity for some people. *(page 210)*

Reynolds v. Sims the 1964 Supreme Court ruling that state legislatures must apportion their representatives according to the ''one person, one vote'' principle. *(page 640)*

rider an amendment added to a bill having nothing to do with the subject of the bill. *(page 369)*

''right'' on the political spectrum, referring to people who hold conservative views. *(page 229)*

right-to-work law a state law that allows a worker to obtain and keep a job without being required to join a union. *(page 576)*

Roosevelt Corollary the 1904 corollary to the Monroe Doctrine in which the United States reserved the right to interfere in the internal affairs of any American nation that could not pay its debts or maintain order. *(page 540)*

rule by law a system in which the law applies to government officials as much as to ordinary citizens, and public officials must make decisions based on the law, not on personal opinions or wishes. *(page 19)*

''rule of four'' the agreement of four of the nine Supreme Court justices needed for a case to be heard on appeal. *(page 474)*

Rules Committee the committee which regulates the calendar of the House of Representatives. *(page 368)*

S _____

''salutary neglect'' Britain's policy of non-interference in its American colonies' internal affairs in order to increase the colonies' productivity and value. *(page 36)*

sample in polling terms, a small group of people who accurately represent a universe. *(page 238)*

sampling error the range of accuracy of the results of a random sample poll. *(page 239)*

sanctions punishment or show of disapproval, often in the form of economic and trade restrictions on an offending country. *(page 372)*

schedule the part of a constitution that states how and when the document will be ratified. *(page 635)*

school board the governing body of a school district. *(page 697)*

school district an area within a state defined by a local or state government to run the public schools within that area. *(page 697)*

scientific polling the determination of public opinion through precise sampling and statistical methods. *(page 238)*

secede a state's act of leaving the Union. *(page 97)*

Secretariat the executive branch of the United Nations. *(page 558)*

Security Council the division of the UN that has the main responsibility of maintaining the peace; consists of five permanent member nations and ten nations elected for two-year terms. *(page 556)*

sedition (sih-DISH-un) conduct or language that stirs up rebellion or advocates the overthrow of a government. *(page 151)*

segregation the legal separation of one group from another, usually on a racial basis. *(page 196)*

select committee a temporary congressional committee created for a specific purpose not handled by a standing committee. *(page 361)*

selectmen a group of elected officials who supervise a town's affairs. *(page 696)*

self-incrimination the giving of testimony that might implicate oneself in criminal activity. *(page 177)*

senatorial courtesy the custom that senators will not confirm a presidential nomination opposed by both senators from the state of the appointee or

by the senior senator of the President's party. *(page 80)*

Senior Executive Service a high level group of government executives receiving higher salaries than persons under the GS rating, but with less job security. *(page 442)*

seniority length of service. *(page 355)*

sentence the punishment decided by a court. *(page 505)*

''separate but equal'' a doctrine established in *Plessy v. Ferguson* upholding segregation as long as public facilities were equal. *(page 197)*

separation of powers the division of governmental power among separate branches. *(page 63)*

sequester to isolate jury members during a particularly sensitive trial. *(page 504)*

severance tax a state tax imposed on the extraction of natural resources from the state's land or water. *(page 679)*

shadow Cabinet a group of Britain's opposition party members who are ready to take control of the government if an election is held and their party wins a majority of seats in Parliament. *(page 760)*

Sherman Antitrust Act an 1890 law that made it illegal for businesses to set up monopolies. *(page 568)*

shield law a law that establishes conditions under which journalists are not required to testify or reveal confidential sources of information. *(page 159)*

single-issue group interest groups that focus their attention almost entirely on one issue. *(page 257)*

single-member district a district in which only the candidate with the largest number of votes wins election. *(page 273)*

slander defamation in spoken form. *(page 153)*

slate a list of persons to be appointed or elected to office. *(page 387)*

small claims court a minor court that hears civil cases involving relatively small sums of money (usually under $1,000). *(page 654)*

Smith Act a sedition law which made it a crime to advocate the violent overthrow of any government in the United States, attempt or conspire to commit rebellion, or organize or join any organization advocating rebellion. *(page 152)*

social contract an agreement among the members of a society to create a state and obey its government. *(page 8)*

social insurance federal assistance programs that are funded by personal contributions and are available to those who have paid into them. *(pages 518, 614)*

socialism the economic system which advocates government ownership of the basic means of production. *(page 747)*

Social Security a federal social insurance program begun in 1935 to provide retirement support for American workers. *(page 614)*

socioeconomic having a combination of social and economic characteristics. *(page 313)*

solar power power produced from the energy generated by the sun's rays. *(page 607)*

Solicitor General the Justice Department's legal officer who decides which cases the federal government will appeal to the Supreme Court and who will represent the government before the Court. *(page 496)*

"solid South" the one-party southern states which consistently voted overwhelmingly for Democratic candidates from the late 1800's on. *(page 279)*

solid waste garbage and trash. *(page 599)*

sovereign immunity the principle of law that a sovereign government cannot be sued. *(page 469)*

sovereignty (SAHV-ur-en-tee) a state's right to rule itself. *(page 5)*

Soviet bloc the cold war term for the Soviet Union and its East European "satellites." *(page 543)*

Speaker of the House the member of the majority party in the House of Representatives who presides over the legislative body. *(page 356)*

special district a unit of local government set up to provide services that a local government does not or cannot handle, such as fire protection, water supply, soil conservation, sanitation, and irrigation. *(page 697)*

special session an emergency congressional meeting called by the President when Congress is adjourned or in recess. *(page 353)*

speech-plus a speech in combination with some kind of action, such as marching, singing, picketing, or chanting slogans. *(page 150)*

split ticket a vote cast on one ballot for candidates of two or more different parties. *(page 285)*

spoils system a system of patronage by which government jobs are awarded on a political party basis. *(page 438)*

sponsor the member of Congress who introduces a bill. *(page 364)*

Stamp Act a law passed by Parliament in 1765 which placed a tax on all printed materials. *(page 37)*

standing committee permanent congressional committee that deals with bills about particular subjects. *(page 360)*

stare decisis (STAH-ray dih-SIGH-sis) the principle by which the Supreme Court's ruling on one case is used as a model in deciding similar cases. *(page 480)*

state an independent political unit characterized by population, territory, government, and sovereignty. *(page 5)*

State of the Union Address the annual message delivered before Congress in which the President outlines legislative priorities for the session to come. *(page 400)*

states' rights the theory that the states should have the power to nullify any actions of the federal government that run contrary to the states' interests. *(page 96)*

statutory law the detailed rules of government passed by a legislature. *(page 78)*

straight party ticket a vote cast on one ballot for all the candidates of the same party. *(page 285)*

status quo the present or existing state of affairs, usually favored by conservatives. *(page 229)*

straw poll an informal survey of public opinion. *(page 237)*

strict construction an interpretation of the Constitution holding that the powers of the federal government are strictly defined. *(page 88)*

strip mining a method of mining coal by stripping away rock and topsoil material (instead of digging a shaft) to reach coal lying close to the surface. *(page 600)*

subcommittee a division of a standing congressional committee. *(page 360)*

subdivision the way land is divided and prepared for sale and occupancy. *(page 725)*

subpoena (suh-PEA-nah) a court order requiring a person to appear as a witness. *(page 182)*

subsidy (SUB-sih-dee) a grant given by the government to reduce the cost of something. *(page 566)*

substantive due process principle which ensures that laws must be reasonable and fair to all citizens. *(page 169)*

suffragist a supporter of the extension of voting rights, especially for women. *(page 212)*

summit meeting a meeting of

two or more heads of state. *(page 544)*

sumptuary tax a tax on items such as tobacco and alcoholic beverages that are considered extravagant or unnecessary. *(page 679)*

sunbelt the region stretching across the U.S. from the southeastern Atlantic coast to southern California. *(page 338)*

sunshine law a law requiring government agencies to hold open meetings and to notify the public of those meetings in advance. *(page 159)*

superpower a powerful, influential nation with many allies. *(page 538)*

Supplemental Security Income (SSI) a social program designed to provide uniform benefits to needy persons by giving them a minimum income. *(page 625)*

supremacy clause Article VI, Clause 2, which states that the Constitution is the supreme law of the land. *(page 67)*

surplus an extra supply. *(page 582)*

surveillance (ser-VAY-lunts) close observation of an individual suspected of illegal activity. *(page 174)*

suspect classification a questionable classification based on race or national origin. *(page 208)*

symbolic speech conveying a message by replacing words with actions and objects. *(page 151)*

syndicalism a form of socialism which calls for labor unions to replace the capitalist economic system and take over the state. *(page 748)*

T ────────────────

table to make a parliamentary motion to kill a bill. *(page 369)*

takeover the act of one company buying another. *(page 569)*

target price the estimated market price for agricultural

commodities established by the Department of Agriculture. *(page 583)*

tax base the thing or value on which taxes are levied. *(page 717)*

territorial court a court, corresponding to a federal district court, established by Congress under its authority to govern U.S. territories. *(page 468)*

tight money monetary policy in which money is taken out of circulation to fight inflation. *(page 533)*

Title IX a stipulation of the Education Amendments of 1972 requiring all schools receiving federal funds to give male and female students equal opportunities in instruction and extracurricular activities. *(page 218)*

tort a wrongful act that injures persons or their property. *(page 493)*

totalitarianism an extreme form of authoritarian government in which the ruler or ruling group attempts to reshape the state, the people, and the society to conform to an idea or plan. *(page 14)*

town the primary unit of local government in colonial New England; a unit of local government similar to a city. *(page 695)*

town manager a professionally trained manager who is elected or appointed by a town's selectmen to oversee daily operations of the town. *(page 696)*

town meeting an annual meeting open to all of a town's qualified voters to decide the basic policies of the town. *(page 696)*

township a county subdivision dating back to colonial times. *(page 696)*

toxic waste the by-products of chemical manufacturing that are poisonous. *(page 597)*

treaty a formal agreement between nations. *(page 408)*

true bill a grand jury's agreement

with a prosecutor that the evidence in a case warrants a trial. *(page 176)*

trust a form of business that unites several companies into one organization, often creating a monopoly. *(page 568)*

two-party system a political system in which two major groups with differing political philosophies compete for control of the government. *(page 271)*

U ────────────────

"uncontrollable" expenditures payments established as a result of past policies committing lawmakers to spending in such areas as support for the sick, elderly, and poor. *(page 524)*

underwriting guaranteeing a loan by agreeing to take responsibility if the borrower fails to pay it back. *(page 566)*

unemployment compensation a government payment, established under the Social Security Act of 1935, to persons who lose their job through no fault of their own. *(page 579)*

unicameral having one legislative house. *(page 43)*

union shop a place of employment in which workers are required to join a union after being hired. *(page 576)*

unitary government a form of government in which the central government has authority over all political subdivisions. *(page 12)*

universe referring to public opinion polls, the population to be studied. *(page 238)*

urbanization the percent of a population living either in cities of more than 2,500 people or in the suburbs of cities of 50,000 or more. *(page 665)*

urban renewal the rebuilding or improvement of declining downtown areas. *(page 712)*

user's fee a source of local

revenue collected for the consumption of some service, such as metered water or electricity. *(page 720)*

utopian a person who believes that an ideal society can be created. *(page 748)*

V ————————————

variance permission granted to free property owners from zoning restrictions under certain circumstances. *(page 724)*

venue (VEN-yoo) the location of a trial. *(page 503)*

verdict the decision in a trial. *(page 505)*

veterans' preference the practice of adding bonus points to the civil service examination scores of honorably discharged veterans and of disabled veterans. *(page 441)*

veto the power of a chief executive to prevent a bill from becoming law. *(page 66)*

Virginia Plan a plan designed by Edmund Randolph which favored a strong national government with three branches and a bicameral legislature. *(page 51)*

Virginia Statute of Religious Liberty principle of religious toleration established in Virginia to provide freedom of religion and separation of church and state. *(pages 142, 143)*

Voting Rights Act (1965) an act that allowed federal officials to ensure African Americans the right to vote. *(page 204)*

W ————————————

ward a part of a voting district set up by a state and divided by a local government; larger than a precinct. *(page 311)*

War Powers Act (1973) law which restricts the President's use of American troops abroad unless Congress declares war, a law authorizes such action, or there is a national emergency. *(page 412)*

warrant a court order that authorizes law-enforcement officials to make an arrest, search a person or place, or take property as evidence. *(page 171)*

welfare state a system in which the state assumes primary responsibility for the welfare of its citizens by providing benefits such as free medical care, free education, guaranteed income, and pensions. *(page 750)*

Whigs a political party which split from the Democratic-Republicans and opposed the policies of Andrew Jackson. *(page 278)*

whip an assistant floor leader in Congress. *(page 356)*

White House Office the ''command post'' of the executive branch whose members advise the President on congressional and public relations and foreign affairs. *(page 423)*

white primary a type of primary election, declared unconstitutional in 1944, in which African Americans were prohibited from voting on the grounds that the Fifteenth Amendment applied only to general elections. *(page 309)*

will a legal document made out by people to direct what they want done with their property after they die. *(page 655)*

withholding an automatic deduction from wages or salary used to pre-pay income tax. *(page 515)*

worker's compensation payments required by law to be made to an employee with a work-related injury or illness. *(page 579)*

"workfare" social programs that require welfare recipients to take jobs in order to receive benefits. *(page 625)*

write-in candidate a person who fails to get on the ballot and whose name is written in on election day. *(page 294)*

writ of *certiorari* (sir-shee-uh-RARE-ee) an order from the Supreme Court to a lower court to prepare and send records of a case for review. *(page 474)*

Z ————————————

zones of privacy areas where Americans can expect to be free from government interference in their lives. *(page 188)*

zoning making regulations for the use or occupancy of land. *(page 722)*

INDEX

This index includes references not only to the text but to the pictures *(p)*, charts and graphs *(c)*, and maps *(m)* as well.

Indiana, 338, 340, *c814, c817;* revnues, 679; state constitution, *c637;* voting requirements, *c324*
Indians (North American). *See* American Indians
indictment, 176, 500
individual liberty, 19, 33
individual worth, 18–19
Indonesia, 602
industrial corporations, *c571*
Industrial Revolution, 735–736
Industrial Workers of the World (IWW), 748
industry. *See* business; commerce; economy
INF. *See* Intermediate-range nuclear forces
inflation, 527, 529, 532–533
Information Agency, U.S. (USIA), 552
information, 439, 500; freedom of, 159
inherent powers, 90
initiative process of legislation, 261, 636, 645
injunction, 156, 492
Inner Cabinet, 430
innocence, presumption of, 185
INS. *See* Immigration and Naturalization Service
insurance, regulation of, 100
integration. *See* desegregation; discrimination; segregation
intercontinental ballistic missile (ICBM), 554–555
interest groups, 246–263, 431, 472; agricultural, 249, *p250,* 252–254, *c253; amicus curiae,* 261, 476, 496; business, *c253;* characteristics of, 248; civil rights groups, 255, *c256;* class action suits of, 261; conflicting interests and, 249; direct legislation, 261–262; economic, 252–255; electioneering, 260; environmental protection groups, *c256,* 595; funding of, 250; goals of, 252–258; grassroots campaigns, 260; influencing elections, 259–260, 269; judging effectiveness, 249; labor, 249, *c253;* lobbying, 258–259; as measure of public opinion, 236; nature of, 248–250; organization and resources of, 249–250; political action committees, 260; professional, 252, *c253;* public interest groups, *c256,* 257; religious groups, 255–257, *c256;* single-issue groups, 257–258, *c257;* social action, 255–257, *c256;* use of propaganda, 261; veterans' rights groups, 255. *See also* lobby groups
interim committees, 642
Interior, U.S. Department of the, 206, 428, 431, 590, 592, 594, 608;

services of, 455
Intermediate-range Nuclear Forces (INF), 555
Internal Revenue Service (IRS), 145, 460, 469, 515–517, *p515*
International Court of Justice, UN, 495, *c557,* 558
International Criminal Police Organization (INTERPOL), 456
international law, 495, 548
international trade, 566, 630
International Trade Administration (ITA), 449
International Union, United Auto., etc. v. Johnson Controls, 217
interstate commerce, 93, 99–100, 676
Interstate Commerce Act (1887), 527, 567–568
Interstate Commerce Commission (ICC), 432, 434, 568, 571
interstate compact, 106
interventionism, 540
Intolerable Acts, 39
inversion, 596
investigations, limits on, 170–175, 510-10–510-11
Iowa, 298, *c814, c817;* executive branch, 646; federal disaster relief in, 405; public policy of, 666, 669; state constitution, *c637;* voting requirements, *c324*
Iran, 15, 416, 546, 558, 602; American hostages in, 430; arms trading scandal, *p334,* 335, 424; public opinion of, 228, *c416*
Iran-*contra* affair, *p330, p334,* 335, *c416,* 546
Iraq, *p216,* 406, 410, *p410,* 411–412, 416, 510–15, 554–555, 558, *p558*
iron curtain, 543
iron triangles, 431
IRS. *See* Internal Revenue Service
isolationism, 539–540
Israel, *c315,* 407, 749
Italy, 271, 314, *c315,* 316, 541, 735, 748, 749
item veto, 404, 651

J

Jackson, Andrew, 277, 278, 293, 399, *c403, c810;* Cabinet of, 428; style of, 413; spoils system and, 438
Jackson Board of Education, Wygant v., 211
Jackson, Jesse, 296, *p296,* 298, 300, 381
Jackson, Rachel Donelson Robards, *c811*
Jackson, Robert H., 140, 477
Jackson, William, 49, 51
Jaffree, Wallace, v., 146, *c510-8*
Jamestown (Virginia), 30
Japan, 271, *c315,* 380, 406, 541,

630, 736, 741
Japanese Americans, 208–209, *p209,* 261
Japanese Pact (1951), 553
Jay, John, 39, 55, 56, *c476*
JCS. *See* Joint Chiefs of Staff
Jefferson, Martha Skelton, *c811*
Jefferson, Thomas, 3, 19, 29, 33, 40, 43, 44, 49, 68, *p80,* 86–88; *p88,* 96, 142, 143, 267, 276–277, 352, 388–389, 402, *c403,* 405–406, 417, 427, 563, *c810, c811;* amnesty and, 404; Inaugural Address, 277
Jehovah's Witnesses, 144, 147–148, 255
Jenner-Butler Bill (1958), 484–485
Jepsen, Roger, 343
Jews, *p145,* 162–163, *c256,* 283; restrictive covenants against, 204; and U.S. foreign policy, 539
Jim Crow laws, 196, *p196*
Job Corps' Civilian Conservation Centers, 455
job discrimination, 204, 217–218, 248
Job Training Partnership Act, 457
Johnson, Andrew, 385, 402, *c403, c810, c811;* amnesty and, 404–405; impeachment, *p115*
Johnson, Claudia Alta Taylor, *c813*
Johnson Controls, International Union, United Auto, etc. v., 217
Johnson, Eliza McCardle, *c811*
Johnson, Lyndon B., 95, 203–204, 209, 280, 290–291, 296, 358, 384, *p386,* 398, *p399, c403,* 406, *c812, c813;* Cabinet of, 428, 429; characteristics of, *c414;* power of persuasion, 415; Supreme Court appointments, 482; use of negative political advertising, 307; Vietnam War, 411; war on poverty, 615, 619
Johnson, Richard M., *c811*
Johnson, Samuel, 488
Johnson, Texas v., 151
Johnson, William Samuel, 52
Joint Chiefs of Staff (JCS), 424, 450, 548
joint committees, 642
Jones & Laughlin Steel Corp., National Labor Relations Board v., 100
Jones v. Mayer, 195
Jordan, Barbara, statement on impeachment, 799
Jordan, Hamilton, 425
Journal (William Jackson), 51
judges, 466–467, *p471;* compensation of, 470–471; constitutional provisions for, 470, 471; impeachment of, 470; length of terms, 64; lower court, 473; selection of, 471–473; state, 657–659
judicial activism, 480

INDEX

INDEX

INDEX

Acknowledgments

Text Credits

Grateful acknowledgment is made to authors, publishers, and other copyright holders for permission to reprint (and in some selections to adapt slightly) copyright material listed below.

77 From "Immigration Bill's OK Could Be Salvation of Our Ideals" by Jody Powell, in the *Houston Post,* July 9, 1986. Copyright © 1986 by the Los Angeles *Times* Syndicate. Reprinted by permission of Joseph L. (Jody) Powell. **77** From "A Missed Chance for True Economic Reform" by Gary S. Becker, *Business Week,* December 1, 1986. **192** Reprinted from "I Have A Dream" by permission of Joan Daves. Copyright © 1963 by Martin Luther King, Jr. **226** From *Public Opinion and American Democracy* by V.O. Key, Jr. Copyright © 1961, Alfred A. Knopf, Inc. Reprinted by permission of The Trustees of the Luella Gettys Key Trust. **232** Adapted from *The Civic Culture: Political Attitudes and Democracy in Five Nations* by Gabriel A. Almond and Sidney Verba. Copyright © 1963 by Princeton University Press. **234** From "The Role of the Elementary School in Political Socialization" by Robert D. Hess and David Easton, *The School Review,* LXX, June 1962. Copyright © 1962. Reprinted by permission of The University of Chicago Press. **246** From *Democracy in America* by Alexis de Tocqueville, edited by Phillips Bradley, translated by Henry Reeve, revised by Francis Bowen. Copyright © 1980. Reprinted by permission of Alfred A. Knopf, Inc. **255** From *Why We Can't Wait* by Martin Luther King, Jr. Copyright © 1963, 1964 by Martin Luther King, Jr. Used by permission of Joan Daves. **268, 269, 417** From *Parties and Politics in America* by Clinton Rossiter. Copyright © 1960, Cornell University. Reprinted by permission of Cornell University Press. **307** From "The Constitutional Convention Is 'Still in Session'," by Curtis J. Sitomer, *The Christian Science Monitor,* April 13, 1987. Copyright © 1987, The Christian Science Publishing Society. All rights reserved. Reprinted by permission of *The Christian Science Monitor.* **308** From *To Praise Our Bridges: The Autobiography of Fannie Lou Hamer.* **353** From "Freshman Congressmen: Finding Their Place on the Hill" by Allan Dodds Frank, *Family Weekly,* June 1, 1980. Reprinted by permission of Congressman Kent Hance of Texas. **355** Adapted from *Congressional Procedures and the Policy Process,* by Walter J. Oleszek. Copyright ©

1984. Reprinted by permission of Congressional Quarterly, Inc. **415** From *Presidential Power: The Politics Leadership from FDR to Carter* by Richard E. Neustadt. Copyright © 1980. Reprinted by permission of Macmillan Publishing Company, New York. **415** From *The State of the Presidency* by Thomas E. Cronin. Copyright © 1975, Little, Brown and Company. **474** From *The Court Years: 1939–1975* by William O. Douglas. Copyright © 1980, Random House, Inc. Reprinted by permission of Random House, Inc. **480** From *The Judicial Process,* by Henry J. Abraham. Copyright © 1957. Reprinted by permission of Oxford University Press. **482** From *The Diaries of Felix Frankfurter,* edited by Joseph P. Lash. Copyright © 1975 by Joseph P. Lash. Reprinted by permission of W.W. Norton & Co., Inc., New York, N.Y. **483** From "Confirm Judge Thomas, But Don't Let Him Forget His Origins" by Birdia M. Churchwell, *Houston Post,* September 11, 1991. Copyright © 1991. Reprinted by permission of the author. **483** From "Cynical Thomas Bid Should Be Rejected" by Thomas Kleven, *Houston Post,* September 1, 1991. Copyright © 1991. Reprinted by permission of the author. **510–2** From "El Chicano y the Constitution: The Legacy of *Hernandez v. Texas* Grand Jury Discrimination" by Lorenzo Arredondo and Donato Tapia in University of San Francisco *Law Review,* Volume 6, Number 1, October 1971. Copyright © 1972 by University of San Francisco *Law Review.* Reprinted by permission of University of San Francisco *Law Review.* **510–2** From "A Child's Faith" by Roger Wilkins, *The Washington Post Magazine,* June 28, 1987. Reprinted by permission of the author. **510–3** From "Unequal Partners" by Elizabeth Rose Bird in *The Washington Post Magazine,* June 28, 1987. Copyright © 1987 by Elizabeth Rose Bird. **520** From "Soaring National Debt—What It Really Means" by Patricia Scherschel and Robert Morse, *U.S. News & World Report,* Sept. 16, 1985. Copyright © 1985. Reprinted by permission of U.S. News & World Report, Inc. **551** From *The Hunt for Red October* by Tom Clancy. Copyright © 1984 by the United States Naval Institute. Published by the Naval Institute Press, Annapolis, Maryland. **588** From *Silent Spring* by Rachel Carson. Copyright © 1962, Rachel Carson. Reprinted by permission of Houghton Mifflin Company. **688** From *Weekly Articles,* Nov. 15, 1925. Reprinted by permission of The Will Rogers Memorial. **697** From *Remarkable Providences 1600–1760,* edited by John Demos.

Copyright © 1972 by John Demos. Reprinted by permission of George Braziller, Inc., New York. **732** From *Capitalism and Freedom* by Milton Friedman. Copyright © 1962. Reprinted by permission of The University of Chicago Press. **741** From "Neo-Protectionism" by David Peterson, *Vital Speeches of the Day,* Feb. 1, 1987. Copyright © 1987. Reprinted by permission of City News Publishing Co. **795** From *The Life and Writings of Frederick Douglass,* edited by Philip Foner. Copyright © 1955, 1983, International Publishers Co., Inc. Reprinted with permission. **797** From "A New Pentecost: A Vision for the Archdiocese of San Antonio" by Most Reverend Patricio F. Flores, Archbishop of San Antonio. Copyright © 1981 by Patricio F. Flores. Reprinted by permission of the author. **799** From "Who Then Will Speak for the Common Good?" by Barbara Jordan, *Vital Speeches of the Day,* Aug. 15, 1976. Copyright © 1976. Reprinted by permission of City News Publishing Co. **804** From "Inaugural Address" (1990) by David Dinkins. Reprinted by permission. **805** From *Visit to America* by Jawaharlal Nehru. Copyright © 1950. Reprinted by permission of Harper & Row Publishers, Inc.

Art Credits

Cover: Design concept by Design Plural, Inc. Photos: *Front Cover (top left to bottom right):* Tony Stone World Wide/Chicago Ltd./Robert E. Daemmrich; Tony Stone World Wide/Chicago Ltd./ David R. Frazier; Tony Stone World Wide/Chicago Ltd./Marc Pokempner; Tony Stone World Wide/ Chicago Ltd./Robert E. Daemmrich. *Spine:* Tony Stone World Wide/Chicago Ltd./Alan Smith. *Back Cover (top left to bottom right):* Tony McCarty/Black Star; Tony Stone World Wide/Chicago Ltd./Dom Smetzer; Tony Stone World Wide/Chicago Ltd./Robert E. Daemmrich.

Bill of Rights furnished by: Maryland State Archives, GOVERNOR AND COUNCIL (U.S. Bill of Rights) MSA S 1170.

Title Page and half title: Photo: Grant LeDuc/Stock Broker

Maps and diagrams by David L. Fuller/Earth Surface Graphics. Charts on pp. 13, 65, 207, 322, 376, 388, 423, 510, 514, 521, 569, 672, 686, 721, 741 by Neil Pinchin Design.

Maps on pp. 806–809 by Donnelly Cartographic Services.

Black line illustrations by Terry Presnall.

Speaking Out portraits by James E. Tennison; pp. 797 and 804, Barbara Higgins Bond.

Civic Literacy artwork by Gary Hoover.

Calligraphy by Paul Breeden.

As Others See Us photo by Jean Pierre Pieuchot.

vi see page 4 **vii** see page 124 **viii** see page 299 **x** AP/Wide World Photos, New York **xi** see page 472 **xii** see page 510-10 **xiii** see page 577 **xiv** see page 650 **xv** see page 771 **1** Stephen R. Brown/TSM **2** © Robert E. Daemmrich/Tony Stone Worldwide **4** © Arthur Grace/Sygma **9** AP/Wide World Photos **10** Hiroyuki Matsumoto/Black Star (inset) © Elliott Varner Smith **13** Mark Peters/Sipa Press **14** The Granger Collection **15** © Alon Reininger/Contact Press Images/Woodfin Camp **16** Bob Mahoney/The Picture Group **17** Grant LeDuc/The Stock Broker **18** Lou Jones **22** Bettmann Archive **23** AP/Wide World Photos **27** AUTH copyright 1989 Philadelphia Inquirer. Reprinted with permission of Universal Press Syndicate. All rights reserved. **28** Medford Taylor/Focus Virginia **31** The Granger Collection **32** The Granger Collection **35** Cary Wolinsky/Stock, Boston **36** E.R. Degginger, FPSA **37** The Granger Collection **38** Historical Pictures Services **51** James Blank/FPG (inset) James Madison (detail), by Frothingham after Stuart. National Portrait Gallery, Washington, D.C. **56** Courtesy of The New-York Historical Society **59** MIKE PETERS reprinted by permission of UFS, Inc. **60** David Marie/Folio, Inc. **62** Reuters/ Bettmann **67** Mark Segal/Folio, Inc. **68** Architect of the Capitol (inset) John Marshall (detail), by J.R. Lambdin after Henry Inman. National Portrait Gallery, Washington, D.C. **72** Bettmann Archive **74** Frank Johnston/Black Star **79** © Paul Conklin **80** Historical Paintings Collection, Continental Insurance Companies **83** © 1990 William Costello/The Lowell Sun. **84** David Pollack/The Stock Market **88** The Granger Collection **89** The Granger Collection **90** David Muench/H. Armstrong Roberts **93** Alon Reininger/Contact Press Images **96** Joanna B. Pinneo/Black Star **97** "Webster's Reply to Senator Hayne" (located in Faneuil Hall), Courtesy of the City of Boston Art Commission **100** The Granger Collection **102** Larry Mulvehill/Photo Researchers, Inc. **106** Port Authority of New York and New Jersey **109** Cartoon by Dennis Renault, Sacramento Bee. Reprinted by permission **110** Reuters/Bettmann **112** The Granger Collection **113** The Granger Collection **114** (bottom) Robert Llewellyn (top) The Granger Collection **115** (bottom) Culver Pictures, Inc. (top) The Granger Collection **116** Dennis Brack/Black Star **117** The Granger Collection **118** (bottom) Bettmann Archive (top) The Granger Collection **119** The Granger Collection **120** Library of Congress **121** (bottom) The Granger Collection (top) Bettmann Archive **122** (bottom) Frank Scherschel, Life Magazine © Time-Warner, Inc. (top) Bettmann Archive **124** (bottom) Randy Duchain/The Stock Market (top) The Granger Collection **125** Historical Pictures Services **127** Historical Pictures Services **129** The Granger Collection **130** The Granger Collection **131** The Granger Collection **132** Library of Congress **133** The Granger Collection **134** Bettmann Archive **136**

UPI/Bettmann Newsphotos **137** Robert Llewellyn **139** Larry Lee/Tony Stone Worldwide, Inc. **140** Michael Nelson/FPG International **142** Ed Bohon/Fran Heyl & Associates **144** Sepp Seitz/Woodfin Camp & Associates **145** Blair Seitz/Photo Researchers, Inc. **147** MacDonald/The Picture Cube **149** Grant LeDuc/The Stock Broker **151** Kusel/Sipa Press **152** © Nina Berman/Sipa Press **154** AP/Wide World Photos. **156** Caroline Brown/Fran Heyl & Associates **157** Gabe Palmer/The Stock Market **158** The Granger Collection **160** © Bob Daemmrich **162** Leonard Freed/Magnum Photos **165** Cartoon by Jim Borgman, 1990, Cincinnati Enquirer. Reprinted with special permission of King Features Syndicate, Inc. **166** Steve Liss, Time Magazine. Time-Warner, Inc. **168** UPI/Bettmann **171** David Falconer/Bruce Coleman, Inc. **174** (right) Everett J. Johnson/Folio, Inc. (inset) Erich Hartmann/Magnum Photos **176** Gary Lansman/Folio, Inc. **178** James Ballard & Associates **181** James Pickerell/Black Star **182** Michel Heron/Woodfin Camp & Associates **183** Flip Schulke, Life Magazine. Time-Warner, Inc. **184** Paul S. Conklin **187** Stephen Ferry/Gamma-Liaison **191** Cartoon by Scott Stantis. Reprinted by permission of The Commercial Appeal **192** ©Jeffrey Markowitz/Sygma, New York **195** The Granger Collection **196** Leonard Freed/Magnum Photos **199** Kindra Clineff **200** Carl Iwaski, Life Magazine. Time-Warner, Inc. **201** Photo courtesy of the Norman Rockwell Museum at Stockbridge. Printed by permission of the Norman Rockwell Family Trust. Copyright © 1964 the Norman Rockwell Family Trust. **203** Francis Miller, Life Magazine. © 1963 Time-Warner, Inc. **205** Daniel Brody/Stock, Boston **206** John Running/Stock, Boston **209** Library of Congress **210** Cary Wolinksy/Stock, Boston **212** Culver Pictures, Inc. **216** AP/Wide World Photos **218** Ellis Herwig/The Picture Cube **221** Clay Bennett, St. Petersburg Times. Reprinted by permission of the artist. **222** © 1991 Bert Andrews **223** Fredrik D. Bodin **224** © Michael Abramson/Sipa Press **227** Stephen R. Brown/The Stock Market **231** ©Catherine Ursillo/Photo Researchers, Inc. **233** ©Don Goode/Photo Researchers, Inc. **235** © Robert McElroy/Woodfin Camp & Associates **237** © Renato Rotolo/Gamma Liaison Network, New York. **238** © Elliott Varner Smith **239** UPI/Bettmann **241** Grant LeDuc/The Stock Broker **245** Chris OBrion, courtesy Potomac News **247** E. Alan McGee/FPG International **248** David Falconer/Folio, Inc. **249** Stephen Ferry/Gamma-Liaison **250** © John Ficara/Woodfin Camp & Associates **254** © Al Stephenson/Picture Group **255** Wally McNamee/Woodfin Camp & Associates **259** The Granger Collection **261** Caroline Brown/Fran Heyl & Associates **265** © 1989 Wayne Stayskal, Tampa Tribune. Reprinted by permission of Wayne Stayskal. **266** Shepard Sherbell/The Picture Group **268** Historical Pictures Service, Inc. **270** Bob Kramer Studio **273** Shelly Katz/Black Star **278** The Granger Collection **281** AP/Wide World Photos **289** Cartoon by Dan Wasserman. Copyright 1984, Boston Globe. Distributed by Los Angeles Time Syndicate.

Reprinted with permission. **290** Daniel Brody/Stock, Boston **293** Read D. Brugger/The Picture Cube, Inc. **294** The Granger Collection **295** Peter Blakely/Picture Group, Inc. **296** R. McElroy/Woodfin Camp & Associates **297** © 1991 Rick Friedman/Black Star **299** ©Wally McNamee/Woodfin Camp & Associates **300** Robert Maass/Sipa Press **301** © 1991 Janice Rubin Photography **303** AP/Wide World Photos (inset) Museum of American Political Life, University of Hartford **305** Ira Wyman/Sygma **309** Eve Arnold/Magnum Photos **316** Jeff Dunn/The Picture Cube **319** Cartoon by Richard Crowson. Copyright © 1991. Reprinted by permission of the Wichita Eagle **320** Mark Peters/Black Star Cartoon by Politiken/Copenhagen/World Press Review. Reprinted by permission of World Press Review. **321** Bruno Barrey/Magnum Photos (inset) Bob Kramer Studio **325** Diego Goldberg/Sygma **327** (bottom) Stuart Krasner/Uniphoto (top) Everett C. Johnson/Folio, Inc. **329** David Marie/Folio, Inc. **330** Dennis Brack/Black Star **333** David Marie/Folio, Inc. **334** James Colburn/Photoreporters, Inc. (inset) Dennis Brack/Black Star **336** Trippet/Sipa Press **345** Grant LeDuc/The Stock Broker **349** Cartoon by Jim Borgman, 1990, Cincinnati Enquirer. Reprinted with special permission of King Features Syndicate, Inc. **350** John Troha/Black Star **354** Dennis Brack/Black Star **358** Fred Ward/Black Star **361** Trippett/Sipa Press **362** Dennis Brack/Black Star **367** © John Ficara 1988/Woodfin Camp & Associates **369** Michael J. Petty/Uniphoto **370** Dennis Brack/Black Star **371** Architect of the Capitol **375** © Jerry Barnettt. Courtesy, The Indianapolis News **376** H. Armstrong Roberts **377** Jeff Gnass/West Stock **378** Courtesy of the White House **381** UPI/Bettmann Newsphotos **382** Courtesy of The White House Historical Association **386** UPI/Bettmann Newsphotos **392** Reuters/Bettmann **395** Copyright © 1976 by Herblock in The Washington Post **396** UPI/Bettmann Newsphotos **399** UPI/Bettmann Newsphotos **402** Wally McNamee/Woodfin Camp & Associates **405** AP/Wide World Photos **407** Sygma News Photos **408** © Diana Walker/Gamma Liaison Network, New York **410** Eric Bouvet/Gamma-Liaison **414** (bottom left) Herbert C. Hoover by Douglas Chandor, The National Portrait Gallery, Smithsonian Institution (bottom right) Calvin Coolidge by Joseph E. Burgess, The National Portrait Gallery, Smithsonian Institution (top left) Franklin D. Roosevelt by Oskar Stoessel, The National Portrait Gallery, Smithsonian Institution (top right) Warren G. Harding by Margaret Lindsey Williams, The National Portrait Gallery, Smithsonian Institution **419** Cartoon by Bill Mauldin. Reprinted with permission from the Chicago Sun-Times. **420** Dennis Brack/Black Star **426** Trippett/Sipa Press **429** © James Colburn/Photoreporters **433** Dave Davis/FPG International **434** G. Mathison/Sygma News Photos **436** NASA **439** Grant LeDuc/The Stock Broker **442** Chris Jones/The Stock Market **445** Cartoon by Dan Wasserman. Copyright, Boston Globe. Distributed by Los Angeles Times Syndicate. Reprinted with permission. **446** Cartoon by Mitchell/ The Australian/© 1991 Cartoonists & Writers Syndicate. Reprinted by permission. **448** Tom Tracy/The Stock Shop **449** David Moore/Black Star **450** Chuck Feil/Stock, Boston **451** Gregg Eisman **452** C.B. Jones/Taurus Photos, Inc. **453** Barbara Alper/Stock, Boston **454** John Lawlor/The Stock Market **455** Tom Tracy/The Stock Shop **456** David York/The Stock Shop **457** Robert Llewellyn **459** Stanley Rowin/The Picture Cube **460** J. Pozarik/Gamma-Liaison **461** R. Krubner/H. Armstrong Roberts **462** Fred Ward/Black Star **464** Jack Swenson/Tom Stack & Associates **471** Windjammer/FPG International (inset) Henry Ortega **472** © Ken Heinen 1986 **475** AP/Wide World Photos, New York. **477** © Ken Heinen **479** © Jerry Jacka **484** Linda L. Creighton, U.S. News and World Report **487** Cartoon by Jeff MacNelly, 10/2/91. Reprinted by permission: Tribune Media Services **488** © Theo Westenberger **490** Art Resource **493** Julian Calder/Woodfin Camp & Associates **495** David Bartruff/FPG International **496** Western History Collection, University of Oklahoma **498** Larry Mulvehill/Photo Researchers, Inc. **501** Grant LeDuc/The Stock Broker **505** Copyright © by Universal Pictures, a Division of Universal City Studios, Inc. Courtesy of MCA Publishing Rights, a Division of MCA, Inc. **506** Tom Campbell/FPG International **509** ROB ROGERS reprinted by permission of UFS, Inc. **510-2** (top right) © D. Goldberg/Sygma News Photos **510-3** (lower bottom) © 1987 Ben Boblett (top right) © A. Knudsen/Sygma News Photos **510-4** (top right) © Le. Segretain/Sipa Press **510-5** (bottom front) © Peter A. Silva, 1990/Picture Group (bottom right) © Dana Fineman/Sygma News Photos **510-6 to 7** Ralph J. Brunke Photography (bottom right) © David Murray/Sipa Press (top right) © Chris Carroll/Onyx **510-7** (top right) AP/Wide World Photos. **510-8** (top right) © Rob Crandall/Picture Group **510-9** (bottom) Photograph by Ted Thai, Time Warner, Inc. (top right) © Christopher Fitzgerald/Picture Group **510-10** (bottom center) © Ken Reagan/Camera Five (top right) © Joe Towers 1989/The Stock Market **510-11** (bottom left) UPI/Bettmann **510-12** (bottom left) © Alexandra Avakian/Woodfin Camp & Associates (top right) AP/Wide World Photos, New York. **510-13** (top right) UPI/Bettmann Newsphotos **510-14** (bottom) Department of Defense, Bethesda, MD (top right) © Patrick Piel/Gamma-Liaison. **510-15** (right center) © Marty Katz/Sipa Press **510-16** (bottom center) © Gregory Neisler/The Image Bank (top right) © Thomas Braise/The Stock Market **510-17** (top right) © Alon Reininger/Woodfin Camp & Associates **510-18** (center right) © Bob Daemmrich/Sygma News Photos (top center) © Bill Gentile/Sipa Press **510-19** (bottom left) © Bill Gentile/Sipa Press (top right) © Wesley Boxce/Sipa Press (bottom left) **510-20** © Peter Miller/The Image Bank (top right) © Bob Daemmrich **510-21** (top right) © Richard Hutchings/Photo Researchers, Inc. **510-22** (top right) © Randy Davey/Picture Group **510-23** (bottom left) Steve Smith/Time Magazine (top right) P.F. Bentley/Time Magazine **510-24** (bottom left) AP/Wide

World Photos (top right) © Rob Crandall/Picture Group (inset) UPI/Bettmann Newsphotos **510-25** (bottom right) © Steve Starr/Picture Group **510-26** (bottom) © Christian Simonpietri/Sygma News Photos **510-27** (bottom center) Doug Jennings/AP/Wide World Photos (top right) © Stephen J. Krasemann/Photo Researchers, Inc. **510-28** (bottom right) © John Ficara/Woodfin Camp & Associates (top right) Courtesy, African American Images **510-29** (left) Courtesy, Kenneth Clark (bottom left) H. Armstrong Roberts **510-30** (bottom center) © 1990 Viviane Moos/The Stock Market (top right) Thomas Kristich/Time Magazine **510-31** (bottom left) Thomas Kristich/Time Magazine (bottom right) © Lori Grinker/Woodfin Camp & Associates (top left) Thomas Kristich/Time Magazine **510-32** (center) © Greg Smith/Sipa Press (lower center) AP/Wide World Photos (top center) © Robert E. Daemmrich/Tony Stone Worldwide **511** Tom Ebenhoh/Black Star **512** George Contorakes/The Stock Market **515** © Peter Chapman **516** J.L. Atlan/Sygma News Photos **517** Grant LeDuc/The Stock Broker **519** Donald C. Dietz/Stock, Boston **525** Diana Walker/Gamma-Liaison **528** UPI/Bettmann Newsphotos **529** Stacy Pick/Stock, Boston **532** AP/Wide World Photos **535** © Michael Ramirez. Courtesy, Copley News Service, San Diego. **536** © 1993 Sal DiMarco/Black Star **539** "View of Whampao" by Youqua. Peabody Museum of Salem **540** The Granger Collection **541** Bettmann Archive **544** UPI/Bettmann Newsphotos **547** Ron Edmonds/AP/Wide World Photos **549** F. Lieberman/Folio, Inc. **552** Susan Van Etten/Taurus Photos, Inc. **554** B. Markel/Gamma-Liaison **558** © Walker/Gamma Liaison **561** ©Signe Wilkinson, Philadelphia Daily News. Courtesy, Cartoonists & Writers Syndicate, New York. **562** Charlton Photos **565** Mike Yamashita/Woodfin Camp & Associates **566** Gabe Palmer/The Stock Market **568** Culver Pictures, Inc. **570** Bernard Gotfryd/Woodfin Camp & Associates **575** Mike Maple/Woodfin Camp & Associates **577** Alan Pogue/Black Star **578** Lewis W. Hine Memorial Collection **580** Bettmann Archive **583** John Marshall **584** J.P. Laffont/Sygma News Photos **587** By Dana Summers © 1986, Washington Post Writers Group. Reprinted with permission. **588** Peter Fronk/Tony Stone Worldwide **591** (bottom) William Waterfall/The Stock Market (top) Tom Bean/The Stock Market **592** (top) Peter Pearson/Tony Stone Worldwide **594** AP/Wide World Photos (inset) AP/Wide World Photos **595** Dan Budnick/Woodfin Camp & Associates **597** Steve Woit/Picture Group **598** AP/Wide World Photos **602** ©Alain Nogués/Sygma **606** (bottom right) Fred Ward/Black Star (center left) Thomas Braise/The Stock Market (center right) Sal Maimone/Shostal/Superstock (top left) Roy Morsch/The Stock Market **611** Reprinted by permission of Joe Heller, Green Bay Press-Gazette **613** Four By Five/Superstock **615** J.P. Laffont/Sygma News Photos **619** Ira Wyman/Sygma **620** Walter Hodges/West Stock, Inc. **621** Ellis Herwig/The Picture Cube **623** Julie O'Neil **629** Cartoon by Dick Locher, Chicago Tribune. Reprinted by permission: Tribune Media Services **630** Courtesy, Sony Corporation of

America **631** Doris DeWill/Tony Stone Worldwide **632** Camera Hawaii, Inc. **635** Bettmann Archive **636** Jeffry W. Myers/Stock, Boston (inset) USDA **638** Charles Gupton/Georgia State Capitol **643** Nebraska Unicameral (inset) Phil Johnson, Omaha World Herald **644** Fred Kaplan/Black Star **647** State of Alabama Bureau of Tourism and Travel/Vickie Smith **648** AP/Wide World Photos, New York. **649** Grant LeDuc/The Stock Broker **650** AP/Wide World Photos, New York. **651** Paul Conklin **652** Office of the Secretary of State of California **655** Walter Chandola Photography **656** David R. Frazier Photo Library **658** © Kennedy/TexaStock **661** Bruce Plante/The Chattanooga Times **662** University of Wisconsin **665** James Blank/FPG International **666** Chris Springman/The Stock Market **668** Bob Riddell/Tony Stone Worldwide **669** Richard Wood/Taurus Photos, Inc. **670** Spencer Swanger/Tom Stack & Associates **674** Frank J. Staub/The Picture Cube **676** Mark Antman/The Image Works **678** Robert Frerck/Tony Stone Worldwide **681** James Colburn/Photoreporters, Inc. **682** Hiroyuki Matsumoto/Black Star **685** Bruce Plante/The Chattanooga Times **686** ©Anticoli-Nicozzi-Nusca/Gamma Liaison Network, New York. **687** Ed Bohon/The Stock Market **688** Martin Rogers/Stock, Boston **690** Lucien Niemeyer **695** Dan McCoy/Rainbow **696** Hanson Carroll/FPG International **701** Courtesy, Alexander Penelas, County Commissioner, Dade County, Fl. **704** © 1993 Bart Bartholomew/Black Star, New York. **707** Cartoon by Paul Conrad, 5/15/91. Copyright, 1991, Los Angeles Times. Reprinted by permission. **708** Robert Srenco/FPG International **712** J. Neubauer/FPG

International **713** Grant LeDuc/The Stock Broker **714** Maxwell MacKenzie/Uniphoto Picture Agency **718** Buddy Pettit/FPG International **720** Alan Carey/The Image Works **726** George Gardner/The Image Works **729** © Rob Rogers. Reprinted by permission of UFS, Inc., New York. **730** Courtesy, Sovfoto **731** Peter Baker/FPG International **732** J. Messerschmidt/FPG International **737** Grant LeDuc/The Stock Broker **738** Stephanie Maze/Woodfin Camp & Associates **739** John Troha/Black Star **743** UPI/Bettmann Newsphotos **745** © 1991 Lisa Quinones/Black Star **746** AP/Wide World Photos **748** UPI/Bettmann Newsphotos **749** Joan & Milton Mann/Cameraman International **750** Paolo Koch/Photo Researchers, Inc. **753** Cartoon by Jim Borgman, 1989. Cincinnati Enquirer. Reprinted with special permission of King Features Syndicate, Inc. **754** © Andy Hernandez/Sipa Press **757** Adam Woolfitt/Woodfin Camp & Associates **759** ©Charles Thatcher/Tony Stone Worldwide **760** Dowen/F.S.P./Gamma-Liaison **761** Lee Snider/Photo Images **763** Mexican Government Tourism Office **764** Jonathan Meyers/FPG International, Inc. **765** © Sergio Dorantes/Sygma. **766** © Louise Gubb/JP Pictures. **768** Tom Haley/Sipa Press **769** Culver Pictures, Inc. **770** © Sygma News Photos **771** AP/Wide World Photos **772** Lee Celano/Sipa Press **775** © 1992 David Horsey Seattle Post-Intellegencer. Reprinted with special permission of North American Syndicate. **776** © Bernard Gotfryd 1988/Woodfin Camp & Associates **782** Reprinted with special permission of King Features Syndicate, Inc. **790** from THE HERBLOCK GALLERY Simon and Schuster, 1964.

TEACHER'S PROFESSIONAL HANDBOOK

Consulting Editor

Betty Dean
Educational consultant/former teacher, Bellaire High School
Houston, Texas

CONTENTS

THE MULTICULTURAL CHALLENGE

Bartley L. McSwine

Bartley L. McSwine is Coordinator of Secondary Education at Chicago State University and Associate Professor in the Department of Curriculum and Instruction. He formerly served as Professor of Multicultural Methods at the University of North Texas.

Multicultural education can be defined on several levels. It is simultaneously an organic educational process, a movement for social reform, and a goal toward which a society must strive if it is to become a truly democratic and pluralistic society.

As an organic educational process, multicultural education views culture as the basic ingredient out of which all human society evolves. Empirical research shows that culture determines not only *what* we learn, but *how* we learn. In other words, culture literally structures how we view our world. Our languages, eating habits, religious practices, and even thoughts are in some respects all unique to our cultural group. Multicultural education recognizes and attempts to utilize the unique cultural characteristics of each ethnic group.

Multicultural education is also a growing movement for social reform. The number of immigrants coming to this country is rising, as is the number of large city school systems that are now made up primarily of minority group and immigrant children. Cities such as Dallas and Los Angeles, which even two decades ago had predominantly white public school systems, now serve mostly minority populations. One American in four currently defines himself or herself as Hispanic or nonwhite. By the year 2020 the number of United States residents who are Hispanic or nonwhite will have more than doubled, while the white population will have increased very little, if at all.

The increase in the nonwhite population has led to demands that more cultures and cultural values be included in the education process. Traditional curricula have ignored the histories and contributions of minority groups, to the detriment of the children. A growing chorus of voices is calling for inclusion of these elements.

Strategies for Multicultural Teaching

Secondary classroom teachers may want to consider the following broad strategies for the addition of ethnic content to their classroom syllabus or lesson plans. James Banks has defined four levels at which such integration may be attempted.

The Contributions Approach. Level 1 involves including ethnic heroes and various aspects of their culture in the curriculum. Therefore, individuals such as Barbara Jordan and Daniel Inouye should be discussed along with traditional mainstream leaders like Thomas Jefferson, Franklin Roosevelt, and George Bush. Elements unique to each individual's cultural background would also be discussed. Banks cautions, however, that this approach leaves the basic goals and structure of the mainstream curriculum unchanged.

The Ethnic Additive Approach. Level 2 involves including new concepts, themes, and perspectives in the curriculum without changing its basic structure, purpose, or characteristics. It is often accomplished by the addition of a book, a unit, or a course to the curriculum. Thus, for example, a book on Spanish colonial law and administration might be used to supplement the unit on the foundations of American government.

The Transformation Approach. Level 3 alters the curriculum's basic goals and structure through the perspectives that are presented to students. It enables students to view concepts and issues from several ethnic points of view. The mainstream Anglo perspective then becomes only one perspective among many. The chapter on civil rights, for example, examines laws protecting the rights of *all* Americans.

The Social Action Approach. Level 4 attempts to make students active participants in the educational process. For example, in covering political campaigning, students may not only examine the ways that candidates use the media, but may focus on how the candidates target specific ethnic groups with certain messages. Case studies might be used that focus on campaigns by African American or Hispanic candidates. The teacher should keep in mind, however, that at Level 4, the primary goal is to have students develop critical analytical and thinking skills to ensure high cognitive and affective functioning on the part of each student.

In summary, the multicultural challenge is the challenge of taking American education beyond a monocultural focus to the incorporation of all the ethnic and racial groups that make up the American cultural mosaic. It is the challenge of making every classroom a model of cultural pluralism where every child is cherished for his or her unique ability to contribute to the development of a truly democratic society.

STRATEGIES FOR STUDENTS ACQUIRING ENGLISH

Argelia Arizpe Guadarrama

Argelia Arizpe Guadarrama is Coordinator for English to Speakers of Other Languages in Pharr-San Juan-Alamo Schools (Texas).

Many language-minority students are faced with the challenge of learning through a language other than their mother tongue. They need to develop the language skills required for participating in all aspects of schooling, while they strive to keep pace with native-speaking classmates in content mastery as well.

Issues in Language and Content Instruction

How Is Language Acquired? Current theory suggests that language is acquired when we understand what is said or read. Steven Krashen writes that language is acquired by "getting comprehensible input" (*Principles and Practices in Second Language Acquisition*, Prentice-Hall, 1982). Instruction that includes clues, such as pictures, graphs, charts, and games, is more likely to be understood because these clues help support the oral or written words. Another assumption supported by strong empirical evidence is that language is acquired more readily when we do something with it, such as gathering information, problem solving, or thinking critically about ideas.

How Is Content Learned? Many of the major professional organizations involved in K–12 education are calling for curriculum and instructional reform to promote more student interaction, the recognition of student diversity, and critical thinking in the classroom. The National Council for the Social Studies (NCSS) is calling for more multicultural awareness among social studies teachers as well as more recognition of cultural and ethnic contributions to the subject.

Language Instruction and Government

The integrated approach helps both the language and content teacher to determine on which concepts to focus, how to present those concepts, and how to promote language development among their students. Chapter Planner pages, which appear before each chapter in the Teacher's Annotated Edition of **Government in America**, include Students Acquiring English activities that meet the following major objectives:

1. To develop proficiency in academic English through presentation and activities using **Government in America** as the content base.
2. To teach students learning strategies that can help them become more independent learners capable of thinking critically.
3. To provide a basis for understanding the value of United States citizenship and prepare a background for those who may wish to obtain it.

Each activity includes language-learning strategies, so that the classroom teacher who is not a language specialist can still implement them effectively.

Games. Games provide a very real, understandable, and enjoyable method of achieving many of the language and learning objectives. They help to reinforce newly acquired information and review material that has been previously covered. The games described in these activities make an excellent reward to encourage students to cooperate, help them relax, and provide a source of motivation.

Creating Visuals. The preparation of posters, graphs, or bulletin boards by the students will enhance their comprehension. The creation of the poster for Chapter 8 is an example of a cooperative activity that develops vocabulary and an appreciation for various communities.

Grouping. The ability to identify and analyze critical attributes is a skill that starts with the Chapter 1 activity, which directs students to use newspapers to form a bulletin board on government services.

Role Playing. By assuming other personae, the students can feel safer: inhibitions are relieved, and students are often more receptive to corrections. In the course of acting, language flows, and the students will take risks that are not taken in traditional classroom exercises. Be careful not to make too many corrections—they can be confusing and cause frustration. Students may also be encouraged to imitate a character from one of the movies recommended in the Listening/Speaking sections.

Resources

For more information, write or call: Center for Applied Linguistics; 1118 22nd Street, N.W.; Washington, D.C. 20037; (202) 429-9292; and Teachers of English to Speakers of Other Languages (TESOL); 1600 Cameron Street, Suite 300; Alexandria, Virginia 22314; (703) 836-0774.

This essay discusses creative strategies that teachers can use to enhance their teaching of American government. The first part looks at cooperative learning—the grouping of students into teams that work together to solve problems, complete projects, and perform other classroom work. The second part deals with graphic organizing—using diagrams to convey information and concepts from the text in a visual form.

COOPERATIVE LEARNING

Cooperative learning offers both social and academic benefits. Often cooperative learning groups are a more enjoyable method of learning for teachers and students. Having each student contribute to a small group builds self-esteem. When properly structured, cooperative groups tend to promote positive relations among students of different abilities and ethnic backgrounds. Cooperative groups have also been particularly beneficial for students acquiring English, enabling them to take a positive role within a heterogeneous group.

One of cooperative learning's most significant benefits is that students learn to work as a team. By varying activities, cooperative groups can promote the development of creativity and critical thinking skills.

Basic Elements of Cooperative Learning
According to D. W. Johnson and R. T. Johnson, leaders in cooperative learning, this approach has five basic elements:

1. Face-to-face interaction. The teacher structures the groups so that students are sitting face-to-face through every aspect of the assignment. Such an arrangement ensures the depth of interaction that is a critical element of the learning group. This physical structuring promotes a group dynamic of encouragement, helping, and sharing.

2. Positive interdependence. This has been termed the "sink or swim" method; students understand that they must work together in order to complete the assignment. A teacher can structure positive interdependence within a group in several ways. By requiring a group to share resources, teachers ensure that students depend upon one another for specific information with which to complete the assignment. By establishing mutual goals, teachers encourage students to make sure that all members of the group learn the material. By giving joint rewards, teachers ensure that all group members have a vested interest in the group's meeting stated criteria. By having assigned roles, all students feel a sense of belonging to and being needed by the group.

3. Individual accountability. It is essential for teacher and students to understand that individual accountability must be built into the structure of cooperative learning groups; otherwise, there is too great a danger of one or two students having to do the work for the entire group. The teacher may assess individual performance in a variety of ways; for example, by giving tests to individual students or choosing a student at random to provide the answer. Students may also be graded for their interpersonal skills while the group is functioning.

4. Interpersonal and small group skills. Social skills are essential to effective group cooperation. Students do not enter a group with mastery of these skills; they must be taught. Skills range from the basic level of taking turns, listening carefully, and encouraging other group members, to the more difficult level of making decisions, resolving conflicts, communicating complex ideas, and building trust.

5. Group processing or evaluation. Students should consider how well their group functioned and how well they met their goals; teachers can evaluate the positive accomplishments and needs of each group and of the class as a whole.

How to Implement Cooperative Learning
The keys to success are a clearly defined and explained structure and careful implementation.

1. Specify objectives. Identify objectives for both the academic content and the collaborative skills you want students to learn. The following are some suggestions of activities and projects that lend themselves to a cooperative learning format.

- Create maps.
- Write diary or journal entries.
- Paraphrase or rewrite historical documents.
- Make audiotapes or videotapes.
- Create illustrated timelines.
- Conduct written or oral interviews.
- Interpret a cartoon or draw an original cartoon.
- Create a museum project.
- Complete worksheets as a group activity.
- Improvise skits.

2. Organize learning groups. Structure the groups according to the nature of the assignment, the amount of experience that students have had with cooperative learning, and the time period in which the assignment needs to be completed. In general, you will make three decisions regarding the groups: size, composition, and duration. Group size generally ranges from two to six students, and cooperative learning theorists recommend placing students of high, middle, and low abilities in the same group. Another goal is to create a mix of students who differ in race, sex, and socioeconomic class. This intentional grouping builds positive relations among students who might never get to know each other otherwise.

You may decide to introduce cooperative learning by assigning students to groups or you may choose to set up the groups with some student input. Ask students to list three students with whom they would like to work. Then, in assigning students to groups, make sure each student gets to work with at least one named partner. Students who have not been named can be assigned across groups. This method allows inclusion of students who tend to be isolated when traditional choosing of groups takes place.

You should change groups from time to time. However, do allow groups to remain together long enough for members to develop facility in working with one another.

3. Set groups in motion. After dividing your students into groups, explain clearly what their academic task is. You also need to identify the group skill you want them to develop. Structure interdependence into the lesson. Provide limited materials so that resources must be shared—for example, one pencil and one answer sheet or one resource card per group. Assign roles to ensure that each student participates in the group. Typical roles are recorder, researcher, presenter, moderator, and supplies/equipment person. Explain to students that each member must contribute to the group product for both the individual and the group to receive full credit. Here are some ways to account for individual participation in the group:

- Require input from each student at every stage.
- Call on any student at random to explain responses that the group writes or produces.
- Have each student initial his or her parts of all written work.
- Test students individually and either count scores separately or average the group's scores.

Reward good group effort to reinforce the concept of "All for one and one for all." If individual accountability is the "stick" of cooperative learning, group rewards are the "carrot."

4. Monitor groups. Watch the interactions of the groups to see if they are on target both academically and socially. Intervene, if necessary, to help students get back to work, but act as a facilitator, not a referee.

5. Evaluate the process. Ask yourself and your students how well the groups worked together. Evaluation is the final step in implementing cooperative learning groups. End the cooperative learning lesson several minutes early each session to allow students time to reflect on positive interactions as well as needs for group improvement. You may also wish to share the results of your observations with the class, being careful to focus on positive rather than negative behaviors.

You may choose to videotape cooperative groups in your classroom at an early stage of the year, and then several months later, to compare the degree of collaboration within groups. Share these viewings with the class as you continue to look for ways to improve group functioning.

Cooperative Learning Outcomes

Because a cooperative learning activity has both academic and social objectives, you need to look for outcomes in both areas. You also need to consider outcomes for individuals as well as for groups. (Be careful, however, not to emphasize social outcomes for less able students and academic outcomes for more able students. All students need practice in both areas.)

Analysis One way to look at the outcomes of a cooperative learning activity is to fill in a four-celled table such as this:

	Academic Objective	**Social Objective**
Group		
Individual		

With this information, you can see at a glance what your students have accomplished. From there you can determine the areas in which they need further development.

Grading Techniques Grading techniques depend on the nature of the assignment. A set of facts to be mastered gets a percentage score. To grade a more complex group activity, you might use a letter grade or even a Pass/No Pass for the group. If each student has been responsible for a single element of the project, you may grade each element individually and then average the grades.

Team Techniques for Cooperative Learning

Cooperative learning groups lend themselves to several team techniques that make learning more fun.

1. Group investigation Students work in teams to prepare a presentation or project to share with the class. Students form teams based on a shared interest in the topic and divide the work so that each student on a team has a definite task to perform.

Uses: This strategy is helpful to students in synthesizing information from several sources, including interviews and library research.

Benefits: Promotes organizational and presentation skills; helps students direct their own learning.

2. Jigsaw In the jigsaw strategy each member of the team becomes "expert" about a particular topic related to a larger team project. Team members then share information to prepare a presentation or solve a problem. Following are the main steps:

1. Identify several manageable topics related to a larger topic or concept.
2. Set up an "expert" group for each topic made up of one member from each team.
3. Have expert groups research their topic.
4. Experts return to their original teams and share what they have learned.
5. You may assign the teams a particular format for presenting their findings, or you may let teams select for themselves the formats they wish to use.

Uses: The jigsaw approach is particularly effective in helping students to prepare for informed debate or to acquire and present new information.

Benefits: Promotes interdependence; helps students find connections among concepts and bodies of information.

Teaching Tips in Cooperative Learning

1. Troubleshooting
- Are students not ready to work in larger groups?
- Have social expectations been well established?
- Are requirements or time limits more than students can cope with?
- Is the grading system used more punitive than rewarding?
- Remember, if it's not fun, something is wrong.

2. Role of Teacher
- Classroom shifts from teacher-directed to student-centered learning.
- Teacher acts as coach and facilitator.
- Teacher must check degree of student learning, particularly when students are introducing information to other group members.
- Except in the jigsaw technique, teacher presents material.

3. When to Use Cooperative Learning
- Cooperative groups are appropriate for review, studying, and culminating projects.
- It is best to begin with small groups and simple assignments, and then build as students and teacher become comfortable.

4. Range of Collaborative Skills from Simple to More Complex
- Get into cooperative groups quietly.
- Talk quietly in groups.
- Stay with group.
- Ask for help if necessary.
- Check to be sure everyone understands.
- Remember that you share a mutual goal with all members of your group.
- Everyone contributes.
- Listen to fellow group members.

Further Reading

Aronson, E., et al. The Jigsaw Classroom. *Sage Publications, 1978.*

Dishon, D. and P. W. O'Leary. A Guidebook for Cooperative Learning: A Technique for Creating More Effective Schools. *Learning Publications, Inc., 1984.*

Johnson, D. W., R. T. Johnson, E. J. Holubec, and P. Roy. Circles of Learning: Cooperation in the Classroom. *Association for Supervision and Curriculum Development, 1984.*

Kagan, S. Cooperative Learning: Resources for Teachers. *Resources for Teachers, 1989.*

Slavin, R. E., et al., eds. Learning to Cooperate, Cooperating to Learn. *Plenum Press, 1985.*

TEACHING AND LEARNING WITH GRAPHIC ORGANIZERS

Why is advertising so successful? It uses strong, simple images and a few clear words to convey a single idea. While teaching history is a much more complex undertaking, we can borrow some of advertising's visual power to help students make sense out of the mass of information we give them to learn.

What Are Graphic Organizers?

Graphic organizers use simple shapes and common symbols to diagram key pieces of information. From the arrangement of shapes and symbols, students can see at a glance the relationship between or among those pieces of information. Instead of memorizing a lot of seemingly unconnected facts that tell "what," they can see the "why" that relates the facts. Understanding the relationship provides a context for remembering. It makes the facts make sense.

Imagine yourself as a student who must learn how the Supreme Court decides cases it has heard for a test tomorrow. Your assignment is to read the text section "The Supreme Court Decides Difficult Cases." You might outline this information to help you remember it, or you might take notes. A third possibility is to draw a graphic organizer. After reading and thinking, you might sketch something like this:

In drawing this graphic organizer, you have had to figure out what are the main points, sequence them in chronological order, and show cause-and-effect relationships. Using critical thinking skills, you have drawn meaning out of the information you have read. Creating the graphic organizer has helped you learn; reviewing for the test will be a lot easier with this visual shorthand.

Types of Graphic Organizers

A graphic organizer can be any kind of diagram that organizes information in a meaningful way. However, government lends itself well to a few basic patterns. Five of these patterns are shown and described here. They are a flow chart, an organization chart, a Venn diagram, a web, and a tree. The simpler you keep them, the better: four or five pieces of information are a good amount; eight should be the maximum. More than eight pieces of information becomes difficult to remember.

1. Flow Chart As the Supreme Court example shows, a flow chart clearly illustrates a sequence of events. It can also show cause-and-effect relationships that happen in sequence. The text section "The Criminal Justice System Enforces the Law" in Chapter 18 can be nicely summarized with this type of graphic organizer.

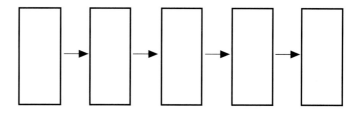

2. Organization Chart Use an organization chart to show power relationships. Place the person or group with the most power at the top of the pyramid, and then add as many intermediate levels as you need. Chapter 16 suggests several organization diagrams—for the Executive Office, Executive Departments, and other executive agencies.

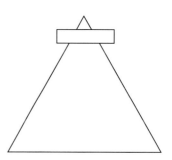

3. Venn Diagram The overlapping circles of a Venn diagram make it easy to compare and contrast two things. In the text, the chapter on federalism compares and contrasts national and state powers. To transfer this information to the Venn diagram, write what the state and federal governments have in common in the overlapping segment. In the outside segments, list their differences. (Students might recognize this diagram from their math class as representing the intersection of two sets.)

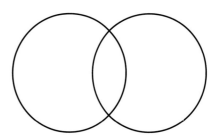

4. Web   Use the web to show the relationship between a main idea and supporting details, an event and its multiple causes, or a whole and its parts. For example, you might use a web to organize information on interest groups. You would write "Types of Interest Groups" in the center, and put one variety at the end of each strand.

5. Tree   The tree chart, with its spreading branches, is a graphic presentation of an outline: the main subject, or "trunk," is divided into categories, which are further divided into subcategories. Students are familiar with using tree charts to describe genealogy, but a tree is also an excellent image to use for mapping organizations.

Graphic Organizers in the Classroom

You may want to create graphic organizers, using the small diagrams on these pages as models, for use as generic overhead transparencies. Fill them in with specific information as teaching aids for your lessons, adding arrows or other symbols as you see fit. Please note that also available with **Government in America** is a book of teaching transparencies, many of which are ready-to-use graphic organizers based on sections of the text.

You can also teach your students the valuable study skill of making their own graphic organizers. Challenge them to design a graphic organizer for a particular text passage or body of information. Students must read the passage, decide what kind of information it is, and then select the appropriate type of graphic organizer to represent it visually. They may modify the original format in any way they think will show the information most clearly. This makes an excellent cooperative learning activity, for it requires students to reason together and taps the skills of those who are more visual and kinesthetic learners.

The process of creating a graphic organizer is as valuable a learning tool as the product. And the product, of course, is worth a thousand words.

VOCABULARY STRATEGIES

Henry Ward Beecher, the nineteenth century theologian, once described words as "pegs to hang ideas on." In no subject is that more true than in American government. Many important concepts and ideas are introduced through key terms and phrases, and the student who learns these terms is well on the way to mastery of the subject material.

The task of learning new terms, however, is often seen as dry and not appealing to students. This essay presents strategies that will spark interest in vocabulary acquisition, by describing games you can use in the classroom to review words and terms introduced in specific sections and chapters.

Using Games to Enhance Vocabulary

Research shows that students not only have fun, but are highly motivated by playing games. Games provide opportunities for learner-centered instruction, and can be used as cooperative learning activities. For games to be a useful tool, however, teachers need to follow some basic rules that apply to all the games described here.

- Before introducing a game to the class, be sure you are completely familiar with its description and rules.
- Make certain that each team is made up of students at different ability levels.
- Penalize disruptive teams. You may also set up a reward system for groups that follow the rules.
- Keep score. Appoint an impartial student to record scores on the chalkboard where all can see.
- Take the first answer given and give points only if the answer is correct according to your definition.
- Reward winning teams with privileges, such as release from a homework assignment.
- The teacher serves as referee or umpire in making final decisions.

GOVERNMENT BINGO

This game can be used to review vocabulary terms from a section or chapter. If you use the bingo board shown below, you will need at least 24 vocabulary terms.

Organization: Individual players.

Length: 10–15 minutes.

Preparation: Write each definition of a vocabulary term on a separate slip of paper and put the slips of paper in a box. Have students copy the bingo board shown below (or create a smaller grid if you are using fewer vocabulary terms) on a piece of paper. Students should write a different vocabulary term in each empty space on the grid. Encourage the students not to keep the terms in the order in which they appear in the text. Have students trade their bingo boards with their neighbors, so that each student is using a board made by another student. Then ask students to cut up another piece of paper into 24 pieces that can be used to cover a space on their bingo grid.

Goal: To cover either one row or column, or all the spaces on the grid.

Rules of Play:

1. At random, pull one of the slips of paper from the box and read aloud the definition. Put that slip of paper in a separate pile.
2. Students should examine their bingo boards to match the vocabulary term defined. If they find the correct vocabulary term, they may cover the space with a small piece of paper. Remind students that the center space is considered filled.
3. Continue reading aloud the definitions. The first student to fill in a complete row or column (or the entire grid if that is the goal) should call out "Government."
4. Check to see if the terms the student has covered are correct by comparing them with the pile of read definitions.

Game Design:

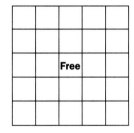

WIDE WORLD OF SPORTS

These games are based on popular sports played by professional and school teams. Depending on the season or student preference you may have the class play "Football," "Basketball," "Hockey," "Baseball," or "Soccer." The description that follows is of "Football," but the same basic rules apply for the other sports games.

Organization: Two teams.

Length: 20–30 minutes.

Preparation: Game boards can be drawn on a transparency and projected by an overheard projector or the boards may be drawn on the chalkboard. A football-shaped marker or chalk mark is needed to show team progress.

Use all vocabulary and key terms from at least one chapter. (It is better to have at least 30 terms for these games.) Write each term on a different slip of paper and label the paper either "run" or "pass." Label other slips of paper "fumble," "interception," and "penalties" for 5, 10, and 15 yards. Arrange the slips of paper in a pile.

(Note: For games other than "Football," follow the same basic idea, creating a board that looks like the correct playing field. Use appropriate labels for vocabulary terms and penalties—"single," "double," "double play," "pop-up fly ball caught" in "Baseball," for example.)

Goal: To score the most points.

Rules of Play:

1. Divide the class into teams. Then have them choose their team names and turn their seats to face each other. Select team captains. Toss a coin to see which team begins.

2. The game starts with the ball on the 50-yard line. Take the slip of paper on the top of your pile and ask the first student on the starting team to define the "run" or "pass" term.

3. If the student answers correctly, move the marker ten yards (one space on the board) toward the end zone. (If the game is "Basketball," a correct answer is worth a basket; in "Baseball," a base.) If the student is unable to answer, allow a second "down" by having the next team member try. You can allow four downs or a lesser number, if you wish, but if no team member gives a correct definition, the ball moves on to the other team.

4. If a player gets a slip of paper labeled "fumble" or "interception," the ball moves to the other team. The marker is moved in the case of "penalties."

5. Play the game for a specified "quarter," returning the ball to the 50-yard line at half time.

Game Design:

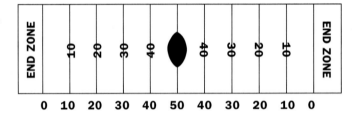

OLYMPIC PASSWORD

This game can be used for quick review of section vocabulary terms. It is played by four students at a time, so you may wish to have the rest of the class play along silently while listening to the clues given by the players.

Organization: Teams of two students. A class of 30, for example, would have fifteen teams. (Teams may wish to choose to represent specific countries in this "Olympic" competition.)

Length: 10–15 minutes.

Preparation: Draw a "tree" to keep track of how teams are doing and post it in your classroom. Fill in the tier of "trial heats" by randomly choosing teams to compete against each other. Before each competition, write each key term on two separate sheets of paper.

Goal: To win the gold (most points).

Game Design:

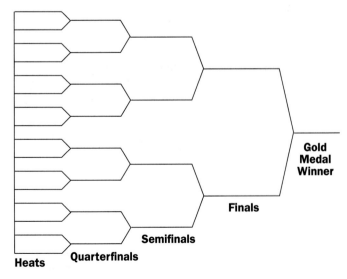

Rules of Play:

1. Have the two competing teams sit in front of the class, with teammates facing each other. Toss a coin to see who goes first.
2. Give one player on each team a paper with the same key term on it, making sure that their teammates cannot see the term.
3. The player holding the term on the first team gives a one-word clue to his or her teammate, who has a chance to guess the term. If he or she guesses correctly, that team gets the point. If not, the person with the term on the other team gets to give a one-word clue. Teams take turns giving clues until the term is guessed.
4. Give the next term to the two players who guessed during the first round and have them present the clues to their teammates. The team that started the guessing for the first term should now go second. Have the players take turns giving clues and starting first until all the terms have been guessed.
5. The team with the most points wins the heat, and continues to the quarterfinals. (Ties may be broken by bonus terms taken from another lesson.)
6. Teams should progress up the "tree" until the class has gold, silver, and bronze medalists.

BOARD GAME PLAY

The construction of a board game can be assigned as a project to cooperative learning groups, as well as to individual students or partners. Descriptions on board spaces should be connected to the unit the class is studying.

Organization: Teams of four to six students. One member is designated the "Mover," another the "Thrower," a third the "Spokesperson."

Length: 30–40 minutes.

Preparation: Have each group of students design a board game. You may wish to have them base the design on the sample shown below, or let them make it up entirely. Games may be used to review units, and different groups may be responsible for different units of the text. (For example, a board game for Unit One could illustrate the writing of the Constitution, with the "Start" labeled *Constitutional Convention Convenes* and the "Goal" labeled *Constitution Ratified.*)

Before beginning the game, make a list of vocabulary words from the chapter or unit you are reviewing. You will also need one die for players to use to determine the number of spaces they may move.

Goal: To reach the end of the board first.

Rules of Play:

1. Have each team choose a different marker—buttons, chalk, candy, etc.—and have the Movers put their markers at the starting space on the board. Have Throwers throw the die to determine the order of play.
2. Give the first team a vocabulary word or term and allow teammates time to confer over the answer. The Spokesperson should then give the team's definition. (If anyone else answers, the team loses its turn.) If correct, the Thrower throws the die and the Mover moves the corresponding number of spaces. If the definition is incorrect, the term goes to the next team for definition.
3. Continue play until all teams have reached the end of the board.

Game Design:
Here is one possible game board outline for a game based on running for the presidency.

White House

Announce Candidacy

Accolade
Accolade Inc.
5300 Stevens Creek Blvd.
San Jose, CA 95129

AIT
Agency for Instructional
Technology
P.O. Box A
1111 W. 17th St.
Bloomington, IN 47402

Annenberg
The Annenberg/CPB
Collection
Dept. CA 93
P.O. Box 2345
South Burlington, VT
05407-2345

Barr
Barr Films
P.O. Box 7878
12801 Schabarum Ave.
Irwindale, CA 91706-7878

BFA
SEE Phoenix Learning
Resources

BS
Brøderbund Software
500 Redwood Blvd.
Novato, CA 94948

Bullfrog
Bullfrog Films, Inc.
P.O. Box 149
Oley, PA 19547

Carousel
Carousel Film & Video
260 Fifth Ave.
Room 405
New York, NY 10001

CENFPD
Center for Public Dialogue
10615 Brunswick Ave.
Kensington, MD 20895

C Guild
Cinema Guild
1697 Broadway
Suite 802
New York, NY 10019

Churchill
Churchill Media
6901 Woodley Ave.
Van Nuys, CA 91406-4844

Coronet
Coronet/MTI Film & Video
Modern Curriculum Press
4350 Equity Dr.
P.O. Box 2649
Columbus, OH 43216

CRM
CRM Films Ltd.Partnership
2215 Faraday Ave.
Carlsbad, CA 92008–7295

EBEC
Encyclopaedia Britannica
Educational Corp.
310 South Michigan Ave.
Chicago, IL 60604

EDACT
Educational Activities, Inc.
P.O. Box 392
Freeport, NY 11520

Films
Films, Inc./PMI
Ravenswood Ave.
Chicago, IL 60640–1199

Focus
Focus Media, Inc.
485 S. Broadway
Suite 12
Hicksville, NY 11801

FRI
First Run/Icarus Films
153 Waverly Place
6th Floor
New York, NY 10014

Intellimation
Intellimation
Library for the Macintosh
Department 2SCK
P.O. Box 219
Santa Barbara, CA 93116

LCA (Coronet)
SEE Coronet

McGraw-Hill (CRM)
SEE CRM

MECC
MECC
6160 Summit Dr. N.
Minneapolis, MN 55430

MIS
Moody Institute of Science
12000 E. Washington Blvd.
Whittier, CA 90606

MTI (Coronet)
SEE Coronet

MTPS
Modern Talking Picture
Service
5000Park St., North
St. Petersburg, FL 33709

NGS
National Geographic
Society Educational
Services
1145 17th Street N.W.
Washington, D.C.
20036–4688

NTS
National Technical
Information Service
(formerly NAVC)
U.S. Department of
Commerce
5285 Port Royal Road
Springfield, VA 22161

OD
Optical Data Corp.
30 Technology Dr.
Warren, NJ 07059

Paramount
Paramount Pictures
5555 Melrose Ave.
Hollywood, CA 90038

Parthenon (Paramount)
SEE Paramount

PBS
PBS Video
Public Broadcasting
Service
1320 Braddock Place
Alexandria, VA
22314–1698

PCGlobe
SEE Brøderbund

Phoenix
Phoenix Learning
Resources
2349 Chassee Dr.
St. Louis, MO 63146

PSUAVS
Audio-Visual Services
Pennsylvania State
University
Special Services Bldg.
1127 Fox Hill Rd.
University Park, PA 16803

PSC
Project SERAPHIM
Clearinghouse
University of Wisconsin
Chemistry Dept.
Madison, WI 53706

Pyramid
Pyramid Film and Video
P.O. Box 1048
Santa Monica, CA 90406

Queue
Queue, Inc.
338 Commerce Dr.
Fairfield, CT 06430

Scholastic
Scholastic Software
P.O. Box 7502
Jefferson City, MO 65102

Time-Life Video
Time-Life Video
777 Duke St.
Alexandria, VA 22314

Time-Warner
Time-Warner, Inc.
75 Rockefeller Plaza
New York, NY 10019

TS
Tom Synder Productions
80 Coolidge Hill Rd.
Watertown, MA 02172

UCEMC
University of California at
Berkeley
Extension Media Center
2000 Center St.
4th Floor
Berkeley, CA 94704

UWA
Classroom Support
Services
University of Washington
23 Kane Hall, DG-10
Seattle, WA 98195